Abnormal Psychology and Modern Life
Ninth Edition

Robert C. Carson
Duke University

James N. Butcher
University of Minnesota

 HarperCollins*Publishers*

Sponsoring Editor: Laura Pearson
Developmental Editor: Joanne M. Tinsley
Project Coordination, Text and Cover Design: Proof Positive/Farrowlyne
   Associates, Inc.
Cover Illustration/Photo: (front top) Hill Gallery, Burmingham, Michigan;
   (center, bottom, back cover, and spine) Collection de l'Art Brut, Lausanne
Photo Researcher: Leslie Coopersmith
Production Manager: Michael Weinstein
Compositor: Black Dot Graphics
Printer and Binder: R. R. Donnelley & Sons Company
Cover Printer: The Lehigh Press, Inc.

Abnormal Psychology and Modern Life, Ninth Edition

Library of Congress Cataloging-in-Publication Data

Carson, Robert C., 1930–
     Abnormal psychology and modern life / Robert C. Carson, James N.
Butcher.—9th ed.
         p.   cm.
     Includes bibliographical references and index.
     ISBN 0-673-46488-1 (student ed.)
     ISBN 0-673-46617-5 (teacher ed.)
     1. Pyschiatry. I. Butcher, James Neal, 1933–   . II. Title.
     [DNLM: 1. Mental Disorders. 2. Psychopathology. WM 100 C321a]
RC454.C275 1991
616.89--dc20
DNLM/DLC
for Library of Congress   91-20863
                                                              CIP

91 92 93 94 9 8 7 6 5 4 3 2 1

Contents in Brief

Contents

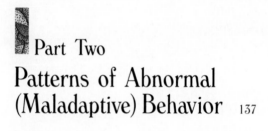

Part Two
Patterns of Abnormal (Maladaptive) Behavior   137

Chapter 5
Stress and Adjustment Disorders   138

Chapter 6
Anxiety-based Disorders   180

■ Chapter 7
Psychological Factors and Physical Illness   228

■ Chapter 8
Personality Disorders   262

■ Chapter 9
Substance-Use and Other Addictive Disorders   294

■ Chapter 10
Sexual Disorders and Variants   340

■ Chapter 11
Mood Disorders and Suicide   380

■ Chapter 12
The Schizophrenias and Delusional Disorders   426

■ Chapter 13
Organic Mental Disorders   476

■ Chapter 14
Mental Retardation and Developmental Disorders 502

■ Chapter 15
Behavior Disorders of Childhood and Adolescence 534

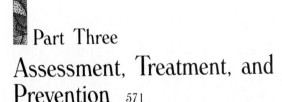

▨ Part Three
Assessment, Treatment, and Prevention 571

■ Chapter 16
Clinical Assessment 572

■ Chapter 17
Biologically Based Therapies   604

■ Chapter 18
Psychologically Based Therapies   626

■ Chapter 19
Contemporary Issues in Abnormal Psychology   672

Preface

As instructors who have used earlier versions of this text will readily perceive, the pace of developments in the field of abnormal behavior on both the conceptual and empirical fronts has accelerated substantially in recent years. This quickening pace requires an almost constant scanning of the pertinent literature in order to ensure that important milestones and trends will not be missed in the avalanche of information that the investigators and scholars of the field produce and place before us. As textbook authors committed to educating our readers comprehensively in the best that contemporary research and thinking has to offer, our involvement in this ninth edition of *Abnormal Psychology and Modern Life* has been a taxing enterprise. It has also been an enormously exciting one because the task has obliged us to immerse ourselves in this rapidly evolving field at a level we suspect would be unlikely under any less compelling circumstances.

The sheer density of new challenges and advances in the four years since we completed the eighth edition has required us to rethink and restructure our approach across a broad front. For example, concern with issues of taxonomy and classification of mental disorders, never far beneath the surface, has become a dominating theme recently as we struggle toward the creation of a new system, the fourth edition of the *Diagnostic and Statistical Manual of Mental Disorders* (DSM-IV). Meanwhile, we have witnessed the development of important new insights in numerous substantive areas, such as the pervasive character of posttraumatic stress disorders and the mechanisms underlying human adaptational failure in response to stress; the limitations of the genetic model of mental disorder; the nature of degenerative brain changes in Alzheimer's disease; the origins and consequences of drug abuse, particularly cocaine; and the profound impact of child abuse on the long-term adjustment of victims, to mention only a few.

In response to these developments as well as to reviewer input, the structure of the ninth edition has been extensively revamped. Most immediately apparent here is the addition of one chapter, expanding the total to 19. This addition was necessitated by our recognition that it was no longer possible to combine mental retardation and organic mental disorders in a single chapter and do justice to each of these topics. They now appear in separate chapters, enabling us to expand our coverage of both developmental (Axis II childhood) disorders, in which mental retardation is included, and the organic mental syndromes. In regard to the latter, we have more thoroughly examined the increasingly important problem of Alzheimer's dementia; we have also been able to introduce what we have learned to date about the newly recognized AIDS dementia complex, a widespread complication of AIDS infection.

A new chapter sequence was devised for Part Two (Patterns of Abnormal [Maladaptive] Behavior) of the ninth edition, one that better emphasizes conceptual relatedness as the various disorders of abnormal psychology are sequentially addressed. Thus, problems of behavioral medicine and the psychogenesis of physical disease are discussed immediately following the examination of stress and the anxiety-based disorders. Personality, substance-use, and sexual disorders are then taken up in an uninterrupted sequence involving conduct problems. We move next to the mood and schizophreniform disorders. The organic mental disorders then come into focus, followed by two chapters devoted to the specific types of psychopathology usually becoming manifest prior to adolescence.

Within chapters, all material has been updated with respect to new findings and developing trends at the conceptual level. Particular updating effort has been devoted to those disorders on which new and productive attention has been focused since the last edition, such as posttraumatic stress disorder (Chapter 5), multiple personality disorder (Chapter 6), and dementia of the Alzheimer's type (Chapter 13). Relating in particular to the first two of these, we have expanded at many points throughout the text our coverage of the etiologic significance of childhood trauma, in keeping with our dramatically enhanced recognition of the tragic dimensions of childhood abuse, both sexual and general, in our society.

We have also become even more critical of the too facile interpretations of the major disorders now increasingly offered to the general public—for example, that schizophrenia has been proven to be a unitary entity always caused by brain disease (usually of genetic origin), or that one can "cure" the profoundly human experience of depression by resorting to drugs. In each of these cases, as in many others, we invite the reader to weigh the evidence with us. Usually, as in these instances, it is found wanting.

For the first time in four decades the name of James Coleman is missing from the cover and title page of *Abnormal Psychology and Modern Life*. Although this change reflects the inevitability of change in human affairs, we cannot forego this opportunity to express our gratitude and admiration for the signal contribution our senior mentor made to higher education in the field of abnormal psychology. Like most psychologists of our generation, our own introduction to the field was enhanced by the scholarship, wisdom, and profound humanity of the man who brought this now classic text into being.

One of Coleman's abiding strengths, perhaps his major one, as a leading author in abnormal psychology was that he never succumbed to the temptation of oversimplification. This is an extremely challenging and complex field, as challenging and complex as are broader but intimately related questions pertaining to the fundamental origins of human behavior. While other authors in the field took "positions," and most to a greater or lesser extent reviewed evidence selectively and followed particular viewpoints, Coleman could be counted on to give every viewpoint its due and to emphasize an unbiased reporting of empirical findings—even when the "facts," as was often the case, led to no coherent, unqualified conclusions. A reputation for comprehensive analysis had thus been earned well before the present authors became involved with the text.

Much has changed in the field of abnormal psychology since we assumed major responsibility for this work, and indeed we can point to many areas where genuine advances in knowledge have been achieved. Nevertheless, it remains true that many basic issues are at least as puzzling now as they were when we began preparation for the sixth edition some 15 years ago. True to the tradition of this text, we have tried from the outset to be unstinting in identifying these areas of continuing perplexity and in rejecting premature closure on matters for which the empirical evidence remains equivocal. The ninth edition is in this essential respect no exception.

Our experience is that many more such unsettled questions remain than is commonly acknowledged. In this era of quick summaries, thumbnail sketches, and selectivity in reported evidence, our approach may seem to some unduly detailed and at times skeptical. Nevertheless, "telling it like it is" has remained one of our foremost objectives. We reject out of hand any notion that such an objective is inappropriate for a college textbook.

We do think this book will challenge students; the field, we reiterate, is itself challenging. We also hope it will inspire them to demand more of themselves, of the mental health professions, and of our society than has characterized our history in the area of coping effectively with mental disorder. Within the broad boundaries that we give to the study and treatment of abnormal behavior, a cogent argument can be made that nothing is more important to the advancement—even the survival—of humankind.

◼ Ancillaries

The ancillaries for this text are many, and we will provide a brief overview here.

For the Student

A *Study Guide* by Mary Koss (University of Arizona) provides chapter overviews, key terms, learning objectives, and extensive study questions and self-tests.

SuperShell Computerized Tutorial by David Lutz (Southwest Missouri State University) is an interactive text-related program for IBM and compatibles, featuring multiple-choice, true-false, and completion quizzes, as well as chapter outlines and flash cards for key terms and concepts.

The *Brief Casebook in Abnormal Psychology* by Judith Rosenberger (Hunter College) and Edith Gould (Psychoanalytic Institute of the Post Graduate Center for Mental Health—New York City) provides a set of 13 case studies covering a wide range of psychological disorders.

Computerized Case Simulations by Matthew E. Lambert (Texas Tech University) is a new interactive program in which the student can take the role of a therapist to assess, diagnose, and treat fictional clients for various disorders.

For the Instructor

In addition to the ancillaries for students, a complete set of ancillary materials is available from our publisher for instructors who adopt this book.

An *Instructor's Manual* by Frank J. Prerost (Western Illinois University) gives overviews, lists of key terms, learning objectives, abstracts with discussion questions, recommended readings, discussion and lecture ideas, as well as activities and projects for each chapter.

Videos from "THE WORLD OF ABNORMAL PSYCHOLOGY," a new thirteen part telecourse, produced by the Annenberg/CPB Project in conjunction with Toby Levine Communications, Alvin H. Perlmutter, and HarperCollins Publishers, are available with accompanying literature on how to incorporate the videos into classroom lectures.

HarperCollins Video in Abnormal Psychology, features interviews with clients at the Western Missouri Mental Health Center, conducted by David S. Holmes (University of Kansas). The 80-minute video contains eight separate interviews and offers an exceptionally clear depiction of a wide range of symptoms covered in the text. Print materials are available with the video.

A *Test Bank,* written by David Lutz (Southeast Missouri State University) contains over 100 multiple-choice and essay questions per chapter. Questions are keyed to learning objectives in the study guide and instructor's manual, and are referenced according to difficulty level and cognitive type.

TestMaster, the computerized version of the test bank, is also available for IBM PC and MAC compatibles. The program allows you to customize your own tests on a built-in word processor that lets you delete, add, and revise questions as necessary.

GRADES is a classroom management program that lets you store data for up to 200 students and calculate average scores, grading curves and individual grades. For IBM PCs and compatibles.

For more information on the ancillaries and their availability, please contact your local Harper-Collins representative or write the company at the address on the copyright page.

◼ Acknowledgments

No project of this magnitude, which on this occasion included the coordinate development of a series of documentary videotapes, could be brought to fruition without the dedicated efforts of numerous talented people. We particularly note the gracious and competent reception we have received from our new publishers, HarperCollins. Those individuals making direct contributions are named in the following paragraphs. We want here to single out for a special note of praise and appreciation our developmental editor, Joanne Tinsley. Indeed, we

believe that her editorial wisdom and taste and her unfailing organizational skill are central to whatever success the current edition enjoys, just as they have been for four of its predecessors.

Also at HarperCollins, we would like to thank Susan Driscoll, Editor-in-Chief; Laura Pearson, Acquisitions Editor; Michael Weinstein, Full Service Manager; Paula Cousin, Project Editorial Supervisor; and Otis Taylor, Marketing Manager, for their enthusiastic support of and attention to the development of the ninth edition. Our Photo Researcher Leslie Coopersmith delighted us with her sensitive graphic depictions of what we were trying to say. Bob Olander, Project Editor, and Ann Skuran, Designer, at Proof Positive/Farrowlyne Associates were superb and unflappable in the hectic and demanding role of managing, under pressured time constraints, the conversion of our sometimes chaotic manuscript copy into printed pages.

Numerous others also contributed materially to our efforts as authors. Carolyn L. Williams provided timely references and some of the case material used in the text. We also benefited significantly from the comments offered by reviewers of the previous edition and of various versions and parts of the manuscript for the current one. They are:

Lewis R. Aiken
Pepperdine University

G. Dale Baskett
Tuskeegee University

Ernest E. Beckham
University of Oklahoma

Lorna S. Benjamin
University of Utah

Ira H. Bernstein
University of Texas/Arlington

James F. Calhoun
University of Georgia

Lee Anna Clark
Southern Methodist University

Lorry J. Cology
Owens Technical College

Eric Cooley
Western Oregon State

Barry Edelstein
West Virginia University

Robert Emmons
University of California/Davis

Peter R. Finn
Indiana University

Sheila Fling
Southwest Texas State

Robert L. Gossette
Hofstra University

Robert Holmstrom
George Washington University

D. Lamar Jacks
Sante Fe Community College

Fred A. Johnson
University of the District of Columbia

Edward Katkin
State University of New York/Stony Brook

Karl G. Krisac
Delaware County College

Michael J. Lambert
Brigham Young University

Arnold LeUnes
Texas A&M University

Muriel Lezak
Oregon Health Sciences University

Patrick E. Logue
Duke University

James E. Maddux
George Mason University

Lisa McCann
Traumatic Stress Institute

Linda D. Nelson
University of California/Orange

Richard Neufeld
University of Western Ontario

Marcia Ozier
Dalhousie University

Robert W. Payne
University of Victoria

Harold A. Ries
California State University/Sacramento

Alexander Rosen
University of Illinois/Chicago

Michael J. Ross
St. Louis University

Dennis P. Saccuzzo
San Diego State University

John R. Schallow
University of Manitoba

Milton Simmons
University of Tennessee/Martin

Art Skibbe
Appalachian State University

Barry D. Smith
University of Maryland/College Park

T. Gale Thompson
Bethany College

Elliot S. Valenstein
University of Michigan

William Van Ornum
Marist College

Herman A. Walters
University of Montana

Charles Wenar
Ohio State University

Fred Whitford
Montana State University

Logan Wright
University of Oklahoma

Finally, we thank once again the members of both of our immediate families, who endured without complaint the substantial privations of presence, residual energy, and focused attention necessarily entailed in an authorship task of this magnitude.

R.C.C.
J.N.B.

To the Student

A number of features have been incorporated into this book to help you learn about abnormal psychology. Another goal is to enable you to develop a balanced yet critical perspective that should serve you well in future pursuits.

Chapter outlines introduce each chapter and provide an overview of what is to come. **Chapter summaries** provide a broad overview of the chapter and can be read for preview purposes before you read the chapter and for review purposes after you've read and studied the chapter.

Key terms appear in boldface type when first introduced and defined in the text. For each chapter, key terms are also placed after the summary in a page-referenced composite list; at the end of the text, the terms are again listed and defined in an expanded glossary.

Highlight boxes expand on or summarize important text content. An in-text reference to each box tells you when you should read each Highlight.

Unresolved Issues sections appear before the summary for each chapter. These sections bring the field alive by examining some of the challenges and dilemmas facing researchers. They are a great source for term paper topics or extra credit work.

The **DSM-III-R,** a classification system for abnormal behavior that you will read about in Chapter 1 and use throughout this book, is printed for ready reference on the back endsheets of your book.

Case studies of individuals with various behavior disorders appear throughout the book. These cases provide real-life examples of the clinical pictures of the many disorders you will read about. Some are brief excerpts; others are quite detailed analyses. In any case, they serve not only to make what you're reading about more real, but also to remind you of the human factor so intimately a part of the subject matter of this text. In scanning the text, you can spot case studies by the pale screen behind the type; cases also sometimes appear in Highlight boxes.

Patient art appears on the cover and in the chapter openers, with a brief biographical sketch of the artist. **Photos,** too, are used throughout to visually enhance the key concepts of the text; in many cases, these photos are of individuals who have actually been diagnosed as having a disorder. We hope the art and the photos will serve not only to instruct but also to humanize your study of abnormal behavior.

At the end of the book, you will find a **Glossary** that contains definitions to words that appear in boldface type in the text and to other terms commonly encountered in this or other psychology texts; you can use the glossary as a general reference tool and as a study aid for the course. You will find here, too, the **Subject** and **Name Indexes** in which you can find quickly any topic or individual discussed in the book. The boldface page numbers in the **Subject Index** indicate where key terms are first discussed in-depth. A listing of **References** appears at the end of the text; should you wish to further examine any of the citations that appear in the text proper, this is where you will find the information you need.

A *Study Guide* by Mary Koss can assist you in organizing and mastering the material you are studying. It includes chapter overviews, learning objectives, a list of key terms, study questions, and multiple-choice self-test quizzes that should prepare you for class exams. If the *Study Guide* is not available at the bookstore, ask the bookstore manager if he or she can order a copy for you.

A **Mailer** appears on the last printed page of your text. This is your opportunity to provide us with your thoughts on how this text has worked for you. We hope you will take time to complete this brief questionnaire; we have relied on student input over the years to improve each edition of *Abnormal Psychology and Modern Life*.

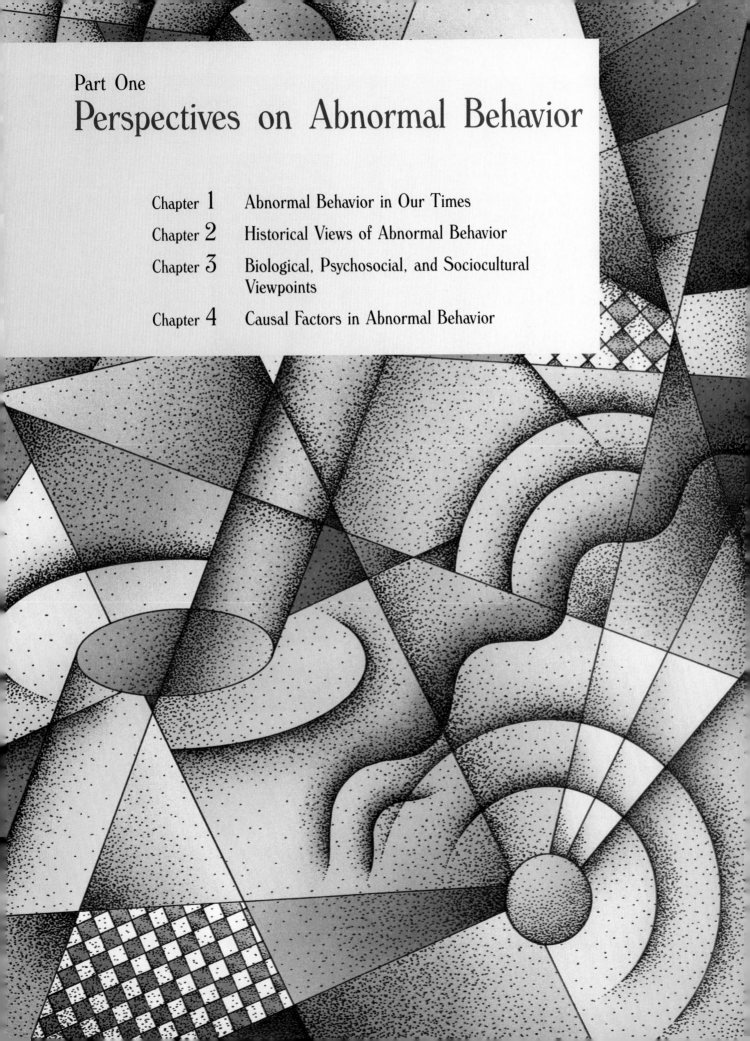

Part One
Perspectives on Abnormal Behavior

Chapter 1
Abnormal Behavior in Our Times

Miguel Hernandez, *Odalisques* (1947–1948). Hernandez (1893–1957), a Spaniard of working-class background, was interned in a concentration camp in France for fighting on the Republican side during the Spanish Civil War. He drew his first designs during his imprisonment in the camp. After his release, Hernandez began to work in oil, eventually to the exclusion of almost all other activities. He spent the last ten years of his life in Paris under a cloud of loneliness and spiritual exhaustion. This strikingly warm and harmonious painting is all the more remarkable for having been created by one who endured such difficult personal trials.

In studying abnormal psychology, we set our sights squarely on the worst that can happen when human beings find themselves confronted by challenges or demands that exceed their coping resources, by problems that are just too great. Consider the following cases:

> *A*lbert G., a 62-year-old university professor at a small college in the Midwest, was immensely popular and well regarded by everyone who knew him. Students flocked to his classes; his professional colleagues sought his consultation and scholarly views; and he wrote, when his moods permitted, with penetrating insight and unusual candor. With such high praise and with obvious success, why did he kill himself—a victim of deep personal despair? He had lived a tidy and conscientious life, always concerned about how he was viewed by others. Although dwelling alone, he had had several close friends, yet no one knew of the personal plight he apparently had experienced. No one around him, even his closest associates, had been aware of the depth of his despondent moods. The suicide left everyone in the community wondering about the psychological forces that could prompt someone as promising as Albert to end his life.

Many people live their lives, or episodes of their lives, in suffering and desperation, unable to cope with challenges that are too great. Abnormal psychology is concerned with these difficulties of human adaptation and with investigating ways in which they may be prevented or reversed.

3

*S*ue D., a 38-year-old attorney, acknowledged to her treatment group that she did not know how long she had had a problem with alcohol and tranquilizer abuse. She had become painfully aware of her problems when she had "hit bottom." She described the evening when she had gone to dinner with some friends and had lingered afterward in the restaurant bar to have a few drinks. She had drunk a great deal more than she had intended (as was often the case) and had gotten into a heated argument with other patrons and the manager of the bar. Sue explained how the situation had deteriorated. Objects had been thrown, the police had been called, and she had been arrested for public drunkenness and abuse of police officers. The police then had taken her to a detoxification center at the county hospital—the same hospital where she served as chief counsel for the law firm at which she worked. Sue told her group that the hospital administrator had been incensed, and the law firm partners had been embarrassed and outraged. Sue had been given the option of leaving the law firm or seeking treatment; she had chosen the latter and had begun a new phase of her life. She had entered a treatment program and was trying to understand how she had allowed her life to shatter as it had.

*M*anuel D., a 22-year-old Hispanic American, lived in a predominantly Spanish community in a large California city. One evening, after four teenagers in another car on the highway had allegedly made obscene gestures to him, he followed their car for some distance until they stopped. He then accosted the group and, with a revolver, killed one youth, and wounded another. What prompted him to engage in such destructive behavior? Although he lived in a tough neighborhood in which youth gangs were prominent, he was not a gang member. He had acted alone in the shooting. Drug and alcohol screening, conducted shortly after the incident, was negative. A search of his background showed that he had had several previous incidents of personal violence, a record of arrests, and a previous commitment to a psychiatric hospital for suspicious and threatening behavior. What factors underlaid his lack of impulse control and his violent acts toward other people?

To an extent, when we study cases such as these we see a distorted picture of human adaptation, one emphasizing the failings of psychological resourcefulness rather than the inspiring heights it more often attains. But in looking at these failings, we also learn something of their sources and the ways in which they may be prevented or reversed. We find that these failings are scientifically lawful; they are understandable and even, within reason, predictable and controllable. This knowledge about behavior problems allows us to expand our scientific understanding of abnormal psychology. Perhaps one day we may reach the point where irrational behavior that leads to persistent self-defeat and threatens group survival is no longer of serious concern. But before we reach that point, we have much to learn. We will begin our study of abnormal psychology by examining some popular views on the makeup of individuals with psychological problems.

POPULAR VIEWS OF ABNORMAL BEHAVIOR

Examples of mental disorders that we have heard or read about are apt to give us a distorted, perhaps even a chamber-of-horrors impression of abnormal behavior. In truth, less spectacular maladjustments are far more common. Popular beliefs about abnormal behavior thus tend to be based on atypical, exaggerated, and often unscientific descriptions.

Mental disorders of one kind or another have been a favorite topic of writers for many centuries, and the public's changing conceptions of mental disorders have been strongly influenced by popular literary and dramatic works. Though certainly not the first to explore this area, William Shakespeare is especially notable for having created a number of characters whose actions resemble certain behaviors we now associate with officially recognized clinical patterns—characters such as Lady Macbeth (obsessive-compulsive behavior), King Lear (paranoia), Iago (antisocial personality), Ophelia (depression/melancholy), and Othello (obsessive, paranoid jealousy).

The fascination with abnormal behavior has continued in modern writing, often in autobiographies. Examples include Mark Vonnegut's *The Eden Express* (1975), in which the author describes his own acute schizophrenic breakdown, and Hannah Green's *I Never Promised You a Rose Garden* (1964), which describes her treatment by a gifted therapist for a more chronic form of the same disorder. Stuart

In Shakespeare's play Hamlet the heroine Ophelia—driven mad with grief upon learning of the death of her father—drowns herself in a pond. Ophelia is one of a number of Shakespeare's memorable characters who suffer greatly from mental disorder and confusion.

Sutherland, a distinguished British psychologist, presents an account of his own psychotic episode in *Breakdown* (1977). An earlier autobiographical account of psychosis, *A Mind That Found Itself* (1908/1970) by Clifford Beers, played a significant role in the development of the mental hygiene movement in the United States. The Beers book, in part a chilling account of the conditions in mental hospitals around the turn of the century, foreshadowed equally disturbing modern accounts by Mary Jane Ward in *The Snake Pit* (1946) and by Ken Kesey in his fictionalized (but in many ways poignantly accurate) *One Flew Over the Cuckoo's Nest* (1962). Fortunately, the horrible conditions described by these writers have been rectified in many contemporary mental hospitals, although in many cases the problems may have been transferred unwittingly to the deplorable conditions of the many mentally ill who are homeless or who live in substandard community-based nursing facilities.

We seem to have an insatiable curiosity about bizarre behavior, and—in addition to accounts we read in books—most of us avidly seek and devour newspaper, radio, and TV accounts on the subject. Though we surely learn some things from these accounts, we also may be narrowing our perspective because the popular media typically simplify issues, appearing to give answers when, in fact, they barely succeed in posing the correct questions. The daily press regularly carries stories about seemingly demented people and often seeks to legitimize these stories by citing mental health professionals who more often than not have never examined these people. Such armchair diagnoses are useless (and probably unethical) in the majority of cases.

As a result of such exposure in literature and the media, you are likely to have a more than passing acquaintance with abnormal behavior. You may already have reached conclusions about its causes and its treatment. In most instances, however, we simply do not yet have sufficient information to permit valid conclusions about causal factors and treatment options, and the misinformation that is

The public's changing conceptions of mental disorders have been strongly influenced by popular literary and dramatic works. Shown here is a still from the film version of Ken Kesey's One Flew Over the Cuckoo's Nest, a classic account of the disturbing, dehumanizing conditions in mental hospitals.

HIGHLIGHT 1.1

Some Popular Myths and Misconceptions Concerning Mental Disorder and Abnormal Behavior

Myth	Fact
Abnormal behavior is invariably bizarre.	The behavior of most individuals diagnosed with a mental disorder is usually indistinguishable from that of "normal" people.
Normal and abnormal behavior are different in kind.	Few if any types of behavior displayed by mental patients are unique to them. Abnormality consists largely of a poor fit between behavior and the situation in which it is enacted.
As a group, former mental patients are unpredictable and dangerous.	A typical former mental patient is no more volatile or dangerous than a "normal" person. The exceptions to this rule generate much publicity and give a distorted picture.
Mental disorders are associated with fundamental personal deficiencies and hence they occur because individuals fail to correct a deficit.	So far as we know, everyone shares the potential for becoming disordered and behaving abnormally.
Appropriate attitudes toward mental disorder include awe and fearfulness about one's own foibles and vulnerability.	Mental disorders are natural adaptive processes that are comprehensible within this context. The majority of people have an excellent chance of never becoming disordered and of recovering completely should the unlikely happen.

readily available can cloud one's perspective. Therefore it is wise to suspend any preconceived beliefs about abnormal psychology until we consider the evidence. Look, too, at *HIGHLIGHT 1.1* for an overview of the more common misconceptions people are likely to have about abnormal behavior.

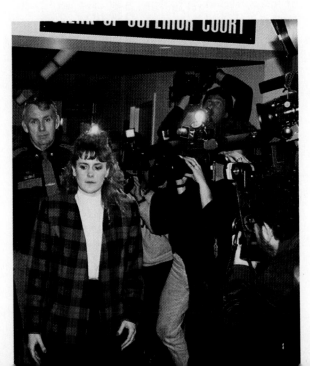

We tend to find sensationalistic accounts of bizarre behavior compelling. Witness the media furor over the recent case of 23-year-old Pamela Smart, found guilty of conspiring with her 16-year-old lover to murder her husband. The mixture of sex, scheming, and murder in the setting of a quiet New Hampshire town dominated news reporting for weeks. Cases such as these are likely to give us a narrow perspective of abnormal behavior because the information we get from press and TV stories may be simplified or distorted.

WHAT DO WE MEAN BY ABNORMAL BEHAVIOR?

To assess, treat, and prevent abnormal behavior, it is important to develop definitions of normal and abnormal and to specify criteria for distinguishing one from the other. Unfortunately, making such distinctions is not always easy to do. The word *abnormal* literally means "away from the normal," which implies deviation from some clearly defined norm. But what is the norm? In the case of physical illness, the norm is the structural and functional integrity of the body; here, the boundary lines between normality and pathology are usually (but not always) clear. For psychological disorder, however, we have no ideal model or even normal model of human functioning to use as a base of comparison. Thus we find considerable confusion and disagreement as to just what is or is not normal, a confusion aggravated by our changing values.

In the final analysis, any definition of abnormal must be somewhat arbitrary. Definitions tend to represent one of two broad perspectives. One view is that the concepts of normal and abnormal are meaningful only with reference to a given culture: abnormal behavior is behavior that deviates from society's norms. The other view—which is the one we advocate—is that behavior is abnormal if it interferes with the well-being of the individual and the group. Let us look more closely at each of these perspectives.

■ Abnormal Behavior as a Deviation from Social Norms

According to Ullmann and Krasner (1975), *abnormal* is simply a label given to behavior that deviates from social expectations. They maintain that behavior cannot be considered abnormal as long as society accepts it. As *cultural relativists,* they reject the concept of a sick society in which the social norms themselves might be viewed as pathological.

A critical example is whether an obedient Nazi concentration camp commander would be considered normal or abnormal. To the extent that he was responding accurately and successfully to his environment and not breaking its rules, much less coming to the professional attention of psychiatrists, he would not be labeled abnormal. Repulsive as his behavior is to mid-twentieth-century Ameri-

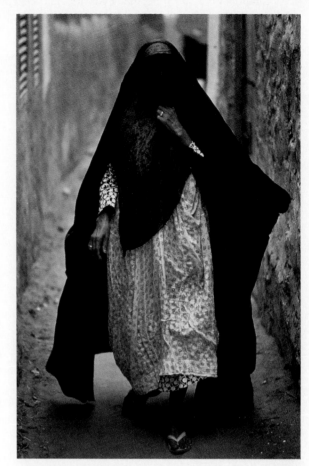

What is considered abnormal or deviant behavior in one society may be quite normal in another. We might consider this Arab woman's style of dress to be abnormal, but in her society it is the norm. What we consider normal may not be normal for everyone.

cans, such repulsion is based on a particular set of values. Although such a person may be held responsible for his acts—as Nazi war criminals were—the concept of abnormality as a special entity does not seem necessary or justified. If it is, the problem arises as to who selects the values, and this, in turn, implies that one group may select values that are applied to others. This situation of one group's values being dominant over others is the fascistic background from which the Nazi camp commander sprang. (Ullmann & Krasner, 1975, p. 16)

The acceptance of complete cultural relativism simplifies the task of defining abnormality: behavior is abnormal if—and only if—the society labels it as such (Scheff, 1984). But serious questions can be raised about the validity of this definition. It rests on the questionable assumption that social acceptance makes behavior normal—that one set of values is as good as another for human beings to adopt. It then follows that the task of the psychotherapist is to ensure that patients conform to the norms their society views as appropriate, regardless of the values on which these norms are based.

Cultural relativists maintain that behavior cannot be considered abnormal as long as society accepts it. In this context, is the behavior of a concentration camp guard—such as these German guards leading Jewish prisoners to a Nazi concentration camp —abnormal if he is conforming to the norms of his environment?

◼ Abnormal Behavior as Maladaptive

Although some degree of social conformity is essential to group life, we believe that the best criterion for determining the normality of behavior is not whether society accepts it, but whether it fosters individual and group well-being. When we use the term *well-being* we mean more than maintenance and survival. The term also implies growth and fulfillment—the actualization of potentialities. According to this criterion, **abnormal behavior** is *maladaptive behavior*. Even behavior that conforms to societal values is abnormal if it interferes with functioning and growth and if it is self-defeating.

So defined, abnormal behavior includes the more traditional categories of mental disorders— alcoholism and schizophrenia, for example—as well as prejudice and discrimination, wasteful use of natural resources, pollution of air and water, irrational violence, and political corruption, regardless of whether such actions are condemned or condoned by a given society. All of these actions represent maladaptive behavior that impairs individual or group well-being. Typically they lead to personal distress, and often they bring about destructive group conflict as well.

In defining abnormal behavior as maladaptive, we are making two value assumptions: (a) survival and actualization are worth striving for on both individual and group levels; and (b) human behavior can be evaluated in terms of its consequences for these objectives. As with the assumptions underlying cultural relativism, these value assumptions are open to criticism on the grounds that they are arbitrary. But unless we value the survival and actualization of the human race, there seems little point in trying to identify abnormal behavior or do anything about it. We can thus claim that our position is ultimately pragmatic.

In assessing, treating, and preventing abnormal behavior, mental health personnel are concerned not only with the maladaptive behavior itself, but also with the family, community, and society. From this perspective, therapy is defined not solely in terms of helping individuals adjust to their personal situations—no matter how frustrating or abnormal —but also in terms of alleviating group and societal conditions that may be causing or maintaining the maladaptive behavior.

Before we move on, you should be aware of several distinct but closely related professional fields concerned with the study of abnormal behavior and mental health. The distinction among them is often hard to draw precisely, for even though each has its own functions and areas of work, the discoveries in one field are constantly influencing and contributing to the thinking and work in others.

Abnormal psychology, or **psychopathology,** has long been referred to as that part of the field of psychology concerned with the understanding, treatment, and prevention of abnormal behavior. Within the area of applied psychology, **clinical psychology** is the discipline broadly concerned with the study, assessment, treatment, and prevention of abnormal behavior. **Psychiatry** is the corresponding field of medicine; it is thus closely related to clinical psychology, the chief difference being that psychiatrists tend to conceptualize abnormal behavior and its treatment in medical rather than behavioral terms. **Social work** is concerned with the analysis of social environments and with providing services that help individuals adjust in both family and community settings.

Most research in abnormal behavior is conducted by psychologists, in keeping with their primarily academic roots—the Ph.D. continues to be the most common degree among clinical psychologists. A relatively small proportion of psychiatrists, chiefly those in academic settings (such as medical schools), also do research, typically after obtaining specialized research training. Research activity is not usually conducted by social workers or other types of mental health professionals.

CLASSIFYING ABNORMAL BEHAVIOR

Traditionally, the study of abnormal behavior focuses on three distinct but often overlapping categories: (a) the nature of the abnormality, (b) the factors that cause or influence its occurrence, and (c) the methods developed for reducing or eliminating the behavior. As you will see, although much of the discussion in this text is organized around these categories, and although the categories are readily defined, it is still often difficult to understand completely the nature, causes, and treatment of abnormal behavior.

Describing the nature of abnormal behavior, also known as defining its **clinical picture,** is critical to understanding the cause and treatment of the behavior. Considerable attention has been paid to obtaining accurate clinical pictures because they serve as scientific guideposts, often pointing to important areas of needed research. For these descriptions to be helpful, they must organize the observed data in a systematic way, one that enables us to use the descriptions as diagnostic and treatment tools. In other words, good clinical pictures allow us to *classify* abnormal behavior.

Classification is important in any science, whether we are studying plants, planets, or people. With an agreed-upon classification system, we can be confident that we are communicating clearly. If someone says to you, "I saw a collie running down the street," you probably have an accurate idea of what the collie looked like—not from seeing it but rather from your knowledge of dog classifications.

In abnormal psychology, classification involves the delineation of various types, or categories, of maladaptive behavior. Classification is the necessary first step toward introducing some order into our discussion of the nature, causes, and treatment of such behavior. It enables communication about particular clusters of behavior in agreed-upon and meaningful ways. For example, we cannot conduct research on background causal factors in a given disorder unless we begin with a more or less clear definition of the behavior under examination. We need that clarity first of all to select proper research subjects. There are other reasons for "diagnostic" classifications, too, such as enabling adequate statistical counts of the incidence of various disorders or meeting the needs of medical insurance companies (which insist on having formal diagnoses before they will authorize payment of claims).

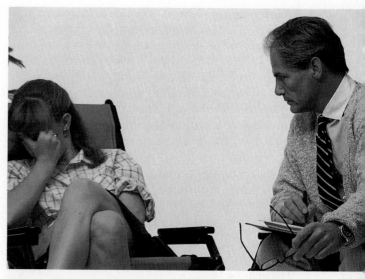

Mental health practitioners, in looking for the nature, causes, and treatment of maladaptive behavior, use diagnostic classifications. To diagnose a patient's problem, they must consider whether the patient shows a specific number of symptoms that fit a given diagnostic category.

It is important to keep in mind that all classification is the product of human invention—it is, in essence, a matter of making generalizations based on what has been observed. Even when observations are precise and carefully made, generalizations go beyond them by making inferences about underlying similarities and differences. In abnormal psychology, it is important to keep in mind that formal classification is accomplished only through precise techniques of psychological, or clinical, assessment —techniques that have been refined over the years. We will examine these techniques in Chapter 16, after we have looked thoroughly at the nature of abnormal behavior. In short, it is helpful first to understand the nature and causal factors underlying abnormal behavior before studying how to assess it.

Granting that all classification systems are fundamentally arbitrary, some of them are much better than others in helping us organize and discuss our observations. We base a classification system's usefulness on its reliability and validity. **Reliability** is the degree to which a test or measuring device produces the same result each time it is used to measure the same thing. In the context of classification, it is a measure of the extent to which different observers can agree that a behavior "fits" a given diagnostic category. If observers cannot agree, it may mean that the classification criteria are not precise enough to determine whether the disorder is present or absent. In contrast, **validity** refers to the extent to which a measuring instrument actually measures what it claims to measure. In the case of classification, validity is determined by whether the diagnostic category tells us something important or basic about the disorder. If, for example, we diagnose a person as schizophrenic, we should be able to infer from the classification information the characteristics that differentiate the person from others considered normal or from those suffering from different mental disorders, characteristics that go beyond the observations leading to the diagnosis. Validity presupposes reliability. We will encounter the important concepts of reliability and validity again when we discuss psychological assessment techniques in Chapter 16.

■ DSM Classification of Mental Disorders

The most widely used classification scheme for mental disorders in the United States is the *Diagnostic and Statistical Manual of Mental Disorders,* Third Edition Revised, put together by the American Psychiatric Association (1987). It is referred to in brief as **DSM-III-R.** There also exists a worldwide classification system called the *International Classification of Diseases,* Ninth Edition (World Health Organization, 1979), or ICD-9, which covers all diseases and disorders, both physical and mental. Both the American Psychiatric Association and the World Health Organization have worked closely over the years to ensure compatibility between their classification systems. For example, with the publication of DSM-III in 1980, a clinical modification of the mental disorders section of the ICD-9 was written to accommodate many of the DSM-III changes. Some differences remain, however; the ICD-9-CM (the CM was adopted to indicate the clinical modification) retains a number of categories that have since been dropped from DSM-III-R. These differences show that the process of classification is an ongoing search for a better, more effective system.

Each successive edition of DSM has sought to improve its clinical usefulness for professionals who diagnose and treat patients. Efforts have been directed specifically at overcoming the weaknesses in reliability and validity encountered with its predecessors. The distinctive innovation in DSM-III (and DSM-III-R) is its attempt to use only "operational" criteria for defining the different disorders included in the classification system. This innovation means that the DSM system specifies the exact behaviors that must be observed for a given diagnostic label to be applied. In a typical case, a specific number of signs or symptoms from a designated list must be

present before a diagnosis can properly be assigned. In other words, efforts have been made to remove subjective elements from the diagnostic process.

To the extent this goal can be achieved, diagnostic reliability is substantially improved. On the other hand, the use of stricter criteria can cause much abnormal behavior to be assigned to "wastebasket" or residual categories such as "psychotic disorders not elsewhere classified." When this occurs, validity suffers, since a category so broad can give only generalities about disorders within it.

DSM-III-R evaluates an individual's behavior according to five dimensions, or *axes*. The first three axes assess an individual's present condition:

I. The particular maladaptive symptoms, or clinical psychiatric syndromes, such as schizophrenia

II. Any long-standing personality problems (adults) or specific developmental problems (children and adolescents)

III. Any medical or physical disorders that may also be present

More than one diagnosis may be recorded on Axes I and III and, in exceptional instances, on Axis II. A person may have multiple psychiatric symptoms or medical diseases (Axes I and III, respectively), and may have more than one personality disorder diagnosed on Axis II.

The last two DSM-III axes are used to assess broader aspects of an individual's situation, one dealing with the stressors that may have contributed to the current disorder and the other dealing with how well the individual has been coping in recent months.

IV. The severity of psychosocial stressors

V. The level of adaptive functioning

Axes I and II, which list the categories of mental disorders, are provided in full on the endsheets of this book. These categories may be regarded for purposes of clarity as fitting into several broad groupings, each containing several subgroupings:

1. *Organic mental disorders* refer to disorders involving gross destruction or malfunctioning of brain tissue (as in Alzheimer's disease) and a wide range of other conditions based on brain pathology. These disorders are described in Chapter 13.

2. *Substance-use disorders* involve problems such as drug and alcohol abuse. These are discussed in Chapter 9.

3. *Disorders of psychological or sociocultural origin* have no known brain pathology as a primary causal factor, as in anxiety (Chapter 6), psychophysiologic (Chapter 7), psychosexual (Chapter 10), and personality (Chapter 8) disorders. The **functional psychoses**—that is, severe mental disorders for which a specific organic pathology has not been demonstrated—such as major mood disorders (Chapter 11) and schizophrenia (Chapter 12), are also traditionally included here, although it appears increasingly likely that certain types of brain dysfunction sometimes help cause them.

4. *Disorders usually arising during childhood or adolescence* include mental retardation and special problems, such as early infantile autism and pervasive developmental disorders, that may occur in children and that warrant separate categorization (Chapter 14), as well as other problems of childhood, such as hyperactivity and conduct disorders (Chapter 15).

In referring to mental disorders, several qualifying terms are commonly used. **Acute** is a term used to describe disorders of relatively short duration, usually under six months. In some contexts, it also connotes behavioral symptoms of high intensity. **Chronic** refers to longstanding and usually permanent disorders, but the term can also be applied generally to low-intensity disorders since long-term difficulties are often of this sort. **Mild, moderate,** and **severe** are terms that describe the severity of a disorder. **Episodic** is used to describe disorders that tend to recur, as with some mood and schizophrenic patterns.

Axis III of DSM-III-R is often used in conjunction with an Axis I diagnosis of psychological factors affecting physical condition. An Axis III diagnosis, which requires a medical examination, is used when a diagnostician has reason to believe that a psychological factor is contributing in some way to a physical disease—for example, problems with dependency are often thought to be associated with gastric ulcers. Axis III itself can be used for any physical disorder that accompanies a psychiatric one, whether or not the two are related.

Axes IV and V were new to the DSM-III and revised in DSM-III-R. They provide a framework for assessing an individual's life situation (Axis IV) and recent ability to cope with it (Axis V). Axis IV (presented in *HIGHLIGHT 1.2*) has a six-point scale for rating the severity of psychosocial factors—either acute events or enduring circumstances—that may be placing an individual under stress and contributing to the current disorder. The scale can

be used for both adults and children. Levels range from *none* at one end of the scale to *catastrophic* at the other. Axis V (presented in *HIGHLIGHT 1.3*) has a ninety-point scale for rating an individual's current global level of functioning. A clinician is also encouraged to use the same scale to rate the highest level of functioning in past years. Here the levels range from good functioning in all areas through levels of impairment to conditions considered dangerous. Both these scales can help ensure that when different clinicians talk about either stress severity or "good" adjustments, for example, they are talking about the same thing.

As an example of an extended DSM-III-R diagnosis, let us consider the case of Albert, the university professor described in the opening pages of this chapter. His diagnosis might be as follows:

Axis I
    Major depressive disorder
Axis II
    Compulsive personality disorder
Axis III
    None
Axis IV
    Level of psychosocial stressors: 3 (moderate)
Axis V
    Global functioning: 60 (moderate difficulty)

Axes IV and V are significant additions. Knowing the demands that have been on an individual is important for understanding the problem behavior that has developed. Knowing an individual's general level of success in meeting these demands in the recent past can help a clinician make an appropriate and realistic treatment plan and can give him or her an idea of what to expect. Some clinicians, however, object to the routine use of these axes for insurance forms and the like on the grounds that such use unnecessarily compromises a patient's right to privacy. Because of such concerns, Axes IV and V are now considered optional for diagnosis and in fact are rarely used in most clinical settings.

■ The Development of DSM-IV

Discussion is currently underway to develop the next version of the diagnostic classification system (DSM-IV), which is planned for publication in 1993 (Frances, Widiger, & Pincus, 1989). One of the main goals of the revision is to coordinate the DSM diagnostic categorization system with the International Classification of Disease System (which is also in revision and to be designated ICD-10). Another reason for periodic revisions of the DSM is that using diagnostic systems reveals

HIGHLIGHT 1.2

Axis IV Scale for Rating the Severity of Psychosocial Stressors

Code	Term	Adult Examples	Child or Adolescent Examples
1	None	No apparent psychosocial stressor or enduring circumstances	No apparent psychosocial stressor or enduring circumstances
2	Mild	Break-up with boyfriend or girlfriend or child leaving home; family arguments; job dissatisfaction	Break-up with boyfriend or girlfriend; family arguments; overcrowded living quarters
3	Moderate	Marriage or marital separation; loss of job; marital discord; serious financial problems	Suspension from school; birth of sibling; chronic parental discord; disabling illness in parent
4	Severe	Divorce; birth of a child; unemployment; poverty	Divorce of parents; unwanted pregnancy; harsh or rejecting parents; multiple foster home placement
5	Extreme	Death of a spouse; serious illness; victim of rape; ongoing physical or sexual abuse	Sexual or physical abuse; death of a parent; recurrent sexual or physical abuse
6	Catastrophic	Death of a child; suicide of a spouse; hostage or concentration camp experience	Death of both parents; chronic, life-threatening illness
0		Inadequate information or no change in condition	

Adapted from DSM-III-R (APA, 1987, p. ii).

their inadequacies in terms of reliability and validity. Thus there is a need to incorporate refinements in the system that improve the understanding of patient problems and enable the communication of ideas and research findings through an agreed-upon language. One important goal in the revision of DSM-III-R is to incorporate an ongoing, multisite research program to make revisions in the system (Spitzer & Williams, 1988).

■ The Limitations of DSM Classifications

Not all writers and practitioners subscribe to the DSM classification system. Even the coauthors of this book view the DSM classifications from somewhat different perspectives and with different de-

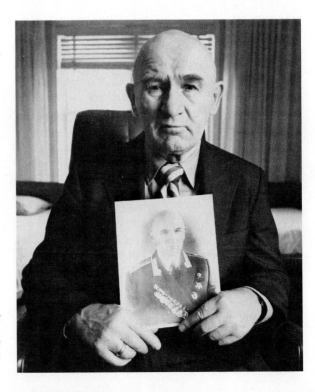

Pyotr Grigorenko is one of a number of Soviet dissidents who have been committed to mental hospitals because of their dissent. Grigorenko was a highly honored Red Army general before his dissent led Soviet doctors to incarcerate him. After finding asylum in America, Grigorenko was evaluated and found to be sane.

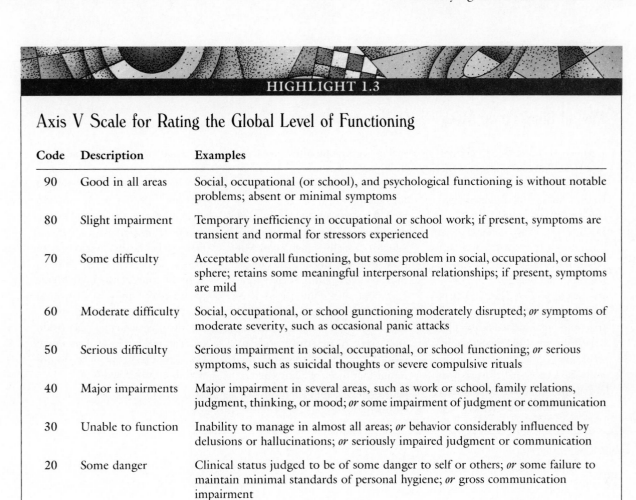

HIGHLIGHT 1.3

Axis V Scale for Rating the Global Level of Functioning

Code	Description	Examples
90	Good in all areas	Social, occupational (or school), and psychological functioning is without notable problems; absent or minimal symptoms
80	Slight impairment	Temporary inefficiency in occupational or school work; if present, symptoms are transient and normal for stressors experienced
70	Some difficulty	Acceptable overall functioning, but some problem in social, occupational, or school sphere; retains some meaningful interpersonal relationships; if present, symptoms are mild
60	Moderate difficulty	Social, occupational, or school gunctioning moderately disrupted; *or* symptoms of moderate severity, such as occasional panic attacks
50	Serious difficulty	Serious impairment in social, occupational, or school functioning; *or* serious symptoms, such as suicidal thoughts or severe compulsive rituals
40	Major impairments	Major impairment in several areas, such as work or school, family relations, judgment, thinking, or mood; *or* some impairment of judgment or communication
30	Unable to function	Inability to manage in almost all areas; *or* behavior considerably influenced by delusions or hallucinations; *or* seriously impaired judgment or communication
20	Some danger	Clinical status judged to be of some danger to self or others; *or* some failure to maintain minimal standards of personal hygiene; *or* gross communication impairment
10	Persistent danger	Person judged to be a persistent danger to self or others; *or* inability to maintain minimal standards of hygiene; *or* recent serious suicidal act having clear expectation of death

Adapted from DSM-III-R (APA, 1987, p. 12).

grees of respect for their utility (see the Unresolved Issues section at the end of this chapter for more on this issue). One of the major problems in the DSM classification system is that the categories *describe* rather than *explain*. It is all too easy to believe that something has been explained when, in fact, it has only been named. When we apply the term *schizophrenic* to an individual's behavior we have not said anything about how that pattern came into being— only that the person's behavior resembles that of individuals we have defined as schizophrenic.

A second limitation is that only individual behavior is covered. Disturbed families, delinquent subcultures, and violence-prone societies show maladaptive behavior that does not fit into a scheme made for classifying individuals. Classifying only individual behavior as abnormal implies that when

individuals do not fit smoothly into their social milieu, it is the individuals who are at fault and must change. This attitude casts the mental health profession in the role of preserving the status quo, no matter how abnormal the status quo might be. The Soviet Union has made this possibility a terrifying reality by "diagnosing" dissidents as mentally disturbed and forcing "hospitalization" and "treatment" upon them.

As we examine specific disorders later in the text, we will try to overcome this limitation by examining the role that pathogenic families and other groups play in causing and maintaining maladaptive behavior. As you will see, this behavior does not occur in a vacuum but, in part, is a response to the social context in which an individual lives (Hooley, 1985; Weary & Mirels, 1982).

Mental Illness as a Myth

Psychiatrist Thomas Szasz (born 1920) has been an outspoken critic of current practices and labels within the field of abnormal psychology (Szasz, 1961, 1970). In his writings, Szasz contends that mental illness is a myth and that traditional treatment can be more harmful than helpful.

According to Szasz, most of the disorders treated by psychiatrists and other mental health professionals are not illnesses. Instead, he claims, they are simply individual traits or behaviors that deviate from what our society considers morally or socially normal. They are caused by problems in living—by unmet personal needs or by stressful relationships, for example.

Szasz believes that traditional psychiatric treatment harms many people by labeling them as ill. Not only does this labeling encourage these people to fulfill society's expectations and thus act in irresponsible ways, but it also implies that they must become patients and accept treatment in order to change. In Szasz's view, this means that they are being encouraged to think and behave in ways considered normal by psychiatrists rather than to attack the social causes of their problems.

More recently, Sarbin and Mancuso (1980) have developed a related attack on the specific concept of schizophrenia, thought by many to be the most serious of all mental disorders. These authors liken the concept of schizophrenia to that of the unicorn, a mythical animal of antiquity. Schizophrenia, they say, is not a proper medical diagnosis but instead is a moral label given to people who do not behave in prescribed ways.

■ The Problem of Labeling

Some researchers have pointed out another equally important limitation to diagnostic classification: a psychiatric diagnosis is nothing more than a label applied to a defined disorder. The label does not describe a *person,* but rather some behavioral pattern associated with that person's current level of functioning. Yet once a label has been assigned, it may close off further inquiry. It is all too easy—even for professionals—to accept a label as an accurate and complete description of an individual rather than of that person's behavior. It is hard then to look at the person's behavior objectively, without preconceptions about how he or she will act. These expectations can influence even the simplest interactions and treatment choices.

Once an individual is labeled, he or she may accept a redefined identity and play out the expectations of that role. ("I'm a substance abuser, therefore everyone expects me to take drugs.") This tendency can be harmful because of the pejorative and stigmatizing implications of many psychiatric labels—implications that have the power to transform social identities and "mark" people as second-class citizens with severe, often debilitating limitations (Jones et al., 1984; Sarbin & Mancuso, 1970). Obviously, the effects on a person's morale and self-esteem can be devastating. (For a look at how some psychologists have responded to these problems, see *HIGHLIGHT 1.4*).

Interestingly, other researchers have concluded that "labeling," per se, does not necessarily imply that people are going to act negatively toward a former patient simply because he or she has been mentally ill (Cockerham, 1981; Rabkin, 1972). In fact, some writers have stated that former mental patients can avoid negative reactions from people by simply behaving differently. In this view, labeling actually has little impact on people's attitudes toward mental illness (Segal, 1978). In opposition to this view and reaffirming the role of labeling on the social rejection of former mental patients, Link, Cullen, Frank, and Wozniak (1987) found that placing labels of mental illness on a person did influence others to judge that individual as "dangerous" and to seek social distance from the individual. The relative impact of labeling on views toward mental illness is an active debate within the field of abnormal psychology, and one can find considerable research and emotional commitment to both sides of the argument.

Clearly, it is important for professionals to be very cautious in the diagnostic process, in their use of labels, and in ensuring confidentiality with respect to both. A related change has developed over

Gladys Burr (shown here with her lawyer) is a tragic example of the dangers of labeling. Involuntarily committed by her mother (apparently because of some personalilty problems) in 1936 at the age of 29, Ms. Burr was diagnosed as psychotic and was later declared to be mentally retarded. Though a number of IQ tests administered from 1946 to 1961 showed her to be of normal intelligence, and though a number of doctors stated that she was of normal intelligence and should be released, she was confined in a residential center for the mentally retarded or in a state boarding home until 1978. Though a court did give her a financial award in compensation, surely nothing can compensate for 42 years of unnecessary and involuntary commitment.

the past 40 years regarding the person who goes to see a mental health professional. For years the traditional term for such a person has been *patient,* which is closely associated with a medically "sick" person and a passive stance, waiting for a doctor's cure. Today many professionals prefer the term *client* because it implies more responsibility and participation on the part of an individual for bringing about his or her own recovery.

■ The Extent of Abnormal Behavior

What is the rate of mental disorder in society today? Or, to put it another way, how many people actually have psychological disorders? The frequency or infrequency of particular disorders are important considerations for a number of reasons. For one, researchers in the mental health field need to have a clear understanding of the nature and extent of abnormal behaviors in order to conduct research into their causes. In addition, mental health practitioners need to know whether the problems they are dealing with are relatively common or rare in order

to evaluate the appropriateness of treatment measures. Finally, mental health planners need to have a clear picture of the nature and extent of psychological problems being faced by society in order to determine how resources can be most effectively allocated.

Before we can discuss the extent of mental disorders in society we must clarify how psychological problems are counted. **Epidemiology** (specifically, mental health epidemiology) is the study of the distribution of mental disorders in a given population. A key component of an epidemiological survey is determining the magnitude of the problem being studied. There are several ways of doing this. The term **prevalence** refers to the rate of active cases that can be identified at a given point in time. It is to be distinguished from the term **incidence,** which is the occurrence rate of a given disorder in a given population. For example, "point" prevalence refers to the proportion of actual cases in a given population at a particular

Practitioners are concerned with how often various mental health problems occur in the population at large. Epidemiologists can provide answers because they study the distribution of mental disorders in a given population. Statistical information about the prevalence and incidence of disorders is important as a basis for devising appropriate interventions.

point in time—say on May 9, 1991. Incidence refers to the proportion of people in a population who have at some time been diagnosed as having the disorder and includes recovered cases. Incidence rates are normally reported as an individual's lifetime risk of contracting the disorder in question.

A large-scale epidemiological study sponsored by the National Institutes of Mental Health (NIMH) has provided us with perhaps the most reliable and valid information about the prevalence of mental disorders in contemporary society (Regier et al., 1988). The NIMH catchment area epidemiological study surveyed 18,571 individuals from five communities: Baltimore, New Haven, St. Louis, Durham, and Los Angeles. They found that about 15.4 percent of the population suffer from substance abuse problems or mental disorders in any given month. They also concluded that 33 percent of the individuals sampled are likely to have some psychological disorder or substance abuse problem in their lifetimes.

The NIMH study also provided information on specific issues or disorders:

1. There appear to be substantial differences in the lifetime prevalence for various disorders (the probability of a person ever having a certain disorder) in the five sites studied. For example, the prevalence rate for simple phobia in Baltimore was more than twice the rate in St. Louis and three times the rate in New Haven (Robins et al., 1984).

2. One-month prevalence studies show that disorders vary in frequency. The most common specific disorders were phobia (6.2%), dysthymia or depression (3.3%), major depressive episode (2.2%) and alcohol abuse or dependence (2.8%).

3. Rates of disorder differ between men and women. Men have a greater preponderance of substance abuse disorder (6.3% as opposed to 1.6% in women) and personality disorder (.8% as opposed to .02% in women); women appear to develop relatively more major mood disorder (6.6% as opposed to 3.5% in men), anxiety disorder (9.7% as opposed to 3.6% in men), and somatization disorder (.1% as opposed to an insignificant percentage in men).

Another recent epidemiological study provided important information about the development of mental disorders in "healthy" individuals. Vaillant and Schnurr (1988) conducted a follow-up study of 188 healthy men who had been studied for 50 years. They found that the incidence rates for mental disorders in this group were similar to the rates

The decline in psychiatric populations in public mental health facilities has been linked to the current problems of homelessness in the United States.

found in other studies—20 to 25 percent of the men had developed psychological disorders at some point. Fourteen percent were alcoholic and 6 percent had developed depressive disorders.

Most individuals with psychological problems do not get hospitalized in a large state or county psychiatric institution. Recent information from the U.S. Department of Health and Human Services (1990) indicates that admission to mental hospitals has decreased substantially over the past 35 years. Inpatient hospitalization constituted 77 percent of all mental health episodes in 1955 but decreased to only 27 percent in 1986. Long-term psychiatric care in inpatient facilities has been steadily declining over the past decades, as noted in *HIGHLIGHT 1.5.* This trend, often referred to as *deinstitutionalization,* will be discussed more extensively in Chapter 19. Individuals experiencing psychological problems are more likely to receive treatment in outpatient facilities. However, evidence suggests that only about 25 percent of individuals with psychological problems actually receive any treatment at all (Robins et al., 1984).

RESEARCH IN ABNORMAL PSYCHOLOGY

The facts and ideas presented in this book are products of the powerful methods of research used to study maladaptive human behavior. You are

HIGHLIGHT 1.5

Changing Patterns of Mental Health Admissions

In 1986 one-third fewer patients were in America's large, isolated state and county mental hospitals than at the end of 1969. The trend toward fewer patients began shortly after the peak year for admissions, 1955. Fifty percent fewer patients are in state mental health facilities today than in 1955 (Lee & Goodwin, 1987). This dramatic decline in occupied state and county mental hospital beds is due to several factors, including (a) the introduction of a host of potent drugs that suppress severe mental symptoms; (b) the recognition of the debilitating and antitherapeutic effects of long-term hospitalization and the attendant deinstitutionalization movement; (c) the introduction of community health centers and related community facilities to care for individuals on an outpatient basis; and (d) the increased availability of alternate care facilities, such as nursing homes for the aged.

The decline in psychiatric populations in state and county facilities has been linked to the current problems of homelessness in the United States (see Chapter 19). This decline in admissions to traditional psychiatric hospitals has also been accompanied by an *increase* in admissions to other psychiatric facilities, such as private psychiatric hospitals, Veterans Administration facilities, and nonfederal general psychiatric services. The actual net effect has been a steady *increase* in overall hospital admissions during the past several decades. Data show that mental health problems continue to require a great deal of our health resources to manage. In 1985 most states spent daily between $20.00 and $40.00 per capita for mental health care. The daily per capita cost of mental health services varied, however, from $10.51 in Iowa to $90.12 in New York.

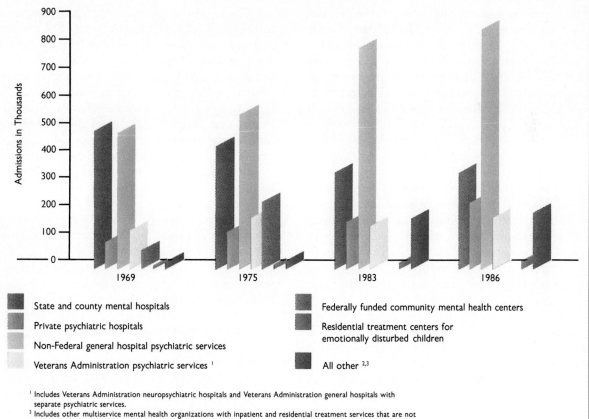

State and county mental hospitals

Private psychiatric hospitals

Non-Federal general hospital psychiatric services

Veterans Administration psychiatric services [1]

Federally funded community mental health centers

Residential treatment centers for emotionally disturbed children

All other [2,3]

[1] Includes Veterans Administration neuropsychiatric hospitals and Veterans Administration general hospitals with separate psychiatric services.
[2] Includes other multiservice mental health organizations with inpatient and residential treatment services that are not elsewhere classified.
[3] Beginning in 1983 a definitional change sharply increased the number of multiservice mental health organizations while decreasing the number of freestanding psychiatric outpatient clinics.

probably already familiar with scientific methods in general and likely have been exposed to their uses in various areas of psychology. Certain issues and problems arise in applying these methods to understanding the nature, causes, and treatment of abnormal behavior; thus some review is appropriate before we move on. Our review will be organized around (a) direct observation of behavior, (b) sampling and generalization, (c) correlation and causation, (d) experimental strategies, (e) case studies, and (f) retrospective and prospective strategies.

◼ Observation of Behavior

Whatever we are observing—be it the overt actions of an organism, certain of its measurable internal behaviors (e.g., its physiological processes), or verbal reports about human inner processes or events —the focus of psychology is always on observing behavior. Of course, all of us observe our own overt behavior and certain of our inner events, such as thoughts and feelings. But self-observation of one's inner processes has distinct limits as a data base for psychological science, in large part because the observations are one's own, hidden from direct confirmation by anyone else. Science normally demands such confirmation by others. This constraint has been a source of considerable difficulty for the discipline of psychology throughout its history.

The **observational method** is a systematic technique by which observers are trained to watch and record behavior without bias. This technique has helped to ensure the scientific integrity of observational research, but obstacles still remain.

In the field of abnormal psychology, psychologists must inevitably make use of a subject's verbal reports or "observations" of his or her inner experience; we cannot directly observe the subject's thoughts and feelings. In most situations, a subject will be cooperative and truthful. But even assuming a sincere attitude, often a subject will be unable to make crucial observations. The determinants of behavior are many, and they operate at many levels of functioning; not all of them are within the range of a person's conscious awareness.

To make sense of observed behavior, psychologists generate **hypotheses,** more or less plausible ideas to explain something—in this case, behavior. All empirical sciences use hypotheses, although these hypotheses appear to be more closely tied to observable phenomena in the more established physical sciences. For example, the concept of electricity is actually hypothetical. Scientists have only observed the effects of this presumed entity, but these effects are extremely reliable and predictable;

One of the ways psychologists generate hypotheses about behavior and determine therapeutic approaches is through observation, a systematic technique for watching and recording behavior. Observing and making sense of behavior, however, is highly dependent on a practitioner's point of view. What one psychologist "observes" in watching a child, as in the photo here, may not be what another observes, and both may arrive at effective, if differing, treatments.

hence we believe in the real existence of electricity. Most people have less confidence in a construct such as the ego.

These considerations are particularly important in the study of abnormal behavior. For the most part, we understand the behavior of the people we meet, at least to the extent necessary to carry on ordinary social interactions. Even when we observe something unexpected in a person's behavior, we can usually empathize enough to have a sense of the factors that have contributed to the behavior. Almost by definition, however, abnormal behavior is unintelligible to the majority of persons observing it. Abnormal behavior does not seem governed by the same principles we generally understand, and our minds are therefore attracted to extraordinary explanations of it—to extraordinary hypotheses. Whether or not these hypotheses can account satisfactorily for abnormal behavior is open to question, but it is clear that we need them in order to begin to understand. Behavior never explains itself, whether it is normal or abnormal.

Several competing hypotheses exist to explain the highly complex behavior patterns we find in abnormal behavior. In fact, these hypotheses tend to cluster together in distinctive approaches or viewpoints. These general viewpoints are described in Chapter 3. For now, we wish merely to emphasize that all forms of psychological inquiry begin with observations of behavior, and that much of the subject matter of abnormal psychology is built on hypotheses that account more or less adequately for observed behavior. These hypotheses are important because they frequently determine the therapeutic approaches used to counter an abnormality. For example, suppose we are confronted with someone who washes his or her hands 60 to 100 times a day, causing serious injury to the skin and underlying tissues. If we conclude that this behavior is a result of subtle neurological damage, we would try to discover the nature of the individual's disease in the hope of administering a cure. If we view the behavior as the symbolic cleansing of sinful thoughts, we would try to unearth and address the sources of the person's excessive scrupulousness. If we regard the hand-washing "symptom" as merely the product of unfortunate conditioning or learning, we would devise a means of counterconditioning to eliminate the offending behavior. These different approaches are based on different conceptualizations of the causes of the abnormal behavior. Without such conceptualizations—if we are limited merely to observing behavior itself—we would be left with no means of grasping difficult-to-understand behavior.

■ Sampling and Generalization

Research in abnormal psychology is concerned with gaining enhanced understanding and, where possible, control of abnormal behavior. Although we can occasionally get important leads from the intensive study of a single case of a given disorder, such a strategy rarely yields enough information to allow us to reach firm conclusions. The basic difficulty with this strategy is that we cannot know whether our observations pertain to the disorder, to unrelated characteristics of the person with the disorder, to some combination of these factors, or even to characteristics of the observer. It is also possible that the particular abnormality might arise from different internal sources in different people, a circumstance that could be detected only by studying a number of people who exhibit the behavior.

For these reasons, we generally place greater reliance on research studies using groups of individuals who show roughly equivalent abnormalities of behavior. Typically, several people in such studies share one characteristic (the problematic behavior) while varying widely on others. We can then infer that anything else they have in common, such as excessively punitive parents, may be related to the behavioral abnormality—provided, of course, that the characteristic is not widely shared by people who do not have the abnormality. If the abnormality arises from different sources in different people (which might in itself be an important finding), we would probably have considerable dif-

ficulty identifying with precision the patterns underlying the abnormality. In fact, difficulties of this sort are impeding our progress in respect to several of the disorders we will consider in later chapters. For example, it seems increasingly likely that the disordered behavior known as schizophrenia has multiple patterns of causation that vary from one affected person to another.

If we wanted to research the problem of compulsive hand-washing, for example, a first step would be to determine criteria for identifying persons affected with the alleged condition. Presumably, these criteria would cover such areas as the frequency of hand-washing and the degree of impairment caused by it. We would then need to find people who fit our criteria. Obviously, we could never hope to study all of the people in the world who meet our criteria; we would use instead a technique called **sampling,** in which we would select as subjects a limited number of hand-washers who appear to be representative of the much larger group of compulsive hand-washers. From our study of this group, we would hope to generalize our findings to the larger group. To ensure validity, it is important that every person in the larger group have an equal chance of being included in the group we intend to study. Usually, we can only approximate this degree of rigor in choosing research samples.

As we have learned from the results of poorly designed public opinion polls, nonrepresentative sampling can produce erroneous conclusions about the larger group we wish to study. For example, if our research group of hand-washers did not adequately represent the socioeconomic statuses of compulsive hand-washers in general, we might attribute some characteristic to hand-washers that is in fact more true of persons in a given socioeconomic group.

Even if our study group were thoroughly representative, there would always be the possibility that our findings about, for example, the family backgrounds of our hand-washers would be similar to findings about other selected groups, or even about persons in general. If such were the case, we would have wasted our own and our subjects' time. Thus researchers use a **control group,** a sample of people who do not exhibit the disorder being studied but who are comparable in all other respects to the **criterion group,** members of which do exhibit the disorder. Typically, the control group is psychologically "normal" according to specified criteria. We can then compare the two groups in certain areas—such as reported parental punishment practices—to determine if they differ. They would in fact almost certainly differ because of chance factors, but we have powerful statistical techniques to determine whether or not such factors are truly significant. If we found, for example, that compulsive hand-washers had significantly more severe parental punishment in their backgrounds, as reported, than the "normals," we might conclude that severe parental punishment in childhood is associated with later compulsive hand-washing. This hypothesis, of course, assumes that the people in our study have reported their backgrounds accurately, a sometimes dubious assumption.

Though a dysfunctional family relationship may be a correlate of some form of abnormal behavior, this is not necessarily a causal factor because there may be many other ways of accounting for a particular mental disorder.

■ Correlation and Causation

The mere **correlation,** or association, of two or more variables can never by itself be taken as evidence of **causation,** that is, a relationship in which a preceding variable causes other variables. This is an important distinction to bear in mind, especially so in the field of abnormal psychology. Returning to our hypothetical hand-washing study, for instance, we could not legitimately conclude that severe parental punishment is a causal factor in the emergence of compulsive hand-washing among adults. There are simply too many alternative ways to account for such an association, including the possibility that hand-washers are more prone than others to exaggerate the level of punishment to which their parents subjected them.

Many studies in abnormal psychology show that two (or more) things regularly occur together, such as poverty and retarded intellectual development, or depression and reported prior stressors. Such variables may well be related to one another in some kind of causal context, but the relationship could take a variety of forms:

- Variable *a* causes variable *b* (or vice versa).
- Variable *a* and variable *b* are both caused by variable *c*.
- Variables *a* and *b* are both involved in a complex pattern of variables influencing *a* and *b* in similar ways.

Coming from a broken home, for instance, has been established as a significant correlate of many forms of abnormal behavior. Yet we cannot conclude that such families cause abnormality because many other potential causes of abnormality are statistically associated with parental separation or divorce—socioeconomic stress, marital disharmony, alcoholism in one or both parents, a move to a new neighborhood or school, the effort to adjust to a single parent's new love relationships, and so forth. Unfortunately, such complexity is the rule rather than the exception that we find when attempting to understand how abnormal behavior becomes established.

Recently developed statistical techniques (such as path analysis) that take into account how variables "predict" and are related to one another through time are frequently helpful in disentangling correlated factors. These techniques give us much greater confidence in our causal inferences. A relatively simple application of path analysis was made in a study by Mednick et al.(1978) of high-risk children. The study found that an adult outcome of schizophrenia was statistically linked with both obstetrical complications at birth and the presence of subtle autonomic nervous system impairment. Path analysis confirmed that the impact of the birth complications was dependent on the influence of the nervous system damage; in other words, obstetrical complications were involved with schizophrenia only to the extent that they were accompanied by nervous system impairment observed in childhood. This study strongly suggested a causal chain beginning with birth difficulties and leading to neurological dysfunction, which in turn increased the likelihood of schizophrenia.

However great their problems in pinning down causal relations, correlational studies can be a powerful and rich source of inference; they often suggest causal hypotheses and occasionally provide crucial data that confirm or refute these hypotheses. As a measure of their usefulness, we need only reflect on what the science of astronomy would be without correlational studies, since astronomers cannot manipulate the variables they study, such as stars and planets.

Correlational studies have been useful in many areas of abnormal psychology, but especially so in determining epidemiological patterns. Epidemiological research attempts to establish the pattern of occurrence of certain disorders (in our case, mental disorders) in different times, places, and groups of people. Where we find significant variations in the incidence or prevalence of a disorder, we ask why. In some cases, the answer will be obvious or trivial, as in the observation that the diagnosis of mental retardation increases suddenly among six-year-olds (i.e., children facing their first real intellectual challenge, in school). But in other cases, the question leads, if not to the unequivocal identification of causal factors, at least to promising avenues for investigation.

Observations that, for example, a particular disorder is highly associated with a particular causal factor but is uncorrelated with others may help us identify possible causal factors in other disorders; such observations make certain hypotheses more likely and others less so and thus maximize the efficiency with which the search for understanding continues. In the next section, we review methodological approaches that have a higher promise of exactitude than correlational studies as well as the enhanced problems and risks of actively intervening in people's lives.

■ Experimental Strategies

Scientific research is most rigorous, and its findings most reliable, when it employs the full power of the **experimental method.** In such cases, scientists control all factors, except one, that could have an effect on a variable or outcome of interest; then they actively manipulate that one factor. If the outcome of interest is observed to change as the manipulated factor is changed, the factor can be regarded as a cause of the outcome.

Unfortunately, the experimental method cannot be applied to many problems of abnormal psychology because of practical and ethical restraints. Suppose, for example, we wanted to use the experimental method to determine whether parental punitiveness causes compulsive hand-washing. But for ethical constraints, our ideal approach would be to choose at random two groups of young children for a longitudinal study (a study in which subjects are examined over an extended period of time). In one group, the children's parents would be taught to be highly punitive in their child-rearing practices; the other group of parents would be left to their own devices. We would carefully monitor the two groups of children until they reached an age considered beyond risk for the development of new cases of compulsive hand-washing. At that point, we would assess in a systematic way the prevalence of

hand-washing compulsions in the two groups, hypothesizing that the ill-treated children would have a significantly higher rate of the disorder. Such a study would be good—although logistically demanding—science, but it would of course be ethically unacceptable to treat people in this callous and destructive way.

The ethical constraints on using the experimental method to search for causes can sometimes be circumvented or reduced by employing models of abnormal behavior. Experiments of this kind are generally known as **analogue studies**—studies in which a researcher attempts to simulate the conditions under investigation. These experiments establish the causes of maladaptive behavior by (a) inducing the behavior in subhuman species or (b) inducing the behavior in humans, if the behavior is of trivial import, temporary, or reversible (for example, inducing temporary depression by having normal subjects concentrate on negative thoughts). Apart from what many would regard as undiminished ethical problems in much research of this sort, the major scientific problem is of course to establish major commonality between the contrived behavior and the real thing as it occurs "naturally." By and large, such analogue studies have failed to make convincing connections.

A case in point is the hypothesis that learned helplessness is a cause of depression in humans (Seligman, 1975). Laboratory experiments with dogs demonstrated that, when subjected to repeated experiences of painful, unpredictable, inescapable shock, these animals lost their ability to learn a simple escape routine to avoid further shock; they just sat and endured the pain. Seligman argued from this observation that human depression (which he equated with the reaction of the "helpless" dogs) is a reaction to the experience of noncontingency between one's behavior and the outcomes of that behavior—that is, to learned helplessness. There ensued a large number of learned helplessness experiments on human subjects, all attempting to induce mild and reversible depressions, with results that can only be called disappointing. Subjects often did not respond with helplessness to noncontingency situations, many of them actually showing enhanced effort (facilitation) following the frustrating experiences (see the February 1978 issue of *Journal of Abnormal Psychology*, Volume 87).

Reacting to these disappointing results, Seligman and colleagues (Abramson et al., 1978) modified the learned helplessness theory of depression. They suggested that a noncontingency experience should have a depression-inducing effect only on those persons prone to interpret failure-to-cope

Analogue studies in which generalizations are made from laboratory models to the real world may fail to make convincing connections. Results of testing—using rats, mice, dogs, or monkeys, for example, in a laboratory setting—may not hold up when extended to humans.

experiences in a negative way—specifically by attributing them to personal (internal) characteristics that are pervasive (global) and relatively permanent (stable). Of course, it could be (and indeed has been) argued that people having such negative thoughts may already be depressed, experiences of helplessness notwithstanding. In fact, the possibility that depressed feelings precede and cause such negative attitudes, rather than the other way around, continues to be a viable alternative to the modified learned helplessness theory (Carson, 1989; Cochran & Hammen, 1985; Peterson, Villanova, & Raps, 1985).

This ongoing research on learned helplessness and human depression illustrates the hazards involved in generalizing from laboratory models to the real world. As is often the case, the learned helplessness analogue generated much research and thereby clarified certain aspects of an important psychopathological problem. For example, further research showed that mere noncontingency is not a cause of depression in otherwise "normal" persons; that people react differently than dogs; and that helplessness may be an effect rather than a cause of depression. To that extent, it has been a productive venture. At the same time, like many other analogue models in the field, it has proven to be flawed and even misleading.

If the role of the experimental method in establishing the causes of abnormal behavior must necessarily be a limited one, no such restriction applies to its role in the evaluation of treatment approaches. On the contrary, the sophisticated use of experimental techniques in determining the efficacy of different therapies for a given disorder remains an indispensable tool.

It is a relatively simple and straightforward matter to set up a study in which a treatment is given to a designated group of patients and withheld from a similar group of patients. Should the former group show significantly more improvement than the latter, we can have confidence in the treatment's effectiveness. Of course, special techniques must often be employed in such treatment research to ensure that the two groups are in fact comparable in every respect. Once a treatment has proved effective, it can subsequently be employed for members of the original control group, leading to improved functioning for everyone. When this *waiting list control group* strategy is deemed inadvisable, as it sometimes is for ethical and other reasons (Imber et al., 1986), a research design may call for a comparison of two or more treatments in different equivalent groups. Such comparative outcome research has much to recommend it (VandenBos, 1986) and is being utilized increasingly.

Fortunately, we have made great progress in the statistical control of variables that do not yield readily to the classic form of experimental control. Statistical controls, in effect, allow us to adjust for otherwise uncontrolled variables. For example, the incidence of certain mental disorders appears to vary with socioeconomic status. Using statistical controls, we can "correct" our results for any differences in socioeconomic status existing between our experimental and control groups. The same effect could be achieved by experimental control if we could ensure that socioeconomic statuses in our control group existed in exactly the same proportions as those in the pathological group we wish to study, but such a proportional distribution might be difficult to achieve. An additional problem could create difficulty. If we insist that socioeconomic statuses in our control group exactly mirror those in the experimental group rather than those in the general population, then our control group may no longer be representative of the general population.

■ Clinical Case Studies

Despite the growing use of experimental methods, most instances of a given disorder are still studied individually, using the traditional clinical case study method. A **case study** is an in-depth examination of an individual or family that draws from a number of data sources, including interviews and psychological testing. The clinical investigator, who is usually also a patient's therapist, intensively observes an individual's behavior and marshals background facts that may be pertinent when attempting to formulate the case. A case study includes a set of hypotheses about what is causing the problem and a guide to treatment planning. These hypotheses and therapies may be revised as necessary based on a patient's response to treatment interventions. This strategy is sometimes called an *N=1 experiment,* especially when the precise relationships between treatment interventions and patient responses are systematically monitored. While much can be learned when skilled clinicians use the case study method, the information thus acquired can also be seriously flawed, especially if one seeks to apply it to other cases involving an apparently similar abnormality. When there is only one observer, and when the observations are made in a relatively uncontrolled context, there is a distinct possibility that erroneous conclusions will be drawn.

Retrospective Versus Prospective Strategies

In one of the most important developments in recent years, the more or less standard **retrospective research** (research that looks backward from the present) has been supplemented by **prospective research** that focuses, before the fact, on individuals who have a higher-than-average likelihood of becoming psychologically disordered. As we saw in our example of compulsive hand-washers, there are certain difficulties in attempting to reconstruct the pasts of people already experiencing a disorder; it is hard to disentangle the effects of the present disorder from the effects of past events and to trace a clear cause-and-effect relationship. Nevertheless, this has been the standard method of causal investigation: we observe the behavioral abnormality and then comb the backgrounds of afflicted individuals for commonalities that might have caused it. Apart from the fact that a disordered person may not be the most accurate or objective source of information, such a strategy invites investigators to discover what they expect to discover about the background factors theoretically linked to a disorder. One way around these difficulties is to utilize documents and records dated before the emergence of the disorder. While this strategy has on occasion been productively employed, it obviously depends on the accidental availability of the precise information needed.

We can have much more confidence in our causal hypotheses when they look ahead instead of backward and when they correctly predict the individuals in a group who will develop a particular form of disordered behavior—or, alternatively, which of two groups will prove to have been at risk. It is logistically difficult, of course, to follow various unselected groups from childhood into adulthood in the numbers required to produce a suitable "yield" of various adult disorders. Hence, in a typical instance, children sharing a risk factor known to be associated with relatively high rates of subsequent breakdown are studied over the course of years. Those who do break down are compared with those who do not in the hope that crucial differentiating factors will be discovered. The method is not without certain difficulties, however, including uncertainties about what constitutes risk and how the selected risk factor may interact with other factors. In addition, prospective studies have so far failed to produce striking and unequivocal results. Despite these reservations, the very invention of the method and its widespread deployment in many long-term, ongoing research projects is probably indicative of a genuine maturing of the field (Garmezy, 1978c). Serious researchers in abnormal behavior are aware of the magnitude of the challenges facing them, and as a group they are no longer confident that easy answers are lying about ready to be discovered by an enterprising but impatient investigator. Such a high level of confidence was never justified in the first place, in that it seriously underestimated the complex nature of human behavior.

THE ORIENTATION OF THIS BOOK

Psychology is an unusual science in that the human mind is both the agent and the object of study. The difficulty is one of reflexivity: in our study we are using the very instrument—the mind—that we hope to understand. Keeping a proper perspective in such a situation is and will continue to be problematic. Can we fashion an approach to abnormal behavior that is scientific and humanistic in the best senses of both of these terms? This book is an attempt in that direction, but the course is to a large extent uncertain and uncharted.

In this text we will study abnormal behavior and its place in contemporary society. Although we will deal with all the major categories of mental disorders, we will focus on those patterns that seem most relevant to a broad, basic understanding of maladaptive behavior. While we will not hesitate to include the unusual or bizarre, our emphasis will be on the unity of human behavior, ranging from normal to abnormal.

Throughout this text we assume that a sound and comprehensive study of abnormal behavior should be based on the following concepts:

1. *A scientific approach to abnormal behavior.* Any comprehensive view of human behavior must draw upon concepts and research findings from a variety of scientific fields. Of particular relevance are genetics, biochemistry, neurophysiology, sociology, anthropology, and of course psychology. Common scientific concepts, such as causal processes, control groups, dependent variables, placebos, and theories, will figure in our discussion. Special emphasis will be placed on the application of learning principles to the understanding and treatment of mental disorders.

In this general context, you are encouraged to take a critical and evaluative attitude toward the research findings presented in this text and in other sources. When properly conducted, scientific research provides us with information that has a high probability of being accurate, but many research findings are subject to bias and open to serious questions. We must appreciate as well the special problems involved when we attempt to turn the light of scientific inquiry on ourselves. While science may not have all the answers, it is also true that we have not yet pushed science to its limits. The problems we face in moving toward the twenty-first century are too important to afford ourselves the luxury of ignorance and uncritical analysis.

2. *An awareness of our common human concerns.* Science cannot touch on many of the experiences and problems common to human existence. Insights into hope, faith, courage, love, grief, despair, death, and the quest for values and meaning are not obtainable in a laboratory. Rather, we must turn to literature, drama, autobiographical accounts, and even art, history, and religion to seek a greater understanding of these aspects of human psychological functioning. Although these sources of insight strike a common chord in all of us, it is important to distinguish the information gained through them from the information obtained through scientific observation.

3. *Respect for the dignity, integrity, and growth potential of the individual.* A basic orientation of this book is described well in the opening statement of the *Ethical Principles of Psychologists,* formulated by the American Psychological Association: "Psychologists respect the dignity and worth of the individual and strive for the preservation and protection of fundamental human rights" (1990, p. 390). Implicit in this statement is a view of individuals not merely as products of their past conditioning and present situation, but as potentially active agents as well—people who can develop and use

their capacities for building the kind of life they choose and a better world for humankind.

In attempting to provide a perspective on abnormal behavior, we will focus not only on how maladaptive patterns are perceived by clinical psychologists and other mental health personnel, but also on how such disorders feel to and are perceived by the individuals experiencing them. In dealing with the major patterns of abnormal behavior, we will focus on four significant aspects of each: the *clinical picture, causal factors, treatments,* and *outcomes.* In each case, we will examine the evidence for *biological, psychosocial* (psychological and interpersonal), and *sociocultural* factors.

Since this is a psychology book, much of our focus will be on the psychosocial factors involved in abnormal behavior. This focus is apt as well because it is the psychosocial area that presents especially challenging adaptational problems for the future. We are less well equipped for rapid advance in this area than in the biomedical arena, which continues to develop at a rate more equal to that of the culture generally. Yet even in respect to our physical health, there are increasing signs that ultimate solutions will depend on a far greater sophistication about ourselves as psychosocial as opposed to biological entities. The advances in biomedicine to which we have become accustomed are not likely to bail us out—at least not in the foreseeable future. For example, it is not presently conceivable that a prescription medication or a brain operation might be fashioned that will convert a person lacking in both cognitive and social skills into one capable of effortlessly negotiating the complexities of modern life.

Most of this book will be devoted to a presentation of well-established patterns of abnormal behavior and to special problem behaviors of our time that are more controversial but directly relevant. Initially, however, we will trace the development of contemporary views of abnormal behavior from early beliefs and practices, outline several attempts to explain what makes human beings "tick," and review the general causes of abnormal behavior in modern life.

Later, after a series of chapters on various problem behaviors, we will devote four chapters to modern methods of assessment and treatment. These chapters will include a discussion of the potential of modern psychology and allied sciences for preventing mental disorders and for helping humankind achieve a more sane and harmonious world.

At the close of his journeys, Tennyson's Ulysses says, "I am part of all that I have met." It is the authors' hope that, at the end of your journey through this book, you will have a better understanding of human experience and behavior—and that you will consider what you have learned to be a meaningful part of your own life experience.

UNRESOLVED ISSUES
on Classification

Of the several sources of potential confusion facing a student of abnormal psychology, none is likely to be more perplexing or fundamental than the manner in which abnormal behavior is segmented into various types. It will be of some comfort, we hope, to know that even the "experts" differ in the value they place on the current diagnostic classification scheme—the categories of DSM-III-R and what promise to be the quite similar ones of DSM-IV (Carson, in press-b; Widiger et al., in press).

Unfortunately, both reliability and validity have proven extraordinarily difficult to achieve in the classifications used in abnormal psychology. This is due in no small part to the enormous complexity of human behavior. But it is also due, according to some observers, to our having chosen an inadequate model for describing behavioral abnormalities. This model is essentially a medical or disease metaphor for conceptualizing abnormal behavior. By this we mean that abnormal behavior has been viewed as the outward manifestation of a corresponding type of illness or disease. But is it? While we are not troubled by the notion of a diseased brain, what possible meaning, on close examination, can we assign to the concept of a diseased mind? They are not, after all, the same thing.

Despite the fact that every genuine human disease shows a certain level of individual variation, it also has at its core a fundamental and invariant pathophysiology that can be described with increasing precision with advances in biomedical knowledge. Thus we know that the pain associated with the coronary heart disease known as angina is produced by an insufficient oxygen supply to the heart muscle, due to blocked coronary arteries. Armed with this knowledge, we can discriminate between two or more diseases even when their surface characteristics may share certain similarities —for example, between angina and indigestion.

To use another example, a fever of 101 degrees tells us that something is wrong with a physical organism, perhaps a flu infection; a fever of 104 degrees tells us that something is *very* wrong, such

as pneumonia. A physician is usually able, by using various diagnostic signs and perhaps laboratory findings, to pinpoint with great accuracy the nature of the underlying pathophysiology.

Personal despondency at the level of a diagnosable mental depression also tells us that something is wrong, and in severe cases that something is *very* wrong. But what? Generally, we would be right in concluding that something has gone awry in the person's self-perceived ability to cope with some life dilemma. Consistent with this observation is the fact that serious depressive feelings often complicate many other forms of disorder, both mental and physical. Beyond that, however, the situation is notably clouded; despite occasional claims to the contrary, we have no laboratory test to give us a more reliable answer, nor is it obvious that a more precise answer is possible. From this perspective, one depression is pretty much like any other, except for minor variations in expression and, like fever, in severity. The DSM-III-R, however, specifies several separate categories of depression, largely based on surface characteristics—despite the fact that there is little convincing evidence of fundamental differences among them, apart from severity. (The severity dimension, incidentally, also has no obvious breaks, or discontinuities.) We know of no one who seriously suggests that it would be useful to designate fever to be itself a separate disease, or to try to discriminate among qualitatively different kinds of fever, yet this is what the DSM does with depression.

As the example of depression illustrates, the DSM attempts to treat mental disorder as consisting of a variety of discrete (discontinuous) categories. Implicit in this approach is the idea that each of the

DSM-III-R treats depression as consisting of a variety of discrete types, even though the evidence to support this view still eludes us. The question of whether efforts to differentiate disorders in this way are meaningful is an unresolved issue in the field of abnormal psychology.

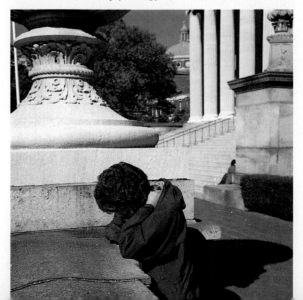

categories has a unique underlying core and a definable boundary separating it from other categories, as in the case of true diseases (Millon, in press). The fact that we cannot identify the features of the core except by uncertain inference from surface characteristics is attributed to a temporary lack of knowledge, a lack that supposedly will be overcome by future research. Meanwhile, the exact boundary of each category will remain uncertain and will have to be approximated by somewhat arbitrary rules to achieve a satisfactory separation from other categories.

There is considerable disagreement and doubt about the possibility of our ever finding such a precisely definable and constant array of causal factors at the core of each mental disorder included in the DSM classification. The only exceptions may be those relatively few disorders that are in fact related to brain diseases, the so-called organic mental disorders. Thus, lacking a constant core for each purported disorder, it becomes difficult to know if our efforts to differentiate one sort of disorder from another are in fact correct or even meaningful.

As noted by Widiger and Frances (1985a), there appear to be three basic approaches currently possible to classify abnormal behavior: the categorical, the dimensional, and the prototypal. A **categorical approach,** as we have seen, assumes that (a) all human behavior can be sharply divided into the categories *normal* and *abnormal,* and (b) there exist discrete, non-overlapping classes or types of abnormal behavior, often referred to as "mental" illnesses or diseases. The categorical approach bears a close affinity to the identification of diagnosable physical illnesses such as pneumonia, coronary thrombosis, diabetes, and so on. As already suggested, some professionals believe that this approach is inappropriate for most types of mental disorder, which do not seem to be discrete. It is, however, the one officially used.

The dimensional and prototypal approaches differ fundamentally in the assumptions they make, particularly in respect to the requirement of discrete classes of behavior. In a **dimensional approach,** it is assumed that a person's typical behavior is the product of differing strengths or intensities of behavior along several definable dimensions, such as mood, emotional stability, aggressiveness, gender identity, anxiousness, interpersonal trust, clarity of thinking and communication, social introversion, and so on. The important dimensions, once established, would be the same for everyone. In this conception, people differ from one another in their configuration or profile of these dimensional traits (each ranging from very low to very high), not in terms of surface indications of some presumed "illness." Normal could be discriminated from

abnormal, then, by precise statistical criteria applied to dimensional intensities. Returning to our example of depression, a person's level of depression would probably need to be included as one of the basic trait measures in any serious attempt to use a dimensional strategy for organizing abnormal behavior and for "diagnosing" individual disorders.

DSM-III-R Axes IV and V are examples of dimensional scales. These axes, however, are not directed to the definition of types of disorders, but rather to certain qualifying features of disorders as diagnosed.

Of course, in taking a dimensional approach it would be possible—perhaps even likely—to discover that such profiles tend to cluster together in types, and even that some of these types are correlated, though imperfectly, with recognizable sorts of gross behavioral malfunctions, such as anxiety disorders or depression. It is highly unlikely, however, that any individual's profile would exactly fit a narrowly defined type, or that the types identified will not have some overlapping features. This brings us to the matter of a prototypal approach.

A *prototype* (as the term is used here) is a conceptual entity depicting an idealized combination of characteristics, ones that more or less regularly occur together in a less perfect or standard way at the level of empirical reality. Prototypes are actually an aspect of our everyday thinking and experience; we can all generate in our mind's eye a prototypal apple, while recognizing that we have never seen nor ever will see two identical apples. Thus no item in a prototypally defined group may actually have all of the characteristics of the defining prototype, although it will have many of the more central of them. It is also possible that a certain item may be an exemplar, in part at least, of more than one prototype within a given domain. A dog whose parents are, let us say, a purebred collie and a purebred golden retriever will show both prototypal organizations in its appearance. Unlike the often forced categorical separations of the DSM-III-R, prototypes are not mutually exclusive. A given prototype may blend into another with which it shares many characteristics—perhaps especially its more peripheral ones, such as redness in apples.

Some psychologists believe that by adopting a **prototypal approach** we could wed some of the advantages of the categorical and the dimensional approaches while avoiding the disadvantages of each (the dimensional approach, for example, is cumbersome and inconvenient for routine clinical use). Use of such a "hybrid" (Millon, in press) approach implies, however, that we should expect to find few if any pure exemplars of diagnostic groupings, as well as much blurring of the boundaries between them. This, of course, would make communication for researchers and clinicians more difficult. For advocates of a prototypal approach, however, this drawback is necessary to attain more validity and a classification system that better represents what mental disorder really involves.

There is reason to believe in fact that the more recent versions of the DSM, including the projected DSM-IV, *have* moved closer to a prototypal model without explicitly acknowledging this to be the case (Carson, in press). In the DSM-III-R, for example, multiple diagnoses within Axes I and II are not only permitted, but encouraged.

Though many psychologists have reservations about the prevailing classificatory and diagnostic procedures, most do not recommend that these procedures be summarily abandoned or ignored. While far from ideal, they constitute the standard language of the field for both formal (especially research-based) and informal communication. Familiarity with the system in use is thus vital for the serious student. We hope, however, that this discussion has given you a more sophisticated perspective on the classificatory issues facing the field.

▌SUMMARY

In our contemporary culture, people constantly face a bewildering assortment of challenges and pressures, many of which may stymie their efforts to live happy, fulfilling, and purposeful lives. Psychologists are ethically committed to helping people succeed in these efforts, but psychologists too must face certain obstacles, in particular those beliefs and preconceptions that impede progress in their understanding of mental disorder, its prevention, and its proper treatment.

Students beginning serious study of abnormal psychology are likely to hold preconceptions about the field that are widely shared by others. In part, this is due to certain popular images of mental disorders that have persisted over time, but it is also due to the great attention that the media has focused on the subject in recent years and to the willingness of mental health professionals to supply offhand accounts of behavior disorders and their treatment. Much of this exposure has accurately depicted limited aspects of the field, but some of it has distorted other aspects, causing widespread misconceptions about mental disorders and the people who suffer from them.

The most certain way to avoid misconception and error is to adopt a scientific attitude and approach to the study of abnormal behavior. This involves, among other things, the habit of suspending judgment until pertinent facts are known, the employment of objective and reliable methods of observation, and the development of a valid system for classifying the phenomena being studied. Progress has been made in all these areas, but abnormal psychology continues to be a complex and challenging field. Much work remains to be done, even in so basic an area as classification. We still lack even a universally accepted definition of abnormality, although we, the authors, argue for one that emphasizes outcomes of behavior in terms of the good that is accomplished for an individual or a group.

A scientific approach to abnormal behavior also involves a focus on research and research methods, including an appreciation of the distinction between what is observable and what is hypothetical, or inferred. Much of the content of abnormal psychology falls into the latter category. Research on abnormal conditions, if it is to produce valid results, must be done on people who are truly representative of the pathological groups to which they purportedly belong—a requirement that is often difficult to satisfy. We must also remain alert to the fact that mere correlation does not establish a causal relationship between the variables in question. Researchers use experimental methods and prospective research designs to resolve questions of causality, but these approaches are not always appropriate and may not always be effective. The individual case study method, despite its weaknesses, remains a frequently used investigative technique.

Science, of course, does not have all the answers. Any approach to the field must also recognize the significance of more simply human concerns, such as the feelings of despair or of hope that are such crucial elements in the total picture of normal and abnormal functioning.

▌Key Terms

abnormal behavior (p. 8)
abnormal psychology (p. 8)
psychopathology (p. 8)
clinical psychology (p. 8)
psychiatry (p. 8)
social work (p. 8)
clinical picture (p. 9)
reliability (p. 9)
validity (p. 9)
DSM-III-R (p. 10)
functional psychoses (p. 11)
acute (p. 11)
chronic (p. 11)
mild (p. 11)
moderate (p. 11)
severe (p. 11)
episodic (p. 11)
epidemiology (p. 15)

prevalence (p. 15)
incidence (p. 15)
observational method (p. 18)
hypotheses (p. 18)
sampling (p. 19)
control group (p. 19)
criterion group (p. 19)
correlation (p. 20)
causation (p. 20)
experimental method (p. 21)
analogue studies (p. 21)
case study (p. 22)
retrospective research (p. 23)
prospective research (p. 23)
categorical approach (p. 26)
dimensional approach (p. 26)
prototypal approach (p. 26)

Chapter 2
Historical Views of Abnormal Behavior

Baya, *Village au Palmier* (1950?). Baya (b. 1931) was born to a family in the Kabyle tribal group near the north African city of Algiers. Orphaned at the age of 5, she was taken to live in the city proper, where she began to paint and sculpt for her own amusement. In 1950 she married into a traditional Algerian family and immediately ceased her creative efforts. In 1963 a retrospective of her work at the national museum in Algiers induced Baya to begin painting again, but the pieces done since that time have been clearly influenced by popular Algerian art and so cannot be properly considered "Art Brut."

The history of our efforts to understand abnormal behavior is a fascinating one. Certainly, many of our misconceptions about mental disorders have their roots in the past, but it is equally true that many modern scientific concepts and treatments have their counterparts in approaches tried long ago. For example, free association—a technique used in twentieth-century psychoanalytic therapy to allow repressed conflicts and emotions to enter conscious awareness—is described by the Greek playwright Aristophanes in his play *The Clouds* (423 B.C.). Interestingly enough, the scene in which Socrates tries to calm and bring self-knowledge to Strepsiades is complete with a couch. Nineteenth-century psychiatrists attempted to use electricity to cure mental disorders almost a century before electroconvulsive therapy became an accepted form of biologically based treatment. (See Chapter 17 for more on early electrical stimulation instruments.)

In this chapter, we will trace the evolution of popular views and treatments of psychopathology from ancient times to the twentieth century. In a broad sense, we will see an evolution from beliefs we view today as superstition to those based on scientific awareness—from a focus on supernatural causes to a knowledge of natural causes. The course of this evolution has not been a steady movement forward; on the contrary, it has often been marked by brief periods of great advancement or unique individual contributions followed by long years of inactivity or unproductive backward surges. (A summary of many of the people we will discuss and their contributions appears later in this chapter.)

As we will see, current views of abnormal behavior have been shaped by the prevailing attitudes of past times and the advances of science. Each has contributed to the growth—and often the stagnation—of the other. For example, during certain periods in ancient Greece, the body was considered sacred. Researchers were thus prevented from performing human autopsies, which did little to advance understanding of human anatomy or biological processes. Much later, during the nineteenth and early twentieth centuries, the belief that a biological (medical) solution was needed to cure mental disorders thwarted investigation into psychological causes. Even today, with the renewed emphasis upon biological causes and treatments, the focus on psychological causation and treatment is sometimes undervalued.

The advances in understanding and treatment of abnormal behavior become all the more remarkable when viewed against a persistent resurfacing of ignorance, superstition, and fear. And if we think that we have today arrived at a knowledgeable and humane approach to treating the mentally ill, we should think again. We are still bound by many culturally conditioned constraints; for many, attitudes toward people who are different are still formed, at least in part, by superstition and fear.

ABNORMAL BEHAVIOR IN ANCIENT TIMES

Although human life presumably appeared on earth some 3 million or more years ago, written records extend back only a few thousand years. Thus our knowledge of our early ancestors is limited.

The earliest known treatment of abnormal behavior was that practiced by Stone Age cave dwellers some half-million years ago. For certain forms of mental disorders, probably those in which an individual complained of severe headaches and experienced convulsive attacks, a shaman (medicine man) appears to have treated the disorder by means of an operation that later came to be called **trephining.** This operation was performed with stone instruments and consisted of chipping away a circular area of the skull until it was cut through. The opening, called a trephine, presumably allowed the evil spirit that was causing the trouble to escape. In some cases, trephined skulls of primitive people show

Stone Age cave dwellers used a technique called trephination to treat mental disorders. With a stone instrument, a medicine man would produce a hole in the skull of a patient, allowing the "evil spirits" causing the disturbance to be driven out.

signs of healing, indicating that the patient survived the operation and lived for many years afterward (Selling, 1943).

Two Egyptian papyri dating from the sixteenth century B.C. have provided some of the earliest written evidence of the treatment of diseases and behavior disorders. The Edwin Smith papyrus (named after its nineteenth-century discoverer) contains detailed descriptions of the treatment of wounds and other surgical operations. In it, the brain is described—possibly for the first time in history—and the writing clearly shows that the brain was recognized as the site of mental functions. We may think this remarkable for the sixteenth century B.C.; it becomes even more remarkable once we realize that this papyrus is believed to be a copy of an earlier work from about 3000 B.C. The Ebers papyrus provides another perspective on treatment. It covers internal medicine and the circulatory system but relies more on incantations and magic for explaining and curing diseases that had unknown causes. Although surgical techniques may have been used, they were probably coupled with prayers and the like that reflected the prevailing view of the origin of behavior disorders, to which we now turn.

▪ Demonology, Gods, and Magic

References to abnormal behavior in the early writings of the Chinese, Egyptians, Hebrews, and Greeks show that they generally attributed such behavior to a demon or god who had taken possession of an individual. This belief is not surprising if we remember that "good" and "bad" spirits were widely used to explain lightning, thunder, earthquakes, storms, fires, sickness, and many other events that otherwise seemed incomprehensible. It was a simple and logical step to extend this theory to peculiar and incomprehensible behavior as well.

The decision as to whether the "possession" involved good spirits or evil spirits usually depended on an individual's symptoms. If a person's speech or behavior appeared to have a religious or mystical significance, it was usually thought that he or she was possessed by a good spirit or god. Such individuals were often treated with considerable awe and respect, for it was thought that they had supernatural powers.

Most possessions, however, were considered to be the work of an angry god or an evil spirit, particularly when an individual became excited or overactive and engaged in behavior contrary to religious teachings. Among the ancient Hebrews, for example, such possessions were thought to

Exorcism as a treatment for mental illness still has appeal today, not only in fictionalized accounts, but even in practice. Amid much controversy, an exorcism performed on a 16-year-old emotionally disturbed girl, known as Gina, was recently shown on the television program "20/20." Gina can be seen here, being restrained, and having a cross pressed to her cheek during the exorcism. The state of her mental health after the exorcism is not known. This televised ritual underscored the deep-seated and powerful belief in demonology, even in contemporary society.

represent the wrath and punishment of God. Moses is quoted in the Bible as saying, "The Lord shall smite thee with madness." Apparently this punishment was thought to involve the withdrawal of God's protection and the abandonment of the individual to the forces of evil. In such cases, every effort was made to rid the person of the evil spirit. Jesus reportedly cured a man with an "unclean spirit" by transferring the devils that plagued him to a herd of swine who, in turn, became possessed and "ran violently down a steep place into the sea" (Mark 5:1–13).

The primary type of treatment for demonic possession was **exorcism,** which included various techniques for casting an evil spirit out of an afflicted person. These techniques varied considerably but typically included magic, prayer, incantation, noisemaking, and the use of various horrible-tasting concoctions, such as purgatives made from sheep's dung and wine. More severe measures, such as starving or flogging, were sometimes used in extreme cases to make the body of a possessed person such an unpleasant place that an evil spirit would be driven out. We will look more closely at exorcism as the treatment of choice in the Middle Ages later in this chapter. The continuing popularity of movies and books on possession and exorcism suggests that these primitive ideas still have appeal today.

The task of exorcising was originally in the hands of shamans, but was eventually taken over in Egypt and Greece by priests, who apparently served as holy people, physicians, psychologists, and magicians. Many of their cures remained based in magical rites. Although these priests typically believed in demonology and used established exorcistic prac-

tices, many of them began to treat people with mental disturbances in a more humane way. For example, in the temples of the god Asclepius in ancient Greece, the priests had patients sleep in the temple. Supposedly, the dreams they had there would reveal what they needed to do to get better. The priests supplemented prayer and incantation with kindness, suggestion, and recreational measures, such as plays, riding, walking, and harmonious music.

■ Early Philosophical and Medical Concepts

The Greek temples of healing ushered in the Golden Age of Greece under the Athenian leader Pericles (461–429 B.C.). During this time, considerable progress was made in the understanding and treatment of mental disorders. Interestingly, this progress was made in spite of the fact that Greeks of this time considered the human body sacred and thus little could be learned of human anatomy or physiology. During this period the Greek physician Hippocrates (460–377 B.C.), often referred to as the father of modern medicine, received his training and made substantial contributions to the field.

Hippocrates   Hippocrates denied that deities and demons intervened in the development of illnesses and insisted that mental disorders had natural causes and required treatments like other diseases. His position was unequivocal: "'For my own part, I do not believe that the human body is ever befouled by a God'" (in Lewis, 1941, p. 37). Hippocrates believed that the brain was the central organ of intellectual activity and that mental disor-

Hippocrates' (460–377 B.C.) belief that mental disease was the result of natural causes and brain pathology was revolutionary for its time.

ders were due to brain pathology. He also emphasized the importance of heredity and predisposition and pointed out that injuries to the head could cause sensory and motor disorders.

Hippocrates classified all mental disorders into three general categories—mania, melancholia, and phrentis (brain fever)—and gave detailed clinical descriptions of the specific disorders included in each category. He relied heavily on clinical observation, and his descriptions, which were based on daily clinical records of his patients, were surprisingly thorough. Hippocrates considered dreams to be important in understanding a patient's personality. On this point, he not only elaborated on the thinking set forth by the priests in the temples of Asclepius, but also was a harbinger of a basic concept of modern psychodynamic psychotherapy.

The treatments advocated by Hippocrates were far in advance of the exorcistic practices then prevalent. For the treatment of melancholia, for example, he prescribed a regular and tranquil life, sobriety and abstinence from all excesses, a vegetable diet, celibacy, exercise short of fatigue, and bleeding if indicated. He also believed in the importance of the environment and often removed his patients from their families.

Hippocrates' emphasis on the natural causes of diseases, clinical observation, and brain pathology as the root of mental disorders was truly revolutionary. Like his contemporaries, however, Hippocrates had little knowledge of physiology and could still be far from the truth. He wrongly believed that hysteria (the appearance of physical illness in the absence of organic pathology) was restricted to women and was caused by the uterus wandering to various parts of the body, pining for children. For this "disease," Hippocrates recommended marriage as the best remedy. He also wrongly believed in the existence of four bodily fluids or *humors*—blood, black bile, yellow bile, and phlegm. In his work *On Sacred Disease,* he stated that when the humors were adversely mixed or otherwise disturbed, physical or mental disease resulted: " 'Depravement of the brain arises from phlegm and bile; those made from phlegm are quiet, depressed and oblivious; those from bile excited, noisy and mischievous' " (in Lewis, 1941, p. 37). Although the concept of humors went far beyond demonology, it was too crude physiologically to be of much therapeutic value. Yet in its emphasis on the importance of bodily balances to mental health, it may be seen as a precursor of today's focus on the need for biochemical balances to maintain normal brain functioning and good health.

Plato and Aristotle   The problem of dealing with mentally disturbed individuals who have committed criminal acts was studied by the Greek philosopher Plato (429–347 B.C.). He wrote that such persons were in some "obvious" sense not responsible for their acts and should not receive punishment in the same way as normal persons: ". . . someone may commit an act when mad or afflicted with disease. . . . [If so,] let him pay simply for the damage; and let him be exempt from other punishment." Plato also made provision for mental cases to be cared for in the community as follows: "If anyone is insane, let him not be seen openly in the city, but let the relatives of such a person watch over him in the best manner they know of; and if they are negligent, let them pay a fine . . ." (Plato, n.d., p. 56). In making these humane suggestions, Plato was addressing issues with which we are still grappling today—for example, the issue of *insanity* as a legal defense. **Insanity** is a legal term for mental disorder that implies a lack of understanding as required by law and therefore a lack of responsibility for one's acts and an inability to manage one's affairs. Even today the question of whether an individual's mental condition at the time of a crime is relevant to a legal defense is widely debated (we will return to this issue in Chapter 19).

In addition to his emphasis on the humane treatment of the mentally disturbed, Plato contributed to a better understanding of human behavior by pointing out that all forms of life, human included, were motivated by physiological needs, or "natural appetites." He viewed psychological phenomena as responses of the whole organism, reflecting its internal state. He also seems to have anticipated Freud's insight into the functions of fantasies and dreams as substitute satisfactions; he concluded that in dreams, a person could satisfy desires through imagery because the higher faculties no longer inhibited the "passions." In his *Republic,* Plato emphasized the importance of individual differences in intellectual and other abilities, pointing to the role of sociocultural influences in shaping thinking and behavior. He also included a provision for "hospital" care for individuals who developed beliefs that were contrary to the broader social order. These antagonistic individuals would be removed and housed separately so that their minds could be altered. These individuals would have periodic conversations analogous to psychotherapy to promote the health of their souls (Milns, 1986). Despite these modern ideas, however, Plato shared the belief of his time that mental disorders were in part divinely caused.

The celebrated Greek philosopher Aristotle (384–322 B.C.), who was a pupil of Plato, wrote extensively on mental disorders. Among his most lasting contributions to psychology are his descriptions of consciousness. He, too, anticipated Freud in his view of "thinking" as directed striving toward the elimination of pain and the attainment of pleasure. On the question of whether mental disorders could be caused by psychological factors such as frustration and conflict, Aristotle discussed the possibility and rejected it; his lead on this issue was widely followed. Aristotle generally believed the Hippocratic theory of disturbances in the bile. For example, he thought that very hot bile generated amorous desires, loquacity, and suicidal impulses.

Later Greek and Roman Thought   Hippocrates' work was continued by some of the later Greek and Roman physicians. Particularly in Alexandria, Egypt (which became a center of Greek culture after its founding in 332 B.C. by Alexander the Great), medical practices developed to a high level, and the temples dedicated to Saturn were first-rate sanatoriums. Pleasant surroundings were considered of great therapeutic value for mental patients, who were provided with constant activities, including parties, dances, walks in the temple gardens, rowing along the Nile, and musical concerts. Physicians of this time also used a wide range of therapeutic measures, including dieting, massage, hydrotherapy, gymnastics, and education, as well as some less desirable practices, such as bleeding, purging, and mechanical restraints.

One of the most influential Greek physicians was Galen (A.D. 130–200), who practiced in Rome. Although he elaborated on the Hippocratic tradition, he did not contribute much that was new to the treatment or clinical descriptions of mental disorders. Rather, he made a number of original contributions concerning the anatomy of the nervous system. (These findings were based on dissections of animals; human autopsies were still not allowed.) Galen also maintained a scientific approach to the field, dividing the causes of psychological disorders into physical and mental categories. Among the causes he named were injuries to the head, alcoholic excess, shock, fear, adolescence, menstrual changes, economic reverses, and disappointment in love.

Roman medicine reflected the characteristic pragmatism of the Roman people. Roman physi-

Galen (A.D. 130–200) believed that psychological disorders could have either physical causes, such as injuries to the head, or mental causes, such as disappointment in love.

cians wanted to make their patients comfortable and thus used pleasant physical therapies, such as warm baths and massage. They also followed the principle of *contrariis contrarius* (opposite by opposite)—for example, having their patients drink chilled wine while they were in a warm tub.

Although historians generally consider the fall of Rome at the end of the fifth century to be the dividing line between ancient and medieval times, the "Dark Ages" in the history of abnormal psychology began much earlier, with Galen's death in A.D. 200. The contributions of Hippocrates and the later Greek and Roman physicians were soon lost in the welter of popular superstition, and though some exceptions can be found, most of the physicians of Rome returned to some sort of belief in demonology as an underlying factor in abnormal behavior.

■ Views During the Middle Ages

In Islamic countries during medieval times, the more scientific aspects of Greek medicine survived. The first mental hospital was established in Baghdad in A.D. 792; it was soon followed by others in Damascus and Aleppo (Polvan, 1969). In these hospitals, the mentally disturbed received humane treatment. The outstanding figure in Islamic medicine was Avicenna (c. A.D. 980–1037), called the

"prince of physicians" (Campbell, 1926) and author of *The Canon of Medicine,* perhaps the most widely studied medical work ever written. In his writings, Avicenna frequently referred to hysteria, epilepsy, manic reactions, and melancholia. The following story shows his unique approach to the treatment of a young prince suffering from a mental disorder:

A certain prince was afflicted with melancholia, and suffered from the delusion that he was a cow . . . he would low like a cow, causing annoyance to everyone, . . . crying "Kill me so that a good stew may be made of my flesh," finally . . . he would eat nothing. . . . Avicenna was persuaded to take the case. . . . First of all he sent a message to the patient bidding him be of good cheer because the butcher was coming to slaughter him, whereat . . . the sick man rejoiced. Some time afterwards Avicenna, holding a knife in his hand, entered the sickroom saying, "Where is this cow that I may kill it?" The patient lowed like a cow to indicate where he was. By Avicenna's orders he was laid on the ground bound hand and foot. Avicenna then felt him all over and said, "He is too lean, and not ready to be killed; he must be fattened." Then they offered him suitable food of which he now partook eagerly, and gradually he gained strength, got rid of his delusion, and was completely cured. (Browne, 1921, pp. 88–89)

Unfortunately, most Western medical practitioners of Avicenna's time dealt with mental patients in a far different way. The advances made by the thinkers of antiquity had little impact on the ways most people approached abnormal behavior.

During the Middle Ages in Europe (about A.D. 500–1500), scientific inquiry into abnormal behavior was limited, and the treatment of psychologically disturbed individuals was more often characterized by ritual or superstition than by attempts to understand an individual's condition. In contrast to Avicenna's era or to the period of enlightenment during the seventeenth and eighteenth centuries, the Middle Ages can largely be characterized as void with respect to scientific thinking and the humane treatment of the mentally disturbed. A similar sequence of events occurred in other parts of the world, as can be seen in *HIGHLIGHT 2.1*.

Mental disorders were quite prevalent throughout the Middle Ages, especially so toward the end of the period, when medieval institutions, social structures, and beliefs began to change drastically. During this time, supernaturalistic explanations of the causes of mental illness grew. Within this environment, it obviously was difficult to make great

Islamic physician Avicenna (980–1037) approached the treatment of mental disorder with humane practices, unknown by Western medical practitioners of the time.

HIGHLIGHT 2.1

Early Views of Mental Disorders in China

Tseng (1973) traced the development of Chinese concepts of different mental disorders by reviewing their descriptions and recommended treatments in historical medical documents. For example, the following passage is taken from an ancient Chinese medical text supposedly written by Huang Ti (c. 2674 B.C.), the third legendary emperor. Historians now believe that the text was written at a later date, possibly during the seventh century B.C.:

The person suffering from excited insanity initially feels sad, eating and sleeping less; he then becomes grandiose, feeling that he is very smart and noble, talking and scolding day and night, singing, behaving strangely, seeing strange things, hearing strange voices, believing that he can see the devil or gods. . . . (p. 570)

Even at this early date, Chinese medicine was based on a belief in natural rather than supernatural causes for illnesses. For example, in the concept of Yin and Yang, the human body, like the cosmos, is divided into positive and negative forces that both complement and contradict each other. If the two forces are balanced, the result is physical and mental health; if they are not, illness will result. Thus treatments focused on restoring balance: "As treatment for such an excited condition withholding food was suggested, since food was considered to be the source of positive force and the patient was thought to be in need of a decrease in such force" (p. 570).

Chinese medicine reached a relatively sophisticated level during the second century, and Chung Ching, who has been called the Hippocrates of China, wrote two well-known medical works around A.D. 200. Like Hippocrates, he based his views of physical and mental disorders on clinical observations, and he implicated organ pathologies as primary causes. However, he also believed that stressful psychological conditions could cause organ pathologies, and his treatments, like those of Hippocrates, utilized both drugs and the regaining of emotional balance through appropriate activities.

As in the West, Chinese views of mental disorders regressed to a belief in supernatural forces as causal agents. From the later part of the second century through the early part of the ninth century, ghosts and devils were implicated in "ghost-evil" insanity, which presumably resulted from possession by evil spirits. The "Dark Ages" in China, however, were not as severe—in terms of the treatment of mental patients—nor as long lasting as in the West. A return to biological, somatic (bodily) views and an emphasis on psychosocial factors occurred in the centuries that followed.

---

strides in the understanding and treatment of abnormal behavior. However, as Schoeneman (1984) puts it, "Demonology did not triumph as a theory of insanity, but coexisted with naturalistic etiologies and treatments derived from Galenic humoural theory and folk medicine" (p. 301). Although the influence of theology was growing rapidly, "sin" was not always cited as a causal factor in mental illness. For example, Kroll and Bachrach (1984) examined 57 episodes of mental illness, ranging from madness and possession to alcohol and epilepsy. They found sin implicated in only 9 cases (16%).

To understand better this elusive period of history, let us look at two events of the times— mass madness and exorcism—to see how they relate to views of abnormal behavior.

Mass Madness   During the last half of the Middle Ages, a peculiar trend emerged in abnormal behavior. It involved the widespread occurrence of group behavior disorders that were apparently cases of hysteria. Whole groups of people were affected simultaneously.

Dancing manias (epidemics of raving, jumping, dancing, and convulsions) were reported as early as the tenth century. One such episode, occurring in Italy early in the thirteenth century, was recorded by physicians of the time whose records were reviewed by medical historian H. E. Sigerist. He wrote the following:

[It] occurred at the height of the summer heat. . . . People, asleep or awake, would suddenly jump up,

In this painting, The Removal of the Stone of Folly, by Pieter Brueghel, we can see one of the more severe medieval methods of treating the psychologically disturbed. Patients were bound and holes were bored into their skulls in order to remove stones thought to be the cause of insanity.

feeling an acute pain like the sting of a bee. Some saw the spider, others did not, but they knew that it must be the tarantula. They ran out of the house into the street, to the market place, dancing in great excitement. Soon they were joined by others who like them had been bitten, or by people who had been stung in previous years. . . .

Thus groups of patients would gather, dancing wildly in the queerest attire. . . . Others would tear their clothes and show their nakedness, losing all sense of modesty. . . . Some called for swords and acted like fencers, others for whips and beat each other. . . . Some of them had still stranger fancies, liked to be tossed in the air, dug holes in the ground, and rolled themselves into the dirt like swine. They all drank wine plentifully and sang and talked like drunken people. . . . (1943, pp. 103, 106–107)

Known as **tarantism** in Italy, this dancing mania later spread to Germany and the rest of Europe, where it was known as **St. Vitus's dance.** The behavior was similar to the ancient orgiastic rites by which people had worshiped the Greek god Dionysus. These rites had been banned with the advent of Christianity, but they were deeply embedded in the culture and were apparently kept alive in secret gatherings (which probably led to considerable guilt and conflict). Then, with time, the meaning of the dances changed. The old rites reappeared, but they were attributed to symptoms of the tarantula's bite. The participants were no longer sinners

but the unwilling victims of the tarantula's spirit. The dancing became the "cure" and is the source of the dance we know today as the *tarantella.*

Isolated rural areas were also afflicted with outbreaks of **lycanthropy**—a condition in which people believed themselves to be possessed by wolves and imitated their behavior. In 1541 a case was reported in which a lycanthrope told his cap-

This fifteenth-century engraving shows peasant women overcome by St. Vitus's dance.

Mass disorders seem to occur during periods of widespread public fear and stress, such as that felt by these West Bank Palestinian schoolgirls, who developed the same mysterious physical symptoms in April of 1983. Although Arab leaders at first suspected the girls had been the victims of an Israeli poison plot, it was later thought that psychological factors had played an important role in the appearance of their symptoms.

tors, in confidence, that he was really a wolf but that his skin was smooth on the surface because all the hairs were on the inside (Stone, 1937). To cure him of his delusions, his extremities were amputated, following which he died, still uncured.

Mass madness occurred periodically into the seventeenth century but apparently reached its peak during the fourteenth and fifteenth centuries—a period noted for oppression, famine, and pestilence. During this period, Europe was ravaged by a plague known as the Black Death, which killed millions (some estimates say 50 percent of the population of Europe died) and severely disrupted social organization. Undoubtedly, many of the peculiar cases of mass madness were related to the depression, fear, and wild mysticism engendered by the terrible events of this period. People simply could not believe that frightening catastrophes such as the Black Death could have natural causes and thus could be within our power to control, prevent, or even create. On the other hand, many investigators today believe that mass madness during the Middle Ages was the result of ergotamine poisoning caused by bad grain.

So-called mass hysteria occasionally occurs today; the affliction usually mimics some type of physical disorder, such as fainting spells or convulsive movements. In 1982, after a nationwide story about some Chicago-area residents poisoned by Tylenol capsules, California health officials reported a sudden wave of illness among some 200 people who drank soda at a high school football game. No objective cause for the illness could be found, and officials speculated that most sufferers had been experiencing a kind of mass hysteria related to the Tylenol incident (UPI, 1982). Another

case of apparent mass hysteria occurred among hundreds of West Bank Palestinian girls in April of 1983. This episode threatened to have serious political repercussions because some Arab and Israeli leaders initially thought that the girls had been poisoned by Israelis; health officials later concluded that psychological factors had played a key role in most of the cases. As in many such instances, the initial failure to control inflammatory reactions to the incident was due to a communications breakdown (Hefez, 1985; *Time* April 18, 1983, p. 52).

Exorcism   In the Middle Ages, treatment of the mentally disturbed was left largely to the clergy. Monasteries served as refuges and places of confinement. During the early part of the medieval period, the mentally disturbed were, for the most part, treated with considerable kindness. "Treatment" consisted of prayer, holy water, sanctified ointments, the breath or spittle of the priests, the touching of relics, visits to holy places, and mild forms of exorcism. In some monasteries and shrines, exorcisms were performed by the gentle "laying on of hands." Such methods were often joined with vaguely understood medical treatments derived mainly from Galen, which gave rise to prescriptions such as the following: "For a fiend-sick man: When a devil possesses a man, or controls him from within with disease, a spewdrink of lupin, bishopswort, henbane, garlic. Pound these together, add ale and holy water" (Cockayne, 1864–1866).

As exorcistic techniques became more fully developed, emphasis was placed on Satan's pride, which was believed to have led to his original downfall. Hence, in treating persons possessed by a

As the notion spread in the Middle Ages that madness was caused by Satanic possession, exorcism became the treatment of choice.

devil, the first goal was to strike a fatal blow to the devil's pride—to insult him. This strategy involved calling the devil some of the most obscene epithets that imagination could devise, and the insults were usually supplemented by long litanies of cursing:

May all the devils that are thy foes rush forth upon thee, and drag thee down to hell! . . . May god set a nail to your skull, and pound it in with a hammer, as Jael did unto Sisera! . . . May . . . Sother break thy head and cut off thy hands, as was done to the cursed Dagon! . . . May God hang thee in a hellish yoke, as seven men were hanged by the sons of Saul! (Thesaurus Exorcismorum)

This procedure was considered highly successful in the treatment of possessed persons. A certain bishop of Beauvais claimed to have rid a person of five devils, all of whom signed an agreement stating that they and their subordinate imps would no longer persecute the possessed individual (A. D. White, 1896).

Interestingly, there has been a resurgence of superstition in contemporary society. Today one can find those who believe that supernatural forces cause psychological problems and that "cures" should involve exorcism to rid people of unwanted characteristics or "spells." Some practicing clinical psychologists actually incorporate exorcism into their treatment programs for some clients.

■ Witchcraft and Mental Illness: Fact or Fiction?

Fifteenth- and sixteenth-century Europe witnessed extensive witch-hunts in which many individuals were accused of and punished for deviating from the Christian faith. Possessed people were supposed to have made a pact with the devil, consummated by signing in blood a book presented to them by Satan, which gave them certain supernatural powers. It was believed that these people could cause pestilence, storms, floods, sexual impotence, and injuries to their enemies; could turn milk sour; and could rise through the air, ruin crops, and turn themselves into animals. In short, they were witches.

These beliefs were not confined to simple serfs but were held and elaborated on by most of the important clergy of the period. No less a man than Martin Luther (1483–1546), the German leader of the Protestant Reformation, came to the following conclusions:

The greatest punishment God can inflict on the wicked . . . is to deliver them over to Satan, who with God's permission, kills them or makes them to undergo great calamities. Many devils are in woods, water, wildernesses, etc., ready to hurt and prejudice people. When these things happen, then the philosophers and physicians say it is natural, ascribing it to the planets.

[People] are possessed by the devil in two ways; corporally or spiritually. Those whom he possesses corporally, as mad people, he has permission from God to vex and agitate, but he has no power over their souls." (Colloquia Mensalia [Table Talk])

It has long been thought that, during this period, many mentally disturbed people were accused of being witches and thus were punished and often killed (e.g., Zilboorg & Henry, 1941). But more recent interpretations have questioned the extent to which this situation was the case. Schoeneman (1984), for example, in a review of the literature, points out that "the typical accused witch was not a mentally ill person but an impoverished woman with a sharp tongue and a bad temper [the majority of witches who were punished were women] . . ." (p. 301). He goes on to say that "witchcraft was, in fact, never considered a variety of possession either by witch hunters, the general populace, or modern historians . . ." (p. 306). To say "never" may be overstating the case; clearly, some mentally ill individuals were punished as witches. Otherwise, as you will see in the next section, why did some physicians

This French engraving of "moonstruck" women dancing in the town square illustrates the commonly held belief that the moon could affect behavior.

and thinkers go to great lengths to expose the fallacies of the connection? In the case of witchcraft and mental illness, the confusion may be due, in part, to a confusion about demonic possession. As can be seen in the quote from Luther's *Colloquia Mensalia*, there were two types of demonically possessed people—those corporally possessed were considered mad; those spiritually possessed were likely considered witches. With time, the distinctions between these two categories may have blurred in the eyes of historians, thus resulting in a less-than-accurate perception that witchcraft and mental illness were connected more frequently than was the case.

The changing view of the relationship between witchcraft and mental illness points up an even broader issue—the difficulties of interpreting historical events accurately. We will discuss this issue in more depth in the Unresolved Issues section at the end of the chapter.

THE GROWTH TOWARD HUMANITARIAN APPROACHES

During the latter part of the Middle Ages and the early Renaissance, scientific questioning reemerged and a movement emphasizing the importance of specifically human interests and concerns began—a movement (still with us today) that can be loosely referred to as *humanism*. Consequently, the superstitious beliefs that had retarded the understanding and therapeutic treatment of mental disorders began to be challenged.

■ The Resurgence of Scientific Questioning in Europe

Paracelsus, a Swiss physician (1490–1541), was an early critic of superstitious beliefs about possession. He insisted that the dancing mania was not a possession but a form of disease, and that it should be treated as such. He also postulated a conflict between the instinctual and spiritual nature of human beings, formulated the idea of psychic causes for mental illness, and advocated treatment by "bodily magnetism," later called hypnosis (Mora, 1967). Although Paracelsus rejected demonology, his view of abnormal behavior was colored by his belief in astral influences (*lunatic* is derived from the Latin word *luna* or "moon"). He was convinced that the moon exercised a supernatural influence over the brain—an idea, incidentally, that persists among some people today. Paracelsus defied the medical and theological traditions of his time; he often burned the works of Galen and others of whom he disapproved. Had he been more restrained and diplomatic in his efforts, he might have exerted more influence over the scientific thinking of his day. Instead, he became known more for his arrogance than for his scientific advances.

During the sixteenth century, Teresa of Avila, a Spanish nun who was later canonized, made an extraordinary conceptual leap that has influenced thinking to the present day. Teresa, in charge of a group of cloistered nuns who had become hysterical and were therefore in danger from the Spanish Inquisition, argued convincingly that her nuns were not possessed but rather were "as if sick" (*comas enfermas*). Apparently, she did not mean that they were sick of body. Rather, in the expression "as if," we have what is perhaps the first suggestion that a mind can be ill just as a body can be ill. It was a momentous suggestion, which apparently began as a kind of metaphor but was, with time, accepted as fact: people came to see mental illness as an entity, and the "as if" dropped out of use (Sarbin & Juhasz, 1967).

Johann Weyer (1515–1588) wrote against the prevalent beliefs in witchcraft and decried the persecution of the mentally ill.

Teresa of Avila, a sixteenth-century Spanish nun, had a major influence on the conception of mental illness in her era when she insisted that the hysterical nuns in her care were not possessed, but were "as if sick." This argument paved the way for the view that the mind can be sick like the body.

Johann Weyer (1515–1588), a German physician and writer who wrote under the Latin name of Joannus Wierus, was so deeply disturbed by the imprisonment, torture, and burning of people accused of witchcraft that he made a careful study of the entire problem. About 1563 he published a book, *The Deception of Demons,* which contains a step-by-step rebuttal of the *Malleus maleficarum,* a witch-hunters handbook published in 1486 for use in recognizing and dealing with those suspected of being witches. In it, he argued that a considerable number, if not all, of those imprisoned, tortured, and burned for witchcraft were really sick in mind or body and, consequently, that great wrongs were being committed against innocent people. Weyer's work received the approval of a few outstanding physicians and theologians of his time. Mostly, however, it met with vehement protest and condemnation.

Weyer was one of the first physicians to specialize in mental disorders, and his wide experience and progressive views justify his reputation as the founder of modern psychopathology. Unfortunately, however, he was too far ahead of his time. He was scorned by his peers, many of whom called him "Weirus Hereticus" and "Weirus Insanus." His works were banned by the Church and remained so until the twentieth century.

Perhaps there is no better illustration of the developing spirit of scientific skepticism in the sixteenth century than the works of the Oxford-educated Reginald Scot (1538–1599). Scot devoted his life to exposing the fallacies of witchcraft and demonology. In his book, *Discovery of Witchcraft*, published in 1584, he convincingly and daringly denied the existence of demons, devils, and evil spirits as the cause of mental disorders:

"These women are but diseased wretches suffering from melancholy, and their words, actions, reasoning, and gestures show that sickness has affected their brains and impaired their powers of judgment. You must know that the effects of sickness on men, and still more on women, are almost unbelievable. Some of these persons imagine, confess, and maintain that they are witches and are capable of performing extraordinary miracles through the arts of witchcraft; others, due to the same mental disorder, imagine strange and impossible things which they claim to have witnessed." (in Castiglioni, 1946, p. 253)

King James I of England, however, came to the rescue of demonology, personally refuted Scot's thesis, and ordered his book seized and burned.

The clergy, however, were beginning to question the practices of the time. For example, St. Vincent de Paul (1576–1660), at the risk of his life, declared: "Mental disease is no different to bodily disease and Christianity demands of the humane and powerful to protect, and the skillful to relieve the one as well as the other."

In the face of such persistent advocates of science, who continued their testimonies throughout the next two centuries, demonology and superstition gave ground. These advocates gradually paved the way for the return of observation and reason, which culminated in the development of modern experimental and clinical approaches.

■ The Establishment of Early Asylums and Shrines

From the sixteenth century on, special institutions called **asylums,** meant solely for the care of the mentally ill, grew in number. The early asylums were begun as a way of removing from society troublesome individuals who could not care for themselves. Although scientific inquiry into understanding abnormal behavior was on the increase, most early asylums, often referred to as *madhouses,* were not much better than concentration camps. The unfortunate residents lived and died amid conditions of incredible filth and cruelty.

Early Asylums   In 1547 the monastery of St. Mary of Bethlehem at London was officially made into a mental hospital by Henry VIII. Its name soon was contracted to *Bedlam,* and it became widely known for its deplorable conditions and practices. The more violent patients were exhibited to the public for one penny a look, and the more harmless inmates were forced to seek charity on the streets of London in the manner described by Shakespeare: "Bedlam beggars, who, with roaring voices . . . Sometimes with lunatic bans, sometime with prayers Enforce their charity" (*King Lear*, Act II, Scene iii).

Such hospitals for the mentally ill were gradually established in other countries. The San Hipolito, established in Mexico in 1566 by philanthropist Bernardino Alvares, was the first mental hospital established in the Americas. The first such hospital in France, La Maison de Charenton, was founded in 1641 in a suburb of Paris. A mental hospital was established in Moscow in 1764, and the notorious Lunatics' Tower in Vienna was constructed in 1784. This structure was a showplace in Old Vienna, an ornately decorated round tower within which were square rooms. The doctors and "keepers" lived in the square rooms, while the patients were confined in the spaces between the walls of the rooms and the outside of the tower. The patients were put on exhibit to the public for a small fee.

These early asylums were primarily modifications of penal institutions, and the inmates were treated more like beasts than like human beings. The following passage describes the treatment of the chronically insane in La Bicêtre, a hospital in Paris. This treatment was typical of the asylums of the period and continued through most of the eighteenth century.

The patients were ordinarily shackled to the walls of their dark, unlighted cells by iron collars which held them flat against the wall and permitted little movement. Ofttimes there were also iron hoops around the waists of the patients and both their hands and feet were chained. Although these chains usually permitted enough movement that the patients could feed themselves out of bowls, they often kept them from being able to lie down at night. Since little was known about dietetics, and the patients were presumed to be animals anyway, little attention was paid to whether they were adequately fed or to whether the food was good or bad. The cells were furnished only with straw and

From the sixteenth century on, an accepted treatment for people with mental disorders was confinement in asylums like this, the Bethlehem Royal Hospital in London. The hospital's name was soon contracted to Bedlam, a synonym for the uproar and confusion within its walls. This view of Bedlam is from Hogarth's Rake's Progress. In the eighteenth century, it was considered entertaining to view the lunatics, as the two ladies of fashion shown here are doing.

were never swept or cleaned; the patient remained in the midst of all the accumulated ordure. No one visited the cells except at feeding time, no provision was made for warmth, and even the most elementary gestures of humanity were lacking. (Modified from Selling, 1943, pp. 54–55)

In the United States, the Pennsylvania Hospital at Philadelphia, completed under the guidance of Benjamin Franklin in 1756, provided some cells or wards for mental patients. The Public Hospital in Williamsburg, Virginia, constructed in 1773, was the first hospital in the United States devoted exclusively to mental patients. The treatment of mental patients in the United States was no better than that offered by European institutions. Zwelling's (1985) review of Public Hospital's treatment methods show that, initially, the philosophy of treatment involved the view that patients needed to choose rationality over insanity. Thus the treatment

techniques were aggressive, aimed at restoring a "physical balance in the body and brain." These techniques were designed to intimidate patients; they included powerful drugs, water treatments, bleeding and blistering, electrical shocks, and physical restraints. For example, a violent patient might be plunged into ice water or a listless patient into hot water; frenzied patients might be administered drugs to exhaust them; or any patient might be bled in order to drain their system of "harmful" fluids. Early estimates of the cure rate for patients at the hospital were only about 20 percent.

Even as late as 1830, new patients had their heads shaved, were dressed in straitjackets, put on sparse diets, compelled to swallow some active purgative, and placed in dark cells. If these procedures did not quiet unruly or excited patients, more severe measures, such as starvation, solitary confinement, cold baths, and other torturelike methods, were used (Bennett, 1947).

The Geel Shrine   There were a few bright spots in this otherwise bleak situation. Out of the more humane Christian tradition of prayer, laying on of hands (or holy touch), and visits to shrines, there arose several great shrines where treatment by kindness and love stood out in marked contrast to prevailing conditions. The shrine at Geel in Belgium, visited since the thirteenth century, is probably the most famous. Legend has it that hidden in the forest of Geel is the body of a young princess who, upon the death of her mother, had dedicated her life to the poor and mentally disturbed. She was later slain by her incestuous father. Years later, five lunatics who spent the night in the forest recovered their mental health. Villagers believed that the princess, reincarnated as St. Dymphna, was responsible for the cures. Pilgrimages to Geel were organized for the mentally sick; many of the patients stayed on to live with the local inhabitants (Karnesh & Zucker, 1945). The colony of Geel has continued its work into modern times (Aring, 1974, 1975b; Belgian Consulate, 1990). Today, a new psychiatric hospital has been built in Geel, and nearly 1000 mental patients live in private homes with "foster families," work in community-based centers, and suffer few restrictions other than not drinking alcohol. Many types of mental disorders are represented, including schizophrenia, affective disorder, antisocial personality, and mental retardation. Ordinarily, patients remain in Geel until they are considered recovered by a supervising therapist. It is unfortunate that the great humanitarian work of this colony—and the opportunity it affords to study the treatment of patients in a family and community setting—has received so little recognition.

Humanitarian Reform

Clearly, by the late eighteenth century, most mental hospitals in Europe and America were in need of reform. The humanitarian treatment of patients received great impetus from the work of Philippe Pinel (1745–1826) in France.

Pinel's Experiment   In 1792, shortly after the first phase of the French Revolution, Pinel was placed in charge of La Bicêtre in Paris. In this capacity, he received the grudging permission of the Revolutionary Commune to remove the chains from some of the inmates as an experiment to test his views that mental patients should be treated with kindness and consideration—as sick people and not as vicious beasts or criminals. Had his experiment proved a failure, Pinel might have lost his head, but fortunately it was a great success. Chains were removed; sunny rooms were provided; patients were permitted to exercise on the hospital grounds; and kindness was extended to these poor beings, some of whom had been chained in dungeons for 30 years or more. The effect was almost

This painting shows Philippe Pinel supervising the unchaining of inmates at La Bicêtre hospital. Pinel's experiment represented both a great reform and a major step in divising humanitarian methods of treating disorders.

miraculous. The previous noise, filth, and abuse were replaced by order and peace. As Pinel said: "The whole discipline was marked with regularity and kindness which had the most favorable effect on the insane themselves, rendering even the most furious more tractable" (Selling, 1943, p. 65).

The reactions of these patients when all their chains were removed for the first time was telling. One patient, an English officer who had years before killed a guard in an attack of fury, tottered outside on legs weak from lack of use, and for the first time in some 40 years saw the sun and sky. With tears in his eyes he exclaimed, "Oh, how beautiful!" (Zilboorg & Henry, 1941, p. 323). When night came, he voluntarily returned to his cell, which had been cleaned during his absence, to fall peacefully asleep on his new bed. After two years of orderly behavior, including helping to handle other patients, he was pronounced recovered and permitted to leave the hospital. Pinel himself was once saved from a mob that accused him of antirevolutionary activities by a soldier whom he had freed from asylum chains.

Pinel was later given charge of La Salpêtrière hospital, where the same reorganization was instituted with similar results. La Bicêtre and La Salpêtrière hospitals thus became the first modern hospitals for the care of the insane. Pinel's successor, Jean Esquirol (1772–1840), continued Pinel's good work at La Salpêtrière and, in addition, helped establish ten new mental hospitals. These hospitals put France in the forefront of humane treatment for the mentally disturbed and "signalled the end of the indiscriminate mixture of paupers and criminals, the physically sick, and the mentally deranged" (Rosenblatt, 1984, p. 246).

Tuke's Work in England   At about the same time that Pinel was reforming La Bicêtre, an English Quaker named William Tuke (1732–1822) established the York Retreat, a pleasant country house where mental patients lived, worked, and rested in a kindly religious atmosphere (Narby, 1982). This retreat represented the culmination of a noble battle against the brutality, ignorance, and indifference of his time. Some insight into the difficulties and discouragements he encountered may be gleaned from a simple statement he made in a letter regarding his early efforts: "All men seem to desert me." This statement is not surprising when we remember that the belief in demonology was still widespread and that as late as 1768 Protestant leader John Wesley declared that "the giving up of witchcraft is in effect the giving up of the Bible." The belief in demonology was too strong to be conquered overnight.

As word of Pinel's amazing results spread to England, Tuke's small force of Quakers gradually gained support from John Connolly, Samuel Hitch, and other great English medical psychologists. In 1841 Hitch introduced trained nurses into the wards at the Gloucester Asylum and put trained supervisors at the head of the nursing staffs. These innovations, quite revolutionary at the time, were of great importance not only in improving the care of mental patients but also in changing public attitudes toward the mentally disturbed.

Rush and Moral Management in America
The success of Pinel's and Tuke's humanitarian experiments revolutionized the treatment of mental patients throughout the Western world. In the United States, this revolution was reflected in the work of Benjamin Rush (1745–1813), the founder of American psychiatry. While associated with the Pennsylvania Hospital in 1783, Rush encouraged more humane treatment of the mentally ill; wrote the first systematic treatise on psychiatry in America, *Medical Inquiries and Observations upon the Diseases of the Mind* (1812); and was the first American to organize a course in psychiatry. But even he did not escape entirely from established beliefs of his time. His medical theory was tainted with astrology, and his principle remedies were bloodletting and purgatives. In addition, he invented and used a

Benjamin Rush (1745–1813) founded American psychiatry and encouraged more humane treatment of the mentally ill. He was the first American to write a systematic treatise on psychiatry and to organize a course on the subject.

Before the straitjacket became the chief means of controlling unmanageable patients, various diabolical restraining devices were commonly used in mental institutions, even after reform had begun. The chained patient was a familiar sight; the "crib" shown here was an immobilizing device used during the 1880s in the New York Insane Asylum to control violent patients.

device called "the tranquilizer," which was probably more torturous than tranquil for patients. Despite these limitations, we can consider Rush an important transitional figure between the old era and the new.

During the early part of this period of humanitarian reform, the use of **moral management**—a wide-ranging method of treatment that focused on a patient's social, individual, and occupational needs—became relatively widespread. This approach, which stemmed largely from the work of Pinel and Tuke, began in Europe during the late eighteenth century and in America during the early nineteenth century. As Rees (1957) has described the approach:

The insane came to be regarded as normal people who had lost their reason as a result of having been exposed to severe psychological and social stresses. These stresses were called the moral causes of insanity, and moral treatment aimed at relieving the patient by friendly association, discussion of his difficulties, and the daily pursuit of purposeful activity; in other words, social therapy, individual therapy, and occupational therapy. (pp. 306–307)

Changes at Williamsburg's Public Hospital reflected this change in attitude. First, the hospital was renamed the Williamsburg Lunatic Asylum to reflect "the view that the mentally ill were innocent victims who required protection from society" (Zwelling, 1985, p. 30). Treatment regimens were also changed. There were fewer physical restraints, more open wards, and opportunities to practice positive activities such as farming and carpentry. Social activities, some involving members of the opposite sex, were incorporated into the daily activities of the patients.

Moral management achieved an almost incredible level of effectiveness—all the more amazing because it was done without the benefit of the antipsychotic drugs so prevalent today and because many of the patients were probably suffering from syphilis, the then-incurable disease of the central nervous system. In the 20-year period between 1833 and 1853, Worcester State Hospital's discharge rate for patients who had been ill less than one year prior to admission was 71 percent. Even for patients with a longer preadmission disorder, the discharge rate was 59 percent (Bockhoven, 1972).

Despite its relative effectiveness, moral management was nearly abandoned by the latter part of the nineteenth century. The reasons were many and varied. Among the more obvious ones were the ethnic and racial prejudice that came with the rising immigrant population, leading to tension between staff and patients; the failure of the movement's leaders to train their own replacements; and the overextension of hospital facilities, reflecting the misguided belief that bigger hospitals would differ from smaller ones only in size.

Two other reasons for the demise of moral management are, in retrospect, truly ironic. One was the rise of the **mental hygiene movement,** which advocated a method of treatment that focused almost exclusively on the physical well-being of hospitalized mental patients. Although the creature comforts of patients may have improved under the mental hygienists, the patients received no help for their mental problems and thus were condemned subtly to helplessness and dependency.

The use of moral management included less use of restraint and the practice of positive activities and socializing. This photo from the turn of the century shows male patients taking their leisure. Moral management had profoundly positive effects on a great many patients, and it was certainly a more humanitarian practice than the methods that had preceded it.

Advances in biomedical science also contributed to the demise of moral management and the rise of the mental hygiene movement. These advances fostered the notion that all mental disorders would eventually yield to biological explanations and biologically based treatments. Thus the psychological and social environment of a patient was considered largely irrelevant; the best one could do was keep the patient comfortable until a biological cure was discovered. Needless to say, the anticipated biological cure-all did not arrive, and by the late 1940s and early 1950s discharge rates were down to about 30 percent. We do better today, with discharge rates above 90 percent, but these improved rates are a recent development due to many factors, including advances in drug therapy and a trend to release many patients for continued care in their communities. The fact that the care in the community often does not meet acceptable standards is an issue we will address in Chapter 19.

Notwithstanding its negative effects on the use of moral management, the mental hygiene movement has accounted for many humanitarian accomplishments.

Dix and the Mental Hygiene Movement

Dorothea Dix (1802–1887) was an energetic New England schoolteacher forced into early retirement because of recurring attacks of tuberculosis. In 1841 she began to teach in a women's prison. Through this contact she became acquainted with the deplorable conditions in jails, almshouses, and asylums. In a "Memorial" submitted to the Congress of the United States in 1848, she stated that she had seen

more than 9000 idiots, epileptics and insane in the United States, destitute of appropriate care and protection . . . bound with galling chains, bowed beneath fetters and heavy iron bails attached to drag-chains, lacerated with ropes, scouraged with rods and terrified beneath storms of execration and cruel blows; now subject to jibes and scorn and torturing tricks; now abandoned to the most outrageous violations. (Zilboorg & Henry, 1941, pp. 583–584)

As a result of her findings, Dix carried on a zealous campaign between 1841 and 1881 that aroused people and legislatures to do something

Dorothea Dix (1802–1887) was a tireless reformer who made great strides in changing public attitudes toward the mentally ill.

about the inhuman treatment accorded the mentally ill. Through her efforts, the mental hygiene movement grew in America: millions of dollars were raised to build suitable hospitals, and 20 states responded directly to her appeals. Not only was she instrumental in improving conditions in American hospitals, but she directed the opening of 2 large institutions in Canada and completely reformed the asylum system in Scotland and several other countries. She is credited with establishing 32 mental hospitals, an astonishing record considering the ignorance and superstition that still prevailed in the field of mental health. She rounded out her career by organizing the nursing forces of the northern armies during the Civil War. A resolution presented by the United States Congress in 1901 characterized her as "among the noblest examples of humanity in all history" (Karnesh & Zucker, 1945, p. 18).

Retrospective criticism of Dix's work has questioned the importance of her contributions and has attributed several negative consequences to her efforts (Bockhoven, 1972; Dain, 1964). Later critics have claimed that establishing hospitals for the mentally ill and increasing the number of people in them created overcrowded facilities and custodial care. Housing patients in institutions away from society, these critics have claimed further, interfered with the treatment of the day (moral therapy) and deferred the search for more appropriate and effective treatments for mental disorders (Bockhoven, 1972). These criticisms, however, do not consider the context in which Dix's contributions were made (see the Unresolved Issues discussion on page 50). Dix's advocacy of the humane treatment of the

mentally ill should be considered in light of the cruel treatment common at the time (Viney & Bartsch, 1984), and we believe her efforts warrant considerable praise for their results.

THE FOUNDATIONS OF TWENTIETH-CENTURY VIEWS

It is difficult to partition modern views of abnormal behavior into discrete, uniform attitudes or to trace their historical precedents without appearing arbitrary and overly simplistic. Much that has happened in the nineteenth and twentieth centuries is the subject of the next chapter; however, a brief, selective overview here will bring us into the twentieth century and set the scene for Chapter 3.

■ Changing Attitudes Toward Mental Health

By the end of the nineteenth century, the mental hospital or asylum—"the big house on the hill"— with its high turrets and fortresslike appearance, had become a familiar landmark in America. In it, mental patients lived under semiadequate conditions of comfort and freedom from abuse. To the general public, however, the asylum was an eerie place, and its occupants a strange and frightening lot.

Little was done by the resident psychiatrists— then called *alienists,* in reference to treating the "alienated," or insane—to educate the public to reduce the general fear and horror of insanity. A principal reason for this silence, of course, was that early psychiatrists had little actual information to impart.

Gradually, however, important strides were made toward changing the general public's attitude toward mental patients. In America, the pioneering work of Dix was followed by that of Clifford Beers (1876–1943), whose book, *A Mind That Found Itself,* was published in 1908. Beers, a Yale graduate, described his own mental collapse and told of the bad treatment he received in three typical institutions of the day. He also explained his eventual recovery in the home of a friendly attendant. Although chains and other torture devices had long since been given up, the straitjacket was still widely

Clifford Beers (1876–1943) used his own experiences of incarceration in mental institutions to wage a campaign of public awareness about the need for changes in the attitudes toward and treatment of mental patients.

used as a means of "quieting" excited patients. Beers experienced this treatment and supplied a vivid description of what such painful immobilization of the arms means to an overwrought mental patient:

No one incident of my whole life has ever impressed itself more indelibly on my memory. Within one hour's time I was suffering pain as intense as any I ever endured, and before the night had passed that pain had become almost unbearable. My right hand was so held that the tip of one of my fingers was all but cut by the nail of another, and soon knife-like pains began to shoot through my right arm as far as the shoulder. If there be any so curious as to wish to get a slight idea of my agony, let him bite a finger tip as hard as he can without drawing blood. Let him continue the operation for two or three minutes. Then let him multiply that effect, if he can, by two or three hundred. In my case, after four or five hours the excess of pain rendered me partially insensible to it. But for nine hundred minutes— fifteen consecutive hours—I remained in that strait-jacket; and not until the twelfth hour, about breakfast time the next morning, did an attendant so much as loosen a cord. (Beers, pp. 127–128)

After Beers recovered, he began a campaign to make people realize that such treatment was no way to handle the sick. He soon won the interest and support of many public-spirited individuals, including the eminent psychologist William James and the "dean of American psychiatry," Adolf Meyer.

■ The Growth of Scientific Research

While the mental hygiene movement was gaining ground in the United States during the latter years of the nineteenth century, great technological discoveries were occurring both at home and abroad. These advances helped begin what we know today as the scientific, or experimentally oriented, view of abnormal behavior and the application of scientific knowledge to the treatment of disturbed individuals.

The most immediately apparent advances were in the study of the biological and anatomical factors underlying both physical and mental disorders. A major biomedical breakthrough, for example, came with the discovery of the organic factors underlying general paresis—syphilis of the brain—one of the most serious mental illnesses of the day. General paresis produced paralysis and insanity and typically caused death within two to five years. The investigation into the causes of paresis and the finding of a cure—in essence, infecting a sufferer with malarial fever—stretched over a period of nearly 100 years, as outlined in *HIGHLIGHT 2.2*. Though today we have penicillin as an effective, simpler treatment of paresis, the early malarial treatment represented, for the first time in history, a clear-cut conquest of a mental disorder by medical science. The field of abnormal psychology had come a long way—from superstitious beliefs to scientific proof of how brain pathology can cause a specific disorder. This breakthrough raised great hopes in the medical community that organic bases would be found for many other mental disorders—perhaps for all of them.

Despite the emphasis on biological causation, the scientific investigation into psychological factors and human behavior was progressing, too. In 1879 Wilhelm Wundt (1832–1920) established the first experimental psychology laboratory at the University of Leipzig. While studying the psychological factors involved in memory and sensation, Wundt and his colleagues devised many basic experimental methods and strategies. Early contributors to the empirical study of abnormal behavior were directly influenced by Wundt; they followed his experimental methodology and also used some of his research strategies to study clinical problems. For example, a student of Wundt's, J. McKeen Cattell (1860–1944), brought Wundt's experimental methods to the United States and used them to assess individual differences in mental processing. He and other students of Wundt's work established research laboratories throughout the United States.

Events Leading to the Discovery of Organic Factors in General Paresis

Scientific discoveries do not occur overnight; usually they require the combined efforts of many scientists over extended periods of time. In addition, such discoveries rarely proceed sequentially from point *a* to point *z*. Rather, they often result from an uncoordinated process in which many scientists pursue dead-end hypotheses, go off on tangents, refuse to accept "evidence," experience crises in their thinking, and so on.

Abbreviated descriptions of the events leading to scientific discoveries often fail to capture the excitement, intrigue, and frustration that enter the process. With this caution in mind, we identify here ten key steps in the long effort to find a cure for general paresis.

1. In 1825 French physician A. L. J. Bayle differentiated general paresis as a specific type of mental disorder. Bayle gave a complete and accurate description of the symptom pattern of paresis and convincingly presented his reasons for believing paresis to be a distinct disorder.

2. In 1857 Esmarch and Jessen reported on paretic patients known to have had syphilis and concluded that the syphilis caused the paresis.

3. In 1869 Argyll-Robertson in Scotland described the failure of the pupillary reflex (failure of the pupil to narrow under bright light) as diagnostic of the involvement of the central nervous system in syphilis.

4. In 1897 Viennese psychiatrist Krafft-Ebing conducted experiments involving the inoculation of paretic patients with matter from syphilitic sores. None of the patients developed secondary symptoms of syphilis, which led to the conclusion that they must previously have been infected. This crucial experiment established the relationship of general paresis to syphilis.

5. In 1905 Schaudinn discovered that *Spirochaeta pallida* is the cause of syphilis.

6. In 1906 von Wassermann developed a blood test for syphilis. This development made it possible to check for the presence of the deadly spirochetes in the bloodstream of an individual before the more serious consequences of infection appeared.

7. In 1908 Plant applied the Wasserman test to the cerebrospinal fluid to indicate whether or not the spirochete had invaded a patient's central nervous system.

8. In 1909 Ehrlich, after 605 failures, developed the arsenical compound arsphenamine (which he thereupon called *606*) for the treatment of syphilis. Although 606 proved effective in killing the syphilitic spirochetes in the bloodstream, it was not effective against the spirochetes that had penetrated the central nervous system.

9. In 1913 Noguchi and Moore verified that the syphilitic spirochete was the brain-damaging agent in general paresis. They discovered these spirochetes in a postmortem study of the brains of patients who had suffered from paresis.

10. In 1917 Wagner-Jauregg, chief of the psychiatric clinic of the University of Vienna, introduced the malarial fever treatment of syphilis and paresis. He inoculated nine paretic patients with the blood of a soldier who was ill with malaria and found marked improvement in three patients and apparent recovery in three others.

Wilhelm Wundt (1832–1920) established the first experimental psychology laboratory, which led others to use scientific methods to investigate psychological processes, including mental disorders.

It was not until 1896, however, that another of Wundt's students, Lightner Witmer (1867–1956), combined research with application and established the first American psychological clinic at the University of Pennsylvania. Witmer's clinic focused on the problems of mentally deficient children, both in terms of research and therapy. Other clinics were soon established. One clinic of note was the Chicago Juvenile Psychopathic Institute (later called the Institute of Juvenile Research), established in 1909 by William Healy (1869–1963). Healy was the first to describe juvenile delinquency as a symptom of urbanization and not as a result of inner psychological problems. In so doing, he was among the first to seize upon a new area of causation—environmental, or sociocultural, factors.

By the first decade of the twentieth century, psychological laboratories and clinics were burgeoning, and a great deal of research was being generated. The rapid and objective communication of scientific findings was perhaps as important in the development of modern psychology (or any science) as the collection and interpretation of research findings. This period saw the origin of many scientific journals for the dissemination of research and theoretical discoveries. Two notable publications in the field of abnormal psychology were the *Journal of Abnormal Psychology,* founded by Morton Prince in 1906, and *The Psychological Clinic,* founded by Lightner Witmer in 1907. As the years have passed, the number of journals has grown. The American Psychological Association now publishes over 20 scientific journals, many of which focus on research

into abnormal behavior and personality functioning. The many avenues available for communicating new findings ensures that important discoveries will become widely known. Yet the very amount of information available can cause confusion and controversy, as we shall see in Chapter 3. We may have left supernatural beliefs behind, but we have moved into something far more complex in trying to determine the role of natural factors—be they biological, psychological, or sociocultural—in abnormal behavior. For a recap of some of the key contributors to the field of abnormal psychology, see *HIGHLIGHT 2.3*

UNRESOLVED ISSUES
on Interpreting Historical Events

One would think that trying to look back in history to get a picture of events that occurred long ago would not be all that difficult a task—that it would be a simple matter of reviewing some history books and some publications from the time in question. Any number of obstacles, however, can stand in the way of our gaining an accurate picture of the attitudes and behaviors of people who lived hundreds of years ago. This has certainly been the case with our views of the Middle Ages.

The foremost problem in retrospective psychological analysis is that we cannot rely on direct observation, a hallmark of psychological research. Instead, we must turn to written documents or historical surveys of the times. Though these sources are often full of fascinating information, they may not reveal directly the information we seek; we must therefore extrapolate "facts" from the information we have, which is not always an easy task. We are restricted in our conclusions by the documents or sources available to us; attempting to learn about a people's subtle social perceptions hundreds of years ago by examining surviving church documents or biographical accounts is less than ideal. First, we view these documents out of the context in which they were written. Second, we do not know whether the authors had ulterior motives or what they were—that is, what the real purposes were behind the documents. Kroll and Bachrach (1984), in their review of historical misinterpretations of the Middle Ages, point to the "propaganda element" that existed during the Middle Ages (as it still does today). For example, many historians have conclud-

Major Figures in the Early History of Abnormal Psychology

The Ancient World

Hippocrates (460–377 B.C.) A Greek physician who believed that mental disease was the result of natural causes and brain pathology rather than demonology.

Plato (429–347 B.C.) A Greek philosopher who believed that mental patients should be treated humanely and should not be held responsible for their actions.

Aristotle (384–322 B.C.) Greek philosopher and pupil of Plato who believed in the Hippocratic theory that various agents, or humors, within the body, when imbalanced, were responsible for mental disorders. Aristotle rejected the notion of psychological factors as causes of mental disorders.

Galen (A.D. 130–200) A Greek physician and advocate of the Hippocratic tradition who contributed much to our understanding of the nervous system. Galen divided the causes of mental disorders into physical and mental categories.

The Middle Ages

Avicenna (980–1037) An Islamic physician who adopted principles of humane treatment for the mentally disturbed at a time when Western approaches to mental illness were the opposite.

Martin Luther (1483–1546) A German theologian and leader of the Reformation who held the belief, common to his time, that the mentally disturbed were possessed by the devil.

Paracelsus (1490–1541) A Swiss physician who rejected demonology as a cause of abnormal behavior. Paracelsus believed in psychic causes of mental illness.

The Sixteenth Through the Eighteenth Centuries

Teresa of Avila (16th century) A Spanish nun who argued that mental disorder was an illness of the mind.

Johann Weyer (1515–1588) A German physician who argued against demonology and was ostracized by his peers and the Church for his progressive views.

Reginald Scot (1538–1599) An Englishman who refuted the notion of demons as the cause of mental disorders and was castigated by King James I.

Philippe Pinel (1745–1826) A French physician who pioneered the use of moral management in La Bicêtre and La Salpêtrière hospitals in France, where mental patients were treated in a humane way.

William Tuke (1732–1822) An English Quaker who established the York Retreat, where mental patients lived in humane surroundings.

Benjamin Rush (1745–1813) An American physician and founder of American psychiatry who used moral management, based on Pinel's humanitarian methods, to treat the mentally disturbed.

The Nineteenth and Early Twentieth Centuries

Dorothea Dix (1802–1887) An American teacher who founded the mental hygiene movement in the United States, which focused on the physical well-being of mental patients in hospitals.

Clifford Beers (1876–1943) An American who campaigned to change public attitudes toward mental patients after his own experiences in mental institutions.

Wilhelm Wundt (1832–1920) A German scientist who established the first experimental psychology laboratory in 1879 and subsequently influenced the empirical study of abnormal behavior.

J. McKeen Cattell (1860–1944) An American psychologist who adopted Wundt's methods and studied individual differences in mental processing.

Lightner Witmer (1867–1956) An American psychologist who established the first psychological clinic in the United States, focusing on problems of mentally deficient children. He also founded the journal *The Psychological Clinic* in 1907.

William Healy (1869–1963) An American psychologist who established the Chicago Juvenile Psychopathic Institute and advanced the idea that mental illness was due to environmental or sociocultural factors.

ed erroneously that people of the Middle Ages considered sin as a major causal factor in mental illness. This wrong conclusion may have been due in part to writings that invoked God's punishment if the victims of illnesses were enemies of the authors. Apparently, historians did not take note of the fact that if the victims were friends of the authors, sin was typically not mentioned as a causal factor (Kroll & Bachrach, 1984). Such writings, of course, are biased, but we may have no way of knowing this. The fewer the sources surveyed, the more likely any existing bias may go undetected.

In other cases, concepts important to historical interpretation may have quite a different meaning to us today than they did in the past. Or the meaning may simply be unclear. Kroll and Bachrach (1984) point out that the concept of "possession"—so critical to our views of the Middle Ages—is

a very vague and complex concept for which we have no helpful natural models. Our language fails us, except for colourful analogies and metaphors. Just as the term "nervous breakdown" means different things to different people, so too "possession" means and meant many different things, and un-doubtedly had a different range of meanings to medieval persons from what it has to us. (p. 510)

This kind of uncertainty can make definitive assessments of the happenings during the Middle Ages difficult—if not impossible.

Bias can come into play during interpretation, also. Our interpretations of historical events or previously held beliefs can be colored by our own views of normal and abnormal. In fact, it is difficult to conduct a retrospective analysis without taking current perspectives and values as a starting point. For example, our modern beliefs about the Middle Ages have led, says Schoeneman (1984), to our contemporary misinterpretation that, during the fifteenth and sixteenth centuries, the mentally ill were typically accused of being witches. For most of us, this interpretation—albeit a wrong one— makes sense simply because we do not understand the medieval perspective on witchcraft.

Although reevaluations of the Middle Ages have minimized the views that demonology, sin, and witchcraft played a key role in the medieval understanding of mental illness, it is also clear that in some cases, these concepts *were* associated with mental illness. Wherein lies the truth? It appears that the last word has not been written on the Middle Ages, nor on any period of our history, for that matter. At best, historical views—and, therefore, retrospective psychological studies—must be held as working hypotheses that are open to change as new perspectives are applied to history or "new" historical documents are discovered.

SUMMARY

The development of modern views on psychopathology has not followed a straight evolutionary path. We can, however, trace a general movement away from superstitious and "magical" explanations of abnormal behavior toward more reasoned, scientific explanations.

Early superstitions were followed by the emergence of medical concepts in many places, such as Egypt and Greece; many of these concepts were developed and refined by Roman physicians. With the fall of Rome near the end of the fifth century A.D., most Europeans returned to superstitious views, which dominated popular thinking about mental disorders for over 1000 years. In the fifteenth and sixteenth centuries, it was still widely believed that mentally disturbed people were possessed by a devil.

During the latter stages of the Middle Ages and early Renaissance, a spirit of scientific questioning reappeared in Europe, and several noted physicians spoke out against inhumane treatments, arguing that "possessed" individuals were actually "sick of mind" and should be treated as such. With this recognition of a need for the special treatment of disturbed people came the founding of various "asylums" toward the end of the sixteenth century. However, with institutionalization came the isolation and maltreatment of mental patients; slowly, this situation was recognized, and in the eighteenth century, further efforts were made to help afflicted individuals by providing them with better living conditions and kind treatment.

The nineteenth and early twentieth centuries witnessed a number of scientific and humanitarian advances. The work of Philippe Pinel in France, William Tuke in England, and Benjamin Rush and Dorothea Dix in the United States prepared the way for several important developments in contemporary abnormal psychology. Among these developments were the gradual acceptance of mental patients as afflicted individuals who needed and deserved professional attention; the success of biomedical methods as applied to disorders such as general paresis; and the growth of scientific research into the biological, psychological, and sociocultural roots of abnormal behavior.

Understanding the history of viewpoints on psychopathology, with its forward steps and reverses, helps us understand the emergence of modern concepts of abnormal behavior. This knowledge also provides us with a perspective for understanding new and future advances.

■ Key Terms

trephining (p. 30)

exorcism (p. 31)

insanity (p. 32)

tarantism (p. 36)

St. Vitus's dance (p. 36)

lycanthropy (p. 36)

asylums (p. 41)

moral management (p. 45)

mental hygiene movement (p. 45)

Chapter 3
Biological, Psychosocial, and Sociocultural Viewpoints

Paul Goesch, *Dream Fantasy*. Goesch, a native of
East Germany, made his name both as an architect
and as a painter. After several years of successful architectural practice, he quit to devote all his time to painting. He
was institutionalized in 1921 and lived in psychiatric
institutions until 1940, when he was murdered by the Nazis.

We have a strong tendency to look for explanations, to seek final answers. Even in the most exact of the scientific disciplines, however, we rarely find ultimate answers. In the preceding chapter, for example, we examined many interpretations developed over the centuries to explain the sources of deviant behavior, from beliefs in supernatural possession to theories of naturally occurring factors. Alternative viewpoints of the causes and treatments of abnormal behavior emerge because no single existing approach sufficiently accounts for or explains abnormal behavior. Different perspectives develop in an effort to better explain the complex phenomena under study. Each of these viewpoints focuses on important facets of behavior, though each falls short of standing alone as the "complete" explanation. In this chapter, we will look at several viewpoints that dominate today's approaches to understanding abnormal behavior and that form the basis for the types of therapy we will discuss in Chapters 17 and 18. All these viewpoints derive from the events described in Chapter 2, and, since we can expect them to continue evolving to meet new ideas and discoveries, they may well represent tomorrow's "history."

Students are often perplexed by the fact that, in the behavioral sciences, there are several competing explanations for the same thing. In general, the more complex the phenomena being investigated, the greater the number of viewpoints that emerge, all attempting to explain the phenomena. Inevitably, not all these viewpoints will be equally valid. As you will see, the applicability of a viewpoint is often determined by the extent to which it helps an observer understand a given phenomenon.

Clearly, the viewpoints to be discussed here help many professionals explore abnormal behavior. They help people understand disorders on three broad fronts: their clinical pictures (the symptoms of the disorders), their causal factors, and their treatments. In each case, these orientations help people organize the observations they have made, provide a system of thought in which to place the observed data, and suggest areas of focus. They can also blind people to evidence that may call for a change of orientation.

Typically, theoretical orientations in science retain a strong hold over their adherents, even in the face of disconfirming evidence and alternative explanations of observable phenomena. They do so until some new insight is achieved that resolves the problems left unsolved by the conflicting interpretations of the empirical data. These new insights constitute *paradigm shifts,* fundamental reorganizations of how people think about an entire field of science (Kuhn, 1962).

Sigmund Freud, for example, was responsible for a major shift in the focus of abnormal psychology; later, as seems to be the ultimate fate of all such shifts, major aspects of Freud's theory came under attack. Though we cannot yet say with certainty where the next paradigm shift will take us, it appears likely that the biological viewpoint will have significant impact. Let us hope, however, that adherents of a biological perspective have learned from their predecessors. Recall that during the mental hygiene movement many believed that a biological cure-all for mental illness would be found; thus psychosocial or sociocultural efforts to treat abnormal behavior were put on the back burner. We are still waiting for this biological "cure." Though today we can be more certain that biology will play a major role in the treatment of many behavior disorders, we know, too, that if the biological viewpoint is to become a dominant force, its adherents need to incorporate into its tenets a variety of well-established findings in the psychosocial and sociocultural areas.

Many researchers and practitioners in abnormal psychology do not subscribe to a single view or theoretical perspective. Rather, they take an *eclectic* approach, drawing on what they see as the best principles or techniques from two or more viewpoints. This approach seems to work better in practice than in theory; regardless, it reflects a growing trend by some practitioners not to be bound to any one viewpoint. We will return to this issue in the Unresolved Issues section of this chapter.

But first we must understand the major viewpoints of abnormal behavior. Our survey will be descriptive, comprehensive, and, we hope, objective. We do not intend to advocate one viewpoint over another; rather, we will present information about the structure and ideology of each perspective. It will be up to you to decide on your particular preference, if any, as you become more knowledgeable about the field. We will first consider the biological viewpoint. From there we will move on to several psychosocial approaches, including the psychodynamic, behavioristic, cognitive-behavioral, humanistic, and interpersonal perspectives. We will

look briefly, too, at the sociocultural viewpoint and the importance of accounting for traits that stem from being reared in a cultural background different from the majority culture. Finally, in this chapter's Unresolved Issues section, we will investigate avenues leading toward the integration of theories.

THE BIOLOGICAL VIEWPOINT

Many professionals in the field, especially those with biological backgrounds, focus on the biophysical processes that have gone awry in affected people. This approach represents the **biological viewpoint.** In its most extreme form, this viewpoint, also referred to as the **medical model,** focuses on mental disorder as a medical disease, the primary symptoms of which are behavioral rather than physiological or anatomical. Mental disorder is thus viewed as a disease of the central nervous system that is either inherited or caused by some brain pathology. Neither psychological factors nor the psychosocial environment of an individual are believed to play a causal role in the mental disorder. A less extreme version of the biological viewpoint allows for other causal factors but focuses on the biochemical processes that have become imbalanced (for whatever reason) and are disrupting the normal behavior of an individual. These two versions of the biological viewpoint mirror, respectively, the early and more recent developments in the field, which are discussed in the following sections.

The Roots of the Biological Viewpoint

We can look far back into our history (as we did in Chapter 2) and find individuals who suspected that organic factors played a role in psychopathology. To find the more direct roots of our current views, however, we need not look back very far.

The Establishment of Brain Pathology as a Causal Factor   With the emergence of modern experimental science in the early part of the eighteenth century, knowledge of anatomy, physiology, neurology, chemistry, and general medicine increased rapidly. These advances led to the gradual identification of the biological, or organic, pathology underlying many physical ailments. Scientists began to focus on diseased body organs as the cause of physical ailments. It was only another step for these people to assume that mental disorder was an illness based on the pathology of an organ—in this case, the brain.

In 1757 Albrecht von Haller (1708–1777), in his *Elements of Physiology,* emphasized the importance of the brain in psychic functions and advocated postmortem dissection to study the brains of the insane. The first systematic presentation of this viewpoint, however, was made by the German psychiatrist Wilhelm Griesinger (1817–1868). In his textbook *The Pathology and Therapy of Psychic Disorders,* published in 1845, Griesinger insisted that all mental disorders could be explained in terms of brain pathology.

During this time, scientists discovered the organic cause of general paresis, which we discussed in Chapter 2. Other successes followed. The brain pathology in cerebral arteriosclerosis and in the senile mental disorders was established by Alois Alzheimer and other investigators. Eventually, the organic pathologies underlying the toxic mental disorders (those severe mental disorders caused by toxic substances such as lead), certain types of mental retardation, and other mental illnesses were discovered.

It is important to note here that although the discovery of the organic bases of mental disorders may have addressed the *how* behind causation, it did not, in most cases, address the question of *why.* This situation is sometimes true to this day. For example, although we know what causes certain "presenile" mental disorders—brain pathology—we do not yet know why some individuals are afflicted and others not. Nonetheless, we can predict quite accurately the courses of these disorders. This ability is due not only to a greater understanding of the organic factors involved, but also, in large part, to the work of a follower of Griesinger, Emil Kraepelin (1856–1926).

The Beginnings of a Classification System

Kraepelin played a dominant role in the early development of the biological viewpoint. His textbook, *Lehrbuch der Psychiatrie,* published in 1883, not only emphasized the importance of brain pathology in mental disorders but also made several related contributions that helped establish this viewpoint. The most important of these contributions was his system of classification, which became the forerunner of today's DSM-III-R (discussed in Chapter 1). Kraepelin noted that certain symptom patterns occurred regularly enough to be regarded as specific types of mental disease. He then proceeded to describe and clarify these types of mental disorders,

Emil Kraepelin (1856–1926), by integrating clinical data, worked out one of the first systematic classification systems, a forerunner of the modern DSM-III-R.

working out a scheme of classification that is the basis of our present system. The integration of the clinical material underlying this classification was a herculean task and represented a major contribution to the field of psychopathology.

Kraepelin saw each type of mental disorder as separate and distinct from the others and thought that the course of each was as predetermined and predictable as the course of measles. Thus the outcome of a given type of disorder could presumably be predicted even if it could not yet be controlled. Such conclusions led to widespread interest in the accurate description and classification of mental disorders.

Advances Achieved as a Result of Early Biological Views   Although early biologically based thinking was perhaps too widely adopted before its limitations were recognized, it represented the first great advance of modern science toward the understanding and treatment of mental disorder. In turn, there was an enormous research effort to discover specific causes of disorders that would yield to specific medical treatments; researchers looked for damage or disease in particular sections of the brain to find the causes underlying different disorders. Such efforts necessarily involved differentiating various forms of abnormality, leading to a promising system for classifying separate disorders. These were substantial accomplishments.

Not all of the consequences of this early thinking were positive, however. Because the disorders best understood in terms of then-available knowledge were ones in which brain damage or deterioration were a central feature (as in general paresis), there naturally developed an expectation that all abnormal behavior would eventually be explained by reference to gross brain pathology. To be sure, organic mental disorders do occur (and we will describe them in Chapter 13), but the vast majority of abnormal behavior is not clearly associated with physical damage to brain tissue. Nonetheless, the medical model—a conceptual model that is inappropriate for much abnormal behavior—became stubbornly entrenched by these early but limited successes.

It is important to note that a medical-model orientation is not limited to biological viewpoints on the nature of mental disorder. It has also extended into psychosocial theorizing by adopting a *symptom/underlying-cause* point of view. This point of view assumes that abnormal behavior, even though it may be psychological (rather than biological) in nature, is a symptom of some sort of underlying, internal pathology or "illness"—just as a fever is a symptom of an underlying infection. As we will discuss later in the chapter, Freud, who was a physician, took this approach in developing his psychoanalytic theory of abnormal behavior.

■ Modern Biological Thinking

As we have discussed, the disorders first recognized as having biological or organic components were those associated with gross destruction of brain tissue. These disorders were *neurological diseases*— that is, they resulted from the disruption of brain functioning by physical or chemical means and often involved a psychological or behavioral aberration. We should distinguish between neurological diseases and the abnormal mental states (such as delusions) that sometimes accompany them; neurological damage does not necessarily result in abnormal behavior.

Likewise, bizarre thought content is probably never, in itself, the direct result of brain damage. Clearly, a neurologically damaged person will have many challenges to overcome, and these challenges will probably be all the more difficult because of his or her limited cognitive resources for coping with them. Such a person's behavioral *impairment* (such as memory loss) is readily accounted for by structural damage to the brain, but it is not so apparent how such damage produces the sometimes bizarre *content* of the person's behavior. For example, we can understand how the loss of neurons in general paresis could lead to difficulties in executing certain tasks, but the fact that an individual claims to be Napoleon is not likely to be the result simply of a loss of neurons. So far as we know, there are no "I

am (or am not) Napoleon" neurons in the brain. Such behavior must be the product of some sort of functional integration of many different neural structures, some of which have been "programmed" by past experience.

In addition, many conditions temporarily disrupt the information-processing capabilities of the brain without inflicting permanent damage or death to the neural cells involved—for example, brain inflammation or high fever. In these cases, normal functioning is altered by the context (especially the chemical context) in which the neural cells operate. The most routine example here is alcohol intoxication. In this condition, behavior that would normally be inhibited is given free rein, only to be regretted the morning after.

In sum, we now realize that many processes short of brain damage can affect the functional capacity of the brain and thus change behavior. Adequate brain functioning is dependent on the efficiency with which an excited nerve cell, or neuron, can transmit its "message" across a synapse to the next neuron in an established pathway in the brain. These interneuronal (or transsynaptic) transmissions are accomplished by chemicals called **neurotransmitters** that are released into the synaptic gap by the presynaptic neuron (see *HIGHLIGHT 3.1* on page 61). Some neurotransmitters increase the likelihood that the postsynaptic neuron will "fire" (produce an impulse), while others inhibit the impulse. Whether or not the neural message is successfully transmitted to the postsynaptic neuron depends on the concentration of certain neurotransmitters within the synaptic cleft. This situation can be complicated by the fact that the cleft is normally bathed in various other biochemical substances that may or may not have transmitter properties. The belief that *biochemical imbalances* in the brain can result in abnormal behavior is the basic tenet of the biological perspective today. Some adherents of this view even suggest that psychological stress can bring on biochemical imbalances.

We will now look briefly at two key areas of research surrounding biochemical imbalances that are contributing to the resurgence of the biological viewpoint: (a) behavior genetics and (b) biophysical therapies. We will then discuss these topics in relation to causal factors in Chapter 4.

Behavior Genetics   Genes affect biochemical processes and thereby the structure and physiologic functioning of organisms. Though behavior is never determined exclusively by genes, organisms are genetically programmed through biochemical processes to adapt, physically and behaviorally, to their environments. In general, the more complex the organism, the greater its built-in capacity to meet and overcome the challenges of its environment. It requires little imagination to suppose that because of genetic endowment, some humans have a greater or lesser adaptive capacity than others. This idea has many unfortunate sociopolitical and racial overtones, and it has occasionally been misused by both scientists and politicians. Nonetheless, substantial evidence shows that some mental disorders have a hereditary component. The genetic transmission of traits from one generation to the next is, by definition, a biological process. Thus, the many recent studies suggesting that heredity is an important causal factor in several disorders, particularly depression and schizophrenia (Neale & Oltmanns, 1980; Paykel, 1982a) and alcoholism (Cloninger et al., 1986; Li et al., 1987), support the biological viewpoint.

We are still far from understanding the extent to which genetically determined hormone levels influence human behavioral tendencies. Our most advanced knowledge in this area has to do with gender-related behaviors. Building on the earlier work of Money and Ehrhardt (1972), several investigators have convincingly reported that the brain pathways that determine behavior in males and females differ in certain ways because chromosomal differences cause each sex to produce different hormones or hormone levels (Ehrhardt & Meyer-Bahlburg, 1981; MacLusky & Naftolin, 1981; McEwen, 1981; Rubin, Reinisch, & Haskett, 1981).

It also seems possible that many broad temperamental features of newborns and children are genet-

ically determined—for example, social introversion. Some characteristics also appear to be both familial and consistent over time. In an extensive study of identical twins reared apart being conducted at the University of Minnesota, Bouchard and his colleagues (1990) concluded that a great many psychological characteristics had a high genetic component. For example, their data suggested that about 70 percent of the variation in people's intelligence could be attributed to genetic endowment. Moreover, they also reported that personality characteristics had considerably more of a genetic basis than had been believed before. They concluded that

for almost every behavioral trait so far investigated, from reaction time to religiosity, an important fraction of the variation among people turns out to be associated with genetic variation. . . . We infer that the diverse cultural agents of our society, in particular most parents, are less effective in imprinting their distinctive stamp on the children developing within their spheres of influence—or are less inclined to do so—than has been supposed. (p. 227)

The idea that temperament affects mental health is an ancient one, and it is a key element in the modern biological approach to mental disorders. The importance of genetic factors in forming adult personality has been demonstrated in a study by Pogue-Geile and Rose (1985). They used a longitudinal research design with college-aged twins to study genetic factors in personality. The research group initially identified 203 same-sex

This set of identical twins from Bouchard's University of Minnesota study of the roles of genetics versus environment provides some striking support for the prominence of the genetic influence. Jim Springer (left) and Jim Lewis (right) were separated four weeks after their birth in 1940. They grew up 45 miles apart in Ohio. After they were reunited in 1979, they discovered they had some eerie similarities: both chain-smoked Salems, both drove the same model blue Chevrolet, both chewed their fingernails, and both had dogs named Toy. Further, they had both vacationed in the same neighborhood in Florida. When tested for such personality traits as sociability and self-control, they responded almost identically.

twins from the undergraduate population at Indiana University. The researchers then determined which twins were identical and conducted preliminary psychological testing, using the Minnesota Multiphasic Personality Inventory (MMPI), to assess their personalities. They initially tested 101 identical pairs and 102 nonidentical pairs. The researchers retested the twins 4½ years later to determine the consistency of personality factors over time. They were able to obtain complete follow-up MMPIs on 133 twin pairs (71 identical pairs of which 25 pairs were male, and 62 nonidentical pairs of which 24 pairs were male). The researchers found that genetic inheritance, as measured by the differences between the identical and nonidentical twins, was related to the performance of individuals on several personality dimensions (particularly social maladjustment, depression, unusual thinking, and anxiety). Even here, however, the biological factor did not operate alone. Different environmental experiences appeared to have important mediating effects on personality, shown by the similar results on personality measures for many pairs of both nonidentical and identical twins.

Biophysical Therapies   With few exceptions, advances in the understanding and treatment of mental disorders languished during the first third of this century. At the same time, discharge rates from mental hospitals declined and resident populations of such hospitals rose at an alarming pace. These trends were due to a simple fact: the medical model of abnormal behavior had not fulfilled its promise. Biological interventions based on theories such as the nutritional or infectious basis of mental disorders had not proven successful at curing large numbers of patients (Valenstein, 1986).

Then, beginning in the 1930s, new therapies were introduced that produced significant behavioral changes in some patients. One of these then-revolutionary techniques, electroconvulsive therapy (ECT), is still in use today. ECT produces a convulsion in a patient by passing an electric current through his or her brain. In certain instances, this treatment results in a patient's prompt return to normal functioning. How electroconvulsive therapy works is still not fully understood, although some promising research has been done in this area (Abrams & Essman, 1982). It is generally believed that the loss of consciousness produced by the electrical current produces a confused state that disrupts previously disturbing thoughts, thereby allowing a patient to "reconstruct" his or her thinking along more adaptive lines. Biologically

speaking, the electric current presumably disrupts the biochemistry of the brain and somehow returns it to a more appropriate biochemical balance. Though more will be said about ECT and other biological treatment approaches in Chapter 17, we should point out here that ECT is considered an extreme form of therapy and is quite controversial today.

More importantly, since the 1950s we have witnessed many new and often dramatic developments in the use of drugs to treat mental disorders —in particular, the more severe ones. In contrast to the situation with ECT, we have a good understanding of how these medications produce their beneficial effects. We know at least to some extent what biochemical changes are caused by taking these drugs, and we can evaluate those effects by noting behavioral changes that occur with a patient. For example, phenothiazines are known to reduce confused thinking and block intrusive thoughts. We can evaluate such changes by determining a patient's altered modes of thinking following various dosages of the medication. As we will see throughout this text, research on the mediating effects of medications have led to many intriguing hypotheses about the chemical imbalances that accompany, and may be causally related to, various disorders. Most of these hypotheses are concerned with the nature of neurotransmission, which is graphically depicted in *HIGHLIGHT 3.1*.

The Impact of the Biological Viewpoint

Biological discoveries have profoundly affected the way we think about human behavior. We now recognize the important role of biochemical factors and innate characteristics, many of which are genetically determined, in both normal and abnormal behavior.

The host of new drugs that dramatically and quickly alter the severity and course of certain mental disorders has brought renewed attention to the biological viewpoint, not only in scientific circles but also in the popular media. Biological treatments seem to have more immediate results than other available therapies, and the hope is that they may in most cases lead to a "cure-all"— immediate results with seemingly little effort.

However, we must remind ourselves again that few, if any, mental afflictions are independent of people's personalities or of the problems they face in trying to live their lives. We will examine viewpoints that emphasize these psychosocial and sociocultural considerations in the pages that follow. Keep in mind that many clinicians and researchers are eclectic in practice: they incorporate seemingly different

HIGHLIGHT 3.1

Neurotransmission and Abnormal Behavior

The synapse is the action site for several therapies used in combating abnormal behavior. The axonal endings of one neuron lie near the dendritic endings of the next neuron. As an impulse reaches the end of its axon, it stimulates the release of neurotransmitters. The neurotransmitters are released through the terminal portion of the axon into the space between the axon and the dendrite of the next neuron. The neurotransmitters thus stimulate that dendrite to initiate an impulse. The neurotransmitters are quickly destroyed by an enzyme, such as monoamine oxidase, or they are returned to storage vesicles in the axonal button by a "reuptake" mechanism, so that the second neuron does not continue firing in the absence of a real impulse. Certain medications act to increase or decrease the concentrations of pertinent neurotransmitters in the synaptic gap.

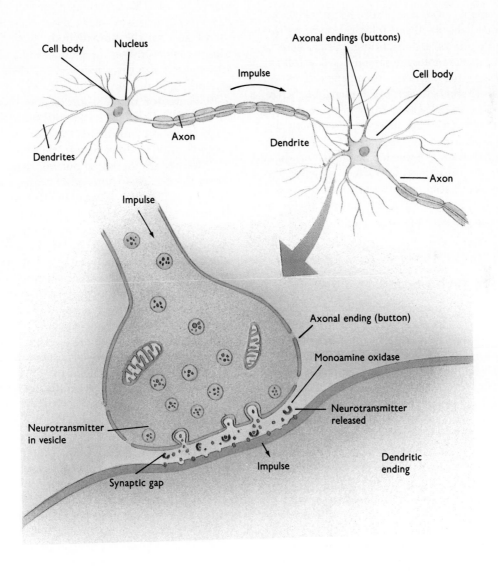

elements of biological, psychological, and sociocultural viewpoints in their work. One problem, however, is that eclecticism is easier in practice than in theory. The challenge remains to integrate these varying perspectives into a theoretically consistent general system of psychopathology. We will return to this challenge in more depth in this chapter's Unresolved Issues section.

THE PSYCHOSOCIAL VIEWPOINTS

There are many more psychosocial interpretations of abnormal behavior than biological ones, reflecting the difficulty of understanding humans as people and not just as biological organisms. The following sections will examine five perspectives on human nature and behavior: psychodynamic, behavioristic, cognitive-behavioral, humanistic, and interpersonal. Although these viewpoints represent distinct and sometimes conflicting orientations, they are in many ways complementary. All of them emphasize the importance of early experience and an awareness of social influences and psychological processes within an individual—hence the term **psychosocial viewpoints** as a general descriptive label.

◼ The Psychodynamic Perspective

The first steps toward understanding psychological factors in mental disorders were taken by Sigmund Freud (1856–1939). During five decades of observation, treatment, and writing, Freud developed a theory of psychopathology that emphasized the inner dynamics of unconscious motives, called the **psychoanalytic perspective.** The methods he used to study and treat patients are called **psychoanalysis.** Over the last half century, other clinicians have modified and revised Freud's theory, resulting in new **psychodynamic perspectives.** These perspectives contain many of the same assumptions and viewpoints as Freud's original theory, but they differ from classical psychoanalysis in some important respects (for example, Adler rejected Freud's emphasis on sexuality in favor of social motivation). We will review some of these perspectives later in this section.

In reviewing the psychodynamic perspective, we will divide our discussion into an examination of (a) the roots of psychodynamic thought, (b)

Freud and the beginnings of psychoanalysis, (c) the basic principles of psychoanalysis, (d) newer psychodynamic perspectives, and (e) the impact of the psychodynamic perspective on our views of human nature.

The Roots of Psychodynamic Thought
We find the roots of psychoanalysis in a somewhat unexpected place—the study of hypnosis, especially in its relation to hysteria. Hypnosis, an induced state of relaxation in which an individual is highly open to suggestion, first came into widespread use in late eighteenth- and early nineteenth-century France.

Mesmerism.   Our story starts with Anton Mesmer (1734–1815), a German physician who further developed Paracelsus' ideas about the influence of the planets on the human body (see Chapter 2). Mesmer believed that the planets affected a universal magnetic fluid in the body, the distribution of which determined health or disease. In attempting to find cures for mental disorders, Mesmer concluded that all people possessed magnetic forces that could be used to influence the distribution of the magnetic fluid in other people, thus effecting cures.

Mesmer attempted to put his views into practice in Vienna and various other towns, but it was in Paris in 1778 that he gained a broad following. There he opened a clinic in which he treated all kinds of diseases by "animal magnetism." In a dark room, patients were seated around a tub (a *baquet*) containing various chemicals, and iron rods protruding from the tub were applied to the affected areas of the patients' bodies. Accompanied by music, Mesmer appeared in a lilac robe, passing from one patient to another and touching each one with his hands or his wand. By this means, Mesmer was reportedly able to remove hysterical anesthesias and paralyses. He also demonstrated most of the phenomena later connected with the use of hypnosis.

Eventually branded a charlatan by his medical colleagues, Mesmer was forced to leave Paris and he quickly faded into obscurity. His methods and results, however, were at the center of scientific controversy for many years—in fact, **mesmerism,** as his technique came to be known, was as much a source of heated discussion in the early nineteenth century as psychoanalysis became in the early twentieth century. This discussion led to a renewed interest in hypnosis itself as an explanation of the "cures" that took place.

The Nancy School.   Liébeault (1823–1904), a French physician who practiced in the town of Nancy, used hypnosis successfully in his practice.

Anton Mesmer believed that the distribution of magnetic fluid in the body was responsible for determining health or disease. He further thought that all people possessed magnetic forces that could be used to influence the distribution of fluid in others, thus effecting cures. In this painting of Mesmeric therapy, Mesmer stands at the back, on the right, holding a wand. Mesmer was eventually branded a fraud by his colleagues, but he did demonstrate most of the phenomena later connected with the use of hypnosis.

Also in Nancy at the time was a professor of medicine, Bernheim (1840–1919), who became interested in the relationship between hysteria and hypnosis. His interest was the result of Liébeault's success in curing by hypnosis a patient who Bernheim had been treating unsuccessfully by more conventional methods for four years (Selling, 1943). Bernheim and Liébeault worked together to develop the hypothesis that hypnotism and hysteria were related and that both were due to suggestion (Brown & Menninger, 1940). Their hypothesis was based on two lines of evidence: (a) phenomena observed in hysteria, such as paralysis of an arm, inability to hear, or anesthetic areas in which an individual could be stuck with a pin without feeling pain (all of which occurred when there was apparently nothing organically wrong), could be produced in normal subjects by means of hypnosis; and (b) the same symptoms also could be removed by means of hypnosis. Thus it seemed likely that hysteria was a sort of self-hypnosis. The physicians who accepted this view ultimately came to be known as the **Nancy School.**

Meanwhile, Jean Charcot (1825–1893), who was head of the Salpétrière Hospital in Paris and the leading neurologist of his time, had been experimenting with some of the phenomena described by the mesmerists. As a result of his research, Charcot disagreed with the findings of the Nancy School and insisted that degenerative brain changes led to hysteria. In this, Charcot was eventually proved wrong, but work on the problem by so outstanding a scientist did a great deal to awaken medical and scientific interest in hysteria.

The dispute between Charcot and the Nancy School was one of the major debates of medical history, during which many harsh words were spoken on both sides. The adherents of the Nancy School finally triumphed, representing the first recognition of a psychologically caused mental disorder. This recognition spurred more research on the behavior underlying hysteria and other disor-

It took some time before Jean Charcot (1825–1893), the leading neurologist of his time, believed that there might be a causal relationship between self-hypnosis and hysteria. Once convinced, however, he did much, through research and lectures about hypnosis, such as the one shown here, to promote interest in the role psychological factors may play in mental disorders.

ders. Soon the data suggested that psychological factors were also involved in anxiety states, phobias, and other psychopathologies. Eventually, Charcot himself was won over to the new point of view and did much to promote the study of psychological factors in various mental disorders.

The debate as to whether mental disorders are caused by biological or psychological factors continues to this day. The Nancy School/Charcot debate represented a major step forward for psychology, however. Toward the end of the nineteenth century, it was clear that mental disorders could have either psychological bases or biological bases, or both. With this recognition, a major question remained to be answered: How do the psychologically based mental disorders actually develop?

The Beginnings of Psychoanalysis   The first systematic attempt to answer this question was made by Sigmund Freud. Freud was a brilliant young Viennese physician who specialized in neurology and received an appointment as lecturer on nervous diseases at the University of Vienna. In 1885 he went to study under Charcot and later became acquainted with the work of Liébeault and Bernheim at Nancy. He was impressed by their use of hypnosis with hysterical patients and came away convinced that powerful mental processes could remain hidden from consciousness.

On his return to Vienna, Freud worked in collaboration with another physician, Joseph Breuer (1842–1925), who had introduced an interesting innovation in the use of hypnosis with his patients.

Unlike hypnotists before him, he directed his patients to talk freely about their problems while under hypnosis. The patients usually displayed considerable emotion, and on awakening from their hypnotic states felt considerably relieved. Because of the emotional release involved, this method was called **catharsis.** This simple innovation in the use of hypnosis proved to be of great significance: it not only helped patients discharge their emotional tensions by discussing their problems, but it also revealed to the therapist the nature of the difficulties that had brought about certain symptoms. The patients, upon awakening, saw no relationship between their problems and their hysterical symptoms.

Thus was made the discovery of **the unconscious**—that portion of the mind that contains experiences of which a person is unaware—and with it the belief that processes outside of a person's awareness can play an important role in the determination of behavior. In 1893 Freud and Breuer published their joint paper, *On the Psychical Mechanisms of Hysterical Phenomena,* which was one of the great milestones in the study of psychodynamics.

Freud soon discovered, moreover, that he could dispense with hypnosis entirely. By encouraging patients to say whatever came into their minds without regard to logic or propriety, Freud found that patients would eventually overcome inner obstacles to remembering and would discuss their problems freely. Two related methods allowed him to understand patients' conscious and unconscious

Sigmund Freud (1856–1939), the founder of psychoanalysis, emphasized the role of unconscious processes in the determination of behavior. He abandoned the use of hypnosis for the techniques of free association and dream analysis to help patients achieve insight into their problems.

Joseph Breuer (1842–1925) used the cathartic method to help patients discharge emotional tensions by discussing their problems. The discussion would usually reveal the nature of the difficulties that had brought about neurotic symptoms.

thought processes. One method, **free association,** involved having patients talk freely about themselves, thereby providing information about their feelings, motives, and so forth. A second method, **dream analysis,** involved having patients record and describe their dreams. These techniques helped analysts and patients gain insights and achieve a more adequate understanding of emotional problems.

Freud devoted the rest of his long and energetic life to the development and elaboration of psychoanalytic principles. His views were formally introduced to American scientists in 1909, when he was invited to deliver a series of lectures at Clark University by the eminent psychologist, G. Stanley Hall, who was then president of the university. These *Introductory Lectures on Psychoanalysis* created a great deal of controversy and helped popularize psychoanalytic concepts among scientists as well as the general public.

The Basics of Psychoanalysis   The actual techniques involved in psychoanalysis are based on the general principles underlying Freud's theory of personality; they are very complex. We shall not attempt to deal with them in detail here. For our purposes, a general overview of the principles of classical psychoanalysis should suffice. For those wishing more information, good resources include Alexander's (1948) *Fundamentals of Psychoanalysis* or any of Freud's original works.

Id, ego, and superego.   Freud theorized that an individual's behavior results from the interaction of three key parts or subsystems within the personality or psyche: the id, ego, and superego.

The **id** is the source of instinctual drives, which are inherited and considered to be of two opposing types: (a) *life instincts,* which are constructive drives primarily of a sexual nature, and which constitute the **libido,** the basic energy of life; and (b) *death instincts,* which are destructive drives that tend toward aggression, destruction, and eventual death. Freud used the term *sexual* in a broad sense to refer to almost anything pleasurable, from eating to painting. The id is completely selfish, concerned only with the immediate gratification of instinctual needs without reference to reality or moral considerations. Hence it is said to operate in terms of the **pleasure principle.** While the id can generate mental images and wish-fulfilling fantasies, referred to as the **primary process,** it cannot undertake the realistic actions needed to meet instinctual demands.

Consequently, a second part of the personality, as viewed by Freud, develops—the **ego.** The ego mediates between the demands of the id and the realities of the external world. The basic purpose of the ego is to meet id demands, but in such a way as to ensure the well-being and survival of an individual. This role requires the use of reason and other intellectual resources in dealing with the external world, as well as the exercise of control over id

During his only visit to the United States, in 1909, Freud delivered a series of lectures to American scientists at Clark University. Among those in the front row here are William James (third from the left), G. Stanley Hall (sixth from the left), Freud (seventh), and Carl Jung (eighth).

demands. The ego's adaptive measures are referred to as the **secondary process,** and the ego is said to operate in terms of the **reality principle.** Freud viewed id demands, especially sexual and aggressive strivings, as inherently in conflict with the rules and prohibitions imposed by society.

Since the id-ego relationship is merely one of expediency, Freud postulated a third key subsystem —the **superego.** The superego is the outgrowth of the taboos and moral values of society. It is essentially what we refer to as the *conscience;* it is concerned with right and wrong. As the superego develops, it becomes an additional inner control system that copes with the uninhibited desires of the id. The superego also operates through the ego system and strives to compel the ego to inhibit desires that are considered wrong or immoral.

Freud believed that the interplay of id, ego, and superego is of crucial significance in determining behavior. Often, inner conflicts arise because the three subsystems are striving for different goals. These conflicts are called **intrapsychic conflicts** and, if unresolved, lead to mental disorder.

Anxiety, defense mechanisms, and the unconscious. The concept of anxiety—generalized feelings of fear and apprehension—is prominent in the psychoanalytic viewpoint. Freud distinguished among three types of anxiety, or "psychic pain," that people can suffer: (a) *reality anxiety,* arising from dangers or threats in the external world; (b) *neurotic anxiety,* caused by the id's impulses threatening to break through ego controls into behavior that will be punished in some way; and (c) *moral anxiety,* arising from a real or contemplated action that is in conflict with an individual's superego and thus arouses feelings of guilt.

Anxiety is a warning of impending danger as well as a painful experience, so it forces an individual to take corrective action. Often, the ego can cope with anxiety through rational measures; if these do not suffice, however, the ego resorts to irrational protective measures that are referred to as **ego-defense mechanisms** and are described in *HIGHLIGHT 3.2.*

These defense mechanisms discharge or soothe anxiety, but they do so by helping an individual push painful ideas out of consciousness rather than by dealing directly with a problem. For the individual, this results in a distorted view of reality.

A key concept of psychoanalytic principles, as we have seen, is the *unconscious.* Freud thought that the conscious part of the mind represents a relative-ly small area, while the unconscious part, like the submerged part of an iceberg, is the much larger portion. In the depths of the unconscious are the hurtful memories, forbidden desires, and other experiences that have been *repressed*—that is, pushed out of consciousness. Unconscious material continues to seek expression when ego controls are temporarily lowered under hypnosis, or in fantasies, dreams, slips of the tongue, and so forth. Until such unconscious material is brought to awareness and integrated into the ego structure—for example, through psychoanalysis—it presumably leads to irrational and maladaptive behavior.

Psychosexual stages of development.   Freud con-ceptualized five **psychosexual stages of develop-ment.** Each stage is characterized by a dominant mode of achieving libidinal (sexual) pleasure:

- *The oral stage.* During the first two years of life, the mouth is the principal erogenous zone; an infant's greatest source of gratification is sucking.

- *The anal stage.* From age 2 to age 3, the membranes of the anal region provide the major source of pleasurable stimulation.

- *The phallic stage.* From age 3 to age 5 or 6, self-manipulation of the genitals provides the major source of pleasurable sensation.

- *The latency stage.* In the years from 6 to 12, sexual motivations recede in importance as a child becomes preoccupied with developing skills and other activities.

- *The genital stage.* After puberty the deepest feelings of pleasure come from heterosexual relations.

Freud believed that appropriate gratification during each stage is important if an individual is not to be *fixated* at that level. For example, he main-tained that an infant who does not receive adequate oral gratification may be prone to excessive eating or drinking in adult life.

In general, each stage of development places demands on an individual and arouses conflicts that must be resolved. One of the most important conflicts occurs during the phallic stage, when the pleasures of self-stimulation and accompanying fan-tasies pave the way for the **Oedipus complex.** Oedipus, according to Greek mythology, unknow-ingly killed his father and married his mother. Each young boy, Freud thought, symbolically relives the Oedipus drama. He has incestuous cravings for his mother and views his father as a hated rival; howev-er, he also fears his father and especially is afraid that his father may harm him by removing his penis. This **castration anxiety** forces the boy to repress his sexual desire for his mother and his hostility toward his father. Eventually, if all goes well, the boy identifies with his father and comes to have only harmless affection for his mother.

The **Electra complex** is the female counterpart of the Oedipus complex. It is based on the view that each girl experiences penis envy and wants to possess her father and replace her mother. While the boy renounces his lust out of fear of castration, no such threat can realistically be posed for the girl. Her emergence from the complex is more mild and less complete than the boy's. She essentially settles for a promissory note: one day she will have a man of her own who can give her a baby—a type of penis substitute.

For either sex, resolution of this conflict is considered essential if a young adult is to develop satisfactory heterosexual relationships. In short, the psychoanalytic perspective holds that about the best we can hope for is a compromise among our warring inclinations, from which we will realize as much instinctual gratification as possible with mini-mal punishment and guilt. It thus presents a pessi-mistic and deterministic view of human behavior that minimizes rationality and freedom of self-determination. On a group level, it interprets vio-lence, war, and related phenomena as the inevitable products of the aggressive and destructive instincts present in human nature.

The demands of the id are evident in early childhood. Accord-ing to Freud, babies pass through an oral stage, in which sucking is a dominant pleasure.

Summary Chart of Ego-Defense Mechanisms

Mechanism	Example
Denial of reality. Protecting the self from an unpleasant reality by the refusal to perceive or face it.	A smoker concludes that the evidence linking cigarette use to health problems is scientifically worthless.
Fantasy. Gratifying frustrated desires by imaginary achievements.	A socially inept and inhibited young man imagines himself chosen by a group of women to provide them with sexual satisfaction.
Repression. Preventing painful or dangerous thoughts from entering consciousness.	A mother's occasional murderous impulses toward her hyperactive two-year-old are denied access to awareness.
Rationalization. Using contrived "explanations" to conceal or disguise unworthy motives for one's behavior.	A fanatical racist uses ambiguous passages from Scripture to justify his hostile actions toward minorities.
Projection. Attributing one's unacceptable motives or characteristics to others.	An expansionist-minded dictator of a totalitarian state is convinced that neighboring countries are planning to invade.
Reaction formation. Preventing the awareness or expression of unacceptable desires by an exaggerated adoption of seemingly opposite behavior.	A man troubled by homosexual urges initiates a zealous community campaign to stamp out gay bars.
Displacement. Discharging pent-up feelings, often of hostility, on objects less dangerous than those arousing the feelings.	A woman harassed by her boss at work initiates an argument with her husband.
Emotional insulation. Reducing ego involvement by protective withdrawal and passivity.	A child separated from her parents because of illness and lengthy hospitalization becomes emotionally unresponsive and apathetic.
Intellectualization (isolation). Cutting off affective charge from hurtful situations or separating incompatible attitudes by logic-tight compartments.	A prisoner on death row awaiting execution resists appeals on his behalf and coldly insists that the letter of the law be followed.

Newer Psychodynamic Perspectives   In seeking to understand his patients and develop his theories, Freud was chiefly concerned with the workings of the id, its nature as a source of energy and the manner in which it could be channeled or transformed. Later theorists, notably including his daughter Anna Freud (1895–1982), were much more concerned with how the ego performed its central functions as the "executive" of personality. This second generation of psychodynamic theorists refined and elaborated on the ego-defense reactions.

Contemporary approaches focus on neither the nature of the id nor the ego, but rather on the objects toward whom the child has directed these impulses and which the child has introjected (incorporated) into his or her own personality. *Object* in this context refers to the symbolic representation of another person in the child's environment, most often a parent. The concept of **introjection,** a difficult one for most students, refers to an internal process in which the child incorporates symbolically, through images and memories, some person viewed with strong emotion. For example, the child might internalize the image of a parent's scowling face. Later, this symbol, or object, can influence how a person experiences events and behaves.

Mechanism	Example
Undoing. Atoning for or magically trying to dispel unacceptable desires or acts.	A teenager who feels guilty about masturbation ritually touches a doorknob a prescribed number of times following each occurrence of the act.
Regression. Retreating to an earlier developmental level involving less mature behavior and responsibility.	A man whose self-esteem has been shattered reverts to childlike "show-off" behavior and exhibits his genitals to young girls.
Identification. Increasing feelings of worth by affiliating oneself with a person or institution of illustrious standing.	A youth-league football coach becomes excessively demanding of his young players in emulation of an authoritarian pro football coach.
Overcompensation. Covering up perceived weaknesses by emphasizing a desirable characteristic or making up for frustration in one area by overgratification in another.	A dangerously overweight woman goes on eating binges when she feels neglected by her husband.
Acting out. Engaging in antisocial or excessive behavior without regard to negative consequences as a way of dealing with emotional stress.	An unhappy, frustrated sales respresentative has several indiscriminate affairs without regard to the negative effects of the behavior.
Splitting. Viewing oneself or others as *all* good or bad without integrating positive or negative qualities into the evaluations; reacting to others in an "all or none" manner rather than considering the full range of their qualities.	A conflicted manager does not recognize individual qualities or characteristics of her employees. Instead, she views them as all good or all bad, seeing most of them as all bad.
Sublimation. Channeling frustrated sexual energy into substitutive activities.	A sexually frustrated artist paints wildly erotic pictures.
Fixation. Attaching oneself in an unreasonable or exaggerated way to some person, or arresting emotional development on a childhood or adolescent level.	An unmarried, middle-aged man still depends on his mother to provide his basic needs.

Based on Anna Freud (1946); DSM-III-R (1987).

The earliest development of this **object-relations** emphasis in psychodynamic thought took place in the 1930s in England under the leadership of Melanie Klein, W. R. D. Fairbairn, and D. W. Winnicott. These theorists developed the general notion that internalized objects could have various conflicting properties—such as exciting or attractive versus hostile, frustrating, or rejecting—and moreover that these objects could split off from the central ego and maintain independent existences, thus giving rise to inner conflicts. For example, a child might internalize images of a punishing father; that image would then become a harsh self-critic. An individual experiencing such splitting among internalized objects is, so to speak, "the servant of many masters" and cannot therefore lead an integrated, orderly life.

The work of Margaret Mahler (1897–1985) in the United States complemented and added additional insights to this approach (see, for example, Mahler, 1976). Mahler pointed out that, for a very young child, objects are not differentiated with respect to self versus other. Only gradually does a child gain an internal representation of self as distinct from representations of other objects. Only gradually is object constancy achieved (in which, for

Anna Freud (1895–1982) elaborated the theory of ego-defense mechanisms and pioneered the psychoanalytic treatment of children.

Margaret Mahler (1897–1985) elaborated the object-relations approach, which many see as the main focus of contemporary psychoanalysis.

instance, the mother of yesterday is seen as the same object as the mother of today). This process involves a developmental phase of **separation-individuation,** the successful completion of which is essential for the achievement of personal maturity.

Many other American analysts have, in recent years, become advocates of the object-relations point of view. Among them is Otto Kernberg, noted especially for his studies of both borderline and narcissistic personalities (see Chapter 7). Kernberg's view is that the borderline personality, whose chief characteristic is instability (especially in personal relationships), is an individual who is unable to achieve a full and stable personal identity (self) because of an inability to integrate and reconcile pathological internalized objects.

These newer developments in psychodynamic therapy emphasize interpersonal relationships and how the quality of early relationships affects a person's subsequent ability to achieve fulfilling adult interactions. These ideas have developed largely independently of the psychodynamic mainstream and have assumed importance in their own right. They will be addressed further in a later section on the interpersonal perspective.

Impact of the Psychodynamic Perspective

In historical perspective, Freudian psychoanalysis can be seen as the first systematic, psychodynamic approach to show how human psychological processes can result in mental disorders. Much as the biological perspective had replaced superstition

with organic pathology as the suspected cause of mental disorders, the psychoanalytic perspective replaced brain pathology with exaggerated ego defenses as the suspected cause of at least some mental disorders.

Freud greatly advanced our understanding of both normal and abnormal behavior. Many of his original concepts have become fundamental to our thinking about human nature and behavior. Two of Freud's contributions stand out as particularly noteworthy.

1. He developed techniques such as free association and dream analysis for becoming acquainted with both the conscious and unconscious aspects of mental life. The data thus obtained led Freud to emphasize (a) the dynamic role of unconscious motives and ego-defense processes, (b) the importance of early childhood experiences in later personality adjustment and maladjustment, and (c) the importance of sexual factors in human behavior and mental disorders. Although, as we have said, Freud used the term *sexual* in a much broader sense than usual, the idea struck a common chord, and the role of sexual factors in human behavior was finally brought out into the open as an appropriate topic for scientific investigation.

2. He demonstrated that certain abnormal mental phenomena occur in the attempt to cope with difficult problems and are simply exaggerations of normal ego-defense mechanisms. This realization that the same psychological principles apply to both normal and abnormal behavior dissipated much of the mystery and fear surrounding mental disorders. Patients could be mentally disordered, but could also have dignity as human beings.

The psychodynamic perspective has come under attack from many directions—from other perspectives as well as from theorists within the psychodynamic tradition. Two important criticisms of psychoanalytic theory center around its failure as a scientific theory to explain abnormal behavior. First, it fails to recognize the scientific limits of personal reports of experience as the primary mode of obtaining information. Second, there is a lack of scientific evidence to support many of its explanatory assumptions or the effectiveness of its therapy. Freudian theory in particular has been criticized for an overemphasis on the sex drive; for undue pessimism about basic human nature; for an exaggeration of the role of unconscious processes; and for failing to consider motives toward personal growth and fulfillment. The second generation of psychodynamic theorists did much to overcome these objections. Criticisms surrounding the scientific validity of psychodynamic approaches remain, however. In addition, today's psychodynamic therapies have been criticized for neglecting the role of cultural differences in shaping behavior and because they frequently take months, and even years, to complete, which is very expensive for a client.

The Behavioristic Perspective

While psychoanalysis dominated thought about abnormal behavior in the early part of this century, another school—behaviorism—was emerging to challenge its supremacy. Behavioristic psychologists believed that the study of subjective experience—through the techniques of free association and dream analysis—did not provide acceptable scientific data, because such observations were not open to verification by other investigators. In their view, only the study of directly observable behavior and the stimuli and reinforcing conditions that "control" it could serve as a basis for formulating scientific principles of human behavior.

The **behavioristic perspective** is organized around a central theme: the role of learning in human behavior. Although this perspective was initially developed through research in the laboratory rather than through clinical practice with disturbed individuals, its implications for explaining and treating maladaptive behavior soon became evident.

Roots of the Behavioristic Perspective

The origins of the behavioristic view of abnormal behavior and its treatment are tied to experimental work on the form of stimulus-response learning known as **conditioning.** This work began with the discovery of the conditioned reflex by Russian physiologist Ivan Pavlov (1849–1936). Around the

Ivan Pavlov (1849–1936), a pioneer in demonstrating the part conditioning plays in behavior, is shown here with his staff and some of the apparatus used to condition reflexes in dogs.

turn of the century, Pavlov demonstrated that a dog would learn to salivate to a nonfood stimulus, such as a bell, after the stimulus had been regularly accompanied by food.

Pavlov's discovery, which came to be known as *classical conditioning,* excited a young American psychologist, John B. Watson (1878–1958), who was searching for objective ways to study human behavior. Watson reasoned that if psychology were to become a true science, it must abandon the subjectivity of inner sensations and other "mental" events and limit itself to what could be objectively observed. What better way to do this than to observe systematic changes in behavior brought about simply by rearranging stimulus conditions? Watson thus changed the focus of psychology to the study of overt behavior, an approach he called *behaviorism.*

Watson, a man of impressive energy and demeanor, saw great possibilities in behaviorism, and he was quick to point them out to his fellow scientists and a curious public. He boasted that, through conditioning, he could train any healthy child to become whatever sort of adult one wished. He also challenged the psychoanalysts and the more biologically oriented psychologists of his day by suggesting that abnormal behavior was the product of unfortunate, inadvertent earlier conditioning and could be modified through reconditioning.

By the 1930s Watson had made an enormous impact on American psychology. Watson's approach placed heavy emphasis on the role of the social environment in conditioning personality development and behavior, both normal and abnormal. Today's behavioristically oriented psychologists still accept the basic tenets of Watson's doctrine, although they are more cautious in their claims.

While Watson was studying stimulus conditions and their relation to behavioral responses, E. L. Thorndike (1874–1949) and subsequently B. F. Skinner (1904–1990) were exploring the other side of the conditioning coin—the fact that, over time, the consequences of behavior tend to influence behavior. Behavior that *operates* on the environment is *instrumental* in producing certain outcomes, and those outcomes, in turn, determine the likelihood that the behavior will be repeated on similar occasions. This type of learning came to be called *instrumental* or *operant conditioning.*

The principles of conditioning had been worked out enough by 1950 that in that year John Dollard and Neal Miller published their classic work *Personality and Psychotherapy,* which essentially reinterpreted psychoanalytic theory in the terminology of learning principles. In essence they asserted that the ungoverned pleasure-seeking impulses of Freud's id were merely an aspect of the principle of reinforcement (the behavior of all organisms being determined by the maximization of gratification and minimization of pain); that anxiety was merely a conditioned fear response; that repression was

John B. Watson (1878–1958) changed the focus of psychology from the study of inner sensations to the study of outer behavior, an approach called behaviorism.

E. L. Thorndike (1874–1949) formulated the law of effect—a seemingly simple observation that rewarded responses are strengthened and unrewarded responses are weakened—which had implications for controlling human behavior.

B. F. Skinner (1904–1990) formulated the concept of operant conditioning in which reinforcers could be used to make a response more or less probable and frequent.

merely conditioned thought-stoppage; and so on. The groundwork was thus laid for a behavioristic assault on the prevailingly psychodynamic doctrines of the time. Early efforts to apply learning principles in the treatment of abnormal behavior, such as those by Salter (1949) and Wolpe (1958), were met with much resistance by the well-entrenched supporters of psychoanalysis; it was not until the 1960s and 1970s that behavioral therapy became established as a powerful way of viewing and treating abnormal behavior.

Basics of the Behavioristic Perspective

As we have noted, **learning**—the modification of behavior as a consequence of experience—provides the central theme of the behavioristic approach. Since most human behavior is learned, the behaviorists have addressed themselves to the question of how learning occurs. In trying to answer this question, they have focused on the effects of environmental conditions (stimuli) on the acquisition, modification, and possible elimination of various types of response patterns—both adaptive and maladaptive.

Classical and operant conditioning. A specific stimulus may come to elicit a specific response through the process of **classical conditioning.** For example, although food naturally elicits salivation, any stimulus that reliably precedes the presentation of food will also elicit salivation. In this case, food is the *unconditioned stimulus,* and salivation is the *unconditioned response.* A stimulus that precedes food delivery and eventually elicits salivation is called a *conditioned stimulus.* Conditioning has occurred when presentation of the conditioned stimulus alone elicits salivation (called the *conditioned response*). Pavlov, for instance, sounded a tone (the soon-to-be conditioned stimulus) just before he presented food (the unconditioned stimulus) to his dogs. After several tone-food pairings, the dogs salivated (the conditioned response) to the tone (the conditioned stimulus) alone. The dogs had learned that the tone was a reliable predictor of food delivery. The hallmark of classical conditioning is that the response is elicited by the conditioned stimulus.

The chief importance of classical conditioning in abnormal psychology is the fact that many responses of the autonomic nervous system, including those relating to fear or anxiety, can be conditioned. Thus one can learn a fear of the dark if fear-producing stimuli (such as frightening dreams

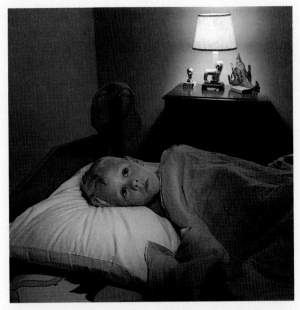

Fear, which is a response of the autonomic nervous system, can be conditioned. Fear of the dark, for example, can be learned if frightening encounters or experiences happen under conditions of darkness.

or fantasies) occur regularly during conditions of darkness.

In **operant (or instrumental) conditioning,** an individual learns how to achieve a desired goal. The goal in question may be to obtain something that is rewarding or to avoid something that is unpleasant. Here a response typically precedes the desired stimulus, as when an individual kicks a coffee machine that has failed to function. If the kick causes the machine to produce coffee, the next time it does not work, the person will probably kick it again. As we grow up, operant learning becomes an important mechanism for discriminating between what will prove rewarding and what will prove unrewarding—and for acquiring the behaviors essential for coping with our world.

Unfortunately, there is no guarantee that what we learn will be accurate or useful. Thus we may learn to value things that seem attractive but actually will hurt us; we may fail to learn techniques necessary for coping; or we may learn coping patterns such as helplessness, bullying, or other irresponsible behaviors that are maladaptive rather than adaptive.

Reinforcement. Essential to both classical and operant conditioning is **reinforcement**—the strengthening of a new response by manipulating its relationship with a particular stimulus. This stimulus can be either pleasant or aversive. In operant conditioning, a behavior is strengthened by being repeatedly associated either with a pleasant stimulus or with the avoidance of an aversive stimulus. For example, a child may learn a certain response if it has in the past produced a reinforcer (such as candy) or avoided a punisher (such as a spanking). Initially a high rate of reinforcement may be necessary to establish a response, but lesser rates are usually sufficient to maintain it. In fact, a learned response appears to be especially persistent when reinforcement is intermittent—when the reinforcing stimulus does not invariably follow the response—as demonstrated in gambling when occasional wins seem to maintain high rates of response. However, when reinforcement is consistently withheld over time, the conditioned response—whether classical or operant—eventually extinguishes. In short, the subject stops making the response; this process is known as **extinction.**

A special problem arises in extinguishing a response in situations where a subject has been conditioned to anticipate an aversive event and to respond by avoiding it. For example, a boy who has been bitten by a vicious dog may develop a *conditioned avoidance response* in which he consistently avoids all dogs. When he sees a dog, he feels anxious; avoiding contact lessens his anxiety and is thus reinforcing. As a result, his avoidance response is highly resistant to extinction. It also prevents him from having experiences with friendly dogs that could bring about reconditioning. In later discussions, we will see that conditioned avoidance responses play a role in many patterns of abnormal behavior.

Generalization and discrimination.   In both classical and operant conditioning, when a response is conditioned to one stimulus or set of stimulus conditions, it can be evoked by other, similar stimuli; this process is called **generalization.** A person who fears bees, for example, may generalize that fear to all flying insects.

A process complementary to generalization is **discrimination,** which occurs when an individual learns to distinguish between similar stimuli and to respond differently to them. The ability to discriminate may be brought about through *differential reinforcement.* For example, since red strawberries taste good and green ones do not, a conditioned discrimination will occur if an individual has experience with both. According to the behavioristic perspective, complex processes like perceiving, forming concepts, and solving problems are all based on this basic discriminative process.

The concepts of generalization and discrimination have many implications for the development of maladaptive behavior. While generalization enables us to use past experiences in sizing up new situations, the possibility always exists of making inappropriate generalizations—as when a troubled youth fails to discriminate between friendly and hostile "joshing" from peers, or when a child of wealthy parents learns to regard all rich people with respect, whatever the source of their wealth. In some instances, a vital discrimination may be beyond an individual's capability—as when a bigoted person deals with others as stereotypes rather than as individuals—and may lead to inappropriate and maladaptive behavior.

Impact of the Behavioristic Perspective

By means of relatively few basic concepts, behaviorism attempts to explain the acquisition, modification, and extinction of all types of behavior. Maladaptive behavior is viewed as essentially the result of (a) a failure to learn necessary adaptive behaviors or competencies, such as how to establish satisfying personal relationships; or (b) the learning of ineffective or maladaptive responses. Maladaptive behavior is thus the result of learning that has gone awry and is defined in terms of specific, observable, undesirable responses.

For the behaviorist, the focus of therapy is thus on changing specific behaviors—eliminating undesirable reactions and learning desirable ones. For example, therapists can have considerable impact with the application of learning principles in the area of social skills training (Liberman, Mueser, & DeRisi, 1989). A number of *behavior-modification techniques* have been developed, based on the systematic application of learning principles, many of which are described in *HIGHLIGHT 3.3.* Additional examples of these techniques will be given in later chapters.

The behavioristic approach has been heralded for its precision and objectivity, for its wealth of research, and for its demonstrated effectiveness in changing specific behaviors. A behavioral therapist specifies what behavior is to be changed and how it is to be changed; later, the effectiveness of the therapy can be evaluated objectively by the degree to which the stated goals have been achieved. On the other hand, the behavioristic perspective has been criticized for being concerned only with symptoms, for ignoring the problems of value and meaning that may be important for those seeking help, and for denying the possibility of choice and self-direction.

The behavioristic tradition has been expanded to focus on human thought processes (as will be

Some Behavior–Modification Techniques Based on Learning Principles

Learning Principle	Technique	Example
Behavior patterns are developed and established through repeated association with positive reinforcers.	Use of positive reinforcement to establish desired behavior	Paul and Lentz (1977) successfully rehabilitated a group of chronic mental patients by providing them with tokens contingent on desirable behavior. The tokens could subsequently be used to "purchase" food, pleasant surroundings, etc.
The repeated association of an established behavior pattern with aversive stimuli results in avoidance behavior.	Use of aversive stimuli to eliminate undesirable behavior (aversive conditioning)	Rolider and Van Houten (1985) suppressed tantrum behavior in a 5-year-old psychotic boy and inappropriate behavior in a 10-year-old retarded boy through use of a delayed punishment procedure. Parents tape-recorded tantrums or inappropriate behavior that occurred in daily school settings, then later played back portions of the tape while administering punishment. Punishment consisted of response suppression (holding the child in a corner) and firm verbalizations. The tape-recorder-mediated procedure produced greater reductions in tantrums than verbal punishment alone.
When an established behavior pattern is no longer reinforced, it tends to be extinguished.	Withdrawal of reinforcement for undesirable behavior	Liberman and Raskin (1971) reported improvement in the treatment of depression by instructing family members of a depressed person to provide attention for constructive behavior but to ignore depressive behavior.
Avoidance behavior will be inhibited or reduced if the conditions that provoke it are repeatedly paired with positive stimuli.	Desensitization to conditions that elicit unreasonable fear or anxiety	Rimm and Lefebvre (1981) cited the successful treatment of phobias concerning loud noises and high places in a 45-year-old air force veteran. The treatment, known as systematic desensitization, consisted of having the man repeatedly imagine fearful scenes relating to his phobias while in a state of deep relaxation.
A specified behavior can be established gradually if successive approximations of the behavior are reinforced.	Shaping of desired behavior	Blount et al. (1984) successfully used shaping and modeling procedures to teach children to swallow pills required for their treatment. They used graduated sizes of candy, a vitamin pill, and a placebo capsule as training stimuli; and they used toys to reinforce the child to swallow a training stimulus. In the initial training session, the child was seen without parents present. The experimenter first modeled the swallowing behavior, then reminded the child of the correct steps to use in swallowing the pill. When the child successfully swallowed two training stimuli, the toy was given as reinforcement. After the child learned to swallow the pills, he or she was tested with the parents present. The child was followed-up in the home for three weeks immediately after training and again at three months. Five out of six children successfully learned to take their medications.
Reinforcement can operate to modify covert behavior (cognitions) as well as overt behavior.	Cognitive restructuring	Goldfried, Linehan, and Smith (1978) told highly anxious subjects to imagine being in an anxiety-arousing test situation and then presented them with instructions for reducing their anxiety. Subjects not only learned to react to test situations with less anxiety but reponded to other social circumstances with more adaptive attitudes.

discussed in the next section). Even with this trend, however, the most ardent behaviorists continue to emphasize the potential use of modern science and technology for planning a better world. In his famous novel, *Walden Two* (1948), and its nonfiction version, *Beyond Freedom and Dignity* (1971), Skinner depicted the utopian world he believed would result from the systematic application of learning principles and behavior-modification procedures to world problems. He (1974) stated the matter succinctly: "In the behavioristic view, man can now control his own destiny because he knows what must be done and how to do it" (p. 258). Skinner does not explain how people who have no choices could choose to exert such control.

Whatever its limitations and paradoxes, the behavioristic perspective has had and continues to have a tremendous impact on contemporary views of human nature, behavior, and psychopathology.

John Dollard (1900–1980) was a pioneer in shifting the focus on the nature of psychological functioning from overt behavior to the underlying cognitions assumed to be producing that behavior.

■ The Cognitive–Behavioral Perspective

The behavioristic perspective was a reaction to the subjectivism of an earlier era in psychology. It sought to banish private mental events from psychological study because they were unobservable and therefore unsuitable for scientific research. Some proponents of behaviorism even refused to use such terms as *mind* and *thought*. Although there were some who rejected behaviorism, it quickly gained wide acceptance among psychologists. As a result, the constraints imposed by the behavioristic point of view inhibited the development of cognitive psychology for three decades after the 1920s.

The Basics of the Cognitive-Behavioral Perspective   Since the 1950s, psychologists, including some learning theorists, have focused on **cognitive processes**—the thoughts, images, and techniques involved with information processing— and their impact on behavior. In many respects, the current emphasis on the cognitive aspects of human behavior is a reaction to the mechanistic nature of the behavioral viewpoint.

Developments in clinical psychology have paralleled this reorientation of the larger field. In many instances, this reorientation has been led by individuals who were formerly identified with the behavioral tradition. A number of theorists have diverged from a somewhat mechanistic, purely learning-based approach to understanding abnormal behavior to an approach that incorporates human thought processes. This approach, referred to as the *cognitive*

or **cognitive-behavioral perspective,** focuses on thought and information-processing processes as they apply to distorted thinking and maladaptive behavior. Unlike behaviorism's focus on overt behavior, the cognitive view treats thoughts as "behaviors" and thus brings them into focus as appropriate and relevant events from which to obtain empirical data.

The pioneering work of John Dollard (1900–1980) and Neal Miller (b. 1909), in their efforts to scientifically study and apply learning principles to psychodynamic processes, focused on cognitive concepts to explain abnormal behavior. They considered cognition—for example, using symbolic processes to visualize and label emotions and problems—an important process in gaining control over maladaptive behaviors.

Another pioneering theorist, George Kelly (1905–1966), contributed substantially to the cognitive viewpoint. Kelly developed a personality theory in which he postulated that people build **personal constructs**—uniquely individual ways of perceiving other people and events. People then use these personal constructs to interpret events around them. For example, the way a person describes or interprets a comment made by an acquaintance can produce emotional upset even though the comment was neutral and not intended to hurt. It is the meaning an individual attaches, filtered through his or her own personal constructs, that results in negative feelings and an emotional reaction.

Another learning theorist, Albert Bandura (b. 1925), has placed considerable emphasis on the

Neal Miller (b. 1909), along with John Dollard, reinterpreted psychoanalytic theory into the language of learning principles in their classic work, Personality and Psychotherapy.

George Kelly (1905–1966) was another cognitive-behavioral theorist who linked maladaptive behavior to the way people use personal constructs—how they interpret events around them.

Albert Bandura (b. 1925) stressed that people learn more by internal than external reinforcement; they can visualize the consequences of their actions and influence their environment rather than rely exclusively on environmental reinforcements.

cognitive aspects of learning. Bandura has stressed that human beings regulate their behavior by internal symbolic processes—thoughts. That is, they learn by *internal reinforcement*. We prepare ourselves for difficult tasks, for example, by visualizing what the consequences would be if we did not perform them. Thus we take our automobiles to the garage in the fall and have the antifreeze checked because we can "see" ourselves stranded on a road in the winter. We do not always require external reinforcement to alter our behavior patterns; with our cognitive abilities we can solve many problems internally. Bandura (1974) has gone so far as to say that human beings have "a capacity for self-direction" and that recognition of this capacity "represents a substantial departure from exclusive reliance upon environmental control" (pp. 861, 863).

The development of a cognitive-behavioral viewpoint distinct from behaviorism is not surprising. A hallmark of clinical behavioristic practice has always been the precise identification of specific problem behaviors, followed by the use of techniques directed specifically at those behaviors. This is in contrast to, for example, psychodynamic practice, which assumes that diverse problems are due to a limited array of intrapsychic conflicts (such as an unresolved Oedipus complex) and tends not to focus treatment techniques directly on a person's particular problems or complaints. Behaviorally oriented therapies, such as *systematic desensitization* (described in Chapter 18), have from the outset relied heavily on asking clients to conjure up images in their minds, certainly a process that is cognitive

in nature. Cognitive-behavioral theoreticians and clinicians have simply shifted their focus from overt behavior itself to the underlying cognitions assumed to be producing that behavior. The issue then becomes one of altering the maladaptive cognitions.

Today many behaviorally-oriented clinicians and researchers are incorporating cognitive processes, including imagery and self-awareness, into their pictures of psychological functioning. To a large extent, cognitive-behavioral clinicians are concerned with their client's self-statements—with what these people say to themselves by way of interpreting their experiences. For example, people who interpret what happens in their lives as a negative reflection of their self-worth are likely to feel depressed. A cognitive-behavioral clinician would approach this situation with a variety of techniques designed to alter the negative cognitive bias the client harbors (see, for example, Beck, Emery, & Greenberg, 1985; Kendall & Braswell, 1985; Meichenbaum, 1977). The most widely used cognitive-behavioral therapies, Ellis' Rational Emotive Therapy and Beck's Cognitive-Behavioral Treatment, will be described in greater detail in Chapter 18.

The Impact of the Cognitive-Behavioral Perspective The cognitive-behavioral viewpoint has had a powerful impact on contemporary clinical psychology. Many researchers and clinicians support the principle of altering human behavior through changing the way people view or think about themselves and others. Many traditional behaviorists, however, are skeptical of the cognitive-behavioral viewpoint. Skinner (1990), in his last major address, remained true to his theories over the years. He questioned the move away from principles of operant conditioning and toward cognitive behaviorism. He reminded his audience that cognitions are not observable phenomena and cannot, as such, be relied on as solid empirical data. Though Skinner is gone, this debate will surely continue.

■ The Humanistic Perspective

The **humanistic perspective** focuses on freeing people from disabling assumptions and attitudes so that they can live fuller lives. Its emphasis is thus on growth and self-actualization rather than on curing diseases or alleviating disorders; its practitioners do not typically deal with individuals suffering from serious mental disorders.

The humanistic perspective has been influenced by both the behavioristic and the psychodynamic perspectives, but it is in significant disagreement with both. The behavioristic perspective, with its focus on the stimulus situation and observable behavior, is seen as an oversimplification that underrates the importance of an individual's psychological makeup, inner experience, and potential for self-direction. Humanistic psychologists also disagree with the negative picture of human nature presented by psychoanalytic theory and its stress on the overwhelming power of irrational, unconscious impulses. Instead, the humanistic perspective views basic human nature as "good," emphasizes present conscious processes—paying less attention to unconscious processes and past causes—and places strong emphasis on peoples' inherent capacity for responsible self-direction. Humanistic psychologists think that much of the empirical research designed to investigate causal factors is too simplistic to uncover the complexities of human behavior. Thus the humanistic perspective tends to be as much a statement of values—how we *ought* to view the human condition—as it is an attempt to account for human behaviors, at least among persons beset by personal problems.

Some psychologists have raised objections to the use of the term *humanistic* to describe the more experientially-oriented therapies because it implies that other approaches demean individuals or view humans as objects with which to tinker. All approaches, of course, ultimately aim at helping people to be happier and more effective; all approaches are "humanistic" in this sense, just as all are interested in changing behavior and thus recognize the importance of learning. Their labels indicate their special focuses but do not imply that they exclude all other factors.

The Roots of the Humanistic Perspective

The humanistic perspective has been heavily influenced by outstanding psychologists such as William James, Gordon Allport, Abraham Maslow, Gardner Murphy, Carl Rogers, and Fritz Perls. Although some of its roots extend deep into the history of psychology—as well as philosophy, literature, and education—others are of more recent origin. The humanistic approach emerged as a major perspective in psychology during the 1950s and 1960s when many middle-class Americans began to feel materially affluent and spiritually empty. (A related movement—the existential perspective—is described in *HIGHLIGHT 3.4*.)

The humanistic approach recognizes the importance of learning and other psychological processes that have traditionally been the focus of research, but, as noted above, it is optimistically concerned with an individual's future rather than his or her past. This perspective is also concerned with processes about which we have as yet little scientific information—love, hope, creativity, values, meaning, personal growth, and self-fulfillment. Inevitably, its formulations are less based on empirical observation than those of behaviorism. In essence, humanistic psychologists feel that modern psychology has failed to address many of the most significant problems of human existence.

The Basics of the Humanistic Perspective

Though not readily subject to empirical investigation, certain underlying themes and principles of humanistic psychology can be identified. These views are described in the following sections.

The self as a unifying theme.   In the first comprehensive textbook on psychology, published in 1890, William James included a discussion of the consciousness of self. This concept was later dropped by the behaviorists because the self could not be observed by an outsider. Though the behaviorists have again incorporated cognitive aspects of human behavior into their perspective, it was the humanists of the 1950s and 1960s who focused their perspective on the concept of self.

Among humanistic psychologists, Carl Rogers (1902–1987) developed the most systematic formulation of the **self-concept,** based largely on his pioneering research into the nature of the psychotherapeutic process. Rogers (1951, 1959) stated his

The Existential Perspective

During the middle part of this century, as the humanistic perspective was becoming an influential force in the field of psychology, a related intellectual movement (centered in Europe) was also beginning to have a notable impact. This movement was called *existentialism*, a philosophical outlook with roots in the work of such existential thinkers as Martin Heidegger and Søren Kierkegaard.

The existential perspective resembles humanism in its emphasis on the uniqueness of each individual, the quest for values and meanings, and the existence of freedom for self-direction and self-fulfillment. The existential perspective, however, represents a less optimistic view of human beings and places more emphasis on the irrational tendencies and the difficulties inherent in self-fulfillment—particularly in a modern, bureaucratic, and dehumanizing mass society. In short, living is much more of a "confrontation" for the existentialists than for the humanists. Existential thinkers also place considerably less faith in modern science, being more concerned with the inner experiences of an individual in his or her attempts to understand and deal with the deepest human problems. The following paragraphs summarize some of the basic tenets of existentialism:

1. *Existence and essence.* A basic theme of existentialism is that our existence is a given, but what we make of it—our essence—is up to us. An adolescent boy who defiantly blurts out, "Well, I didn't ask to be born," is stating a profound truth, but in existential terms it is completely irrelevant. Whether he asked to be born or not, he is in the world and answerable for himself—for one human life. What he makes of his essence is up to him. It is his responsibility to shape the kind of person he is to become and to live a meaningful and constructive life.

2. *Choice, freedom, and courage.* Our essence is created by our choices, because our choices reflect the values on which we base and order our lives. As Sartre said, "I am my choices." In choosing what sort of people to become, we have absolute freedom; even refusing to choose represents a choice. Thus the locus of value is within each individual. We are inescapably the architects of our own lives.

3. *Meaning, value, and obligation.* A central theme in the existential perspective is the will-to-meaning. This trait is considered a basic human characteristic and is primarily a matter of finding satisfying values and guiding one's life by them. As we have noted, this is a difficult and highly individual matter, for the values that give one life meaning may be quite different from those that provide meaning for another. Each of us must find our own pattern of values. This orientation should not be interpreted as purely nihilistic or selfish. Existentialism also places strong emphasis on our *obligations* to each other. The most important consideration is not what we can get out of life but what we can contribute to it. Our lives can be fulfilling only if they involve socially constructive values and choices.

4. *Existential anxiety and the encounter with nothingness.* A final existential theme, *nonbeing,* or *nothingness,* adds an urgent and painful note to the human situation. In its ultimate form, nothingness is death, which is the inescapable fate of all human beings. The awareness of our inevitable death and its implications for our living can lead to *existential anxiety*—a deep concern over whether we are living meaningful and fulfilling lives. We can overcome our existential anxiety and deny victory to nothingness by living a life that counts for something. If we must perish, we can at least resist our death—living in such a way that nothingness will be an unjust fate.

This philosophy has clear implications for students of abnormal psychology. Existential psychologists focus on the importance of establishing values and acquiring a level of spiritual maturity worthy of the freedom and dignity bestowed by one's humanness. It is the avoidance of such central issues that creates corrupted, meaningless, and wasted lives. Much abnormal behavior, therefore, is seen as the product of a failure to deal constructively with existential despair and frustration.

Before the turn of the twentieth century, William James (1842–1910) set the stage for the humanistic perspective by discussing the concept of self in his book, Principles of Psychology.

Gordon Allport (1897–1967) believed that personality traits were actual forces in a person that could be used to explain the consistency of his or her behavior.

Abraham H. Maslow (1908–1970) devoted more than two decades to showing the potentialities of human beings for higher self-development and functioning.

views in a series of propositions that may be summarized as follows:

- Each individual exists in a private world of experience of which the I, me, or myself is the center.

- The most basic striving of an individual is toward the maintenance, enhancement, and actualization of the self.

- An individual reacts to situations in terms of the way he or she perceives them, in ways consistent with his or her self-concept and view of the world.

- A perceived threat to the self is followed by a defense—including a tightening of perception and behavior and the introduction of self-defense mechanisms.

- An individual's inner tendencies are toward health and wholeness; under normal conditions, a person behaves in rational and constructive ways and chooses pathways toward personal growth and self-actualization.

In using the concept of self as a unifying theme, humanistic psychologists emphasize the importance of individuality. Because of the great human potential for evaluation and learning and the great diversity in genetic endowments and experience, each person is unique. In studying human nature, psychologists are thus faced with the dual task of describing the uniqueness of each person and identifying the characteristics that all people share.

A focus on values and personal growth. Humanistic psychologists emphasize values and the process of value choices in guiding our behavior and achieving meaningful and fulfilling lives. They consider it crucial that each of us develop values based on our own experiences and evaluations rather than blindly accepting the values of others; otherwise, we deny our own experiences and lose touch with our own feelings.

To evaluate and choose for ourselves requires a clear sense of our own identity—the discovery of who we are, what sort of person we want to become, and why. Only in this way can we become **self-actualizing,** meaning that we are achieving our full potential.

According to the humanistic view, psychopathology is essentially the blocking or distortion of personal growth and the natural tendency toward physical and mental health. Such blocking or distortion is generally the result of one or more of these causal factors: (a) the exaggerated use of ego-defense mechanisms that leave an individual increasingly out of touch with reality; (b) unfavorable social conditions and faulty learning; and (c) excessive stress.

A positive view of human nature and potential. In contrast to the psychoanalytic and behavioristic perspectives, the humanistic approach takes a much more positive view of human nature and potential. Despite the myriad instances of violence, war, and cruelty that have occurred since ancient times, humanistically oriented psychologists conclude that under favorable circumstances humans tend to be

Carl Rogers (1902–1987) contributed significantly to the humanistic perspective with his systematic formulation of the concept of self, which emphasizes the importance of individuality and a striving towards what Rogers called self-actualization.

Fritz Perls (1893–1970) was influential in the development of therapeutic procedures for enhancing human experiencing and functioning, particulary in the context of confrontation groups.

friendly, cooperative, and constructive. Selfishness, aggression, and cruelty are viewed as pathological behaviors resulting from the denial, frustration, or distortion of basic human nature. Though people can be misled by inaccurate information, handicapped by social and economic deprivation, and overwhelmed by the complexity of human life, they still tend to be rational creatures. People try to find meaning in their experiences, to act and think in consistent ways, and to follow standards and principles they believe are good. According to this view, humans are not passive automatons but active participants in life with some measure of freedom for shaping their personal destinies and the destinies of their social groups.

Impact of the Humanistic Perspective

The major impact of the humanistic perspective has been its emphasis on our capacity for full functioning as human beings. In a sense, the humanistic perspective has introduced a new dimension to our thinking about abnormal behavior. Abnormality is seen as a failure to develop our tremendous potentials as human beings—as a blocking or distortion of our natural tendencies toward health and personal growth rather than as abnormality or deviance. In fact, Maslow (1962, 1969) has even expressed concern about the "psychopathology of the normal"—that is, the disappointing and wasteful failure of so many "normal" people to realize their potentialities as human beings.

Therapy, according to this way of thinking, is not a means of moving an individual from maladjustment to adjustment, but of fostering growth

The humanistic approach takes a positive view of human nature and potential. Humanistically oriented psychologists believe that under favorable circumstances, human propensities are in the direction of friendly, cooperative, and constructive behavior. According to this view, we are active participants in life with some measure of freedom for shaping our personal destiny.

Alfred Adler (1870–1937) was a student of Freud who took issue with psychoanalytic theory for its neglect of social factors as determinants of behavior. Adler believed that people were inherently social beings motivated primarily by the desire to belong to and participate in a group. His work laid the foundation for the interpersonal perspective.

Erich Fromm (1900–1980) focused on the orientations that people adopt in their interactions with others. He believed that these basic orientations to the social environment were the bases of much psychopathology.

Karen Horney (1885–1952) was trained in Freudian theory, but she rejected Freud's demeaning psychoanalytic view of women. She believed that "femininity" was a product of the culturally determined social learning that most women experience.

toward a socially constructive and personally fulfilling way of life. As might be expected, humanistic psychologists are keenly interested in encounter groups, awareness training, and other experiential techniques for promoting individual growth, building satisfying relationships, and finding effective methods of coping.

The humanistic perspective has been criticized for its diffuseness, for its lack of scientific rigor, and for its high expectations. Although some psychologists view its goals as grandiose, others see them as useful descriptions of the challenging long-range tasks that confront psychology today.

■ The Interpersonal Perspective

We are social beings, and much of what we are is a product of our relationships with others. It is logical to expect that much of psychopathology reflects this fact—that psychopathology is rooted in the unfortunate tendencies we have developed while dealing with our interpersonal environments. It is also true that abnormal behavior has its chief impact on our relationships with other people. Hence it should not be surprising that many theorists conclude that abnormal behavior is best understood by analyzing our relationships, past and present, with other people. This is the focus of the **interpersonal perspective.**

Roots of the Interpersonal Perspective

The roots of the interpersonal perspective lie clearly in the psychodynamic movement. The defection in 1911 of Alfred Adler (1870–1937) from the psychoanalytic viewpoint of his teacher, Freud, grew out of Adler's emphasis on social rather than inner determinants of behavior. Adler objected to the prominence Freud gave to instincts as the basic driving forces of personality. In Adler's view, people were inherently social beings motivated primarily by the desire to belong to and participate in a group.

Over time, a number of other Freudian theorists took issue with psychoanalytic theory for its neglect of crucial social factors. Among the best known of these theorists were Erich Fromm (1900–1980) and Karen Horney (1885–1952). Fromm focused on the orientations, or dispositions (exploitive, for example), that people adopted in their interactions with others. He believed that these basic orientations to the social environment were the bases of much psychopathology. Horney independently developed a similar view and, in particular, vigorously rejected Freud's demeaning psychoanalytic view of women (for instance, the idea that women experience penis envy). According to Horney, "femininity" was a product of the culturally determined social learning that most women experienced.

Erik Erikson (b. 1902) elaborated and broadened Freud's psychosexual stages into more socially oriented concepts. Erikson described conflicts that occurred at eight stages, each of which could be resolved in a healthy or unhealthy way.

The interpersonal model is based largely on the work of Harry Stack Sullivan (1892–1949), who believed that personality had meaning only in relation to interaction with others.

Erik Erikson (b. 1902) also extended the interpersonal aspects of psychoanalytic theory. He elaborated and broadened Freud's psychosexual stages into more socially oriented concepts, describing conflicts that occurred at eight stages, each of which could be resolved in a healthy or unhealthy way. For example, during the oral stage, a child may learn either basic trust or basic mistrust. Although these conflicts are never fully resolved, failure to develop toward the appropriate pole of each conflict handicaps an individual during later stages. Trust, for instance, is needed for later competence in many areas of life. A clear sense of identity is necessary for a satisfying intimacy with another person; such intimacy, in turn, is important for becoming a nurturing parent.

Contemporary psychodynamic thought has partially responded to the challenges leveled by these socially oriented theorists. The psychodynamic tradition has become much more interpersonal in focus, largely due to the influence of the object-relations approach. In fact many foresee the possibility of a harmonious integration of the psychodynamic with the more distinctly social and interpersonal viewpoints (Fine, 1979). Still, classical psychodynamic theory continues to emphasize the primacy of libidinal energies and intrapsychic conflicts, an emphasis that many interpersonally oriented theorists find objectionable.

Currently the dominant interpersonal theory is that developed by Harry Stack Sullivan (1892–1949), an American psychiatrist. The section that follows treats his theory in detail.

Sullivan's Interpersonal Theory   While the thinking of many individuals had nourished the roots of interpersonal theory, Sullivan offered a comprehensive and systematic theory of personality that was explicitly interpersonal.

Sullivan (1953) maintained that the concept of personality had meaning only when defined in terms of an individual's characteristic forms of relating to others. He argued that personality development proceeded through various stages involving different patterns of interpersonal relationships. Early in life, for example, a child becomes socialized mainly through interactions with parents. Later, during a gradual emancipation from parents, peer relationships become increasingly important. In young adulthood, intimate relationships are established, culminating typically in marriage. Failure to progress satisfactorily through these various stages paves the way for maladaptive behavior.

In this developmental context, Sullivan was concerned with the anxiety-arousing aspects of interpersonal relationships during early childhood. Because an infant is completely dependent on parents and siblings, called **significant others,** for meeting all physical and psychological needs, a lack of love and care leads to insecurity and anxiety. Sullivan emphasized the role of early childhood relationships in shaping the self-concept, which he saw as constructed largely out of the appraisals of significant others. For example, if a little girl perceives that others are rejecting her, she may view herself in a similar light and develop a negative self-image that almost inevitably leads to maladjustment.

The pressures of the socialization process and the continual appraisals by others lead a child to label some personal tendencies as the *good-me* and others as the *bad-me*. It is the bad-me that is associated with anxiety. With time, an individual develops a **self-system** that protects him or her from such anxiety through the control of awareness —the person simply does not attend to elements of experience that cause anxiety. If severe anxiety is aroused by some especially frightening aspect of self-experience, the individual perceives it as the *not-me,* totally screening it out of consciousness or even attributing it to someone else. Such actions, however, lead to an incongruity between the individual's perceptions and the world as it really is, which may result in maladaptive behavior. Here we can see a similarity between Sullivan's views and those of Freud, Rogers, and the cognitive-behavioral psychologists.

The good-me and bad-me constructs are especially important aspects of a much broader and more profound idea—that all mental processing concerning ourselves, others, and our relationships with them is influenced by precedents, or prototypes, established in earlier relationships. These mental prototypes, which Sullivan called *personifications,* determine how we perceive current relationships. We each have our own ideas about the characteristics, behaviors, and interactions we expect of our moms, teachers, lovers, and friends. Unfortunately, this means that we may distort events involving important current relationships. When such distortions are severe, relationships become complicated and confusing. Because these distortions shape our behavior toward other people, they tend to become self-fulfilling. The result can be anxiety and, ultimately, dissolution of certain relationships.

Features of the Interpersonal Perspective

Many subdisciplines of the social sciences and psychiatry have contributed to the interpersonal perspective in recent years. Some of these contributions are described briefly in the following sections.

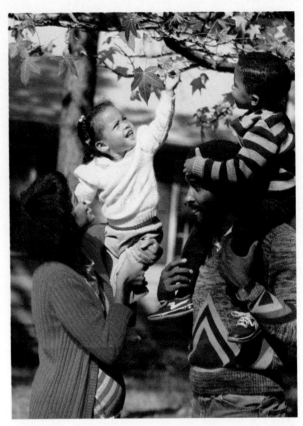

One way of viewing interpersonal relationships is in terms of social roles. In family relationships, each person has certain role expectations—in terms of obligations, rights, duties, and so on—that the others are expected to meet. If a member of the family significantly diverges from his or her expected role, interpersonal complications are likely to occur.

Social exchange and roles.   Two ways of viewing our relationships with other people are helpful in understanding both satisfying and hurtful interactions. First, the **social-exchange** view, developed largely by Thibaut and Kelley (1959) and Homans (1961), is based on the premise that we form relationships with each other to satisfy our needs. Each person in a relationship wants something from the other, and the exchange that results is essentially like trading or bargaining. When we feel that we have entered into a bad bargain—that the rewards are not worth the costs—we may attempt to work out some compromise or simply terminate the relationship.

A second way of viewing interpersonal relationships is in terms of **social roles.** Whether we are teachers, or doctors, or patients, we subscribe to certain behaviors. While we each lend a personal interpretation to our roles, there are usually limits to the "script," beyond which we are not expected to go. Similarly, in intimate personal relationships, each person has certain role expectations—in terms of obligations, rights, duties, and so on—that the other person is expected to meet. If one spouse, for example, fails to live up to the other's role expectations, or if the husband and wife have different conceptions of what a "wife" or "husband" should be or do, serious complications are likely to occur.

Causal attribution in interpersonal relations. Another contribution to the interpersonal approach is **attribution theory** (Bem, 1972; Heider, 1958; Weary & Mirels, 1982), which simply refers to the process of assigning causes to things that happen. We may attribute external causes, such as rewards or punishments; or we may assume that the causes are internal—that they are traits within ourselves or others. These causes are not seen but are assumed to exist as underlying realities. Assuming them helps us explain our own or other people's behaviors and makes it possible to predict what we or others are likely to do in the future.

For example, if a person does something mean, we may assume that he or she has a quality of meanness and expect it to cause mean behavior in the future. Or if a person fails a test, he or she may attribute the failure to stupidity as a personal trait. On the other hand, if the person attributes the failure to ambiguous test questions or unclear directions, he or she is looking to the environment as a cause and not to his or her own abilities.

Attribution theorists say that attributions are important in relationships because they form the basis for continuing evaluations and expectations. However inaccurate the attributions may be, they become important parts of our view of the world and tend to become self-fulfilling. They can also make us see other people and ourselves as unchanging and unchangeable, leading us to be inflexible in our relationships. Obviously, these ideas are similar to Sullivan's notion of personifications.

Communication and interpersonal accommodation. **Interpersonal accommodation** is the process in which two people develop patterns of communication and interaction that enable them to attain common goals, meet mutual needs, and build a satisfying relationship. People use many cues, both verbal and nonverbal, to interpret what is really being said to them. If individuals in a close relationship have a tangle of unresolved misunderstandings and conflicts, they will probably have trouble communicating clearly and openly with each other. In fact, the final phase of a failing

marriage is often marked by an almost complete inability of the partners to communicate. Sullivan believed that faulty communication is far more common than most people realize, especially in family interactions on an emotional level.

In addition to establishing and maintaining effective communication, interpersonal accommodation involves other adjustments, such as determining mutually satisfying role relationships, resolving disagreements constructively, and dealing adequately with external demands. Sullivan thought that interpersonal accommodation is facilitated when the motives of the individuals in a relationship are complementary, as when two people are strongly motivated to give and receive affection. When interpersonal accommodation fails and a relationship does not meet the needs of one or both partners, it is likely to be characterized by conflict, dissension, and eventually dissolution. The principles of interpersonal behavioral accommodation have been analyzed at length by Benjamin (1982), Carson (1969, 1979), Kiesler (1983), Leary (1957), and Wiggins (1982).

Impact of the Interpersonal Perspective
The interpersonal perspective views unsatisfactory relationships in the past or present as the primary causes of many forms of maladaptive behavior. Such relationships may extend back to childhood, as

Interpersonal accommodation is the process in which two people evolve patterns of communication and interaction that enable them to attain common goals, meet mutual needs, and build a satisfying relationship.

when a boy's self-concept is distorted by parents who tell him he is worthless or by rigid socialization measures that make it difficult to integrate the bad-me into his self-concept. Poor relationships may also result from self-defeating games that individuals learn to play, from uncomfortable roles they are given, from faulty assumptions about the causes of their own or others' behaviors, or from unsuccessful attempts to separate from parents and other adults in order to become a fully functioning adult.

In the area of diagnosis, many supporters of the interpersonal perspective believe that the reliability and validity of psychological diagnoses can be improved if a new system based on interpersonal functioning is developed. Some work and thinking underlying these efforts is described in HIGHLIGHT 3.5.

The focus of interpersonal therapy is on alleviating problem-causing relationships and on helping individuals achieve more satisfactory relationships. Such therapy is concerned with verbal and nonverbal communication, social roles, processes of accommodation, causal attributions (including those supposedly motivating the behavior of others), and the general interpersonal context of behavior. The therapy situation itself can be used as a vehicle for learning new interpersonal skills.

Like the humanistic viewpoint, the interpersonal approach is handicapped by incomplete information. As a result, many of Sullivan's concepts and those of later investigators lack adequate scientific grounding. Despite such limitations, the interpersonal perspective has focused attention on the key role an individual's close relationships play in determining whether behavior will be effective or maladaptive.

To review, each of the psychosocial perspectives on human behavior—psychodynamic, behavioristic, cognitive-behavioral, humanistic, and interpersonal—contributes to our understanding of psychopathology, but none alone seems to account for the complex variety of human maladaptive behavior. Each perspective has a substantial amount of evidence to support it, yet each one also depends on generalizations from limited events and observations. In attempting to explain a complex disorder such as alcoholism, for example, the psychodynamic principles focus on intrapsychic conflict and anxiety; the behavioristic principles focus on faulty learning and environmental conditions that may be exacerbating or maintaining the condition; the cognitive-behavioral principles focus on maladaptive thinking, including deficits in problem solving and information processing; the humanistic principles focus on the ways in which an individual's struggles with values, meaning, and personal growth may be contributing to the problem; and the interpersonal principles focus on difficulties in a person's past and present relationships.

Thus adopting one perspective or another has important consequences: it influences our perception of maladaptive behavior, the types of evidence we look for, and the way in which we are likely to interpret data. In later chapters, we will discuss relevant concepts from all these viewpoints, and in many instances, we will contrast different ways of explaining and treating the same behavior.

THE SOCIOCULTURAL VIEWPOINT

By the beginning of the twentieth century, sociology and anthropology had emerged as independent scientific disciplines and were making rapid strides toward understanding the role of sociocultural factors in human development and behavior. Early sociocultural theorists included such notables as Ruth Benedict, Ralph Linton, Abram Kardiner, Margaret Mead, and Franz Boas. Their investigations and writings showed that individual personality development reflected the larger society—its institutions, norms, values, ideas, and technologies—as well as the immediate family and other groups. Studies also made clear the relationship between sociocultural conditions and mental disorders—between the particular stressors in a society and the types of mental disorders that typically occur in it. Further studies showed that the patterns of both physical and mental disorders in a given society could change over time as sociocultural conditions changed. These discoveries have added another dimension to modern perspectives concerning abnormal behavior.

Uncovering Sociocultural Factors Through Cross–cultural Studies

The relationships between maladaptive behavior and sociocultural factors such as poverty, discrimination, or illiteracy are complex. It is one thing to observe that an individual with a psychological disorder has come from a harsh environment. It is quite another thing, however, to show empirically

HIGHLIGHT 3.5

Toward an Interpersonal Diagnostic System

While acknowledging that the DSM-III-R diagnostic system is an improvement over its predecessors, Clinton McLemore and Lorna Benjamin (1979; Benjamin, 1982) argue that it is fundamentally flawed in at least three ways: (a) it still requires a diagnostician to make impressionistic clinical judgments; (b) it still categorizes human beings by reference to certain broadly defined "illnesses"; and, especially, (c) it almost totally neglects the social context in which maladaptive behavior occurs. They note that abnormality is typically displayed by the way in which a person relates to others: "We submit that rigorous and systematic description of social behavior is uniquely critical to effective definition and treatment of the problems that bring most individuals for psychiatric or psychological consultation" (p. 18).

The solution, according to these authors, is to seek the careful and rigorous development of a diagnostic system organized around disordered forms of interpersonal functioning rather than alleged entities of mental disorder. Building on the work of earlier investigators, they suggest that the beginnings of such a system should incorporate dimensions of autonomy-interdependence, friendliness-hostility, and (where the situation is one of high interdependence between a person and others) dominance-submission. Since the most important and central of the behaviors associated with traditional (DSM) psychiatric diagnoses involve precisely these dimensions, they argue, it should be possible to include virtually all DSM-III-R diagnoses within this more systematic and potentially more meaningful framework. For example, the DSM-III-R diagnosis of major depression might, in interpersonal terms, be described as a position of appeasement (hostile submission) toward another person's stance of accusation and blame (hostile dominance), which leads to internalized self-accusation and blame (hostile domination of self). The narcissistic personality disorder, on the other hand, might be viewed as a hostile assertion of autonomy ("Ignore it, pretend it's not there"), which leads to a preoccupation with oneself and one's own affairs and a reversion to fantasy as a principal means of gratification.

and unequivocally that these circumstances were both *necessary* and *sufficient* conditions for producing the later disorder. The **sociocultural viewpoint** is thus concerned with the impact of the social environment on mental disorder.

Evidence that sociocultural factors have influenced personality adaptation or resulted in abnormal behavior is compelling but difficult to verify. It is virtually impossible to conduct controlled experiments. Both economic and ethical restraints prevent investigators from rearing children with similar genetic or biological traits in diverse social or economic environments in order to find out which variables, if any, play a part in the individual adjustment.

However, natural occurrences have provided laboratories for researchers. Groups of human beings have been exposed to very different environments, from the Arctic to the tropics to the desert. These societies have developed different means of economic subsistence and different types of family structures for propagating the species under different and often adverse conditions. Human groups have developed highly diverse social and political systems. Nature has indeed done social scientists a great favor by providing such a wide array of human groups for study.

Yet an investigator who attempts to conduct crosscultural research is plagued by numerous technological and methodological problems. Some of these are (a) the different languages and thought systems; (b) the political and cultural climates that prevent objective inquiry; (c) the difficulties in finding appropriately trained local scientists to collaborate in the research and prevent the researcher's ethnocentric attitudes or values from distorting the findings; and (d) the high costs of large scale crosscultural research.

In the earliest cross-cultural studies, Western-trained anthropologists observed the behavior of "natives" and considered those behaviors in the context of Western scientific thought. One of the er. For example, she noted that some cultures valued cataleptic and trancelike states. Thus she concluded that normality was simply a culturally defined concept.

Early research also found that some types of abnormal behavior occurred only in certain cultures. Several of these "culture-bound" behaviors are described in *HIGHLIGHT 3.6*.

These and other early anthropological findings led many investigators to take a position of **cultural relativism** concerning abnormal behavior. According to this view, one cannot apply universal standards of normality or abnormality to all societies. In fact, for a time many people accepted the anthropologist's veto: any general principle could be rejected if a contrary instance somewhere in the world could be demonstrated. For example, schizophrenia would no longer be viewed as abnormal if its symptoms were somewhere accepted as normal behavior.

This extremely relativistic view of abnormal behavior is not widely held (Strauss, 1979). As noted earlier, the biological viewpoint is the dominant force in the fields of psychiatry and abnormal psychology today. Whether this perspective is accepted or not, it is generally recognized that the more severe types of mental disorder described in Western psychology are found and considered maladaptive in societies throughout the world. When individuals become so mentally disordered that they can no longer control their behavior, perform their expected roles, or even survive without special care, their behavior is considered abnormal in any society.

Research supports the view that many psychological disturbances are universal, appearing in most cultures studied (Al-Issa, 1982; Carpenter & Strauss, 1979; Cooper et al., 1972; Murphy, 1976; World Health Organization, 1975). For example, although the incidences and symptoms vary, the behaviors we call schizophrenia can be found among almost all peoples, from the most primitive to the most technologically advanced. Recent studies have also shown that certain psychological symptoms, as measured by the Minnesota Multiphasic Personality Inventory (MMPI, see Chapter 16), were consistently found among similarly diagnosed clinical groups in other countries (in Turkey by Savacir & Erol, 1990; in China by Cheung & Song, 1989).

Sociocultural influences, however, cannot be disregarded. Although some universal symptoms appear, there is reason to believe that cultural factors influence abnormal behavior. The cultural relativists, though a minority voice, raise the unimpeacha-

Margaret Mead (1901–1978), the world-famous anthropologist, spent years studying other societies and amassing cross-cultural data. Her Coming of Age in Samoa *(published in 1928) gave a favorable picture of many aspects of life in a "primitive" society and was influential in establishing an attitude of cultural relativism among many scientists and thinkers. Here she is pictured meeting with schoolchildren in New Guinea.*

earliest attempts to apply Western-based concepts in other cultures was the classic study of Malinowski (1927), *Sex and Repression in Savage Society.* In this work, he attempted to explain the behavior of "savages" through the use of the then dominant principles of psychoanalysis. Malinowski found little evidence among the Trobriand Islanders of any Oedipal conflicts as described by Freud. He concluded that the sexually based behavior postulated by psychoanalytic theory was not universal but rather was a product of the patriarchal family structure in Western society.

Shortly thereafter, Ruth Benedict (1934) pointed out that even the Western definitions of abnormality might not apply to behavior in other cultures. Citing various ethnographic reports, she indicated that behavior considered abnormal in one society was sometimes considered normal in anoth-

Unusual Patterns of Behavior Considered to Be Culture-bound Disorders

Name of Disorder	Culture	Description
Amok	Malaya (also observed in Java, Philippines, Africa, and Tierra del Fuego)	A disorder characterized by sudden, wild outbursts of homicidal aggression in which an afflicted person may kill or injure others. This rage disorder is usually found in males who are rather withdrawn, quiet, and inoffensive prior to the onset of the disorder. Stress, sleep deprivation, extreme heat, and alcohol are among the conditions thought to precipitate the disorder. Several stages have been observed: typically in the first stage the person becomes more withdrawn; then a period of brooding follows in which a loss of reality contact is evident. Ideas of persecution and anger predominate. Finally, a phase of automatism or *Amok* occurs, in which the person jumps up, yells, grabs a knife, and stabs people or objects within reach. Exhaustion and depression usually follow, with amnesia for the rage period.
Anorexia nervosa	Western nations (particularly the U.S.)	A disorder occurring most frequently among young women in which a preoccupation with thinness produces a refusal to eat. This condition can result in death (see Chapter 8).
Latah	Malay	A fear reaction often occurring in middle-aged women of low intelligence who are subservient and self-effacing. The disorder is precipitated by the word *snake* or by tickling. It is characterized by *echolalia* (repetition of the words and sentences of others) and *echopraxia* (repetition of the acts of others). A disturbed individual may also react with negativism and the compulsive use of obscene language.
Koro	Southeast Asia (particularly Malay Archipelago)	A fear reaction or anxiety state in which a person fears that his penis will withdraw into his abdomen and he will die. This reaction may appear after sexual overindulgence or excessive masturbation. The anxiety is typically very intense and of sudden onset. The condition is "treated" by having the penis held firmly by the patient or by family members or friends. Often the penis is clamped to a wooden box.
Windigo	Algonquin Indian hunters	A fear reaction in which a hunter becomes anxious and agitated, convinced that he is bewitched. Fears center around his being turned into a cannibal by the power of a monster with an insatiable craving for human flesh.
Kitsunetsuki	Japan	A disorder in which victims believe that they are possessed by foxes and are said to change their facial expressions to resemble foxes. Entire families are often possessed and banned by the community. This reaction occurs in rural areas of Japan where people are superstitious and relatively uneducated.
Taijin kyofusho (TKS)	Japan	A relatively common psychiatric disorder in Japan in which an individual develops a fear of offending or hurting other people through being awkward in social situations or because of an imagined physical defect or problem. The excessive concern over how a person presents himself or herself in social situations is the salient problem.

Based on Kiev (1972), Kirmayer (1991), Lebra (1976), Lehmann (1967), Simons and Hughes (1985) and Yap (1951).

ble point that human biology does not operate in a vacuum. Cultural demands serve as primary causal factors and modifying influences in psychopathology. Fabrega (1989) recently questioned the pervasive biological reductionism used as an explanatory model, arguing that contemporary relativistic perspectives explain how physiological behavior results in part from an individual's experiences. The role a particular sociocultural factor plays in producing abnormal behavior largely depends on the amount of stress it creates for an individual (Al-Issa, 1982; Sue & Sue, 1987). For example, children growing up in an oppressive society that offers few rewards and many hassles are likely to experience more stress and thus be more vulnerable to disorder than children growing up in a society that offers ample rewards and considerable social support. Growing up during a period of great fear, such as during a war, a famine, or a period of persecution, can make a child vulnerable to psychological problems.

Sociocultural factors also appear to influence what disorders develop, the forms that they take, and their courses. How a disordered individual is treated and what is expected from a patient can influence whether the individual recovers or becomes chronically disordered (Murphy, 1982). A good example of this point is a comparison study of psychiatric patients from Italy, Switzerland, and the United States carried out by Butcher and Pancheri (1976). Patients grouped according to diagnostic categories produced similar general personality patterns on the MMPI. However, the Italian patients also showed an exaggerated pattern of physical complaints significantly greater than that of the Swiss and the American patients, regardless of clinical diagnosis.

This finding was consistent with earlier work by Opler and Singer (1959) and Zola (1966). For example, Zola examined symptom expression in two samples of second-generation American patients (Italian and Irish) at an ear-nose-throat clinic in Boston. When patients were matched on the basis of their actual physical illnesses, Zola found that the Italian patients made more complaints than the Irish. He attributed this difference to a defense mechanism, which he called *dramatization,* that led the Italian patients, once identified as ill, to exaggerate or dramatize their physical problems to a greater extent than the Irish patients.

In another study, Kleinman and Good (1985) surveyed the experience of depression across cultures. Their data show that important elements of depression in Western societies—for example, the acute sense of guilt typically experienced—do not appear in other cultures. They point out that the symptoms of depression (or dysphoria), such as

sadness, hopelessness, unhappiness, lack of pleasure with the things of the world and with social relationships has dramatically different meaning in different societies. For Buddhists, taking pleasure from things of the world and social relationships is the basis of all suffering; a willful dysphoria is thus the first step on the road to salvation. For Shi'ite Muslims in Iran, grief is a religious experience, associated with recognition of the tragic consequences of living justly in an unjust world; the ability to experience dysphoria fully is thus a marker of depth of person and understanding. Some societies, such as the Kaluli of Papua New Guinea, value full and dramatic expression of sadness and grieving. (p. 3)

Kleinman (1986) traced the different ways that Chinese people (in Taiwan and in the People's Republic of China) deal with stress compared to Western individuals. He found that in Western societies depression was a frequent reaction to individual stress. In China, on the other hand, he noted a relatively low rate of reported depression. Instead, the effects of stress were more typically manifested in physical problems, such as fatigue, weakness, and other complaints.

These findings illustrate an important point— the need for greater study of the cultural influences on psychopathology. This neglected area of research may yet answer many questions about the origins and courses of behavior problems (Draguns, 1979; Marsella et al., 1985). Yet, even with strong evidence of the cultural influences on psychopathology, many professionals may fail to adopt an appropriate cultural perspective when dealing with mental illness. Clark (1987) notes a reluctance of "mainstream" psychologists and psychiatrists to incorporate the cross-cultural perspective in their research and clinical practices even when their patients or subjects are from diverse cultures. In a shrinking world, with instant communication and easy transportation, it is crucial for our sciences and professions to take a world view. In fact, Kleinman and Good consider cultural factors so important to our understanding of depressive disorders that they have urged the psychiatric community to incorporate another Axis in the DSM diagnostic system to reflect cultural factors in psychopathology.

■ Sociocultural Influences in Our Own Society

As we narrow our focus to our own society, we find a number of early studies dealing with the relation of social factors to the nature and incidence of mental disorder. For example, in a pioneering 1939 study, Faris and Dunham found that a disproportionate number of the schizophrenic patients admitted to mental hospitals came from the lower socio-economic areas of a large city. The rate of admission decreased according to how far patients lived from these deteriorating sections of the city. Later surveys have consistently found a relationship between social class and psychopathology (e.g., Dohrenwend & Dohrenwend, 1974).

Other researchers have investigated a wider range of subgroups (such as urban-rural, ethnic, religious, and occupational) in relation to mental disorders. An extensive study of mental disorders in Texas conducted by Jaco (1960) found that the incidence of psychoses was three times higher in urban than in rural areas and higher among the divorced and separated than among the married or widowed. Several studies found that the highest rates of mental disorders were in the areas of large cities that were undergoing rapid and drastic social changes (Blazer et al., 1985; Bloom, Asher, & White, 1978; Dooley & Catalano, 1980). It must be emphasized, however, that these are merely correlational findings and thus not evidence of causal relationships.

As was noted in Chapter 1, the study of the incidence and distribution of physical and mental disorders in a population (as in the research just cited) is called *epidemiology*. The epidemiological approach implicates not only the social conditions and high-risk areas that are correlated with a high incidence of given disorders, but also the groups for whom the risk of pathology is especially high—for example, refugees from other countries (Vega and Rumbaut, 1991). Throughout this text we will point out many high-risk groups with respect to suicide, drug dependence, and other maladaptive behavior patterns. This information provides a basis for formulating prevention and treatment programs; in turn, the effectiveness of these programs can be evaluated by means of further epidemiological studies.

With the gradual recognition of sociocultural influences, what was previously an almost exclusive concern with individual patients has broadened to include a concern with societal, communal, familial, and other group settings as factors in mental disorders. It is now clear that a person's maladaptive behavior might be caused not only by personal problems but also by abnormal conditions in the surrounding social environment.

Sociocultural research has led to programs designed to improve the social conditions that foster maladaptive behavior and to community facilities for the early detection, treatment, and long-range prevention of mental disorder. In Chapter 19 we will examine some clinical facilities and other programs—both governmental and private—that have been established as a result of community efforts.

UNRESOLVED ISSUES
on Theoretical Viewpoints

The viewpoints described in this chapter are theoretical constructions devised to orient psychologists in the study of abnormal behavior. As a set of hypothetical guidelines, each viewpoint speaks to the importance and integrity of its own position to the exclusion of other explanations. Most psychoanalytically-oriented clinicians, for example, value those traditional writings and beliefs consistent with Freudian or later psychodynamic theory, and they minimize or ignore the teachings of opposing viewpoints; they would likely adhere to prescribed practices of psychoanalysis in their therapy and not use other methods, such as desensitization therapy.

Theoretical integrity and adherence to a systematic viewpoint has a key advantage: it provides a consistent approach to orient one's practice or research efforts. Once mastered, the methodology can guide a practitioner or researcher through the complex web of human problems. It can also provide direction and considerable reassurance that one's approach is relevant and effective. Theoretical adherence has its disadvantages, however. In excluding other possible explanations, it can blind researchers to other factors that may be equally important.

The fact is that none of the theories to date address the whole spectrum of abnormality—they are each limited by their focus. Two general trends have occurred as a result. The first involves *revisions* of an original theoretical doctrine by expanding or modifying some elements of the system. The second involves making use of two or more diverse approaches in a more general, *eclectic* approach. We will now examine how effectively each of these trends brings order to theoretical complexity.

1. *The revision of theoretical viewpoints.* The emergence of diverse viewpoints to explain abnormal behavior has led to criticisms of each viewpoint and thus to attempts to accommodate these criticisms. There are many examples of such corrective interpretations, such as Adler's or Jung's modification of Freudian theory or the more recent cognitive-behavioral approach in behavior therapy. But many of the early Freudian theorists did not accept the neo-

Freudian additions, and many classical behavior therapists today do not accept the revisions proposed by cognitive behaviorists. Therefore, theoretical viewpoints tend to multiply and coexist—each with its own proponents—rather than being assimilated into previous views. In effect, "revisions" of an original doctrine tend to survive as new, alternative interpretations of psychopathology. The result is a cumbersome backdrop of myriad theoretical viewpoints from which to study abnormal behavior. Of course, this situation complicates communication among psychologists who may hold to different perspectives. In addition, it is more difficult for a person to evaluate the scope and nature of any research or treatment because a complete understanding requires an awareness of the perspective from which the research or the treatment is initiated. With so many different perspectives, it is impossible to have a clear grasp of them all.

2. *The eclectic approach.* As the research engendered by different perspectives has gradually led to a better understanding of mental disorders, it has become increasingly apparent that explanations based on single viewpoints are likely to be incomplete. Usually, the interaction of several causal factors (biological, psychosocial, and sociocultural) produces the disorders that we see. For example, an individual may have a biological predisposition to severe mood swings but may function well until some severe crisis brings on a depressive state. Gradually, investigators have come to realize that even where brain damage is present, a patient's psychological reaction to it and to the resulting change in his or her life are of vital importance in determining an overall clinical picture. It is also apparent that the emotional support of family members—as well as the kind of situation to which a patient will return after discharge from the hospital—are significant factors in determining a favorable outcome. Likewise, research has found that the use of biological therapies—such as antidepressant drugs or electroconvulsive shock—sometimes produces dramatic results even for mental disorders that are apparently the result of psychological rather than biological factors. Finally, the symptoms, prognosis, and reaction to a treatment for a certain disorder may all vary somewhat for individuals from different cultural backgrounds.

In practice, many psychologists have responded to the existence of many perspectives by adopting an eclectic stance—that is, they accept working ideas from several existing viewpoints and use them all as practicable. For example, a psychologist using an eclectic approach might accept causal explanations from psychoanalytic theory while applying techniques of anxiety reduction derived from behavior therapy. Purists in the field—those advocates of a single viewpoint—are skeptical about eclecticism, claiming that the eclectic approach tends to lack integrity and produces a "crazy quilt" of activity with little rationale and inconsistent practice. This criticism may be true, but the approach certainly works for many psychologists.

Typically, those using an eclectic approach make no attempt to synthesize the theoretical perspectives. The approach seems to work best in practice rather than in theory; the underlying principles of many of the theoretical perspectives are incompatible as they now stand. Thus the eclectic approach still falls short of the final goal, which is to tackle the theoretical clutter and develop a single, comprehensive, internally consistent viewpoint that accurately reflects what we know empirically about abnormal behavior. It may be unrealistic to expect a single theoretical viewpoint to be broad enough to explain abnormal behavior in general and specific enough to accurately predict the symptoms and causes of specific disorders. Nevertheless, such a unified viewpoint is the challenge for the next generation of theorists in the field of abnormal psychology. Perhaps some reader of this chapter will confront this challenge and perform the necessary synthesis for a clearer conceptual picture of psychopathology.

SUMMARY

Abnormal psychology is a relatively young scientific discipline that contains many points of view on the interpretation and treatment of abnormal behavior. The early biological viewpoint focused on neurological brain damage as a model for the understanding of abnormality. We now see that model as limited even for the cases to which it most clearly applies. Modern biological thinking about mental disorders has focused on the biochemistry of brain functioning. Investigations in this area show much promise for advancing our knowledge of how the mind and the body interact to produce maladaptive behavior, particularly in respect to the more severe disorders.

The psychosocial viewpoints on abnormal behavior, dealing with human psychology rather than biology, necessarily are more varied than the biological perspective. The oldest of these perspectives is Freudian psychoanalysis. For many years this view has been preoccupied with questions about libidinal energies and their containment, but more recently it has shown a distinctly social or interpersonal thrust under the direction of object-relations theory. Psychoanalysis and closely related approaches are termed *psychodynamic* in recognition of their attention to inner, often unconscious forces. An integration of psychodynamic and interpersonal perspectives (as suggested by Sullivan's work) would seem possible as we move into the future.

The behavioristic perspective, which is rooted in the desire to make psychology an objective science, was slow in overcoming a dominant psychodynamic bias, but in the last 25 years has established itself as a significant force. Behaviorism focuses on the role of learning in human behavior, and views maladaptive behavior as a failure of learning. Its therapeutic methods have achieved excellent results, and its ability to accommodate itself to the current dominance of cognitive thinking in psychology ensures its continued growth and importance.

Initially a spinoff from (and in part a reaction against) the behavioristic perspective, the cognitive-behavioral viewpoint attempts to incorporate the complexities of human cognition in a rigorous, learning-based framework. This viewpoint attempts to alter maladaptive thinking and improve people's abilities to solve problems and to plan. As we will discuss in Chapter 18, the treatment procedures incorporating cognitive processes are highly effective in dealing with many behavioral problems.

The humanistic perspective does not chiefly concern itself with the origins and treatments of severe mental disorders. Rather, it focuses on the conditions that can maximize functioning in individuals who are just "getting along." It views abnormality as a failure to develop individual human potential. As such, it has to do with personal values and personal growth.

The originators of the interpersonal perspective were defectors from the psychoanalytic ranks who took exception to the Freudian emphasis on the internal determinants of motivation and behavior. As a group, interpersonal theorists have emphasized that important aspects of human personality have social or interpersonal origins. This viewpoint sees unsatisfactory relationships in the past or present as the primary causes of maladaptive behaviors. The most fully articulated and important interpersonal theories are those of Harry Stack Sullivan.

Any comprehensive approach to the study of human behavior—normal or abnormal—must take account of the sociocultural context in which a given behavior occurs. Cultural influences on psychopathology are important in understanding the origin and course of a behavioral problem. The sociocultural viewpoint is concerned with the social environment as a contributor to mental disorder.

Finally, we are still a long way from the goal of a complete understanding of abnormal behavior. The many theoretical perspectives that exist have given us a start, and a good one at that—but they fall short. To obtain a more comprehensive understanding of mental disorder, we must draw on a variety of sources, including the findings of genetics, biochemistry, psychology, sociology, and so forth. Clearly, none of the theories currently available is complete; we do not have an integrated, theoretically consistent view of abnormal behavior that is widely accepted. It rests upon future generations of theorists to devise a general theory of psychopathology, if indeed one is possible.

■ Key Terms

biological viewpoint (p. 56)
medical model (p. 56)
neurotransmitters (p. 58)
psychosocial viewpoints (p. 62)
psychoanalytic perspective (p. 62)
psychoanalysis (p. 62)
psychodynamic perspectives (p. 62)
mesmerism (p. 62)
Nancy School (p. 63)
catharsis (p. 64)
the unconscious (p. 64)
free association (p. 65)
dream analysis (p. 65)
id (p. 65)
libido (p. 65)
pleasure principle (p. 65)
primary process (p. 65)
ego (p. 65)
secondary process (p. 66)
reality principle (p. 66)
superego (p. 66)
intrapsychic conflicts (p. 66)
ego-defense mechanisms (p. 66)
psychosexual stages of development (p. 67)
Oedipus complex (p. 67)
castration anxiety (p. 67)
Electra complex (p. 67)
introjection (p. 68)
object-relations (p. 69)

separation-individuation (p. 70)
behavioristic perspective (p. 71)
conditioning (p. 71)
learning (p. 73)
classical conditioning (p. 73)
operant (or instrumental) conditioning (p. 73)
reinforcement (p. 73)
extinction (p. 74)
generalization (p. 74)
discrimination (p. 74)
cognitive processes (p. 76)
cognitive-behavioral perspective (p. 76)
personal constructs (p. 76)
humanistic perspective (p. 78)
self-concept (p. 78)
self-actualizing (p. 80)
interpersonal perspective (p. 82)
significant others (p. 83)
self-system (p. 84)
social exchange (p. 84)
social roles (p. 84)
attribution theory (p. 85)
interpersonal accommodation (p. 85)
sociocultural viewpoint (p. 87)
cultural relativism (p. 88)

Chapter 4
Causal Factors in Abnormal Behavior

Eddie Arning, *Untitled.* Arning (b. 1898), a native of Texas, was committed to a state mental hospital while in his mid–twenties because of his violent behavior and depression. At the age of 64, he was found mentally stable and was moved to a nursing home. It was at this point that Arning began to make highly schematic crayon drawings, first of recollections of his family life and later of images he saw in newspaper and magazine ads. Sadly, Arning's creative inspiration seemed to leave him when he was released from the nursing home at age 78, and he stopped drawing.

Abnormal behavior almost never arises suddenly, out of the blue, in a person with a faultless biological and psychological makeup—if any such person ever existed. Rather, we can usually see—although often only in retrospect—the pattern of factors that made an individual vulnerable to abnormality. At the very least, we can usually piece together a number of hypotheses about these background factors.

It is a reasonable assumption that all of us harbor **vulnerabilities,** factors that under certain circumstances make us susceptible to behaving abnormally. Whether or not we ever do appears to depend on the nature, number, and degree of these vulnerabilities; on the way they combine in any given individual and on the nature and severity of the life challenges we face. Commenting on the enormous complexity and widespread individual differences implied here, Meehl (1978, 1989) has suggested that severe mental breakdown is often the result of "bad luck." He notes, however, that such a conclusion does not justify the abandonment of our efforts to understand, prevent, and treat mental disorder.

In the preceding chapter, we described several *theoretical* viewpoints concerning abnormal behavior, each of which focuses on different origins or background events that contribute to maladaptive behavior. In brief, the biological viewpoint emphasizes various organic conditions that can impair brain functioning and lead to psychopathology. Of the psychosocial viewpoints, the psychodynamic focuses on intrapsychic conflicts that lead to anxiety; the behavioristic, on faulty learning; the cognitive-behavioral, on information processing processes involved in distorted thinking; the humanistic, on blocked or distorted personal growth; and the interpersonal, on unsatisfactory relationships. Finally, the sociocultural viewpoint focuses on pathological social conditions. In this chapter we will look at the *empirical* evidence concerning the origins, in general terms, of our human vulnerabilities, reviewing available research on the subject. Unfortunately, there is often little discernible relationship between theoretical perspectives and the sorts of causal or risk factors that can be studied using empirical methods. This situation results from the difficulty of formulating these theoretical propositions into terms clear enough to permit empirical investigation. Before proceeding with a review of the evidence, however, we must give some additional attention to the concept of causation in abnormal behavior.

PERSPECTIVES ON CAUSATION

Central to the field of abnormal psychology are questions about what causes some people to behave maladaptively in some situations for varying periods of time. These questions not only challenge us to deepen our appreciation of the human condition, but they also address practical considerations in prevention, assessment, and treatment. Equipped with a knowledge of the specific causes for given classes of disorder, we could more efficiently help to avoid conditions that lead to disorder and perhaps reverse those that maintain it. Somewhat less obviously, we could better classify and diagnose disorders if we clearly understood the causal sequences leading to diverse disordered outcomes rather than relying on clusters of apparently similar behavior, as we for the most part do now.

Although understanding the causes of abnormal behavior is clearly a desirable goal, it is enormously difficult to achieve because human behavior is so complex. Even the simplest of human behaviors, such as speaking or writing a word, is the product of literally thousands of prior events—only some of which are understood, and then frequently only in the vaguest of ways. Understanding a person's life in causal terms, even an utterly "adaptive" life, is an incomplete project of enormous magnitude; when the life is a maladaptive one, we can assume the task is even more difficult. As a result, many investigators now prefer to speak of *risk factors* (variables correlated with an abnormal outcome) rather than of *causes*. Nevertheless, causes remain the ultimate quarry.

In attempting to analyze the causal factors in abnormal behavior, it will be helpful to consider (a) the distinctions between primary, predisposing, precipitating, and reinforcing causes; (b) the problem of feedback and circularity in abnormal behavior; and (c) the concept of diathesis-stress as a broad causal model of abnormal behavior.

Primary, Predisposing, Precipitating, and Reinforcing Causes

Regardless of one's theoretical perspective, several terms can be used to specify the role a factor plays in the **etiology,** or causal pattern, of abnormal behavior. A **primary cause** is a condition that must exist for a disorder to occur—syphilis of the brain is an example in the case of general paresis. A primary cause is a necessary but not always sufficient factor in abnormality. Many recognized disorders appear not to have primary causes. A **predisposing cause** is a condition that comes before and paves the way for a later occurrence of disorder under certain conditions; an example is parental rejection, which could predispose a child toward difficulty in handling close personal relationships later. A **precipitating cause** is a condition that proves too much for an individual and triggers a disorder; an example is a crushing disappointment. Often a precipitating cause seems insignificant and related only tangentially, if at all, to a primary or predisposing cause. In short, it is the straw that breaks the camel's back. For example, leaving the cap off the toothpaste may be a minor annoyance in a basically well-adjusted family, but the same act can cause a full-fledged argument in a family already experiencing major difficulties in communicating. Finally, a **reinforcing cause** is a condition that tends to maintain maladaptive behavior that is already occurring. An example is the extra attention, sympathy, and removal from unwanted responsibility that often come when a person is "ill"; these pleasant experiences may contribute to a delay in recovery. Reinforcing causes have received a great deal of attention in recent years, especially among behaviorally-oriented psychologists.

In a given case, a primary cause may be either absent or unknown, or two or more factors may share primary responsibility. Likewise, the exact patterning of primary, predisposing, precipitating, and reinforcing causes may be far from clear; a given factor or event may contribute to a disorder in more than one way. For example, the death of a parent can be both a primary and a precipitating factor in a child's subsequent grief reaction; it might also predispose the child to severe reactions to losses in adulthood.

As this example suggests, serious adjustment challenges early in life, whatever their nature, may predispose a person toward specific difficulties later in life. In other words, all the causal factors just discussed (including primary, precipitating, and

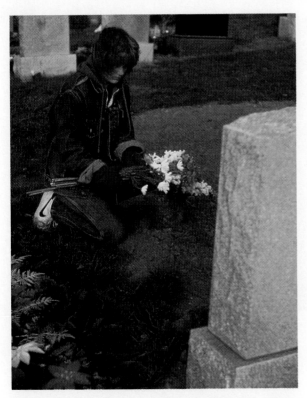

Serious adjustment challenges, such as the death of a loved one, may predispose a person toward later difficulties in life.

reinforcing factors) can act as predisposing factors; that is, they may play important roles in increasing a person's vulnerability to disorder. (For our purposes, the terms *predisposition* and *vulnerability* can be used interchangeably.) A parent's overprotective behavior, for example, could become a reinforcing cause for fearfulness and timidity in a child, so that the child would be less well equipped than others to manage the rigors of adulthood. Such a child would be more predisposed, more vulnerable, to breakdown when his or her resources are seriously challenged.

■ Feedback and Circularity in Abnormal Behavior

Traditionally in the sciences, the task of determining cause-and-effect relationships has focused on isolating the condition X (cause) that could be demonstrated to lead to condition Y (effect). For example, when the alcohol content of the blood reaches a certain level, alcoholic intoxication occurs. Where more than one causal factor is involved, the term **causal pattern** has been used. Here conditions

A, B, C, etc. lead to condition Y. In either case, this concept of cause follows a simple linear model in which a given variable or set of variables leads to a result either immediately after or later in time. Classical physicists had adopted this essential causal model until it was shown to be inadequate for the much more complex universe discovered by twentieth-century physicists.

In the behavioral sciences, and particularly in abnormal psychology, such simple cause-and-effect sequences are very rare. This rarity results not only because we usually must deal with a multitude of interacting causes, but also because we often have difficulty distinguishing between what is cause and what is effect. The concept of self-regulating systems can be applied here. A *self-regulating system* is one in which effects operate as causes for new effects, as when room temperature determines whether or not a home thermostat will signal the furnace to put out more heat. In abnormal behavior, the effects of feedback and the existence of mutual, two-way influences must be taken into account. Consider the following situation:

> *A husband and wife are undergoing counseling for difficulties in their marriage. The husband accuses his wife of drinking excessively, while the wife accuses her husband of rejecting her and showing no affection. In explaining her frustrations to the therapist, the wife views the situation as "I drink because my husband rejects me." The husband sees the problem differently: "I reject my wife because she drinks too much."*
>
> *Over time, a vicious circle has developed in which the husband has increasingly withdrawn as his wife has increasingly lost control of her drinking. It is extremely difficult, if not impossible, to differentiate cause from effect. Rather, the problem has become a vicious circle: each person influences and maintains the behavior of the other.*

Even more subtle confoundings of cause and effect are regularly encountered in the lives of disturbed people. Consider the following scenario:

> *A boy with a history of disturbed interactions with his parents routinely misinterprets the intentions of his peers as being hostile. He*

In abnormal psychology, we often have difficulty distinguishing between what is cause and what is effect. For example, in problems between marital partners, a vicious circle may develop in which each person influences and maintains the behavior of the other. A wife who feels her husband is rejecting her may become increasingly hostile, and the husband may become more withdrawn as his wife's hostility increases, making it virtually impossible to differentiate cause from effect.

develops defensive strategies to counteract the supposed malevolence of those around him, such as the surly rejection of others' efforts to be friendly, which efforts he misconstrues as patronizing. His behavior is difficult for others to deal with, even if those others in fact have benign intentions at the outset. Confronted by the boy's prickly behavior, however, they become defensive, hostile and rejecting, thus confirming and strengthening the boy's distorted expectations. In this manner, each opportunity for new experience and new learning is in fact subverted and becomes another encounter with a social environment that seems perversely and persistently hostile—exactly in line with the boy's expectations.

These not-so-hypothetical situations illustrate that our concepts of causal relationships must take into account the complex factors of feedback, information exchange (communication), patterns of interaction, and circularity.

■ The Diathesis–Stress Model

Throughout the rest of this chapter, we will deal chiefly with predispositional causes of maladaptive behavior in their biological, psychosocial, and sociocultural contexts. A predisposition toward developing a given disorder is termed a **diathesis**. Most mental disorders are conceived (probably rightly) as the product of stress operating on an individual who harbors a diathesis for the type of disorder that emerges. Hence we adopt here what is commonly known as a **diathesis-stress model** of abnormal behavior, which is little more than a recognition of the rather obvious fact that disorder results when a challenge exceeds a particular organism's capacity to meet it. The model should be viewed merely as a conceptual convenience. It has little analytical precision or predictive utility in individual cases of disorder, because it is usually impossible to identify pathogenic diatheses or stressors independently of one another or of an occurrence of maladaptive behavior.

Stress, the response of an organism to adjustive demands made upon it, will be the focus of Chapter 5. Inevitably, however, we will find ourselves referring to stress and *stressors* (the adjustive demands themselves) in our discussion of diatheses because these concepts are so closely related. Indeed, as already suggested, the presence of a diathesis often can be inferred only after some stressful circumstances have led to a breakdown of adaptive behavior. Often, the factors contributing to the development of a diathesis are themselves highly potent stressors, as when a child is physically abused by parents and thereby acquires a predisposition to become a child abuser later in life.

Since stress is the response of an organism to an adjustive demand, it follows that the consequences of stress depend on the coping resources available to

HIGHLIGHT 4.1

Predisposing Causes of Depressive Reactions to Rape

Atkeson et al. (1982) assessed depressive responses to rape in a group of 115 victims of sexual assault, following them for a period of 12 months after the occurrences of the crime. Most of these women experienced depressive emotions immediately following the assaults, but as a group, they were not significantly more depressed than a nonvictim control group at the 4-month follow-up. However, a subgroup of these victims continued to be depressed even at the 12-month follow-up. Demographic variables such as age and socioeconomic factors were found to be related to subsequent depression (older and poorer women being the more affected). Surprisingly, the levels of trauma experienced during the rapes had no detectable effect on long-term depressive symptomatologies. Adequate support immediately after the rapes did appear to lessen long-term effects.

The strongest determinants of adjustment in the long-term post-rape period were associated with the victim's level of prior functioning. Less functional individuals were much more vulnerable to depression after having been raped than were their more functional counterparts. Women who already had had psychological problems of one sort or another, especially including depression, anxiety, and obsessive-compulsive behavior, were slower to recover from rapes. Additionally, problems with sexual relationships generally and with physical health seem to have hampered rapid recoveries from the stress of rapes. Research on the general effects of rape on its victims (e.g., Koss, 1983) suggests that they may sometimes be exacerbations of preexisting tendencies.

---

an individual undergoing an adjustive challenge. Thus one way of viewing vulnerability is in terms of a lack of resources needed to overcome a challenge. This way of viewing vulnerability is general but does have merit, as can be seen in the research, described in *HIGHLIGHT 4.1*, on differential rates of recovery from the experience of rape.

The more specific concept of diathesis refers to a vulnerability to a particular disorder, or a tendency to respond in a particular way to adjustive failure. In other words, an individual is likely to be at special risk for developing the disorder in question should stress exceed current coping resources.

In sum, we can distinguish between causes of abnormal behavior that lie within and are part of the biological makeup or prior experience of a person— diathesis, vulnerability, or predisposition—and those that pertain to current challenges in a person's life, generally termed stressors. A reinforcing cause, for example, would be a special type of stressor. It will be useful to keep these distinctions in mind as we explore the sources of our vulnerabilities in the following sections. Although we will be discussing biological, psychosocial, and sociocultural factors separately, it will also be important to keep in mind that their interaction is critical.

BIOLOGICAL CAUSAL FACTORS

Biological factors influence all aspects of our behavior, including our intellectual capabilities, basic temperament, primary reaction tendencies, stress tolerance, and adaptive resources. Thus a wide range of biological conditions—such as faulty genes, diseases, endocrine imbalances, malnutrition, injuries, and other factors that interfere with normal development and functioning—are potential causes of abnormal behavior.

In this section we will focus on four categories of biological factors that seem particularly relevant to the development of maladaptive behavior: (a) genetic defects; (b) constitutional liabilities; (c) brain dysfunction; and (d) physical deprivations or disruptions. Each of these categories encompasses a number of conditions that influence the quality and functioning of our bodies. They are not necessarily independent of each other, and they may—and most likely do—occur in varying combinations in given individuals.

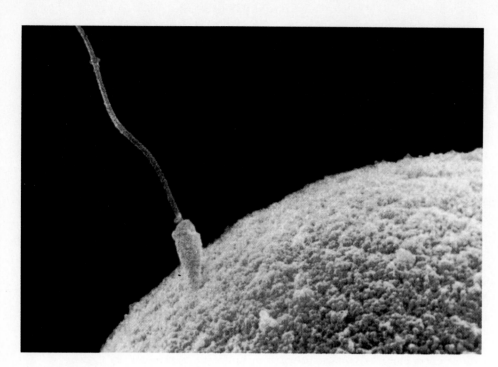

Inheritance begins at conception when the male sperm cell penetrates and fertilizes the female egg cell. The resulting embryo receives a genetic code that provides potentialities for development and behavior throughout a lifetime.

■ Genetic Defects

The essential characteristics of human inheritance are basically the same for all people of all racial and ethnic groups. The specific features of genetic endowment, however, vary widely. Except for identical twins, no two humans have ever begun life with the same endowment. Thus heredity not only provides the potentialities for development and behavior typical of the species, but it is also an important source of individual differences. In general, heredity determines not the specifics of human behavior but rather the ranges within which characteristic behavior can be modified by environmental or experiential influences.

Inheritance begins at conception, when the egg cell of a female is fertilized by the sperm cell of a male, and the resulting embryo receives a genetic code that provides potentialities for development and behavior throughout a lifetime. Since our behavior is inevitably influenced by our biological inheritance, it should hardly be surprising that certain vulnerabilities have their sources at this basic level. Some inherited defects cause structural abnormalities that interfere directly with the normal development of the brain. Other more subtle defects can leave a person susceptible to even the most severe mental disorders. These subtle influences are usually transmitted in the genetic code itself, showing up as metabolic or biochemical variations from an ideally functional norm. The form of mental retardation known as phenylketonuria (PKU), for example, is produced by a genetic error that prevents the adequate metabolization of a chemical compound present in many foods. Other genetic defects are believed to affect adversely the delicate regulation of brain biochemistry. In other words, the individual may inherit faulty genes.

Chromosomal Anomalies   The chainlike structures within a cell nucleus that contain the genes are **chromosomes.** Advances in cellular biological research have enabled us to readily detect **chromosomal anomalies**—irregularities in the chromosomal structure—even before birth, thus making it possible to study their effects on future development and behavior. The first major breakthrough in this area was the discovery that most normal human cells have 46 chromosomes containing the genetic materials in which the hereditary plan—the overall guide for development—is encoded. When fertilization takes place, the normal inheritance consists of 23 pairs of chromosomes, one of each pair from the mother and one from the father. Twenty-two of these chromosome pairs are called **autosomes;** they determine by their biochemical action general anatomical and physiological characteristics. The remaining pair, the **sex chromosomes,** determine an individual's sex. In a female both of these sex chromosomes—one from each parent—are designated as **X chromosomes.** In a male the sex chromosome from the mother is an X, but that from the father is a **Y chromosome.**

Research in developmental genetics has shown that abnormalities in the structure or number of the chromosomes are associated with a wide range of malformations and disorders. For example, Down syndrome is a type of mental retardation in which there is a *trisomy* (a set of three chromosomes instead of two) in chromosome 21. Here the extra chromosome is the primary cause of the disorder. A predisposing cause in Down syndrome is parental age at conception; the probability of this defect rises sharply with the age of the mother (especially after 40) and less sharply but still significantly with the age of the father (Hook, 1980; Stene et al., 1981). Fortunately, this predisposing factor manifests itself only rarely in Down syndrome, but the risk reaches 1 in 50 for a mother in her 40s (Holvey & Talbot, 1972).

Anomalies may also occur in the sex chromosomes, producing a variety of complications that may predispose a person to develop abnormal behavior. For example, Klinefelter's syndrome also involves 47 chromosomes, but in this case the pathogenic element is an extra X chromosome. These XXY individuals have male body structures (although they are usually infertile) and a predominantly male gender identity. They are, however, far more likely than males with the usual 46 chromosomes to develop several kinds of psychopathology, such as juvenile delinquency and problems arising from gender identity confusion (Wright, Schaefer, & Solomons, 1979). Such individuals are said to be at high risk for these outcomes.

Studies by Sergovich et al. (1969) and Hanerton et al. (1975) indicate that the incidence of observable chromosomal abnormalities in newborns is approximately one half of 1 percent. The exact causes of chromosomal anomalies are not yet fully understood. Some have evidently been passed on from one or both of the parents; some apparently are due to errors that occur in the combining of egg and sperm at conception; and still others are caused by aberrant embryo development after conception.

A search for chromosomal irregularities in schizophrenia and other nonorganic psychoses has not proved fruitful, and none of the chromosomal anomalies thus far observed has been directly related to such disorders. Even in the case of Down syndrome, where a trisomy has been identified, it is estimated that 65 percent of the fetuses thus affected spontaneously abort (Creasy & Crolla, 1974). The potential effects of extreme chromosomal irregularities are largely unknown because they ordinarily result in an embryo's death. Nearly 50 percent of stillborn infants have such chromosomal abnormalities (Poland & Lowry, 1974).

One thing appears certain: females are less susceptible to defects from sex-linked disorders because they have two X chromosomes. If one proves faulty, the other member of the pair generally can handle the work of development. Nevertheless, females are sometimes born with a missing chromosome (XO, called Turner's syndrome) or an extra sex chromosome (XXX), either of which may produce abnormalities. Since males normally have a single X chromosome paired with a single Y chromosome, a defect in either may mean trouble. For a summary of some of the known chromosomal abnormalities that can occur, see *HIGHLIGHT 4.2.*

Faulty Genes   It is important to distinguish between chromosomal irregularities, which can now usually be directly observed, and genetic faults (abnormalities of specific genes), which can exist in the absence of obvious chromosomal deviations. **Genes** are the long molecules of DNA (deoxyribonucleic acid) that form at various locations on a chromosome. Individual genes may contain information that causes bodily processes to malfunction, as in the PKU example cited earlier. Unfortunately, we cannot yet predict with any great certainty the occurrence of most such malfunctions.

Through the use of electron microscopes, however, we can study the internal structure of genes, and by complicated gene mapping techniques we can gain information concerning the code that regulates the development and functioning of an organism. This code is carried by the biochemical constituents of the DNA molecule's now-familiar spiraling ladder—the double helix (see *HIGHLIGHT 4.3).* Genes carry the instructions for specific body traits, such as eye color and blood type. They also provide the assembly instructions for organ development. Thus they are the specific units or bearers of an individual's biological inheritance.

Some genes are **dominant genes;** their instructions are activated even if the other member of the pair carries contradictory instructions. **Recessive genes** have instructions that are not carried out unless an individual has inherited two of them, one from each parent. In the field of abnormal psychology, however, genetic influences rarely express themselves in such simple, straightforward ways. This results because behavior, unlike some physical characteristics such as eye color, is not determined exclusively by genetic endowment: it is a product of the environment's interaction with the structural and functional characteristics of an organism.

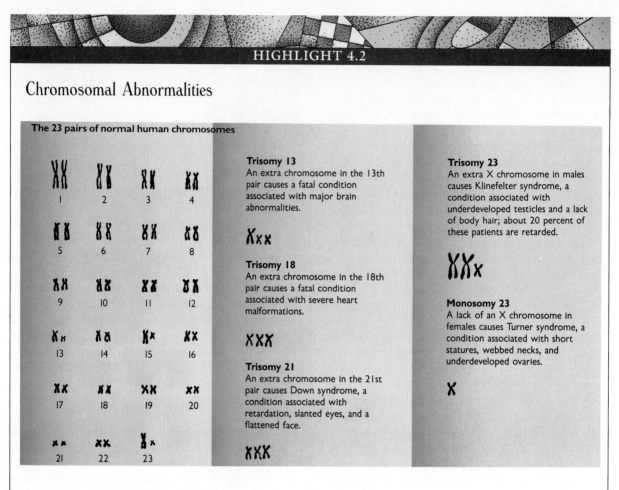

Adapted from a *Chicago Tribune* graphic; *Chicago Tribune,* February 6, 1983.
Data from "It's Not Too Late for a Baby: For Women and Men over 35" by Sylvia P. Rubin.

Genes can affect behavior only indirectly, through their influence on the physical and chemical properties of a body, whose development they regulate in concert with other factors in their environments. Gene "expression," therefore, is normally not a simple or direct outcome of the information encoded in DNA, but is rather the end product of an intricate and involved process that may be influenced by the internal (and likely the external) environment. Unqualified statements about the inheritance of certain mental disorders—sometimes made even by authorities who should know better —must therefore be viewed with a degree of caution; they are almost always untrue in any literal sense (Carson & Sanislow, 1992).

The few instances in which relatively straightforward predictions of mental disorders can be made on the basis of known laws of inheritance invariably involve gross neurological impairment. In such cases, abnormal behavior arises, in part, as a consequence of a central nervous system malfunction. Examples of these rare disorders include Huntington's chorea (a type of brain degeneration beginning in the young or middle adult years) and Tay-Sachs disease (a disorder of fat metabolism causing mental retardation and early death, found mostly among people of European Jewish ancestry). Generally, such disorders occur where there is a pairing of two recessive genes, each of which contains the faulty code.

It appears likely that many of the most interesting (if still largely obscure) genetic influences in abnormal behavior do not usually involve dominant and recessive relationships in one or only a few gene pairs. Rather, most researchers believe that pathogenic genetic influences typically operate *polygenically,* that is, through the action of many genes together in some sort of additive or interactive fashion (e.g., Faraone & Tsuang, 1985). A genetically vulnerable individual has inherited a large

The Double Helix

The DNA double helix molecule is depicted in the figure below. The bases of the two strands point toward one another, joined by the "rungs" of the twisting ladderlike form. The helical form is stabilized because these rungs always consist of one purine (adenine [A] or guanine [G]) and one pyrimidine (thymine [T] or cystocine [C]) "base pair" of molecules, which form a hydrogen bond between them; every A is paired with a T, and every G is paired with a C. The genetic code itself depends on the sequencing of these base pairs of molecules. Though we do not know exactly how it occurs, aberrations in the pairing of the molecules result in biochemical malfunctioning, which may, in turn, affect bodily structure and function. The extremely small size of DNA's structure is indicated by scale in nanometers (nm). A nanometer is one-billionth of a meter. The diameter of the helix is maintained at 2 nanometers.

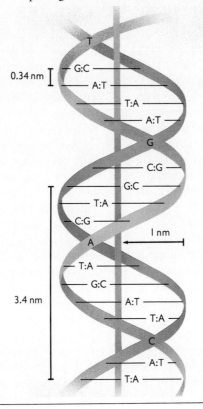

number of these genes that collectively represent faulty heredity. These faulty genes, in turn, may lead to errors in the regulation of brain chemistry that predispose the individual to later difficulties.

Although marked advances have been made in identifying faulty genetic endowment (including the location of the faulty genes responsible for certain physical anomalies), we are not yet able to isolate specific defects on the genes themselves. Therefore most of the information we have on the role of genetic factors in mental disorders is based not on studies of genes, but on studies of individuals genetically related to one another. This pedigree, or family history, method requires that an investigator observe samples of relatives of each *proband* or *index case* (the subject, or carrier, of the trait in question) in order to see whether the incidence increases in proportion to the degree of hereditary relationship. In addition, the incidence of the trait in a normal population is compared (as a control) with its incidence among the relatives of the index cases.

Such research is much more difficult and complicated to carry out than it may at first appear. The history of research in this area, particularly with regard to schizophrenia, is littered with exaggerated conclusions and biased reports. For example, many studies have been made of the rates at which schizophrenia in one monozygotic (genetically identical) twin predicts schizophrenia in the other (Gottesman & Shields, 1972). These rates are called **concordance rates.** Reports from such studies have varied between 6 percent and 86 percent. An accurate figure, it now appears, would be somewhat under 50 percent, but this figure is hard to interpret because twins, especially identical twins, almost always share similar environments as well as heredity. Even if identical twins are separated from birth they are likely to have more similar environments than, say, separated dizygotic (fraternal) twins because, being of the same sex, appearance, and so on, they affect the environment in more similar ways. Nevertheless, identical twins do have sufficiently different experiences to produce measurable effects on personality development (Baker & Daniels, 1990), which is consistent with the observation that many monozygotic twins are *discordant* for schizophrenia—that is, if one twin becomes schizophrenic the other does not necessarily become so as well. Thus firm and stable conclusions about the magnitude of genetic contribution to mental disorders are hard to come by.

The main point here is that in many instances of schizophrenia (and probably in certain other mental disorders), there seems to be a modest but inexactly quantified hereditary component—an innate vulnerability. As was noted in Chapter 3, evidence of this type supports the resurgent biological viewpoint. Whether an individual with this pathogenic makeup will develop schizophrenia is determined by many factors that operate after conception. We still do not know much about these other factors and how they interact with genetic endowment. In Chapter 12 we will address in greater detail this matter of genetic influences in schizophrenia.

Given a favorable life situation, an individual's inherited vulnerability to a certain disorder probably will never result in abnormal behavior. The evidence suggests that in a genetically predisposed person, the most likely outcome is nonoccurrence of the disorder, as is proven in the most conservaive possible fashion by routine findings of monozygotic twin concordance rates of under 50 percent. In the area of physical disease, there are also many examples of genetic predispositions that never become observable diseases; these include predisposi-

tions for diabetes, hypertension, coronary heart disease, and some forms of cancer (Bergsma, 1974; Kaiser Foundation, 1970).

■ Constitutional Liabilities

The term **constitutional liability** is used to describe any detrimental characteristic that is either innate or acquired so early—often in the prenatal environment—and in such strength that it is functionally similar to a genetic characteristic. Physique, physical handicaps, and basic reaction tendencies are among the many traits included in this category. Our focus will be on the role of these constitutional factors in the etiology of maladaptive behavior.

Physique   Though some early research sought to establish a direct link between physique and psychopathology—for example, between muscular physique and criminal behavior (Glueck & Glueck, 1968; Sheldon, 1954)—most data suggest that the link, if any, is not primarily biological but is rather a product of social learning. A muscular person, for instance, may learn that aggression often pays off.

A look at everyday situations shows that physique and other aspects of physical appearance do play an important role in personality development and adjustment. Beauty, for example, is highly valued in our society. One need only attend a social gathering, watch television, or note the billions of dollars spent each year on cosmetics to see the influence of beauty on people's behavior and on their feelings about themselves and others. It is reasonable to assume that, on the whole, physically attractive people have advantages in life not shared by the less attractive; indeed, mental disorder has been found to be correlated with judged unattractiveness (Napoleon, Chassin, & Young, 1980).

Even the mistaken impression that one is unattractive may enhance the risk of disorder (Noles, Cash, & Winstead, 1985). Some data suggest that attractiveness may facilitate recovery from disorder (Farina et al., 1986). The power of this variable, neglected until recently in psychological research, is illustrated in an intriguing experiment by Snyder, Tanke, and Berscheid (1977). These investigators demonstrated that college males who believed they were talking on the telephone to an attractive female behaved quite differently from those who believed they were talking to an unattractive female. (The subjects had been shown false photographs of their "partners" that had previously been judged as to attractiveness.) Interestingly, the females as-

Beauty is highly valued in our society. Children, such as these young girls putting on makeup, understand at an early age that being physically attractive is an important advantage in life.

sumed to be attractive responded to the greater interest shown them and were rated by independent judges (listening to recordings of the conversations) as in fact being attractive, a good example of the circularity in causation mentioned earlier. On the other hand, the females assumed to be unattractive responded to their telephone partners' behavior in ways that led the judges to rate them as unattractive. What had been reality only in the minds of the male subjects became "reality" in the behavior of their unknown female partners.

This study suggests that other people's reactions to our real or imagined characteristics may determine our own behavior, often in ways that conform to their expectations. Further confirmation of this point has been provided by Christensen and Rosenthal (1982). Their study provided male and female college students with arbitrary expectations concerning strangers with whom they were asked to interact. The behavior of the strangers did indeed conform to the students' expectations. Interestingly, males tended to produce stronger conforming behaviors in their partners, while female partners were more likely to conform to expectations. As Jones (1990) has shown in a detailed examination of the entire field of person perception, effects of this kind are both widespread and subtle in human interactions. People are rarely aware of the extent to which their own expectancy-based behaviors produce the expected behavior in others. Biases or stereotypes about physical attri-

butes (such as, "redheads have fiery tempers") therefore stand a better than chance likelihood of being confirmed.

Physical Handicaps   Embryologic abnormalities or environmental conditions operating before or after birth may result in physical defects. A defect that a child is born with is called a **congenital defect.** Some time ago it was estimated that 5 out of every 100 babies born in this country had such defects (Wright et al., 1979). About a third of these defects were considered to be inherited; another sixth were thought to be due to drugs or disease; the causes of the rest—about half in all—were unknown, though an indeterminate proportion may also have been hereditary. It is likely that these figures have now changed somewhat in light of such factors as the increased use of cocaine by pregnant women. Some defects are apparent at birth, while others—such as brain anomalies, endocrine disturbances, and heart defects—may go undetected for months or years. Often such anomalies are minor, but more serious congenital defects constitute one of the five leading causes of death during childhood, accounting for over half a million deaths yearly. It is estimated that nearly half of the deaths occurring in pediatric hospitals are due to structural disorders with significant genetic components (Wright et al., 1979).

The most common birth difficulty associated with later mental disorders (including mental retar-

The most common birth difficulty associated with later mental disorders is low birth weight, which is defined as a birth weight in the range of 5 pounds or less. Low birth weight is most often a factor in premature births, but it can also occur in full-term babies. Some of the risk factors associated with low birth weight may be lessened if the infant is given special treatment, such as stroking and massage, in the first month after birth. Unfortunately, many such infants are not given this care because they tend to spend their early days in incubators.

dation, hyperactivity, and emotional disturbances) is low birth weight, which is defined as a birth weight in the range of 5 pounds or less. This problem is most often a factor in premature births, but can also occur in full-term births. Prenatal conditions that can lead to premature birth and to low birth weight include nutritional deficiencies, disease, exposure to radiation, drugs, emotional stress, or the mother's excessive use of alcohol or tobacco.

It appears that the risk factor associated with low birth weight may be lessened by special treatment of the infant, such as systematic stroking and massage, during the first postnatal month (Rice, 1977). Unfortunately, the likelihood that such treatment will occur is not high since high-risk infants tend to spend their early days mostly in incubators because of their uncertain viability.

Mothers who experience severe emotional stress during pregnancy appear to have a much higher incidence of premature deliveries. Even in the case of full-term babies, severe maternal stress seems to be associated with hyperactivity in the fetus during later pregnancy, and with feeding difficulties, sleep disorders, irritability, and other problems after birth (Blau et al., 1963; Sontag, Steele, & Lewis, 1969). As might be expected, socioeconomic status is related to fetal and birth difficulties, the incidence being several times greater among mothers on lower socioeconomic levels (Robinson & Robinson, 1976).

A fetus, and especially a fetal brain, is not so well protected as many investigators once thought; a variety of biological and psychological conditions affecting a mother during pregnancy can have profound effects on a child's development and adjustment. Considerable evidence suggests that children whose earliest development is thus compromised are at significant risk for a variety of later maladaptive behaviors (e.g., Rutter et al., 1970). Such difficulties may be the direct result of impaired brain function (Breslau, 1990), or they may reflect diminished abilities to handle life challenges.

Primary Reaction Tendencies   Newborns differ in how they react to particular kinds of stimuli. Some are startled by slight sounds or cry if sunlight hits their faces; others are seemingly insensitive to such stimulation. These reactions differ from baby to baby and are examples of **primary reaction tendencies,** characteristic behaviors that appear to have been established prior to any extensive interaction with the environment. These behaviors are regarded as constitutional rather than genetic because they are likely due to more than genetic influences alone; prenatal environmental factors may also play a role in their development. They include such things as sensitivity to stimuli, temperament, and activity level (Rothbart, 1981). Longitudinal studies have shown that reaction tendencies are relatively enduring from infancy to young adulthood and beyond (e.g., Kagan et al., 1984).

Studies suggest that even the differences in behavior between men and women may be due in part to primary reaction tendencies caused by hormonal influences on the developing nervous system. Though we know that sex-typing and other social learning experiences may override such influences, vestiges of biological determination may yet remain and show up in gender-related primary reaction tendencies (Ehrhardt & Meyer-Bahlburg, 1981; Money & Ehrhardt, 1972; Pervin, 1978; Rubin, Reinisch, & Haskett, 1981). Sex differences that fall into this category may be cognitive, affective, or behavioral. After a careful review of the then-available evidence, Pervin (1978) concluded, in part, as follows:

In cognitive functioning, there is no evidence of overall differences in intelligence but considerable evidence suggesting differences in special abilities. Females tend to perform better than males on tests of verbal ability while males tend to perform better than females on tests of mathematical ability and the manipulation of spatial relationships. . . . The differences between the sexes tend to be small and the overlap between the sexes great.

[In] the realm of affective functioning . . . enough studies have reported differences in activity level [higher for males], fearfulness [higher for females], and emotional responses to frustration [higher for males] to suggest that basic differences in affective functioning may exist. . . .

In overt behavioral functioning, the evidence suggests that males are higher in aggression and dominance behavior while females are higher in dependence and nurturance behavior. . . . The evidence for a difference in aggression seems to be most reliable since it comes from a variety of sources—evolutionary, crosscultural, developmental, and biological-hormonal. . . . (pp. 176–177)

Since Pervin's review a variety of new evidence questions the suggestion of a basic gender difference in verbal versus mathematical-spatial abilities. Researchers have, however, raised no serious challenge to the notion of gender differences (on average) in affectivity or dominance and aggression.

Primary reaction tendencies also include characteristic ways of reacting to stress. Some infants react to changes in routine or other stressors by running fevers; others, by having digestive disorders; still others, by developing sleep disturbances. Several investigators have attempted to relate such primary reaction vulnerabilities to stress and maladaptive behavior.

In a classic longitudinal study of infant development, Chess, Thomas, and Birch (1965) found that 7 to 10 percent of all babies are "difficult"—they show irregular patterns of eating, sleeping, and bowel movement; tend to cry a great deal and to show predominantly negative moods; and are inclined to be irritable and have difficulty adjusting to changes. These researchers concluded that since mothers do not gain the satisfactions they expected from having such babies, the temperamental difficulties become overlaid and complicated by unsatisfactory mother-infant relationships. In recent follow-up work with adopted children, Maurer, Cadoret, and Cain (1980) confirmed the link between membership in the "difficult" group and later childhood adjustment difficulties. In extreme cases, a difficult child can contribute to its own abuse and maltreatment and thus increase its vulnerability. For example, in a study of infants who were either abused or neglected, Crittenden (1985) found that the abused children tended to be "difficult," contributing thereby to repetitive parental abuse.

Thomas, Chess, and Birch (1968) have made the important point that a poor "fit" between a child's temperament and the structure and flexibility of environmental demands, particularly those within the home, can lead to "dissonant stress." Such stress in turn can lead to a behavioral disturbance that may partly reflect the child's temperament. The problem is complicated if the child also suffers from developmental deviations such as mental retardation. Such deviations increase the likelihood of behavior disorders and thus make a "good fit" between temperament and environmental conditions even more crucial. A number of factors may thus help determine the links between constitutional features and subsequent behavior disorders (Buss & Plomin, 1975; Maziade et al., 1990; Thomas & Chess, 1977).

Other longitudinal studies (e.g., Mednick, Schulsinger, & Schulsinger, 1975) have followed children believed to be at high risk due to abnormal prenatal conditions or to parents with serious problems. As was noted in Chapter 1, such studies have potential advantages in clarifying causal patterns. They start with subjects who have not yet developed a disorder and try to predict which ones will succumb, or, as in the preceding case, they watch what actually happens and try to identify the conditions that seem to push a child in one direction or another. These studies are demanding and expensive, however, and can encounter many unforeseen difficulties. Thus most of our evidence still comes from research in which individuals who have already developed a disorder are studied, and the researcher must reconstruct a picture of the probable causes.

Incomplete though our knowledge is, we can conclude that childhood disturbance is often followed by adult disturbance. The specific form of childhood problem, however, does not clearly indicate the particular nature of adult difficulties (Fish,

1975; Hanson Gottesman, & Meehl, 1977; Meehl, 1978; Roff, 1960, 1963). To at least some extent, early manifestations of vulnerability seem to be diffuse and nonspecific; what later abnormality will result, in terms of the specific adult diagnosis, is hard to predict. For example, a child who shows delinquent behavior may later be diagnosed as a schizophrenic, but delinquency is not necessarily a predictor of schizophrenia.

■ Brain Dysfunction

The unique aspect of human inheritance is an immeasurably superior brain. It has been described as the most highly organized apparatus in the universe, consisting of some 10 billion nerve cells, or neurons, with countless interconnecting pathways as well as myriad connections with other parts of the body. The human brain provides a fantastic communication and computing network with tremendous capabilities for learning and storing experiences; for reasoning, imagining, and problem solving; and for integrating the overall functioning of the organism. The human brain makes possible our enormous adaptability to varied and changing conditions of existence, but it often does so at a price—a price being paid mostly by those people who live with mental disorders. The nervous systems of lower organisms are not nearly so flexibly adaptive, but they are also much less likely to go awry or lead to behavior that is maladaptive.

As we discussed in Chapter 2, a major scientific breakthrough in psychopathology came when researchers proved that general paresis was related to definite destruction of brain tissue. We now realize that significant damage or loss of brain tissue places a person at risk for psychopathology.

Gross brain pathology (that is, physical malformation of or damage to the brain) is a known causal factor in only about 25 percent of mentally retarded people who acquire the condition before or at birth. Likewise, severe brain injuries due to early childhood accidents are relatively infrequent. In fact, gross brain pathology in children or young adults is not a major factor contributing to psychiatric disorder (Eisenberg, 1990). The incidence of such damage increases notably among the elderly, owing chiefly to the aging process itself (often resulting in Alzheimer's disease) or to associated cardiovascular insufficiency, both of which will be discussed in Chapter 13. It is estimated that at least 17 percent of people above the age of 65 have significant brain damage (Kolata, 1981a). Brain damage sometimes leads to a demented condition and increases vulnerability by making a person less able to cope. At the same time, the person is often quite aware of his or her disability, and this awareness can be a significant source of stress. Thus it is not surprising that some 5 percent of people over age 60 develop distinctly psychopathologic symptoms, such as delusions, and are diagnosed as having organic mental disorders (Dohrenwend et al., 1980). These elderly patients typically occupy a substantial proportion (about 20 percent overall) of the beds in mental hospitals.

Gross brain pathology, in which there are observable defects in brain tissue, is only a small part of the brain pathology "story." Much research is currently under way to correlate specific neurotransmission irregularities (presumed diatheses) with certain mental illnesses, such as major mood disorders. Clearly, the normal functioning of the brain is dependent on a delicately balanced biochemical system. Some people may be genetically prone under stress to experience disruptions in this delicate balance; these disruptions, in turn, would make them vulnerable to brain malfunctions and therefore to serious psychopathologies. We will have much more to say about such matters in subsequent chapters.

Even more subtle deficiencies of brain function, such as those involved in attention deficit disorders and specific learning disabilities in children, may enhance vulnerability to subsequent disorders of a more serious and pervasive sort, particularly when a child's difficulties remain undiagnosed and remedial efforts are not undertaken. Too often in such cases these difficulties are attributed to intelligence or "character" defects in the child, such as stupidity or laziness, leading to severe impairments in self-esteem and a blunted desire to try new or challenging tasks. Such a child may have well-entrenched psychological problems by adolescence, by which point, ironically, the original disorder may no longer be in evidence. The occurrence of "soft" neurological signs (such as slightly abnormal reflexes), fairly common in these children, is a probable risk factor for even so severe a disorder as schizophrenia.

■ Physical Deprivation or Disruption

Although we do not fully understand the processes involved, we do know that digestive, circulatory, and other bodily functions work to maintain the body's physiological equilibrium and integration. The mechanisms for ensuring normal blood chemistry, for maintaining constant body temperature, and for combating invading microorganisms strive to preserve *steady states*—to maintain physiological activity within a range essential to efficient functioning and survival. This process is generally referred to as **homeostasis.** For example, if we are cold, we shiver; if we are too hot, we sweat.

Injuries and diseases that result in pain and infirmity strike all of us from time to time and upset our normal equilibrium. The psychological repercussions from such events, often underestimated, can be profound. Depressions, for example, frequently accompany significant physical illnesses, in part because illnesses painfully remind us of the limits of our control over our lives. Should a disability be permanent or a recovery long delayed, it may be difficult or even impossible for a person's body to become reorganized around a new steady state.

Also, obvious physical disabilities may result in social stigmatization that is itself demoralizing and destabilizing, leaving a person vulnerable to still other types of stress (Jones et al., 1984). Even without such unfortunate events, many people rou-tinely experience challenges to their equilibriums. In the following sections, we deal with two such situations: deprivation of basic physiological needs and nonoptimal levels of stimulation.

Basic Physiological Needs   The most basic human requirements are those for food, oxygen, water, sleep, and the elimination of wastes. In order to survive and meet adjustive demands, people must constantly renew themselves through rest and by taking in nutrients to replace materials used up in the process of living. Prolonged interference with such renewal weakens people's resources for coping with even normal demands and makes them vulnerable to special stresses. Prisoners have sometimes been "broken" by nothing more persuasive than the systematic prevention of sleep or deprivation of food over a period of several days.

Experimental studies of volunteers who have gone without sleep for periods of 72 to 98 hours show increasing psychological problems as the sleep loss progresses—including disorientation for time

The effects of sleep deprivation are obvious in the before and after photos of the subjects shown here. These subjects volunteered for an experiment in which they went without sleep for periods of 72 to 98 hours. The subjects showed increasing psychological problems as their sleep loss progressed, including disorientation for time and place and feelings of depersonalization.

and place and feelings of depersonalization. As Berger (1970) has summarized it, "One thing is sure . . . we must sleep in order to stay sane" (p. 70).

Studies of dietary deficiencies have pointed to marked changes in psychological functioning, the exact changes depending largely on the type and extent of the deficiencies. Some of these effects were demonstrated in a pioneering study of semistarvation carried out by Keys (1950) and his associates during World War II, a study that probably will never be repeated.

During the semistarvation period in the Keys et al. (1950) experiment, the hunger drive became the most important factor affecting the subjects' behavior. The men became unsociable, frequently ignoring such amenities as table manners.

Thirty-two conscientious objectors served as volunteer subjects. The men were first placed on adequate diets for three months. They were then given low-caloric diets characteristic of European famine areas for a period of six months, followed by a three-month period of nutritional rehabilitation.

During the six-month period of semistarvation, the men had an average weight loss of 24 percent. At the same time, they also showed dramatic personality and behavioral changes. They became irritable, unsociable, and increasingly unable to concentrate on anything but food. In some instances they resorted to stealing food from one another and lying in attempts to obtain additional food rations. Other psychological changes included apathy, loss of pride in personal appearance, and feelings of inadequacy. By the close of the experiment, there was a marked reduction or disappearance of their interest in sex, and the predominant mood was one of gloom and depression. Food dominated the men's thoughts, conversations, and even daydreams. They pinned up pictures of chocolate cakes instead of pretty women. In some cases, they went so far as to replan their lives in the light of their newly acquired respect for food. The investigators concluded that by the end of the twenty-fifth week, hunger had become the dominant influence in the men's behavior.

The long-term compromise of cognitive functioning has been demonstrated in a group of former World War II and Korean War POWs who had lost 35 percent or more of their original body weight while in captivity (Sutker, Galina, & West, 1990). In ordinary life, chronic deprivation may result in lowered resistance to stress. Insufficient rest, inad-

equate diet, or attempts to carry a full work load under the handicap of a severe cold, fatigue, or emotional strain may interfere with our ability to cope and predispose us to personality disorganizations.

Perhaps the most tragic deprivation is seen in young children who are malnourished. If they survive, the scars of vulnerability are likely to remain for life. Severe malnutrition, which is associated with a host of other potentially damaging variables such as parental neglect and limited access to health care (Brozek & Schurch, 1984), not only impairs physical development and lowers resistance to disease, but also stunts brain growth and results in markedly lowered intelligence (Amcoff, 1980; Cravioto & DeLicardie, 1975; Winick, 1976). Peterson (1978) has noted that thiamine, niacin, and vitamin B_{12} deficits may lead to organic brain syndromes.

In a postmortem study of infants who had died of malnutrition during their first year of life, Winick (1976) found the total brain cell content to be 60 percent below that of normal infants. Further research on animals showed a similar effect in the offspring of malnourished mothers (Winick & Rosso, 1973). Babies who undergo severe malnutrition but survive suffer the permanent stunting of brain growth because the brain's fastest growth

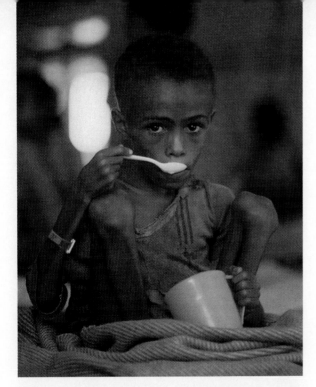

Severe malnutrition, which can be observed in this Ethiopian child, not only impairs physical development and lowers resistance to disease, but also stunts brain growth and results in markedly lowered intelligence.

occurs from about five months before until ten months after birth. In a random sample of areas in ten American states where 75 to 80 percent of the resident families were living either in poverty or close to it, the U.S. Public Health Service found that 15 percent of all children studied showed evidence of physical and mental retardation associated with malnutrition (reported in Winick, 1976).

Malnutrition because of faulty diet, resulting in a wide range of physical disorders and generally lowered resistance to stress, is found even in lower middle-income families (Reice, 1974). Among adults, Robinson and Winick (1973) have reported on the higher incidence of psychoses and other mental disturbances among individuals who follow crash diets to achieve rapid weight losses. In some cases, such reactions result from disappointed expectations: weight losses do not solve long-standing psychological and social problems (Knittle et al., 1982). Nevertheless, changes in mental status can be directly produced by severe nutritional deficiencies (Baker & Lyen, 1982).

Stimulation and Activity   We have known for some time that healthy mental development depends on a child's receiving adequate amounts of stimulation from the environment. Since the 1940s (Spitz, 1945), a number of researchers have described a "hospitalism" syndrome among under-

stimulated, institutionalized infants. The syndrome leads an alarming proportion of these children simply to waste away and die. Psychological vulnerabilities induced by too little stimulation clearly can be substantial; we shall explore these predispositions in the upcoming discussion of psychosocial factors. It also seems probable, however, that the physical development of the brain is adversely affected by an insufficient environment (Shapiro, 1968). Numerous animal studies demonstrate enhanced biological development produced by conditions of special stimulation (Wright et al., 1979), including positive changes in brain chemistry and anatomy (Diamond, 1988; Krech, 1966; Krech, Rosenzweig, & Bennett, 1962; Rosenzweig et al., 1968).

On the other hand, there are limits to how much stimulation is beneficial to a developing organism. We know that sensory overload can impair adult functioning (Gottschalk, Haer, & Bates, 1972) and that excessive life changes are correlated with physical illness. Although we might assume that infants and children are similarly affected, we unfortunately have no solid research on this issue.

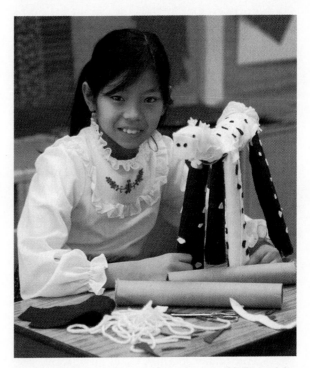

Healthy mental development depends on a child's receiving adequate amounts of stimulation from the environment. Providing enjoyable, creative, tactile activities for children, like the art project this young girl is involved in, can influence psychological development. Such stimulation may also enhance brain development.

In general each individual seems to have an optimal level of stimulation and activity that may vary over time, but that must be maintained for normal psychological functioning. Under excessive pressure, we may strive to reduce the level of input and activity. On the other hand, under some conditions—such as boredom—we may strive to increase the level of stimulation by doing something engaging. In Chapter 8, we will see that certain personality types, such as antisocial personalities, have higher than average needs for excitement.

PSYCHOSOCIAL CAUSAL FACTORS

We begin life with few built-in patterns and a great capacity to learn from experience. We may use our experiences to develop perspectives that can help us face challenges resourcefully and resiliently. Unfortunately, such a happy outcome is by no means guaranteed—not even for people who are biologically and constitutionally sound.

In this section we will examine the psychosocial factors that make people vulnerable to disorder. Psychosocial factors are those developmental influences that may handicap a person psychologically, making him or her less resourceful in the struggle to cope.

What we know about psychosocial causal factors is less precise and reliable than our knowledge of biological predispositions. Even though there are a host of psychosocially-based theoretical perspectives (as were summarized in Chapter 3), few of them are helpful in pinpointing the causal factors contributing to mental disorders in individual cases. It is much more difficult to measure and quantify the psychosocial aspects of an individual than the biological ones. Nonetheless, we will examine here what we do know about psychosocial factors, beginning with a brief examination of the central role played by our perceptions of ourselves and our world. From there we will move to a review of more specific influences that may distort the cognitive structures on which good psychological functioning is dependent. We will focus on early deprivation and trauma, inadequate parenting, pathogenic family structures, and maladaptive peer relationships. Such factors typically do not operate alone. They interact with each other and with other psychosocial factors; with particular genetic and constitutional factors; and with particular settings or environments.

Self-perception and Cognitive Maps

Fundamental to determining what we know, want, and do are some basic assumptions that we make about ourselves, our world, and the relationship between the two. These assumptions make up our frames of reference—our **cognitive maps,** or **schemas**—concerning the universe and our place in it. Because what we can learn or discern directly through our senses can provide, at best, only an inadequate representation of "reality," we need extensive cognitive frameworks to fill in the gaps and make sense out of what we can observe. Our personal cognitive maps are our guides, one might say, through the complexities of living in the world as we understand it. These maps include our views on what we are, what we might become, and what is important to us. Other aspects concern our notions of the various roles we occupy or might occupy in the social fabric, such as woman, man, student, parent, physician, American, older person, and so on. An individual's cognitive map also can be

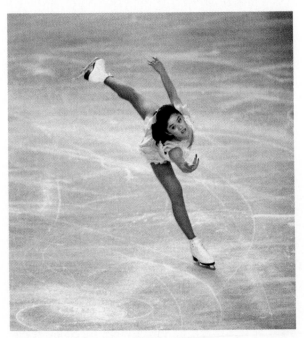

Our cognitive maps—our frames of reference concerning our place in the world—are influenced by the roles we occupy. How we perceive ourselves in relation to these roles may result in effective behavior or may make us vulnerable to disorder. A key element of this young woman's cognitive map is likely to be her role as a skater. If she focuses on the grace, athleticism, and self-discipline required to be a skater, her cognitive map is a source of healthy functioning. If she views skating as something that is lonely and stressful, her cognitive map may be a source of psychological vulnerability.

construed as his or her **self-identity:** what that person is as distinguished from other persons; what he or she knows and believes; what he or she holds dear and reveres; what meaning his or her existence has. One aspect of these cognitive systems, the *love map* (Money, 1986; Money & Lamacz, 1989) is at the root of our sexual orientation and our erotic relationship to an idealized partner, as discussed in Chapter 10. Vital though they are to effective and organized behavior, our cognitive maps are also, regrettably, key sources of our psychological vulnerabilities, many of which can predispose us to abnormal behavior.

Parts of our cognitive maps may be valid, some invalid; other parts may be true for us but not for others; still other parts may be held with varying degrees of conviction, and they may be more or less explicit and conscious. Although our daily decisions and behavior are in large part shaped by our frames of reference, we may be quite unaware of the assumptions on which they are based—or even of having made assumptions at all. We think that we are simply seeing things the way they are. We do not often consider the fact that other pictures of the "real" world might be possible or that other rules for "right" might exist. Some people (e.g., Scheff, 1984) have even suggested we may be unable to achieve this level of detachment from our most fundamental assumptions. Thus many of our thoughts, actions, and feelings are based on internalized rules and ways of seeing the world that we would be hard-pressed to articulate or define.

On the one hand, the self can be seen as a set of rules for processing information and for selecting behavior alternatives; on the other hand, it can be seen as the product of those rules—a sense of selfhood, or self-identity (Vallacher, Wegner, & Hoine, 1980). Deficiencies or deviations in either aspect of the development of the self can make one vulnerable to disorder. For example, if a person's information-processing rules differ in major respects from those of his or her peers, then that person's "reality" will be correspondingly different and may lead to rejection, isolation, despair, and disorder. Similarly, should an individual's self-identity require propping up by membership in an eccentric cult, or should its perceived contents be so amorphous or fragmented that they must be continuously inferred from the intense reactions of partners in serial love relationships (as in many cases of borderline personality disorder, Chapter 7), the individual will be at serious risk of a breakdown.

As Vallacher et al. (1980) have put it, we look *through* the rules of the self—rarely *at* them. For this reason, the rules, once established, may be hard to identify, and it may be difficult to deliberately change them. New experiences tend to be assimilated into our existing cognitive frameworks, even if the new information has to be reinterpreted or distorted to make it fit. We tend to cling to existing assumptions and reject or change new information that is contradictory to them. **Accommodation**—changing our existing frameworks to make it possible to incorporate discrepant information—is more difficult and threatening, especially when important assumptions are challenged. Accommodation is, of course, a basic goal of psychosocial therapies—explicitly in the case of the cognitive and cognitive-behavioral variants, but deeply implicated in virtually all other approaches as well. This process makes major therapeutic change a difficult task.

An individual's failure to acquire appropriate principles or rules in cognitive organization can affect future vulnerability. Indeed, about 75 percent of so-called mentally retarded persons—who as a group are at high risk for mental disorder—are intellectually disabled not because of defective brain tissue, but rather because their neural tissue has been insufficiently "programmed" to manage the complexities of modern life. Failure at this level—whether the inadequate programming involves academic, employment, or social skills—results in a person's being less able than others to cope effectively with adjustive demands.

Essentially, these issues involve learning, and they grow in importance as children progress beyond the simple conditioning that characterizes the infancy period. Although children in a given culture show similarities in what they learn, they also show marked differences. Mischel (1973) has identified five learning-based differences that become apparent early in childhood: (a) children have acquired different levels of competency in different areas; (b) they have learned different concepts and strategies for coding and categorizing their experiences, and they thus "process" new information differently; (c) although they have all learned that certain things follow from certain others, what they have learned to expect is quite different, depending on their unique experiences; (d) they have learned to find different situations attractive or disagreeable and thus to seek quite different things; and (e) they have learned different ways of coping with impulses and regulating their behavior—they have developed a characteristic "style" of dealing with life's demands. Differences in these general areas continue through childhood and into the adult years and help shape later learning.

These learned variations make some children far better prepared than others for further learning and personal growth. The ability to make effective use of new experience depends very much on the degree to which past learning has created cognitive structures that facilitate the integration of the novel or unexpected. A well-prepared child will be able to assimilate or when necessary accommodate new experience in ways that will be productive of growth; a child with less adequate cognitive foundations may be confused, unreceptive to new information, and psychologically vulnerable. It is mainly for this reason that most theories of personality development emphasize the importance of early experience in shaping the main directions that an individual's coping style will take.

A good example is afforded by modern research on the cognitive antecedents of psychological depression. The onsets of most such depressions, including severely incapacitating ones, have been linked repeatedly with the prior occurrence of negative life events, such as illness, divorce, or serious financial setbacks. Negative events are inevitable in all of our lives, and most of us muddle through them in one way or another without becoming psychological casualties. Substantial evidence shows that people who respond to such events with clinically diagnosable depressions are in some sense "primed" to respond in this way because of the ways in which they process the negative happenings. While the details of such a negative "set" are still being researched, they seem to involve a kind of overreaction and overgeneralization as to the meaning of negative events, one that was learned much earlier and may have remained relatively dormant for many years. The ultimate source of these maladaptive learnings is often unclear, but some evidence suggests that traumatic experiences, such as the death of a parent in childhood, may encourage their acquisition.

The example just given reminds us that the events making up one child's experiences may be vastly different from those of another, and that many such events are neither predictable nor controllable. At one extreme are children who develop in stable and lovingly indulgent environments within families that buffer them, as far as possible, from the harsher realities of the world; at the other extreme are children whose developmental experiences consist of constant exposure to frightening events, sometimes including unspeakable cruelties. We see the effects of such different experiences in the corresponding cognitive maps of adults: some present a world that is uniformly loving, unthreatening and benign, which of course it is not; others resemble a jungle in which minimal safety and perhaps even life itself is constantly in the balance,

also a distortion for most adults. Given a preference in terms of likely outcomes, most mental health professionals would opt for the former of these maps, but in fact neither is optimal as a blueprint for engaging the real world; both represent serious adaptive deficits.

Fear or *anxiety* (fear in the absence of objective danger) occupies a place close to the conceptual center of psychopathology; it is also the central problem in a number of the specific mental disorders to be discussed in later chapters of this book. While we are accustomed to viewing anxiety as an emotion or affect, recent research and thinking (e.g., Barlow, 1988; Beck, Emery, & Greenberg, 1985) have emphasized a substantial cognitive component in the genesis and experience of the crippling types of anxiety seen in clinical situations. Barlow (1988), in fact, characterizes anxiety as "a diffuse cognitive-affective structure" whose "essence is *arousal-driven apprehension*" (p. 235). Apprehension, of course, has a substantial cognitive component of expectation, the expectation that one is soon going to have an unpleasant experience—in the extreme, perhaps even the experience of dying.

In Barlow's well-researched model, arousal drives apprehension, but apprehension (expectation) also, importantly, drives arousal. While this model acknowledges the likely contribution of some sort of biological vulnerability to stressful circumstances, it stresses the importance of experience with negative outcomes perceived to be unpredictable and uncontrollable, based on a focused review of pertinent human and animal research. Restated in terms of the present discussion, a clinically anxious person is someone whose cognitive map includes strong possibilities that terrible things over which he or she has no control may happen unpredictably. It is not difficult to imagine developmental scenarios that would lead to a life map having these elements as prominent characteristics.

Finally, it appears that some uncontrollable experiences to which children are subjected are so overwhelming and contradictory that it is impossible to construct a coherent cognitive map within which they can be assimilated. This situation is perhaps seen most clearly in cases of multiple personality disorder (MPD), where the separate personalities develop separate cognitive maps that may be completely walled off from one another. Indeed, in one recently reported instance, the original "person," having been repeatedly raped by a stepfather at age 2, simply ceased to exist; she was "replaced" by a host of alter personalities that were better able to manage the bizarre and terrifying events of the child's life (Chase et al., 1990). We have in fact learned in recent years that MPD (discussed in Chapter 6) may be associated with repeated, traumatic sexual abuse in childhood. The main point here is that a fragmented selfhood, whatever its origin—and it is frequently traumatic —invites the development of abnormal behaviors.

■ Early Deprivation or Trauma

Fortunately, experiences of the intensity and persistence just noted, while more common than was thought only a decade ago, are nevertheless relatively rare. There are, however, other kinds of experiences that, while less dramatic and chilling, may leave children with deep and sometimes irreversible psychic scars. The deprivation of needed resources normally supplied by parents or parental surrogates is one such circumstance.

Parental deprivation refers to an absence of adequate care from and interaction with parents or their substitutes during the formative years. It can occur even in intact families where, for one reason or another, parents are unable (for instance, because of mental disorder) or unwilling to provide for a child's needs for close and frequent human contact. The children of parents experiencing severe depressions, for example, are at enhanced risk for disorder themselves (Downey & Coyne, 1990), at least partly because depression makes for inept parenting —notably including inattentiveness to a child's needs (Gelfand & Teti, 1990). The most severe manifestations of deprivation, however, are usually seen among abandoned or orphaned children who may either be institutionalized or placed in a succession of unwholesome foster homes.

We can interpret the consequences of parental deprivation from several psychosocial viewpoints. Such deprivation might result in fixation at the oral stage of psychosexual development (Freud); it might interfere with the development of basic trust (Erikson); it might retard the attainment of needed skills because of a lack of available reinforcements (Skinner); it may preempt self-actualizing tendencies with maintenance and defensive requirements (Rogers, Maslow); or it might stunt the development of the child's capacity for relatively anxiety-free exchanges of tenderness and intimacy with others (Sullivan). Any of these viewpoints might in a given instance be the best way of conceptualizing the problems that arise, or some combination of them may be superior to any one in the insight it affords. Most generally, however, we see the victims of such experiences as acquiring dysfunctional cog-

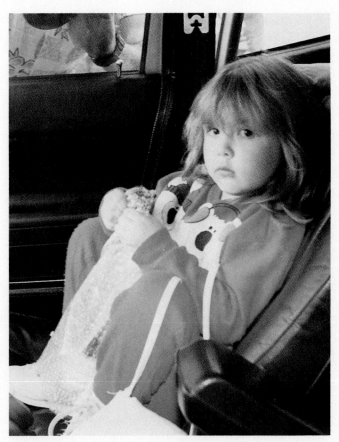

Parental deprivation refers to an absence of adequate care from and interaction with parents or their substitutes during the formative years. Its most severe manifestations are usually seen among abandoned or orphaned children. Parental deprivation can take other forms, however, as in the case of 4-year-old Rachel Rauser, whose father allegedly tried to sell her to her aunt and uncle. Rachel was turned over to her stepmother.

nitive maps. On such maps, the basic stability, trustworthiness, and affection of the world and of relationships are represented, if at all, to be uncertain and thus unworthy of serious investment or commitment.

From any viewpoint, the effects of parental deprivation can be serious. Faulty development has often been observed in infants experiencing deprivation. Many studies have focused on the role of the mother, but all such studies are essentially concerned with warmth and stimulation, whether it comes from the mother, the father, or institutional staff members.

Institutionalization   In an institution, as compared with an ordinary home, there is likely to be less warmth and physical contact; less intellectual, emotional, and social stimulation; and a lack of encouragement and help in positive learning. A much-referenced study by Provence and Lipton (1962) compared the behavior of infants living in institutions with that of infants living with families. At 1 year of age, the institutionalized infants showed general impairments in their relationships to people, rarely turning to adults for help, comfort, or pleasure and showing no signs of strong attachments to any person. These investigators also noted a marked retardation of speech and language development, emotional apathy, and impoverished and repetitive play activities. In contrast to the babies living in families, the institutionalized infants failed to show the personality differentiation and learning that "can be thought of both as accomplishments of the first year of life and as the foundation upon which later learning is built" (p. 161). With more severe and pervasive deprivation, development may be even more retarded.

The long-range effects of severe early deprivation are suggested by the early findings of Beres and Obers (1950) in their study of 38 adolescents who had been institutionalized between the ages of about 3 weeks and 3 years. At the time of the study, 16 to 18 years after discharge from the orphanage, 4 were diagnosed as psychotic, 21 as having character (or "personality") disorders, 4 as mentally retarded, and 2 as neurotic. Only 7 were judged to have achieved satisfactory personal adjustments. In general, it appears that "affectionless psychopathy"—characterized by the inability to form close interpersonal relationships and often by antisocial behavior—is a syndrome commonly found among children who have been institutionalized at an early age, particularly before the age of 1 year.

These early findings have been confirmed in a review of more recent research on child abandonment by Burnstein (1981). Burnstein concludes that abandoned children are at high risk for psychological disturbances and that excessive levels of aggressiveness, rebelliousness, and disobedience are especially likely. Such behaviors suggest interpersonal anxieties that are defended against by the adoption of "antiweak," "antitrust" orientations to the world. The long-range prognosis for children suffering early and prolonged parental deprivation is considered unfavorable (Rutter, 1972; Tizard & Rees, 1975; Wolkind, 1974).

Although some earlier estimates of the pathological effects of such deprivation were exaggerated, it is now clear that many children deprived of normal parenting in infancy show maladaptive personality development. The extent to which early deprivation can be made up for by abundant love and attention at a later time is not yet known. It does appear, however, that attachment to a particular adult (typically the mother)—once considered the essential element in healthy development—may not, in fact, be the critical factor. Research by Leiderman and Leiderman (1974) comparing *monomatric* with *polymatric* (one mother versus multiple mother) households, and by Kagan, Kearsley, and Zelazo (1976) on the effects of early placement in quality day-care settings, failed to show any substantial deficits in multiple-mothered children. Belsky and Steinberg (1978) and Scarr (1984) reached a similar conclusion concerning quality alternate care settings. The operative word here is *quality,* however, and as many dual-career couples have learned to their dismay, it may be difficult to find quality day-care centers.

In sum, whether maladaptive personality development can be reversed probably depends on a number of factors, including the duration of prior deprivation and the quality and time of therapeutic enrichment efforts. It is clear that, if the deprivation continues, any movement toward more adaptive personality development becomes increasingly difficult as a child gets older (Freedman, Kaplan, & Sadock, 1976; Skolnick, 1986). After some period of time a child's cognitive map no longer accommodates new experiences, in part because the child's expectations of abandonment make it difficult for even well-meaning others to convincingly disconfirm them; most of us do not have an unending supply of patience in confronting persistent and surly mistrust.

An institutional environment may be detrimental to young children, but the defects of such settings can be overcome by the quality of care they provide. These children in a day-care center, judging by their surroundings, are in an enriched setting. Studies have shown that placement in quality day-care settings has no substantial impact on children's personality development.

Deprivation in the Home   By far the greatest number of infants subjected to parental deprivation are not separated from their parents, but rather suffer from inadequate or distorted care at home. In these situations parents typically neglect or devote little attention to their children and are generally rejecting.

The effects of such deprivation may be devastating. The early work of Ribble (1944, 1945), for example, showed that rejecting, indifferent, or punishing mothers may cause tense, unsatisfied, and negative behavior in their infants at a very early age. In fact, Bullard and his associates (1967) delineated a "failure to thrive" (FTT) syndrome that "is a serious disorder of growth and development frequently requiring admission to the hospital. In its acute phase it significantly compromises the health and sometimes endangers the life of the child" (p. 689). In a follow-up study conducted eight months to nine years after the hospitalization of such children for treatment, Bullard found that almost two-thirds of the subjects showed evidence "either of continued growth failure, emotional disorder, mental retardation, or some combination of these" (p. 681).

The effects of deprivation vary considerably from infant to infant; in some societies, practices that we would expect to be permanently damaging are not. For example, Kagan (1973) compared the development of year-old Guatemalan Indian infants with that of American-raised infants. Due to the custom of the culture, Guatemalan Indian infants spend their first year in a psychologically impoverished environment. Kagan found that they were, by comparison, severely retarded in their development. After the first year, however, the environment of these infants was enriched, and by age 11, they performed as well or better than American children on problem-solving and related intellectual tasks.

Prolonged neglect may have serious long-term effects even where a child shows minimal immediate difficulties. For example, Roff and Knight (1981) conducted a follow-up study of individuals averaging 43.7 years of age who had had adjustment difficulties as children and who had become schizophrenic in young adulthood. They found that childhood parental neglect was significantly associated with relatively poor long-term outcomes. These outcomes also appeared to have been due to serious family disorganization and disruption, factors that we will discuss later.

Parental rejection of a child is closely related to deprivation and may be demonstrated in various ways—by physical neglect, denial of love and affection, lack of interest in the child's activities and

Parental rejection may underlie a child's attempt to run away from home. Other behaviors exhibited by children who are victims of parental rejection are a tendency to be overly aggressive and prone to impulsive behavior, diminished intellectual functioning, excessive fears, and an inability to form meaningful relationships.

achievements, harsh or inconsistent punishment, failure to spend time with the child, and lack of respect for the child's rights and feelings. In a minority of cases, it also involves cruel and abusive treatment. Parental rejection may be partial or complete, passive or active, or subtly or overtly cruel.

Regardless of its specific nature or intensity, parental rejection has been associated with a more or less specific pattern of development in its victims. These children often have a tendency to be overly aggressive and prone to impulsive behavior (Lefkowitz et al., 1973; Patterson, 1979; Pemberton & Benady, 1973; Sears, Maccoby, & Levin, 1957). Pringle (1965) reported that adults who had experienced significant rejection in childhood had serious difficulty in giving and receiving affection, and Yates (1981) found that severely abused children lacked the capacity to form meaningful relationships, a trait common to adult narcissistic personalities (see Chapter 8). Wolfe, Gentile, & Wolfe (1989), in a follow-up study of 71 sexually abused children, have likened the outcomes observed to those of posttraumatic stress disorder (see Chapter 5). Other reported behaviors associated with parental rejection include diminished intellectual functioning (Hurley, 1965), excessive fears (Poznanski, 1973), and running away from home (Stierlin, 1973).

A large proportion of parents who reject or abuse their children have themselves been the victims of parental rejection (Kaplun & Reich, 1976; Wright et al., 1979), with corresponding effects on their cognitive maps. In this sense, lack of love has been referred to as a communicable disease. Rejection, of course, is not a one-way street; a child may also reject or otherwise cause unusual stress for his or her parents (Crittenden, 1985; Wolfe, 1985). This pattern sometimes occurs when the parents belong to a low-status minority group of which the child is ashamed. Although the results of such rejection have not been studied systematically, it appears that children who reject their parents deny themselves needed models, loving relationships, and other essentials for the healthy development of their cognitive maps.

Childhood Trauma   Most of us have had one-time traumatic experiences that temporarily shattered our feelings of security, adequacy, and worth and influenced our perceptions of ourselves and our environment. The term **psychic trauma** is used to describe any aversive (unpleasant) experience that inflicts serious psychological damage on an individual. The following illustrates such an incident.

I believe the most traumatic experience of my entire life happened one April evening when I was 11. I was not too sure of how I had become a member of the family, although my parents had thought it wise to tell me that I was adopted. That much I knew, but what the term adopted meant was something else entirely. One evening after my step-brother and I had retired, he proceeded to explain it to me—with a vehemence I shall never forget. He made it clear that I wasn't a "real" member of the family, that my parents didn't "really" love me, and that I wasn't even wanted around the place. That was one night I vividly recall crying myself to sleep. That experience undoubtedly played a major role in making me feel insecure and inferior.

Traumas of this magnitude are apt to leave psychological wounds that never completely heal. As a result, later stress that reactivates these wounds may be particularly difficult for an individual to handle and often explains why one person has difficulty with a problem that is not especially stressful to another. Psychic traumas in infancy or early childhood are especially damaging for the following reasons:

1. *Children, almost by definition, have limited coping resources and are relatively helpless in the face of threat.* They are therefore more readily overwhelmed by traumas than an older person would be. Conditioned responses, which in cognitive terms are *acquired expectancies* that a particular event will follow from another, are readily established in situations that evoke strong emotions; such responses are often highly resistant to extinction. Thus one traumatic experience of almost drowning in a deep lake may be sufficient to establish a fear of water that endures for years or a lifetime.

2. *Conditioned responses stemming from traumatic experiences may generalize to other situations.* A child who has learned to fear water may also come to fear riding in boats and other situations associated with even the remotest possibility of drowning.

3. *Traumatic situations tend to result in strong and automatic conditioning that is relatively resistant to cognitive reappraisal.* Consequently, exposure to similar situations tends to reactivate an affective-cognitive structure of intense apprehension that usurps a person's attention and thereby prevents a rational review of the actual risk confronting the person. Young children are thus especially prone to acquiring intense anxieties that remain resistant to modification even as their resources for coping undergo tremendous growth during their subsequent development.

The aftereffects of early traumatic experiences depend heavily on the support and reassurance given a child by parents or other significant people. This support appears particularly important when the trauma involves an experience that arouses strong feelings of inadequacy and self-devaluation, such as being ridiculed for stuttering or clumsiness. For a look at the factors of vulnerability that may be involved when children are separated from their parents, see *HIGHLIGHT 4.4*

Many psychic traumas in childhood, though highly upsetting at the time, probably have minor long-term consequences. Some children are less vulnerable than others and show more resilience and recoverability from hurt (Crittenden, 1985). Not all children who experience a trauma—for example, a parent's death (Barnes & Prosen, 1985; Crook & Eliot, 1980)—exhibit discernible long-term effects. However, a child exposed to repeated early psychic traumas, such as physical abuse (Crittenden, 1985) or incestuous advances (Owens,

Separation from Parents as a Traumatic Experience

Bowlby (1960, 1973) has summarized the effects on children from 2 to 5 years old of being separated from their parents during prolonged periods of hospitalization. He cited three stages of their separation experiences:

1. *Initial protest*—characterized by increased crying, screaming, and general activity.
2. *Despair*—included dejection, stupor, decreased activity, and general withdrawal from the environment.
3. *Detachment*—followed discharge from the hospital and reunion with their mothers; characterized by indifference and sometimes even hostility toward their mothers.

The effects of long-term or permanent separation from one or both parents are complex. When the separation occurs as early as 3 months after birth, an infant's emotional upset seems to be primarily a reaction to environmental change and strangeness, and he or she usually adapts readily to a surrogate parent. But once attachment behavior has developed, the emotional hurt of separation may be deeper and more sustained, and a child may go through a period of bereavement and have greater difficulty adjusting to the change. It appears that the age at which an infant is most vulnerable to long-term separation or loss is from about 3 months to 3 years. The long-term consequences of such loss appear to depend not only on the time of its occurrence, but also on the child in question, the previous relationship with the parent, and the quality of subsequent parental care.

The magnitude of this problem is indicated by the statistic that well over 10 million children in the United States have lost at least one parent through separation, divorce, or death.

1984), is likely to show a disruption in normal personality development. Even though subsequent experiences may have a moderating influence, the detrimental effects of such early traumas may never be completely overcome, partly because experiences that would provide the necessary relearning are selectively avoided. A child whose cognitive map does not include the possibility that others can be trusted does not venture out toward others far enough to learn that some people in the world are in fact trustworthy.

◼ Inadequate Parenting

All the psychosocial viewpoints on abnormal behavior focus attention on the behavioral tendencies a child acquires in the course of early social interaction with others—chiefly parents or parental surrogates. While their explanations vary considerably, all the viewpoints accept the general principle that certain deviations in parenting can have profound effects on a child's subsequent ability to cope with life's challenges.

You should keep in mind that a parent-child relationship is always bidirectional in respect to influence. As with any continuing relationship, the behavior of each person affects the behavior of the other. Some children are easier to love than others; some parents are more sensitive than others to an infant's needs. It is often hard to say which person was originally the most responsible for certain interactional patterns.

In occasional cases, we are able to identify characteristics in an infant that have been largely responsible for an unsatisfactory relationship between parent and child. One example is the difficult baby, described by Chess and her associates (see page 107), a baby whose irregularities may help establish a mutually unsatisfying relationship between parent and child.

Another example is the withdrawn, unresponsive, autistic child (described more fully in Chapter 14). It has been observed that the parents of such children often seem cold, emotionally reserved, and "intellectual." Early researchers had blamed this parental coldness and distance for their children's autism—thereby adding guilt to the problems these

Parents play a critical role in their children's growth toward physical and psychological competence. Though a parent-child relationship is bidirectional—the behavior of each person affects the behavior of the other—the influence of a parent on a child is likely to be more important in shaping the child's behavior than vice versa.

parents already were facing. Infantile autism is now recognized by most authorities as usually related to a congenital neurological deficit in children; evidently, parents restrict their emotional involvement, often unconsciously, as a way of coping with their profoundly unresponsive children (Schopler, 1978). Other evidence suggests that some of the disturbances commonly found in the parents of schizophrenic patients are a reaction to their children's disturbances, rather than the other way around (Carson, 1984).

In most cases, however, the influence of a parent on his or her child is likely to be more important in shaping a child's behavior than vice versa. Several specific patterns of parental influence appear with great regularity in the backgrounds of children who show certain types of faulty development that enhance the likelihood of adaptive breakdown. Some of these patterns will be discussed in the following sections.

Overprotection and Excessive Restriction

Overprotective parents may watch over their children constantly, protect them from the slightest risk, overly clothe and medicate them, and make decisions for them at every opportunity. In essence, they smother their children's growth. With recent societal changes favoring dual-career parenting and the placement of young children in nursery schools or other day-care centers, the problem of overprotection probably occurs less frequently than it once did. It is doubtful, however, that it has disappeared from the scene, especially because overprotective parents most likely resist alternate care options.

Although fathers have been known to overprotect their children, the problem is probably more common among mothers (Weintraub & Frankel, 1977). Such maternal reactions represent a type of behavior in which a mother attempts, through contact with her child, to live out a cognitive map whose "mother" component has problematic features. She may, for example, attempt to gain satisfactions that are better pursued in relations with other adults or her husband. One common pattern, usually involving a male child, is the encouragement of excessive closeness and intimacy, to the extent that the father of the child may develop distinct feelings of resentment for playing "second fiddle." A corollary syndrome sometimes occurs between fathers and daughters.

In a study of the family backgrounds of children referred to a child guidance clinic, Jenkins (1968) found that those youngsters characterized as overanxious were likely to have an infantilizing, overprotective mother. Similarly, in his study of children with excessive fears, Poznanski (1973) found a dependent relationship on an overprotective mother to be a key reason for the fears. Roff and Knight (1981), in a longitudinal study (mentioned earlier) of middle-aged men who had experienced schizophrenic episodes, found that maternal overanxiousness and overprotectiveness, as well as maternal neglect, predicted poor outcomes.

In shielding a child from every danger, an overprotective parent fails to provide the opportunities the child needs for reality testing and the development of essential competencies. In addition, the overprotective behavior implies that the parent regards the child as weak, fragile, and incapable of coping with everyday problems, qualities that may then be incorporated in the child's emerging self-identity. A "sissy" reputation among the child's peers is a frequent complication of this pattern. It is not surprising that such children often reach adolescence and young adulthood feeling inadequate and threatened by a dangerous world.

Closely related to overprotection is restrictiveness. Here parents rigidly enforce unduly restrictive rules and standards and give a child little autonomy or freedom for growing in his or her own way. Parental restrictiveness is of course one of the most commonly heard complaints, whether justified or not, of adolescence—an age range whose major developmental task is the achievement (ambivalently desired) of autonomous selfhood. Restrictiveness may foster well-controlled, socialized behavior, but it can also nurture fearfulness, dependency, submission, repressed hostility, and some dulling of intellectual striving (Baumrind, 1971; Becker, 1964). Often, too, extreme behavior on the part of an adolescent is a way of rebelling against severe restrictions. In the overcontrolled hostility syndrome (Megargee, 1966), a history of extreme restrictions on anger and appropriate forms of aggression may lead to an impulsive, murderous attack.

Unrealistic Demands   Some parents place excessive pressures on their children to live up to unrealistically high standards. For example, a child may be expected to excel in school and all other activities. If the child has the capacity for exceptionally high-level performance, things may work out; but even then the child may be under such sustained pressure that little room is left for spontaneity or development as an independent person.

Typically, however, such a child is never quite able to live up to parental expectations and demands. Nothing the child does seems good enough.

If the child raises a grade of C to a B, rather than giving praise, the parents may ask why it was not an A. Effort only brings more painful frustration and self-devaluation. Those parents who promote feelings of failure by their excessive demands also tend to discourage further effort on the child's part. Almost invariably such a child feels hopelessly in the wrong league: "I can't do it, so why try?"

One need only observe a child's eager "Watch me, Daddy," while demonstrating some new achievement, to understand how important parental recognition for new skills is to healthy development. Research studies, such as the investigation of the antecedents of children's self-respect carried out by Coopersmith (1967), have shown that high parental expectations are both common and helpful for a child's development, particularly when they encourage reasonable achievement strivings. Such expectations, however, need to be realistically set for the capabilities and temperament of each child. A child who is repeatedly rebuffed in his or her efforts to gain approval and self-esteem is unlikely to develop effective coping techniques.

Often, unrealistic parental demands focus on moral standards—particularly with regard to sex, alcohol, and related matters. For example, parents may instill in a child the view that masturbation or any other sexual activity is sinful and can lead only to moral and physical degeneration. The child who accepts such parental standards, unmodulated by the influence of his or her peer group, may face many guilt-arousing and self-devaluating conflicts.

Parental expectations are common and helpful for a child's development, but they need to be realistically set for the capabilities and temperament of each child. A child who is repeatedly rebuffed in his or her efforts to gain approval and self-esteem is unlikely to develop effective coping techniques.

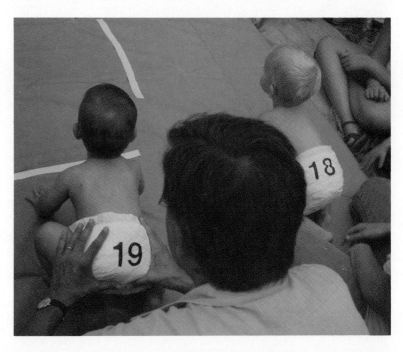

In still other instances, parental demands are unrealistically low; the parents do not care what happens as long as the child stays out of trouble. Coopersmith (1967) found that the children of such parents had significantly lower achievement and self-esteem levels than children whose parents had high but realistic expectations for them. Thus unrealistic expectations and demands—either too high, too low, or distorted and rigid—can help cause a faulty self-identity.

Overpermissiveness and Indulgence   Sometimes one or both parents will cater to a child's slightest whims and, in so doing, fail to teach and reward desirable standards of behavior. In essence, the parent surrenders the running of the home to an uninhibited son or daughter. As noted in an amusing fashion by comedian Bill Cosby (1986), children seem to have a perverse tendency to exploit any such parental weaknesses.

Pollack (1968), for example, has quoted a permissive father who finally rebelled at the tyranny of his 9-year-old daughter, and, in a near tantrum, exploded with, "I want one thing clearly understood—I live here, too!" (p. 28). Similarly, one of the authors has observed a 3-year-old girl essentially demolish the living room of a neighbor's home in full view of her doting mother. When the mother finally intervened, she was repeatedly struck and kicked by this little tyrant, who was in turn not punished in any way for her behavior.

Overly indulged children are characteristically spoiled, selfish, inconsiderate, and demanding. Sears (1961) found that much permissiveness and little discipline in a home were correlated positively with antisocial, aggressive behavior, particularly during middle and later childhood. Unlike rejected, emotionally deprived children, indulged children enter readily into interpersonal relationships, but they exploit people for their own purposes in the same way that they have learned to exploit their parents. In dealing with authority, such children are usually rebellious because they have had their own way for so long. Overly indulged children also tend to be impatient, to approach problems in an aggressive and demanding manner, and to find it difficult to accept present frustrations in the interests of long-range goals (Baumrind, 1971, 1975). In short, they have cognitive maps with extended "entitlement" features.

The fact that their pampered status at home does not transfer automatically to the outside world may come as a great shock to indulged youngsters. Confusion and adjustive difficulties may occur when "reality" forces them to reassess their assumptions about themselves and the world. When they fail to do so in an adequate manner, as is often the case, their adult lives are littered with repeated interpersonal failures and eventual frustration and disillusionment.

Faulty Discipline   Parenthood is one of the most important and demanding commitments adults undertake, yet they are usually ill prepared for it. Despite the increasing availability of special programs, such as parent effectiveness training, and a variety of sophisticated books on the subject, most parents still rely primarily on what they learned from their own parents, who may or may not have been ideal models (Wright et al., 1979). Disciplining children is a particularly controversial and confusing topic for most parents (Baumrind, 1975). Many simply abdicate the responsibility. In other cases, parents have resorted to excessively harsh discipline, convinced that if they "spare the rod" they will spoil the child. And in still other cases, parents behave inconsistently, punishing children one day and ignoring or even rewarding them the next for the same behavior. Depressed adults, as might be expected, have several deficiencies as parents, one of which is ineptness in disciplining their children (Gelfand & Teti, 1990).

There is no question that well-placed permissiveness can be good, encouraging a child's creativity. Overpermissiveness and lack of discipline, however, tend to produce a spoiled, inconsiderate, aggressive child—and an insecure one as well. On the other hand, overly harsh discipline may have a variety of harmful effects, including a fear and hatred of the punishing person, a lack of initiative or spontaneity, and a mistrust of others. When accompanied by rigid moral standards, overly severe discipline is likely to result in a seriously repressed child who lacks spontaneity and warmth and devotes much effort toward controlling impulses that are, in fact, natural. Such children often subject themselves to severe self-recrimination and self-punishment for real or imagined mistakes and misdeeds. They may also apply the same standards to the behavior of their peers, thus earning reputations as "prudes" or worse. Overly severe discipline, combined with restrictiveness, also may lead to rebellion and socially deviant behavior as children grow older and are subjected to outside influences that are incompatible with parental views and practices.

When severe discipline takes the form of physical punishment—as opposed to the withdrawal of approval and privileges—the result tends to be increased aggressive behavior on the part of a child (Eron et al., 1974; Faretra, 1981; Patterson, 1979). Apparently, physical punishment provides a model of aggressive behavior that the child emulates and incorporates into his or her own cognitive map. Researchers and clinicians, in only recently discovering the tragic proportions of physical child abuse, have also discovered that abusers were almost always abused themselves as children.

Inconsistent discipline makes it difficult for a child to establish stable values for guiding behavior. A child who is punished one time and ignored and rewarded the next time for the same behavior does not learn what behavior is appropriate. Deur and Parke (1970) found that children with a history of inconsistent reward and punishment for aggressive behavior were more resistant to punishment and to the extinction of their aggressive behavior than were children who had experienced more consistent discipline. This study supports earlier findings showing a high correlation between inconsistent discipline and later delinquent and criminal behavior.

In the past, discipline was conceived as a method for both punishing undesirable behavior and preventing or deterring such behavior in the future. Discipline is now thought of more positively as providing needed structure and guidance for promoting a child's healthy growth. Such guidance provides a child with a cognitive map that is richly representative of the outcomes actually meted out by the world, contingent on a person's behavior. The person thus informed has a sense of control over these outcomes and is free to make deliberate choices. For example, Baumrind (1975) has found that authoritative discipline is associated with children's development of general competencies for dealing with others and with their environments. When coercion or punishment is deemed necessary, it is important that a parent make clear exactly what behavior is considered inappropriate; it is also important that the child know what behavior is expected, and that positive and consistent methods of discipline be worked out for dealing with infractions. In general, a child should be granted autonomy commensurate with his or her level of maturity and ability to use it constructively. As competent parents would doubtless agree, this judgment is not always easy to make.

Inadequate and Irrational Communication

Parents sometimes discourage a child from asking questions and in other ways fail to foster the information exchange essential for helping the child develop essential competencies. Limited and inade-

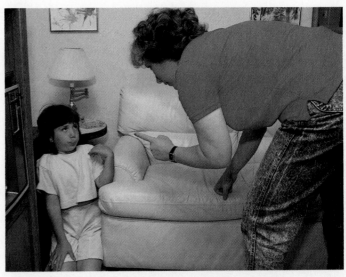

The question of disciplining children is a particularly difficult one for most parents. Inconsistent discipline makes it difficult for a child to establish stable values for guiding behavior. When punishment is deemed necessary, a parent should make it clear what behavior was considered inappropriate. The child should also be told what behavior is expected. Positive and consistent methods of discipline should be worked out for rewarding appropriate behavior and for dealing with infractions.

quate communication patterns have commonly been attributed to economically disadvantaged families, but these patterns are not restricted to any socioeconomic level.

Inadequate communication may take a number of forms. Some parents are too busy or preoccupied with their own concerns to listen to their children and to try to understand the conflicts and pressures they are facing. As a consequence, these parents often fail to give needed support and assistance, particularly when there is a crisis. Other parents have forgotten that the world often looks different to a child or adolescent—rapid social change can lead to a communication gap between generations.

In other instances, faulty communication may take more deviant forms in which messages become completely garbled because a listener distorts, disconfirms, or ignores a speaker's intended meaning. The following case study is a good example of such pathological communication. The setting is a meeting in a hospital involving a schizophrenic young man, his parents, and his therapist. Prior to the meeting, the patient had sent his mother a Mother's Day card containing the inscription, "For Someone Who's Been Like a Mother to Me." We pick up the conversation following a confrontation between mother and son concerning the obliquely hostile inscription:

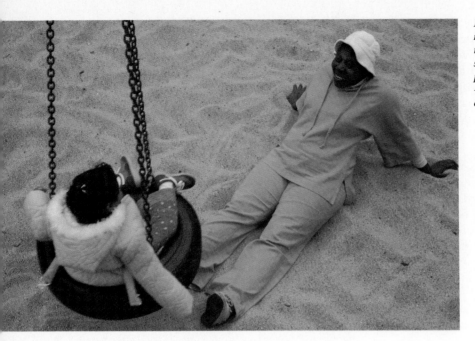

Encouraging children to ask questions, taking the time to listen to their concerns, and trying to understand the conflicts and pressures they are facing are important ways that parents—and in this photo, a grandparent—can help children to develop essential competencies.

Patient: *Well, I meant to sting you just a tiny bit by that outside phrase.*

Mother: *You see I'm a little bit of a psychiatrist too, Simon, I happen to be—(laughing). So I felt so—when you talked to [the therapist] I brought along that card—I wanted to know what's behind your head. And I wanted to know—or you made it on purposely to hurt me—well, if you did, I—I . . .*

Patient: *(interrupting) Not entirely, not entire . . .*

Mother: *(interrupting and overlapping) I'll take all—Simon, believe me. I'll take all the hurt in the world if it will help you—you see what I mean?*

Therapist: *How can you . . .*

Mother: *(continuing) Because I never meant to hurt you—Huh?*

Therapist: *How can you hurt anybody who is perfectly willing to be hurt? (short pause)*

Father: *What's that?*

Mother: *I uh—a mother sacrifices—if you would be—maybe a mother you would know too. Because a mother is just a martyr, she's sacrificing—like even with Jesus with his mother—she sacrificed too. So that's the way it goes on, a mother takes over anything what she can help . . .*

Therapist: *(interrupting) What mother?*

Mother: *(continuing) . . . her children.*

Patient: *(interrupting and overlapping) Well, uh, I'll tell you Ma—listen, Ma, I didn't mean to—to sting you exactly that outside part there.*

Therapist: *Well, you said so.*

Patient: *Oh, all right, but it—it wasn't that exactly. No, I'm not giving ground—uh—it's hard to explain this thing. Uh—uh—what was I going to say? Now I forgot what I was going to say (short pause). I mean I felt that this—this is what I mean, uh—that I felt that you could have been a better mother to me than you were. See there were things.*

Mother: *Uh . . .*

Father: *Well you said . . .*

Patient: *(interrupting) You could have been better than you were. So that's why—that's that—I felt—it was, uh—uh, was all right to send it that way.*

Mother: *Well, if you meant it that way that's perf—that's what I wanted to know—and that's all I care, you see. But I still say, Simon, that if you would take your father and mother just like they're plain people—you just came here and you went through life like anybody else went through—and—and don't keep picking on them and picking them to pieces—but just leave them alone—and go along with them the way they are—and don't change them—you'll be able to get along with everybody, I assure you.*

Patient: *(interrupting) I mean after all a card is a*

> card—why I'd—it seems to me kind of silly (anguish in his voice and near weeping) to bring that thing in here—they have sold them at the canteen, Ma . . .
>
> **Therapist:** *Are you anxious now . . .*
>
> **Patient:** *Why . . .*
>
> **Therapist:** *Are you anxious now because she said . . .*
>
> **Patient:** *I shouldn't be blamed for a thing like that, it's so small . . .*
>
> **Mother:** *(overlapping) I'm not blaming you.*
>
> **Patient:** *(continuing) I don't even remember exactly what the thing was.*
>
> **Mother:** *(overlapping) Well, that's all I wanted to know (laughs).*
>
> **Patient:** *(continuing) I didn't want to—to—to—to blame you or nothing."* (Haley, 1959, p. 360)

This conversation continued in similar fashion until the patient conceded that what he had meant by the inscription was that his mother had been a *real* mother to him. This concession produced a considerable reduction in general tension, but it was, of course, at the expense of what might have proved a useful confrontation with reality.

Such deviant forms of intrafamilial communication are often found in the families of schizophrenic individuals. Although other types of unusual parent-child relations are also seen in such cases, many investigators believe that communication deviance has a special relevance for schizophrenia (Carson & Sanislow, 1992; Goldstein & Strachan, 1987). It is still not definitely established, however, that such communication patterns have causal significance; they may be only correlations. It is possible, for example, that the presence of a schizophrenic or preschizophrenic child in a household might induce parents to communicate in strangely ineffective ways.

In any event, the types of deviant communication often found in the households of schizophrenic individuals are quite varied. They include fragmented and amorphous ways of communicating, erotic overtones between parent and child, difficulties in maintaining a focus of attention, inability to establish closure about a topic, and undue amounts of hostile and critical attention focused on the member who is at risk for a schizophrenic episode (Liem, 1980). Before we move on to broader issues of family structure, *HIGHLIGHT 4.5* summarizes faulty parent-child relationships.

■ Pathogenic Family Structures

The pathogenic parent-child patterns so far described, such as parental rejection, are rarely found in severe form unless the total familial context is abnormal. Thus pathogenic family structure is an overarching risk factor that increases an individual's vulnerability to particular stressors. A parent's repeated incestuous assaults on a child, for example, can hardly escape a spouse's detection; somewhat incredibly, and very sadly, it is not at all unusual to discover that the spouse does not intervene. In the Roff and Knight (1981) longitudinal study of persons who became schizophrenic in early adulthood, two types of mothering—neglectful and overprotective—were found to be common among those individuals who had poor long-term outcomes. It was also demonstrated, however, that each of these patterns of mothering occurred in a particular type of disordered family structure. This finding confirmed earlier reports concerning two family patterns that had appeared especially predictive of a schizophrenic outcome in offspring. Maternal neglect was found to be associated with a *discordant* family pattern, whereas maternal anxiety and overprotectiveness was associated with a *disturbed* one. Each of these family structures is described in the following sections, including a description of the potential pathogenic effects of disrupted families.

Discordant and Disturbed Families   In a **discordant family,** one or both of the parents is not gaining satisfaction from the relationship. One spouse may express feelings of frustration and disillusionment in hostile ways such as nagging, belittling, and doing things purposely to annoy the other person. Value differences, a common source of conflict and dissatisfaction, may lead to serious disagreements about a variety of topics, including sexual behavior and how money is spent. Whatever the reasons for the difficulties, seriously discordant relationships of long standing are likely to be frustrating, hurtful, and generally pathogenic in their effects on the adults and their children. Children who grow up in discordant families are likely to find it difficult to establish and maintain marital and other intimate relationships.

In a **disturbed family,** one or both of the parents behave in grossly eccentric or abnormal ways and may keep the home in constant emotional turmoil. Such families differ greatly, but it is common to find (a) parents who are fighting to maintain their own equilibrium and are unable to give children the love and guidance they need; (b) grossly irrational communication patterns as well as

Summary Chart of Faulty Parent-Child Relationships

Undesirable Condition	Typical Effect on Child's Personality Development
Rejection	Anxiety, insecurity, low self-esteem, negativism, hostility, attention-seeking, loneliness, jealousy, and slowness in conscience development
Overprotection and excessive restriction	Submissiveness, lack of self-reliance, dependence in relations with others, low self-evaluation, some dulling of intellectual striving
Overpermissiveness and indulgence	Selfishness, demanding attitude, inability to tolerate frustration, rebelliousness toward authority, excessive need of attention, lack of responsibility, inconsiderateness, exploitativeness in interpersonal relationships
Unrealistic demands	Lack of spontaneity, rigid conscience development, severe conflicts, tendency toward guilt and self-condemnation if there is failure to live up to parental demands
Faulty discipline: Lack of discipline	Inconsiderateness, aggressiveness, and antisocial tendencies
Harsh, overly severe discipline	Fear or hatred of parent, little initiative or spontaneity, lack of friendly feelings toward others
Inconsistent discipline	Difficulty in establishing stable values for guiding behavior; tendency toward highly aggressive behavior
Inadequate and irrational communication	Tendency toward confusion, lack of an integrated frame of reference, unclear self-identity, lack of initiative, self-devaluation

The exact effects of faulty parent-child relationships on later behavior depends on many factors, including the age of the child, the constitutional and personality makeup of the child at the time, the duration and degree of the unhealthy relationship, the child's perception of the relationship, and the total family setting and life context, including the presence or absence of alleviating conditions and whether or not subsequent experiences tend to reinforce or correct early damage. There is no uniform pattern of pathogenic family relationship underlying the development of later psychopathology, but the conditions we have discussed often act as predisposing factors.

faulty parental models; and (c) almost inevitably, the entanglement of children in the parents' emotional conflicts.

Lidz et al. (1965) described two similar patterns in the family backgrounds of many schizophrenic patients they studied. They called these patterns (a) **marital schism,** in which both parents are constantly embroiled in deep-seated conflicts; and (b) **marital skew,** in which the healthier marital partner, in the interest of minimizing open disharmony, essentially accepts and supports the frequently bizarre beliefs and behaviors of his or her spouse.

Marital schism and skew are roughly equivalent, respectively, to discordant and disturbed family patterns. In either instance, the children in such families are caught up in an unwholesome and irrational psychological environment.

Disrupted Families   A third type of family pattern that may be pathogenic is the disrupted family. A **disrupted family** is incomplete as a result of death, divorce, separation, or some other circumstance. Due partly to a growing cultural acceptance of divorce, more than a million divorces now occur yearly in the United States, with a rate of increase averaging about 8 percent per year. These statistics provide a sobering commentary on the difficulties of maintaining extended intimate relationships.

Unhappy marriages are difficult, but ending a marital relationship can also be enormously stressful, both mentally and physically. Divorced and separated individuals are overrepresented among psychiatric patients, although the direction of the causal relationship is not always clear. In their comprehensive review of the effects of marital disruption, Bloom, Asher, & White (1978) concluded that such disruption is a major source of psychopathology, physical illness, death, suicide, and homicide.

Divorce can have traumatic effects on children, too. Feelings of insecurity and rejection may be aggravated by conflicting loyalties and, sometimes, by the spoiling the children receive while staying with one of the parents—maybe not the one they would prefer to be with. Some children, however, adjust quite well to the divorce of their parents, particularly those who were relatively well-adjusted or very young prior to the breakup (Kurdek et al., 1981; Wallerstein, 1984).

It has been commonly assumed that the loss of a father is more traumatic for a son than for a daughter, but some doubt has been raised about this assumption. It is now believed that the absence of a father has adverse effects on the formation of a secure gender identity for both girls and boys (Hetherington, Cox, & Cox, 1978). For example, Hetherington (1973) found that "the effects of father absence on daughters appear during adolescence and manifest themselves mainly as an inability to interact appropriately with males" (p. 52). Similarly, Roy (1985) has found a small but significant association of adult depression with permanent separation from either parent prior to age 17, irrespective of gender.

The long-range effects of family disruption on a child may vary greatly—they may even be favorable compared to the effects of remaining in a home torn by marital conflict and dissension (Hetherington et al., 1978). Detrimental effects may be minimized if a substitute for the missing parent is available, if the remaining family members compensate for the missing parent and reorganize the family into an effectively functioning group, or if a successful remarriage follows that provides an adequate environment for child rearing. Above all, the remaining parent (usually the mother) can help children work through the crisis by coping well with his or her own emotional upset while addressing the children's needs—an extremely demanding task that some divorced parents understandably cannot master.

Unquestionably, parental separation or divorce involves great stresses for children; it is hardly surprising that some succumb to these stresses and develop maladaptive responses. Delinquency and other abnormal behaviors are much more frequent among children and adolescents from disrupted homes than among those from intact families, although it may be that a contributing factor here is prior or continuing parental strife (Rutter, 1971, 1979). We are beginning to learn, however, that we are not always justified in inferring that a disrupted home has caused some maladaptive behavior. For example, since both broken homes and delinquency are more common among families in lower socioeconomic circumstances, it may be that disrupted homes and childhood deviance are each largely caused by the stresses of poverty and exclusion from society's mainstream.

■ Maladaptive Peer Relationships

Relationships with family members, particularly parents or parental surrogates, clearly have a profound effect on a child's coping resources that often continues into the adolescent and early adult years (and sometimes beyond). Another important set of relationships begins in the preschool years—those involving age-mates, or peers. Normally, these neighborhood or school relationships involve a much broader range of possible experiences than do the more constrained and established intrafamilial relationships, including sibling relations. When a child ventures into a world relatively bereft of adult monitoring and supervision, he or she is faced with a number of complicated and unpredictable challenges whose solution is largely in the child's own hands. The potential for failure is considerable.

Children at this stage are hardly masters of the fine points of human relationships or diplomacy. Empathy—the appreciation of another's situation, perspective, and feelings—is at best only primitively developed, as can be seen in a child who turns on and rejects a current playmate when a more favored candidate arrives. The child's own immediate satisfaction tends to be the preemptive goal of any interaction, and there is only an uncertain recognition that cooperation and collaboration may bring even greater benefits. The assessments a child makes

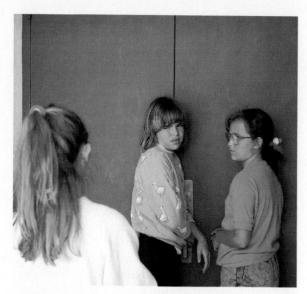

Juvenile socializing is a risky business in which a child's hard-won prestige in a group is probably perceived as being constantly in jeopardy. Actually, reputation and status in a group tend to be stable. Thus, in spite of deviations from characteristic behavior, popular youngsters will tend to remain "stars" and socially rejected ones will tend to remain "rejects."

of others in the juvenile society also tend to be centered on the other's potential contribution to the child's own sense of well-being. Should an assessment be negative, it is apt to be accompanied by actions whose directness, sometimes including physical assault, would affront the sensibilities of most adults. Even when physical retaliation is inconvenient or problematic, a resourceful youngster may recruit a coalition of peers who proceed to heap uncommonly cruel forms of social abuse and rejection on the offender, as when a victim is surrounded and taunted concerning some alleged shortcoming.

In short, juvenile socializing is a risky business in which a child's hard-won prestige in a group is probably perceived as being constantly in jeopardy. Actually, reputation and status in a group tends to be persistent, even in the face of substantial changes in characteristic behavior. We may surmise that this status inertia is a useful buffer for a child who, while occasionally lapsing into unacceptable behavior, has amassed considerable status "credits" in his or her peer group. But what of the child who has few or no credits, who has perhaps already become an object of ridicule, contempt, or unrelenting social rejection? Few options are available to such a youngster in this unforgiving social environment; the role of "goat" is as sticky as that of "star."

It requires but a moment's reflection on one's own childhood experience to recognize that such social casualties are by no means rare in the juvenile peer situation. A classic instance is that of the socially rejected girl who, in adolescence, becomes the neighborhood "easy make" in a desperate but ill-fated bid for attention and affection. This substantial minority of youngsters seems somehow ill-equipped for the rigors and competition of the school years, most likely by virtue of constitutional factors and deficits in the psychosocial climate of their families. Given the limited paths available, large numbers of them withdraw from their peers; others, also in large numbers (especially among males), develop intransigent hatreds and resentments, turn against their "tormenters," and adopt physically intimidating and aggressive life-styles. The neighborhood bully and the menacing schoolyard loner are examples. Neither of these routes, of course, solves such children's problems—quite the contrary—nor do they bode well for good mental health outcomes (e.g., Hartmann et al., 1984; Kupersmidt, Coie, & Dodge, 1990; Roff & Wirt, 1984).

Fortunately, there is another side to this coin. If peer relations have their developmental hazards, they can also be sources of key learning experiences that stand an individual in good stead for years, perhaps for a lifetime. For a resourceful youngster, the give-and-take, the winning and losing, the successes and failures of the school years provide superb training in coming to grips with the real world and with his or her developing self—its capabilities and limitations, its attractive and unattractive qualities. The experience of intimacy with another, a friend, has its beginning in this period of intense social involvement. A child reveals things to, and checks out things with, a friend that could never be revealed to any other person, thus laying the groundwork for intimate exchanges and the recognition of the commonalities and differences among people. In short, peer relations during the school years, in the best of circumstances, afford a marvelous opportunity for honing and rounding out a child's cognitive map.

If all has gone well in the early juvenile years, a child emerges into adolescence with a considerable repertoire of knowledge and skills relating to human interaction. Such a youth can effectively adapt his or her behavior to the requirements of a situation and communicate, as appropriate, his or her thoughts and feelings to others. Practice and experience in intimate communication with others makes possible a transition from attraction, infatuation, and mere sexual curiosity to genuine love and commitment. These and a multitude of other resources acquired while negotiating among peers can be strong bulwarks against frustration, demoralization, despair, and mental disorder. A youth who, for one reason or another, has not had access to the rich store of learning available in peer interactions during the school years will find it difficult to compensate for this experience deficit in later years and will be more vulnerable than those who participated fully.

Although the scenario just outlined seems reasonable, it lacked until recently a strong empirical research foundation. In fact, the developmental period it addresses had been largely ignored by the major personality theorists, Erickson and Sullivan being notable exceptions. In the last 25 years, however, research into the risk factors associated with youngsters' peer relations has been developing at an accelerating pace, and, as a result, we have been nailing down some significant facts. Some of the more important of these findings are briefly summarized in the following sections.

Popularity   By far the most consistent correlate of popularity among juveniles is being seen as friendly and outgoing (Hartup, 1983). The causal relationship between popularity and friendliness is indeterminate and probably complexly involved with other variables, such as intelligence and physical attractiveness. The other side of the coin, peer rejection, is also only partly understood. One large factor is an excessively demanding or aggressive approach to ongoing peer activities, but this factor by no means characterizes the behavior of all children rejected by their peers. A smaller group of children is apparently rejected because of their own social withdrawal. The remaining large group is rejected for unknown reasons; evidently some of the antecedents of rejectability are quite subtle (Coie, 1990).

Status Invariance   A child's sociometric position in a group tends, in the absence of intervention, to remain stable, especially by the fifth grade and beyond. Although there are exceptions to this general rule, "stars" tend to remain stars and "rejects," rejects (Coie & Dodge, 1983). Moreover, a child of given status in one group will tend to replicate that status in a new group in a relatively short time; childhood peer status, it appears, is portable (Coie & Kupersmidt, 1983).

Early Sources of Rejection   A number of studies have attempted to identify why some children are persistently rejected by their peers. As already suggested, many of these children have poor entry skills in seeking to join ongoing group activities: they draw attention to themselves in disruptive, task-irrelevant ways; make unjustified aversive comments to others; and frequently become the focal point of verbal and physical aggression (Coie & Kupersmidt, 1983; Dodge, 1983; Putallaz & Gottman, 1983). More generally, Dodge and colleagues (1980; Dodge & Newman, 1981; Dodge & Frame, 1982; Dodge, Murphy, & Buchsbaum, 1984) have described these children as taking offense too readily and as unjustifiably attributing hostile intent to the bantering actions of their peers, escalating confrontations to unintended levels. In the end, rejection leads to social isolation, often self-imposed (Dodge, Coie, & Brakke, 1982; Hymel & Rubin, 1985; Ladd, 1983). Coie (1990) has recently pointed out that such isolation is likely to have serious consequences because it deprives a child of further opportunities to learn the "rules" of social behavior and interchange, rules that become increasingly

If all has gone well in childhood peer relationships, an adolescent has gained a considerable repertoire of knowledge and skills relating to human interaction. Such a youth can effectively adapt his or her behavior to the requirements of a situation and can appropriately communicate his or her thoughts and feelings.

sophisticated and subtle with increasing age. Repeated social failure is the usual result, with further damaging effects on self-confidence and self-esteem.

Adult Outcomes   Both logic and research findings lead to a similar conclusion: a child who fails to establish a satisfactory relationship with peers during the developmental years is deprived of a crucial set of background experiences. We would expect such a child to have an increased likelihood of coping with failure and adaptive breakdown as the various challenges of the adult years present themselves. Again, the relevant research, recently surveyed by Kupersmidt, Coie, & Dodge (1990), supports this assumption. Peer social problems in childhood have been linked to a variety of breakdowns in later adaptive functioning, including schizophrenia, school dropout, crime, and increased general involvement with mental health services. While these correlational data do not in themselves permit strong causal inferences, they constitute important links in a highly plausible causal chain.

SOCIOCULTURAL CAUSAL FACTORS

As we discussed in Chapter 3, the sociocultural viewpoint grew out of observations on the varying value and behavior patterns among different cultural groups. These observations increased insight into the power of social and cultural forces to shape behavior and personality. We also noted that a number of cultures and subcultures seem to protect their members from the more serious forms of personal misery and disorganization, as shown by incidence rates that are markedly below worldwide averages. Other cultures—southern Ireland, for example—have above-average incidence rates for certain disorders (Torrey, 1979; Torrey et al., 1984). We can assume that these differences occur because the cultures themselves in some way either protect their members from disorder or instill within them a measure of vulnerability.

For reasons of temperament, conditioning, and other individual factors, not all people adopt the prevailing cultural patterns. These people may escape some of the culture's detrimental influences but may also miss the protection of the more adaptive ones. This situation is especially common in Western society, where we are exposed to many competing values and patterns. The following sections will emphasize that, in our society, several social and cultural influences may act to increase our vulnerabilities to the development of abnormal behaviors. We will begin by discussing the role of culture in determining an individual's behavior pattern. We will then turn to particular factors in the sociocultural environment that may increase vulnerability: low socioeconomic class, disorder-engendering social roles, prejudice and discrimination, economic and employment problems, and social change and uncertainty.

The Sociocultural Environment

In much the same way that we receive a genetic inheritance that is the end product of millions of years of biological evolution, we also receive a sociocultural inheritance that is the end product of thousands of years of social evolution. The significance of this inheritance was well pointed up by Aldous Huxley (1965):

The native or genetic capacities of today's bright city child are no better than the native capacities of a bright child born into a family of Upper Paleolithic cave-dwellers. But whereas the contemporary bright baby may grow up to become almost anything—a Presbyterian engineer, for example, a piano-playing Marxist, a professor of biochemistry who is a mystical agnostic and likes to paint in water colours—the paleolithic baby could not possibly have grown into anything except a hunter or food-gatherer, using the crudest of stone tools and thinking about his narrow world of trees and swamps in terms of some hazy system of magic. Ancient and modern, the two babies are indistinguishable. . . . But the adults into whom the babies will grow are profoundly dissimilar; and they are dissimilar because in one of them very few, and in the other a good many, of the baby's inborn potentialities have been actualized. (p. 69)

Because each group fosters its own cultural patterns by systematically teaching its offspring, all its members tend to be somewhat alike—to conform to certain basic personality types. Individuals reared among headhunters become headhunters; individuals reared in societies that do not sanction violence learn to settle their differences in nonviolent ways. In New Guinea, for example, Margaret Mead (1949) found two tribes—of similar racial origin and living in the same general geographical area—whose members developed diametrically opposed characteristics. The Arapesh were a kindly, peaceful, cooperative people, while the Mundugumor were warlike, suspicious, competitive, and vengeful. Such differences appear to be social in origin.

The more uniform and thorough the education of the younger members of a group, the more alike they will become. Thus in a society characterized by a limited and consistent point of view, there are not the wide individual differences typical in a society like ours, where children have contact with diverse, often conflicting, beliefs. Even in our society, however, there are certain core values that most of us consider essential.

Subgroups within a general sociocultural environment—such as family, sex, age, class, occupational, ethnic, and religious groups—foster beliefs and norms of their own, largely by means of **social roles** that their members learn to adopt. Expected role behaviors exist for a student, a teacher, an army officer, a priest, a nurse, and so on.

The extent to which role expectations can influence development is well illustrated by masculine and feminine roles in our own society and their effects on personality development and on behavior. In recent years, a combination of masculine and feminine traits (**androgyny**) has often been proclaimed to be psychologically ideal for both men and women. Many people, however, continue to show evidence of having been strongly affected by assigned masculine and feminine roles. Moreover, there is accumulating evidence that the acceptance of gender-role assignments has substantial implications for mental health. In general, studies show that low "masculinity" is associated with maladap-

tive behavior and vulnerability to disorder for either biological sex, possibly because this condition tends to be strongly associated with deficient self-esteem (Carson, 1989). Baucom (1983), for example, has shown that high-feminine-sex-typed (low masculinity) women tend to reject opportunities to lead group problem-solving situations. He likens this effect to learned helplessness, which, as we have seen, has in turn been suggested as a causal factor in anxiety (Barlow, 1988) and depression (Abramson et al., 1978).

An individual, being a member of various subgroups, is subject to various role demands. These social roles, of course, change as group memberships—or positions in various groups—change. In fact, an individual's life can be viewed as a succession of roles—child, student, worker, spouse, parent, and senior citizen. The various groups may allow a person considerable leeway in role behavior, but there are limits. Conformity to role demands is induced by the use of positive and negative reinforcers—money, prestige, status, punishment, or loss of membership in a group—as well as through instruction. When social roles are conflicting, unclear, or uncomfortable, or when an individual is unable to achieve a satisfactory role in a group, healthy personality development may be impaired—just as when a child is rejected by juvenile peer groups.

Each individual interacts with various people and groups, typically beginning with family members and gradually extending to peer group members and other significant people. Much of an

An individual's life can be viewed as a succession of roles—child, student, worker, spouse, parent, and so on. When social roles are conflicting, unclear, or uncomfortable, healthy personality development may be impaired. The extent to which role expectations can influence development is well illustrated by "masculine" and "feminine" sex roles in our own society and their effects on personality development and characteristic behavior.

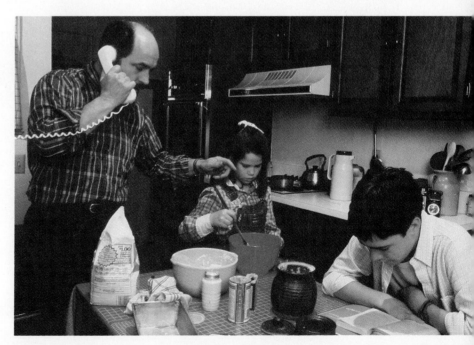

individual's personality development reflects experiences with these key people. Relationships formed in a Boy Scout troop, for example, will likely have effects on development quite different from relationships formed in a delinquent gang. The behavior patterns children learn depend heavily on which models they observe, whose expectations they are trying to meet, and what rewards are forthcoming for their behavior.

Pathogenic Societal Influences

Since each of us belongs to different subgroups and experiences different interpersonal relationships, we each participate in the sociocultural environment in a unique way. In the situations that follow, different social roles and experiences can be seen as significant influences in the development of maladaptive behaviors.

Low Socioeconomic Status   In our society, an inverse correlation exists between socioeconomic status and the prevalence of abnormal behavior—the lower the socioeconomic class, the higher the incidence of abnormal behavior (Eron & Peterson, 1982). The strength of the correlation seems to vary with different types of disorder, however. Some disorders may be related to social class only minimally or perhaps not at all. For example, the incidence of schizophrenia is inversely correlated with social class, while that of mood disorders bears a less

distinct relationship to class and, if anything, may tend in the opposite direction.

We do not understand all the reasons for the more general inverse relationship. Undoubtedly some inadequate and disturbed people slide down to the lower rungs of the economic ladder and remain there; these people will often have inadequate and disturbed children. At the same time, more affluent people are better able to get prompt help or to conceal their problems.

In addition, it is almost certainly true that people living in poverty encounter more, and more severe, stressors in their lives than do people in the middle and upper classes, and they usually have fewer resources for dealing with them. As Kohn (1973) has pointed out, the conditions under which lower-class youngsters are reared tend to inhibit the development of the coping skills needed in our increasingly complex society. Thus the tendency for abnormal behavior to appear more frequently in lower socioeconomic groups may be at least partly due to predispositional coping deficits.

Disorder-engendering Social Roles   An organized society, even an "advanced" one, sometimes asks its members to perform roles in which the prescribed behaviors are either deviant themselves or may produce maladaptive reactions. A soldier who is called upon by his superiors (and ultimately by his society) to deliberately kill and maim other human beings may subsequently develop serious feelings of guilt. He or she may also have

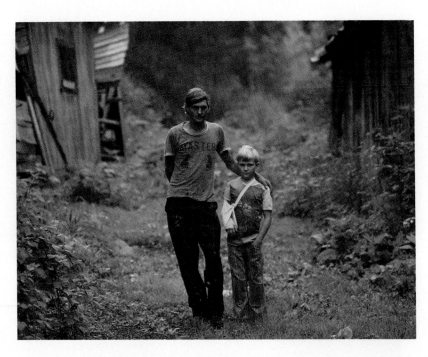

In our society, the lower the socioeconomic class, the higher the incidence of abnormal behavior. The conditions under which lower-class youngsters are reared tend to inhibit the development of coping skills. Many individuals, however, emerge from low socioeconomic environments with strong, highly adaptive personalities and skills.

latent emotional problems resulting from the horrors commonly experienced in combat and hence be vulnerable to disorder. As a nation, we are still struggling with the many problems of this type that have emerged among veterans of the Vietnam War, whose rates of abnormality have been well above national averages (Strayer & Ellenhorn, 1975). As a group, these veterans are expected to have continuing problems well into the future (Horowitz & Solomon, 1978). In fact, the DSM-III diagnosis of posttraumatic stress disorder was created largely in response to the problems of these veterans of the Vietnam War.

Militaristic regimes and organizations are especially likely to foster problematic social roles. Military and civilian officials in Germany during the Nazi Holocaust and in the Soviet Union during Stalin's collectivization of rural areas in the 1930s (Conquest, 1986) willingly participated in history's most heinous and cold-blooded mass murders. Some American street gangs demand extreme cruelty and callousness on the part of their members. Well-organized terrorist groups, feeling that the world is ignoring their just claims, train their members for hostage-taking, mass destruction, and murder.

In a famous experiment, Zimbardo and his associates (1975) demonstrated the power of "guard" and "prisoner" roles to quickly produce extremely maladaptive behavior in otherwise normal persons. As an unintended consequence, the study's subjects learned some things about themselves that they may have been better off not knowing. In fact, the study had to be prematurely ended because of its disturbing effects on the subjects.

There is, of course, no easy answer to the problems of violence and coercion in the modern world; people will often resort to force when other remedies fail, as demonstrated by the seemingly unending turmoil in the Middle East. As long as such actions are taken, many people will be subjected to conditions of extraordinary stress and will feel compelled to enact difficult and painful social roles. In some cases, the end result will be psychological disorder.

Prejudice and Discrimination   Vast numbers of people in our society have been subjected to demoralizing stereotypes and overt discrimination in areas such as employment and education. We have made progress in race relations since the 1960s, but the lingering effects of mistrust and discomfort among various ethnic and racial groups can be clearly observed on almost any college campus. For the most part, students socialize informally only with members of their own subcultures, despite the attempts of many well-meaning college administrators to break down the barriers. The tendency of students to avoid crossing these barriers needlessly limits their educational experiences and probably contributes to continued misinformation about prejudice toward others.

We have also made recent progress in recognizing the demeaning and often disabling social roles our society has historically assigned to women. Again, though, much remains to be done. Many more women than men seek treatment for various emotional disorders, notably depression; mental health professionals believe this fact is a consequence both of the vulnerabilities (such as passivity and dependence) intrinsic to the traditional roles assigned to women, and of the special stressors with which many modern women must cope (being full-time mothers, full-time homemakers, and full-time employees) as their traditional roles rapidly change.

Economic and Employment Problems
Economic difficulties and unemployment have repeatedly been linked to enhanced vulnerability and thus to elevated rates of abnormal behavior (Dooley & Catalano, 1980). Recession and inflation coupled with high unemployment are sources of chronic anxiety for many people. Unemployment has placed a burden on a sizable segment of our population, bringing with it both financial hardships and self-devaluation. In fact unemployment can be as debilitating psychologically as it is financially (Nelson, 1974). In recent years the economic plight of the nation's small farmers has produced widespread fear and discouragement in this group. Similarly, the changing economic situation of America's traditional major manufacturing industries has displaced tens of thousands of skilled workers for whom comparable employment simply does not exist. As a society, we have yet to solve the human problems such major economic shifts entail, and some would hold that we have not even begun to engage them. The philosophies of free enterprise and rugged individualism run deep in American culture and politics, and they are in fact shared by many of the victims of these displacements. The result is self-blame and personal demoralization.

Periods of extensive unemployment are typically accompanied by increases in certain types of maladaptive behavior, such as depression, suicide, and crime (Brenner, 1973). Hardest hit by economic and employment problems are those at the bottom of the social ladder, who are already handicapped by poor education, poor nutrition, broken or unstable families, inadequate housing, feelings of helplessness, and a sense of rejection by the larger society—all of this in the midst of a culture that indulges itself in crass displays of affluence. It is small wonder that some members of these groups are enticed by the dangerous but lavish life-style and elevated status afforded by the sale of illegal drugs.

Even for many people who are employed, a major source of demoralization is job dissatisfaction. Job dissatisfaction is related to anxiety, tension, and a wide range of psychophysiologic disorders. It has also been linked to impaired marital and family relationships.

Whatever the possibilities for job satisfaction in an increasingly complicated society, the demand for it seems to be increasing (Gartner & Riessman, 1974). People no longer see money alone as an adequate return for their investment of time and energy; they also desire meaningful employment and the integration of education, work, and leisure into a fulfilling life pattern. The difficulties of achieving this goal adds yet another frustrating dimension to the job picture: many people may realize their career ambitions and still find themselves unhappy or disillusioned with their work.

Social Change and Uncertainty   The rate and pervasiveness of change today are different from anything our ancestors ever experienced. All aspects of our lives are affected—our educations, our jobs, our families, our leisure pursuits, our finances, and our beliefs and values. Constantly trying to keep up with the numerous adjustments demanded by these changes is a source of constant and considerable stress. In fact, Toffler (1970) proposed the term *future shock* to describe the profound confusion and emotional upset resulting from too-rapid social change.

Simultaneously, we confront inevitable crises as the earth's consumable natural resources dwindle and as our environment becomes increasingly noxious with pollutants—while environmentalists vie with those who feel their jobs will be threatened by tighter controls. No longer are Americans confident that the future will be better than the past or that technology will solve all our problems. On the contrary, our attempts to cope with existing problems increasingly seem to create new problems that are as bad or worse. The resulting despair, demoralization, and sense of helplessness are well-established predisposing conditions for abnormal reactions to stressful events (Dohrenwend et al., 1980; Frank, 1978).

Environmental pollution is one aspect of contemporary life that is threatening to our sense of well-being. The uncertainty people feel about a future clouded by problems of such large magnitude can increase vulnerability to abnormal behavior.

UNRESOLVED ISSUES
on Causation

For people sharing particular forms of maladaptive behavior, we have made substantial progress in identifying certain background factors, often called *risk factors,* that they tend to have in common (usually with many exceptions). For example, persons diagnosed as schizophrenic are found, at a higher than normal rate, to have close relatives suspected of having the disorder—suggesting genetic predisposition as a possible causal element. In order someday to predict with accuracy who is at risk for and who will develop schizophrenia, we must discover as many of these relationships as possible, even if we do not yet know how they are causally related to the disorder.

Thus we know that individuals born to schizophrenic mothers are at a quantifiable risk for schizophrenia, but we do not know the mechanisms accounting for the increased probability of schizophrenia; a genetic connection is only one of several possibilities. Moreover, if we did have such knowledge, it would be of limited help in understanding the many schizophrenics who have no history of schizophrenia in their family backgrounds. And, of course, we would still have to account for the many people born to schizophrenic mothers who never develop the disorder. Evidently, there is more than one causal pathway that can lead to schizophrenia, and this situation appears to be the rule rather than the exception across the broad spectrum of behavioral abnormalities.

Thus in undertaking a causal analysis of an individual case of disorder, we rarely have any precise, reliable knowledge about how the person got from "there" to "here." Even the exceptions, largely limited to those disorders in which true primary causes have been established, can leave us baffled when observing diverse outcomes. For example, general paresis cannot occur in the absence of an untreated (or unsuccessfully treated) syphilitic infection; yet only a small percentage of people with advanced syphilis exhibit the full general paretic syndrome. What then are the additional conditions leading to the disorder? We can make educated guesses, but in the end, we often do not know.

Causal analysis is difficult in part because of our dependence on essentially *correlational* methods. The mere association of one variable with another cannot by itself establish a causal connection between them. Would the full use of *experimental* methods on etiological questions—ethical issues aside—be an assured way of gaining the information we need? Probably not.

In essence, investigators using the experimental method systematically varies one factor or variable (or at most a few) while controlling all others, and then observes the outcome in respect to the phenomena of interest—in our case, the occurrence of some type of abnormal behavior. The method derives from classical physics, where the task is to understand the behavior of matter, and in that context it has been fruitful. Increasingly, however, physicists are recognizing its limitations, as they probe more deeply into phenomena that do not yield to simple cause-and-effect analysis. Human behavior is probably even more complex.

We are thus coming to the conclusion that most disorders, especially beyond childhood, are the result of many causal factors—biological, psychosocial, and sociocultural—that for any person may be unique, or at least not widely shared in major groupings of other people. If this conjecture proves true in terms of future research findings, then we are faced with a truly intimidating task that we cannot solve with our currently available scientific tools. In brief, the problem is this: if common causal patterns cannot be found in individuals supposedly sharing the same disorder, then we have no obvious means of distinguishing between an attribute of an individual as opposed to an attribute of a disorder. Our considerable knowledge of the general factors correlated with one or another disorder at the group level provides clues about causal influences in individual cases, but it never completes the individual causal picture. A rather large array of "unexplained" influences almost always remains. Nor is it obvious at present what new methodology we need to move beyond this stymied position.

Meanwhile, we suspect that the individual case study method, for all its imprecision and shortcomings (described in Chapter 1), will remain an indispensable tool for assessing causal patterns and sequences. The absence—one might even say the inconceivability—of cookie-cutter, universally applicable patterns to account for most disorders also means that sound, experienced clinicianship is not likely to be replaced by technological advances.

SUMMARY

In most instances the occurrence of abnormal or maladaptive behavior is the joint product of an individual's vulnerability (diathesis) to disorder and of certain stressors that challenge an individual's coping resources. Such vulnerabilities are generally considered predisposing causes. Predisposing causal influences are the focus of this chapter, although other types of causes (primary, precipitating, and reinforcing) are discussed. In practice it is often difficult to make distinctions between these various types of causes.

Predisposing causes of mental disorder may be classified as biological, psychosocial, and sociocultural. While these three classes can interact with each other in complicated ways, certain known causes are especially related to each.

In examining biologically-based vulnerabilities, we must consider genetic endowment (including chromosomal irregularities), constitutional factors, primary reaction tendencies, and various disruptions of the biological system. All of these essentially physical disturbances can create conditions that make a person vulnerable to disorder.

For psychosocially determined sources of vulnerability, the situation is somewhat more blurred. It is clear, however, that a person's frame of reference, or cognitive map (including its *self*-identity component), plays a central role as both an information-processing system and as a collection of attributions and values concerning the world and that person's personal identity. The efficiency, accuracy, and coherence of a person's cognitive map appears to be an important bulwark against breakdown. Sources of psychosocially determined vulnerability include early social deprivation, severe emotional trauma, inadequate parenting, and dysfunctional peer relationships.

Sociocultural variables are also important sources of vulnerability, or, conversely, of resistance to it. The incidence of particular disorders varies widely among different cultures; unfortunately, we know little of the specific factors involved in these variations. In our own culture, certain prescribed roles, such as those relating to gender, appear to be more predisposing to disorder than others. Low socioeconomic status is also associated with greater risk for various disorders, possibly because it is often difficult for economically distressed families to provide their offspring with sufficient coping resources. Additionally, certain roles evolved by given cultures may in themselves be maladaptive, and certain large-scale cultural trends, such as rapid technological advance, may increase stress while lessening the effectiveness of traditional coping resources.

Finally, the intimidating nature of the search for a complete understanding of the causes of vulnerability leaves little room for complacency despite the very real progress made in identifying general factors at the group level. It is not clear how we will approach the problem of the individual patterning of these causal factors.

■ Key Terms

vulnerabilities (p. 95)
etiology (p. 96)
primary cause (p. 96)
predisposing cause (p. 96)
precipitating cause (p. 96)
reinforcing cause (p. 96)
causal pattern (p. 97)
diathesis (p. 98)
diathesis-stress model
    (p. 98)
chromosomes (p. 100)
chromosomal anomalies
    (p. 100)
autosomes (p. 100)
sex chromosomes (p. 100)
X chromosomes (p. 101)
Y chromosome (p. 101)
genes (p. 101)
dominant genes (p. 101)
recessive genes (p. 101)

concordance rates (p. 104)
constitutional liability
    (p. 104)
congenital defect (p. 105)
primary reaction tendencies
    (p. 106)
homeostasis (p. 109)
cognitive maps (schemas)
    (p. 112)
self-identity (p. 113)
accommodation (p. 113)
psychic trauma (p. 118)
discordant family (p. 125)
disturbed family (p. 125)
marital schism (p. 126)
marital skew (p. 126)
disrupted family (p. 126)
social roles (p. 131)
androgyny (p. 131)

Part Two
Patterns of Abnormal (Maladaptive) Behavior

Chapter 5
Stress and Adjustment Disorders

Josef Schneller (Sell), *The Next World, Myriad-Resurrection.* Schneller (1878–?) was an architectural draftsman by trade. He was committed to a mental institution in 1907 with psychosis marked by delusions and hallucinations that involved his senses of smell and touch. Some of Schneller's work has sadistic–masochistic images of women in a setting that is part school, part prison, and part convent. Other works convey his interest in fantasy, magic, and architecture.

Any one of us may break down if the going gets tough enough. Under conditions of overwhelming stress, even a previously stable individual may develop temporary (transient) psychological problems. That is, the individual may experience a lowering or breakdown of integral, adaptive functioning. This breakdown may be sudden, as in the case of an individual who has gone through a severe accident or fire, or it may be gradual, as for a person who has been subjected to prolonged periods of tension and self-esteem loss culminating in a marital breakup. Usually a person recovers once a stressful situation is over, although in some cases there may be long-lasting damage to his or her self-concept and an increased vulnerability to certain types of stressors —today's stress can be tomorrow's vulnerability. In the case of an individual who is quite vulnerable to begin with, of course, a stressful situation may precipitate more serious and lasting psychopathology.

In Chapter 4 we focused on the diathesis, or vulnerability, half of the diathesis-stress model of abnormal behavior; we saw that our vulnerabilities can predispose us to abnormal behavior. In this chapter we will focus on the role of stress as a precipitating causal factor in abnormal behavior. We will see that, at times, the impact of stress depends not only on its severity, but on an individual's preexisting vulnerabilities as well. It is important to note here that a duality exists in the relationship between diathesis and stress: many of the factors that contribute to diatheses are also sources of stress. This duality is especially true of psychosocial factors, such as emotional deprivation, inadequate parenting, and the like. In this chapter our focus will be on the *precipitating* nature of stress; in Chapter 4 we focused on its *predisposing* nature.

We will first look at what stress is, the factors that affect it, and how we react to it. Then we will turn to some specific situations that result in severe stress and examine their effects on adjustment. We will then examine severe, catastrophic stress situations that predispose a victim to the development of posttraumatic stress disorders. In the last part of the chapter, we will look at attempts made by mental health workers to intervene in the stress process— either to prevent stress reactions or to limit their intensity and duration once they have developed.

STRESS AND STRESSORS

Life would be simple indeed if our needs were automatically gratified. As we know, many obstacles, both personal and environmental, prevent this ideal situation. Such obstacles place adjustive demands on us and can lead to stress. The term *stress* has typically been used to refer both to the adjustive demands placed on an organism and to the organism's internal biological and psychological responses to such demands. To avoid confusion, we will refer to adjustive demands as **stressors,** to the effects they create within an organism as **stress,** and to efforts to deal with stress as **coping strategies.** Note that separating these constructs is a somewhat arbitrary action; as Neufeld (1990) has pointed out, stress is a byproduct of coping. For the purpose of study, however, making the distinction can be of help. What is important to remember in the long run is that the two concepts—stress and coping—are interrelated and dependent on each other.

All situations, positive and negative, that require adjustment are stressful. Thus, according to Canadian physiologist Hans Selye (1956; 1976a), the notion of stress can be broken down further into positive stress, **eustress,** and negative stress, **distress.** (In most cases, the stress experienced during a wedding would be eustress; during a funeral, distress.) Both types of stress tax an individual's resources and coping skills, though distress typically has the potential to do more damage. In the following sections, we will look at (a) categories of stressors; (b) factors predisposing an individual to stress; and (c) the unique and changing stressor patterns that characterize each person's life.

Categories of Stressors

Adjustive demands, or stressors, stem from a number of sources. These sources represent three basic categories: frustrations, conflicts, and pressures. Though we will consider these categories separately, they are closely interrelated.

Frustrations   When a person's strivings are thwarted, either by obstacles that block progress toward a desired goal or by the absence of an appropriate goal, frustration occurs. Frustrations can be particularly difficult for an individual to cope with because they often lead to self-devaluation, making the person feel that he or she has failed in some way or is incompetent.

A wide range of obstacles, both external and internal, can lead to frustration. Prejudice and discrimination, unfulfillment in a job, and the death of a loved one are common frustrations stemming from the environment; physical handicaps, lack of needed competencies, loneliness, guilt, and inadequate self-control are sources of frustration based on personal limitations.

Selye distinguished between two types of stress: eustress (positive stress) and distress (negative stress). The stress experienced during a wedding is eustress; during a funeral, distress. In general, distress has greater potential for causing difficulties in adjustment.

Conflicts   In many instances stress results from the simultaneous occurrence of two or more incompatible needs or motives: the requirements of one preclude satisfaction of the others. In essence we have a choice to make, and we experience conflict while trying to make it. Conflicts with which everyone has to cope may be classified as approach-avoidance, double-approach, and double-avoidance types.

1. *Approach-avoidance conflicts* involve strong tendencies to approach and to avoid the same goal. Perhaps an individual wants to join a high-status group but can do so only by endorsing views contrary to his or her personal values; or a former smoker may want to smoke during a party but realizes that doing so may jeopardize his or her long-term status as a nonsmoker. Approach-avoidance conflicts are sometimes referred to as mixed-blessing dilemmas because some negative and some positive features must be accepted regardless of which course of action is chosen. Roth and Cohen (1986) point out that being inflexible in making these choices—that is, in always choosing an approach strategy or an avoidance strategy—can be maladaptive. When dealing with a stressor, sometimes the best method of coping is to approach it; at other times, the best thing to do is to avoid it.

2. *Double-approach conflicts* involve choosing between two or more desirable goals, such as which of two movies to see on one's only free night of the week. To a large extent, such simple plus-plus conflicts result from the inevitable limitations in one's time, space, energy, and resources; they are usually handled in stride. In more complex cases, however, as when an individual is torn between two good career opportunities or between present satisfactions and future ones, decision making can be difficult and stressful. Though the experience may cause more eustress than distress, the stress is still real and the choice difficult; in either case, the individual gives up something.

3. *Double-avoidance conflicts* are those in which the choices are between undesirable alternatives, such as either going to a party when you would rather stay home or being considered impolite if you cancel at the last moment. Neither choice will bring satisfaction, so the task is to decide which course of action will be least disagreeable—that is, least stressful.

Classifying conflicts in this manner is somewhat arbitrary, and various combinations among the different types are perhaps the rule rather than the exception. Thus a double-approach conflict between alternative careers may also have its approach-avoidance aspects because of the responsibilities that either will impose. Regardless of how we categorize conflicts, they represent a major source of stress that can often become overwhelming in intensity.

Pressures   Stress may stem not only from frustrations and conflicts, but also from pressures to achieve specific goals or to behave in particular ways. In general, pressures force a person to speed up, intensify effort, or change the direction of goal-oriented behavior. All of us encounter many everyday pressures, and we often handle them without undue difficulty. In some instances, however, pressures seriously tax our coping resources, and if they become excessive, they may lead to maladaptive behavior.

Pressures can originate from external or internal sources. Students may feel under severe pressure to make good grades because their parents demand it, or they may submit themselves to such pressure because they want to get into graduate school. The long hours of study, the tension of examinations, and the sustained concentration of effort over many years result in considerable stress for many students (Bolger, 1990), as shown in *HIGHLIGHT 5.1*.

Occupational demands can also be highly stressful, and many jobs make severe demands in terms of responsibility, time, and performance.

Pressure is a significant source of stress. Certain occupations make severe demands in terms of responsibility, time, and performance. Workers who experience unusually high degrees of stress, such as air-traffic controllers, may have an increased vulnerability to disease or disorder.

Examinations and Anxiety

Many students preparing for important, career-determining examinations, such as the Graduate Records Exam (GRE) or the Medical College Admissions Test (MCAT), experience considerable anxiety as the examination date approaches. Bolger (1990) obtained self-reported anxiety ratings on 50 premedical students for 17 days before and 17 days after the MCAT examination. As shown in the following figure, the experience of anxiety was clearly greater in the days preceding the examination—with peak anxiety occurring as the examination day approached. Individuals who were prone to using maladaptive coping mechanisms, such as wishful thinking or self-blame, tended to show increased maladaptive behavior and increased anxiety under high stress. Performance on the examination, however, did not appear to be related to the use of various coping strategies to deal with the stress—that is, those students who used maladaptive behaviors did not appear to do worse on the exam.

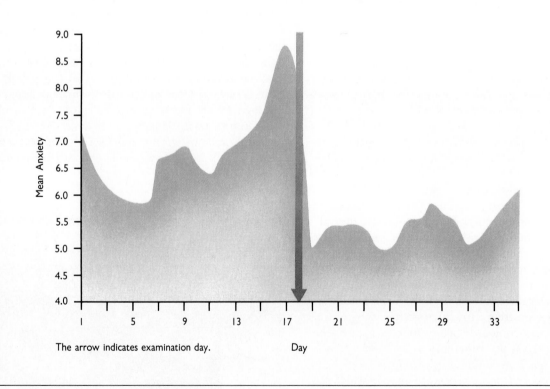

The arrow indicates examination day.

Day

Carruthers (1980) has noted that some occupations, such as coal mining, airplane flying, or auto racing, apparently place individuals under unusually high levels of stress, which result in vulnerabilities to heart disease. Carruthers has pointed out that our "stone-age biochemistry and physiology has in several important respects failed to adapt to [our] present-age situation" (p. 11). In almost any job, if an individual is not interested in or well suited to the work, occupational demands are likely to be a major source of stress, regardless of the actual job demands. Pressures that people experience in times of economic recession can have considerable impact on their psychological adjustments. In a study on individual vulnerability to economic stress, Aldwin and Revenson (1986) interviewed workers who had been laid off from their jobs; they found, not surprisingly, consistent patterns of depressed moods and chronic frustration.

It appears that a given situation may involve elements of all three categories of stressors—frustration, conflict, and pressure. The following case illustrates this point:

A premed student whose lifelong ambition was to become a doctor received rejection letters from all the medical schools to which he had applied. This unexpected blow left him feeling depressed and empty. He felt extreme frustration over his failure and conflict over what his next steps should be. He was experiencing pressure from his family and peers to try again, but he was also overwhelmed by a sense of failure. He felt so bitter that he wanted to drop everything and become a beach bum or a blackjack dealer in Las Vegas. The loss of self-esteem he was experiencing left him with no realistic backup plans and little interest in pursuing alternative careers.

Although a particular stressor may predominate in any situation, we rarely deal with an isolated demand. Instead, we usually confront a continuously changing pattern of interrelated and sometimes contradictory demands.

■ Factors Predisposing an Individual to Stress

The severity of stress is gauged by the degree to which it disrupts functioning. For example, an individual will experience severe disruption of both physiological and psychological processes if deprived of food for a long time.

The actual degree of disruption that occurs or is threatened depends partly on a stressor's characteristics and partly on an individual's resources—both personal and situational—and the relationship between the two. The following sections examine the factors that predispose us to react poorly to external demands.

The Nature of a Stressor   The impact of a stressor depends on its importance, duration, cumulative effect, multiplicity, and imminence. Although most stressors are dealt with as a matter of course, stressors that involve important aspects of an individual's life—such as the death of a loved one, a divorce, a job loss, or a serious illness—tend

to be highly stressful for most people (Grant et al., 1981; Holmes & Rahe, 1967; Rahe & Arthur, 1978; Zilberg, Weiss, & Horowitz, 1982). Furthermore, the longer a stressor operates, the more severe its effects. Prolonged exhaustion, for example, imposes a more intense stress than does temporary fatigue. Also, stressors often appear to have a cumulative effect (Singer, 1980). A married couple may maintain amicable relations through a long series of minor irritations or frustrations only to dissolve the relationship in the face of one "last straw"—a precipitating stressor.

Encountering a number of stressors at the same time also makes a difference. If a man has a heart attack, loses his job, and receives news that his son has been arrested for drug abuse—all at the same time—the resulting stress will be more severe than if these events occurred separately.

In difficult situations, including those involving conflicts, the severity of stress usually increases as the need to deal with the demand approaches. In a classic study, Mechanic (1962) found that although graduate students thought about their examinations from time to time and experienced some anxiety during the three months prior to the tests, they did not demonstrate intense anxiety until the examinations were nearly upon them. Similar experiences have been reported by sports parachutists as the hour of their next jump approached (Epstein & Fenz, 1962, 1965). People anticipating other stressful situations—such as major surgery—have found that the severity of stress increased as the time for the ordeal approached (Janis & Leventhal, 1965).

Finally, the symptoms of stress intensify when a person is more closely involved in a traumatic situation. Pynoos et al. (1987) conducted an extensive investigation of children's symptoms and behavior one month after a shooting incident in a schoolyard (one child was killed and several others wounded when a sniper randomly fired into the playground). A total of 159 children from the school were interviewed. Depending on where they were—on the playground, in the school, in the neighborhood, on the way home, absent from school, or out of the vicinity—the children experienced different stress levels. Children on the playground, closest to the shooting, had the most severe symptoms, whereas children on vacation or who were not at school during the shooting experienced no symptoms.

An Individual's Perception and Tolerance of Stress   Most of us are well aware that, in some cases, one person's stressor is another person's "piece of cake." The different reactions can be due to both a individual's perception of threat and his or her stress tolerance.

Perception of threat.   If a situation is seen as threatening, it is highly stressful, especially if a person believes that his or her resources for dealing with the situation are inadequate—whether they really are or not. A person who is generally unsure of his or her adequacy and worth is much more likely to experience threat than a person who feels generally confident and secure (except, of course, in objectively stressful situations, such as rape, when all people would experience extreme stress).

Often, new adjustive demands that have not been anticipated and for which no ready-made coping strategies are available will place an individual under severe stress. To avoid this stress, the training of emergency workers, such as police and firefighters, normally involves repeated exposure to controlled or contrived stressors until coping patterns have become second nature. Likewise, recovery from the stress created by major surgery can be markedly facilitated when a patient is given realistic expectations beforehand (MacDonald & Kuiper, 1983). The same sense of adequacy and control can be achieved by choosing a stressful situation voluntarily, rather than having it be imposed by others or occur unexpectedly (Averill, 1973). The importance of having a sense of control has been noted by Paterson and Neufeld (1987): "Control appears to moderate the effects of stress by allowing the individual to alter the stress response directly or to select a response that will alter or avert the threatened event" (p. 413).

Understanding the nature of a stressful situation, preparing for it, and knowing how long it will last all lessen the severity of the stress when it does come. Of course, we continually create new stressors that make preparation and anticipation difficult at best. Two recent nuclear disasters are cases in point: the Chernobyl nuclear disaster in the Soviet Union in 1986 and the 1979 nuclear accident at Three Mile Island in Pennsylvania. Koscheyev (1990) reported high levels of stress and lowered psychological functioning among workers at the plant following the Chernobyl accident. Sixty percent of the workers were experiencing psychological symptoms a year after the accident. Victims of the Three Mile Island nuclear accident were showing physical effects from the experience, such as high blood pressure, more than a year after its occurrence (Baum, Gatchel, & Schaeffer, 1983).

Stress tolerance.   If a person is marginally adjusted, the slightest frustration or pressure may be

Stress tolerance may be increased by the environmental support of a prescibed course of action. Thus the training of emergency personnel, such as these Coast Guard trainees, often involves repeated exposure to controlled or contrived stressors until coping patterns have become second nature.

highly stressful. The term **stress tolerance** refers to a person's ability to withstand stress without becoming seriously impaired.

Both biologically and psychologically, people vary greatly in overall vulnerability to stressors. In addition, different people are vulnerable to different stressors. Emergencies, disappointments, and other problems that one person can take in stride may prove incapacitating to another. As we have seen, early traumatic experiences can leave an individual especially vulnerable to certain stressors.

External Resources and Social Supports
Considerable evidence suggests that positive social and family relationships can moderate the effects of stress on an individual and can reduce illness and early death (Monroe & Steiner, 1986). Conversely, the lack of external supports—either personal or material—can make a given stressor more potent and weaken an individual's capacity to cope with it. A divorce or the death of a person's mate evokes more stress if he or she is left feeling alone and

unloved than if the person is surrounded by people he or she cares about and feels close to. Siegel and Kuykendall (1990), for example, found that widowed men who attended church or temple experienced less depression than those who did not. In this study spouse loss was related to depression more in the men than in the women. The reasons for this finding remain unclear, though others have found similar results as well (e.g., Stroebe & Stroebe, 1983). It could be that the women had more social resources available to them from the outset, which may have reduced their vulnerability to depression.

In other situations, an individual may be adversely affected by other family members who are experiencing problems. The level of tension for all family members can be increased if one individual experiences extreme difficulty, such as a chronic or life-threatening illness or a psychiatric disability. Yager, Grant, and Bolus (1984) concluded that the intensity of an individual's own psychological symptoms was related to that of his or her spouse; a person showed more emotional symptoms if his or her spouse was psychologically disturbed.

Environmental supports are a complex matter, however, and behavior by an individual's family or friends that is intended to provide support may actually increase the stress. In his study of graduate students facing crucial examinations, Mechanic (1962) compared the effects of different types of spousal behavior. Though the study was conducted 30 years ago, the findings are still relevant today:

In general, spouses do not provide blind support. They perceive the kinds of support the student wants and they provide it. The [spouse] who becomes worried about examinations also may provide more support than the spouse who says, "I'm not worried, you will surely pass." Indeed, since there is a chance that the student will not pass, the person who is supportive in a meaningful sense will not give blind assurance. . . . Often a statement to the effect, "Do the best you can" is more supportive than, "I'm sure you are going to do well." The latter statement adds to the student's burden, for not only must he fear the disappointment of not passing, but also the loss of respect in the eyes of his spouse. (p. 158)

Often the culture offers specific rituals or courses of action that support individuals as they attempt to deal with certain types of stress. For example, most religions provide rituals that help the bereaved through their ordeals, and in some faiths, confession and atonement help people deal with stresses related to guilt and self-recrimination.

In sum, the interaction between the nature of a stressor and an individual's resources for dealing with it largely determines the severity of stress. However great a challenge, it creates little stress if an individual can easily handle it.

■ Individual Stressor Patterns over Time

Each individual faces a unique pattern of adjustive demands. This fact is partly due to differences in the way people perceive and interpret similar situations, but also, objectively, no two people are faced with exactly the same pattern of stressors. Each person's age, sex, occupation, economic status, personality, competencies, and family situation help determine the demands he or she will face. The stressor pattern a child faces will differ in many ways from that of an older person, and the pattern faced by a carpenter will differ from that of a business executive.

Sometimes, key stressors in a person's life center around a continuing, difficult life situation. These stressors are considered *chronic*, or long-lasting. A person may be frustrated in a boring and unrewarding job from which there is seemingly no escape, suffer for years in an unhappy and conflictful marriage, or be severely frustrated by a physical handicap or a long-term health problem.

Stressor patterns often change with time—either predictably, as when we enter different life periods, or unpredictably, as when an accident, a death in the family, or a drastic social change makes new demands. Also, the type of stressors vary. Some of these changes bring only minor stress, while others place us under severe or excessive stress. Regardless of severity, the stressor patterns we face today are somewhat different from those we faced a week ago, and they will be different in the future from what they are now. The total pattern at any time determines the part any one stressor will play and how much difficulty we are likely to have coping with it—and the way that we cope with stressors over time shapes the course of our lives.

From time to time, most of us experience periods of especially *acute* (sudden and intense) stress. The term **crisis** is used to refer to times when a stressful situation approaches or exceeds the adaptive capacities of an individual or group. Crises are often especially stressful because the coping techniques we typically use do not work.

A crisis may center around a traumatic divorce, an episode of depression in which a person seriously considers suicide, or the aftermath of an injury or disease that forces difficult readjustments in a person's self-concept and way of life. Estimates of how

From time to time, most of us experience periods of intense stress brought on by some sort of crisis. The outcome of such crises can have a profound effect on a person's subsequent adjustment. Consider the case of Renee Katz (left). Ms. Katz, a music student who played the piano and flute, was pushed in front of a subway train and lost her right hand. Though the hand was reattached, she was not able to pursue her musical career. Instead, after undergoing physical and occupational therapy to regain some strength in her mangled hand, Ms. Katz became an occupational therapist in order to help those who, like her, needed some rehabilitative help. In this case, severe personal trauma was followed by a positive adjustment to a new situation.

often such crises occur in the life of the average person range from about once every ten years to about once every two years. In view of our complex and rapidly changing society, the latter estimate may be more realistic.

The outcome of such crises has a profound influence on a person's subsequent adjustment. An effective new method of coping developed during a crisis may be added to the person's repertoire of coping behaviors; the inability to deal adequately with the crisis may impair the person's ability to cope with similar stressors in the future because of the expectation of failure. For this reason **crisis intervention**—providing psychological help in times of severe and special stress—has become an important element in contemporary treatment and prevention approaches. We will discuss such intervention in more detail in Chapter 19.

It is important to remember that life changes, even some positive ones, place new demands on us and thus may be stressful. The faster the changes, the greater the stress. Early research efforts on life changes focused on developing scales that could measure the relationship between stress and possible physical and mental disorders. Holmes and his colleagues (Holmes & Holmes, 1970; Holmes & Rahe, 1967; Rahe & Arthur, 1978), for example, developed the Social Readjustment Rating Scale, an objective method for measuring the cumulative stress to which an individual has been exposed over a period of time. This scale measures life stress in terms of "life change units" (LCU): the more stressful the event, the more LCUs assigned to it. At the high end of the scale, "death of a spouse" rates 100 LCUs and "divorce" rates 73 LCUs; at the low end of the scale, "vacation" rates 13 LCUs and

"minor violations of the law" rates 11 LCUs. Holmes and his colleagues found that individuals with LCU scores of 300 or more for recent months were at significant risk for getting a major illness within the next two years. In another effort, Horowitz and his colleagues (Horowitz, Wilner, & Alvarez, 1979) developed the Impact of Events Scale. This scale measures an individual's reaction to a stressful situation by first identifying the stressor and then posing a series of questions to pinpoint how he or she is coping.

In the past ten years, these life stress scales have been criticized for numerous methodological problems. For example, a number of criticisms have targeted the items selected for different scales, the subjectivity of the scoring, the failure to take into account the relevance of items for the populations studied, and the reliance on the subjects' memory of events (Monroe, 1983; Schroeder & Costa, 1984; Zimmerman, 1983). Perhaps the most problematic aspect of life events scales is that they provide only a general indicator of distress and do not assess specific types of disorders. This vagueness has not helped researchers gather specific information on various disorders. Another significant limitation of life event scales, and one that eats away the foundation of these studies, is that they tend to measure chronic problems rather than reactions to specific environmental events (Depue & Monroe, 1986). Despite these limitations, however, the weight of evidence supports the stressfulness of life changes (Maddi, Bartone, & Puccetti, 1987).

With an awareness that research in this area is sometimes flawed, let us examine, in the following sections, some of the ways individuals cope with stressful events.

COPING STRATEGIES

Evidence suggests that some particularly hardy individuals may be relatively immune to stressors that would impair most people's functioning (Kobasa, 1979). In general, however, increased levels of stress threaten an individual's well-being and produce automatic, persistent attempts to relieve the tension. Stress forces a person, in short, to do something. What is done depends on many influences. Sometimes inner factors—such as a person's frame of reference, motives, competencies, or stress tolerance—play the dominant role in determining his or her coping strategies; at other times, environmental conditions—such as social demands and expectations—are of primary importance. Any stress reaction, of course, reflects the interplay of inner strategies and outer conditions—some more influential than others, but all working together to make the individual react in a certain way. In the following section, we will consider some general principles of adjustive behavior and coping; then we will examine some characteristic stages that occur when an individual's adaptive functioning is threatened.

General Principles of Coping with Stress

In reviewing certain general principles of coping with stress, it is helpful to conceptualize three interactional levels. On a biological level, there are immunological defenses and damage-repair mechanisms; on a psychological and interpersonal level, there are learned coping patterns, self-defenses, and support from family and friends; and on a sociocultural level, there are group resources, such as labor unions, religious organizations, and law-enforcement agencies.

The failure of coping efforts on any of these levels may seriously increase an individual's vulnerability on other levels. For example, a breakdown of immunological defenses may impair not only bodily functioning, but psychological functioning as well; chronically poor psychological coping patterns may lead to peptic ulcers or other diseases; or the failure of a group on which a person depends may seriously interfere with his or her ability to satisfy basic needs.

In coping with stress, a person is confronted with two challenges: (a) to meet the requirements of the stressor, and (b) to protect the self from psychological damage and disorganization. When a person feels competent to handle a stressful situation, a **task-oriented response** is typical—that is, behavior is directed primarily at dealing with the requirements of the stressor. Typically, this response means the individual objectively appraises the situation, works out alternative solutions, decides on an appropriate strategy, takes action, and evaluates feedback. The steps in a task-oriented response—whether the actions turn out to be effective or ineffective—are generally flexible enough to enable an individual to change course.

Task-oriented responses may involve making changes in one's self, one's surroundings, or both, depending on the situation. The action may be overt—as in showing one's spouse more affection—or it may be covert—as in lowering one's level of aspiration. The action may involve retreating from the problem, attacking it directly, or trying to find a workable compromise. Any of these actions are appropriate under certain circumstances. For instance, if one is faced with a situation of overwhelming physical danger, such as a forest fire, the logical task-oriented response might well be to run.

When a person's feelings of adequacy are seriously threatened by a stressor, a **defense-oriented response** tends to prevail—that is, behavior is directed primarily at protecting the self from hurt and disorganization, rather than at resolving the situation. Typically, the person using defense-oriented responses has forsaken more productive task-oriented action in favor of an overriding concern for maintaining the integrity of the self, however ill-advised and self-defeating the effort may prove to be.

There are two common types of defense-oriented responses. The first consists of responses such as crying, repetitive talking, and mourning that seem to function as psychological damage-repair mechanisms. The second type consists of the so-called ego- or self-defense mechanisms introduced in Chapter 3 (p. 66). These mechanisms, including such responses as denial and repression, relieve tension and anxiety and protect the self from hurt and devaluation. They protect an individual from external threats, such as failures in work or relationships, and from internal threats, such as guilt-arousing desires or actions. They appear to protect the self in one or more of the following ways: (a) by denying, distorting, or restricting an individual's experience; (b) by reducing emotional or self-involvement; and (c) by counteracting threat or damage. Often, of course, a given defense mechanism may offer more than one kind of protection.

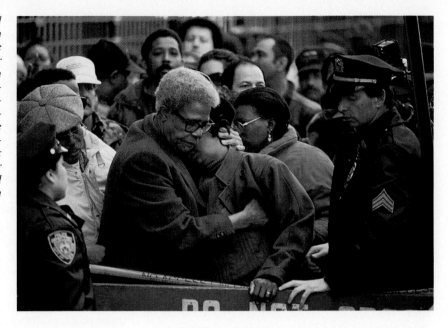

Two ways that we may choose to deal with a stressful situation are through task-oriented behavior, in which we try to resolve the situation, or through defense-oriented behavior, in which we protect ourselves from psychological damage and disorganization. The couple weeping and holding each other in this photo have witnessed a fire in a Bronx discotheque that left 87 dead. They cannot change or resolve the situation. Their reactions are defense-oriented, used to help them cope with the hurt of an overwhelming stressor.

These defense mechanisms are ordinarily used in combination rather than singly, and often they are combined with task-oriented behavior. We all use them to some extent for coping with the problems of living. In fact, Gleser and Sacks (1973) have concluded that we tend to be fairly consistent in the particular mechanisms we use. Ego-defense mechanisms are considered maladaptive when they become the predominant means of coping with stressors.

Decompensation Under Excessive Stress

As we have seen, stressors challenge a person's adaptive resources, bringing into play both task- and defense-oriented reactions. Most of the time these varied reactions are successful in containing a threat. When stressors are sustained or severe, however, a person may not be able to adapt and may experience lowered integrated functioning and eventually a breakdown. This lowering of adaptive functioning is referred to as **decompensation.** Whether stress becomes "excessive" depends, as we have seen, not only on the nature of a stressor, but also on an individual's tolerance for stress and available resources for coping with it. In the following section we will deal with some of the generalized effects of excessive stress. Then we will move on to specific forms of decompensation on biological, psychological, and sociocultural levels.

The Effects of Severe Stress   Stress is a fact of life, and our reactions to stress can give us

competencies we need and would not develop without being challenged to do so. Stress can be damaging, however, if certain demands are too severe for our coping resources or if we believe and act as if they are. Severe stress can exact a high cost in terms of lowered efficiency, depletion of adaptive resources, wear and tear on the system, and, in extreme cases, severe personality and physical deterioration—even death.

Lowering of adaptive efficiency.   On a physiological level, severe stress may result in alterations that can impair the body's ability to fight off invading bacteria and viruses. On a psychological level, the perception of threat leads to an increasingly narrow perceptual field and rigid cognitive processes. It thus becomes difficult or impossible for the individual to see the situation objectively or to perceive the alternatives actually available. This process often appears to be part of suicidal behavior.

Our adaptive efficiency may also be impaired by the intense emotions that commonly accompany severe stress. Acute stage fright may disrupt our performance of a public speech; examination jitters may lead us to fail an exam despite adequate preparation. In fact, high levels of fear, anger, or anxiety may lead not only to impaired performance, but to behavior disorganization.

Depletion of adaptive resources.   In using its resources to meet one severe stressor, an organism may suffer a lowering of tolerance for other stressors. Selye (1976b) demonstrated that successions of noxious stimuli can have lethal effects on animals. It appears that an organism's coping resources are limited: if they are already mobilized against one stressor, they are less available against others. This finding helps explain how sustained psychological stress can lower biological resistance to disease and vice versa. Interestingly, prolonged stress may lead to either pathological overresponsiveness to stressors—as illustrated by the "last straw" response—or to pathological insensitivity to stressors, as shown by a loss of hope or extreme apathy. In general, severe and sustained stress on any level leads to a serious reduction in an organism's overall adaptive capacity.

Wear and tear on the system.   Most of us probably believe that even after a very stressful experience, rest can completely restore us. In his pioneering studies of stress, however, Selye has found evidence to the contrary:

Experiments on animals have clearly shown that each exposure leaves an indelible scar, in that it uses up reserves of adaptability which cannot be replaced. It is true that immediately after some harassing experience, rest can restore us almost to the original level of fitness by eliminating acute fatigue. But the emphasis is on the word almost. Since we constantly go through periods of stress and rest during life, even a minute deficit of adaptation energy every day adds up—it adds up to what we call aging. (1976, p. 429)

When pressure is severe and long-lasting, adjustment problems such as excessive worry may become chronic and eventually lead to physical changes such as high blood pressure. Davidson and Baum (1986) studied the effects of stress over a five-year period. In a follow-up to the study mentioned earlier on p. 144, they found that individuals exposed to the March 1979 nuclear accident at Three Mile Island, even five years after the incident, showed symptoms of high stress such as elevated blood pressure and the presence of urinary noradrenaline (often associated with a persistent arousal state). These people also reported more intense psychological symptoms of stress, such as intrusive thoughts, than residents in the control community.

Biological Decompensation   It is difficult to specify the exact biological processes underlying an organism's response to stress. A model that helps explain the course of biological decompensation under excessive stress is the **general adaptation syndrome,** introduced by Selye (1956; 1976b). Selye found that the body's reaction to sustained and excessive stress typically occurs in three major phases: (a) *alarm reaction,* in which the body's

defensive forces are "called to arms" by the activation of the autonomic nervous system; (b) *stage of resistance,* in which biological adaptation is at the maximum level in terms of bodily resources used; and (c) *exhaustion,* in which bodily resources are depleted and the organism loses its ability to resist so that further exposure to stress can lead to illness and death. A diagram of this general adaptation syndrome is shown in *HIGHLIGHT 5.2.*

When decompensation does not run its entire course (resulting in the death of an organism), maintenance mechanisms attempt to repair damage and reorganize normal function. If the stress has resulted in extensive damage, this restorative process is often a matter of reorganizing remaining resources, but a permanent lowering of the previous level of integration and functioning remains.

Psychological Decompensation   Personality decompensation under excessive stress is somewhat easier to specify. It appears to follow a course resembling that of biological decompensation and may, in fact, involve specific biological responses.

1. *Alarm and mobilization.* First an individual's resources for coping with a stressor are alerted and mobilized. Typically involved at this stage are emotional arousal, increased tension, heightened sensitivity, greater alertness (vigilance), and determined efforts at self-control. At the same time, the individual undertakes various coping measures—which may be task-oriented or defense-oriented or a combination of the two—in attempts to meet the emergency. During this stage, symptoms of maladjustment may appear, such as continuous anxiety and tension, gastrointestinal upset or other bodily diseases, and lowered efficiency—signs that the mobilization of adaptive resources is inadequate.

2. *Resistance.* If stress continues, an individual is often able to find some means for dealing with it and thus to resist psychological disintegration. Resistance may be achieved temporarily by concerted, task-oriented coping measures; the use of ego-defense mechanisms may also be intensified during this period. Even in the resistance stage, however, indications of strain may exist, including psychophysiologic symptoms and mild reality distortions. During the late phases of this stage, the individual tends to become rigid and to cling to previously developed defenses rather than trying to reevaluate the stressor situation and work out more adaptive coping patterns.

3. *Exhaustion.* In the face of continued excessive stress, an individual's adaptive resources are deplet-

HIGHLIGHT 5.2

Selye's General Adaptation Syndrome (GAS)

The general adaptation syndrome (GAS), shown in the diagram below, graphically illustrates a typical individual's general response to stress. In the first phase (alarm reaction), the person shows an initial lowered resistance to stress or shock. If the stress persists, the person shows a defensive reaction or resistance (resistance phase) in an attempt to adapt to stress. Following extensive exposure to stress, the energy necessary for adaptation may be exhausted, resulting in the final stage of the GAS—collapse of adaptation (exhaustion phase).

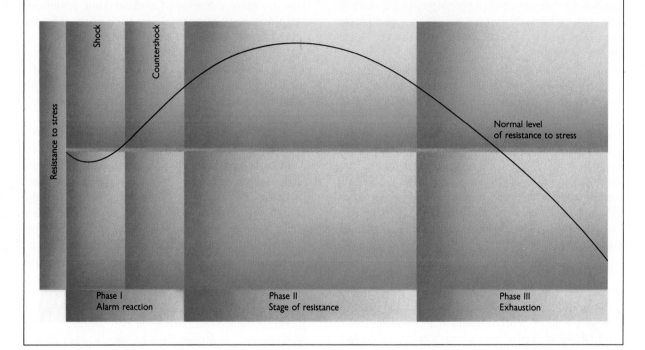

ed and the coping patterns called forth in the stage of resistance begin to fail. As the stage of exhaustion begins, integration is lowered and exaggerated and inappropriate defensive measures are introduced. The latter reactions may be characterized by psychological disorganization and a break with reality, involving delusions and hallucinations. These delusions appear to represent increasingly disorganized thoughts and perceptions along with desperate efforts to salvage psychological integration and self-integrity by restructuring reality. Metabolic changes that impair normal brain functioning may also be involved in delusional and hallucinatory behavior. Eventually, if the excessive stress continues, the process of decompensation proceeds to a stage of complete psychological disintegration—perhaps involving continuous uncontrolled violence, apathy, stupor, and eventually death. Siegel (1984) found this pattern among 31 hostage victims whose cases he analyzed. Those who had been held under conditions of isolation, visual deprivation, physical restraint, physical abuse, and threat of death typically experienced hallucinations.

As we will see, relatively severe psychological decompensation may be precipitated by sudden and extreme stress; but more often, decompensation is a gradual, long-term process. Typically, of course, treatment measures are instituted before decompensation runs its course. Such measures may increase an individual's adaptive capabilities or alleviate a stressor situation so that the process of decompensation is reversed.

Sociocultural Decompensation   Although social science has made only modest inroads into the understanding of group pathology, it appears that the concept of decompensation is just as applicable here as on the biological and psychological levels. In the face of wars, economic problems, and other internal and external stressors that surpass their adjustive capabilities, societies may undergo varying degrees of decompensation. At such times societies often resort to extreme measures in their attempts to maintain their organization and resist disintegration. The historian Toynbee and other writers have depicted this process while describing the decline and fall of civilizations throughout history.

In completing our immediate discussion of decompensation, it should be emphasized that the outcome in a given situation—on biological, psychological, and sociocultural levels—depends on the extent to which any damage can be repaired and remaining resources reorganized. In some instances, an individual or group's functional level may be permanently lowered following excessive stress; in other cases, with successful problem resolution, the individual or group may attain a higher level of integration and functioning than before the episode.

ADJUSTMENT DISORDER: REACTIONS TO COMMON LIFE STRESSORS

Research literature and clinical observations on the relationship between stress and psychopathology are so substantial that the role of stressors in symptom development is now formally emphasized in diagnostic formulations (Brett, Spitzer, & Williams, 1988). In DSM-III-R, for example, a diagnostician can specify on Axis IV (shown on p. 12) the specific psychosocial stressors facing an individual. The Axis IV scale is particularly useful in relation to two Axis I categories: adjustment disorder and posttraumatic stress disorder (acute, chronic, or delayed). Both of these disorders involve patterns of psychological and behavioral disturbances that occur in response to identifiable stressors. The key

differences between the two disorders lie not only in the severity of the disturbances, but also in the natures of the stressors and the time frames during which the disorders occur. In both disorders, the stressors supposedly can be identified as causal factors and specified on Axis IV.

An individual whose response to a common stressor—such as marriage, divorce, childbirth, or losing a job—is maladaptive *and* occurs within three months of the stressor can be said to have an **adjustment disorder.** The individual's reaction is considered maladaptive if he or she is unable to function as usual or if the person's reaction to the particular stressor is excessive. Usually, the individual's maladjustment lessens or disappears when (a) the stressor has subsided or (b) the individual learns to adapt to the stressor. Should the symptoms continue beyond six months, DSM-III-R recommends that the diagnosis be changed to some other mental disorder. As will be evident, the reality of adjustment disorders does not always adhere to such a strict time schedule.

We might well ask here, "What would be considered a normal response to a stressor?" The answer seems a bit elusive by DSM criteria. Clearly, not all reactions to stressors are adjustment disorders. What seems to push a reaction into this category is the inability to function as usual—and yet this criteria is true for many other disorders as well. We will not resolve this uncertainty any time soon; it is perhaps more important to recognize that *adjustment disorder* is probably the least stigmatizing and mildest diagnosis a therapist can assign to a client, and it is frequently used by therapists for insurance purposes.

We will look now at some of the stressor situations that typically cause adjustment disorders: unemployment, bereavement, and divorce or separation. We will then turn to stressor situations that can lead to posttraumatic stress disorder: major life problems such as life-threatening traumatic events, rape, military combat, imprisonment, being held hostage, and forced relocation.

Stress from Unemployment

Managing the stress associated with unemployment requires great coping strength, especially for people who have previously earned an adequate living. The negative impact of losing one's job and being unable to find suitable employment has been common in the last decade. The economic decline of the automobile, steel, oil, gas, electronics, and small-scale farming industries especially has transformed many thriving communities into depressed areas and many industrious employees into unemployed or underemployed individuals. In almost any community one can find numerous workers who have been laid off from jobs they had held for many years and who are facing the end of their unemployment compensation. The following case is typical of the problems that unemployment can bring:

David C., a 49-year-old construction foreman who was married and had two children attending college, had worked for a large building construction firm since he graduated from high school. One afternoon in May of 1982, his company, without warning, filed for bankruptcy, closed down its remaining job sites, and began to liquidate its resources.

David was stunned. The unexpected changes in his life were not easy for him to face. Early efforts to find other employment were met only with frustration because other construction companies were experiencing similar economic problems and layoffs.

After a few weeks his savings were depleted, and he took a step he never dreamed possible: he applied for unemployment compensation. This action was a tremendous blow to his self-esteem. He had always been self-sufficient and had taken great pride in being a hard worker and a good provider for his family. He was particularly upset at not being able to pay the tuition and living costs for his two sons in college and he felt a great sense of failure when they remained on their summer jobs rather than returning to school. His wife, who had never worked outside the home since their marriage, took a job in a local department store to meet some of the family's living expenses.

After some searching David seemingly gave up on finding a job and began to spend more time in bars. His drinking problems intensified. When he returned home in the evenings he sulked around the house and rebuffed most attempts by other family members to socialize or communicate. During this period family arguments were so frequent that Joel, his eldest son, felt that he couldn't tolerate the tension any more and enlisted in the army. In February, eight months after he lost his job, David saw a notice in the newspaper indicating that a local company was taking applications for 25 construction jobs

the following Monday. He arrived at the company's employment office early on Monday morning only to find that there were about 3000 other applicants ahead of him—some who had arrived the day before and had stood in line all night in the bitter cold. He left the lot dejected. That same week the bank initiated foreclosure proceedings on his house because he had not made a mortgage payment in seven months. He was forced to sell his house and move into an apartment.

For the next year David still could not find work in his community. Finally, after he had exhausted his unemployment benefits, he and a fellow employee left their families and moved to another city in the Southeast to find work. David planned to have his wife follow him when he got settled. She, however, had by that time been enjoying some success on her job and refused to move away. After several months of living apart, David's wife filed for a divorce. No further information is available on David.

Unemployment is becoming a common experience in today's society—plant closings, layoffs, and hostile takeovers all result in work-force reductions, often in management-level positions. Some population subgroups—especially young minority males—live in a permanent economic depression, more pervasive and just as debilitating as the Great Depression was for the white majority. Unemployment among blacks (12.2%) is almost twice that for whites (6.3%) (Department of Labor, 1991). Indeed, for young black men, the unemployment rates today are over twice those for whites during the 1930s (Lebergott, 1964). The long-range psychological consequences of this situation can be great. Some people can deal with setbacks such as David experienced and can adapt without suffering long-range adjustment difficulties once the initial stressful situation has ended. For others, however, unemployment can have serious long-term effects.

The impact of chronic unemployment on an individual's self-concept, sense of worth, and feeling of belongingness is shattering—especially in an affluent society. The vulnerability of our population's lower socioeconomic segment to unemployment helps explain why this segment contributes a disproportionately high number of individuals to penal institutions and mental hospitals.

Recently, a number of employee-based intervention programs have been initiated to counsel and assist displaced workers. Maida, Gordon, and

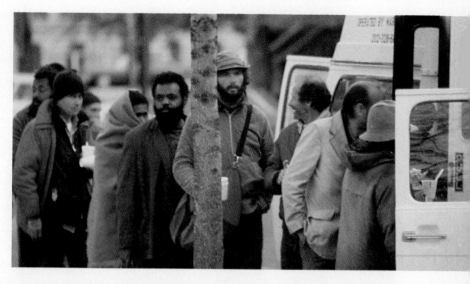

Managing the stress associated with unemployment requires great coping strength. Some people can deal with setbacks and can adapt without suffering long-range adjustment difficulties once the initial stressful situation has ended. The impact of chronic unemployment, however, can be shattering and can have serious long-term effects.

Farberow (1989) provide a valuable survey of the issues that affect these newly unemployed individuals and describe many problems resulting from transitional stress and chronic unemployment. They also explore several intervention strategies—such as increasing support networks, out-placement counseling, stress counseling, and more—that can reduce the psychological impact of job loss and promote more effective coping strategies.

■ Stress from Bereavement

When someone close to us dies, we are psychologically upended. Often the first reaction is disbelief. Then, as we begin to realize the significance of the death, our feelings of sadness, grief, and despair (even, perhaps, anger at the departed person) frequently overwhelm us.

Grief over the loss of a loved one is a natural process that allows the survivors to mourn their loss and then free themselves for life without the departed person. The following description of the normal grief process (*uncomplicated bereavement* in DSM-III-R terms) was provided by Janis et al. (1969):

Typically, the normal grief pattern following the loss of a loved one begins with a period of numbness and shock. Upon learning of the death, the person reacts with disbelief. For several days his feelings may be blunted and he may be in a semi-dazed state, punctuated by episodes of irritability and anger. In some instances the protest reactions take the extreme form of outbursts of impotent rage, as when adult brothers and sisters bitterly blame one another for having failed to do something that might have prolonged the life of their elderly parent. This initial phase usually ends by the time of the funeral, which often can release the tears and feelings of despair that had been bottled up in the grief-stricken person. Thereafter, a very intense grief reaction ensues: The mourner weeps copiously, yearns for the lost person, and wishes he had been more helpful and considerate while the loved one was still alive. . . . Attacks of agitated distress are likely to alternate with periods of more silent despair, during which the sufferer is preoccupied with memories of the dead person.

For many days and perhaps weeks the mourner remains somewhat depressed and apathetic, expresses a general sense of futility, and becomes socially withdrawn, although he still goes through the motions of carrying out his usual social obligations. During this period of despair, he is likely to suffer from insomnia, psychosomatic [psychologically induced] intestinal disorders, loss of appetite, restlessness, and general irritability. A tendency to deny the fact of the death may persist for many weeks; the mourner continues to think of the dead person at times as still alive and present in the house. There is also a tendency to idealize the dead person in memory and . . . to seek companionship mainly with persons who are willing to limit their conversation to talking about him.

The mourner is usually able to return to work and resume other daily activities, such as talking with friends and relatives, after about two or three weeks. But he may continue to withdraw from certain types of social affairs that used to give him pleasure. After a month or two the most acute

When someone close to us dies, we are psychologically upended. Our first reaction is often disbelief. Then, as we begin to realize what has happened, we are often overcome by feelings of sadness, grief, despair, and even anger. In general, grief over the loss of a loved one is a natural process that seems to allow the survivors to mourn their loss and then free themselves for life without the departed person.

symptoms begin to subside, but there may still be residual sadness, yearning, and attacks of acute grief during the ensuing months. (pp. 179–180)

Some individuals do not go through the typical process of grieving, perhaps because of their personality makeups or as a consequence of their particular situations. An individual may, for instance, be expected to be stoical about his or her feelings or may have to manage the family's affairs. Other individuals may develop exaggerated or prolonged depressions after their normal grieving processes should have ended (a normal grieving process should last no longer than one year). Such pathological reactions to death are more likely to occur in people who have a history of emotional problems or who harbor a great deal of resentment and hostility toward the deceased, thus experiencing intense guilt. They are usually profoundly depressed and may, in some instances, be suffering from major depression (see Chapter 11 for more on this). The following case illustrates an extreme adjustment disorder with withdrawal or pathological grief reaction (and, in this instance, a positive outcome):

*N*adine, a 66-year-old former high school teacher, lived with Charles, age 67, her husband of 40 years (also a retired teacher). The couple had been nearly inseparable since they met — they even taught at the same schools during most of their teaching careers. They lived in a semirural community where they had worked and had raised their three children, all of whom had

married and moved to a large metropolitan area about 100 miles away. For years they had planned their retirement and had hoped to travel around the country visiting friends. A week before their fortieth anniversary, Charles had a heart attack and, after five days in the intensive care unit, had a second heart attack and died.

Nadine took Charles's death quite hard. Even though she had a great deal of emotional support from her many friends and her children, she had great difficulty adjusting. Elaine, one of her daughters, came and stayed a few days and encouraged her to come to the city for a while. Nadine declined the persistent invitation even though she had little to do at home. Friends called on her frequently, but she seemed almost to resent their presence. In the months following the funeral, Nadine's reclusive behavior persisted. Several well-wishers reported to Elaine that her mother was not doing well and was not even leaving the house to go shopping. They reported that Nadine sat alone in the darkened house — not answering the phone and showing reluctance to come to the door. She had lost interest in activities she had once enjoyed.

Greatly worried about her mother's welfare, Elaine organized a campaign to get her mother out of the house and back to doing the things she had formerly enjoyed. Each of Nadine's children and their families took turns visiting and taking her places until she finally began to show interest in living again. In time, Nadine agreed to come to each of their homes for visits. This proved a therapeutic step since Nadine had always been *fond of children and took pleasure in the time spent with her eight grandchildren—she actually extended the visits longer than she had planned.*

The loss of a close family member can significantly affect a survivor's life for months. Over a period of two years, Shanfield and Swain (1984) studied parents who had lost an adult child in a traffic accident. They found that the parents continued to grieve intensely and had higher-than-expected emotional symptoms and physical complaints for months after their losses. Rinear (1988) studied the grief processes of parents who had lost one of their children through homicide and found severe, long-term effects, including lingering fears over what might happen to their other children.

■ Stress from Divorce or Separation

The deterioration or ending of an intimate relationship is a potent stressor and a frequent reason why people seek psychological treatment. Divorce, though more generally accepted today, is still a tragic and usually stressful outcome to a once close and trusting relationship. We noted in Chapter 4 that marital disruption is a major source of vulnerability to psychopathology: individuals who are recently divorced or separated are markedly over-represented among people with psychological problems.

Many factors make a divorce or separation unpleasant and stressful for everyone concerned: the acknowledgment of failure in a relationship important both personally and culturally; the necessity of "explaining" the failure to family and friends; the loss of valuable friendships that often accompanies the rupture; the economic uncertainties and hardships that both partners frequently experience; and, when children are involved, the problem of custody—including court battles, living arrangements, and so on.

After the divorce or separation, new problems typically emerge. The readjustment to a single life, perhaps after many years of marriage, can be a difficult experience. Since in many cases it seems that friends as well as assets have to be divided, new friendships need to be made. New opposite-sex relationships may require a great deal of personal change. Even when the separation has been relatively agreeable, new strength to adapt and cope is needed. Thus it is not surprising that many people

seek counseling after the breakup of a significant relationship. The following case illustrates how the stress in a marital breakup can adversely affect a capable and generally well-functioning person.

Janice was a 33-year-old manager of an office that employed over 50 people. She had always been competent and had received a great deal of satisfaction from her career. For several months, however, she had been quite upset and depressed about her marital situation and had been unable to sleep. She had lost 12 pounds because of her poor appetite and was experiencing painful burning feelings in her stomach; she was worried about having ulcers.

Janice's marriage (her second) had begun to show signs of trouble almost from the start. Shortly after the wedding two years before, her husband's drinking had increased. He often stayed out late and on two occasions did not come home at all. Usually he lied about his whereabouts. For the first few months Janice was tolerant of his transgressions, trying to make this second marriage work. Her husband, who she regarded as a charming person that she "couldn't stay mad at," was always forgiven, and they "had a great time making up." In the most recent incident, however, he had returned late at night with "evident traces of another woman." This was the last straw, and Janice moved out.

The intense stress she was experiencing over the breakup of the marriage appeared to be directly related to her sense of failing in life for a second time. Her first marriage had ended in divorce after her husband of seven years developed a severe drinking problem, stayed away from home a great deal, and frequently abused her physically.

Janice's marital problems did not interfere with her performance at work, but, in addition to depression and physical problems, she began to experience problems with her teenage daughter. As a result she entered psychotherapy, hoping it would help her know herself better and understand why she had married two "losers."

Janice, diagnosed as having an adjustment disorder with anxious mood, was seen in cognitive-behavioral therapy for about six months. During that time she gained a great deal of insight into her motivation for marrying alcoholics: she wished to "save" them from themselves. Janice's father had been an alcoholic and had died when she was a teenager—from chronic drinking. During therapy Janice was able to "resist" taking her husband back and was able to feel more comfortable about living with her daughter.

POSTTRAUMATIC STRESS DISORDER: REACTIONS TO SEVERE LIFE STRESSORS

In **posttraumatic stress disorder (PTSD),** the stressor is unusually severe (that is, outside the realm of typical human experience) and is psychologically traumatic—for example, a life-threatening situation, the destruction of one's home, seeing another person mutilated or killed, or being the victim of physical violence. Posttraumatic stress disorder includes the following symptoms:

1. The traumatic event is persistently reexperienced by the individual—he or she may have intrusive, recurring thoughts or repetitive nightmares about the event.
2. The individual persistently avoids stimuli associated with the trauma; for example, he or she tries to avoid activities related to the incident or blocks out the memory of certain aspects of the experience. Situations that recall the traumatic experience provoke anxiety.
3. The individual may experience persistent symptoms of increased arousal, such as chronic tension and irritability, often accompanied by insomnia, the inability to tolerate noise, and the complaint that "I just can't seem to relax."
4. The individual may experience impaired concentration and memory.
5. The individual may experience feelings of depression. In some cases he or she may withdraw from social contact and avoid experiences that might increase excitation—commonly manifested in the avoidance of interpersonal involvement, loss of sexual interest, and an attitude of "peace and quiet at any price."

In DSM-III-R no separate category exists for stress disorders, and posttraumatic stress disorder is categorized under the anxiety disorders. Clearly, PTSD includes elements of anxiety—generalized feelings of fear and apprehension—but since PTSD bears such a close relationship to the experience of stress, we cover it here and follow in Chapter 6 with coverage of the more traditional anxiety disorders.

The diagnosis of posttraumatic stress disorder is not given unless the symptoms last for at least one month. The diagnosis can be further specified in terms of when the symptoms begin. If the symptoms begin within six months of the traumatic event, then the reaction is considered to be *acute.* If the symptoms begin more than six months after the traumatic situation, the reaction is considered to be *delayed.* The delayed version of PTSD is less well defined and more difficult to diagnose than disorders that emerge shortly after the precipitating incident. Some authorities have even questioned whether a delayed reaction should be diagnosed as a posttraumatic stress disorder at all; instead, some would categorize such a reaction as some other anxiety-based disorder. It is important to keep in mind that the criteria for posttraumatic stress disorder specify that the reaction last for at least one month; if the length of the reaction is less than that, it would be considered a "normal" stress reaction to a clearly threatening situation.

We will look now at some general principles underlying reactions to catastrophic events. Then we will turn to some specific stressor events that can cause posttraumatic stress.

Reactions to Catastrophic Events

With few exceptions, people exposed to plane crashes, automobile accidents, explosions, fires, earthquakes, tornadoes, sexual assaults, or other terrifying experiences show psychological "shock" reactions—transient personality decompensation. The symptoms may vary greatly, depending on the nature and severity of the terrifying experience, the degree of surprise, and the personality makeup of the individual. Consider the following examples: over half of the survivors of the disastrous Coconut Grove nightclub fire—which took the lives of 492 people in Boston in 1942—required treatment for severe psychological shock (Adler, 1943). When two commuter trains collided in Chicago in 1972, leaving 44 people dead and over 300 injured, the tragedy also left scores of people with feelings of fear, anxiety, and guilt; more than 80 of them attended a voluntary "talk session" arranged by the University of Chicago's psychiatric adult outpatient clinic (Uhlenhuth, 1973). Psychological evaluations of 8 of the 64 survivors of the collision of two jet planes on Santa Cruz de Tenerife Island in 1977,

The aftermath of catastrophic events, such as the destruction of one's home by a tornado, may bring about psychological reactions including initial shock, passivity, repetitive retelling of the experience, and sometimes long-lasting or delayed symptoms of stress, such as recurrent nightmares.

in which 580 people died, indicated that all eight suffered from serious emotional problems stemming directly from the accident (Perlberg, 1979).

A **disaster syndrome** has been delineated that appears to characterize the reactions of many victims of such catastrophes (see *HIGHLIGHT 5.3*). This syndrome may be described in terms of the reactions during the traumatic experience; the initial reactions after it (the acute posttraumatic stress); and the long-lasting or late-arising complications (the chronic or delayed posttraumatic stress).

The Disaster Syndrome   A victim's initial responses following a disaster typically involve three stages: (a) the *shock stage,* in which the victim is stunned, dazed, and apathetic; (b) the *suggestible stage,* in which the victim tends to be passive, suggestible, and willing to take directions from rescue workers or others; and (c) the *recovery stage,* in which the individual may be tense and apprehensive and show generalized anxiety, but gradually regains psychological equilibrium—often showing a need to repetitively tell about the catastrophic event. It is in the third stage that posttraumatic stress disorder may develop.

These three stages are well illustrated in the *Andrea Doria* disaster, in which 52 persons died and over 1600 were rescued.

On July 25, 1956, at 11:05 P.M., the Swedish liner Stockholm smashed into the starboard side of the Italian liner Andrea Doria a few miles off Nantucket Island, . . . During the phase of initial shock the survivors acted as if they had been sedated . . . as

though nature provided a sedation mechanism which went into operation automatically. [During the phase of suggestibility] the survivors presented themselves for the most part as an amorphous mass of people tending to act passively and compliantly. They displayed psychomotor retardation, flattening of affect, somnolence, and in some instances, amnesia for data of personal identification. They were nonchalant and easily suggestible. [During the stage of recovery, after the initial shock had worn off and the survivors had received aid,] they showed . . . an apparently compulsive need to tell the story again and again, with identical detail and emphasis. (Friedman & Linn, 1957, p. 426)

In some cases, the clinical picture may be complicated by intense grief and depression. When an individual feels that his or her own personal inadequacy contributed to the loss of loved ones in a disaster, the picture may be further complicated by strong feelings of guilt, and the posttraumatic stress may last for months. This pattern is well illustrated in the following case of a husband who failed to save his wife in the jet crash at Tenerife in 1977.

Martin's story is quite tragic. He lost his beloved wife of 37 years and blames himself for her death, because he sat stunned and motionless for some 25 seconds after the [other plane] hit. He saw nothing but fire and smoke in the aisles, but he roused himself and led his wife to a jagged hole above and behind his seat. Martin climbed out onto the wing and reached down and took hold of his wife's hand, but "an explosion from within literally blew her out

Mount Saint Helens and the Disaster Syndrome

Can psychological responses to disasters result in diagnosable mental disorders, such as depression, generalized anxiety disorder, or schizophrenia? This point is debated among researchers. Dohrenwend and Egri (1981) are among those who find clear evidence of mental disorders among individuals who were "normal" prior to a stressful event. On the other side, Depue and Monroe (1986) and McFarlane (1986) have noted that psychological problems following stress tend to occur most frequently among individuals who were previously maladjusted or vulnerable to problems prior to the stress. Methodological problems and the absence of reliable predisposing personality measures on disaster victims limit research in this area; consequently, a definitive conclusion is difficult to reach. One recent field study by Shore, Tatum, and Vollmer (1986) provided some weight to the position that stress in response to a natural disaster can produce psychological disorder even in victims who were not at risk for developing disorder before the disaster. They conducted an epidemiological study of the Mount Saint Helens disaster victims in an effort to further understand the disaster syndrome—the

dazed, confused state of victims following a disaster.

In May of 1980 Mount Saint Helens violently erupted, producing volcanic flow, ash fall, and flooding that resulted in great property damage and loss of life. This catastrophic situation placed many people in the surrounding Washington state area at great risk of property loss, injury, and even death for a time following the eruption. The researchers surveyed residents whose homes had suffered significant damage as determined through tax assessor records. The families who experienced the most damage as a result of the eruption were further subdivided, after the interviews, into *high-* (N = 138) and *low-* (N = 410) exposure-to-stress categories on the basis of the amount of damage suffered or whether loss of life was involved. They also surveyed residents from a control community (N = 477) in Oregon that was similar in demographic characteristics but had not been affected by the eruption or floods. In each case one household member (between the ages of 18 and 79) was interviewed in his or her home between 38 and 42 months after the disaster. The interviews were conducted by trained personnel following the diagnostic

interview schedule based on DSM-III.

The researchers found that a significantly higher number of DSM-III diagnosable disorders occurred in individuals exposed to high levels of stress following the Mount Saint Helens eruption. Specifically, there was a greater prevalence of generalized anxiety, major depression, and posttraumatic stress disorder in the high-exposure subjects. The study also found some tendency for older females to be more vulnerable to disorder.

The results of this study do not unequivocally support the idea that disaster-related stress produces psychological disorders because the researchers had no prestress measures on the groups. Assuming that the two groups were in fact equal on psychopathology prior to the volcanic eruption, then these data do suggest that a natural disaster can produce psychological disorder among individuals who are not at risk for disorder on the basis of their prestress adjustment. Evidence did indicate that the *amount* of stress, in the form of high exposure, was associated with diagnosed clinical disorder.

of my hands and pushed me back and down onto the wing." He reached the runway, turned to go back after her, but the plane blew up seconds later. . . .

[Five months later] Martin was depressed and bored, had "wild dreams," a short temper and became easily confused and irritated. "What I saw there will terrify me forever," he says. He told [the psychologist who interviewed him] that he avoided

television and movies, because he couldn't know when a frightening scene would appear. (Perlberg, 1979, pp. 49–50)

In some instances the guilt of the survivors seems to center around the belief that they deserved to survive no more or perhaps even less than those who died. As one flight attendant explained after the crash of a Miami-bound jet in the Florida Everglades that took many lives, "I kept thinking, I'm alive. Thank God. But I wondered why I was spared. I felt, it's not fair . . ." (*Time*, Jan. 15, 1973, p. 53).

Sometimes individuals who undergo terrifying experiences exhibit symptoms of stress that may endure for weeks, months, or even years. The experience of extreme posttraumatic symptoms is not uncommon. In a recent review and comparison of all published disaster research in which estimates of postdisaster psychopathology were included, the average effect was that 17 percent of individuals showed psychological adjustment problems in the aftermath of the disaster (Rubonis & Bickman, 1991). Shore, Vollmer, and Tatum (1989) studied the prevalence rates of posttraumatic stress disorder in two northwestern communities and found a lifetime prevalence rate of posttraumatic stress reaction, according to DSM-III criteria, to be about 3 percent for both men and women.

Recurrent nightmares and the typical need to tell the same story about the disaster again and again appear to be mechanisms for reducing anxiety and desensitizing the self to the traumatic experience. Tension, apprehensiveness, and hypersensitivity appear to be residual effects of the shock reaction and to reflect the person's realization that the world can become overwhelmingly dangerous and threatening. As we have seen, feelings of guilt about having failed to protect loved ones who perished may be quite intense, especially in situations where some responsibility can be directly assigned.

The posttraumatic stress may be more complicated in cases of physical mutilation that necessitate changes in one's way of life. It may also be complicated by the psychological effects of disability compensation or damage law suits, which tend to prolong posttraumatic symptoms (Egendorf, 1986; Okura, 1975).

Causal Factors in Posttraumatic Stress

Most people function relatively well in catastrophes, and, in fact, many behave with heroism (Rachman, 1978). Whether someone develops posttraumatic stress disorder or not depends on a number of factors. Some research suggests that preexisting personality factors are more relevant at low and moderate levels of stress, and less relevant for more extreme traumatic experiences; for the latter, the nature of the traumatic stressor itself appears to account for most of the stress-response variance (for example, Ursano, Boydstun, & Wheatley, 1981). In other words, everyone has a breaking point, and at sufficiently high levels of stress the average person can be expected to develop some psychological difficulties (which may be either short-lived or long-term) following a traumatic

event. Other researchers suggest that preexisting factors may play a greater role even at high levels of stress. For example, McFarlane (1988) studied fire fighters over a period of months after an intensely traumatic experience fighting a brushfire. He concluded that though an extremely traumatic event can trigger multiple psychiatric problems, the trauma is insufficient to explain the onset of disorder. The existence of posttraumatic symptoms can only be explained by considering the individual's biological makeup; preexisting psychological problems, such as low self-esteem; emotional insecurity; interpersonal skill deficits; and the social context of recovery.

In all cases of posttraumatic stress, conditioned fear—the fear associated with the traumatic experience—appears to be a key causal factor. Thus prompt psychotherapy following a traumatic experience is considered important in preventing conditioned fear from establishing itself and becoming resistant to change.

Treatments and Outcomes

Supportive therapy and proper rest (induced by sedatives if necessary) usually can alleviate symptoms that lead to posttraumatic stress disorder. Repetitive talking about the experience and constantly reliving it in fantasies or nightmares may serve as built-in repair mechanisms to help an individual adjust to the traumatic event. As Horowitz has concluded from his own experimental findings and an early review of available literature,

A traumatic perceptual experience remains in some special form of memory storage until it is mastered. Before mastery, vivid sensory images of the experiences tend to intrude into consciousness and may evoke unpleasant emotions. Through such repetitions the images, ideas, and associated affects may be worked through progressively. Thereafter, the images lose their intensity and the tendency toward repetition of the experience loses its motive force. (1969b, p. 552)

In general, the more stable and better integrated a personality and the more favorable an individual's life situation, the more quickly he or she will recover from a severe stress reaction.

Many people who experience a disaster benefit from at least some psychological counseling, no matter how brief, to begin coping with their experiences. Brom, Kleber, and Defares (1989) conducted a controlled study of the effectiveness of brief therapy with individuals experiencing PTSD and found that treatment immediately following the traumatic event significantly reduced the PTSD

HIGHLIGHT 5.4

Counseling for Disaster Workers

In September 1978 an airliner collided with a private airplane in the vicinity of the San Diego airport, killing all 137 passengers aboard the two planes and 7 people on the ground. Unlike many other air disasters, the wreckage and remains of the victims were not scattered widely but were instead concentrated in an area smaller than a city block. The force with which the planes struck the ground left few recognizable aircraft parts or human beings.

Disaster workers called to the scene to give aid and clear away the debris were generally unprepared for the calamity they witnessed. One police officer reported that "it was like stepping suddenly into hell. . . . We were standing in a pile of human tissue mixed with tiny pieces of airplane" (Davidson, 1979a). Several hundred police officers and fire fighters worked five days in temperatures that soared over 100 degrees to clean up the area. Most of the people involved in the cleanup operation—even veterans of many years of police work—were

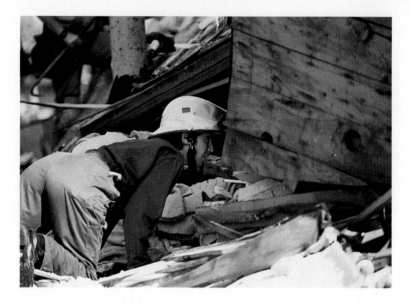

stunned by the horrible circumstances. Apparently one reason why such experienced people were so adversely affected by the situation was that "it looked very different from what people expected a plane crash to look like—they had no frame of reference for such a calamity and really lost their equilibrium" (Davidson, 1979b). Many developed psychological symptoms—depression, loss of

appetite, inability to sleep, and anxiety.

To help the disaster workers, a group of psychologists from the San Diego area offered free psychological counseling. Within a few days of the accident, over 30 police officers and fire fighters along with about 50 civilians sought counseling. Interestingly, few relatives or friends of people who perished in the crash sought

symptoms. Sixty percent of the treated individuals showed improvement while only 26 percent of the untreated group improved. They also found, however, that treatment did not benefit everyone and that some individuals maintained their PTSD symptoms even after therapy was terminated.

Treatment is often required, too, for disaster area workers, as can be seen in *HIGHLIGHT 5.4*. Many people called to the scene of a disaster to assist victims later experience posttraumatic stress disorder themselves. Bartone et al. (1989) found that workers who provide support to bereaved

families of disaster victims are at risk for increased illness, psychiatric symptoms, and negative psychological well-being for up to a year following the disaster. They also reported a dose-response effect relating disaster intensity with later psychological symptoms in assistance workers following an air disaster. (That is, the closer one is to the disaster, the more intense and disabling the reaction is.) They found that social supports, including high morale and cohesive group relationships, lessen the amount and intensity of posttraumatic symptoms among disaster workers.

help, presumably because many of the victims were not San Diego residents. Several reasons were given for why so many police officers—a group traditionally skeptical of mental health professionals and wary of being viewed by their superiors as "weird"—sought help: (a) many officers developed unexpected problems as a result of this experience; (b) these officers had no effective outlet for the feelings of anger and frustration they were experiencing; (c) their superior officers indicated that it would be appropriate for them to discuss their feelings with professional psychologists; and (d) the counseling was set up outside of the police department's influence, thus assuring anonymity.

The counseling—crisis intervention therapy (see Chapter 18)—focused on providing support and reassurance and allowing individuals to vent their pent-up or unmanageable emotions. For most of the individuals involved, this brief crisis intervention was effective in providing symptom relief. A few individuals, however, required more extensive, long-term psychotherapy. The following description is of a 42-year-old police officer who suffered a severe reaction to the stress of the San Diego air crash.

Don had been a model police officer during his 14 years on the force. He was highly evaluated by his superiors, had a master's degree in social work, and had attained the rank of sergeant. While patrolling in a squad car, he heard that there had been an accident, and he quickly drove to the scene to give aid to any survivors. When he arrived he wandered around "in a daze" looking for someone to help—but there was only destruction. He later remembered the next few days as a bad dream.

He was quite depressed for several days after the cleanup, had no appetite, couldn't sleep, and was impotent. Images and recollections of the accident would come to him "out of nowhere." He reported having a recurring dream in which he would come upon an airplane crash while driving a car or flying a plane. In his dream, he would rush to the wreckage and help some passengers to safety.

Don decided that he needed help and sought counseling. Because of his deteriorating mood and physical condition, he was placed on medical leave from the police force. Eight months after the accident he was still in therapy and had not returned to work. During therapy it became apparent that Don had been experiencing a great deal of personal dissatisfaction and anger prior to the crash. His prolonged psychological disorder was not only a result of his anguish over the air crash but also a vehicle for expressing other problems. (Davidson, 1979a)

Based on Davidson, 1979a, 1979b; O'Brien, 1979.

We will explore now several instances of posttraumatic stress disorder, examining both the immediate and long-range effects of several debilitating situations: rape, military combat, imprisonment as a POW or in a concentration camp, detainment as a hostage, and displacement from one's homeland.

■ The Trauma of Rape

The experience of rape inflicts severe trauma on a victim. *Rape* is a criminal act of violence in which sexual relations, typically intercourse, are forced on one person by another. In most cases, the victim is a woman.

Our concern here is with a victim's response to rape, which can vary depending on a number of factors. In a "stranger" rape—one in which the victim does not know the offender—the victim is likely to experience strong fear of physical harm and death. In an "acquaintance" rape the reaction is apt to be slightly different (Ellison, 1977). In such a situation the victim not only may feel fear, but also may feel that she has been betrayed by someone she had trusted. She may feel more responsible for what happened and experience greater guilt. She may also be more hesitant to seek help or report the rape to the police out of fear that she will be held partially responsible for it.

The age and life circumstances of a victim may also influence her reaction (Notman & Nadelson, 1976). For a young child who knows nothing about sexual behavior, rape can lead to sexual scars and confusion, particularly if the child is encouraged to forget about the experience without thoroughly talking it over first (Browne & Finkelhor, 1986). For young adult women, rape can increase the conflicts over independence and separation that are normal in this age group. In an effort to be helpful, parents of these victims may encourage various forms of regression, such as moving back to the family home, which may prevent mastery of this developmental phase. Married rape victims with children face the task of explaining their experience to their children. Sometimes the sense of vulnerability that results from rape leaves a woman feeling temporarily unable to care for her children.

Husbands and boyfriends can also influence rape victims' reactions by their attitudes and behavior. Rejection, blaming, uncontrolled anger at the offender, or insistence on a quick resumption of sexual activity can increase victims' negative feelings.

In a recent formulation of the stress women experience following rape, McCann (1988) found empirical evidence of problems in five areas of functioning: (a) physical disturbances, including hyperarousal; (b) emotional problems, such as anxiousness, depressed mood, and low self-esteem; (c) cognitive dysfunctioning, including disturbed concentration and the experience of intrusive thoughts; (d) atypical behavioral acts, such as aggressive, antisocial actions and substance abuse; and (e) interference in social relationships, including sexual problems, intimacy problems, and further victimization.

Coping Behavior of Rape Victims   The research on rape victims soon after their rapes has provided clear insights into the emotional turmoil and psychological processes they go through in coping with their experiences (Burgess & Holmstrom, 1974, 1976; Holmstrom & Burgess, 1975; McCombie, 1976; Meyer & Taylor, 1986; Roth & Lebowitz, 1988). The following sections summarize these findings and integrate the feelings and problems women experience at different points of their traumas.

Anticipatory phase.   This period occurs before an actual rape when an offender "sets up" a victim and the victim begins to perceive that a dangerous situation exists. In the early minutes of this phase, the victim often uses defense mechanisms such as denial to preserve an illusion of invulnerability. Common thoughts are "Rape could never happen to me" or "He doesn't really mean that."

Impact phase.   This phase begins with a victim's recognition that she is actually going to be raped and ends when the rape is over. The victim's first reaction is usually intense fear for her life, a fear much stronger than her fear of the sexual act itself. Symonds (1976) has described the paralytic effect of intense fear on victims of crime, showing that this fear usually leads to varying degrees of disintegration in the victim's functioning and possibly to complete inability to act. Roth and Lebowitz (1988) found that the sexual trauma "confronts the individual" with emotions and images that are difficult to manage and may have long-term adjustment consequences. When the victim later recalls her behavior during the assault, she may feel guilty about not reacting more efficiently, and she needs to be reassured that her actions were normal. Major physiological reactions such as vomiting sometimes occur during this phase, but victims who try to simulate such reactions in order to escape generally discover that they cannot produce them voluntarily.

Posttraumatic recoil phase.   This phase begins immediately after a rape. Burgess and Holmstrom (1974, 1976) observed two emotional styles among the rape victims they interviewed in hospital emergency rooms. Some victims exhibited an *expressed style* where feelings of fear and anxiety were shown through crying, sobbing, and restlessness. Others demonstrated a *controlled style* in which feelings appeared to be masked by a calm, controlled, subdued facade. Regardless of style, most victims felt guilty about the way they had reacted to the offender and wished that they had reacted faster or fought harder. (Excessive self-blame has been associated with poor long-term adjustment [Meyer & Taylor, 1986].) Feelings of dependency were increased, and victims often had to be encouraged and helped to call friends or parents and make other arrangements. Physical problems, such as general tension, nausea, sleeplessness, and trauma directly related to the rape, were common.

Reconstitution phase.   This phase begins as a victim starts to make plans for leaving the emergency room or crisis center. It ends, often many months later, when the stress of the rape has been assimilated, the experience shared with significant others, and the victim's self-concept restored. Certain behaviors and symptoms are typical during this phase.

1. Motor activity, such as changing one's telephone number and moving to a new residence, is common. The victim's fear is often well justified at this point because, even in the unlikely event that the offender has been arrested and charged with rape, he is often out on bail.
2. Frightening nightmares in which the rape is relived are common. As the victim moves closer toward assimilating the experience, the content of the dreams gradually shifts until the victim successfully fights off the assailant.
3. Phobias—including fear of the indoors or outdoors (depending on where the rape took place), fear of being alone, fear of crowds, fear of being followed, and sexual fears—have been observed to develop immediately following rape.

Counseling Rape Victims   The women's movement has played a crucial role in establishing specialized rape counseling services, such as rape crisis centers and hotlines. Rape crisis centers are often staffed by trained paraprofessionals who provide general support for a victim, both individually and in groups. Crisis centers also have victim advocacy services in which a trained volunteer accompanies a victim to a hospital or police station, helps her understand the procedures, and assists her with red tape. The advocate may also accompany the victim to meetings with legal representatives and to the trial—experiences that tend to temporarily reactivate the trauma of the rape.

In a study of the counseling needs of rape victims, Mezey and Taylor (1988) reported that rape victims needed to better understand the trauma situation and desired information about how they could cope with their dramatically altered lives. They also found that rape victims wanted to talk with other women who had gone through similar experiences.

Long-term Effects   Whether a rape victim will experience serious psychological decompensation depends to a large extent on her past coping skills and level of psychological functioning. A previously well-adjusted woman usually will regain her prior equilibrium, but rape can precipitate se-

vere pathology in a woman with psychological difficulties (Atkeson et al., 1982; Meyer & Taylor, 1986; Santiago et al., 1985). Keep in mind that this general finding is not true in every case—clearly the nature of the crime and the adequacy of therapy are critical factors contributing to a victim's recovery. What we are saying is that research does point to a correlation between previous psychological functioning and recovery from a rape experience.

As for long-term effects, comparisons of women who have been raped with those who have not indicate that, though victims feel that their rapes have had and continue to have impacts on them, generally no significant differences in overall psychological adjustment exist between victims and nonvictims (Oros & Koss, 1978). When problems do continue, or when they become manifest later in a delayed posttraumatic stress disorder, they are likely to involve anxiety, depression, withdrawal, and heterosexual relationship difficulties (Gold, 1986; Koss, 1983; Meyer & Taylor, 1986; Santiago et al., 1985).

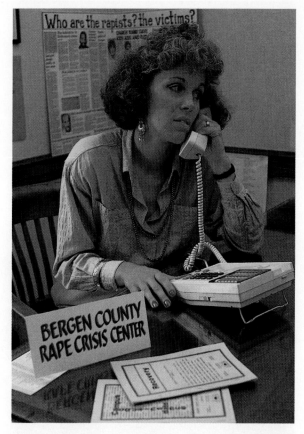

Rape crisis centers provide both psychological counseling and advocacy services with the intent of helping rape victims cope with their crisis and its aftermath. Such intervention can have a significant impact on psychological recovery from rape.

■ The Trauma of Military Combat

At any given time wars or armed conflicts are taking place in some parts of the world. Shaw (1990) recently noted that "war is a constant of history." War continues to take an incredible toll on human lives and economic resources, often leaving large numbers of victims in its wake. The consequences of war on survivors, both civilian and military, are often great. Many individuals who have been involved in war's turmoil can experience devastating psychological problems for months or even years following the conflict. Much research has accumulated on the psychological effects of war.

During World War I, traumatic reactions to combat conditions were called *shell shock*, a term coined by a British pathologist, Col. Frederick Mott (1919), who regarded these reactions as organic conditions produced by minute brain hemorrhages. It was gradually realized, however, that only a small percentage of such cases represented physical injury from the concussion of exploding shells or bombs. Most victims were suffering instead from the general combat situation, with its physical fatigue, ever-present threat of death or mutilation, and severe psychological shocks. During World War II traumatic reactions to combat passed through a number of classifications, such as *operational fatigue* and *war neuroses*, before finally being termed *combat fatigue* or *combat exhaustion* in the Korean and Vietnam wars.

Even the latter terms were none too aptly chosen, since they implied that physical exhaustion played a more important role than was usually the case. They did, however, serve to distinguish such disorders from other psychological disorders that happened to occur under war conditions but might well have occurred in civilian life—for example, among individuals showing histories of maladaptive behaviors that were aggravated by the stress of combat. Most soldiers who became psychological casualties because of combat had adjusted satisfactorily to civilian life and to prior military experiences.

It has been estimated that in World War II, 10 percent of Americans in combat developed combat exhaustion; however, the actual incidence is not known because many soldiers received supportive therapy at their battalion aid stations and were returned to combat within a few hours. Records were kept mainly on soldiers evacuated from the front lines who were considered the most seriously disturbed cases. Of the just over 10 million people accepted for military service during World War II, approximately 530,000—a little over 5 percent—were given medical discharges for neuropsychiatric reasons (including combat exhaustion, psychosis, neurosis, and other personality disorders that made them unsuitable for military life). In fact combat exhaustion caused the single greatest loss of personnel during that war (Bloch, 1969). During the Korean War the incidence of combat exhaustion dropped from an initial high of over 6

It has been estimated that in World War II, 10 percent of Americans in combat developed combat exhaustion. The stress of combat clearly took its toll on this Marine who had just finished two days of heavy fighting in the Pacific.

percent to 3.7 percent; 27 percent of medical discharges were for psychiatric reasons (Bell, 1958). In the Vietnam War the figure dropped to less than 1.5 percent for combat exhaustion, with a negligible number of discharges for psychiatric disorders (Allerton, 1970; Bourne, 1970).

Reasons advanced to explain the decrease in combat exhaustion during the Vietnam War include (a) better medical care near the front lines; (b) the sporadic nature of the fighting, in which brief intensive encounters were followed by periods of relative calm and safety—as contrasted with the weeks and months of prolonged combat that many soldiers went through in World War II and the Korean War; and (c) a policy of rotation after 12 months of service (13 months for Marines).

However, research has shown a high prevalence of posttraumatic stress disorder for Vietnam veterans. Though combat exhaustion was not as great a factor as in previous wars, combat-related stress apparently manifested itself later. Adopting research methodology developed in the study of genetic inheritance, Goldberg et al. (1990) studied identical twins who were in the military during the Vietnam War but who experienced different degrees of combat exposure. Some members of the twin pairs had served in Southeast Asia (SEA) and others had not; the latter served as the control group. Using military service records, the researchers identified 2092 pairs of male-male identical twins who agreed to cooperate in the study. These twins were surveyed to determine their exposure to stressful combat situations using an objective demographic and experience questionnaire. The researchers placed individuals into combat-exposure groups as follows: 950 twin pairs had not served in SEA; 427 twin pairs included two individuals who had served in SEA; 715 twin pairs included one twin who had served in SEA and one who had not. The presence or absence of PTSD symptoms was assessed by having each twin complete a health survey containing 12 items that dealt with their specific military experiences. The questionnaire followed the DSM-III-R PTSD symptom cluster and enabled the researchers to determine the presence of posttraumatic symptoms. The researchers based their determinations on the belief that PTSD can be diagnosed "when an individual reports a traumatic event outside the normal range of human experience and at least one symptom of reexperiencing the event, at least three symptoms of avoidance, and at least two symptoms of increased arousal." (p. 1228)

Marked differences in the prevalence of PTSD were found between the groups that had served in SEA and those that had not. The twin pair group that had not served in SEA reported low rates of PTSD symptoms (4.3 to 12.3 percent) compared with the group in which both pairs had served in SEA (14.4 to 28.2 percent). The most interesting comparison was in the discordant group in which one twin had served in SEA and the other had not. In this group the twins not serving in SEA reported low rates of PTSD (from 4.8 to 12.2 percent), similar to the group of twins that had not served in SEA. Those twins from the discordant pair who had actually served in SEA reported high rates of PTSD (from 15.8 to 30.6 percent), similar to the twin group in which both pairs had served in SEA.

A further analysis was conducted to assess the relationship between the degree of combat exposure and the later development of posttraumatic stress disorder. The researchers found a clear intensity effect in the later development of PTSD symptoms. Individuals who had experienced high levels of combat had a greater prevalence of posttraumatic stress symptoms than those who had had lower levels of combat exposure.

Clinical Picture in Combat-related Stress

The specific symptoms of combat-related stress vary considerably, depending on the type of duty, the severity and nature of the traumatic experience, and the personality of the individual.

A recent study evaluating different dimensions of posttraumatic stress disorder according to the type of war-related stress experienced was conducted by Laufer, Brett, and Gallops (1985). They surveyed 251 Vietnam veterans and, on the basis of the veterans' self-reports, grouped them according to three levels of experienced stress: (a) exposed to combat; (b) exposed to abusive violence in combat; and (c) participated in abusive violence in combat. They found that different degrees of stress symptoms were reported by individuals who had been exposed to different types of war trauma. Exposure to combat and exposure to violence were found to be associated with later experiences of posttraumatic symptoms, including intrusive imagery, hyperarousal, numbing, and cognitive disruption. Participation in abusive violence was most highly associated with more severe pathologies marked by cognitive disruptions, such as depression. The authors concluded that the clinical picture of posttraumatic stress disorder varies depending on the stressors experienced. Patients who have experienced particular types of war stress are likely to present specific types of symptoms, and not all PTSD patients present identical symptoms.

Despite variations in experience, however, the general clinical picture was surprisingly uniform for soldiers who had developed combat stress in different wars. The first symptoms had been a failure to maintain psychological integration, with increasing irritability and sensitivity, sleep disturbances, and often recurrent nightmares. The following diary covers a period of about six weeks of combat in the South Pacific during World War II and illustrates the cumulative effect of combat stresses on an apparently stable personality.

"*Aug. 7, 1942. Convoy arrived at Guadalcanal Bay at approximately 4 A.M. in the morning. Ships gave enemy a heavy shelling. At 9 A.M. we stormed the beach and formed an immediate beachhead, a very successful landing, marched all day in the hot sun, and at night took positions and rested. Enemy planes attacked convoy in bay but lost 39 out of 40 planes.*

"*Aug. 8, 1942. Continued march in the hot sun and in afternoon arrived at airport. Continued on through the Jap village and made camp for the night. During the night Jap navy attacked convoy in battle that lasted until early morning. Enemy had terrific losses and we lost two ships. This night while on sentry duty I mistook a horse for a Jap and killed it.*

"*Aug. 19, 1942. Enemy cruiser and destroyer came into bay and shelled the beach for about two hours. The cruiser left and the destroyer hung around for the entire morning. We all kept under shelter for the early afternoon a flying fortress flew over, spotting the ship and bombed it, setting it afire we all jumped and shouted with joy. That night trouble again was feared and we again slept in foxholes.*

"*Aug. 21, 1942. The long awaited landing by the enemy was made during the night 1500 troops in all and a few prisoners were taken and the rest were killed. Bodies were laying all over the beach. In afternoon planes again bombed the Island [Here the writing begins to be shaky, and less careful than previously.]*

"*Aug. 28, 1942. The company left this morning in higgins Boats to the end of the Island, landed and started through thick jungle and hills. It was hot and we had to cut our way through. In afternoon we contacted the japs. our squad was in the assault squad so we moved up the beach to take positions the enemy trapped us with machine gun and rifle fire for about two hours. The lead was really flying. Two of our men were killed, two were hit by a hand greade and my corporal received a piece of shrampnel in back, — was wounded in arm, out of the squad of eight we have five causitry. We withdrew and were taken back to the Hospital.*

"*Sept. 12, 1942. Large jap squadron again bombed Island out of 35 planes sent over our air force knocked down 24. During the raid a large bomb was dropped just sevety yards from my fox hole.*

"*Sept. 13, 1942. At one o'clock three destroyers and one cruiser shelled us contumally all night. The ships turned surch lights all up and down the beach, and stopped one my foxhole seveal time I'm feeling pritty nervese and scared, afraid I'll be a nervas reack befor long. slept in fox hole all night not much sleep. This morning at 9:00 we had another air raid, the raid consisted of mostly fighter planes. I believe we got several, this afternoon. we had another raid, and our planes went out to met them, met them someplace over Tulagi, new came in that the aircraft carries wasp sent planes out to intersept the bombers. This eving all hell broke lose. Our marines contacted enemy to south of us and keep up constant fire. . . .*

"*Sept. 14, 1942. This morning firing still going on my company is scaduted to unload ships went half ways up to dock when enemyfire start on docks, were called back to our pososeion allon beach, company called out again to go after japs, hope were lucker than we were last time [part of this illegible]. Went up into hills at 4:00 P.M. found positions, at 7.00 en 8 sea planes fombed and strifed us, 151942 were strifed biy amfibious planes and bombed the concussion of one through me of balance and down a 52 foot hil. I was shaking likd a leaf. Lost my bayanut, and ran out of wathr. I nearves and very jumpy, hop I last out until morning. I hope sevearly machine s guns ore oping up on our left flank there going over our heads.*

"*Sept. 16. this morning we going in to take up new possissons we march all morning and I am very week and nerves, we marched up a hill and ran in to the affaul place y and z company lost so many men I hardly new what I was doing then I'm going nuts.*

"*Sept. 17. don't remember much of this day.*

"*Sept. 18. Today I'm on a ship leaving this awful place, called Green Hell. I'm still nearves and shakey.*" (Stern, 1947, pp. 583–586)

In the Vietnam War, soldiers were seldom exposed to prolonged periods of shelling and bombardment; combat reactions were typically more sudden and acute as a result of some particularly overwhelming combat experience.

The recorded cases of combat-related stress among soldiers in various wars show that the common sympton usually has been overwhelming anxiety. In comparison, it is interesting to note that most wounded soldiers have shown less anxiety or physical symptoms, even minor ones (Merbaum & Hefez, 1976).

In fact it is not unusual for soldiers to admit that they have prayed to be hit or to have something "honorable" happen to them to remove them from battle. When approaching full recovery and the necessity of returning to combat, injured soldiers sometimes show prolonged symptoms or delayed traumatic reactions of nervousness, insomnia, and other symptoms that were nonexistent when they were first hospitalized.

Causal Factors in Combat Stress Problems

In a combat situation, with the continual threat of injury or death and repeated narrow escapes, a person's ordinary coping methods are relatively useless. The adequacy and security the individual has known in the relatively safe and dependable civilian world are completely undermined. However, we must not overlook the fact that most soldiers subjected to combat have not become psychiatric casualties, although most of them have evidenced severe fear reactions and other symptoms of personality disorganization that were not serious enough to be incapacitating. In addition, many soldiers have tolerated almost unbelievable stress before they have broken, while others have become casualties under conditions of relatively slight combat stress or even as noncombatants—for example, during basic training.

In order to understand traumatic reactions to combat, we need to look at factors such as constitutional predisposition, personal maturity, loyalty to one's unit, and confidence in one's officers—as well as at the actual stress experienced.

Biological factors.   Do constitutional differences in sensitivity, vigor, and temperament affect a soldier's resistance to combat stress? They probably do, but little actual evidence supports this assumption. We have more information about the conditions of battle that tax a soldier's emotional and physical stamina. Add other factors that often occur in combat situations—such as severe climatic conditions, malnutrition, and disease—to the strain of continual emotional mobilization, and the result is a general lowering of an individual's physical and psychological resistance to all stressors.

Psychosocial factors.   A number of psychological and interpersonal factors may contribute to the overall stress experienced by soldiers and predispose them to break down under combat. Such factors include reductions in personal freedom, frustrations of all sorts, and separation from home and

Many factors may contribute to traumatic reactions to combat —constitutional predisposition, personal immaturity, compromised loyalty to one's unit, diminished confidence in one's officers, as well as the actual stress experienced. Thus, although combat situations completely undermine a person's ordinary coping methods, some soldiers can tolerate great stress without becoming psychiatric casualties, while others may break down under only slight combat stress.

fewer combat exhaustion symptoms—except in cases of permanent mutilation. Apparently a wound, in providing an escape from a stressful combat situation, removes the source of anxiety. A similar finding was reported among Israeli soldiers hospitalized during the Yom Kippur War. (The Yom Kippur War began on October 6, 1973, the Jewish Holy Day of Atonement [Yom Kippur], when Egyptian and Syrian forces attacked Israel in an effort to regain control of the Sinai Peninsula and the Golan Heights. A cease-fire was agreed to on October 23, and on November 11, a peace agreement calling for talks to resolve differences was signed.) Those soldiers hospitalized for physical injuries—even severe ones such as paralysis or loss of limb—showed no appreciable psychological disturbances. In contrast, those hospitalized because of psychiatric problems —such as severe depression, thought disorders, and obsessiveness—were quite disturbed about their loved ones. Central, of course, are the many stresses arising from combat, including constant fear, unpredictable circumstances, the necessity of killing, and prolonged harsh conditions.

An individual's personality is an important determinant of adjustment to military experiences. Personality characteristics that lower an individual's resistance to stress or to particular stressors may be important in determining his or her reactions to combat. Personal immaturity—sometimes stemming from parental overprotection—is commonly cited as making a soldier more vulnerable to combat stress. Worthington (1978) found that American soldiers who experienced problems readjusting after they returned home from the Vietnam War also tended to have had greater difficulties before and during their military service than soldiers who adjusted readily.

In their study of the personality characteristics of Israeli soldiers who had broken down in combat during the Yom Kippur War, Merbaum and Hefez (1976) found that over 25 percent reported having had psychological treatment prior to the war. Another 12 percent had experienced difficulties previously in the six-day Israeli-Arab war of 1967. Thus about 37 percent of these soldiers had clear histories of some personality instability that may have predisposed them to break down under combat stress. On the other hand, the other soldiers who broke down —over 60 percent—had not shown earlier difficulties and would not have been considered to be at risk for such breakdown.

A background of personal maladjustment does not always make an individual a poor risk for withstanding combat stress. Some individuals are so accustomed to anxiety that they cope with it more or less automatically, whereas soldiers who are feeling severe anxiety for the first time may be terrified by the experience, lose their self-confidence, and go to pieces. It has also been observed that sociopaths (antisocial personalities, according to DSM-III-R), though frequently in trouble during peacetime service for disregarding rules and regulations, have often demonstrated good initiative and effective combat aggression against the enemy. However, the soldiers who function most effectively and are most apt to survive combat usually come from backgrounds that fostered self-reliance, the ability to function in a group, and ready adjustment to new situations (Bloch, 1969; Borus, 1974; Grinker, 1969; Lifton, 1972).

Sociocultural factors.   Several sociocultural factors play an important part in determining an individual's adjustment to combat. These general factors include clarity and acceptability of war goals, identification with the combat unit, esprit de corps, and quality of leadership.

An important consideration is how clear and acceptable the war's goals are to an individual. In general, war goals have a supportive effect on a soldier if they can be concretely integrated into the soldier's values in terms of his or her "stake" in the war and the worth and importance of what he or she is doing. Another important factor is a person's identification with the combat unit. The soldier who is unable to identify with or take pride in his or her group lacks the feeling of "we-ness" that helps maintain stress tolerance. Lacking this identity, a soldier stands alone, psychologically isolated and less able to withstand combat stress. In fact the stronger the sense of group identification, the less chance that a soldier will break down in combat. Feelings of esprit de corps influence an individual's morale and adjustment to extreme circumstances. Finally, the quality of leadership and confidence in one's unit are of vital importance in a soldier's adjustment to combat. If a soldier respects his or her leaders, has confidence in their judgment and ability, and can accept them as relatively strong parental or sibling figures, the soldier's morale and resistance to stress are bolstered. On the other hand, lack of confidence or dislike of leaders is detrimental to morale and to combat stress tolerance.

It also appears that returning to an unaccepting social environment can increase a soldier's vulnerability to posttraumatic stress. For example, in a one-year follow-up of Israeli men who had been psychiatric war casualties during the Yom Kippur War, Merbaum (1977) found that they not only continued to show extreme anxiety, depression, and extensive physical complaints, but in many instances they appeared to have become more disturbed over time. Merbaum hypothesized that their psychological deterioration had probably been due to the unaccepting attitudes of the community; in a country so reliant on the strength of its army for survival, considerable stigma is attached to psychological breakdown in combat. Because of the stigma, many of the men were experiencing not only isolation within their communities, but also self-recrimination about what they perceived as failure on their own parts. These feelings exacerbated the soldiers' already stressful situations.

Long-term Effects of Posttraumatic Stress
In some cases, soldiers who have experienced combat exhaustion may show symptoms of posttraumatic stress for sustained periods of time, as is graphically detailed in *HIGHLIGHT 5.5.* In cases of delayed

Residual Effects of Posttraumatic Stress Among Outpatients at a VA Clinic

Twenty years after the end of World War II, Archibald and Tuddenham (1965) conducted a follow-up study of the residual effects of posttraumatic stress in 62 combat exhaustion cases. The following chart compares the incidence of several symptoms in this group and in 20 veterans who had not suffered combat exhaustion during the war. In addition to the symptoms listed here, the more severe combat exhaustion cases revealed various other symptoms, including difficulties in work and family relationships, social isolation, and narrowing of interests. Alcoholism was a problem for about 20 percent of both groups.

In many cases symptoms had appeared to clear up when the stress was over, only to reappear in chronic form later. It seems evident that intense and sustained stress can lead to lasting symptoms even if the victims receive follow-up care. Although the combat exhaustion veterans were receiving assistance at a Veterans Administration outpatient psychiatric clinic, they were not receiving additional disability compensation as a result of their prolonged stress reactions.

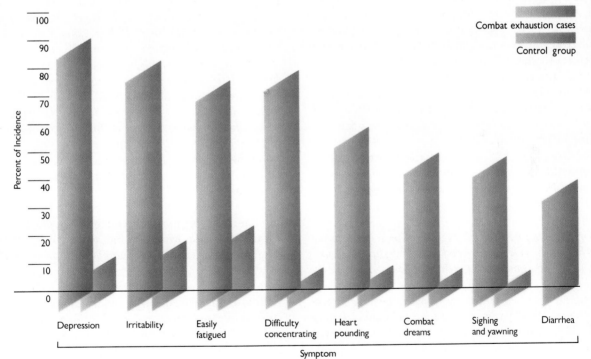

Chart adapted from Archibald and Tuddenham (1965), omitting statistics for noncombat psychiatric military cases.

In March 1986, Michael Dean, a Vietnam veteran, and the woman he lived with, Caroline Hull, fed sleeping pills to her three children. Hull then took sleeping pills herself. When Hull and her children were unconscious, Dean shot each of them in the heart and set the house on fire. He then shot himself. Letters from Dean and Hull described the deaths as an act of protest for the forgotten veterans of the Vietnam War and their families. Dean, who had been depressed and moody after his return from the war, was considered by many doctors to be a clear example of posttraumatic stress syndrome.

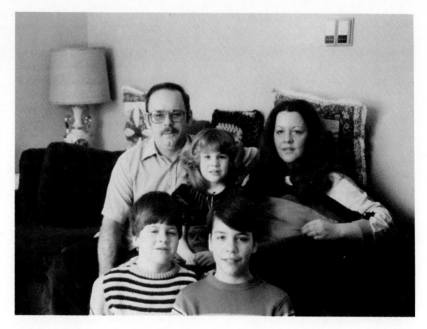

posttraumatic stress, some soldiers who have stood up exceptionally well under intensive combat situations have experienced posttraumatic stress only upon their returns home, often in response to relatively minor stresses that they had handled easily before. Evidently, these soldiers have suffered long-term damage to their adaptive capabilities, in some cases complicated by memories of killing enemy soldiers or civilians that are tinged with feelings of guilt and anxiety (Haley, 1978; Horowitz & Solomon, 1978; Polner, 1968).

Shatan (1978) illustrated the effects of posttraumatic stress disorder on Vietnam veterans with the story of Dwight Johnson, who had won the Medal of Honor in Vietnam:

Jon Nordheimer's front-page New York Times story [1971] sensitively described Sgt. Dwight Johnson's apathy and alienation, his demoralization by unemployment, and his suspicion that he was being exploited by the army, even when he was in the hospital. His government's highest martial honor weighed heavily around his neck each time he was praised for slaughter—and thereby forced to recall that he was the sole survivor of his tank crew, buddies during eleven months of warfare. While the army used him in recruiting drives, empty promise piled upon empty promise and his cynicism grew.

Johnson had been placed in restraints and narcotized for 24 hours immediately after his final day of combat—the action for which he received the supreme distinction. Yet, 48 hours later, he was back in the U.S. with a non-psychiatric discharge. His emotional difficulties received no official interest

until he became a "hot property." His treatment began more than a year after his return home, at the Valley Forge Army Hospital. There he was diagnosed as suffering from "depression caused by post-Vietnam adjustment problems."

On several occasions, he asked his psychiatrist how society would react if he were to respond to the black dilemma in Detroit with the same uncontrolled ferocity that had earned him the highest recognition in battle. He found his ultimate answer, not in a distant jungle but on the floor of a hometown grocery. There he lived out his haunting fantasies and nightmares of being killed at point blank range. (pp. 46–47)

Similarly, the long-term effects of posttraumatic stress were shown in a follow-up study of 92 combat veterans of the Vietnam War. Polner (1968) cited a number of cases in which combat experiences continued to disturb the veterans after their returns to civilian life. In most instances the difficulties appeared to center around guilt feelings over killing. For example, one veteran said, "I can't sleep, I'm a murderer." He continued,

"We were outside Bac Lieu, out on an eight-man patrol along with 15 ARVNs [South Vietnamese soldiers]. Our orders were to move ahead and shoot at anything suspicious. My God, how I remember that damned day! It was hot and sticky. The mosquitoes were driving me crazy. And there was this boy, about 8 or 9. He had his hand behind his back, like he was hiding something. 'Grab him,' someone screamed, 'he's got something!' I made a move for

him and his hand moved again. 'Shoot!' I fired. Again and again, until my M-2 was empty. When I looked he was there, all over the ground, cut in two with his guts all around. I vomited. I wasn't told, I wasn't trained for that. It was out-and-out murder. . . .

"You know I killed nine people as an adviser." (p. 12)

Many of the other veterans interviewed by Polner, however, felt that they had simply done their duty in a worthwhile cause.

In another study of Vietnam returnees, Strange and Brown (1970) compared combat and noncombat veterans who were experiencing emotional difficulties. The combat group showed a higher incidence of depression and of difficulties in their close interpersonal relationships. They also showed a higher incidence of aggressive and suicidal threats but did not actually carry them out. In a later study of Vietnam veterans who were making a satisfactory readjustment to civilian life, DeFazio, Rustin, and Diamond (1975) found that the combat veterans *still* reported certain symptoms twice as often as the noncombat veterans. Based on a questionnaire obtained from 207 veterans who had been out of the armed forces for over five years, DeFazio et al. found the following percentages of combat veterans still reporting symptoms: (a) frequent nightmares—68 percent; (b) quick temper—44 percent; (c) many fears—35 percent; (d) worries about employment—35 percent; (e) difficulties with emotional closeness—35 percent; (f) quick fatigue—32 percent. In a more recent study, Solomon (1989) found that combat veterans reported more stress symptoms over a three-year period than did a control group. The symptoms of combat stress, however, diminished over time.

In some cases a significant incident may precipitate a chronic reaction. A case reported by Christenson et al. (1981) shows how a later event may trigger past traumas and result in serious adjustment problems.

Mr. A, a 55-year-old divorced man, was admitted with severe anxiety, multiple somatic complaints, feelings of hopelessness, somatovegetative signs of depression, and suicidal ideations. He had required psychiatric hospitalization for "nerves" shortly after his discharge from the service at the end of World War II. He subsequently had a good adjustment and a stable marriage and work history. Three years before this admission, Mr. A abruptly left his job as an emergency room technician and began drinking heavily. Eventually his wife left him, and the actual signing of divorce papers precipitated the symptoms that led to his admission.

It was only after another patient on the ward began talking of his difficulties during World War II that Mr. A revealed the following history. He had been stationed in the South Pacific and had survived two battles in which his ship had been destroyed and many people around him violently killed. Shortly after these events, his unit was instructed that island children were being wired as human bombs, and an order was issued to shoot all children approaching the camp. When Mr. A was on duty, he had been forced to shoot a 10-year-old boy. After this incident, Mr. A began having nightmares of exploding shells, violent scenes of people being killed, and scenes of himself killing the boy. These cleared over a period of a few years.

Mr. A's recent deterioration (3 years ago) came after an episode at work in the emergency room where he was told to clean up a child in one of the rooms. He was unaware that the child (a 9-year-old boy) was already dead when he was brought to the emergency room. When Mr. A discovered that the boy was dead, he was horrified, left work, and never returned. His nightmares resumed, but he felt unable to discuss these war episodes with his wife. At times, he would wake up screaming and throw his wife to the floor to "cover" her from exploding shells. It was this unexplained behavior that forced their separation.

During this hospital stay, Mr. A was able to talk about these war episodes for the first time in 35 years. He actively participated in a small therapy group of World War II veterans that focused on the veterans ventilating their feelings about traumatic war experiences. Mr. A was also treated with 150 mg h.s. of doxepin [an antidepressant administered at bedtime].

Gradually, Mr. A's depression cleared, and he claimed he was less anxious than at any time since the war. He was sleeping through the night without nightmares. Mr. A made appropriate arrangements to resume his most recent job and had an optimistic view of the future. He identified the opportunity to openly discuss his war experiences as the most important factor in his recovery. (p. 984)

The nature and extent of this delayed posttraumatic stress disorder are somewhat controversial (Burstein, 1985). Reported cases of delayed stress syndrome among Vietnam combat veterans are often difficult to relate explicitly to combat stress because these individuals may also have other significant adjustment problems. Individuals experiencing adjustment difficulties may erroneously attribute their present problems to specific incidents from their past, such as experiences in combat. The wide publicity recently given to delayed posttraumatic stress disorder has made it easy for clinicians to "find" a precipitating cause in their patients' backgrounds; indeed, the frequency with which this disorder has recently been diagnosed in some settings suggests that its increased use is as much a result of its plausibility and popularity as of its true incidence.

■ The Trauma of Being a Prisoner of War or in a Concentration Camp

Although some individuals adjust to the stress of being a prisoner of war or in a concentration camp (especially if part of a supportive group), the past shows us that the toll on most prisoners is great. About half of the American prisoners in Japanese POW camps during World War II died during their imprisonment; an even higher number of prisoners of Nazi concentration camps died. Those who survived the ordeal often sustained residual organ-

ic and psychological damage along with a lowered tolerance to stress of any kind.

Without question, reentry to society is difficult for former POWs and concentration camp survivors. They must adjust to the sudden and major changes in their lives and to the social changes that took place during their imprisonments.

The residual damage to survivors of Nazi concentration camps was often extensive and commonly included anxiety, insomnia, headaches, irritability, depression, nightmares, impaired sexual potency, and "functional" diarrhea (which occurs in any situation of stress, even relatively mild stress). Such symptoms were attributed not only to the psychological stressors but also to biological stressors, such as head injuries, prolonged malnutrition, and serious infectious diseases (Eitinger, 1964, 1969, 1973; Sigal et al., 1973; Warnes, 1973).

Among returning POWs, psychological problems were often masked by the feelings of relief and jubilation that accompanied release from confinement. Even when there was little evidence of residual physical pathology, however, survivors of prisoner-of-war camps commonly showed impaired resistance to physical illness, low frustration tolerance, frequent dependence on alcohol and drugs, irritability, and other indications of emotional instability (Chambers, 1952; Goldsmith & Cretekos, 1969; Hunter, 1978; Strange & Brown,

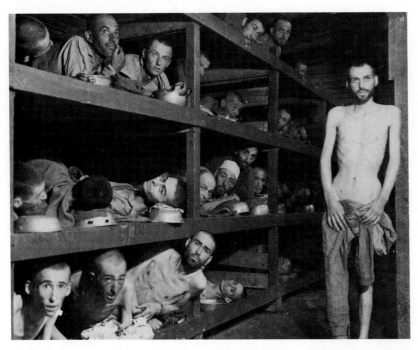

The physical and psychological stresses of life in Nazi concentration camps left permanent scars on many of those who survived the ordeal. When samples of concentration camp survivors who did not undergo psychotherapy have been studied, however, they have been shown to be resilient and well-functioning over time. Elie Wiesel, pictured here on the second tier of prisoners (the second man behind the man with the bandaged head), was liberated from Buchenwald and went on to win the Nobel Peace Prize in 1986.

HIGHLIGHT 5.6

Failure to Readjust After Captivity: A Case of Diathesis or Stress?

When the POWs held in North Vietnam were finally released in 1973, most Americans felt relieved that the Vietnam War was at last over. The prisoners who returned—some after many years of captivity—were welcomed back into society. A few of the returning prisoners, however, found the United States to be as hostile an environment as a North Vietnamese POW camp.

One such soldier, Jerry L., returned to the United States to find himself facing a possible court-martial on charges of collaboration with the enemy. His alleged behavior during captivity had received adverse publicity, and Jerry's friends and relatives reacted by treating him with coldness and suspicion. Shortly after his return, Jerry died of self-inflicted gunshot wounds.

Two psychologists were asked by the district attorney's office to construct a "psychological autopsy" to clear up the circumstances

surrounding the unexpected death. In conducting their investigation, Selkin and Loya (1979) encountered resistance from Jerry's family and from the military. Jerry's wife and other family members believed that the government had mistreated Jerry and that his death was related to the military's lack of support and medical attention, plus the extreme anxiety caused by the collaboration charges. As a result the family was at first reluctant to provide information about Jerry's early life, though they later became more cooperative. Meanwhile, military officials initially refused to release Jerry's records—though they, too, finally decided to cooperate.

Selkin and Loya discovered that Jerry had been following what appeared to be a "suicidal life course that had begun long before the war in Vietnam" (p. 89). For years Jerry had tended to drink heavily when under stress

and had a history of delinquency and other maladjustments. Despite this history the military had provided Jerry with little psychiatric attention after his release from the POW camp. Although he spoke briefly with a "partially trained" psychiatrist, he was not offered psychological help or a psychiatric follow-up after he returned home. It was apparent that "no one in any official capacity made an honest attempt to understand him or take a careful look at his life situation" (p. 90).

This investigation indicates both the relationship of prior psychological problems to adjustment after captivity and the importance of the environment to the successful repatriation of prisoners of war. A few days after the psychological autopsy was completed, the government dropped all charges against other POWs who had been accused of collaborating with the enemy.

1970; Wilbur, 1973). In a retrospective study of psychological maladjustment symptoms following repatriation, Speed et al. (1989) interviewed a large sample of former POWs and found that half of them reported symptoms that met DSM-III criteria for PTSD in the year following their releases from captivity.

Another measure of the toll taken by the prolonged stress of being in a POW or concentration camp is the higher death rate after return to civilian life. Among returning World War II POWs from the Pacific area, Wolff (1960) found that within the first six years, nine times as many died from tuberculosis as would have been expected in civilian life, four times as many from gastrointestinal disorders, over twice as many from cancer, heart disease, and suicide, and three times as many from

accidents. Eitinger (1973) has reported comparable figures for concentration camp survivors. The case of one Vietnam POW is examined in HIGH-LIGHT 5.6.

Aware that problems may show up years after release, military psychologists and psychiatrists have been following representative groups of Vietnam War POWs on a long-term basis with yearly checkups. These former POWs differ from those in earlier wars in that they were almost all flight crew personnel, which meant that they were officers and somewhat older than the rank-and-file combat personnel. In the examination made two years after their return, it was found that the longer the imprisonment, the more likely a person was to develop psychiatric problems (O'Connell, 1976). Other factors that seemed to predispose individuals to later problems were harsh POW treatment and isolation while captured (Hunter, 1976). The most frequent problems requiring psychological help were depression and marital difficulties (Hunter, 1978, 1981).

A great deal has been written about the long-term adjustment problems of concentration camp survivors. Some writers, for example Krystal (1968) and Niederland (1968) (who based their views on the survivors of death camps who later sought psychological treatment), have contended that concentration camp survivors carry psychological scars with them for the rest of their lives. Other writers have concluded that these emotional scars are so profound that they can be transmitted to the survivors' children (Epstein, 1979; Schneider, 1978). We must bear in mind, however, that most of the conclusions about the psychopathologies of concentration camp survivors and their children are based on people who are undergoing or have undergone psychotherapy. The observations that long-term adjustment problems persist, as noted by some writers, may be valid for particular individuals and may support the idea that some people do not deal effectively with life after experiencing severe life stress. These clinical studies, however, cannot be viewed as representative. The biased nature of their samples (psychotherapy patients) precludes generalizations about concentration camp survivors as a whole. In fact, when community (nonpsychiatric) samples of concentration camp survivors are studied they have been shown to be remarkably resilient and well functioning over time (Kahana, Harel, and Kahana, 1988; Leon et al., 1981).

■ The Trauma of Being Held Hostage

Hostage-taking seems to increase each year. Not only are politically driven hostage-taking situations becoming more frequent, but kidnappings in the United States for economic or other motives also seem on the rise. Clearly such situations can produce disabling psychological symptoms in victims (Danto, 1990). The following case reported by Sonnenberg (1988) describes a man who experienced a horrifying ordeal that left him with intense symptoms of anxiety and distress for months following the incident.

Mr. A. was a married accountant, the father of two, in his early thirties. One night, while out performing an errand, he was attacked by a group of youths. These youngsters made

him get into their car, and took him to a deserted country road.

There they pulled him from the car and began beating and kicking him. They took his wallet, began taunting him about its contents (they had learned his name, his occupation, and the names of his wife and children), and threatened to go to his home and harm these family members. Finally, after brutalizing him for several hours, they tied him to a tree, one youth held a gun to his head, and after he begged and pleaded for his life, the armed individual pulled the trigger. The gun was empty, but at the moment the trigger was pulled this victim defecated and urinated in his pants. Then the youths untied him and left him on the road.

This man slowly made his way to a gas station he had seen during his abduction, and called the police. I was called to examine him, and did so at intervals for the next 2 years. The diagnosis was PTSD. He had clearly experienced an event outside the range of normal human experience, and was at first re-experiencing the event in various ways: intrusive recollections, nightmares, flashbacks, and extreme fear upon seeing groups of unsavory looking youths. He was initially remarkably numb in other respects: he withdrew from the members of his family and lost interest in his job. He felt generally estranged and detached. He expected to die in the near future. There were also symptoms of increased psychophysiologic arousal: poor sleeping, difficulty concentrating, exaggerated startle response, and when we first spoke about his abduction in detail, he actually soiled himself at the moment he described doing so during the original traumatic experience.

This man received treatment during the next 2 years from another psychiatrist, consisting of twice-weekly intensive individual psychotherapy sessions and the concurrent administration of a tricyclic antidepressant. The individual psychotherapy consisted of discussions that focused on the sense of shame and guilt this man felt over his behavior during his abduction. He wished he had been more stoic and had not pleaded for his life. With the understanding help of his psychotherapist, he came to see that he could accept responsibility for his behavior during his captivity, that his murderous rage at his abductors was understandable, as was his desire for revenge and that his response to his experience was not remarkable compared with what others might have done and

Being held hostage, like this blind-folded American in Iran, and subjected to both physical and mental abuse is an experience that seems to be on the rise. Victims of other traumatic situations outside the range of normal human experience may exhibit disabling psychological symptoms months and years after the ordeal is over.

felt. Eventually he began to discuss his experience with his wife and friends, and by the end of the 2 years over which I followed him, he was essentially without symptoms, although he still became somewhat anxious when he saw groups of tough-looking youths. Most importantly, his relationship with his wife and children was warm and close, and he was again interested in his work. (p. 585)

The Trauma of Forced Relocation

Being uprooted from home is a threatening event that violates a person's sense of security. In recent years at Love Canal in New York, at Times Beach in Missouri, at Bhopal in India, and at Chernobyl in the USSR, families found their homes and themselves exposed to deadly toxins that had contaminated the environment. The danger forced these families to relocate. It is not surprising that, in such circumstances, the accompanying stress can be severe.

Imagine, then, the trauma of refugees who are forced not only to leave their homes but also their homelands and to face the stress of adapting to a new and unfamiliar culture. For those who come to the United States, the "land of opportunity" may seem a nightmare rather than a haven. Such was the case for Pham, a 34-year-old Vietnamese refugee

who killed his sons and himself. Because Pham had no past history of mental disorder and seemed to function reasonably well, it is likely that he was experiencing symptoms of poor adaptation to his new environment.

Pham's ordeal began with a comfortable life in a wealthy Vietnamese family and a good job as a Saigon pharmacist. It ended after six months in the United States in a small two-bedroom apartment in Washington, D.C. The county police called it a murder-suicide.

Police believe that the refugee, a lab technician in a local community college's work-study program, administered the poison to his own family and then took his own life. Only Pham's wife survived the administration of the poison.

Two seven-page suicide notes, one in Vietnamese and one in English, began, "To whom it may concern. We committed suicide by cyanide. The reason is that I lost my mind I cannot live here like a normal person. . . . "

Pham, according to relatives, had been depressed over what he considered his financial and social failures in America. He was despondent over having to study five years to become a pharmacist here and about his difficulties communicating in English.

Pham was a dutiful son who had never been away from home before leaving for Thailand. He was homesick for his native country and for the parents who remained behind.

"He had a lot of expectations about America," said one relative, "he just could not cope." (Adapted from the Washington Star, December 8, 1980)

Pham's suffering is not unique. It is estimated that more than 16 million refugees exist in today's world, mostly from third-world or developing countries, with only about 11 percent of them relocating in developed nations like the United States and Canada (Brandel, 1980). Most refugees move between third-world countries; for example, more than 1.5 million Kurdish refugees from Iraq have either fled to Iran or live near the Iraq-Turkey border in makeshift living quarters.

In the United States, recent refugees have come from many countries—Poland, the Soviet Union, Iran, Cuba, Haiti, Laos, Vietnam, and Cambodia. The largest group of refugees currently entering the United States is from the Soviet Union—over 40,000 immigrants a year (U.S. Committee for Refugees, 1990). The Southeast Asians who began arriving in America after 1975 perhaps had the most difficult adjustment. Although many of these individuals were functioning well in their homeland and, in time, became successful and happy American citizens, others have had difficulty adjusting (Westermeyer, Williams, & Nguyen, 1991). For example, in a 10-year longitudinal study of Hmong

refugees from Laos, Westermeyer, Neider, and Callies (1989) found that many refugees had made considerable progress in their acculturation. Many had improved economically—about 55 percent were employed with incomes approaching those of the general population. The percentage of people initially living on welfare had dropped from 53 percent to 29 percent after ten years. As a group, psychological adjustment had also improved, with symptoms of phobia, somatization, and low self-esteem showing the most positive changes. Considerable problems remain, however. Many refugees still have not learned the language, some seemingly have settled permanently onto the welfare rolls, and some show symptoms—such as anxiety, hostility, and paranoia—that have changed little over the period studied. Although many refugees have adapted to their new culture, many are still experiencing considerable adjustment problems even after ten years in the United States.

PREVENTION OF STRESS DISORDERS

If we know that extreme or prolonged stress can produce maladaptive psychological reactions that have predictable courses, is it possible to intervene early in the process to prevent the development of emotional disorder? When an unusually stressful situation is about to occur, is it possible to "inoculate" an individual by providing information about

Being forced out of one's home is a threatening event that violates one's sense of security. The physical suffering of the Kurdish refugees from Iraq, recently forced to flee to Iran or to the mountains near the Iraqi-Turkish border because of Saddam Hussein's brutality, has been well-documented, but the psychological trauma can only be imagined.

likely stressors ahead of time and suggesting ways of coping with them? If preparation for battle stressors can help soldiers avoid breakdowns, why not prepare other people to effectively meet anticipated stressors?

One researcher, Janis, did just this with patients about to undergo dangerous surgery. His findings provide a substantial base for preventive efforts aimed at reducing the emotional problems of patients following their surgery (Janis, 1958; Janis et al., 1969).

Janis (1958) conducted interviews before and after surgery to determine the relationship between preoperative fear and adjustment after surgery. He found that patients with moderate fear did better than those with either extreme or little fear. Those who greatly worried about suffering pain or being mutilated by the surgery exhibited, after surgery, extreme anxiety, emotional outbursts, and fearfulness about participating in postoperative treatment. Those who showed very little anticipatory fear displayed afterward an acute preoccupation with their vulnerability and were often angry and resentful toward the staff for being "mistreated." Those patients who were moderately fearful before surgery were the most cheerful and cooperative during the postoperative treatment.

An important finding in Janis's work is that individuals who are outwardly calm and appear to feel invulnerable to real danger are likely to have more postcrisis problems than individuals who have been "part-time worriers" beforehand. Janis suggested that the "work of worrying" may involve processes similar to the "work of mourning" following bereavement. In this case, however, it is accomplished before a trauma, helping an individual understand and work through the dangerous and aversive situation and be emotionally ready to adjust to it when it comes. Later studies, too, have shown that when patients are prepared for surgery by being given accurate information about the procedures and a warning about the pain they will experience, they are less likely to have severe emotional reactions following surgery (Egbert et al., 1964).

Work in cognitive-behavioral therapy has focused on **stress inoculation training** to prepare individuals for difficult events (Beech, Burns, & Sheffield, 1982; MacDonald & Kuiper, 1983; Meichenbaum & Cameron, 1983). This training prepares individuals to tolerate an anticipated threat by changing the things they say to themselves before the crisis.

A three-stage process is employed. The first stage provides information about the stressful situation and about ways people can deal with such dangers. In the second stage, self-statements that promote effective adaptation—for example, "Don't worry, this little pain is just part of the treatment"—are rehearsed. In the third stage, the individual practices making such self-statements while being exposed to a variety of ego-threatening or pain-threatening stressors, such as unpredictable electric shocks, stress-inducing films, or sudden cold. This last phase allows the person to apply the new coping skills learned earlier. We shall discuss stress-inoculation training and the use of self-statements in greater detail in Chapter 19.

UNRESOLVED ISSUES

on the Politics of Posttraumatic Stress Disorder

This chapter has addressed the role of stress in producing psychological disorders. A considerable amount of research has substantiated the link between severe stress or trauma and subsequent psychological problems. Individuals may react to stressful situations in ways that are quite disabling. Many symptoms of posttraumatic stress disorder can interfere with psychological functioning, at least for a time, and can require considerable adaptive effort to

In recent years, for better or for worse, psychological disability as a result of posttraumatic stress disorder has become a popular avenue of defense in both civil and criminal cases. Although this defense has been legitimately employed in many cases, it has also been misused by generously "broadening" the concept of posttraumatic stress disorder.

Posttraumatic stress is frequently used as a defense in court cases to justify criminal acts. A recent case illustrates the sometimes loose connection between PTSD and deviant behavior.

In January 1987 an employee of an air cargo company, who had been fired from his job the day before, returned to the office dressed in army fatigues and carrying a sawed-off shotgun. He chased several employees away from the office and took his former supervisor hostage. He held his supervisor at gunpoint for about 1½ hours, making him beg for his life. During this time he fired about 21 shots at desks, computers, and windows, destroying a great deal of property. Once the hostage-taking situation ended, the former employee was arrested on charges of property destruction and assault with a deadly weapon. He reportedly claimed that he was extremely distraught and was suffering a post-traumatic stress disorder. He explained that he had just viewed the movie Platoon, which brought back horrible memories of Vietnam and had resulted in his becoming enraged. However, a check of his background and military records showed that he had never been in Vietnam and had actually spent his service time in a low stress, noncombat environment.

The posttraumatic syndrome is also being increasingly used in civil court cases, such as those involving compensation and personal injury. For example, in one case (*Albertson's Inc.* v. *Workers' Compensation Appeals Board of the State of California,* 1982), a bakery employee was awarded damages because her boss's comments to her caused her great embarrassment. The court concluded that job harassment was a sufficient cause of psychological damage and stress, and it was thus compensable. In another case a police officer filed a compensation claim because his job had created a great deal of stress for him. The police officer was not awarded a stress-related disability; the court ruled that when a person accepts a job as a police officer, he or she accepts the stress that accompanies it. The court did, however, award compensation payments for his physical disability (ulcers) as a result of the stressful job (*Egeland* v. *City of Minneapolis,* 1984).

Establishing legal justification for the "stress defense" is an interesting exercise, often involving considerable imagination if not out-and-out myth-making. Whether a stressor is causally linked to a specific psychological disorder—thereby warranting compensation in disability cases or commanding leniency in criminal trials—is often difficult to substantiate and usually involves expert witness testimony by psychiatrists or psychologists. In most situations both sides in a case rely on expert testimony to support their side. However, the most important factor, from the standpoint of legal precedent, is that there must be sufficient evidence that the alleged stressor was clearly related to the behavior in question.

When circumstances clearly involve a significant psychological stressor, the opposing side may attempt to lessen the perception of its responsibility for stress effects in order to reduce liability in the

case. The most dramatic example of this tactic involves the litigation following the 1985 Delta Airlines crash in Dallas, which resulted from the pilot's inability to control the aircraft because of wind shear. In an apparent effort to limit the liability of claims against the airline, the legal staff employed by the airline's insurer conducted private investigations on many of the victims and survivors to show that their problems actually preceded the crash. For example, in the case of one passenger who was killed, the insurer's attorneys argued that the man and his wife had been having marital problems and that the baby born to his wife four days after the crash was not actually his. The lawyers concluded that, because the man's marriage was on the rocks, they shouldn't have to pay much for his death. In another trial the attorneys argued that another passenger who was killed in the crash was a homosexual who probably would have died of AIDS anyway—thus limiting their liability ("60 Minutes," Feb. 15, 1987). These tactics are certainly questionable, but we must keep in mind that our legal system requires a lawyer to do everything legally possible to defend his or her client. In the Delta Airlines cases, the lawyers' tactics may be more indicative of the fact that definitively proving the existence of posttraumatic stress disorder remains exceedingly difficult.

Seeking psychological damages for alleged stress, whether justified or contrived, will probably continue as a legal strategy in court cases. Because symptoms of stress disorders are not uniform, and disabilities following stressful events are not easily predictable, it is likely that the problem of clearly establishing causal links between stressors and claimed symptoms will continue to plague our courts.

SUMMARY

Many factors influence an individual's response to stressful situations. The impact of stress depends not only on its severity, but also on the individual's preexisting vulnerabilities. An individual's response to conflict situations may be viewed differently depending on whether the conflicts are approach-avoidance, double-approach, or double-avoidance. A wide variety of psychosocial stressors exists, and a person can respond to them in different ways. In attempting to deal with stressful events, for instance, an individual may react with task-oriented or defense-oriented responses. The effects of extreme or prolonged stress on a person can bring about extensive psychological problems.

The DSM-III-R classifies individual problems in response to stressful situations under two categories: adjustment disorders and posttraumatic stress disorder (included with the anxiety disorders). Several relatively common stressors (prolonged unemployment, loss of a loved one through death, and marital separation or divorce) may produce a great deal of stress and psychological maladjustment, resulting in adjustment disorder. More intense psychological disorders in response to trauma or excessively stressful situations (such as rape, military combat, imprisonment, being held hostage, relocation, or other disasters) may be categorized as posttraumatic stress disorder. These disorders may involve a variety of symptoms, including intrusive thoughts and repetitive nightmares about the event, intense anxiety, avoidance of stimuli associated with the trauma, increased arousal manifested as chronic tension, irritability, insomnia, impaired concentration and memory, and depression. If the symptoms begin six months or more after the traumatic event, the diagnosis is *delayed* posttraumatic stress disorder. Many factors contribute to breakdown under excessive stress, including the intensity or harshness of the stress situation, the length of the traumatic event, the individual's biological makeup and personality adjustment prior to the stressful situation, and the ways in which the person manages problems once the stressful situation is over. In many cases the symptoms recede as the stress diminishes, especially if the individual is given supportive psychotherapy. In extreme cases, however, there may be residual damage or the disorder may be of the delayed variety, not actually occurring until some time after the trauma.

The treatment of stress-related psychological problems is most effective when intervention is applied early. Crisis intervention therapy, a brief problem-focused counseling approach, may aid a victim of a traumatic event in readjusting to life after the stressful situation has ended. In some situations it may be possible to prevent maladaptive responses to stress by preparing an individual in advance to deal with the stress. This approach to stress management has been shown to be effective in cases where the individual is facing a known traumatic event, such as major surgery or the breakup of a relationship. In these cases a professional attempts to prepare the individual in advance to cope better with the stressful event through developing more realistic and adaptive attitudes about the problem.

Posttraumatic stress disorder has been used frequently in recent criminal and civil court cases to explain deviant behavior or to justify compensation for perceived damages. The extent to which this psychological disorder has been successfully used in court has varied. In some situations, especially when extreme trauma has been involved, the maladaptive behavior is readily explainable in terms of the traumatic event. In other situations, however, a causal link between maladaptive behavior and a traumatic event has been difficult to establish.

◼ Key Terms

stressors (p. 140)
stress (p. 140)
coping strategies (p. 140)
eustress (p. 140)
distress (p. 140)
stress tolerance (p. 144)
crisis (p. 145)
crisis intervention (p. 146)
task-oriented response (p. 147)
defense-oriented response (p. 147)

decompensation (p. 148)
general adaptation syndrome (p. 149)
adjustment disorder (p. 151)
posttraumatic stress disorder (PTSD) (p. 156)
disaster syndrome (p. 157)
stress inoculation training (p. 177)

Chapter 6
Anxiety–based Disorders

Vojislav Jakíc, *Les Effrayants Insectes Cornus*. Jakíc (b. 1932), the son of a Montenegrin priest, was raised in a small town in Serbia. Ostracized as a boy by his peers because of his ethnic background, he developed an introverted personality. While at school, Jakíc became aware of his artistic ability. He began art studies in Belgrade at the age of 20. Thereafter, his life was marked by chronic illness, poverty, and lack of recognition, as well as by increasing paranoia.

In our discussion of stress and different reactions to it, we dealt primarily with stable people who had been subjected to excessive stressor demands. In this chapter we will look at disorders in which maladaptive reaction patterns—the beginnings of which are often evident early in life—have resulted in persistent vulnerability to experience fear or anxiety when facing *everyday* problems. In these cases ordinary methods of coping, including the "normal" use of ego-defense mechanisms, have proven inadequate, and an individual either experiences disabling anxiety or increasingly relies on more extreme defensive reactions. Although these defenses may help ward off acute feelings of threat, they exact a high price in ineffective and self-defeating behavior.

Neurotic behavior—the exaggerated use of avoidance behaviors and defense mechanisms—is clearly maladaptive. It does not, however, typically involve gross distortion of reality or marked personality disorganization, nor is it likely to result in violence to the individual or to others. Rather, we are dealing here with individuals who are typically fearful, ineffective, unhappy, and often guilt-ridden; they do not ordinarily require hospitalization but nevertheless are in need of therapy. Incidence rates are difficult to determine, but it has been estimated that between 8 and 25 percent of American adults—a reasonable guess is some 30 million people—suffer from one of the many variants of neurotic disorder (Dohrenwend et al., 1980; National Institute of Mental Health, 1985b; Robins et al., 1984).

The term **neurosis** was coined by Englishman William Cullen and first used in his *System of Nosology,* published in 1769, to refer to disordered sensations of the nervous system. It reflected the long-held belief that neurological malfunction must be involved in neurotic behavior. This belief endured until the time of Freud, himself a neurologist, who postulated that neurosis stems from intrapsychic conflict rather than a physically disordered nervous system. Specifically, Freud held that neurosis is the outcome of an inner conflict involving an unbearable wish (approach tendency of the id) and the ego's and superego's prohibitions against its expression (avoidance tendency). **Anxiety**—a general feeling of fear and apprehension—is central to this formulation. It is both a signal provided by the ego that a dangerous impulse has been activated and the motivational force behind the deployment of

181

Most people handle everyday problems—such as the demands of their family—with a variety of "normal" ego-defense mechanisms. Individuals with anxiety-based disorders, on the other hand, experience disabling fear or rely on extreme defensive reactions in response to life stress.

defenses. Thus for Freud neurosis consists of an intrapsychic approach-avoidance conflict, psychological in nature. It is acquired during a developmental process involving excessive, impulse-generated anxiety and maladaptive efforts to cope with it. The symptoms traditionally ascribed to neurosis are the outward manifestations of the conflict raging within. Over time Freud's conception of neurosis has tended to become its definition.

As we will see, the prominence Freud gave to anxiety is readily understood when we consider the frequency and intensity with which anxiety is manifested in many of the disorders traditionally classified as *neurotic*. The other components Freud claimed as intrinsic to neurosis are typically much less obvious. As such, Freud's overall views on the nature of neuroses have come under attack as being too theoretical, referring as they do to essentially unobservable inner states and events. The original meaning of the term *neurotic* also became clouded as it entered the popular lexicon. Responding to these concerns, the authors of DSM-III and its 1987 revision (DSM-III-R) pursued the theoretically neutral course of abandoning (except in parenthetical phrases) the term *neurosis* and its derivatives. Instead, they favored descriptions of specific symptom syndromes, most of which had previously been considered as diverse manifestations of a generic "neurotic" condition. These syndromes are now grouped into three general classes according to the predominant symptoms overtly displayed: anxiety, somatoform, or dissociative.

The new DSM classification has provoked some controversy from those committed to a psychody-namic, especially Freudian, position because many consider the concept of neurosis the crowning achievement of psychoanalytic theory. That is, some have seen the change as a broad attack on their fundamental ideological tenets (Bayer & Spitzer, 1985; Millon, 1986). We will address this matter again in the Unresolved Issues section, but such questions ultimately must and will be settled, if at all, on the basis of superior empirical evidence. In the meantime these questions should perhaps not be co-opted by issues of nomenclature. By the same token, we find ourselves not quite ready to join in a fervent rejection of all things psychodynamic that we detect in some of our colleagues, as will be clear in this chapter. Our decision to retain the overarching term *neurosis* (and its derivatives) is in part a concession to this conservative bent but is also motivated by our lingering doubts that the disorders to be considered here are as discrete and discontinuous as current nomenclature suggests. In particular many of them seem to be driven and fueled by anxiety, even where anxiety may not be a striking or obvious element in their clinical pictures.

Given this hypothesis, we will begin by discussing the nature of anxiety as an emotional state to which humans seem all too vulnerable. We will then move to a description of the DSM categories subsumed under anxiety, somatoform, and dissociative disorders. From there we will consider whether or not less severe or asymptomatic forms of these disorders exist in the guise of neurotic styles. We will then look at specific causal factors in this range of disorders, typical methods of treatment, and treatment outcomes.

THE ANXIETY–RESPONSE PATTERN

The task of defining *anxiety* in explicit terms is a difficult one. Most of us have an intuitive appreciation of what anxiety is, based largely on direct experience with the obtrusive and usually quite unpleasant inner state the term signifies. The experience, including its perceived autonomic nervous system components, shares many properties with that of fear; in the case of the latter, however, the source or the instigating circumstances are normally quite clear to us and we know that the danger would be regarded as objectively real by most people. With anxiety, we frequently cannot specify clearly what the danger is, and if we can, we are painfully aware that others do not understand the "problem." It is as though we are anticipating some dreadful happening not objectively predictable from our actual circumstances, a quality recognized in the widespread use of the term *apprehension* to describe the state.

Animal experimentation going back many decades has established that the basic fear-response pattern is highly conditionable—that is, it can readily be transferred to previously neutral stimuli by promptly and repeatedly linking the occurrences of these stimuli with painful events, such as electric shocks. Of course, few human infants or children are subjected to electric shocks, but many have experiences that are inherently fear-inspiring; and, as we have increasingly discovered in recent years, some have unspeakably cruel and terrifying experiences visited upon them by disturbed parents or other adults. In such situations a wide variety of inherently non-noxious stimuli may come, accidentally as it were, to serve as cues that something threatening and unpleasant is about to happen. The stimuli thus become, themselves, fear-invoking. In addition, we have at the human level the enormously complicating feature of a richly elaborate mental life, such that fleeting impressions, thoughts, images, and indeed even acquired mental associations to them may (like the external stimuli in animal experiments) become capable of eliciting the fear-response pattern—or what in this case would be experienced as *anxiety*. In this scenario any type of stimulus, mental or physiological, regularly preceding a full-blown anxiety episode would be expected to acquire in itself the tendency to elicit anxiety.

This relatively straightforward and doubtless somewhat oversimplified account of the origins of human anxiety is consistent in its main outlines with the conclusions reached in a comprehensive analysis recently offered by David Barlow (1988). Barlow presents a model of the genesis of anxiety as involving biological, psychological, and environmental events that, when "lined up" in a mutually facilitative way, become a self-sustaining feedback system—an **anxiety-response pattern** of sorts. The cognitive and emotional core of this system, strengthened by repeated "alarm" experiences (physiological arousal cues) in contexts construed as unpredictable and uncontrollable, becomes stored in long-term memory. There it may undergo further pathological elaboration through the formation of new associative networks. Once the pattern is established, its automatic nature makes it immune to rational processing, and cognitive reappraisals based on new experiences are difficult to arrange. At an advanced stage, then, systematic therapeutic intervention to disrupt the feedback system becomes a challenging task. That task is complicated by the fact

that, by this point, many severely anxiety-prone patients will have developed an array of avoidant-defensive behaviors, typically with redundant back-ups, that are in themselves maladaptive and that effectively defeat countermeasures. A phobic patient, for example, will usually have developed a multitude of behavioral strategies to make certain that he or she does not confront the anxiety-provoking circumstance, thus ensuring a lack of corrective experience regarding its benign nature. It will be useful to bear in mind these general features of the anxiety-response pattern as we proceed to examine the recognized clinical disorders of which it is the core element.

ANXIETY DISORDERS

An **anxiety disorder,** as the term suggests, has an unrealistic, irrational fear of disabling intensity at its core and also as its principal and most obvious manifestation. DSM-III-R recognizes seven basic types of anxiety disorder: panic disorder, agoraphobia, phobias of "social" or of "simple" type, obsessive-compulsive disorder, generalized anxiety disorder, and posttraumatic stress disorder. The last of these, basically a delayed reaction to traumatic stressors, was discussed in the preceding chapter and will not be considered here.

Anxiety disorders are relatively common. In the New Haven-Baltimore-St. Louis Epidemiologic Catchment Area program sponsored by the National Institute of Mental Health, phobia was the most common psychiatric disorder reported for women and the second-most common (behind alcohol abuse or dependence) for men. Among women, obsessive-compulsive disorder had a prevalence rate exceeded only by phobia and certain mood disorders (Myers et al., 1984; Robins et al., 1984). Projecting the figures for panic, phobic, and obsessive-compulsive disorders to the entire American population yields a combined estimate of about 15 million cases (National Institute of Mental Health, 1985).

Panic Disorder and Agoraphobia

Diagnostically, **panic disorder** is defined and characterized by the occurrence of one or more "unexpected" panic attacks not triggered by the sufferer's being the focus of others' attentions. The person must have experienced at least four attacks in a four-week period, or, in the case of fewer attacks, must have been fearful of recurrence for at least a month. An attack is defined in terms of a lengthy list of symptoms (such as shortness of breath, palpitations, sweating, dizziness, fear of dying, fear of "going crazy") of which the person must have at least four for the experience to qualify as a full panic episode. Such attacks are normally unexpected in the sense that they do not appear to be provoked by identifiable components of the immediate situation. Their initial appearance, however, often follows earlier-appearing feelings of distress (Lelliott et al., 1989) or some highly stressful life circumstance, such as the loss of an important relationship (Foa, Steketee, & Young, 1984; Pollard, Pollard, & Corn, 1989). A panic attack typically subsides within a few minutes, but the stark terror of those minutes normally precludes any reassurance of a quick end. These two features—the characteristic brevity and the marked intensity of the reaction—distinguish panic disorder from other types of anxiety problems.

The specific fear in **agoraphobia** is that of being in places or situations from which escape would be physically or psychologically difficult, or in which immediate help would be unavailable in the event of some untoward reaction, particularly a panic attack. In short, what agoraphobics fear is fear. They usually fear travel in general, and they commonly avoid cars, buses, airplanes, subway trains, and so on.

Mary, the woman shown here, is riding an escalator as part of her therapy in overcoming her agoraphobia. The specific fear in agoraphobia is that of being in places or situations from which escape would be physically or psychologically difficult. Agoraphobic individuals typically avoid crowded situations, standing in line, and vehicles of transportation.

These individuals are even apt to be uncomfortable venturing outside their homes alone. Other typical sources of difficulty include being in crowded situations or standing in lines.

Agoraphobia is a frequent complication of panic disorder, but it can also occur in the absence of prior attacks whose intensity would merit the designation *panic*. In the latter instance a common pattern is that of a gradually spreading fearfulness in which more and more aspects of the environment outside the home acquire threatening properties, a condition informally referred to as *pan-phobia*. In severe cases agoraphobia becomes a terribly confining disorder in which an individual is unable to go beyond the narrow confines of home, or even particular parts of the home.

We consider panic disorders and agoraphobia together because accumulating research evidence suggests that they share some basic properties, including a possible genetic linkage (Noyes et al., 1986). Many people with an agoraphobic pattern report a history of repetitive panic attacks. It appears that in at least some cases agoraphobia develops as a secondary reaction to the experience of panic. That is, an individual fears being "out on the town," especially alone, because he or she is terrified of having a panic attack in public. The DSM-III-R recognizes this link by providing for diagnoses of agoraphobia with and without a history of prior panic attacks. In the former instance, in fact, the primary diagnosis would be that of panic disorder (with agoraphobia).

The case of Anne Watson is in many respects typical of panic disorder with agoraphobia:

*M*s. *Watson, married mother of two and age 45 at her first clinic contact, experienced her first panic attack some two years earlier, several months after the sudden death of an uncle to whom she had been extremely close while growing up. While returning home from work one evening she had the feeling that she couldn't catch her breath. Immediately thereafter her heart began to pound, she broke out in a cold sweat, and she had a sense of unreality. Feeling immobilized by a leaden quality in her legs, she became certain she would pass out or die before she could reach home. Soliciting help from a passerby, she was able to engage a cab, directing the driver to take her to the nearest hospital emergency room. Her ensuing physical examination revealed no abnormalities apart from a slightly elevated heart rate, which subsided to* normal limits before the examination was completed. She regained composure rapidly and was able to return home on her own.

Four weeks later, after the incident had been all but forgotten, Ms. Watson had a second similar attack while at home preparing a meal. Four more occurred in the next several weeks, all of them surprises, and she began to despair about discovering their source. She also noticed that she was becoming anxious about the probability of additional attacks. Consultation with the family physician yielded a diagnosis of "nervous strain" and a prescription for antianxiety medication. The medication made Ms. Watson calmer, but seemed to have no effect on the continuing panics. She discovered alcohol was even more effective than the medication in relieving her tension and began to drink excessively, which only increased the worry and concern of her husband.

As the attacks continued, Ms. Watson began to dread going out of the house alone. She feared that while out she would have an attack and would be stranded and helpless. She stopped riding the subway to work out of fear she might be trapped in a car between stops when an attack struck, preferring instead to walk the 20 blocks between her home and work. She also severely curtailed her social and recreational activities—previously frequent and enjoyed—because an attack might occur, necessitating an abrupt and embarrassing flight from the scene. When household duties and the like required brief driving excursions, she surreptitiously put these off until she could be accompanied by one of the children or a neighbor. Despite these drastic alterations of life-style and her growing unhappiness and desperation, however, she remained her normal self when at home or when her husband accompanied her away from home.

On the advice of the family physician, Ms. Watson began psychotherapy sessions with a psychiatrist. While she found these sessions, which were entirely verbal and nonspecific in focus, helpful in a number of ways, they had no apparent effect on the frequency or intensity of her panic attacks. About a year later she read an article describing a clinic program for agoraphobia. She decided to apply.

The clinic program was engaged in an evaluation of the efficacy of antidepressant medication (imipramine [Tofranil]) in the treatment of panic disorder, encouraging reports of which had be-gun to appear in the professional literature. After some initial difficulties in establishing an optimal dosage level, Ms. Watson ceased reporting further panic attacks. Within eight months she had resumed all of her former activities, stopped drinking, and reduced her antianxiety medication to a minimal level. She was enjoying life again and reported being back to her "old self." (Adapted from Spitzer et al., 1983.)

It should be noted that the relatively rapid resolution of Ms. Watson's difficulties through the use of antidepressant medication is not necessarily typical. Although these drugs do sometimes suppress panic attacks, their precise mode of action in doing so is unknown. Also, troublesome side effects (such as blurring of vision) are common in such treatment, causing many patients to tolerate recommended dosages poorly and thus to stop taking the drugs (Mavissakalian & Perel, 1989). Many behaviorally oriented clinicians question the wisdom of using these potent medications as the initial treatment for difficulties of this sort; they point to the established efficacy of certain specialized programs that treat patients through controlled exposure to the avoided situations (e.g., Barlow & Waddell, 1985; Barlow & Cerny, 1988). We will have more to say about treatment issues in a later section.

■ Other Phobic Disorders

Traditionally, a **phobia** is a persistent and disproportionate fear of some specific object or situation that presents little or no actual danger to a person. Recalling our earlier discussion on the nature of the anxiety-response pattern, phobia victims literally but involuntarily "psyche" themselves into their problems. This traditional concept is most closely approximated by the DSM-III-R diagnosis of **simple phobia**. The clinical picture in this type of problem is described in the next few paragraphs.

The following list of the common phobias and their objects will give some hint of the variety of situations and events around which simple phobias may be centered:

Acrophobia—high places
Algophobia—pain
Astraphobia—storms, thunder, and lightning
Claustrophobia—closed places
Hematophobia—blood
Monophobia—being alone

Mysophobia—contamination or germs

Nyctophobia—darkness

Ochlophobia—crowds

Pathophobia—disease

Pyrophobia—fire

Syphilophobia—syphilis

Zoophobia—animals or some particular animal

Some of these phobias involve an exaggerated fear of things that most of us fear to some extent, such as darkness, fires, disease, spiders, and snakes. Others, such as phobias of open places or crowds, involve situations that do not elicit fear in most people. Some evidence (e.g., Cook, Hodes, & Lang, 1986; Tomarken, Mineka, & Cook, 1989) suggests that phobic reactions to objectively fearful objects are more readily acquired and less readily extinguished than those to more benign stimuli.

Phobic disorders are more common among adolescents and young adults than among older people. They are also, as earlier indicated, more frequently diagnosed in females than in males, possibly because strong fears have traditionally been more compatible with female roles than with male roles in our society. Of course, most of us have minor irrational fears, but in phobic disorders such fears are intense and interfere with everyday activities. For example, phobic individuals may go to great lengths to avoid entering a small room or passageway, even when they must. People who suffer from phobias usually admit that they have no real cause to fear the object or situation, but they say that they cannot help themselves. If they attempt to approach the phobic situation, they are overcome with anxiety, which may vary from mild feelings of uneasiness and distress to a full-fledged anxiety attack verging on panic.

Phobic individuals usually show a wide range of other symptoms in addition to their phobias, such as tension headaches, back pains, stomach upsets, dizzy spells, and fears of "cracking up." At times of more acute panic, such individuals often complain of depersonalization phenomena and of feelings of unreality, strangeness, and "not being themselves." Depression frequently accompanies phobias, and many patients report serious interpersonal difficulties, some of them doubtless the result of the impatience of significant others with the victims' irrational fears. In some instances, phobics also have serious difficulty in making decisions—a condition that Kaufmann (1973) somewhat facetiously called *decidophobia*. Here we may be touching on a seeming connection between phobias and obsessions.

The particular phobias that develop are often influenced by cultural factors. For example, a phobia of flying was quite unlikely until we entered the age of commercial air travel. In some cases, phobic

Phobias come in many shapes and sizes. Fear of flying is such a common phobia that a number of classes and programs have been developed to help aerophobics, such as the man shown here, overcome their fears. The woman on the ferris wheel is exhibiting the intense fear of height that is characteristic of acrophobia.

reactions may also be obsessive, as when a persistent, obsessive fear of contamination dominates a neurotic individual's behavior and consciousness. In such a case the DSM-III-R requires consideration of an *obsessive-compulsive* diagnosis (to be discussed in a subsequent section). In certain instances a phobia is a rather transparent displacement; a person substitutes a more "acceptable" fear-inspiring object or situation for one whose acknowledgment would be difficult or painful. The classic example here is that of a woman who develops a phobia of public places because of a fear that she may yield to the blandishments of men who may try to "pick her up."

Regardless of how it begins, phobic behavior tends to be reinforced by the reduction in anxiety that occurs each time an individual avoids a feared situation. In addition, phobias may be maintained in part by secondary gains (benefits derived from being disabled), such as increased attention, sympathy, and some control over the behavior of others. For example, a phobia of driving may enable a homemaker to escape from responsibilities outside the home, such as grocery shopping or transporting children to and from school. If the homemaker should also happen to feel chronic anger toward her unhelpful spouse, who must now pick up these chores, so much the better for phobia maintenance. Phobias, then, in addition to being primary manifestations of irrational, acquired fears, may sometimes serve the interests of seemingly remote objectives, although usually without the sufferer's awareness. Since the net effect of phobias, especially the more expansive ones, is to render the victim "helpless," they draw our attention in particular to a secondary gain hypothesis involving the avoidance of adult independence and responsibility. Our experience has frequently (but not always) confirmed such a hypothesis in careful clinical assessment, where it may also appear that other members of a family have a stake in maintaining the phobic individual's helplessness. The sometimes complicated ways in which phobic behavior may become involved in other personal and interpersonal issues is illustrated in the following case:

An intelligent, well-educated married woman in her mid-30s complained of marked fear, bordering on panic, of driving her auto in unfamiliar neighborhoods, riding in elevators, flying, and entering tall buildings and shopping centers. During the initial interview she revealed that she had had these fears for some 18 years. For this entire period, except since her marriage two years earlier, she had been in almost continuous treatment. A succession of reputable therapists had employed widely differing modes of intervention, including psychoanalysis and certain behavior therapy techniques. None of these measures had brought significant relief, and by this point the patient had become so adept at "managing" therapists that she could usually maintain their interest in "taking care of her" over considerable periods without seriously attempting to resolve her difficulties. At the outset, then, the situation appeared rather unpromising for a renewed attempt at therapy.

The history revealed a long series of dependent relationships, chiefly with males (including male therapists), culminating in marriage to an older, previously married professional man. Initially the husband had appeared "strong" although somewhat given to tyrannical outbursts; over time, this strength proved to be largely an illusion. As the husband's appearance of strength had evaporated, the wife's phobic symptoms had returned and increased in severity over time, driving her back into therapy once again. With the wife's increase in phobic symptoms, the husband's life had become more frantic and hectic, since he had had to assume many of the household responsibilities she could no longer perform. The marital relationship had deteriorated rapidly under the assault of these conflicting interests. This collapse was accelerated in the wife's case by the emergence of increasingly disabling symptoms and in the husband's by a return after long abstinence to excessive alcohol consumption, accompanied by verbal and moderate physical abuse of his now "helpless" wife.

A relatively clear understanding of the intermeshing of these contributory factors, together with some confidence (in light of her history) that standard treatment would almost certainly fail, encouraged the therapist to intervene forcefully into this complicated situation. For example, he largely ignored the patient's fears and insisted on discussing her relationship with her husband, who was also summoned to attend some therapy sessions. As was expected, the patient became markedly dependent on the therapist as her condition improved—to the extent that she continued to complain of phobias even after her phobic behavior had essentially disappeared. Meanwhile, her marital situation became more stable as she came to accept and even be sympathetic toward her husband's insecurities.

At the point where a relative marital tranquility and mutual support had been reestablished, the therapist, after weighing options and possible consequences, unilaterally terminated further therapy sessions; this unusual step was taken to abort the client's growing dependency on the therapist. He assured the surprised and doubtful client that there was no need for further therapy and that any remaining fears would clear up spontaneously. Several weeks later, the client telephoned to say cheerfully that, in fact, they had. Informal long-term follow-up indicates that this client continues to do well.

Although some phobias, once established, remain fairly circumscribed, others, as we have seen, tend to "spread" or generalize to additional situations, possibly because of an "incubation" effect that is thought to occur with some types of anxiety (Eysenck, 1976). The following case illustrates this spreading effect:

An 18-year-old woman had been given strict "moral" training concerning the evils of sex, and she associated sexual relations with vivid ideas of sin, guilt, and hell. This basic orientation was reinforced when she was beaten and sexually attacked by a young man on her fifteenth birthday. Nevertheless, when the young man she was dating kissed her and "held her close," it aroused intense sexual desires. These desires were extremely guilt arousing, however, and led to a chain of avoidance behaviors. First she stopped seeing the man in an effort to get rid of her "immoral" thoughts; then she stopped all dating; then she began to feel uncomfortable with any young man she knew; and finally she became fearful of any social situations where men might be present. At this point, her life was largely dominated by her phobias and she was so "completely miserable" that she requested professional help.

The case just described verges, in DSM terms, into **social phobia.** Criteria for this diagnosis emphasize (a) a fear of situations in which one is exposed to focused scrutiny by others, and (b) the corollary fear that one may do something or act in such a manner as to risk humiliation or embarrassment. Probably a far more common type of social

Social phobia consists of a fear of being in situations in which one is exposed to focused scrutiny by others and the corollary fear that one may do something or act in such a manner as to risk humiliation or embarrassment. The most common type of social phobia is probably stage fright, which can render performance virtually impossible in some cases.

phobia is what is commonly known as stage fright, which can mount to levels rendering performance impossible or at least markedly impaired. The following case is illustrative:

An intelligent, recently-divorced mother of two young children sought consultation because she "froze" whenever asked to audition for membership in local orchestral groups. An accomplished cellist, performing with this instrument had been one of her few reliable sources of satisfaction, self-esteem, and genuine recreation during her adult years. She had tried various methods of self-help, including commercially available tape recordings purporting to teach relaxation, to no avail. On initial interview, she appeared unusually tense and anxious, and it rapidly became clear that she regarded the interview as another "performance" in which she was under scrutiny. A gently-framed invitation for her to consider this "hypothesis" produced confirmation but no discernible tension reduction.

The client suggested hypnosis as a treatment approach in an obvious effort to circumvent the discomfort she felt in relating to the therapist in normal conversation. The therapist was willing to consider this mode but suspected that the question of her hypnotizability would be experienced as another performance demand resulting in the characteristic disabling anxiety. A brief test of hypnotic responsivity confirmed this suspicion.

There was no change in situational anxiety level in a series of brief additional appointments deliberately planned to desensitize the client to the treatment situation; in fact, the client canceled and rescheduled several of these. Finally, the client was provided with a tailor-made (with the therapist as trainer) relaxation-training tape and instructions to practice on a regular basis at home, recontacting the therapist when she felt she had made some progress and was ready for the next step. She has not been heard from since.

Many of us show some compulsive behavior, but people with compulsive disorders feel compelled to perform repeatedly some act that seems pointless and absurd even to them and that they in some sense do not want to perform, such as washing one's hands as often as six times each hour.

Fortunately, the type of treatment complication encountered here, where the client's principal difficulty negatively impacts the treatment process, is not especially typical for the treatment of social phobia. On the contrary, a relatively good treatment outcome for this disorder can normally be anticipated, although especially intense fears of negative evaluation, as in this case, may limit long-term treatment efficacy (Mattick, Peters, & Clarke, 1989).

■ Obsessive–Compulsive Disorder

An **obsession** is a persistent preoccupation with a certain mental content, typically an idea or a feeling. A **compulsion** is an impulse to engage in some behavior experienced as irresistible. Thus in **obsessive-compulsive disorder** (OCD) individuals feel compelled to think about something that they do not want to think about or to carry out some action, often pointlessly ritualistic, seemingly against their own will. These individuals, usually having high levels of manifest anxiety, realize that their behavior is irrational but cannot seem to control it. The DSM-III-R diagnosis requires that this involuntary behavior cause marked distress to an individual,

consume excessive time, or interfere with occupational or social functioning.

Estimates from the Epidemiologic Catchment Area study, expanded to five widely dispersed American communities, indicate that obsessive-compulsive disorder is more prevalent than was once thought. Specifically, the lifetime prevalence rate (which somewhat underestimates the incidence rate because as yet unaffected younger subjects remain at risk) of OCD in this composite sample was 2.5 percent, with divorced (or separated) and unemployed people being somewhat overrepresented (Karno et al., 1988). This figure translates to a U.S. population estimate in excess of 6 million cases. Also contrary to earlier reports suggesting a preponderance of OCD among females, these newer figures show no gender difference after correcting for marital status. The disorder is not uncommon in children, where its symptoms are strikingly similar to those of adult cases (Swedo et al., 1989). As Nemiah (1967) has pointed out, obsessive-compulsive behaviors cover a wide range:

The phenomena may be manifested psychically or behaviorally; they may be experienced as ideas or as impulses; they may refer to events anticipated in the future or actions already completed; they may express desires and wishes or protective measures

against such desires; they may be simple, uncompli-
cated acts and ideas or elaborate, ritualized patterns
of thinking and behavior. . . . (p. 916)

Most of us have experienced minor obsessive thoughts, such as persistent thoughts about a coming trip or a haunting melody that we cannot seem to get out of our minds. In the case of obsessive reactions, however, the thoughts are much more persistent, appear irrational to the individual, and interfere considerably with everyday behavior. Neurotic obsessive thoughts may center around a variety of topics, such as a concern over bodily functions, committing immoral acts, attempting suicide, or even finding the solution to some seemingly unsolvable problem. Particularly common are obsessive thoughts of committing some immoral act. A wife may be obsessed with the idea of poisoning her husband; a daughter may constantly imagine pushing her mother down a flight of stairs.

Even though obsessive thoughts are usually not carried out in action, they remain a source of often excruciating torment to an individual. This pattern is well illustrated in a classic case described by Kraines (1948) of a woman who

complained of having "terrible thoughts." When
she thought of her boyfriend she wished he were
dead; when her mother went down the stairs, she
"wished she'd fall and break her neck"; when her
sister spoke of going to the beach with her infant
daughter, the patient "hoped that they would both
drown." These thoughts "make me hysterical. I
love them; why should I wish such terrible things to
happen? It drives me wild, makes me feel I'm crazy
and don't belong to society; maybe it's best for me
to end it all than to go on thinking such terrible
things about those I love." (p. 183)

As is the case with obsessive thoughts, many of us show some compulsive behavior—stepping over cracks in sidewalks, checking to see that a door is locked immediately after having locked it, or making multiple backups of our computer files—but without the degree of compulsiveness of a neurotic individual. Most of us also resort to minor obsessive-compulsive patterns under severe pressure or when trying to achieve goals that we consider of critical importance. Many historical figures have shown an "obsessive-compulsive" adherence to their goals despite discouragement and ridicule: Columbus persisted for 18 years in his efforts to secure financial backing for his expedition to "India," and Darwin assembled evidence for 22 years

before he would present his ideas on evolution. Goal-directedness is a distinguishing feature of such persistence.

In contrast, people with compulsive disorders feel compelled to perform repeatedly some act that seems pointless and absurd even to them and that they in some sense do not want to perform. These compulsive acts vary from relatively mild ritual-like behavior, such as checking to be sure that the free ends of a shoelace are exactly the same length, to more extreme behavior, such as washing one's hands as often as six times each hour. They can involve actual physical acts or can be essentially cognitive in nature, involving feelings and thoughts (see *HIGHLIGHT 6.1*). The performance of the compulsive act or the ritualized series of acts usually brings a feeling of reduced tension and satisfaction (Carr, 1971; Hodgson & Rachman, 1972). On the other hand, anxiety mounts if the person tries to resist the compulsion.

An obsessive-compulsive disorder is considered maladaptive because it represents irrational and exaggerated behavior in the face of stressors that are not unduly upsetting to most people. In addition, such patterns reduce the efficiency and flexibility of behavior and the capability for self-direction. Generally, people exhibiting such behavior are characterized by feelings of inadequacy and insecurity, rigid and perfectionistic conscience development, a tendency toward feelings of guilt, and high vulnerability to threat. In short, these people appear chronically overaroused, unable to relax (Turner et al., 1985).

As in all of the anxiety disorders, certain maladaptive personality characteristics show up at greater than expected rates in the backgrounds of affected people. Significantly, a large proportion of obsessive-compulsive individuals are found to have been unusually preoccupied with issues of control long before their symptoms appeared. These individuals often have histories suggesting marked discomfort in any situation in which they felt they were not in control of the events immediately around them. The following case is illustrative:

Prior to his hospitalization, this patient had
his life ordered in minute detail. He arose in the
morning precisely at 6:50, took a shower, shaved,
and dressed. His wife had breakfast ready precise-
ly at 7:10 and followed a menu that he worked
out months in advance. At exactly 7:45, he left
for the office where he worked as an accountant.
He came home precisely at 5:55, washed, read

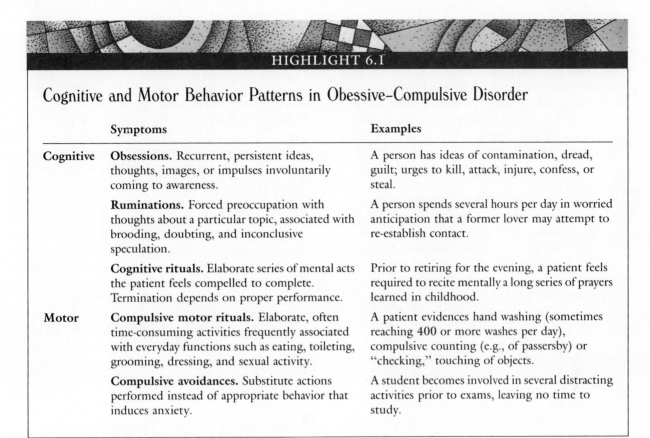

HIGHLIGHT 6.1

Cognitive and Motor Behavior Patterns in Obessive–Compulsive Disorder

	Symptoms	Examples
Cognitive	**Obsessions.** Recurrent, persistent ideas, thoughts, images, or impulses involuntarily coming to awareness.	A person has ideas of contamination, dread, guilt; urges to kill, attack, injure, confess, or steal.
	Ruminations. Forced preoccupation with thoughts about a particular topic, associated with brooding, doubting, and inconclusive speculation.	A person spends several hours per day in worried anticipation that a former lover may attempt to re-establish contact.
	Cognitive rituals. Elaborate series of mental acts the patient feels compelled to complete. Termination depends on proper performance.	Prior to retiring for the evening, a patient feels required to recite mentally a long series of prayers learned in childhood.
Motor	**Compulsive motor rituals.** Elaborate, often time-consuming activities frequently associated with everyday functions such as eating, toileting, grooming, dressing, and sexual activity.	A patient evidences hand washing (sometimes reaching 400 or more washes per day), compulsive counting (e.g., of passersby) or "checking," touching of objects.
	Compulsive avoidances. Substitute actions performed instead of appropriate behavior that induces anxiety.	A student becomes involved in several distracting activities prior to exams, leaving no time to study.

the evening paper, and had dinner precisely at 6:30, again as per menu. His schedule was equally well worked out for evenings and weekends, with a movie on Tuesday, reading on Wednesday, rest on Monday and Thursday, and bridge on Friday. Saturday morning he played golf and Sunday morning and evening he attended church. Saturday evening usually involved having guests or visiting others. He was also fastidious in his dress. Each shirt had to be clean and unwrinkled, his suit pressed every two days, and so on. His demands, of course, also meant close supervision of his wife, who was inclined to be easygoing and was upset when he "blew up" at the smallest variation from established routine.

By means of his carefully ordered existence, the patient had managed to make a reasonably successful adjustment until he became involved in a business deal with a friend and lost a large sum of money. This loss proved too much for him and led to a severe anxiety reaction with considerable agitation and depression, necessitating hospitalization.

In this case we assume that the patient's need to be in utter control of his life was driven by anxiety over being controlled by something or someone else. When his ordered existence in fact failed to protect him from another's exploitation, he fell apart.

Quite often the intense concern with self-imposed control in a pre-obsessive-compulsive person takes the form of exaggerated perfectionism or concerns that his or her actions may lead to terrible consequences. The following case illustrates this characteristic and also indicates how intractable and persistent this disorder may become:

A 32-year-old high school cooking teacher developed marked feelings of guilt and uneasiness, accompanied by obsessive fears of hurting others by touching them or by their handling something she had touched. She dreaded having anyone eat anything she had prepared, and if students in her cooking class were absent, she was certain they had been poisoned by her cook-

ing. In addition, she developed the obsessive notion that a rash at the base of her scalp was a manifestation of syphilis, which would gnaw at her brain and make her a "drooling idiot."

Accompanying these obsessive fears were compulsions consisting primarily of repeated hand-washings and frequent returns to some act already performed, such as turning off gas or water, to reassure herself that the act had been done right.

In treatment the patient was self-centered but highly sensitive and conscientious. She had graduated from college with honors and considered herself highly intelligent. About three years before her present difficulties she had married a noncollege man of whom she had been ashamed because of his poor English, bad table manners, and lack of other characteristics she thought important to a good social showing. As a result she had rejected him in her thinking and behavior and had treated him in what she now considered a cruel manner. On one occasion she had also been unfaithful to him, which was directly opposed to her moral upbringing and values.

Over a period of time, however, she came to realize that he was a fine person and that other people thought highly of him despite his lack of social polish. In addition, she gradually came to the realization that she was very much in love with him. At this point she began to reproach herself for her cruel treatment. She felt that he was a truly wonderful husband, and that she was completely unworthy of him. She was sure her past cruelty and unfaithfulness could never be forgiven. "Heaven knows that every word he says is worth fifty words I say. If I were real honest and truthful I would tell my husband to leave me."

In some cases of obsessive-compulsive disorder, the preexisting behavior seems to involve problems in the control of aggression. Many parents, for instance, have fleeting thoughts and fantasies about harming their children. Fortunately, these thoughts are only rarely expressed in action, and most such parents are amused or at least not frightened by these impulses. Others are less successful in managing their hostility, as the following case illustrates:

A farmer developed obsessive thoughts of hitting his 3-year-old son on the head with a hammer. The father was completely unable to

explain his "horrible thoughts." He stated that he loved his son very much and thought he must be going insane to harbor such thoughts. In the treatment of this case, it was revealed that the patient's wife had suffered great pain in childbirth and had since refused sexual relations with him for fear of again becoming pregnant. In addition, she lavished most of her attention on the son, and their previously happy marriage was now torn with quarreling and bickering.

It appears here that the farmer could not be sufficiently assertive either to allow himself to experience his resentment toward his son or to confront his wife on needed changes in their relationship. His feelings could emerge only in seemingly automatic, alien thoughts. As with neuroses in general, persons having OCD seem unable to take the direct steps needed to diminish or resolve their difficulties; on the contrary, they regularly dig deeper holes for themselves.

■ Generalized Anxiety Disorder

Unlike other neurotic patterns, generalized anxiety disorder does not include in its behavioral profile any effective anxiety-avoidance mechanisms. Thus although victims of other disorders to some extent allay their anxieties, feelings of threat and anxiety are the central feature of generalized anxiety disorder.

Generalized anxiety disorder is characterized by chronic excessive worry, traditionally described as free-floating anxiety. While the disorder is common, precise prevalence rates are unavailable. DSM-III-R criteria specify that the worry must last at least six months and not be confined to a single life circumstance. Its content may not be related to another, concurrent Axis I disorder, such as the possibility of a panic attack. The subjective experience of worry must also be accompanied by at least six of the following symptoms:

Motor tension
- Trembly, twitchy, "shaky" feeling
- Tense, aching, sore muscles
- Restlessness
- Easy fatigability

Vigilance and scanning
- "Keyed up," "on edge" feeling
- Exaggerated startle response
- Difficulty sleeping

- Concentration problems
- Irritability

Autonomic hyperactivity
- Shortness of breath, feeling of "smothering"
- Rapid pulse, palpitations
- Sweating, clammy hands
- Dry mouth
- Dizziness, lightheadedness
- Nausea, diarrhea, other gastrointestinal distress
- Hot flashes or chills
- Frequent urination
- Trouble swallowing, lump in throat

Although the diagnostic criteria in this clinical picture are silent about occasional flare-ups of intense anxiety (indistinguishable from "panic" as previously described), such attacks are known to be quite common—as indeed they are in the anxiety disorders generally (Barlow et al., 1985).

Individuals suffering from generalized anxiety disorder live in a relatively constant state of tension, worry, and diffuse uneasiness. They are oversensitive in interpersonal relationships and frequently feel inadequate and depressed. Usually they have difficulty concentrating and making decisions, dreading to make a mistake. The high level of tension they experience is often reflected in strained postural movements, overreaction to sudden or unexpected stimuli, and continual nervous movements. Commonly, they complain of muscular tension, especially in the neck and upper shoulder region, chronic mild diarrhea, frequent urination, and sleep disturbances that include insomnia and nightmares. They perspire profusely and their palms are often clammy; they may show cardiovascular changes such as elevated blood pressure and increased pulse rate. They may experience breathlessness and heart palpitations for no apparent reason.

No matter how well things seem to be going, individuals with generalized anxiety disorder are apprehensive and anxious. Their vague fears and fantasies—some examples of which are given in *HIGHLIGHT 6.2*—combined with their general sensitivity keep them continually upset, uneasy, and discouraged. Not only do they have difficulty making decisions, but after decisions have been made they worry endlessly over possible errors and unforeseen circumstances that may prove the decisions wrong and lead to disaster. They have no appreciation of the logic most of us use in concluding that it is pointless to torment ourselves about possible outcomes over which we have absolutely no control.

Generalized anxiety disorder is characterized by chronic unrealistic or excessive worry. Individuals suffering from generalized anxiety disorder live in a relatively constant state of tension, worry, and diffuse uneasiness.

The lengths to which they go to find things to worry about are remarkable; as fast as one cause for worry is removed, they find another, until relatives and friends lose patience with them.

Even after going to bed, people who suffer from generalized anxiety disorder are not likely to find relief from their worries. Often, they review each mistake, real or imagined, recent or remotely past. When they are not reviewing and regretting the events of the past, they are anticipating all the difficulties that may arise in the future. Then, after they have crossed and recrossed most of their past and future bridges and managed to fall asleep, they frequently have anxiety dreams—dreams of being choked, being stabbed with knives, falling from high places, or being chased by murderers, with the horrible sensation that their legs will move only in slow motion. *HIGHLIGHT 6.3* provides an idea of the frequency with which individuals experiencing this disorder report various symptoms.

Many of these individuals show mild depression as well as chronic anxiety (Barlow, 1988; Downing & Rickels, 1974; Prusoff & Klerman, 1974). This finding is not unexpected in view of their generally gloomy outlook on the world. Nor is it surprising that excessive use of tranquilizing drugs, sleeping pills, and alcohol often complicates the clinical picture in generalized anxiety disorder.

As the following two cases illustrate, this disorder often results from the breakdown of previously functional but fragile defensive systems:

Fantasies of Anticipated Harm in Anxiety Disorders

In a study of 32 anxiety-neurotic individuals, Beck, Laude, and Bohnert (1974) found unrealistic expectations and fantasies of harm associated with these patients' heightened levels of anxiety and with anxiety attacks. The degree of anxiety was related to the severity and the perceived likelihood of the anticipated harm.

These expectations and fanta-sies centered around both physical and psychological dangers—such as being involved in an accident, becoming sick, being violently attacked, failing, and being humiliated or rejected by significant others. In this context, the following examples are instructive.

Often the fantasies and images reported by a given patient were related to past personal experienc-es. For example, in the following cases, the homemaker had experienced the death of a close friend and the artist's mother had died of a heart attack. These investigators concluded that the expectations and fantasies of anxious patients "not only hold up mirrors to their psychopathology but provide entry points for treating it" (p. 325).

Patient	Fantasy of Anticipated Harm	Stimuli Triggering Anxiety
Physician Male, age 32	Fear of sudden death	Any gastrointestinal symptoms
Teacher Male, age 25	Fear of inability to function as a teacher and of ending up on skid row	Anticipation of giving lecture
Homemaker Female, age 30	Fear of physical catastrophe happening to member of family	Sirens, news of deaths, fires, accidents, etc.
Student Male, age 26	Fear of psychological harm, school failure, rejection of everyone, illness	Schoolwork, confrontation with people, any physical symptom
Laborer Male, age 35	Continuous visual fantasies of accident, fear of imminent death	Any noises that might suggest danger (e.g., traffic noises)
Psychologist Male, age 40	Fear of heart attack, cerebral hemorrhage, fainting in public and subsequent disgrace	Physical sensations in chest or abdomen, back pains, hearing about heart attacks
Artist Female, age 35	Fear of heart attacks	Exertion, anticipation of exertion, reading or hearing about heart attacks
Student Male, age 18	Fear of appearing foolish and subsequent rejection by others	Contact with or anticipated contact with others

Thomas G., a 44-year-old Protestant minister, upon discovery of his wife's infidelity, began to experience chronic anxiety. He was quick to take the blame for the failure of the marriage, sure that his inattentiveness to the needs of his wife and children had driven her away. Yet he was angry at her for creating a public embarrassment for him. He was contemplating a divorce, but such an action would violate his moral convictions. He was also torn by the feeling that because his marriage had failed, he had failed the church, and must resign from the ministry. He loved his work so much, however, that he could not imagine being without it.

During the week before he came for therapy, he had been unable to sleep, lying awake worrying about his problems. He could not eat and complained of a strong burning sensation in his stomach and feelings of being constantly choked up. He was unable to think clearly enough to prepare his sermon for Sunday or to follow through on several commitments he had previously made.

Rev. G.'s present stress only exaggerated problems he had had for many years. He reported that he had always been an insecure and dependent person who found a great deal of emotional support in the church and in his strong, indepen-

HIGHLIGHT 6.3

Frequency of Symptoms in 100 Cases of Generalized Anxiety Disorder

Affective/Somatic	%	Cognitive/Behavioral	%
Unable to relax	97	Difficulty concentrating	86
Tense	86	Fear losing control	76
Frightened	79	Fear being rejected	72
Jumpy	72	Unable to control thoughts	72
Unsteady	62	Confusion	69
Weakness all over	59	Mind blurred	66
Hands (only) sweating	52	Inability to recall	55
Terrified	52	Sentences disconnected	45
Heart racing	48	Blocking in speech	45
Face flushed	48	Fear of being attacked	35
Wobbly	45	Fear of dying	35
Sweating all over	38	Hands trembling	31
Difficult breathing	35	Body swaying	31
Urgent need to urinate	35	Stuttering	24
Nausea	31		
Diarrhea	31		
Faint/dizzy feeling	28		
Face is pale	24		
Feeling of choking	14		
Actual fainting	3		

Adapted from Beck and Emery (1985, pp. 87–88).

---

dent wife. She was a "take charge" person who had always handled all their personal matters, including shopping for his clothes. Any thought of an end to either his marriage or his position with the church made him extremely anxious and insecure—but now it seemed that continuing in the marriage and in his current position would be intolerable.

In short, the minister was able to function when surrounded by familiar supports but became overwhelmed when he was forced to face the necessity of leading a self-directed life. His reaction was an exacerbation of long-standing difficulties, not merely an adjustment disorder in response to a stressful event.

Specifically, we see in this case substantial evidence of a dependent personality organization preceding and in all likelihood contributing causally to Thomas G.'s anxiety disorder. The following case represents a pattern similar in basic structure, although involving a rather different type of preexisting personality organization:

Dr. H. J., a second-year resident in internal medicine at a major university medical center, referred himself for therapy in connection with his growing problems in coping with anxiety. He dated the onset of these difficulties to his acceptance of an invitation to join an elite cardiology team at the conclusion of his first year of postdoctoral training. The team consisted of a small, hand-picked group of senior resident physicians, two brilliant younger medical faculty members, and the leader, who was world famous for his basic discoveries in cardiovascular functioning and his innovations in the assessment and treatment of cardiovascular disease. The team collaborated in various cutting edge research projects and in managing the care of a large number of seriously ill patients. "Graduation" from this team was a virtual guarantee of a high-profile career in cardiovascular medicine, but the demands were great and the rate of attrition notoriously high for those who joined.

On initial assessment, Dr. J., who was manifestly tense, complained of never being entirely free of a sense of impending disaster, although he could not further specify the nature of this anticipated catastrophe. The thought of being involuntarily terminated from his envied position on the cardiology team, earlier a source of intense anxiety, had "on one or two occasions lately," he acknowledged, provided him momentary feelings of relief. He noted a number of signs of autonomic hyperarousal that he experienced on virtually a daily basis, emphasizing in particular excessive sweating, which had become a source of embarrassment. He was medicating himself for persistent attacks of diarrhea. He complained of an inability to attain a refreshing level of sleep even on those rare occasions when he could count on a few uninterrupted, off-duty hours, and his few waking "leisure" hours were filled with restless irritability. He was greatly concerned about his wife's growing complaints of loneliness, and he was fearful she would leave him; however, he expressed a sense of helplessness about being able to alter the situation.

Dr. J.'s request for therapy was precipitated by three additional concerns of more recent origin: (a) He had experienced his first panic attack several evenings ago and had fled from an intensive care unit for which he had been the sole responsible physician, an understanding nurse having had to cover for his absence. (b) He had noticed that the "requirement" (actually, a team expectancy) of remembering without recourse to notes the full background and updated details of every patient under the team's care, never easy, had lately become impossible. (3) He was concerned that his ever-increasing use of antianxiety medication (Valium) would be noticed or lead to drug dependency.

Exploration of Dr. J.'s background revealed he was the adopted child of an otherwise childless couple of modest circumstances. He had been adopted shortly after birth and knew nothing of his biological parentage. While his adoptive parents were extremely loving and had made him "the center of their world," Dr. J. vividly recalled the shock he had experienced when, in his early teens, he had been informed he was adopted. This information had mortified him

and had engendered in him a vague, irrational, unshakable sense of being "different," "not quite right," and, in the final analysis, unacceptable as a human being. Apparently in consequence of this imagined basic flaw, Dr. J. thereafter had placed himself on a life course of unforgiving and ruthless pursuit of perfection.

A decidedly "average" young man, academically and otherwise, prior to learning of his adoption, J. had astonished his parents, his teachers, and his friends by his sudden transformation into a grim and dourly serious, incredibly organized, coldly efficient "nerd." As his social life had deteriorated, partly because he had had little time for anything other than his studies and partly because he had developed an annoying tendency to be bossy, critical, and aloof, his school performance had improved enough to place him at the head of his large high school class. He had been appointed valedictorian in his senior year, by which time he had determined he would become a physician.

Dr. J. had continued on essentially the same course through college and medical school. He had been somewhat resentful that financial constraints had precluded his matriculation at the most prestigious educational institutions, but he had consoled himself with the thought that, with his now customary relentless application, he could easily outdistance "the competition" in the schools he attended. And he had, receiving various academic honors and awards throughout. While working at a part-time service job in college, he had met the woman he would subsequently marry; although plain in appearance, she came from an extremely wealthy and socially prominent family. By Dr. J.'s account, this courtship had been remarkable for its decidedly unpassionate character.

Dr. J.'s performance as a medical student, possibly aided by his recently acquired family connections, had resulted in his being accepted into the highly acclaimed internal medicine residency of his choice. His unsparing diligence and exactitude in fulfilling duties during his first year had led to his being asked to join the elite cardiology team already described. Significantly, Dr. J. reported that, from the first, he never had felt "good enough" to be a member of this team.

Treatment of Dr. J. was made contingent on his agreeing to a programmed withdrawal from antianxiety medication. It involved a combined behavioral-interpersonal-cognitive approach, in the course of which he came to see that his "flaw" *was no more a flaw than was his attempted compensation for it (being "super doc," as he put it) a true aspiration. In due course he resigned from the cardiology team, acknowledging that his former team colleagues might well be "better" than he in terms of their motivation and expertise in that particular field. He decided to complete his residency in internal medicine, however, because he felt it was a good basis for practicing family medicine. This new goal, he recognized, was related to his discovery of a need for "real contact" with people, including his wife. As his anxiety diminished and he began to permit himself the satisfactions of such contact, his compulsive ordering and organizing of the most minute details of his life gradually fell away. A long-suppressed passion for freshwater fishing (which he had enjoyed as a boy with his adoptive father) reappeared.*

By mutual agreement between Dr. J. and his therapist, treatment was terminated 15 months following its initiation, at which point Dr. J. and his wife were anticipating the arrival of their first child. He was virtually free of all anxiety symptoms.

The cases of Reverend G. and Dr. J. raise an important and somewhat controversial issue. Prior to their anxiety disorder breakdowns, the personality organization of each may have qualified them for DSM-III-R, Axis II personality disorder diagnoses (to be considered in Chapter 8). Specifically, Reverend G. might have been considered to have had a *dependent* and Dr. J. an *obsessive-compulsive* personality disorder. The observation of Axis I disorders seeming to develop out of already existing Axis II disorders is extremely common, and is in fact an important reason why personality disorders are recognized in the diagnostic nomenclature. On the other hand, however, as in these two cases, the later-developing symptomatic difficulties (generalized anxiety disorder) could reasonably be conceived as part of and continuous with an underlying anxiety-driven personality disorder. In other words, what may look like (and even meet criteria for) an Axis II personality disorder might sometimes more profitably be conceived as part of an essentially anxiety-based process, one many would describe as neurotic in nature. We will address this issue further in the pages that follow.

As a group, the anxiety disorders, while clearly outside the normal range, rarely strike us as utterly strange or exotic—probably because we have all at

one time or another experienced relatively strong fears or apprehensions that we could not rationally explain. And, as was noted, most of us are not even strangers to mild obsessive and compulsive phenomena. In the following sections we take up neurotic patterns that are more remote from the experience of most people.

SOMATOFORM DISORDERS

Soma means "body," and **somatoform disorders** involve anxiety-based neurotic patterns in which individuals complain of bodily symptoms that suggest the presence of physical problems, but for which no organic bases can be found. Such individuals are typically preoccupied with their state of health and with various presumed disorders or diseases of bodily organs. Though no organic bases exist, these individuals sincerely believe their symptoms are real and serious, and they should not be confused with people who feign physical illness (malingerers) in order to obtain some special treatment. "Functional" somatic symptoms, in which psychological problems are manifested in sincere complaints of physical dysfunction, are extremely common (Kellner, 1985); they represent a large proportion of the clientele of primary care physicians.

In our discussion, we will focus on four more or less distinct somatoform patterns: somatization disorder, hypochondriasis, somatoform pain disorder, and conversion disorder. Although all four involve the neurotic development or elaboration of physical disabilities, the patterns of causation and the most effective treatment approaches may differ somewhat. DSM-III-R includes a fifth syndrome, body dysmorphic disorder, in which there is a preoccupation with some imagined defect in one's physical appearance. While this problem doubtless occurs with significant frequency and sometimes with such severity as to approach delusion, it seems to be fundamentally different in character from the classic somatoform patterns. It will not be considered in this section.

Somatization Disorder

Somatization disorder is characterized by multiple complaints of physical ailments over a long period, beginning before age 30, that are inadequately explained by independent findings of physical illness or injury. A diagnostician need not be con-

Qualifying Symptoms for the Diagnosis of Somatization Disorder

DSM-III-R diagnostic criteria for somatization disorder include the specification that at least 13 of the 35 symptoms listed below have at some time been a focus of significant complaint by an individual. The items appearing in boldface may be used to "screen" for the disorder; the reported occurrence of any two of them establishes a high likelihood of the presence of the full syndrome.

Gastrointestinal symptoms
1. **Vomiting** (other than during pregnancy)
2. Abdominal pain (other than while menstruating)
3. Nausea (other than motion sickness)
4. Bloating (gassy)
5. Diarrhea
6. Intolerance of (gets sick from eating) several different foods

Pain symptoms
7. **Pain in extremities**
8. Back pain
9. Joint pain
10. Pain during urination
11. Other pain (not including headaches)

Cardiopulmonary symptoms
12. **Shortness of breath when not exerting self**
13. Palpitations
14. Chest pain
15. Dizziness

Conversion or pseudoneurological symptoms
16. **Amnesia**
17. **Difficulty swallowing**
18. Loss of voice
19. Deafness
20. Double vision
21. Blurred vision
22. Blindness
23. Fainting or loss of consciousness
24. Seizure or convulsion
25. Trouble walking

26. Paralysis or muscle weakness
27. Urinary retention or difficulty urinating

Sexual symptoms (occurring for most of the person's life following commencement of opportunities for sexual activity)
28. **Burning sensation in sex organs or rectum, *not* during sexual intercourse**
29. Sexual indifference
30. Pain during intercourse
31. Erectile dysfunction

Female reproductive symptoms (judged by the person to be more frequent or more severe than in most women)
32. **Painful menstruation**
33. Irregular menstrual periods
34. Excessive menstrual bleeding
35. Vomiting throughout pregnancy

vinced that these claimed illnesses actually existed in a patient's background history; the mere reporting of them is sufficient. The DSM-III-R provides a list of 35 symptoms (summarized in *HIGHLIGHT 6.4*) that qualify as possible indicators of somatization disorder. To qualify, the symptoms must be reported as having been severe enough to require medication, to require consulting a physician, or to cause an alteration in life-style.

The differences between somatization disorder and hypochondriasis (discussed in the following section), are none too clear in the DSM-III-R diagnostic manual, apparently because the two disorders (if they are in fact distinct) are closely related. The main differences seem to be that hypochondriasis may have its onset after age 30; that the abnormal health concerns characteristic of hypochondriasis need not focus on any particular set of symptoms nor on a profusion of them; and that a hypochondriacal person mostly focuses on the idea that he or she has a serious disease, claims of explicit symptoms or physical disabilities being secondary to this concern.

The somatization disorder diagnosis, new to DSM-III in 1980, has not as yet been subjected to the extensive clinical and research scrutiny characteristic of other somatoform disorders. It is apparently based on long clinical experience with a certain group of medical patients who seem almost never to be entirely "well," even though clear identification of specific organ malfunctions often (although not always) proves to be elusive. The pattern was earlier known as *Briquet's syndrome.*

Hypochondriasis

One of the most frequently seen somatoform patterns is **hypochondriasis,** which is characterized by an individual's multiple complaints about possible physical illness where no evidence of such illness can be found. Hypochondriacal complaints are usually not restricted to any physiologically coherent symptom pattern; rather, they express a preoccupation with health matters and unrealistic fears of disease. Although hypochondriacal people repeatedly seek medical advice, their fears are not in the least lessened by their doctors' reassurances—in fact they are frequently disappointed when no physical problem is found.

Individuals with this disorder may complain of uncomfortable and peculiar sensations in the general area of the stomach, chest, head, genitals, or anywhere else in the body. They usually have trouble giving a precise description of their symptoms, however. They may begin by mentioning pain in the stomach, which on further questioning is not really a pain but a gnawing sensation, or perhaps a feeling of heat, or of pressure, whose locus may now on more careful observation migrate to a neighboring portion of the abdomen, and so on. The mental orientation of these individuals keeps them constantly on the alert for new symptoms, the description of which may challenge the capacity of mere language to communicate.

Hypochondriacal patients are likely to be avid readers of popular magazines on medical topics and are apt to feel certain that they are suffering from every new disease they read or hear about. They are major consumers of over-the-counter (and often virtually worthless) remedies touted in ads as being able to heal vaguely described problems such as "tired blood" or "irregularity." Tuberculosis, cancer, exotic infections, and numerous other diseases are readily diagnosed by these individuals. Their morbid preoccupation with bodily processes, coupled with their often limited knowledge of medical pathology, leads to some interesting diagnoses. One patient diagnosed his condition as "ptosis of the transvex colon," and added, "If I am just half as bad off as I think, I am a dead pigeon."

This attitude appears to be typical: such individuals are sure they are seriously ill and cannot recover. Yet—and this is revealing—despite their exaggerated concerns over their health, they do not usually show the fear or anxiety that might be expected of those suffering from such horrible ills. In fact they are usually in good physical condition. Nevertheless, they are not **malingering,** that is, consciously faking symptoms; they are sincere in their conviction that their symptoms represent real illness, although an attentive listener may get the impression that something more is being communicated in these complaints.

A classic illustration of the shifting symptoms and complaints in a severe case of hypochondriasis is presented in the following letter that a hospitalized patient wrote to her anxious relatives:

Hypochondriacal individuals are preoccupied with health matters and unrealistic fears of disease. They are convinced that they have symptoms of physical illness, but their complaints typically do not conform to any coherent symptom pattern, and they usually have trouble giving a precise description of their symptoms.

"Dear Mother and Husband:

"I have suffered terrible today with drawing in the throat. My nerves are terrible. My head feels queer. But my stomach hasn't cramped quite so hard. I've been on the verge of a nervous chill all day, but I have been fighting it hard. It's night and bedtime, but, Oh, how I hate to go to bed. Nobody knows or realizes how badly I feel because I fight to stay up and outdoors if possible. . . .

"The long afternoons and nights are awful. There are plenty of patients well enough to visit but I'm in too much pain.

"The nurses ignore any complaining. They just laugh or scold.

"Eating has been awful hard. They expect me to eat like a harvest hand. Every bite of solid food is agony to get down, for my throat aches so and feels so closed up. . . .

"My eyes are bothering me more.

"Come up as soon as you can. My nose runs terribly every time I eat.

"The trains and ducks and water pipes are noisy at night.

Annie"
(Menninger, 1945, pp. 139–140)

Hypochondriacal individuals often show a morbid preoccupation with digestive and excretory functions. Some keep charts of their bowel movements, and most are able to give detailed information concerning diet, constipation, and related matters. Many, as earlier suggested, use a wide range of self-medications of the type frequently advertised on television. However, they do not show losses or distortions of sensory, motor, and visceral functioning that occur in conversion disorder (to be discussed in a later section); nor do their complaints have the bizarre delusional quality—such as "insides rotting away" or "lungs drying up"—that typically occurs in psychotic disorders.

Most of us as children learn well the lesson that, when sick, special comforts and attention are provided and, furthermore, that one is excused from a number of responsibilities or, at least, is not expected to perform certain chores up to par. This lesson has proved exceptionally alluring and persistent for a hypochondriacal adult. Such an adult is in effect saying, (a) "I deserve more of your attention and concern," and (b) "You may not legitimately expect me to perform as a well person would." Typically these messages are conveyed with more than a touch of angry rebuke or whining, inconsolable demand.

In short, hypochondriasis may be viewed as a certain type of interpersonal communication as well as a disorder involving abnormal preoccupation with disease. Treatment of the latter in the absence of an appreciation of the former frequently produces clinical frustration, if not exasperation.

■ Somatoform Pain Disorder

Somatoform pain disorder is characterized by the report of severe and lasting pain. DSM-III-R specifies a duration of at least six months. Either no physical basis is apparent, or the reaction is greatly in excess of what would be expected from the physical pathology. In approaching this phenomenon it is important to understand that pain is always a sensation registered in a patient's mental experience; there is in fact no perfect correlation between the occurrence or intensity of pain (as reported in the general population) and tissue damage or irritation. This partial independence of physical damage and psychological experience evidently makes possible the considerable effectiveness of purely psychological treatment for pain that has a definite physical basis (Keefe & Williams, 1989). Because, like all other experience, pain is ultimately always private, we have no way of gauging with certainty the actual extent of a patient's pain. This fundamental unclarity is wholly insufficient to justify the conclusion that a patient is faking or exaggerating his or her pain, although such a judgment is regrettably frequent among clinicians. Somatoform pain disorder is fairly common among psychiatric patients (Katon, Egan, & Miller, 1985) and is more often diagnosed among women.

The reported pain may be vaguely located in the area of the heart or other vital organs, or it may center in the lower back or limbs. (Tension headaches and migraines are not included here, since they involve demonstrable physiological changes, such as muscle contractions.) People with psychogenic pain disorders flirt with an invalid life-style. They tend to "doctor-shop" in the hope of finding both a physical confirmation of their pain and some medication to relieve it. This behavior continues even if several visits to doctors fail to indicate any underlying physical problem. Sadly enough, in many cases somatoform pain patients actually wind up being disabled—either through addiction to pain medication or through the crippling effects of surgery they have been able to obtain as treatment for their condition.

Although technically a disorder should be diagnosed as a somatoform pain disorder only when no adequate organic basis for the pain can be found, some vaguely related injury or physical problem may be discovered in a pain patient's medical history. Usually, however, the past incident serves more as perceived justification for the patient's physical concern rather than as a predisposing factor to it.

Conversion Disorder

Conversion disorder, earlier called *hysteria,* involves a neurotic pattern in which symptoms of some physical malfunction or loss of control appear without any underlying organic pathology. It is one of the most intriguing and baffling patterns in psychopathology, and we still have much to learn about it.

As we mentioned in Chapter 2, the term *hysteria* was derived from the Greek word meaning "uterus." It was thought by Hippocrates and other ancient Greeks that this disorder was restricted to women, and that it was caused by sexual difficulties, particularly by the wandering of a frustrated uterus to various parts of the body because of sexual desires and a yearning for children. Thus the uterus might lodge in the throat and cause choking sensations, or in the spleen, resulting in temper tantrums. Hippocrates considered marriage the best remedy for the affliction, and ironically—as Freud's subsequent experience with Victorian-era women showed—he may in some instances have been right.

Freud used the term *conversion hysteria* for these disorders because he believed that the symptoms were an expression of repressed sexual energy— that is, the psychosexual conflict was seen as *converted* into a bodily disturbance. For example, a conflict over masturbation might be "solved" by developing a paralyzed hand. This was not done consciously, of course, and the person was not aware of the origin or meaning of the physical symptom.

In contemporary psychopathology, reactions of this type are no longer interpreted in Freudian terms as the "conversion" of sexual conflicts or other psychological problems into physical symptoms. Rather, the physical symptoms are now usually seen as serving a defensive function, enabling an individual to escape or avoid a stressful situation without having to take responsibility for doing so. The term *conversion* has been retained, however.

Conversion disorders were once relatively common in civilian and especially in military life. In World War I, conversion disorder was the most frequently diagnosed psychiatric syndrome among soldiers; it was also relatively common during World War II. Conversion disorder typically occurred under highly stressful combat conditions and involved men who would ordinarily be considered stable. Here, conversion symptoms—such as being paralyzed in the legs—enabled a soldier to avoid an anxiety-arousing combat situation without being labeled a coward or being subjected to court-martial.

During World War I, conversion disorder was the most frequently diagnosed psychiatric syndrome among soldiers. It enabled soldiers to avoid anxiety-arousing combat situations, the severity of which is evident in this scene on the western front.

Today conversion disorders constitute only some 5 percent of all neurotic disorders treated. Interestingly enough, their decreasing incidence seems to be closely related to our growing sophistication about medical and psychological disorders: a conversion disorder apparently loses its defensive function if it can be readily shown to lack an organic basis. In an age that no longer believes in such phenomena as being struck blind or suddenly afflicted with an unusual and dramatic paraplegia, the cases that occur now increasingly simulate more exotic physical diseases that are harder to diagnose, such as convulsive seizures or gastrointestinal ailments. Even psychologically sophisticated people have been known to develop conversion symptoms under stress, however, as the following case shows:

A 29-year-old physician in the first year of a psychiatric residency was experiencing a great deal of stress from problems in both his personal life and his hospital work. His marriage was deteriorating and he was being heavily criticized by the rather authoritarian chief of psychiatry for allegedly mismanaging some treatment cases. Shortly before he was to discuss his work in an important hospital-wide conference being conducted by the chief psychiatrist, he had an "attack" in which he developed difficulty in speaking and severe pains in his chest. He thought his condition was probably related to a viral infection, but physical findings were negative.

Here we see with particular clarity how a conversion symptom may serve the function of escape from unwanted responsibility.

The range of symptoms in conversion disorder is practically as diverse as for physically based ailments. In describing the clinical picture in conversion disorder, it is useful to think in terms of three categories of symptoms: sensory, motor, and visceral.

Sensory Symptoms   Any of the senses may be involved in sensory conversion reactions. The most common forms are as follows:

Anesthesia—loss of sensitivity

Hypesthesia—partial loss of sensitivity

Hyperesthesia—excessive sensitivity

Analgesia—loss of sensitivity to pain

Paresthesia—exceptional sensations, such as tingling

You may be wondering why somatoform pain disorder, given its essential similarity to the symptoms just listed, is not included here as merely another form of sensory conversion disorder. Why is it a separate category? The DSM-III-R offers no satisfactory answer to this question. It may be that it was given separate status because it appears to occur far more frequently than other conversion phenomena.

Some idea of the range of sensory symptoms that may occur in conversion disorders can be gleaned from Ironside and Batchelor's (1945) study of hysterical visual symptoms among airmen in World War II. They found blurred vision, photophobia (extreme sensitivity to light), double vision, night blindness, a combination of intermittent visual failure and amnesia, deficient stereopsis (the tendency to look past an object during attempts to focus on it), restriction in the visual field, intermittent loss of vision in one eye, color blindness, jumbling of print during attempts to read, and failing day vision. They also found that the symptoms of each airman were closely related to his performance duties. Night fliers, for example, were more subject to night blindness, while day fliers more often developed failing day vision. The results of a later study of student military aviators who developed conversion disorders are reported in HIGHLIGHT 6.5.

The other senses may also be subject to a wide range of disorders. A puzzling and unsolved question in hysterical blindness and deafness is whether individuals actually cannot see or hear, or whether the sensory information is received but screened from consciousness (Theodor & Mandelcorn, 1973). In general, the evidence supports the latter hypothesis, that the sensory input is screened from consciousness.

Motor Symptoms   Motor conversion reactions also cover a wide range of symptoms, but only the most common need be mentioned here.

Paralysis conversion reactions are usually confined to a single limb, such as an arm or a leg, and the loss of function is usually selective. For example, in "writer's cramp," a person cannot write but may be able to use the same muscles in shuffling a deck of cards or playing the piano. Tremors (muscular shaking or trembling) and tics (localized muscular twitches) are common. Occasionally, symptoms include contractures, which usually involve flexing of the fingers and toes, or rigidity of the larger joints, such as the elbows and knees. Paralyses and contractures frequently lead to walking disturbances. A person with a rigid knee joint may be forced to

HIGHLIGHT 6.5

Conversion Reactions in Student Naval Aviators

Mucha and Reinhardt (1970) reported on a study of 56 student aviators with conversion reactions who were assessed at the U.S. Naval Aerospace Medical Institute in Pensacola, Florida. In the group, representing 16 percent of a total population of 343 patients at the institute, four types of symptoms were found. These were, in order of frequency: visual symptoms (most common), auditory symptoms, paralysis or paresthesias (prickling sensations) of extremities, and paresthesia of the tongue.

Generally, the 56 students came from middle-class, achievement-oriented families. The fathers of 80 percent of them were either high school or college graduates and were either professional men or white-collar workers. Interestingly enough, 89 percent of the cases had won letters in one or more sports in high school or college; all were college graduates

and presently were flight students, officer candidates, or officers.

Commenting on the relatively high incidence of conversion reactions among the patients at the institute, Mucha and Reinhardt emphasized three conditions which they considered of etiological significance:

1. *Unacceptability of quitting.* In the students' previous athletic training, physical illness had been an acceptable means of avoiding difficult situations, whereas quitting was not. Moreover, the present training environment tended to perpetuate this adaptation, since the military is also achievement-oriented and does not tolerate quitting as a means of coping with stress situations.

2. *Parental models and past experience.* Seventy percent of the parents of these students had had significant illnesses affecting the

organ system utilized in the students' disorders; and a majority of the students had had multiple physical symptoms prior to enlistment—often as a result of athletic injuries.

3. *Sensitization to the use of somatic complaints.* As a result of their previous experience, the students were sensitized to the use of somatic complaints as a face-saving means of coping with stressful situations.

When faced with the real stress of the flight training program and with frequent life-or-death incidents they resorted to this unconscious mechanism to relieve the stress and to avoid admitting failure. To admit failure would be totally unacceptable to the rigid demands of their superegos. (p. 494)

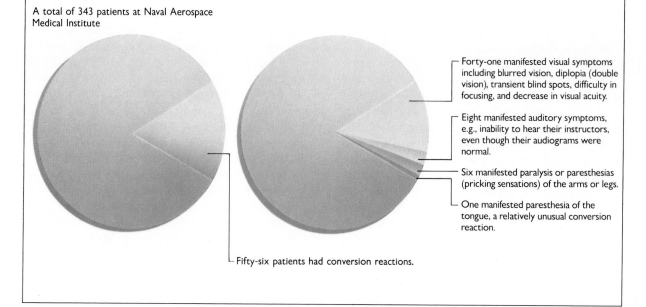

A total of 343 patients at Naval Aerospace Medical Institute

Forty-one manifested visual symptoms including blurred vision, diplopia (double vision), transient blind spots, difficulty in focusing, and decrease in visual acuity.

Eight manifested auditory symptoms, e.g., inability to hear their instructors, even though their audiograms were normal.

Six manifested paralysis or paresthesias (pricking sensations) of the arms or legs.

One manifested paresthesia of the tongue, a relatively unusual conversion reaction.

Fifty-six patients had conversion reactions.

throw his or her leg out in a sort of arc as he or she walks. Another walking disturbance is *astasia-abasia,* in which an individual can usually control leg movements when sitting or lying down, but can hardly stand and has a grotesque, disorganized walk, with both legs wobbling about in every direction.

The most common speech-related conversion disturbances are *aphonia,* in which an individual is able to talk only in a whisper, and *mutism,* in which he or she cannot speak at all. Interestingly enough, a person who can talk only in a whisper can usually cough in a normal manner. In true laryngeal paralysis both the cough and the voice are affected. Aphonia is a relatively common conversion reaction and usually occurs after some emotional shock, whereas mutism is relatively rare. Occasionally, symptoms may involve convulsions, similar to those in epilepsy. People with such symptoms, however, show few of the usual characteristics of true epileptics—they rarely, if ever, injure themselves in falls, their pupillary reflex to light remains unaffected, they are able to control excretory functions, and they do not have attacks when alone.

Visceral Symptoms   Visceral conversion reactions also cover a wide range of symptoms, including headaches, "lump in the throat" (formerly known as *globus hystericus*) and choking sensations, coughing spells, difficulty in breathing, cold and clammy extremities, belching, nausea, vomiting, and so on. Occasionally, persistent hiccoughing or sneezing occurs.

Actual organic symptoms may be simulated to an almost unbelievable degree. In a pseudoattack of acute appendicitis, a person not only may evidence lower-abdominal pain and other typical symptoms, but also may have a temperature far above normal. Conversion-reaction cases of malaria and tuberculosis have also been cited in the literature. In the latter, for example, an individual may show all the usual symptoms—coughing, loss of weight, recurrent fever, and night sweats—without actual organic disease. Numerous cases of pseudopregnancy have been reported, in which menstruation may cease, the abdominal area and breasts may enlarge, and the woman may experience morning sickness.

Because the symptoms in conversion disorder can simulate almost every known disease, accurate diagnosis can be a problem. However, in addition to specialized medical techniques, several criteria are commonly used for distinguishing between conversion disorders and organic disturbances:

1. A certain *belle indifference,* in which the patient describes what is wrong in a rather matter-of-fact way, with little of the anxiety and fear that would be expected in a person with a paralyzed arm or loss of sight. Mucha and Reinhardt (1970) reported that all of the 56 student fliers in their study (p. 203) showed this pattern, seeming to be unconcerned about long-range effects of their disabilities. In itself, however, unconcernedness cannot be taken as a reliable sign of conversion; some stoic individuals having genuine organic pathology display a similar disregard.

2. The frequent failure of the dysfunction to conform clearly to the symptoms of the particular disease or disorder. For example, little or no wasting away or atrophy of a "paralyzed" limb occurs in paralyses that are conversion reactions, except in rare and long-standing cases.

3. The selective nature of the dysfunction. For example, in conversion blindness, an individual does not usually bump into people or objects; "paralyzed" muscles can be used for some activities but not others; and uncontrolled contractures usually disappear during sleep.

4. The interesting fact that under hypnosis or narcosis (a sleeplike state induced by drugs) the symptoms can usually be removed, shifted, or reinduced by the suggestion of the therapist. Similarly, if the individual is suddenly awakened from a sound sleep, he or she may be tricked into using a "paralyzed" limb.

Where conversion symptoms are superimposed on an actual organic disorder, making a diagnosis may become difficult. It is usually fairly easy, however, to distinguish between a conversion reaction and frank malingering. Malingerers are consciously perpetrating frauds by faking the symptoms of diseases, and this fact is reflected in their demeanors. Individuals with conversion disorders are usually dramatic and apparently naive; they are concerned mainly with the symptoms and willingly discuss them. If inconsistencies in their behaviors are pointed out, they are usually unperturbed. To the contrary, malingerers are inclined to be defensive, evasive, and suspicious; they are usually reluctant to be examined and slow to talk about their symptoms, lest the pretense be discovered. Should inconsistencies in their behaviors be pointed out, malingerers immediately become more defensive.

Thus conversion disorder and malingering are considered distinct patterns, although sometimes they overlap.

The phenomenon of *mass hysteria,* as typified by outbreaks of St. Vitus's dance and biting manias during the Middle Ages, is a form of conversion disorder that has become a rarity in modern times. As we saw in Chapter 2, however, some outbreaks do still occur (for some recent examples, see page 37). In all cases, suggestibility clearly plays a major role—a conversion reaction in one individual rapidly spreads to others.

In the development of a conversion disorder, the following chain of events typically occurs: (a) a desire to escape from some unpleasant situation; (b) a fleeting wish to be sick in order to avoid the situation (this wish, however, is suppressed as unfeasible or unworthy); and under additional or continued stress, (c) the appearance of the symptoms of some physical ailment. The individual sees no relation between the symptoms and the stress situation. The particular symptoms that occur are usually those of a previous illness or are copied from other sources, such as symptoms observed among relatives, seen on television, or read about in magazines. The symptoms may also be superimposed on an existing organic ailment, associated with anticipated secondary gains, or symbolically related to the conflict situation.

Sometimes, conversion disorders seem to stem from feelings of guilt and the necessity for self-punishment. In one case, for example, a female patient developed a marked tremor and partial paralysis of the right arm and hand after she had physically attacked her father. During this incident she had clutched at and torn open his shirt with her right hand, and apparently the subsequent paralysis represented a sort of symbolic punishment of the "guilty party," while preventing a recurrence of her hostile and forbidden behavior.

Conversion symptoms often develop following an accident or injury from which an individual hopes to receive financial compensation. These reactions usually occur after accidents in which an individual might have been seriously injured but is actually only shaken up or slightly injured. Later, in discussions with family or friends, it may be agreed that the individual would have had a strong legal case if there had been an injury. "Are you sure you are all right? Could you possibly have injured your back? Perhaps there is something wrong with it." Indeed, the recent advertising practices of some law firms have involved precisely this approach. With

the aid of a "sympathetic" lawyer (whose fee often will be determined by the size of the monetary award), the individual may proceed to file suit for injury compensation.

In such cases it is especially hard to distinguish between a malingerer's deliberate simulation of injury and the unconscious deception of an individual suffering from conversion disorder (Lewis, 1974). It may well be that this dichotomy itself is misleading. Apparently many conversion disorder cases include a combination of the two, in which conscious acting is superimposed on unconscious acting or role playing. In any event, the patient in such cases often shows an amazingly rapid recovery once there has been "proper" compensation for the "injuries."

Whatever specific causal factors may be involved, however, the basic motivational pattern underlying conversion disorder seems to be to avoid or reduce anxiety-arousing stress by getting sick—thus converting an intolerable emotional problem into a face-saving physical one. Once this response is learned, it is maintained because it is repeatedly reinforced—both by anxiety reduction and by the interpersonal gains (in terms of sympathy and support) that result from being sick.

DISSOCIATIVE DISORDERS

Like somatoform disorders, **dissociative disorders** appear mainly to be ways of avoiding anxiety and stress and of gratifying secret needs. Both disorders also permit a person to deny personal responsibility for his or her "unacceptable" wishes or behavior. In the case of dissociative disorders, however, the person avoids the stress by dissociating—in essence by escaping from his or her own personal identity. Dissociative patterns include psychogenic amnesia and fugue states, multiple personality, and depersonalization. A generalized conception of these patterns appears in *HIGHLIGHT 6.6.* These patterns are generally not so well researched or understood as those already described; hence our coverage of them will be relatively brief.

Psychogenic Amnesia and Fugue

Amnesia is partial or total inability to recall or identify past experience. It may occur in neurotic

HIGHLIGHT 6.6

Continuum of Dissociative Processes and States

The following figure is a graphic representation of the manner in which Ross (1989, p. 80) conceives dissociation's fundamental role in mental disorders of varying types and severities. Thus a simple form of dissociative process is involved in normal dis- sociative states, whereas complex dissociation processes characterize MPD, all the more where many and changing alter personalities are poorly integrated with one another (called "polyfragmented" MPD). Notice that Ross includes conversion disorder on this con- tinuum, the symptoms of which are also conceived to be dissociat- ed parts of the self. While this idea is not prominent in contemporary writings on conversion disorder, much historical precedence exists for it.

SIMPLE								COMPLEX
	Normal dissociation	Psychogenic amnesia	Psychogenic fugue	Partial MPD	Dual personality	Complex MPD	Polyfragmented MPD	
		Conversion disorder	Atypical dissociative disorder					

Note: MPD = multiple personality disorder

---

and psychotic disorders and in brain pathology, including brain injury and diseases of the central nervous system. If the amnesia is caused by brain pathology, it usually involves an actual *retention* failure. That is, either the information is not regis- tered and does not enter memory storage, or, if stored, it cannot be retrieved; it is truly and almost always permanently lost (Hirst, 1982).

Psychogenic amnesia, on the other hand, is usually limited to a failure to *recall.* The "forgot- ten" material is still there beneath the level of consciousness, as becomes apparent under hypnosis or narcosis interviews, and in cases where the amnesia spontaneously clears up. Four types of psychogenic amnesia are recognized: *localized* (a person remembers nothing that happened during a specific period—usually the first few hours follow- ing some traumatic event); *selective* (a person forgets some but not all of what happened during a given period); *generalized* (a person forgets his or her entire life history); and *continuous* (a person remem- bers nothing beyond a certain point in the past). The latter two types occur rarely.

As we have noted, psychogenic amnesia is fairly common in initial reactions to intolerably traumatic experiences, such as those occurring during combat conditions and immediately after catastrophic events. Some neurotically functioning individuals, however, develop such amnesias in the face of stressful life situations with which most people deal more effectively.

In typical psychogenic amnesic reactions, indi- viduals cannot remember their names, do not know how old they are or where they reside, and do not recognize their parents, relatives, or friends. Yet their basic habit patterns—such as their abilities to read, talk, perform skilled work, and so on— remain intact, and they seem quite normal aside from the amnesia.

In this amnesic state, a person may retreat still further from real-life problems by going away in what is called a **fugue state.** A fugue reaction is a defense by actual flight—an individual is not only amnesic, but also wanders away from home, often assuming a partially or completely new identity. Days, weeks, or sometimes even years later, such

This woman, dubbed "Jane Doe," was emaciated, incoherent, partially clothed, covered by insect and animal bites, and near death when discovered by a Florida park ranger in September 1980. Her recovery was further complicated by a rare form of psychogenic amnesia, generalized amnesia, in which she had lost the memory of her name, her past, and her ability to read and write. Judging from her accent, linguistic experts said the woman was probably from Illinois. Although interviews conducted under the effect of drugs revealed that the woman had apparently had a Catholic education, her few childhood memories were so common that they were meaningless. In a dramatic attempt to recover her past, Jane Doe and her doctor appeared on "Good Morning America" and appealed to her relatives to step forward. The response was overwhelming, and authorities came to believe that Jane Doe was the daughter of a couple from Roselle, Illinois, whose daughter had gone to the Ft. Lauderdale area to open a boutique. Their last contact with their daughter had been a phone call in 1976. Despite the couple's certainty, Jane Doe was never able to remember her past.

individuals may suddenly find themselves in strange places, not knowing how they got there and with apparently complete amnesia for their fugue periods. Their activities during their fugues may vary from merely going on a round of motion pictures to traveling across the country, entering a new occupation, and starting a new way of life.

The pattern in psychogenic amnesia is essentially the same as in conversion disorder, except that instead of avoiding some unpleasant situation by

getting sick, a person avoids thoughts about the situation or in the extreme leaves the scene. Apparently, virtually any type of inner conflict involving wishes that are unacceptable to a person and are therefore anxiety-arousing may serve as the basis of an amnesic reaction and its elaboration into fugue. The threatening information becomes inaccessible, owing either to some sort of automatic cognitive blockage or to deliberate suppression. In patterns involving suppression, individuals apparently tell themselves that they will not remember some traumatic event or situation; subsequently they try to believe and behave as though they actually are amnesic. For example, in a study of 98 amnesia cases, primarily among military personnel, Kiersch (1962) found 41 to be of this seemingly "feigned" ("factitious" in DSM-III-R terminology) type.

People experiencing psychogenic amnesia are typically egocentric, immature, highly suggestible individuals who are faced with extremely unpleasant situations from which they see no escape. Often, they previously had experienced conscious impulses to "forget" and run away but were too inhibited to accept that solution. Eventually, however, the stress becomes so intolerable that they suppress large segments of their personalities and all memory for the stressful situations, thus allowing more congenial patterns to carry on. As O'Neill and Kempler (1969) have pointed out, psychogenic amnesia is highly selective and involves only material that is basically intolerable or threatening to the self.

During a dissociative fugue reaction, an individual appears normal and is able to engage in complex activities. Normally the activities chosen reflect a rather different life-style from the previous one, the rejection of which is usually transparent. This behavior is well illustrated in the following case:

Burt Tate, a 42-year-old short-order cook in a small-town diner, was brought to the attention of local police following a heated altercation with another man at the diner. Questioned by the police, he gave his name as Burt Tate and indicated that he had arrived in town several weeks earlier. However, he could produce no official identification and could not tell the officers where he had previously lived and worked. No charges were proffered and no arrest made, but Burt was asked to accompany the officers to the emergency room of a local hospital so that he might be examined, to which request he agreed.

Burt's physical examination was negative for evidence of recent head trauma or any other medical abnormality, and there was no indication of drug or alcohol abuse. He was oriented as to current time and place, but manifested no recall of his personal history prior to his arrival in town. He did not seem especially concerned about his total lack of a remembered past. He was kept in the hospital overnight for observation and discharged the following day.

Meanwhile, the police instituted missing-person search procedures and discovered that Burt matched the description of one Gene Saunders, a resident of a city some 200 miles away who had disappeared a month earlier. The wife of Mr. Saunders was brought to the town and confirmed the real identity of "Burt," who, now noticeably anxious, stated that he did not recognize Mrs. Saunders.

Prior to his disappearance, Gene Saunders, a middle-level manager in a large manufacturing firm, had been experiencing considerable difficulties at work and at home. A number of stressful work problems, including failure to get an expected promotion, the loss through resignation of some of his staff, failure of his section to meet production goals, and increased criticism from his superior—all occurring within a brief time frame—had upset his normal equanimity. He had become morose and withdrawn at home, and had been critical of his wife and children. Two days before he had left he had had a violent argument with his 18-year-old son, who'd declared his father a "failure" and had stormed out of the house to go live with friends. (Adapted from Spitzer et al., 1989, pp. 215–216.)

■ Multiple Personality Disorder

Multiple personality is a dissociative reaction, usually with identifiable stressor precipitants, in which a patient manifests two or more complete systems of personality. Each system has distinct, well-developed emotional and thought processes and represents a unique and relatively stable personality. The individual may change from one personality to another at periods varying from a few minutes to several years, though shorter time frames are more common. The personalities are usually dramatically different; one may be carefree and fun-loving, and another quiet, studious, and serious.

Needs and behaviors inhibited in the main or basic personality are usually liberally displayed by the others.

Dual and multiple personalities have received a great deal of attention and publicity in fiction, television, and motion pictures. Actually, however, they were until recently relatively uncommon in clinical practice. Prior to about the last 15 years, in fact, only slightly more than 100 cases could be found in the psychological and psychiatric literature. Their occurrence seems to have increased dramatically in recent years. No wholly satisfactory explanation exists for such a change in the occurrence base rate. Some of the increase, however, may be artifactual, the product of increased acceptance of the diagnosis by clinicians, who traditionally have been somewhat skeptical of the astonishing behavior these patients often display—such as undergoing sudden and dramatic shifts in personal identity before one's eyes. More females than males are diagnosed as having the disorder, with the ratio being about nine to one (Ross, 1989).

A more substantive and disturbing reason for the apparent increase in cases of multiple personality disorder (MPD) is offered by Ross (1989), who attributes it in part to an increasingly "sick" society in which child abuse, especially sexual abuse by adults, has become rampant. If Ross's suggestion about the deterioration of society is arguable, his observation that MPD is commonly preceded by childhood abuse is almost certainly not. While it is somewhat amazing that this connection was not generally recognized until about 1984, there is now no reasonable doubt about the reality of this association. Since childhood sexual abuse is a far more common occurrence for females than for males, there may be a relationship here with the gender discrepancy in diagnosis. The issue of abuse is addressed in further detail later in this section.

As already suggested, the question of malingering has dogged the diagnosis of MPD for at least a century. These doubts are reinforced by the suspicion that clinicians, by virtue of undue fascination with the problem and unwise use of techniques such as hypnosis, are sometimes responsible for eliciting these phenomena in highly suggestible patients. The latter criticism has a modest ring of truth, but it fails adequately to account for all of the observations reported—such as the elaborate pretreatment personal histories with which alternate personalities are commonly endowed. Cynicism about the concept of MPD has also been encouraged by the frequency with which it is used by defendants and their attorneys to escape punishment for crimes

("My other personality did it."). This defense was used in the famous case of the "Hillside Strangler," Kenneth Bianchi (Orne, Dinges, & Orne, 1984).

It is also true, as Spanos, Weekes, and Bertrand (1985) have clearly demonstrated, that normal college students can be induced by suggestion to exhibit some of the phenomena seen in MPD, including the adoption of a second personality. Such role-playing demonstrations are interesting in various ways, but they do not answer, nor even convincingly address, the question of the reality of MPD. That college student subjects might be able to give a convincing portrayal of a person with a broken leg would not, after all, establish the nonexistence of broken legs.

Our own view of the controversy surrounding MPD, as was suggested previously in our discussion of conversion versus malingering, is that it rests on a dichotomous way of thinking that is itself false. The increasing knowledge about normal mental and cognitive processes, such as the widespread evidence of separate (dissociated) memory subsystems and nonconscious active mental processing, strongly suggests that much highly organized mental activity is carried on in the "background," outside of awareness—analogous in some ways to computer multitasking (Hintzman, 1990). Accordingly, questions about whether a given behavior is consciously *or* unconsciously mediated, genuine *or* feigned, intended *or* unintended, deliberate *or* spontaneous, and so on are in the final analysis usually unanswerable as asked. So far as we can tell, the human mind does not operate in these dichotomous ways. In addition, such oversimplifications distract us from the task of understanding how it is that individuals go about solving the often difficult problems they have with managing and somehow integrating their extant mental contents with the challenges of their everyday lives. Is MPD "real?" Perhaps, but that is not to say we believe elements of theatrical pretense are never a part of this interesting and complex disorder.

The number of alter personalities in MPD varies, but in two substantial series of cases evaluated by questionnaire it averaged an amazing 15 (Ross, 1989). Alter personalities are usually strikingly different from the primary personality, suggesting that the alters express rejected parts of the original self. Alter characteristics are also highly varied, but certain "roles" are extremely common in the alter repertoires of MPD patients. These include the roles of Child, Protector, and Persecutor; an Opposite Sex alter, who may share one of these other roles, is also present in a majority of

cases (Ross, 1989). These various types of role behaviors are discernible in *HIGHLIGHT 6.7*, which attempts to outline the kinds of cognitive structures regularly observed to be operating in cases of MPD. Normally, alters know of the existence of the primary personality and of each other, but the primary personality is not "permitted" knowledge of these others occupying his or her space, time, and body. Mutual and unidirectional amnesias among the alters also sometimes occur. Interestingly, very often one alter personality knows "everything" and, if cooperative, may be a valuable consultant for the therapist.

Wolfe, Gentile, and Wolfe (1989), in a recent study evaluating 71 sexually abused children, have likened their reactions to posttraumatic stress disorder. Evidence is building impressively in support of the notion that MPD is largely a type of posttraumatic dissociative disorder, one whose principal manifestation is the development of partially independent (dissociated) subsystems that constitute, in themselves, coherent personality organizations. The existence of these semiautonomous subpersonalities appears to serve important adaptive and coping functions for individuals who were severely and repeatedly traumatized as children, particularly (although not exclusively) by incestuous sexual abuse. Concerning the latter, 79.2 percent of Ross and colleagues' (1989) 236 cases, and 83.0 percent of Putnam and colleagues' (1986) 100 cases of MPD reported childhood abuse of a specifically sexual nature. The figures for other types of physical abuse were not far behind, suggesting that as children most of these individuals had lived in environments characterized by marked brutality. It is thought that the tendency to dissociate as a method of coping begins while victimization is in process—"This is not happening to *me*."

The cruelty that some MPD patients suffered as children is almost unbelievable. A compelling illustration is the well-known case of Sybil, who was the subject of both a well-researched biography (Schreiber, 1973) and a feature motion picture. The case is briefly summarized here.

By the time of her adult years, Sybil reportedly had developed 15 alter personalities. Some of these were relatively minor characters, one was a baby, and two late developers were men. From infancy through late childhood, Sybil had been brutalized, sexually tortured, and nearly murdered by her psychotic (schizophrenic) mother,

Core Assumptions Characteristic of Multiple Personality Disorder and Associated Cognitive Distortions

Different parts of the self are separate selves.
- We have different bodies.
- I could kill (or slash, burn, force to overdose) her and be unaffected myself.
- Her behavior is not my responsibility.
- The abuse never happened to me.
- They're not my parents.

The victim is responsible for the abuse.
- I must be bad; otherwise it wouldn't have happened.
- If I had been perfect, it wouldn't have happened.
- I deserved to be punished for being angry.
- If I were perfect, I would not get angry.
- I never feel angry—she is the angry one.
- She deserves to be punished for allowing the abuse to happen.
- She deserves to be punished for showing anger.

It is wrong to show anger (or frustration, defiance, etc.).
- When I showed anger I was abused.
- If I never show anger, I will not be abused.
- I deserve to be punished for being angry.
- If I were perfect, I would not get angry.
- I never feel angry—she is the angry one.

- She deserves to be punished for allowing the abuse to happen.
- She deserves to be punished for feeling anger.

The past is present.
- I am 8 years old.
- The abuse is still happening.
- I am scared.
- The doctor is going to abuse me now.
- No one will protect me.

The primary personality can't handle the memories.
- We have to keep the memories.
- You can't tell her about us.
- If she has to remember, we will make her crazy.
- If she remembers, she won't like us.
- The abuse never happened.
- They must be sick to think those things happened.
- My parents are not like that.
- She is weak—I am strong.

I love my parents but she hates them.
- She is the bad one.
- You have to get rid of her.
- Nobody could ever be friends with her (or like her).
- She wants to hurt me.

The primary personality must be punished.
- It's her fault the abuse happened.

- She deserves all the bad things that happen to her.
- Everything bad that happens to her happens because she is bad.
- She has suffered enough—she would be better off if I killed her.
- I can punish her and be unaffected myself.
- I (the punishing alter) was never abused.
- Nobody would ever want to be close to me (persecutor alter).
- I am unlovable.

I can't trust myself or others.
- People have always abused me.
- I always end up choosing abusive relationships.
- I want to be abused.
- My parents were never consistent with me.
- Previous doctors wouldn't believe me (concerning abuse history and diagnosis).
- Whenever people get close to me, they leave.
- She trusted before and she got hurt.
- We won't let anyone get close to her.
- I can't trust her—she gets herself in situations she can't handle.

Adapted from Ross, 1989, pp. 126–130.

while her proper, hypocritical, and detached father managed persistently to convince himself—contrary to overwhelming evidence—that nothing untoward was happening in his family.

In the course of 11 years of ultimately successful treatment by a devoted and tenacious therapist, Sybil's extraordinary history—confirmed by her father when the outraged therapist forcefully confronted him—was gradually pieced together. The following are some highlights from that history:

The parents, engaging in extensive sexual activity nightly, made no obvious effort over the first nine years of her life to shield Sybil, who shared the same bedroom, from these experiences. In the daytime, neither parent was physically affectionate toward the other, and both held forth often and vociferously on the evils of sex. An additional twist on this bizarre situation was that Sybil frequently observed her mother molesting little girls she was supposedly baby-sitting, in the course of certain "games" she would suggest they play together. Also, on one occasion Sybil inadvertently discovered her mother engaged in mutual genital manipulation with three teenage girls in the neighborhood.

Beginning when Sybil was not yet a year old, her mother regularly performed certain morning rituals on her. These varied considerably but included such things as tying her up in various ways, suspending her from the ceiling by means of a light bulb cord, administering unneeded, adult-sized enemas to her with cold water, and forcing her to take potent laxatives with the prohibition that the child not use the bathroom; if she soiled herself she was beaten. The mother laughed during all of this; Sybil cried until she was 3½, then cried no more.

One morning ritual that her mother took great pains to carry out in an orderly fashion involved placing Sybil on the kitchen table and forcefully inserting various objects, including sharp metal ones, into her vagina. She explained to the child continuously from 6 months of age that she was only preparing her for "what men do to you." Needless to say, the child's vaginal canal was seriously injured by these ministrations, and permanent scarring of her genitalia to the point of probable sterility was observed in adult gynecological exams.

When Sybil's mother determined that actual punishment was in order because of misbehavior, she would become even more dangerous. The child would be slapped with enough force to

knock her to the floor, or she might be flung across the room—on one occasion with such violence as to dislocate her shoulder. On another occasion Sybil's larynx was fractured with a blow delivered to her neck. She was also seriously burned with a hot flat iron and was nearly asphyxiated with a scarf tied tightly around her neck. In addition to these more deliberate inflictions of injury the child suffered many "accidents," such as a drawer violently closed on her hand. These numerous injuries were explained with vague references of the "kids will be kids" variety, a fabrication that was not seriously challenged by either Sybil's father or the family physician. Her mother's all-too-credible threats kept Sybil from revealing the truth to anyone.

On one occasion Sybil's mother nearly succeeded in killing her daughter. She placed her in a well-stocked wheat crib above her husband's shop "to play," and elevated the retractable stairs so that escape was impossible. Anyone with a rural background would know well the considerable danger of smothering in an entrapment of this kind, and in fact Sybil, buried in wheat and having difficulty breathing, thought she was going to die. She was saved by her father's unexpected return from work and his curiosity about the retracted stairs. Sybil's mother denied to her concerned husband any knowledge of how the child had got into the wheat crib, suggesting that it may have been done by a certain neighborhood bully, who of course also denied any knowledge of the incident.

The more recently publicized case of Truddi Chase and her "troops," a total of 92 separately identifiable personalities, is more typical in involving a male stepfather as the abuser, but no less revolting in its depiction of years of sadistic cruelty and heinous sexual victimization—beginning in this case at age 2. Frighteningly (but apparently of common occurrence in these cases), Truddi's mother did not effectively intervene to terminate the abuse for 14 years. Meanwhile, Truddi Chase, the original personality and the designated main author of the remarkable book, *When Rabbit Howls* (Chase et al. 1990), apparently ceased to exist; she has been "asleep" since age 2, having been replaced by "the troops."

The troops, the actual authors, are an astounding assortment of characters, many of them extremely talented and articulate, who participated in a program of treatment with psychotherapist Robert

One of the most well-known recent illustrations of multiple personality disorder is the case of Truddi Chase, who developed 92 personalities by the time she was an adult. Truddi's history of unspeakably brutal treatment by her stepfather and the subsequent manifestation of the "troops" is in keeping with the growing evidence that severe and repeated childhood trauma, both physical and sexual, is a significant factor in the occurrence of multiple personality disorder.

A. Phillips, Ph.D. The currently main personality is an employed adult woman, divorced and the mother of one child, a daughter. Prior to her treatment she had experienced continual dizziness, temper tantrums, and periods of blackout, but knew nothing of the others inhabiting her body. These other personalities include the following:

- Rabbit, mentioned in the book's title, who does not communicate except by howling in pain
- Mean Joe, the principal Protector, who is 11 feet tall
- Miss Wonderful, a model of human perfection
- Elvira, somewhat wild and irresponsible
- Twelve, a sensitive and artistic child
- Black Katherine, the assertive caretaker of Twelve and the other children
- Sewer Mouth, another woman who expresses rage in explicit language

- Ean the Irishman, who offers obscure commentary in a thick brogue
- The Front Runner, who keeps track of and reports on the other troops

The treatment undertaken by Dr. Phillips was apparently successful in achieving a workable "integration" of these diverse and fragmented personifications.

The question arises as to whether or not MPD occurs in the absence of a history of chronic childhood trauma. Ross (1989), who has had much clinical experience with MPD, allows that there may be such atraumatic cases of the disorder, but that he has personally never seen one where MPD was well-established and complexly organized. An unequivocal answer to the question is not easily obtained owing to an understandable and well-documented resistance among MPD patients to remembering events of this kind. In the absence of definitive information, our guess is that significantly disruptive MPD does occur in people whose backgrounds are unremarkable with respect to abuse. We would expect in such cases, however, to see evidence of other factors encouraging the development of dissociative tendencies.

■ Depersonalization Disorder

A relatively more frequent dissociative disorder that occurs predominantly in adolescents and young adults is **depersonalization disorder,** in which there is a loss of the sense of self. Individuals with this disorder feel that they are, all of a sudden, different—for example, that they are other people or that their bodies have drastically changed and have become, perhaps, quite grotesque. Frequently, the altered states are reported as out-of-body experiences in which individuals feel that they are, for a time, floating above their physical bodies and observing what is going on below. Mild forms of the experience are extremely common and are no cause for alarm. Reports of out-of-body experiences have included perceptions of visiting other planets or relatives who are in other cities. The disorder is often precipitated by acute stress resulting from an infectious illness, an accident, or some other traumatic event, as in the following case:

Charlotte D., a recently separated 19-year-old woman, was referred to an outpatient mental health service by her physician because she had experienced several "spells" in which her mind left her body and went to a strange place in another state. The first instance had occurred two months earlier, a few days after her husband had left her without explanation. Since then, she had had four episodes of "traveling" that had occurred during her waking state and had lasted for about 15 to 20 minutes. She described her experiences as a dreamy feeling in which her arms and legs were not attached to her body and other people around her were perceived as zombielike. Typically she felt dizzy and had pains in her stomach for hours after each spell.

Individuals who experience depersonalized states, and they are many, are usually able to function entirely normally between episodes. With more severe manifestations, as in the preceding case, the experience can be quite frightening and understandably causes a victim to become anxiously concerned about imminent mental collapse. Mostly such fears are unfounded, but the person might well profit from some professional help in dealing with the precipitating stressors and for reducing anxiety. A diagnostic problem may nevertheless arise because feelings of depersonalization sometimes are in fact early manifestations of impending decompensation and the development of frankly psychotic states of a schizophreniform type, discussed in Chapter 12.

NEUROTIC STYLES

As was earlier noted, the strategy employed in recent DSMs in creating discrete categories for the syndromes described above is probably a good one from a diagnostic perspective. Abandonment of the *concept* of neurosis may be premature on other counts, however. It has robust research and clinical support; it continues to be employed by numerous workers in the field; and it remains a useful way to conceptualize many of the behaviors described not only in this chapter but elsewhere in the text.

In this section we will explore the possibility that neurotic patterns can exist in the absence of the relatively dramatic symptom syndromes described in preceding sections. In this context, we will introduce the notion of neurotic "styles." Personal misery and ineffectiveness are not, after all, dependent on the presence of obtrusive "symptoms." We will illustrate this point with a brief consideration of the manner in which neurotic styles can influence interpersonal processes.

No precise equivalent to the concept of **neurotic style** has ever been included in the formal Axis I DSM categories. It is unlikely that one will be because these styles, as general "symptomless" ways of coping with anxiety, do not warrant the status of formally recognized mental disorders. By *symptomless,* we mean that neurotic styles do not entail disabilities that would be obvious to everyone. Rather, they involve general ways of behaving that interfere with an individual's effectiveness and ability to satisfy personal needs, and are in this sense somewhat akin to Axis II personality disorders. We include them here for two reasons: (a) many individuals who seek the services of mental health practitioners are less troubled by specific clinical symptoms per se than by unsatisfactory interpersonal relationships caused by neurotic styles; and (b) an understanding of neurotic styles should enhance our understanding of the established DSM categories of neurotic symptom disorders, since generalized neurotic behavior patterns often accompany these specific disorders (as a recall of several of the cases presented earlier will confirm). Concerning this point, Shapiro (1965) has written: "Every reader with clinical experience and, for that matter, every sensitive person will know that [neurotic] symptoms or outstanding pathological traits regularly appear in contexts of attitudes, interests, intellectual inclinations and endowments, and even vocational aptitudes and social affinities with which the given symptom or trait seems to have a certain consistency" (p. 3).

In other words, disabling neurotic symptoms are usually embedded within a broader context of related personal characteristics. As we will see, many of these characteristics seem to arise from the same sources as do the symptoms. An example at this point may help clarify.

A 30-year-old man, married and with two children, was referred to a psychologist because of a persistent paralysis of his left arm and hand. Though the paralysis had developed following an auto accident, no evidence of organic damage would account for it. It was diagnosed as a conversion disorder. The man's history revealed that he had been dependent on an aunt who had raised him but who had subsequently died when he was 15. He had responded by making a show of self-sufficiency, but his work history as an adult had been marred by a series of dissatisfactions and changes of employment—primarily because he invariably had grown to feel that not enough was being done for him by his employers. Prior to the accident, his marital relationship had also become disrupted because his wife, having become more independent, was spending less time at home. The patient had bitterly complained that she was not being a "good mother" for her children.

Despite making a somewhat halfhearted attempt to resolve his difficulties in psychotherapy, treatment progress was reported as slow. The paralysis continued, and the patient appeared to have settled comfortably into the role of helpless victim. (Adapted from Spitzer et al., 1983.)

We see here the interplay between the patient's life-style prior to the accident and the particular symptom he developed in response to increased stress and the "opportunity" the accident afforded. Dependency appeared to be the principal theme both before and afterward. As we will see, neurotic dependency of this sort is usually the product of the *inhibition,* by anxiety, of independent, autonomous behavior (Hine, 1971; Hine et al., 1972, 1983). We will now consider how inhibition functions in neurotic styles.

■ The Role of Inhibition in Neurotic Styles

As indicated earlier, a person can be conditioned to respond with anxiety (or fear) to certain non-noxious stimuli. The person may then respond in the same way to other stimuli having similar properties. Once the anxiety-response pattern is established, the individual will learn to avoid the stimuli that provoke it. In a neurotic process, certain of an individual's own *behaviors,* or even the person's thoughts of engaging in them, will evoke the anxiety response. These anxiety-inspiring behaviors are then avoided or inhibited. Should such behaviors be important or essential for good adjustment, the affected person may be deprived of the means to function effectively in the world.

Let us suppose, for example, that a child is born to parents who do not tolerate aggressive behavior in any form, so much so that they repeatedly threaten to abandon their child anytime she displays normal childhood levels of aggressive conduct. It is

possible that such a child would learn to respond with strong anxiety to the more "aggressive" elements of her behavioral repertoire, or to any internal demand (motivational impulse) or external need to act aggressively. In other words, she would have pronounced inhibitions with respect to aggression and perhaps even related behavior, such as normal assertiveness. Here we may introduce the notion of an inhibited behavior *system*—a cluster of related behaviors that act as anxiety-eliciting stimuli. Insofar as aggressive or assertive behaviors are in some situations appropriate and adaptive, this child will have an important gap in her adaptive repertoire as she grows into adulthood.

The scenario given here is hypothetical, and we do not mean to suggest that all such anxieties are learned in this or comparable ways. In fact it is often difficult to determine precisely the sources of a neurotic person's special fears concerning the enactment of certain types of behavior. As suggested earlier, we certainly cannot rule out a constitutional element as a possibility, and indeed Shapiro's (1965) discussion of neurotic styles strongly hints at constitutional origins.

In any event, as the preceding example illustrates, one important characteristic of a person with a neurotic style is a deficit in behavioral repertoire. That is, certain types of behavior that seem adaptive and even expected in certain circumstances do not occur. They are blocked or inhibited by the anxiety their expression would cause. Dr. J., in the case described earlier, did not have egalitarian, easygoing, "passive" responses in his repertoire prior to his anxiety disorder breakdown. Two other characteristics often seen accompanying such deficits deserve brief mention, partly because of their importance as diagnostic clues:

1. A tendency for a person to behave, often in an inflexible and exaggerated manner, in ways that are the seeming opposite of the "missing" behaviors. Evidently, this is a defense used by the person to further lessen the likelihood of expressing, or perhaps even recognizing the existence of, the behavior system that is inhibited by anxiety. In the case of neurotic inhibition of aggressive behavior, for example, we might be struck by a person's extreme and unfailing agreeableness, even in situations that would seem to call for a vigorous defense of self—for example, in being unjustly humiliated by a bullying superior.

2. The failure of neurotic defenses to contain fully either the anxiety underlying them or some indirect evidence of the inhibited behavior system. Hence a person who develops a neurotic style will often show overt signs of anxiety, such as excessive sweating or muscular tension, while attempting to pursue his or her well-practiced defensive stance. Total success in blocking the expression of inhibited behavior systems is rarely, if ever, achieved. A trained observer, or even an especially sensitive layperson, will usually be able to detect in the person a tendency for the inhibited system to reveal itself, but normally only in indirect ways. The behavior of a client of one of the authors provides an instructive example. The client, a well-educated man who was a victim of severe aggression inhibition, repeatedly interrupted the therapist's comments with "respectful" requests that the therapist define the meaning of the relatively common words he was using, the client claiming to have a "poor vocabulary." The therapist's own increasing annoyance with these interruptions ultimately provided the clue to understanding. As subsequently confirmed by the client, his constant requests for interpretation of vocabulary items were his way of expressing his "aggressive" feelings that the therapist was acting like a "pompous ass." So much for the self-esteem hazards of the therapist's trade!

We will now briefly examine four inhibition patterns common to neurotic styles that can be seen in our own culture: aggression/assertion, responsibility/independence, compliance/submission, and intimacy/trust. Our illustrations should be considered as models or prototypes, much oversimplified for pedagogic reasons. They are based to a considerable extent on the analyses of Hine and colleagues (1971, 1972, 1983).

Aggression/Assertion Inhibition   The problems associated with this form of neurotic style have been illustrated already. A person with this neurotic style is markedly uncomfortable in any situation in which aggressive, self-assertive actions would seem to be reasonable responses. Instead, the person rigidly clings to a typically cooperative, agreeable, and "forgiving" stance, showing little or no hostile response to even extreme provocation. The anger and hostility presumably felt at some levels are largely stifled, though their intensities may build over time in the face of continued provocation. Physical and psychological problems (such as hypertension or compulsive behavior) are common long-term results. Fortunately less common is the so-called overcontrolled hostility syndrome (Megargee, 1966), in which buried anger and resent-

ment may lead to a sudden outburst of incredibly intense violence. Out of such circumstances are bred tales of, say, the much-admired Eagle scout who one day hacks his mother to death with an axe.

Responsibility/Independence Inhibition

Some individuals acquire in the course of their development a marked, anxiety-driven aversion to exercising personal independence or legitimate authority over others. Situations or events calling for assertions of independence or authority are, for these people, occasions of painful stress and anxiety. Hence such persons normally arrange their lives to minimize the likelihood they will be called on for displays of strength and autonomous action. They may, for example, prove to be incompetent at many of life's most simple tasks. Related to and normally accompanying these traits is a notable submissiveness and a clinging dependency on others. Few people can tolerate such childlike dependency indefinitely, and therefore such a person's relationships usually turn out to be unsatisfactory and short-lived. The development of symptoms consistent with this "helpless" state is a typical complication of this neurotic style.

Compliance/Submission Inhibition   Individuals who fear tendencies to comply or submit constitute a significant proportion of the "rebels" within our own and other cultures. They tend to reject ready-made solutions to personal problems offered by various professional, religious, and media figures, and also solutions imposed by authorities, legitimate or not. Presumably, people with this form of anxiety have learned that reliance on "established" authorities, parental or otherwise, leads to far greater disasters than does reliance on themselves. Accordingly, they become anxious and rebellious when they are required (or are motivated) to obey or "go along."

Compliant, submissive, and dependent behaviors are appropriate to many life circumstances—such as when one has a serious physical illness or when a legitimate authority frustrates one's plans—but these responses exact an enormous cost in anxiety from an individual who fears submission. Such an individual may display intense, inappropriate "strength" in the form of defiance, noncompliance with legitimate authority, inability to accept help in adversity, dangerous risk taking, and exaggerated wariness about letting anyone else be in control.

Traits of this sort are of course highly valued in American folklore. For example, Butch Cassidy and

Compliant, submissive, and dependent behaviors are appropriate to many life circumstances, but an individual who fears submission may display defiance, noncompliance with established authority (parental or otherwise), dangerous risk taking, and exaggerated wariness about letting anyone else be in control.

the Sundance Kid enraptured sophisticated movie audiences of the 1970s as much as similar film cowboys had since virtually the beginnings of the movie industry. More recent versions are Augustus McCrae and Woodrow Call of the novel and television series *Lonesome Dove*. It is certainly true that, in moderation, such traits can be functionally adaptive. When they are based on unrealistic fears of submission, however, they rarely can be contained within the moderate range. The result is often behavior that is unsatisfying, self-defeating, and on occasion dangerous to health and physical survival. For example, a person who cannot submit, comply, and depend on others during the treatment period immediately following a heart attack will have a significantly diminished life expectancy.

Intimacy/Trust Inhibition   People who feel unusually strong anxiety over establishing close personal attachments with others typically need relationships of mutual trust and intimacy at least as much as the rest of us. Indeed, they may spend inordinate amounts of time and energy in seeking them. However, at a crucial point in a relationship —perhaps when it seems to be going especially well or when an enhanced commitment is demanded— such a person suddenly becomes wary and retreats. Explicit suspiciousness and cynicism about the other's sincerity frequently enter the picture at this point, and the often bewildered other is more or less forcefully driven away. In cases of severe intimacy/ trust inhibition, this sequence is played out rapidly, with the result that few if any potential relationships

ever really get off the ground. When the problem is this severe, even more serious psychopathology tends to develop. In milder instances, a person can manage an occasional long-term relationship, although in such cases the person usually maintains a certain aloofness and distance.

As was mentioned earlier, neurotic styles often turn out to be similar in their manifest, overt aspects to certain of the DSM personality disorders, which are the subject of Chapter 8. In fact Horowitz and colleagues (1984) have used the term "personality styles" to refer to this class of problems. For example, the overt manifestations of neurotic intimacy/trust inhibition are as a practical matter often indistinguishable from those of the Axis II avoidant personality disorder. The distinction is at the conceptual level of imputed etiology; as we will see, "personality" disorders are conceived to be merely the aberrant developments of certain personality traits—not defensive behaviors driven by unrealistic fear (anxiety), as in neurotic styles.

■ Interpersonal Aspects of Neurotic Styles

As the preceding descriptions illustrate, individuals who develop neurotic styles can create not only frustration and misery for themselves, but also serious problems for people with whom they interact. Typically, people who behave neurotically do not have large networks of enduring relationships, and they tend to be quite dependent (although not necessarily in any obvious way) on the few they have. Consequently, most relatively non-neurotic people sooner or later find it unappealing to attempt to deal with the conflicting and unrelenting demands placed on them by their neurotic partners. For reasonably well-functioning individuals who are drawn to neurotically functioning people, it is literally a "no win" situation. For example, a man may find that a woman with compliance/submission inhibition is in many respects an "ideal" partner; she will "take charge" of all situations and will not allow herself or her mate to be taken advantage of or controlled. Yet the man in such a relationship might well find it difficult never to have his suggestions taken seriously, never to be allowed to take the lead. Hence the typical experience of a neurotic person is that relationships fall by the wayside, which may be yet another source of anxiety and insecurity.

Relationships need not turn out this way, however, particularly if the prospective friend or lover is also neurotic in a complementary way. For example, two people with aggression/assertion inhibitions may sustain a satisfying relationship because both are so frightened of aggression that neither presents a hint of provocation to the other. The relationship is characterized by a level of "understanding" and "niceness" that astounds external observers, although such observers may also be aware of a certain lack of zest and spontaneity in the interactions of the mutually inhibited pair. In effect they protect each other from their darker sides.

Other types of mutually neurotic, sustainable relationships readily come to mind. For example, a person with responsibility/independence inhibition married to a person with compliance/submission inhibition may find that the marriage results in a reasonably stable standoff. Of course, the relationship is apt to be punctuated by stormy episodes because, as we have seen, the inhibited portion of a neurotic individual's behavioral repertoire is unlikely to remain totally and permanently in abeyance. Thus even in cases of this kind of "perfect match," the upshot can often be a major crisis, sometimes ending in divorce court.

An obvious implication of these remarks is that relationships maintained on the basis of neurotic complementarity are vulnerable to disruption should one of the parties undergo therapy. Hafner (1984), for example, identified a group of husbands who experienced negative reactions when their wives, through therapy, overcame the "helplessness" of agoraphobia.

THE DEVELOPMENT AND MAINTENANCE OF NEUROTIC BEHAVIORS

In our preceding discussion we described the basic nature of neurotic disorders, noting that they may be manifested in certain characteristic symptoms, in general behavioral styles, or both. We presented a variety of specific neurotic patterns. Now let us focus more closely on relevant causal factors and give some attention to treatment considerations and to the outcomes that may be expected.

As we have seen, Freud considered anxiety to be the central problem in neurosis, a conclusion echoed over the years by many writers of widely differing theoretical persuasions. It is also basically the approach we have taken in seeking to conceptualize the varied behavioral phenomena traditionally classified as "neurotic." To understand these disorders, then, we need to understand the origins of relatively severe anxiety and of the inefficient and self-defeating modes often used to cope with it. We will approach these issues from biological, psychosocial, and sociocultural perspectives.

Biological Factors

The precise role of genetic and constitutional factors in neurotic behavior has not been delineated. Ample evidence from army records and civilian studies indicates that the incidence of neurotic patterns is much higher in the family histories of neurotic individuals than in the general population. The extent to which such findings reflect the effects of heredity is not known, however. Other explanations for these correlations are readily available, such as the likelihood that symptom modeling occurs among family members. For example, in the chronic multiple phobia case described earlier (page 187), the client's mother had also suffered lifelong phobic reactions and had sought actively to transmit her fears to her daughter.

In a study of concordance rates of neurotic disorders in identical and fraternal twins in the military, Pollin et al. (1969) found that among identical twins, the rate was only one and a half times as high as it was among fraternal twins. Since the environmental backgrounds of identical twins are likely to be more similar than those of fraternal twins, these investigators concluded that heredity plays a minimal role in the development of neurotic behaviors. After evaluating the evidence, Cohen (1974) came to a similar conclusion: "the concept of a genetically based disease or defect cannot provide a satisfactory explanation for the diversity and variability of most neurotic phenomena" (p. 473). Barlow (1988) has thoroughly reviewed the evidence on the heritability of the anxiety disorders, concluding that genetic factors seem modestly implicated, but only in the sense of contributing to some generalized vulnerability.

Sex, age, glandular functioning, and other physiological factors have also been investigated without clearly illuminating the causal picture. It is known, of course, that stress tolerance is lowered by loss of sleep, poor appetite, and increased irritability associated with prolonged emotional tension—but such conditions are by no means exclusive to the neurotic disorders. A more promising possibility centers around constitutional differences in ease of anxiety-response conditioning, as was suggested earlier. For example, extreme sensitivity and autonomic lability (instability) may predispose an individual to a "surplus" of conditioned fears and hence to avoidance behavior. Or it may be that some individuals are more prone biologically to experience the physiological disruptions underlying the anxiety experience.

Along these lines, several investigators have shown that infusions of sodium lactate or sodium bicarbonate (e.g., Gorman et al., 1989; Hollander et al., 1989; Liebowitz et al. 1984, 1985), or the inhalation of carbon dioxide (e.g., Woods et al., 1986, 1987), can produce panic attacks in panic disorder patients at a much higher rate than in normal subjects. While such observations are consistent with the notion that panic disorder patients have some sort of elevated biological vulnerability to evocation of the panic pattern, a much simpler explanation pertains to the subjective effects produced by these procedures. Namely, they mimic the physiological cues normally preceding a panic attack. Panic disorder patients, being familiar with these prodromal cues, apparently "misinterpret" the latter type of experience as beginning panic. As noted earlier in our discussion of anxiety-response dynamics, such a misinterpretation would be expected often to lead to a full-blown panic attack. In other words, sensitivity to lactate or CO_2 is more likely a *consequence* than a cause of the panic experience. Along somewhat similar lines, Ley (1988) has suggested that panic attacks are produced by physiological cues resulting from unnoticed hyperventilation in panic-prone patients.

In general it would be somewhat surprising to discover that innate features of physiologic reactivity and temperament have no role in predisposing individuals to the anxiety response or to particular ways of managing it when it occurs. As yet, however, the evidence is inconclusive; a great deal more research is needed to clarify the possible role of constitutional and other biological factors in the development of neurotic disorders.

■ Psychosocial Factors

The psychological and interpersonal causal factors that we reviewed in Chapter 4 as predisposing an individual to develop specific maladaptive behaviors are especially applicable to neurotic behaviors. Relevant here are early psychic trauma, pathogenic parent-child and family patterns, and disturbed interpersonal relationships.

Additionally, each of the psychosocial viewpoints summarized in Chapter 3 has posed a hypothesized origin of neurosis and neurotic behaviors. We list some of the more explicit of these in the following sections.

Anxiety-Defense   As we have noted, neurotic disorders have traditionally been explained within the framework of anxiety-defense, as originally proposed by Freud and elaborated by later investigators. According to this view, threats stemming from internal or external sources elicit intense anxiety; this anxiety in turn leads to the exaggerated use of various ego-defense mechanisms and to maladaptive behaviors. Although today other causal factors, such as cognitive elaboration, are also taken into account, this view still has broad generality and explanatory power, as illustrated in earlier sections of this chapter. As we have already indicated, however, it is now thought that virtually any human propensity —not just primitive sexual and aggressive impulses —may become blocked or inhibited by anxiety, leading to essentially defensive (and ultimately maladaptive) behaviors. This view does not in itself address the *sources* of such maladaptive anxiety, but it seems likely that many of them relate to faulty conditioning and learning, to which we now turn.

Faulty Learning   In more recent years, faulty learning, a major focus of the behavioral perspective, has become the most widely used explanation for both the development and the maintenance of neurotic behaviors. Faulty learning is seen in the acquisition of maladaptive anxiety responses and modes of coping with stressful situations. It is also

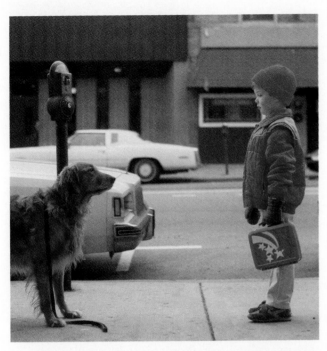

The fear associated with a stimulus such as a large dog may, through generalization, be associated with other similar stimuli, leading to a phobia of all dogs, big or small.

seen in the typical failure of neurotic individuals to learn the competencies and attitudes needed for dealing with normal life problems. For individuals who feel basically inadequate and insecure in a competitive and hostile world, making the effort to become competent is especially difficult; relying on defensive and avoidant life-styles is less threatening and brings enough short-term alleviation of anxiety to be repeatedly reinforced.

The principles of simple learning, or conditioning, may in certain instances account for the acquisition of irrational fears and anxieties in the first place. As noted earlier, the physiological arousal pattern associated with fear has been shown in countless experiments to be readily conditioned to previously neutral stimuli. These stimuli then act as expectancy cues signaling that painful events will follow. In fact, some evidence suggests that people who are already anxious overestimate the strength or reliability of contingencies of this kind; that is, a potentially threatening stimulus is perceived as more likely to be followed by an aversive event than is actually the case (Tomarken, Mineka, & Cook, 1989). Furthermore, through *generalization,* the newly acquired fear may spread to other, similar stimuli, including internal ones, such as motives to engage in certain actions. The generalization process seems especially pertinent to certain phobias in which there occurs a "displacement" of anxiety

from one situation to another having similar elements or characteristics.

The powerful role of learning in the development of neurotic behaviors was supported in a survey by Ost and Hugdahl (1981). These investigators administered questionnaires to 106 adult phobic patients concerning, among other things, the purported origins of their fears. In describing the situations they considered as sources of their phobias, 58 percent cited conditioning experiences, and another 17 percent described situations that were based on indirect or "vicarious" learning. Such observations may be but an aspect of the more general problem of traumatic events sensitizing individuals to the unpredictable and uncontrollable nature of negative life events. Pollard, Pollard, and Corn (1989), for example, have shown the onset of panic attacks to be related to the prior occurrence of such events. Relatedly perhaps, Sanderson, Rapee, and Barlow (1989) have shown that a sense of control, even an illusory one, may decrease the likelihood of laboratory-induced panics.

An important point to consider in any discussion of acquired or learned fears (anxieties) is that, almost certainly, some stimuli more readily come to elicit fear than do others. This too is an aspect of a far more general principle that we have come to appreciate only in recent years: what can be learned efficiently is to a considerable extent limited and species-specific. The term *preparedness* has been used to refer to the likelihood that humans are biologically predisposed to develop certain types of fears (Cook, Hodes, & Lang, 1986; Seligman & Hager, 1972). For example, we seem much more likely to acquire a fear of snakes than a fear of grapefruits. Thus any listing of commonly observed types of phobias, while it is apt to be extensive, is also finite. Lelliott et al. (1989) note in this connection that 81 percent of the first panic attacks experienced by a series of agoraphobic patients occurred in places having strong "extraterritorial" (unfamiliar environmental) cues.

Conditioning is by no means the only way in which people can learn irrational fears. Abundant evidence exists that much human learning, including the learning of fears, is *observational* in nature. Frightening events in which a person in no way participates may nevertheless become the occasion for marked and persistent fear arousal. How many people have had their enjoyment of the beach marred by having seen the movie *Jaws* or one of its sequels? Similarly, as noted earlier, fears can be transmitted from one person to another by a *modeling* process: merely observing the fear of another in a given situation may cause that situation to become a fearful one for the observer. For example, if a child's parents prove to be more or less uniformly anxious in situations calling for assertive behavior, that child might well grow up with a similar maladaptive anxiety. Of course, the same result might be accomplished via a conditioning process if the parents routinely punish the child for any show of assertiveness.

Blocked Personal Growth   We have noted the emphasis placed by the humanistic perspective on values, meaning, personal growth, and self-fulfillment; we have also seen how stressful one's life situation can become when it is devoid of meaning and hope, as depicted by reports of former inmates of concentration and POW camps. In any case, lack of meaning and blocked personal growth often appear to stem from a lack of needed competencies and resources or a feeling that duty requires one to remain in a self-stifling role. As a result, an individual's main efforts are devoted to simply trying to meet basic needs, rather than to personal growth and development. According to the humanistic perspective, such a life-style can ultimately bring feelings of anxiety, hostility, and futility—feelings that may inspire neurotic behaviors.

Pathogenic Interpersonal Relationships
As we have seen, certain interactions within families and other early relationships can set the stage for children to develop neurotic life-styles in later life. For example, parents who overprotect or indulge their children may prevent them from developing the independent, effective coping techniques required in their adult years. Or insecure parents may instill their own excessive concerns with ailments into their children, which is a common background feature in somatoform disorders (Kellner, 1985). Much of what a person becomes in later life—attitudes, values, and often even particular symptoms—can be traced to interactions within the family during the formative years.

It is apparent that the preceding views of psychosocial causation are interrelated and may apply in varying degrees to a given case. This is an important point to remember. Though we may have focused at times on one or another feature of a person's behavior, in most cases all of the concepts discussed above are helpful in understanding the development of neurotic behavior.

■ Sociocultural Factors

Reliable data on the incidence of neurotic disorders in other societies is meager. Kidson and Jones (1968) failed to find classical neurotic patterns among the aborigines of the Australian western desert; but they did note that as these groups were increasingly exposed to modern civilization, hypochondriacal concerns and other somatic complaints occurred. In general, however, it appears that conversion disorder is more common among the people of underdeveloped countries, while anxiety and obsessive-compulsive disorders are more common in technologically advanced societies.

In our own society, neurotic disorders are found among all segments of the population. Significant differences, however, seem to exist in the incidence and types of patterns manifested by particular subgroups. In general, neurotic individuals from the lower educational and socioeconomic levels appear to show a higher than average incidence not only of conversion disorder but also of aches, pains, and other somatic symptoms. Neurotic individuals from the middle and upper classes, on the other hand, seem especially prone to anxiety and obsessive-compulsive disorders—with such subjective symptoms as "unhappiness" and general feelings of dissatisfaction with life. Phobias and the more serious dissociation disorder of multiple personality, as we have seen, are far more common in women than in men, although it is not yet certain that these differences are due to sociocultural variables.

Although there has been little systematic research on how specific sociocultural variables affect the development of neurotic disorders, it seems clear that the social environment influences both an individual's likelihood of developing a neurotic reaction and the particular form that reaction is most likely to take. Thus as social conditions continue to change in our own society and elsewhere, we can expect corresponding changes in both the incidence and prevailing types of neurotic behavior.

TREATMENTS AND OUTCOMES

The treatment of neurotic disorders may involve a wide range of goals and procedures. Treatment may be aimed at alleviating distressing symptoms, changing an individual's basically defensive and avoidant life-style, or both; it may include drug therapy or psychotherapy, or some combination of these approaches. Anxiety (excluding obsessive-compulsive), phobic, and conversion disorders usually respond more readily to treatment than do other more complex neurotic patterns, but the outlook here is, in general, favorable. Andrews and Harvey (1981) have reanalyzed the data on overall outcomes of psychosocial therapy specifically as these data relate to neurotic disorders. They have used a technique known as *meta-analysis* (Smith, Glass, & Miller, 1980), a description of which may be found in Chapter 18. Results from 81 controlled studies involving the treatment of neurotic individuals indicated that the average client who had received treatment was more functional than nearly 80 percent of comparably disordered, untreated control clients evaluated at the same time. Also, the relapse rate for treated clients during two years following therapy was insignificant.

For present purposes, we shall keep our discussion brief and focused on the aspects of treatment that are particularly relevant to neurotic behavior. These therapies will be more thoroughly examined in Chapters 17 and 18.

■ Pharmacological (Drug) Therapies

"Psychopharmacological agents are the most widely prescribed, widely misprescribed, most frequently abused, and probably the most advertised of all the pharmaceuticals available to the practicing clinician. They clearly occupy a role at or near the center of medical practice" (Levenson, 1981, p. xi).

As the preceding statement attests, many patients seen by medical practitioners are neurotic individuals seeking relief from their "nervousness" and their various functional (psychogenic) physical problems. Most often in such cases minor tranquilizing drugs such as Valium or Xanax are prescribed. These drugs are used—and misused—for tension relief and for relaxation; they also reduce subjective anxiety and may stabilize emotional reactivity. Neurotic individuals also frequently attempt to control their anxiety or other symptoms by self-medication with nonprescription drugs, including alcohol.

Available statistics indicate that some 70 percent or more of neurotic patients show some symptom relief following drug therapy, and most of them are able to function more effectively (Bassuk, Schoonover, & Gelenberg, 1983; Covi et al., 1974; Engelhardt, 1974; Prusoff & Klerman, 1974). These drugs, however, can have undesirable side effects—such as drowsiness—and in some cases a patient develops an increasing tolerance for and persistent dependence on a drug. In addition, many people expect too much of a treatment that is merely palliative, and the masking of their symptoms may discourage them from seeking needed psychotherapy.

We earlier took note in the case of Anne Watson of the use of antidepressant medication to control panics and agoraphobia. While the evidence is still somewhat fragmentary, this approach looks promising and has led to speculation (e.g., Breier, Charney, & Heninger, 1984) concerning a possible biological connection between depression and panic (and agoraphobic) disorders. As also noted earlier, antidepressant drug side effects can be a serious problem (Mavissakalian & Perel, 1989).

Recently the drug Clomipramine has been suggested as an effective biological treatment for obsessive-compulsive disorder (e.g., Benkelfat et al., 1989). It appears in fact to reduce the intensity of this disorder's symptoms, but we have not yet seen convincing evidence of marked and lasting therapeutic potency.

■ Psychological Therapies

Individual psychotherapies, behavior therapy, family therapy, and multimodal therapy have been used to treat neurotic disorders.

Individual Psychotherapies   These therapies are oriented toward helping individuals achieve greater understanding of themselves, their problems, and their relationships, and toward developing healthier attitudes and better coping skills. The various types of therapy included in this general category differ somewhat in their specific goals and procedures—each reflecting the particular psychosocial perspective on which it is based—but all stress the need for self-understanding, a realistic frame of reference, a satisfying pattern of values, and the development of effective techniques for coping with adjustive demands.

These objectives sound deceptively easy to achieve—actually they share a number of stumbling blocks. First is the problem of creating a therapeutic situation in which neurotic individuals feel safe enough to lower their defenses; explore their innermost feelings, thoughts, and assumptions; and begin to recognize the possibility of other options. Second is the problem of providing opportunities for neurotic individuals to learn new ways of perceiving themselves and their world, and to see new ways of coping. Third is the problem of helping them transfer what they have learned in the therapy situation to real life; even when they understand the nature and causes of their self-defeating behavior and have learned that more effective coping techniques are available, they may still be "unable to risk the initial venture into the heretofore out-of-bounds area of living" (Salzman, 1968, p. 465). Fourth is the problem of changing the conditions in their life situations that may be reinforcing and thus maintaining the neurotic life-styles. For example, a domineering and egocentric husband who will not participate in a therapy program may tend to block his wife's efforts toward self-direction and make it more difficult for her to give up her insecure, neurotic behavior. He may even manage to sabotage the entire treatment program.

The behavior patterns we have called neurotic styles seem especially amenable to treatments emphasizing an interpersonal approach, since these conditions are manifested chiefly in interpersonal difficulties. Interpersonal therapies tend to be active and confrontative in focusing on how to alter maladaptive interpersonal behavior. Hence they tend to be efficient and relatively brief (Anchin & Kiesler, 1982; Carson, in press-a).

Behavior Therapies   As we have seen, behavior therapies focus on (a) removing specific symptoms or maladaptive behaviors; (b) developing needed competencies and adaptive behaviors; and (c) modifying environmental conditions that may be reinforcing and maintaining maladaptive behaviors. In this last context, Bandura (1969) has stated, "A treatment that fails to alter the major controlling conditions of the deviant behavior will most certainly prove ineffective" (p. 50). In general, behavior therapy approaches have an excellent record of efficacy in the neuroses (Smith, Glass, & Miller, 1980).

The behavior therapy most commonly used in the treatment of neurotic behaviors is controlled exposure to anxiety-producing circumstances. Here clients are placed—symbolically or increasingly under "real life" conditions—in those situations they

Systematic desensitization is frequently used to help people overcome simple phobias, such as the fear of snakes. In this type of therapy, patients are placed in a series of situations, each closer to the situation that would provoke the most anxiety, while they practice relaxation techniques to counter their anxiety. Here, a number of patients have progressed from handling rubber snakes (upper left) and peering at snakes through glass (center top) to actually handling living but harmless snakes. Note that some patients first handle the snakes while wearing rubber gloves.

find most threatening. In the variant known as systematic desensitization, an attempt is made to associate the fear-producing situations with states that reduce anxiety, such as relaxation. Other forms of "guided exposure" to fear-producing stimuli also continue to show much promise (Barlow, 1988), perhaps particularly where a "self-efficacy" component is emphasized (Williams, S. L., Turner, & Peer, 1985). A combination of exposure and (compulsive) response prevention, illustrated in *HIGHLIGHT 6.8* may be the most effective approach to the difficult problem of obsessive-compulsive disorders (Steketee & Foa, 1985). In addition, Klosko et al. (1990) have recently reported a well-designed study showing that a particular behavior therapy program emphasizing exposure is significantly superior to antianxiety medication in the treatment of panic disorder.

As we saw in our discussion of specific types of neurotic disorders, some maladaptive behaviors—such as conversion paralyses—may be extinguished by removing reinforcements that have been maintaining the behavior, while simultaneously providing reinforcements for more responsible coping patterns. Other maladaptive behaviors can sometimes be removed by mild aversive conditioning (Bandura, 1969, 1973; Stern, Lipsedge, & Marks, 1973). Here, too, the conditioning works best when combined with reinforcements of more adaptive alternative behaviors (Sturgis & Meyer, 1981).

As noted in Chapter 3, many behaviorists in recent years have been using behavior therapy techniques to change cognitive behavior (Mahoney, 1974; Meichenbaum, 1977). Individuals who are experiencing neurotic problems, such as anxiety attacks, may be viewed as behaving anxiously in response to internal thoughts and beliefs (cognitions). Here a therapist attempts to change the neurotic behavior by changing the individual's inner thoughts and beliefs that may be causing or reinforcing the behavior. This process is called *cognitive mediation*. With encouraging preliminary results, Beck and colleagues (1985) have extended to the anxiety disorders their well-known work on the cognitive-behavioral treatment of depression. We will discuss cognitive-behavioral therapy in more detail in Chapter 18.

Although behavior therapy is usually directed toward changing specific "target behaviors"—such as removing phobias—it often seems to have more far-reaching positive results (Marks, 1978). A client who overcomes a specific phobia gains confidence in his or her ability to overcome other problems. Ultimately, the individual learns that coping effectively with adjustive demands is more rewarding

Often pathogenic family interactions maintain neurotic behaviors in individuals. Family therapy emphasizes treating family systems rather than focusing primarily on individuals.

than trying to avoid them. Thus although cognitive-behavioral therapies usually focus more on modifying a patient's internal cognitions and behavior therapy focuses more on the removal of specific target behaviors, the outcomes of these two forms of therapy (and others) are often comparable (Sloane et al., 1975; Smith et al. 1980; Stiles et al., 1986).

Family Therapy   Often pathogenic family interactions keep a neurotic individual in a continually "sick situation." As Melville (1973) has expressed it, "In a family there is no such thing as one person in trouble" (p. 17). As a consequence of such findings, increasing emphasis has been placed on treating family systems rather than focusing primarily on individuals (Fox, 1976; Gurman & Kniskern, 1978).

Multimodal Therapy   As this term, coined by Lazarus (1981, 1985), implies, a combination of varied approaches may be used in the treatment of a given individual for neurotic behaviors. In fact increasing evidence (see, for example, Goldfried, 1980; Goldfried & Safran, 1986) shows that professional therapists are lessening their strong allegiances to particular therapies and are increasingly willing

Treatment of Obsessive–Compulsive Disorder with Exposure and Response Prevention

Steketee and Foa (1985) present the following case as an illustration of their recommended approach to the treatment of obsessive-compulsive disorders. The patient, June, was a 26-year-old recently married nursing graduate who complained of washing and cleaning problems so severe that she was unable to seek work in her profession. On initial evaluation she was agitated and distressed, feeling helpless to control her need to take at least two 45-minute showers daily and, in addition, to wash her hands some 20 times a day for five minutes. She also spent a great deal of time wiping various objects with alcohol. Inquiry soon determined that she was terrified of becoming "contaminated," particularly by bird, animal, or human feces, which she took great pains to avoid. She also had problems with garbage and with dead animals on the roadway. Previous treatment by sys-

tematic desensitization, tranquilizing drugs, and "cognitive restructuring" had been ineffective. Her marriage was now threatened owing to her husband's frustration with her excessive cleanliness.

Exposure treatment. The therapist and patient worked together to create a hierarchy of upsetting stimuli, rating them on a scale of 1 through 100 according to their capacities to evoke disgust and the impulse to wash. For example, the patient gave ratings of 100 to touching dog feces (if unable to wash immediately), 90 to automobile tires (which may have contacted a dead animal), and 40 to the outside doorknob of a public bathroom (the inside doorknob rated 80). Subsequently, in treatment sessions three times weekly, June was instructed to expose herself deliberately to these stimuli either in guided fantasy (in vitro) or directly (in vivo),

beginning with those rated relatively low in the hierarchy and moving gradually to the more severely threatening ones.

In addition to the exposures conducted during therapy sessions, "homework" was liberally assigned. Subjective ratings of discomfort were carefully monitored during these encounters. On one occasion well into treatment, the therapist drove with the patient to a place where she had observed a dead cat on the roadside and insisted that the patient approach the "smelly" corpse and touch it with a stick. The stick and a pebble lying close by were presented to the patient with the instruction that she keep them in her pocket and touch them frequently throughout the day. The patient was also told to drive her car past the spot on subsequent days.

The therapist made "home visits" to assist the patient in facing her problems in that setting,

to learn and to employ techniques they formerly criticized. For example, a therapist could use an interpersonal therapeutic strategy to defeat a client's neurotic style while employing behavior therapy techniques to eradicate particular symptoms. In our judgment, this "ecumenical" trend in psychosocial treatment represents a maturing of the field, and we strongly applaud it.

No matter which therapeutic techniques are employed, it often requires a great deal of courage and persistence on a neurotic individual's part to face problems realistically and give up the defensive and avoidant life-style that has helped alleviate feelings of inadequacy, anxiety, and even stark

terror. For some, this seems too great a task, and they present themselves in such a way as to put the whole responsibility for their immediate well-being and happiness on their therapists. For these individuals, palliative drug therapy may be the only recourse.

Despite the difficulties involved, however, powerful forces are aligned on the side of psychotherapy. For one thing, neurotic individuals who seek help are usually experiencing considerable inner distress, so they are motivated to change. When helped, in a supportive environment, to understand their problems and learn more effective and satisfying ways of coping with them, they usually find the touching contaminated objects and places (such as a porch railing soiled with pigeon droppings) and contaminating (by unwashed touch) clean ones. Systematic exposure continued until the patient appeared at ease with a particular confrontation and her discomfort rating concerning it dropped to the 40 to 50 range.

Response prevention. After obtaining June's commitment to the full treatment procedure (which had previously been explained) in the fourth session, the therapist instituted a no washing rule. Specifically, the patient was to remain unwashed for a period of five days, after which she could take a ten-minute shower to be followed by another wash-free five days. As anticipated, June was notably upset by this proposed regimen and strongly doubted she could carry it off. The therapist was encouraging but insistent, promising support through the

hard times, and the patient was successful in curbing her frequent impulses to wash. A transition to "normal washing and cleaning behavior" was instituted shortly before the end of the planned 15 therapy sessions. This plan consisted of one 10-minute shower per day and hand-washings not to exceed six per day at mealtimes, after bathroom use, and after touching clearly soiled or greasy objects.

Because June's discomfort ratings remained somewhat high (maximum 70, but only briefly) following the planned 15 sessions, a few additional follow-up sessions were given. In an evaluation nine months following the initiation of treatment, June described herself as "definitely a lot better . . . maybe 80 percent." She acknowledged that she still had obsessions "once every week or two" (such as "driving over someone"), but she was now em-

ployed and her relationship with her husband was much improved. She felt she was living a "normal life."

As Steketee and Foa pointed out, obsessive-compulsive disorders rarely remit completely; even a successfully treated patient will usually have some residual obsessive problems or rituals, as in June's case. The treatment undertaken here was of course direct and rigorous and was based on a behavioral formulation. It appears to have been the treatment of choice. One can only speculate on how June would have fared under the care of a psychoanalyst, particularly in view of the pronounced "anal" character (signalled by her preoccupation with dirt and feces) of her symptoms.

courage to see it through. Although outcomes vary considerably, it appears that from 70 to 90 percent of the people who receive appropriate kinds of help for their neurotic behavior benefit from it (Lambert, Shapiro, & Bergin, 1986).

In concluding our discussion of neurotic disorders, several additional points should be mentioned. Fear of committing suicide is a common neurotic symptom, but the actual incidence of suicide among neurotic individuals does not appear to be higher than for the general population. Nor do the life spans of these individuals appear to be adversely affected by their chronic tension and somatic disturbances, unless these disturbances re-

sult in pathologic organ changes (to be discussed in Chapter 8). As to whether neurotic behavior is likely to develop into psychotic behavior, the answer seems to be a definitive no. In only 5 percent or fewer of neurotic behavior cases does excessive stress lead to severe personality decompensation and psychotic patterns.

Finally, people often ask how a neurotic style affects creativity and productiveness. Many authors have described neurotic individuals as "pleasantly different," and more likely than a "normal" person to be innovative and productive. In general, however, the evidence indicates that by relying on defensive strategies, neurotic individuals reduce their potential for positive accomplishments as well as their enjoyment of life.

UNRESOLVED ISSUES
on the Anxiety-based Disorders

The framers of DSM-III (affirmed by those of DSM-III-R) dropped the category *neurosis* because they thought it had accumulated excess meaning beyond what could reliably be demonstrated regarding the clinical phenomena of anxiety, somatoform, and dissociative disorders. These disorders are now listed as distinct major categories in themselves. This conservative step leaves open for further investigation the questions of the natures and etiologies of these behavioral anomalies. While it has provoked considerable objection because it has been widely interpreted as an attack on psychodynamic thinking (to which the notion of neurosis is central), the move is defended by its protagonists as emphasizing a proper theoretical neutrality in respect to such matters as the etiologies of the disorders in question. As we have indicated, we find the latter reasoning sound and have no quarrel with the new taxonomy on this score.

The basic question of the validity and generality of the "neurosis" model remains, however; it cannot be dismissed or resolved by a change in terminology. Unfortunately, it seems unlikely that it will be resolved in a timely fashion by the preferable route of skillfully conducted empirical research. It is difficult, if not impossible, at present to conceive of a definitive study or program of studies that would establish the anxiety-defense internal-conflict interpretation of most of these disorders as incontrovertibly right or wrong. Hence it is a judgment call, and one on which serious, competent investigators and clinicians honestly differ.

While we find the anxiety-defense model a useful and heuristic one, our commitment to it is a loose and flexible one. Moreover, we think it fits to varying degrees such reliable empirical observation as we have in regard to the conditions described in this chapter. In general it appears to clearly apply in respect to neurotic styles and some anxiety disorders, such as obsessive-compulsive behavior. Its adequacy as an integrating model for the somatoform and dissociative disorders is also variable within these classes, but overall less certain. Presumably it was just such uncertainty that caused the authors of DSM-III to limit their approach to the descriptive level. Obviously we have much to learn

in this area, including a more complete understanding of the predisposing factors that influence an individual's "choice" of maladaptive reaction pattern.

Finally, although we have made impressive progress in fashioning demonstrably effective treatment approaches to these conditions, there remains the puzzling question of why they do not, in effect, cure themselves. Inasmuch as they generate considerable misery for the persons affected, and inasmuch as we know behavior tends to maximize pleasant consequences and minimize pain, how is it that these usually self-defeating behaviors persist— often over many years? Freud was acutely aware of this paradox, although his attempted solution of it—a somewhat magical concept of "repetition compulsion" (a hypothesized drive causing persons to return to and relive traumas of the past)—did little to clarify the issue. Another attempted explanation involving a presumed prepotency of immediate over delayed consequences (for example, prompt anxiety reduction), while more promising, tends to founder on the routine observation that humans seem at least as much influenced by long-term as short-term satisfactions. Were it otherwise, indeed, we might have to close down our more demanding colleges. We suspect that the main answer lies in the often complex and distorted "feedback loops" a neurotic person tends to set up with a usually unwitting social environment, such that the environmental response in some way reinforces and maintains the maladaptive behavior. Obviously we are touching here on problems relating to therapy, and we shall return to this intriguing issue in Chapter 18.

SUMMARY

This chapter has been concerned with maladaptive behavior patterns that appear to have *anxiety* as their bases. Sometimes these patterns, while not involving disabling symptoms as such, act to inhibit behaviors that would be appropriate, effective, and adaptive in certain situations. We have termed these conditions *neurotic styles*. In other cases, anxiety, or defenses against it, gives rise to disabling symptoms. Formerly these symptom disorders were officially called *neuroses*, but recent versions of the DSM have largely abandoned this term. We have chosen to retain the term *neurotic* for its pedagogic and descriptive advantages, although acknowledging that the basic issue remains unresolved. Neurotic symptom disorders, on careful assessment, often turn out to be related to preexisting neurotic styles.

Of the neurotic symptom disorders, the anxiety disorders are those in which, for some reason, a person has been unable to develop means of controlling and containing relatively severe anxiety. The anxiety thus surfaces in overt, fearful behavior. In somatoform disorders, an individual "somatizes" anxiety (diverts it to the body), causing psychologically based disabilities, preoccupations with illnesses, or both. In dissociative disorders, anxiety causes aspects of an individual's personality to "split off" and function more or less independently of the core self. To a large extent, somatoform and dissociative symptoms are conceived as defenses against experiencing the full impact of anxiety.

Researchers have identified a number of neurotic styles. Four relatively common neurotic styles are those involving inhibition of aggression/assertion, responsibility/independence, compliance/submission, and intimacy/trust behaviors.

The experience of anxiety in neurotic disorders is indistinguishable from strong fear, and indeed some of these problems have their origins in terrifying circumstances. Most neurotic individuals, however, do not have identifiable, rational, realistic sources of current anxieties. Most such anxieties are believed to be acquired through conditioning or other learning mechanisms, although some people may be constitutionally predisposed to acquire such responses.

Many neurotic people are treated by physicians, often with drugs designed to allay anxiety. Such treatment is essentially palliative in nature, and it is not without dangers. A number of alternative means of achieving anxiety reduction are available. In general, psychosocial treatments, which typically aim at solving a person's problems, have a reasonably good record with the neurotic disorders. However, some neurotic people fail to achieve satisfactory benefits from any form of treatment. The persistence of neurotic disorders in the face of the miseries to which they give rise remains a puzzling paradox.

■ Key Terms

neurotic behavior (p. 181)
neurosis (p. 181)
anxiety (p. 181)
anxiety-response pattern (p. 183)
anxiety disorder (p. 183)
panic disorder (p. 183)
agoraphobia (p. 184)
phobia (p. 185)
simple phobia (p. 185)
social phobia (p. 188)
obsession (p. 189)
compulsion (p. 189)
obsessive-compulsive disorder (p. 189)
generalized anxiety disorder (p. 192)
somatoform disorders (p. 197)
somatization disorder (p. 197)
hypochondriasis (p. 199)
malingering (p. 199)
somatoform pain disorder (p. 200)
conversion disorder (p. 201)
dissociative disorders (p. 205)
amnesia (p. 205)
psychogenic amnesia (p. 206)
fugue state (p. 206)
multiple personality (p. 208)
depersonalization disorder (p. 212)
neurotic style (p. 213)

Chapter 7
Psychological Factors and Physical Illness

Carlo, *Personnage au Visage Vert et aux Cheveux Longs.* Carlo (b. 1916) grew up in the Italian province of Verona, where he was put to work as an agricultural worker at the age of 9. As a child, he showed evidence of a solitary nature, preferring in general the company of his dog to that of other people. During the war, he suffered a series of psychological shocks that undermined an already-fragile psychological condition. Subject to delirium and visions of persecution, Carlo entered a psychiatric hospital in 1947. Since 1957, working in a small artist's studio provided by the hospital, he has devoted himself to creating complex, stylized drawings of animals and humans.

Traditionally, the medical profession has concentrated clinical and research efforts on understanding and controlling anatomical and physiological factors in disease. In psychopathology, on the other hand, interest has centered primarily on the discovery and remedy of psychological factors that are associated with mental disorders. Today we realize that both these approaches are limited: although a disorder may be primarily physical or primarily psychological, it is always a disorder of the whole person—not just of the body or the psyche.

Fatigue or a bad cold may lower tolerance for psychological stress; an emotional upset may lower resistance to physical disease; maladaptive behavior, such as excessive alcohol use, may contribute to the impairment of various organs, like the brain and liver. Furthermore, an individual's overall life situation has much to do with the onset of a disorder, its form, duration, and prognosis.

Recovery is apt to be more rapid for a patient eager to get back to work and to accustomed interactions with significant others than for the one who will be returning to a frustrating job or an unpleasant home. In short, an individual is a bio-psychosocial unit.

There seems little doubt, too, that sociocultural influences affect the types and incidences of disorders found in different groups. The ailments to which people are most vulnerable—whether physical, psychological, or both—are determined in no small part by when, where, and how they live.

Behavioral medicine is the broad interdisciplinary approach to the treatment of physical disorders thought to have psychological factors as major aspects of their causal patterns (Gentry, 1984a). The field includes professionals from many disciplines—including medicine, psychology, and sociology—who seek to incorporate biological, psychological, and sociocultural factors into a total picture. Its emphasis, however, is essentially on the role psychological factors play in the occurrence, maintenance, and prevention of physical illness.

Because we are dealing here with largely **psychogenic illnesses** (psychologically induced or maintained diseases), it is only natural that psychologists have found this an area of major interest. **Health psychology** is the subspecialty within the behavioral medicine approach and within the generic discipline of psychology that deals specifically with psychology's contributions to the diagnosis, treatment, and prevention of these psychological components of physical illnesses (Bradley & Prokop, 1981; Weiss, Herd, & Fox, 1981). Currently developing at a rapid pace, the field has already evolved some of the trappings of a new and independent profession (G. C. Stone et al., 1987).

A behavioral medicine approach examines the broad biopsychosocial context of the following problem areas (adapted from Gentry, 1984a):

1. *Etiology.* How do critical life events, characteristic behavior, and personality organization predispose an individual to physical illness?

2. *Host resistance.* How are the effects of stress reduced by resistance resources, such as coping styles, social supports, and certain personality traits?

3. *Disease mechanisms.* How is human physiology altered by stressors, particularly those arising from maladaptive behavior? What effects are produced in such systems as the immune, the gastrointestinal, and the cardiovascular?

4. *Patient decision making.* What are the processes involved in the choices individuals make with respect to such matters as hazardous life-styles, health care decisions, and adherence to preventive regimens?

5. *Compliance.* What factors—biomedical, behavioral, self-regulative, cultural, social, and interpersonal (for example, factors in the practitioner-patient relationship)—determine compliance with sound medical advice?

6. *Intervention.* How effective are psychological measures, such as health education and behavior modification, in altering unhealthy life-styles and in directly reducing illness and illness behavior at both individual and community levels?

From this perspective, then, *any* instance of physical illness should occasion a review of the context in which the specific pathogen or primary cause is operating. To do so is to use a behavioral medicine approach; properly applied, it multiplies the tools available for interventions whose efficacy often extends beyond any immediate crisis to conditions both prior and subsequent to such events.

We might, for example, ask whether emotional factors may have lowered the resistance of a tuberculosis patient and hence contributed to the onset of the disease. We might also ask how the individual will react to the life changes brought about by the disease. Some patients apparently give up when medically the chances seem good that they will recover. Others with objectively more serious organic pathologies recover or survive for long periods of time. Dunbar, a pioneer in the field, concluded that it is often "more important to know what kind of patient has the disease than what kind of disease the patient has" (1943, p. 23).

Before DSM-III, psychogenic illnesses were categorized as *psychophysiologic disorders* (and before that as *psychosomatic disorders*); the focus in these earlier times was on specific body system diseases, such as peptic ulcer, traditionally thought to have psychological origins. In 1980 (with the adoption of DSM-III), the category of psychophysiologic disorders was dropped (and it remained so in DSM-III-R), partly because of the newer perspective that emphasizes the psychological component of all physical illnesses. That is, the attempt to specify particular diseases as having psychological components in their etiology or maintenance came to be seen as both limiting and misleading, because it was increasingly understood that the absence of such components in any disease would be quite rare. As we have seen, in DSM-III-R patients are now rated separately on different axes for psychiatric symptoms (Axis I), developmental and personality disorders (Axis II), and accompanying physical disorders (Axis III). Thus there is no place on the first two axes for the classic psychosomatic disorders.

To permit some sort of psychiatric coding for the many diseases that we now recognize may involve psychological contributions, Axis I provides a category called *psychological factors affecting physical condition.* This category should be used when a physical disorder, coded on Axis III, involves psychological factors that have either definitely or probably played a significant role in initiating or exacerbating the illness. Obviously, this decision is intended to be left to the diagnostician's judgment, because no sharp line of demarcation exists between a significant and a less significant role for psychological factors.

In this chapter, after a broader consideration of the role of psychological factors in both health and illness, we will look at coronary heart disease and the eating disorders known as anorexia and bulimia, which have special contemporary significance. From there, we will move to brief considerations of other physical illnesses having strong psychological components. Then we will examine possible causal factors, and, finally, highlight several treatment approaches in this rapidly developing area.

GENERAL PSYCHOLOGICAL FACTORS IN HEALTH AND DISEASE

Research has repeatedly shown that mental and emotional processes are somehow implicated both in good health and in most physical diseases. Definitive proof of such relationships, however, and a beginning knowledge of what is happening in the body, are relatively recent accomplishments. The boundaries of this field seem virtually limitless. As Ader and Cohen (1984) have put it: "As a result of research in psychosomatic and behavioral medicine, it has become clear that there is probably no major organ system or [physical] homeostatic defense mechanism that is not subject to the influence of interactions between psychological and physiological events" (p. 117).

In this section we will outline the main phenomena relating to psychosocial influences on biological health in general, specifying, where possible, the mechanisms involved. We will begin our survey with observations on health, attitudes, and coping. We move from there to an examination of the autonomic nervous system and its potential effects on health. We then move to what may eventually be recognized as the most basic and general topic in this area—the immune system and the compromise of its functioning by psychological states and events. The section ends with a brief discussion of life-style and its implications for physical health maintenance.

Health, Attitudes, and Coping Resources

The sometimes devastating effects of hopeless and helpless attitudes on organic functioning have long been known, partly through anthropological research on voodoo deaths and similar phenomena. Today many surgeons will delay a major operation until they are convinced that a patient is reasonably optimistic about the outcome, and optimism in a more positive, everyday sense seems to buffer against disease (Scheier & Carver, 1987). Likewise, harboring an "explanatory style" of helplessness in the face of adversity is associated with poor health outcomes, as shown in an interesting study of hall-of-fame baseball players by Peterson and Seligman (1987). Such negative attitudes in this group of athletes (as assessed by their verbatim statements

The relationship between mental and emotional processes and good health is now well documented. Positive emotions may produce a certain immunity to physical disease. Likewise, chronic negative styles of coping with ordinary frustrations of life, such as being stuck in traffic, may enhance the risk of disease.

reported in newspapers and other sources) were significantly associated with health problems following their active playing years. In the literature, too, are numerous reports of apathy deaths in situations such as concentration and prisoner-of-war camps. Every year we hear reports of "unexplained" deaths among people who believed themselves to be in hopeless circumstances—for example, after having ingested poisonous substances in dosages that were actually too small to be lethal. Such phenomena have been extensively reviewed by both Seligman (1975) and Jones (1977).

Less dramatically but in many ways of equal or greater importance, the effects of multiple life changes on a variety of illnesses have been amply documented (e.g., Elliott, 1989), as outlined in Chapter 5. To cite only two examples, Rahe (1974) noted a study on the health status of physicians that demonstrates a marked correspondence between health problems experienced and the amount of change-related stress undergone in an immediately preceding period. Similarly, in a study of 192 men between the ages of 30 and 60, Payne (1975) found that long-standing physical and psychological health problems were related to larger degrees of life changes, even when the changes had been favorable. Some evidence suggests, however, that the negative health effects of positive life changes are limited, interestingly, to individuals having prior low self-esteem (Brown & McGill, 1989). Evidently, it is the amount of adjustment required following change that overtaxes such individuals' resources, and good things happening to people who do not expect them may constitute significant adjustment challenges.

In other instances, the particular nature of an individual's coping resources is itself suspect. The most familiar example here is the Type A behavior pattern. When certain ordinary frustrations of life (such as having to wait in line) habitually provoke extremes of behavior (such as rage), a person is designated "Type A." A large body of evidence, some of it reviewed later in this chapter, has implicated a component of this coping style as a significant risk factor for coronary heart disease. More generally, any type of chronic negative affect or emotion seems to enhance the risk of disease (Friedman & Booth-Kewley, 1987b).

Often it appears that any severe stress serves to facilitate, precipitate, or aggravate a physical disorder in a person already predisposed to it. This assumption is in keeping with the diathesis-stress model we discussed in Chapter 4. A person who is allergic to a particular protein may find resistance further lowered by emotional tension; similarly, as we will see, when an invading virus has already entered a person's body—as is thought to be the case in multiple sclerosis, for example—emotional stress may interfere with the body's normal defensive forces or immunological system.

In like manner, any stress may tend to aggravate and maintain certain disorders, such as migraine headaches (Levor et al., 1986). Day (1951), another pioneer in psychosomatic disorders, once pointed out, "To develop chronic active pulmonary tuberculosis a person needs some bacilli, some moderately inflammable lungs . . . and some internal or external factor which lowers the resistance to the disease." He noted further that unhappiness was among the stressors that could lower resistance.

The relationship between psychological factors and good health has also been well-documented (e.g., Jones, 1977); that is, positive emotions often seem to produce a certain immunity to physical disease or to be associated with speedy and uncomplicated recoveries when disease does strike (O'Leary, 1985). In fact, this reality complicates efforts to determine the true effectiveness of new treatment techniques, such as new drugs. A patient who *believes* a treatment is going to be effective has a much better chance of showing improvement than does one who is neutral or pessimistic—even when the treatment is subsequently shown to have no direct or relevant physiological effects. This reaction has become known as the **placebo effect,** and it

accounts in part for the controversies that arise periodically between the scientific community and the general public regarding the efficacy of certain drugs or other treatments.

It has even been suggested that, had it not been for the placebo effect, the medical profession as we know it would not have survived to the present century, because until this century practitioners in fact had little else to offer disease sufferers; indeed, specific treatments were as often as not harmful. The profession's survival and prosperity from ancient times is to a large extent a demonstration of the power of "faith" in healing (Shapiro & Morris, 1978). Thus the fundamental intimacy of the mind and body is perhaps nowhere better documented than in health and illness.

■ Autonomic Excess and Tissue Damage

Our cave-dwelling ancestors had much need for organ systems that could rapidly prepare their bodies for the intense life-or-death struggles that were the daily fare of their existence. Nature provided these in the form of a rather elaborate apparatus for dramatically enhancing energy mobilization on a short-term basis. The pertinent physiological events, chiefly involving the autonomic nervous system, were termed the "flight or fight" pattern by Walter Cannon (1929), underscoring its apparent function either in fleeing danger or subduing an aggressor. In describing the pattern, Cannon noted that, with the advance of civilization, it has become to a degree obsolete; in fact he referred to certain psychosomatic disorders as "diseases of civilization." Because contemporary human beings rarely have the concrete options of either physically fleeing or attacking a threat, no effective avenue exists for the prompt discharge of high states of physiologic readiness to perform extraordinary physical feats. In Cannon's view (and the views of many contemporary investigators), this state of affairs, when unduly repetitive or long-continued, produces tissue breakdown—that is, disease, such as ulcers and hypertension.

Autonomic nervous system arousal involves many component processes, some of them subtle or even "silent" in terms of ready accessibility to observation. With increasing levels of arousal, we can see many of the more dramatic manifestations: increased breathing and heart rate, increased perspirating, increased muscle tone, and flushing; a keen observer will note pupillary dilation, enhancing vision. With adequate instrumentation, we could also observe, for example, increased blood pressure, the dumping of sugar reserves into the blood, redistribution of blood pooled in the viscera to the peripheral or "voluntary" musculature, and enhanced secretion of powerful neurotransmitter substances. All of these changes are sometimes referred to collectively as the *alarm reaction* (Selye, 1976b),[1] the first phase of the general adaptation syndrome (Chapter 5). They are the body's response to a "battle stations" signal from the brain. Such a system was not evolved for dealing with trifling circumstances, and it is hardly surprising that such widespread and potent effects, if not permitted to subside (and the system to remain for the most part at rest), might over time lead to organic structural alterations of a pathological sort.

Coming to a similar conclusion, the early psychosomatic theorists, notably including Flanders Dunbar (1943) and Franz Alexander (1950), reasoned that chronic *internal* sources of threat could place physical health in serious jeopardy. In other words, unremitting psychological conflict of the type found in anxiety-related disorders (Chapter 6), which by its very nature would preclude arousal

Internal bodily changes similar to those caused by stress can be induced by carefully monitored physical activity. This patient on a treadmill can be observed for such things as increased heart rate and blood pressure to determine how much arousal may be a threat to physical health.

discharge, might actually cause physical damage to vital organs. These early theorists appear to have been largely on the right track, although—as so often happens in psychology and in science generally—many of their more detailed conceptions have proven inaccurate or oversimplified.

■ Psychosocial Factors and the Immune System

Although autonomic nervous system events often dominate the alarm stage of the general adaptation syndrome, they are joined in due course, often quite rapidly, by a complex array of other bodily processes. These processes contain or, if possible, eliminate the threat posed. This reaction is the beginning of Selye's stage of resistance, where the protective resources of an organism are mobilized to detect the nature of a threat and to deploy countermeasures against it. To use a simple example, if you burn your finger while cooking, your "alarm" reaction is followed promptly by transport to the site of the injury of a variety of substances that tend to limit damage and initiate tissue repair. We say "tend" in the above sentence because in this instance, as in many other more important ones, the damage-control mechanism sometimes overshoots the mark, exceeding the requirements of adequate defense and producing new problems of its own making. Thus the recommended first aid of cold application for minor burns has as its purpose the *inhibition* of an excessive defense process. We do much the same thing, incidentally, when we take common-cold remedies to inhibit mucus production in the nasal and sinus passages.

The examples just cited illustrate an important point: just as the psyche's defensive resources can display "adaptiveness" without "intelligence," so too can the body's defensive resources be both marvelously attuned to protection and at the same time clumsy and self-defeating. This paradox has important implications in many areas of medicine, such as organ transplantation. Here the body's defenses against invasion by "foreign" protein may actually destroy the life-sustaining new organ.

Considered biomedically, a crucial component of an organism's resistance-stage equipment is the immune system, whose basic properties are outlined in the next section.

---

[1]This usage of the term is somewhat incorrect. In Selye's original formulation of the general adaptation syndrome, the alarm reaction is not necessarily observable, as when it occurs in response to an intruding infectious microorganism.

Elements of the Human Immune System

While much remains to be learned about the details of immunologic functioning, particularly in regard to psychosocial influences, certain broad outlines are now fairly well understood. What follows is a brief summary of the workings of the system insofar as they are known or strongly suspected, based on contemporary research.

The **immune system** is an organism's principal means of maintaining its integrity when faced with the intrusion of foreign substances, such as bacteria, viruses, or tumors. The primary components of the immune system are the blood, thymus, bone marrow, spleen, and lymph nodes. Of the blood's principal components, the serum (a soluble medium) and the white blood cells are especially important in immune function. The serum is made up of large protein molecules and water; it is the medium by which the body transports its defenses.

The white blood cells, also called leukocytes, contain much of the body's defense system. They can be further divided into subpopulations (each with specialized functions) and are found in the thymus, spleen, and lymph nodes and in the blood itself. White blood cell subpopulations include B-cells, T-cells, macrophages (literally, big eaters), and natural killer cells, which have inherent properties destructive to foreign protein. While the role of these cells in immune functioning is often quite direct, certain of them also secrete various chemical substances that have a more indirect effect in regulating, orchestrating, and enhancing the total immune response.

Immune function is traditionally divided into two branches, humoral and cellular. The humoral branch refers to the activity of B-cells and the antibodies they produce. Cellular immune function, on the other hand, is mediated by T-cells, whose effects, while widespread, do not include antibody production. When an organism is invaded by an **antigen**—that is, a substance recognized as foreign—B- and T-cells become activated and multiply rapidly, deploying the various forms of counterattack mediated by each type of cell. In the process of defense, a subset of memory cells becomes "programmed" to recognize the particular antigen (or substances that mimic it in important respects), the code being retained for any subsequent reexposure. Thus the organism is "sensitized" for future rapid deployment of specific defensive processes. This sensitization process can also go awry, as in the sometimes serious reactions certain people have to minimally threatening foreign substances to which they have previously been exposed. Bee stings are a good example of this type of reaction: for some people who have become sensitized to bee sting venom, subsequent exposure to it can produce a life-threatening condition known as anaphylactic shock.

B-cells, which are formed in the bone marrow, perform their defensive function by producing antibodies that circulate in the blood serum. B-cell (or humoral immune) functioning is involved chiefly with protection against the more common varieties of bacterial infection.

T-cells develop to maturity in the thymus and mediate immune reactions that, while slower, are far more extensive and direct in character. While T-cells do not produce or secrete antibodies, they are capable of secreting chemicals (lymphokines) that have toxic and other effects on other cells. These cells mainly generate an attack that is highly specific to a given invading antigen.

Particular types of T-cells, called helper cells, signal B-cells to turn on antibody production and other immune cells to seek and destroy the invading antigen. The T_4 helper cell, principal target of the AIDS (HIV-1) virus, plays a crucial early role in the detection and precise identification of foreign protein. Randomly circulating macrophages encounter such protein, fragments of which then become attached to the cells' surfaces. The immune response is initiated when a T_4 cell, marvelously equipped for analyzing the threat and alerting other components of the system to its presence, collides with one of these contaminated macrophages and "reads" the antigen code on its surface. The T_4 cell is thus a vital part of an organism's first line of defense against invaders, such as viruses, that escape antibody destruction by gaining access to the interior of host cells (McCutchan, 1990).

The devastating and unrelenting effects of AIDS, an unusually virulent disease, can be attributed to the fact that HIV-1, by invading the T_4 (also called Cluster Determinant$_4$) and certain other immune cells, participates in the cellular proliferation its own invasion sets off. Furthermore, the virus destroys or functionally impairs not only the cells it invades but other T_4 cells as well in some manner not yet understood. It also attacks the circulating macrophages essential to the T_4's immunological effectiveness. In due course the T-cell defense system is severely weakened by a drastic depletion of its component members. Hence a victim is rendered highly vulnerable to a multitude of potentially dangerous antigens that would promptly be detected and destroyed in an immunocompetent person. For this reason the infections and tumors acquired by AIDS patients are said to be "opportunistic."

Antibodies to the AIDS virus, which are detectable in the blood of exposed people, are compromised in their effectiveness because the virus lives in

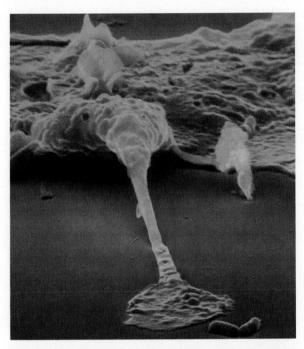

A macrophage reaches out to eat bacteria. Macrophages are important components of the immune system because they initiate the action of B-cells and T-cells against bacterial, or antigen, invasion.

a protected intracellular habitat. One can hardly imagine a killer entity better designed than HIV-1 to frustrate efforts to deter it by methods that are not in themselves dangerous to a victim. This awesome scourge underscores our utter dependence on a well-functioning immune system for health maintenance.

In summary, the front line of immune defense is contained within the highly differentiated system of white cells that circulate freely in the blood or remain as resident reinforcements in the lymph nodes. One of its two main divisions, the B-cell (or humoral), mediates the production of antibodies—circulating immunoglobulin substances of high specificity whose main role is detecting the presence of and destroying invading bacteria. The other and far more complicated main division—mediated by several descendant forms of the progenitor T-cell—includes the following among its functions: (a) direct and indirect (in concert with other elements such as macrophages) destruction of certain types of antigens, especially nonbacterial ones; and (b) regulation and in certain instances activation of the other, antibody-based division of the defense system. The immune system's response to antigen invasion is thus generalized and intricately orchestrated, requiring the intact functioning of numerous components. A much-simplified illustration of the system appears in *HIGHLIGHT 7.1.*

Psychosocial Compromise of the Immune Response

The virulence of the AIDS virus is such that psychosocial factors were originally thought to play little or no role in the resultant immune breakdown and death. More recent research suggests that this conclusion may have been premature (Kiecolt-Glaser & Glaser, 1988). For example, Antoni et al. (1990) report preliminary results indicating that behavioral interventions, such as aerobic exercise, had positive psychological and immunocompetence effects among groups of uninfected high-risk and early-stage infected gay men. If such results can be maintained over time they may show how to prevent HIV from gaining a sustainable foothold after exposure, or to slow the progress of the disease following established infection. In light of the serious toxicity of the antiviral drugs known to deter the progress of HIV infection, the discovery of more benign, noninvasive (and less expensive) treatment methods would be of tremendous help in containing the disease's effects and improving the quality of life of infected individuals.

The role of psychosocial factors in respect to many other less fearsome disease-producing antigens may be considerable. Recent evidence from a wide variety of sources, reviewed by Antoni et al. (1990) and Geiser (1989), strongly suggests that psychosocial factors can have an important effect on the functional status of the immune system at any point in time. In particular, psychosocial stressors and the mental states associated with them may depress immune function to the point of enhancing vulnerability to virtually any antigen to which a person is concurrently exposed. It seems extremely likely, for example, that some such mediating mechanism is involved in the observed relationship between stressful life changes and subsequent physical illnesses (Geiser, 1989; Koranyi, 1989; Rogers, 1989; also see *HIGHLIGHT 5.2*, p. 150).

Obviously, the central nervous system would somehow be involved in mediating effects of this kind. These observations have led to the development of the relatively new field of **psychoneuroimmunology,** which explores psychological influences on the nervous system's control of immune responsiveness. Although still in its infancy and hampered for obvious reasons in mounting a full-scale experimental assault on some outstanding questions (such as the risks associated with purposely introducing antigens into the blood streams of experimental subjects), the field has developed in a rapid and impressive manner.

Fortunately for research progress, it is possible to estimate at least the earliest phases of immune responsiveness (for example, enhanced reproduc-

Star Wars in Microcosm: The Body's Exquisitely Organized Defense System

Below is a simplified schematic of the cellular functioning of the human immune system. The immune system is normally brought into action upon detection of the presence of a foreign, "nonself" substance—an *antigen* (An)—say the *Streptococcus* bacterium often responsible for sore throat. *Phagocytes,* or *macrophages,* eating cells that wander about in the blood serum, attempt to ingest the invader, leaving identifying parts of it embedded in their own membranes. In due course, one of these foreign-substance-containing phagocytes chances to make contact with a circulating *helper T-cell* (T_h) of the T_4 variety whose surface antibody code happens to match the foreign material cap-

tured on the phagocyte membrane. This chance meeting initiates the more dramatic phases of the immune response.

The helper T-cell with the matching molecule (and hence the essential information identifying the Streptococcal invader) begins to divide, as do succeeding generations of daughter cells. These distinctive cells, shortly numbering in the thousands and each containing essentially a copy of the invading antigen, migrate to various regions and mediate, in addition, the large-scale production of targeted *cytotoxic T-cells* (T_c) and *B-cells*. The latter in turn produces *antibodies* specifically coded to bind to the offending *Streptococci* and render them vul-

nerable to easy attack by other cells, such as macrophages.

Meanwhile, the antigen/ antibody complex combines with a group of proteins known as *complements* to stimulate the secretion of histamine and the production of fever, both of which serve additional defensive functions but also make us feel ill.

If all goes well, and it usually does eventually even without antibiotic treatment, *suppressor T-cells* (T_s) assume a dominant role and turn off the system. If neither antibiotic medication nor the natural immune defense is successful in curbing the infection, serious medical consequences may ensue, even with so common an antigen as *Streptococcus.*

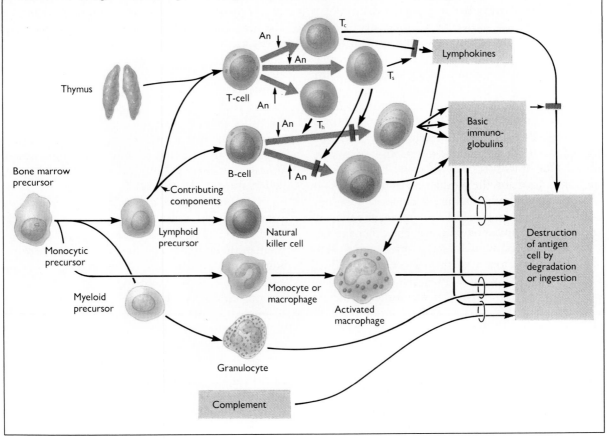

tion of various types of white cells) from laboratory examination of blood samples. This investigative strategy has been used effectively in demonstrating, for example, the suppression of white blood cell reproduction following sleep deprivation, marathon running, space flight, death of a spouse, and during psychological depression (Schleifer, Keller, & Stein, 1985; Schleifer et al., 1989; Vasiljeva et al., 1989). Immune responsiveness has been shown to vary with even normal, diurnal mood variations (A. A. Stone et al., 1987). A group of researchers at Ohio State University has repeatedly demonstrated the compromise of white blood cell proliferation, including diminished natural killer cell activity, among medical students undergoing stress (Glaser et al., 1985, 1987). Natural killer cells are believed to play a key role in tumor surveillance and the control of viral infections.

Granting the likelihood that stressors, in particular psychosocial or "mental" ones, can impair the immune response, a conclusion supported by the weight of evidence (Antoni et al., 1990; Jemmott & Locke, 1984), intriguing questions remain about the pathway or pathways of influence that may be involved. Until fairly recently, most researchers were convinced that the primary pathway was the hypothalamus-pituitary-adrenocortical (HPA) axis. According to this hypothesis, the processing of stressful events in the brain causes hypothalamic activation of the pituitary, which in turn stimulates the adrenal cortex to secrete excessive levels of adrenocortical hormones (steroids). Certain of the latter substances are known to have negative (as well as some positive) effects on immune functioning. Hence the hypothesis, while largely speculative, remains somewhat attractive.

Nevertheless, more recent research findings and conceptual refinements have turned up a host of strong competitors to the HPA interpretation. For example, we now know that a number of other hormone substances, including growth hormone, testosterone, and estrogen, are responsive to stressor conditions and also affect immune competence. The same is true of a variety of neuropeptides, including endorphins. The link between psychosocial stressors and the immune system may be even more direct, however. The discovery of nerve endings in thymus, spleen, and lymph nodes, tissues literally teeming with white blood cells, suggests the possibility of direct neural control of the secretion of immunologic agents. Along somewhat similar lines, it is now known that white blood cell surfaces contain receptors for circulating neurotransmitter substances (Rogers, 1989). We must assume that the presence of such structures on these cells is not a gratuitous freak of nature, but rather that the cells respond in some way to messages conveyed by the brain-regulated substances. Finally, and perhaps most unexpectedly, immunosuppression can be classically conditioned (Ader & Cohen, 1984)—that is, it can be *learned* as a response to previously neutral stimuli, just as Pavlov's dogs learned to salivate to a tone. Conceivably, even mental stimuli such as thoughts could thus come to activate immunosuppression if they were regularly paired with immunosuppressive events (operating as unconditioned stimuli).

In sum, we have a wealth of potential ways to eventually understand the relationship between psychosocial stressors and immunosuppression. Our guess is that such an understanding will turn out to be very complicated.

Much circumstantial evidence shows, in keeping with Selye's postulate of a state of exhaustion, that the resources of the immune system and other "resistance" mechanisms are not infinitely replenishable. In other words, these defensive resources apparently may under certain circumstances be used up at a rate faster than they can be replaced by the body's compensatory metabolism. Indeed, Selye held that this metabolic regulatory mechanism might itself become impaired as demands placed on it over a lifetime accumulate, resulting ultimately in aging and death. In any event, the weight of evidence strongly suggests that the adequacy of the immune response to a particular antigen diminishes proportionally with the quantity and intensity of other stressors simultaneously impinging on an organism, including other, unrelated illnesses. Among its other strengths, this conception nicely integrates the vast amount of data we have associating much physical illness, notably including infectious diseases, with the occurrence of antecedent stressful events (Elliott, 1989; Koranyi, 1989; Maddi, Bartone, & Puccetti, 1987).

Note that the stressful events referred to in the preceding sentence are largely psychosocial rather than physical in meaning and presumed impact on a recipient—for example, death of a spouse, change in employment status, marital difficulties, and so on. In short, we find the evidence compelling, if not conclusive, that psychosocial stressors temporarily impair the immune response and thereby contribute substantially to the development of many physical illnesses.

While efforts to relate specific stressors to specific physical diseases have not generally been successful, stress is becoming a key underlying theme in our understanding of the development and course of virtually all organic illness. Stress may serve as a predisposing, precipitating, or reinforcing factor in the causal pattern, or it may merely aggravate a condition that might have occurred anyway. Often stress appears to speed up the onset or increase the severity of a disorder, and to interfere with the body's immunological defenses and other homeostatic functions. Presuming we all have one organ system somewhere in our bodies that is at maximum relative vulnerability, a high, chronic level of stress puts us at risk for a breakdown of that organ system, and perhaps others, sooner or later.

◼ Life-style as an Added Factor in Health Maintenance

Today a great deal of attention is being paid to the role of life-style in the development or maintenance of many health problems. Numerous aspects of the way we live are now considered influential in the development of some severe physical problems: diet—particularly overeating and consuming too many high-fat, low-fiber foods; lack of exercise; smoking cigarettes; excessive alcohol and drug use; constantly facing high-stress situations; and even ineffective ways of dealing with day-to-day problems are but a few of the many life-style patterns that are viewed as contributing causes. This growing awareness of the role individual factors play in susceptibility to disease, its impact and course, has resulted in more attention to life-style by both physicians and psychologists working in health care settings (Engel, 1977; O'Leary, 1985; Oldenburg, Perkins, & Andrews, 1985; Weiner, 1977). Particularly in this area of life-style factors, health psychology—which focuses heavily on prevention and health maintenance—is growing rapidly. New efforts are being made to determine more precisely what role personality or life-style factors play in the genesis and course of disease. Finding the answers becomes all the more important when we realize that life-style factors—habits or behavior patterns presumably under our own control—are believed to play a major role in three of the leading causes of death in this country: coronary heart disease, automobile accidents, and alcohol-related deaths (National Center for Health Statistics, 1982).

We cannot help but be struck by the rather sobering observation of Knowles (1977), who takes the position that most people are born healthy and suffer premature death and disability only as a result of personal misbehavior and unnecessarily pathogenic environmental conditions. He believes that most health problems could be drastically reduced if only

It is generally recognized that personal life-style influences psychophysiologic well-being.

no one smoked cigarettes or consumed alcohol and everyone exercised regularly, maintained optimal weight on a low-fat, low-refined carbohydrate, high-fiber content diet, reduced stress by simplifying their lives, obtained adequate rest and recreation, . . . drank fluoridated water, followed the doctor's orders for medication and self-care once disease was detected, and used available health resources. (p. 1104)

Before anyone rushes to alter radically his or her life-style according to the rather Spartan regimen outlined by Knowles, it should be pointed out that the connection between many life-style habits or patterns and physical illness may not be as strong as some advocates suggest. In many cases the connection, though seemingly proven in a statistical sense, is relatively weak and usually one of correlation, with the force of the argument based more on common sense than definitive data. For example, the extent to which rates of physical diseases, such as coronary heart disease, can be controlled or reduced through such means as reducing dietary cholesterol has not been conclusively established. Nevertheless, the stakes are sufficiently high that it would seem imprudent to tempt fate by ignoring one's cholesterol intake.

Even in cases where virtual proof of causation exists, it is difficult for many individuals to alter significantly their life-styles to reduce their risk for disease—an incentive that may be remote for people not experiencing current health difficulties. Significant and lasting change is generally hard for people, and this is especially true where available rewards are immediate and powerful, as in the case of addictions (Chapter 9). The high and sustained motivation necessary to achieve reliable self-control often proves fragile. Some of the most well-established risk factors, such as cigarette smoking, are thus not easy habits to alter, even when the connection between the habit and the disease is direct and seemingly evident. After having two heart attacks and surgery to remove a cancerous lung, one man continued to smoke two and a half packs of cigarettes a day even though he frequently said, "I know these things are killing me a little at a time . . . but they have become so much a part of my life I can't live without them!"

PSYCHOSOCIAL FACTORS IN SPECIFIC DISEASE PROCESSES

The debilitating effects of stressful life circumstances and of harmful life-style habits tend to be relatively diffuse and nonspecific in terms of the organ systems adversely affected and the diseases for which risk is ultimately enhanced. Excessive autonomic activity, persistent negative emotional states, diminished immune competence, or even "bad habits" such as cigarette smoking typically compromise a person's functioning in several different ways and may therefore be implicated in a range of disease processes. Complementing such generalized influences are a host of more specific factors that help determine whether or not a given individual will acquire a particular illness or disease at some time. Most obvious among these are certain innate predispositions to develop a disease, often inherited ones, and levels of exposure to pertinent pathogenic agents, such as noxious chemicals in the workplace. In addition, contemporary research (see e.g., Friedman & Booth-Kewley's (1987b) quantitative review) increasingly implicates factors of personality and interpersonal functioning as having causal roles in the development of certain physical illnesses. The present section undertakes a selective survey of apparent instances of the latter.

As we have seen, the idea that personality traits might be causally related to the development of one or another type of physical illness is by no means

new. Until fairly recently, however, evidence for such relationships was based mainly on unsystematic and often rather casual observations. This evidence has now been supplemented, at least in some instances, with quite rigorously developed data that render the implicated causal hypotheses highly plausible, if not compelling. In the following sections we will review in some detail certain widespread conditions that are the focus of much contemporary psychophysiologic research and theorizing— coronary heart disease and the eating disorders known as anorexia nervosa and bulimia. Then we shall move on to a brief survey of several other illnesses classically considered to have strong psychogenic aspects.

Coronary Heart Disease and the Type A Behavior Pattern

Coronary heart disease (CHD) is a potentially lethal blockage of the arteries supplying blood to the heart muscle, or myocardium. Its chief clinical manifestations are (a) angina pectoris, severe chest pain signalling that the delivery of oxygenated blood to the affected area of the heart is quantitatively insufficient for its current work load; (b) myocardial infarction, functionally complete blockage of a section of the coronary arterial system, resulting in death of the myocardial tissue supplied by that arterial branch; and (c) disturbance of the heart's electrical conduction consequent to arterial blockage, resulting in disruption or interruption of the heart's pumping action, often leading to death. Many instances of sudden cardiac death, in which victims have no prior history of CHD symptoms, are attributed to "silent" CHD (see HIGHLIGHT 7.2).

While deaths from CHD have declined dramatically in recent years, this decline has occurred at the end of a long period, comprising most of the twentieth century, of rising CHD-related mortality in the United States. CHD retains today the dubious distinction of being the nation's number one killer, despite spectacular advances in treatment (such as coronary artery bypass surgery) and markedly enhanced appreciation of risk factors, some of which (elevated serum cholesterol, smoking, lack of exercise, obesity, and hypertension, for example) are potentially reversible.

The known biological risk factors for CHD explain less than half of the CHD-related outcomes people actually experience. In other words, much of the causal pattern for CHD development (or, for that matter, for its failure to develop) remains shrouded in mystery. Noting this circumstance, cardiovascular researchers have increasingly turned their attention to possible nonbiological contributions to the disease's development—to psychosocial and personality factors—emulating in this respect some eminent forebears. Englishman William Harvey, the discoverer of circulation, was writing of "affections of the mind" that generate problems in heart function as early as 1628. The distinguished Canadian physician Sir William Osler, in landmark lectures on cardiology published in 1892, explicitly related the development of CHD to "the worry and strain of modern life" and "the high pressure" under which people live. Attempts to refine and precisely specify the psychological contribution to the disease's development continue to the present day, for the most part in the context of identifying the crucial components of what M. Friedman and Rosenman (1959) first labeled the **Type A behavior pattern.**

As conceptualized by Friedman and Rosenman, the Type A pattern is a complex set of behaviors that may be observed in certain individuals under appropriately stressful or challenging circumstances. The pattern, they said, involves excessive competitive drive in the absence of well-defined goals, impatience or time urgency, and hostility. It manifests itself in accelerated speech and motor activity. The

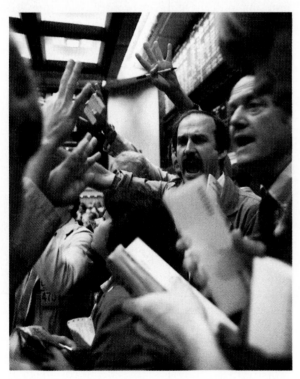

The Type A behavior pattern may be observed in certain individuals under stressful or challenging circumstances. The pattern involves excessive competitiveness, impatience, hostility, and accelerated speech and motor activity.

pattern is best assessed and measured, according to these investigators, by means of a structured interview devised for this purpose (Rosenman, 1978). The contrasting Type B pattern, to which little descriptive attention has been paid, is negatively defined in terms of the absence of Type A characteristics. Various questionnaire-type approaches to the assessment of Type A behavior have also been developed, of which the Jenkins Activity Survey for Health Prediction (Jenkins et al., 1971) has been most popular among researchers.

Unfortunately, the various assessment measures for the A/B typology are not as strongly intercorrelated as one might wish. This situation suggests continuing problems in the construct's definition and the likelihood that differing measurement approaches emphasize different components of the Type A pattern as originally described. This measurement problem may be the principal reason why a few studies have failed to find a Type A-CHD relationship (Fischman, 1987). Moreover, as Krantz and Glass (1984) have noted, some evidence shows that not all components of the Type A pattern are equally predictive of CHD or even of differing pathological manifestations within the CHD syndrome (for example, angina versus infarction). Overall, some consensus has developed that the pattern's hyperaggressivity/hostility component, perhaps in association with status insecurity and inhibition of overt expressions of anger, is the one most closely correlated with demonstrable coronary artery deterioration (M. Friedman & Ulmer, 1984; Krantz & Glass, 1984; Williams et al., 1980; Williams, Barefoot, & Shekelle, 1985; Wood, 1986).

However, considerable conceptual and empirical uncertainties remain regarding the measurement of the A/B-Type variable and identification of its most significant components. Booth-Kewley & H. Friedman (1987), after a careful review of the pertinent evidence, have suggested that anxiety and depression are as important as anger and hostility in the correlational network that includes CHD development. Further, a recent longitudinal study by Hearn, Murray, & Luepker (1989) tends to negate any role for hostility. These authors contacted, in 1985 through 1986, 1313 men, or their surviving relatives, who had completed the Minnesota Multiphasic Personality Inventory, or MMPI (see Chapter 16) as university freshmen in 1953. The MMPI can be scored for a special, relatively well-validated scale measuring subject hostility (Ho). The subjects, divided according to those scoring high and low on the Ho scale, or their relatives were interviewed (by telephone) about their intervening health statuses. Hostility, as measured by the Ho

HIGHLIGHT 7.2

Heart Attack

We have all heard the old story about the faint-hearted guard dog who, on being told "Attack," had one. *Attack* is now a common word in our vocabulary, as well it should be since heart attacks kill over half a million Americans each year. The incidence of heart disease among Americans is one of the highest in the world; about 30 million people are affected. (Some countries have a higher rate, including France, or a lower one, such as Japan.) But what is a heart attack? Technically, it is the result of a *myocardial infarction*—that is, a blockage of the arteries that feed the heart. (The lighter areas in the photo indicate blockage.)

When such an artery is blocked, the oxygen-starved muscles of the heart begin to die. Depending on how much of the heart is damaged and how badly, the results can vary from almost complete recovery to death. Blockage of the coronary vessels that feed the heart is usually caused by one of three things: a clot lodged in the vessel, a prolonged contraction of the vessel walls, or atherosclerosis.

Atherosclerosis is the result of the buildup of a number of substances, such as fat, fibrin (formed in clots), parts of dead cells, and calcium. These substances reduce the elasticity of the vessel, and by decreasing its diameter, they raise blood pressure, just as you raise the pressure in a garden hose by holding your thumb over the end. No one knows what causes atherosclerosis, but a number of things can speed its development, such as

smoking cigarettes and, probably, eating animal fat and cholesterol. Other factors include age, hypertension, diabetes, stress, heredity, gender (males have more heart attacks), and a Type A behavior pattern.

The warnings of heart attack are often (but not always) (1) a pain that spreads along the shoulders, arm, neck, or jaw; (2) sudden sweating; (3) a heavy pressure and pain in the center of the chest; and (4) nausea, vomiting, and shortness of breath. The symptoms may come and go.

People who have not developed a strong and efficient cardiovascular system through exercise are particularly susceptible to *angina pectoris* (chest pain), which occurs when the heart fails to receive enough blood, particularly during times of stress or exercise. It should not be confused with a true heart attack, although it may forecast one in the future.

The pain may be relieved by stopping the unusual exercise or by reducing the stress levels. Blood flow to the heart can be increased by an exercise program or by surgically inserting vessels from other parts of the body (a coronary bypass). Certain chemicals, such as nitroglycerin, also dilate the heart's vessels and increase the circulation of blood there.

Another form of heart attack results in a phenomenon called *sudden death*. The death may be due to chaotic and uncoordinated contractions of the ventricles, often brought on by an unanticipated myocardial infarction. The contractions do not move blood along and, after a few spasms, the heart may stop entirely. Many people afflicted in such a way mysteriously fall dead in their tracks. Some however, can be saved if they are helped in time.

In fact, victims of any form of heart attack stand a much greater chance of surviving if they are treated immediately. In many metropolitan areas, citizens are being trained in cardiopulmonary resuscitation (CPR) to help restore a victim's circulation in such emergencies. CPR continues the flow of blood to the brain, where sensitive tissues die quickly without oxygen. In Seattle, Washington, with an extensive citizen-training program, passersby have performed about one-third of the city's resuscitations. Their success rate is higher than that of professionals because they usually reach victims sooner.

Adapted from *Biology: The world of life,* Robert A. Wallace (Glenview, Ill.: Scott, Foresman and Company, 1987).

scale, did not in fact predict subsequent CHD-related illness, CHD mortality, or total mortality from all causes over the 33-year period involved.

In spite of these continuing conceptual and measurement uncertainties, it remains difficult to dispute the original evidence that the general cluster of reactions identified as the Type A pattern is a significant predictor of CHD, independent of other risk factors. While several studies support such a conclusion, two in particular stand out because their prospective designs circumvent many of the interpretation problems attending less powerful investigative strategies. (For example, inquiry about personality factors occurring after a diagnosis of CHD could lead to retrospective distortion based on preconceived notions of a coronary-prone personality type.) The first of these prospective studies is known as the Western Collaborative Group Study (WCGS) project, in which some 3150 healthy men between the ages of 35 and 59 on entry were typed as to A or B status and followed for a period of eight and a half years. Type As were found to be approximately twice as likely as Type Bs to have developed CHD (angina or myocardial infarctions) during the follow-up period. This differential remained even when other risk factors were statistically eliminated from consideration. When the data for a younger group of men (ages 39 to 49 on entry into the project) were considered separately, CHD was proportionately six times more prevalent among Type As than Type Bs (Rosenman et al., 1975). The findings also linked the Type A pattern to recurrent myocardial infarctions (Jenkins, Zyzanski, & Rosenman, 1976) and to sudden cardiac death (M. Friedman et al., 1973).

We should note in passing that Ragland and Brand (1988) have called into question the WCGS study's conclusions on the basis of their finding that people who died from a heart attack subsequent to their first ones were more likely to be Bs than As. It seems to us, however, that such a finding does not negate the original conclusions. Also to be noted is that those Type As who were maximally at risk were already dead when the data on subsequent attacks was analyzed, leaving behind a sample of subjects biased in favor of CHD deaths among Bs. Nobody ever held that A or B status was the only determinant of death from CHD.

The second prospective study to be considered here was an aspect of the well-known Framingham Heart Study, now in its fourth decade and involving long-term follow-up of a large sample of male and female individuals from that Boston suburb. Some 1700 coronary-free subjects were typed as to A or B status in the mid-1960s. Analysis of the data for CHD occurrence during an eight-year follow-up

period not only confirmed the major findings of the WCGS project but extended them to women as well. In fact the two-fold increase in CHD risk reported for Type A men was almost exactly replicated for Type A women. Somewhat curiously, the CHD-Type A association among males in this study was limited to those of white-collar socioeconomic status (Haynes et al., 1980). See *HIGHLIGHT 7.3* for a graph summarizing these results.

Taken together, these and other studies meet most of the stringent criteria established by epidemiologists to justify the assumption of a cause-effect relationship in disease genesis. That is, the evidence overall suggests that some aspect of the Type A behavior pattern, possibly one involving general negative affect that remains unexpressed (Endicott, 1989; H. Friedman & Booth-Kewley, 1987a), is more or less directly implicated in the development of a potentially lethal organic deficit (CHD) among some individuals. It is important to note, too, however, that this area is under active investigation and heated debate. Clearly, many factors are involved in the causal chain of CHD.

The theoretical importance of the preceding findings for advancing our understanding of basic processes underlying CHD is considerable. Beyond that, they raise the possibility of saving lives by devising preventive therapeutic interventions to alter the Type A reaction pattern (or more precisely its negative affect component) in persons at risk. To date, however, little formal or systematic work in this area has been reported.

■ The Anorexic and Bulimic Syndromes

Anorexia nervosa and bulimia, which are normally considered separate syndromes, are coded (separately) as eating disorders of adolescence and adulthood in DSM-III-R. In fact neither syndrome occurs in appreciable numbers prior to adolescence, and onset after age 25 is rare. Also, the overwhelming preponderance of victims are female—on the order of 20 to 1. This figure suggests that, for reasons not yet fully understood, "femaleness" may be an intrinsic factor in these disorders. Further, it suggests that males exhibiting similar anomalies in eating behavior may therefore not represent true instances, in other essential respects, of these presumed clinical entities. In any event, little of a systematic nature is known about such males and hence we will confine ourselves here to typical cases involving girls or young women. Anorexia, in particular, is often an intractable and dangerous disorder, with a mortality rate near 5 percent (Szmukler & Russell, 1986).

The Type A Behavior Pattern and Coronary Heart Disease

The following graph depicts the percent incidence of coronary heart disease (CHD) over an eight-year period among subjects of the Framingham Heart Study.

Subjects are distinguished according to age, sex, occupation (men only), and Type A versus Type B behavior pattern. Note the substantial rise in CHD among Type

A women and men of white-collar occupations over their Type B counterparts. The failure to confirm this finding among blue-collar males remains unexplained.

Anorexia nervosa has been officially recognized as a distinct disorder for at least a century. The central features of the syndrome are an intense abhorrence of obesity coupled with the often absurd complaint that one is "fat"; loss of at least 25 percent of original body weight (or, in those under 18, significant weight loss and a discrepancy from average projected weight gain that together constitute a 25 percent shortfall); and unremitting refusal to maintain weight within the lower limits of normal for age and height. Associated features that are usually present include cessation of menstruation and marked overactivity. Brief binges of overeating followed by self-induced vomiting or other purging practices are also common, constituting one of several links with bulimia.

Anorexic girls usually describe their mothers in unflattering terms: excessively dominant, intrusive, overbearing, and markedly ambivalent. We must register caution here, however, in light of the possibility that mothers respond in these ways to the self-starvation of their children. By contrast, anorex-

ic girls usually describe their fathers as "emotional absentees." Most clinicians who work with anorexic individuals are in fact impressed with the extent to which family dynamics seem to contribute to the disorder. Along this line, Humphrey (1989) has analyzed the interactions of families with an anorexic daughter using the Structural Analysis of Social Behavior (SASB; Benjamin, 1974), a highly systematic, quantitative technique for measuring the nature of interpersonal relationships. The parents of these young women were found to communicate with their daughters in abnormally complicated ways, providing "double messages" that at once communicated both nurturant affection and disqualification of the daughters' attempts to express themselves. In turn, the anorexic daughters displayed behaviors that wavered between self-expression and submission to the leads provided by parents.

Anorexia often begins when life changes require new or unfamiliar skills concerning which the person feels inadequate, such as occurs when going off

Though this anorexic woman's appearance is shocking to us, she is likely convinced that she is "fat." This distorted view of the true nature of one's body weight is a central feature of anorexia nervosa, along with a refusal to maintain weight within the normal limits for age and height. Anorexia often begins as an extension of normal dieting, but what distinguishes a normal dieter from one who converts dieting into a dangerous activity remains a mystery.

to college, getting married, or even reaching puberty. Often the disorder begins as an extension of normal dieting, which is common among young women. What distinguishes the normal dieter from the one who converts dieting into a dangerous flirtation with disaster remains a mystery. The case of Mary S., including her marked activity despite dwindling energy resources and her unfailing denial of the growing seriousness of her condition, is in most respects fairly typical of the anorexic syndrome:

*M*ary S., aged sixteen and one-half years, grew disgusted with a close friend who began to put on weight by eating candy. The two girls agreed to go on a reducing diet, although Mary weighed only 114 pounds. A year later she

graduated from high school and obtained a job as a stenographer. She began to lead a very busy life, working every day, and going dancing at night with a young man who paid her attention. As her activities increased, her weight loss became more apparent, and soon her menses disappeared. Up to this time her dieting had been a voluntary control of eating, but now her appetite failed. Some months later one of the patient's sisters lured her boyfriend from her. Mary began to feel tired, and had to force herself to keep active. The onset of dizzy spells caused her to consult a doctor, who suggested a tonsillectomy. After the operation she refused to eat, but continued her active pace, including dancing every night. She now weighed 71 pounds. Two months later she became so dizzy and weak that she could no longer walk, and was finally brought to the hospital weighing 63 pounds. In three days, two and a half years after beginning her diet, Mary S. was dead of bronchopneumonia. (Nemiah, 1961, p. 10)

Recurrent episodes of seemingly uncontrollable binge eating, with full awareness of the pattern's abnormality and with much secrecy, shame, guilt, and self-deprecation concerning it, are the hallmarks of *bulimia,* now relabeled **bulimia nervosa** in DSM-III-R. Victims normally have pronounced fears that they will be unable to stop eating voluntarily; are preoccupied with weight gain; and engage in frequent attempts to lose weight by severe methods, such as fasting, self-induced vomiting, and overuse of laxatives and diuretics. While extreme weight fluctuations are common among bulimics, many successfully avoid obvious obesity and are able to conceal their problems from families, associates, and friends. Bulimia is thus a quite specific and distinctive syndrome and should be distinguished from the more common and demographically far less specific problem of overeating and obesity per se, which is discussed in Chapter 11. Unlike anorexia nervosa, its specific recognition as a psychiatric syndrome is relatively recent—it is not mentioned in the DSM-II of 1968.

The term *bulimarexia* was coined in 1976 by Boskind-White and White (1983) upon their discovering a large group of young women with distinctive dietary problems whose syndromes, they felt, differed significantly from either anorexia or bulimia, as these terms were then generally understood. These authors acknowledge (1986) that, with the inclusion of the purging phenomenon in the DSM-III bulimia definition, the terms *bulimia* and *bulimarexia* have become essentially interchangeable. While we have opted for the shorter term here, Boskind-White & White's (1983) rich clinical descriptions of the "bulimarexic" syndrome may be unsurpassed (see *HIGHLIGHT 7.4* for an example), and they add much to our understanding of these unfortunate young women. They emphasize a common core of psychological attributes involving perfectionism; obsessive concern with food and body proportions; low self-esteem; social withdrawal; and excessive preoccupation with pleasing others, if necessary to their own detriment.

Both anorexia nervosa (Strober, 1986) and bulimia (Boskind-White & White, 1986) have undergone a marked rise in incidence in the United States over at least the past three decades. Numerical estimations of incidence are therefore difficult to pin down. For females, onset of the disorder within the age range of 12 to 18 is probably in excess of 1 in 250. Foreyt (1986) estimates the incidence of bulimia to be "as high as" 15 percent in college-aged women.

Most authorities agree that these eating disorders have their origins in psychological problems that somehow become focused on food ingestion and body proportions. Many believe that our contemporary cultural preoccupation with an ideal of thinness encourages the rise in eating disorders we in fact seem to be experiencing. The fact that these syndromes are overwhelmingly more common in females than males is explained, in part, by the greater pressure for thinness experienced by females, as demonstrated in a clever study by Fallon & Rozin (1985). Using figure drawings as stimuli, these authors found that (a) women judged their "current figure" as too heavy; (b) men believed women liked heavier female figures than they in fact did; and (c) women believed men liked thinner female figures than they in fact did. Overall, men were satisfied and women dissatisfied with their own current figures as personally judged. While this self-devaluating perceptual bias in women hardly seems a complete explanation for their markedly disproportionate vulnerability to serious eating disorders, the likelihood is high of its making some contribution to that outcome (Hsu, 1989). Fashion magazines and the like, with their depictions of the ideal woman as malnourished in appearance, undoubtedly exacerbate the effect.

As Garner (1986) convincingly argues, the current trend of considering anorexia and bulimia to be psychologically dissimilar disorders may be seriously misleading. Not only do anorexic and bulimic individuals typically share many psycholog-ical traits, such as perfectionism and dysfunctional thought processes, they also share the same goal of maintaining suboptimal body weights. Moreover, a given patient may often move between the two syndromes at different times in her quest for ultimate thinness. Most anorexic and bulimic individuals come from socioeconomically advantaged backgrounds. The perfectionism and overachievement typical of anorexic patients were illustrated in a recent study by Dura and Bornstein (1989), who showed the school achievements of a group of hospitalized anorexic adolescents to be well above those predicted from their IQ scores.

Comparable underlying psychodynamics have also been described for anorexic and bulimic patients. The Humphrey (1989) study on family interactions in anorexia mentioned earlier contained a bulimic subject group. Disturbed family dynamics involving an undercutting of the daughter's autonomy (here within a context of excessive family enmeshment) were also observed for young women having this form of eating disorder. The general picture of family dysfunction in bulimia was also confirmed by Scalf-McIver and Thompson (1989) in a questionnaire study of college women showing bulimic eating patterns. In short, both anorexic and bulimic individuals seem deeply but ambivalently involved with their parents in power struggles concerning autonomy and identity.

Bruch (1986), who until her recent death was generally considered the world's leading authority on anorexia, saw the genuine anorexic person (she believed there were many "me too" facsimiles) as attempting to camouflage an undeveloped and amorphous selfhood by being different, even unique, in a special and fiercely "independent" way. She reportedly doubted that bulimia existed as a basic entity independent of anorexia or possibly even of some other unrelated syndrome (Foreyt, 1986). Boskind-White and White (1983, 1986), although seeing anorexic and bulimic individuals as struggling with similar personal and family issues, consider the typical bulimic person to be at a relatively more advanced stage of identity development, having achieved a measure of independence from family and been at least minimally successful in peer relations. The establishment of a truly autonomous selfhood, including a mature approach to sexuality, however, remains a difficult hurdle for both groups of women—although bulimic women as a group may be more likely to have had extensive sexual experiences (Coovert, Kinder, & Thompson, 1989).

Granting apparent psychological origins, persistent anorexia or bulimia leads eventually to serious

A Bulimic's Morning

Nicole awakens in her cold dark room and already wishes it was time to go back to bed. She dreads the thought of going through this day, which will be like so many others in her recent past. She asks herself the same question every morning: "Will I be able to make it through the day without being totally obsessed by thoughts of food, or will I blow it again and spend the day binge-ing?" She tells herself that today she will begin a new life, today she will start to live like a normal human being. However, she is not at all convinced that the choice is hers.

She feels fat and wants to lose weight, so she decides to start a new diet: "This time it'll be for real! I know I'll feel good about myself if I'm thinner. I want to start my exercises again because I want to make my body more attractive."

Nicole plans her breakfast, but decides not to eat until she has worked out for a half hour or so. She tries not to think about food since she is not really hungry. She feels anxiety about the day ahead of her. "It's this tension," she rationalizes. That is what is making her want to eat.

Nicole showers and dresses and plans her schedule for the day—classes, studying, and meals. She plans this schedule in great detail, listing where she will be at every minute and what she will eat at every meal. She does not want to leave blocks of time when she might feel tempted to binge.

"It's time to exercise, but I don't really want to; I feel lazy. Why do I always feel so lazy? What happened to the will power I used to have?"

Gradually, Nicole feels the binge-ing signal coming on. Half-heartedly she tries to fight it, remembering the promises she made to herself about changing.

She also knows how she is going to feel at the end of the day if she spends it binge-ing. Ultimately, Nicole decides to give into her urges because, for the moment, she would rather eat.

Since Nicole is not going to exercise, because she wants to eat, she decides that she might as well eat some "good" food. She makes a poached egg and toast and brews a cup of coffee, all of which goes down in about thirty seconds. She knows this is the beginning of several hours of craziness!

After rummaging through the cupboards, Nicole realizes that she does not have any binge food. It is cold and snowy outside and she has to be at school fairly soon, but she bundles up and runs down the street. First she stops at the bakery for a bagful of sweets —cookies and doughnuts. While munching on these, she stops and buys a few bagels. Then a quick run to the grocery store for grano-

Boskind-White and White (1983, pp. 29–32).

physical problems relating both to starvation and the dire methods often employed to purge food following a binge. These patients routinely suffer from anemia; dehydration; deficiencies in essential vitamins, minerals, and electrolytes; chronic urinary and bowel difficulties; hypoglycemia; endocrine abnormalities; and potentially serious alterations in cardiovascular functioning. Amenorrhea is virtually always present in anorexia and is common in bulimia as well. At some point in the process, biological factors seem to develop their own demands, taking the behavior beyond conscious control and making it exceedingly difficult to reverse, as we will see later in the chapter in our discussion of treatment measures. One school of thought holds that hypothalamic functioning is altered by deliberate selfstarvation, resulting finally in autonomous dysregulation of both appetite and menstruation, and yielding the typical advanced clinical picture (Bemis, 1978; Walsh, 1980).

Like CHD, these disorders of the basic drive for nutritional sustenance are dangerous and have become commonplace in modern American society. Also like CHD, we have yet to devise a reliably effective means of preventing or reversing the psychological substrates that encourage their development and maintenance. As we will see later, however, progress is being made on both these fronts.

The main issues addressed thus far in this chapter have had a decidedly contemporary focus, and deliberately so. We have sought to introduce the topic of psychological influences on health by discussing some currently high-profile concerns in both the public and professional sectors. We have la and milk. At the last minute, Nicole adds several candy bars. By the time she is finished, she has spent over fifteen dollars.

Nicole can hardly believe that she is going to put all of this food, this junk, into her body; even so, her adrenaline is flowing and all she wants to do is eat, think about eating, and anticipate getting it over with. She winces at the thought of how many pounds all of this food represents, but knows she will throw it up afterward. There is no need to worry.

At home Nicole makes herself a few bowls of cereal and milk, which she gobbles down with some of the bagels smothered with butter, cream cheese, and jelly (not to mention the goodies from the bakery and the candy bars which she is still working on). She drowns all of this with huge cups of coffee and milk, which help speed up the process even more. All this has taken no

longer than forty-five minutes, and Nicole feels as though she has been moving at ninety miles an hour.

Nicole dreads reaching this stage, where she is so full that she absolutely has to stop eating. She will throw up, which she feels she has to do but which repels her. At this point, she has to acknowledge that she's been binge-ing. She wishes she were dreaming, but knows all too well that this is real. The thought of actually digesting all of those calories, all of that junk, terrifies her.

In her bathroom, Nicole ties her hair back, turns on the shower (so none of the neighbors can hear her), drinks a big glass of water, and proceeds to force herself to vomit. She feels sick, ashamed, and incredulous that she is really doing this. Yet she feels trapped—she does not know how to break out of this pattern. As her stomach empties, she steps on and off the

scale to make sure she has not gained any weight.

Nicole knows she needs help, but she wants someone else to make it all go away. As she crashes on her bed to recuperate, her head is spinning. "I'll never do this again," she vows. "Starting tomorrow, I'm going to change. I'll go on a fast for a week and then I'll feel better."

Unfortunately, deep inside, Nicole does not believe any of this. She knows this will not be the last time. Reluctantly, she leaves for school, late and unwilling to face the work and responsibilities that lie ahead. She almost feels as though she could eat again to avoid going to school. She wonders how many hours it will be until she starts her next binge, and she wishes she had never gotten out of bed this morning.

---

also tried to give due attention to the contextual, system-level thinking that is growing in the health field (for example, organ failure is not a discrete, isolated event). As we have seen, the behavioral medicine approach explicitly embodies such a far-reaching perspective, calling into question much of traditional medicine's exclusive concern with the pathophysiology of individual organs when (*after*) disease strikes (Weiner & Fawzy, 1989).

We have also seen, however, that various medical pioneers have from time to time called attention to the influence of psychosocial factors, chiefly emotional ones, in causing or maintaining physical illness. By the 1950s this thinking had become strongly wedded to the psychoanalytic tradition. As was noted earlier, these ideas involved quite specific causal hypotheses concerning certain diseases that

came to be considered "psychosomatic" in nature —organic dysfunctions produced by aberrant emotional processes.

As a group, these early notions shared the joint problems of being both too specific and too general. They frequently specified the exact type of psychological "conflict" presumed to underlie a given disease, and they tended to assume that this alleged conflict was both necessary and sufficient in causing any instance of the disease. For example, asthma was conceived as "suppressed crying" caused by an impulse to cry joined with a need to inhibit it, both propensities relating in turn to a fear of abandonment. We now know that asthma can have many causes, that it probably does not occur in the absence of a biologically based predisposition, and that any emotional factors involved in precipitating an attack tend to be quite idiosyncratic to the victim (A. Alexander, 1977, 1981; Knapp, 1989). Comparable ideas relating a number of other illnesses to rather fanciful and specific psychogenic hypotheses also lost credibility when subjected to rigorous empirical evaluation.

Despite the general failure of this "psychosomatic specificity" approach, there were some exceptions—not so much in the sense of detailed confirmations as in that of establishing modest associations between certain illnesses and certain emotional states (much as in the relatively more recent case of CHD and some still imprecisely identified component of the Type A pattern). We will now briefly examine three illnesses that have continued to attract attention in this regard: essential hypertension or high blood pressure, peptic ulcers, and persistently recurrent headaches.

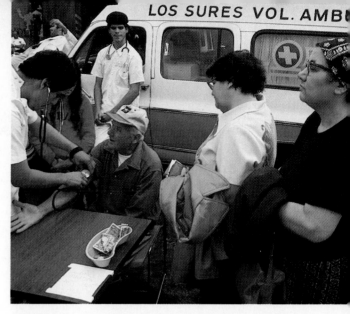

High blood pressure is an insidious and dangerous disorder, but it is easy and painless to detect by means of the familiar inflated arm cuff. It is common to see mobile units at shopping centers and the like, offering free blood pressure checks.

◼ Essential Hypertension

During states of calm, the beat of the heart is regular, the pulse is even, blood pressure is relatively low, and the visceral organs are well supplied with blood. With stress, however, the vessels of the visceral organs constrict, and blood flows in greater quantity to the muscles of the trunk and limbs— part of the flight or fight pattern described earlier. With the tightening of the tiny vessels supplying the visceral organs, the heart must work harder. As it beats faster and with greater force, the pulse quickens and blood pressure mounts. Usually, when the crisis passes, the body resumes normal functioning and the blood pressure returns to normal. Under continuing emotional strain, however, high blood pressure may become chronic.

About 12 percent of Americans suffer from chronically high blood pressure, or **hypertension.** Preexisting organic factors account for only some 5 to 10 percent of hypertension cases (Byassee, 1977); the large remainder are given the designation **essential hypertension,** meaning no physical cause is known. Although Wing and Manton (1983) have reported a reduced incidence of deaths due to hypertension, it nevertheless is the primary cause of more than 60,000 deaths each year and a major predisposing factor in another 1 million or more deaths a year from strokes and cardiovascular diseases, including CHD (Coates et al., 1981). It is also a risk factor in kidney failure, blindness, and a number of other physical ailments. For reasons that are not entirely clear but apparently relate in part to diet, the incidence of hypertension is about twice as high among blacks as among whites (Anderson & Jackson, 1987; Edwards, 1973; Mays, 1974), mak-

ing it a more serious health problem in this population than even sickle-cell anemia.

Unlike the other disease states we have dealt with, there are usually no symptoms to signal high blood pressure. Sufferers experience no personal distress. In severe cases, some people complain of headaches, tiredness, insomnia, or occasional dizzy spells—symptoms often easy to ignore—but most people suffering from hypertension receive no warning symptoms. In fact, Nelson (1973) reported on one survey encompassing three middle-class neighborhoods in Los Angeles that revealed that a third of the adults tested had high blood pressure; only half of them had been aware of it. As Mays (1974) has described the situation, "In most instances . . . the disease comes as silently as a serpent stalking its prey. Someone with high blood pressure may be unaware of his affliction for many years and then, out of the blue, develop blindness or be stricken by a stroke, cardiac arrest or kidney failure" (p. 7).

Since there is no such thing as benign hypertension, high blood pressure is an insidious and dangerous disorder. Ironically, it is both simple and painless to detect by means of the familiar inflated arm cuff, automatic versions of which are now widely available for self-testing at shopping centers and the like.

In some cases a physical cause of hypertension can be identified. For example, it may be attributable to a narrowing of the aorta or one of its arteries, to the excessive use of certain drugs, or to dietary factors. The normal regulation of blood pressure, however, is so complex that when it goes awry in a particular case, identifying the causal factors can be extremely difficult (Herd, 1984). Kidney dysfunction, for example, may be a cause or an effect of dangerously elevated pressures—or both.

Obesity, long suspected as an etiological factor, has emerged as a possible underlying factor in several other known correlates of hypertension, such as poor diet and lack of exercise (Ostfeld & D'Atri, 1977). Obesity, of course, can also be a factor contributing to the current level of experienced stress.

A number of investigators have shown that chronic hypertension may be triggered by emotional stress. For example, a highly stressful job markedly increases the risk of high blood pressure (Edwards, 1973). The stresses of inner-city life—as well as dietary factors such as excessive salt intake—have been identified as probably playing a key role in the high incidence of hypertension among black people (Anderson & Jackson, 1987; Mays, 1974).

The classical psychoanalytic interpretation of hypertension is that affected people suffer from "suppressed rage," and scattered evidence supports this hypothesis (Gentry et al., 1982; Spielberger et al., 1985; Stone & Hokanson, 1969). Although there is a high incidence of hypertension in the black inner-city population, among whom suppressed hostility might be expected to run high (Harburgh et al., 1973), the suppressed-rage hypothesis cannot be said to be firmly established in respect to all, or even necessarily a majority, of affected persons. Findings by Esler et al. (1977) suggest that, in the subgroup of hypertensive people who do show suppressed hostility, it is often accompanied by high levels of submissiveness, overcontrol, and guilt.

A variant of the suppressed-rage hypothesis has been proposed by McClelland (1979). According to this view, an affected individual is driven not so much by rage and the need to suppress it as by power motives and the need to inhibit their expression. Unexpressed anger is then a frequent accompaniment. In a well-conceived study designed to test these ideas, McClelland found that personality measures of "need for power" and "activity inhibition" were indeed jointly associated with elevated blood pressures. Moreover, he demonstrated that this inhibited power motive syndrome in men in their 30s accurately predicted elevated blood pressure and signs of hypertensive disease in these same men 20 years later.

Perhaps we will find that neither rage nor power motives per se are critical elements in essential hypertension. What is common to the findings of McClelland and earlier work is the inhibition or suppression of strong, emotion-laden urgings to perform certain acts that are poorly tolerated by polite society. The common factor, in other words, might be that of a poor match between individual drives and internalized societal restraints. Conflictual states of this sort were examined in some detail in our earlier discussion of neurotic processes (Chapter 6).

■ Peptic Ulcers

Peptic ulcers were first observed in Western culture during the early part of the nineteenth century. The term derives from *pepsin,* an important component of the acid stomach juices that aid in the early phases of digestion. These ulcerations of the stomach or upper intestine (the duodenum) were first found primarily in young women, but a shift occurred in the second half of the nineteenth century, and in the twentieth century men became far more prone to peptic ulcers than women. Today the sex ratio appears to be equalizing, and incidence and prevalence figures show a downward trend. The epidemiologic data suggest that incidence trends mirror the transformation from rural to urban living in different societies, declining in the posturbanization period (Thompson, 1982). Approximately 10,000 Americans die every year from peptic ulcers (Whitehead et al., 1982).

The ulcer itself results from an excessive flow of the stomach's acid-containing digestive juices, which eat away the lining of the stomach or duodenum, leaving a craterlike wound. Although dietary factors, diseases, and other organic conditions may also lead to ulcers, it is now recognized that worry, repressed anger, resentment, anxiety, dependency, and other negative emotional states may be causally involved in many cases. A high activity level, in particular, has been found to be a frequent correlate of gastric lesions (Weiss, 1984). Conceivably, any of these factors might contribute to a breakdown of the stomach's mucosal lining, which seems to be the immediate cause of ulcer formation. The result is that the stomach begins to digest itself.

It has long been believed that conflicts centering on dependency needs are especially likely to be found in individuals who develop ulcers. In support of this belief we have available a landmark study, the scope of which has not since been equaled (Weiner et al., 1957):

Relying on prior evidence of a high rate of gastric secretion in ulcer-prone individuals, as indicated in part by a high level of pepsinogen in the blood serum, Weiner and his colleagues tested a population of 2073 army draftees and chose for study those men found to be maximum and minimum gastric secreters. These were groups of men, in other words, who should be at maximum and minimum risk for ulcer formation by virtue of constitutional predisposition.

Membership in one or the other group did in fact predict the incidence of ulcer formation during the stress of basic training. Of perhaps even greater importance, however, is the fact that a battery of psychological tests also correctly predicted the pepsinogen-level group in which recruits would fall, and even correctly identified at an above-chance level which high-pepsinogen recruits would develop ulcers. These test results showed evidence of major unresolved dependency (in Freudian terms "oral") conflicts, with resultant frustration and suppressed hostility.

The most important point established by this study was that neither a high pepsinogen level nor dependency conflicts was alone responsible for peptic ulcer development. Taken together, however, they constituted a pathogenic predisposition that, on exposure to a special stressor (basic training), could be expected to challenge the equilibrium of an individual, thus producing an abnormally high risk of ulcer formation. Strang (1989), reviewed a variety of other research findings and found that they generally support dependency issues as having special relevance in the pathogenesis of ulcers.

The dependency of an ulcer-prone individual is not always obvious at the behavioral level. In fact such an individual may seem to be quite independent or autonomous, even excessively hard-driving in terms of surface behavior. We also have little doubt that psychological factors other than unresolved dependency conflicts can be involved in the development of ulcers. Animal experiments, for example, suggest that gastric lesions are most likely to occur when an organism's attempts to cope with a challenge produce little or no useful feedback to guide future responding (Weiss, 1984). Human situations having these characteristics are readily imagined, but as yet we have no solid evidence relating them to ulcer development.

◼ Recurrent Headaches

Although headaches can result from a wide range of organic conditions, the majority of them—about nine out of ten—seem to be related to emotional tension. More than 50 million Americans suffer from tension or migraine headaches, with the overall incidence apparently being higher among women than men. In one survey, Andrasik, Holroyd, and Abell (1979) found that 52 percent of a large group of college students reported headaches at least once or twice a week.

Research in this area has focused primarily on **migraine,** an intensely painful headache that recurs periodically. Although typically involving only one side of the head, migraine is sometimes more generalized; it may also shift from side to side. Migraine was described extensively by medical writers of antiquity, but the cause of the pain remained a mystery until the 1940s, when interest was focused on the pain-sensitive arteries of the head. The typical migraine occurs in two phases. First, there is a markedly reduced flow of blood (and hence oxygen) to certain parts of the brain. Although this reduced blood flow is not associated with pain, many victims experience it as an "aura" that predictably leads to the painful second phase. This second phase is characterized by a sudden rush of blood to the previously deprived areas, causing rapid expansion of the affected arteries and stimulation of local nerve endings. This stimulation produces the distinctive migraine pain.

It has also been shown that a variety of experimentally induced stressors—frustrations, excessive demands for performance, and threatening interviews—cause vascular dilation among migraine sufferers but not among other people. *HIGHLIGHT 7.5* traces the course of a headache induced during a discussion that evoked hostile feelings in the subject—a migraine sufferer.

The vast majority of headaches are so-called **simple tension headaches.** These, too, involve stress and vascular changes, but the changes are thought to be different from those in migraine headaches. With simple tension headaches, emotional stress seems to lead to contraction of the muscles surrounding the skull; these contractions,

Emotional tension seems to be the cause of nine out of ten headaches. More than 50 million Americans suffer from tension or migraine headaches.

Migraine Headaches

The side-view drawing of the head below shows the location of pain-sensitive cranial arteries. The dotted lines mark the areas where a headache is felt as various parts of the arteries dilate.

The graph traces the course of a headache induced during a discussion that evoked feelings of hostility in the subject. Both the changes in the amplitude of the artery pulsations and the corresponding increase and decrease in the intensity of the pain reported are shown. The headache was completely relieved by means of an injection that the subject believed would end the suffering but which actually could have had no physical effect.

Temporal artery pulsations   Headache gone

Intensity

10 +
8 +
6 +
4 +
2 +

0   10:45   11:00   11:35   11:47   11:55   Noon

Interview

1 cc. normal saline subcu.

Adapted from Wolff (1948, 1953).

From *Wolff's headache and other head pain,* Fourth Edition, by Donald J. Dalessio. Copyright © 1980 by Oxford University Press, Inc. Reprinted by permission.

in turn, result in vascular constrictions, which cause headache pain. We should note here, however, that with the more precise measurement techniques now available, the evidence for the physiological differences between migraine and tension headaches is being drawn into question (Blanchard & Andrasik, 1982). Though further studies are needed, it may be that the physiological processes are similar for the two types of headaches and that the difference is rather one of degree, with migraine involving greater vascular disruption. Certainly it is true that many people suffer headaches that appear to have both vascular and muscular origins.

Both tension and migraine headaches usually appear during adolescence and recur periodically during stressful times. The pain can often be relieved with analgesics, with muscle-relaxant drugs, or with certain relaxation-inducing psychological procedures (Blanchard et al., 1990a). These latter procedures include **biofeedback,** a technique in which a person is taught to influence his or her own physiological processes (Blanchard et al., 1990b). Of the two types, migraine headaches are usually more painful and slower to respond to treatment than simple tension headaches.

The presumed psychological predispositions for psychogenic headaches are less clear than in the case of other disorders considered in this chapter. Also, the interaction of personality factors with particular types of stressors appears to be especially important for headache sufferers (Levor et al., 1986). However, clinicians increasingly seem to agree that it is important to the typical headache-prone person to feel in control of events impinging on him or her. Such individuals are usually described as highly organized and perfectionistic (Williams, 1977). In one instance, a highly skilled nurse, who specialized in the demanding field of cardiac emergencies, was subject to excruciatingly severe migraine attacks. She went to a clinic for therapy but was so bent on maintaining control of virtually every aspect of the therapeutic relationship that she managed to sabotage it with a regularity astonishing to both herself and her therapist.

In a study by Andrasik et al. (1982), the traditional belief that migraine sufferers show higher levels of depression, passivity, nonassertiveness, hostility, and high-achievement strivings was not supported. Psychological tests of migraine sufferers revealed psychologically normal profiles. Instead, the tension headache sufferers showed the greatest psychopathology. This finding suggests that tension headaches might be more indicative of psychological problems per se than migraine headaches.

In focusing, as we have in this section, on certain diseases in which a psychogenic contribution to etiology seems especially likely, we do not intend to exclude by omission the possibility—indeed likelihood—that other specific diseases may sometimes have identifiable psychogenic roots. As in the case of asthma mentioned earlier, however, we suspect that in most such instances, some sort of biological predisposition will turn out to be a necessary element in the total causal pattern. Within this constraint, the literature indicates several additional candidates for continued scrutiny in search of specific psychogenic mediators. These diseases include: certain allergies and skin eruptions; chronic diarrhea and ulcerative colitis; rheumatoid arthritis; Raynaud's disease (a potentially serious local vasoconstriction that may interrupt the blood supply to certain body parts); diabetes; menstrual irregularities and other endocrine disturbances (see, e.g., Levitan, 1989; Sandhu & Cohen, 1989); and chronic disturbances of the sleep cycle.

PSYCHOGENIC PHYSICAL DISEASE: ADDITIONAL ETIOLOGIC CONSIDERATIONS

In the foregoing pages we have explored at a general level the manner in which negative thinking and attitudes, autonomic excess, stressor-induced immunosuppression, and health-endangering life-sty-

les can compromise a person's biological integrity. From there, we proceeded to discuss apparently specific psychogenic contributions, insofar as these are known, to the etiology of five extremely common and sometimes life-threatening physical conditions: coronary heart disease, eating disorders (anorexia and bulimia), essential hypertension, peptic ulcers, and recurrent headaches. We also noted that this listing is by no means exhaustive in cataloging the physical ills that may have psychogenic roots.

In this section we return to a more general level of analysis to complete our picture of psychological causation in physical illness. We will be particularly concerned with the problem of specificity—of why, under stress, one individual develops anorexia, another hypertension, and still another migraine headaches. For the sake of economy and convenience, we will generally refer to such stress-related conditions as psychogenic illnesses or diseases, even though it should be clear that other etiological factors, particularly predisposing biological ones, are inevitably involved. We begin the discussion at the level of biological predisposition.

■ Biological Factors

Obviously, biological factors are involved in all disease. We focus here on those factors likely to have a role in determining the adequacy of a person's response to stressor circumstances.

Genetic Factors   In general, understanding of genetic contributions to diseases believed to have strong psychogenic origins remains limited (Kidd & Morton, 1989). The field involves many perplexities, including the mind-boggling difficulties of differentiating genetic contributions to (a) an underlying physical vulnerability for acquiring the disease in question; (b) the psychological makeup of the individual and his or her stress tolerance; and (c) the nature of any interaction between (a) and (b).

Research by Gregory and Rosen (1965) has demonstrated that the brothers of ulcer patients are about twice as likely to have ulcers as comparable members of the general population. Relatedly, Rotter et al. (1979) have presented evidence of genetic cotransmission of both high pepsinogen serum levels and peptic ulcers. Increased frequencies of hypertension, migraine, and other reactions have also been reported for close relatives of people with these disorders.

Although social learning (for example, children modeling the inadequate coping skills of their parents) could be a factor in such family resemblances, research evidence on this point is equivocal, and genetic factors cannot be ruled out. In fact it would probably be difficult to discover any human disease in which genetic factors could be ruled out entirely.

An interesting separation of genetic and psychological influences is contained in the findings of Liljefors and Rahe (1970), who studied the role of life stress in coronary heart disease among twins. The subjects consisted of 32 pairs of identical male twins between 42 and 67 years of age, in which only one twin in each pair suffered from coronary heart disease. The genetic contribution in such twinships is of course constant for each pair, thus controlling for this factor. The investigators found that the twins suffering from heart disease were more work oriented, took less leisure time, had more home problems, and in general experienced greater dissatisfactions in their lives than their healthier twin brothers. Such a finding represents a rather compelling case for psychosocial contribution to the development of CHD, but the study's design cannot rule out a genetic contribution as well. The latter could still be a *necessary*, but not *sufficient*, condition for CHD pathology. According to this scenario, both twins may have been at genetic risk for CHD—its actual "expression" then being determined by an excess of psychosocial disorganization in one of the pair's members. Interpretive complexities of this sort are the rule rather than the exception in trying to estimate the magnitude of genetic influences here as well as in other areas of psychopathology.

Differences in Autonomic Reactivity and Somatic Weakness   In our earlier discussion (Chapter 4) of vulnerability and causal factors, we noted that individuals vary significantly in primary reaction tendencies. Even very young infants reveal marked differences in their sensitivities to aversive stimuli; some infants react to such stressors by developing fevers, others by digestive upsets, and still others by sleep disturbances. Such differences in reactivity continue into adult life and presumably help account for individual differences in susceptibility to psychogenic diseases, and for the types of diseases a given individual is most likely to develop.

In connection with the latter point, Wolff (1950) suggested that people can be classified as "stomach reactors," "pulse reactors," "nose reactors," and so on, depending on what kinds of physical changes stress characteristically triggers in them. For example, a person who has an inherited tendency to respond to stressors with increased cardiac output and vasoconstriction may be at special risk for chronic hypertension (Friedman & Iwai,

1976). A person who reacts with increased secretion of stomach acids will be more likely to develop peptic ulcers (Strang, 1989).

Sometimes a particular organ is especially vulnerable because of heredity, illness, or prior trauma. A person who has inherited or developed a "weak" stomach will be prone to gastrointestinal upsets during anger or anxiety. Presumably, the weakest link in the chain of visceral organs will be the organ affected. Caution must be exercised, however, to avoid ex post facto reasoning, because it would not be safe to conclude that when a particular organ system is affected it must have been weak to begin with. Also, as we will see, conditioning may play a key role in determining which organ system is involved.

Disruption of Corticovisceral Control Mechanisms   Other biological explanations have focused on the role of central control mechanisms in regulating autonomic functioning. According to one hypothesis, the corticovisceral control mechanisms of the brain may fail in their homeostatic functions, so that an individual's emotional response is exaggerated in intensity and his or her physiological equilibrium is not regained within normal time limits (Halberstam, 1972; Lebedev, 1967; Schwartz, 1989). Such control failures might well be central to deficient hypothalamic regulation of *both* the autonomic nervous system and the adrenocortical hormones of the endocrine system, which may be involved in the body's immunity to disease. More generally, we have seen that breakdowns in a number of different pathways can compromise immune competence during the brain's processing of stressor events.

In assessing the role of biological factors in psychogenic diseases, most investigators would take into consideration each of the factors we have described. Perhaps the greatest emphasis at present would be placed on a person's characteristic autonomic activity, the vulnerability of affected organ systems, and possible constitutionally-based or acquired alterations in the control mechanisms of the brain that normally regulate autonomic and endocrinologic functioning.

■ Psychosocial Factors

Though evidence suggests that psychological factors play a prominent role in the causal picture of many diseases, it is still not altogether clear what factors are involved or how they exert their effects. Factors that investigators have emphasized include personality characteristics (including failure to learn adequate coping patterns), interpersonal relationships, and learning in the autonomic nervous system.

Personality Characteristics

The work of Dunbar (1943, 1954) and a number of other early investigators raised the hope of identifying specific personality factors associated with certain psychophysiologic disorders—for example, noting that rigidity, high sensitivity to threat, and chronic underlying hostility are typical among those who suffer from hypertension. The ability to delineate ulcer types, hypertensive characters, and so on would, of course, be of great value in understanding, assessing, and treating the pertinent illnesses—and perhaps even in preventing them.

As we have seen, however, later research evidence has suggested that such an approach is oversimplified. For example, although Kidson (1973) found hypertensive patients as a group to be significantly more insecure, anxious, sensitive, and angry than a nonhypertensive control group, a sizable number of the control-group members also showed these characteristics. Similarly, the tendency for Type A behavior (or some limited component of it) to be associated with CHD and heart attacks must be tempered with the observation that most Type As do not have coronary problems, and some Type Bs do (see figures in *HIGHLIGHT 7.3*).

So even though personality makeup seems to play an important role, we still do not know why some individuals with "predisposing" personality characteristics do not develop a particular disease; nor can we account adequately for the wide range of personality makeups among individuals who suffer from that same condition. Usually, we can at best conclude only that particular personality factors are weakly but significantly correlated with the occurrence of certain illnesses.

Normally, when individuals are subjected experimentally to frustrating experiences, their blood pressures rise and their hearts beat more rapidly. If they are then given an opportunity to express physical or verbal aggression against the frustrator, their blood pressures and heart rates rapidly return to normal. If they are permitted only fantasy aggression or no aggression at all, however, their bodies return much more slowly to normal physiological functioning (Hokanson & Burgess, 1962). Thus, besides looking at people's abilities to cope with the stress of frustrations or conflicts or whatever, it seems necessary to consider their abilities to deal adequately with the accompanying emotional tensions.

Interpersonal Relationships

In our previous discussions we have repeatedly noted the destructive effects that stressful interpersonal patterns—including marital unhappiness and divorce—may have on personality adjustment. Such patterns may also influence physiological functioning. In fact, death rates from varied causes, including physical disease, are markedly higher in people who have recently undergone marital problems or divorce than in the general population (Bloom, Asher, & White, 1978).

Loss of a spouse through death also puts the survivor at risk. In an extensive review of the literature, Stroebe and Stroebe (1983) concluded that men are slightly more adversely affected by the death of their wives than women are by the death of their husbands. For example, in an earlier study of widowers, Parkes, Benjamin, and Fitzgerald (1969) reported that during the six-month period following the death of their wives, the widowers' death rate was 40 percent above the expected rate. In fact the incidence of cardiac deaths among these men was so high that the investigators referred to this pattern as "the broken-heart syndrome."

Lynch (1977), in a book entitled *The Broken Heart,* argues convincingly that the relatively high incidence of heart disease in industrialized communities stems in part from the absence of positive human relationships. He notes that heart disease and other illnesses are more prevalent among individuals lacking human companionship and for whom loneliness is common. This group includes not only those people who have recently lost a spouse through death but also single or divorced individuals.

Other studies have focused on the role of pathogenic family patterns. For example, studies have found that the mothers of asthmatic patients have in many cases felt ambivalent toward these children and tended to reject them, while at the same time being overprotective and unduly restrictive of the children's activities (Lipton, Steinschneider, & Richmond, 1966; Olds, 1970). Because individuals coming out of such family backgrounds tend to be overdependent and insecure, it would hardly be surprising if they should react with chronic emotional mobilization to problems that do not seem threatening to most people. On the other hand, as we have seen, a strictly psychogenic interpretation of asthma is questionable. Severe asthma is a terrifying and life-threatening disorder. It would not be surprising on this basis alone to discover that asthmatic children are overdependent and insecure, or that their mothers tend to become ambivalent, protective, and restrictive after the asthma appears.

Complementing the work of Humphrey (1989) mentioned earlier, Kog and Vandereycken (1985) found substantial evidence of controlling relationships and parental discord in the families of eating disorder patients. They also noted a high incidence of physical illness, mood disorder (see Chapter 11), and alcoholism (Chapter 9) in these families.

Learning in the Autonomic Nervous System Although Pavlov and many subsequent investigators have demonstrated that autonomic responses can be conditioned—as in the case of salivation—it was long assumed that an individual could not learn to control such responses "voluntarily." We now know that this assumption was wrong. Not only can autonomic reactivity be conditioned involuntarily via the classical Pavlovian model, but operant learning in the autonomic nervous system can also take place.

Thus the hypothesis has developed that certain physical disorders may arise through accidental reinforcement of symptom and behavioral patterns. "A child who is repeatedly allowed to stay home from school when he has an upset stomach may be learning the visceral responses of chronic indigestion" (Lang, 1970, p. 86). Similarly, an adolescent girl may get little or no attention from being "good," but if she starves herself to the point of severe weight loss she may become the center of attention. If this pattern is continued, she might learn to avoid weight gain at all costs and correspondingly learn a profound aversion to food. The increasing alarm of her parents and others would presumably serve as a potent reinforcement for her to continue in her dangerous ways regarding food ingestion.

Although causal factors other than conditioning are now thought to play a role in most cases of psychogenic illness, it seems clear that regardless of how a physical symptom may have developed, it may be elicited by suggestion and maintained by the reinforcement provided by **secondary gains,** indirect benefits derived from the illness behavior. The role of suggestion was demonstrated by a study in which 19 of 40 volunteer asthmatic subjects developed asthma symptoms after breathing the mist of a salt solution that they were told contained allergens, such as dust or pollen. In fact, 12 of the subjects had full-fledged asthma attacks. When the subjects then took what they thought was a drug to combat asthma (actually the same salt mist), their symptoms disappeared immediately (Bleeker, 1968). This study clearly shows the effect of suggestion on an autonomically mediated response. Why the other 21 subjects remained unaffected is not clear.

In short, it appears that some physical disorders may be acquired, maintained, or both in much the same way as other behavior patterns. Indeed, this finding is a basic tenet of behavioral medicine and health psychology, one aspect of which examines how various behavior modification and psychotherapeutic techniques can alter overt and covert reactions to physical disease processes (Bradley & Prokop, 1982; Gentry, 1984b; G. C. Stone et al., 1987; Williams & Gentry, 1977).

■ Sociocultural Factors

As we have seen, the incidence of specific disorders, both physical and mental, varies in different societies, in different strata of the same society, and over time. In general, what Cannon (1929) called diseases of civilization do not occur among nonindustrialized societies like the aborigines of the Australian Western Desert (Kidson & Jones, 1968), the Navajo Indians of Arizona, or certain isolated groups in South America (Stein, 1970). As these societies are exposed to social change, however, gastrointestinal, cardiovascular, and other psychogenic diseases begin to make their appearances. There is evidence of change in the nature and incidence of such disorders in Japan paralleling the tremendous social changes that have taken place there since World War II (Ikemi et al., 1974). For example, the incidence of hypertension and coronary heart disease has increased markedly with the post-war westernization of Japanese culture.

After an extensive review of the literature within our society, Senay and Redlich (1968) found that psychogenic diseases did not respect social class or other major sociocultural variables. Similarly, Kahn (1969) found that, contrary to folklore, only a small number of executives develop peptic ulcers; in fact, blue-collar workers who are dissatisfied with their jobs are more likely to develop ulcers than successful business executives who are moving up the corporate ladder.

The phenomenon of eating disorders poses fascinating sociocultural questions for which answers are largely lacking. We still have no entirely satisfactory explanation of the seeming epidemic of eating disorders recently among young American women, although it appears likely that changing sociocultural factors are somehow implicated. It seems doubtful that the cultural preference for thinness, which for women was well-established at a time when eating disorders were quite rare, provides a complete answer. Although the combination of high achievement striving and middle-class socioeconomic origins is consistent from a sociocultural standpoint, it is not clear what role that combination, or either factor separately, plays in the increasing incidence and prevalence of dietary dyscontrol. For that matter, we do not have a confident understanding of the tremendous gender imbalance in the occurrence of these syndromes, although again sociocultural factors are likely to be involved. Perhaps the time has come for us to make a serious effort to unearth and eradicate the seemingly impossible demands we as a society have created for that now large group of young women who are at high risk for these dangerous disorders.

In general, it appears that any sociocultural conditions that markedly increase life stress tend to play havoc with the human organism and lead to an increase in disease as well as other physical and mental problems.

TREATMENTS AND OUTCOMES

Though a particular environmental stressor may have been a key causal factor in the development of a physical illness, removal of this stressor, even combined with learning more effective coping techniques, may be insufficient for recovery if organic changes have taken place; such changes may have become chronic and irreversible.

Treatment therefore begins by assessing the nature and severity of the organic pathology as well as the roles of psychosocial and organic factors in the total causal pattern. In hypertension, for example, the role of dietary factors may far outweigh that of current psychosocial stressors in causation and maintenance. Dietary patterns, however, reflect cultural patterns and attitudes—that all-important life-style—that also may have to be reckoned with. Thus a thorough assessment involving the past and present roles of biological, psychosocial, and sociocultural factors is essential to the development of an effective treatment program.

Except for conditions involving serious organic pathology, treatment methods are similar to those for anxiety-based disorders; the outcomes are likewise reasonably favorable. Instead of going into detail concerning the methods of treatment and the outcomes for each type of disorder, we shall briefly summarize the general treatment measures currently used. More detailed discussion of these therapies can be found in Chapters 17 and 18.

Biological Measures

Aside from immediate and long-range medical measures, such as emergency care for bleeding ulcers or bypass surgery for coronary heart disease, biological treatment can involve the use of mild tranquilizers aimed at reducing emotional tension. Such drugs, of course, do not deal with the stressful situation or the coping reactions involved. By alleviating emotional tension and distress symptoms, however, they may provide an individual with an opportunity to regroup his or her coping resources. Of course, health professionals must guard against too readily prescribing tranquilizers to insulate patients against everyday stress that they might be better off facing and resolving in some manner. Some patients may also come to rely too much on their prescriptions for easy "cures," and such palliative, symptomatic treatment may divert needed attention from a persistently destructive life-style.

Other drugs, such as those used to control high blood pressure, are prescribed on a more specific basis. Recent reports suggest that antidepressant medication may have a modest role in the treatment of bulimia (Hughes et al., 1986; Mitchell et al., 1990), although we are troubled by the absence of a convincing theoretical rationale to support this type of intervention. A change of diet may be indicated in certain of the psychogenic diseases, including peptic ulcers, migraine headaches, and hypertension. Acupuncture is still considered a largely experimental approach for alleviating certain types of symptoms (such as the pain of tension and migraine headaches) because of problems in disentangling specific from nonspecific placebo effects.

Psychosocial Measures

In treating psychosocially mediated physical diseases, one-on-one, verbally oriented psychotherapies—aimed at helping patients understand their problems and achieve more effective coping techniques—have been (with certain exceptions) relatively ineffective. The cognitive-behavioral therapy variant, however, has shown considerable promise in the treatment of bulimia (Agras et al., 1989) and psychogenic headaches (Blanchard et al., 1990a, 1990b). Bulimic individuals have also recently been found to respond quite positively to intensive, specifically structured group therapy

Dylan is a boy suffering from severe and throbbing migraine headaches that may last for days. Here he is receiving biofeedback treatment for his migraines. With biofeedback, people are taught to change and control internal bodily processes once thought to be involuntary. Though generally failing to live up to the hype it generated when first introduced two decades ago, biofeedback is showing modest success in treating migraine.

(Mitchell et al., 1990). As might be expected, family therapy has shown some promising results in the case of anorexia nervosa (Minuchin, 1974); rather than singling out the individual, family therapy examines the whole family structure and patterns of communication. Those structures that are thought to be preventing the individual from developing positive relationships within the family (resulting in personal maladjustment) are then targeted for change.

It is interesting to note here that, although classical psychoanalytic theory has emphasized associations between emotions and pathological visceral states, it has had little impact on the treatment of psychogenic physical disorders (Agras, 1982). That is, psychoanalytic approaches have not derived treatment methods that can reverse or prevent the disease process in predictable ways. Also somewhat ironically (in light of its focus on altering physiological states), biofeedback treatment for psychogenic diseases, though showing modest success (for example, in treating migraine [Blanchard et al., 1990b]), has generally failed to live up to the hype it generated when first introduced some two decades ago. In general, its effects are so small and transient as to lack substantial clinical significance, and they rarely exceed those that can be obtained in simpler (and cheaper) ways, as by providing systematic relaxation training (Reed, Katkin, & Goldband, 1986). In fact it is not clear that biofeedback is anything more than an elaborate means to teach patients to relax.

Behavior Therapy   Behavior-modification techniques are based on the assumption that because autonomic responses can be learned, they can also be unlearned via extinction and differential

reinforcement. In one rather famous case, the patient, June C., was a 17-year-old girl who had been sneezing every few seconds of her waking hours for a period of 5 months. Medical experts had been unable to help her, and Kushner, a psychologist, volunteered to attempt treatment by behavior therapy.

Dr. Kushner used a relatively simple, low power electric-shock device, activated by sound—the sound of June's sneezes. Electrodes were attached to her forearm for 30 minutes, and every time she sneezed she got a mild electric shock. After a ten-minute break, the electrodes were put on the other arm. In little more than four hours, June's sneezes, which had been reverberating every 40 seconds, stopped. Since then, she has had only a few ordinary sneezes, none of the dry, racking kind that had been draining her strength for so long. "We hope the absence of sneezes will last," said Dr. Kushner cautiously. "So do I," snapped June. "I never want to see that machine again." (Time, 1966, p. 72)

In a follow-up report, Kushner (1968) stated that a program of maintenance therapy had been instituted, and at the end of 16 months the intractable sneezing had not recurred.

Many studies have examined the effects of various behavioral relaxation techniques on selected psychogenic illnesses. Results obtained have been variable, though generally encouraging. For example, simple tension headaches have proven quite amenable to general relaxation treatment procedures (Blanchard et al., 1990a; Cox, Freundlich, & Meyer, 1975; Tasto & Hinkle, 1973). The same kinds of procedures have not been quite as effective when used to treat essential hypertension (Blanchard et al., 1979; Schwartz, 1978; Surwit, Shapiro, & Good, 1978), especially in comparison with medication (Wadden, et al., 1985).

The potential of behavior therapy alone in treating psychogenic physical disorders remains to be established. A great deal of work is continuing in this area, and it looks promising. It may turn out that the greatest contribution of behavioral approaches will be in the area of altering self-injurious "habits," such as smoking and excessive alcohol use, in systematic programs that teach self-control and life-style alteration (Blanchard & Andrasik, 1982; Goldfried & Merbaum, 1973; Weisenberg, 1977). Such programs may have particular importance in recovery from heart attack (Oldenburg, Perkins, & Andrews, 1985). Relatedly, some success has been reported in modifying Type A life-styles using a group therapy approach (Fischman, 1987).

In sports, behavioral relaxation techniques are used as a means of reducing stress and enhancing performance. Here the University of Wisconsin football team goes through a relaxation exercise before a game.

Cognitive-Behavioral Treatment Some cognitive-behavioral techniques have also been used to treat stress-related illnesses. In one study, these techniques were shown to be effective at reducing maladaptive behaviors—such as rushing, impatience, and hostility—characteristic of Type A personalities (Jenni & Wollersheim, 1979). In two studies designed to teach patients how to cope better with life stresses that precipitated headaches, researchers showed that stress-management techniques could decrease the frequency of headaches (Holroyd & Andrasik, 1978; Holroyd, Andrasik, & Westbrook, 1977). More generally, Kobasa (1985) and colleagues are experimenting with cognitive-behavioral methods to increase "hardiness," the ability to withstand stressful circumstances and remain healthy. Though we will look at these techniques in more detail in Chapter 18, they basically involve teaching individuals to use more effective coping skills to lower their experiences of stress and thus reduce the occurrences of symptoms.

■ Combined Treatment Measures

To be treated successfully, psychogenic diseases usually require prompt medical attention for physical symptoms combined with psychosocial therapeutic intervention to alter or reduce the maladaptive behavioral factors underlying the disorder. The treatment for anorexia nervosa clearly illustrates the need for combined medical and psychological measures. If an anorexic individual's condition becomes

life-threatening, extreme measures must be taken to nourish the patient. Typically, hospitalization is necessary in an emergency of this sort. The patient may initially be fed intravenously, but because the disorder is apparently under voluntary control, therapy must ultimately focus not only on weight gain but also on the psychological factors underlying the patient's refusal to eat.

Several treatment approaches have been successful in promoting weight gain among anorexic patients. One includes making a patient stay in isolation, earning privileges—such as time for socializing—only as she gains weight. Leon (1983) describes this scenario:

Given the compliant, perfectionistic behavioral characteristics of many anorexics, it might not be surprising that once the youngster has made the decision to eat in order to gain relief from isolation or to gain a variety of social and other reinforcers, she compliantly follows the daily weight gain criteria set up for her and systematically gains weight. It has been my experience, however, in viewing charts of the weight histories of many treated anorexics, that their weight precipitously plummets once they are released from the hospital. Thus, compliance with the treatment regimen has brought relief from the aversiveness of the hospital situation and has also affected hospital discharge. (Leon, 1983)

As Leon suggests, then, in many cases therapy achieves no significant long-term normalization in eating patterns, even when drastic measures are taken in response to life-threatening crises. This major drawback results if the therapy focuses single-mindedly on just the immediate need to gain weight. Leon goes on to say,

The crucial issue of the regulation of food intake as one of several treatment goals is under-scored by the fact that some anorexics after release from the hospital continue eating until the point of obesity or develop bulimia-vomiting patterns to control their weight. Thus, treatment should also address the personal concerns about self-control over one's body and one's environment, and other difficulties related to family interactions that the anorexic might be attempting to cope with through self-starvation.

This conclusion seems related to an earlier finding by Halmi, Falk, and Schwartz (1981) in which data suggested that treatment choice did not seem to be a factor in successful weight gain for hospitalized patients: they typically gained weight regardless of the treatment technique employed.

Though the obvious goal, both short- and long-term, is to get an anorexic patient to gain weight, therapy for psychological adjustment may be far more important and far more elusive for long-term success. In the end, as Bruch (1988) has noted in a posthumously published book on the subject, lasting therapeutic results in anorexia may involve nothing less than a patient's rediscovery of *herself.* Such a goal is unlikely to be achieved by merely technical interventions that cause the patient temporarily to put on a few pounds.

Lucas, Duncan, and Piens (1976) reported on an interesting therapeutic setting developed at the Mayo Clinic and designed to deal with both the physiological and psychological needs of an anorexic patient. Their approach was a combined medical-psychiatric effort, with a coordinated team of professionals who focused on the problems of malnutrition as well as on the psychological family problems in each case. The first step in their treatment efforts was to remove the anorexic person from the home. The individual was placed in an inpatient ward where the nutritional problems were dealt with by staff members who monitored food intake. The patient was given social rewards—such as time with peers—for appropriate food consumption. Group psychological treatment with a supportive orientation was provided, in which the patient was allowed to express her thoughts, concerns, and fears. While the inpatient treatment program was in progress, the staff also worked with the family in an effort to resolve the family behaviors that might be encouraging the patient's anorexic behavior. This approach thus combined medical efforts with individual and family therapy.

Behavioral approaches to health maintenance are important in systematic programs that teach self-control and life-style change. The stop-smoking class pictured here helps smokers break their habit by holding their cigarettes in an uncomfortable way.

■ Sociocultural Measures

Sociocultural treatment measures are targeted more toward preventive efforts and are typically applied to selected populations or subcultural groups thought to be at risk for developing disorders. Within these groups, efforts are made to alter certain life-style behaviors to reduce the overall level of susceptibility to a disorder. For example, cigarette smoking is associated with increased risk for lung cancer and heart disease; to reduce the general risk of these scourges, efforts might be made to reduce or prevent cigarette smoking in groups that are vulnerable to the smoking habit—such as adolescents. Similarly, some correlation appears to exist between high-cholesterol diets and coronary heart disease; at high risk here are middle-aged men, and efforts might be made to alter their diets to reduce the rate of coronary heart disease in the total population. Obviously, such intervention efforts involve substantial amounts of persuasive appeal—often employing the media and, in the case of smoking, even restrictive changes in quasi-legal federal regulations (such as airline passenger smoking policies).

An excellent example of a community-based, prevention-oriented program aimed at reducing the incidence of atherosclerotic disease (a predisposing factor in coronary heart disease) comes from Finland. The North Karelia Project, named after the province in which it was conducted, was a large-scale effort that included 60,000 "subjects" (the province residents) and involved several types of community intervention efforts.

The overall goal was to promote greater public awareness of the high-risk factors—especially cigarette smoking and high serum cholesterol levels thought to be caused by eating high-fat foods—in atherosclerotic disease. Then the effort was made to get individuals to reduce these risk factors by smoking less and eating low-fat foods. Project staff (a) provided information through the mass media—such as a seven-session TV course aimed at reducing smoking—and through public meetings; (b) organized existing health-care services and initiated new ones to focus on eliminating high-risk factors by forming self-help groups; (c) trained community leaders, such as teachers, to work on the program; (d) promoted the distribution and sale of healthy, low-fat foods; and (e) devised a method by which they could measure the effects of the program (McAlister et al., 1980; Puska, 1983; Puska et al., 1979).

Early results were encouraging. The intervention program was shown to lower effectively the coronary heart disease risk in the population: death from heart disease fell 27 percent for men and 42 percent for women. A self-report survey on smoking behavior indicated that participants had reduced their cigarette consumption; significant reductions were also found in serum cholesterol levels.

As we learn more about the role of biological, psychosocial, and sociocultural factors in the etiology of disease, it becomes increasingly possible to delineate high-risk individuals and groups—such as heart-attack-prone personalities with chronic negative affects and groups living in precarious and rapidly changing life situations. This ability, in turn, enables treatment efforts to focus on early intervention and prevention. In this context, counseling programs—aimed at fostering changes in maladaptive life-styles of individuals and families and at remedying pathological social conditions—seem eminently worthwhile.

UNRESOLVED ISSUES
on Psychological Factors and Illness

The many reports in the research literature of severe illnesses or deaths attributed to the *attitudes* of hopelessness or helplessness, including documented cases of apparent voodoo deaths, continue to puzzle and confound us. If we assume the reliability of the primary observations, we might account for some of these events on the basis of a possibly lethal autonomic system "storm" provoked by severe fright, or, in more delayed reactions, by reference to immunosuppression and the compromise of defenses against virulent antigens present in the body or the local environment. Neither of these proposed mechanisms, however, can reasonably be invoked to explain every reported case. To further complicate matters, there are many seemingly reliable reports of instances in which unexplained remissions of terminal illnesses have occurred following attitude changes emphasizing patients' mastery and control over their pathological processes.

Most of us remain somewhat skeptical concerning phenomena of this type, but our skepticism is in large part the product of our continuing ignorance concerning the fundamentals of mind-body interaction. We still find ourselves struggling, for example, with the problem of how an *idea,* such as "I am going to master my illness," might be transformed into the *physical processes* that must underlie, let us say, tumor regression. None of the proposed solutions to this age-old philosophical dilemma can

claim to be proven, and in fact the question may be fundamentally insoluble within a scientific context.

Closely related and equally vexing are a host of other psycho-physical interactions entailed in the notion of psychogenesis. Among the foremost is the issue of the control of immunocompetence by events that may be stressors to one person but not to another. The designation "stressor" is not as a general rule inherent in an event itself but is rather assigned somehow by a stressed person as he or she cognitively processes the event. To put it another way, the person, in reacting stressfully, is responding to the *meaning* the event is perceived to have, not to its objective, physical characteristics. We need therefore ultimately to understand how this subjective meaning somehow produces the multitude of physical events we must assume are involved in immune-reaction inhibition. The task promises to be a formidable one.

The discovery of the conditionability of immunosuppression, which may appear promising in this regard, is probably a different case. Although the procedure involved may be viewed as one in which the occurrence of a conditioned stimulus acquires the "meaning" that ingestion of an immunosuppressant substance is soon to follow (as tone signified the arrival of food to Pavlov's dogs), the use of an immunosuppressant substance as the "unconditioned stimulus" may make the demonstration irrelevant to our everyday trials and tribulations. We say "may" here because we are not completely certain. We assume, however, that stress normally *is* the unconditioned stimulus for immunosuppression, which still leaves us with the problem of idiosyncracy in what are perceived as "stressors."

Moving now to a more mundane level, our rapidly developing knowledge concerning psychological influences in health and illness is not matched by equally impressive advances in the areas of prevention and treatment of psychogenic disease. While some strides have been made in limited areas, our overall impression is that, thus far, our efforts in this arena have been feeble and to a large extent unimaginative. We have not, for example, figured out reliable ways of getting people to alter life-styles we know to be unhealthy. Though our species has had eons of experience with the bereavement process, now known to be a substantial risk to physical health, we have not yet devised effective means of easing the enormous stress of this common experience. Indeed there is little evidence that we have even tried to solve this problem on a scientific basis, apparently owing to the unproven assumptions that such stress is inevitable, and that nothing effective could ever be found to alleviate it.

▌SUMMARY

Research has clearly established that emotional factors influence the development of many physical disorders and play an important role in the course of disease processes. The official Axis I diagnosis, Psychological Factors Affecting Physical Condition (new to the DSM-III and unchanged in DSM-III-R), is an acknowledgment of our enhanced appreciation of the widespread nature of such effects. Likewise, the relatively new field of behavioral medicine has its origins in the general recognition of these influences and seeks to extend our conceptions of disease beyond the traditional medical preoccupation with the physical breakdown of organs and organ systems.

At the most general level, the influence of psychological variables on health is seen in excessive autonomic nervous system responses to stressor conditions, sometimes resulting directly in organ damage. It is also seen in the increasing evidence that psychosocial challenges can impair the immune system's ability to respond, leaving a person more vulnerable to disease-producing agents. Damaging habits and life-styles are also known to enhance risk for physical disease.

Psychogenic vulnerability to particular diseases may be somewhat specific in nature, although not so specific as early doctrines implied. The distressingly common coronary heart disease and the increasingly common eating disorders known as anorexia nervosa and bulimia nervosa seem to be cases in point. The Type A behavior pattern, or rather one or more of its components, is now well-established as an independent risk factor for CHD, and the two eating disorders have been somewhat less compellingly associated with deficiencies in achieving au-

tonomy. Evidence relating to specific psychosocial factors in the etiology of other physical diseases—notably hypertension, peptic ulcers, and recurrent headaches—continues to show promise.

Biological factors, including genetic vulnerabilities, excessive autonomic reactivity, and possible organ weaknesses, must of course continue to be given prominent attention in the search for etiological patterns. They must also be a part of treatment considerations whenever physical disease occurs, regardless of strong evidence of psychological contributions to its development.

A common factor in much psychosocially mediated physical disease is inadequacy in an individual's coping resources for managing stressful life circumstances. Our own culture seems particularly rich in providing these challenges, whereas we have made only limited progress in learning how to instill hardiness in our citizenry and thereby prevent many needless physical breakdowns. Psychosocial treatment measures, typically used (if at all) only after illness is discovered, are showing considerable promise. However, the more exciting challenge will be to devise more, and more effective, psychosocial interventions that prevent breakdowns in the first place.

▌Key Terms

behavioral medicine (p. 229)
psychogenic illnesses (p. 229)
health psychology (p. 229)
placebo effect (p. 232)
immune system (p. 234)
antigen (p. 234)
psychoneuroimmunology (p. 235)
coronary heart disease (CHD) (p. 239)
Type A behavior pattern (p. 240)

anorexia nervosa (p. 243)
bulimia nervosa (p. 244)
hypertension (p. 248)
essential hypertension (p. 248)
peptic ulcers (p. 249)
migraine (p. 250)
simple tension headaches (p. 250)
biofeedback (p. 251)
secondary gains (p. 255)

Chapter 8
Personality Disorders

Gaston Duf, *Pâûlíhinêle gânsthêrs vitrês–he* (1949).
As a child, Duf (b. 1920) was frequently terrorized by
his father, often seeking the protection of his mother. When
his parents finally married, Duf, then 18, reacted violently.
After two suicide attempts, he was institutionalized in 1940.
He began his artistic career while in the asylum, painting
strange, powerful animals, as well as comically propor-
tioned, motley human figures like this one.

It is probably meaningless to speak of an end product in the developmental process; people continue to change throughout their lives. Healthy adjustment through the life cycle is, after all, chiefly a matter of flexibly adapting to the changing demands, opportunities, and limitations associated with different life stages. Nevertheless, a person's broadly characteristic traits, coping styles, and ways of interacting in the social environment emerge during development. These traits normally crystalize into established patterns by the end of the adolescent years. They represent the individual's **personality**—the unique pattern of traits and behaviors that characterize the individual.

For most of us, our adult personality is attuned to the demands of society. In other words, we readily comply with societal expectations. In contrast, there are certain individuals who, although not necessarily displaying obvious symptoms of disorder, nevertheless seem somehow ill-equipped to become fully functioning members of society—any society. For these individuals, personality formation has been so warped that they are unable to perform adequately the varied roles expected of them by their societies. These people might be diagnosed as having **personality disorders,** or **character disorders.**

Personality disorders typically do not stem from debilitating reactions to stress, as in posttraumatic stress disorder, nor from disabling defenses against anxiety, as in the neurotic disorders. Rather, the disorders to be examined here stem largely from the development of immature and distorted personality patterns, which result in persistently maladaptive ways of perceiving, thinking about, and relating to the world. These maladaptive approaches usually significantly impair functioning and in some cases cause subjective distress. Often these patterns of personality and behavior are recognizable by adolescence and continue into adult life.

The category of personality disorders is broad, with behavioral problems that differ greatly in form and severity. On the mildest end of the spectrum we find individuals who generally function adequately but would be described by their relatives or associates as troublesome or eccentric. They have characteristic ways of approaching situations and people that make them difficult to get along with, yet they are often quite capable or even gifted in some ways. At the other end of the spectrum are individuals

263

We might consider Michael Jackson eccentric because of the unusual way he dresses or his rumored multiple plastic surgeries, but eccentric behavior alone does not necessarily indicate a personality disorder. People with personality disorders tend to be at the extreme of a continuum of unusual behavior; they live aberrant lives that others find confusing, exasperating, unpredictable, and unacceptable. Their behavior typically causes at least as much difficulty in the lives of others as in their own lives.

whose extreme and often unethical "acting out" against society makes them less able to function in a normal setting; many are incarcerated in prisons or maximum security hospitals, but some are able to manipulate others and keep from getting caught.

The prevalence of personality disorders is unknown, since many individuals with such disorders never come in contact with mental health or legal agencies. Estimates of the prevalence of one personality disorder, antisocial personality, were reported in an epidemiological study to be 2.1 percent, 2.6 percent, and 3.3 percent in the three study sites (Robins et al., 1984). Many individuals become identified through the correctional system or through court-ordered psychological evaluations stemming from family problems such as physical abuse. Others eventually show up in alcohol treatment programs. Although we have no accurate estimates as to what percentage of incarcerated individuals would be classified as having personality disorders, it is believed that the figure would be quite high. Reich, Yates, and Nduaguba (1989) reported an 11.1 percent prevalence rate for DSM-III-R personality disorders in prison inmates.

Personality disorders are an area of active research in the field today. To support this statement we need only point out that Gorton and Akhtar (1990) surveyed articles on personality disorders published between 1985 and 1988; they found over 1000 articles on the subject. In this chapter, we will consider several types of disordered personalities that have been identified and then examine one of them—antisocial personality—in greater detail to give you an idea of the extensive research in this area.

Personality disorders are often a factor in several disorders that will be considered in other chapters, such as alcoholism (Chapter 9), sexual deviations (Chapter 10), and delinquency (Chapter 15). Although conduct disorders and juvenile delinquency do in fact sometimes represent the early stages of a lifelong process of personality disorder, they often do not; much of the acting-out behavior of adolescence, including much delinquency, is limited to the adolescent years. Thus we will discuss conduct disorders and delinquency with the other special disorders of childhood and adolescence. Finally, the behavioral patterns associated with personality disorders can be similar to those determined primarily by the residual effects of head injuries or other brain pathologies. In such cases, these behaviors are evidence of organic brain disorders, which we consider in Chapter 13. These qualifications aside, let us move on to an examination of personality disorders.

PERSONALITY DISORDERS

Personality disorders are chiefly, although not exclusively, characterized by problems in which individuals typically cause at least as much difficulty in the lives of others as in their own lives. Such people live aberrant lives that others find confusing, exasperating, unpredictable, and, in varying degrees, unacceptable—although rarely as bizarre or out of contact with reality as those people with psychotic disorders (to be discussed in Chapters 11 and 12). People with personality disorders do not suffer unduly from anxiety or depression. Their persistent behavioral deviations seem to be intrinsic to their personalities; for one reason or another they develop in an aberrant manner and do not learn to take part in mutually respectful and satisfying social relationships.

In the past, these persistent disorders were thought to center around personality characteristics referred to as **temperament** or **character traits,** suggesting the possibility of hereditary or constitutional influences. More recently, environmental and social factors, particularly learning-based habit patterns, have been receiving more attention as possible causal elements. The possibility of genetic transmission of these disorders, however, particularly antisocial personality, has been once again receiving strong support in the research literature.

The definition of personality disorders in DSM-III-R is as follows:

Personality traits are enduring patterns of perceiving, relating to, and thinking about the environment and oneself, and are exhibited in a wide range of important social and personal contexts. It is only when personality traits are inflexible and maladaptive and cause either significant functional impairment or subjective distress that they constitute Personality Disorders. The manifestations of Personality Disorders are often recognizable by adolescence or earlier and continue throughout most of adult life, though they often become less obvious in middle or old age.

The diagnostic criteria for the Personality Disorders refer to behaviors or traits that are characteristic of the person's recent (past year) and long-term functioning since early adulthood. The constellation of behaviors or traits causes either significant impairment in social or occupational functioning or subjective distress.

The diagnosis of a Personality Disorder should be made only when the characteristic features are typical of the person's long-term functioning and are not limited to discrete episodes of illness. (American Psychiatric Association, 1987, p. 335)

The behavior patterns of personality disorders are rather new to clinical texts and diagnostic manuals; they were not clearly described until the publication of the American Psychiatric Association's first *Diagnostic and Statistical Manual* (DSM-1) in 1952. Before that, they were regarded as "disorders of character" found in people who were otherwise essentially normal—problems "without psychosis" (Murray, 1938).

In the DSM-III-R, the personality disorders are coded on a separate Axis II because they are regarded as being different enough from the standard psychiatric syndromes (which are coded on Axis I) to warrant separate classification. Axis II represents long-standing personality traits that are inflexible and maladaptive and that cause social or occupational adjustment problems or personal distress. The traits included on Axis II are reaction patterns so deeply embedded in the personality structure (for whatever reason) that they are extremely resistant to modification. Though an individual might be diagnosed on Axis II only, he or she could

instead be diagnosed on both Axes I and II, which would reflect the existence of both a currently active mental disorder and a more chronic, underlying personality disorder.

A special caution is in order regarding the personality disorders. Perhaps more misdiagnoses occur here than in any other categories. There are a number of reasons for this problem. One is that personality disorders are not as sharply defined as other diagnostic categories; no clear set of criteria exists for them. To ensure the reliability of the diagnosis, more precise operational criteria are needed for each disorder (Tyrer, 1988).

A second reason is that the diagnostic categories are not mutually exclusive: often an individual will show characteristics of more than one type of personality disorder, which makes diagnosis difficult (Blashfield & Breen, 1989; Gorton & Akhtar, 1990; Widiger & Frances, 1985). For example, an individual might show the suspiciousness, mistrust, avoidance of blame, and guardedness of paranoid personality disorder, along with the withdrawal, absence of friends, and aloofness that characterize schizoid personality disorder.

A third reason for diagnostic problems is that the personality characteristics that define personality disorders are dimensional in nature—that is, they range from normal expressions to pathological exaggerations and can be found, on a smaller scale and less intensely expressed, in many normal individuals (Frances, 1980). For example, liking one's work and being conscientious about the details of one's job does not make one an obsessive-compulsive personality, nor does being economically dependent automatically make a spouse a dependent personality. Applying diagnostic labels to people who are functioning well enough to be outside a hospital setting is always risky; it is especially so where the diagnosis involves judgment about characteristics that are also common in normal individuals.

A fourth reason is that personality disorders are defined by inferred traits or consistent patterns of behavior rather than by objective behavioral criteria. On Axis I, for example, there are objective behavioral criteria for drug intoxication or somatization disorder, but on Axis II dependent or compulsive personality patterns are inferred from consistencies in behavior. Personality disorders thus require more judgment in classification than do many Axis I disorders.

These problems can lead to unreliability of diagnoses and in fact they often do (Gorton and Akhtar, 1990). Someday a more objective scheme for the personality disorders may be devised that accounts for the problems described here. In the meantime, however, the categorical system of symptoms and traits will continue to be used with the recognition that it is more dependent on the observer's judgment than one might wish. Several theorists have attempted to deal with the problems inherent in categorizing personality disorders (Cloninger, 1987; Millon, 1981; Tyrer, 1988; Widiger & Frances, 1985); however, no clearly consistent theoretical view on the classification of personality disorders currently exists. With these cautions, we will look now at the elusive and often exasperating clinical features of the personality disorders.

■ Clinical Features of Personality Disorders

The several special types of personality disorders are classified according to the particular characteristics (dependence, avoidance, and so on) that are most prominent, although, as we have seen, in given cases these dividing lines are often unclear. These characteristics, in turn, predict what kind of disordered relationships can be expected. Although we will look individually at the several types of personality disorders that have been delineated, let us look first at a number of features they all seem to have in common:

1. Perhaps most characteristic is a pattern of disrupted personal relationships. Whether narcissistic or dependent or passive-aggressive, individuals with personality disorders usually leave a trail of disturbed personal relationships marked by difficulties they have caused others.

2. Personality disorders are generally long-standing and marked by behaviors that are considered troublesome to others. There are not usually "episodes" of pathological behavior that can be identified, but rather persistent patterns of recurring problems.

3. Personality disorders are often associated with other negative life outcomes, such as addictive disorders and criminal or illegal behaviors. For example, Khantzian and Treece (1985) found that the entire range of personality disorders was represented among individuals who became addicted to narcotics.

4. Whatever the particular trait patterns affected individuals have developed (obstinacy, covert hostility, or suspiciousness, for example), these patterns color each new situation and lead to a repetition of

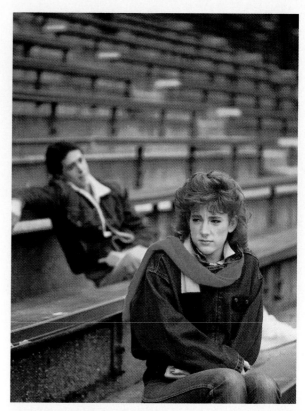

One common feature of personality disorders is a pattern of disturbed personal relationships.

the same maladaptive behaviors. For example, a dependent person may wear out a relationship with someone, such as a spouse, by incessant and extraordinary demands; after that partner leaves, the person may go immediately into another dependent relationship and repeat the behavior. Thus personality disorders are marked by considerable consistency over time, with no apparent learning from previous troubles.

5. It follows from the preceding feature that many of these disorders are in a sense disorders of reputation: they are marked by the imprints they make on others rather than by any psychic pain felt by the affected individuals. In many cases, these individuals are known not by what they have reported to clinicians but by the reports of others. People with certain disorders, such as antisocial personality disorder, rarely take the initiative in seeking therapy and, when referred for therapy by others, have little or no motivation to profit from it. Instead, they are likely to disrupt or sabotage it—or leave it if possible.

6. Finally, the behavioral patterns reflected in personality disorders are highly resistant to change. Many of these individuals neither seek to change nor to accommodate the demands other people place on them to alter their behaviors.

All these characteristics lead to the fractured relationships that are the hallmark of the personality disorders.

■ Types of Personality Disorders

The DSM-III-R personality disorders are grouped into three clusters on the basis of similarities among the disorders. Many people meet the criteria for more than one personality disorder.

Cluster I includes paranoid, schizoid, and schizotypal personality disorders. Individuals with these disorders often seem odd or eccentric, although their unusual behavior takes quite different forms.

Cluster II includes histrionic, narcissistic, antisocial, and borderline personality disorders. Individuals with these disorders have in common a tendency to be dramatic, emotional, and erratic. Their impulsive behavior, often involving antisocial activities, is more colorful, more forceful, and more likely to get them into contact with mental health or legal authorities than the behaviors characterizing disorders in the first cluster.

Cluster III includes avoidant, dependent, obsessive-compulsive, and passive-aggressive personality disorders. Unlike in the other clusters, anxiety and fearfulness are often part of these disorders, making it difficult in some cases to distinguish them from anxiety-based disorders. Because of their anxieties, individuals suffering from these disorders are more likely to seek help.

Two new personality disorders—self-defeating and sadistic personality disorders—are listed in DSM-III-R in the appendix under the heading *proposed diagnostic categories needing further study.* Individuals with these disorders are typically involved in interpersonal interactions that are characterized by abusiveness. These disorders, as we will see, are controversial because there is some potential for misuse or misapplication and because some professionals have considered them inappropriate and biased toward women. A summary of the personality disorders and their characteristics is presented in *Highlight 8.1.*

Paranoid Personality Disorder   Individuals with **paranoid personality disorder** typically are suspicious, hypersensitive, rigid, envious, and argumentative. They tend to see themselves as blameless, instead finding fault for their own mistakes and failures in others—even to the point of ascribing

evil motives to others. Such individuals are constantly expecting trickery and looking for clues to validate their expectations, while disregarding all evidence to the contrary. They are keenly aware of power and rank, envious of those in high places, and disdainful of those who seem weak or soft. It is important to keep in mind that paranoid personalities are not psychotic; that is, they are in clear contact with reality. Another disorder, paranoid schizophrenia, to be discussed later in the book, may have some symptoms found in paranoid personality. Paranoid schizophrenics have additional problems, however, including loss of reality contact and extreme behavioral deterioration, such as delusions and hallucinations.

The following case demonstrates well the behaviors characteristic of paranoid personality disorder:

A 40-year-old construction worker believes that his coworkers do not like him and fears that someone might let his scaffolding slip in order to cause him injury on the job. This concern followed a recent disagreement on the lunch line when the patient felt that a coworker was sneaking ahead and complained to him. He began noticing his new "enemy" laughing with the other men and often wondered if he were the butt of their mockery. He thought of confronting them, but decided that the whole issue might just be in his own mind, and that he might get himself into more trouble by taking any action.

The patient offers little spontaneous information, sits tensely in the chair, is wide-eyed and carefully tracks all movements in the room. He reads between the lines of the interviewer's questions, feels criticized, and imagines that the interviewer is siding with his coworkers. He makes it clear that he would not have come to the personnel clinic at all except for his need for sleep medication.

He was a loner as a boy and felt that other children would form cliques and be mean to him. He did poorly in school, but blamed his teachers—he claimed that they preferred girls or boys who were "sissies." He dropped out of school, and has since been a hard and effective worker; but he feels he never gets the breaks. He believes that he has been discriminated against because of his Catholicism, but can offer little convincing evidence. He gets on poorly with bosses and coworkers, is unable to appreciate joking around, and does best in situations where he can work and have lunch alone. He has

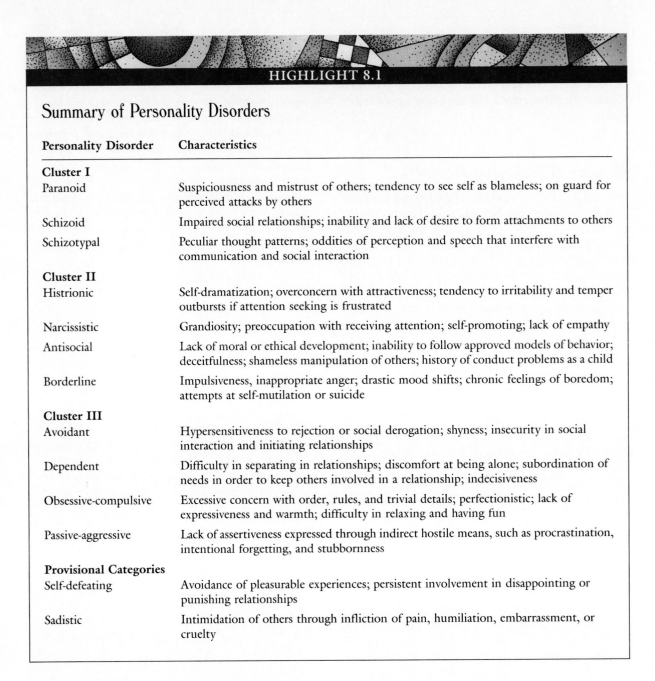

HIGHLIGHT 8.1

Summary of Personality Disorders

Personality Disorder	Characteristics
Cluster I	
Paranoid	Suspiciousness and mistrust of others; tendency to see self as blameless; on guard for perceived attacks by others
Schizoid	Impaired social relationships; inability and lack of desire to form attachments to others
Schizotypal	Peculiar thought patterns; oddities of perception and speech that interfere with communication and social interaction
Cluster II	
Histrionic	Self-dramatization; overconcern with attractiveness; tendency to irritability and temper outbursts if attention seeking is frustrated
Narcissistic	Grandiosity; preoccupation with receiving attention; self-promoting; lack of empathy
Antisocial	Lack of moral or ethical development; inability to follow approved models of behavior; deceitfulness; shameless manipulation of others; history of conduct problems as a child
Borderline	Impulsiveness, inappropriate anger; drastic mood shifts; chronic feelings of boredom; attempts at self-mutilation or suicide
Cluster III	
Avoidant	Hypersensitiveness to rejection or social derogation; shyness; insecurity in social interaction and initiating relationships
Dependent	Difficulty in separating in relationships; discomfort at being alone; subordination of needs in order to keep others involved in a relationship; indecisiveness
Obsessive-compulsive	Excessive concern with order, rules, and trivial details; perfectionistic; lack of expressiveness and warmth; difficulty in relaxing and having fun
Passive-aggressive	Lack of assertiveness expressed through indirect hostile means, such as procrastination, intentional forgetting, and stubbornness
Provisional Categories	
Self-defeating	Avoidance of pleasurable experiences; persistent involvement in disappointing or punishing relationships
Sadistic	Intimidation of others through infliction of pain, humiliation, embarrassment, or cruelty

switched jobs many times because he felt he was being mistreated.

The patient is distant and demanding with his family. His children call him "Sir" and know that it is wise to be "seen but not heard" when he is around. At home he can never comfortably sit still and is always busy at some chore or another. He prefers not to have people visit his house and becomes restless when his wife is away visiting others. (Spitzer et al., 1981, p. 37)

This pervasive suspiciousness and mistrust of other people leave a paranoid personality prone to numerous difficulties and hurts in interpersonal relationships. These difficulties typically lead the individual to be continually "on guard" for perceived attacks by others.

Schizoid Personality Disorder   Individuals with **schizoid personality disorder** usually show an inability to form social relationships and a lack of interest in doing so. Such individuals are unable to express their feelings and are seen by others as cold and distant; they often lack social skills and can be classified as *loners,* with solitary interests and occupations.

Early theorists considered a schizoid personality to be a likely precursor to the development of schizophrenia. This viewpoint has been challenged in recent times, however (Seiver, 1986). Research studies on the possible genetic transmission of schizoid personality have failed to establish either a link between the two disorders or the hereditary basis of schizoid personality (Kety et al., 1975; Slater, 1953). Seiver (1986), in his theoretical comparison of the schizoid and schizotypal personality disorders (to be considered in the next section), considered the schizotypal personality to be more closely linked genetically to schizophrenia; however, as we will see, the evidence for this linking is also contradictory.

The following case of a schizoid personality illustrates a fairly severe personality problem in a man who had been functioning adequately as judged both by occupational criteria and by his own standards of "happiness." When he sought help, it was at the encouragement of his supervisor and his physician.

Bill D., a highly intelligent but quite introverted and withdrawn 33-year-old computer analyst, was referred for psychological evaluation by his physician, who was concerned that Bill might be depressed and unhappy. At the suggestion of his supervisor, Bill had recently gone to the physician for rather vague physical complaints and because of his gloomy outlook on life. Bill had virtually no contact with other people. He lived alone in his apartment, worked in a small office by himself, and usually saw no one at work except for the occasional visits of his supervisor to give him new work and pick up completed projects. He ate lunch by himself and about once a week, on nice days, went to the zoo for his lunch break.

Bill was a lifelong loner; as a child he had had few friends and always had preferred solitary activities over family outings (he was the oldest of five children). In high school he had never dated and in college had gone out with a woman only once—and that was with a group of students after a game. He had been active in sports, however, and had played varsity football in both high school and college. In college he had spent a lot of time with one relatively close friend—mostly drinking. However, this friend now lived in another city.

Bill reported rather matter-of-factly that he had a hard time making friends; he never knew what to say in a conversation. On a number of occasions he had thought of becoming friends with other people but simply couldn't think of the right words, so "the conversation just died." He reported that he had given some thought lately to changing his life in an attempt to be more "positive," but it never had seemed worth the trouble. It was easier for him not to make the effort because he became embarrassed when someone tried to talk with him. He was happiest when he was alone.

In short, the central problem of the schizoid personality is an inability to form attachments to other people. It is as though the needs for love, belonging, and approval fail to develop in these individuals—or if they do, they are somehow obliterated at an early stage. The result is a profound barrenness of interpersonal experience.

Schizotypal Personality Disorder   Individuals with **schizotypal personality disorder** are seclusive, oversensitive, and eccentric in their communication and behavior. They tend to be egocentric and frequently see chance events as related to themselves. Though both schizotypal and schizoid personalities are characterized by behavioral patterns of isolation and withdrawal, the two can be distinguished in that schizotypal personality—but not schizoid personality—also involves oddities of thought, perception, or speech. Though reality contact is usually maintained, highly personalized and superstitious thinking are characteristic of individuals with a schizotypal personality. Their oddities in thinking, talking, and other behaviors are similar to those often seen in more severe forms in schizophrenic patients; in fact, they are sometimes first diagnosed as exhibiting simple or latent schizophrenia. Widiger, Frances, and Trull (1987) found that the cognitive malfunctioning symptoms included in schizotypal personality disorder, such as cognitive perceptual problems, magical thinking (for example, belief in telepathy and superstitions), ideas of reference (the belief that conversations or gestures of others refer to oneself), recurrent illusions (the distortion of a person or event) odd speech, and suspicious beliefs were more useful in making a clinical diagnosis than social isolation, inadequate rapport, and social anxiety. A genetic association with schizophrenia is widely suspected (Seiver, 1986); in fact the term *schizotypal* is an abbreviation for "schizophrenic genotype" (Rado, 1956). However, evidence for a genetic link with schizophrenia is not conclusive (Neale & Oltmanns, 1980). The following case is fairly typical:

> *A* 41-year-old male was referred to a community mental health center's activities program for help in improving his social skills. He had a lifelong pattern of social isolation, and spent hours worrying that his angry thoughts about his older brother would cause his brother harm. He had previously worked as a clerk in civil service, but had lost his job because of poor attendance and low productivity.
>
> On interview the patient was distant and somewhat distrustful. He described in elaborate and often irrelevant detail his rather uneventful and routine daily life. He told the interviewer that he had spent an hour and a half in a pet store deciding which of two brands of fish food to buy, and explained their relative merits. For two days he had studied the washing instructions on a new pair of jeans—Did "Wash before wearing" mean that the jeans were to be washed before wearing the first time, or did they need, for some reason, to be washed each time before they were worn? He did not regard concerns such as these as senseless, though he acknowledged that the amount of time spent thinking about them might be excessive. When asked about his finances, he could recite from memory his most recent monthly bank statement, including the amount of every check and the running balance as each check was written. He knew his balance on any particular day, but sometimes got anxious if he considered whether a certain check or deposit had actually cleared. He was very sensitive to questions put by the interviewer, reading in criticism where none was intended. (Spitzer et al., 1981, p. 234)

The distinguishing feature of a schizotypal person is peculiar thought patterns, which are in turn associated with a loosening—although not a complete rupture—of ties to reality. The individual appears to lack some key integrative competence of the sort that enables most of us to "keep it all together" and move our lives toward some personal goals. As a result, many basic abilities, such as being able to communicate clearly, are never fully mastered, and the individual tends to drift aimlessly and unproductively through the adult years.

Histrionic Personality Disorder   Individuals with **histrionic personality disorder** typically show immaturity, excitability, emotional instability, a craving for excitement, and self-dramatization (an attention-seeking device that is often seductive in nature). Sexual adjustment is usually poor and interpersonal relationships are stormy. These individuals often exhibit dependence and helplessness and are quite gullible. Usually they are self-centered, vain, and overconcerned about approval from others, who see them as overly reactive, shallow, and insincere. The following case illustrates the histrionic personality pattern:

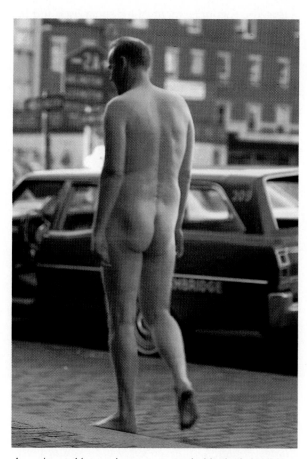

Attention-seeking tactics are common in histrionic behavior.

Pam, a 22-year-old secretary, was causing numerous problems for her supervisor and co-workers. According to her supervisor, Pam was unable to carry out her duties without constant guidance. Seemingly helpless and dependent, she would overreact to minor events and job pressures with irritability and occasional temper tantrums. If others placed unwanted demands on her, she would complain of physical problems, such as nausea or headaches; furthermore, she frequently missed work altogether. To top it off, Pam was flirtatious and often demandingly seductive toward the men in the office.

As a result of her frequent absenteeism and her disruptive behavior in the office, Pam's supervisor and the personnel manager recommended that she be given a psychological evaluation and counseling in the Employee Assistance Program. She went to the first appointment with the psychologist but failed to return for follow-up visits. She was finally given a discharge notice after several incidents of temper outbursts at work.

Both Pam's physical complaints and her seductive behavior are examples of attention-seeking tactics commonly found in the histrionic personality pattern. When these tactics fail to bring about the desired result, irritability and temper outbursts typically follow.

Narcissistic Personality Disorder   Individuals with **narcissistic personality disorder** show an exaggerated sense of self-importance and a preoccupation with receiving attention. Ronningstam and Gunderson (1989) reported that grandiosity was the most stable and generalizable criterion for diagnosing narcissistic patients. They reported that the common components of narcissistic personality included a search for recognition, disregard for society's values and rules, and crimes committed because of rage or to avoid defeat. Individuals with narcissistic personality disorder have a chronically fragile, low self-esteem (Svrakic, 1990) and a strategy for asserting their own self-worth so that they and others do not recognize their own basic frailties. Their sense of entitlement is frequently a source of astonishment to others, although they themselves regard their lavish expectations as merely their just dues. By and large, they do not permit others to be genuinely close to or to become

dependent on them. They behave in stereotypical ways (for example, with constant self-references and bragging) to gain the acclaim and recognition that feeds their grandiose expectations. These tactics, to those around them, appear to be excessive efforts to make themselves look good.

Akhtar (1989) considers six areas of functioning to be central to narcissistic personality disorder: (a) a narcissistic individual has a basic sense of inferiority, which underlies a preoccupation with fantasies of outstanding achievement; (b) a narcissistic individual is unable to trust and rely on others and thus develops numerous, shallow relationships to extract tributes from others; (c) a narcissistic individual shows a superficial commitment to excellence—instead he or she has an aimless orientation toward superficial interests. Such a person is often socially charming and successful, however, and is preoccupied with appearances; (d) a narcissistic individual has a shifting morality—always ready to shift values to gain favor. He or she may, however, show to the outside world a calculated sense of modesty; (e) a narcissistic person is unable to remain in love, showing an impaired capacity for a committed relationship. Consequently, marital instability and promiscuity are prominent; (f) although he or she may impress others with knowledge and decisiveness, a narcissistic person's information base is often limited to trivia. Such a person characteristically shows "headline intelligence," knowing only sketchy details, yet is able to use language to enhance his or her self-esteem and impress others.

Narcissistic personalities share another central element—they are unable to take the perspective of others, to see things other than "through their own eyes." In more general terms, they lack the capacity for empathy, which is an essential ingredient for mature relationships. In this sense all children begin life as narcissists and only gradually acquire a perspective-taking ability. For reasons that are far from entirely understood, some children do not show normal progress in this area, and indeed, in extreme cases, show little or none. The latter grow up to become adult narcissistic personalities. The following case is illustrative:

A 25-year-old, single graduate student complains to his psychoanalyst of difficulty completing his Ph.D. in English Literature and expresses concerns about his relationships with women. He believes that his thesis topic may profoundly increase the level of understanding in his discipline and make him famous, but so far he has not been able to get past the third chapter. His mentor does not seem sufficiently impressed with his ideas, and the patient is furious at him, but also self-doubting and ashamed. He blames his mentor for his lack of progress, and thinks that he deserves more help with his grand idea, that his mentor should help with some of the research. The patient brags about his creativity and complains that other people are "jealous" of his insight. He is very envious of students who are moving along faster than he and regards them as "dull drones and ass-kissers." He prides himself on the brilliance of his class participation and imagines someday becoming a great professor.

He becomes rapidly infatuated with women and has powerful and persistent fantasies about each new woman he meets, but after several experiences of sexual intercourse feels disappointed and finds them dumb, clinging, and physically repugnant. He has many "friends," but they turn over quickly, and no one relationship lasts very long. People get tired of his continual self-promotion and lack of consideration of them. For example, he was lonely at Christmas and insisted that his best friend stay in town rather than visit his family. The friend refused, criticizing the patient's self-centeredness; and the patient, enraged, decided never to see this friend again. (Spitzer et al., 1981, pp. 52–53)

The narcissistic personality disorder is more frequently observed in men than in women (Akhtar & Thompson, 1982). Individuals with narcissistic personality patterns may not seek psychological treatment because they view themselves as nearly perfect and in no need of personal change. Those who do enter treatment often do so at the insistence of another person, such as a husband or wife, and may terminate therapy prematurely—particularly if their therapist is confrontational and questions their self-serving behavior. Most of what is known about narcissistic personality disorder has emerged from psychoanalytic therapy and later egoanalytic writings (Kernberg, 1984; Kohut & Wolff, 1978). The psychodynamic treatment approach appears to be the most viable therapy because a long-term treatment relationship seems needed to bring about changes in these patients' persistent self-oriented patterns (Kernberg, 1989).

Antisocial personalities violate the rights of others through aggressive behavior and seldom show any loyalty toward others or remorse for cruel behavior. They may have enough charm and intelligence to carry out elaborate schemes for conning people. Such behavior is typified by Giovanni Vigliotto, who was convicted of defrauding one of his 105 wives. Vigliotto would allegedly marry a lonely, middle-aged woman, get control of her assets, and then, setting a date for a rendezvous in another city, disappear. Several of his wives said of him that he was charming, friendly, and warm. Though he admitted to marrying 105 women over a 33-year span, Vigliotto denied swindling anyone.

Antisocial Personality Disorder   Individuals with **antisocial personality disorder** continually violate the rights of others through aggressive, antisocial behavior, without remorse or loyalty to anyone. Some antisocial personalities have enough intelligence and social charm to devise and carry out elaborate schemes for conning large numbers of people. Impostors fit into this category. Because this pattern has been studied more fully than the others, it will be examined in some detail later in this chapter. A brief clinical description should suffice here.

Mark, a 22-year-old, came to a psychology clinic on court order. He was awaiting trial for car theft and armed robbery. His case records revealed that he had a long history of arrests beginning at age 9, when he had been picked up for vandalism. He had been expelled from high school for truancy and disruptive behavior. On a number of occasions he had run away from home for days or weeks at a time—always returning in a disheveled and "rundown" condition. To date he had not held a job for more than a few days at a time, even though his generally charming manner enabled him to readily obtain work. He was described as a loner, with few friends. Though

*initially charming, Mark usually soon antago-
nized those he met with his aggressive, self-
oriented behavior.*

*Mark was generally affable and complimen-
tary during the therapy session. At the end of it,
he enthusiastically told the therapist how much
he'd benefited from the counseling and looked
forward to future sessions.*

*Mark's first session was his last. Shortly after
it, he skipped bail and presumably left town to
avoid his trial.*

Borderline Personality Disorder   Individuals with **borderline personality disorder** show a
pattern of behavior that resembles features of both
the personality disorders and some of the more
severe psychological disorders, particularly the affective disorders (Chapter 11) and schizophrenia
(Chapter 12). The designation of "borderline" personality is applied because the symptoms fall on the
border between the personality disorders and the
more extreme mood disorders and schizophrenia.
Although they are usually aware of their circumstances and surroundings, borderline personalities
may have short episodes in which they appear to be
out of contact with reality and experience delusions
or other psychotic-like symptoms, such as recurrent
illusions, magical thinking, and paranoid beliefs
(O'Connell et al., 1989).

Individuals with borderline personalities are
frequently impulsive and unpredictable, angry,
empty, and unstable. They have chronic feelings of
boredom and a low tolerance for frustration. Their
extreme instability is reflected in drastic mood
shifts and erratic, self-destructive behaviors, such as
binges of gambling, sex, alcohol use, eating, or
shoplifting. They commonly have a history of intense but stormy relationships, typically involving
overidealizations of friends or lovers that later end
in bitter disillusionment and disappointment (Gunderson & Singer, 1986). They typically display
intense anger outbursts with little provocation, and
they may show disturbances in basic identity that
preoccupy them and produce a basically negative
outlook. Feeling slighted, they might, for example,
become verbally abusive toward loved ones or
might threaten suicide over minor setbacks. Suicide
attempts, often flagrantly manipulative, are frequently part of the clinical picture (Fine & Sansone,
1990), and self-mutilation is one of the most discriminating signs for borderline personality
(Widiger et al., 1986). The following case illustrates
the frequent risk of suicide and self-mutilation
among borderline personalities:

*A 26-year-old unemployed woman was re-
ferred for admission to a hospital by her therapist
because of intense suicidal preoccupation and
urges to mutilate herself by cutting herself with a
razor.*

*The patient was apparently well until her
junior year in high school, when she became
preoccupied with religion and philosophy, avoided friends, and was filled with doubt about who
she was. Academically she did well, but later,
during college, her performance declined. In
college she began to use a variety of drugs,
abandoned the religion of her family, and*

*The women shown here have been
diagnosed as having borderline
personalities. They have been in
some kind of therapy for at least
five years and have made enormous progress. Nonetheless, in
this therapy group, Linda (center)
describes how at times she gets so
angry that she cuts herself. Self-
mutilation is one of the most discriminating signs for borderline
personality.*

seemed to be searching for a charismatic religious figure with whom to identify. At times massive anxiety swept over her and she found it would suddenly vanish if she cut her forearm with a razor blade. Three years ago she began psychotherapy, and initially rapidly idealized her therapist as being incredibly intuitive and empathic. Later she became hostile and demanding of him, requiring more and more sessions, sometimes two in one day. Her life centered on her therapist, by this time to the exclusion of everyone else. Although her hostility toward her therapist was obvious, she could neither see it nor control it. Her difficulties with her therapist culminated in many episodes of her forearm cutting and suicidal threats, which led to the referral for admission." (Spitzer et al., 1981, pp. 111–112)

Clinical observation of people whose behavior meets the criteria of borderline personality disorder points strongly to a problem of achieving a coherent sense of self as a key predisposing causal factor. These people somehow fail to complete the process of achieving an articulated self-identity and hence do not really become individuals. This lack of individualization leads to complications in interpersonal relationships.

Avoidant Personality Disorder   Individuals with **avoidant personality disorder** are hypersensitive to rejection and apprehensive of any sign of social derogation; such individuals readily see ridicule or disparagement where none was intended. Lifelong patterns of limited social relationships and reluctance to enter into social interactions are common. These individuals are too fearful of criticism and rebuff to seek out other people, yet they desire affection and are often lonely and bored. Unlike schizoid personalities, they do not enjoy their aloneness: their inability to relate comfortably to other people causes acute distress and low self-esteem, as shown by the following case:

Sally, a 35-year-old librarian, lived a relatively isolated life and had few acquaintances and no close personal friends. From childhood on, she had been very shy and had withdrawn from close ties with others to keep from being hurt or criticized. Two years before she entered therapy, she had had a date to go to a party with an acquaintance she had met at the library. The moment they had arrived at the party, Sally had

felt extremely uncomfortable because she had not been "dressed properly." She left in a hurry and refused to see her acquaintance again. It was because of her continuing concern over this incident that—two years later—Sally decided to go into therapy, even though she dreaded the possibility that the psychologist would be critical of her.

In the early treatment sessions, she sat silently much of the time, finding it too difficult to talk about herself. After several sessions, she grew to trust the therapist, and she related numerous incidents in her early years in which she had been "devastated" by her alcoholic father's obnoxious behavior in public. Though she had tried to keep her school friends from knowing about her family problems, when this had become impossible she instead had limited her friendships, thus protecting herself from possible embarrassment or criticism.

When Sally first began therapy, she avoided meeting people unless she could be assured that they would "like her." With therapy that focused on enhancing her assertiveness and social skills, she made some progress in her ability to approach and talk with people.

Sally's extreme need to avoid situations in which she might be embarrassed is the keynote of the avoidant personality. Life is full of risks, yet such individuals cannot face even the slightest risk of embarrassment or criticism. They want guarantees of success before they will participate—and if they cannot have them, they just will not play the game.

The diagnosis of avoidant personality is not without its critics, particularly with regard to how well it can be distinguished from schizoid personality disorder (Livesley, West, & Tanney, 1985). The diagnostic criteria for avoidant personality have been thought to blend imperceptibly with two other categories—schizoid and dependent personalities. Trull, Widiger, and Frances (1987), however, in a diagnostic study of personality disorder in an inpatient facility, found that these disorders were clearly distinguishable. The key difference is that avoidant personality is associated with being hypersensitive, shy, and insecure, while schizoid personality is characterized by being indifferent, aloof, and cold. The more difficult distinction is between dependent and avoidant personalities. In this case, a dependent personality has great difficulty separating in relationships, while an avoidant personality has problems initiating them.

Some research (e.g., Alden & Capp, 1988) suggests that an avoidant personality may be a biologically based disorder that is reinforced by environmental factors to become a highly stable and chronic behavioral pattern (Kagan, Reznick, & Snidman, 1988). However, efforts to modify avoidant personality behaviors have recently been undertaken with some success; this success calls into question the nature of any biological causal factor. Alden (1989), for example, reported on a controlled study of structured behavioral treatment in which the treated group of avoidant clients showed significant improvements in terms of self-esteem and a reduction in social reticence. However, in spite of their noticeable improvements, the avoidant clients, at the end of treatment, still had not achieved normal levels of social functioning. This limited success of treatment and poor prognosis for behavioral change was confirmed in a recent study by Stravynski et al. (1989). They found that social skills training was not effective in reducing avoidant behavior.

Dependent Personality Disorder   Individuals with **dependent personality disorder** show extreme dependence on other people and acute discomfort—even panic—at having to be alone. These individuals usually build their lives around other people and subordinate their own needs to keep these people involved with them. They lack self-confidence and feel helpless even when they have actually developed good work skills or other competencies. They function well as long as they are not required to be on their own. The following case is one in which a woman with a dependent personality experienced such distress following desertion by her husband that she sought help:

Sarah D., a 32-year-old mother of two and a part-time tax accountant, came to a crisis center late one evening after Michael, her husband of a year and a half, abused her physically and then left home. Although he never physically harmed the children, he frequently threatened to do so when he was drunk. Sarah appeared acutely anxious and worried about the future and "needed to be told what to do." She wanted her husband to come back and seemed rather unconcerned about his regular pattern of physical abuse. At the time, Michael was an unemployed resident in a day treatment program at a halfway house for paroled drug abusers that taught abstinence from all addictive substances through harassment and

group cohesiveness. He was almost always in a surly mood and "ready to explode."

Although Sarah had a well-paying job, she voiced great concern about being able to make it on her own. She realized that it was foolish to be "dependent" on her husband, whom she referred to as a "real loser." (She had had a similar relationship with her first husband, who had left her and her oldest child when she was 18.) Several times in the past few months, Sarah had made up her mind to get out of the marriage but couldn't bring herself to break away. She would threaten to leave, but when the time came to do so, she would "freeze in the door" with a numbness in her body and a sinking feeling in her stomach at the thought of "not being with Michael."

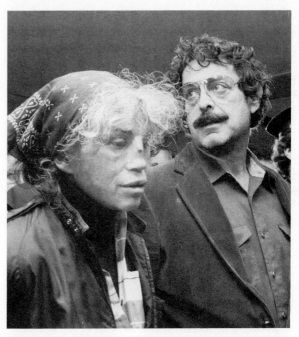

Dependent personalities may tolerate emotional or physical abuse in order to avoid being abandoned. Their lack of self-confidence is so extreme that they passively allow other people to take over the major decisions in their lives. Hedda Nussbaum exhibited such behavior in her relationship with her lover Joel Steinberg. He physically abused Hedda and their illegally adopted daughter Lisa for years. On the last night of 6-year-old Lisa's life, when Steinberg beat her and left her comatose on the bathroom floor all night, Hedda did nothing to help Lisa. Hedda testified against Joel at the trial for the murder of Lisa in exchange for not being prosecuted herself. Once a competent person with a job as a children's book editor, Hedda had become so unable to function without Joel, though he abused her, that she tolerated the abuse of Lisa as well, ultimately sharing the responsibility for her death. Steinberg was convicted of first-degree manslaughter and is currently serving his sentence.

As a result of their lack of confidence, dependent personalities passively allow other people to take over the major decisions in their lives—such as where they will live and work, what friends they will have, and even how they will spend their time. These individuals typically appear "selfless" and bland, since they usually feel they have no right to express even mild individuality.

Obsessive-Compulsive Personality Disorder   Individuals with **obsessive-compulsive personality disorder** show excessive concern for rules, order, efficiency, and work, coupled with an insistence that everyone do things their way and an inability to express warm feelings. Such individuals tend to be overinhibited, overconscientious, overdutiful, and rigid, and to have difficulty relaxing or doing anything just for fun. They are usually preoccupied with trivial details and poor allocations of time.

The behavior patterns of this disorder are somewhat similar to those of neurotic compulsive disorders. In obsessive-compulsive disorder, however, an individual suffers from the persistent intrusion of particular undesired thoughts (obsessions) or actions (compulsions) that are a source of extreme anxiety because the individual recognizes that they are irrational but cannot seem to control them. Obsessive-compulsive personalities have whole lifestyles characterized by obstinacy and compulsive orderliness. Although they may be anxious about getting all their work done in keeping with their exacting standards, they are not anxious about their compulsiveness itself (Pollack, 1979). An example of obsessive-compulsive personality is reflected in the following case:

Alan appeared to be well suited to his work as a train dispatcher. He was conscientious, perfectionistic, and attended to minute details. However, he was not close to his coworkers and, reportedly, they thought him "off." He would get quite upset if even minor variations to his daily routine occurred. For example, he would become tense and irritable if coworkers did not follow exactly his elaborately constructed schedules and plans. If he became tied up in traffic, he would beat the steering wheel and swear at other drivers for holding him up.

In short, Alan got little pleasure out of life and worried constantly about minor problems. His rigid routines were impossible to maintain, and he often developed tension headaches or stomachaches when he couldn't keep his complicated plans in order. His physician, noting the frequency of his physical complaints and his generally perfectionistic approach to life, referred him for a psychological evaluation. Psychotherapy was recommended to him, although the prognosis for significant behavioral change was considered questionable. He did not follow up on the treatment recommendations because he felt that he could not afford the time away from work.

Other people tend to view obsessive-compulsive personalities as rigid, stiff, cold, and even disorganized—in spite of their frequent and extensive preoccupation with the details in their lives.

Passive-Aggressive Personality Disorder   One of the most controversial of the personality disorder diagnoses is that of **passive-aggressive personality disorder.** The reasons for this controversy are twofold. First, the diagnosis is conceptually ambiguous: that is, a person is considered both passive and actively aggressive at the same time—two seemingly contradictory behaviors. Second, empirical support of the reliability and validity of this diagnosis is limited (Penna, 1986). Individuals with this disorder typically express hostility in indirect and nonviolent ways, such as procrastinating, pouting, "forgetting," or being obstructionistic, stubborn, or intentionally inefficient. Passive-aggressive individuals resent and manage not to comply with demands others make on them; the behavior is most apparent in their work situations but also occurs in their social relationships. Resentment of authority figures, coupled with a lack of assertiveness, is typical.

The passive-aggressive personality pattern is shown in the following case of marital therapy. Though the marital problems were the major focus of the initial sessions, Wanda's adjustment difficulties required additional attention.

David and Wanda had met through a singles travel club and had been initially attracted to each other because of their mutual interest in travel and dancing. After a brief courtship, they had married. Two successive pregnancies had left them with two lovely children but little time or money to pursue their interests.

In the early sessions, David, a 29-year-old sales representative, complained that Wanda, a

28-year-old homemaker, was a "great procrasti-nator" and that she kept the house a "shambles." Apparently, Wanda also often "forgot" to cook, sometimes because she became preoccupied with a book or a puzzle. She was often unaware of the time and fed the children late; in addition, she often did not have dinner ready when David came home. On the other hand, after some prodding, Wanda revealed that she found herself in an intolerable situation. She was unhappy with her marriage; she saw her husband as a selfish, picky person who was obsessive about the cleanliness of the house and the preparation of the meals, and who was unaware of the difficulties of caring for two young children. It was clear from these early sessions that David and Wanda were frustrated in their marriage and each harbored great resentments toward the other.

In subsequent therapy sessions, it became apparent that Wanda's problems were consistent with a lifelong pattern and not just the result of her present situation. She was a rather passive and nonassertive person who had difficulty making her objections known to others. She had great difficulty making her feelings known to David about her disappointments in the marriage. Instead, she dealt with her frustration through indirect means—intentional inefficiency. She related several incidents in her life in which she had had periods of ineffective functioning or, as she called it, stubbornness. Inevitably, these periods had occurred during times of frustration. For example, her parents had hoped she would pursue a career in music, as they had; rather than tell them she had no desire to be a musician, she instead could "just never seem to complete" her university assignments and eventually had flunked out of school.

In addition to the marital therapy sessions, it was recommended that Wanda also be seen in individual psychotherapy to explore further her personal adjustment problems. As for the maintenance of the house, it was recommended that, for the time being at least, they hire outside help.

In sum, we can see in a passive-aggressive personality a pattern of never confronting a problem situation directly. This characteristic way of reacting to a problem is really no solution at all. It is frustrating for others, who must deal with the inefficient behavior usually without knowing the real reason for it; and it is frustrating for the individual, because it typically does not productively resolve the problem.

Self-defeating Personality Disorder   The **self-defeating personality disorder** (often called masochistic personality disorder) is an extensive pattern of behavior characterized by an individual's avoidance of pleasurable experiences and persistent involvement in disappointing relationships. Individuals with this disorder seemingly choose relationships or situations that lead to disappointment, failure, or mistreatment even though better options are available. These individuals appear to be almost magnetically drawn to punishing relationships and seemingly discourage or reject the attempts of others to help them extricate themselves from these painful experiences.

Self-defeating personalities fail to accomplish tasks or goals that are crucial to their personal objectives in spite of the fact that they have the ability to perform them. If they do achieve personal recognition or accomplishments, these individuals might react by feeling depressed or guilty or by engaging in some inappropriate behavior rather than feeling self-enhanced as most people would. They avoid opportunities for pleasure or success and are reluctant to admit to enjoyment.

Self-defeating individuals elicit rejecting responses from others and then feel hurt or scorned by them. For example, a man who makes fun of his wife in public may provoke her to make a negative response. He then feels devastated over the spouse's rejection.

Self-defeating personality disorder is a provisional diagnostic category that is included in the appendix of DSM-III-R. It is there because many clinicians believe that no other personality disorder is adequate to describe this pattern of personality disturbance in which an individual is drawn to relationships in which he or she will suffer. Reich (1989) found that the behavioral and symptomatic criteria for self-defeating personality disorder were somewhat difficult to apply because of clear overlap with other disorders, such as avoidant, dependent, and especially borderline personalities. Reich also concluded, however, that diagnosis, though difficult, could be applied effectively.

Fuller and Blashfield (1989) evaluated whether the proposed personality disorder—the self-defeating, or masochistic, personality disorder—was needed to classify the behaviors in question, or whether patients with these problems could be classified using another DSM-III-R category. They found that the behaviors in question did not fall into an existing category and thus suggested that the proposed category was needed.

The authors of DSM-III-R attempted to incorporate criteria that would distinguish self-defeating personality disorder from normal reactions to being victimized or abused (Kass et al., 1989). Nevertheless, the category of self-defeating personality disorder has met with considerable objection from vocal critics, particularly some feminist action groups, which view it as having antifemale biases. For example, representatives of Women in Psychology have made the point that the diagnostic label *self-defeating personality disorder* misplaces the blame for abusive relationships onto women who are actually the victims of abuse (Fisher, 1986). Fuller & Blashfield (1989) evaluated the question of whether this proposed disorder might be vulnerable to gender bias when applied as a diagnosis. They found no evidence for bias, but the extent to which the usefulness of the diagnosis in clinical practice outweighs the criticism of bias has yet to be determined. It is likely that additional research will be required to assure critics of the objectivity of this proposed disorder.

Sadistic Personality Disorder   Another proposed diagnostic category in the appendix of DSM-III-R is **sadistic personality disorder,** which is defined by a pervasive pattern of cruel, demeaning, and aggressive behavior toward other people. It is usually evident by early adulthood. Individuals with this disorder have a history of using physical cruelty to inflict pain on other people, usually for the satisfaction of seeing them suffer. They might humiliate, demean, or embarrass other people in social situations, or they might attempt to get other people to do what they want by intimidation. Sadistic individuals tend to restrict the autonomy of other people with whom they are involved in close relationships; they will, for example, not let others go out unaccompanied. They are characteristically fascinated with violence, weapons, martial arts, or torture.

As with the self-defeating disorder, some critics have expressed concern that the sadistic disorder might be used to disadvantage women. For example, having a diagnostic label *sadistic personality disorder* for individuals who have committed violent crimes against women may tend to excuse these abusive individuals by attributing their behavior to their being disordered.

An additional argument advanced by Women in Psychology in response to the new diagnostic categories, which they consider antiwomen, is that they are not based on scientific research and do not represent advances in our understanding of behavior disorders. Whether these proposed diagnostic categories will eventually be fully substantiated by research is yet to be determined.

■ Causal Factors in Personality Disorders

Establishing the causal factors in personality disorders has not progressed far, partly because such disorders were not even included in the official diagnostic classifications before 1952 and partly because they are less amenable to thorough study. Many individuals with these disorders are never seen by clinical personnel. Typically, those who do come to the attention of clinicians or legal authorities have already developed a full-blown disorder, so that only *retrospective* study is possible—that is, going back through what records may exist in an effort to reconstruct the chain of events that may have led to the disorder. As we have seen, researchers have more confidence in *prospective* studies, in which groups of individuals are observed before a disorder appears and followed over a period of time to see which individuals develop problems and what causal factors have in fact been present.

Research on causal factors in disordered personalities is also made difficult by the fact that, for the most part, general personality traits rather than specific behavioral patterns are being studied in the personality disorders. It is hard to identify the point at which, for example, great attention to detail ceases to be within the normal range and becomes characteristic of compulsive personality.

Of possible biological factors, it has been suggested that the constitutional reaction tendencies that infants display (high or low vitality, special sensitivity, and so on) may predispose them to the development of particular personality disorders. In addition, some research suggests that genetic factors may be important for the development of paranoid personality (Kendler & Gruenberg, 1982) and borderline personality (Loranger et al., 1982). The constitutional basis for the personality disorders remains largely hypothetical, however, with the possible exception of antisocial personality, to be discussed later in this chapter.

Among psychological factors, early learning is usually assumed to contribute the most in predisposing an individual to develop a personality disorder, yet the "data" in support of this belief are based largely on speculation and inference. Some research has suggested that abuse in childhood may be related to the development of personality disorders. Ogata et al. (1990) found that 71 percent of borderline patients reported having been abused as children, while only 22 percent of depressed patients reported having been abused. However, except for antisocial personality, research has simply not sufficiently established particular antecedents for these disorders.

Sociocultural factors contributing to personality disorders are even less well defined. We do know that the incidence and form of psychopathology in general vary somewhat with time and place, and some clinicians believe that personality disorders have increased in American society in recent years (Smith, 1978). If this claim is true, we can expect to find the increase related to changes in our culture's general priorities and activities. Is our emphasis on impulse gratification, instant solutions, and pain-free benefits leading more people to develop the self-centered life-styles that we see in more extreme forms in the personality disorders? Only further research can clarify this issue.

■ Treatments and Outcomes

Personality disorders seem especially resistant to therapy. For example, speaking of antisocial personalities, Ellis (1977) pointed out that

[they] are exceptionally difficult to treat with psychotherapy. They only rarely come for treatment on a voluntary basis; and when they are treated involuntarily, they tend to be resistant, surly, and in search of a "cure" that will involve no real effort on their part. Even when they come for private treatment, they are usually looking for magical, effortless "cures," and they tend to stay in treatment only for a short period of time and to make relatively little improvement. (p. 259)

In many cases, people with personality disorders who are seen clinically are there as part of another person's treatment—as, for example, in couple counseling, where a partner identified as the "patient" has a spouse with a personality disorder. Or a child referred to a child guidance center may have a parent with a personality disorder. In these cases, of course, the problems of the so-called patient may be due in no small measure to the great strain caused by the family member with severe personality disorder. A narcissistic father, who is so self-centered and demanding of attention from others that family relationships are constantly strained, leaves little room for small children to grow into self-respecting adults. Likewise, a mother whose typical manner of responding to others is through passive-aggressive maneuvers, such as procrastination, obstruction, and pouting, may create an unhealthy family atmosphere that distorts a child's development.

A child subjected to such extreme, inescapable, and often quite irrational behavior on the part of one or both parents may become the weak link that breaks, bringing the family into therapy. Many a child or family therapist has quickly concluded after seeing a child in a family context that psychological attention, if it is to be effective at all, must be focused on the parental relationships. The following case clearly illustrates this problem:

Mrs. A. brought her 7-year-old son, Christopher, to a mental health center for treatment because he was fearful of going out and recently had been having bad nightmares. Mrs. A. sought help at the recommendation of the school social worker after Chris refused to return to school. She voiced a great deal of concern for Chris and agreed to cooperate in the treatment by attend-

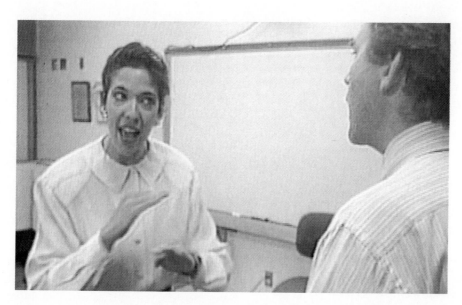

As part of an interesting training program for psychotherapists, the actress shown here is being trained to behave in ways characteristic of an individual with narcissistic personality, for example, by being self-centered and demanding of attention. She will then act out her role in mock therapy sessions with would-be psychotherapists.

ing parent effectiveness training sessions. However, she seemed quite reluctant to talk about getting her husband involved in the treatment. After much encouragement, she agreed to try to bring him to the next session, but he adamantly refused to participate. Mrs. A described him as a "very proud and strong-willed man" who was quite suspicious of other people. She felt that he might be afraid people would blame him for Chris's problems. She reported that he had been having a lot of problems lately—he had seemed quite bitter and resentful over some local political issues and tended to blame others (particularly minorities) for his problems. He refused to come to the clinic because he "doesn't like social workers."

After several sessions of therapy, Mrs. A. confessed to her therapist that her husband's rigid and suspicious behavior was disrupting the family. He would often come home from work and accuse her of, for example, "talking with Jewish men." He was a domineering person who set strict house rules and enforced them with loud threats and intimidation. Both Mrs. A. and Chris were fearful of his tyrannical demands, but his suspicious nature made it difficult for them to explain anything to him. Mrs. A. also felt a great deal of sympathy for her husband because she felt that deep down inside he was frightened; she reported that he kept numerous guns around the house and several locks on the doors for protection against outsiders, whom he feared.

Because they usually enter treatment only at someone else's insistence and do not believe that they need to change, individuals with personality disorders typically put the responsibility for treatment on others and are adept at avoiding the focus of therapy themselves. In addition, the difficulties they have in forming and maintaining good relationships generally tend to make a therapeutic relationship stormy at best. The pattern of acting out, typical in their other relationships, is carried into the therapy situation, and instead of dealing with their problems at the verbal level, they may become angry at their therapist and loudly disrupt the sessions. Goldberg et al. (1986) reported high dropout rates for some types of personality disordered patients. These patients may also behave in socially inappropriate ways outside the sessions to show their therapist that the therapy is not working.

When questioned about such behavior, these individuals often drop out of treatment or become

even more entrenched in their defensiveness. In some cases, however, confrontation can be quite effective. For individuals who become identified with their therapy group, or who are sufficiently "hooked" into couple therapy not to flee the sessions when their behavior comes under scrutiny, the intense feedback from peers or spouse often is more acceptable than confrontation by a therapist in individual treatment (Gurman & Kniskern, 1978; Lubin, 1976).

In some situations, therapeutic techniques must be modified. For example, recognizing that traditional individual psychotherapy tends to encourage dependency in people already too dependent, Leeman and Mulvey (1974) developed a treatment strategy in individual outpatient therapy for altering a dependent individual's basic life-style instead of fostering it. First, they would inform a patient at the outset that the therapy would be brief. Next, they made it clear that they "would not assume responsibility for managing the patient's life" (p. 36) and that they expected strength on the part of the patient "both to tolerate feelings and to behave in more adaptive and self-satisfying ways" (p. 36). Therapy sessions were then kept focused on relationships outside of therapy rather than on the treatment relationship, and demands were made on the patient to *change* his or her behavior—not just to understand it. Several highly dependent patients, including one "veteran" of ten years of individual psychotherapy, responded favorably to this treatment, and most reported that they were doing much better two and a half years later.

In general, therapy for individuals with severe personality disorders may be more effective in situations where acting-out behavior can be constrained. Outpatient treatment is often not promising because severe acting out can disrupt the course of treatment. The tenacity of these disorders and the failure of individuals either to profit from ordinary therapy or to learn from their life experiences is shown in the following case of an individual diagnosed as a passive-aggressive personality:

Charles, age 29, appeared to be a highly successful salesperson in a large retail shoe store. He was a handsome, friendly, and outgoing person who quickly impressed customers and gained ready admirers. His relationships with coworkers and employers, however, were an entirely different matter. He was a disorganized person who couldn't keep the bookkeeping and stock in order. He was a procrastinator who promised everything but delivered nothing. He responded to criticism by his employers with smiles and promises but was never able to get organized. He never expressed anger toward his supervisor or disgruntled customers but seldom fulfilled their demands.

One evening, after he had been criticized for his sloppiness, he was directed to straighten out his "mess" and lock up the store after everyone else had left. He failed to comply and actually left the store open with the lights on. This was the last straw for his employers, and Charles was fired.

Over the years, his stubborn and passive-aggressive actions had lost him several other jobs. In each situation, he had been able to secure a sales position quite readily, but in short order his behavior had angered his employers and the ensuing criticisms had made him even more intractable.

Finally, he entered therapy at his wife's insistence because of marital problems. His behavior toward his wife was similar to his behavior in other personal relationships: he was obstinate and unyielding even though he always smiled and never lost his temper. After only two weeks in therapy, he began to miss sessions until, after a month, he stopped coming altogether because "he had to look for work."

Treatment prognosis (outcome) for borderline personality disorder patients is typically considered to be guarded because of their long-standing problems and extreme instability. Because borderline patients are usually difficult to manage due to their behavioral problems and acting out tendencies, treatment often involves a judicious use of both psychological and biological treatment methods (Swenson & Wood, 1990). Cowdry and Gardner (1988) found that some borderline personality patients can be effectively treated with the drug tranylcypromine (Parnate), an MAO inhibitor for use in treatment of depression (see *HIGHLIGHT 17.3*), as an adjunct to psychological treatment. They concluded that pharmacotherapy aided in the reduction of mood and behavior in borderline patients. Treatment of borderline patients typically requires optimal flexibility on the part of a therapist to shift from a psychological to a medications-based treatment approach (Stone, 1990).

As might be expected, research comparing treatment outcomes for borderline, bipolar mood disorder, and schizophrenic patients found significantly better results for the bipolar and borderline patients than for the schizophrenic patients (McGlashan, 1986). Adjustment after discharge from the hospital was, nevertheless, rocky for the borderline patients, and they frequently required further hospitalization.

ANTISOCIAL PERSONALITY

As we have seen, the outstanding characteristics of antisocial personality disorder are a marked lack of ethical or moral development and an apparent inability to follow approved models of behavior. Basically, these individuals are unsocialized and seemingly incapable of significant loyalty to other people, groups, or social values. These characteristics often bring them into repeated conflict with society. The terms **psychopathic personality** and **sociopathic personality** are also commonly used in referring to this disorder.

The category called *antisocial personality* includes a mixed group of individuals: unprincipled business people, shyster lawyers, quack doctors, high-pressure evangelists, crooked politicians, impostors, drug pushers, a sizeable number of prostitutes, and assorted criminals. Few of these individuals find their way into community clinics or mental hospitals. A larger number are confined in penal institutions, but a history of repeated legal or social offenses is not sufficient justification for assuming that an individual is sociopathic. In point of fact, a large number of sociopathic individuals manage to stay out of correctional institutions, although they tend to be in constant conflict with authority (see *HIGHLIGHT 8.2*).

The prevalence of antisocial personality disorder—as reported in one large-scale epidemiological study (Robins et al., 1984)—is between 3.9 and 4.9 percent for males and less than .07 percent for females. Onset is in early childhood for males but typically not until puberty for females.

The Clinical Picture in Antisocial Personality

Often intelligent, spontaneous, and likeable on first acquaintance, antisocial personalities are deceitful and manipulative, callously using others to achieve their own ends. Often they seem to live in a series of

Wanted: Everyday Psychopaths

Most studies of antisocial personalities have been conducted on institutionalized individuals, leaving us ignorant about the far larger number who never get caught. Widom (1977) tried an ingenious approach for reaching this larger group. She ran advertisements in the local newspapers which read:

Are you adventurous? Psychologist studying adventurous, care- *free people who've led exciting, impulsive lives. If you're the kind of person who'd do almost anything for a dare and want to participate in a paid experiment, send name, address, phone, and short biography proving how interesting you are to. . . . (p. 675)*

Widom had hoped to attract antisocial individuals and apparently did just that. When given a bat- tery of tests, those who responded turned out to be similar in personality makeup to institutionalized psychopathic individuals. Although she did not go further than a personality assessment of these individuals, her method suggests a way of making contact with samples of uninstitutionalized antisocial personalities.

---

present moments, without consideration for the past or future. The following example is illustrative:

> *Two 18-year-old youths went to visit a teenager at her home. Finding no one there, they broke into the house, damaged a number of valuable paintings and other furnishings, and stole a quantity of liquor and a television set. They sold the TV to a mutual friend for a small sum of money. On their apprehension by the police, they at first denied the entire venture and then later insisted that it was all a "practical joke." They did not consider their behavior particularly inappropriate, nor did they think any sort of restitution for damage was called for.*

Also included in the general category of antisocial individuals are hostile, sociopathic people who are prone to acting out impulses in remorseless and often senseless violence. In other cases, antisocial individuals show periods of reliability and are capable of assuming responsibility and pursuing long-range goals, but they do so in unethical ways with a complete lack of consideration for the rights and well-being of others.

Only individuals 18 or over are diagnosed as antisocial personalities. According to the DSM-III-R classification, this diagnosis is made if the following criteria are met: (a) at least three instances of deviant behavior, such as theft, vandalism, or unusually aggressive actions, occur before age 15;

(b) at least four behavioral problems, such as financial irresponsibility, illegal occupation, ineffective functioning as a parent, or poor work history, occur after age 15, with no period longer than five years without such a problem; (c) the antisocial behavior endures, with no "remission" lasting longer than five years (unless the person is incapacitated or imprisoned); and (d) the antisocial behavior is not a symptom of another mental disorder.

To fill in the clinical picture, let us begin by summarizing characteristics that antisocial personalities tend to share. We will then describe a case

Delinquency can sometimes be a prelude to the development of antisocial personality disorder in adulthood. In many cases, however, delinquent behavior ends with adolescence.

that illustrates the wide range of behavioral patterns that may be involved.

Common Characteristics   While all the characteristics examined in the following sections are not usually found in a particular case, they are typical of antisocial personalities in general.

Inadequate conscience development.   Antisocial personalities are unable to understand and accept ethical values except on a verbal level. They make glib verbalizations and claims of adherence to high moral standards that have no apparent connection with their behavior. In short, though their intellectual development is typically normal or above, their conscience development is severely retarded or nonexistent.

Antisocial personalities tend to "act out" tensions and problems rather than worry them out. Their apparent lack of anxiety and guilt, combined with the appearance of sincerity and candor, may enable them to avoid suspicion and detection for stealing and other illegal activities. They often show contempt for those they are able to take advantage of—their "marks."

Irresponsible and impulsive behavior.   Antisocial individuals generally have a callous disregard for the rights, needs, and well-being of others. They have learned to take rather than earn what they want. Prone to thrill seeking and deviant and unconventional behavior, they often break the law impulsively and without regard for the consequences. They seldom forego immediate pleasure for future gains and long-range goals. They live in the present, without realistically considering either past or future. External reality is used for immediate personal gratification. Unable to endure routine or to shoulder responsibility, they frequently change jobs. Several studies have shown that antisocial personalities have high rates of alcoholism (Lewis, Robins, & Rice, 1985; Lewis, Cloninger, & Pais, 1983).

Ability to impress and exploit others.   Often antisocial individuals are charming and likeable, with a disarming manner that easily wins friends. Typically, they have a good sense of humor and an optimistic outlook. Though frequent liars, they usually will seem sincerely sorry if caught in a lie and promise to make amends—but not do so. They seem to have good insight into other people's needs and weaknesses and are adept at exploiting them. For example, many psychopathic individuals engage in unethical sales schemes in which they use their charm and the confidence they inspire in others to

Serial killer Ted Bundy, here shown on a TV monitor outside Florida State prison, exhibited antisocial behavior at its most extreme and dangerous. He had considerable good looks, charm, and intelligence, which masked violent impulses, manipulativeness, and a total lack of remorse for his victims. Bundy's clean-cut image, which he used to get close to his victims—all young women whom he sexually abused and then murdered—was so convincing as to be chilling when the magnitude of his acts became apparent. Bundy was electrocuted in Florida in 1989.

make "easy money." They readily find excuses and rationalizations for their antisocial conduct, typically projecting the blame onto someone else. Thus they are often able to convince other people—as well as themselves—that they are free of fault.

Rejection of authority.   Antisocial individuals behave as if social regulations do not apply to them: they do not play by the rules of the game. Frequently they have a history of difficulties with educational and law-enforcement authorities. Yet although they often drift into criminal activities, they are not typically calculating, professional criminals. Despite the difficulties they get into and the punishments they may receive, they go on behaving as if they are immune from the consequences of their actions.

Inability to maintain good relationships.   Although initially able to win the liking and friendship of other people, antisocial personalities are seldom able to keep close friends. Irresponsible and egocentric, they are usually cynical, unsympathetic, ungrateful, and remorseless in their dealings. They seemingly cannot understand love in others or give it in return. As Horton, Louy, and Coppolillo (1974) have expressed it, the psychopathic personality "continues to move through the world wrapped in his separateness as though in an insulator, touched rarely and never moved by his fellow man" (p. 622).

Antisocial personalities pose a menace not only to chance acquaintances but also to their family and friends. Violence toward family members is common. Herman (1986) reported that antisocial personality was the only clinical diagnosis found to be unusually frequent among males who were abusive toward others.

Manipulative and exploitive in sexual relationships, antisocial individuals are irresponsible and unfaithful mates. Although they often promise to change, they rarely do so for any considerable length of time.

Many of the preceding characteristics may be found in varying degrees in maladjusted individuals, in those dependent on drugs, and in those showing other maladaptive behavior patterns. In the case of antisocial personalities, however, these characteristics are extremely pronounced and occur apart from other "symptoms" of psychopathology. Whereas most maladjusted individuals, for example, are beset by worry and anxiety and have a tendency to avoid difficult situations, antisocial personalities act on their impulses fearlessly, with little or no thought for the difficulties they may be incurring.

Patterns of Behavior   The antisocial personality disorder is illustrated in the following case study published by Hare (1970):

Donald S., 30 years old, has just completed a three-year prison term for fraud, bigamy, false pretenses, and escaping lawful custody. The circumstances leading up to these offenses are interesting and consistent with his past behavior. With less than a month left to serve on an earlier 18-month term for fraud, he faked illness and escaped from the prison hospital. During the ten months of freedom that followed he engaged in a variety of illegal enterprises; the activity that resulted in his recapture was typical of his method of operation. By passing himself off as the "field executive" of an international philanthropic foundation, he was able to enlist the aid of several religious organizations in a fund-raising campaign. The campaign moved slowly at first, and in an attempt to speed things up, he

arranged an interview with the local TV station. His performance during the interview was so impressive that funds started to pour in. However, unfortunately for Donald, the interview was also carried on a national news network. He was recognized and quickly arrested. During the ensuing trial it became evident that he experienced no sense of wrongdoing for his activities. He maintained, for example, that his passionate plea for funds "primed the pump"—that is, induced people to give to other charities as well as to the one he professed to represent. At the same time, he stated that most donations to charity are made by those who feel guilty about something and who therefore deserve to be bilked. This ability to rationalize his behavior and his lack of self-criticism were also evident in his attempts to solicit aid from the very people he had misled. Perhaps it is a tribute to his persuasiveness that a number of individuals actually did come to his support. During his three-year prison term, Donald spent much time searching for legal loopholes and writing to outside authorities, including local lawyers, the Prime Minister of Canada, and a Canadian representative to the United Nations. In each case he verbally attacked them for representing the authority and injustice responsible for his predicament. At the same time he requested them to intercede on his behalf and in the name of the justice they professed to represent.

While in prison he was used as a subject in some of the author's research. On his release he applied for admission to a university and, by way of reference, told the registrar that he had been one of the author's research colleagues! Several months later the author received a letter from him requesting a letter of recommendation on behalf of Donald's application for a job.

Donald was the youngest of three boys born to middle-class parents. Both of his brothers led normal, productive lives. His father spent a great deal of time with his business; when he was home he tended to be moody and to drink heavily when things were not going right. Donald's mother was a gentle, timid woman who tried to please her husband and to maintain a semblance of family harmony. When she discovered her children engaged in some mischief, she would threaten to tell their father. However, she seldom carried out these threats because she did not want to disturb her husband and because his reactions were likely to be dependent on his mood at the time; on some occasions he would fly into a rage and beat the children and on others he would administer a verbal reprimand, sometimes mild and sometimes severe.

By all accounts Donald was considered a willful and difficult child. When his desire for candy or toys was frustrated he would begin with a show of affection, and if this failed he would throw a temper tantrum; the latter was seldom necessary because his angelic appearance and artful ways usually got him what he wanted. Similar tactics were used to avoid punishment for his numerous misdeeds. At first he would attempt to cover up with an elaborate facade of lies, often shifting the blame to his brothers. If this did not work, he would give a convincing display of remorse and contrition. When punishment was unavoidable he would become sullenly defiant, regarding it as an unjustifiable tax on his pleasures.

Although he was obviously very intelligent, his school years were academically undistinguished. He was restless, easily bored, and frequently truant. His behavior in the presence of the teacher or some other authority was usually quite good, but when he was on his own he generally got himself or others into trouble. Although he was often suspected of being the culprit, he was adept at talking his way out of difficulty.

Donald's misbehavior as a child took many forms including lying, cheating, petty theft, and the bullying of smaller children. As he grew older he became more and more interested in sex, gambling, and alcohol. When he was 14 he made crude sexual advances toward a younger girl, and when she threatened to tell her parents he locked her in a shed. It was about 16 hours before she was found. Donald at first denied knowledge of the incident, later stating that she had seduced him and that the door must have locked itself. He expressed no concern for the anguish experienced by the girl and her parents, nor did he give any indication that he felt morally culpable for what he had done. His parents were able to prevent charges being brought against him. Nevertheless, incidents of this sort were becoming more frequent and, in an attempt to prevent further embarrassment to the family, he was sent away to a private boarding school. . . .

When he was 17, Donald left the boarding school, forged his father's name to a large check, and spent about a year traveling around the world. He apparently lived well, using a combination of charm, physical attractiveness, and false pretenses to finance his way. During subsequent years he held a succession of jobs, never staying at any one for more than a few months. Throughout this period he was charged with a variety of crimes, including theft, drunkenness in a public place, assault, and many traffic violations. In most cases he was either fined or given a light sentence.

His sexual experiences were frequent, casual, and callous. When he was 22 he married a 41-year-old woman whom he had met in a bar. Several other marriages followed, all bigamous. In each case the pattern was the same: he would marry someone on impulse, let her support him for several months, and then leave. One marriage was particularly interesting. After being charged with fraud Donald was sent to a psychiatric institution for a period of observation. While there he came to the attention of a female member of the professional staff. His charm, physical attractiveness, and convincing promises to reform led her to intervene on his behalf. He was given a suspended sentence and they were married a week later. At first things went reasonably well, but when she refused to pay some of his gambling debts he forged her name to a check and left. He was soon caught and given an 18-month prison term. As mentioned earlier, he escaped with less than a month left to serve.

It is interesting to note that Donald sees nothing particularly wrong with his behavior, nor does he express remorse or guilt for using others and causing them grief. Although his behavior is self-defeating in the long run, he considers it to be practical and possessed of good sense. Periodic punishments do nothing to decrease his egotism and confidence in his own abilities, nor do they offset the often considerable short-term gains of which he is capable. However, these short-term gains are invariably obtained at the expense of someone else. In this respect his behavior is entirely egocentric, and his needs are satisfied without any concern for the feelings and welfare of others. (Hare, 1970, pp. 1–4)

The repetitive behavior pattern shown by Donald is common among individuals diagnosed as having an antisocial personality. Interestingly, many antisocial individuals do eventually settle down to responsible positions in their community. Furthermore, Brantley and Sutker (1984), in reviewing the literature on people with an antisocial personality, point out that—although much of the literature has focused on their negative aspects—these individuals also have positive qualities; as a group they seem to be

robust, socially facile and ingenious in many situations. . . . In fact, there are . . . data on which to build a case for their capacity to respond with appropriate emotional expression in most interpersonal situations. Certainly, the extreme cases among groups in which individuals are diagnosed as antisocial personality or sociopathic may represent the epitome of distaste for authority as well as disregard for the wishes of significant others in their lives. Among their ranks, however, are daring, adventuresome, resourceful persons who may have capabilities to outperform so-called normals when the going gets rough.

It is interesting to note that though high intelligence is characteristic of antisocial personality disorder, intelligence also seems to serve as a protective factor for most individuals at risk for antisocial behavior. Kandel et al. (1988), for example, found that many individuals predisposed to antisocial personality never get involved in criminal behavior because they become more reinforced by schooling. Thus they presumably focus their energies on more socially accepted behaviors.

■ Causal Factors in Antisocial Personality

As is the case with all the personality disorders discussed here, the causal factors in antisocial personality are still not fully understood. Our perspective is complicated by the fact that the causal factors involved appear to differ from case to case, as well as from one socioeconomic level to another. However, more research has been conducted on the antisocial personality than on any of the other personality disorders, so we do at least have a broader basis of data on which to draw. Contemporary research in this area has variously stressed the causal roles of constitutional deficiencies, the early learning of antisocial behavior as a coping style, and the influence of particular family and community patterns.

Biological Factors   Because an antisocial individual's impulsiveness, acting out, and intolerance of discipline tend to appear early in life, several investigators have focused on the role of biological factors as causative agents in antisocial behaviors. The following sections focus on some of these biological factors.

Deficient emotional arousal.   Research evidence indicates that a primary reaction tendency typically found in antisocial individuals is a deficient emotional arousal; this condition presumably renders them less prone to fear and anxiety in stressful situations and less prone to normal conscience development and socialization.

In an early study, for example, Lykken (1957) concluded that antisocial individuals have fewer inhibitions about committing antisocial acts because they suffer little anxiety. Similarly, Eysenck (1960) concluded that antisocial individuals are less sensitive to noxious stimuli and have a slower rate of conditioning than normal individuals. As a result, antisocial individuals presumably fail to acquire many of the conditioned reactions essential to normal avoidance behavior, conscience development, and socialization. Support for this viewpoint is found in a study by Chesno and Kilmann (1975), who concluded that sociopathic individuals, unlike normal people, "were relatively unsuccessful in acquiring active avoidance responses" (p. 150).

Hare (1970) and other later investigators have reported comparable findings with respect to antisocial individuals' lack of normal fear and anxiety reactions and failure to learn readily from punishments. The latter point merits qualification, however. Schmauk (1970) confirmed earlier observations that such individuals were less adept than nonantisocial individuals in learning to avoid physical and social punishments, but found them to be more adept than normal people in learning to avoid the loss of money—a type of punishment that was apparently *meaningful* to them. These findings are more understandable when it is added that the individuals observed in the experiment were inmates of a penal institution where physical and social punishments were relatively mild for most forms of misbehavior, whereas money was both hard to come by and valuable for obtaining niceties beyond the grim prison fare.

In addition, it should be noted that although the lack of normal emotional arousal may be based on constitutional deficiencies, it may also be based partially on learning. Antisocial individuals often manage to avoid the full consequences of their antisocial behavior by such devices as lies and plausible excuses, dramatic shows of remorse, and empty but convincing promises of "good" behavior in the future. In fact, the absence of anxieties attributed to these individuals has been questioned by Vaillant (1975), who believes that they have simply learned to handle their anxieties differently. In Vaillant's view, rather than succumb to their anxieties like individuals with anxiety-based disorders, they conceal them and in most cases find ways to escape from them. When they cannot flee, they may experience anxieties, but they hide their feelings. Vaillant believes that this concealment of anxieties was learned because the parents could not tolerate their own anxieties. He points out that escaping from anxiety-arousing situations is an immature behavior, such as is found in adolescence.

Stimulation seeking.   In his study of criminally antisocial individuals, Hare (1968) reported that they operate at low levels of arousal and are deficient in autonomic variability. He considered these characteristics—together with their lack of normal conditioning to noxious and painful stimuli—indicative of a "relative immunity" to stimulation, which in turn would likely prompt them to seek stimulations and thrills as ends in themselves. In a study comparing antisocial and normal individuals, Fenz (1971) also found that the former seemed to have an insatiable need for stimulation. Several other investigators, using Zuckerman's sensation-seeking scale (a scale that measures such characteristics [Zuckerman, 1972, 1978]), have noted that individuals involved in antisocial behaviors—such as prison escapes (Farley & Farley, 1972), drug use (Kilpatrick et al., 1976), and recurrent arrests among skid-row alcoholics (Malatesta, Sutker, & Treiber, 1981)—have higher sensation-seeking scores and low tolerances for boredom.

Such findings support the earlier view of Quay (1965), who concluded that antisocial behavior is, in essence, an extreme form of stimulation-seeking behavior:

The psychopath is almost universally characterized as highly impulsive, relatively refractory to the effects of experience in modifying his socially troublesome behavior, and lacking in the ability to delay gratification. His penchant for creating excitement for the moment without regard for later consequences seems almost unlimited. He is unable to tolerate routine boredom. While he may engage in antisocial, even vicious, behavior, his outbursts frequently appear to be motivated by little more than a need for thrills and excitement. . . . It is the impulsivity and the lack of even minimal tolerance for sameness which appear to be the primary and distinctive features of the disorder. (p. 180)

Such extreme stimulation seeking does not bode well in the total context of a personality also characterized as impulsive, lacking in judgment, deficient in inner reality and moral controls, and seemingly unable to learn from punishment and experience. Though further investigation is needed, it seems plausible that stimulation seeking "unchecked by conditioned fear response is a two-edged sword for antisocial behavior" (Borkovec, 1970, p. 222).

There is evidence that individuals involved in antisocial behaviors, such as playing with dangerous weapons, have an insatiable need for stimulation.

Deficits in cognitive functioning. Gorenstein (1982) raised the possibility that antisocial individuals have deficits in cognitive processes, such as attention to detail, reflecting dysfunctioning in the frontal-lobe area of the brain. He found that antisocial individuals tested in a psychiatric setting performed poorly on several cognitive measures of frontal lobe functioning compared to nonantisocial individuals. However, Hare (1984) disputed these results on grounds that the particular diagnostic procedures were inappropriate for testing frontal lobe functioning. In an attempt to replicate the Gorenstein study using similar procedures to test frontal-lobe functioning in a prison population, Hare did not find differences between antisocial and nonantisocial individuals. Hare suggested that narcotics abuse among antisocial individuals could explain the discrepant results. Gorenstein (1987), in a reanalysis of his data, found that the original findings held when narcotics abuse was controlled. Until more conclusive findings are available, the most appropriate conclusion appears to be that antisocial individuals in psychiatric settings exhibit cognitive or neurological deficits although many such individuals in prison do not.

Genetic influence. MacMillan and Kofoed (1984) provided an interesting sociobiological theory as a causal explanation for antisocial personality. Their view assumes a genetic influence on predispositions for particular behaviors. They maintain that because the goal of natural selection involves the spreading of genes into the next generation, an individual who maximizes the number of his or her offspring by "courting and copulating with multiple mates" is demonstrating the general characteristic of the "most fit" (in the Darwinian sense) of the species. In this scheme, antisocial personalities, especially males, are likely to be most successful in propagation. They are charming, have a lack of guilt and remorse, and are usually promiscuous. Moreover, they are likely to misrepresent themselves, in terms of status and resources, to quickly impress others in forming relations. MacMillan and Kofoed refer to this behavior as the "cheating strategy" and suggest that many individuals with antisocial personality disorders are generally adept at manipulating women for their own purposes. The validity of this viewpoint has not been studied; however, it provides some interesting leads for researchers to follow in further studies of antisocial personality. For example, it might be fruitful to assess the interpersonal attraction and "cheating" skills of antisocial personalities and relate these findings to other known aspects of antisocial behavior.

Family Relationships   Perhaps the most popular generalization about the development of an antisocial personality is the assumption of some form of early disturbance in family relationships. The following sections explore some of these disturbances.

Early parental loss and emotional deprivation. A number of early studies reported that an unusually high number of antisocial individuals had experienced the trauma of losing a parent at an early age—usually through the separation or divorce of their parents. For example, Greer (1964) found that 60 percent of one group of antisocial individuals he studied had lost a parent during childhood, as contrasted with 28 percent for a control group of other psychologically maladjusted individuals and 27 percent for a control group of normal subjects.

Because many normal people have experienced the loss of a parent at an early age, it seems that considerably more than parental loss is required to produce an antisocial personality. In reviewing the available evidence, Hare (1970) suggested that the factor of key significance was not the parental loss per se, but rather the emotional disturbances in family relationships created before the departure of a parent.

This point is supported by Wolkind (1974), who found a high incidence of "affectionless psychopathy" in a group of 92 institutionalized children. In many of these cases, the antisocial disorder seemed to have been caused by pathogenic family situations prior to the children's being placed in an institution.

Parental rejection and inconsistency. A number of studies have attempted to relate parental rejection and inconsistent discipline to inadequate socialization and antisocial personality. After an extensive review of the available literature, McCord and McCord (1964) concluded that severe parental rejection and lack of parental affection were the primary causes of antisocial personality.

Another aspect of this theory has been pointed out by Buss (1966), who concluded that two types of parental behavior foster antisocial personality. In the first, parents are cold and distant toward a child and do not allow a warm or close relationship to develop. A child who imitates this parental model will become cold and distant in later relationships;

although the child learns the formal attributes and amenities of social situations, he or she does not develop empathy for others or become emotionally involved with them.

The second type of parental behavior involves inconsistency, in which parents are capricious in supplying affection, rewards, and punishments. Usually they are inconsistent in their own role enactments as well, so that a child lacks stable models to imitate and fails to develop a clear-cut sense of self-identity. Often these parents reward not only "superficial conformity" but also "underhanded nonconformity"—that is, nonconformity that goes undetected by outsiders. Thus they reinforce behaviors that lead to antisocial behavior. Similarly, when parents are both arbitrary and inconsistent in punishing a child, avoiding punishment becomes more important than receiving rewards. Instead of learning to see behavior in terms of right and wrong, the child learns how to avoid blame and punishment by lying or other manipulative means.

In Chapter 4, we noted that slow conscience development and aggression are among the damaging effects of parental rejection and inconsistent discipline. We also noted that children subjected to inconsistent rewards and punishments for aggressive behavior were more resistant to efforts to extinguish the behavior than were children who experienced more consistent discipline. It seems desirable, however, to exercise caution in using parental rejection and inconsistency as basic explanations of antisocial personalities. For one, these same conditions have been implicated in a wide range of later maladaptive behaviors. In addition, many children coming from such family backgrounds do not become antisocial personalities or evidence other serious psychopathology. Thus further explanation is needed.

Faulty parental models and family interactions. In an early study of 40 male antisocial personalities, Heaver (1943) emphasized the influence exerted by faulty parental models—typically a mother who overindulged her son and a father who was highly successful, driving, critical, and distant.

Greenacre (1945) added a number of details that have been supported by later studies of antisocial individuals from middle-class families. The father is typically a successful and respected member of the community and is distant and fear inspiring to his children. The mother, on the other hand, is indulgent, pleasure loving, frivolous, and often tacitly contemptuous of her husband's importance. When such families are heavily dependent on the approval and admiration of their communities—as in the case of some clergy and politicians—it is crucial that they maintain the illusion of a happy family by concealing and denying any evidence of bickering or scandal. Thus the children learn that appearances are more important than reality, and they, too, become part of the show-window display, where a premium is put on charm and impressing others rather than on competence and integrity. This need to please and to win social approval for their parents' sake seems to bring out a precocious but superficial charm in some of these children, together with great adroitness in handling people for purely selfish ends.

A son in such a family cannot hope to emulate his successful and awe-inspiring father, but, aware that the high evaluation that is placed on his father extends to himself, he develops a feeling of importance and of being exempt from the consequences of his actions. Frequently the prominence of the father does, in fact, protect the child from the ordinary consequences of antisocial behavior. If we add one additional factor—the contradictory influence of a father who tells his son of the necessity for responsibility, honesty, and respect for others, but who himself is deceitful and manipulative—we appear to have a family background capable of producing a middle-class antisocial personality.

Supporting this explanation is Hare's (1970) finding of a high incidence of psychopathic personalities—particularly fathers—in the families of children who later manifest such behavior themselves. In this context, Hare concluded that "at least part of a psychopath's behavior results from modeling another individual's psychopathic behavior" (p. 107).

The intermittent reinforcement of short-term gains and success in avoiding punishment also make the antisocial life-style especially resistant to change. With relative freedom from anxiety, guilt, and remorse, little motivation exists to learn different patterns.

Sociocultural Factors   Antisocial personality is thought to be more common in lower socioeconomic groups. Although we have emphasized the part played by constitutional and family factors, it appears that social conditions such as those found in our urban ghettos also produce their share of antisocial individuals. An environment characterized by the breakdown of social norms and regulations,

An environment characterized by the breakdown of social norms, disorganization, undesirable peer models, and alienation may produce antisocial personalities.

disorganization, undesirable peer models, and pervasive alienation from and hostility toward the broader society seems to produce inadequate conscience development, lack of concern for others, and destructive behavior. On a family level, the picture is often aggravated by broken homes, parental rejection, and inconsistent discipline. These family situations lead to distrust, a confused sense of personal identity, self-devaluation, and feelings of hurt and hostility. The end result may be overtly aggressive behavior, directed especially at the representatives of "conventional" society.

In one high school in a disadvantaged area, two youths held a teacher while a third poured gasoline over him and set him on fire. Fortunately, another teacher came to the rescue and was able to extinguish the flames before the teacher was seriously burned. The youths were apprehended and detained in a juvenile facility because they were under 18 years of age. Interviewed by a social worker, they showed no remorse for their act, did not consider it wrong, and were disappointed that they had not succeeded in killing the teacher. The youths were not in any of his classes, nor did they know him personally. The apparent leader of the group stated that "Next time we'll do it right, so there won't be nobody left around to identify us."

Melges and Bowlby (1969) have pointed out that such individuals believe other people cannot be counted on and see their own futures as out of their hands. In essence, they feel helpless and hopeless— as well as resentful and hostile—in relation to their aversive life situations. Seeing no possible way they can make it, they lash out to make others suffer too.

Another possible explanation for the development of an antisocial personality has been suggested by Smith (1978). Smith believes that antisocial orientations are encouraged and rewarded by the materialistic, competitive, marketplace values of our capitalistic society. Antisocial individuals, he feels, simply carry these prevalent tendencies to extremes. While this view offers a plausible explanation for some typically antisocial behaviors, such as manipulativeness, superficial charm, and concern only for outward appearances, it does not seem sufficient to explain the extreme lawlessness and destructive behaviors that also accompany this disorder.

Although some cultural groups appear to have a relatively high rate of antisocial personality among their members, others have relatively low rates. Among the Hutterites, members of a relatively isolated religious sect who live on large communal farms in the Midwest, there is a negligible incidence of antisocial personality disorder. Perhaps the close-knit social structure with its strong emphasis on traditional values punishes or fails to reinforce the expression of antisocial behaviors. In addition, the adults to whom this group's children are exposed during their early development provide nonpsychopathic role models. The low rate of antisocial disorders among the Hutterites may also result from a natural selection process in which individuals who have deviant social characteristics leave the group so that neither they nor their offspring contribute to the statistics.

In summary, antisocial personalities are a mixed group of individuals who nevertheless have certain characteristics in common. Although the causal factors are not clear and may differ from case to case, varying combinations of biological, psychosocial, and sociocultural factors appear to be involved.

■ Treatments and Outcomes in Antisocial Personality

Because most individuals with antisocial personalities do not exhibit obvious psychopathology and can function effectively in many respects, they seldom come to the attention of mental hospitals or clinics. Those who run afoul of the law may participate in rehabilitation programs in penal institutions, but usually they are not changed by them. Even if more and better therapeutic facilities were available, effective treatment would still be a challenging task.

In general, traditional psychotherapeutic approaches have not proven effective in altering antisocial personalities. For example, in a treatment program for opiate addicts, those individuals with diagnosed personality disorders were the most difficult to treat and had the most negative outcomes—that is, they got worse or failed to improve (Woody et al., 1985). Factors inherent in antisocial individuals' personalities—the inability to trust, to feel as others do, to fantasize, and to learn from experience—apparently make the prognosis for psychotherapy very poor (Charney, 1979). Nor have biological treatment measures for psychopathic personalities—including electroconvulsive therapy or drugs—fared any better.

Perhaps the most promising treatment approach for antisocial personalities is behavioral therapy. Behavioral therapists have dealt successfully with specific antisocial behaviors, and their techniques appear to offer promise of more effective treatment (Bandura, 1969; Sutker, Archer, & Kilpatrick, 1979).

On the basis of a now-classic review of research findings, Bandura (1969) suggested three steps that can be used to modify antisocial behavior through the application of learning principles: (a) the withdrawal of meaningful reinforcements for antisocial behavior, and, where appropriate, the use of punishment for such behavior; (b) the modeling of desired behavior by *change agents*—the therapist and other behavioral models who are admired—and the use of a graded system of rewards or reinforcers for imitating such behavior; and (c) the reduction of material incentives and rewards as the individual's behavior is increasingly brought under the control of self-administered, symbolic rewards. Essentially, the objective is to effect the gradual transfer of evaluative and reinforcement functions from the environment to the antisocial individual by helping him or her develop inner controls that minimize the need for external ones.

An important facet of this approach is providing situations in which one individual's improved behavior becomes a model for others in treatment. Patients can thus function as change agents for each other while furthering the long-range modification of their own behaviors. Such a program requires a controlled situation in which the therapist can administer or withhold reinforcement and the individual cannot run away.

The necessity of having a controlled situation seems paramount for greater success in treatment. When treating antisocial behavior, we are dealing with a total life-style rather than with a specific maladaptive behavior, like a phobia, which can be targeted for treatment. Without a controlled situation, the intermittent reinforcement of short-term gains and successful avoidance of punishments, combined with a lack of anxiety and guilt, leave an antisocial individual with little motivation to change.

Vaillant (1975), for example, believes that antisocial individuals can be effectively treated *only* in settings where behavioral control is possible—in other words, treating sociopaths on an outpatient basis is doomed to failure. He has found control necessary, also, to prevent self-destructive behaviors and to overcome these individuals' fears of intimacy. Like other investigators, he has concluded that punishment is ineffective for controlling antisocial behavior and that severely antisocial individuals "should work for liberty, not pay for past mistakes."

Vaillant also pointed out that one-to-one therapeutic relationships (even meeting several times a week) were rarely adequate to change sociopathic behavior. What seemed to work best was group membership that provided both an opportunity to learn to care for others and a place to be accepted by peers.

Fortunately, many antisocial personalities improve after the age of 40 even without treatment, possibly because of weaker biological drives, better insight into their self-defeating behaviors, and the cumulative effects of social conditioning. Such individuals are often referred to as "burned-out psychopaths." Hare, McPherson, and Forth (1988) recently confirmed the hypothesis that antisocial individuals tend to burn out over time. They followed up a group of male antisocial personalities and tracked their criminal careers beyond age 40. They found a clear and dramatic reduction in criminal behavior after age 40. They were quick to note, however, that even with this reduction in criminal behavior, over 50 percent of these individuals continued being arrested after age 40. Even with the prospect that they might eventually engage in less destructive behavior, antisocial individuals can create a great deal of havoc before they reach 40—as well as afterward if they do not change. In view of the distress and unhappiness they inflict on others and the social damage they cause, it seems desirable—and more economical in the long run—to put increased effort into the development of effective treatment programs.

UNRESOLVED ISSUES
on Axis II of DSM-III-R

While reading this chapter, you may have had some difficulty in capturing a clear, distinctive picture of each of the personality disorders. Possibly, as you studied the descriptions of the different disorders, the characteristics and attributes of some of them, say the schizoid personality disorder, seemed to blend with other conditions, such as the schizotypal or avoidant disorders. You certainly are not alone in this difficulty. Even expert clinicians often disagree and will arrive at different conclusions about an Axis II diagnosis on the same patient. In other words, Axis II diagnoses are considerably less reliable than diagnoses made for Axis I disorders.

Axis II diagnoses are unreliable for several reasons. One major difficulty lies in the classification process used in grouping the disorders. As noted in Chapter 1, some aspects of the diagnostic process are best thought of in terms of dimensions of behavior rather than categories of behavior. The personality processes classified on Axis II are dimensional in nature; that is, the data on which Axis II classifications are made are underlying personality traits that vary in individuals in terms of degree. For example, the trait of suspiciousness, central to paranoid personality disorder, can be viewed as a personality dimension on which essentially all people can be rated or given scores. The scores might range, on an illustrative "scale of suspiciousness," as follows:

Extremely Low	Low	Average	High	Extremely High

| 0 | 10 | 20 | 30 | 40 | 50 | 60 | 70 | 80 | 90 | 100 |

It is rather arbitrary to take the presence of "suspiciousness" as a criterion of paranoid personality disorder since it exists, to some extent, as a trait in virtually everyone. No attempt is made in the DSM-III-R categorization to quantify this trait or provide a means of grading the degree of suspiciousness; instead, all traits are forced into discrete categories or types.

A second problem inherent in Axis II classifications involves the fact that traits that are highly correlated with other traits may be seen as symptoms and treated as though they are mutually exclusive behaviors for a personality disorder. However, the same or other correlated traits may be used in the classification of other, different diagnoses. For example, suspiciousness, a defining characteristic of paranoid personality, may be correlated with avoidance, which is a defining characteristic of avoidant personality disorder. The DSM-III-R personality disorders are thus not based on mutually exclusive criteria.

Both researchers and clinicians are somewhat dissatisfied with Axis II. This situation is due, in part, to the difficulties in applying the system and to its relative unreliability. Penna (1986), for example, called Axis II "one of the most unsatisfactory links in DSM-III." He concluded that the specificity of the criteria for disorders varies widely and results in low confidence in the application of some personality disorder categories. Moreover, in actual clinical practice, the multiaxial system is seldom applied to its fullest. While Axis I is usually recorded on patients' charts (because it is required for insurance and administrative purposes), other axes, including Axis II, are frequently omitted because their concepts are vague and because they are viewed as inessential to the immediate classification requirements.

The developers of DSM-III made an important theoretical leap when they recognized the importance of weighing premorbid personality factors in the clinical picture and thus developed the second axis. Practiced employment of the Axis II concepts can lead to a better understanding of a case, particularly with regard to treatment outcomes. Strong, ingrained personality characteristics can work against treatment interventions. The use of Axis II forces a clinician to attend to these long-standing and difficult-to-change personality factors in planning treatment.

What can be done to resolve the difficulties with Axis II? One possible solution involves the psychiatric community's giving up on the typological approach to classification in favor of a dimensional approach and developing rating methods that would take into account the relative "amounts" of given traits shown by patients. It is not likely, however, that the dimensional approach to personality measurement will supplant the present categorical system, because sound quantitative rating would likely involve far too much time for most busy clinicians to apply it. In addition, as we saw in Chapter 1, medically oriented practitioners have a pronounced preference for categorical diagnosis.

If the present categorical classification system continues to be used, a clearer set of classification rules is needed to make the categories more accurate and more mutually exclusive. The classification rules should be made more exhaustive and incorporate behaviors that do not overlap with other categories. Such an undertaking, while scientifically desirable, would doubtless be extremely difficult— perhaps, in the final analysis, impossible. There appear to be few if any "pure" clusters for grouping people's behaviors into the type of neat pigeonholes ideally required by the categorical approach.

In sum, the ultimate status of Axis II in future editions of the DSM is uncertain. Many problems inherent in using typological classes for essentially dimensional behavior (traits) have yet to be resolved. Whether Axis II will survive in its present form and remain an integral part of future diagnosis is, according to some predictions, open to debate.

SUMMARY

Personality disorders, in general, appear to be extreme or exaggerated patterns of personality traits that predispose an individual to troublesome behavior—often of an interpersonal nature. A number of personality disorders have been delineated in which there are persistent maladaptive patterns of perceiving, thinking, and relating to the environment. Three general clusters of personality disorders have been described. Individuals with paranoid, schizoid, and schizotypal personality disorders seem odd or eccentric; individuals with histrionic, narcissistic, antisocial, and borderline personality disorders share a common tendency to be dramatic, emotional, and erratic; and individuals with avoidant, dependent, obsessive-compulsive, and passive-aggressive personality disorders, unlike those with the previous disorders, show fearfulness or tension as in anxiety-based disorders. Two new and somewhat controversial personality disorders are listed for further study in the appendix of DSM-III-R: the self-defeating and sadistic personality disorders. The acceptability and utility of these disorders by practicing clinicians has not yet been determined. Each of these disorders reflect characteristics such as immaturity, self-centeredness, lack of feeling for others, manipulativeness, and a tendency to act out and to project blame for problems and frustrations onto others.

For many of the personality disorders, little research into causality has been conducted. One of the most notable of the personality disorders is the antisocial, or psychopathic, personality. In this disorder, an individual is callous and unethical, without loyalty or close relationships, but often with superficial charm and intelligence. Both constitutional and learning factors seem to be important in causing the disorder. Some evidence suggests that genetic factors may predispose an individual to develop this disorder. Unlike the anxiety-based disorders described in Chapter 6, an antisocial individual does not appear to experience anxiety. The disorder often begins and is recognized in childhood or adolescence, but only individuals who are 18 or over are given the diagnosis of antisocial personality.

Treatment of these individuals is difficult, because they rarely see any need for self-change and tend to blame other people for their problems. Traditional psychotherapy is typically ineffective, but where control is possible, as in institutional settings, newer methods incorporating meaningful reinforcement and behavioral modification have had some success.

Key Terms

personality (p. 263)
personality disorders (character disorders) (p. 263)
temperament (character traits) (p. 264)
paranoid personality disorder (p. 267)
schizoid personality disorder (p. 268)
schizotypal personality disorder (p. 269)
histrionic personality disorder (p. 270)
narcissistic personality disorder (p. 271)
antisocial personality disorder (p. 272)
borderline personality disorder (p. 273)
avoidant personality disorder (p. 274)
dependent personality disorder (p. 275)
obsessive-compulsive personality disorder (p. 276)
passive-aggressive personality disorder (p. 276)
self-defeating personality disorder (p. 277)
sadistic personality disorder (p. 278)
psychopathic personality (sociopathic personality) (p. 281)

Chapter 9
Substance-Use and Other Addictive Disorders

Guillaume Pujolle, *Les Aigles—La Plume d'Oie* (1940). Pujolle (1893–?) was born in the Haute-Garonne area in France. A joiner by trade, he was torn by emotional conflicts and was eventually admitted to a hospital in Toulouse. He began to draw in 1935. His pictures (such as the one here) have a dream-like, fluid appearance, composed as they are of a mosaic of broad, undulating strips of color.

Cambyses, King of Persia in the sixth century B.C., has the dubious distinction of being one of the first alcoholics on record. People of many other early cultures, including the Egyptian, Greek, and Roman, made extensive and often excessive use of alcohol. Beer was first made in Egypt around 3000 B.C. The oldest surviving wine-making formulas were recorded by Marcus Cato in Italy almost a century and a half before the birth of Christ. About 800 A.D., the process of distillation was developed by an Arabian alchemist, thus making possible an increase in both the range and the potency of alcoholic beverages.

Addictive behavior, behavior based on the pathological need for a substance or activity, may involve the abuse of substances, such as alcohol or cocaine, or the excessive ingestion of high-caloric food, resulting in extreme obesity. Addictive behavior is one of the most pervasive and intransigent mental health problems facing our society today. Addictive disorders represent disorders of self-control and can be seen all around us: in extremely high rates of alcoholism, in tragic exposés of cocaine abuse among star athletes and entertainers, and in reports of the "epidemic" proportions of eating disorders.

The most commonly used problem drugs are the **psychoactive drugs,** those drugs that affect mental functioning: alcohol, barbiturates, minor tranquilizers, amphetamines, heroin, and marijuana. Some of these drugs, such as alcohol, can be purchased legally by adults; others, such as the barbiturates, can be used legally under medical supervision; still others, such as heroin, are illegal.

The diagnostic classification of addictive or psychoactive substance-use disorders is divided into two major categories. First, psychoactive substance-induced organic mental disorders and syndromes (the latter of which are included within the organic mental disorders) are those conditions that involve *organic impairment* resulting from the ingestion of psychoactive substances. These conditions involve such factors as **toxicity,** the poisonous nature of the substance (leading to, for example, amphetamine delusional disorder, alcoholic intoxication, or cannabis delirium), or physiologic changes in the brain due to vitamin deficiency (resulting in, for example, alcohol disorder involving amnesia, also known as Korsakoff's syndrome).

A number of addictive disorders are covered in the second category, which focuses on the maladaptive *behaviors* resulting from regular and consistent use of a substance and includes psychoactive substance-abuse and -dependence disorders. This category is further subdivided into two general groups: substance abuse and substance dependence. **Psychoactive substance abuse** generally involves a pathological use of a substance resulting in potentially hazardous behavior, such as driving while intoxicated, or in continued use despite a persistent social, psychological, occupational, or health problem. **Psychoactive substance dependence** includes more severe forms of substance-use disorders and usually involves a physiological need for a substance. Dependence in these disorders means that an individual will show either **tolerance** for a drug or **withdrawal symptoms** when the drug is unavailable. (Tolerance refers to the need for increased amounts of a substance to achieve the desired effects; withdrawal symptoms are physical symptoms, such as sweating, tremors, and tension, that accompany abstinence from the drug.)

The increasing problem of substance abuse and dependence in our society has drawn both public and scientific attention. Although our present knowledge is far from complete, investigating these problems as maladaptive patterns of adjustment to life's demands, with no social stigma involved, has led to clear progress in understanding and treatment. Such an approach, of course, does not mean that an individual bears no personal responsibility in the development of a problem; the widespread notion that drug dependence and abuse can be viewed as forms of "disease" does not imply that the individual is a passive participant in the addiction process. Individual life-styles and personality features are thought by many to play important roles in the development of addictive disorders and are central themes in some types of treatment.

In addition to the abuse and dependence disorders that involve particular substances, there are disorders that have all the features of an addictive condition, such as excessive eating, but do not involve substances with chemically addicting properties (Orford, 1985). Two of these disorders, excessive overeating and pathological gambling, are discussed in this chapter because the maladaptive behaviors involved and the treatment approaches shown to be effective suggest that they are quite similar to the various drug-use and drug-induced disorders.

ALCOHOL ABUSE AND DEPENDENCE

The terms *alcoholic* and *alcoholism* have been subject to some controversy and are used differently by various groups. The World Health Organization, for instance, uses the term *alcoholic* to refer to any person with life problems related to alcohol. The National Council on Alcoholism, on the other hand, uses a more restrictive definition; certain diagnostic signs delineating the extent and severity of abuse must be present for an individual to be classified as an alcoholic. Some behavioral researchers recommend a still more restrictive definition; they prefer to use the term *problem drinker* for most alcohol abusers, conceptualizing drinking as a continuum, with alcoholics constituting a small subgroup at one extreme and nondrinkers at the other (Miller, 1979; Miller & Caddy, 1977). In this chapter we will use the definition of The President's Commission on Mental Health (1978), which uses the term **alcoholic** to refer to an individual with a serious drinking problem, whose drinking impairs his or her life adjustment in terms of health, personal relationships, and occupational functioning. Likewise, the term **alcoholism** refers to a dependence on alcohol that seriously interferes with life adjustment.

However defined, alcoholism is a major problem in the United States. Per capita alcohol consumption increased nearly 50 percent over the past generation (Heckler, 1983). Alcohol is the most commonly abused substance in the United States; approximately 7 percent of all adults age 18 or older, about 10 million people, are problem drinkers (Smith, 1989). Yet only about 1 million of these individuals currently receive treatment for their drinking problems.

The potentially detrimental effects of excessive alcohol use—for an individual, his or her loved ones, and society—are legion. The life span of the average alcoholic is about 12 years shorter than that of the average citizen, and alcohol now ranks as the third major cause of death in the United States, behind coronary heart disease and cancer. Over 37 percent of alcohol abusers suffer from at least one coexisting mental disorder (Rovner, 1990). Organic impairment, including brain shrinkage, occurs in a high proportion of alcoholics (Lishman, Jacobson, & Acker, 1987).

About 10 percent of alcoholics commit suicide (Miles, 1977), and over 18 percent are found to

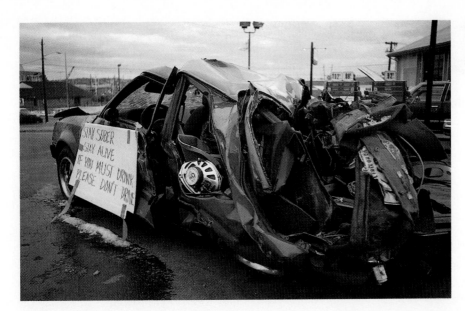

Alcohol is associated with over half of the deaths and serious injuries suffered in automobile accidents in the United States each year.

have a history of suicide attempts (Black et al., 1986). Recent research (Murphy, 1988; Rich et al., 1988) has reaffirmed the strong relationship found between substance abuse and suicide. The increased suicide rates among the young during the 1970s and 1980s have been tied to alcohol and drug abuse. Gomberg (1989) reported that, of women experiencing psychological difficulties, a significantly higher percentage with alcohol problems (40%) had attempted suicide than had women without alcohol problems (8.8%). In a follow-up study of mortality in psychiatric outpatients, Martin et al. (1985) found that alcoholics were in the group of disorders with highest mortality rates. Bengelsdorf (1970a) has pointed out that ". . . its abuse has killed more people, sent more victims to hospitals, generated more police arrests, broken up more marriages and homes, and cost industry more money than has the abuse of heroin, amphetamines, barbiturates, and marijuana combined" (p. 7).

In addition to the serious problems they create for themselves, excessive drinkers pose serious difficulties for others. About 10 percent of all deaths each year are related to alcohol abuse (Smith, 1989). Alcohol abuse is associated with over half the deaths and major injuries suffered in automobile accidents each year, and with about 50 percent of all murders, 40 percent of all assaults, 35 percent or more of all rapes, and 30 percent of all suicides. About one out of every three arrests in the United States are related to alcohol abuse. Alcohol-related accidents are, in fact, the leading cause of death among college-age people (NIDA, 1981). The financial drain imposed on the economy by alcoholism is estimated to be over $49.4 billion a year, in large part composed of losses to industry from absenteeism, lowered work efficiency, accidents, and the costs involved in the treatment of alcoholics. Alcohol use has also been found to play a role in victimization. A recent study showed that 46 percent of homicide victims in the city of Los Angeles had detectable blood-alcohol levels, and in 30 percent of the victims, the count of alcohol in their blood qualified them as legally drunk (Goodman et al., 1986). The authors hypothesized that alcohol could increase the likelihood of risk taking and could result in provocative behavior on the victim's part. In a follow-up study of alcoholics, Polich, Armor, and Braiker (1981) found that 14.5 percent of their subjects had died during the 4½-year period since the study began. These deaths were attributed to alcohol-related conditions, such as cirrhosis, suicide, gastrointestinal hemorrhage, and automobile accidents.

Alcoholism in the United States cuts across all age, educational, occupational, and socioeconomic boundaries. It is considered a serious problem in industry, in the professions, and in the military; it is found among such seemingly unlikely candidates as priests, airline pilots, politicians, surgeons, law enforcement officers, and teenagers. The once popular image of the alcoholic as an unkempt resident of skid row is clearly inaccurate. Further myths about alcoholism are noted in *HIGHLIGHT 9.1*.

The great majority of problem drinkers are men and women who are married and living with their families, who hold jobs—often important ones—and who are accepted members of their communities. Although alcoholism has traditionally been considered to be more common among males than females, alcohol abuse among women appears to be

HIGHLIGHT 9.1

Some Common Misconceptions About Alcohol and Alcoholism

Fiction	Fact
Alcohol is a stimulant.	Alcohol is actually a nervous system depressant.
You can always detect alcohol on the breath of a person who has been drinking.	It is not always possible to detect the presence of alcohol. Some individuals successfully cover up their alcohol use for years.
One ounce of 86-proof liquor contains more alcohol than two 12-ounce cans of beer.	Actually two 12-ounce cans of beer contain *more* than an ounce of alcohol.
Alcohol can help a person sleep more soundly.	Alcohol may actually interfere with sound sleep.
Impaired judgment does not occur before there are obvious signs of intoxication.	In fact, impaired judgment can occur long before motor signs of intoxication are apparent.
An individual will get more intoxicated by mixing liquors than by taking comparable amounts of one kind—e.g., bourbon, Scotch, or vodka.	It is the actual amount of alcohol in the bloodstream rather than the mix that determines intoxication.
Drinking several cups of coffee can counteract the effects of alcohol and enable a drinker to "sober up."	Drinking coffee does not affect the level of intoxication.
Exercise or a cold shower helps speed up the metabolism of alcohol.	Exercise and cold showers are futile attempts to increase alcohol metabolism.
People with "strong wills" need not be concerned about becoming alcoholics.	Alcohol is seductive and can lower the resistance of even the "strongest will."
Alcohol cannot produce a true addiction in the same sense that heroin can.	Alcohol has strong addictive properties.
One cannot become an alcoholic by drinking just beer.	One can consume a considerable amount of alcohol by drinking beer. It is, of course, the amount of alcohol that determines whether one becomes an alcoholic.
Alcohol is far less dangerous than marijuana.	There are considerably more individuals in treatment programs for alcohol problems than for marijuana abuse.
In a heavy drinker, damage to the liver shows up long before brain damage appears.	Heavy alcohol use can be manifested in organic brain damage before liver damage is detected.
The physiological withdrawal reaction from heroin is considered more dangerous than is withdrawal from alcohol.	The physiological symptoms accompanying withdrawal from heroin are no more frightening or traumatic to an individual than alcohol withdrawal.

growing. The commonly used incidence figure of 5 males to 1 female is considered a conservative estimate (Smith, 1989). A survey by Celentano and McQueen (1978) showed that of 81 percent of the men who drank alcohol, 26 percent considered themselves heavy drinkers; of 68 percent of the women who drank, 8 percent considered themselves heavy drinkers. It appears, too, that problem drinking may develop during any life period from early childhood through old age. Mann, Chassin, and Sher (in press) report that 64.9 percent of their sample of high school students indicated a moderate use of alcohol and 18.8 percent of these reported a misuse of alcohol. Some evidence also indicates that the rates of alcoholism among rural populations, particularly rural blacks, is higher than among urban dwellers. Blazer, Crowell, and George (1987) recently conducted an epidemiological survey showing that adults living in rural communities disclosed almost twice as many alcohol-related problems as a matched sample of urban residents.

■ The Clinical Picture of Alcohol Abuse and Dependence

The Roman poet Horace, in the first century B.C., wrote lyrically about the effects of wine: "It discloses secrets; ratifies and confirms our hopes; thrusts the coward forth to battle; eases the anxious mind of its burthen; instructs in arts. Whom has not a cheerful glass made eloquent! Whom not quite free and easy from pinching poverty!" Unfortunately, the effects of alcohol are not always so benign or beneficial. According to a Japanese proverb, "First the man takes a drink, then the drink takes a drink, and then the drink takes the man."

Alcohol is a depressant that affects the higher brain centers, impairing judgment and other rational processes and lowering self-control. As behavioral restraints decline, a drinker may indulge in the satisfaction of impulses ordinarily held in check. Some degree of motor incoordination soon becomes apparent, and the drinker's discrimination and perception of cold, pain, and other discomforts are dulled. Typically the drinker experiences a sense of warmth, expansiveness, and well-being. In such a mood, unpleasant realities are screened out and the drinker's feelings of self-esteem and adequacy rise. Casual acquaintances become the best and most understanding of friends, and the drinker enters a generally pleasant world of unreality in which worries are temporarily left behind.

When the alcohol content of the bloodstream reaches 0.1 percent, the individual is considered to be intoxicated. Muscular coordination, speech, and vision are impaired, and thought processes are confused. Even before this level of intoxication is reached, however, judgment becomes impaired to such an extent that the person misjudges his or her condition. For example, drinkers tend to express confidence in their ability to drive safely long after such actions are in fact quite unsafe. Although it differs somewhat between individuals, when the blood-alcohol level reaches approximately 0.5 percent, the entire neural balance is upset and the individual passes out. Unconsciousness apparently acts as a safety device, because concentrations above 0.55 percent are usually lethal. *HIGHLIGHT 9.2* provides additional information on alcohol levels in the blood and their effects on individual behavior.

In general, it is the amount of alcohol actually concentrated in the bodily fluids, not the amount consumed, that determines intoxication. The ef-

fects of alcohol, however, vary for different drinkers, depending on physical condition, gender, amount of food in the stomach, and duration of the drinking. In addition, alcohol users may gradually build up a tolerance for the drug so that ever-increasing amounts may be needed to produce the desired effects. Drinkers' attitudes are important, too: although actual motor and intellectual abilities decline in direct ratio to the blood concentration of alcohol, many people who consciously try to do so can maintain *apparent* control over their behavior, showing few outward signs of being intoxicated even after drinking relatively large amounts of alcohol.

Exactly how alcohol works on the brain is not yet fully understood, but several physiological effects are common. One is a tendency toward increased sexual stimulation but, simultaneously, lowered sexual performance. As Shakespeare wrote in *Macbeth,* alcohol "provokes the desire, but it takes away the performance."

Second, an appreciable number of problem drinkers also experience blackouts—lapses of memory. At first these occur at high blood-alcohol levels, and individuals may carry on rational conversations and engage in other relatively complex activities but have no trace of recall the next day. For heavy drinkers, even moderate drinking can elicit memory lapses.

A third curious phenomenon associated with alcoholic intoxication is the hangover, which many drinkers experience at one time or another. Some

Drinkers' attitudes can influence the effects of alcohol. At BARLAB, a mock bar used as part of a University of Washington class, students feel and act drunk even though they are unknowingly drinking beer that does not contain alcohol.

Alcohol Levels in the Blood After Drinks Taken on an Empty Stomach by a 150–pound Male Drinking for One Hour

Effects	Time for Alcohol to Leave the Body (Hours)	Alcohol Concentration in Blood (Percent)	Amount of Beverage
Slight changes in feeling	1	0.03	1 highball (1½ oz. whiskey) *or* 1 cocktail (1½ oz. whiskey) *or* 5½ oz. ordinary wine *or* 1 bottle beer (12 oz.)
Feeling of warmth, mental relaxation	2	0.06	2 highballs *or* 2 cocktails *or* 11 oz. ordinary wine *or* 2 bottles beer
Exaggerated emotion and behavior—talkative, noisy, or morose	4	0.07	3 highballs *or* 3 cocktails *or* 16½ oz. ordinary wine *or* 4 bottles beer
Clumsiness—unsteadiness in standing or walking	6	0.12	4 highballs *or* 4 cocktails *or* 22 oz. ordinary wine *or* 6 bottles beer
Gross intoxication	10	0.15	5 highballs *or* 5 cocktails *or* 27½ oz ordinary wine *or* ½ pint whiskey

Calories

5½ oz. wine	115
12 oz. beer	170
1½ oz. whisky	120

Note: Blood-alcohol level following given intake differs according to a person's weight, the length of the drinking time, and the person's sex.

Time, April 22, 1974, p. 77.

observers consider the hangover to be a mild form of withdrawal. As yet, no one has come up with a satisfactory explanation or remedy for the symptoms of headache, nausea, and fatigue characteristic of the hangover.

Development of Alcohol Dependence   Excessive drinking can be viewed as progressing insidiously from early- to middle- to late-stage alcoholism, although some alcoholics do not follow this progressively developing pattern. (*HIGHLIGHT 9.3* presents some of the common early warning signs

of excessive drinking.) Alcohol dependence is reached when symptoms of alcohol tolerance or alcohol withdrawal can be identified. Some investigators view alcohol dependence as recognizable through a number of related symptoms of alcohol use. In their extensive study of the "natural course of alcoholism," Polich et al. (1981) evaluated the presence of alcohol-dependence symptoms among drinkers in their sample of identified alcoholics and found the following percentages of individuals reporting the occurrence of certain symptoms in a 30-day period:

Early Warning Signs of Drinking Problems

1. *Frequent desire*—increase in desire, often evidenced by eager anticipation of drinking after work and careful attention to maintaining supply.
2. *Increased consumption*—increase that seems gradual but is marked from month to month. An individual may begin to worry at this point and lie about the amount consumed.
3. *Extreme behavior*—commission of various acts that leave an individual feeling guilty and embarrassed the next day.
4. *"Pulling blanks"*—inability to remember what happened during an alcoholic bout.
5. *Morning drinking*—either as a means of reducing a hangover or as a "bracer" to help start the day.

A person who exhibits this pattern is well on the road to abusive drinking. The progression is likely to be facilitated if there is environmental support for heavy or excessive drinking from the person's spouse, job situation, or sociocultural setting.

- Tremors (had the "shakes")   31
- Morning drinking (had a drink as soon as they woke up)   41
- Loss of control (tried to stop drinking but couldn't)   32
- Blackouts (memory lapses)   29
- Missing meals (missed a meal because of drinking)   42
- Continuous drinking (12 hours or more)   37
- One or more of the above symptoms   64

The researchers concluded that these secondary symptoms of dependence could not be viewed as isolated events but rather as related problems.

Chronic Alcohol Use and Dependence

Although many investigators have maintained that alcohol is a dangerous systemic poison even in small amounts, in moderate amounts it is not harmful to most people and may actually be beneficial to reduce the tensions of everyday life (HEW, 1974). For pregnant women, however, even moderate amounts are believed to be dangerous; in fact, no safe level has been established, as is discussed in *HIGHLIGHT 9.4*.

For individuals who drink immoderately, the clinical picture is highly unfavorable. For one, the alcohol that is taken in must be assimilated by the body, except for about 5 to 10 percent that is eliminated through breath, urine, and perspiration. The work of assimilation is done by the liver, but when large amounts of alcohol are ingested, the liver may be seriously overworked and eventually suffer irreversible damage. In fact, over time, an excessive drinker has a 1-in-10 chance of developing cirrhosis of the liver, a pathological condition in which liver cells are irreparably damaged and replaced by fibrous scar tissue. This results in the death of over 63,000 people each year (Smith, 1989).

Alcohol is also a high-calorie drug. A pint of whiskey—enough to make about 8 to 10 ordinary cocktails—provides about 1200 calories, which is approximately half the ordinary caloric requirement for a day. Thus consumption of alcohol reduces a drinker's appetite for other food. Because alcohol has no nutritional value, the excessive drinker often suffers from malnutrition. Furthermore, heavy drinking impairs the body's ability to utilize nutrients, so the nutritional deficiency cannot be made up by popping vitamins. The excessive intake of alcohol also impairs the activity of the white blood cells in fighting disease and is associated with a greatly increased risk of cancer (HEW, 1974).

In addition to the other problems, an excessive drinker usually suffers from chronic fatigue, oversensitivity, and depression. Initially, alcohol may seem to provide a useful crutch for dealing with the stresses of life, especially during periods of acute stress, by helping screen out intolerable realities and enhancing the drinker's feelings of adequacy and worth. The excessive use of alcohol becomes counterproductive, however, resulting in lowered feelings of adequacy and worth, impaired reasoning and judgment, and gradual personality deterioration. Behavior typically becomes coarse and inappropriate, and the drinker assumes increasingly less responsibility, loses pride in personal appearance, neglects spouse and family, and becomes generally

Fetal Alcohol Syndrome: How Much Drinking Is Too Much?

Research indicates that heavy drinking by expectant mothers can affect the health of unborn babies. Newborn infants whose mothers drank heavily during pregnancy have been found to have frequent physical and behavioral abnormalities. For example, such infants are lighter and smaller than average and sometimes show facial and limb irregularities (Jones & Smith, 1975; NIMH, 1978a; Jones, Smith, & Hansen, 1976; and Streissguth, 1976). In fact, *The Third Report on Alcohol and Health* (HEW, 1978) reports that alcohol abuse in pregnant women is the third-leading cause of birth defects (the first two being Down syndrome and spina bifida, the latter referring to the incomplete formation and fusion of the spinal canal).

How much drinking endangers a newborn's health? The HEW report warns against drinking more than one ounce of alcohol per day or the equivalent (two 12-ounce cans of beer or two 5-ounce glasses of wine, for example). The actual amount of alcohol that can safely be ingested during pregnancy is not known, but it is clear that existing evidence for fetal alcohol syndrome is strongest when applied to heavy alcohol users rather than light to moderate users (Kolata, 1981b). Nonetheless, the American Medical Association (1982) has approved a report recommending that pregnant women abstain from using alcohol as the "safest course" until safe amounts of alcohol consumption can be determined.

touchy, irritable, and unwilling to discuss the problem.

As judgment becomes impaired, an excessive drinker may be unable to hold a job and generally becomes unqualified to cope with new demands that arise. General personality disorganization and deterioration may be reflected in loss of employment and marital breakup. By this time, the drinker's general health is likely to have deteriorated, and brain and liver damage may have occurred. For example, Golden et al. (1981) found significant structural changes in the left hemisphere of the brains of chronic alcoholics. Lishman (1990) indicated that evidence is beginning to show that an alcoholic's brain could be accumulating diffuse organic damage—even in cases in which no extreme organic symptoms are evident. Goldman, Williams, and Klisz (1983) found that alcoholics over age 40 failed to recover from visual-spatial brain dysfunction as readily as did younger alcoholics, and they were less able to compensate for impairments. Svanum and Schladenhauffen (1986) found extensive alcohol consumption to be associated with an increased amount of neurological deficit in later life.

Psychoses Associated with Alcoholism

Several acute psychotic reactions fit the diagnostic classification of substance-induced disorders. These reactions may develop in individuals who have been drinking excessively over long periods of time or who have a reduced tolerance for alcohol for other reasons—for example, because of brain lesions. Such acute reactions usually last only a short time and generally consist of confusion, excitement, and delirium. They are often called alcoholic psychoses because they are marked by a temporary loss of contact with reality. Two commonly recognized psychotic reactions will be briefly described.

Among those who drink excessively for a long time, a reaction known as *alcohol withdrawal delirium* (formerly known as *delirium tremens*) may occur. This reaction can happen during a prolonged drinking spree or on the withdrawal of alcohol after prolonged drinking. The delirium usually is preceded by a period of restlessness and insomnia during which a person may feel generally uneasy and apprehensive. Slight noises or sudden moving objects may cause considerable excitement and agitation. The full-blown symptoms include (a) disorientation for time and place in which, for example, a person may mistake the hospital for a church or jail, no longer recognize friends, or identify hospital attendants as old acquaintances; (b) vivid hallucinations, particularly of small, fast-moving animals like snakes, rats, and roaches, which are clearly localized in space; (c) acute fear, in which these animals may change in form, size, or color in terrifying ways; (d) extreme suggestibility, in which a person can be made to see almost any animal if its presence is

The effects of fetal alcohol syndrome can be both dramatic and long-lasting. This child suffers from permanent physical abnormalities because his mother drank alcohol while pregnant.

The subject was brought forcibly to the psychiatric ward of a general hospital after he had fired his shotgun at 3:30 A.M. while "trying to repel an invasion of cockroaches." On admission, he was confused and disoriented and had terrifying hallucinations involving "millions and millions" of invading cockroaches. He leaped from his bed and cowered in terror against the wall, screaming for help and kicking and hitting frantically at his imaginary assailants. When an attendant came to his aid, he screamed for him to get back out of danger or he would be killed too. Before the attendant could reach him, he dived headlong on his head, apparently trying to kill himself.

The subject's delirium lasted for 3½ days, after which he returned to a state of apparent normality, apologized profusely for the trouble he had caused everyone, stated he would never touch another drop, and was discharged. On his way home, however, he stopped at a bar, had too much to drink, and on emerging from the bar, collapsed on the street. This time he sobered up in jail, again apologized for the trouble he had caused, and, extremely remorseful, was released with a small fine. What happened to him beyond that time is unknown.

merely suggested; (e) marked tremors of the hands, tongue, and lips; and (f) other symptoms, including perspiration, fever, a rapid and weak heartbeat, a coated tongue, and foul breath.

The delirium typically lasts from three to six days and is generally followed by a deep sleep. When a person awakens, few symptoms—aside from possible slight remorse—remain, but frequently the individual is badly scared and may not resume drinking for several weeks or months. Usually, however, drinking is eventually resumed, followed by a return to the hospital with a new attack. The death rate from withdrawal delirium as a result of convulsions, heart failure, and other complications once approximated 10 percent (Tavel, 1962). With newer drugs such as chlordiazepoxide, however, the current death rate during withdrawal delirium and acute alcoholic withdrawal has been markedly reduced. The following is a brief description of a 43-year-old male withdrawal delirium patient:

A second alcohol-related psychosis is the disorder referred to as *alcohol amnestic disorder* (formerly known as *Korsakoff's psychosis*). This condition was first described by the Russian psychiatrist Korsakoff in 1887. The outstanding symptom is a memory defect (particularly with regard to recent events), which is sometimes accompanied by falsification of events (confabulation). Individuals with this disorder may not recognize pictures, faces, rooms, and other objects that they have just seen, although they may feel that these people or objects are familiar. Such people increasingly tend to fill in their memory gaps with reminiscences and fanciful tales that lead to unconnected and distorted associations. These individuals may appear to be delirious, delusional, and disoriented for time and place, but ordinarily their confusion and disordered actions are closely related to their attempts to fill in memory gaps. The memory disturbance itself seems related to an inability to form new associations in a manner that renders them readily retrievable. Such a reaction usually occurs in older alcoholics, after many years of excessive drinking.

The symptoms of this disorder are now thought to be due to vitamin B (thiamine) deficiency and other dietary inadequacies. Although it has been generally believed that a diet rich in vitamins and minerals generally restores a patient to more normal physical and mental health, recent evidence suggests otherwise. Lishman (1990) reported that Korsakoff's psychosis did not respond well to thiamine replacement. Some memory functioning appears to be restored with prolonged abstinence. However, some personality deterioration usually remains in the form of memory impairment, blunted intellectual capacity, and lowered moral and ethical standards.

Recently, the American Public Health Association (*The Nation's Health,* 1986) has proposed that vitamin B be added to all alcoholic beverages to prevent these deficiencies. Concentrations of thiamine to prevent malnutrition would not adversely affect the taste or the appearance of alcoholic beverages yet would help prevent the occurrence of alcohol amnestic disorder. Whether this measure will eventually be approved is uncertain.

■ Causes of Alcohol Abuse and Dependence

In trying to identify the causes of problem drinking, some researchers have stressed the role of genetic and biochemical factors; others have pointed to psychosocial factors, viewing problem drinking as a maladaptive pattern of adjustment to the stress of life; still others have emphasized sociocultural factors, such as the availability of alcohol and social approval of excessive drinking. As with most other forms of maladaptive behavior, it appears that there may be several types of alcohol dependence, each with somewhat different patterns of biological, psychosocial, and sociocultural causal factors. Recently, a committee of experts from the National Academy of Sciences (Institute of Medicine, 1990) concluded that identifying a single cause for all types of alcohol problems is unlikely.

Biological Factors   In an alcohol-dependent person, cell metabolism has adapted itself to the presence of alcohol in the bloodstream and now demands it for stability. When the alcohol in the bloodstream falls below a certain level, withdrawal symptoms occur. These symptoms may be relatively mild—involving a craving for alcohol, tremors, perspiration, and weakness—or more severe—with nausea, vomiting, fever, rapid heartbeat, convulsions, and hallucinations. The shortcut to ending them is to take another drink. Once this point is reached, each drink serves to reinforce alcohol-

Alcohol abuse knows no age, educational, occupational, or socioeconomic boundaries. Bill Shoemaker's outstanding career as a jockey—with the most wins in horse-racing history—ended with an automobile accident that left him paralyzed. Shoemaker was alone in the car and driving drunk.

seeking behavior because it reduces the unpleasant symptoms. An unusual craving could result from a genetic vulnerability. The possibility of a genetic predisposition to developing alcohol-abuse problems has been widely researched. Cotton (1979)—in a review of 39 studies of families of 6251 alcoholics and 4083 nonalcoholics who had been followed over 40 years—reported that almost one third of alcoholics had at least one parent with an alcohol problem. More recently, a study of children of alcoholics by Cloninger et al. (1986) reported strong evidence for the inheritance of alcoholism. They found that, for males, having one alcoholic parent increased the rate of alcoholism from 11.4 percent to 29.5 percent, and having two alcoholic parents increased the rate to 41.2 percent. For females with no alcoholic parents, the rate was 5.0 percent; for those with one alcoholic parent, the rate was 9.5 percent; and for those with two alcoholic parents, it was 25.0 percent. However, it should be kept in mind that the majority of individuals in the study did not have alcoholic parents. Also, such studies do not rule out environmental influences, such as modeling.

An interesting problem for researchers in the search for causal factors in substance abuse is how to determine if the behavior being investigated is antecedent to the drinking or caused by the drinking itself. One approach to understanding the precursors to alcoholism is to study the behavior of individuals who are at high risk for substance abuse but who are not yet affected by alcohol—prealcoholic personalities. An alcohol-risk personality has been described by Finn (1990) as an individual (usually an alcoholic's child) who has an inherited predisposition toward alcohol abuse and who is impulsive, prefers taking high risks, is emotionally unstable, has difficulty planning and organizing behavior, has problems in predicting the consequences of his or her actions, has many psychological problems, finds that alcohol is helpful in coping with stress, does not experience hangovers, and finds alcohol rewarding.

Research has shown that prealcoholic men show different physiological patterns than nonalcoholic men in several respects. Prealcoholic men are more sensitive to stress-response dampening (lessened experience of stress) with alcohol ingestion than nonalcoholic men (Finn & Pihl, 1987; Finn, Zeitouni, & Pihl, 1990). They also show different alpha wave patterns on EEG (Stewart, Finn, & Pihl, 1990). Prealcoholic men as defined by the personality characteristics described in the preceding paragraph were found to show larger conditioned physiological responses to alcohol cues than were individuals who were considered at a low risk for alcoholism, according to Earlywine and Finn (1990). These results suggest that prealcoholic men may be more prone to develop tolerance for alcohol than low risk men.

In support of possible genetic factors in alcoholism, some research has suggested that certain ethnic groups, particularly Orientals and American Indians, have abnormal physiological reactions to alcohol. Fenna et al. (1971) and Wolff (1972) found that Oriental and Eskimo subjects showed a hypersensitive reaction, including flushing of the skin, a drop in blood pressure, and nausea, following the ingestion of alcohol. The relatively lower rates of alcoholism among Oriental groups are tentatively considered to be related to a faster metabolism. Schaefer (1977, 1978), however, questioned these and other metabolism studies as a basis for interpreting cultural differences in alcoholism rates. Using more explicit criteria of metabolism rate, he found no differences in alcohol metabolism between a group of Reddis Indians and a group of northern European subjects. He concluded that further research into metabolism rate differences

and sensitivity to alcohol needs to be integrated with studies focusing on relative stress in various cultures.

The role genetics play in the development of alcoholism remains unclear. We will return to this topic in the Unresolved Issues section at the end of the chapter.

Psychosocial Factors   Not only do alcoholics become physiologically dependent on alcohol, they develop a powerful psychological dependence as well. Because excessive drinking is so destructive to an individual's total life adjustment, the question arises as to why psychological dependence is learned. A number of psychosocial factors have been advanced as possible answers.

Psychological vulnerability.   Is there an "alcoholic personality"—a type of character organization that predisposes a given individual to turn to the use of alcohol rather than to some other defensive pattern of coping with stress? In efforts to answer this question, investigators have reported that potential alcoholics tend to be emotionally immature, to expect a great deal of the world, to require an inordinate amount of praise and appreciation, to react to failure with marked feelings of hurt and inferiority, to have low frustration tolerance, and to feel inadequate and unsure of their abilities to fulfill expected male or female roles. Morey, Skinner, and Blashfield (1984) have shown that individuals at high risk for alcoholism development were significantly different in personality, especially in terms of showing more impulsivity and aggression, from those at low risk for abusing alcohol.

The two psychopathological conditions that have been most frequently linked to addictive disorders are depression (Lutz & Snow, 1985; Weissman et al., 1977; Woodruff et al., 1973) and antisocial personality (Cadoret et al., 1985; Seixas & Cadoret, 1974; Stabenau, 1984). By far, most of the research has related antisocial personality and addictive disorders, with about 75 to 80 percent of the studies showing an association between the two (Alterman, 1988; Grand et al. 1985).

While such findings provide promising leads, it is difficult to assess the role of specific personality characteristics in the development of alcoholism. Certainly many people with similar personality characteristics do not become alcoholics, and others with dissimilar ones do. The only characteristic that appears common to the backgrounds of most problem drinkers is personal maladjustment, yet most maladjusted people do not become alcoholics. An alcoholic's personality may be as much a result as a cause of his or her dependence on alcohol—for example, the excessive use of alcohol may lead to depression, or a depressed person may turn to the excessive use of alcohol, or both.

Stress, tension reduction, and reinforcement.   A number of investigators have pointed out that the typical alcoholic is discontented with his or her life and is unable or unwilling to tolerate tension and stress. In this view, anyone who finds alcohol to be tension-reducing is in danger of becoming an alcoholic, even without an especially stressful life situation. If this were true, however, we would expect alcoholism to be far more common that it is, since alcohol tends to reduce tension for most people who use it. In addition, this model does not explain why some excessive drinkers are able to maintain control over their drinking and continue to function in society while others are not.

At the opposite end of the spectrum are investigators who reject the view that alcoholism is a learned maladaptive response, reinforced and maintained by tension reduction. They point out that the long-range consequences of excessive drinking are too devastating, far outweighing its temporary relief value. However, as Bandura (1969) has pointed out, "This argument overlooks the fact that behavior is more powerfully controlled by its immediate, rather than delayed, consequences, and it is precisely for this reason that persons may persistently engage in immediately reinforcing, but potentially self-destructive behavior . . ." (p. 530).

Cox and Klinger (1988) describe a *motivational model of alcohol use* that places a great deal of responsibility on the individual. According to this view, the final common pathway of alcohol use is motivation; that is, a person decides, consciously or unconsciously, whether to consume a particular drink of alcohol. Alcohol is consumed to bring about affective changes, such as the mood-altering effects, and even indirect effects, such as peer approval. In short, alcohol is consumed because it is reinforcing to the individual.

Finally, much data in the literature suggest that for certain individuals, alcohol reduces the magnitude of response to stressful situations, thereby reinforcing the drinking of alcohol. Levenson et al. (1980) found that alcohol had a dampening effect on an individual's feeling of immediate stress. It thus seems that alcoholics drink to feel better at a particular moment, even though they may know they will feel worse later.

Marital and other intimate relationships.   Excessive drinking often begins during crisis periods in marital or other intimate personal relationships, particularly crises that lead to hurt and self-devaluation. For example, in an important early study of 100 middle- and upper-class women who were receiving help at an alcoholism treatment center, Curlee (1969) found that the traumas that appeared to trigger the women's drinking problems were related to changes or challenges in their roles as wives or mothers, such as divorce, menopause, or children leaving home (the so-called empty-nest syndrome). Many women appear to begin their immoderate drinking during their late thirties and early forties when such life-situation changes are common.

A husband who lives with an alcoholic wife is often unaware of the fact that, gradually and inevitably, many of the decisions he makes every day are based on the expectation that his wife will be drinking. In a case such as this, the husband is becoming "drinking-wife oriented." These expectations, in turn, may make the drinking behavior more likely. Thus one important concern in many treatment programs today involves identifying *codependency* in alcohol-abusing relationships. That is, such programs try to identify the personality or life-style factors in a relationship that serve to promote, maintain, or to justify the drinking behavior of an alcoholic. Eventually an entire marriage may center around the drinking of an alcoholic spouse. In some instances, the husband or wife may also begin to drink excessively, possibly through the reinforcement of such behavior by the drinking mate or to blank out the disillusionment, frustration, and resentment that are often elicited by an alcoholic spouse. Of course, such relationships are not restricted to marital partners but may also occur in those involved in love affairs or close friendships.

Excessive use of alcohol is the third most frequent cause of divorce in the United States (and often a hidden factor in the two most common causes—financial and sexual problems). People who abuse alcohol are about seven times more likely to be divorced or separated than nonabusers (Levitt, 1974). The deterioration in such people's interpersonal relationships, of course, further augments the stress and disorganization in their life situations.

Sociocultural Factors   In a general sense, our culture has become dependent on alcohol as a social lubricant and a means of reducing tension. Thus numerous investigators have pointed to the role of sociocultural as well as physiological and psychological factors in the high rate of alcohol abuse and dependence among Americans. It is of interest to note here the conclusions of Pliner and Cappell (1974) concerning the reinforcing effects of social

Drunken college students on spring break have become a symbol of springtime. Our society reinforces the role of alcohol in promoting gaiety and fun—witness any beer commercial—but the reinforcement of social drinking can lead some people to excessive alcohol use.

drinking in our society, in which liquor has come to play an almost ritualistic role in promoting gaiety and pleasant social interaction.

According to the present results, if it is the case that much of the early drinking experience of . . . individuals takes place in such convivial social settings, drinking will be likely to become associated with positive affective experiences. This reinforcing consequence may in turn make drinking more probable in the future. Thus, to the extent that a social context can enhance the attraction of alcohol, for some individuals it may play a crucial role in the etiology of pathological patterns of alcohol consumption. (p. 425)

Bales (1946), in a classic study, outlined three cultural factors that play a part in determining the incidence of alcoholism in a given society: (a) the degree of stress and inner tension produced by the culture; (b) the attitudes toward drinking fostered by the culture; and (c) the degree to which the culture provides substitute means of satisfaction and other ways of coping with tension and anxiety. This outline has been borne out by cross-cultural studies.

The importance of the stress level in a given culture is shown in studies of preliterate societies. In a pioneering study of 56 such societies, Horton (1943) found that the greater the insecurity level of the culture, the greater the amount of alcohol consumption—due allowance having been made for the availability and acceptability of alcohol.

Rapid social change and social disintegration also seem to foster excessive drinking. For example, the U.S. Public Health Service's Alaska Native Medical Center reported excessive drinking to be a major problem among Eskimos in many places in rural Alaska (*Time,* April 22, 1974). This problem was attributed primarily to rapid change in traditional values and ways of life, in some cases approaching social disintegration.

The effect of cultural attitudes toward drinking is well illustrated by Muslims and Mormons, whose religious values prohibit the use of alcohol, and by orthodox Jews, who have traditionally limited its use largely to religious rituals. The incidence of alcoholism among these groups is minimal. In comparison, the incidence of alcoholism is high among Europeans, who comprise less than 15 percent of the world's population yet consume about half the alcohol (Sulkunen, 1976). Interestingly, Europe and six countries that have been influenced by European culture—Argentina, Canada, Chile, Japan, the United States, and New Zealand—make up less than 20 percent of the world's population yet consume 80 percent of the alcohol (Barry, 1982). The French appear to have the highest rate of alcoholism in the world, approximately 15 percent of the population. France has both the highest per capita alcohol consumption and the highest death rate from cirrhosis of the liver (Noble, 1979). Thus it appears that religious sanctions and social customs can determine whether alcohol is one of the coping methods commonly used in a given group or society.

In sum, we can identify many reasons why people drink—as well as many conditions that can predispose them to do so and reinforce drinking behavior—but the combination of factors that result in a person's becoming an alcoholic are still unknown.

■ Treatments and Outcomes

Unfortunately, many alcoholics refuse to admit they have a problem or to seek assistance before they "hit bottom"—which, in many cases, is the grave. When alcoholics are confronted with their drinking problem they may react with denial or become angry at the "messenger" and withdraw from this person. At times, however, such a confrontation has the desired effect, as in the case of Don Shelby, a Minneapolis television newscaster, who described in the following manner the day, March 31, 1980, when he went on the air drunk:

"I had done that before, so you at home didn't know, but there was no hiding this," Shelby said. *"Incomprehensible. It was incredibly embarrassing to me, but I want to tell you the kind of embarrassment Ron Handberg suffered.*

"Ron Handberg is the general manager of the television station, the man who hired me. He was humiliated beyond words that I had done that to him and his television station. Ron Handberg wanted to fire me and I wanted to be fired. I didn't want to be forced to walk down the street and have people see my face and realize what I had done," Shelby said.

"Mr. Handberg invited me into his office and complained that he could not fire me, because under certain rules and regulations he was forced to offer me treatment, and he despised my guts.

"He told me that the company would pay for my treatment, and I'd be given some time off and I could come back to work and resume my duties.

"Mr. Handberg said he was also authorized to tell me that if I refused treatment I would be fired and he would spend the rest of his natural life seeing to it that I was never employed in television again," Shelby said.

"I decided to enter treatment and the rest is history, as they say. Six years later, I am coanchor of the 10 p.m. news. That's a remarkable story, a story of recovery, and a story of Ron Handberg," Shelby said.

Since Shelby's recovery, eight other people at the station were identified and helped "short of humiliation," and each one of those individuals has climbed either the reportorial or executive ladder. (Bloomington Sun Current, June 16, 1986)

A multidisciplinary approach to the treatment of drinking problems appears to be most effective because the problems are often complex, thus requiring flexibility and individualization of treatment procedures. Also, an alcoholic's needs change as treatment progresses.

Formerly it was considered essential for the treatment of a problem drinker to take place in an institutional setting, removing the individual from a probably aversive life situation and making possible more control over his or her behavior. However, an increasing number of problem drinkers are now being treated in community clinics, especially drinkers who do not require hospitalization for withdrawal treatment. In fact, one survey of treatment facilities (ADAMHA, 1982) found that most alcoholics are treated on an outpatient basis, which appears to be as effective as inpatient treatment (Miller & Hester, 1986). When hospitalization is required, the length of the hospital stay is often short—an average of roughly 28 days. (In some treatment programs, stays are now being limited to 7 to 14 days.) Halfway houses are also being used increasingly to bridge the gap between institutionalization and return to the community and to enhance the flexibility of treatment programs.

Treatment program objectives include physical rehabilitation, control over alcohol-abuse behavior, and development of an individual's realization that he or she can cope with the problems of living and lead a much more rewarding life without alcohol. Although traditional treatment programs usually include the goal of abstinence from alcohol, some current programs are attempting to promote controlled drinking as a treatment goal for some problem drinkers.

Biological Approaches   Biological approaches include a variety of treatment measures ranging from detoxification procedures to medication use. In acute intoxication, the initial focus is on detoxification (the elimination of alcoholic substances from an individual's body), on the treatment of withdrawal symptoms, and on a medical regimen for physical rehabilitation. These steps can best be handled in a hospital or clinic, where drugs, such as chlordiazepoxide, have largely revolutionized the treatment of withdrawal symptoms. Such drugs overcome motor excitement, nausea, and vomiting, prevent withdrawal delirium and convulsions, and help alleviate the tension and anxiety associated with withdrawal. Concern is growing, however, that the use of tranquilizers at this stage does not promote long-term recovery. Accordingly, some detoxification clinics are exploring alternative approaches, including a gradual weaning from alcohol instead of a sudden cutoff.

Medications are also used in the treatment of alcoholism. Maintenance doses of mild tranquilizers are used at times on patients withdrawing from alcohol to reduce anxiety and help them sleep. Such use of tranquilizers may be less effective than no treatment at all, however. Usually patients must learn to abstain from tranquilizers as well as from alcohol, because they tend to misuse both. Further, under the influence of tranquilizers, they may even return to alcohol use.

Disulfiram (Antabuse), a drug that causes violent vomiting when followed by ingestion of alcohol, may be administered to prevent an immediate return to drinking. However, such deterrent therapy is seldom advocated as the sole approach, because pharmacological methods alone have not proven effective in treating alcoholism. For example, since the drug is usually self-administered, an alcoholic may simply discontinue the use of Antabuse when he or she is released from a hospital or clinic and begin to drink again. In fact, the primary value of drugs of this type seems to be their ability to interrupt the alcoholic cycle for a period of time, during which therapy may be undertaken. Uncomfortable side effects may accompany the use of Antabuse; for example, alcohol-based after-shave lotion can be absorbed through the skin, resulting in an individual becoming ill.

Psychosocial Approaches   Detoxification is optimally followed by psychosocial measures, including family counseling and the use of community resources relating to employment and other aspects of an individual's social readjustments. Although individual psychotherapy is sometimes effective, the focus of psychosocial measures in the alcoholism treatment more often involves group therapy, environmental intervention, behavioral therapy, and the approach used by Alcoholics Anonymous.

Group therapy.   In the rugged give-and-take of group therapy, alcoholics are sometimes forced to face their problem and recognize its possible disastrous consequences, but they also begin to see new possibilities for coping with it. Often, but by no means always, this double recognition paves the way for learning more effective methods of coping and other positive steps toward dealing with their drinking problem.

In some instances, the spouses of alcoholics and even their children may be invited to join in group therapy meetings. In other situations, family treatment is itself the central focus of therapeutic efforts. In the latter case, an alcoholic individual is seen as a member of a disturbed family in which all the members have a responsibility for cooperating in treatment. Because family members are frequently the people most victimized by the alcoholic's addiction, they often tend to be judgmental and punitive, and the alcoholic, who has already passed harsh judgment on himself or herself, tolerates this further source of devaluation poorly. In other instances, family members may unwillingly encourage

an alcoholic to remain addicted, as, for example, when a wife with a need to dominate her husband finds that a continually drunken and remorseful spouse best meets her needs.

Environmental intervention.   As with other serious maladaptive behaviors, a total treatment program for alcoholism usually requires measures to alleviate a patient's aversive life situation. As a result of their drinking, alcoholics often become estranged from family and friends and either lose or jeopardize their job. Typically the reaction of those around them is not as understanding or supportive as it would be if they had a physical illness of comparable magnitude. Simply helping alcoholics learn more effective coping techniques may not be enough if their social environment remains hostile and threatening. For alcoholics who have been hospitalized, halfway houses—designed to assist them in their return to family and community—are often important adjuncts to their total treatment program.

Relapses and continued deterioration are generally associated with a lack of close relationships with family or friends, or with living in a stressful environment. In general, it appears unlikely that an alcoholic will remain abstinent after treatment unless the negative psychosocial factors that operated in the past are dealt with.

Behavioral therapy.   One interesting and often effective form of treatment for alcohol-abuse disorders is behavioral therapy, of which several types exist. One is *aversive conditioning*, involving the presentation of a wide range of noxious stimuli with alcohol consumption in order to suppress drinking behavior. For example, the ingestion of alcohol might be paired with an electrical shock. The Romans used a similar technique by placing a live eel in a cup of wine; forced to drink this unsavory cocktail, an alcoholic presumably would feel disgusted and from then on be repelled by wine.

Today a variety of pharmacological and other deterrent measures can be used in behavioral therapy after detoxification. One approach involves an intramuscular injection of emetine hydrochloride, an emetic. Before experiencing the nausea that results from the injection, a patient is given alcohol, so that the sight, smell, and taste of the beverage become associated with severe retching and vomiting. With repetition, this classical conditioning procedure acts as a strong deterrent to further drinking—probably in part because it adds an immediate and unpleasant physiological consequence to the more general socially aversive consequences of excessive drinking.

These paintings were done by W., a 40-year-old male with a history of alcoholism, loss of employment, and hospitalization for treatment. His interest in painting, which gradually became the key aspect of his treatment program at an alcoholism treatment center, also led to a new way of life following his discharge. In the painting on the left, W. depicted alcoholism as a magnetlike vise that drew and crushed his consciousness. He symbolized his feelings in sober periods between drinking sprees as the chained tree, and the nebulous higher power to which he looked for help as a descending dove. The egg and the eye, a motif W. used in earlier work to depict his unrealistic view of alcohol, are merged into a straining muscular arm reaching back to the more placid past and unattainable dream castles—that is, futile quests with which W. associated his past abuses of alcohol. In the painting on the right, the overriding concept is of constructive action. Three portals are depicted, one leading to a world "blown to hell" (left); another with two entrances (right), one leading downward to an abyss, the other to barrenness; and a third in the shape of a cross (middle), symbolic of hope, that leads upward to a pleasant landscape, representing a goal or purpose.

Mild electrical stimulation is another of the aversive-conditioning techniques. This method presumably enables a therapist to maintain more exact control of the aversive stimulus, reduces possible negative side effects and medical complications, and can even be administered by means of a portable apparatus that can be used by a patient for self-reinforcement. Using a procedure that paired electrical stimulation with drinking-associated stimuli, Claeson and Malm (1973) reported successful results—no relapses after 12 months—in 24 percent of a patient group consisting mostly of advanced-stage alcoholics.

Another aversive approach, called *covert sensitization,* involves extinguishing drinking behavior by conditioning an individual to associate it with noxious mental images (Cautela, 1967). Positive results have been reported, with reduction of drinking for a time. The long-term effects of covert sensitization, however, generally have not been impressive. To expect stimuli such as images (which are under an individual's control) to change a deeply ingrained life pattern is perhaps unrealistic. Covert sensitization procedures might be effectively used as an early step, with other treatment procedures then employed while a person remains abstinent. The most important effect of any type of aversion therapy with alcoholics seems to be this temporary extinction of drinking behavior, making it possible for other psychosocial methods to be used effectively (Davidson, 1974).

One of the most promising contemporary procedures for treating alcoholics is the cognitive-behavioral approach recommended by Marlatt (1985) and Lang and Marlatt (1983). This approach combines cognitive-behavioral strategies of intervention with social-learning theory and modeling of behavior. The approach, often referred to as a *skills-training procedure,* is usually aimed at younger problem drinkers who are considered to be at risk for developing more severe drinking problems because of alcoholism in their family history or their heavy current consumption level. This approach relies on such techniques as imparting specific knowledge about alcohol, developing coping skills in situations associated with increased risk of alcohol use, modifying cognitions and expectancies, and acquiring stress-management skills.

Other behavioral techniques have also received attention in recent years, partly because they are based on the hypothesis that some problem drinkers need not give up drinking altogether but can learn to drink moderately (Gottheil et al., 1982; Lang & Kidorf, 1990; Miller, 1978). Several approaches to learning controlled drinking have been attempted (Lloyd & Salzberg, 1975), and research has suggested that some alcoholics can learn to control their alcohol intake (Miller, 1978; Miller & Caddy, 1977). Miller et al. (1986) evaluated the results of four long-term follow-up studies of controlled-drinking treatment programs. They reported a clear trend of increased numbers of abstainers and relapsed cases at long-term follow-up. However, a consistent percentage (15 percent) of individuals across the four studies controlled their drinking. The researchers concluded that controlled drinking was more likely to be successful in individuals with less severe alcohol problems. The finding that some individuals are able to maintain some control over their drinking after treatment (and not remain totally abstinent) was also reported by Polich and colleagues (1981). They found that 18 percent of the alcoholics they studied had reportedly been able to drink socially without problems during the six-month follow-up of treatment.

One promising approach to teaching alcoholics self-control over drinking was reported by Lovibond and Caddy (1970). They conducted blood-alcohol discrimination training sessions, which were aimed at getting alcoholics to control drinking by becoming aware of intoxicating levels of alcohol in their blood. Miller and Munoz (1976) and Miller (1978) used behavioral self-control training to teach alcoholics to monitor and reduce their alcohol intake. Patients kept records of their drinking behavior, and the therapy sessions focused on determining blood-alcohol concentration based on their intake. Strategies for increasing future intake control were discussed along with identifying alternatives to alcohol consumption. Self-control training techniques, in which the goal of therapy is to get alcoholics to reduce alcohol intake without necessarily abstaining altogether, have a great deal of appeal for some drinkers. It is difficult, of course, for individuals who are extremely dependent on the effects of alcohol to abstain totally from drinking. Thus many alcoholics fail to complete traditional treatment programs. The idea that they might be able to learn to control their drinking and at the same time enjoy the continued use of alcohol might serve as a motivating element (Lang & Kidorf, 1990).

Whether alcoholics who have learned to recognize intoxicating levels of alcohol and to limit their intake to lower levels will maintain these skills in the long run has not been sufficiently demonstrated. Most workers in the field still assume that total abstinence should be the goal for all problem drinkers. Some groups, such as Alcoholics Anonymous, are adamant in their opposition to programs aimed at controlled drinking for alcohol-dependent individuals.

Alcoholics Anonymous.   A practical approach to alcoholism that has reportedly met with considerable success is that of Alcoholics Anonymous (AA). This organization was started in 1935 by two individuals, Dr. Bob and Bill W. in Akron, Ohio. Bill W. recovered from alcoholism through a "fundamental spiritual change," and immediately sought out Dr. Bob, who, with Bill's assistance, achieved recovery. They in turn began to help other alcoholics. Since that time, AA has grown to over 10,000 groups with over 1 million members. In addition, AA groups have been established in many other countries.

Alcoholics Anonymous operates primarily as a nonprofessional counseling program in which both person-to-person and group relationships are emphasized. AA accepts both teenagers and adults with drinking problems, has no dues or fees, does not keep records or case histories, does not participate in political causes, and is not affiliated with any religious sect, although spiritual development is a key aspect of its treatment approach. To ensure anonymity, only first names are used. Meetings are devoted partly to social activities, but consist mainly of discussions of the participants' problems with alcohol, often with testimonials from those who have recovered from alcoholism. Recovered members usually contrast their lives before they broke their alcohol dependence with the lives they now live without alcohol. We should point out here that the term *alcoholic* is used by AA and its affiliates to refer either to individuals who currently are drinking excessively or to people who have recovered from such problems but must, according to AA philosophy, continue to abstain from alcohol consumption in the future. That is, one is an alcoholic for life, whether or not one is drinking—one is never "cured" of alcoholism.

An important aspect of AA's rehabilitation program is that it lifts the burden of personal responsibility by helping alcoholics accept that alcoholism, like many other problems, is bigger than they are. Henceforth, they can see themselves not as weak-willed or lacking in moral strength, but rather simply as having an affliction—they cannot drink —just as other people may not be able to tolerate certain types of medication. By mutual help and

Family relationships are severely threatened by an alcoholic family member. In some instances, the spouses and children of alcoholics may be invited to join in therapy, and family treatment may itself be the central focus of therapeutic efforts. Because family members are frequently the people most victimized by an alcoholic's addiction, they often tend to be judgmental and punitive. They also may unknowingly encourage an alcoholic to remain addicted. Therapy can help them to gain an understanding of the nature of alcoholism and to learn ways of helping an alcoholic family member deal with his or her problem.

reassurance through a group composed of others who have shared similar experiences, many alcoholics acquire insight into their problems, a new sense of purpose, greater ego strength, and more effective coping techniques. Continued participation in the group, of course, helps prevent the crisis of a relapse.

Affiliated movements, such as Al-Anon family groups and Ala-Teen, are designed to bring family members together to share common experiences and problems, to gain understanding of the nature of alcoholism, and to learn techniques for helping an alcoholic individual deal with his or her problem.

The generally acknowledged success of Alcoholics Anonymous is based primarily on anecdotal information rather than objective study of treatment outcomes. Brandsma et al. (1980), however, included an AA program in their extensive comparative study of alcoholism treatments. The success of this treatment method with severe alcoholics was quite limited. One important finding was that the AA method had high dropout rates compared to other therapies. Apparently many alcoholics are unable to accept the quasi-religious quality of the sessions and the group testimonial format that is so much a part of the AA program. The individuals who were assigned to the AA group subsequently encountered more life difficulties and drank more than individuals in other treatment groups.

Results of Treatment   Statistics on the long-range outcomes of alcoholism treatments vary considerably, depending on the population studied and on the treatment facilities and procedures employed. They range from low rates of success for hard-core alcoholics to recoveries of 70 to 90 per-

cent where modern treatment and aftercare procedures are used. Rounsaville et al. (1987) reported that psychopathology was influential in treatment outcomes for alcoholics. Individuals who were also diagnosed as having a personality disorder or affective disorder tended to have poorer outcomes in alcohol treatment than those for whom the diagnosis was simply alcoholism.

In their extensive four-year follow-up of a large group of treated alcoholics, Polich et al. (1981) found that the course of alcoholism after diverse treatment methods was variable:

There is no single pattern, and no definite path, characterizing the 4-year history of alcoholics in this study. Instead, we find remission, frequent relapse, and diverse forms of behavior among alcoholics. Our conclusions about the course of alcoholism depend upon recognizing these multidimensional and highly diverse features of alcoholic behavior. (p. 201)

In some respects, the findings of this study were not encouraging and seemed to point to the difficulty of treating alcoholics. Only 7 percent of the total sample (922 males) abstained from alcohol use throughout the four-year period, and 54 percent continued to show alcohol-related problems. (In addition, 36 percent of the sample demonstrated alcohol-dependence symptoms, and another 18 percent showed adverse consequences—such as arrests —from drinking.)

On the positive side, however, the Polich et al. study can be viewed as demonstrating a clear beneficial effect of treatment for some individuals. Although 54 percent showed drinking problems at follow-up, over 90 percent of the subjects had had serious drinking problems at the beginning of treatment—a significant reduction. Interestingly, although only 7 percent of the alcoholics had been able to abstain from drinking for the full four-year period, others had abstained for shorter periods. For example, 21 percent had abstained for one year or more, and an additional 7 percent had abstained for six months. An impressive finding, and one that will fuel the controlled-drinking versus total-abstinence controversy, was that 18 percent of the alcoholics had been able to drink without problems during the six-month period before follow-up.

The outcome of treatment is most likely to be favorable when an individual realizes that he or she needs help, when adequate treatment facilities are available, and when alcohol-use reduction (as opposed to strict abstinence) is an acceptable treatment goal. However, Fontana and Dowds (1975) reported a "honeymoon effect" following treatment of severe alcohol abuse. They found a frequent pattern of decreased alcohol consumption with a return to initial drinking levels at a six-month follow-up.

Great progress has been made in alcoholism treatment by the introduction of employee programs in both government and industry. Such programs have proven highly effective in detecting drinking problems early, in referring drinkers for treatment, and in ensuring the effectiveness of aftercare procedures. When we realize that an estimated 5 percent of the nation's work force are alcoholics, and an additional 5 percent are considered alcohol abusers, it is apparent that such programs can have a major impact on coping with the alcohol problem in our society (Alander & Campbell, 1975).

In their study of various treatments of chronic, severe alcohol problems, Brandsma et al. (1980) found that direct treatment—whether professional or paraprofessional, insight-oriented or rational-behavior therapy—was more effective than an untreated control condition. The investigators randomly assigned chronic alcoholics to treatment groups—insight-oriented therapy, rational behavior therapy, Alcoholics Anonymous, self-help (paraprofessional) therapy—or to a nontreatment control group. One important finding was that professional treatment was more effective than non-professional treatment, although either of the two major therapeutic orientations (insight-oriented versus rational-behavior therapy) was equally effective. As noted above, Alcoholics Anonymous was the least effective, partly due to a high dropout rate.

Clearly no miracle cure for alcoholism is available. Nevertheless, it appears that the great majority of alcoholics may find a treatment program that can be tailored to their needs and provide a good chance for recovery.

Relapse Prevention One of the greatest problems in the treatment of addictive disorders, such as alcoholism or any of the conditions described in this chapter, is maintaining abstinence or self-control once the behavioral excesses have been checked. Most alcohol treatment programs show high success rates in "curing" the addictive problems, but many programs show lessening rates of abstinence or controlled drinking at various periods of follow-up. Many treatment programs do not pay sufficient attention to the important element of maintaining effective behavior and preventing relapse into previous maladaptive patterns.

In recent years, some researchers have been focusing on the problem of relapse prevention by examining the thought processes that lead an abstinent individual back into the self-indulgent patterns that originally got him or her in trouble. The cognitive-behavioral approach to relapse prevention by Marlatt and his colleagues (Cummings, Gordon, & Marlatt, 1980; Marlatt & Gordon, 1980, 1985) shows great promise in this area.

The cognitive-behavioral view holds that the definition of relapse behavior should be broadened beyond the previously held notion that people resume drinking because of a "craving" based on vaguely understood physiological needs. Instead, the behaviors underlying relapse are "indulgent behaviors" and are based on an individual's learning history. When an individual is abstinent or has an addiction under control, he or she gains a sense of personal control over the indulgent behavior. The longer the person is able to maintain this control, the greater the sense of achievement—the self-efficacy or confidence—and the greater the chance that he or she will be able to cope with the addiction and maintain control.

However, according to Marlatt, an individual may violate this rule of abstinence through a gradual, perhaps unconscious, process rather than through the sudden "falling off the wagon" that constitutes the traditional view of craving and relapse. In the cognitive-behavioral view, an individual may inadvertently make a series of mini-decisions, even while maintaining abstinence, that begin a chain of behaviors making relapse inevitable. For example, an abstinent alcoholic who buys a quart of bourbon just in case his friends drop by or a dieting obese woman who changes her route to work to include a pass by the bakery are both unconsciously preparing the way for relapse. Marlatt refers to these minidecisions that place an individual at risk as "apparently irrelevant decisions." These decisions are easy for the individual to make, since they do not appear to be related to the abstinent behavior; however, they lead the individual into a situation in which some form of relapse is likely to occur.

Another type of relapse behavior involves the "abstinence violation effect," in which even minor transgressions are seen to have drastic significance by the abstainers. The effect works this way: an abstinent individual may hold that he or she should not, under any circumstance, transgress or give in to the old habit. Abstinence-oriented treatment programs are particularly guided by this prohibitive rule. What happens, then, when an abstinent man becomes somewhat self-indulgent and takes a drink offered by an old friend? He may lose some of the sense of self-efficacy, the confidence needed to control his drinking. Since the vow of abstinence has been violated, he may feel guilty about giving in to the temptation and rationalize that he "has blown it and become a drunk again, so why not go all the way?"

Marlatt and his colleagues recommend a cognitive-behavioral treatment program for preventing relapse. Clients are taught to recognize the apparently irrelevant decisions that serve as early warning signals of the possibility of relapse. High-risk situations are targeted, and the individuals learn to assess their own vulnerability to relapse. Clients are also trained to be prepared for the abstinence violation effect, and, if they do relapse, not to become so discouraged that they lose their confidence. Some cognitive-behavioral therapists have employed a "planned relapse" phase in the treatment to supervise an individual's cognitive behavior and to help the client through this important problem area.

DRUG ABUSE AND DEPENDENCE

Aside from alcohol, the psychoactive drugs most commonly associated with abuse and dependence in our society appear to be (a) narcotics, such as opium and its derivatives; (b) sedatives, such as barbiturates; (c) stimulants, such as cocaine and amphetamines; (d) antianxiety drugs, such as benzodiazepines; and (e) hallucinogens, such as LSD and PCP. (These and other drugs are summarized in *HIGHLIGHT 9.5.*) Caffeine and nicotine are also drugs of dependence, and disorders associated with tobacco withdrawal and caffeine intoxication are included in the DSM-III-R diagnostic classification system; we will deal with them briefly in our present discussion.

Though they may occur at any age, drug abuse and dependence are most common during adolescence and young adulthood (Smith, 1989). Clinical pictures vary markedly, depending on the type, amount, and duration of drug use; the physiological and psychological makeup of the individual; and, in some instances, the social setting in which the drug experience occurs. Thus it appears most useful to deal separately with some of the drugs that are more commonly associated with abuse and dependence in contemporary society.

It should be noted that the most common action of all drugs—even those that are medically prescribed—is the alteration of cell metabolism. Typically, this change in cellular action is a temporary one designed to help combat a patient's problem. Nevertheless, the changes that drugs bring about in target cells are in a direction *away* from normal functioning. Thus medication does not result in cells performing "better than ever." Of course, some drugs, such as hormones, do replace or supplement substances that are normally present in the body, and in this sense they may improve the normal functioning of various organs and cells; but in general, drugs tend to block some important function of cells. Hence it is best to keep drug use to a minimum.

■ Opium and Its Derivatives (Narcotics)

People have used opium and its derivatives for over 5000 years. Galen (A.D. 130–201) considered theriaca, whose principal ingredient was opium, to be a panacea:

It resists poison and venomous bites, cures inveterate headache, vertigo, deafness, epilepsy, apoplexy, dimness of sight, loss of voice, asthma, coughs of all kinds, spitting of blood, tightness of breath, colic, the iliac poisons, jaundice, hardness of the spleen, stone, urinary complaints, fevers, dropsies, leprosies, the trouble to which women are subject, melancholy and all pestilences.

Even today, opium derivatives are still used for some of the conditions Galen mentioned.

Opium is a mixture of about eighteen nitrogen-containing agents known as *alkaloids.* In 1805 the alkaloid present in the largest amount (10 to 15 percent) was found to be a bitter-tasting powder that could serve as a powerful sedative and pain reliever; it was named **morphine** after Morpheus, god of sleep in Greek mythology. The hypodermic needle was introduced in America about 1856, allowing morphine to be widely administered to soldiers during the Civil War, not only to those wounded in battle but also to those suffering from dysentery. As a consequence, many Civil War veterans returned to civilian life addicted to the drug, a condition euphemistically referred to as "soldier's illness."

Scientists concerned with the addictive properties of morphine hypothesized that one part of the morphine molecule might be responsible for its analgesic properties (that is, its ability to eliminate pain without inducing unconsciousness) and another for its addictiveness. Thus at about the turn of the century, it was discovered that if morphine were treated by an inexpensive and readily available chemical called *acetic anhydride,* it would be converted into another powerful analgesic called **heroin.** Heroin was hailed enthusiastically by its discoverer, Heinrich Dreser (Boehm, 1968). Leading scientists of his time agreed on the merits of heroin, and the drug came to be widely prescribed in place of morphine for pain relief and related medicinal purposes. However, heroin was a cruel disappointment, for it proved to be an even more dangerous drug than morphine, acting more rapidly and more intensely and being equally if not more addictive. Eventually, heroin was removed from use in medical practice.

As it became apparent that opium and its derivatives—including codeine, which is used in some cough syrups—were perilously addictive, the United States Congress enacted the Harrison Act in 1914. Under this and later acts, the unauthorized sale and distribution of certain drugs became a federal offense; physicians and pharmacists were held accountable for each dose they dispensed. Thus, overnight, the role of a narcotic user changed from that of addict—which was considered a vice, but tolerated—to that of criminal. Unable to obtain drugs through legal sources, many turned to illegal ones, and eventually to other criminal acts as a means of maintaining their suddenly expensive drug supply. The number of addicts in the United States declined, however, and stayed near 40,000 for several decades.

During the 1960s, there was a rapid increase in heroin use. An estimated 150,000 or more addicts lived in New York City alone, with some 300,000 in the country as a whole—and public attention was focused on the "heroin epidemic" (Bazell, 1973; Greene & Dupont, 1974). Fortunately, the actual number of heroin users has diminished steadily since 1975 (Smith, 1989). Heroin-related hospital admissions have decreased in recent years from 47 percent of total drug-related admissions to 37 percent.

Effects of Morphine and Heroin   Morphine and heroin are commonly introduced into the body by smoking, snorting (inhaling the powder), eating, "skin popping," or "mainlining," the last two being methods of introducing the drug via hypodermic injection. Skin popping refers to injecting the liquefied drug just beneath the skin, and mainlining to injecting the drug directly into the bloodstream. In the United States, a young addict usually moves from snorting to mainlining.

Among the immediate effects of mainlined or snorted heroin is a euphoric spasm (the rush) lasting 60 seconds or so, which many addicts compare to a sexual orgasm. This rush is followed by a high, during which an addict typically is in a lethargic, withdrawn state in which bodily needs, including needs for food and sex, are markedly diminished; pleasant feelings of relaxation, euphoria, and reverie tend to dominate. These effects last from 4 to 6 hours and are followed—in addicts—by a negative phase that produces a desire for more of the drug.

The use of opium derivatives over a period of time usually results in a physiological craving for the drug. The time required to establish the drug habit varies, but it has been estimated that continual use over a period of 30 days is sufficient. Users then find that they have become physiologically dependent on the drug in the sense that they feel physically ill when they do not take it. In addition, users of opium derivatives gradually build up a tolerance to the drug so that even larger amounts are needed to achieve the desired effects.

When people addicted to opiates do not get a dose of the drug within approximately 8 hours, they start to experience withdrawal symptoms. The character and severity of these reactions depend on many factors, including the amount of the narcotic habitually used, the intervals between doses, the duration of the addiction, and especially the addict's health and personality.

Contrary to popular opinion, withdrawal from heroin is not always dangerous or even very painful. Many addicted people withdraw without assistance. Withdrawal can be an agonizing experience for some people, however. Initial withdrawal symptoms usually include a running nose, tearing eyes, perspiration, restlessness, increased respiration rate, and an intensified desire for the drug. As time passes, the symptoms become more severe, usually reaching a peak in about 40 hours. Typically a feeling of chilliness alternates with vasomotor disturbances of flushing and excessive sweating, vomiting, diarrhea, abdominal cramps, pains in the back and extremities, severe headache, marked tremors, and varying degrees of insomnia. Beset by these

Psychoactive Drugs Commonly Involved in Drug Abuse

Classification	Drugs	Effects
Sedatives	Alcohol (ethanol)	Reduce tension Facilitate social interaction "Blot out" feelings or events

	Barbiturates
	   Nembutal (pentobarbital)
	   Seconal (secobarbital)
	   Veronal (barbital)
	   Tuinal (secobarbital
	     and amobarbital)
		Reduce tension

Stimulants	Amphetamines
	   Benzedrine (amphetamine)
	   Dexedrine (dextroamphetamine)
	   Methedrine (methamphetamine)
		Increase feelings of alertness and confidence
		Decrease feelings of fatigue
		Stay awake for long periods

	Cocaine (coca)	Decrease feelings of fatigue Increase endurance Stimulate sex drive

Narcotics	Opium and its derivatives
	   Opium
	   Morphine
	   Codeine
	   Heroin
		Alleviate physical pain
		Induce relaxation and pleasant reverie
		Alleviate anxiety and tension

	Methadone (synthetic narcotic)	Treatment of heroin dependence

Psychedelics and hallucinogens	Cannabis
	   Marijuana
	   Hashish
		Induce changes in mood, thought, and
		   behavior

	Mescaline (peyote) Psilocybin (psychotogenic mushrooms) LSD (lysergic acid diethylamide-25)	"Expand" one's mind
	PCP (phencyclidine)	Induce stupor
Antianxiety drugs (minor tranquilizers)	Librium (chlordiazepoxide) Miltown (meprobamate) Valium (diazepam) Others, e.g., Compōz (scopolamine)	Alleviate tension and anxiety Induce relaxation and sleep

In reviewing this list, it is important to note that it is by no means complete; for example, it does not include new drugs, such as Ritalin, which are designed to produce multiple effects; it does not include the less commonly used volatile hydrocarbons, such as glue, paint thinner, gasoline, cleaning fluid, and nail-polish remover, which are highly dangerous when sniffed for their psychoactive effects; and it does not include the antipsychotic and antidepressant drugs, which are

discomforts, an individual refuses food and water, and this, coupled with the vomiting, sweating, and diarrhea, results in dehydration and a weight loss of as much as 5 to 15 pounds in one day. Occasionally, symptoms may include delirium, hallucinations, and manic activity. Cardiovascular collapse may also occur and can result in death. If morphine is administered, the subjective distress experienced by an addict ends, and physiological equanimity is restored in about 5 to 30 minutes.

Medical Usage	Tolerance	Physiological Dependence	Psychological Dependence
No	Yes (reverse tolerance later)	Yes	Yes
Yes	Yes	Yes	Yes
Yes	Yes	No	Yes
No	No (minimal)	No	Yes
Yes, except heroin	Yes	Yes	Yes
Yes	Yes	Yes	Yes
No, except in research	No—possible reverse tolerance (marijuana)	No	Yes
No	No	No	Yes
Yes	Yes	Yes	Yes

abused, but relatively rarely. We shall deal with these and the anti-anxiety drugs in our discussion of drug therapy in Chapter 17. It also should be emphasized that abuses of various kinds can occur with both prescriptive and non-prescriptive drugs, and with both legal and illegal drugs. In all cases, drugs should be used with great care.

If an addict stops taking heroin, the withdrawal symptoms will usually be on the decline by the third or fourth day, and by the seventh or eighth day will have disappeared. As the symptoms subside, the individual resumes normal eating and drinking and rapidly regains lost weight. An additional hazard exists now in that after withdrawal symptoms have ceased, the individual's former tolerance for the drug also disappears, and death may result from taking the former large dosage.

Several investigators have reported a stable pattern of controlled heroin use (Harding et al., 1980; Zinberg, 1980). These researchers have found that some users tend to both limit and control their use of the drug.

In some cases, individuals may have enough self-control to use opiates without allowing them to interfere with their work and ruin their life; but the danger in the use of such drugs—especially heroin—is great. Kirsch (1974) noted that occasional, not hard-core, narcotics users were overrepresented to a great degree among heroin overdose cases treated in the emergency room of a New York hospital. In general, tolerance builds up so rapidly that larger and more expensive amounts of the drug are soon required, and withdrawal treatments are likely to do little to end the problem. Most addicted individuals—even after withdrawal—find it extremely difficult to break their dependence. Biochemical alterations appear to be at least partly responsible for an individual's continued craving for the narcotic even after completion of a withdrawal treatment.

Typically the life of a narcotic addict becomes increasingly centered around obtaining and using drugs, so the addiction usually leads to socially maladaptive behavior as the individual is eventually forced to lie, steal, and associate with undesirable companions to maintain a supply of drugs. Many addicts resort to petty theft to support their habits, and some female addicts turn to prostitution as a means of financing their addictions.

It should be noted that narcotic drugs introduced during pregnancy can have seriously damaging effects on the development of infants after birth. Householder et al. (1982) reviewed the effects of narcotics addiction in mothers and the subsequent problems of their offspring. They concluded that in later childhood these children showed increasingly frequent disturbances of activity level, attention span, sleep pattern, and socialization.

Along with the lowering of ethical and moral restraints, addiction has adverse physical effects on an individual's well-being. An inadequate diet, for example, may lead to ill health and increased susceptibility to a variety of physical ailments. The use of unsterile equipment may also lead to various problems, including liver damage from hepatitis and, in some groups, transmission of the AIDS virus. In addition, the use of such a potent drug without medical supervision and government controls to assure its strength and purity can result in fatal overdosage. Injection of too much heroin can cause coma and death. In fact, over 10,000 heroin addicts have died through heroin overdose (Smith, 1989), and in one short period between January and June 1988, more than 867 deaths associated with heroin

Mainlining heroin, or injecting it with a needle, gives an immediate "rush," often compared to a sexual orgasm, followed by a high lasting from 4 to 6 hours in which feelings of relaxation, euphoria, and reverie are prominent.

overdose were reported in the United States (Project DAWN, 1988).

Usually, however, addiction to opiates leads to a gradual deterioration of well-being. The ill health and general personality deterioration often found in opium addiction do not result directly from the pharmacological effects of the drug, but are usually products of the sacrifice of money, proper diet, social position, and self-respect as an addict becomes more desperate to procure the required daily dosage. For example, Westermeyer (1982b), in a book detailing his experiences treating opium addicts in Southeast Asia during the 1960s, concludes that long-term opium use has clear dangers in terms of a person's health and the social and economic deprivation it can bring to the user's entire family. On the other hand, a narcotic addict with financial means to maintain both a balanced diet and an adequate supply of drugs without resorting to criminal behavior may maintain his or her drug dependence over many years without the usual symptoms of physical or mental disorder.

Causal Factors in Opiate Abuse and Dependence   No single causal pattern fits all addictions to narcotic drugs. A study by Fulmer and Lapidus (1980) concluded that the three most frequently cited reasons for beginning to use heroin were pleasure, curiosity, and peer pressure. Pleasure was the single most widespread reason—given by 81 percent of addicts. Other reasons, such as life stress, personal maladjustment, and sociocultural conditions, also play a part (Bry, McKeon, & Pandina, 1982).

Alexander and Hadaway (1982) argued convincingly that opiate addiction could be more sufficiently explained by an "adaptive" orientation than by the traditional view that people become addicted by being "exposed" to opiates. They cited evidence that simply using heroin or other opiates for a period of time is not sufficient cause for continued, addictive use of the substance—many people have not, even after prolonged use, been compelled to continue. Alexander and Hadaway concluded that "opiate users are at risk of addiction only under special circumstances, namely, when faced with severe distress and with no more salubrious way of coping than by habitual use" (p. 367).

Although the following categorization of causal factors is somewhat artificial, it does provide a convenient means of ordering our discussion.

Neural bases for physiological addiction.   Research teams have isolated and studied receptor sites for narcotic drugs in the brain (Goldstein et al., 1974; Pert & Snyder, 1973). Such receptor sites are specific nerve cells into which given psychoactive drugs fit like keys into the proper locks. This interaction of drug and brain cells apparently results in a drug's action, and in the case of narcotic drugs, may lead to addiction. Research shows that there are different neurotransmitter receptor sites that produce the various effects of these drugs—for example, pleasurable euphoria or painkilling and tranquillizing action (Bloom, 1983; Gold & Rea, 1983).

The human body produces its own opiumlike substances, called **endorphins,** in the brain and pituitary gland. These substances are produced in response to stimulation and are believed to play a role in an organism's reaction to pain (Akil et al., 1978; Bolls & Fanselow, 1982). Some investigators have suspected that endorphins may play a role in drug addiction, speculating that chronic underproduction of endorphins may lead to a craving for narcotic drugs. Hollt et al. (1975) experimented on animals to determine whether drugs like heroin or methadone influence endorphin production by causing actual changes in the receptor sites; they found only transient changes and no modification of the underlying receptor mechanisms. Research on this issue has not yet been extensive; however, some indication that endorphins may be a factor in addiction was suggested in a study by Su et al.

(1978). These researchers attempted to block methadone withdrawal by administering endorphins and found that endorphins were moderately effective in reducing withdrawal symptoms.

Research on the role of endorphins in drug addiction has generally been inconclusive and disappointing. According to Watson and Akil (1979), before the anatomical and physiological bases of addiction and drug tolerance can be understood, many complex problems of measurement must be resolved.

Addiction associated with pain relief.   Many patients are given narcotic drugs, such as morphine, to relieve pain during illness or following surgery or serious injury. The vast majority of such patients never develop an addiction, and when their medication is discontinued, they do not again resort to the use of morphine. Those narcotic addicts who blame their addiction on the fact that they used drugs during an illness usually show personality deficiencies that may have predisposed them to drug use—such as immaturity, low frustration tolerance, and the ability to distort and evade reality by way of a flight into drug-induced fantasy.

Addiction associated with psychopathology.   A high incidence of antisocial personalities has been found among heroin addicts. In a comparison between a group of 45 young institutionalized male addicts and a control group of nonaddicts, Gilbert and Lombardi (1967) found that distinguishing features were "the addict's antisocial traits, his depression, tension, insecurity, and feelings of inadequacy, and his difficulty in forming warm and lasting interpersonal relationships" (p. 536). Similarly, in a study of 112 drug abusers admitted to Bellevue Psychiatric Hospital in New York, Hekimian and Gershon (1968) found that heroin users usually showed antisocial personality characteristics. Meyer and Mirin (1979) found that opiate addicts were highly impulsive and showed an inability to delay gratification. Kosten and Rounsaville (1986) reported that about 68 percent of heroin abusers were also diagnosed as having a personality disorder. As in the case of alcoholism, however, it is essential to exercise caution in distinguishing between personality traits before and after addiction; the high incidence of psychopathology among narcotics addicts may in part result from, rather than precede, the long-term effects of addiction.

Addiction associated with sociocultural factors.   In our society a so-called narcotics subculture exists in which addicts can obtain drugs and protect themselves against society's sanctions. Apparently the majority of narcotics addicts participate in this drug culture. The decision to join this culture has important future implications, for from that point on addicts will center their activities around their drug-user role. In short, addiction becomes a way of life.

With time, most young addicts who join the drug culture become increasingly withdrawn, indifferent to their friends (except those in the drug group), and apathetic about sexual activity. They are likely to abandon scholastic and athletic endeavors and to show a marked reduction in competitive and achievement strivings. Most of these addicts appear to lack good sex-role identification and to experience feelings of inadequacy when confronted with the demands of adulthood. While feeling progressively isolated from the broader culture, their feelings of group belongingness are bolstered by continued association with the addict milieu; at the same time, they come to view drugs both as a means of revolt against authority and conventional values and as a device for alleviating personal anxieties and tensions.

Treatments and Outcomes   Treatment for heroin addiction is initially similar to that for alcoholism in that it involves building up an addict both physically and psychologically and providing help through the withdrawal period. Addicts often dread the discomfort of withdrawal, but in a hospital setting it is less abrupt and usually involves the administration of a synthetic drug that eases the distress.

After withdrawal has been completed, treatment focuses on helping a former addict make an adequate adjustment to his or her community and abstain from the further use of narcotics. Traditionally, however, the prognosis has been unfavorable. Despite the use of counseling, group therapy, and other measures, only about 13 percent of people discharged from government rehabilitation programs in England did not become readdicted (Stephens & Cottrell, 1972). These and comparable findings from studies in the United States have led to the hypothesis that withdrawal does not remove the craving for heroin and that a key target in treatment must be the alleviation of this craving.

An approach to dealing with the physiological craving for heroin was pioneered by a research team at the Rockefeller University in New York. Their approach involved the use of the drug methadone in conjunction with a rehabilitation program (counseling, group therapy, and other procedures) directed toward the "total resocialization" of addicts (Dole & Nyswander, 1967; Dole, Nyswander, & Warner, 1968). **Methadone hydrochloride** is a synthetic narcotic that is related to heroin and is equally addictive physiologically. Its usefulness in treatment lies in the fact that it satisfies an addict's craving for heroin without producing serious psychological impairment, if only because it is administered as a "treatment" in a formal clinical context.

As a result of impressive preliminary findings, the federal government in 1972 agreed to a licensing program for physicians and clinics using methadone in the treatment of narcotics addicts. As methadone treatment has become more widely employed, however, the question as to whether methadone alone is sufficeint to rehabilitate narcotics addicts has been raised. Research on whether providing psychological treatment along with methadone contributes to a successful outcome has been contradictory. A recent, well-controlled study to evaluate the effectiveness of providing psychotherapy in addition to methadone maintenance found that psychotherapy added little to treatment outcome. Patients randomly assigned to the methadone treatment group with no psychotherapy were doing as well at follow-up over 2½ years later as patients who had received psychotherapy along with methadone (Rounsaville et al., 1986). The researchers found that many former addicts improved in social (73 percent) and psychological (61 pecent) functioning with little ancillary treatment.

The practice of weaning an addict from heroin only to addict him or her to another narcotic drug that may be required for life is also questionable. Methadone advocates might respond that addicts on methadone can function normally and hold jobs—not possible for most heroin addicts. In addition, methadone is available legally, and its quality is controlled by government standards. Nor is it necessary to increase the dosage over time. In fact, some patients can eventually be taken off methadone without danger of relapse to heroin addiction. Many heroin addicts can undergo methadone treatment without initial hospitalization, and during treatment they are able to hold jobs and function in their family and community settings (Newman & Cates, 1977).

Improvements in methadone maintenance treatment over the past few years have increased its attractiveness for treating heroin abusers and have improved its overall success rates. Milby (1988) reported that consistent gains have been made in the improvement rates for methadone maintenance over the past 20 years: from 39.7 percent reported in studies from 1970 to 1975, 54.9 percent in studies during the years between 1976 and 1980, and 76.3 percent in studies reported since 1980. The increased success rates for methadone treatment have been attributed to the use of additional drugs like clonidine (an antihypertensive drug used to treat essential hypertension and prevent headache), which aid in the detoxification process and reduce the discomfort of withdrawal symptoms.

■ Barbiturates (Sedatives)

In the 1930s, powerful sedatives called **barbiturates** were introduced. Although barbiturates have legitimate medical uses, they are extremely dangerous drugs commonly associated with both physiological and psychological dependence and with lethal overdoses.

Effects of Barbiturates   Barbiturates are widely used by physicians to calm patients and induce sleep. They act as depressants—somewhat like alcohol—to slow down the action of the central nervous system. Shortly after taking a barbiturate, an individual experiences a feeling of relaxation in which tensions seem to disappear, followed by a physical and intellectual lassitude and a tendency toward drowsiness and sleep—the intensity of such feelings varies depending on the type and amount of the barbiturate taken. Strong doses produce sleep almost immediately; excessive doses are lethal because they result in paralysis of the brain's respiratory centers.

Excessive use of barbiturates leads to increased tolerance as well as to physiological and psychological dependence. It can also lead to a variety of undesirable side effects, including sluggishness, slow speech, impaired comprehension and memory, extreme and sudden mood shifts, motor incoordination, and depression. Problem solving and decision making require great effort, and an individual usually is aware that his or her thinking is "fuzzy." Prolonged, excessive use of barbiturates can lead to brain damage and personality deterioration. Unlike opiates, tolerance of barbiturates does not increase the amount needed to cause death. This fact means that users can easily ingest fatal overdoses, either intentionally or accidentally. Indeed, barbiturates are associated with more overdoses and suicides than any other drug.

Causal Factors in Barbiturate Abuse and Dependence   Though many young people experiment with barbiturates, or downers, most do not become dependent. In fact, the individuals who do become dependent on barbiturates tend to be middle-aged and older people who often rely on them as "sleeping pills" and who do not commonly use other classes of drugs (except, possibly, alcohol and the minor tranquilizers). Often these people are referred to as *silent abusers* because they take the drugs in the privacy of their homes and ordinarily do not become public nuisances. Barbiturate dependence usually seems to occur in emotionally maladjusted individuals who seek relief from feelings of anxiety, tension, inadequacy, and the stresses of life.

Barbiturates are commonly used with alcohol. Some users claim they can achieve an intense high—a kind of controlled hypersensitivity—by combining barbiturates, amphetamines, and alcohol. However, one possible effect of combining barbiturates and alcohol is death, because each drug *potentiates* (increases the action of) the other. This situation was true in the case of Judi, described in *HIGHLIGHT 9.6*.

Treatments and Outcomes   As with many other drugs, it is often essential in treatment to distinguish between barbiturate intoxication, which results from the toxic effects of overdosage, and the symptoms associated with drug withdrawal. With barbiturates, withdrawal symptoms are more dangerous, severe, and long-lasting than in opiate withdrawal. A patient going through barbiturate withdrawal becomes anxious and apprehensive and manifests coarse tremors of the hands and face; additional symptoms commonly include insomnia, weakness, nausea, vomiting, abdominal cramps, rapid heart rate, elevated blood pressure, and loss of weight. Between the sixteenth hour and the fifth day, convulsions may occur. An acute delirious psychosis often develops, which may include symptoms similar to those found in withdrawal delirium.

For individuals used to taking large dosages, the withdrawal symptoms may last for as long as a month, but usually they tend to abate by the end of the first week. Fortunately, the withdrawal symptoms in barbiturate addiction can be minimized by administering increasingly smaller doses of the barbiturate itself or another drug producing similar effects. The withdrawal program is still a dangerous one, however, especially if barbiturate addiction is complicated by alcoholism or dependence on other drugs.

■ Amphetamines and Cocaine (Stimulants)

In contrast to barbiturates, which depress or slow down the action of the central nervous system, amphetamines and cocaine have chemical effects that stimulate or speed it up.

Amphetamines   The earliest **amphetamine** to be introduced—Benzedrine, or amphetamine sul-

One Girl Who Gambled with Barbiturates and Lost

Judi A. was a young, attractive girl from a middle-class family who apparently was seeking something that eluded her. She died of an overdose of barbiturates. The newspaper account of her death began with a statement from the autopsy report:

"The unembalmed body for examination is that of a well-developed, well-nourished Caucasian female measuring 173 cm. (68 inches), weighing 100–110 pounds, with dark blonde hair, blue eyes, and consistent in appearance with the stated age of. . . ."

Judi A. had lived only 17 years, 5 months and 27 days before her nude body was found on a grimy bed which had been made up on the floor of a rundown apartment in Newport Beach [California].

The inside of her mouth and her tongue were a bright red. The fingers of both hands were stained with the same color. . . . A small pill was found on the bed near the body, another was discovered on the floor.

Judi's death was classified as an accident because there was no evidence that she intended to take her own life. Actually it was about as accidental as if she'd killed herself while playing Russian roulette.

Judi didn't intentionally take too many reds. She was familiar with them, had taken them before, knew what to expect. She'd even had an earlier scare from a nonfatal overdose.

But her mind, clouded by the first few pills, lost count and she ingested a lethal number. She was dying before she swallowed the last pill. . . . (Hazlett, 1971, p. 1)

A complete investigation was ordered, in which it came to light that Judi had taken drugs when she had been unhappy at home, apparently often feeling unloved and unwanted. Following her parents' divorce, she had lived with her grandparents—who seemed to have been unaware of her drug problem and hence had not attempted to help her with it.

Judi had escalated the odds against herself by combining barbiturates with alcohol. Her friends said she had not been particularly different from the other girls they knew, most of whom also took pills in combination with beer or wine. In Judi's case, however, the combination had been lethal. She had not been able to find the something that had eluded her, but she had ultimately found death.

---

fate—was first synthesized in 1927 and became available in drugstores in the early 1930s as an inhalant to relieve stuffy noses. However, the manufacturers soon learned that some customers were chewing the wicks in the inhalers for "kicks." Thus the stimulating effects of amphetamine sulfate were discovered by the public before the drug was formally prescribed as a stimulant by physicians. In the late 1930s two newer amphetamines were introduced—Dexedrine (dextroamphetamine) and Methedrine (methamphetamine hydrochloride, also known as speed). The latter preparation is a far more potent stimulant of the central nervous system than either Benzedrine or Dexedrine and hence is considered more dangerous. In fact its abuse is lethal in an appreciable number of cases.

Initially these preparations were considered to be "wonder pills" that helped people to stay alert and awake and to function temporarily at a level beyond normal. During World War II, military interest was aroused in the stimulating effects of these drugs, and they were used by both Allied and German soldiers to ward off fatigue (Jarvik, 1967). Similarly, among civilians, amphetamines came to be widely used by night workers, long-distance truck drivers, students cramming for exams, and athletes striving to improve their performances. It was also discovered that amphetamines tend to suppress appetite, and they became popular with people trying to lose weight. In addition, they were often used to counteract the effects of barbiturates or other sleeping pills that had been taken the night before. As a result of their many uses, amphetamines were widely prescribed by doctors.

Today amphetamines are used medically for curbing the appetite when weight reduction is desirable; for treating individuals suffering from narcolepsy—a disorder in which people cannot prevent themselves from continually falling asleep during the day; and for treating hyperactive children. Curiously enough, amphetamines have a calming rather than a stimulating effect on many of these youngsters. Amphetamines are also sometimes prescribed for alleviating mild feelings of depression, relieving fatigue, and maintaining alertness for sustained periods of time.

Since the passage of the Controlled Substance Act of 1970 (DEA, 1979), amphetamines have been classified as Schedule II controlled substances—that is, drugs with high abuse potential that require a prescription for each purchase. As a result, medical use of amphetamines has declined in recent years, and they are more difficult to obtain legally. Nevertheless, it is apparently easy to find illegal sources of amphetamines, which thus remain among the most widely abused drugs.

Causes and effects of amphetamine abuse.   Despite their legitimate medical uses, amphetamines are not a magical source of extra mental or physical energy, but rather serve to push users toward greater expenditures of their own resources—often to a point of hazardous fatigue. In fact athletes have damaged their careers by using speed to try to improve their stamina and performance (Furlong, 1971). Although amphetamines are psychologically but not physiologically addictive, the body does build up tolerance to them rapidly. Thus habituated users may consume pills by the mouthful several times a day, whereas such amounts would be lethal to nonusers. In some instances, users inject the drug to get faster and more intense results. To get high on amphetamines, people may give themselves from 6 to 200 times the daily medical dosage usually prescribed for dieters.

For a person who exceeds prescribed dosages, amphetamine consumption results in heightened blood pressure, enlarged pupils, unclear or rapid speech, profuse sweating, tremors, excitability, loss of appetite, confusion, and sleeplessness. In some instances the jolt to body physiology from "shooting" (injecting) Methedrine can raise blood pressure enough to cause immediate death. In addition, the chronic abuse of amphetamines can result in brain damage and a wide range of psychopathology, including a disorder known as amphetamine psychosis, which appears similar to paranoid schizophrenia. Suicide, homicide, assault, and various other acts of violence are associated with amphetamine abuse. In the United States, Ellinwood (1971) studied 13 people who committed homicide under amphetamine intoxication and found that, in most cases, "the events leading to the homicidal act were directly related to amphetamine-induced paranoid thinking, panic, emotional lability (instability), or

lowered impulse control" (p. 90). A study of 100 hospital admissions for amphetamine intoxication revealed that 25 of the subjects had attempted suicide while under the influence of amphetamines (Nelson, 1969).

Treatments and outcomes.   Withdrawal from amphetamines is usually painless physically, because physiological addiction is absent or minimal. In some instances, however, withdrawal on a cold turkey basis from the chronic, excessive use of amphetamines can result in cramping, nausea, diarrhea, and even convulsions (AMA, 1968a).

Psychological dependence is another matter, however, and abrupt abstinence commonly results in feelings of weariness and depression. The depression usually reaches its peak in 48 to 72 hours, often remains intense for a day or two, and then tends to lessen gradually over a period of several days. Mild feelings of depression and lassitude may persist for weeks or even months after the last dose. If brain damage has occurred, residual effects may also include impaired ability to concentrate, learn, and remember, with resulting social, economic, and personality deterioration.

Cocaine   Like opium, **cocaine** is a plant product discovered and used in ancient times. It was widely used in the pre-Columbian world of Mexico and Peru (Guerra, 1971). It has been endorsed by such diverse figures as Sigmund Freud and the legendary Sherlock Holmes. Because of its exorbitant price, cocaine has become known as the "high" for the affluent. Its use increased significantly in the United States during the 1980s to the point that it was considered epidemic, especially among middle- and upper-income groups. Hospital admissions for cocaine abuse nearly doubled between 1978 and 1981 (NIDA, 1981). In a recent follow-up study of young adults (ages 15 to 16) who had been surveyed nine years earlier about drug use, Kandel et al. (1986) found that 37 percent of males and 24 percent of females surveyed had tried cocaine. Recent statistics (NIDA, 1990) suggest that the number of Americans who are "occasional cocaine users" is declining: 45 percent in the last two years and 72 percent since 1985. It may be that drug use is becoming unfashionable in the health-conscious middle- and upper-socioeconomic classes. The number of hardcore cocaine users, however, especially those in poverty-ridden inner-city neighborhoods, is increasing.

Like the opiates, cocaine may be ingested by sniffing, swallowing, or injecting. Also like the opiates, it precipitates a euphoric state of four to six hours' duration, during which a user experiences feelings of confidence and contentment. However, this blissful state may be preceded by headache, dizziness, and restlessness. When cocaine is chronically abused, acute toxic psychotic symptoms may occur, similar to those in acute schizophrenia—a user encounters frightening visual, auditory, and tactual hallucinations, such as the "cocaine bug" (Post, 1975).

Unlike the opiates, cocaine stimulates the cortex of the brain, inducing sleeplessness and excitement as well as stimulating and accentuating sexual processes. Consequently, some individuals have been known to administer cocaine to others as an aid to seduction. To complicate matters, Rolfs, Goldberg, and Sharrar (1990) found that cocaine abusers, because of their high sexual promiscuity, were at risk for contracting syphilis.

Dependence on cocaine also differs somewhat from dependence on opiates. It was believed until recently that tolerance was not increased appreciably with cocaine use. However, acute tolerance has now been demonstrated, and some chronic tolerance may occur as well (Fischman & Schuster, 1982; Jones, 1984). The previous view that cocaine abusers did not develop physiological dependence on the drug also has been changing. Recently, Gawin and Kleber (1986) demonstrated that chronic abusers who become abstinent develop uniform, depression-like symptoms, but the symptoms are transient. These states are usually followed by a period of dysphoria. Kleinman et al. (1990) reported that 47 percent of cocaine abusers were found to be clinically depressed, and many also reported symptoms of phobic behavior.

The psychological and life problems experienced by cocaine users are often great. In a 2½-year follow-up study of cocaine users and nonusers, Kosten, Rounsaville, and Kleber (1988) found that users (particularly those whose use increased over the span of the study) had significantly more psychosocial problems than nonusers. These problems included employment, family, psychological, and legal matters. Many life problems experienced by cocaine abusers result, in part, from the considerable amounts of money that are required to support their habits. Kleinman et al. (1990) reported that most of the cocaine abusers in their sample were spending in excess of $1000 per month to buy the drug.

Finally, cocaine use can be fatal—a recent study showed that cocaine-related deaths almost tripled between 1985 and 1988, with a total of 1033 deaths nationwide in the first six months of 1988, excluding New York City (Project DAWN, 1988). This point was dramatically illustrated during a period of ten days in the summer of 1986 when two well-known athletes, Len Bias, an all-American basketball player, and Don Rogers, a star running back for the Cleveland Browns, died after taking cocaine.

Psychological dependence on cocaine, like addiction to opiates, often leads to an obsession with procuring the drug, concurrent with a loss of social approval and self-respect. The following case illustrates this pattern:

The subject was a strikingly pretty, intelligent woman of 19 who had divorced her husband two years previously. She had married at the age of 16 and stated that she was terribly in love with her husband but he had turned out to be cruel and brutal. The woman was too ashamed of her marital failure (her parents had violently opposed the marriage and she had left home against their will) to return to her home. She had moved away from her husband and had gotten a job as a cocktail waitress in the same bar where her husband had been accustomed to taking her. She had been severely depressed, and several of his friends had insisted on buying her drinks to cheer her up. This process had continued for almost a year, during which she drank excessively but managed to hold her job. Following this, she had met a man in the bar where she worked who had introduced her to cocaine, assuring her that it would cheer her up and get rid of her blues. She stated that it both "hopped me up and gave me a feeling of peace and contentment." For a period of several months, she had purchased her cocaine from this same man until she had become ill with appendicitis and had been unable to pay the stiff prices he asked. Following an appendectomy, she had been induced to share his apartment as a means of defraying her expenses and ensuring the supply of cocaine, which she had now become heavily dependent on psychologically. She stated that she had felt she could not work without it. During this period, she had had sexual relations with the man although she had considered it immoral and had severe guilt feelings about it. This pattern had continued for several months until her "roommate" had upped his prices on the cocaine, on the excuse that it had been getting more difficult to obtain. He had suggested that she might be able to earn enough money to pay for it if she were not so prudish about whom she slept with. At this time, the full significance of where her behavior was leading seems to have dawned on her and she had come voluntarily to a community clinic for assistance.

Many celebrities—actors, musicians, politicians, sports figures—have become involved in cocaine use. Tragically, the activities of many of these individuals have led to drug-related problems and drug abuse. Former Mayor Marion Barry of Washington, D.C., made headlines for months after he was arrested while using cocaine in a hotel room with a young woman who had turned FBI informer. Through her, the FBI was able to videotape the encounter; we can clearly see Barry smoking crack in the portion of the tape shown here. His prominence as a public figure put the pervasive use of cocaine in the spotlight; about one million other, less prominent, Americans have also tried crack.

A new "supercharged" variety of cocaine, with the street names of *crack* and *rock*, made its appearance in the United States during the mid-1980s and became an immediate sensation among drug users. The high from crack is immediate and intense. It is estimated that over 1 million Americans have tried crack. The resulting human problems have been dramatic. Crack is believed to be one of the most dangerous drugs introduced to date because of its immediate addicting properties and its health risks (Smith, 1989). The devastation this drug can cause to a user is illustrated in the following case:

> *E*va is a 16-year-old patient at New York City's Phoenix House drug rehabilitation center who got hooked on crack two years ago. The product of a troubled middle-class family, she was already a heavy drinker and pot smoker when she was introduced to coke by her older brother, a young dope pusher. "When you take the first toke on a crack pipe, you get on top of the world," she says.
>
> She first started stealing from family and friends to support her habit. She soon turned to prostitution and went through two abortions before she was 16. "I didn't give a damn about protecting myself," she said. "I just wanted to get high. Fear of pregnancy didn't cross my mind when I hit the sack with someone for drugs." (Time, 1986)

The modifications in DSM-III-R diagnostic classification reflect a significant increase in our knowledge of cocaine's addictive properties. A new disorder, cocaine withdrawal, is described, which involves symptoms of depression, fatigue, disturbed sleep, and increased dreaming.

Treatment for psychological dependence on cocaine does not differ appreciably from that for other drugs that involve physiological dependence. Kosten (1989) reported that effective cocaine-abuse treatment includes the use of medications, such as desipramine, to reduce cravings and the use of psychological therapy to insure treatment compliance. The feelings of tension and depression that accompany absence of the drug have to be dealt with during the immediate withdrawal period.

▪ LSD and Related Drugs (Hallucinogens)

The **hallucinogens** are drugs whose properties are thought to induce hallucinations. In fact, however, these preparations do not so often "create" sensory images as distort them, so that an individual sees or hears things in different and unusual ways. These drugs are often referred to as *psychedelics*. The major drugs in this category are LSD (lysergic acid diethylamide), mescaline, and psilocybin. Not long ago, PCP, or "angel dust," became popular as well. Our present discussion will be restricted largely to LSD because of its unusual hallucinogenic properties.

LSD   The most potent of the hallucinogens, the odorless, colorless, and tasteless drug **LSD** can produce intoxication with an amount smaller than a grain of salt. It is a chemically synthesized substance first discovered by the Swiss chemist Hoffman in 1938. Hoffman was not aware of the potent hallucinatory qualities of LSD until some five years after his discovery, when he swallowed a small amount. This is his report of the experience:

Last Friday, April 16, 1943, I was forced to stop my work in the laboratory in the middle of the afternoon and to go home, as I was seized by a peculiar restlessness associated with a sensation of mild dizziness. On arriving home, I lay down and sank into a kind of drunkenness which was not unpleasant and which was characterized by extreme activity of imagination. As I lay in a dazed condition with my eyes closed (I experienced daylight as disagreeably bright) there surged upon me an uninterrupted stream of fantastic images of extraordinary plasticity and vividness and accompanied by an intense kaleidoscope-like play of colors. This condition gradually passed off after about two hours." (Hoffman, 1971, p. 23)

Hoffman followed up this experience with a series of planned self-observations with LSD, some of which he described as "harrowing." Researchers thought LSD might be useful for the induction and study of hallucinogenic states or "model psychoses," which were thought to be related to schizophrenia. About 1950, LSD was introduced into the United States for purposes of such research and to ascertain whether it might have medical or therapeutic uses. Despite considerable research, however, LSD has not proven therapeutically useful.

After taking LSD, a person typically goes through about eight hours of changes in sensory perception, lability of emotional experiences, and feelings of depersonalization and detachment. The peak of physiological and psychological effects usually occurs between the second and fourth hours. Physiological effects include increased heart rate, elevation of blood pressure, and faster and more variable breathing.

An LSD "trip" is not always pleasant. It can be extremely traumatic, and the distorted objects and sounds, the illusory colors, and the new thoughts can be menacing and terrifying. For example, Rorvik (1970) has cited the case of a young British law student who tried to "continue time" by using a dental drill to bore a hole in his head while under the influence of LSD. In other instances, people undergoing "bad trips" have set themselves aflame, jumped from high places, and taken other drugs that proved lethal in combination with LSD.

An interesting and unusual phenomenon that may occur following the use of LSD is a **flashback,** an involuntary recurrence of perceptual distortions or hallucinations weeks or even months after taking the drug. These experiences appear to be relatively rare among individuals who have taken LSD only once—although they do sometimes occur. One recent study found that continued effects on visual function were apparent at least two years following LSD use. Abraham and Wolf (1988) reported that individuals who had used LSD for a week were shown to have reduced visual sensitivity to light during dark adaptation and showed other visual problems compared to control individuals who had never used the drug.

Despite the possibility of adverse reactions, LSD was widely publicized during the 1960s, and a number of relatively well-known people experimented with it and gave glowing accounts of their "trips." In fact, during this period, an "LSD movement" was under way, based on the conviction that the drug could "expand the mind" and enable one to use talents and realize potentials previously undetected. No evidence exists that LSD enhances creative activity: no recognized works of art have been produced under the influence of the drug or as a consequence of a psychedelic experience. Although several artists have claimed improved creativity stemming from their LSD experiences, objective observers recognize few, if any, improvements in the work of these artists (AMA, 1968a). It should be pointed out, too, that though users of LSD do not develop physiological dependence, some chronic users have developed psychological dependence in the sense that they focus their life around LSD experiences.

For acute psychoses induced by LSD intoxication, treatment requires hospitalization and is primarily a medical matter. Often the outcome in such cases depends heavily on an individual's personal stability prior to taking the drug; in some cases, prolonged hospitalization may be required. Fortunately, brief psychotherapy is usually effective in treating psychological dependence on LSD and in preventing the recurrence of flashbacks that may still haunt an individual as a result of a bad trip. As in the case of trauma experienced in combat or civilian disasters, therapy is aimed at helping the individual work through the painful experience and integrate it into his or her self-structure.

Mescaline and Psilocybin   Two other well-known hallucinogens are mescaline and psilocybin. **Mescaline** is derived from the small, disclike growths (mescal buttons) at the top of the peyote cactus; **psilocybin** is obtained from a variety of "sacred" Mexican mushrooms known as *Psilocybe mexicana*. These drugs have been used for centuries in the ceremonial rites of native peoples living in

Mexico, the American southwest, and Central and South America. In fact, they were used by the Aztecs for such purposes long before the Spanish invasion. Both drugs have mind-altering and hallucinogenic properties, but their principal effect appears to be enabling an individual to see, hear, and otherwise experience events in unaccustomed ways—transporting him or her into a realm of "nonordinary reality." As with LSD, no definite evidence shows that mescaline and psilocybin actually "expand consciousness" or create new ideas; rather, they seem primarily to alter or distort experience.

▪ Marijuana

Although **marijuana** may be classified as a mild hallucinogen, there are significant differences in the nature, intensity, and duration of its effects as compared with those induced by LSD, mescaline, and other major hallucinogens. Marijuana comes from the leaves and flowering tops of the hemp plant, *Cannabis sativa*. The plant grows in mild climates throughout the world, including parts of India, Africa, Mexico, South America, and the United States. In its prepared state, marijuana consists chiefly of the dried green leaves—hence the colloquial name *grass*. It is ordinarily smoked in the form of cigarettes (reefers, or joints) or in pipes, but it can also be baked into brownies and other foods. In some cultures the leaves are steeped in hot water and the liquid is drunk, much as one might drink tea. Marijuana is related to a stronger drug, **hashish,** which is derived from the resin exuded by the cannabis plant and made into a gummy powder. Hashish, like marijuana, may be smoked, chewed, or drunk.

Both marijuana and hashish use can be traced far back into history. Cannabis was apparently known in ancient China (Blum, 1969; Culliton, 1970) and was listed in the herbal compendiums of the Chinese emperor Shen Nung, written about 2737 B.C. Until the late 1960s, marijuana use in the United States was confined largely to members of lower socioeconomic minority groups and to people in entertainment and related fields. In the late 1960s, however, its use among the youth of our society dramatically increased, and during the early 1970s it was estimated that over half the teenagers and young adults in America had experimented with marijuana in social situations, with about 10 percent presumably going from occasional to habitual use. Recently, Kandel et al. (1986) reported that among 24- and 25-year-old subjects, about 78 percent of males and 69 percent of females had tried marijuana.

Effects of marijuana   The specific effects of marijuana vary greatly, depending on the quality and dosage of the drug, the personality and mood of the user, the user's past experiences with the drug, the social setting, and the user's expectations. However, considerable consensus exists among regular users that when marijuana is smoked and inhaled, an individual gets high. This state is one of mild euphoria distinguished by increased feelings of well-being, heightened perceptual acuity, and pleasant relaxation, often accompanied by a sensation of drifting or floating away. Sensory inputs are intensified. Often a person's sense of time is stretched or distorted, so that an event lasting but a few seconds may seem to cover a much longer span. Short-term memory may also be affected, as when one notices a bite taken out of a sandwich but does not remember having taken it. For most users, pleasurable experiences, including sexual intercourse, are reportedly enhanced. When smoked, marijuana is rapidly absorbed and its effects appear within seconds to minutes but seldom last more than two to three hours.

Marijuana may lead to unpleasant as well as pleasant experiences. For example, if an individual takes the drug while in an unhappy, angry, suspicious, or frightened mood, unsavory feelings may be magnified. With higher dosages and with certain unstable or susceptible individuals, marijuana can produce extreme euphoria, hilarity, and overtalkativeness; it can also produce intense anxiety and depression as well as delusions, hallucinations, and

Group counseling is a common treatment for psychological dependence on drugs. In the give and take of group therapy, individuals may be able to face the consequences of their addiction and to see new possibilities for coping with it.

other psychotic-like behavior. Recent evidence (Tien & Anthony, 1990) suggests a strong relationship between daily marijuana use and the occurrence of self-reported psychotic symptoms.

Marijuana's short-range physiological effects include a moderate increase in heart rate, a slowing of reaction time, a slight contraction of pupil size, bloodshot and itchy eyes, a dry mouth, and an increased appetite. Furthermore, Braff et al. (1981) reported that marijuana induces memory dysfunction and a slowing of information processing. Continued use of high dosages over time tends to produce lethargy and passivity. In such cases marijuana appears to have a depressant and a hallucinogenic effect. The effects of long-term and habitual marijuana use are still under investigation, although a number of possible adverse side effects have been related to the prolonged, heavy use of marijuana.

Marijuana has often been compared to heroin, but the two drugs have little in common with respect either to tolerance or to physiological dependence. Marijuana does not lead to physiological dependence, as heroin does, so discontinued use is not accompanied by withdrawal symptoms. Marijuana can, however, lead to psychological dependence, in which an individual experiences a strong need for the drug whenever he or she feels anxious and tense.

■ Caffeine and Nicotine

Two quite common addictions to legally available and widely used substances, caffeine and nicotine, are included in the DSM III-R. Although these addictions do not represent the extensive and self-destructive problems found in the drug and alcohol disorders previously described, they are important physical and mental health problems in our society for several reasons: (a) These drugs are easy to abuse. It is easy to become addicted to them because they are widely used and most people are exposed to them early in life. (b) These drugs are readily available to anyone desiring to use them; in fact, it is usually difficult, because of peer pressure, to avoid using them in our society. (c) Both caffeine and nicotine have clearly addictive properties; use of them promotes further use, until they become a needed commodity in one's daily life. (d) It is difficult to quit using these drugs both because of their addictive properties and because they are so embedded in the social context (nicotine use, however, is falling out of favor in many settings). (e) The extreme difficulty most people have dealing with

the withdrawal symptoms when trying to "break the habit" often produce considerable frustration. (f) Finally, the health problems and side effects of these drugs have been widely noted. One in seven deaths in the United States is associated with cigarette consumption (USDHHS, 1988).

Because of their tenacity as habits and their contributions to many major health problems, we will examine each of these addictions in more detail.

Caffeine   Caffeine is a chemical compound found in many commonly available drinks and foods. Although the consumption of caffeine is widely practiced and socially promoted in contemporary society, problems can occur as a result of excessive caffeine intake. The negative effects of caffeine involve intoxication rather than withdrawal. Unlike with other drugs, such as alcohol or nicotine, withdrawal from caffeine does not produce severe symptoms, except for headache, which is usually mild.

Caffeine-induced organic mental disorder (also referred to as Caffeinism), as described in DSM-III-R, involves symptoms of restlessness, nervousness, excitement, insomnia, muscle twitching, and gastrointestinal complaints. It follows the ingestion of caffeine-containing substances, such as coffee, tea, cola, or chocolate. The amount of caffeine that results in intoxication differs among individuals; however, consumption of over 1 gram of caffeine could result in muscle twitching, cardiac arrythmia, agitation, and rambling thinking. Consumption of 10 grams of caffeine can produce seizures, respiratory failures, and death.

Nicotine   Nicotine is a poisonous akaloid that is the chief active ingredient in tobacco; it is found in such items as cigarettes, chewing tobacco, and cigars, and is even used as an insecticide.

Strong evidence indicates a nicotine dependency syndrome (USDHHS, 1988). Nicotine-induced organic mental disorder, as it is called in DSM-III-R, results from ceasing or reducing the intake of nicotine-containing substances after an individual has acquired physical dependence on them. The diagnostic criteria for nicotine withdrawal include (a) the daily use of nicotine for at least several weeks; and (b) the following symptoms after nicotine ingestion is stopped or reduced: craving for nicotine; irritability, frustration, or anger; anxiety; difficulty concentrating; restlessness; decreased heart rate; and increased appetite or weight gain. Several other physical concomitants are associated with withdrawal from nicotine, including decreased metabolic rate, headaches, insomnia, tremors, increased coughing, and impairment of performance on tasks requiring attention.

These withdrawal symptoms usually continue for several days to several weeks, depending on the extent of the nicotine habit. Some individuals report a desire for nicotine continuing for several months after they have quit smoking. In general, nicotine withdrawal symptoms operate in a manner similar to other addictions—they are "time limited and abate with drug replacement or gradual reduction" (Hughes, Higgins, & Hatsukami, 1990, p. 381).

Treatment of nicotine withdrawal Over the past 25 years, since the Surgeon General's report that detailed the health hazards of smoking cigarettes, numerous treatment programs have been developed to aid smokers in quitting (Lando, in press; Schwartz, 1987; USDHHS, 1989). Quit-smoking programs use many different methods, including social support groups; various pharmacologic agents, which replace cigarette consumption with other safer forms of nicotine, such as candy or gum; self-directed change, which involves giving individuals guidance as to how they can change their own behaviors (Abrams et al., in press); and professional treatment using psychological procedures such as behavioral or cognitive-behavioral interventions (Lando, in press).

In general, tobacco dependency can be successfully treated (USDHHS, 1989), and most of the quit-smoking programs enjoy some success, averaging about a 20 to 25 percent success rate, when evaluated by objective criteria. Lando (in press) concluded that "no *single* treatment suitable for all smokers has emerged," and Schwartz (1987) found that smokers tend to prefer self-help and minimal-contact treatments over more intensive treatment programs.

OTHER ADDICTIVE DISORDERS: HYPEROBESITY AND PATHOLOGICAL GAMBLING

Not all addictive disorders involve the use of substances with chemical properties that induce dependency. People can develop "addictions" to certain activities that can be just as life-threatening as severe alcoholism and just as damaging, psychologically and socially, as drug abuse. We include two

such disorders in this chapter—hyperobesity and pathological gambling. They are similar to other addictions in their behavioral manifestations, their etiologies, and their resistance to treatments.

■ Hyperobesity

To get an idea of how extensive the problem of obesity is, just look around and count the number of individuals who are seriously overweight. Weiss (1984), defining hyperobesity as 20 percent in excess of desirable weight, estimates that from 15 to 16 million Americans fall into this category. In addition, Weiss reports that obesity is a serious but often overlooked health problem in the United States today. Stewart and Brook (1983) found, in a survey of 5817 Americans aged 14 to 61, that 10 percent were moderately overweight and 12 percent severely overweight.

In this discussion, we are concerned with **hyperobesity**—often called morbid obesity—which we define as being 100 pounds or more above ideal body weight. Such obesity is not simply unattractive; it can be a dangerous, life-threatening disorder, resulting in such conditions as diabetes, musculoskeletal problems, high blood pressure, and other cardiovascular diseases that may place an individual at high risk for a heart attack. Although some cases of extreme obesity result from metabolic or hormonal disorders, most obese individuals simply take in more calories than they burn off.

Obesity, as a disorder, may be placed in several diagnostic categories, depending on which characteristics are being emphasized. If we focus on the physical changes, for example, we may view obesity as having both psychological and physical components. Many clinicians, however, view the central problem not as the excessive weight itself, but as the long-standing habit of overeating. Thus obesity resulting from gross, habitual overeating is considered to be more like the problems found in the personality disorders—especially those involving loss of control over an appetite of some kind (Kurland, 1967; Leon et al., 1978; Orford, 1985).

Causes of Persistent Overeating What prompts people to overeat to the point of obesity, despite an awareness of the detrimental health effects and a consciousness of the strong social prejudice in favor of the "body beautiful"? Several potential causal factors have been explored; although results are not conclusive, biological and learning factors seem to be of great importance.

Biological factors.   Some people seem able to eat high-calorie foods without significant weight gain, while others become overweight easily and engage in a constant struggle to maintain their weight. Most people gain weight with advancing age, but this gain could be related to reduced activity and to the fact that older people are likely to continue their earlier eating habits even though they need fewer calories. As already indicated, some individuals have metabolic or endocrine anomalies that can produce obesity at any age, though these cases seem to be relatively rare.

Adult obesity is related to the number and size of the adipose cells (fat cells) in the body (Weiss, 1984). Individuals who are obese have markedly more adipose cells than people of normal weight. When weight is lost, the size of the cells is reduced, but not their number. Some evidence suggests that the total number of adipose cells stays the same from childhood on (Crisp et al., 1970). It is possible that overfeeding infants and young children may cause them to develop more adipose cells and may thus predispose them to weight problems in adulthood.

Psychosocial factors.   Factors other than biological endowment play an important role in obesity (Newman et al., 1990). In many cases the key determinants of excessive eating and obesity appear to be family behavior patterns. In some families, the customary diet or an overemphasis on food may produce obesity in many or all family members. In such families, a fat baby may be seen as a healthy baby, and there may be great pressure on infants and children to eat more than they want. In other families, eating (or overeating) becomes a habitual means of alleviating emotional distress.

Several psychological views address the causes of gross habitual overeating. Some of these views are discussed in the following paragraphs:

1. According to the psychodynamic view, obese individuals are fixated at the oral stage of psychosexual development (Bychowski, 1950). They are believed to orient their lives around oral gratification (through excessive eating) because their libidinal energies and psychological growth have not advanced to a more mature level.

This view has been elaborated by Bruch (1973), who distinguishes between developmental obesity and reactive obesity. She sees developmental obesity as a childhood response to parental rejection or other severe disturbances in the parent-child relationship. Supposedly, the parents compensate for their emotional rejection by overfeeding and overprotecting the child. Such children never learn to distinguish different internal signals because their parents respond to all signs of distress by giving them food. Bruch sees this pattern as leading to a distorted perception of internal states—that is, not knowing when enough food has been ingested.

Reactive obesity is defined by Bruch as obesity that occurs in adults as a reaction to trauma or stress. Here, individuals are thought to use the defense mechanism of overeating to lessen their feelings of distress or depression. Though this view may be depicted as "truth" in countless cartoons and sitcoms, the research findings are inconclusive.

2. According to the *externality hypothesis,* eating is under the control of external cues rather than an individual's internal state. Whereas hunger and its satisfaction dictate the eating patterns of most people, obese people are seen as being at the mercy of environmental inducements. Regardless of how recently or amply they have eaten, they may be prompted to eat again simply by the sight or smell of food. This reliance on external cues is pointedly illustrated in the complaint of an obese 29-year-old patient:

I crave food . . . everywhere I go, whatever I do, I am reminded of food. Today after breakfast, I rode to work on the bus. The advertisements made me so hungry that I had to stop at the coffee shop for rolls before I went into the office. When I watch TV, I find myself constantly eating—I want everything. I can't stop. My big downfall is "munchies"— peanuts, potato chips, brownies. Going to the grocery store, I lose control and before you know it I have to get another grocery cart—and the first one is just full of junk. I can sit down in the evening to write a letter and before I know it the jar of peanuts is completely gone!

Other investigators, however, reject the externality hypothesis. Rodin (1974) found obese people no more sensitive to external cues than people of normal weight. Leon and Roth (1977), too, in a review of research on this hypothesis, found the evidence highly equivocal.

3. The simplest explanation—and therefore the easiest to accept—seems to be found in the behavioral view. According to this view, a person's weight gain and his or her tendency to maintain excessive weight can be explained quite simply in terms of learning principles (Jordan & Levitz, 1975; Leon & Chamberlain, 1973; Stuart, 1971b).

For all of us, eating behavior is determined in part by conditioned responses to a wide range of environmental stimuli. For example, people are encouraged to eat at parties and movies, while watching TV, and even at work. Eating is reinforced in all these situations, and it is difficult to avoid the many inducements to eat. Thus a wide assortment of seemingly avoidable reinforcers and conditioned stimuli enter the lives of most Americans.

Obese people, however, have been shown to be conditioned to more cues—both internal and external—than people of normal weight. Anxiety, anger, boredom, and social inducements all may lead to overeating. Eating in response to such cues is then reinforced because the taste of good food is pleasurable and the individual's emotional tension is reduced. This reinforcement increases the probability that overeating will continue and worsen.

With such frequent overfeeding, obese people may then learn not to respond to satiety cues, no longer feeling full when they have had enough. Meanwhile, physical activity, because its short-term effects are often aversive rather than pleasant, tends not to be reinforced, especially as pounds accumulate. Thus obese individuals may become less and less active.

Sociocultural factors.   Different cultures have different concepts of human beauty. Some value slimness; others, a rounded contour. In some cultures, obesity is valued as a sign of social influence and power. Within our own society, obesity seems to be related to social class, occurring six times as often in lower-class adults and nine times more often in lower-class youngsters. (Stunkard et al., 1972). Obesity may be related to high-carbohydrate diets in lower-class families, however.

Treatment of Hyperobesity   Losing weight is a preoccupation of many Americans; diet books, dietary aids, and weight-loss programs are big business. Diet plans abound, with new programs emerging as often as clothing fads. The success rates of most of these devices and programs are quite low. In fact Stuart (1967) reported that the average outcome from diets is a regaining of 105 percent of the weight lost (Stuart, 1967). Cyclic loss and regaining can even be dangerous because it may do serious damage to the cardiovascular system, further compounding the problem.

Most obese patients who seek professional help have failed on many diets in the past. Some of the most successful dietary programs are the self-control behavioral management programs, conduct-ed in groups and including follow-up booster sessions (Kingsley & Wilson, 1977).

A number of weight-loss group programs are conducted by commercial organizations like TOPS (Take Off Pounds Sensibly) and Weight Watchers (Bumbalo & Young, 1973). These programs provide strong group pressures to reduce weight by public praise of weight losses and public disapproval and "punishments" for failures. Thus they provide community support and encouragement to maintain better eating habits. Individuals who remain with these group programs lose about 14 pounds on the average (Garb & Stunkard, 1974); however, less than a third of those who begin the programs stay for 24 months.

Fasting or starvation diets under medically controlled conditions generally produce weight losses in hyperobese patients—with some studies reporting losses of over 100 pounds (Leon, 1976). This method of rapid weight loss, however, may involve several dangerous potential complications, such as hypertension, gout, and kidney failure (Munro & Duncan, 1972; Runcie & Thompson, 1970). Two eating disorders, anorexia nervosa and bulimia (discussed in Chapter 7), involve an excessive preoccupation with weight loss.

Another questionable medical treatment of hyperobese patients has centered on the use of *anorexigenic drugs* to reduce appetite. Diet pills, such as amphetamines, suppress the desire for food and, as a result, have been used extensively. Again, however, maintenance of weight loss once the diet pills are gone often becomes a problem.

Moreover, diet pills often present an additional problem of their own. As we have seen, amphetamines are addicting substances and are particularly dangerous when used in combination with other substances, such as alcohol. The general ineffectiveness of amphetamines for long-term weight control plus their high abuse potential has made these drugs of doubtful value in weight-reduction programs.

The most effective psychological treatment procedures for extremely obese patients are behavioral management methods, which teach individuals to take off weight gradually through reduced food intake and exercise (Jeffery, Wing, & Stunkard, 1978). A number of methods using positive reinforcement, self-monitoring, and self-reward can produce moderate weight loss over time. In general these procedures, based on positive reinforcement, are more effective than classical conditioning procedures, such as aversive conditioning in which shock or unpleasant thoughts may be paired with eating behavior (Leon, 1976).

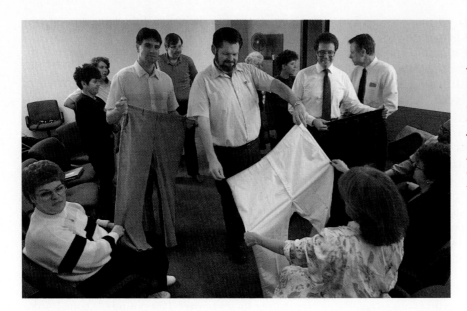

Some of the most successful dietary programs are the self-control behavioral management programs, conducted in groups. Here dieters show how much weight they have lost by proudly displaying pants they can no longer wear. Programs like this provide strong group pressures to lose weight through public praise of successes and support and encouragement for maintaining better eating habits.

The treatment of extremely obese patients is often a difficult and frustrating task for all concerned. Even with the most effective treatment procedures, failures abound, partly due to the necessity of self-motivation in treatment.

In one case involving a 15-year-old high school student named Beth, a variety of treatment and counseling approaches were used, including a token reward system for eating balanced meals with smaller portions. Though she reportedly complied with the point system and earned rewards for the first three weeks, she nevertheless lost little weight. She said that she had cut down on high-calorie snacks but was still eating large portions at mealtimes. The treatment sessions focused on problems occurring in her school and with her family that were related to her eating habits. Ways of maintaining her diet were explored, as were issues concerning the decision to eat and her commitment to change. The primary emphasis was on self-control and self-management techniques. She was also taught a system of self-monitoring of her food intake. After 16 treatment sessions over a period of five months, Beth had only decreased her weight from an original 208½ pounds to 207¼ pounds. The therapist confronted her with her apparent lack of commitment and pointed out the difference between wanting to lose weight and wanting to change her eating style. Two weeks later,

Beth came to the final session having decided that the freedom to eat what she wanted was more important to her at that point in her life than changing her eating patterns.

The poor outcome in this example illustrates the tenacity of extreme obesity. As in Beth's case, many patients lose interest in their remote goal and choose to remain obese rather than make the difficult and persistent effort required to lose weight and keep it off.

A promising cognitive-behavioral treatment approach for eating disorders has been explored by Garner (1986). This approach emphasizes how the symptom pattern of obesity logically follows from faulty assumptions individuals make and their beliefs about their bodies. The cognitive-behavioral approach is not incompatible with other treatment approaches and allows exploration of early developmental issues, interpersonal conflicts, faulty family interaction patterns, and biological factors. In this approach a patient (a) is taught to monitor his or her own thinking, especially the pattern of faulty beliefs; (b) is helped to recognize the connection between faulty thoughts and maladaptive eating behaviors; (c) is taught to seek evidence for the faulty beliefs underlying the overeating; and (d) is taught to gradually substitute more realistic and appropriate views of his or her own behaviors based on objective evidence.

Garner's cognitive-behavioral approach follows two "tracks" in assisting a patient to alter his or her eating patterns. The first track involves normalizing the patient's eating behavior and physical condition; the second track involves assisting the patient to assess his or her faulty thoughts and actions (Garner, 1986). Evidence on the effectiveness of this approach awaits further research.

■ Pathological Gambling

Gambling is usually defined as wagering on games or events in which chance largely determines the outcome. In modern societies, money is typically the item of exchange; in other societies, seashell currency, beads, jewelry, and food are often used. The ancient Chinese frequently wagered hairs of their heads—and sometimes even fingers, toes, and limbs—on games of chance (Cohen & Hansel, 1956). Regardless of the item of exchange, gambling seems to be an enduring human proclivity. Judging from written history and the studies of anthropologists, gambling has occurred and continues to occur almost universally and among all social strata.

Pathological gambling, also known as compulsive gambling, is an addictive behavior in which gambling disrupts an individual's life. Although this behavior pattern does not involve a chemically addictive substance, it can be considered an addictive disorder because of the personality factors that tend to characterize compulsive gamblers, the difficulties attributable to compulsive gambling, and the treatment problems involved. Like other addictions, pathological gambling involves behavior maintained by short-term gains despite long-term disruption of an individual's life.

Clinical Picture in Pathological Gambling

Gambling in our society takes many forms, including casino gambling, betting on horse races (legally or otherwise), numbers games, lotteries, dice, bingo, and cards. The exact sums that change hands in legal and illegal gambling are unknown, but it has been estimated that habitual gamblers in the United States lose more than 20 billion dollars each year.

If one were to define gambling in its broadest sense, even investing in the stock market might be considered a game of chance. Sherrod (1968) has pointed to the need for a clearer definition of terms: "If you bet on a horse, that's gambling. If you bet you can make three spades, that's entertainment. If you bet cotton will go up three points, that's business. See the difference?" (p. 619).

In any event, gambling appears to be one of our major national pastimes, with some 50 percent of the population gambling at one time or another on anything from Saturday night poker games to the outcome of sporting events. Usually, such gambling is a harmless form of social entertainment; an individual places a bet and waits for the result. Win or lose, the game is over. But while most people can gamble and then get on with their life, an estimated 6 to 10 million Americans get "hooked" on gambling (see *HIGHLIGHT 9.7*). Whatever an individual gambler's situation, a recent survey confirmed that compulsive gambling significantly affects the social, psychological, and economic well-being of the gambler's family (Lorenz & Shuttlesworth, 1983). In fact, a recent study by Blaszczynski, McConaghy, and Frankova (1989) found that a high proportion of pathological gamblers commit crimes that are related to gambling.

Causal Factors in Pathological Gambling

Although a few psychologists and psychiatrists have dealt with the topic of pathological gambling, little systematic research has been done, and the causal factors are not yet well understood. Pathological gambling seems to be a learned pattern that is highly resistant to extinction. Often a person who becomes a pathological gambler won a substantial sum of money the first time he or she gambled; chance alone would dictate that a certain percentage of individuals would have such "beginner's luck." Bolen and Boyd (1968) considered it likely that the reinforcement an individual received during this introductory phase is a significant factor in later pathological gambling. Because anyone is likely to win from time to time, the principles of intermittent reinforcement could explain an addict's continued gambling despite excessive losses. Bolen and Boyd were struck particularly by the similarity between slot-machine players and Skinner's laboratory pigeons; the latter, placed on a variable reinforcement schedule, "repetitively and incessantly pecked to the point of exhaustion and eventual demise while waiting the uncertain appearance of their jackpot of bird seed" (1968, p. 629).

Despite their awareness that the odds are against them, and despite the fact that they rarely or never repeat their early success, compulsive gamblers continue to gamble avidly. To "stake" their gambling, they often dissipate their savings, neglect their families, default on bills, and borrow money from friends and loan companies. Eventually, they may resort to writing bad checks, embezzlement, or

A Case of Pathological Gambling

John was a 40-year-old, rather handsome man with slightly graying hair who managed an automobile dealership for his father. For the previous two years, he had increasingly neglected his job and was deep in debt as a result of his gambling activities. He had gambled heavily since he was about 27 years old. His gambling had occasioned frequent quarrels in his first marriage and finally a divorce. He had married his second wife without telling her of his problem, but it eventually had come to light and had created such difficulty that she had taken their two children and had returned to her parents' home.

John joined an encounter group in the stated hope that he might receive some assistance with his problem. In the course of the early group sessions, he proved to be an intelligent, well-educated man who seemed to have a good understanding of his gambling problem and its self-defeating nature. He stated that

he had started gambling after winning some money at the horse races. This experience convinced him that he could supplement his income by gambling judiciously. However, his subsequent gambling—which frequently involved all-night poker games, trips to Las Vegas, and betting on the races—almost always resulted in heavy losses.

In the group, John talked about his gambling freely and coherently—candidly admitting that he enjoyed the stimulation and excitement of gambling more than sexual relations with his wife. He was actually rather glad his family had left because it relieved him of certain responsibilities toward them and alleviated his guilt for neglecting them. He readily acknowledged that his feelings and behavior were inappropriate and self-defeating, but he stated that he was "sick" and that he desperately needed help.

It soon became apparent that although John was willing to talk

about his problem, he was not prepared to take constructive steps in dealing with it. He wanted the group to accept him in the role of a pathological gambler who could not be expected to "cure" himself. At the group's suggestion, he attended a few meetings of Gamblers Anonymous but found them "irrelevant." It was also suggested that he try aversive therapy, but he felt this would not help him.

While attending the group sessions, John apparently continued to gamble and continued to lose. After the eighth encounter group session, he did not return. Through inquiry by one of the members, it was learned that he had been arrested for embezzling funds from his father's business, but that his father had somehow managed to have the charges dropped. John reportedly then left for another state and his subsequent history is unknown.

---

other illegal means of obtaining money, feeling sure that their luck will change and that they will be able to repay what they have taken. Whereas others view their gambling as unethical and disruptive, they are likely to see themselves as taking "calculated risks" to build a lucrative business. Often they feel alone and resentful that others do not understand their activities.

In a pioneering and well-controlled study of former pathological gamblers, Rosten (1961) found that as a group they tended to be rebellious, unconventional individuals who did not seem to fully understand the ethical norms of society. Half of the group described themselves as "hating regulations." Of 30 men studied, 12 had served time in

jail for embezzlement and other crimes directly connected with their gambling. Rosten also found that these men were unrealistic in their thinking and prone to seek highly stimulating situations. In the subjects' own words, they "loved excitement" and "needed action." Although the men admitted that they had known objectively the all-but-impossible odds they faced while gambling, they had felt that these odds did not apply to them. Often they had the unshakable feeling that "tonight is my night"; typically, they had also followed the so-called Monte Carlo fallacy—that after so many losses, their turn was coming up and they would hit it big. Many of the men discussed the extent to which they had "fooled" themselves by elaborate rationalizations.

For example, one gambler described his previous rationalizations as covering all contingencies: "When I was ahead, I could gamble because I was playing with others' money. When I was behind, I had to get even. When I was even, I hadn't lost any money" (Rosten, 1961, p. 67).

It is of interest to note that within a few months after the study, 13 of Rosten's 30 subjects either had returned to heavy gambling, had started to drink excessively, or had not been heard from and were presumed to be gambling again.

Later studies strongly support Rosten's findings. They describe pathological gamblers as typically immature, rebellious, thrill seeking, superstitious, and basically psychopathic (Bolen & Boyd, 1968; Bolen, Caldwell, & Boyd, 1975; Custer, 1982; and Graham, 1978a). The most comprehensive study is that of Livingston (1974), who observed, interviewed, and tested 55 mostly working-class men who had joined Gamblers Anonymous to try to stop gambling. Livingston found that these men often referred to their "past immaturity" in explaining their habitual gambling. They also described themselves as having a "big ego" and acknowledged a strong need for recognition and adulation from others.

Although these men had usually been able to cover their losses early in their gambling careers, the course was downhill, leading to financial, marital, job, and often legal problems. Eventually, things got so bad that it seemed the only way out of their difficulties was the way they got into them—by gambling.

A study by Graham (1978a) compared the psychological test performance of pathological gamblers with that of alcoholics and heroin addicts. The three groups of addicts showed many similar characteristics. The individuals in each group were self-centered, narcissistic, tense, nervous, and anxious; they overreacted to stress and were pessimistic and brooding. They were characterized by acting out, impulsive behavior; they had periodic outbursts of anger, were frustrated with their own lack of achievement, were reluctant to open up emotionally for fear of being hurt, often showed superficial remorse, and were passive-dependent and manipulative. They stated a desire to "turn over a new leaf" but showed a poor prognosis for behavioral change in traditional therapy. These similarities suggest that common personality characteristics may be involved as predisposing factors in the three disorders.

Cultural factors also appear to be important in developing gambling problems. Recently reported

A famous case of the destructive nature of gambling is that of Pete Rose, whose long and record-breaking career in baseball was tarnished when he was convicted for betting on the sport. It is difficult to fathom why someone with such fame, talent, and success would be so careless as to risk it all by gambling. The causal factors in pathological, or compulsive, gambling are not well understood, but we do know that compulsive gamblers will continue to gamble avidly, even at risk of personal disasters; their thinking is unrealistic and their behavior is sensation-seeking and oblivious to ethical norms.

research with Southeast Asian refugee populations highlights the role of cultural influences in gambling. Pathological gambling is one of the most serious, yet most common, problems shown by Southeast Asian refugees, particularly those from Laos, in adapting to resettlement countries. The problem of out-of-control gambling among refugees has been underestimated in the past because health-service-needs surveys have been typically directed at surveying participation in mental health programs. New surveys of mental health problems that have focused on *key informants*—that is, knowledgeable, concerned, and observant leaders in refugee communities—have reported almost epidemic problems with gambling (Aronoff, 1987; Ganju & Quan, 1987). For example, Aronoff (1987) reported that 54 percent of informants in the Laos group reported gambling as a significant problem. This problem is among the most serious adaptation difficulties for refugees because family members who gamble away the limited resources available to them (for example, food stamps) can place even greater pressure on their efforts to adapt to a new culture.

Pathological gambling problems are not new to Southeast Asians because gambling is reportedly common among these groups in their own cultures. However, these problems have apparently become more intensified and more widespread in this country. Reasons for these increased gambling problems include the following: (a) social sanctions that worked to control excessive gambling in Southeast Asia appear no longer to operate; (b) the stress levels that refugees experience are high, and gambling serves temporarily to relieve cares; reportedly, when they are in their gambling houses or "casinos," many refugees feel, at least temporarily, as though they are still in their native lands; (c) many individuals have a great deal of time on their hands because they are unable to find employment, and gambling helps pass the time; and (d) finally, of course, gambling lures refugees with the possibility of great rewards and the opportunity to regain all they lost during migration.

Professionals working in refugee mental health programs have become increasingly concerned with the extent of gambling problems in refugee families. Because these problems are not brought to the mental health clinics, they are often not dealt with in treatment.

Treatments and Outcomes   Treatment of pathological gamblers is still a relatively unexplored area. However, Boyd and Bolen (1970) have reported on a study in which eight pathological gamblers and their spouses were treated together through group psychotherapy—an approach based on the finding that a pathological gambler's marital relationship is generally chaotic and turbulent, with the spouse frequently showing seriously maladaptive behavior patterns also. Gambling ceased in three of these cases and almost completely stopped in the other five. The extent to which changes in the gamblers' marital relationships influenced the treatment outcomes can only be surmised—six of the eight couples showed significant improvements. Other treatment approaches, including aversion therapy and covert sensitization (Cotler, 1971) and cognitive-behavioral therapy (Bannister, 1975) have been tried with individual cases, but further studies are needed before we can evaluate the potential effectiveness of psychotherapy in treating this disorder.

Some pathological gamblers who want to change find help through membership in Gamblers Anonymous. This organization was founded in 1957 in Los Angeles by two pathological gamblers who found that they could help each other control their gambling by talking about their experiences. Since then, groups have been formed in most major American cities. The groups are modeled after Alcoholics Anonymous, and they view those who gamble as personally responsible for their own actions. The only requirement for membership is an expressed desire to stop gambling. In group discussions, members share experiences and try to gain insights into the irrationality of their gambling and to realize its inevitable consequences. As with Alcoholics Anonymous, members try to help each other maintain control and prevent relapses. Unfortunately, only a small fraction of pathological gamblers find their way into Gamblers Anonymous. Of those who do, only about 1 in 10 manages to overcome the addiction to gambling (Strine, 1971).

A novel inpatient treatment program for pathological gamblers has been developed at the Brecksville, Ohio, Veterans' Administration Medical Center (1981). This program, initiated in 1972, has helped many individuals and has served as a model for many other hospitals.

The Brecksville treatment program for pathological gamblers, which lasts for a minimum of 28 days, is integrated into the alcohol treatment program. Five inpatient beds in the 55-bed unit are set aside for pathological gamblers. Alcoholics and gamblers are housed together and share many common program elements because their problems are viewed as quite similar.

It may seem that inpatient hospital treatment for a "social" problem such as pathological gambling is an overly drastic and unwarranted measure. In a number of circumstances, however, such measures seem necessary. For example, a gambler might be depressed or be experiencing severe panic or desperation and may present a possible suicide risk; or the individual may have allowed his or her health to deteriorate; or the individual's legal situation might require confinement; or in some areas of the country, the individual may not have access to outpatient attention for his or her gambling behavior (for example, there may not be a local chapter of Gamblers Anonymous).

The treatment goals for these pathological gamblers include abstinence from gambling, major life-style changes, participation in Gamblers Anonymous programs, and, because gambling behavior is viewed as "trivial" and of no social value, the acquisition of more adaptive forms of recreation.

A variety of treatment approaches are used during an individual's hospital stay: (a) the ward is managed according to strict rules of discipline and any deviation from the rules may result in discharge from the hospital; (b) group therapy is provided; (c) workshops devoted to helping the resident learn more adaptive living skills are offered; (d) educational lectures related to gambling problems are given; (e) attendance at AA and Gamblers Anonymous meetings is required; and (f) the individual is expected to get involved in planned recreational activities.

Pathological gambling, as an addictive disorder, is on the increase in the United States (Custer, 1982). Furthermore, liberalized gambling legislation has permitted state-operated lotteries, horse racing, and gambling casinos in an effort to increase state tax revenues. In the context of this apparent environmental support and "official" sanction for gambling, it is likely that pathological gambling will increase substantially as more and more people "try their luck." Given that pathological gamblers are resistant to treatment, it is likely, too, that our future efforts toward developing more effective preventive and treatment approaches will need to be increased as this problem continues to grow.

UNRESOLVED ISSUES
on the Genetics of Alcoholism

Several recent research efforts suggest a possible genetic predisposition toward alcoholism (Tarter, 1988). One source of evidence has come from studies of alcoholics' children who were placed for adoption early in life and did not come under the environmental influences of their biological parents. Several such studies can be found to support the genetic viewpoint. For example, Goodwin et al. (1973) found that children of alcoholic parents who had been adopted by nonalcoholic foster parents had nearly twice the number of alcohol problems by their late twenties as did a control group of adopted children whose real parents were not alcoholics. In another study, Goodwin and his colleagues (1974) compared the sons of alcoholic parents who were

adopted in infancy by nonalcoholic parents with those raised by their alcoholic parents. Both adopted and nonadopted sons later evidenced high rates of alcoholism—25 percent and 17 percent respectively. These investigators concluded that being born to an alcoholic parent, rather than being raised by one, increased the risk of a son's becoming an alcoholic.

Another approach to exploring a possible genetic basis in alcoholism has focused on finding underlying mechanisms for the transmission of alcohol abuse or susceptibility to alcoholism. For example, researchers have attempted to determine if individuals who have a genetic "risk" for alcoholism—such as children of alcoholics—show signs of a predisposition toward alcoholism. Evidence for increased alcoholism risk includes such factors as a decreased intensity of subjective feelings of intoxication, a decrease in motor performance, and less body sway after alcohol ingestion. Along with these behavioral indices, increases in prolactin (a pituitary hormone) levels after low doses of alcohol has been thought to occur in individuals with a predisposition to alcohol-abuse disorders. Research into these risk factors in alcohol predisposition typically involves obtaining a sample of highly susceptible individuals, such as children of alcoholics, and a sample of controls, and then determining if certain variables (one or more of the risk factors) distinguish the groups. Recent research by Schuckit and Gould (1988) has reported that alcohol susceptibility indicators significantly separate sons of alcoholics from matched controls.

The evidence on the genetic basis of alcoholism continues to be debated, however, and other experts are not convinced of the primary role of genetics in alcoholism development. Searles (1988) points to the ambiguous evidence for the genetics of alcoholism and cautions against interpreting genetics as a causal factor in the development of alcoholism. Negative results have been found in both adoptive studies and in studies designed to follow-up the behavior of high-risk individuals. It is clear that the great majority of children who have alcoholic parents do not themselves become alcoholics—whether or not they are raised by their real parents. The successful outcomes—that is, children of alcoholics who make successful life adjustments—have not been sufficiently studied (Heller, Sher, & Benson, 1982). In one study of high-risk children of alcoholics, a group of young men 19 to 20 years of age who were presumably at high risk for developing alcoholism were carefully studied for symptoms of psychopathology. Schulsinger and colleagues (1986) found no differences in psychopathology or alcohol-abuse behavior from a control sample similar to the general population. In another study of high-risk individuals, Alterman, Searles, and Hall (1989) failed to find differences in drinking behavior or alcohol-related symptoms between a group of high-risk subjects (those who had alcoholic fathers) and a group of non-high-risk subjects.

We do not know the possible role genetic factors play in the etiology of alcoholism. Available evidence suggests that they might be important as predisposing causes, or that they might contribute to constitutional factors in alcoholism development. Of course, a constitutional predisposition to alcoholism could be acquired as well as inherited. It is not known whether acquired conditions, such as endocrine or enzyme imbalances, increase an individual's vulnerability to alcoholism.

The evidence for a genetic basis of alcoholism is ambiguous at best. At present, it appears that the genetic interpretation of alcoholism remains an attractive hypothesis; however, additional research is needed for us to hold this view with confidence.

SUMMARY

Addictive disorders—such as alcohol or drug abuse, extreme overeating, and pathological gambling—are among the most widespread and intransigent mental health problems facing us today. Alcohol- and drug-abuse problems can be viewed as psychoactive substance-induced organic mental disorders and syndromes or as psychoactive substance-abuse and -dependence disorders. Many problems of alcohol or drug use involve difficulties that stem solely from the intoxicating effects of the substances. Dependence occurs when an individual develops a tolerance for the substance or exhibits withdrawal symptoms when the substance is not available. Several psychoses related to alcoholism have been identified: idiosyncratic intoxication, withdrawal delirium, chronic alcoholic hallucinosis, and dementia associated with alcoholism.

Drug-abuse disorders may involve physiological dependence on substances, such as opiates—particularly heroin—or barbiturates; however, psychological dependence may occur with any of the drugs that are commonly used today—for example, marijuana or cocaine.

A number of factors are considered important in the etiology of alcoholism. Although the data are not conclusive, it appears that genetic factors may play some role in causing susceptibility, as may other biological factors, such as metabolic rates and sensitivity to alcohol. Psychological factors—such as psychological vulnerability, stress, and the desire for tension reduction—and marital and other relationships are also seen as important etiologic elements in alcohol-use disorders. Although the existence of an "alcoholic personality type" has been disavowed by most theorists, personality factors apparently play an important role in the development and expression of addictive disorders. Finally, sociocultural factors may predispose individuals to alcoholism.

Possible causal factors in drug abuse include the influence of peer groups, the existence of a so-called drug culture, and the availability of drugs as tension reducers or as pain relievers. Some recent work has explored a possible physiological basis for drug abuse. The discovery of endorphins, morphinelike substances produced by the body, has raised speculation that a biochemical basis to drug addiction may exist.

The treatment of individuals who abuse alcohol or drugs is generally difficult and often fails. Many reasons can be found for this poor prognosis: the abuse may reflect a long history of psychological difficulties; interpersonal and marital distress may be involved; and financial and legal problems may be present. In addition, all such problems may be operating on an individual who denies that problems exist and is not motivated to work on them.

Several approaches to the treatment of chronic alcoholism or drug abuse have been developed. Frequently, the situation requires biological or medical measures—for example, medication to deal with withdrawal symptoms and withdrawal delirium, or dietary evaluation and treatment for malnutrition. Psychological therapies, such as group therapy and behavioral interventions, may be effective with some alcoholic or drug-abusing individuals. Another source of help for alcoholics is widely available through Alcoholics Anonymous; however, the extent of successful outcomes with this program has not been sufficiently studied.

Most treatment programs show high success rates in "curing" addictive problems, but show lowered success rates at follow-up. Recent work in the area of relapse prevention has contributed new insights into the problems of self-control once addictive behaviors have been checked. Part of this approach involves making an individual aware of factors that can lead to relapse and preparing him or her to deal with these phenomena. Most treatment programs require that an individual remain abstinent; however, over the past 15 years, research has suggested that some alcoholics can learn to control their drinking while continuing to drink socially. The controversy surrounding controlled drinking remains unresolved.

Not all addictive disorders involve the use of substances such as alcohol or drugs. Some individuals eat to excess, endangering their health. Others gamble to such an extent that they wreck their lives and damage or destroy their family relationships. These disorders—hyperobesity and pathological gambling—involve many of the same psychological mechanisms that seem to underlie chronic alcoholism or drug addiction. Treatment approaches found to be effective for alcoholism and drug abuse appear to work about the same with obese clients and pathological gamblers. Many of the same difficulties, especially concerning response to treatment and relapse, also plague the treatment of obese individuals and compulsive gamblers.

■ Key Terms

addictive behavior (p. 295)
psychoactive drugs (p. 295)
toxicity (p. 295)
psychoactive substance abuse (p. 296)
psychoactive substance dependence (p. 296)
tolerance (p. 296)
withdrawal symptoms (p. 296)
alcoholic (p. 296)
alcoholism (p. 296)
opium (p. 314)
morphine (p. 314)
heroin (p. 315)
endorphins (p. 319)
methadone hydrochloride (p. 320)

barbiturates (p. 321)
amphetamine (p. 321)
cocaine (p. 323)
hallucinogens (p. 325)
LSD (p. 325)
flashback (p. 326)
mescaline (p. 326)
psilocybin (p. 326)
marijuana (p. 327)
hashish (p. 327)
caffeine (p. 328)
nicotine (p. 328)
hyperobesity (p. 329)
pathological gambling (p. 333)

Chapter 10
Sexual Disorders and Variants

Gaston Teuscher, *Dessin* (1976). The son of a soldier in the Swiss army and a midwife of French ancestry, Teuscher (1903–?) at an early age developed an ambivalent attitude toward women, an attitude that he traced back to his parents' strong desire to have a girl. He never married, and devoted much of his life to esoteric mathematical and philosophical pursuits. Teuscher began producing sketches and drawings in 1974. He worked at a prodigious rate on bits of crumpled paper, stained tablemats—that is, on whatever materials came immediately to hand.

At the lower levels of the evolutionary scale, animal reproductive processes are not sexual and seem to be essentially preprogrammed and more or less "automatic." The individuals of a species show little variation in their reproductive functioning.

As we move up the scale, reproduction becomes sexual in nature, and by the time we reach the higher animals, we see the reproductive process richly infused with behavioral distinctiveness. Organisms differ considerably in their sexual behaviors and selectively choose mates. Sexual functioning also incorporates other behavioral characteristics, such as a dominance hierarchy and aggressiveness in the case of males.

This expanding repertoire of reproductive behavior continues up to the human level, but the gap between humankind and even the highest of the other animals is huge. It is paralleled only in the advantage humans enjoy in intellectual power by their possession of conceptual language.

Several dimensions of variation underlie this evolutionary progression in reproductive behavior. The most important of these, for our concerns, is the increasing freedom from rigidly programmed, instinctual, stereotyped forms of sexual behavior. For example, the human female is free from recurrent, biologically based cycles of heat and nonreceptivity. Of perhaps even greater importance is the enormously increased adaptability in human sexual needs themselves. With a loosened connection between sex and procreation, human sexual behavior is no longer simply the expression of instinct but has become at least as much a matter of *learned* patterns of attraction, activity, and consummation. To put it another way, human sexuality has largely come under the control of "higher" neural processes. It is primarily recreational and only incidentally procreational for most people.

As in numerous other areas of human activity, these gains in flexibility and adaptability, while having unquestioned species advantages, have come at some cost. Although human sexuality has much more variety than that of any other species, sexuality at the human level is also more likely to go awry. While much sexual variation adds zest and richness to our lives, enhances our happiness, and may intensify our bonds to each other, it may also cause profound misery or worse for the individuals involved, for those close to them, and, in the case of certain deviations, for countless victims.

Money (1986) has suggested the concept of the **lovemap** to refer to the pattern of an individual's own erotic attachments and preferences, his or her idealized scenario for sexual fulfillment. Some lovemaps become distorted or "vandalized" (Money & Lamacz, 1989) in the course of development, leading to a variety of maladaptive outcomes. We will be employing this useful concept in some of the discussion that follows. It is formally defined as

> . . . a developmental representation or template, synchronously functional in the mind and the brain, depicting the idealized lover, the idealized love affair, and the idealized program of sexuoerotic activity with that lover, projected in imagery and ideation, or in actual performance." (Money & Lamacz, 1989, p. 43)

The lovemap is analogous to a person's native language in its developmental and cognitive representational qualities. Its basic properties are thought to be largely settled prior to puberty and, once settled, highly resistant to change. Lovemaps vary on a number of dimensions, of which an important one is relative simplicity versus complexity.

This chapter is concerned with "abnormalities" of human sexuality. They fall naturally into two distinct classes. The *sexual dysfunctions* involve inhibitions in sexual desire or problems with psychophysiological functioning in the sexual response cycle; premature ejaculation in males is an example. The *sexual variants* or *deviations* include those forms of sexual behavior that fall outside the range of generally accepted sexual activity, such as exhibitionism or sexual sadism. In our discussion, we make a further distinction between victimless sexual variants and those that involve injury, force, or nonconsent.

It should be noted that not all forms of sexual abnormality, especially those in which no one is victimized, are considered disorders requiring treatment. Neither are all sexual disorders seen as inevitably causing additional difficulties in other aspects of a person's personal life. Conversely, some abnormalities, such as incest, are considered crimes rather than psychological disorders and thus do not appear in the official (that is, the DSM) classification system, presumably because manifestations of disorder are not legally punishable. Obviously, however, many behaviors can be both crimes and manifestations of disorder, and because we need not here concern ourselves with such legal niceties, we will discuss some disorders that are also crimes by statutory definition.

Human societies have generally exhibited a kind of "double vision" regarding sexual behavior. On the one hand, they typically have rather elaborate systems, often legally codified, limiting sexual behavior and directing that sexual acts shall encompass only certain narrowly defined "proprieties" with partners having specified characteristics—that is, one's opposite-sex spouse. On the other hand, societies have informal expectations that these limits will be regularly and routinely exceeded by at least the more venturesome of their members. It is only in recent times, thanks largely to the pioneering work of Kinsey and his associates (1948, 1953), that we have come to understand that personal problems with sexuality and deviations from formal propriety are widespread and at times extreme within our own culture.

As is implied in these observations, issues pertaining to sexual behavior tend to arouse strong emotional and attitudinal responses and inspire much concern about public regulation and control of individual behavior. In our own culture public concern about sexual matters is never far beneath the surface, a fact that can be and has been exploited by shrewd political campaign managers. It is difficult in such a climate to maintain a scholarly, objective approach to matters of human sexual behavior and its abnormalities. Nevertheless, that is our intent in this chapter. We are not so arrogant as to assume complete success in this intention, nor so naive as to imagine we can avoid offending some readers.

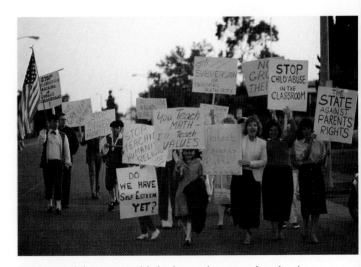

Issues pertaining to sexual behavior, such as sex education in the schools, tend to arouse strong emotional and attitudinal responses and inspire much concern about the public regulation and control of individual behavior.

SEXUAL DYSFUNCTIONS

The term **sexual dysfunction** refers to impairment either in the desire for sexual gratification or in the ability to achieve it. With some exceptions, such impairments occur in the absence of anatomical or physiological pathology and are based on faulty psychosexual adjustment and learning. They vary markedly in degree and, regardless of which partner is alleged to be dysfunctional, the enjoyment of sex by both parties in a relationship is typically adversely affected; both are prevented from approximating the conditions of their respective lovemaps. Certain types of sexual dysfunction, such as erectile disorder, occur with significant frequency in homosexual relationships, but research in this domain is seriously lacking. Thus we will focus on the heterosexual context.

Like sexuality in general, sexual dysfunctions were until recently either ignored entirely by polite society or—if discussed at all—were the subject of turgid medical treatises written by authors who were usually as ill-informed and prejudiced as their readers. Then, with the popularization of Freudian thought, an era gradually developed in which all manner of difficulties in sexual functioning (and some that were not even "difficulties" in the normally accepted sense) were said to be the result of unconscious conflicts of childhood origin—requiring years of psychoanalytic treatment to resolve. We now know, thanks again to precedent-breaking and courageous work—chiefly by Masters and Johnson (1966, 1970, 1975)—that the common sexual dysfunctions are both more numerous and less complex and mysterious than had once been believed. We will first describe several of the most common ones and then discuss issues of causation and treatment. *HIGHLIGHT 10.1* summarizes the dysfunctions we will be covering here.

■ Dysfunctions Affecting Males

Here we will briefly discuss several dysfunctions that may affect men: erectile insufficiency, premature ejaculation, and inhibited male orgasm.

Male Erectile Disorder   Inability to achieve or maintain an erection sufficient for successful sexual intercourse—formerly known as *impotence* —is known clinically as *erectile insufficiency,* or in DSM terms, **male erectile disorder.** In **primary erectile insufficiency,** a man has never been able to sustain an erection long enough to accomplish a satisfactory duration of penetration—usually defined as including intravaginal ejaculation. In **secondary erectile insufficiency,** a man has had at least one successful attempt at coitus but is presently unable to produce or maintain the required level of penile rigidity. Primary insufficiency is a relatively rare disorder, but it has been estimated that half or more of the male population has experienced the secondary variety of erectile insufficiency on at least a temporary basis, especially in the early years of sexual exploration.

Prolonged or permanent erectile insufficiency before the age of 60 is relatively rare and is often due to psychological factors, notably anxiety-induced interference by distracting, dysfunctional thoughts concerning "performance" (Barlow, 1986, 1988). In fact, according to the findings of Kinsey and his associates, only about one-fourth of males become impotent by the age of 70 and even here many cases have psychological components in their causal patterns. More recent studies have indicated that men and women in their 80s and 90s are quite capable of enjoying intercourse (Burros, 1974; Kaplan, 1975; Masters & Johnson, 1975). It appears that in some cases men who experience difficulties in their later years may simply be complying with the societal expectation of declining performance (Tollison & Adams, 1979). On the other hand, the vascular, neurological, and hormonal factors that support adequate erectile functioning do undergo impairment with advancing age in many men (Mohr & Beutler, 1990). The lessened reliability of the erectile response may lead to the type of dysfunctional cognitions already noted, thus exacerbating the difficulty. Erectile problems are notoriously self-perpetuating, with every "failure" psychologically enhancing the likelihood of further ones.

We have probably underestimated in recent years the proportion of erectile problems having some pathophysiologic involvement, formerly considered to be as low as 15 percent (Kaplan, 1975). More recent data suggest that the figure may actually be close to 50 percent (Mohr & Beutler, 1990; Tiefer & Melman, 1989), which at a minimum implies the necessity of a thorough assessment of contributory medical conditions. Thus a diagnosis of psychogenic causation does not by itself rule out an element of physiologic malfunction, or vice versa. These organic conditions can be quite varied and can include certain types of vascular disease, diabetes, neurological disorders, kidney failure, hormonal irregularities, and excess blood levels of certain drugs, including alcohol (Tiefer & Melman, 1989; Wagner & Green, 1981).

HIGHLIGHT 10.1

Sexual Dysfunctions

Dysfunctions	Characteristics
Male dysfunctions	
Male erectile disorder	An inability to achieve or maintain an erection (formerly known as impotence)
Premature ejaculation	An unsatisfactorily brief period between the beginning of sexual stimulation and the occurrence of ejaculation
Inhibited male orgasm	An inability to ejaculate during intercourse (also known as retarded ejaculation)
Female dysfunctions	
Female sexual arousal disorder	Nonresponsiveness to erotic stimulation both physically and emotionally (formerly known as frigidity)
Vaginismus	An involuntary muscle spasm at the entrance to the vagina that prevents penetration and sexual intercourse
Inhibited female orgasm	A difficulty in achieving orgasm, either manually or during sexual intercourse
Dysfunctions of both sexes	
Dyspareunia	Painful coitus—may have either an organic or psychological basis
Sexual desire disorders:	
Hypoactive sexual desire disorder	Little or no sexual drive or interest
Sexual aversion disorder	Total lack of interest in sex and avoidance of sexual contact

Distinguishing between psychogenic and organically caused insufficiency for diagnostic purposes is at best a complicated process. The normal male has several erections per night, associated with periods of REM (rapid eye movement) sleep. Some researchers have suggested that organically based insufficiency can be distinguished from psychogenic by noting an absence of these nocturnal erections. However, it now appears that many other factors must also be evaluated in order to establish a proper diagnosis, because the nocturnal penile tumescence (NPT) procedure has been found, by itself, to produce both false positive and false negative results that are unacceptably high (Mohr & Beutler, 1990; Wagner, 1981). An important implication of these assessment difficulties is that we have probably, once again, made the common error of assuming a mutually exclusive dichotomy (organic versus psychogenic), where such pure cases may in fact be the exception rather than the rule (Tiefer & Melman, 1989).

Premature Ejaculation   Often psychologically related to erectile insufficiency, **premature ejaculation** refers to an unsatisfactorily brief period between the commencement of sexual stimulation and the occurrence of ejaculation. The consequences include failure of the female partner to achieve satisfaction and, often, acute embarrassment for the male with disruptive anxiety about recurrence on future occasions. An exact definition of prematurity is not possible, however, partly because of pronounced variations in both the likelihood and the latency of female orgasm in sexual intercourse. LoPiccolo (1978) suggested that an inability to tolerate as much as four minutes of stimulation without ejaculation is a reasonable indicator that a man may be in need of sex therapy. This suggested guideline is subject to numerous qualifications, however, including the age of a client—the alleged "quick trigger" of the younger male being more than a mere myth (McCarthy, 1989). Not surprisingly, premature ejaculation is most likely when previous abstinence has been lengthy (Spiess, Geer, & O'Donohue, 1984). This fact suggests the use of masturbation as a form of self-treatment for the difficulty, but, somewhat curiously, few premature ejaculators discover or make use of this coping method.

In sexually normal men the ejaculatory reflex is to a considerable extent under voluntary control. They monitor their sensations during sexual stimulation and are somehow able, perhaps by judicious use of distraction, to forestall the point of ejaculatory inevitability until they decide to "let go" (Kaplan, 1987). Premature ejaculators are for some reason unable to use this technique effectively, probably in many cases because their anxiety prevents adequate monitoring of their current stage in the sexual response buildup leading to orgasm. As in the case of erectile difficulties, failures in control lead to increased anxiety in subsequent opportunities, and thus increased likelihood of failures.

Inhibited Male Orgasm   It is interesting that, while problems of female orgasmic dysfunction have received wide attention in the popular press, one rarely hears public mention of the corollary problem in males. It is not a topic high on the locker room agenda, and indeed sexually active women seem to have a more realistic appreciation of its prevalence than do most men. As a result, many males suffering from **inhibited male orgasm**—that is, retarded ejaculation or the inability to ejaculate during intercourse—are condemned to worry needlessly about their supposedly unique defect, a type of worry likely to worsen the problem. In fact, relatively few cases of inhibited male orgasm are seen by sex therapists, but our own clinical experience suggests that the problem is much more widespread than this observation would seem to indicate, a conclusion shared by Apfelbaum (1989) and by Kaplan (1974). It appears that many men are too embarrassed by the problem even to contemplate therapy for it.

Instances of complete ejaculatory incompetence are rare. Most men who have difficulty ejaculating intravaginally during intercourse can nevertheless achieve orgasm by other means of stimulation, notably through solitary masturbation. In milder cases a man can ejaculate in the presence of a partner, but only by means of manual or oral stimulation (Kaplan, 1987). Retarded ejaculation may even be partner-specific; that is, it occurs only with a particular partner but not with others (Apfelbaum, 1989). The problem is therefore largely one of psychological inhibition or overcontrol, and it appears relatively specific to the circumstance of vaginal containment of the penis. It thus seems obvious that substantial "symbolic" and interpersonal elements exist in the typical instance of this dysfunction.

◼ Dysfunctions Affecting Females

Female sexual dysfunctions somewhat parallel the male sexual dysfunctions. The following sections will discuss arousal insufficiency, vaginismus, and orgasmic dysfunction.

Female Sexual Arousal Disorder   Formerly and somewhat pejoratively referred to as *frigidity,* **female sexual arousal disorder** is in many ways the female counterpart of erectile insufficiency (DSM-III-R lists both as *sexual arousal disorders*). It is often accompanied by an absence of sexual arousal feelings and an unresponsiveness to most or all forms of erotic stimulation. Its chief physical manifestation is a failure to produce the characteristic swelling and lubrication of the vulva and vaginal tissues during sexual stimulation, a condition that may make intercourse quite uncomfortable.

Fortunately, true primary nonresponsiveness to erotic stimuli (where a woman has never experienced arousal to any form of stimulation) is rare; it may also be untreatable in terms of currently available intervention techniques. Most often, then, we are dealing here with a dysfunction that, while it may be stubbornly entrenched, is at least to some minimal extent situational. A woman with this disorder is not so much lacking in the capacity for sexual responsiveness as she is inhibiting for some reason a responsiveness that might otherwise be full and gratifying. The possible reasons for this inhibition run the gamut from early sexual traumatization to excessive and distorted socialization about the evils of sex to dislike of or disgust with a current partner's sexuality.

Vaginismus   An involuntary spasm of the muscles at the entrance to the vagina (not due to a physical disorder) that prevents penetration and sexual intercourse is called **vaginismus.** Evidently these muscles are readily conditionable to respond with intense contraction to stimuli associated with impending penetration. In some cases, women who suffer from vaginismus also have arousal insufficiency, possibly as a result of conditioned fears associated with earlier traumatic sexual experiences. In other cases, however, they are sexually responsive, but are still afflicted with this disorder. It is not always possible to identify the "unconditioned stimuli" presumed to have been involved in the acquisition of vaginismus (Kaplan, 1987), probably because the disorder is sometimes "overdetermined" in the sense of having multiple causal links (Leiblum, Pervin, & Campbell, 1989). This form of sexual dysfunction is relatively rare, but, when it occurs, it is likely to be extremely distressing for both an affected woman and her partner (Leiblum et al., 1989; Tollison & Adams, 1979).

Inhibited Female Orgasm   Many women who are readily sexually excitable and who otherwise enjoy sexual activity nevertheless experience **inhibited female orgasm**—greater or lesser difficulty in achieving orgasm, whether manually or through intercourse. Of these women, many do not routinely experience orgasm during sexual intercourse without direct supplemental stimulation of the clitoris; indeed this pattern is so common that it can hardly be considered dysfunctional. A small percentage of women are able to achieve orgasm *only* through direct mechanical stimulation of the clitoris, as in vigorous digital manipulation, cunnilingus (oral stimulation), or the use of an electric vibrator. Even fewer are unable to have the experience under any known conditions of stimulation; this condition is called **primary orgasmic dysfunction,** analogous to primary erectile insufficiency in males.

The diagnosis of orgasmic dysfunction is complicated by the fact that the subjective quality of orgasm varies widely among women, within the same woman from time to time, and depending on mode of stimulation. Thus precise evaluations of occurrence and quality are difficult (Singer & Singer, 1978). The criteria to be applied are also unclear in the vast middle range of orgasmic responsiveness. Most clinicians agree that a primary anorgasmic woman needs treatment, and that a woman at the other extreme who routinely climaxes with relatively brief intercourse, or perhaps even with only breast stimulation or fantasy, does not. Differences of opinion become notable, however, as we move away from these extremes into the range in which most women's experiences actually fall (Kaplan, 1987). Our own view is that this question is best left to a woman herself to answer; if she is dissatisfied about her responsiveness, and if there is a reasonable likelihood that treatment will help, then it should be provided on request.

■ Dysfunctions Affecting Both Sexes

Certain dysfunctions are, at least on surface presentation, common to both sexes. Their underlying causes, however, may differ somewhat between men and women.

Dyspareunia   Painful coitus, or **dyspareunia,** can occur in males but is far more common in females (Lazarus, 1989). This is the form of sexual dysfunction most likely to have an organic basis—for example, in association with infections or structural pathology of the sex organs. It often has a psychological basis, however, as in the case of a woman who has an aversion to sexual intercourse and experiences her displeasure as intense physical discomfort; in such cases the designation *functional* is used. Understandably, dyspareunia is often asso-

ciated with vaginismus. This form of sexual dysfunction is rare.

Sexual Desire Disorders   Researchers have delineated two types of sexual desire disorders. The first is **hypoactive sexual desire disorder.** As distinguished from sexual arousal disorder (male erectile disorder or female arousal disorder), it is a dysfunction in which either a man or a woman shows little or no sexual drive or interest. It is assumed in most cases that the biological basis of the sex drive remains unimpaired, but that for some reason sexual motivation is blocked. These people usually come to the attention of clinicians only at the request of their partners, who typically complain of an insufficient frequency of sexual interaction. This fact exposes one problem with the diagnosis, because it is known that preferences for frequency of sexual contact vary widely among otherwise "normal" individuals. Who is to decide what is "not enough"? DSM-III-R explicitly indicates that this judgment is left to the clinician.

Nevertheless, there do appear to be some people who are almost totally lacking in sexual desire. In extreme cases, sex actually becomes psychologically aversive, and warrants a diagnosis of **sexual aversion disorder,** the second type of sexual desire disorder. Formerly considered rare and largely limited to females, sexual desire disorder diagnoses have in recent years become fairly common and are applied relatively often to males (Rosen & Leiblum, 1989). Doubtless this change is due at least in part to changing role expectations, of which more will be said later.

■ Causal Factors in Sexual Dysfunctions

Both sexual desire and genital functioning may be affected by a wide range of organic conditions, including injuries to the genitals, disease, fatigue, excessive alcohol consumption, and abuse of certain drugs, such as tranquilizers. Most cases of sexual dysfunction, however, are more likely due to psychosocial rather than physical causes. Although specific causal factors may vary considerably from one type of sexual dysfunction to another, the following psychosocial factors are commonly found.

Faulty Learning   In some nonindustrialized societies, older members of a group instruct younger members in sexual techniques before marriage. In our society, though we recognize that sexual behavior is (with certain proscriptions) an impor-

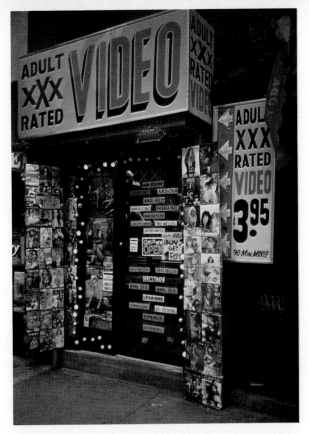

In our society, the learning of sexual techniques and attitudes is too often left to chance, which may include such sources as X-rated video shops. As a result, a great number of people acquire faulty information and expectations that can impair their sexual enjoyment and adequacy. Sexual dysfunction is a problem for many different kinds of people from all walks of life.

tant aspect of life, the learning of sexual techniques and attitudes is too often left to chance. The result is that many young people start out with faulty expectations and a lack of needed information or harmful misinformation that can impair their sexual adequacy and enjoyment. In fact, Kaplan (1974) has concluded that couples with sexual problems are typically practicing insensitive, incompetent, and ineffective sexual techniques; this conclusion is readily endorsed by most investigators in the field (Leiblum & Rosen, 1989a; LoPiccolo & LoPiccolo, 1978; Tollison & Adams, 1979).

In our society, many people, but especially women (being at risk for pregnancy), have been subjected to early training that depicts sexual relations as lustful, dirty, and evil. The attitudes and inhibitions thus established can lead to a great deal of anxiety, conflict, and guilt about sexual relations, whether in or out of marriage. Faulty early conditioning may also have taken the form of indoctrination in the idea that a woman has a primary responsibility to satisfy a man sexually—and therefore to suppress her own needs and feelings. Masters and Johnson (1970) considered such faulty learning to be the primary cause of orgasmic dys-

function in females. In vaginismus, a somewhat different conditioning patterning has occurred, leading a female to associate vaginal penetration with pain—either physical, psychological, or both. This conditioned defensive reflex comes into operation when penetration is attempted by a sexual partner (Kaplan, 1975; Leiblum, Pervin, & Campbell, 1989).

Although males may also be subjected to early training emphasizing the evils of sex, such training apparently is in general a far less important factor for them. However, another type of faulty early conditioning may be a key factor in premature ejaculation: males typically have their first and often extensive sexual experiences in solitary masturbation, and such masturbatory sessions are likely to be highly efficient in the achievement of orgasm and ejaculation. A young male may thus train his sexual response cycle in this mode of rapid, direct, and altogether "impersonal" discharge, thereby paving the way for prematurity in his later love relationships (McCarthy, 1989).

Researchers have also observed the seemingly opposite pattern in which premature ejaculators report markedly subnormal masturbatory activity on moral or religious orthodoxy grounds. Such young men are also unlikely to have alternative outlets other than involuntary nocturnal emissions, and may thus experience lengthy periods of ejaculatory inactivity. Since it is known that a lengthy interval following the last ejaculation increases the likelihood of a precipitous emission, these men are at high risk for an awkward incident should an acceptable opportunity for sexual experience present itself.

In other instances, initial difficulties in sexual functioning have led to conditioned anxieties that in turn have impaired subsequent performances. We will elaborate on this point in the section that follows.

Feelings of Fear, Anxiety, and Inadequacy
In a study of 49 adult males with erectile disorders, Cooper (1969) found anxiety to be a contributing factor in 94 percent of the cases and the primary problem for those whose erectile problems had started early. Many subsequent investigators have confirmed this essential observation. Similarly, Kaplan (1974) concluded from her studies that "a man who suffers from impotence is often almost unbearably anxious, frustrated, and humiliated by his inability to produce or maintain an erection" (p. 80). Males who suffer from premature ejaculation may also experience acute feelings of inadequacy— and often feelings of guilt as well—stemming from

their lack of control and inability to satisfy their sexual partners via intercourse.

Females may also feel fearful and inadequate in sexual relations. A woman may be uncertain whether her partner finds her sexually attractive, and this may lead to anxiety and tension that interfere with her sexual enjoyment. Or she may feel inadequate because she is unable to have an orgasm or does so infrequently; we have seen many women who have permitted such problems to undermine severely their sense of themselves, their identities as complete women. Sometimes a woman who is not climaxing will pretend to have orgasms to make her sexual partner feel fully adequate. The longer a woman maintains such a pretense, however, the more likely she is to become confused and frustrated; in addition, she is likely to resent her partner for being so insensitive to her real feelings and needs. This in turn only adds to her sexual difficulties.

From a more general viewpoint, Masters and Johnson (1975) concluded that most sexual dysfunctions are due to crippling fears, attitudes, and inhibitions concerning sexual behavior, often based on faulty early learning and then exacerbated by later aversive experiences. In a more recent review of the accumulated evidence, Beck and Barlow (1984) played down the role of anxiety per se—which can actually enhance sexual performance in males—emphasizing instead the cognitive distractions frequently associated with anxiety in dysfunctional people. A follow-up laboratory study (Abrahamson, Barlow, & Abrahamson, 1989) confirmed that dysfunctional men with erectile problems differ from their more functional counterparts chiefly in being readily and specifically distracted by cues about their performance, resulting in decreased penile rigidity during erotic stimulation. These self-defeating thoughts about performance encourage the adoption of a "spectator role" in sexual relations, making wholehearted participation impossible.

Interpersonal Problems   Interpersonal problems may cause a number of sexual dysfunctions. Lack of emotional closeness can lead to erectile or orgasmic problems. An individual may be in love with someone else, may find his or her sexual partner physically or psychologically repulsive, or may have hostile feelings from prior misunderstandings, quarrels, and conflicts. A one-sided interpersonal relationship—in which one partner does most of the giving and the other most of the receiving—can lead to feelings of insecurity and resentment with resulting impairment in sexual performance (Friedman, 1974; Leiblum & Rosen, 1989a; Lobitz & Lobitz, 1978; Simon, 1975).

For a female, lack of emotional closeness often appears to result from intercourse with a partner who is a "sexual moron"—rough, unduly hasty, and concerned only with self-gratification. As Kaplan (1974) pointed out,

Some persons have as much difficulty giving pleasure as others do in receiving it. These individuals don't provide their partners with enough sexual stimulation because they lack either the knowledge and sensitivity to know what to do, or they are anxious about doing it. (p. 78)

In other instances, an individual may be hostile toward and not want to please his or her sexual partner. This situation seems to occur rather frequently in unhappy marital or other intimate relationships. In such relationships, channels of communication have largely broken down and sexual relations continue as a sort of habit or duty or simply to gratify one's own sexual needs.

Physiologically, people are capable of experiencing orgasm with any personally acceptable partner. However, Switzer (1974) aptly pointed to a generally agreed-on conclusion: "Orgasm has especially delightful overtones when you're with a person whom you love and when you can abandon yourself" (p. 36).

Changing Male-Female Roles and Relationships   An increase in erectile problems was reported during the 1970s that a number of investigators have related to two phenomena occurring during that period: (a) the increasing changes being achieved by the women's movement in our society, and (b) the growing awareness of female sexuality (Burros, 1974; Heiman & Grafton-Becker, 1989; Leiblum & Rosen, 1989b). These trends have led women to want and expect more from their lives, including their sexual relationships. Women no longer accept the older concept of being the passive partner in sex, and many are taking a more assertive and active role in sexual relations.

This new role appears to threaten the image many men have of themselves as the supposedly "dominant" partner who takes the initiative in sexual relations (Steinmann & Fox, 1974). In fact some men appear to regard sexually assertive women who play an active role in sex as "castrating females" (Kaplan, 1974). In addition, the greater assertiveness and expectancy of women makes many men feel that they are under pressure to perform. As Ginsberg, Frosch, and Shapiro (1972) expressed it early on, "This challenge to manhood is most apparent in a sexually liberated society where women are not merely available but are perceived as demanding satisfaction from masculine performance" (p. 219). The distracting thoughts such a challenge may inspire in an insecure man may result not only in impaired male performance but even in erectile failure.

Changing male-female roles in sexual relationships also place greater demands on women. The expectation of taking an active rather than a passive role may cause a woman to make unrealistic demands on her own sexual responsiveness—such as expecting to have a highly pleasurable orgasm each time she engages in sexual relations. Such demands are likely to lead to some degree of unfulfilled desires, confusion, and self-devaluation, which in turn impair actual sexual performance. This situation seems especially true when a female assumes a "spectator's role" and almost literally monitors her own sexual performance, thus depriving it of spontaneity and naturalness.

Finally, our enhanced awareness of sexually transmitted diseases—fueled by the seemingly relentless advance of the deadly AIDS virus—has added an increment of anxiety to many sexual encounters both casual and otherwise (Leiblum & Rosen, 1989b). The relatively carefree promiscuity of the 1960s and 1970s has increasingly and wisely given way to concerns about "safe sex" with partners whose sexual (and drug-use) histories place them outside of the known high-risk groups. Monogamy and sexual exclusivity have made dramatic comebacks. The adolescent's sense of invulnerability and immortality has been not so gently shaken, probably for the better. The condom, once widely rejected as inhibiting spontaneity (or the appearance of it) and decreasing pleasure, is now heralded as essential equipment for many prudent adolescents and young adults—male and female—who still "cruise." In short, we are clearly in the midst of a new sexual revolution, one involving life and death decisions, and thus one whose constraints all but the foolhardy will heed. It is still too early to tell what effect these dramatic changes will have on the incidence and prevalence of sexual dysfunctions. Conceivably, the added anxiety and suspicion created by the AIDS epidemic will be counterbalanced by the positive effects that may come with expectations of more enduring and committed relationships.

■ Treatments and Outcomes

The treatment of sexual dysfunctions, too, has undergone nothing less than a revolution during the lifetime of today's young adults. Once regarded as difficult and intractable therapeutic challenges,

most instances of sexual dysfunction are now readily treated with new techniques that are still being developed and improved. Generally, these techniques include direct methods of attack on the dysfunctions themselves, usually with high levels of gentle and affectionate partner participation. For example, a couple may be given instruction and guided practice in overcoming, by vigorous stimulation, orgasmic inhibition in one of the partners; or vaginismus may be treated with intravaginal insertion, by the male partner, of cylindrical objects of gradually increasing circumference until the excessive vaginal contractions cease. As a result of these newer approaches, success rates approaching 90 percent or more for some dysfunctions have become quite routine (Andersen, 1983; Kaplan, 1987; Leiblum & Rosen, 1989a; LoPiccolo & Stock, 1986; Tollison & Adams, 1979; Zilbergeld & Kilmann, 1984).

The turning point in sex therapy is uniformly considered to be the publication in 1970 of Masters and Johnson's *Human Sexual Inadequacy,* the product of an eleven-year search to develop truly effective treatment procedures for the common dysfunctions, both male and female. The success rates claimed by this team of dedicated clinical researchers astonished the professional community and rapidly led to the widespread adoption of their general approach, which combined elements of traditional and behavioral therapy in a framework emphasizing, as already noted, direct intervention aimed at the dysfunctions themselves.

Although the early confidence inspired by Masters and Johnson's reported results has waned somewhat (Leiblum & Pervin, 1980; Leiblum & Rosen,

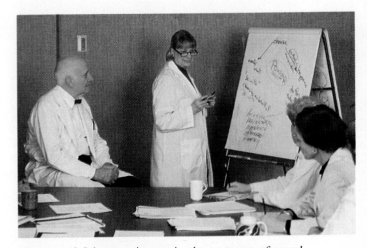

Masters and Johnson, pioneers in the treatment of sexual dysfunction, emphasize the importance of removing crippling fears, misconceptions, and inhibitions about sex and fostering attitudes toward and participation in sexual behavior as a pleasurable, natural, and meaningful experience.

1989b; LoPiccolo & Stock, 1986; Vandereycken, 1982; Zilbergeld & Evans, 1980), their work has unquestionably unleashed a ground swell of new therapeutic techniques. Despite differences in emphasis and methods, there seems to be general agreement on the importance of removing crippling misconceptions, inhibitions, and fears, and on fostering attitudes toward sexual behavior as a pleasurable, natural, and meaningful experience.

Because of the manner in which sexual dysfunctions are presented and described by those suffering from them, it is easy to lose sight of a crucial issue emphasized by Masters and Johnson and by virtually all those who have followed in their footsteps. That is, sexual dysfunctions are not normally disorders of individuals, but rather of relationships between individuals. Thus the new treatments for sexual dysfunctions typically involve *both* parties to a relationship in which a disorder manifests itself. Joseph LoPiccolo (1978) put it this way:

It must be stressed that all sexual dysfunctions are shared disorders; that is, the husband of an inorgasmic woman is partially responsible for creating or maintaining her dysfunction, and he is also a patient in need of help. Regardless of the cause of the dysfunction, both partners are responsible for future change and the solution of their problems. (p. 3)

With competent treatment, success rates vary between approximately 30 and 100 percent, depending in part on the individual or couple and on the nature of the problem. For example, Masters and Johnson (1970) and Kaplan (1975) have reported success rates approaching 100 percent for the treatment of premature ejaculation and vaginismus, but considerably lower rates for male erectile and female organismic dysfunctions. More recent reviews (Andersen, 1983; Leiblum & Rosen, 1989a; LoPiccolo & Stock, 1986; Zilbergeld & Kilmann, 1984) essentially confirm these relative outcome expectancies but make an important distinction between primary and secondary female orgasmic dysfunction. Treatment of the former, typically beginning with instruction and guided practice in masturbating to orgasm, has a high likelihood of success, while "situational" anorgasmia (where a woman may experience orgasm in some situations, with certain kinds of stimulation, or with certain partners, but not under the precise conditions she desires) often proves intractable.

The more treatment-resistant erectile disorders probably reflect underlying contributory medical problems, the prevalence of which were until recently seriously underestimated. As noted by Mohr & Beutler (1990), the only available recourse for these disorders may be the use of some sort of mechanical aid. Inflatable penile prostheses often prove preferable to implanted prostheses that maintain a constant rigidity, despite the potential disruption the need to inflate them may entail. The combination of a vacuum device (which draws blood into the spongy tissue of the penis) and

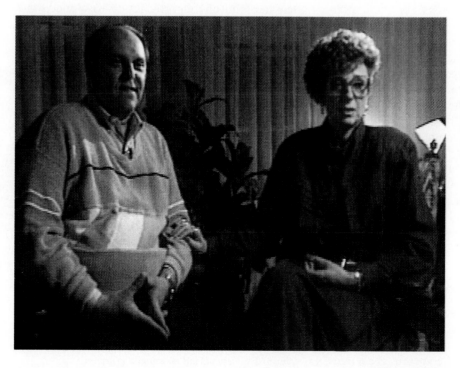

This couple has had successful sex therapy. They are able to laugh now that they have worked out some of their problems. With competent treatment, success rates for the treatment of sexual dysfunctions vary between approximately 30 and 100 percent, depending in part on an individual or couple and on the nature of the problem.

constricting rubber or plastic rings at the base of the penis (which keeps it there under pressure) shows considerable promise for some men whose erectile problems prove resistant to psychological or medical treatments.

The term *competent treatment* should be stressed in any discussion of sex therapy, because the quality of treatment in the several thousand American sex clinics may range from sophisticated psychotherapy to outright charlatanism. Indications are strong, in fact, that unqualified practitioners have entered this field in abundance recently, often charging astronomical fees for their decidedly inexpert services.

VARIANT SEXUAL BEHAVIORS

Human sexual interest may take many channels, especially when for some reason the usual patterning has become blocked. It is hardly surprising then that many people find their principal sexual interests and satisfactions in practices outside the range of what is considered acceptable or normal in a given culture. The sexual drive, which is functionally inseparable from the lovemap in which it is manifested, is normally sufficiently powerful to override all but the most severe social sanctions; thus we see variant sexual needs frequently erupting into variant sexual behavior.

Variant sexual behavior is behavior in which satisfaction is dependent persistently and primarily on something other than a mutually desired sexual engagement with a sexually mature member of the opposite sex. So defined, the domain encompasses a vast array of behavior patterns of arousal and sexual consummation in which the sexual development of an affected individual has for some reason deviated from the standard, adult heterosexual course.

As already observed, the specter of these sexual variants seems peculiarly threatening to many people in our society, and expressions of tolerance for such behavior as homosexuality, for example, can arouse intense emotion. It is certainly true that some forms of sexual variation, such as rape and child molestation, are contrary to the welfare of society and its members. Other forms, however, are in themselves generally victimless and thus constitute no obvious, rationally based threat to the public order—provided of course due precaution is taken to avoid sexually transmitted infections. For this reason, we make a distinction between *victimless* sexual variants—in which the acts involved do not infringe on the rights of noninvolved others and are engaged in by mutually consenting adults who do no physical harm to each other—and sexual deviations that involve nonconsent or assault. In the former category, we place gender identity disorders, uncomplicated male and female homosexuality, most cases of fetishism, and transvestism. The more problematic sexual variants, from the standpoint of the society's welfare of society, include voyeurism, exhibitionism, sexual sadism and masochism, pedophilia, incest, and rape. In most jurisdictions, laws against acts in this category not only exist but are actively enforced.

It is important to reiterate that we have chosen *not* to follow the lead of DSM-III-R in respect to the categories of variant behavior. Specifically, that document excludes incest and rape from consideration as mental disorders. We include these variants because they clearly fall within our definition of abnormal behavior, irrespective of whether they are officially considered to be psychiatric disorders. Our position is that the criminal and the abnormal are separate domains having no necessary relationship to one another; some behaviors, such as rape and incest, can be considered both crimes and abnormalities, while others may be one of these without being the other. Homosexuality, which remains a crime in many jurisdictions and a subject of intense controversy regarding its "abnormality," represents a special case to be discussed in a later section.

A key point—one particularly emphasized by Adams and Chiodo (1984) and Barlow (1974)—deserves mention here. In considering these behaviors, we tend to focus our attention on the variant arousal patterns themselves to the exclusion of other, perhaps equally important, factors that may help cause or maintain variant behaviors. These other factors often include (a) the absence of a normal level of arousal to adults of the opposite sex; (b) significant deficits in the social skills normally needed for initiating successful adult heterosexual relationships (Overholser & Beck, 1986; Segal & Marshall, 1985); and (c) failure to establish a firm psychological gender identity, which in males often manifests itself in concerns about dominance and power.

The importance of this broadened view for both understanding and therapy is illustrated in findings of several studies on therapy for homosexual individuals who wanted to change their sexual orientations. Adams and Sturgis (1977), reviewing the evidence, concluded that multiple-target treatment procedures aimed at the three factors just mentioned plus the variant arousal pattern greatly enhanced the likelihood of successful sexual reorientation therapy, as compared with approaches that focused only on suppression of the variant sexual arousal pattern.

Gender Identity Disorders

As has just been noted, individuals manifesting sexually variant behavior are often to a degree confused, uncertain, or disorganized in their concepts of themselves as males or females. This confusion is seen most explicitly in cases of **gender identity disorder** and in some cases of transvestism (dressing in the clothes of the opposite sex) and homosexuality. But even where outward behavior appears to conform to societal expectations and norms, many people will prove on careful assessment to have unclear or unstable gender identities and to lack appropriate repertoires of gender-role behaviors (Adams & Chiodo, 1984).

Gender Identity Formation   The formation of gender identity and the acquisition of culturally prescribed gender-role behaviors are obviously matters of great complexity, and our understanding of the processes involved is limited. Research by Money and colleagues (1980; Money & Ehrhardt, 1972; Money & Lamacz, 1989), among others, has established that outcomes in this area are powerfully determined by learning—that is, by adapting to a host of psychosocial forces that are normally quite effective in "shaping" a person to be psychosocially male or female. But of course, differing social environments will on occasion produce blends or blurrings of the cultural concepts of maleness and femaleness, and the impact of these environments on a developing child will likely be very strong. Many of the most functional men and women in our society seem to have highly developed masculine *and* feminine traits, as conventionally conceived. Conversely, many of the least functional lack a strong identification with *either* side of this traditional behavioral dichotomy and appear confused or "undifferentiated" with respect to psychosocial gender (Carson, 1983; Orlofsky & O'Heron, 1987; Spence & Helmreich, 1978).

While psychosocial influences seem paramount in determining gender identity and role, mounting evidence from both human and animal studies shows that biological factors are also importantly involved, both generally and in respect to specific preferences for differing forms of sexual expression and satisfaction (Bell, Weinberg, & Hammersmith, 1981; Ehrhardt & Meyer-Bahlburg, 1981; MacLusky & Naftolin, 1981; Money, 1980; Money & Lamacz, 1989; Rubin, Reinisch, & Haskett, 1981).

Considering the incidence of sexually variant behaviors such as transsexualism or homosexuality in the light of a historically strong societal rejection of them, such findings give us a potentially valuable insight into why some individuals remain strongly driven to adopt variant behaviors despite the vigorous and continuing condemnation these behaviors often inspire. It may in fact be that they have little choice in the matter (see *HIGHLIGHT 10.2*).

This apparent absence of choice seems especially true of gender identity disorders, as defined in the DSM-III-R, which recognizes separate adult and childhood forms of a profound rejection of one's anatomical sex. Individuals with this disorder feel themselves to be the victims of some grotesque error of fate in being forced to occupy a body that is alien to their gender-related sense of self.

Often this anatomically discrepant gender identity is accompanied by role behaviors and dress that affirm the desired identity, and, in sexually active adults, by a "homosexual" orientation and partner choice; of course, in this context such a choice (for example, a male transsexual choosing a male partner) is the psychological equivalent of a heterosexual one. Many of these individuals feel driven to seek and submit to surgical and endocrinological interventions that hold some promise of bringing them anatomically closer to their gender identities—a venture that is much more likely, for technical/surgical reasons, to have an objectively satisfactory outcome if the desired conversion is male-to-female rather than the opposite. In children, the disorder may be accompanied by stubborn, irrational beliefs that their anatomies will undergo future changes in the desired direction.

The DSM-III-R also recognizes a type of gender identity disorder among adults that is not accompanied by preoccupation with sex change. Rare in incidence, it is designated as *nontranssexual cross-gender disorder*.

Gender identity disorders are quite rare overall. Their incidence in males is estimated to be somewhat less than 3 per 100,000 and in females just under 1 per 100,000 (Walinder, 1968). These figures do not include children, who typically manifest the disorder before the age of 4, and many of whom yield to pressures and adopt sex-appropriate behavior; the few who do not become adult transsexuals (Adams & Chiodo, 1984).

While the hypothesis of biological causation seems plausible, it is also possible that reverse-gender identity and behavior could be learned. Green (1974) has noted certain psychosocial factors that appear to be common in the backgrounds of transsexual boys, among them parental indifference to or encouragement of "feminine" behavior dur-

HIGHLIGHT 10.2

Transsexualism and a Tangled Relationship

After a lengthy courtship, Bob and Mae Sylvester married in 1972, Mae having concluded that Bob had overcome, through therapy, his wish to dress in women's clothing. Bob knew better, but was so attached to Mae that he tried to tell himself he was "cured" of his transvestism. After a brief period, the urge to cross-dress became so strong that Bob told Mae he wished occasionally to wear women's clothing at home. Mae responded by telling him it made her "physically sick" to see him dress in that manner. Nevertheless, on the advice of a second therapist, Bob resumed regular cross-dressing—but never in Mae's presence. At about this time, Bob successfully ran for election to the St. Paul, Minnesota, city council. During a four-year term as a member of this body, Bob distinguished himself as an effective and dynamic leader.

Meanwhile, Bob and Mae tried, with essentially no success,

to establish a satisfactory sexual relationship. Both agreed that their sex life was a disaster. Their relationship was strained further with the emergence of Bob's second identity, an adolescent girl named Susan. Susan was petulant and demanding, and Mae resented the maternal role into which she was now cast. As Susan developed, she wanted more and more "time" and resisted being Bob for an evening at home. Susan demanded, and got, an adolescent girl's bedroom, decorated in pink and mauve with birds, flowers, ribbons, and a pink canopy over the bed. This was apparently the last straw for Mae, and shortly thereafter, in 1981, the couple separated. Bob could not bear to lose the bedroom, so Mae moved out.

Bob had been aware since childhood of his wish to be female. A life-threatening event in February 1982 brought home to him forcefully his wish "just

once" to make love as a woman. The next week he initiated procedures to undergo a sex change. On March 28, Bob legally became Susan Elizabeth Kimberly. Surgery to provide her with female genitalia was scheduled for 1984. Before the surgery, Ms. Kimberly transformed her social identity exclusively to that of a woman.

Mae Sylvester's initial reaction to these events was similar to grieving—indeed, for her, her husband Bob *had* died. Nevertheless, she maintains an active friendship with Susan Kimberly. The two continue to see each other and to share the (nonsexual) activities both had enjoyed before the divorce and Susan's reversal of gender identity. Mae says that Susan has retained many of the qualities she had found attractive in Bob.

Based on *Minneapolis Tribune*, May 1, 1983, pp. 1A, 4A–6A.

ing the first year, maternal overprotection and domination, being dressed in female clothes by a female family member, and a lack of male friends in the early years. Obviously, some of these factors could be secondary accommodations to a child's displaying effeminate behavior from an early age, and hence are not inconsistent with a biological hypothesis. Of incidental interest, Green (1985) followed up these identity-reversed youngsters and found some 70 percent of them to be homosexually or bisexually oriented as adults.

Sex Reassignment Surgery   Efforts to alter gender identity by means of behavior therapy and other psychotherapeutic procedures have generally proven unsuccessful. As a consequence, transsexu-

als who feel a complete inability to accept their assigned sex identity have requested surgical sex change in increasing numbers during recent years.

The first transsexual operation is said to have been performed by F. Z. Abraham in the 1930s. Although occasional reports of similar operations were forthcoming the next two decades, it was not until 1953, when Hamburger reported the case of Christine Jorgensen, that surgical sex change became well known. Currently, medical centers that offer this service receive numerous requests per year from transsexual individuals to undertake evaluation and management of their cases.

In anatomical males, modern surgical procedures accomplish sex conversion through removal of male organs and their replacement with an artfully designed vagina that apparently works satisfactorily in many cases, sometimes even enabling an individual, now a woman, to achieve coital orgasm. Weekly injections of sex hormones stimulate breast development, give more female texture to the skin, and also lessen beard growth, though electrolysis is usually needed to remove excess hair. Surgery for anatomically female transsexuals generally has been less successful, for although surgeons can remove the breasts, ovaries, vagina, and uterus, and can attach a penis constructed from rib cartilage, plastic, or other material, the makeshift penis does not function normally. Nevertheless, many receiving this surgery report satisfaction with the outcomes (Blanchard, Steiner, & Clemmensen, 1985). Transplants of reproductive organs are not yet possible in either males or females, and the individual will be sterile after surgery.

Various evaluative studies of the outcomes of such operations have been reported. One of the best-known early studies is that of Benjamin (1966). This investigator questioned 50 transsexuals who had crossed the sex line from male to female. Their ages at the time of surgery ranged from 19 to 58, with an average age of 32. Of these subjects, 44 reported contentment sexually and socially with their new roles as women; 5 complained either about their abilities to perform sexually or about their appearances; and 1 was totally dissatisfied with the results. In another study, Pauly (1968) reviewed the postoperative courses of 121 male transsexuals who had received sex-reassignment surgery and found that satisfactory outcomes outnumbered unsatisfactory ones at a ratio of 10 to 1. He also reported previous unsuccessful attempts by psychotherapy to help these patients achieve male gender identities. Comparable results were reported by Green (1974). In a more recent and relatively rigorous assessment, Abramowitz (1986) estimated the psychosocial outcome success rate for transsexual surgery to be about two-thirds overall, the female-to-male variety actually showing a slight advantage; some 10 percent of male-to-female interventions were said to produce serious complications, usually associated with the surgery.

Considerable controversy has raged about sex-conversion surgery, and many physicians as well as other professionals remain opposed to it. Newman and Stoller (1974) have pointed out that occasionally schizophrenics and other mentally disturbed individuals seek sexual reassignment, but that their desire is only transitory. For this and related reasons, it is recommended that those considering sex-reassignment surgery undergo a trial period first during which they receive hormone therapy and live in their new roles to get a clearer understanding of

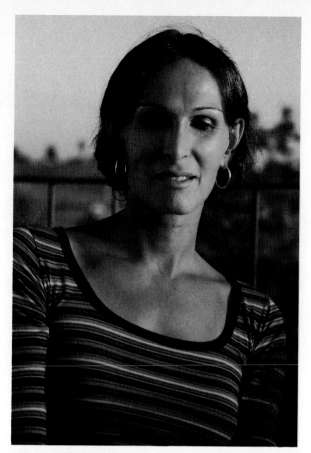

Dr. Richard Raskin, a physician and professional tennis player, became Renee Richards through transsexual surgery.

the many psychological and social adjustments that will be required. Based on his considerable clinical experience with this group, Lothstein (1982, 1983) is also impressed with the prevalence of serious mental disturbances, recommending psychotherapy as the initial treatment of choice. In general, it appears that strict criteria are needed for selecting surgical reassignees (Lothstein, 1982).

■ The Paraphilias

The **paraphilias** are a group of persistent sexual behavior patterns in which unusual objects, rituals, or situations are required for full sexual satisfaction. While mild forms of these activities probably have occurred in the lives of many normal people, a paraphilic person is distinguished by the insistence and relative exclusivity with which his or her sexuality focuses on the acts in question—without which orgasm is often impossible. Paraphilic individuals may or may not have persistent desires to change their sexual preferences.

As described by Money and Lamacz (1989), paraphilic lovemaps tend to be quite stable within individuals but quite variable in character among people having paraphilic tendencies. Some such lovemaps are organized in a quite simple, straightforward manner, while others are complex and richly elaborated, calling for extraordinary preparation and "staging." The playing out of a lovemap may be complete on the first and every subsequent occasion in which it appears, or it may unfold in a series of stages. Some paraphilias require interpersonal formats, and a fortunate paraphilic individual may discover another person with a reciprocally paraphilic lovemap—as in sexual sadomasochism—which may then lead to a lasting although by conventional standards somewhat bizarre love affair. Fairly common is a situation in which a sexually normal person becomes unwittingly involved in a paraphilic person's ritualized sexual program, only gradually discovering that he or she is a mere accessory, a sort of stage prop, in the latter's sexual drama.

The DSM-III-R recognizes nine paraphilias: fetishism, transvestic fetishism, voyeurism, exhibitionism, sexual sadism, sexual masochism, pedophilia, zoophilia (sexual attraction to animals), and frotteurism (rubbing against a nonconsenting person). Of these, we will discuss all but zoophilia, a rare disorder, and frotteurism, a category that is relatively new and not yet satisfactorily researched.

Fetishism   In **fetishism,** sexual interest typically centers on some body part or on an inanimate object, such as an article of clothing. As is generally true for the paraphilias, males are most commonly involved in cases of fetishism; reported cases of female fetishists are extremely rare. The range of fetishistic objects includes hair, ears, hands, underclothing, shoes, perfume, and similar objects associated with the opposite sex. The mode of using these objects to achieve sexual excitement and gratification varies considerably, but it commonly involves kissing, fondling, tasting, or smelling the objects. Fetishism is a victimless sexual variant because, although it sometimes involves crimes such as thievery, its basic nature does not normally interfere with the rights of others, except in an incidental way.

To obtain the required object, a fetishistic person may commit burglary, theft, or even assault. Probably the articles most commonly stolen by fetishistic individuals are women's underthings. One young boy was found to have accumulated over 100 pairs of panties from a lingerie shop when he was apprehended. In such cases the excitement and suspense of the criminal act itself typically reinforce the sexual stimulation and sometimes actually constitute the fetish—the stolen article being of little importance. For example, one youth admitted entering many homes in which the entering itself usually sufficed to induce an orgasm. When it did

not, he was able to achieve sexual satisfaction by taking some "token," such as money or jewelry.

Frequently, fetishistic behavior consists of masturbation in association with a fetishistic object. Here, of course, it is difficult to draw a line between fetishistic activity and the effort to increase the sexual excitation and satisfaction of masturbation through the use of pictures and other articles associated with a desired sexual object. Using such articles in masturbation is a common practice and not usually considered pathological. Where antisocial behavior, such as breaking and entering, is involved, however, the practice is commonly referred to as fetishistic. For example, Marshall (1974) reported a rather unusual case of a young university student who had a "trouser fetish"; he would steal the trousers of teenagers and then use them in physical contact during masturbation. A somewhat different, but not atypical, pattern of fetishism is illustrated by the case of a man whose fetish was women's shoes and legs.

> *T*he fetishist in this case was arrested several times for loitering in public places, such as railroad stations and libraries, watching women's legs. Finally he chanced on a novel solution to his problem. Posing as an agent for a hosiery firm, he rented a large room, advertised for models, and took motion pictures of a number of women walking and seated with their legs displayed to best advantage. He then used these pictures to achieve sexual satisfaction and found that they continued to be adequate for the purpose. (Adapted from Grant, 1953)

Another type of fetishism involves setting fires. Although people who set fires are a mixed group, a sizable number of fires—including some involving loss of life—are set by fetishistic individuals who have come to experience relief of sexual tension from setting and watching fires burn. Such fires include brush and forest fires as well as building fires. Diagnostically, fetishistic fire-setting is included in the DSM-III-R rubric of pyromania, an impulse control disorder.

In approaching the causal factors in fetishism, we should again note that, through learning, many stimuli can come to be associated with sexual excitation and gratification. Probably most people are stimulated to some degree by intimate articles of clothing and by perfumes and odors associated with potential sexual partners. Thus the first prerequisite in fetishism seems to be a conditioning experience. This original conditioning may be quite accidental, as when sexual arousal and orgasm—which are reflexive responses—are elicited by a strong emotional experience involving some particular object or part of the body. More commonly, probably, the conditioning occurs during masturbatory fantasies.

In some instances, however, the associations involved in fetishism are not easy to explain. Bergler (1947) cited an unusual case in which a man's sex life was almost completely absorbed by a fetishistic fascination with automobile exhaust pipes. Nor would just any exhaust pipe do; it had to be in perfect shape, undented and undamaged, and it had to emit softly blowing gases. This fetish became far more attractive to him than sexual behavior with women.

Fetishistic patterns of sexual gratification usually become the preferred patterns only when they are part of a larger picture of maladjustment, at least in the far more common cases involving males; such maladjustment typically involves doubts about one's masculinity and potency, and fear of rejection and humiliation. By fetishistic practices and mastery over an inanimate object—which comes to symbolize a desired sexual object—a man apparently safeguards himself and also compensates somewhat for his feelings of inadequacy.

Transvestic Fetishism   The achievement of sexual arousal and satisfaction by "cross-dressing," that is, dressing as a member of the opposite sex, is called **transvestic fetishism.** It is an uncommon condition in which an individual, usually a male, enjoys excursions into the social roles of the other sex or is markedly distressed by urges to do so. Although a transvestic male, for example, regards himself as a man when dressed as a man, he may

have feelings of being a woman when dressed in women's clothing. A medical researcher and transvestite himself for 35 years expressed it this way: "The transvestite finds that he is both a 'he' and 'she' together—at the same time or alternating from one to the other when opportunity permits or desire compels" (*Los Angeles Times,* September 30, 1973). Because transvestism usually does not directly involve anyone but the cross-dressing individual, it can be considered a victimless sexual variant.

Little is known about transvestism, especially as practiced by females, in whom it appears to be extremely rare. Most reports are based on studies of single male cases, and most of those studied have been in therapy, which may make them an unrepresentative group. Buckner (1970), however, has formulated a description of the "ordinary" male transvestite from a survey of 262 transvestites conducted by the magazine *Transvestia.*

He is probably married (about two-thirds are); if he is married he probably has children (about two-thirds do). Almost all of these transvestites said they were exclusively heterosexual—in fact, the rate of "homosexuality" was less than the average for the entire population. The transvestic behavior generally consists of privately dressing in the clothes of a woman, at home, in secret. . . . The transvestite generally does not run into trouble with the law. His cross-dressing causes difficulties for very few people besides himself and his wife. (p. 381)

The most extensive studies to date of male transvestites' personalities are those of Bentler and Prince (1969, 1970) and Bentler, Shearman, and Prince (1970). These investigators obtained replies

Studies have shown that men who cross dress may actually feel less anxiety and shyness when in their female roles. Though an individual may therefore enjoy excursions into the social roles of the other sex, he may also be markedly distressed by urges to do so, and, if married, his transvestism may also cause difficulties for his wife. Cross dressers are seeking out others of their kind to deal with their special problems in support groups like the one shown here.

to a standardized psychological inventory from a large sample of transvestic people through the cooperation of a national transvestite organization. The transvestic individuals, compared to matched control groups, showed no gross differences on neurotic or psychotic inventory scales. They did, however, present themselves as being more controlled in impulse expression, less involved with other individuals, more inhibited in interpersonal relationships, and more dependent.

Interestingly, it appears that cross-dressing may reduce the strength of some of these aberrant tendencies. Gosslin and Eysenck (1980) asked transvestic males to take a personality test while functioning in regular male clothing and while cross-dressed. "Neuroticism" and "introversion" both declined in the cross-dressed condition. This finding was consistent with subjects' reports of less anxiety and shyness when in their female roles.

It appears that much transvestism can be explained in terms of a simple conditioning model. A male child may receive attention from females in his family who think it is cute for him to dress in feminine attire and hence reinforce this behavior with attention and praise. Such a conditioning process is well portrayed in the case of an adult transvestite studied by Stoller (1974):

"*I* have pictures of myself dressed as a little girl when I was a small child. My mother thought it was cute. She was right. I was a pretty little girl.

"The highlights of my life as a girl came when I was between the ages of 10 and 17. I had an aunt who was childless and wanted to take me through the steps from childhood to young womanhood. She knew of my desires to be a girl. I would spend every summer at her ranch. The first thing she would do was to give me a pixie haircut, which always turned out pretty good since I would avoid getting a haircut for two months before I went to her ranch. She then would take me into the bedroom and show me all my pretty new things she had bought me. The next day, dressed as a girl, I would accompany her to town and we would shop for a new dress for me. To everyone she met, she would introduce me as her 'niece.'

"This went on every year until I was 13 years old. Then she decided I should start my womanhood. I will never forget that summer. When I arrived I got the same pixie haircut as usual but when we went into the bedroom there laid out on the bed was a girdle, a garter belt and bra, size 32AA, and my first pair of nylons. She then took

me over to the new dressing table she had bought me and slid back the top to reveal my very own makeup kit. I was thrilled to death. She said she wanted her 'niece' to start off right and it was about time I started to develop a bust.

"The next morning I was up early to ready myself for the usual shopping trip to town, only this time it was for a pair of high heels and a new dress. I remember I stuffed my bra with cotton, put on my garter belt, and slipped on my nylons with no effort. After all, I became an expert from practice the night before. My aunt applied my lipstick because I was so excited I couldn't get it on straight. Then off to town we went, aunt and 'niece.' What a wonderful day. I shall never forget it." (pp. 209–210)

The adult transvestite who marries faces problems that are well brought out in another case reported by Stoller (1974):

"*We* fell in love and as soon as I felt we could we were married. We have been as happy as two people can be and the best part of it is that she knows all about me and not only accepts me as I am but assists in my transformation and then admires me. . . ."

This is the way the relationship looks at first, when the wife is pleased to see her husband's femininity. She does not know yet that as he becomes a more successful transvestite her enthusiasm will wane. Then he will be hurt that she is no longer interested in his dressing up, his sexual needs, his work. The fighting will start, neither will understand what has happened, and they will divorce. (p. 212)

As we have indicated, transvestic fetishism, like fetishism, causes harm to others only when accompanied by such illegal acts as theft or destruction of property. This is not always the case with the other paraphilias, many of which do contain a definite element of injury or significant risk of injury—physical or psychological—to one or more of the parties involved in a sexual encounter. Typically these practices have strong legal sanctions against them. We shall consider only the most common forms of these paraphilias: voyeurism, exhibitionism, sadism, masochism, and pedophilia.

Voyeurism   The synonymous terms **voyeurism, scotophilia,** and **inspectionalism** refer to the achievement of sexual pleasure through clandestine peeping. Although children often engage in such behavior, it occurs as a sexual offense primarily among young males. These Peeping Toms, as they are commonly called, usually concentrate on females who are undressing or on couples engaging in sexual relations. Frequently they masturbate during their peeping activity.

How do males develop this pattern? First, viewing the body of an attractive female seems to be quite stimulating sexually for many, if not most, males. In addition, the privacy and mystery that have traditionally surrounded sexual activities have tended to increase curiosity about them.

Second, if a boy with such curiosity feels shy and inadequate in his relations with the other sex, it is not too surprising for him to accept the substitute of voyeurism. In this way he satisfies his curiosity and to some extent meets his sexual needs without the trauma of actually approaching a female, and thus without the failure and lowered self-status that such an approach might bring. In fact voyeuristic activities often provide important compensatory feelings of power and secret domination over an unsuspecting victim, which may contribute materially to the maintenance of this pattern. Also, of course, the suspense and danger associated with voyeurism may lead to emotional excitement and a reinforcement of the sexual stimulation. A voyeur does not normally seek sexual activity with those he observes.

If a voyeur is married, as many are, he is rarely well-adjusted sexually in his relationship with his wife.

A young married college student had an attic apartment that was extremely hot during the summer months. To enable him to attend school, his wife worked; she came home at night tired and irritable and not in the mood for sexual relations. In addition, "the damned springs in the bed squeaked." In order "to obtain some sexual gratification" the youth would peer through his binoculars at the room next door and occasionally saw the young couple there engaged in erotic activities. This stimulated him greatly, and he thus decided to extend his peeping to a sorority house. During his second venture, however, he was reported and apprehended by the police. This offender was quite immature for his age, rather puritanical in his attitude toward masturbation, and prone to indulge in rich but immature sexual fantasies.

Although more permissive laws concerning "adult" movies, videos, and magazines have probably removed much of the secrecy from sexual behavior and also have provided an alternative source of gratification for would-be voyeurs, their actual effects on the incidence of voyeurism is a matter of speculation. For many voyeurs these movies and magazines probably do not provide an adequate substitute for secretly watching the sexual behavior of an unsuspecting couple or the "real-life" nudity of a woman who mistakenly believes she enjoys privacy.

Although a voyeur may become somewhat reckless in his behavior and thus may be detected and assaulted by his subjects, voyeurism does not ordinarily have any serious criminal or antisocial aspects. In fact many people probably have rather strong inclinations in the same direction, which are well checked by practical considerations, such as the possibility of being caught, and ethical attitudes concerning the right to privacy. On the other hand, strong voyeuristic tendencies are sometimes accompanied by other, more bizarre elements in a peeper's lovemap that might signal deeper and far more serious problems. For example, one of the authors is involved at this writing in the assessment of a chronic voyeur who preserves over long periods, in plastic baggies, his ejaculate from masturbation. There is a possibility in this case of psychotic disorder.

Exhibitionism The word **exhibitionism** (*indecent exposure* in legal terms) describes the intentional exposure of the genitals to others in inappropriate circumstances and without their consent. The exposure may take place in some secluded location, such as a park, or in a more public place, such as a department store, church, theater, or bus. In cities an exhibitionist often drives by schools or bus stops, exhibits himself while in the car, and then drives rapidly away. In many instances the exposure is repeated under fairly constant conditions, such as only in churches or buses, or in the same general vicinity and at the same time of day. In one case, a youth exhibited himself only at the top of an escalator in a large department store. The sex object too is usually fairly consistent for an individual exhibitionist. For a male offender, this ordinarily involves a young or middle-aged female who is not known to the offender.

In some instances, exposure of the genitals is accompanied by suggestive gestures or masturbatory activity, but more often there is only exposure. Although it is considered relatively rare, a hostile exposer may accompany exhibitionism with aggressive acts and may knock down or otherwise attack a victim. In fact some research indicates a subclass of exhibitionists who may best be considered antisocial personalities, as described in Chapter 8 (Forgac & Michaels, 1982).

Despite the rarity of assaultive behavior in these cases, and the fact that most exhibitionists are anything but the aggressive and dangerous criminals they are often made out to be, an exhibitionistic act nevertheless takes place without the viewer's consent and may be emotionally upsetting, as is indeed the perpetrator's intent. This intrusive quality of the act, together with its explicit violation of propriety norms respecting "private parts," assures condemnation. Thus society considers exhibitionism a criminal offense.

Exhibitionism is the most common sexual offense reported to the police in the United States, Canada, and Europe, accounting for about one-third of all sexual offenses (Rooth, 1974). Curiously enough, it is rare in most other countries. For example, in Argentina only 24 people were convicted of exhibitionism during a five-year period; in Japan only about 60 men are convicted of this offense each year. In still other countries, such as Burma and India, it is practically unheard of.

Exhibitionism is most common during the warm spring and summer months, and most offenders are young adult males. Practically all occupational groups are represented. Usually exhibitionism by males in public or semipublic places is reported to the police, although some women simply ignore such incidents.

Among women, exhibiting the genitals for non-commercial, erotic purposes is so rare that instances sometimes prompt the publication of full case reports in the professional literature (for example, Grob, 1985). Furthermore, these rare occurences are less likely to be reported to the police. Because so little is known about female exhibitionism, the following discussion of causal factors will be limited to male offenders.

In general, cases of exhibitionism appear to fall into one of three categories. These categories are described in the sections that follow.

Personal immaturity.   Witzig (1968) found that about 60 percent of male exhibitionism cases referred by courts for treatment fall into the category of personal immaturity. Here the exhibitionism seems to be based on inadequate information about sex, feelings of shyness and inferiority in approaching potential sexual partners, and puritanical attitudes toward masturbation. Commonly, such exhibitionists have strong bonds to overly possessive

mothers. Often an exhibitionist states that he struggled against the impulse to expose himself in much the same way that an adolescent may struggle against the impulse to masturbate; as sexual or other tensions increased, however, he felt compelled to carry out his exhibitionistic activities. Often an exhibitionist feels guilty and remorseful afterward, particularly if he has achieved ejaculation.

Although over half of all exhibitionists are married, they usually fail to achieve satisfactory sexual and personal relationships with their wives. Witzig (1968) pointed out the following:

These men almost never like to discuss sexual matters with their wives and frequently avoid undressing before them. The idea of living in a nudist colony is a repulsive thought to most exhibitionists, although they are periodically willing to show off their genitals in quite public places. (p. 78)

Many of these offenders state that they married only because of family pressure, often at a late age. Thus we are dealing here with individuals who are essentially immature in their sex-role development, even though they may be well-educated and competent in other life areas.

Closely related to a male exhibitionist's personal immaturity appears to be a second factor: doubts and fears about his masculinity, combined with a strong need to demonstrate masculinity and potency. Apfelberg, Sugar, and Pfeffer (1944), for example, cited the case of an exhibitionist who achieved sexual satisfaction only when he accompanied the exposure of his genitals with a question to his victim as to whether she had ever seen such a large penis. On one occasion, the woman, instead of evidencing shock and embarrassment, scornfully assured him that she had. On this occasion, the defendant stated, he had received no sexual gratification. In general, it appears that the lovemap of an exhibitionist is one that requires the victim to be intimidated by the "awesome" display to which she is an involuntary witness.

It is worth noting that exhibitionism normally takes place in a setting that would not be conducive to having sexual relations—for example, the parking lot of a busy shopping mall. An exhibitionist attempts to elicit a reaction that confirms his masculine "power" without entailing the risk of having to perform adequately in a mutual sexual encounter. Some exhibitionists, to be sure, fantasize that their victims will "take the first step" and approach them for sexual services (Adams & Chiodo, 1984). Because such a reaction is exceedingly unlikely to occur, an exhibitionist is protected from any such real confrontation; most would probably flee were this unlikely event to materialize.

In reviewing the role of personal immaturity and sexual ignorance in exhibitionism, it is interesting to note the conclusion of Rooth (1974) that the "sexual revolution" of the 1960s and 1970s in the Western world may have made matters worse for male exhibitionists: the growing assertiveness of women may make them even more insecure while at the same time they are being bombarded by sexually suggestive material from the "emancipated" mass media, thus increasing their frustration. The impact of these changes on women, both as victims and as potential exhibitionists themselves, has not been studied.

Interpersonal stress and acting out.   Another causal factor is suggested by the high incidence of precipitating stress (Blair & Lanyon, 1981). Often a married exhibitionist appears to be reacting to some conflict or stress situation in his marriage, and his behavior is like a regression to adolescent masturbatory activity. In such instances, an exhibitionist may state that exhibiting himself during masturbation is more exciting and tension-reducing than using pictures of nude women.

An interesting example of stress-induced exhibitionism was published a number of years ago in the autobiography of a prominent National Football League player. Intellectually and physically talented, attractive, wealthy, famous, and married to one of the most beautiful women in the entertainment field, this individual was nevertheless arrested on two occasions for exhibiting himself to preadolescent girls. By his own account, these incidents occurred only during periods of intense pressure, when he felt he was failing in those aspects of his life he most valued—his athletic career and his marriage (Rentzel, 1972).

Exhibitionism without genital arousal may take place following a period of intense conflict over some problem—often involving authority figures—with which an individual feels inadequate to cope.

For example, a Marine who wanted to make a career of the service was having an experience with a superior that made it impossible for him to reenlist. He could not admit to himself that he could be hostile to either the corps or the superior. For the first time in his life, he exposed himself to a girl on the beach. Arrested, he was merely reprimanded and returned to the scene of conflict. A short time later he displayed his genitals to a girl in a parking lot. This time he was placed on probation with the stipulation that he seek treatment, and his enlistment was allowed to terminate in natural sequence. He never repeated the act. He was happily married and seemed to be acting out in this instance a vulgar expression of contempt. (Witzig, 1968, p. 77)

These cases of exhibitionism as expressions of anger and contempt may be partly viewed as a product of societal expectations that men express masculinity by dominating women.

Other psychopathology.   Like other paraphilias, exhibitionism may occur in association with more pervasive forms of psychopathology. Severely mentally retarded youths—both male and female—may exhibit themselves, being apparently unaware or only partially aware that society disapproves of their behavior. Some exhibitionists are older men with senile brain deterioration who evidence a lowering of inner reality and ethical controls.

In other cases, as we have seen, exhibitionism is associated with antisocial personality disorder. Here individuals usually have histories of poor school adjustment and erratic work records; often they have had difficulties with authorities as a consequence of other antisocial acts. Their exhibitionism appears to be just one more form of antisocial behavior, from which they may or may not achieve sexual excitation and gratification. In some instances, exhibitionism is associated with manic or schizophrenic reactions. For example, the only woman in a group of offenders studied by Witzig (1968) typically exposed herself prior to the onset of a full-blown psychotic episode.

Sadism   The term **sadism** is derived from the name of the Marquis de Sade (1740–1814), who for sexual purposes inflicted such cruelty on his victims that he was eventually committed as insane. Although the term's meaning has broadened to denote cruelty in general, we will use it in its restricted sense to mean the achievement of sexual stimulation and gratification by inflicting physical or psychic pain or humiliation on a sexual partner. The practice of "bondage and discipline" (B & D) to enhance sexual excitation and pleasure is a closely related pattern. These elements of a sadist's erotic interest suggest a psychological association with rape (Marshall, Laws, & Barbaree, 1990a), discussed in a later section. The lovemaps of sadistic individuals are thus heavily infused with the inflic-

Mild degrees of sadism and masochism are involved in the sexual foreplay customs of many cultures, and some couples in our own society—both heterosexual and homosexual— regularly engage in such practices. In some cases sexual gratification is obtained from the sadistic practice alone. Sadomasochistic services are even sold in places like the one shown here, complete with racks, pillories, cages, whipping posts, and shackles. Here, people pay $40 to be whipped and abused, and for $20 per half-hour counseling session, can be taught how to practice B & D safely at home.

practice alone. A sadist, for example, may slash a woman with a razor or stick her with a needle, experiencing an orgasm in the process. The peculiar and extreme associations that may occur are shown by the case of a young man who entered a strange woman's apartment, held a chloroformed rag to her face until she lost consciousness, and branded her on the thigh with a hot iron. She was not molested in any other way.

Sometimes sadistic activities are associated with animals or with fetishistic objects instead of other human beings. East (1946) cited the case of a man who stole women's shoes, which he then slashed savagely with a knife. When he was in prison, he was found mutilating photographs that other prisoners kept in their cells by cutting the throats of the women in them. He admitted that he derived full sexual gratification from this procedure.

In other instances, gratification is achieved only if mutilation is performed directly on a victim. Chesser (1971) refers to such offenders as *pathological sadists* and notes that they are often extremely dangerous. The following is such a case:

tion of suffering, or the appearance of it, on their partners.

The pain may be inflicted by such means as whipping, biting, or pinching; the act may vary in intensity, from fantasy to severe mutilation and even murder. Mild degrees of sadism (and masochism) are involved in the sexual foreplay customs of many cultures, and some couples in our own society —both heterosexual and homosexual—regularly engage in such practices. The "golden showers" ritual, for example, in which partners urinate on one another, is a form of foreplay among male homosexuals. Males are ordinarily the "aggressors" in sadistic heterosexual relations, although Krafft-Ebing (1950) early reported a number of cases in which sadists were women; likewise, some contemporary prostitutes specialize in the B & D trade as "dominatrixes." In one unusual case, a wife required her husband to cut himself on the arm before approaching her sexually. She would then suck the wound and become extremely aroused.

In some cases, sadistic activities lead up to or terminate in actual sexual relations; in others, full sexual gratification is obtained from the sadistic

The offender, Peter Kursten, was 47 years old at the time of his apprehension in Düsseldorf, Germany, for a series of lust murders. He was a skilled laborer, well groomed, modest, and had done nothing that annoyed his fellow workers.

Peter came from a disturbed family background, his father having been an alcoholic who had been sent to prison for having intercourse with Peter's older sister. Peter's own earliest sexual experiences were with animals. When he was about 13 years old, he attempted to have intercourse with a sheep, but the animal would not hold still, and he stabbed her with a knife. At that moment he had an ejaculation.

After this experience, Peter found the sight of gushing blood sexually exciting, and he turned from animals to human females. Often he first choked his victim, but if he did not achieve an orgasm, he then stabbed her. Initially he used scissors and a dagger, but later he took to using a hammer or an axe. After he achieved ejaculation, he lost interest in his victim, except for taking measures to cover up his crime.

The offender's sexual crimes extended over a period of some 30 years and involved over 40 victims. Finally apprehended . . . he expressed a sense of injustice at not being like other people who were raised in normal families. (Adapted from Berg, 1954)

The news media have reported more recent cases in which victims have been mutilated and killed in association with sadistic sexual practices. In the early 1970s, a horror story broke concerning the sadistic homosexual murders of 27 teenage boys in Texas. More recently, but prior to the AIDS epidemic, the San Francisco city coroner found it advisable to meet with leaders of the local homosexual community to discuss means of curbing serious injuries and deaths due to sado-masochistic practices within that group (*Time,* May 4, 1981). We do not, however, have enough available case material on which to base definitive conclusions concerning the actual clinical picture or the causal factors involved in cases of sadism reported by the media.

The causal factors in sadism appear roughly comparable to those in fetishism. These factors are listed in the following paragraphs:

1. *Experiences in which sexual excitation and possibly orgasm have been associated with the infliction of pain.* Such conditioned associations may occur under a variety of conditions. In their sexual fantasies many children visualize violent attacks by men on women, and such ideas may be strengthened by newspaper accounts of sadistic assaults on females. Perhaps more directly relevant are experiences in which an individual's infliction of pain on an animal or another person has given rise to strong emotions and, unintentionally, to sexual excitement. We have noted elsewhere the connection between strong emotional stimulation and sexual stimulation, especially during adolescence. Just as in fetishism—where simple conditioning seems to make it possible for almost any object or action to become sexually exciting—conditioning can also be an important factor in the development of sadistic tendencies.

2. *Negative attitudes toward sex.* Sadistic activities may protect individuals with negative attitudes toward sex from the full sexual implications of their behaviors. At the same time, such activities may help certain people express their contempt for and punishment of their partners for engaging in sexual relations. Several early investigators described male sadists as timid, passive, undersexed individuals; they described sadistic behavior as apparently designed to arouse strong emotions in a sex object which, in turn, arouses a sadist and makes orgasm possible. The sadist apparently receives little or no satisfaction if the victim remains passive and unresponsive to the painful stimuli. In fact the sadist usually wants the victim to find the pain exciting, and may even insist that the victim act pleasurably

aroused when being stuck with pins, bitten, or otherwise hurt.

For many sexually inadequate and insecure individuals, the infliction of pain is apparently a "safe" means of achieving sexual stimulation. Strong feelings of power and superiority over a victim may for the time shut out underlying feelings of inadequacy and anxiety.

3. *Association with other psychopathology.* In schizophrenia and other severe forms of psychopathology, sadistic rituals and sexual behavior may result from the lowering of inner controls and from pathologically convoluted symbolic processes. Wertham (1949) cited an extreme case in which a schizophrenic individual with puritanical attitudes toward sex achieved full sexual gratification by castrating young boys and killing and mutilating young girls. He rationalized his actions as being the only way to save them from later immoral behavior.

Masochism   The term **masochism** is derived from the name of the Austrian novelist Leopold V. Sacher-Masoch (1836–1895), whose fictional characters dwelt lovingly on the sexual pleasure of pain. As in the case of the term *sadism,* the meaning of *masochism* has been broadened beyond sexual connotations, so that it includes deriving pleasure from self-denial; from expiatory physical suffering, such as that of the religious flagellants; and from hardship and suffering in general. As we saw in Chapter 8, the recent proposal to incorporate this pattern as an Axis II personality disorder in DSM-III-R provoked a storm of controversy, resulting in the banishment of the diagnosis (now changed to self-defeating personality disorder) to a DSM-III-R appendix of questionable scientific or professional status. Here we will restrict our discussion to the sexual aspects of masochistic behavior.

The clinical picture of masochism is similar to that in sadistic practices, except that the pain is inflicted on the self instead of on others (Sack & Miller, 1975). For example, East (1946) cited the case of a young woman who frequently cut herself on the arms, legs, and breasts; she also inserted pins and needles under her skin. The woman experienced sexual pleasure from the pain and from seeing the blood from the incisions.

Patterns of masochistic behavior may come about through conditioned learning: as a result of early experiences, an individual comes to associate pain with sexual pleasure. For example, Gebhard (1965) cited the case of an adolescent boy who had the fractured bones in his arm hurriedly set without an anesthetic. To comfort the boy, the physician's attractive nurse caressed him and held his head against her breast. As a consequence, he experienced a "powerful and curious combination of pain and sexual arousal," which led to masochistic—as well as sadistic—tendencies in his later heterosexual relations.

Such sayings as "crushed in his arms" or "smothered with kisses" reveal the association commonly made between erotic arousal and pain or discomfort. Thus it is not surprising that many individuals resort to mild sadomasochistic acts, such as biting, in an attempt to increase sexual excitement. For most people, however, such behavior does not result in serious physical injury, nor does it serve as a substitute for normal sexual relations. In actual masochism, by contrast, an individual experiences sexual stimulation and gratification from the experience of pain and degradation in relating to a lover.

In the case of both sadism and masochism, it should be noted that gratification in many instances requires a shared, complementary interpersonal relationship—one sadist and one masochist or, in milder forms, one superior "disciplinarian" and one obedient "slave." Such arrangements are not uncommon in both heterosexual and homosexual relationships (Tripp, 1975). One of the authors has treated a promiscuous male homosexual whose exclusive desire was to be aggressively penetrated anally. Through this act the man sought to relive an exquisitely painful experience in which, as a boy, his father had administered an enema to him, by far the "closest" and most intimate experience he had ever had with this profoundly rejecting man. Here we see an instance in which the lovemap evidently was enormously affected by a single, overwhelmingly powerful experience.

Pedophilia   In **pedophilia** the preferred sex object is a child; the intimacy usually involves manipulation of the child's genitals. Occasionally the child is induced to manipulate the pedophile's sex organ or to engage in fellatio (mouth-genital contact). Sexual intercourse is apparently rare (Adams & Chiodo, 1984), although it is attempted by some pedophiles and often results in injury to the child.

The sexual exploitation and abuse of children might be said to have a long past but a brief history. The ancient Greeks are known to have valued pedophilia, particularly the male homosexual variety, and to have practiced it with considerable enthusiasm. In modern Western culture, until very recently, pedophilic interests have mostly been seen as only moderately "quirky," sometimes amusingly

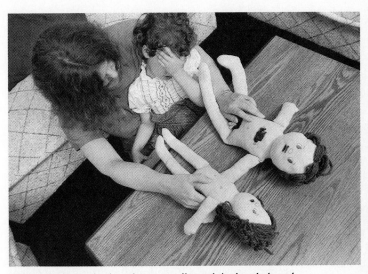

Young children who have been sexually exploited and abused may not be able to verbalize what they have experienced. One way that therapists work with such children is to allow them to demonstrate how they were abused with the use of anatomically correct dolls.

so, as in the novel and motion picture *Lolita*. In general, these activities have been remarkably well tolerated owing to the widespread myths that children suffer no lasting consequences from such encounters, and may indeed benefit from them in some obscurely reasoned way. Organizations and support groups for pedophiles have been open and sometimes quite strident in advocating adult-child sexual relations (Plummer, 1980). This permissiveness even extended only a few years back to the professional and scientific literature on pedophilia, which often emphasized children's seductiveness and their willing and active participation (Stermac, Segal, & Gillis, 1990). Such an observation reminds us of the common legal defense of blaming rape victims for having been raped, and in our judgment merits equal and exceptionless rejection as a factor supposedly mitigating the guilt of the offender.

Over about the past decade a growing body of evidence has suggested the long-term ill effects of subjecting children to the confusion, exploitation, and powerful emotionality of too-early and abrupt sexual engagements with genitally mature people—people occupying other roles as parents, family members, caretakers, and "adults" (who are to be "respected"). We have finally awakened to the terrible psychological scars that may be sustained by these children (Browne & Finkelhor, 1986). Childhood sexual abuse is turning up as a significant risk factor for a substantial proportion of the many mental disorders described in this text—including, ironically, pedophilia involving chiefly male victims (Becker et al, 1989; Herman, 1990). We are not, therefore, dealing with a "fun and games" issue, as some pedophilic propaganda suggests, and the mounting public awareness and outrage concerning the sexual victimization of children seems to us well justified—if more than a bit late in coming.

Offenders are diverse in terms of the act committed; in the intentionality of and general circumstances surrounding the act; and in age, education, and developmental history. Most pedophiles are men, but women occasionally engage in such practices. The average age of these offenders is about 40 years. Many of them are or have been married, and many have children of their own. Indeed, some choose their own children as victims, although there is an increasing trend to differentiate this incest pattern from pedophilia per se (Lanyon, 1986). In an early study of 836 pedophilic offenders in New Jersey, Revitch and Weiss (1962) found that older offenders tended to seek out immature children, while younger offenders preferred pubescent girls between 12 and 15. Girls outnumbered boys as victims more than two to one. Concerning this last observation, more recent data (Abel & Rouleau, 1990) have indicated a higher proportion of male victims. We suspect the discrepancy is due to pedophile sample differences in the two studies, the crucial upshot being that neither girls nor boys can be considered especially "safe" relative to the other sex.

In most cases of pedophilia, a victim is known to an offender, and the sexual behavior may continue over a sustained period of time. Usually no physical coercion takes place, but this can by no means be considered the rule (Abel & Rouleau, 1990). Although in some cases an offender may be encouraged or even "seduced" by his or her victim (a concept we find doubtful, as already noted), Swanson (1968) found provocation or active participation by the victim in only 3 of the 25 cases he studied. Whether or not there is an element of alleged provocation by a victim, the legal onus is quite properly always on an adult offender.

Since pedophiles may subject children to highly traumatic emotional experiences as well as physical injury, legal safeguards to protect children need to be explicit and uncompromising. A serious problem exists, however, in cases where the evidence concerning the occurrence of molestation is equivocal. An alleged offender is sometimes considered guilty until proven innocent, in fact, and a number of people have served time in penal institutions because children or their parents interpreted simple affection as attempted intimacy or molestation. On the other hand, many cases of sexual assault on children undoubtedly go unreported to spare the children further ordeals (Sgroi, 1977).

Researchers have made several attempts to arrive at subtype classifications of pedophiles or of pedophilic activity, but none to date has proved sufficiently reliable or productive of new insights to achieve overall acceptance. The latest of these attempts, so far as we are aware, is one by Knight & Prentky (1990; Knight, Carter, & Prentky, 1989). Their general model is in part hierarchical, having a structure that sometimes branches in proceeding from higher to lower levels.

According to Knight and Prentky, pedophiles and their paraphilic lovemaps vary on a number of dimensions that are to some extent independent of one another. The most important of these dimensions are listed in the following paragraphs:

1. *High versus low fixation.* For those pedophiles considered fixated, sexual activity with children of one or the other sex is virtually their only sexual interest. Others engage in a range of sexual activities and fantasies, both normal and abnormal, and molest children only as another sexual diversion or as the opportunity presents itself.

2. *High versus low social competence.* Regardless of their fixation levels, some pedophiles show little or no deficit in social skills, including those "heterosocial" skills involved in the initiation and maintenance of adult heterosexual relationships. Other pedophiles, evidently the larger group, show deficits that are quite characteristic of paraphiliacs in general. For these pedophiles, the choice of children as love objects usually has obvious compensatory and self-protective features. Many acts of pedophilia are precipitated by events that call into question the perpetrator's adult heterosexual adequacy.

3. *High versus low amount of contact with children.* People with pedophilic interests often arrange their occupational and recreational lives so as to ensure a high degree of contact with children, who of course become potential victims. Thus in recent years the media have reported a rash of arrests and convictions of alleged child molesters who operate alternative child-care facilities. Unfortunately, as a result, innocent individuals have come under unwarranted suspicion. Parents, however, are wise to err on the safe side and to use caution in selecting their child-care arrangements. Some pedophiles, on the other hand, show no particular interest in child-centered activities and appear to choose their victims on other, more opportunistic bases.

4. *Interpersonal versus narcissistic meaning of contact.* In instances of high contact with children, some pedophiles' motives are not exclusively sexual in nature. These individuals (designated "interpersonal" in type) appear genuinely to like children and to enjoy interacting with them in various modes; the sexual contact in these cases is an inappropriate extension of this affectional bonding. Narcissistic high-contact offenders show little evidence of enjoying relations with children for other than the opportunities they may provide for sexual exploitation.

5. *Low versus high physical injury.* According to this scheme of classification, the question of child injury does not normally arise in high-contact pedophilia, probably because such pedophiles usually use seduction instead of force. Low-contact pedophiles, on the other hand, may engage in greater or lesser force or other physically assaultive behaviors with their victims.

6. *Sadistic versus nonsadistic infliction of injury.* Physical injury to a child, mild or serious, may occur unintentionally and incidentally to pedophilic sexual acts, or it may be purposeful and deliberate in character where a pedophile's lovemap requires explicit victim suffering. This suffering might be relatively mild and involve low physical injury but substantial humiliation; it might also be physically dangerous or even fatal. In either case it is likely to leave the surviving victim seriously traumatized psychologically.

In a case known to one of the authors, an offender's sexual satisfaction was uniquely dependent on hearing his boy victims' screams of terror and pain as he violently sodomized them. This man, physically large and of intimidating demeanor, would patrol neighborhoods on a motorcycle in search of victims, who were then frightened into accompanying him to a remote area where the acts would be consummated. Using the scheme just outlined, this case of pedophilia would be described as one involving high fixation, low social competence, low contact, and high physical injury, sadistically motivated.

A number of investigators have also pointed to other severe psychopathology in pedophilic offenders. Some are alcoholic or schizophrenic. Many are older individuals in whom brain deterioration has led to a weakening of normal inhibitory controls. In fact pedophilia and exhibitionism are the most common sexual offenses committed by individuals suffering Alzheimer's or arteriosclerotic brain damage and displaying organic personality syndromes (Chapter 13).

Incest and Rape

In certain respects, the DSM-III-R is a quite conservative document, while in others it may exceed proper boundaries (for example, in the Axis II diagnosis of *developmental arithmetic disorder* in children, which would seem to describe more an educational than a psychiatric problem). Certain sexual deviations, such as incest and rape, are unaccountably (in the authors' judgment) missing from the DSM-III-R classification; this absence seems too conservative. Accordingly, as noted earlier, these two "disorders" are included in what follows even though they are not presently a part of the official psychiatric nomenclature.

Incest   Culturally prohibited sexual relations (up to and including coitus) between family members, such as a brother and sister or a parent and child, are known as **incest**. Although a few societies have approved incestuous relationships—at one time it was the established practice for Egyptian pharaohs to marry their sisters to prevent the royal blood from being "contaminated"—the incest taboo is virtually universal among human societies.

An indication of the risks involved in such inbreeding has been provided by Adams and Neel (1967), who compared the offspring of 18 nuclear-incest marriages—12 brother-sister and 6 father-daughter—with those of a control group matched for age, intelligence, socioeconomic status, and other relevant characteristics. At the end of six months, 5 of the infants of the incestuous marriages had died, 2 were severely mentally retarded and had been institutionalized, 3 showed evidence of borderline intelligence, and 1 had a cleft palate. Only 7 of the 18 infants were considered normal. In contrast, only 2 of the control-group infants were not considered normal—one showing indications of borderline intelligence and the other manifesting a physical defect.

A number of investigators have also maintained that the incest taboo serves to produce greater variability among offspring, and hence to increase the flexibility and long-term adaptability of the population (Schwartzman, 1974).

In our own society, incestuous behavior does occur, but its actual incidence is unknown because it mostly takes place in a family setting (Peters, 1976)

The drawings shown here are all the work of incest victims. Left: a 7-year-old girl engulfed by a maelstrom. Middle: a 9-year-old boy caught in a trap in the middle of a country landscape. Right: a teenage girl threatened by a snake.

and comes to light only when reported to law enforcement or other agencies. It is almost certainly more common than is generally believed, partly because many of the victims do not consider themselves victimized (De Young, 1982; Maisch, 1972). The incidence of "intrafamilial sexual abuse" coming to the attention of professionals approached 100,000 in 1985 (Williams & Finkelhor, 1990). Meiselman (1978) estimated the incidence at 1 or 2 per every 100 people. Kinsey et al. (1948, 1953) reported an incidence of 5 cases per 1,000 people in a sample of 12,000 subjects, and Gebhard et al. (1965) found 30 cases per 1,000 subjects in a group of 3,500 imprisoned sex offenders. In both these latter studies, brother-sister incest was reported as being five times more common than the next most common pattern—father-daughter incest. Mother-son incest is thought to be relatively rare.

In a study of 78 cases of incest, which excluded the brother-sister variety, Maisch (1972) found that the father-daughter and stepfather-stepdaughter varieties accounted for fully 85 percent of the sample; mother-son incest accounted for only 4 percent. Summit and Kryso (1978) estimated that some 36,000 cases of father-daughter incest occur each year in the United States. This estimate may seriously underestimate the actual occurrence (Herman, 1981). In occasional cases, multiple patterns of incest may exist within the same family, and some incestuous fathers involve all of their daughters serially as they become pubescent.

For an understanding of incestuous behavior, it should be noted that incestuous fantasies and desires are common during the adolescent period, and it is not uncommon for fathers to have such feelings toward their daughters. Social mores and prohibitions, however, are usually so deeply ingrained that

the desires are not often acted out. When they are, no single-factor explanation seems to account for it; no characteristic appears universal or near-universal among incestuous fathers, and, contrary to widespread belief, they have usually *not* themselves been sexually abused in childhood (Williams & Finkelhor, 1990).

Bagley (1969) has suggested that several different causal patterns may be involved where incestuous behavior occurs. The following list represents a slight modification of his schema.

1. *Situational incest.* When brothers and sisters share the same bedroom during the preadolescent or adolescent period (which is not uncommon among poorer families), they may tend to engage in sexual exploration and experimentation. In some cases older siblings seduce their younger siblings without any apparent understanding of the social prohibitions or possible consequences.

2. *Incest associated with severe psychopathology.* In the case of psychopathic parents, the incest may simply be part of an indiscriminate pattern of sexual promiscuity. In other individuals, such as alcoholics and psychotics, the incestuous relations may be associated with a lowering of inner controls. Overall, however, only a small minority of incestuous fathers have diagnosable psychiatric disorders, although many show antisocial tendencies of insufficient magnitude to bring them into direct conflict with the law (Langevin et al., 1985; Williams & Finkelhor, 1990).

3. *Incest associated with pedophilia.* Some parents have intense sexual cravings for young children, including their own. It is evident, however, that

HIGHLIGHT 10.3

Sexual Molestation of Young Children

While most incestuous contacts between parents and their children occur after a child has attained puberty, young children—even infants—have been subjected to sexual molestation and abuse by parents or other adults. According to Sgroi (1977), these cases, like those involving adolescents, are markedly underreported. Even in the face of overwhelming evidence, this researcher claims, physicians are extremely reluctant to conclude that a child has been sexually attacked. Apparently it is considered "in bad taste" professionally to draw such a conclusion.

The cases Sgroi uses to illustrate the magnitude of the problem are truly disconcerting. She writes of one city's youngest known rape victim, a child 2 months old; of a 2½-year-old boy and his 4-year-old sister, both of whom acquired acute gonorrhea from their father; of a 17-month-old girl with a torn anus, dead of asphyxiation, with semen in her mouth and throat. In the face of

such horror, one can only applaud Sgroi's attempt to break through the secrecy and "discretion" too often associated with this "last frontier" of child abuse.

Because many cases remain unreported, the actual incidence of child abuse of all types—and especially of sexual abuse—is unknown. In Connecticut, during fiscal years 1973 and 1974, approximately 10 percent of all cases of reported abuse were suspected to involve sexual assault or impropriety—a total of 248 separate incidents. The suspected perpetrators were most often fathers, male relatives, or boyfriends. This finding corroborates an earlier study by DeFrancis (1969). Assuming Connecticut to be representative of the United States as a whole, many thousands of young children are sexually assaulted or abused each year, and all too often the damage is inflicted by their own parents. As indicated in a review of the pertinent research evidence (Browne & Finkelhor, 1986) and our only recently ac-

quired understanding of multiple personality disorder (Chapter 6), the long-term consequences of such abuse can be both extensive and severe. One of the authors is acquainted with the case of a preschool-aged girl who became psychotic, apparently in consequence of her father's protracted sexual molestation. The father, a well-educated and successful middle-level manager, committed suicide when he could no longer successfully deny his culpability.

Sgroi and other advocates for sexually abused children can claim a measure of success in their efforts to direct a spotlight on this long-neglected problem. In recent years a number of states have enacted laws that compel a professional person, under severe penalty, to report to authorized agencies his or her suspicion that child abuse may have occurred. Regrettably, this judgment is often difficult to make, and many cases doubtless still go unreported.

---

pedophilic motivation is not a primary cause of incest, in that most victims are beyond puberty. (A discussion of disturbing exceptions appears in *HIGHLIGHT 10.3*.)

4. *Incest associated with a faulty paternal model.* A father may set an undesirable example for his son by engaging in incestuous relations with his daughters and may encourage his son to do so as well—either at the time with his sisters, or later in life with his own daughters.

5. *Incest associated with family pathology and disturbed marital relations.* In some instances a rejecting wife may actually foster father-daughter incest. Most (but not all) cases of father-daughter

incest, in fact, occur in a setting of marked family disorganization (Lanyon, 1986; Williams & Finkelhor, 1990). Many mothers of father-daughter incest victims have been observed clinically to show incredible levels of inattentiveness in the maintenance of their "ignorance" about the sexual intimacy between their husbands and daughters.

In general, incestuous fathers who come to the attention of authorities do not have a history of sexual offenses or other criminal behavior, nor do they show a disproportionate incidence of prior hospitalization for mental disorders. In fact such fathers tend to restrict their sexual activity to family members, not seeking or engaging in extramarital sexual relations. For example, in his early, intensive study of 12 fathers convicted of incestuous relations with their daughters, Cavillin (1966) reported that only 2 of the 12 had resorted to extramarital relations, despite uniform feelings that they were unloved and rejected by their wives. Such a pattern suggests a certain passivity and lack of venturesomeness among many of these fathers, a picture that has been confirmed fairly regularly in subsequent research (Williams & Finkelhor, 1990). The typical incestuous father's lovemap is thus somewhat paradoxical; it is on the one hand rather cautious and restrictive but on the other does not contain the usual exclusion concerning his own children.

Cavillin further reported that the youngest father in the group was 20 and the oldest 56, with an average age of 39. The average age of the daughters was 13, the youngest being 3 and the oldest 18. Five of the 12 fathers had had a relationship with more than 1 daughter, usually beginning with the oldest; in 11 of the cases the relationships had gone on for some time—from 3 months to 3 years—before being reported by the daughters. In all cases, too, the father felt rejected and threatened by his wife. Cavillin's findings are generally confirmed by Maisch (1972), who studied 78 cases of incest that came to the attention of officials in the Federal Republic of Germany, and by Dixen and Jenkins (1981), Lanyon (1986), and Williams and Finkelhor (1990) in pertinent literature reviews.

Most of us feel a profound repugnance when we hear of fathers seducing, or in rare instances being seduced by, their daughters. Our disgust is certainly appropriate, especially when we consider the future adjustment difficulties many of these girls must face in trying to come to terms with their experiences (Browne & Finkelhor, 1986; Gold, 1986; Owens, 1984). Offit (1981), however, offers us a different, more compassionate view of a father's situation. She described her work with a depressed and lonely man who felt grief for the loss of his married daughter, a daughter who had been the center of his life and his love for 15 years. Like many incestuous fathers, the man described by Offit does not seem, apart from his "perversion," to be a monstrous or evil man. Such descriptions remind us that in our haste to condemn incestuous behavior, we should not assume that all such relationships are tawdry or utterly lacking in genuine feeling or affection. Needless to say, we do not in making this observation intend to convey any tolerance for such profound lapses in parental responsibility.

The psychological effect of an incestuous relationship on a daughter appears to depend on her age at the time of the relationship and on how much anxiety and guilt she experiences. Most girls studied who were still adolescent expressed feelings of guilt and depression over the incestuous behavior. Some girls in this situation turn to promiscuity; others run away from home to escape the stressful environment, and some of these become prostitutes. Later difficulties in adult heterosexual adjustment are extremely common, and incestuous involvement with a father or stepfather appears to inflate the risk of several adult disorders, including multiple personality disorder (Chapter 6) and borderline personality disorder (Chapter 8). It also enhances the likelihood of revictimization by sexual assault or rape (Koss & Dinero, 1989). In some instances no apparent long-range ill effects can be detected (Dixen & Jenkins, 1981; Gold, 1986). Interestingly, in a case treated by one of the authors, a young woman had been continually molested by her father during her childhood and adolescence. She resolutely refused all further sexual contact with him after he provoked her first orgasm. Up to that time, as is apparently often the case, she had not fully grasped the implications of this type of interaction with her father.

Rape   The term **rape** describes sexual activity that occurs under actual or threatened forcible coercion of one person by another. In most states, legal definitions restrict *forcible rape* to forced intercourse or penetration of a bodily orifice by a penis or other object. *Statutory rape* is sexual activity with a person who is legally defined to be under the age of consent (18 in most states). Statutory rape is considered to have occurred regardless of the apparent willingness of an underage partner.

In the vast majority of cases, men rape women. The incidence of forcible rape has increased more rapidly in the last 15 years than that of any other violent crime. Part of the rise, however, as measured by the FBI and other law enforcement agencies, may merely reflect increased reporting by victims and an enhanced likelihood that sexual assaults meeting the definition of "rape" will in fact be recorded as such within local police departments. Even so, the actual incidence of rape is considered to be as much as ten times higher than that reported in FBI *Uniform Crime Report* statistics, which in recent years has approximately 100,000 cases annually.

Many sexually assaulted women remain, for various reasons, reluctant to file complaints with the police and (in the case of students) school officials. Some want to put the whole sickening and degrading experience behind them and not be reminded of it. Others, particularly victims of date rape or where the offender is otherwise known to the victims, have a misguided sense of protecting their attackers or find the role of principal accuser in a major felony very uncomfortable. Still others wish

consent requires:
1) Both Parties are Fully Conscious.
2) Both Parties equally Free to Act.
3) Both Parties have Positively and Clearly Communicated their Intent.

sexual harrassment

RAPE -

In an effort to raise awareness about date rape and sexual harrassment on college campuses, schools are beginning to offer rape-prevention programs, such as this one at Hobart College in New York, in which young men and women are counseled on understanding and avoiding sexual victimization.

to avoid the unfortunate consequences that in the past have often followed a rape complaint. These include social stigmatization and, regrettably, crude and insensitive treatment by some police jurisdictions. There is hope that the gap between actual and reported rapes has been narrowed in recent years as women have banded together to call attention to these widespread assaults, and to protect themselves by doing everything possible to keep rapists from preying on them.

Based on information gathered by the FBI about arrested and convicted rapists, rape, relatively speaking, is a young man's crime. Forty-five percent of all rapists arrested in 1985 were under 25 years of age, and the greatest concentration was in the 18-to-24 age group, accounting for 30 percent of the total. Of the rapists who get into police records, about half are married and living with their wives at the time of the crime. As a group, they come from the low end of the socioeconomic ladder. Typically they are unskilled workers with low intelligence, low education, and low income. How representative they are of all rapists we do not know. The substantial numbers of a certain type of college male who is excessively and sometimes physically coercive (Kanin, 1985; Koss, Gidycz, & Wisniewski, 1987; Koss & Oros, 1982; Lisak & Ross, 1988; Rapaport & Burkhart, 1984) suggests that the basic propensity is not limited to the disadvantaged. One of the authors has assisted in the college expulsion of a student with a history of four documented date rapes; as is apparently typical of the type, he saw nothing wrong with these acts.

Rape tends to be a repetitive activity rather than an isolated act, and most rapes are planned events. In fact, a strong case can be made that rape should be considered a category of paraphilia—not differ-

ent in its essentials from the paraphilias already discussed (Abel & Rouleau, 1990). Another interesting view is that of Herman (1990), who considers it an addiction—with all that this implies in terms of its repetitive nature and the difficulty of treatment. About 80 percent of rapists commit the act in the neighborhoods in which they reside; most rapes take place in an urban setting at night. The specific scene of the rape varies greatly, however. The act may occur on a lonely street after dark, in an automobile in a large shopping center's parking lot, in the elevator or hallway of a building, and in other situations where a victim has little chance of assistance. Rapists have also entered apartments or homes by pretending to be deliverers or repairpersons. In fact, rapes most often occur in the victim's home.

About a third or more of all rapes involve more than one offender, and often they are accompanied by beatings. The remainder are single-offender rapes in which the victim and the offender may know each other; the closer the relationship, the more brutally the victim may be beaten. When a victim struggles against her attacker, she is likely to receive more severe injuries or in rare cases to be killed. On the other hand, one study found that when the victim was able to cry out and run away, she was more likely to be successful in avoiding the rape (Selkin, 1975).

In addition to the physical trauma inflicted on a victim, the psychological trauma may be severe (see Chapter 5, pp. 161–163). One especially unfortunate factor in rape is the possibility of pregnancy; another is the chance of contracting a sexually transmitted disease. A rape may also impact negatively on a victim's marriage or other intimate relationships. The situation is likely to be particularly upsetting to a husband or boyfriend if he has been forced to watch the rape, as is occasionally the case when a victim is raped by the members of a juvenile gang.

The concept of "victim-precipitated" rape, a favorite of defense attorneys and of some police and court jurisdictions, turns out on close examination to be a myth. According to this view, a victim, though often bruised both psychologically and physically—if not worse—is regarded as the *cause* of the crime, often on such flimsy grounds as the alleged provocativeness of her attire, her past sexual behavior, or her presence in a location considered risky (Stermac, Segal, & Gillis, 1990). The attacker, on the other hand, is treated as a brain-dead organism, unable to quell his lust in the face of such irresistible provocation—and therefore not legally responsible for the act. A society as threatened as is ours by rampant sexual assault can ill-afford this type of nonsensical and myth-based jurisprudence; in more than 60 years of combined clinical practice neither of the authors has ever encountered a woman who desired to be raped, nor have we ever heard a convincing account of any such case. Evidence to the contrary notwithstanding, however, the pernicious and dangerous concept that women *want* to be forced into sex is persistent and widespread (Segal & Stermac, 1990).

Women who are repeated victims of rape are especially likely to be suspected of provoking the attacks. In fact such women tend to be significantly dysfunctional in many areas of their lives, and they tend also to be victims in situations other than rape, perhaps including other forms of sexual traumatization (Koss & Dinero, 1989). Far from being the seductresses of popular folklore, they are often more like chronic "losers" with insufficient personal resources to fend off those who would exploit them (Ellis, Atkeson, & Calhoun, 1982; Myers, Templer, & Brown, 1985). It should be pointed out in this context that many college women report having experienced strong unwanted advances from men; such encounters do not imply a special vulnerability to rape (Koss & Oros, 1982).

Rape is a complex act in its antecedent conditions, involving at least factors creating motivation, factors of cognitive distortion, factors influencing inhibitory processes, and factors relating to opportunity (Barbaree, 1990; Darke, 1990; Laws & Marshall, 1990; Malamuth, 1986; Marshall & Barbaree, 1990; Segal & Stermac, 1990). As a group, rapists seem to find violence against women sexually arousing (McFall, 1990; Murrin & Laws, 1990; Quinsey, Chaplin, & Upfold, 1984). Several typologies of rapes and rapists have been proposed, most of them based on inadequate data of questionable representativeness. The system proposed by Groth, Burgess, and Holmstrom (1977) is not only well documented, but apparently has the additional virtue of being able to subsume the types identified in earlier as well as more recent work (e.g., Knight & Prentky, 1990). It is based on the accounts of 133 convicted male rapists and 92 victims of rapes occurring during a limited time period in Massachusetts.

Groth and colleagues, in agreement with many others (e.g., Darke, 1990), noted that rape attacks combine psychological elements of power and anger as well as sexuality. Their strategy was to rank these elements in terms of their apparent prominence for each of the 225 separate accounts of rape available to them. In doing so, they discovered no case in which sexual satisfaction appeared to be the dominant motive of the rapist; that is, all the rapes were characterized as involving either power motives or anger expression more than sexuality on the part of the rapists (see *HIGHLIGHT 10.4*). Evidently a rapist's lovemap has undergone such contortion that "love" is not its most prominent component. Groth et al. also noted that predominantly power- or anger-inspired rapes could each in turn be divided into two subtypes. These subdivisions form the basis of their classification scheme, as described in the following paragraphs:

1. *Power-assertive type.* The essence of a rape in which power motives predominate is that of establishing control over a victim through intimidation; the mode of intimidation used may involve a weapon, physical force without severe injury, or simply threats of harm. The achievement of sexual penetration is regarded as a "conquest." The rape is frequently preceded by fantasies that the victim, once overpowered, will willingly participate with wild abandon. Because reality never matches this fantasy, the rapist is frustrated and is likely to repeat the act compulsively on another occasion. A power-assertive rapist tends to have a history of "hypermasculinity," striving always to assert power and domination over those with whom he comes in contact. We may surmise, of course, that such people in fact have serious questions about their manhood. In Groth and colleagues' sample, 44 percent of the rapes were of the power-assertive variety.

2. *Power-reassurance type.* Like his power-assertive counterpart, a power-reassurance rapist seeks to intimidate and conquer his victim. In this case, however, the underlying sense of weakness, inadequacy, and indistinct gender identity is much more obvious. As in some cases of exhibitionism and pedophilia, the act commonly takes place following some blow to the rapist's fragile ego; the rape is an attempt to repair the damage. Rapes of the power-

The Power, Hostility, and Humiliation Dimensions of Rape

Levine and Koenig (1980) have published transcripts of their interviews with ten incarcerated rapists. The following are verbatim selections from these interviews that reveal the nonsexual components of their assaults on victims.

"It's mostly humiliating the victim, but not hurting or any heavy violence." (p. 25)

"When I was becoming angry . . . I felt I had to have sex at any cost as a reversal of caring. To go as far as I could away from that caring, to cheapen that person." (p. 46)

"I made hate to her." (p. 51)

"I know that I purposely degraded them." (p. 59)

"I fantasized about stabbing her with a knife in the anus—of all places. Just a degrading thought. Put her down and put her in her place for challenging me." (p. 66)

"I think the reason we used to do this [gang rape] was because I like to lower the chicks to me, that's the way I used to think, that I was lowering them and making them look cheap . . . and making them look like dirty tramps. . . . She [the victim] was really humiliated; she was really put down." (pp. 71, 75)

Darke (1990) adds the following rape accounts derived from an analysis of reports to police by victims, witnesses, and offenders:

The assailant used physical violence to subdue his victim. During the assault he said, "Thirteen other guys want to screw you." He also indicated that he was raping her because he couldn't go to a "whorehouse."

The assailant referred to his victim as a "white squaw" and his "slave."

Following physical and sexual assault, the assailant told his victim that she wasn't "worth a shit."

Using physical violence to subdue his 15-year-old victim the assailant then said, "Look at the mess you've gotten yourself into. It was dumb to take a ride from someone you don't know. . . . Have you ever been fucked before?" The victim responded "yes" and the assailant stated, "You should have said no. Are you going to let this happen? Don't you have any respect for yourself?" (p. 64)

---

reassurance type accounted for 21 percent of Groth and colleagues' sample.

3. *Anger-retaliation type.* In comparison with power-oriented rapists, who rarely inflict severe physical damage on their victims, predominantly anger-driven rapists are exceedingly dangerous—sometimes to the point of murdering the women they attack. In such cases, rage, contempt, and hatred dominate the assault, which is usually brutal and violent. Sexual satisfaction, if it occurs at all, is minimal. In fact many anger-dominated rapists view normal sex with revulsion and disgust. Here the rape is an expression of hate toward women in general, and the predominant motive is one of revenge for real or imagined slights suffered at the hands of females. Derogation and humiliation are prominent features of this type of attack. Of the rapes studied by Groth et al., 30 percent were of the anger-retaliation type.

4. *Anger-excitation type.* More than any other, this type of rapist fits the category of *pathological sadist.* His attack is one of eroticized aggression; he derives sexual pleasure, thrills, and excitement not from the sexual elements of his assault but from the suffering of his victim. The anger-excitation type accounted for only 5 percent of Groth and colleagues' sample.

It might seem from the preceding descriptions that rapists as a group are a disturbed segment of the population and that potential rapists should therefore be easy to recognize. This would be an erroneous and possibly dangerous conclusion, however. Although it is true that a certain proportion of rapists are obviously abnormal on a chronic basis—some even being blatantly psychotic—the literature in this area abounds with instances of rape in which, prior to an attack, the rapist had given no hint to the victim of being a sexually assaultive person (Gager & Schurr, 1976; Medea & Thompson, 1974). The apparently widespread occurrence of attempted (and completed) date rape, particularly on college campuses, underscores the same point (Kanin, 1985; Koss, Gidycz, & Wisniewski, 1987; Koss & Oros, 1982; Rapaport & Burkhart, 1984). Whatever rape prevention involves, it is not a matter of informal psychodiagnostic predictions. We know of one university in which women students have taken to listing the names of excessively coercive male dates on dormitory bathroom walls, but of course such a procedure lacks certain safeguards for the falsely accused.

Conviction rates for rape are low and most men who have raped are free in the community. In fact one study of rapists who were in the community found that the men had raped anywhere from 5 to 100 times (Abel et al., 1978). In a more recent study, Abel and colleagues (reported in Abel & Rouleau, 1990) found that 907 separate acts of rape were reported by only 126 nonincarcerated offenders, an average of 7 per offender. Rape, even at its least violent, is a bullying, intrusive violation of another person's integrity, selfhood, and personal boundaries that deserves to be viewed with more gravity—and its victims with more compassion and sensitivity—than is usually the case (Gager & Schurr, 1976; Medea & Thompson, 1974). Much still remains to be done in providing services to these victims (Koss, 1983), many of whom suffer from moderately severe posttraumatic stress disorder (see Chapter 5).

In recent years, new rape laws have been adopted by a majority of states, many of them based on the "Michigan model," which describes four degrees of criminal sexual conduct, with different punishment levels for different degrees of seriousness. In calling the offense *criminal sexual conduct* rather than *rape,* the Michigan law also appropriately places the emphasis on the offender rather than the victim. Unfortunately, the majority of sexual assaults are not reported, and of those that are, less than 10 percent result in conviction (Darke, 1990). Convictions often bring light sentences, and a jail term does not dissuade a substantial number of offenders from repeating their crimes (Furby, Weinrott, & Blackshaw, 1989). The upshot, we reiterate, is that the large majority of rapists are out among us.

■ Treatments and Outcomes

Research concerning the effective treatment of variant sexual behavior has not progressed as far or as rapidly as with the dysfunctions, but there are encouraging signs of progress. As we noted at the beginning of this discussion, we now know that most sexually variant acts are not simply aberrations of sexual arousal. In most instances, we also need to look at an individual's response level to adult heterosexual stimuli, overall social skills with potential and appropriate sexual partners, and adult gender identity development. An important principle embedded in such a program is that it is unrealistic to anticipate an offender giving up an important source of gratification without gaining something comparable in return. Only by taking all these factors into account is it possible to assess a given client's difficulties and fashion treatment procedures for intervening on a broad enough front (Marshall, Laws, & Barbaree, 1990b).

Even when taking all these steps, however, sexually deviant behavior is enormously difficult to treat or to manage if the goal is (as it certainly should be) long-term relapse prevention. Minimally, it may require long-term monitoring and supervision similar to the parole model used by prison administrations. Follow-up data from one study using this approach (Pithers, 1990) is so far encouraging, with a recidivism rate of only 4 percent for combined groups of rapists and pedophiles.

To date, unfortunately, such cutting-edge intervention has been the exception rather than the rule in therapeutic attempts to change variant sexuality, and most treatment efforts still focus on the sexual arousal aspects. Aversive conditioning procedures, in which unpleasant or painful stimuli are paired with the arousal state, though controversial, have proven effective in suppressing problematic arousal variants. Similarly, we know something of how to develop or strengthen arousability to appropriate sexual stimuli (Barlow & Abel, 1976). Surely, we will be able to find ways to teach appropriate social skills where they are lacking; an impressive analysis of what seems needed in this respect, such as enhanced ability to read accurately the "cues" emitted by potential sexual partners (for example, whether a woman is encouraging or discouraging an advance), has recently been contributed by McFall (1990).

Two remaining obstacles appear to exist, both of them major. The first is learning how to strengthen an adult client's gender identity, not necessarily in an exclusively "masculine" or "feminine" direction but more in terms of overcoming amorphousness and immaturity in the individual's sense of being a man or a woman. This promises to be a difficult challenge for clinical research. Having delineated the problem, however, we are in a much better position now than we were even a few short years ago. The second difficult obstacle is that of discovering means to maintain therapeutic gains

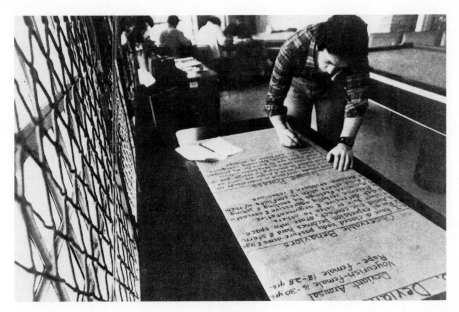

The long-term relapse rate for untreated sex offenders released from prison is about 80 percent. At Oregon State Hospital, a voluntary inpatient treatment program for sex offenders is having some success at reducing this rate through intensive treatment, including psychotherapy and social skills training, various types of behavioral therapy (such as aversive conditioning techniques), and drug therapy to inhibit sexual functioning. Clients continue to be monitored for 18 months after release from prison. This program claims about a 10 percent recidivism rate among offenders who have completed treatment. Here, in one phase of treatment, prisoners must write scenarios of their behavior preceding an assault.

that are made, or prevent relapse. If a more efficient and less costly method than indefinite supervisory contact cannot be devised, we have grave doubts that our society will be willing to bear the expense. Certainly the prison parole system, with its overburdened caseloads and frequent changes of poorly paid and "burned out" personnel, provides little cause for optimism on this front. At least, however, we now understand that the problem of recidivism is central to the reduction and ultimate prevention of sexual victimization.

In the final analysis, of course, the best long-range solution for our society is the eradication or prevention of those conditions that lead to the development of problematic sexual variants. We will address this matter in the Unresolved Issues section at the end of this chapter.

THE HOMOSEXUALITIES

The authors acknowledge some ambivalence about addressing the issue of homosexuality in a text whose title includes the term *abnormal*. This is a sensitive point among some members of the homosexual community, who sincerely feel that in doing so we inevitably contribute to their stigmatization and provide ammunition to "homophobics" and others intent on suppressing homosexual activity and punishing those who engage in it. Indeed, we have been accused of being homophobic ourselves in correspondence from readers of earlier editions. In the final analysis, we think it would be unwise and perhaps professionally irresponsible to inten-

tionally exempt certain behaviors from consideration solely on the grounds that their inclusion generates an unusual degree of unpleasantness. We do think there are serious questions in this area deserving of open discussion.

■ Dilemmas of Classification

On December 14, 1973, by vote of the trustees of the American Psychiatric Association, **homosexuality** (a tendency to direct sexual desires and activities toward people of the same sex) was removed from the list of officially recognized mental disorders. Whatever the motives behind this action—and they appear to have been principled and ethical ones—the voting of a disorder out of existence raises questions concerning the fundamental value of applying a medical perspective to personal and sociobehavioral issues, as was discussed in Chapter 1. We are not here supporting the position that homosexuality should be considered a "mental illness"—quite the contrary, we are pointing up a certain capriciousness sometimes involved in the "diagnosis" of human behavior.

Additional developments have further complicated the situation. First, the intended removal of psychiatric stigma from homosexuality was incomplete. The original version of DSM-III, adopted in 1980, continued to list *ego-dystonic homosexuality* as a mental disorder. This category referred to a situation in which a homosexual orientation was persistently unwanted by a person who had it. The inclusion of subjective distress about one's condition as the defining characteristic of a disorder is a questionable premise. As Adams and Chiodo

(1984) have pointed out, discrepancies between one's values and one's behavior are common aspects of life, but we do not ordinarily think of such discrepancies as deciding, or even raising, questions of mental disorder. In the DSM-III-R of 1987 the picture changed once again. Here what had been called ego-dystonic homosexuality was relegated to an "example" under the category *sexual disorder not otherwise specified,* a sort of wastebasket for various additional deviant behaviors; the intent, it appears, was chiefly cosmetic.

We have some sympathy for the catalogers of official psychiatric disorders, who are faced with highly charged issues that are not resolvable by appeal to either logic or unequivocal evidence— and certainly not in our era by appeal to the old standby of professional authority. We also sympathize with the millions of homosexual people who resent having to defend themselves against attributions of psychiatric illness based on sexual preference, although—as the long list of "paraphilias" indicates—their situation is not unique in this particular respect. It seems clear that we have not heard the last word on the controversy, which, as *HIGHLIGHT 10.5* illustrates, extends to the question of treatment. We suspect that any ultimate resolution will require a substantial reformulation of psychiatry's proper domain as it relates to nonmedical, sociobehavioral issues.

As we have indicated both implicitly and explicitly from the outset, our own notion of abnormal behavior does not always mirror the official psychiatric nomenclature, although the two must obviously overlap at numerous points. Rather, we define abnormality in terms of behavioral maladaptiveness, broadly conceived, and intend thereby no *necessary* attribution of internal psychological derangement

to a maladaptively behaving person. We reject, likewise, any pejorative connotations that anyone would attach to abnormality per se when so defined.

■ Homosexual Heterogeneity

We have used the plural form of *homosexuality* in the title of this section on The Homosexualities because we believe the psychological organization of homosexuality to be extremely heterogeneous, not only between men and women homosexuals but also within these gender categories. That is, we find the evidence inconsistent with the notion that, beyond the obvious same-gender partner choice, one can assign valid attributions to "homosexuals," "gay men," or "lesbian women" considered as classes of people sharing other major psychological commonalities. For example, the relative mix of "nature" (genetic/constitutional) versus "nurture" (environmental) in the causal patterns leading to homosexual orientations appears to vary considerably for both men and women (see, for example, the pertinent work of Money and his associates, 1969, 1972, 1974, 1980, and that of Bell & Weinberg, 1978). At the behavioral level, researchers also note marked variation in the extent to which sexuality per se plays a prominent role in identifying oneself as "homosexual," although in general sexuality is more emphasized among gay men than among lesbian women. In short, the roads leading to homosexuality and the needs served by this mode of sexual expression appear to be many and varied.

Research on homosexual populations has concentrated on gay men. As a result, much less is known about the biopsychosocial correlates of lesbianism. Due to this imbalance, we will here concentrate on homosexuality in males. As will be seen, we do regard certain manifestations of male homosexuality—certain male homosexual lovemaps—to be plainly maladaptive, hence "abnormal."

The issue of **bisexuality** is an interesting one theoretically. As is well known, Freud held that we are all bisexual in the sense of having some basic propensity toward the achievement of sexual satisfaction with partners of either sex. Kinsey and colleagues' (1948) early study seemingly confirmed this view in showing that a significant proportion of the men surveyed admitted to having had homosexual wishes or experiences after the onset of adolescence; 37 percent of male responders, in fact, indicated they had had such a homosexual experience to the point of orgasm.

In interpreting such figures, one must bear in mind that young unmarried American men of the

Homosexuality has existed throughout history. This ancient Greek wall art showing two male lovers at a drinking party is from the tomb of the Diver, at Paestum, near the Gulf of Salerno.

Should Homosexuality Be "Treated"?

The question of whether homosexual people should receive therapy to change their sexual orientations has been one of the key issues in the intense controversy over whether homosexuality is a personality or paraphilic disorder or only a normal sexual variant. In recent years, a number of therapy programs have been developed in which the explicit purpose is that of "reorienting" the sexual needs of homosexual individuals; many of these programs employ aversive conditioning techniques to suppress or eradicate the homosexual arousal pattern. Because the existence of treatment strongly implies that the condition being treated is undesirable, if not pathological, many supporters of the gay liberation movement object to these treatment programs.

This issue was forcefully brought to the attention of psychologists and other mental health professionals by Davison (1976, 1978), a leading researcher in the development of new therapies for sexual difficulties. Davison argues that the very existence of sexual reorientation treatment programs strengthens prejudices against homosexual individuals and increases their self-hatred and embarrassment. Therefore, he concludes, the only ethical course is to stop offering this type of treatment—even to those individuals who voluntarily seek it.

Sturgis and Adams (1978) take the opposing position, arguing that the question of whether homosexuality is abnormal is entirely irrelevant to the question of whether an individual seeking treatment should have access to it. Sturgis and Adams charge that Davison's position will cause therapists to impose their own values —in this case, the belief that homosexuals should not receive treatment—on clients who may not share these values. For Sturgis

and Adams, then, the primary issue is that of the "right to treatment" of those homosexual individuals who desire reorientation therapy. Davison (1978) acknowledges that his position is value-based, but he contends that values are the central consideration in the controversy. He also states that therapists have no absolute responsibility to provide what clients may request.

As seemed likely when this exchange of views first appeared in the professional literature, many sexual reorientation programs have continued to be offered to those who request such treatment. In the meantime, this spirited dialogue between researchers has sharpened the issues and has provoked a wide-ranging and, we think, positive reexamination of attitudes about homosexuality within the professional community.

---

pre-1960s era had few outlets for their abundant sexual energies, and that opportunities for orgasmic experiences with their female peers were severely limited. We suspect, therefore, that the overwhelming majority of these homosexual encounters were ones in which young men submitted passively to the sexual blandishments, usually offers to perform fellatio, of the few openly and aggressively gay men who were well known in virtually every community of any size. It was unusual for the recipients of these acts to consider that *they* were engaging in homosexuality; they were simply, in their conceptions of it, permitting themselves to be serviced by "queers" who for unfathomable reasons liked to do this sort of thing. It is our view therefore that Kinsey and colleagues' figures do not confirm the universality of bisexuality as some sort of fundamental libidinal gender neutrality. What they do suggest, as is now well known from research on prison populations and the like, is that many men denied sexual access

to women can and do "make the best of it" by having sexual relations with other men.

While most people appear capable of engaging in and enjoying homosexual activity at some point in their lives, the overwhelming majority of people, given a choice, prefer heterosexual forms of satisfaction. Among "true" bisexuals—those who are consistently active in both heterosexual and homosexual relationships—some question arises about which, if either, arousal pattern is the more fundamental. Laboratory studies of the arousal patterns of self-designated bisexuals have shown that they in fact respond with stronger arousal to homosexual than to heterosexual stimuli, a finding that holds for both men (Tollison, Adams, & Tollison, 1979) and women (Lamson, 1980). To these findings may be added the observation of Altshuler (1984) that only 1 of 13 self-identified "bisexuals" met reasonable criteria for claiming this designation—these criteria being an approximately equal and random choice in the sex of partners and approximately equal distribution of experienced pleasure with partners of either sex. The exception in Altshuler's sample proved (on independent grounds) to be psychotic. Although much remains to be clarified in this area, the available evidence thus suggests that "bisexuality" is more a label that certain homosexually oriented people apply to themselves than it is a valid description of an equal arousal to both genders.

■ Gay Promiscuity

It is obvious to any but the most prejudiced eyes and minds that being gay does not preclude competence, accomplishment, and significant societal contribution across a vast array of human activity. In particular fields, such as the arts, homosexuality may indeed be associated with extraordinary talent. Much research (Bell, 1974; Bell & Weinberg, 1978; Freedman, 1975; Hooker, 1957; Thompson, McCandless, & Strickland, 1971; Weinberg & Williams, 1974) also clearly demonstrates that gay people as a group do not have disproportionate general psychopathology, especially when we discount problems that are reactive to membership in a sometimes persecuted and despised minority. Many gay individuals lead exemplary, ethical lives of quiet service to humankind, while often maintaining stable, committed, and sexually faithful relationships with their lovers.

Another gay life-style, however, includes problematic features that have escalated immeasurably with the AIDS epidemic in the 1980s. We refer to the preference among some gay men for frequent, largely anonymous, uncommitted, multiple-partner (sometimes in a single evening) sex. Among a certain large subgroup of gays, the value of such casual, multiple-partner sex had become practically a matter of ideologic allegiance prior to the early 1980s, when the connection was definitely made between this life-style and infection with the HIV-1 (AIDS) virus. One of Hooker's (1962) subjects described the life-style poignantly and succinctly: "To be gay is to go to the bar, to make the scene, to look, and look, and look, to have a one-night stand, to never really love or be loved, and to really know this, and to do this night after night, and year after year" (p. 9).

Although pre-1980s adherents to this life-style had, for obvious reasons, much exposure to sexually transmitted diseases (STDs), such as gonococcal infections and syphilis, and although significant numbers of them contracted these diseases, easy access to highly effective antibiotic drugs, such as penicillin, made the risk tolerable. Then, with re-

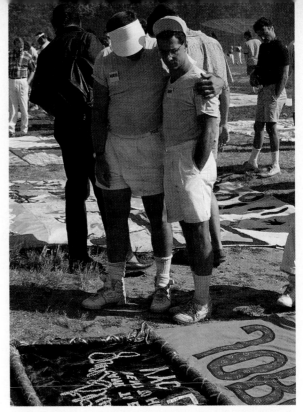

One of the most poignant and sobering memorials to AIDS victims is the AIDS quilt on exhibit around the United States, in which each square of the enormous quilt represents someone who died from AIDS. Many of those victims were homosexuals. Responsible members of the gay community have responded vigorously and tirelessly to the threat of AIDS with efforts to provide vital information, to promote changes in life-style, and to advocate "safe sex." The result has been a leveling off of new cases of HIV infections among gay men, though the disease continues to escalate in other groups.

markable suddenness, HIV-1 appeared—having no cure, a fatal outcome, and a transmission profile that made unprotected (condomless) anal intercourse extremely dangerous for the receptive partner. Ironically and tragically, the appearance of the virus, manifested in large numbers of not-yet-diagnosable infections, coincided with major triumphs of the gay liberation movement. The outcome has been sobering, if not frightening. According to Glasner & Kaslow (1990), prevalence rates of infection (as assessed by blood samples positive for HIV-1) were at 20 to 50 percent in one San Francisco community in 1984; another sample from clientele at an STD clinic had an astounding 70 percent seropositive rate for the period 1978 through 1987.

Once the connection with AIDS became clear, responsible members of the gay subculture responded vigorously and tirelessly with efforts to provide vital information, to promote changes in life-style, and to advocate "safe sex." Their efforts have been rewarded in a definite leveling off of new cases of HIV infections among gay men. Unfortunately, the disease, having gained an established foothold, continues to escalate out of control in other groups.

Evidence also shows that the allures of irresponsible sex are sufficiently strong for some notably immature gay young men that they have modified their behavior little, if at all. For example, Kelly et al. (1990) conducted a recent field study in gay bars in three cities and found that 37 percent of the 526 patrons questioned admitted to engaging in unprotected anal intercourse during the prior 3 months. Of the various risk factors associated with this potentially fatal behavior, such as relative youth, perceived peer pressure, and ignorance of the facts, knowledge of whether or not one had the infection was *not* significantly involved; that is, this knowledge—or the lack of it—made no discernible impact on the decision to engage in condomless anal intercourse. Such findings are, to say the least, deeply disconcerting.

The seemingly compulsive and apparently continuing unprotected sexual promiscuity of a significant group of gay men in this age of literal "fatal attraction" gives us little pause in declaring this behavior to be abnormal, as defined in this text. We should add that we also have no hesitation in coming to exactly the same conclusion about heterosexual behavior that is equally unrestrained as to the known risks, about which more is said in this chapter's Unresolved Issues section.

■ Homosexuality and Society

The centuries-old laws against homosexuality in England were repealed by Parliament in 1967, making private homosexual acts between consenting adults none of the law's business. In the United States, Illinois in 1961 was the first state to repeal existing statutes against private homosexual acts between consenting adults. Many, but not all, other states have since followed suit. Unfortunately, the emergence of AIDS in the 1980s and its original localization in the male homosexual community threatens to halt or even reverse this climate of increased tolerance for gay life-styles.

Certainly, it is in the interest of all to discourage those sexual practices implicated in the spread of the virus, whether in homosexual or heterosexual contexts. It would be tragic, however, if our tendency to "blame the victim" were to result in renewed or more virulent persecution of homosexuals, thereby driving many of them back into the "closet" of secrecy and shame. Apart from the psychological damage that would be inflicted, such a reaction would almost certainly result in an *increased* spread of AIDS. History teaches that the eradication of homosexuality is not a realistic goal for any society, even if it were a worthy one. No evidence suggests

that the social gains heretofore made by "gay liberation" have led to a significant increase in homosexuality or have proven in themselves to be detrimental to the general welfare. In addition, heterosexual interests seem to remain alive and well, so we need have little fear that our species will be decimated by rampant homoeroticism. It could well be decimated by rampant HIV infection. This distinction will be of crucial importance as we face an uncertain future in respect to controlling this deadly threat.

UNRESOLVED ISSUES
on Sexual Disorders and Variants

The unprecedented advances of the past two decades in the treatment of what were previously stubborn problems in sexual functioning should not blind us to the fact that tens of thousands of men and women continue to experience frustration and demoralizing difficulties. Along this line, some researchers suggest that failures to replicate in more recent work the extraordinarily high success rates originally achieved with our new, direct treatment approaches reflect a continuing core of problematic cases; the "easy" ones have now all been successfully resolved, many perhaps even through informed self-help techniques, and hence do not show up in treatment outcome statistics. Whatever the explanation, the search for more effective therapies continues, particularly in the areas of male erectile dysfunction and situational or secondary female anorgasmia. Unfortunately, from a strictly clinical and scientific standpoint, the search must take into account certain societal tolerances and constraints, such as, for example, the controversial and potentially legal consequences of using trained surrogate partners (of *both* sexes) in programs of sex therapy.

Even more difficult and baffling problems continue to plague us, of course, in respect to sexually variant behavior. Of these, perhaps none is more crucial than the relationship between sexuality and aggression, of which we have only the vaguest understanding. The phenomena of rape and sadomasochism, observations of the sexual behavior of some subhuman species, and a growing number of human laboratory studies (e.g., Yates, Barbaree, & Marshall, 1984) suggest that, for males at least, we cannot dismiss the possibility of some sort of synergism being involved at a basic level in these two motivational systems. That is, sexual arousal may enhance the likelihood of aggression, and vice versa. Needless to say, we are not here offering a possible apology or excuse for sexual assault or victimization. To be civilized, after all, is to have control over many urgings of primal origin. Nor do we intend to convey a particular conclusion on the controversial matter of pornography inciting violence, one almost completely confounded by the aggressive or violent themes in much sexually explicit media material. While we are inclined to find censorship repugnant in any form, we think the legally enforced removal of violent, aggressive, sadomasochistic themes from erotica probably would reduce to a measurable extent the prevalence of sexual assaults.

Whatever the origins, it is plain that as a society we are failing in efforts to curb sexual exploitation, victimization, and assault. The extent of our failure becomes all the more agonizing in the face of numerous recent research findings on the often serious short- and long-term consequences for many victims, both child and adult. Apart from enforced physical separation of an offender from his or her victim or potential victims, satisfactory solutions are badly wanting. Surely, at least, we can find ways to improve our services to victims, such as ensuring access to expert counseling. Much work in this area is already underway.

On the offender side, psychotherapeutic intervention may be promising if an offender acknowledges a "problem" and is motivated to work on its resolution, neither of which can be taken for granted. Therapy initiated on court order seems unpromising without an offender's genuine commitment to the process. Radical solutions, such as offender castration, although having a certain emotional appeal for some outraged by these crimes, are often based on fundamental misconceptions about etiology and would, we suspect, more often compound than alleviate the menace. Close monitoring of past offenders shows promise, but it may be too costly on the scale required. We have sound reasons to believe that eliminating child abuse, particularly sexual abuse, would have significant impact in this area. Unfortunately, the time frame for achieving such an objective is generations rather than years. Meanwhile, it seems that we are entitled to a more vigorous form of law enforcement in these areas than has been characteristic of the recent past.

As of February 1989, 85,590 cases of AIDS had been reported in the United States alone; because the average survival period following diagnosis is approximately 11 months, most of these people are already dead. The number of HIV-infected individuals (who, without some dramatic breakthrough in medical research, will acquire AIDS in an average of 8 years following infection) is difficult to estimate, in part because of wide variations in different risk groups and even in different locales. For example, 57 percent of female prostitutes tested in metropolitan (New York) cities in New Jersey were seropositive for HIV-1, whereas this rate was only 1 percent among Atlanta prostitutes. Although rates of seroconversion (that is, new infections) have been declining among gay men, they remained unacceptably high in the latest figures available, and—with the notable exception of transfusion-induced infections—there is little evidence of such decline in other high-risk groups (Glasner & Kaslow, 1990). We are thus dealing with a threat of staggering proportions, one inextricably linked to the manner in which we manage our sexuality.

Such evidence as we have—and it is chiefly anecdotal and informal—indicates that many people have in fact modified their sexual choices and behavior and thus substantially reduced their risk. The increased availability (for example, in college dorm coin dispensers) and use of latex condoms, which have a demonstrated record of prevention (Detels et al., 1988; Fischl et al., 1987), is an encouraging sign of wisdom and maturity. As the history of sexually transmitted diseases painfully reminds us, however, some people will neglect or even refuse to take reasonable precautions. For example, a sexually active undergraduate male recently told one of us in conversation that he would "never" use a condom on the grounds that it "interfered" with his pleasure. What does one do or say in the face of such density and self-indulgence, of such a dangerous denial of common sense, of such *abnormality*?

SUMMARY

In contrast to lower animals, human sexuality is remarkably free of biological constraints and is therefore highly plastic and subject to acquired inhibitions and appetites. The inhibitions are associated chiefly with psychosexual dysfunctions— varied inabilities to achieve satisfaction or to provide it for one's partner. Sexual appetites may involve psychosexual variants or deviations, in which an individual's preferred modes of arousal and gratification are different from conventionally accepted heterosexual patterns and, in some instances, are thought to threaten a group's welfare.

Some such variants, however, are victimless and cause no great harm either to individuals or to society in general.

Some psychosexual dysfunctions involve inhibited sexual desire in either sex. Other dysfunctions are more gender-specific: for males, erectile insufficiency, premature ejaculation, and ejaculatory retardation or incompetence; for females, arousal insufficiency (analogous to erectile insufficiency in a male), vaginismus, orgasmic dysfunction, and dyspareunia. Great strides have been made recently in the treatment of psychosexual dysfunctions in both sexes. Contrary to the situation a quarter-century ago, many people experiencing dysfunctions can now be reassured that, in all likelihood, they will be able to overcome their difficulties with competent professional help.

Of the sexual variants, one of the least understood is gender identity disorder, in which a person feels trapped in a body of the wrong gender. This disorder often results in efforts to have the body altered so as to conform to the person's internal sense of maleness or femaleness. Neither the male nor female pattern is well understood at this time, but it seems likely that both biological and psychosocial factors are implicated in most cases.

The paraphilias are a group of disorders in which sexual satisfaction becomes persistently focused on some unusual object, ritual, or situation. We distinguish between victimless varieties, such as transvestism, and those deviations involving assault or nonconsent, such as exhibitionism. Other paraphilias include fetishism, voyeurism, sadism, masochism, and pedophilia. A persistent rapist may best be conceived as a paraphiliac. Little is known about the development of these deviant practices, but it is strongly suspected that, for the most part, they are due to faulty learning and an inadequate sense of self.

Discussions of incest (especially of the father-daughter type) and rape are also included here, even though neither behavior is recognized in the DSM-III-R. The chief importance of incest, from an abnormal psychology standpoint, is that the child-victim often suffers serious adjustment difficulties in adolescence and adulthood. Contrary to most public opinion, sexual gratification is not the dominant motive in the overwhelming majority of rapes. A desire for power and aggression against women are far more likely to instigate incidents of rape. Many rape victims also sustain long-term reactions that compromise adaptive functioning.

Therapy for the sexual dysfunctions has developed at an impressive pace since the 1970s.

The prognosis for the sexual variants and deviations is, in general, far less optimistic—although, even here, treatment successes do occur, especially where a comprehensive treatment approach is planned and effected.

The DSM-III-R recognizes one type of disorder involving homosexuality—called ego-dystonic homosexuality—in which an individual persistently wishes to change his or her variant sexual orientation. Homosexuality itself is a complex and heterogeneous phenomenon. Both homosexual and heterosexual potentials exist to varying degrees in virtually everyone, but it cannot be said that everyone is fundamentally bisexual. Unlike a "normal" bell-shaped distribution curve, few "bisexuals" are found in the middle portion in terms of behavioral choices made or, probably, satisfaction experienced. Many people claiming to be bisexual are probably homosexual.

Although homosexuality is itself no longer diagnosable as a mental disorder, the authors take the position that one form of the gay life-style emphasizing sexual promiscuity and relative partner anonymity is definitely abnormal within their definition of the term, especially in this age of AIDS.

Unresolved issues in this area include certain dysfunctions, chiefly male erectile and female secondary orgasmic problems, that are proving relatively difficult to treat, and questions of both theoretical and practical import concerning the relationship of sexuality to aggression. Finally, the effect of the growing AIDS crisis on societal attitudes toward sexuality has involved some adaptive life-style changes, but with disturbing exceptions.

■ Key Terms

lovemap (p. 342)
sexual dysfunction (p. 343)
male erectile disorder (p. 343)
primary erectile insufficiency (p. 343)
secondary erectile insufficiency (p. 343)
premature ejaculation (p. 344)
inhibited male orgasm (p. 345)
female sexual arousal disorder (p. 345)
vaginismus (p. 345)
inhibited female orgasm (p. 345)
primary orgasmic dysfunction (p. 346)
dyspareunia (p. 346)
hypoactive sexual desire disorder (p. 346)
sexual aversion disorder (p. 346)
gender identity disorder (p. 352)
paraphilias (p. 354)
fetishism (p. 355)
transvestic fetishism (p. 356)
voyeurism (p. 357)
scotophilia (p. 357)
inspectionalism (p. 357)
exhibitionism (p. 358)
sadism (p. 360)
masochism (p. 362)
pedophilia (p. 363)
incest (p. 365)
rape (p. 368)
homosexuality (p. 373)
bisexuality (p. 374)

Chapter 11
Mood Disorders and Suicide

Heinrich Müller, *The Fly-Man and the Snake*. Müller (1865–1930), a Swiss vineyardist and amateur inventor, was institutionalized as a mental patient at the age of 41. In the hospital, he occupied his time by "experimenting" with bizarre, homemade machines and by drawing disturbing hallucinatory sketches like the one shown here.

Mood disorders are so named because they involve states of positive or negative emotion, or *affect,* that are intense and persistent enough to be clearly maladaptive for significant periods of time. Consider the following case:

A nationally prominent businesswoman in her middle years, noted for her energy and productivity, was unexpectedly deserted by her husband for a younger woman. Following her initial shock and rage, she began to have uncontrollable weeping spells and serious doubts about her business acumen. Decision making, in particular, became an enormous ordeal. Her spirits worsened over a relatively brief period of time, and she began to spend more and more of her time in bed, refusing to deal with anyone. Simultaneously, her alcohol consumption increased to the point that she was seldom entirely sober. Within a period of weeks, serious financial losses were incurred owing to her inability, or refusal, to keep her affairs in order. She felt she was a "total failure," a self-attribution that was entirely resistant to alteration by a review of her considerable achievements; indeed, her self-abnegation gradually spread to all aspects of her life and her personal history. Finally, having become alarmed, members of her family essentially forced her to accept an appointment with a clinical psychologist.

How was the psychologist to deal with this situation? Was something "wrong" with the woman, or was she merely experiencing normal human emotions due to her husband's departure? The psychologist concluded that the woman was suffering from a mood disorder, and treatment was initiated. The diagnosis, based on the severity of the symptoms and the degree of impairment, was major depression. As we shall see, mood-related reactions to distressing events are not limited to relatively mild forms of "adjustment disorder," but may and frequently do include the emergence of the full major depressive syndrome. This source of potential confusion will be further discussed in a later section.

When a mood change, because of its extent, brings about behavior that seriously endangers the affected person's welfare, psychologists and other mental health professionals conclude that the person is disordered. Mood disorders are conceived to be heterogeneous, as is suggested by the many types of depression recognized in the DSM-III-R, listed in *HIGHLIGHT 11.1* Whether or not such elaborate differentiation of depressive disorder is justified is open to question, as we will see in later sections.

In all mood disorders (formerly called *affective disorders*), extremes of *emotion*—soaring elation or deep depression—dominate the clinical picture. By contrast, the schizophrenic and paranoid disorders discussed in the next chapter are predominantly disturbances of thought, or *cognition,* although often they have some distortion of affect, too. In severe cases of any of these disorders, disturbances of both thought and affect may involve **psychotic behavior** (or **psychosis**)—a loss of contact with reality to the extent that a person harbors delusional beliefs or reports bizarre perceptions (hallucinations). Most, but not all, instances of mood disorder fall short of this level of disorganization.

Disordered thought processes are not typical in mood disorders, except where a disorder reaches extreme intensity; even here, though, the disturbed thinking is often circumscribed and seems in some sense "appropriate" to the emotional extremes that the person is experiencing. For example, the delusional idea that one's internal organs have totally deteriorated—an idea sometimes held by severely depressed people—ties in with the mood of a despondent person; in contrast, the idea that one has been chosen by the Deity for a special mission to save humankind is inconsistent with the self-abnegation normally seen in depression. The former type of disordered thinking is termed **mood-congruent thinking,** which means that it is consistent with the predominant mood.

The two key states of mood disorder are **mania,** characterized by intense and unrealistic feelings of excitement and euphoria, and **depression,** which involves feelings of extraordinary sadness and dejection. These states are often conceived to be at opposite ends of a single mood continuum, with normal mood occupying the middle portion. While accurate to a degree, this conception cannot be taken too literally in trying to understand every instance of mood disorder, because in rare cases a patient appears to be both manic and depressed at the same time. Such an observation suggests the aptness of a model involving two independent dimensions, each ranging from mood normality at one pole to either extreme mania or extreme depression at the other.

Depressions of mild intensity are so much a part of our lives that incidence and prevalence figures for them would be difficult to estimate and would probably be meaningless anyway. Of the two types of major mood disorders, **major depression** (a *unipolar* form of disorder in which only depressive episodes occur) is much more frequent, and its occurrence has apparently increased in recent years. The other type, **bipolar disorder** (in which both manic and depressive episodes occur), has decreased. In fact, estimates indicate that some 8 to 10 people in 100—about 25 million Americans—will experience a severe depressive episode at some time in their lives (Brown, 1974). More than 2 million of these will suffer profound depressions (President's Commission on Mental Health, 1978).

Though the great majority of mood disorder cases occur between the ages of 25 and 65, such reactions may occur anytime from early childhood to old age. Lefkowitz and Tesiny (1985) reported a point prevalence rate (cases at a particular point in time) for depression of 5.2 percent among some 3000 third to fifth graders. Poznanski and Zrull (1970) described significant depressive reactions among children ranging from 3 to 12 years of age, and depressions meeting the criteria for designation as *major* have been observed in preadolescent youngsters (Puig-Antich et al., 1985; 1989). A possible early manifestation of the syndrome has recently been observed in the infants of mothers depressed at postpartum (Whiffen & Gotlib, 1989). The occurrence of mood disorders apparently has no upper age limit, and, as we will see, females are considerably more at risk than males.

Fortunate indeed (and probably nonexistent) is the adult who has never experienced at least mild depression from time to time. Research suggests that we can conceive such mild mood disturbances as being largely on the same continuum, at least at the clinical level (what we can actually observe), as the more severe disorders on which this chapter will focus. The differences seem chiefly to be of degree, not of kind, a conclusion supported in a recent review of the pertinent evidence by Free and Oei (1989). At some point along this continuum, however, as we encounter the more extreme or even psychotic phenomena, subtle biological factors likely become implicated, rendering a person in many instances less amenable to psychological treatment approaches. Interestingly, antidepressant medication, the most common biologically-based treatment for depressions, is not particularly useful in treating milder depressions, including milder "major" depressions (Elkin et al., 1989), unless these depressions are accompanied by panic attacks (Stewart et al., 1985).

Our discussion will start with the milder mood disturbances, which are regarded as "normal." From there, we will move to disorders of affect in

HIGHLIGHT 11.1

Varieties of Depression According to DSM–III–R

Diagnosis	Main Features
Organic mood disorder, depressed Primary degenerative dementia with depression Multi-infarct dementia with depression Hallucinogen mood disorder, depressed	The person has notably depressed mood, including symptoms associated with major depression, whose primary cause is considered to be interference with normal brain functioning by some organic process. Where the organic process is known (e.g., multi-infarct dementia), it is specified in the diagnosis on Axis I or III.
Major depression	The person has one or more major depressive episodes in the absence of any manic episode. Symptoms include prominent and persistent depressed mood, accompanied by symptoms such as poor appetite, insomnia, psychomotor retardation, decreased sex drive, fatigue, feelings of worthlessness or guilt, inability to concentrate, and thoughts of death or suicide.
Bipolar disorder, depressed	The person experiences a major depressive episode (as in major depression) and has had one or more manic episodes.
Dysthymia	For the past two years, the person has been bothered all or most of the time by a depressed mood, but not of sufficient severity to meet the criteria for major depression.
Cyclothymia, depressed	At present or during the past two years, the person has experienced episodes resembling dysthymia, but also has had one or more periods of hypomania—characterized by elevated, expansive, or irritable mood not of psychotic proportions.
Adjustment disorder with depressed mood	The person reacts with a maladaptively depressed mood to some identifiable stressor occurring within the past three months. "Uncomplicated bereavement" does not qualify. It is assumed the reaction is temporary.

which an individual's functioning is clearly impaired but in which little or no evidence suggests a pervasive personality breakdown or loss of contact with reality. Finally, we will deal with moderate to severe mood disorders, a group of conditions currently undergoing intensive scientific investigation. Throughout, we will focus primarily on depression, which is much more common than mania.

Suicide is a distressingly frequent and almost always possible outcome of relatively significant depressions. In fact, such episodes are undoubtedly the most common of the predisposing causes leading to suicide. The latter part of this chapter includes a discussion of the varieties, causes, and prevention of suicidal behavior.

MOOD DISTURBANCES AND DISORDERS

Sadness, discouragement, pessimism, and hopelessness about being able to improve matters are familiar feelings to most people. Most of us are prone to move in and out of these states throughout our lives. Depression is unpleasant, even noxious, when we are in it, but it usually does not last long. Sometimes it seems almost to be self-limiting, turning off after a period or after a certain intensity level has been exceeded. As we come out of it, we often experience it as having been in some sense useful: we were stuck, and now we can move on; the former situation was easier to get out of than we thought it could be, and our new perspective encompasses all sorts of possibilities.

This familiar scenario contains certain hints that may be significant to depression generally, including its more severe forms. The more important of these hints are that (a) depression, in its mild form, may actually be adaptive in the long run; (b) much of the "work" of depression seems to involve self-exposure to images, thoughts, and feelings that would normally be avoided; and (c) depression may, at least under some circumstances, be self-limiting. All of these considerations suggest that the capacity to experience depression may be normal—even desirable—provided of course that it is maintained within certain limits of time and intensity. They also suggest the idea of *normal* depressions—depressions we would expect to occur in anyone undergoing certain traumatic but common life events, such as significant personal, interpersonal, or economic losses.

■ Normal Depression

Though the often problematic distinction between "normal" and "abnormal" is especially fuzzy here, any reasonable estimate would suggest that normal depressions far surpass abnormal ones in terms of the numbers of people affected at a given time. Most people suffering from normal depression will not seek or need the specialized services of a mental health professional—although, in doubtful cases, it is certainly better to err on the conservative side and seek such assistance.

Normal depressions are almost always the result of recent stress. In fact, some depressions are considered adjustment disorders (in response to stressors) rather than mood disorders. We discuss such reactions here as well as in Chapter 5 because we doubt such sharp demarcations are justified by the facts. As already noted, many depressions meeting criteria as "major" are clearly related to the prior occurrence of obvious stress (Hammen et al., 1989; Harder et al., 1989; Hirschfeld et al., 1985; Shrout et al., 1989; Winokur, 1985), although this fact tends to be understated or ignored by some biologically-oriented investigators. We will consider some of the milder forms of normal depression in the following sections.

Grief and the Grieving Process   We usually think of grief as the psychological process one goes through following the death of a loved one—a

process that, we have noted, appears to be more damaging for men than women (Stroebe & Stroebe, 1983). Though this may be the most common and intense form of grieving, many other types of loss will give rise to a similar state in an affected person. Loss of a favored status or position (including one occasioned by promotion), separation or divorce, financial loss, the breakup of a romantic affair, retirement, separation from a friend, absence from home for the first time, or even the loss of a cherished pet may all give rise to the symptoms of acute grief.

Whatever the source, this condition has certain characteristic qualities beyond the virtually omnipresent weeping spells. A grieving person will normally "turn off" in response to events that would usually provoke a strong response; figuratively, he or she seems to roll up in a ball, fending off any and all possibilities of additional involvement and hurt by the simple expedient of losing interest in nearly all external happenings. At the same time, the griever often becomes actively involved in fantasies that poignantly depict the now unavailable former situation of satisfaction and gratification. Initially painful, these fantasies, if only by sheer repetition, gradually lose their capacity to evoke pain—a process of response extinction or, as Sullivan (1956) called it, "erasure."

In the typical instance, after a variable interval of a few weeks or months, the ability to respond to the external world is gradually regained, sadness

We usually think of grief as the psychological process one goes through following the death of a loved one. We see grief in the face of this grandmother attending the funeral of her grandson, who died in the Gulf War. Grief may accompany other types of loss as well, such as separation or divorce, romantic break-up, retirement, loss of a job, or even loss of a pet.

abates, zest returns, and a person moves out again into a more productive engagement with the challenges of life. This is the normal pattern. Some people, however, become stuck somewhere in the middle of the sequence, in which case they enter into a more serious psychological status to be described in a later section. P. J. Clayton (1982) estimated that the process of grieving following bereavement is normally completed within one year, during which time a grieving person may experience the "full depressive syndrome" (that is, major depression, to be examined later). If depressive symptoms persist beyond the first year after loss, therapeutic intervention may be called for.

Ignoring for the moment such potential complications, it is easy to see grief as having an adaptive function. In fact the lack of grief under conditions in which it seems warranted would generally be of some concern to a mental health professional. On the other hand, as we discussed in Chapter 7, a prolonged sense of hopelessness may endanger physical health, and eventual recovery and resolution following loss is not a guaranteed outcome (Wortman & Silver, 1989).

Other Normal Mood Variations   Many situations other than obvious loss can provoke depressive feelings, and as we will see, some people seem especially prone to develop depressive responses. It is a commonplace observation, for example, that some doctoral candidates in various fields, including those in clinical psychology, undergo pronounced depressive reactions soon after completion of their final oral exams. A seemingly similar phenomenon is the so-called postpartum depressive reaction of some new mothers (and sometimes fathers) on the birth of a child. Pitt (1982) indicated that as many as 50 percent of women experience at least a mild attack of "the blues" following childbirth, 10 percent of them having reactions of moderately severe depression. Clearly, hormonal readjustments and the like are a key factor here (except for fathers). It is obvious that a psychological component is present as well: it may reflect a letdown after sustained effort and anticipation; or perhaps a person's expectations had failed to include certain realities about the more challenging (overwhelming?) aspects of infant care and dependency, leading to depression rather than to joy; or it may be a feeling of loss—that is, of missing that constant companion in the womb who is now a separate entity.

Many college students experience bouts of mild or serious depression during their college years of supposed freedom and carefree personal growth. Normal depressions among college students were

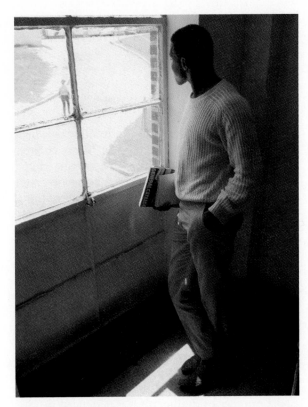

Many college students experience bouts of depression during their college years. The internal and external pressures to get good grades and to achieve can sometimes cause those students who don't make the grade to devalue themselves and to see their lives as having no meaning.

studied by Blatt, D'Afflitti, and Quinlan (1976) in an effort to determine the basic dimensions of the experience. In brief, they found that depression was similar for males and females, and that it involved chiefly three main psychological variables: (a) *dependency*, the sense that one is in dire need of help and support from others; (b) *self-criticism*, the tendency to exaggerate one's faults and to engage in self-devaluation; and (c) *inefficacy*, the sense that events in the world are independent of—not contingent on—one's own actions or efforts. In subsequent work, Blatt and colleagues (1982) focused on the first two of these dimensions, suggesting that there may be two basic types of depressive experience organized around themes of either dependency or self-criticism, inefficacy being common to both. Other investigators, such as Hammen et al. (1985, 1989) and Nietzel and Harris (1990), have contributed independent evidence that such subgroups may indeed exist; that is, some depressed people seem primarily involved with the state of their interpersonal relationships, while others' concerns focus on achievement issues. Because dependency and self-criticism are commonplace among the more severely depressed, these observations lend support to the notion of a continuous severity dimension.

◼ Mild to Moderate Mood Disorders

The point on the severity continuum at which mood *disturbance* becomes mood *disorder* is a matter of clinical judgment. Unfortunately, though criteria exist for exercising this judgment, they are not precise enough to guarantee consensus among different clinicians, and—perhaps more importantly —it is decidedly unclear that any such sharp demarcation would meet the requirement of *validity*—in other words, that it could actually reflect a meaningful point of transition between clinical and nonclinical depression. Although the more severe forms of mood disorder are obviously abnormal to even the casual observer, a gray area exists where a distinction between normal and abnormal is difficult to establish or defend.

It is customary to differentiate the mood disorders along three principal dimensions: (a) *severity* —the number of dysfunctions experienced in various areas of living and the relative degree of impairment evidenced in those areas (for example, sexual performance and satisfaction); (b) *type*—whether depressive, manic, or mixed symptoms predominate; and (c) *duration*—whether the disorder is acute, chronic, or intermittent, with periods of relatively normal functioning between the episodes of disorder. The following discussion reflects these customary divisions, as do the DSM-III-R categories.

DSM-III-R includes three main categories for mood disorders of mild to moderate severity: cyclothymia, dysthymia, and adjustment disorder with depressed mood. Each of these is considered in the following sections.

Cyclothymia   As we have noted, mania is in some ways the mood or affective opposite of depression; it is a state involving excessive levels of excitement, elation, or euphoria, often liberally admixed with components of domination and the assumption of great powers. In its milder forms it is known as **hypomania.** It has long been recognized that certain people are subject to cyclical mood alterations with relative excesses of hypomania and depression that, though substantial, are not disabling. These, in essence, are the symptoms of **cyclothymia.**

Many clinicians feel that cyclothymia is but a milder variant of bipolar disorder (to be discussed later in this chapter), and evidence for this view has

in recent years become quite compelling. For example, Depue and his colleagues have identified a subsyndromal (that is, showing few symptoms) cyclothymic personality organization that is predictive of serious mood disorder episodes (Depue et al., 1981; Goplerud & Depue, 1985; Klein & Depue, 1984, 1985; Klein, Depue, & Slater, 1985, 1986). Specifically, these investigators developed a hypomanic personality inventory scale that postdicted (that is, identified those individuals who had had) not only hypomanic episodes but other maladaptive patterns, including depression, among a group of college undergraduates. This study is significant because it suggests that an identifying personality component is present independent of hypomanic episodes.

Changes in the DSM classification reflect current thinking about cyclothymia. In DSM-I and DSM-II, this pattern was included under the category of personality disorders and was not related to mood disorders per se. The DSM-III-R definition of cyclothymia makes the pattern sound a bit like a junior-grade version of major bipolar disorder, minus certain extreme symptoms and psychotic features, such as delusions. In the depressed phase of cyclothymia, a person's mood is dejected and he or she experiences a distinct loss of interest or pleasure in usual activities and pastimes. In addition, the individual may exhibit sleep irregularity (too much or too little); low energy level; feelings of inadequacy; decreased efficiency, productivity, talkativeness, and cognitive sharpness; social withdrawal; restriction of pleasurable activities, including a relative disinterest in sex; a pessimistic and brooding attitude; and tearfulness.

The hypomanic phase of cyclothymia consists essentially of the opposites of these characteristics, except that the sleep disturbance is invariably one of an apparent decreased need for sleep. As in the case of bipolar disorder, no obvious precipitating circumstance may be evident, and an affected person may have lengthy periods between episodes in which he or she functions in a relatively adaptive manner. In cyclothymia, however, the diagnostic criteria specify at least a two-year span of disturbance for adults and one year for adolescents and children. The following case is illustrative:

A 29-year-old car salesman was referred by his current girl friend, a psychiatric nurse, who suspected he had an Affective [i.e., Mood] Disorder, even though the patient was reluctant to admit that he might be a "moody" person. According to him, since the age of 14 he has experienced repeated alternating cycles that he terms "good times and bad times." During a "bad" period, usually lasting four to seven days, he oversleeps 10–14 hours daily, lacks energy, confidence, and motivation—"just vegetating," as he puts it. Often he abruptly shifts, characteristically upon waking up in the morning, to a three-to-four-day stretch of overconfidence, heightened social awareness, promiscuity, and sharpened thinking—"things would flash in my mind." At such times he indulges in alcohol to enhance the experience, but also to help him sleep. Occasionally the "good" periods last seven to ten days, but culminate in irritable and hostile outbursts, which often herald the transition back to another period of "bad" days. He admits to frequent use of marijuana, which he claims helps him "adjust" to daily routines.

In school, A's and B's alternated with C's and D's, with the result that the patient was considered a bright student whose performance was mediocre overall because of "unstable motivation." As a car salesman his performance has also been uneven, with "good days" canceling out the "bad days"; yet even during his "good days" he is sometimes perilously argumentative with customers and loses sales that appeared sure. Although considered a charming man in many social circles, he alienates friends when he is hostile and irritable. He typically accumulates social obligations during the "bad" days and takes care of them all at once on the first day of a "good" period. (Spitzer et al., 1981, pp. 31–32)

In short, cyclothymia consists of mood swings that, at either extreme, are clearly maladaptive but of insufficient intensity to merit the major disorder designation.

Dysthymia   The symptoms of **dysthymia** are essentially identical to those indicated for the depressed phase of cyclothymia; they include sleep disturbance, low energy level, low self-esteem, concentration difficulties, and pessimism. The main difference is that dysthymically disordered people evidence no tendency toward hypomanic episodes in their life histories. Rather, they exhibit moderate, nonpsychotic levels of depression over a chronic period—that is, at least two years (one year for children and adolescents) of more or less uninterrupted duration. Normal moods may briefly intercede, but they last at most from a few days to a few weeks. As in the case of cyclothymia, no identifiable precipitating event or condition need necessarily be present, though such circumstances are frequently

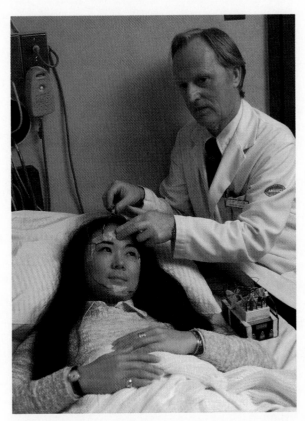

Sleep disturbances are common in both cyclothymia and dysthymia. Studying the brainwave patterns of sleeping cyclothymic and dysthymic patients has helped researchers discover some of the basic patterns underlying these disorders.

observed for depressions of this general type. Indeed, a depressed person tends to elicit reactions from the social environment that will bring about "bad" feelings on a continuous basis (Strack & Coyne, 1983). The following case, which includes obvious self-sustaining features, is typical of this disorder:

A 28-year-old junior executive was referred by a senior psychoanalyst for "supportive" treatment. She had obtained a master's degree in business administration and moved to California a year and a half earlier to begin work in a large firm. She complained of being "depressed" about everything: her job, her husband, and her prospects for the future.

She had had extensive psychotherapy previously. She had seen an "analyst" twice a week for three years while in college, and a "behaviorist" for a year and a half while in graduate school. Her complaints were of persistent feelings of depressed mood, inferiority, and pessimism, which she claims to have had since she was 16 or 17 years old. Although she did reasonably well in college, she constantly ruminated about those students who were "genuinely intelligent." She dated during college and graduate school, but claimed that she would never go after a guy she thought was "special," always feeling inferior and intimidated. Whenever she saw or met such a man, she acted stiff and aloof, or actually walked away as quickly as possible, only to berate herself afterward and then fantasize about him for many months. She claimed that her therapy had helped, although she still could not remember a time when she didn't feel somewhat depressed.

Just after graduation, she married the man she was going out with at the time. She thought of him as reasonably desirable, though not "special," and married him primarily because she felt she "needed a husband" for companionship. Shortly after their marriage, the couple started to bicker. She was very critical of his clothes, his job, and his parents; and he, in turn, found her rejecting, controlling, and moody. She began to feel that she had made a mistake in marrying him.

Recently she has also been having difficulties at work. She is assigned the most menial tasks at the firm and is never given an assignment of importance or responsibility. She admits that she frequently does a "slipshod" job of what is given her, never does more than is required, and never demonstrates any assertiveness or initiative to her supervisors. She views her boss as self-centered, unconcerned, and unfair, but nevertheless admires his success. She feels that she will never go very far in her profession because she does not have the right "connections" and neither does her husband, yet she dreams of money, status, and power.

Her social life with her husband involves several other couples. The man in these couples is usually a friend of her husband. She is sure that the women find her uninteresting and unimpressive, and that the people who seem to like her are probably no better off than she.

Under the burden of her dissatisfaction with her marriage, her job, and her social life, feeling tired and uninterested in "life," she now enters treatment for the third time. (Spitzer et al., 1981, pp. 10–11)

Adjustment Disorder with Depressed Mood

Basically, **adjustment disorder with depressed mood** is behaviorally indistinguishable from dys-

thymia or the depressed phase of cyclothymia. It differs from the latter two conditions in that it does not exceed six months in duration, and it requires the existence of an identifiable (presumably precipitating) psychosocial stressor in the client's life within three months prior to the onset of depression. The justification for making a clinical diagnosis is that the client is experiencing impaired social or occupational functioning, or that the observed stressor would not normally be considered severe enough to account for the client's reaction. There is a difficulty here, of course, because assessing stressor severity is a highly subjective matter. Also, the diagnosis assumes that the person's problems will remit when the stressor ceases or when a new level of adjustment is achieved. This assumption causes further difficulties, because it calls for the diagnostician to predict a benign future course; if enhanced adjustment does not occur, we must assume a continuation of the stressor or a failure of the client to make the "new" adjustment. Presumably, chronic cases of this sort would need to be rediagnosed as dysthymia.

Despite evident problems with this particular set of formal diagnostic criteria, there are doubtless many cases of relatively brief but moderately serious depression (involving definitely maladaptive behavior) that occur in reaction to circumstances generally regarded by most as stressful. (Uncomplicated bereavement, by the way, would not be included under this diagnosis.) The following excerpt from a clinical interview is illustrative of an adjustment disorder with depressed mood.

*P**atient:** Well, you see, doctor, I just don't concentrate good, I mean, I can't play cards or even care to talk on the phone. I just feel so upset and miserable, it's just sorta as if I don't care any more about anything.*

Doctor: You feel that your condition is primarily due to your divorce proceedings?

Patient: Well, doctor, the thing that upset me so, we had accumulated a little bit through my efforts—bonds and money—and he (sigh) wanted one half of it. He said he was going to San Francisco to get a job and send me enough money for support. So (sigh) I gave him a bond, and he went and turned around and went to an attorney and sued me for a divorce. Well, somehow, I had withstood all the humiliation of his drinking and not coming home at night and not knowing where he was, but he turned and divorced me and this is something that I just can't take. I mean, he has broken my health and

*broken everything, and I've been nothing but
good to him. I just can't take it, doctor. There are
just certain things that people—I don't know—
just can't accept. I just can't accept that he would
turn on me that way.*

It should be noted that few, if any, depressions
—including milder ones—occur in the absence of
significant anxiety. In fact the distinction between
depression and anxiety, at clinical levels, may be
difficult. In a recent study involving 470 patients of
mixed diagnoses, their cognitive and symptom profiles for anxiety and depression did in fact show up
as distinct and separable factors, but a fairly substantial group of patients had mixtures of these profiles
(Clark, Beck, & Stewart, 1990). The frequent
"comorbidity" (co-occurrence) of anxiety and depression has also been found in children (Kovacs et
al., 1989). Whatever may turn out to be the reason
for this connection between anxiety and depression
—an interesting question theoretically—a depressed person is often notably fearful and anxious.
Perhaps the person becomes frightened as a consequence of observing the mentally and physically
paralyzing effects of his or her own developing
depression. Alternatively, perhaps a more intrinsic
relationship exists between anxiety and depression,
even at the neurophysiological or neurochemical
level (Roth & Mountjoy, 1982). Some investigators, such as Seligman (1975) and Brown and
Harris (1978), believe that depression may be a
naturally occurring consequence of anxiety, particularly under conditions interpreted as hopeless. In
any event, because of this close association, the
treatment of depression often includes specific
treatment for anxiety as well.

In the range of mild to moderate mood disorders, there are no officially recognized manic or
hypomanic counterparts to dysthymia or adjustment disorder with depressed mood. The implicit
assumption appears to be that all mania-like behaviors must be part of a cyclothymic or bipolar
disorder, or perhaps must exist along a continuum
on which these two conditions fall. Considering
behavior alone, however, any such assumption is
readily challenged. Most clinicians are familiar with
a type of person who is chronically overactive,
dominating, counterdependent, deficient in self-
criticism, perhaps excessively optimistic concerning
the outcome of various plans and schemes, and yet
shows no pronounced history of depressive episodes; such people are by no means rare. It is
unfortunate to assume automatically that this pattern is related to the classic bipolar syndrome. On

the contrary, such people are most often found to
have underlying anxiety that they are attempting to
manage by overactivity in the standard fashion of
neurotic defense, and their problems are perhaps
best considered manifestations of what we have
called compliance/submission inhibition (see
Chapter 6, page 215).

Incidentally, the individuals just described are
unlikely to present themselves initially for treatment at a psychological or psychiatric clinic. The
more common pattern is for them to show up in
medical clinics with a stress-related physical disease,
perhaps as Type A patients with coronary problems
(see Chapter 7).

◼ Moderate to Severe Mood Disorders

We have noted that mood disorders seem to array
themselves along an unbroken continuum of severity; there are no discernible gaps in this continuum
that allow us to distinguish different basic types of
disorder. We must now add a qualification to this
general proposition; the continuum does not quite
tell the whole story. Mood disorders differ, as we
have seen, along the dimensions of severity, type,
and duration. Both severity and type, however, are
often hard to pin down: the *profile,* or pattern, of
symptoms (for example, sleep disturbance, psychomotor retardation or agitation) may vary greatly
from individual to individual and may exist at least
somewhat independently of severity. An obvious
distinction, for example, can be drawn between
manic- and depressive-symptom profiles; but even
within different instances of either mania or depression, different symptom profiles can occur at varying levels of intensity. Far more research attention
has been directed to possible differing types of
depression than mania, and some of the findings are
discussed below.

Major Depression   To a large extent, the diagnostic criteria for major depression involve merely
more intense forms of the symptoms for dysthymia
or the depressive phase of cyclothymia. An affected
person may experience marked sadness of mood,
fatigue, insomnia or hypersomnia (that is, too little
or too much sleep), loss of interest in pleasurable
activities, diminished cognitive capacity, and self-
denunciation to the point of claiming worthlessness
or guilt out of proportion to any past indiscretions.
In addition, the person will often show a decreased
appetite and significant weight loss (or, much more
rarely, their opposites), a slow-down—or, less often, agitation—of mental and physical activity, and
a preoccupation with death and suicide. A majority

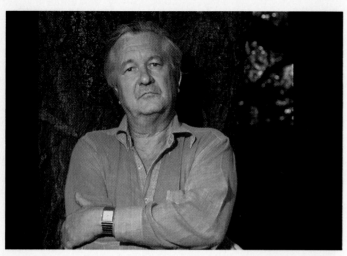

Pulitizer Prize–winning novelist William Styron suffered an episode of depression so severe that it completely disrupted his life for about 9 months. He couldn't concentrate enough to write; couldn't sleep more than four hours a night; lost interest in eating and other activities he had previously found pleasurable, such as walks through the hills around his Connecticut home; believed his life was worthless; and thought about suicide—all symptoms of major depression. When his suicidal impulses became overwhelming, Styron agreed to enter a psychiatric hospital, where his recovery began. He has recounted his experiences in a book titled *Darkness Visible*. He likens the disease to "unimaginable pain—not like the pain of a fractured limb, yet every bit as severe."

(at least five, including either sad mood or loss of pleasure response) of these symptoms must be present all day and nearly every day for two consecutive weeks before the diagnosis is applicable. Psychotic features, such as delusions, hallucinations, or depressive stupor (a mute and unresponsive state), may or may not accompany the other symptoms. Normally, any delusions or hallucinations present are mood-congruent; that is, they involve themes of personal inadequacy, guilt, deserved punishment, death, disease, and so forth. The following conversation between a therapist and a patient illustrates a major depression of moderate severity:

Therapist: Good morning, how are you today?
Patient: (Pause) Well, okay I guess, doctor. . . . I don't know, I just feel sort of discouraged.
Therapist: Is there anything in particular that worries you?
Patient: I don't know, doctor . . . everything seems to be futile . . . nothing seems worthwhile any more. It seems as if all that was beautiful has lost its beauty. I guess I expected more than life

has given. It just doesn't seem worthwhile going on. I can't seem to make up my mind about anything. I guess I have what you would call the "blues."
Therapist: Can you tell me more about your feelings?
Patient: Well . . . my family expected great things of me. I am supposed to be the outstanding member of the family . . . they think because I went through college everything should begin to pop and there's nothing to pop. I . . . really don't expect anything from anyone. Those whom I have trusted proved themselves less than friends should be.
Therapist: Oh?
Patient: Yes, I once had a very good girlfriend with whom I spent a good deal of time. She was very important to me. . . . I thought she was my friend but now she treats me like a casual acquaintance (tears).
Therapist: Can you think of any reason for this?
Patient: Yes, it's all my fault. I can't blame them—anybody that is. . . . I am not worthy of them. I have sinned against nature. I am worthless . . . nobody can love me. I don't deserve friends or success. . . .
Therapist: You sinned against nature?
Patient: Well . . . I am just no good. I am a failure. I was envious of other people. I didn't want them to have more than I had and when something bad happened to them I was glad. Now I am being repaid for my sins. All my flaws stand out and I am repugnant to everyone. (Sighs) I am a miserable failure. . . . There is no hope for me.

For this patient, the most prominent clinical feature—aside from the general mood depression—is self-denunciation, which may have a certain cultural specificity, as we will see.

The most severe form of major depression is the *depressive stupor*, which is characterized by marked psychomotor underactivity. This disorder is illustrated in the following case:

The patient lay in bed, immobile, with a dull, depressed expression on his face. His eyes were sunken and downcast. Even when spoken to, he would not raise his eyes to look at the speaker. Usually he did not respond at all to questions, but sometimes, after apparently great effort, he would mumble something about the "scourge of God." He appeared somewhat ema-

ciated, his breath was foul, and he had to be given enemas to maintain elimination. Occasionally, with great effort, he made the sign of the cross with his right hand. The overall picture was one of extreme vegetative-like immobility and depression.

Two basic subcategories of major depression have been defined: (a) *single episode* (no previous episode of the disorder), and (b) *recurrent* (one or more previous episodes). The type descriptor *melancholic,* described below, may be applied to either. The diagnosis of major depression cannot be made if a patient has ever experienced a manic episode; in such a case, the current depression is viewed as a depressive episode of bipolar disorder. Accordingly, major depression is also known as **unipolar disorder.**

As was suggested earlier, there has been considerable interest recently in attempting to differentiate various types of depression—especially major depression—according to the particular symptom patterns displayed. Such efforts are driven mostly by the hope of discovering differentially effective treatment methods. Thus DSM-III-R requires a specification as to whether or not a major depression is of "melancholic" type. This designation is applied where (in addition to meeting the criteria for major depression) a patient complains of a loss of interest or pleasure in almost all activities, of early morning awakenings, and of increased bad feelings in the morning; shows no evidence of personality disturbance prior to the first major depressive episode; or has had a good response to antidepressant, biologically based therapies in any prior episodes. The chief theoretical importance of the melancholia concept is that it is strongly linked in the psychiatric literature to the idea of *endogenous* causation—that is, to the notion that certain depressions are caused "from within," so to speak, and are unrelated to any events that may currently be impacting a patient's life. We will have more to say about this idea in a later section.

Discriminating major depression from other forms of depressive disorder is not as easy as might be hoped. One complication here is the suggestion that major depression may coexist with dysthymia or other milder forms in some individuals, a condition given the designation "double depression" (Keller & Shapiro, 1982; Keller et al., 1983). The actual data here are more consistent with the notion that some people who are moderately depressed on a chronic basis undergo increased problems from time to time, during which they manifest "major"

symptoms. Also, and perhaps contrary to what one might expect, a major depression is not necessarily a disorder of marked severity. DSM-III-R coding provides for diagnosing major depression where severe (that is, psychotic) features are not present and even—by use of the qualifying phrase *in remission*—where there are currently no notable symptoms at all. Tentatively, then, we doubt the validity of the notion of double depression.

It is plain, in any event, that the diagnostic term *major depression* does not necessarily refer to something observable in the current behavior of a diagnosed person, but possibly to some inferred behavior potential. In current practice, in fact, use of the term normally implies a biological defect or aberration that purportedly renders a person vulnerable to episodes of more or less severe depressive disorder. It is therefore possible to have a major depressive disorder with only mild current symptoms, provided a person has a history of past major depression. By contrast, severe symptoms are almost always considered outward manifestations of a "major" disorder. The concept of major depression is therefore quite problematic because it rests on a pattern of inferences that have been, in our judgment, insufficiently examined.

Overall, we remain unconvinced that there in fact exist several varieties of depression or of major depression representing distinct psychopathological entities. Such differentiation, when it can be accomplished on sound and meaningful grounds, is obviously desirable. We are far from certain, however, that we gain a great deal from the types of differentiations we are presently able to make, limited as they are to certain gross observations about the context, symptom pattern, and severity of the dysphoric mood state.

We think it is reasonable to suggest, for example, that psychological depression may best be conceived as analogous to fever in general medicine. Its occurrence tells us that something is wrong, and with extreme deviation that something is very wrong, but it does not in itself tell us *what* is wrong. Depression in mental dysfunction, like fever in physical dysfunction, is a common phenomenon with a high degree of co-occurrence across many more specifically defined syndromes. Like fever, it should always be taken seriously; but we know of no medical researcher who would advocate mounting a large-scale research effort to discriminate *types* of fever, as opposed to types of pathologic processes with which its occurrence may be associated. Though granting that it is often necessary to treat depression as a problem in and of itself, this is in fact also true of fever; the difference is that with fever we are never entirely satisfied until we have discovered and eradicated its source, whereas with depression we are encouraged to conclude that when it abates the "problem" is solved. If this analogy to fever has any validity, we should find that depression, when successfully treated in a purely symptomatic fashion (that is, without eradicating its cause), has a tendency to recur. Unfortunately, that is too often exactly what happens.

The proportion of patients exhibiting a recurrence of major depression is difficult to estimate reliably because of wide variations in the results of different studies. Coryell and Winokur (1982) tabulated data from the then-available work in this area and reported recurrence figures ranging from 39 to 95 percent of cases, averaging about 63 percent. In an epidemiologic, community-based study, 19.1 percent of subjects having major depression on initial contact were depressed when contacted a year later, whereas 62.2 percent were considered recovered—the remainder of the original sample having been lost. In addition, a history of prior depression predicted depression recurrence or continuance (Sargeant et al., 1990). Probably the best data we have on the question of recurrence has been published recently by Lewinsohn, Zeiss, and Duncan (1989). These investigators interviewed 2046 unipolar depressives concerning previous episodes. Of these subjects, 1130 (55%) reported at least one prior episode, and 173 (8%) reported as many as three. Again, the probability of relapse was a function of the number of prior episodes, and also of the severity of the current episode. Women showed a stronger pattern of recurrence than did men, echoing the gender-related incidence and prevalence figures for depressive disorder.

Different outcomes for depressive disorders also depend importantly on their particular manifestations and several other predictor variables (Gonzales, Lewinsohn, and Clarke, 1985). Despite the variable results from different studies, it is clear that the risk of having additional episodes of major depression is considerable for an individual experiencing a first one. The duration of a given episode is estimated, on average, to be about four months (Perris, 1982).

The traditional view has been that between episodes, a person suffering from a recurrent major mood disorder is essentially normal. This view has been increasingly called into question as more and better research data have become available (Coryell & Winokur, 1982). Indeed, given the frequently devastating effects such episodes have on a person's life circumstances, it would be surprising to find no lasting compromises in personal adjustment. Presumably, such compromises increase with successive episodes. In this connection, Akiskal and Simmons (1985) describe a chronic, residual type of low-grade depression affecting some 10 to 15 percent of people who recover from acute major depressive episodes.

The prospects for "complete recovery" (that is, no recurrence of an episode for a period of five years) from major depression are not particularly encouraging, probably being somewhere around 40 percent (Coryell & Winokur, 1982). As we learn more about managing depression, however, definite possibilities appear for limiting both the severity and the duration of attacks, and increasingly for preventing recurrences. For example, we now know that marital distress—especially as manifested in perceived criticism from the spouse—is a substantial predictor of short-term relapse (Hooley & Teasdale, 1989), and it should prove possible to fashion intervention techniques that lessen the impact of such risk factors.

Bipolar Disorder   As we have seen, depression and mania—despite their seeming opposition—are sometimes closely related. Cyclothymia, described earlier, is a case in point, but a far more dramatic example is the full bipolar syndrome. The sixth-century physician Alexander Trallianus may have been the first to recognize recurrent cycles of mania and melancholia in the same person, thus anticipating by several hundred years Bonet's (1684) "folie mania mélancolique" and Falret's (1854) "folie circulaire." It remained for Kraepelin, however, in 1899, to introduce the term manic-depressive psychosis and to clarify the clinical picture. Kraepelin described the disorder as a series of attacks of elation and depression, with periods of relative normality in between and a generally favorable prognosis.

Bipolar disorder is distinguished from major depression by at least one episode of mania; it is classified as depressive, manic, or mixed, according to the predominant pattern. Even though a patient is exhibiting only manic features, it is assumed that in fact a bipolar disorder exists. Substantial manic or mixed patterns are much less common than the depressive pattern.

The features of the depressive form of bipolar disorder are clinically indistinguishable from those of major depression (Perris, 1982), and we will therefore not describe them in detail here. The essential difference is that these depressive episodes alternate with manic ones, either closely or separated by intervals of relatively normal functioning.

As in the case of the relationship between depressive symptoms of major depression and of cyclothymia, manic symptoms in bipolar disorder tend to be extreme forms of the symptoms associated with the hypomanic phase of cyclothymia. A person who experiences a manic episode has a markedly elevated, euphoric, and expansive mood, often interrupted by occasional outbursts of irritability or even violence—particularly when others refuse to go along with the manic person's antics and schemes. A notable increase in activity occurs, which may appear as an unrelievable restlessness. Mental activity, too, speeds up, so that the individual may evidence a "flight of ideas" and may experience thoughts that "race" through the brain. High levels of verbal output in speech or in writing are common features. Inflated self-esteem is a constant element and at the severe level becomes frankly delusional, so that the person harbors feelings of enormous grandeur and power. The person sleeps only briefly, and in extreme cases hardly at all. Typically, personal and cultural inhibitions loosen, and the individual may indulge in foolish ventures, ignore personal hygiene, make crude and inappropriate sexual advances, or otherwise indicate contempt for conventional restraints and standards of conduct.

The following conversation illustrates a manic episode of moderate severity. The patient is a 46-year-old woman.

During a manic episode, Rodney, shown here, drove his car 120 miles per hour, hit two cars, crashed, stripped off his clothes, and began preaching to passing traffic, thinking he was Christ. He now controls his bipolar disorder with lithium and group therapy.

Doctor: *Hello, how are you today?*
Patient: *Fine, fine, and how are you, Doc? You're looking pretty good. I never felt better in my life. Could I go for a schnapps now. Say, you're new around here, I never saw you before—and not bad! How's about you and me stepping out tonight if I can get that sour old battleship of a nurse to give me back my dress. It's low cut and it'll wow 'em. Even in this old rag, all the doctors give me the eye. You know I'm a model. Yep, I was number one—used to dazzle them in New York, London, and Paris. Hollywood has been angling with me for a contract.*
Doctor: *Is that what you did before you came here?*
Patient: *I was a society queen . . . entertainer of kings and presidents. I've got five grown sons and I wore out three husbands getting them . . . about ready for a couple of more now. There's no woman like me, smart, brainy, beautiful, and sexy. You can see I don't believe in playing myself down. If you are good and know you're good you have to speak out, and I know what I've got.*
Doctor: *Why are you in this hospital?*
Patient: *That's just the trouble. My husbands never could understand me. I was too far above them. I need someone like me with savoir faire you know, somebody that can get around, intelli-*

gent, lots on the ball. Say, where can I get a schnapps around here—always like one before dinner. Someday I'll cook you a meal. I've got special recipes like you never ate before . . . sauces, wines, desserts. Boy, it's making me hungry. Say, have you got anything for me to do around here? I've been showing these slowpokes how to make up beds but I want something more in line with my talents.*
Doctor: *What would you like to do?*
Patient: *Well, I'm thinking of organizing a show, singing, dancing, jokes. I can do it all myself but I want to know what you think about it. I'll bet there's some schnapps in the kitchen. I'll look around later. You know what we need here . . . a dance at night. I could play the piano, and teach them the latest steps. Wherever I go I'm the life of the party.*

This case is particularly illustrative of the inflated self-esteem characteristic of a manic individual. The erotic suggestiveness and impatience with routine seen here are also common features of manic episodes.

The following case description is interesting in its simultaneous and interactive portrayal of two manic patients, one severely disturbed and the other less so. The former, in particular, provides an illustration of the extreme excitement that can occur during a manic episode. The scene is the courtyard of a public mental hospital in the days prior to the advent of effective antimanic medication.

A manic patient had climbed upon the small platform in the middle of the yard and was delivering an impassioned lecture to a number of patients sitting on benches surrounding the platform. Most of the audience were depressed patients who were hallucinating and muttering to themselves and not paying a bit of attention to the speaker. The speaker, however, had an "assistant" in the form of another manic patient who would move rapidly around the circle of benches shaking the occupants and exhorting them to pay attention. If anyone started to leave, the assistant would plump him or her back in a seat in no uncertain terms. In the background were a number of apparently schizophrenic patients who were pacing a given number of steps back and forth, and beyond was a high wire fence surrounding the yard.

The speaker herself was in a state of delirious mania. She had torn her clothing to shreds and was singing and shouting at the top of her voice. So rapidly did her thoughts move from one topic to another that her "speech" was almost a complete word hash, although occasional sentences such as "You goddamn bitches" and "God loves everybody, do you hear?" could be made out. These points were illustrated by wild gestures, screaming, and outbursts of song. In the delivery of her talk, she moved restlessly back and forth on the platform, occasionally falling off the platform in her wild excitement. Her ankles and legs were bleeding from rubbing the edge of the platform during these falls, but she was completely oblivious of her injuries.

Fortunately, the degree of excitement in manic disorders can now be markedly reduced by various drugs, and scenes such as this need no longer occur. The typical stages in a manic episode are summarized in *HIGHLIGHT 11.2.*

Bipolar disorder, like major depression, is typically an intermittent or episodic phenomenon, although with both forms of disorder a relatively small number of patients who otherwise meet diagnostic criteria remain disturbed over long periods of time, even years, and sometimes despite the successive application of all the standard treatment techniques. It is not known whether or not these "refractory" cases represent fundamentally different psychopathological entities (Akiskal & Simmons, 1985).

The diagnostic subcategories for bipolar disorder—mixed, manic, and depressed—refer to particular, present episodes. The latter two of these are self-explanatory; the "mixed" is something of an anomaly. Mixed cases are those in which the full symptomatic picture of both manic and depressive episodes occur, either intermixed or alternating every few days. Such cases do indeed occur, although they are rare.

As we have seen, a person who appears to be depressed cannot be diagnosed as bipolar unless he or she has exhibited at least one manic episode in the past. This means that many people with bipolar disorder whose initial episode or episodes are depressive in nature will be misdiagnosed, at least at the outset and possibly (if no manic episodes are observed) throughout their lives. On the other hand, misdiagnosis is automatically prevented if a person presents distinctly manic symptoms: by DSM-III-R definition, this would be a bipolar disorder, even though some researchers have noted the probable existence of a unipolar type of manic disorder (Andreasen, 1982; Nurnberger et al., 1979). The sometimes arbitrary nature of diagnosis is quite clear in this instance.

People affected with a bipolar disorder seem in many ways to be even more unfortunate than those who suffer from recurrent major depression. On average, they have their first episode at a younger age (25–30 versus 40–45); they suffer from more episodes during their lifetimes (although these episodes tend to be about a month shorter in duration); and they have a substantially higher mortality rate from suicide and other "unnatural" causes (Perris, 1982). The long-term outcomes for the two forms of disorder, however, do not appear to differ greatly, and the probabilities of "full recovery" (that is, being symptom-free for a period of five years) are about equally discouraging—about 40 percent (Coryell & Winokur, 1982). In one recent follow-up study of 73 hospitalized manic patients, 40 percent of them had experienced another manic episode within 1.7 years after discharge, many of them in spite of maintenance lithium therapy (Harrow et al., 1990).

In contrast to the gender neutrality of most types of maladaptive behavior, mood disorders at all levels of severity are more prevalent among women than among men, at a ratio approaching two-to-one overall (Wing & Bebbington, 1985). Though this gender discrepancy is quite marked in the case of major depression, it is less but still discernible for bipolar disorder (Boyd & Weissman, 1982). The diminished discrepancy in bipolar disorder may be related to an apparent tendency for specifically manic episodes to occur less frequently in females (Angst, 1980).

In any event, the finding of a sex differential may have considerable theoretical importance. At

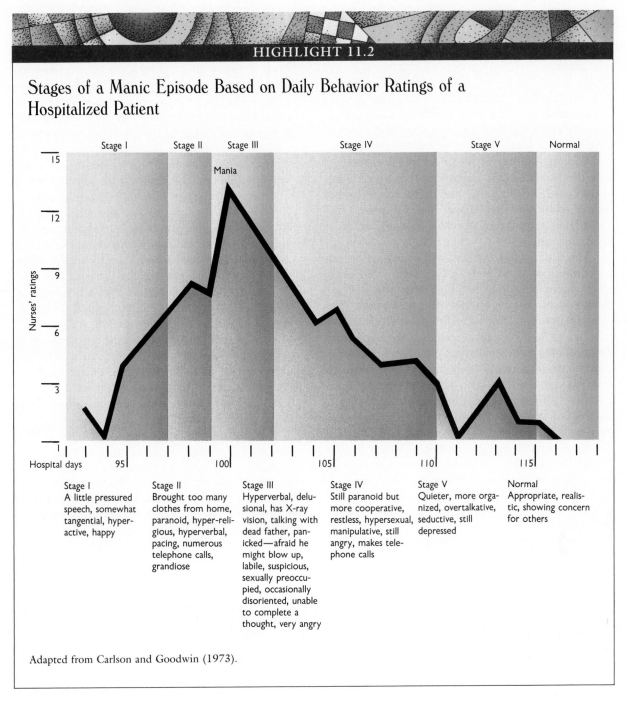

HIGHLIGHT 11.2

Stages of a Manic Episode Based on Daily Behavior Ratings of a Hospitalized Patient

Stage I
A little pressured speech, somewhat tangential, hyperactive, happy

Stage II
Brought too many clothes from home, paranoid, hyper-religious, hyperverbal, pacing, numerous telephone calls, grandiose

Stage III
Hyperverbal, delusional, has X-ray vision, talking with dead father, panicked—afraid he might blow up, labile, suspicious, sexually preoccupied, occasionally disoriented, unable to complete a thought, very angry

Stage IV
Still paranoid but more cooperative, restless, hypersexual, manipulative, still angry, makes telephone calls

Stage V
Quieter, more organized, overtalkative, seductive, still depressed

Normal
Appropriate, realistic, showing concern for others

Adapted from Carlson and Goodwin (1973).

least with respect to unipolar depression, the discrepancy appears to be neither artifactual nor a product of differential psychosocial advantage for men versus women (Amenson & Lewinsohn, 1981; Nolen-Hoeksema, 1987). Though women, especially married ones, frequently report a greater sense of well-being than men (Wood, Rhodes, & Whelan, 1989), they are also for some reason much more prone to experience repeated depressive attacks. It appears that women have more extreme reactions at both ends of this continuum than do men. In fact being unmarried, employed, and without young

children at home are factors that may *reduce* female risk for depression (Wing & Bebbington, 1985). The latter factors would seem to implicate the traditional feminine gender role as possibly pathogenic for depression. This gender role may also contribute to a tendency to ruminate about problems rather than to find ways of distracting oneself from them, as males are more prone to do. The former mode of coping tends to encourage depressive reactions and to be far more common in women than in men (Morrow & Nolen-Hoeksema, 1990; Nolen-Hoeksema, 1987). Although this line of thought is intriguing and consistent with much evidence, we cannot rule out a biological contribution at this time; neither, however, can we positively confirm it.

Schizoaffective Disorder   Occasionally, clinicians are confronted with a patient whose mood disorder is the equal of anything seen in the major depressive or bipolar disorders but whose mental and cognitive processes are so deranged as to suggest the presence of a *schizophrenic* psychosis (see Chapter 12). Such cases are quite likely to be diagnosed as **schizoaffective disorder** under the DSM-III-R category of *psychotic disorders not elsewhere classified*.

The often severe disturbances of psychological functioning seen in these cases, such as mood-incongruent delusions and hallucinations, are indeed reminiscent of schizophrenic phenomena. Unlike schizophrenia, however, the schizoaffective pattern tends to be highly episodic, with a good prognosis for individual attacks and with relatively lucid periods between episodes. The traditional view has also been that schizoaffective patients have a relatively good prognosis for full recovery under the five-year criterion. Recently published follow-up data on these patients, however, cast considerable doubt on such a benign outlook (Coryell et al., 1990a, 1990b). The following case illustrates the mixed picture one sees in this type of disorder:

The patient, Mr. Nehru, is a 32-year-old single, unemployed male who is hospitalized for the fourth time in approximately five years, each episode having had essentially the same features. On interview he is markedly euphoric in mood and his speech is so rapid it is hard to follow. He does much pacing on the hospital ward, where he appears preoccupied with certain religious insights involving the idea that he is the new Messiah—in fact some sort of combination of Jesus, Moses, Vishnu, and Krishna. "Voices" repeatedly confirm to him this extraordinary new identity. His attempts to explain the new religion to others are interrupted by irrelevant distractions that momentarily capture his attention, such as the color match of a doctor's shirt and tie. When limits are placed on his excessively enthusiastic and intrusive behavior, he becomes loud and angry. He states that the hospital is part of a conspiracy to suppress his promulgation of the new religious order, which God has directly inspired him to do.

A native of India, Mr. Nehru migrated to the United States at the age of 13. Recently he had been living with his brother and sister-in-law, who report that his behavior had begun to deteriorate some four weeks prior to hospitalization. Specifically, he was waking up his brother at all hours of the night to discuss religious matters, and he had stopped bathing or changing his clothes. His rehospitalization was precipitated when neighbors complained that he was harassing them in the street with his religious messages.

Mr. Nehru admits that he has been troubled by voices, which he has been hearing throughout the day almost continuously for about five years. Several different voices comment, generally without evaluation, on his ongoing behavior, discussing him in the third person. On occasion they have become insulting, suggesting that he is a fool or a person of limited understanding. The patient states that he is unable to work at a regular job because the voices distract him and prevent him from concentrating on the work to be done. He thus appears to be significantly dysfunctional even in the interludes between his more flagrant episodes.

Between these episodes the patient is described by others as a quiet and somewhat withdrawn person with no remarkable mood deviations. While he reads occasionally, he rarely watches television because of a conviction that television programs often make direct reference to him and his affairs; these references upset him. He is popular in the neighborhood because of his habit of offering help to elderly people in such matters as shopping and yard work.

(Adapted from Spitzer et al., 1989, pp. 64–65)

Mr. Nehru's case actually has an interesting diagnostic twist. Between episodes he meets DSM criteria for schizophrenia, chiefly because of his prominent nonmood-related hallucinations. Within episodes, on the other hand, he consistently presents a classically manic picture that would yield an unqualified diagnosis of bipolar disorder were his interepisode behavior unremarkable or unknown.

As the common diagnostic perplexities of the above case may suggest, the diagnosis of schizoaffective disorder is a controversial one. Some clinicians believe these individuals are basically schizophrenic; others believe they are suffering primarily from mood disorder psychoses; and still others consider their affliction a distinct entity unto itself (Lehmann, 1985). The suggestion that a person might be both schizophrenic and mood disordered concurrently is not generally accepted, apparently owing to the belief that reliability of diagnosis will suffer without sharp discriminations among Axis I disorders. Of course, by attempting to ensure reliability here, we may well be sacrificing validity. It does not strike us as unreasonable to suppose that the co-occurrence of two or more psychiatric disorders is in fact a rather common phenomenon.

■ Causal Factors in Mood Disorders

In considering the development of major mood disorders, we again find it useful to examine the possible roles of biological, psychosocial, and sociocultural factors.

Biological Factors   A biological basis for severe manic and depressive disorders is suggested by the fact that, once a disorder is underway, it often seems to become relatively autonomous until it runs its course or is interrupted by drugs or other interventions. Attempts to establish a biological basis for these disorders have run the familiar gamut from genetic and constitutional factors through neurophysiological and biochemical alterations. Even various related considerations, such as disturbances in the normal cycles of brain activity during sleep or the seasonal variations in ambient light and darkness, have been implicated.

Hereditary predisposition.   The incidence of mood disorders is considerably higher among the blood relatives of individuals with clinically diagnosed mood disorders than in the population at large. Because of the difficulties of disentangling hereditary and environmental influences, however, mere familial concordance can never in itself be taken as conclusive proof of genetic causation. In an early study, Slater (1944) found that approximately 15 percent of the brothers, sisters, parents, and children of "manic-depressive" patients had developed the same disorder, as compared to an expectancy of about 0.5 percent for the general population.

Kallmann (1958) found the concordance rate for these disorders to be much higher for identical than for fraternal twins. Other studies have supported these earlier findings (Mendlewicz, 1985; Perris, 1979).

Twin-based studies such as those just cited have proven useful in many areas of psychological research. Various difficulties with the twin method, however, make it problematic to draw reliable conclusions from them about genetic factors. Among the most basic problems is the fact that identical twins (because they are of the same gender and share similar physical characteristics and appearances, such as physical attractiveness) are likely to *create* more similar environmental reactions to themselves than are fraternal twins or people having any other type of familial relationship. Hence high concordance in psychopathological outcome could as much reflect environmental as genetic commonalities.

Recognition of the inherent problems of twin-based studies led a number of years ago to the *adoption method* of genetic research. This method involves the psychiatric evaluation of people who were adopted out of their biological families at an early age and the comparison of their disorders with those of their biological and adoptive family members. If a predisposition to develop a given disorder is inheritable, it should show up (so the logic goes) more often among biological, as opposed to adoptive, relatives of the affected adoptees.

Of the limited number of adoption studies on mood disorders published thus far, the most adequate is one contributed by Wender et al. (1986). Beginning with Danish samples of 71 mood-disordered subjects and 71 matched normal control adoptees, the close biological and adoptive relatives of these individuals were independently assessed for psychiatric status. With respect to major mood disorders (that is, major depression and bipolar disorder), unipolar depression was eight times more likely to occur among the biological relatives of the depressed subjects as compared with control cases; suicide was fifteen times more likely among biological relatives. By any standard, these are impressive figures.

Based on statistics like these, the case for some hereditary contribution in the causal patterns of at least the major mood disorders is quite strong. The risk for blood relatives of people with bipolar disorders (including an enhanced risk for unipolar disorder) appears to be greater than for relatives of people who suffer from unipolar disorders (Mendlewicz, 1985), but this may merely reflect the likelihood that unipolar disorder is a more diffuse and heterogeneous category (Carson & Carson, 1984). Some researchers have suggested a genetic connection between mood and anxiety disorders, especially agoraphobia and panic disorder (Breier, Charney, & Heninger, 1984; Weissman et al., 1984). A relationship may indeed exist here with the finding that panic attacks are sometimes successfully treated with antidepressant drugs (Stewart et al., 1985).

The incidence of mood disorders is considerably higher among the blood relatives of individuals with clinically diagnosed mood disorders than in the population at large. This family has a history of bipolar disorder spanning four generations, from a woman to her daughter, granddaughter, and a great-grandson, who was diagnosed at only three years of age.

The disproportionately high number of female cases of mood disorder has been cited by some as evidence for genetic predisposition. On the basis of findings indicating higher concordance among female than male members of families, Winokur, Clayton, and Reich (1969) proposed that the gene or genes in question might be located on the X chromosome. If this were universally true, there would be no evidence of father-to-son transmission, because the X chromosome in males can only be inherited from the mother. The investigators in this early study found precisely this anomaly. Since then, however, numerous cases of apparent father-to-son transmission have been reported. The overall picture, reviewed by Nurnberger and Gershon (1982), has thus become somewhat murky and includes at least one confirmation of the Winokur et al. father-son anomaly (Mendlewicz, 1980, 1985). As of this writing, the question remains unresolved.

Finally, we should mention recent work on genetic linkage studies and attempts by gene mapping techniques to locate the chromosomal site of the purportedly implicated gene or genes. One such study, which was widely reported in the popular press several years ago, presented what appeared to be compelling evidence for genetic transmission of a bipolar disorder diathesis. The population involved was the tightly knit Amish community of Lancaster County in southern Pennsylvania (Egeland et al., 1987). Identifying 32 active cases of bipolar disorder in this community of 12,500 members, all of them descendants of a small number of couples immigrating to the area in the early eighteenth century, the investigators were able to document, for *every* case, instances of the disorder in ancestors going back several generations. The 26 documented cases of suicide occurring since 1880 were all traced to just *four* families. Perhaps most importantly, the gene involved was traced to a specific region on chromosome 11, using rather complicated recombinant DNA techniques. Some 63 percent of individuals carrying this gene were said to show at least minimal signs of the disorder.

Reactions to the publication of this study constitute a veritable case history in the premature acceptance of preliminary scientific findings. In fact two other studies (Detera-Wadleigh et al., 1987; Hodkinson et al., 1987) published in the same issue of the same journal in which the Egeland et al. (1987) study was published presented data contradicting the notion of a single gene locus for bipolar disorder. These discrepant studies were almost uniformly ignored at the time by both the media and numerous professional commentators. In any event, it is now clear that daunting methodological problems must be overcome before we can look forward to the effective use of genetic linkage studies to identify specific genes for bipolar disorder, or indeed *any* of the mood disorders (Merikangas, Spence, & Kupfer, 1989). Most importantly, linkage studies are highly dependent on the existence of homogeneous diagnostic groupings. Of the various mood disorders, bipolar disorder is doubtless the best candidate for study in this respect; unfortunately, the precision with which it can at present be delineated appears to fall short of the requirements of this approach.

Overall, no consistent support exists for any specific mode of genetic transmission of the mood disorders, according to a recent comprehensive review by Faraone, Kremen, and Tsuang (1990). These authors do note, however, the continuing possibility of an X-chromosome-linked variant of bipolar disorder.

Biochemical factors. Kraepelin considered manic-depressive psychoses to be toxic, and a good deal of research effort has been directed toward finding possible metabolic alterations and pathologic brain chemistry in individuals with these disorders. Increasingly prominent since the 1960s has been the view that depression and mania both may arise from disruptions in the delicate balance of biochemical substances that regulate and mediate the activity of the brain's nerve cells, or neurons. Certain of these substances, called *neurotransmitters,* mediate the transfer of nerve impulses across the synaptic cleft from one neuron to the next one in a particular neuronal pathway. Emitted by the activated presynaptic neuron, neurotransmitters may either stimulate or inhibit the firing of the next neuron in the chain.

A growing body of evidence suggests that various biological therapies often used to treat severe mood disorders—such as electroconvulsive therapy, potent antidepressant drugs, and lithium carbonate—may affect the concentrations of transmitter substances at the synapse and thus determine the extent to which particular brain pathways are relatively volatile or sluggish in conducting messages. In fact the largely happenstance discovery of these treatments (particularly the antidepressant drugs) and the growing understanding of how they work are what encouraged and now sustain the dominant biochemical conceptions of the etiology of the major mood disorders. They are due, according to this general view, to faulty communication between neurons, caused by disruption of the transmission process.

A bit of history is in order here. Early attention in the 1960s and 1970s focused on two substances of the monoamine class, *norepinephrine* and *5-hydroxytryptamine* (also known as serotonin), because researchers observed that antidepressant medication had the uniform effect of increasing their concentrations at synaptic junctions. This observation led to the theory that depression was due to a depletion and mania to an excess of one or both of these neurotransmitters. It is now clear, based on the known complexity of brain biochemical functioning, that no such straightforward mechanism is

likely to provide the answers we need (Thase, Frank, & Kupfer, 1985; Zis & Goodwin, 1982). Unfortunately, the demise of this theory has not been accompanied by the introduction of a compelling alternative. Recently, research attention in this area has been shifting to a concern with possibly abnormal receptor systems (that is, the large molecules on a postsynaptic neuron to which neurotransmitters bearing the appropriate chemical codes selectively bond) in the major mood disorders (McNeal & Cimbolic, 1986; Sedvall et al., 1986). The yield from such studies, however, as yet provides no firm etiological conclusions.

Though biochemical approaches have not thus far established the case for a primary biological role in the causation of major mood disorders, as many had hoped, biological causation in general remains a viable hypothesis. The case rests essentially on three facts that are beyond reasonable dispute: (a) a predisposition to these disorders may be genetically transmitted; (b) the behavioral symptoms of the disorders often abate promptly with certain biological interventions; and (c) certain profound alterations of bodily function, such as changes in the sleep cycle, often accompany the affective symptoms.

Neurophysiologic and neuroendocrine factors. A collateral goal of biochemical researchers has been to identify subtypes of mood disorder within this heterogeneous domain by establishing differences in treatment effectiveness for different drugs having known effects on various biological systems (e.g., Akiskal, 1979). The success of this line of investigation has so far not been especially impressive. To an extent in fact it has even been overshadowed by developments in other areas of biological research, notably the possible neurophysiologic and neuroendocrine (hormonal) correlates of some distinguishable forms of mood disorder (Thase, Frank, & Kupfer, 1985). For example, it is now clear that some depressed people show disturbances in their electroencephalographic (brain-wave) sleep rhythms, especially in an abnormally brief delay in onset of REM sleep (sleep characterized by rapid eye movements, as well as other organismic changes).

These findings on electroencephalographic indicators of sleep irregularities may be related to a growing body of evidence that some mood disorders are to an extent under seasonal control—that is, that they are responsive to the total quantity of available light in the environment (Rosenthal et al., 1984). More specifically, these individuals, said to have *seasonal affective disorder* (SAD), tend to be depressed in the fall and winter and normal or even hypomanic in the spring and summer (Wehr et al.,

1986). The DSM-III-R acknowledges such seasonal effects by requiring the designation *seasonal pattern,* where appropriate, as a supplement to the diagnosis of bipolar disorder or recurrent major depression. No specification of particular seasons need be involved, however; this appears to have been a wise omission, because it is now known that a minority of SAD patients are reactive to summer rather than winter conditions (Kasper et al., 1989; Wehr & Rosenthal, 1989), a fact that complicates etiologic speculation.

Studies evaluating the potential therapeutic use of controlled exposure to light, even artificial light, for patients with a winter SAD pattern have shown considerable promise (Blehar & Rosenthal, 1989; James et al., 1985; Rosenthal et al., 1984, 1986; Sack et al., 1990; Wehr et al., 1986). In fact a small industry has already developed around the production and sale of therapeutic lighting devices. Though the phenomenon appears genuine and reliable, just how therapeutic light works remains shrouded in controversy (Blehar & Rosenthal, 1989).

With the modern technology of positron emission tomography (PET) scans, it has even proven possible to visualize an anticipated variation in brain metabolic rates, subnormal to supernormal, for depressed and manic states, respectively (Baxter et al., 1985). Findings in this physiological area tend to be scattered, however, and have not yet yielded a coherent conceptual integration or meaning.

Ideas about hormonal influences on mood have a long history. Contemporary thinking (e.g., Stokes & Sikes, 1987) in this area has focused on the hypothalamus-pituitary-adrenocortical influence chain, and in particular on the hormone *cortisol,* which is excreted by the cortex (covering mantle) of the adrenal glands. Blood plasma levels of this substance are known to be elevated in from 50 to 75 percent of seriously depressed patients, suggesting a possible clue of etiological significance. Even more intriguing, however, is the finding that a potent suppressor of plasma cortisol in normal individuals, *dexamethasone,* either fails entirely to suppress or fails to sustain suppression in one- to two-thirds of seriously depressed patients.

These findings, in themselves essentially undisputed, have given rise to the widespread use of the dexamethasone suppression test (DST) in assessing depressed individuals. From this point, however, the issues become murkier. It has been suggested that DST nonsuppressor patients constitute a distinct subgroup among depressed individuals,

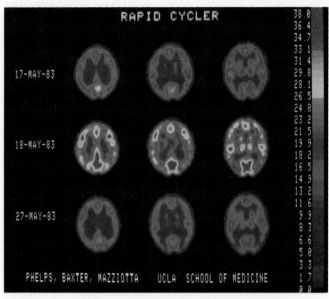

Shown here are positron emission tomographic (PET) scans of identical planes of the brain of a rapid-cycling bipolar patient. The top and bottom sets of planes were obtained on days in which the patient was depressed; the middle set was obtained on a hypomaniac day. Colors of scans correspond to glucose (sugar) metabolic rates in the respective brain areas, the reds and yellows representing high rates and the blues and greens lows.

namely the group sometimes referred to as having the "endogenous" or melancholic form of depression (Carroll, 1982; Kalin et al., 1981). Considerable evidence shows that nonsuppression is in fact correlated with clinical severity and retarded response to treatment (Arana, Baldessarini, & Ornsteen 1985). Also, depressed nonsuppressor patients tend to be older, have better premorbid histories, and have been subject to fewer prior stressors of the more obvious sort than those who show suppression (Zimmerman, Coryell, & Pfohl, 1986). As reviewed by Thase et al. (1985), however, numerous other groups of psychiatric patients exhibit high rates of nonsuppression, calling into question the specificity and hence ultimate diagnostic utility of the DST.

The accuracy, reliability, and validity of the DST are subject to numerous variables that are difficult to control. Ritchie et al. (1985), for example, suggested that many of the conflicting results reported may be traced to poor assessment techniques for estimating plasma cortisol levels. Meanwhile, other reports (e.g., Uhde, Bierer, & Post, 1985) show that cortisol nonsuppression may be due to excessive coffee consumption. It is also possible that nonsuppression is merely a nonspecific indicator of generalized mental distress, an idea supported by the finding that it occurs somewhat routinely in baboons who are socially subordinate (Sapolsky, 1989). As of this writing, the jury is still out on the question of the DST's ultimate value, particularly as it relates to the question of etiology. In their comprehensive review, Arana et al. (1985) cautioned against either excessive enthusiasm or excessive skepticism regarding this line of research. Though this still seems good advice, enthusiasm for the hypothesis has in fact diminished appreciably in the interim.

Psychosocial Factors   Growing awareness of biological factors in the etiology of affective disorders does not, of course, imply that psychosocial factors are irrelevant. In Chapter 4, we outlined various ways in which biological influences may interact with life experience to produce an observed behavior. In the present case, evidence for an important psychological element in most mood disorders is at least as strong as evidence for biological factors. Most likely, then, we are dealing with a complex interaction between the two.

Stress as a causal factor.   In Chapter 7, we learned something of the ways in which psychosocial stressors may lead to altered bodily functioning. We are now in a position to suggest that such stressors may also affect biochemical balances and other conditions in the brain, at least in predisposed people. Barchas and his colleagues (1978), in a summary of research in this area, suggest that psychosocial stressors may cause long-term changes in brain functioning and that these changes may play a role in the development of mood disorders. Essentially the same point has been made by other leading researchers in the field, notably Akiskal (1979) and Kupfer (Thase, Frank, & Kupfer, 1985).

There is no basic incompatibility between biochemical and psychosocial approaches to understanding the mood disorders. In fact, evidence of interactions between biological and psychosocial factors of the kind described here represent a breakthrough of enormous importance in enhancing our understanding of the age-old problem of mind-body interaction. At the same time, this evidence should not blind us to the probability that in some mood disturbances—certainly the milder ones—the contribution of an abnormal biological factor will turn out to be minimal or nonexistent. Pertinent here is the fact that the biological forms of treatment are typically of no value in such conditions. We have also seen that the milder depressions almost always have clear stressor antecedents; the

occurrence of depression following significant losses, for instance, would seem understandable on psychological grounds alone—without the postulation of extraordinary changes in the brain's physical state.

In the case of the more severe mood disorders, too, many investigators, as already noted, have been impressed with the high incidence of aversive life events that apparently serve as precipitating factors. Harder et al. (1989) in fact found no difference between more and less severely depressed patients in regard to the magnitude of prior life stressors. Beck (1967) provided a broad classification of the most frequently encountered precipitating circumstances in depression: (a) situations that tend to lower self-esteem; (b) the thwarting of an important goal or the posing of an insoluble dilemma; (c) a physical disease or abnormality that activates ideas of deterioration or death; (d) single stressors of overwhelming magnitude; (e) several stressors occurring in a series; and (f) insidious stressors unrecognized as such by an affected person.

Paykel (1982b) comprehensively reviewed the earlier literature on life events occurring before episodes of mood disorder and arrived at conclusions generally in agreement with Beck's. In particular, and perhaps not surprisingly, separations from people important in one's life (through death, for example) are strongly associated with the emergence of depressive states, although such losses tend to precede other types of disorder as well. A more recent study by Phifer & Murrell (1986) involving older people (ages 55 and over) confirmed that loss events were associated with the onset of depression but pointed to health problems and minimal sources of social support as having even greater depression-inducing effects in this group.

It may be noted in connection with the last-mentioned finding that the nature of depression-inducing stressors is likely to change over a lifetime, conforming with changing levels of exposure to them and with changing beliefs as to which interests and concerns are more and less vital. Stressors are also likely to differ within age ranges depending on values, needs, personality characteristics, and the like. Hammen et al. (1989), for example, showed that "autonomous" unipolar depressives were more reactive to negative events involving issues of achievement, whereas their more "sociotropic" counterparts reacted mostly to negative events in their relationships with others.

Research data on life events preceding specifically manic attacks are contradictory and inconclusive (Dunner & Hall, 1980). *HIGHLIGHT 11.3*

Stressors Preceding Severe Depression

In an intensive study of 40 depressed patients, Leff, Roatch, and Bunney (1970) found that each patient had been subjected to multiple stressful events prior to early symptoms and to a clustering of such events during the month preceding the actual breakdown in functioning. The chart shows the ten types of stressors most frequently involved.

Strikingly similar to the findings of Leff and her associates are those of Paykel (1973). In this study, which involved 185 depressed patients, it was found that comparable stressful events preceded the onset of the depressive breakdown. In order of significance, these events were categorized as (a) marital difficulties, (b) work moves or changes in work

conditions, (c) serious personal illness, and (d) death or serious illness of an immediate family member. Paykel's (1982) more recent review of findings in this area is generally confirmatory.

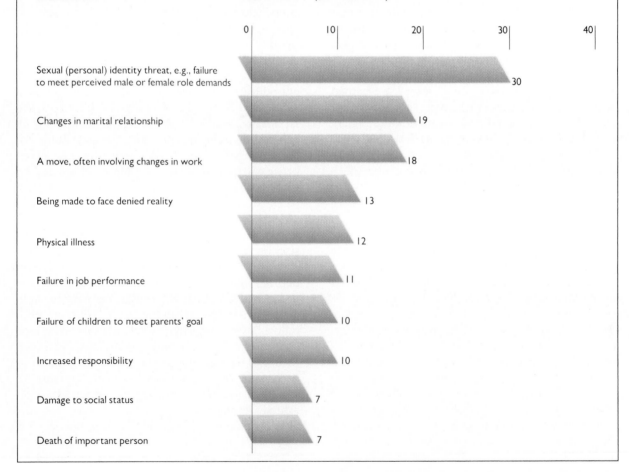

Stressful Event   Patients Affected (from Total of 40)

Stressful Event	Patients Affected
Sexual (personal) identity threat, e.g., failure to meet perceived male or female role demands	30
Changes in marital relationship	19
A move, often involving changes in work	18
Being made to face denied reality	13
Physical illness	12
Failure in job performance	11
Failure of children to meet parents' goal	10
Increased responsibility	10
Damage to social status	7
Death of important person	7

summarizes the stressors that had most often preceded severe depression in one study. An interesting example of the apparent role of aversive life events as precipitating causes in alternating bipolar attacks has been described by Hartmann (1968):

A patient had six severe manic episodes between the ages of 44 and 59, all of which required hospitalization. The patient also had a number of depressive episodes, two of which required hospitalization. Typically this patient tended to be overactive in his general functioning, but during the early autumn he usually either ran for a political office himself or took an active role in someone else's campaign. In the process, he would become increasingly manic; when the ventures led to defeat—which they almost invariably did—he would become depressed in November or December.

Some descriptions of major mood disorders imply that they typically occur *de novo*—out of the blue, so to speak—in the absence of either notable personal distress or significant psychosocial antecedents. This implies that such episodes must be *endogenous*—caused entirely from within—rather than precipitated by life events and circumstances. The idea of endogenous causation is more compatible with the currently strong biomedical model, although instances of major disorder with substantial "situational" components are, as we have seen, quite routine (e.g., Hirschfeld et al., 1985). Because the issue is an important one, we will take a closer look at the evidence to the contrary.

Estimates of the proportion of significant mood disorders that are preceded by precipitating stressors vary from almost none (Winokur & Pitts, 1964) to almost all (Leff, Roatch, & Bunney, 1970; Paykel, 1973). In general, studies that adhere most closely to meticulous background search (e.g., Leff et al., 1970) tend to produce the highest estimates of antecedent stress. A rigorously conducted study of 409 matched pairs of normal and unipolar depressive subjects by Billings, Cronkite, and Moos (1983) provides convincing evidence not only of a greater frequency of prior stressor "events" but also of more chronic sources of psychosocial strain in the depressed group. The "spontaneous" occurrence of mood disorders seems to be at best an infrequent phenomenon, and even where that seems to be the case, we may have overlooked a stressor that was not obvious.

If we take the position—and the available research data seem to justify doing so—that some people are constitutionally more prone than others to develop mood disorders, then it would seem reasonable to suppose that such high-risk individuals would react more intensely to subtle, easily overlooked stressors than would individuals less at risk for these disorders. In addition, if a threshold exists beyond which biological factors play an important role in increasing the intensity of progres-

sive mood deviation, then these high-risk, low-stress cases would exhibit relatively severe symptoms. Unfortunately, there are no data that permit us to evaluate this hypothesis directly and unequivocally.

Predisposing personality and cognitive characteristics.   Beck (1967) argues convincingly that psychosocial stressors provoke severe depressive reactions only in people who already have a negative cognitive set, consisting of negative views of the self, the world, and the future. According to this hypothesis, a stressor merely serves to activate negative cognitions that have heretofore been dormant. The result is an abnormally extreme negative affect. Obviously, Beck's "negative cognitive set" is in the nature of a psychological predisposing variable.

Among factors that might be expected to produce such an underlying negativity would be early parental loss (through death or permanent separation), which Beck in fact reported in his original patient series. Scattered confirmations (and an occasional disconfirmation) of this observation have occurred in research and clinical literature going back many years. Two additional confirmations of a link between adult depression and childhood parental loss have more recently been reported by Barnes and Prosen (1985) and Roy (1985). The weight of evidence appears rather strongly on the positive association side, suggesting that such loss leaves in its wake a long-lasting vulnerability to depression for some individuals. Parental loss through suicide doubtless adds an additional layer of problems for child survivors. Though systematic research on this subject is lacking, moving accounts of the effects of parental suicide on children have recently been presented by Lukas and Seiden (1990), the first author having been himself exposed to such trauma.

We might also expect that exaggerated mood swings in a child would be fostered by observations of similar emotional patterns in his or her parents, and that such behavior would then persist as learned maladaptive response patterns. The high incidence of mood disorders in the families of manic and depressive patients provided greater than average opportunity for such learning.

In their study of 14 depressed children, Poznanski and Zrull (1970) reported that five of the children's parents were depressed at the time of the child's referral; one father had committed suicide, apparently during an episode of depression. Beardslee et al. (1983) and Puig-Antich et al. (1989) have confirmed that parental depression puts children at high risk for many problems, but especially for depression. Finally, Keller et al. (1986) have reported a study on 72 children from families in which at least one parent had a severe mood disorder but no other psychosis. They found that the severity and chronicity of the parents' (especially the mothers') disorders were uniformly associated with adaptive failure and psychiatric diagnoses, including depression, among the children. Of course, a confirmed skeptic could argue that studies such as these merely prove that these disorders are genetically transmitted, but such an argument strains credulity. It seems more likely, in the light of current knowledge, that psychosocial influences would be the deciding factor in such cases, with possibly some contribution from a genetically determined vulnerability.

Attempts to delineate a typical personality pattern for adults who later suffer serious mood disorders have met with limited success. In general, however, manic patients—whatever their childhood backgrounds may have been—are described as ambitious, outgoing, energetic, sociable, and often highly successful, both prior to their breakdown and after remission. As contrasted with members of control groups, they tend to place a higher conscious value on achievement, are conventional in their beliefs, and are deeply concerned about what others think of them. Depressive patients share these characteristics, but they appear to be more obsessive, anxious, and self-deprecatory. They also tend to show an unusually rigid conscience development, which prevents the overt expression of hostile feelings and makes them particularly prone to feelings of guilt and self-blame when things go wrong. A recent finding of low premorbid emotional strength and resiliency (Hirschfeld et al., 1989) suggests that predepressive individuals tend not to take an active approach to problem resolution.

People suffering from bipolar disorder—those destined to experience affective swings between mania and depression—might be expected to share the personality characteristics of both groups, perhaps in alternating phases. Depue et al. (1981) present strong evidence suggesting that this is the case. It must be noted, however, that all such findings are subject to numerous qualifications. Many people who exhibit the traits described will never have a serious mood disorder, and many who do not will develop such a disorder.

Feelings of helplessness and loss of hope.   Investigators of widely differing theoretical orientations have emphasized that feelings of helplessness and hopelessness are basic to depressive reactions. In what is considered the classic treatment of the subject, Bibring (1953), a psychoanalyst, held that the basic mechanism of depression is "the ego's

shocking awareness of its helplessness in regard to its aspirations . . . such that the depressed person . . . has lost his incentives and gives up, not the goals, but pursuing them, since this proves to be useless" (p. 39). A sense of hopelessness may be central in the considerable prevalence of depression among the aged (Fry, 1984). Other investigators have referred to "learned helplessness" in severe depression; presumably an individual, perceiving no likelihood that coping efforts will remove the source of stress, eventually stops fighting and gives up (Hiroto & Seligman, 1975; Seligman, 1973, 1975; Weiss, 1974). Recall that a sense of basic inefficacy does seem to characterize the depressed state. As was discussed in Chapter 1, laboratory experiments have identified conditions that can lead to "learned helplessness," but attempts to relate such conditions directly to clinical depression have not fared well.

Feelings of helplessness and hopelessness and their behavioral consequences have been dealt with from an operant learning standpoint by several investigators. Lazarus (1968) concluded that "depression may be regarded as a function of inadequate or insufficient reinforcers . . . some significant reinforcer has been withdrawn" (pp. 84–85). Similarly, Lewinsohn (1974) concluded that feelings of depression—along with other symptoms of this clinical picture—can be elicited when an individual's behavior no longer results in accustomed reinforcement or gratification. The failure to receive "response contingent positive reinforcement" (RCPR) in turn leads to a reduction in effort and activity, thus resulting in even less chance of coping with aversive conditions and achieving need gratification. The question here, however, is not whether depressed people have low rates of RCPR—they certainly do, almost by definition—but rather whether this is a cause or an effect of the depressed state. The evidence, reviewed by Carson and Carson (1984), suggests that it is an effect, thus illustrating once again the hazards of confusing cause with correlation.

Although the behavioristic perspective seems potentially helpful in understanding depressive reactions, it would seem at first glance less applicable to manic reactions. One might speculate, however, that the manic behavior represents attempts to obtain needed reinforcers via an indiscriminate increase in activity level. As in the case of depressive reactions, however, such reinforcers are not forthcoming. Here the conclusion of Ferster (1973) seems applicable: "It seems likely . . . that any factor which causes a temporary or long-term reduction in positively reinforced ways of acting . . . will also produce bizarre or irrational behavior as a byproduct" (p. 859). Not adequately accounted for in this explanation, however, are the feelings of euphoria that characterize manic reactions.

Extreme defenses against stress. Manic and depressive disorders may be viewed as two different but related defense-oriented strategies for dealing with severe stress.

In the case of mania, individuals try to escape their difficulties by a "flight into reality"—that is, they try to avoid the pain of their inner lives through outer world distractions. In less severe form, hypomania, this type of reaction to stress is shown by a person who goes on a round of parties to try to forget a broken love affair or tries to escape from a threatening life situation by restless action, occupying every moment with work, athletics, sexual affairs, and countless other activities—all performed with professed gusto but with little true enjoyment.

In true mania, this pattern is exaggerated. With a tremendous expenditure of energy, a manic individual tries to deny feelings of helplessness and hopelessness and to play a role of domineering competence. Once this mode of coping with difficulties is adopted, it is maintained until it has spent itself in emotional exhaustion, for the only other alternative is an admission of defeat and inevitable depression. This pattern is well brought out in the following case of a moderately disturbed manic patient:

He neglected his meals and rest hours, and was highly irregular, impulsive, and distractible in his adaptations to ward routine. Without apparent intent to be annoying or disturbing he sang, whistled, told pointless off-color stories, visited indiscriminately, and flirted crudely with the nurses and female patients. Superficially he appeared to be in high spirits, and yet one day when he was being gently chided over some particular irresponsible act he suddenly slumped in a chair, covered his face with his hands, began sobbing, and cried, "For Pete's sake, doc, let me be. Can't you see that I've just got to act happy?" (Masserman, 1961, pp. 66-67)

Unfortunately, as manic disorders proceed, any defensive value they may originally have had is negated, for thought processes are speeded up to a point where an individual can no longer process incoming information with any degree of efficiency. In a manner of speaking, the operator loses control of the computer, resulting in behavior that is highly erratic at best and incomprehensible at the extreme.

In the case of depression, a person apparently gains some relief from an intolerable stress situation by admitting defeat and withdrawing psychologically from the fight. Also, the slowing down of thought processes may serve to decrease suffering by reducing the sheer quantity of painful stimuli to be processed. Any such feelings of relief, however, are gained at the expense of a sense of adequacy and self-esteem and thus are accompanied by marked guilt and self-accusation. Like a soldier who panics and flees from combat, a depressed individual may feel relieved to be out of an intolerable situation but may also feel guilty and devalued.

Because depressive patients tend to blame themselves for their difficulties, they often go over the past with microscopic detail, picking out any possible sins of omission or commission and exaggerating their importance in relation to the present difficulties. They may even accuse themselves of selfishness, unfaithfulness, or acts of hostility that witnesses say did not occur. These self-accusations seem to be attempts to explain and find some meaning for their depression and at the same time achieve some measure of expiation and atonement. The entire process has a certain paradoxical quality: on the one hand, a depressive individual feels unable to determine events that might occur and, on the other hand, tends to accept personal responsibility for all negative events that do occur. Clearly, this pattern requires a degree of cognitive distortion, which is seen even in relatively mild cases.

It may be that the remission of depressive disorders even without treatment occurs because the effort at expiation and atonement has been successful. In such cases, there may be a gradual working through of feelings of unworthiness and guilt in which an individual pays the price for past failures by self-punishment and is thereby cleansed and ready for another go at life.

In bipolar reactions, the shift from mania to depression may tend to occur when the defensive function of the manic reaction breaks down. Similarly, the shift from depression to mania may tend to occur when an individual, devalued and guilt-ridden by inactivity and an inability to cope, finally feels compelled to attempt some countermeasure, however desperate.

Although the view of manic and depressive reactions as extreme defenses seems plausible up to a certain point, it is becoming difficult, as we have seen, to account satisfactorily for the more extreme versions of these states without acknowledging the importance of contributory biological involvement. It seems likely that aberrant biological mechanisms become involved as some level of severity is exceeded, and thereafter the disorder assumes an autonomous course. The effectiveness of biological treatment in alleviating severe episodes lends support to this hypothesis. And yet there remain questions in this area, if only because the impact of manic and depressive behavior on others is so notable and may contribute to the maintenance of this behavior.

Interpersonal effects of mood disorders.   Manic individuals apparently feel that wishing to rely on others or to be taken care of is threatening and unacceptable. Instead, such an individual maintains self-esteem and feelings of adequacy and strength by establishing a social role in which control of other people is possible (Janowsky, El-Yousef, & Davis, 1974).

On the other hand, a depressed individual tends to adopt a role that attempts to place others in the position of providing sympathy, support, and care —and thus reinforcement (Ferster, 1973; Janowsky et al., 1970). Positive reinforcement does not necessarily follow, however. Depressive behavior can, and frequently does, elicit negative feelings and rejection in other people (Coyne, 1976; Gurtman, 1986; Hammen & Peters, 1977, 1978; Hokanson et al., 1989; Howes & Hokanson, 1979). These reactions may remain covert (Stephens, Hokanson, & Welker, 1987). Moreover, such negative reactions are often correctly anticipated by a depressed person (Strack & Coyne, 1983). In fact merely being around a

depressed person may induce depressed feelings in others (Howes, Hokanson, & Loewenstein, 1985).

Coyne (1976) has suggested that the presence or absence of support may depend on whether a depressed individual is skillful enough to circumvent and turn to advantage the negative affect he or she tends to create in other people. Especially if the other people are prone to guilt feelings, a skillful depressive patient may be able to extract considerable sympathy and support, at least over the short term. More commonly, one suspects, the ultimate result is a downwardly spiraling relationship from which others finally withdraw, exacerbating the instigator's depressive state.

Observations such as these raise questions about the extent to which depressive symptoms function as a sort of inept and defeated attempt to exert power over other people. We do not as yet have reliable answers to such questions, although the casual experience of most of us in interacting with depressed people is that of feeling "under pressure," as though we were being accused of lacking in some fundamental empathic quality. Because we usually have no ready response to the vague hint, "So what have you done for me lately?" we are apt to have an unpleasant sense of helplessness ourselves. It is known that depressed people can be quite sensitive about power cues and that they are not averse to the use of power in interpersonal situations (Hokanson et al., 1980).

These and other considerations discussed earlier in the chapter may mean that we should look more closely at issues of power in depression and conceivably in mania as well. Arieti (1982; Arieti & Bemporad, 1980) suggested the existence of two types of depression, one involving submission to a dominant personality (and the consequent failure to thrive as a person), the other concerned with failure to achieve unattainable goals. As already noted, Blatt et al. (1982) presented data supporting such a dichotomy, identifying dependent and self-criticizing depressive modes that correspond to the Arieti subtypes, a characterization in turn supported by other researchers (e.g., Hammen et al., 1989; Nietzel & Harris, 1990). The theme of dominance versus submission is one that may have special import in our attempts to understand those depressions where dependency appears central.

Depressive reactions can often be seen as an individual's attempts to communicate, in pantomime as it were, feelings of angry discouragement and despair—to say, in effect, "I have needs that you are failing to meet." Too often, however, this communication goes unheeded. Thus in failing marriages, which are commonly associated with

Jan (right), shown here with her mother, Phyllis, described her mother's depression this way: "I had really reached the point where I was tired of it all. . . . I didn't want to hear it anymore. . . . You talk about a love-hate relationship, that's exactly what—what I remember feeling. . . ."

depressive reactions, we may see one partner trying to communicate his or her unmet expectations, distress, and dependency and then becoming increasingly depressed and disturbed when the other partner fails to make the hoped-for response. Indeed, probably as often as not, the spouse is observed to respond with increased contempt for what he or she sees as the other's "weakness."

General Sociocultural Factors　The incidence of mood disorders seems to vary considerably among different societies: in some, manic episodes are more frequent, while in others, depressive episodes are more common. In some cultures, particularly China, rates of depression are low but appear to be manifested as somatic symptoms (Kleinman, 1986).

In early studies, Carothers (1947, 1951, 1959) found manic disorders to be fairly common among the East Africans he studied, but depressive disorders relatively rare—the opposite of their incidence in the United States. He attributed the low incidence of depressive disorders to the fact that, in traditional African cultures, individuals have not usually been held personally responsible for failures and misfortunes. The culture of the Kenya Africans, Carothers observed, may be taken as fairly typical in this respect:

Their behavior in all its major aspects is group-determined. Even religion is a matter of offerings and invocations in a group; it is not practiced individually, and does not demand any particular attitude on the part of the individual. Similarly, grief over the death of a loved one is not borne in isolation, but appropriate rites are performed amid great public grieving. In these rites, widowed persons express their grief dramatically in ways prescribed by custom and then resume the tenor of their life as if no bereavement had occurred.

Psychologically speaking, Kenyans receive security because they are part of a larger organism and are not confronted with the problems of individual self-sufficiency, choice, and responsibility that play such a large part in our culture. They do not set themselves unrealistic goals, and they have no need to repress or feel guilty about "dangerous" desires. Their culture actively discourages individual achievement of success, does not consider sexual behavior as evil, and is tolerant of occasional outbursts of aggressive hostility.

In addition, Kenyans feel a great humbleness toward their natural environment, which is often harsh in the extreme. They always expect the worst, and hence can accept misfortunes with equanimity.

Here too, responsibility and blame are automatically placed on forces outside themselves. Although they attempt to counteract misfortune and assure success in their ventures by performing appropriate rituals, the outcome is in the hands of the gods. They are not personally responsible and hence do not ordinarily experience self-devaluation or the need for ego-defensive measures. When excessive stress and decompensation do occur, there tends to be a complete disorganization of personality—as in the hebephrenic type of schizophrenia, which is the most common type of psychotic reaction. (Adapted from Carothers, 1947, 1951, 1953)

Needless to say, much has changed in Africa since Carothers made these observations, and more recent data suggest a quite different picture. In general, it appears that as societies take on the ways of Western culture, their members become more prone to the development of what might be called Western-style mood disorders (Marsella, 1980).

Even in those nonindustrialized countries where depressive disorders are relatively common, they seem less closely associated with feelings of guilt and self-recrimination than in the "developed" countries (Kidson & Jones, 1968; Lorr & Klett, 1968; Zung, 1969). In fact, among several groups of Australian aborigines, Kidson and Jones (1968) found not only an absence of guilt and self-recrimination in depressive reactions, but also no incidence of attempted or actual suicide. In connection with the latter finding, they stated, "The absence of suicide can perhaps be explained as a consequence of strong fears of death and also because of the tendency to act out and project hostile impulses" (p. 415).

These conclusions are generally supported in Marsella's (1980) comprehensive review of the cross-cultural literature concerning depression. Though various methodological problems make it inadvisable at this time to say with certainty that depression occurs less frequently in cultures other than our own, there is little doubt that it generally takes a different form from that customarily seen here. For example, in some non-Western cultures, symptoms of depression lack substantial psychological components, being limited to the so-called vegetative manifestations, such as sleep disturbance, loss of appetite, weight loss, and loss of sexual interest. Interestingly, in some such cultures there is not even a concept of depression that would be reasonably comparable to our own.

In our own society, the role of sociocultural factors in mood disorders is clarifying gradually. It appears that conditions that increase life stress—

such as being a homemaker-mother with young children at home—lead to a higher incidence of these as well as other disorders. In an early study, Jaco (1960) found that although psychotic mood disorders were distributed more evenly in the population than schizophrenia, the incidence was significantly higher among the divorced than among the married, and that it was about three times higher in urban than in rural areas. Subsequent work, such as that by Blazer et al. (1985) on the rural-urban difference and Bloom, Asher, and White (1978) on marital status, has generally confirmed these findings. Some evidence also suggests that the incidence of psychotic depression is higher in the upper socioeconomic classes (Bagley, 1973), though this effect appears limited to bipolar disorder (Boyd & Weissman, 1982). The reasons for this effect are open to speculation, but the elevated depression rates among people of high educational and occupational status has been confirmed in a carefully controlled study (Monnelly, Woodruff, & Robins, 1974). Finally, it should be mentioned that the relatively high percentage of women who suffer from mood disorders may not be universal in all cultures (Rao, 1970).

◼ Treatments and Outcomes

Antidepressant, antipsychotic, and antianxiety drugs are all used with more severely disturbed manic and depressive patients. The role of medication in the mild and moderate forms of depression, as we have seen, is minimal, and such patients are likely to benefit more from appropriate psychological therapies (Beckham & Leber, 1985a; Klerman, 1982).

Lithium carbonate, a simple salt of the lightest elemental metal, was first successfully tried for the treatment of manic disorders in the late 1940s by Cade of Australia, but it was found to have adverse and even dangerous side effects that delayed its acceptance in the United States for nearly 20 years. Thanks to refinements in monitoring blood levels and determining appropriate dosages, however, lithium therapy has now become widely used in the treatment of manic episodes and, more recently, in the treatment of some major depressions as well (Coppen, Metcalfe, & Wood, 1982; Depue & Monroe, 1978; Kramlinger & Post, 1989; Noll, Davis, & DeLeon-Jones, 1985). Some believe that lithium is effective in depression only where the underlying disorder is bipolar in nature.

Lithium therapy is often effective in preventing the cycling between manic and depressive episodes, and susceptible patients are frequently maintained on lithium therapy over long time periods. Until recently lithium was considered an effective preventative for approximately 75 percent of patients suffering repeated bipolar attacks, but some new follow-up data suggest that this figure may be unduly optimistic (Harrow et al., 1990). Unfortunately, too, lithium therapy has some unpleasant side effects, such as lethargy, decreased motor coordination, and gastrointestinal difficulties in some patients. Long-term use has also been associated with kidney malfunction and sometimes permanent kidney damage (Bassuk, Schoonover, & Gelenberg, 1983).

For most seriously depressed patients, the drug treatment of choice is one of the standard antidepressants (called tricyclics because of their chemical structure), such as Tofranil (imipramine). Increasingly, physicians are choosing "second generation" antidepressants from a growing list of such products. One of these, Prozac (fluoxetine), is now extremely popular among physicians in various specialties, and prescriptions for it are being written at a rate that seems clearly excessive; modest distress or unhappiness should not, we think, be an occasion for taking drugs but rather for rigorously examining one's life. When properly prescribed, these drugs are often effective in prevention as well as treatment for patients subject to recurrent episodes (Hollon & Beck, 1978; Mindham, 1982; Noll, Davis, & DeLeon-Jones, 1985).

Unfortunately, antidepressant drugs usually require a week or more to manifest their effects. Thus electroconvulsive therapy (ECT) is often used with patients who present an immediate and serious suicidal risk (Brown, 1974; T. D. Hurwitz, 1974). When selection criteria for this form of treatment are carefully observed (which is by no means guaranteed), a complete remission of symptoms occurs after about four to six convulsive treatments in some 70 to 80 percent of the cases treated (Noll, Davis, & DeLeon-Jones, 1985). Maintenance dosages of antidepressant and antianxiety drugs ordinarily are then used to maintain the treatment gains achieved, until the depression has run its course. If necessitated as a last resort, however, electroconvulsive therapy should be used sparingly because of its distressing side effects, including temporary memory loss and disorientation. Furthermore, compelling evidence shows that, in some cases, ECT produces irreversible brain damage (Breggin, 1979).

In the best of circumstances, the treatment of depression is not confined to drugs or drugs plus electroconvulsive therapy, but is combined with individual and group psychotherapy directed at helping a patient develop a more stable long-range

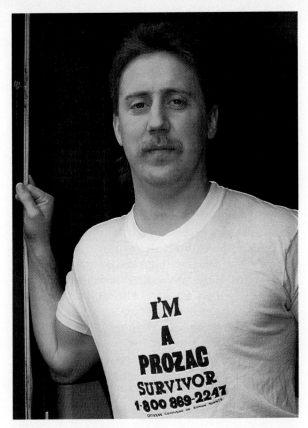

This man claims that he became suicidal after treatment with the antidepressant drug Prozac. Whether or not the drug actually precipitates suicidal impulses in susceptible individuals, the point to be underscored here is that antidepressants are powerful drugs that must be prescribed and used carefully. When care is taken with them, they are said to be effective in prevention as well as treatment for patients subject to recurrent depressive episodes.

adjustment. Studies on the efficacy of the drugs-psychotherapy combination have been reviewed by Klerman and Schechter (1982), Beckham and Leber (1985a), and Conte et al. (1986). The conclusions are most encouraging; apparently, the two broad types of therapy make independent but complementary contributions when combined. Considerable evidence, reviewed by Hollon and Garber (1990), also suggests that appropriate psychotherapy for depression, alone or in combination with drugs, significantly decreases the likelihood of further depressive episodes.

Proposed psychosocial treatments for depression have proliferated at an extraordinary rate over the past few years. In the comprehensive *Handbook of Depression,* edited by Beckham and Leber (1985b), no fewer than seven chapters are devoted to various psychotherapeutic approaches, versus one each for biological-somatic and combined treatments. In addition to depression-focused modifications of classical therapies, a number of specialized systems of psychotherapy have been developed that specifically address the problem of depression. By and large, these psychosocial therapies are intended for outpatient (nonpsychotic) treatment, but they

are increasingly applied in inpatient settings as well (e.g., Salkovskis & Westbrook, 1989).

Two of the best known of these depression-specific psychotherapies are the *cognitive-behavioral approach* of Beck and colleagues (Beck et al., 1979) and the *interpersonal therapy (IPT)* program developed by Klerman, Weissman, and associates (Klerman et al., 1984). Both are relatively brief approaches that focus on here-and-now problems rather than remote causal issues. For example, the cognitive-behavioral technique consists of a highly structured, systematic attempt to reeducate a patient in regard to the aberrant cognitions presumed to underlie a depressed state. The Beck approach has amassed an impressive record of success, even as competitively compared with drug treatment, especially for long-term follow-up (Blackburn et al., 1981; DeRubeis, 1983; Murphy et al., 1984; Rush et al., 1977, 1982; Simons et al., 1986). These conclusions were confirmed in a recent quantitative review (using meta-analysis) of virtually all the pertinent research literature (Dobson, 1989).

The IPT approach, being relatively new, has not been subjected as yet to as extensive an evaluation. The efficacy of both of these psychosocial treatments for depression, however, recently received strong support from the findings of a carefully-designed, multisite study sponsored by the National Institute of Mental Health. In competitive comparison with immediate posttherapy outcomes from antidepressant drug treatment, both these psychosocial treatment approaches proved equally effective for milder cases of major depression, and in some instances even severe ones (Elkin et al., 1989; this important study is further described in Chapter 18). Based on the earlier research mentioned already, we anticipate a distinct advantage for at least the cognitive-behavioral approach over drug therapy when long-term follow-up of these patients is completed.

The more strictly behaviorist approaches have also spawned a number of innovations in the treatment of depression (T. Carson & Adams, 1981; Hoberman & Lewinsohn, 1985). A good example of one such technique, the manipulation of reinforcement contingencies, is presented in the following case study. The patient was a 37-year-old homemaker who had been depressed since the recent death of her mother. The therapist began by observing the patient in her home.

The therapist recorded each instance of "depressive-like" behavior, such as crying, complaining about somatic symptoms, pacing, and withdrawal. He also noted the consequences of these behaviors. Initially, she had a high rate of depressive behaviors and it was noted that members of her family frequently responded to them with sympathy, concern, and helpfulness. During this time, her rate of adaptive actions as a housewife and mother were very low, but she did make occasional efforts to cook, clean house, and attend to the children's needs. . . .

The therapist, in family sessions, instructed her husband and children to pay instant and frequent attention to her coping behavior and to gradually ignore her depressed behavior. They were taught to acknowledge her positive actions with interest, encouragement, and approval. Overall, they were not to decrease the amount of attention focused on the patient but rather switch the contingencies of their attention from "sick woman" to "housewife and mother." Within one week, her depressed behavior decreased sharply and her "healthy" behavior increased.

A clinical experiment was then performed to prove the causal link between her behavior and the responses generated in her family. After the 14th day, the therapist instructed the family members to return to providing the patient with attention and solicitude for her complaints. Within three days, she was once again showing a high level of depressive behavior, albeit not as high as initially. When the focus of the family's attentiveness was finally moved back to her coping skills and away from her miserableness, she quickly improved. One year after termination, she was continuing to function well without depressive symptoms. (Liberman & Raskin, 1971, p. 521)

Other behavioral techniques applied in the treatment of depression include training in progressive goal attainment, decision making, self-reinforcement, social skills, and of course such old standbys as relaxation. In one study, in fact, relaxation training proved to be as effective as cognitive-behavioral therapy for depressed adolescents, with both treatments surpassing in outcomes the waiting-list control condition (Reynolds & Coats, 1986).

Of course, in any overall treatment program, it is important to deal with unusual stressors in a patient's life, because an unfavorable life situation may lead to a recurrence of the depression and may necessitate longer treatment. This point was well made in recent studies that extended to the mood disorders the well-established finding that relapse in

schizophrenia is correlated with certain noxious elements in family life (Hooley, 1986; Hooley, Orley, & Teasdale, 1986). Spouse behavior that can be interpreted by a former patient as criticism seems especially likely to produce depression relapse (Hooley & Teasdale, 1989). Some type of couples or family intervention, described in Chapter 18, might be required in these situations.

Even without formal therapy, as we have noted, the great majority of manic and depressed patients recover from a given episode within less than a year. With modern methods of treatment, the general outlook has become increasingly favorable—so much so that most hospitalized patients can now be discharged within 60 days. Although relapses may occur in some instances, these can now often be prevented by maintenance therapy.

At the same time, the mortality rate for depressed patients appears to be about twice as high as that for the general population because of the higher incidence of suicide (Leonard, 1974; Zung & Green, 1974). Manic patients also have a high risk of death, due to such circumstances as accidents (with or without alcohol as a contributing factor), neglect of proper health precautions, or physical exhaustion (Coryell & Winokur, 1982). Thus, although the development of effective drugs and other new approaches to therapy have brought greatly improved outcomes for patients with mood disorders, the need clearly remains for still more effective treatment methods, both immediate and long-term. Also, a strong need remains to study the factors that put people at high risk for depressive disorders and to apply relevant findings to early intervention and prevention.

SUICIDE

The risk of **suicide**—taking one's own life—is a significant factor in all depressive states. Though it is obvious that people on occasion commit suicide for other reasons, the vast majority of those who complete the act do so during or in the recovery phase of a depressive episode. Paradoxically, the act often occurs at a point when an individual appears to be emerging from the deepest phase of a depressive attack. The risk of suicide is about 1 percent during the year in which a depressive episode occurs, and it raises to 15 percent over the lifetime of an individual who has recurrent episodes (Klerman, 1982). When compared to rates for other possible causes of death—especially in younger age groups—these are substantial figures.

At the present time, suicide ranks among the first ten causes of death in most Western countries. In the United States, estimates show that more than 200,000 people attempt suicide each year and that over 5 million Americans have made suicide attempts at some time in their lives. Official figures show that some 26,000 successful suicides occur each year, meaning that about every 20 minutes someone in the United States commits suicide (Statistical Abstracts of the United States, 1984). Indeed, the problem may be much more serious than these figures suggest, because many self-inflicted deaths are attributed in official records to other "more respectable" causes. Most experts agree that the number of actual suicides is at least two and possibly several times higher than the number officially reported (Wekstein, 1979).

Statistics, however accurate, cannot begin to convey the tragedy of suicide in human terms. As we will see, probably the great majority of people who commit suicide are actually quite ambivalent about taking their own lives. This irreversible choice is often made when they are alone and in a state of severe psychological distress, unable to see their problems objectively or to evaluate alternative courses of action. Thus a basic humanitarian problem in suicide is the seemingly senseless death of an individual who may be ambivalent about living or who does not really want to die. A second tragic concern arises from the long-lasting distress among those left behind that may result from such action. As Shneidman (1969) has put it, "The person who commits suicide puts his psychological skeleton in the survivor's emotional closet . . ." (p. 22). The aptness of this characterization is poignantly confirmed in "survivors'" descriptions of their experiences, as recently investigated by Lukas and H. Seiden (1990). *HIGHLIGHT 11.4* describes some additional insights provided by this work.

In the discussion that follows, we will focus on various aspects of the incidence and clinical picture in suicide, on factors that appear to be of causal significance, on degrees of intent and ways of communicating it, and on issues of treatment and prevention.

■ The Clinical Picture and Causal Pattern

Because the clinical picture and etiology of suicide are so closely interrelated, it is useful to consider these topics under one general heading. This approach will lead us to address the following questions: Who commits suicide? What are the motives for taking one's own life? What general sociocul-

tural variables appear to be relevant to an understanding of suicide?

Who Commits Suicide?   In the United States, the peak age for suicide attempts is between 24 and 44. Historically, three times as many men as women commit suicide, but more women make suicide attempts. Most attempts occur in the context of interpersonal discord or other severe life stress. For females, the most commonly used method is drug ingestion, usually barbiturates; males tend to use methods more likely to be lethal, particularly gunshot, which is probably the main reason that successful suicides are higher among men. Evidence suggests, however, that this long-established pattern may be changing. Data from various Western countries, including the United States, indicate that the incidence of completed suicide has been increasing at a faster rate for women than for men in recent years. Also, more widows than widowers complete the act (Suter, 1976), although this fact seems due mainly to the disproportionate prevalence of widowhood. The precise reasons for these trends are unknown but are doubtless related to the rapid sociocultural changes, including those relating to sex roles, that are now an inescapable part of our lives.

Another perplexing trend is that rates of completed suicide among teenagers and even children seem to be increasing at an alarming pace (Fremouw, de Perczel, & Ellis, 1990; Peck, Farberow, & Litman, 1985; Pfeffer, 1981; Wells & Stuart, 1981). One recent estimate (Spirito et al., 1989) puts the rate of attempted suicide among high school students at between 8 and 9 percent; between 5 and 40 percent of these are believed to be "repeaters." The trend is by no means limited to youngsters from deprived or problematic backgrounds, although they do account for a sizable percentage of the statistics (Miller, Chiles, & Barnes, 1982); suicide rates for children from affluent circumstances also are on the increase. Youthful suicides are especially likely to follow an "epidemic" pattern, wherein particular communities are rocked by a series of self-destruction episodes within a brief time period. Several years ago, for example, seven students attending the same high school in suburban Omaha made suicide attempts in rapid succession, and three of them succeeded (*Time*, February 24, 1986).

Thus while the overall national rate has increased slightly but consistently in recent years, disproportionate increases have occurred among females and among younger members of the population. The greatest increase has been among 15 to 24 year olds; the rate for this age group has essen-

HIGHLIGHT 11.4

"Adjusting" to Suicide: Relationship Trauma Without Closure

Christopher Lukas, himself a childhood suicide survivor, and Henry Seiden (1990), a psychologist, have recently published a sensitive and informed book on suicide survivorship, much of it the product of a survey conducted among people who have endured the experience. The comments that follow are based largely on their findings.

Most of us, fortunately, will never have to cope with the suicide of someone with whom we have shared significant portions of our lives. The involuntary death of a loved one—a parent, a child, a sibling, a spouse, a close friend—through accident or illness often leaves in its wake substantial scars that may never entirely recede. In these cases, however, we are normally spared the additional agony of unanswered and unanswerable questions about the essential cause of the loss and about any role we may have had in bringing it about. For the survivor of a relationship that ends in suicide, questions such as these usually present themselves with a searing, inescapable, and lasting promi-

nence. They can have no final resolution because the one person in the best position to provide answers has deliberately and permanently departed. The first, last, and most central of these unanswered questions for the typical survivor is, why?

Seemingly irresolvable crises are not unique to the situation of the suicide survivor. Everyone's life has its share of them, and every human culture seems to have evolved its own ways of dealing with them. Usually, if not invariably, these coping mechanisms involve substantial communal sharing of the burden, sometimes in formal rituals of one sort or another (such as funerals), but probably more often in less formal exchanges of emotional or material support, information, advice, and counsel from relatives and friends. The professional counselor—shaman, clergy, lawyer, physician, psychotherapist, or similar figure—occupies something of a middle ground here.

The significantly different thing about suicide as an irresolvable crisis, at least in our culture, is

its unacceptability as a topic of reference. Not uncommonly, for example, there is no funeral for the suicide. A survivor, deliberately or not, finds himself or herself complying with the general expectation that the act of self-destruction is not to be openly acknowledged, not even within the immediate family. The typical suicide survivor is thus deprived of the healing properties of sharing by virtue of this conspiracy of silence. He or she must face alone the terrible, wrenching, and ultimately impenetrable question, why? According to the data gathered by Lukas and Seiden, few if any survivors emerge psychologically undamaged from this experience, and only the fortunate are able to conquer fully the psychotoxic residue and move on with their lives unimpeded.

Lukas and Seiden use a "bargain" analogy to analyze the differing coping strategies used by survivors to deal with their special dilemma. These bargains have the function of protecting a survivor from the devastating feelings that would otherwise emerge, but they

---

tially tripled since the mid-1950s, far exceeding its increase as a proportion of the total population (Hendin, 1985). Data from the San Diego Suicide Study suggest that at least some of the increase may be associated with drug abuse (Fowler, Rich, & Young, 1986; Rich, Young, & Fowler, 1986). Suicide ranks as the third most common cause of death for 15 to 24 year olds (the first two are accidents and homicide, respectively; Frederick, 1985).

Most of us feel there is something especially tragic when a young person—physically healthy and having seemingly unlimited potential—undertakes an irreversible, self-destructive action. In fact a sense of hopelessness, strongly correlated with sui-

cide attempts among adults (Beck, Brown, & Steer, 1989; Holden, Medonca, & Serin, 1989), does not appear to be a particularly significant issue in adolescent suicide (Cole, 1989). The motivation to "escape from self" (Baumeister, 1990), on the other hand, possibly has special relevance for this age range; it is discussed further in a later section.

Many college students seem peculiarly vulnerable to the development of suicidal motivations, especially those attending the larger institutions. The rate seems to be higher in large universities than in community colleges and small liberal arts colleges (Peck & Schrut, 1971). The combined stressors of academic demands, social interaction usually also have a hidden "cost" in requiring self-injurious behavior. Some of the more typical of such bargains are as follows:

1. *The long goodbye.* Because survivors often have not had the opportunity to say "good-bye," some become caught up in an unending mourning process in an effort to achieve this type of closure to a relationship. Although severe psychic pain may thereby be avoided, this type of bargain also involves a sort of perpetual moratorium on moving forward with one's life.

2. *Scapegoating.* Here a survivor identifies one or more other people as responsible for the suicide's death, displacing onto them the rage he or she feels toward the actual perpetrator of the act. The hidden cost is that the survivor is prevented from coming to terms with the fact of self-destruction and its meaning.

3. *Guilt as punishment.* Instead of choosing an external scapegoat, some survivors take on to themselves the burden of responsibility for the death; they initiate an interminable self-blame and remain thereafter deep in grief and self-acknowledged guilt.

4. *Cutting off.* Some survivors handle their disruptive emotions by putting a psychological stranglehold on all feelings, turning themselves into emotionless and minimally involved processors of the tasks of living. In one form of this bargain, a survivor loses all tolerance for pleasant experience or joy, turning his or her life, and that of significant others, into a bleak and colorless sequence of emotionally neutral events.

5. *Physical problems.* Here a survivor somatizes the unfinished emotional business of the suicide and becomes preoccupied with various real or imagined illnesses to a crippling degree.

6. *Running.* Some survivors react by involving themselves in endless moves and life changes—in locale, employment, spouses, other relationships, and so on—as a way of distracting themselves from the questions and intensely painful feelings brought about by the suicide. This "running," of course, solves nothing.

7. *Suicide.* Here the bargain—perhaps the saddest of all—is, "Because you died, I'll die." The rage that has no other acceptable target is, finally, turned against the self.

Is there a way out for a survivor? Lukas and Seiden say yes. It is not an easy one, however, not one that accepts the false security of a "bargain." Apparently, no effective substitute exists for facing, working through, and then putting aside the brutal truth of a loved one's suicide, and one's own reactions to it. Fortunately, help is available for doing so, to which these authors provide detailed directions.

problems, and career choices—perhaps interacting with challenges to their basic values—evidently make it impossible for such students to continue making the adjustive compromises their life situations demand. Some 10,000 college students in the United States attempt suicide each year, and over 1,000 of them succeed. For an overview of warning signs for student suicide, see *HIGHLIGHT 11.5*

The greatest incidence of suicidal behavior among college students occurs at the beginning and the end of a school quarter or semester. Echoing the general trend, approximately three times as many female as male students attempt suicide, but more males than females succeed. More than half of those who attempt suicide take pills, about one-third cut themselves, and the remainder—mostly males—use other and more deadly methods, such as hanging, gunshot, or jumping from high places (Klagsbrun, 1976; Ryle, 1969).

Other high-risk groups include depressed people; the elderly (white); alcoholics; separated or divorced people; individuals living alone; migrants; people from socially disorganized areas; members of some Native American tribes (see *HIGHLIGHT 11.6*); and certain professionals, such as physicians, dentists, lawyers, and psychologists (Wekstein, 1979). As might be expected, suicide rates are higher than normal among former mental patients

Warning Signs for Student Suicide

A change in a student's mood and behavior is a significant warning of possible suicide. Characteristically, the student becomes depressed and withdrawn, undergoes a marked decline in self-esteem, and shows deterioration in personal hygiene. These signs are accompanied by a profound loss of interest in studies. Often he or she stops attending classes and stays at home most of the day. Usually, the student's distress is communicated to at least one other person, often in the form of a veiled suicide warning. A significant number of students who attempt suicide leave suicide notes.

When college students attempt suicide, one of the first explanations to occur to those around them is that they may have been doing poorly in school. As a group, however, they are superior students, and though they tend to expect a great deal of themselves in terms of academic achievement and to exhibit scholastic anxieties, their grades, academic competition, and pressure over examinations are not regarded as significant precipitating stressors. Also, though many lose interest in their studies prior to the onset of suicidal behavior and thus receive worse grades, the loss of interest appears to be associated with depression and withdrawal caused by other problems. Moreover, when academic failure does appear to trigger suicidal behavior—in a minority of cases—the actual cause of the behavior is generally considered to be loss of self-esteem and failure to live up to parental expectations, rather than the academic failure itself.

For most suicidal students, both male and female, the major precipitating stressor appears to be either the failure to establish, or the loss of, a close interpersonal relationship. Often the breakup of a romance is the key precipitating factor. It has also been noted that significantly more suicide attempts and suicides are made by students from families that have experienced separation, divorce, or the death of a parent. A particularly important precipitating factor among college males appears to be the existence of a close emotional involvement with a parent that is threatened when the student becomes involved with another person in college and tries to break this "parental knot."

Although most colleges and universities have mental health facilities to assist distressed students, few suicidal students seek professional help. Thus it is of vital importance for those around a suicidal student to notice the warning signs and try to obtain assistance.

Sources drawn on for this description include Hendin (1975), Miller (1975), Murray (1973), Nelson (1971), Pausnau and Russell (1975), Peck and Schrut (1971), Shneidman, Parker, and Funkhouser (1970), and Stanley and Barter (1970).

(Black, Warrack, & Winokur, 1985), and as much as 18 times higher among females who had been diagnosed as schizophrenic (Allebeck & Wistedt, 1986). Both female physicians and female psychologists commit suicide at a rate about three times that of women in the general population; male physicians have a suicide rate about twice that of men in the general population (Ross, 1974; Schaar, 1974; Wekstein, 1979). Finally, those who attempt suicide tend to have traits of submissiveness and high arousability (Mehrabian & Weinstein, 1985). *HIGHLIGHT 11.7* provides more information on people at high risk for suicidal behavior. Summing up, R. Seiden (1974) has called suicide "the number one cause of unnecessary, premature, and stigmatizing death" in the United States.

Other Psychosocial Factors Associated with Suicide   Events, circumstances, and mental states found to be related to the onset of depression are also generally linked to suicidal behavior. Thus, in addition to the sense of hopelessness already mentioned, we find that current stressors (Slater & Depue, 1981), depressed *and* angry feelings (Weissman, Fox, & Klerman, 1973), interpersonal crises of various sorts (Paykel, Prusoff, & Myers, 1975), failure and consequent self-devaluation (Wekstein, 1979), inner conflicts (Menninger, 1938), and the loss of a sense of meaning (Farberow, Shneidman, & Leonard, 1963) all can produce, independently or in combination, a mental state that looks to suicide as a possible way out. Should a person also happen to be drinking excessively at the time (or

HIGHLIGHT 11.6

Native American Tragedy: The Young Men of Wind River

Between August and October of 1985, nine young men, ages 14 to 25, of the Shoshone tribe at Wind River, Wyoming, killed themselves, all by hanging. This devastating rash of self-destruction is some 24 times in excess of the already-established high rate of suicide among Native American males in this age range. What happened at the Wind River reservation? Apart from obvious elements of suggestion and imitation, we may never completely know. The young men themselves left essentially no clues, and no evidence could be found of a suicide pact among them.

A plausible explanation is that Wind River was host to a lethal concentration of the same problems that beset many Native American societies and that impact especially on their young males: marginal status in the larger American society; a dearth of discernible opportunities to "break out" of a stark and bleak existence; rampant unemployment; erosion of ambition in the face of bureaucratically administered "welfare"; and searing boredom, from which available escapes are largely limited to watching television and getting drunk. To these problems can be added, we surmise, the cruel realization of how far this fall has been for the descendants of the proud warriors who once ruled the continent.

As of the date of the news report from which this *HIGHLIGHT* was adapted (*Time*, October 21, 1985), the wave of suicides had apparently subsided. Of interest and possibly of considerable importance, tribal elders fashioned an intervention program emphasizing tribal history, tradition, and the revival of certain healing rituals to which the young were invited and to which they came in large numbers. If a resurgence of cultural identity and pride can halt an epidemic of suicide, can it also give impetus to an attack on the root causes of tribal despair? We hope so.

---

using drugs with similar effects), the danger of successful suicide is markedly increased (Murphy & Wetzel, 1990).

The following, a composite profile of the "average" physician suicide, shows how a number of the above factors can lead a person to suicide:

Statistically, he is a 48-year-old doctor graduated at or near the top of his high-prestige medical school class, now practicing a peripheral specialty associated with chronic problems, where satisfactions are difficult and laggard. Because he is active, aggressive, ambitious, competitive, compulsive, enthusiastic and individualistic, he is apt to be frustrated easily in his need for achievement and recognition, and in meeting his goals. Unable to tolerate delay in gratification, he may prescribe large amounts of anesthetics or psychoactive drugs in his practice. Add a nonlethal annoying physical illness, mood swings,

personal problems with drugs and alcohol— itself a reflection of suicide proneness—in one who may feel a lack of restraints by society, and one who has a likely enough combination to induce significant anxiety and depression, symptoms which not only may require psychiatric treatment, but which also often hamper a worthwhile relationship with a psychiatrist. Self-seeking and self-indulgent, versatile and resourceful, lacking control, he may often resort to hasty, impulsive or immature behavior—possibly suicide. (Ross, 1975, pp. 16–17)

The specific factors leading a person to suicide may take many forms. For example, one middle-aged man developed profound feelings of guilt after being promoted to the presidency of the bank for which he worked; shortly after his promotion, he fatally slit his throat. Such "success suicides" are undoubtedly related to those occasional depressive

HIGHLIGHT 11.7

A "Lethality Scale" for the Assessment of Suicide Potential

In assessing "suicide potentiality," or the probability that a person might carry out a threat of suicide, the Los Angeles Suicide Prevention Center uses a "lethality scale" consisting of ten categories:

1. *Age and sex.* The potentiality is greater if an individual is male rather than female, and is over 50 years of age. (The probability of suicide is also increasing for young adults aged 15 to 24.)

2. *Symptoms.* The potentiality is greater if an individual manifests such symptoms as sleep disturbances, depression, feelings of hopelessness, or alcoholism.

3. *Stress.* The potentiality is greater if an individual is under stress from the loss of a loved one through death or divorce, the loss of employment, increased responsibilities, or serious illness.

4. *Acute versus chronic aspects.* The immediate potentiality is greater when there is a sudden

onset of specific symptoms. The long-term potentiality is greater when there is a recurrent outbreak of similar symptoms, or a recent increase in long-standing maladaptive traits.

5. *Suicidal plan.* The potentiality is greater in proportion to the lethality of a person's proposed method and the organizational clarity and detail of the plan.

6. *Resources.* The potentiality is greater if a person has no family or friends, or if they are unwilling to help.

7. *Prior suicidal behavior.* The potentiality is greater if an individual has made one or more prior attempts or has a history of repeated threats and depression.

8. *Medical status.* The potentiality is greater when an individual has a chronic, debilitating illness or has had many unsuccessful experiences with physicians.

9. *Communication aspects.* The

potentiality is greater if communication between an individual and his or her relatives has been broken off and they reject efforts by the individual or others to reestablish communication.

10. *Reaction of significant others.* Potentiality is greater if a significant other, such as a husband or wife, evidences a defensive, rejecting, punishing attitude and denies that the individual needs help.

The final suicide potentiality rating is a composite score based on weighing each of the ten individual items.

Another interesting approach to the assessment of suicide potentiality involves the use of computers and actuarial methods to predict the risk not only of suicide but also of assaultive and other dangerous behaviors (Griest et al., 1974). Clinicians find this information helpful in making decisions regarding the amount of control needed or the amount of freedom that they can safely allow.

Material concerning the lethality scale is based on information supplied by the Los Angeles Suicide Prevention Center.

episodes that seem to be precipitated by positive life events. More often, suicide is associated with negative events, such as severe financial reverses, loss of social status, imprisonment, or similar situations.

Historically, researchers have proposed several overarching theoretical rationales for seriously suicidal behavior, behavior that has as its unadulterated intent the immediate termination of one's own life. As a group, these theories tend to be rather abstract, even impersonal, and therefore to miss something in depicting the emotional charge of the suicidal act. The essential element here, it seems to us, is that a presuicidal individual intends—even if only at the moment of taking fatal action—to put an end to

conscious experience, permanently and without recourse. The conceivable states of mind that might lead to such a decision are limited in number and one suspects have in common the quality of intolerability, of desperate need for certain and irrevocable escape. Oblivion thus becomes a positive goal. A recent theoretical analysis of suicide offered by Baumeister (1990) captures this notion of escape from intolerable experience. Baumeister conceives suicide as basically an escape from self, or at least self-awareness. In this effort a person achieves a "cognitive deconstruction," which entails both irrationality and disinhibition, such that drastic action becomes acceptable.

General Sociocultural Factors   Suicide rates vary considerably from one society to another. Hungary, with an annual incidence of 44.9 per 100,000, has the world's highest rate. Other Western countries with high rates—20 per 100,000 or higher—include Czechoslovakia, Finland, Austria, Sweden, Denmark, and the (former) Federal Republic of Germany. The United States has a rate of approximately 11.9 per 100,000, which is roughly comparable to that of Canada. Countries with low rates (less than 9 per 100,000) include Greece, Italy, Israel, Spain, and Portugal (World Health Organization, 1982). Among certain groups, such as the aborigines of the western Australian desert, the suicide rate drops to zero—possibly as a result of a strong, culturally determined fear of death (Kidson & Jones, 1968).

Religious taboos concerning suicide and the attitudes of a society toward death are apparently important determinants of suicide rates. Both Catholicism and Muhammadanism strongly condemn suicide, and suicide rates in Catholic and Islamic countries are correspondingly low. In fact most societies have developed strong sanctions against suicide, and many still regard it as a crime as well as a sin.

Japan is one of the few major societies in which suicide has been socially approved under certain circumstances—for example, in response to conditions that bring disgrace to an individual or group. During World War II, many Japanese villagers were reported to have committed mass suicide when faced with imminent capture by Allied forces. There were also reports of group suicide by Japanese military personnel under threat of defeat. In the case of the kamikaze, Japanese pilots who deliberately crashed their explosives-laden planes into American warships during the war's final stages, self-destruction was a way of demonstrating complete personal commitment to the national purpose. It is estimated that 1000 young Japanese pilots destroyed themselves in this exercise of patriotic zeal. Despite the extraordinary effectiveness of this type of attack, one can hardly imagine its being ordered by an American commander, or such an order being obeyed by American pilots.

Societal norms cannot wholly explain differences in suicide rates, however, for the incidence of suicide often varies significantly among societies with similar cultures and also among different subgroups within given societies. For example, it is difficult to account for the marked differences in suicide rates between Sweden and the United States, and we have noted differences in our own society with respect to sex, occupation, and age. In fact the Scandinavian countries, sharing as they do a relatively common ethnic background, cultural pattern, and overall high rates of suicide, pose the puzzling problem of Norway. Here the suicide rate has remained stable and relatively low by world standards for the past century (Retterstøl, 1975)—thus exploding the myth that the high level of social welfare programs in Scandinavia is responsible for encouraging suicide by removing the challenge, and hope, of "making one's own way."

In a pioneering study of sociocultural factors in suicide, the French sociologist Emile Durkheim (1897) attempted to relate differences in suicide rates to differences in group cohesiveness. Analyzing records of suicides in different countries and for different historical periods, Durkheim concluded that the greatest deterrent to committing suicide in times of personal stress is a sense of involvement and identity with other people. More recent studies, including an exceptionally well-designed one by Slater and Depue (1981), tend to confirm this idea.

Durkheim's views also appear relevant to understanding the higher incidence of suicide among subgroups in our society who are subjected to conditions of uncertainty and social disorganization in the absence of strong group ties. In a study sponsored by the National Institute of Mental Health, Hall et al. (1970) found that low-income people from large urban areas have an especially high rate of suicidal gestures and attempts. Similarly, suicide rates have been found to be higher than average among people who are "downwardly mobile" (or who fear they may become so) and among groups undergoing severe social pressures. For example, in 1932 at the height of the Great Depression in the United States, the suicide rate increased from less than 10 to 17.4 per 100,000; during the early years of the severe recession of the mid- and late 1970s, the suicide rate increased to above 12 per 100,000 (NIMH, 1976; Wekstein, 1979). Following the same pattern, we could point to the environmental pressures that appear to contribute to the high rate of suicide among black youth in our society, or to the marked increase in suicide among Eskimo teenagers in Alaska, who find themselves trapped in a sort of no-man's-land between their past culture and assimilation into the "White world" (Parkin, 1974).

■ Suicidal Ambivalence

From the standpoint of intent or motivation, suicide appears to be one method of obtaining relief from an aversive life situation. However, because most people undergoing severe stress do not commit suicide—for example, only a small number of people who are depressed or who develop terminal cancer take their own lives—the question arises as to why an individual uses this method of coping rather than another. This is not an easy question to answer; it involves consideration not only of stress, but also of other aspects of an individual's psychological state at the time of a suicide attempt.

Degree of Intent   The ambivalence that typically accompanies thoughts of suicide finds classic expression in Hamlet's famous soliloquy:

To be, or not to be: that is the question:
Whether 'tis nobler in the mind to suffer
The slings and arrows of outrageous fortune,
Or to take arms against a sea of troubles,
And by opposing end them? To die: to sleep;
No more; and by a sleep to say we end
The heart-ache and the thousand natural shocks
That flesh is heir to, 'tis a consummation
Devoutly to be wish'd. To die, to sleep;
To sleep: perchance to dream: ay, there's the rub;
For in that sleep of death what dreams may come
When we have shuffled off this mortal coil,
Must give us pause. . . .
(Hamlet, Act III, Scene i)

Recognizing that the vast majority of people who contemplate suicide do not in fact kill themselves, some investigators have focused on analyzing the degree of intent associated with suicidal behavior. Thus Farberow and Litman (1970)—echoing Hamlet—have classified suicidal behavior into three categories: "to be," "not to be," and "to be or not to be."

The "to be" group involves individuals who do not really wish to die, but instead want to communicate a dramatic message to others concerning their distress and contemplation of suicide. Their suicide attempts involve minimal drug ingestion, minor wrist-slashing, and similar nonlethal methods. They usually arrange matters so that intervention by others is almost inevitable, although sometimes things go awry. This group is estimated to make up about two-thirds of the total suicidal population. As we have seen, a large—although decreasing—proportion of those who make unsuccessful attempts are women. It seems probable that traditional sex-role socialization of females predisposes many women to feel helpless and to fantasize being rescued—and thus to communicate in this mode (Suter, 1976).

In contrast, the "not to be" group includes people who seemingly are intent on dying. They give little or no warning of their intent to kill

themselves, and they usually arrange the suicidal situation so that intervention is impossible. Although these people use a variety of different methods for killing themselves, they generally rely on the more violent and certain means, such as shooting themselves or jumping from high places. Investigators have estimated that this group makes up only about 3 to 5 percent of the suicidal population. Successful preventive intervention with this group is at best a doubtful goal, even when such a person is protectively incarcerated. In an interesting experiment, a pseudosuicidal "patient" (actually one of the investigators) gained admission to a mental hospital ward on "suicidal status." Though he was supposedly being carefully watched, he discovered multiple opportunities to do himself in (Reynolds & Farberow, 1976).

The "to be or not to be" group constitutes about 30 percent of the suicidal population. It is comprised of people who are ambivalent about dying and tend to leave the question of death to chance, or, as they commonly view it, to fate. Although loss of a love object, strained interpersonal relationships, financial problems, or feelings of meaninglessness may be present, this type of person still entertains some hope of working things out. The methods used for the suicide attempt are often dangerous but moderately slow acting, such as drug ingestion or cutting oneself severely on nonvital parts of the body, thus allowing for the possibility of intervention. The feeling during such attempts can be summed up as, "If I die the conflict is settled, but if I am rescued that is what is meant to be." Often the people in this group lead stormy, stress-filled lives and make repeated suicide attempts.

After an unsuccessful attempt, a marked reduction in emotional turmoil usually occurs. This reduction is not stable, however, and in a subsequent trial by fate, the verdict may well be death. In a follow-up study of 886 people who had made suicide attempts, Rosen (1970) classified them as serious (21 percent) or nonserious (79 percent). During the year following the attempts, the rate of successful suicide was twice as high among the group whose earlier attempts had been classified as serious.

Farberow and Litman's classification is largely descriptive and has little practical value in terms of predicting suicidal behavior. As we indicated, however, it does seem possible to infer the degree of intent from the lethality of the method used—a conclusion strongly supported by the more recent findings of Beck, Beck, and Kovacs (1975). The concept of intent is also a useful reminder that most people who contemplate suicide retain at least some urge to live. Their hold on life, however tenuous, provides the key to successful suicide prevention (Fremouw, de Perczel, & Ellis, 1990).

Communication of Suicidal Intent   Research has clearly disproved the tragic belief that those who threaten to take their lives seldom do so. In fact such people represent a high-risk group in comparison with the general population. In a cross-cultural study, Rudestam (1971) conducted extensive interviews with close friends or relatives of 50 consecutive suicides in Stockholm and Los Angeles and found that at least 60 percent of the victims in both cities had made "direct" verbal threats of their intent. An additional 20 percent had made "indirect" threats.

In a similar study involving suicide deaths in Vienna and Los Angeles, Farberow and Simon (1975) found substantial differences between the two cities. In Los Angeles, 72 percent had made direct references to intent, versus only 27 percent in Vienna; the corresponding figures for indirect references were 25 percent and 2 percent. It thus appears that cultural factors determine to some extent the likelihood that suicidal intent will be "signaled" to others.

Indirect threats typically include references to being better off dead, discussions of suicide methods and burial, statements such as "If I see you again . . . ," and dire predictions about the future.

Whether direct or indirect, communication of suicidal intent usually represents a cry for help. The person is trying to express distress and ambivalence about suicide; the statements are both warnings and calls for help. Unfortunately, the message is often not received or is received with skepticism and denial. The latter pattern is particularly apt to occur when a suicidal person has given repeated warnings but has not made an actual suicide attempt. As a consequence, the recipients of the message may state that they did not think it would happen, or that they thought it might happen but only if the person became much more depressed. In this area, "crying wolf" needs to be taken seriously.

As several investigators have pointed out, many people who are contemplating suicide feel that living may be preferable if they can obtain the understanding and support of their family and friends. Failing to receive it after a suicidal threat, they go on to actual suicide.

Suicide Notes   Several investigators have analyzed suicide notes in an effort to understand better the motives and feelings of people who take their own lives. In a pioneering study of 742 suicides, Tuckman, Kleiner, and Lavell (1959) found that 24 percent left notes, usually addressed to relatives or friends. The notes were either mailed, found on the deceased, or located near the suicide scene. With few exceptions, the notes were coherent and legible. In terms of emotional content, the suicide notes were categorized into those showing positive, negative, neutral, and mixed affect. Of course, some notes showed combinations of these affective components. *HIGHLIGHT 11.8* provides examples of notes showing differing types of emotional content.

Shneidman and Farberow (1957), in another pioneering study, approached the question of suicide notes by comparing 33 notes written by actual suicides with 33 composed by matched subjects who were asked to simulate a presuicidal state. The principal difference between the actual and the fictitious notes was that the actual ones had a greater number of thought units of a "neutral" quality. Evidently, only a genuine writer tends to deal concretely with the idea of actually being gone; thus he or she incorporates much more material of an instructional and admonishing sort to survivors. The genuine writers, however, also expressed more intense feelings of self-blame, hatred, demand, and vengeance.

In another study, Cohen and Fiedler (1974) compared 220 cases of completed suicides who left notes with 813 cases of nonnote suicides. In contrast to the findings of Tuckman et al.—who reported no differences with respect to such variables as sex, race, and marital status—these investigators found that 26 percent of female suicides left notes as contrasted with 19 percent of males. They also found that 40 percent of the separated or divorced females in their sample left notes as contrasted with approximately 31 percent of single females, 25 percent of married females, and 16 percent of widows. Whites left notes almost three times as often as nonwhites. In terms of content, the use of emotional categories corresponded to those reported by Tuckman and his associates—with positive, neutral, mixed, and negative content being used in that order of frequency. In the study by Farberow and Simon (1975) noted earlier, 46 percent of the Los Angeles residents who committed suicide had left notes, but only 18 percent of the Viennese had done so. It appears that the wish to communicate with survivors after the fact varies considerably with a host of demographic and cultural variables.

An understanding of the reasons for or motives underlying note writing (or its absence) could possibly help make the bases of these variations

Types of Suicide Notes

The Tuckman et al. (1959) study classified suicide notes by types of emotional content. A sampling of these various types appears in the following excerpts.

Positive Emotional Content

"Please forgive me and please forget me. I'll always love you. All I have was yours. No one ever did more for me than you, oh please pray for me please." (Tuckman et al., 1959, p. 60)

Negative (Hostile) Emotional Content

"I hate you and all of your family and I hope you never have a peace of mind. I hope I haunt this house as long as you live here and I wish you all the bad luck in the world." (Tuckman et al., 1959, p. 60)

Neutral Emotional Content

*"To Whom It May Concern,
"I, Mary Smith, being of sound mind, do this day make my last will as follows—I bequeath my rings, Diamond and Black Opal to my daughter-in-law, Doris Jones and any other of my personal belongings she might wish. What money I might have in my savings account goes to my dear father, as he won't have me to help him. To my husband, Ed Smith, I leave my furniture and car.*

"I would like to be buried as close to the grave of John Jones as possible." (Darbonne, 1969, p. 50)

Mixed Emotional Content

Dear Daddy,

Please don't grieve for me or feel that you did something wrong, you didn't. I'll leave this life loving you and remembering the world's greatest father.

I'm sorry to cause you more heartache but the reason I can't live anymore is because I'm afraid. Afraid of facing my life alone without love. No one ever knew how alone I am. No one ever stood by me when I needed help. No one brushed away the tears I cried for "help" and no one heard. I love you Daddy, Jeanne

---

clearer. On this point, Cohen and Fiedler (1974) concluded,

Many note writers seem to be motivated to influence the responses of survivors. The desire to be remembered positively by a survivor may account for the large number of statements expressing positive affect. By statements of love and concern, a note writer may try to reassure both the survivor and himself of the worth of their relationship and his own worth as a person. (pp. 93–94)

These investigators, however, as well as Schneidman (1973), expressed disappointment that suicide notes—written by people on the brink of life's greatest mystery—failed to contain any great insights or special messages for the rest of us. As Cohen and Fiedler (1974) expressed it,

The large quantity of references to the concrete, mundane features of everyday life is not congruent with the romantic conception of suicide as a grand, dramatic gesture preceded and accompanied by a corresponding state of the psyche into which the suicide note should serve as a kind of window.

Perhaps all the drama takes place before the action is decided or it is anticipated in the act itself. Whatever role the dramatic elements may play, the large number of references to the commonplace squares best with the conception of suicide notes as communications tailored to the needs of both the suicide and his survivors as these are perceived by the suicide under existing circumstances. (pp. 94–95)

■ Suicide Prevention

The prevention of suicide is extremely difficult. One complicating factor is that most people who are depressed and contemplating suicide do not realize that their thinking is restricted and irrational and that they are in need of assistance. Less than one-third voluntarily seek psychological help; others are brought to the attention of mental health personnel by family members or friends who are concerned because the person appears depressed or has made suicide threats. The majority, however, do not receive the assistance they desperately need. As we have seen, however, most people who attempt suicide do not really want to die and give prior warning of their intentions; if an individual's cry for help can be heard in time, it is often possible to intervene successfully.

Currently, the main thrust of preventive efforts is on crisis intervention. Efforts are gradually being extended, however, to the broader tasks of alleviating long-term stressful conditions known to be associated with suicidal behavior and trying to better understand and cope with the suicide problem in high-risk groups (Fremouw, de Perczel, & Ellis, 1990).

Crisis Intervention   The primary objective of crisis intervention is to help an individual cope with an immediate life crisis. If a serious suicide attempt has been made, the first step involves emergency medical treatment. Typically, such treatment is given through the usual channels—the emergency rooms of general hospitals or clinics. It appears, however, that only about 10 percent of suicide attempts are considered of sufficient severity to warrant intensive medical care; the great majority of people who attempt suicide, after initial treatment, are referred to inpatient or outpatient mental health facilities (Kirstein et al., 1975; Paykel et al., 1974).

When people contemplating suicide are willing to discuss their problems with someone at a suicide prevention center, it is often possible to avert an actual suicide attempt. Here the primary objective is to help these individuals regain their ability to cope with their immediate problems—and to do so as quickly as possible. Emphasis is usually placed on (a) maintaining contact with a person over a short period of time—usually one to six contacts; (b) helping the person realize that acute distress is impairing his or her ability to assess the situation accurately and to choose among possible alternatives; (c) helping the person see that other ways of dealing with the problem are available and preferable to suicide; (d) taking a highly directive and supportive role—for example, fostering a dependent relationship and giving specific suggestions to the person about what to do and what not to do; and (e) helping the person see that the present distress and emotional turmoil will not be endless. When feasible, counselors may elicit the understanding and emotional support of family members or friends; and, of course, they may make frequent use of relevant community agencies. Admittedly, however, these are stopgap measures and do not constitute complete therapy.

In terms of long-range outcomes, people who have made previous suicide attempts are more likely to kill themselves than those who have not, although only about 10 percent of people who unsuccessfully attempt suicide kill themselves at a later

time (Seiden, 1974; Wekstein, 1979; World Health Organization, 1974). As Seiden expressed it, the suicidal crisis "is not a lifetime characteristic of most suicide attempters. It is rather an acute situation, often a matter of only minutes or hours at the most" (p. 2). Because the suicide rate for previous attempters is so much higher than that for the population in general, however, it is apparent that those who have attempted suicide remain a relatively high-risk group.

Farberow (1974) has pointed out that it is important to distinguish between (a) individuals who have demonstrated relatively stable adjustment but have been overwhelmed by some acute stress— about 35 to 40 percent of people coming to the attention of hospitals and suicide prevention centers; and (b) individuals who have been tenuously adjusted for some time and in whom the current suicidal crisis represents an intensification of ongoing problems—about 60 to 65 percent of suicidal cases. For individuals in the first group, crisis intervention is usually sufficient to help them cope with the immediate stress and regain their equilibrium. For individuals in the second group, crisis intervention may also be sufficient to help them deal with the present problem, but with their life-style of "staggering from one crisis to another,"

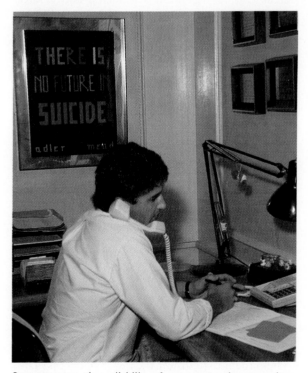

In recent years, the availability of competent assistance at times of suicidal crisis has been expanded through the establishment of suicide prevention centers. These centers are geared toward crisis intervention—usually via 24-hour-a-day availability of telephone contact.

they are likely to require more comprehensive therapy.

During recent years, the availability of competent assistance at times of suicidal crisis has been expanded through the establishment of suicide prevention centers. At present, there are more than 200 such centers in the United States. These centers are geared primarily toward crisis intervention—usually via the 24-hour-a-day availability of telephone contact. Some centers, however, offer long-term therapy programs, and they can refer suicidal people to other community agencies and organizations for special types of assistance. Such suicide prevention centers are staffed by a variety of personnel: psychologists, psychiatrists, social workers, clergy, and trained volunteers. Although initially some doubt existed about the wisdom of using nonprofessionals in the important first-contact role, experience has shown that the empathic concern and peer-type relationships provided by caring volunteers can be highly effective in helping an individual through a suicidal crisis. A guide used by suicide prevention center personnel in gauging the seriousness of suicide threats is provided in *HIGHLIGHT 11.7* on page 416.

It is difficult to evaluate the long-range impact of emergency aid provided by suicide prevention centers, but such facilities seem to have the potential, at least, for significantly reducing suicide rates. The Suicide Prevention Center of Los Angeles has reported that, in comparison with an estimated suicide rate of 6 percent among people judged to be high risks for suicide, the rate has been slightly less than 2 percent among approximately 8000 high-risk people who used their services (Farberow & Litman, 1970).

One difficult problem with which suicide prevention centers must deal is that the majority of people who are seen do not follow up their initial contact by seeking additional help from the center or other treatment agencies. In a follow-up of 53 people who committed suicide after contact with the Cleveland Suicide Prevention Center, Sawyer, Sudak, and Hall (1972) reported that none had recontacted the center just prior to death. They also found that "the interval between the time of last contact with the Center and the time of death ranged from 30 minutes to 32 months with a median interval of 4 months" (p. 232). Since this report was issued, suicide prevention centers have made systematic attempts to expand their services to help them better meet the needs of clients. Thus many centers have introduced long-range after-care or maintenance-therapy programs.

Focus on High-Risk Groups and Other Measures   Many investigators have emphasized the need for broadly based preventive programs aimed at alleviating the life problems of people who, on the basis of statistics, fall into high-risk groups with respect to suicide. Few such programs have actually been initiated, but one approach has been to involve older males—a high-risk group—in social and interpersonal roles that help others. These roles may lessen their frequent feelings of isolation and meaninglessness. Among this group, such feelings often stem from forced retirement, financial problems, the death of loved ones, impaired physical health, and feeling unwanted.

Another innovative approach to dealing with people who are contemplating suicide—and who in this sense represent a high-risk group—was originated by a group of volunteers called the Samaritans, begun in England in 1953 by Reverend Chad Varah. The service extended by the Samaritans is simply that of "befriending." Befrienders offer support to a suicidal person with no strings attached. They are available to listen and help in whatever way needed, expecting nothing in return—not even gratitude. Since their founding, the Samaritans have spread throughout the British Commonwealth and to many other parts of the world, and preliminary findings concerning their effectiveness in suicide prevention seem promising (Farberow, 1974, 1975; Wekstein, 1979).

Other measures to broaden the scope of suicide prevention programs include (a) the use of psychological autopsies (psychological profiles of individuals who have committed suicide); (b) the assessment of high-risk groups' environments, often including their work environments; and (c) the training of clergy, nurses, police, teachers, and other professional personnel who come in contact with many people in their communities. An important aspect of such training is to be alert for suicidal threats. For example, a parishioner might clasp the hand of a minister after church services and intensely say, "Pray for me." Because such a request is quite normal, a minister who is not alert to suicidal cries for help might reply with a simple, "Yes, I will" and turn to the next person in line—only to receive the news a few days later that the parishioner has committed suicide.

Ethical Issues in Suicide Prevention   Most of us respect the preservation of human life as a worthwhile value. Thus suicide is generally considered not only tragic but "wrong." Efforts to prevent suicide, however, also involve ethical problems. If

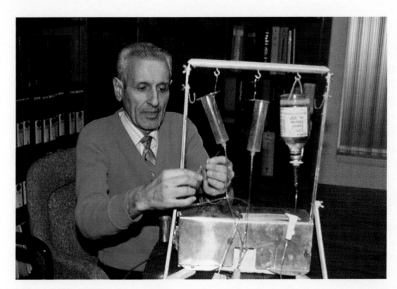

The question of a "right to suicide" is an ethical issue with no easy answers. The issue becomes further clouded in the case of a terminal illness, when a caretaker is faced with the responsibility of a doomed person. One such recent case was that of Janet Adkins, an Alzheimer's patient in the early stages of the disease who decided to take her own life before she became too incapacitated to be able to act for herself. She enlisted the help of Dr. Jack Kevorkian, who had invented a so-called suicide machine, shown here, whereby Ms. Adkins initiated her own suicide through a fatal injection. Though the issue of aiding and abetting a suicide was raised, Dr. Kevorkian was not charged with any crime. The notion of a "suicide machine" further complicates the issue of the right to suicide, and even some who would defend suicide as a reasonable choice under some circumstances feel that such a machine should be illegal.

individuals wish to take their own lives, what obligation—or right—do others have to interfere? This question has been taken seriously by Thomas Szasz (1976), whose view of the problem is captured in the following:

In regarding the desire to live as a legitimate human aspiration, but not the desire to die, the suicidologist stands Patrick Henry's famous exclamation . . . on its head. In effect, he says, "Give him commitment, give him electroshock, give him lobotomy, give him life-long slavery, but do not let him choose death!" By so radically illegitimizing another person's (not his own!) wish to die, the suicide preventor redefines the aspiration of the other as not an aspiration at all. (p. 177)

Needless to say, Szasz's ideas are controversial.

Certainly a persuasive case can be made for the right of people afflicted with a terminal illness, who suffer chronic and debilitating pain, to shorten their agony. But what about the rights of suicidal people who are not terminally ill and who have dependent children, parents, a spouse, or other loved ones who will be adversely affected, perhaps permanently (Lukas & H. Seiden, 1990), by their death? Here a person's "right to suicide," reduced to such nonabstract terms, is not immediately obvious. The right to suicide is even less clear in the case of those who are ambivalent about taking their lives and who might, through intervention, regain their perspective and see alternative ways of dealing with their distress. Still, who has the right to *prevent* another's self-destruction?

Possibly, as has been pointed out by Nelson (1984), the early suicidologists erred in focusing on suicide "prevention." Nelson suggests suicide "intervention" as both a more appropriate term and as descriptive of a more ethically defensible professional approach to suicidal behavior. Suicide intervention, according to this perspective, embodies a more neutral moral stance to suicide than does prevention—it means interceding without the implication of preventing the act—and, in given circumstances, may even hold out the possibility of facilitating the suicidal person's objective.

Here, however, we should reemphasize that the great majority of people who attempt suicide either do not really want to die or are ambivalent about taking their lives; and even for the minority who do wish to die, the desire is often a transient one. With improvement in a person's life situation and a lifting of depression, the suicidal crisis is likely to pass and not recur. As Murphy (1973) has expressed it, "The 'right' to suicide is a 'right' desired only temporarily" (p. 472).

The dilemma becomes intense indeed when prevention requires that an individual be hospitalized involuntarily; when personal items, such as belts and sharp objects, are taken away; and when calming medication is more or less forcibly administered. Sometimes considerable restriction is needed to calm the individual. Not uncommonly, particularly in these litigious times, the responsible clinician feels trapped between threats of legal action on either side of the issue. Undue restriction might lead to a civil rights suit, whereas failure to employ all available safeguards could, in the case of the patient's injury or death, lead to a potentially ruinous malpractice claim initiated by the patient's family (Fremouw, de Perczel, & Ellis, 1990).

Currently, it appears that most practitioners resolve this dilemma by taking the most cautious and conservative course. Thus many patients are hospitalized with insufficient clinical justification. Even where the decision to hospitalize is made on good grounds, however, preventive efforts may be fruitless. For example, in a study of hospitalized people who were persistently suicidal, Watkins, Gilbert, and Bass (1969) reported that "almost one-third used methods from which we cannot isolate them—seven head ramming, two asphyxia by aspiration of paper, one asphyxia by food, and three by exsanguination by tearing their blood vessels with their fingers" (p. 1593). Here again, however, as in the case of terminal illness and suffering, we are talking about a distinct minority of suicide cases.

Admittedly, the preceding considerations do not resolve the issue of a person's basic right to suicide. As in the case of most complex ethical issues, no simple answer is apparent. Unless and until sufficient evidence confirms this alleged right —and society agrees on the conditions under which it may appropriately be exercised—it thus seems the wiser course to encourage existing suicide prevention (intervention) programs and to foster research into suicidal behavior with the hope of reducing the toll in human life and misery taken each year by suicide in our society.

UNRESOLVED ISSUES
on Mood Disorders and Suicide

Despite tremendous advances in recent years, especially but not exclusively at the biological level, the phenomena of human depression continue to challenge us with many enigmas. Biological advances have in fact contributed to one of the foremost of these enigmas in giving rise to persistent suggestions that human depression is not, in a strict sense, "human" at all. It is, according to this view, merely an impersonal breakdown of the "machinery" of the brain; an affected patient is, as it were, a nonparticipant in the process and has no responsibility for either the emergence of the problem or its alleviation. The title, and the substance, of an influential book by psychiatrist Nancy Andreasen (1984), *The Broken Brain,* is as good a statement as

any of this currently popular position in some segments of psychiatry. It predicts a biological treatment revolution "in the 1980s and 1990s," one whose beginnings even at this advanced date we cannot discern. The argument advanced in Andreasen's book contains the seeds of a *reductio ad absurdum* in which, for example, a pill might be prescribed for the "disease" of mourning one's recently deceased child. The human and philosophical implications of the more extremely reductionistic versions of this thesis are, in our judgment, cause for serious concern. Even at a purely pragmatic level, however, this radical view of modern psychiatry's mission has, as we have seen, largely failed to deliver on its inflated promises. Perhaps the time has come for greater restraint among those believing that aberrations of human behavior and personality are reducible to physical malfunctions in the brain that can be set right by tinkering with its parts.

Moving to another but not wholly unrelated matter, serious problems continue in the current taxonomy and nomenclature of the mood disorders. Although there is realistic hope of eventually identifying and isolating a unitary subset of disorders in the bipolar-cyclothymia domain, the remainder of the diagnostic system relating to mood disorders remains in disarray. This situation means that treatment choices are still all too often a matter of "let's see if *this* works." To be sure, many of the impediments to progress in this area relate to its inherent complexities. Others, however, can be traced to researchers' rigidity and prejudices, of which the survival of "endogenous" depression as a concept is, we suspect, an example. As earlier suggested, we think there may be merit in considering depression as analogous to fever, in which case the fine differentiation of subvarieties is a largely pointless exercise, especially where it detracts from a search for the underlying causes of what may be a global and qualitatively uniform (but quantitatively variable) manifestation of psychic distress.

Finally, the vexing ethical problems of whether and to what extent one should intervene in cases of threatened suicide have now been complicated by no less vexing legal ones. As in other areas of professional practice, clinical judgment is no longer the exclusive consideration in intervention decisions. The ramifications of clinical decisions spread widely to matters that were formerly remote or irrelevant, such as the cost of malpractice insurance or the estimated likelihood that a patient or his or her family will sue if the opportunity presents itself. Because this is a societal problem, the solutions—if any—will have to be societal ones.

SUMMARY

Mood disorders (formerly called affective disorders) are those in which extreme variations in mood—either low or high—are the predominant feature. We all experience such variations at mild to moderate levels in the natural course of life. In some instances, however, the extremity of a person's mood in either direction is causally related to behavior that most would consider maladaptive. This chapter describes the official categories of disorder associated with such maladaptive mood variations.

The large majority of these disorders involve some type of mental depression, in which an individual experiences, at the mildest levels, self-depreciation, excessive dependency, and a sense that outcomes are independent of his or her coping efforts. As these problems deepen into disorder, all of these characteristics are intensified, and a person may become preoccupied with feelings of guilt and worthlessness. Often in such cases, basic biological functioning seems to be altered—for example, the sleep pattern may be dramatically altered or the person may become uninterested in food or eating. In the hypomanic or manic variants (for example, in cyclothymia or bipolar disorders in which the current episode is one of being excessively "high"), essentially the opposite pattern exists. Depressive syndromes, however, are much more common than manic ones, and they appear to be much more diffuse and heterogeneous in nature than those in which manic or hypomanic episodes appear in a person's history. In the latter instance, the person is considered to have a (bipolar) predisposition to react in both depressive and manic ways.

Except for certain syndromes that seem secondary to organic brain impairment, the mood disorders are divided into major and nonmajor categories. The major mood disorders are those of major depression and bipolar disorder. Far more common are a variety of depressive (or, less often, hypomanic) conditions that are typically less severe in intensity, including dysthymia, cyclothymia, and adjustment disorder with depressed mood. In general, the efficacy of biologically-based treatments, such as drugs or ECT, is limited to the more severe or major disorders. In the milder forms of mood disorder, psychosocial treatments, of which an increasing variety are available, seem equally or more effective. Combination treatment approaches have shown great promise and may become the treatment of choice for current episodes; considerable evidence suggests that long-term resistance to recurrent depression is best conferred by specialized forms of psychosocial treatment.

Suicide is a constant danger with depressive syndromes of any type or severity. Accordingly, an assessment of suicide risk is essential in the proper management of depressive disorders. A small minority of suicides appears unavoidable—chiefly those of the deliberate "not to be" type. A substantial amount of suicidal behavior (for example, taking slow-acting drugs where the likelihood of discovery is high) is motivated more by a desire for indirect interpersonal communication than by a wish to die. Somewhere between these extremes is a large group of people who are desperately ambivalent about killing themselves and who initiate dangerous actions that they may or may not carry to completion, depending on momentary events and impulses. Most suicide prevention efforts are normally and properly focused on this ambivalent group. Of course, a reasonable and ethical argument can be made that, in certain circumstances, efforts to deter suicide are philosophically questionable.

Key Terms

mood disorders (p. 381)
psychotic behavior (psychosis) (p. 382)
mood-congruent thinking (p. 382)
mania (p. 382)
depression (p. 382)
major depression (p. 382)
bipolar disorder (p. 382)

hypomania (p. 386)
cyclothymia (p. 386)
dysthymia (p. 387)
adjustment disorder with depressed mood (p. 388)
unipolar disorder (p. 391)
schizoaffective disorder (p. 396)
suicide (p. 410)

Chapter 12
The Schizophrenias and Delusional Disorders

Le Voyageur Français, *Le Pays des Météores* (1902–1905). The French Traveler's real name, and most of the details of his life, remain undiscovered. He is thought to have been a professional artist or decorator who was institutionalized at Villejuif, France, for schizophrenia. He painted rather conventional scenes, and then ''signed'' them in the corner with an intricate pattern composed of abstract masses of color. The painting here shows the extremely bizarre effect resulting from the clash of painting and ''signature.''

As we saw in Chapter 11, the mood disorders chiefly involve a disturbance of affect. To the extent that disruptions of perceptual, cognitive, and information-processing mechanisms (such as delusions and hallucinations) occur in the mood disorders, they seem secondary to the more primary mood dysfunction. By and large, the opposite is true in schizophrenic and delusional disorders, where disruption of thought processes is primary, and where often no obvious relationship exists between mood and thinking. This observation, however, does not provide a reliable basis for distinguishing these supposedly separate psychopathological entities. As we have already noted in connection with so-called schizoaffective disorders, many cases fall between the cracks.

With the schizophrenias, we move into a realm of behavioral disorder that represents in many ways the ultimate in psychological breakdown. These disorders include some of the most extreme behaviors to be found in human behavior, and they involve virtually all of the psychopathological processes encountered thus far in this text, plus something more. What that "something more" may be, as we will see, is not readily grasped or defined, but its full expression is clearly within the psychotic range; a schizophrenic individual's whole personality is involved, and there is a more or less sharp break with reality as most of us conceive it.

By and large, schizophrenic people display most of the broad characteristics seen in other types of psychopathology. Identifiable stressors usually precede the onset of their disorders. There is evidence of a genetically transmitted diathesis and, in many cases, a psychosocially disturbed family background. A significant subgroup of these patients have demonstrable neurological anomalies. Usually, people diagnosed as schizophrenic engage in a relatively transparent use of ego-defense mechanisms, and anxiety and panic are common accompaniments of the disorder. Often they are bothered with psychogenic physical ailments of one sort or another, particularly in the early or acute phases of the disturbance. They often show pronounced personality or character deviations prior to breakdown. Finally, they are capable of extremes in mood that are easily the equal of anything seen in the major mood disorders.

Paranoid (delusional) conditions have traditionally been seen as separate processes from those of the schizophrenias, although clinical observers have long noted a tendency for them to occur together; thus we have the classical schizophrenia subtype known as *paranoid schizophrenia*. Contemporary investigators (Brennan & Hemsley, 1984; Magaro, 1981; Meissner, 1981) have confirmed the traditional view, concluding that schizophrenic and paranoid processes are quite distinct. Paranoid forms of thinking sometimes accompany other types of disorder, such as mood, and they may also appear by themselves as relatively uncomplicated delusional states, as will be seen in the latter part of this chapter.

THE SCHIZOPHRENIAS

The schizophrenias are a group of psychotic disorders characterized mainly by gross distortions of reality; withdrawal from social interaction; and disorganization and fragmentation of perception, thought, and emotion. We will focus here on the adult forms of such mental derangements. Similar childhood syndromes will be discussed in Chapter 14. Though the clinical picture may vary widely in people diagnosed as schizophrenic, the disorganization of experience that typifies schizophrenic episodes during the psychotic phase is well illustrated in the following composite description:

Suspicious and frightened, the victim fears he can trust neither his own senses, nor the motives of other people . . . his skin prickles, his head seems to hum, and "voices" annoy him. Unpleasant odors choke him, his food may have no taste. Bright and colorful visions ranging from brilliant butterflies to dismembered bodies pass before his eyes. Ice clinking in a nearby pitcher seems to be a diabolic device bent on his destruction.

When someone talks to him, he hears only disconnected words. These words may touch off an old memory or a strange dream. His attention wanders from his inner thoughts to the grotesque way the speaker's mouth moves, or the loud scrape his chair makes against the floor. He cannot understand what the person is trying to tell him, nor why.

When he tries to speak, his own words sound foreign to him. Broken phrases tumble out over and over again, and somewhat fail to express how frightened and worried he is. (Yolles, 1967, p. 42)

Schizophrenic disorders were at one time attributed to a type of "mental deterioration" beginning early in life. In 1860 the Belgian psychiatrist Morel described the case of a 13-year-old boy who had formerly been the most brilliant pupil in his school but who, over a period of time, lost interest in his studies, became increasingly withdrawn, seclusive, and taciturn, and appeared to have forgotten everything he had learned. He talked frequently of killing his father, and evidenced a kind of inactivity that bordered on stupidity. Morel thought the boy's intellectual, moral, and physical functions had deteriorated as a result of hereditary causes and hence were irrecoverable. He used the term *demence precoce* (mental deterioration at an early age) to describe the condition and to distinguish it from disorders of old age.

The Latin form of this term—*dementia praecox*—was subsequently adopted by the German psychiatrist Emil Kraepelin to refer to a group of conditions that all seemed to have the feature of mental deterioration beginning early in life. Actually, however, the term is somewhat misleading, because the problems usually become apparent not during childhood but during adolescence or early adulthood. In addition, there is no conclusive evidence of permanent mental deterioration in the natural course of most of the disorders subsumed by the term. It appears that both Morel and Kraepelin mistook as a manifestation of progressive brain disease the gradual deterioration of psychosocial functioning that was in fact a result of lengthy incarceration in the bleak and demoralizing mental institutions of the time.

It remained for a Swiss psychiatrist, Eugen Bleuler, to introduce in 1911 a more acceptable descriptive term for this general class of disorders. He used *schizophrenia* (split mind) because he thought the condition was characterized primarily by disorganization of thought processes, a lack of coherence between thought and emotion, and an inward orientation away (split off) from reality. The "splitting" thus does not imply multiple personalities, an entirely different form of disorder discussed in Chapter 6, but a splitting within the intellect, between the intellect and emotion, and between the intellect and external reality.

It is by no means clear that schizophrenia is a unitary process, however. The existence of a single diagnostic label—in this case, *schizophrenia*—does not by itself establish similarity of underlying organization in each case of schizophrenia, any more than does a medical diagnosis of high blood pressure, which can be due to many different underlying conditions. Thus many clinicians today believe that there may be several schizophrenias, quite apart from the classic subtypes such as paranoid and catatonic, with different causal patterns and outcomes (Bellak, 1979). As we will see, there is empirical support for this pluralist view. Interestingly, the title of Bleuler's (1911/1950) masterful treatise on the subject refers to "the Group of Schizophrenias."

Schizophrenic disorders seem to occur in virtually all societies, from the aborigines of the western Australian desert to the remote interior jungles of Malaysia to the most technologically advanced societies. In the United States, the estimated incidence of schizophrenia is slightly under 1 percent of the population. The six-month prevalence rate for schizophrenia (that is, the proportion of people considered to be schizophrenic at any time during a prior six-month period) in the United States at present is estimated to be 0.9 percent of those 18 or older—or about 1.5 million affected people (Locke & Regier, 1985). In recent years schizophrenia has been the primary diagnosis for nearly 40 percent of all admissions to state and county mental hospitals, far outstripping all other diagnostic categories; it has been the second most frequent primary diagnosis (the first being either mood or alcohol-related disorders) for every other type of inpatient psychiatric care, including private hospitals (Manderscheid et al., 1985). During calendar year 1986, approximately 900,000 people received hospital or clinic services in the United States for a primary diagnosis of schizophrenia (Rosenstein, Milazzo-Sayre, & Manderscheid, 1989). Because schizophrenic individuals often require prolonged or repeated hospitalization, they usually constitute about half the patient population for all available mental hospital beds in this country (President's Commission on Mental Health, 1978).

Although schizophrenic disorders sometimes occur during childhood or old age, about three-fourths of all first admissions are between the ages of 15 and 45, with a median age of just over 30. The incidence rate is about the same for males and females. Because of their complexity, their high rate of incidence (especially during the most productive years of life), and their tendency to recur or become chronic, the schizophrenias are considered the most serious of all mental disorders, as well as among the most baffling.

■ A Case Study

We depart somewhat from our usual format in discussing the clinical syndromes to present first a unique and uniquely well-documented case study involving the schizophrenic syndrome. We hope this approach will help you more readily understand the many facets of schizophrenia. The case involves a family of six—two biological parents and their four monozygotic, quadruplet daughters—in which all four daughters became schizophrenic prior to age 25. Some appreciation of just how remarkable this circumstance is can be derived from the combined improbability of viable quadruplicate births, identical heredity, and perfect concordance for schizophrenia; a fairly liberal estimate is that it would occur once in every 1.5 *billion* births. We are indebted for the thorough knowledge we have of this unfortunate family to David Rosenthal (1963) and his colleagues, working under the auspices of the National Institute of Mental Health. For obvious reasons, certain specific but nonessential data, such as names and dates, have been omitted or falsified in the report, and we will honor that consideration in our synopsis. Should you be tempted to jump to the conclusion that these are obviously cases of genetically determined disorder, we counsel keeping an open mind on this point.

Background and Early Years   Some time in the early 1930s, quadruplet girls were born to Mr. and Mrs. Henry Genain, the product of a marriage occasioned by Mr. Genain's threatening to kill the reluctant Mrs. Genain unless she consented to the marriage. Except for their low birth weights, ranging from Nora's 4 lb, 8 oz, to Hester's 3 lb, the girls appeared to be reasonably normal babies, albeit "premature." Hester had to be fitted with a truss (an abdominal compression device) because of a bilateral hernia but was nevertheless discharged from the hospital with her sisters as basically healthy some six weeks after the birth. These were the only children the Genains ever had.

The most pervasive, if not necessarily the most formative, feature of the girls' early life was their fame. From birth, they received a great deal of attention from the media and the public. Early on, in fact, their parents started charging admission (25 cents) to members of the public to visit the home and view the babies, an enterprise that ended when the parents became concerned about the possibility of kidnapping or the transmission of some disease to the children. In subsequent years the children were encouraged in dancing and singing as a team, and they performed often at various functions and at school assemblies. Partly as a result of their "celebrity" status, the girls tended to stick closely together for mutual protection; they even rebuffed children their own age, with the result that they became social isolates. They were encouraged in this social isolation by their parents, who shared strong anxieties about the dangers of "the outside world."

Notwithstanding their genetic identity and physical similarity, the girls were sharply differentiated by their parents virtually from birth. In fact they were treated as though they were two sets of twins—a superior and talented set consisting of Nora and Myra, and an inferior, problematic set consisting of Iris and Hester. Hester—the "runt of the litter"—was regarded from an early age as oversexed. (Possibly because of irritation from her truss, Hester began to masturbate regularly by the age of three, a habit she continued for many years to the considerable dismay of her parents.) Complying with parental attributions, the girls did in fact pair up for purposes of mutual support and intimacy; when threatened from the outside, however, they became a true foursome.

Mr. Genain held a minor political office for more than 20 years, having been pushed into running by his wife. His job was not very demanding, and he spent most of his time drinking and expressing his various fears and obsessions to his family. Prominent among these were fears that break-ins would occur at the home unless he patrolled the premises constantly with a loaded gun, and, especially as the girls developed into adolescence, that they would get into sexual trouble or be raped unless he watched over them with total dedication.

He imposed almost unbelievable restrictions and surveillance on the girls until the time of their breakdowns. Beginning at an early age and persisting through early adulthood, Mr. Genain insisted on being present when his daughters dressed and undressed. He even insisted on watching them change their sanitary pads during menstruation. He was himself sexually promiscuous around town and was reported to have sexually molested at least two of his daughters; quite possibly Myra, who distanced herself from him with singular persistence, was the only one of the girls to escape his attentions in this regard.

Mr. Genain's preoccupation with sexuality, while extreme and almost preemptive of anything else, was at least matched by that of his wife. Mrs. Genain managed to see sexuality and sexual threats in the most innocuous circumstances and yet was curiously impervious to certain real sexual activity occurring practically before her eyes. When the girls complained to her about Mr. Genain's sexual attentions, she dismissed these happenings with the rationale that Mr. Genain was merely testing their virtue; if they objected to his advances, then clearly all was well. Not that she saw Mr. Genain as a paragon of virtue; on the contrary, she recited his many faults of breeding and grossness to anyone who would listen. Nevertheless, she stuck by him to the end (a typically alcoholic end) and largely confirmed and supported his bizarre constructions of reality. Hester, the chronic masturbator, was a particular thorn in her side—all the more so when she discovered that, at about age 12, Hester had apparently seduced Iris into the practice of mutual masturbation, which Iris found pleasing. Apparently unable to think of any more appropriate response to this dilemma, the parents—on the questionable advice of a physician—forced the two girls to submit to clitoral circumcisions, a measure whose drastic quality was exceeded only by its ineffectiveness in altering the offending behavior. In general, however, Mrs. Genain enjoyed the status accorded her as the mother of quadruplets, and she remained unfailingly and overwhelmingly involved in the girls' lives. Most of her affection was reserved for the "good" quads, Nora and Myra.

Adolescence, Young Adulthood, and Breakdown
Except for their extreme social isolation, the girls had a relatively uneventful junior high school experience. They were regarded by their teachers as conforming, hard-working, and "nice," except for some competition among them in respect to grades and adult approval. Hester clearly lagged behind the others, and Iris could not quite keep up with the remaining two in academic performance. Essentially the same pattern continued into high school. In the summer preceding the girls' senior year, Hester, whose behavior had become somewhat peculiar and who was apparently suffering from some type of psychophysiologic gastrointestinal distress, finally became disturbed to the point that her parents could hardly manage her. She was temperamental, often did not seem to know what she was doing, destroyed household furnishings, tore both her own and her sisters' clothing, and on one occasion struck Nora with such force as to render her unconscious. Hester had just turned 18; she never thereafter regained a full measure of effective mental functioning.

The other three girls completed their senior year of high school, engaging in a kind of conspiracy of silence regarding the missing Hester, who remained at home. Outwardly they appeared to be normal adolescents, although they were not permitted to have boyfriends and continued to have various physical difficulties, including menstrual irregularities and persistent enuresis (bed-wetting). Following graduation, they obtained employment as office workers. They continued to be spied on by their suspicious father, however, lest they become involved in sexual liaisons. They were not permitted to date. Of the three, Myra maintained the most independence, defying her father's edict that she not go out at night to meetings and the like.

None of the three young women was comfortable in the world of work, feeling inadequate to the responsibilities heaped on them by allegedly insensitive bosses. Nora was the first to evidence unusual "nervousness," and at age 20 began to have a series of vague physical complaints. She eventually quit her job and took to her bed at home, gradually becoming more disturbed. She stood on her knees and elbows until they became irritated and bled, began to walk and talk in her sleep, and moaned and groaned a great deal, especially at mealtime. Her behavior continued to deteriorate until, at age 22, she underwent her first of several hospital admissions with the diagnosis of schizophrenia. In the meantime, Iris had likewise become increasingly disturbed, also resigning from her job. She was troubled by "spastic colon," vomiting, insomnia, and the belief that people were paying her undue attention. In fact it was later learned that Mr. Genain was at the time greatly attentive to her whereabouts and activities and may have been molesting her. Within several months after Nora's first admission, Iris "just went to pieces." She screamed, was markedly agitated, complained of hearing voices and of people fighting, and drooled at meals, being unable to swallow anything but liquids. She, too, was hospitalized toward the end of her twenty-second year for the first of many times. The diagnosis was schizophrenia.

Myra did not break down until age 24. The onset was similar to that of her sisters: vomiting, panic, insomnia, and waking up at night screaming. Myra resisted hospitalization at this time and, in fact, was not hospitalized until the entire family was shortly thereafter moved to the Clinical Center of the National Institute of Mental Health (NIMH). There, as a unit, they underwent the lengthy and detailed study of which this history is one product. On arrival, Myra was autistic, disordered in thought, and impaired in judgment and reality testing. She was diagnosed as schizophrenic.

It may be significant that in the cases of Nora, Iris, and Myra, deterioration began shortly after an incident in which a man had made rather insistent "improper advances." In paradoxical but characteristic fashion, both parents had minimized the significance of these incidents when the girls complained.

Course and Outcome   By the time they arrived at the Clinical Center at age 24, Nora had

undergone three separate hospital admissions and Iris five. Hester had somehow escaped hospitalization, although she was often bizarre and psychotic at home. With all four of the daughters simultaneously disturbed in varying degrees, the home atmosphere had become truly chaotic.

Once at the NIMH, the sisters were offered varied forms of treatment and care, including the new antipsychotic medications that had recently become available. They remained at the NIMH for three years. At the end of their stay, Myra was the only one capable of attaining a sustainable discharge. The other three sisters were transferred to a state hospital. Mr. Genain had died of liver disease in the interim.

It is important to note that, though the earliest symptoms of the quads were similar in certain respects, the courses and outcomes of their disorders differed markedly and, to some extent, in ways that could have been predicted. The most serious and deteriorated of the classical types of schizophrenia is the *disorganized type* (formerly called *hebephrenic*). In the various diagnoses assigned to them in the course of their hospitalizations, Nora and Myra were never so diagnosed, although Nora was sometimes regarded as having "hebephrenic features." By contrast, Iris and Hester moved through the "milder" *catatonic* and *undifferentiated types* into the disorganized type. The quads' outcomes show a corresponding pattern. At the time of Rosenthal's 1963 report, Myra was working steadily, married, and doing well. Nora was making a marginal adjustment outside of the hospital. Iris was still fluctuating between periods of severe disturbance and relative lucidity in which she could manage brief

In 1981, the Genains performed a rendition of "Alice Blue Gown" at a birthday party held in their honor at the National Institute of Mental Health.

stays outside of the hospital. Hester remained continuously hospitalized in a condition of severe psychosis and was considered essentially a "hopeless case."

It is a tribute to the scientific diligence of the NIMH staff and to David Rosenthal, who has maintained both a human and a scientific interest in this unfortunate family, that we had a follow-up report some 20 years after the original one (DeLisi et al., 1984; Mirsky et al., 1984; Sargent, 1982a). In general, the relative adjustment of the sisters, then in their 50s, remained in 1982 as it was in the 1960s. Myra continued to do well and had two children in the interim. The other three women were living at home with their mother, with Nora continuing to show a higher level of functioning than Iris or Hester. All of the quads were on continuous medication, and even the beleaguered Hester appeared to have overcome to an extent her originally dismal prognosis. It is of considerable interest that newer techniques of neurological assessment showed that Nora had impairments of the central nervous system similar to those of Hester, and yet her outcome seemed far better than that of Hester or even Iris. It is possible that the original pairing of Iris with Hester was inappropriate (at least in the limited sense implied here) and quite destructive of Iris' subsequent psychosocial development. In any event, we see that the quads, despite their identical heredity, array themselves along a considerable range of the possible outcomes associated with schizophrenic breakdown.

Interpretive Comment   We have here, then, four genetically identical women, all of whom have experienced schizophrenic disorders. The disorders, however, have been different in severity, chronicity, and eventual outcome. Obviously these differences must be ascribed to differences in the environments the quads experienced, including their intrauterine environments, which presumably contributed to their modest variations detectable at birth. Clearly Hester, in relative parental disfavor from the beginning, faced the harshest environmental conditions, followed closely by her "twin," Iris. The outcome for these women has been grim. Myra was the most favored youngster and clearly the one who experienced the least objectionable parental attention, partly owing to a greater independence and assertiveness than her sisters displayed. Nora was a close second in this respect but had the misfortune of being her incestuous father's "favorite"; in recent tests, she also proved to have a compromised central nervous system (specifically, an imbalance of metabolic rates in different brain areas) comparable to that of Hester. Though Nora has not done as well as

Myra, she has emerged as clearly superior in functioning to the other two sisters. We see here the enormous power of environmental forces in determining personal destiny.

But let us look again. We have four genetically identical individuals, all of whom became schizophrenic within a period of six years—three of them within a period of some two years. Is this not a compelling case for genetic determination? An independent genealogical history suggests that the quads' father may have harbored some pathogenic genes, which could have been passed on to his daughters. On the other hand, we must ask what might have happened to these girls in the absence of any special genetic impediments. As Rosenthal (1963) points out, their parents failed spectacularly in the most elementary tasks of parenthood. Can we imagine that the Genain sisters would have been reasonably well-adjusted had they possessed no defective genes? This scenario seems rather unlikely.

In the final analysis, a plausible conclusion is that both heredity and environment, operating in some complex and at present mysterious interaction, contributed to the Genain sisters' vulnerabilities. In this instance, unfortunately, it is difficult to make even an estimate of the relative magnitude of the two influences. In some other instances of schizophrenic disorder, one can make a shrewd guess—based on genetic history, developmental experience, and the like—about the relative contribution from each of these two broad sources of behavioral variation. As we have seen, however, and as we will see repeatedly again in this chapter, the central fact always is the interaction between the two. We will refer to the Genains from time to time in the pages that follow.

■ The Clinical Picture in Schizophrenia

Sometimes schizophrenic disorders develop slowly and insidiously. In such cases the early clinical picture may be dominated by seclusiveness, gradual lack of interest in the surrounding world, excessive daydreaming, blunting of affect (diminished emotional responsivity), and mildly inappropriate responses, such as peculiar grimacing or ineptitude in appreciating social proprieties. This symptom pattern has traditionally been referred to as **process schizophrenia**—that is, it develops gradually over a period of time, not in response to obvious discrete stressors, and tends to be long-lasting. The outcome for process schizophrenia is considered generally unfavorable, doubtless partly because the need for treatment is usually not recognized until the behavior pattern has become firmly entrenched. **Poor**

premorbid (preexisting the occurrence of actual disorder) or **chronic schizophrenia** are alternative terms referring to this pattern.

In other instances, the onset of schizophrenic symptoms is quite sudden and dramatic and is marked by intense emotional turmoil and a nightmarish sense of confusion. This pattern, which usually is associated with identifiable precipitating stressors, is referred to as **reactive schizophrenia** (alternatively, **good premorbid** or **acute schizophrenia**). Here the symptoms often clear up in a matter of weeks, though in some cases an acute episode is the prelude to a more chronic pattern.

Today, particularly in the psychiatric literature, the terms **negative-symptom schizophrenia** and **positive-symptom schizophrenia** are being used to refer to the symptom patterns themselves and appear to overlap considerably with the older *process* and *reactive* designations, respectively (Andreasen, 1985). By *negative symptoms* is meant an absence or deficit of behaviors normally present in a person's repertoire, such as affective expression or reactivity to the environment; these symptoms are typically more "subtle." *Positive symptoms,* by contrast, are those in which something has been *added* to a normal repertoire of behavior and experience, such as marked emotional turmoil, motor agitation, delusional interpretation of events, or hallucinations.

Of the Genain quadruplets, Hester—who never seemed quite as well off mentally as her sisters and who seemed to move in imperceptible steps toward increasing deterioration—would be considered a more process (or poor premorbid, or negative-symptom) type. By contrast, Myra, the least disturbed before her breakdown, the last to succumb, and the one whose symptoms, while dramatic, were most circumscribed in time, would be considered a more reactive (good premorbid, positive-symptom) case. Although the experience of the Genains fits this classic dichotomy as it is conceived, there are some serious problems with this conception, as indicated in what follows.

It is sometimes held that antipsychotic medication affects only positive symptoms. This appears to be an erroneous clinical observation, however, since it has been known for many years that negative symptoms, such as social withdrawal, may also respond to these medications (NIMH Psychopharmacology Service Center Collaborative Study Group, 1964). This finding was reconfirmed by Kay & Singh (1989) in a rigorously designed recent study. Another widespread belief is that positive schizophrenia has a better long-term prognosis than negative schizophrenia, but the 36-month follow-up of their patients by Kay and Singh surprisingly indicated the opposite to be the case.

There thus seems to be some confusion concerning the meaning, if any, of this dichotomy. In fact, it is in all likelihood *not* a dichotomy. With rare exception, the available research evidence indicates that the distinctions mentioned in the preceding paragraphs should really be viewed as continua. In regard to positive- versus negative-symptom patterns, instances of schizophrenic disorder can be seen as distributing themselves in the familiar bell-shaped curve, with relatively few falling at either the negative- or positive-symptom extremes and most falling somewhere in the middle. We thus expect a large percentage of schizophrenic patients to display both positive and negative symptoms, as seems in fact to be the case (Guelfi, Faustman, & Csernansky, 1989). Everything considered, therefore, we have considerable doubt that the distinction now designated by the positive/negative rubric is a valid or useful one. Similar reservations have recently been expressed by Andreasen et al. (1990) following a more comprehensive review of the evidence.

Another distinction commonly made by researchers is that between *paranoid* and *nonparanoid symptom patterns* in schizophrenia. In the paranoid pattern, delusions, particularly persecutory or grandiose ones, are a dominant feature; in the nonparanoid forms, delusions, if present at all, tend to be rare, fleeting, and of inconsistent content. Evidence is building that important differences exist between those who exhibit a predominant paranoid symptom pattern and those who exhibit few, or no, or inconsistent paranoid symptoms.

In general, paranoid schizophrenic individuals tend to be more reactive than process in type and to have more benign courses and outcomes (Ritzler, 1981); they are less likely to show the striking kinds of cognitive or attentional deficits seen in other forms of the disorder (Rabin, Doneson, & Jentons, 1979). They may also be genetically less vulnerable to schizophrenia than nonparanoid types (Kendler & Davis, 1981). It has been found, however, that a substantial number of people originally diagnosed as having paranoid forms of schizophrenic disorder are later diagnosed as having nonparanoid ones (Kendler & Tsuang, 1981). Also, there appears to be a small subgroup of paranoid schizophrenic people whose disorders are extremely intractable and chronic. It is of interest to note that all of the Genain sisters exhibited exclusively nonparanoid symptoms during the active phases of their disorders.

Whether positive, negative, paranoid, or nonparanoid in the general sense of these terms, schizophrenia encompasses many specific symptoms that vary greatly over time in an individual's life and from one individual to another. The basic experience in schizophrenia, however, seems to be disorganization in perception, thought, and emotion. The DSM-III-R specifies in concrete terms a list of criteria for the diagnosis, reproduced in *HIGHLIGHT 12.1*. What follows is a more elaborated version of those criteria.

Disorganization of a Previous Level of Functioning

Disorganization of functioning is perhaps the closest we can come to an accepted cardinal sign of schizophrenic breakdown; it distinguishes the schizophrenias from various developmental anomalies, such as infantile autism, in which the person has never attained a degree of integrated behavioral functioning consistent with his or her age. The impairment always occurs in areas of routine daily functioning, such as work, social relations, and self-care, such that observers note that the person is not himself or herself any more.

Disturbance of Language and Communication

First described at length by Bleuler (1911/1950) and often referred to as *formal thought disorder*, communication disturbance, too, is usually considered a prime indicator of a schizophrenic disorder. Basically, an affected individual fails to conform to the semantic and syntactic rules governing verbal communication in the known language—but this failure is *not* attributable to low intelligence, poor education, or cultural deprivation. Meehl (1962) aptly referred to the process as one of "cognitive slippage"; others have referred to it as "derailment" or "loosening" of associations. However labeled, the phenomenon is readily recognized by experienced clinicians: the patient *seems* to be using words in combinations that sound communicative, but in the final analysis, the listener becomes aware of understanding little or nothing of what has been said. Meehl cited as an example the statement, "I'm growing my father's hair"; see *HIGHLIGHT 12.2* for additional examples.

Disturbance of Thought Content

Disturbances in the content of thought typically involve certain standard types of delusion. Prominent among these are the false beliefs that one's thoughts, feelings, or actions are being controlled by external agents; that one's private thoughts are being broadcast indiscriminately to others; that thoughts are being inserted into one's brain by alien forces; that some mysterious agency has robbed one of one's thoughts; or that some innocuous, impersonal environmental event has an intended personal meaning, often termed an "idea of reference." Other absurd convictions, including delusions of grotesque bodily changes, are regularly observed.

Disruption of Perception

Major perceptual disruption often accompanies the criteria already indicated. An apparent breakdown in perceptual filtering is frequently observed wherein the patient seems unable to sort out and properly dispose of the great mass of sensory information to which all of us are exposed in most waking moments. As a result, everything "gets through," overwhelming the meager resources the person has for appropriate information processing. This point is well-illustrated in the following statements of schizophrenic people:

> *"I feel like I'm too alert . . . everything seems to come pouring in at once . . . I can't seem to keep anything out. . . ."*
>
> *"My nerves seem supersensitive . . . objects seem brighter . . . noises are louder . . . my feelings are so intense . . . things seem so vivid and they come at me like a flood from a broken dam."*
>
> *"It seems like nothing ever stops. Thoughts just keep coming in and racing round in my head . . . and getting broken up . . . sort of into pieces of thoughts and images . . . like tearing up a picture. And everything is out of control . . . I can't seem to stop it."*

It is estimated that approximately 50 percent of patients diagnosed as schizophrenic experience this breakdown of perceptual selectivity during the onset of their disorders (Freedman & Chapman, 1973).

Other even more dramatic perceptual phenomena include hallucinations—perceptions for which there are no discernible external stimuli. Hallucinations in the schizophrenias are normally auditory, although they can also be visual and even olfactory. The typical hallucination is one in which a voice (or voices) keeps up a running commentary on the individual's behaviors or thoughts.

Inappropriate Emotion

The schizophrenic syndromes are often said to include an element of clearly inappropriate emotion, or affect. In the more severe or chronic cases, the picture is usually one of apparent *anhedonia* (inability to experience joy or pleasure) and emotional shallowness, or "blunting" (lack of intensity or clear definition). On casual observation, the person may appear virtually emotionless, so that even the most compelling and dramatic events produce at most an intellectual recognition of what is happening. In other instances, particularly in the acute phases, the person may show strong affect, but the emotion clashes

DSM–III–R Diagnostic Criteria for Schizophrenia

A. Presence of characteristic psychotic symptoms in the active phase: either (1), (2), or (3) for at least one week (unless the symptoms are successfully treated):

    (1) two of the following:
        (a) delusions
        (b) prominent hallucinations (throughout the day for several days or several times a week for several weeks, each hallucinatory episode not being limited to a few brief moments)
        (c) incoherence or marked loosening of associations
        (d) catatonic behavior
        (e) flat or grossly inappropriate affect

    (2) bizarre delusions (i.e., involving a phenomenon that the person's culture would regard as totally implausible, e.g., thought broadcasting, being controlled by a dead person)

    (3) prominent hallucinations [as defined in (1)(b) above] of a voice with content having no apparent relation to depression or elation, or a voice keeping up a running commentary on the person's behavior or thoughts, or two or more voices conversing with each other.

B. During the course of the disturbance, functioning in such areas as work, social relations, and self-care is markedly below the highest level achieved before onset of the disturbance (or, when onset is in childhood or adolescence, failure to achieve expected level of social development).

C. Schizoaffective Disorder and Mood Disorder with Psychotic Features have been ruled out, i.e., if a Major Depression or Manic Syndrome has ever been present during an active phase of the disturbance, the total duration of all episodes of a mood syndrome has been brief relative to the total duration of the active and residual phases of the disturbance.

D. Continuous signs of the disturbance for at least six months. The six-month period must include an active phase (of at least one week, or less if symptoms have been successfully treated) during which there were psychotic symptoms characteristic of Schizophrenia (symptoms in A), with or without a prodromal phase, as defined below.

Prodromal phase: A clear deterioration in functioning before the active phase of the disturbance that is not due to a disturbance in mood or to a Psychoactive Substance Use Disorder and that involves at least two of the symptoms listed below.

Residual phase: Following the active phase of the disturbance, persistence of at least two of the symptoms listed below, these not being due to a disturbance in mood or to a Psychoactive Substance Use Disorder.

Prodromal or Residual Symptoms

    (1) marked social isolation or withdrawal

    (2) marked impairment in role functioning as wage earner, student, or homemaker

    (3) markedly peculiar behavior (e.g., collecting garbage, talking to self in public, hoarding food)

    (4) marked impairment in personal hygiene or grooming

    (5) blunted or inappropriate affect

    (6) digressive, vague, overelaborate, or circumstantial speech, or poverty of speech, or poverty of content of speech

    (7) odd beliefs or magical thinking, influencing behavior and inconsistent with cultural norms, e.g., superstitiousness, belief in clairvoyance, telepathy, "sixth sense," "others can feel my feelings," overvalued ideas, ideas of reference

    (8) unusual perceptual experiences, e.g., recurrent illusions, sensing the presence of a force or person not actually present

    (9) marked lack of initiative, interests, or energy

E. It cannot be established that an organic factor initiated and maintained the disturbance.

F. If there is a history of Autistic Disorder, the additional diagnosis of Schizophrenia is made only if prominent delusions or hallucinations are also present.

American Psychiatric Association (1987).

Schizophrenic Writings

The personality decompensation in psychotic reactions is frequently manifested in the content and form of patients' letters and other spontaneous writings. These examples clearly reveal the "loosening" and deviations of thought, the distortion of affect, and the lowered contact with reality so common among schizophrenic individuals. The postcard is a reproduction of a card sent by a paranoid schizophrenic man.

The handwritten excerpts are from a letter written by an 18-year-old woman, also diagnosed as paranoid schizophrenic. As is apparent from the first and last parts of the letter, shown here, the handwriting is of two quite different types, suggestive of the writer's emotional conflict and personality disorganization. Lewinson (1940) included this letter in her study of handwriting characteristics of different types of psychotic patients. Among such patients generally, she found that handwriting typically showed abnormal rhythmic disturbances, with rigidity or extreme irregularity in height, breadth, or depth.

> To: The football department and its members present and future
>   The University of New Mexico, Albuquerque, N. M.
>
> I depend on correct, honest supplementation of this card by telepathy as a thing which will make clear the meaning of this card. There exists a Playing of The Great Things, the correct, the constructive, world or universe politics, out-in-the-open telepathy, etc. According to the Great Things this playing is the most feasible thing of all; but it is held from newspaper advertising and correct, honest public world recognition, its next step, by telepathic forces (it seems), physical dangers, and lack of money. Over 10,000 cards and letters on this subject have been sent to prominent groups and persons all over the world. Correct, honest contact with the honest, out-in-the-open world. This line of thought, talk, etc. rule. The plain and frank. Strangers. The Great Things and opposites idea. References: In the telepathic world the correct playings. Please save this card for a history record since it is rare and important for history.

"Dear Dad" (15.) — Oct 9
—..... Please come to see me immediately. It's very urgent that I see you as quickly as possible.

Just now my insides are rotting with each meal & I have to eat with very disagreeable old hags.

• • • • • • • • •

But it's a matter of life or death & if I don't get any response from you as yet I haven't I swear by that Bible I jump in front of a car. That I'm in need of fun & I am Goddam it. Come up as soon as possible. Here are the Fatal Day & the one Red Letter day, is the one that see do it on when released. Last Chance! Danger
Oct 9, 10, 11, 12, 13 14 15, 16
be a corpse on 16th of the month when I'm out. Goodbye forever
Helen R

with the situation or with the content of his or her thoughts. For example, such a person may laugh uproariously on receiving news of a parent's death. Characteristically, affective "blunting" extends to matters of taste, discretion, and social sensibility— so that, for example, the patient may masturbate in public, seemingly oblivious to other people.

Confused Sense of Self   A schizophrenic person often is perplexed about his or her identity (including gender identity) and, in addition, frequently is confused about the boundaries separating the self from the rest of the world. The latter confusion is often associated with frightening "cosmic" or "oceanic" feelings of being somehow intimately tied up with universal powers, including the deity. It appears to be related to ideas of external control and similar delusions.

Disrupted Volition   Goal-directed activity is almost universally disrupted in schizophrenic individuals, whether due to an intentional flouting of external expectations or to an inability to carry through a course of action. For example, the person may be unable to maintain minimum standards of personal hygiene.

Detached Relationship to the External World   Ties to the external world are almost by definition loosened in the schizophrenic disorders, and in extreme instances, the withdrawal may be nearly total. This detachment is usually accompanied by the elaboration of an inner world in which the person develops illogical and fantastic ideational constructions having little or no relationship to reality as perceived by others. Since the days of Bleuler, this process has generally been referred to as *autism*.

Disturbed Motor Behavior   Various peculiarities of movement are sometimes observed in the schizophrenias; indeed, this is the chief and defining characteristic of catatonic schizophrenia, of which more will be said later. These motor disturbances range from an excited sort of hyperactivity to a marked decrease in all movement or an apparent clumsiness. Also included here are various forms of rigid posturing, mutism, ritualistic mannerisms, and bizarre grimacing.

■ Problems in Defining Schizophrenic Behavior

In an effort to provide for a clear-cut diagnosis of schizophrenia and to sharply distinguish it from mood or other disorders, DSM-III and DSM-III-R criteria are far more exact and explicit than those in earlier DSM editions. Recalling our discussion of these matters in Chapter 1, such an approach almost necessarily enhances diagnostic *reliability* (that is, the agreement on what diagnosis should be assigned). Whether or not it does the same for *validity* (the conceptual and predictive meaningfulness of the diagnosis) depends on the adequacy with which the category, so defined, reflects some natural organization of the behaviors defining the category. Put another way, validity depends on the level of arbitrariness with which the purported entity is defined. Like Goldstein (1983) in a historical review of the *concept* of schizophrenia in light of the then-current DSM-III criteria, we find ourselves unconvinced that DSM-III and the similar DSM-III-R diagnoses of schizophrenia have substantially improved validity.

Persistent problems in the differentiation of mood and schizophrenic disorders, touched on in our Chapter 11 description of schizoaffective disorder, provide an instructive example. A number of factors are involved here. Though DSM-III-R clearly distinguishes, by means of exclusionary language, between mood disorders and schizophrenic disorders, whether these are two discrete and mutually exclusive entities is still open for debate (Lehmann, 1985; Noll, Davis, & DeLeon-Jones, 1985; Wing & Bebbington, 1985). DSM-III and its revision resolved this debate by fiat. One clear result is that the numbers of people considered schizophrenic and mood disordered have changed drastically.

In one study, Winters, Weintraub, and Neale (1981) had 68 DSM-II-diagnosed schizophrenic patients rediagnosed according to DSM-III criteria; only 35 survived the cut, the remainder—nearly half—being allocated mostly to the mood disorders. Comparable findings have been reported by Harrow, Carone, and Westermeyer (1985), whose 111 DSM-II diagnosed schizophrenic patients were reduced to 45 on rediagnosis. Taking such results seriously entails the rather disconcerting conclusion that diagnosed schizophrenic people of the 1980s and 1990s are a *different population* from schizophrenic people of the 1970s. Among many problems, these diagnostic differences call into question the current value of research in "schizophrenia" that began prior to the adoption of DSM-III in 1980—many thousands of studies purporting to teach us important things about the disorder. The drastic change in defining criteria would be defensible, and even laudable, had it been based on dramatic new knowledge refining our understanding of some natural order in this realm of psychopathology. It was not.

Other problems with the current diagnostic criteria for schizophrenia, discussed in detail by Carson and Sanislow (1992), deserve brief mention. A serious one is that they represent a hodgepodge of previously suggested indicators of the presumed entity. You may wish to assess the magnitude of this difficulty by trying to use these criteria (chiefly those included under *A; see HIGHLIGHT 12.1* on page 435) to construct a mental image of the typical schizophrenic person; we suspect that you will encounter unusual frustration in such an exercise. Additionally, the prominent role assigned to hallucinations (especially "voices") in the criteria for schizophrenia involves a basic problem of reliability of observation, since the only possible observer of such private phenomena is the hallucinator, and no other signs are available to corroborate their occurrence. This is an observer, moreover, whose credibility is suspect, if only because he or she hears disembodied voices talking to him or her. We do not raise this puzzle lightly or facetiously: observational consensus, forever unattainable in this context, is the bedrock of scientific understanding.

It should be stated clearly that in taking this critical stand we are not championing or advocating a return to the relatively vague DSM-II definition of schizophrenia; an unreliable category cannot be a *valid* one. But the enhanced reliability of the DSM-III (and DSM-III-R) definition (see, for example, Robins & Helzer, 1986) does not in itself speak to the issue of validity, and we are entitled to a degree of skepticism about a construct that can so radically change in meaning from one edition of the DSM to another. In addition, as we have seen, a close examination of the DSM-III-R criteria for the diagnosis of schizophrenia provides little reassurance that, in the inevitable trade-off between reliability and validity, the latter has not been sacrificed.

In an unusually direct attempt to assess one aspect of validity—namely, the prediction of short-term case outcome—the DSM-III diagnostic criteria for schizophrenia did relatively well in competition with six alternative approaches to diagnosing the disorder; however, all of them did poorly in an absolute sense. That is, they were notably inadequate in predicting the clinical status of patients a mere 6 to 25 months following their intake diagnoses (Endicott et al., 1986). For example, the DSM-III predicted an "overall outcome" measure at a correlational level of +.12, and a measure of "unusual thoughts or perceptual experiences" at +.18. We know of no other data bearing on validity that seriously challenge this rather dismal performance.

The most radical approach to the problem of defining schizophrenia has been advanced by Sarbin and Mancuso (1980; Sarbin, in press), who suggest-

ed, as had Laing (1969) earlier, that there is in fact no such thing as schizophrenia—that the idea is a mythical construction not differing in logical substance from the concept of the unicorn. These authors consider "schizophrenia" to be essentially a "moral verdict" imposed on certain people engaging in unacceptable or unintelligible behavior, rather than a legitimate medical diagnosis. Their argument, admittedly startling, cannot be summarily dismissed when considered thoughtfully and dispassionately. They point out that attributing certain behaviors to a disease entity called schizophrenia does not establish the existence of that entity in the absence of independent, confirmatory evidence, of which little in fact exists, as we will see.

Not even Sarbin and Mancuso deny the existence of the *behaviors* under consideration here, nor do they deny that certain of these behaviors, although not obviously similar to one another, tend to occur together. Such behavior patterns may be analogous to the "syndromes" of symptoms that occur together in various physical (medical) disorders whose underlying causes may not be completely understood—as, for instance, in kidney dysfunctions of undetermined origin. As earlier noted, this is precisely the way in which Bellak (1979) approaches the perplexing problem of defining schizophrenia. He sees the behaviors that we conventionally associate with "schizophrenia" as the "final common pathway" of severe adaptive breakdown, whatever the source of that breakdown. While acknowledging that such issues are far from settled, we think the preponderance of evidence—especially the routine findings of marked heterogeneity among people acquiring the diagnosis—is on Bellak's side. The implication is that some unknown number of relatively distinct pathological processes currently masquerade under the common rubric "schizophrenia." Under this hypothesis, then, it should be possible eventually to disaggregate this overburdened class into its separate and distinct entities. So far, however, little progress has been made on this front.

In any case, it will be clear that the clinical picture in what is called schizophrenia often includes bizarre elements that may be unintelligible to either an affected individual or to external observers. An individual may show peculiarities of movement, gesture, and expression; act out inappropriate sexual and other fantasies; or simply sit apathetically staring into space. We will elaborate on these and other behavioral anomalies in describing the various diagnostic subtypes of schizophrenia.

Clearly not all of the symptoms of schizophrenia occur in every case. In fact, 80 years after the appearance of Bleuler's defining monograph, research has still not revealed a constant, single, universally accepted "sign" of the presence of schizophrenia. Thus the symptom picture may differ markedly from one schizophrenic person to another. Also, the symptom picture may change greatly over time within the same person. Most schizophrenic people "fade in and out of reality" as a function of their own inner state and environmental situation. They might be in "good contact" one day and evidence delusions and hallucinations the next. Likewise, an acute schizophrenic (or *schizophreniform*) reaction may clear up fairly rapidly and never return, or it may progress uninterruptedly to a chronic condition depending on the person and his or her situation.

■ Subtypes of Schizophrenia

Recent editions of the DSM have listed five subtypes of schizophrenia, which are summarized in the *HIGHLIGHT 12.3*. We will focus on four of these in our present discussion: *undifferentiated, catatonic, disorganized,* and *paranoid*. Of these, the undifferentiated and paranoid types are the most common today.

Undifferentiated Type   As the term implies, the diagnosis of **schizophrenia, undifferentiated type** is something of a "wastebasket" category. An individual so diagnosed meets the usual criteria for being schizophrenic—including (in varying combinations) delusions, hallucinations, disordered thoughts, and bizarre behaviors—but does not clearly fit into one of the other types because of a mixed symptom picture. People in the acute, early phases of a schizophrenic breakdown frequently exhibit undifferentiated symptoms, as do those who are in transitional phases from one to another of the standard types, which in fact happens rather often. Each of the Genain sisters was given an undifferentiated diagnosis at least once, and all but Myra received such a diagnosis on several different occasions.

Probably most instances of acute, reactive schizophrenic breakdown occurring for the first time appear undifferentiated in type. However, current diagnostic criteria (that is, DSM-III-R) preclude the diagnosis of schizophrenia and require that of *schizophreniform disorder* (see p. 446) unless there have been signs of the disorder for at least six months, by which time a stable pattern may develop, consistent with a more definite indication of type. Some schizophrenic patients, on the other hand, remain undifferentiated over long time periods. The case of Rick Wheeler is illustrative of the latter course.

Rick Wheeler, 26 years old, neatly groomed, and friendly and cheerful in disposition, was removed from an airplane by airport police because he was creating a disturbance—from his own account probably because he was "on another dimension." On arrest, he was oriented to the extent of knowing where he was, his name, and the current date, but his report of these facts was embedded in a peculiar and circumstantial context involving science fiction themes. Investigation revealed he had been discharged from a nearby state mental hospital three days earlier. He was brought to another hospital by police.

On admission, physical examination and laboratory studies were normal, but Rick claimed he was Jesus Christ and that he could move mountains. His speech was extremely difficult to follow because of incoherence and derailment. For example, he explained his wish to leave the city "because things happen here I don't approve of. I approve of other things but I don't approve of the other things. And believe me it's worse for them in the end." He complained that the Devil wanted to kill him and that his food contained "ground-up corpses." He was born, he claimed, from his father's sexual organs.

Background investigation revealed that Rick's difficulties began, after a successful academic start, in elementary school: "I could comprehend but I couldn't store . . . it's like looking at something but being unable to take it in." He thereafter maintained a D average until he dropped out halfway through his junior year of high school. He had never held a full-time job, and his social adjustment had always been poor. He showed no interest in women until he married, at age 19, a patient he'd met during one of the earliest of some 20 of his hospitalizations, beginning at age 16. A daughter was born from this match, but Rick had lost track of both her and his wife; he had shown no further interest in women. Rick himself was the eldest of five children; there was no known mental disorder in any of his first-degree relatives (that is, siblings and parents).

Unable to maintain employment, Rick had been supported mainly on federal disability welfare—and by virtue of patienthood in public hospitals. His hospital admissions and discharges showed a substantial correlation with his varying financial status; that is, he tended to be released from the hospital around the first of the month, when his welfare check was due, and to be readmitted (or alternatively sent to jail) follow-

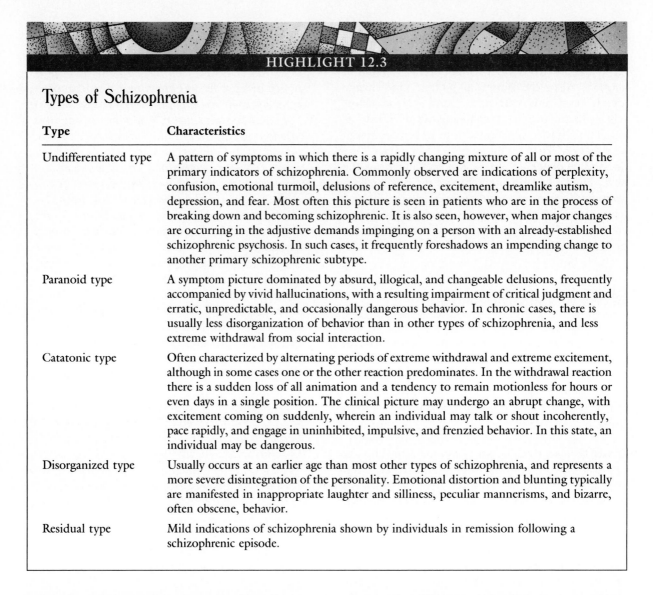

Types of Schizophrenia

Type	Characteristics
Undifferentiated type	A pattern of symptoms in which there is a rapidly changing mixture of all or most of the primary indicators of schizophrenia. Commonly observed are indications of perplexity, confusion, emotional turmoil, delusions of reference, excitement, dreamlike autism, depression, and fear. Most often this picture is seen in patients who are in the process of breaking down and becoming schizophrenic. It is also seen, however, when major changes are occurring in the adjustive demands impinging on a person with an already-established schizophrenic psychosis. In such cases, it frequently foreshadows an impending change to another primary schizophrenic subtype.
Paranoid type	A symptom picture dominated by absurd, illogical, and changeable delusions, frequently accompanied by vivid hallucinations, with a resulting impairment of critical judgment and erratic, unpredictable, and occasionally dangerous behavior. In chronic cases, there is usually less disorganization of behavior than in other types of schizophrenia, and less extreme withdrawal from social interaction.
Catatonic type	Often characterized by alternating periods of extreme withdrawal and extreme excitement, although in some cases one or the other reaction predominates. In the withdrawal reaction there is a sudden loss of all animation and a tendency to remain motionless for hours or even days in a single position. The clinical picture may undergo an abrupt change, with excitement coming on suddenly, wherein an individual may talk or shout incoherently, pace rapidly, and engage in uninhibited, impulsive, and frenzied behavior. In this state, an individual may be dangerous.
Disorganized type	Usually occurs at an earlier age than most other types of schizophrenia, and represents a more severe disintegration of the personality. Emotional distortion and blunting typically are manifested in inappropriate laughter and silliness, peculiar mannerisms, and bizarre, often obscene, behavior.
Residual type	Mild indications of schizophrenia shown by individuals in remission following a schizophrenic episode.

ing some public altercation after his money had run out. Numerous attempts to commit Rick to the hospital indefinitely on an involuntary basis had failed because he was able to appear competent at court appearances. He had, however, been declared incompetent to receive his own checks, and various relatives had stepped forward to handle his finances. Now they are afraid to do so because Rick set his grandmother's house afire, having concluded (erroneously, as it turned out) that she was withholding some of his money. He had also threatened others and had been arrested several times for carrying concealed weapons.

In the latest hospitalization, two different antipsychotic medications were tried over a period of five weeks with no discernible improvement. Rick still claimed supernatural powers and special connections with several national govern-

ments; was still refusing food because of its contamination with ground corpses; and was still threatening bodily harm to people he found uncooperative. A further attempt was made to commit him and to place his affairs under legal guardianship. As Rick had rather boastfully predicted, this attempt failed because of his lucid defense of himself, and the court dismissed the action. He was discharged to a protected boarding house but disappeared four days later. (Adapted from Spitzer et al., 1983, pp. 153– 155)

Fortunately, most patients who show this type of chaotic, undifferentiated pattern do not have the early and slowly developing, insidious onset seen in Rick's case. On the contrary, the breakdown erupts suddenly out of the context of a seemingly unre-

This painting was made by a male patient diagnosed as suffering from undifferentiated schizophrenia. Over a period of about nine years, he did hundreds of paintings in which the tops of the heads of males were always missing, though the females were complete. Although the therapist tried several maneuvers to get him to paint a man's head, the patient never did.

markable life history, usually following some obvious psychic trauma. As we have seen, the initial diagnosis in such cases is schizophreniform disorder, and the episode usually clears up in a matter of weeks or, at most, months. Recurrent episodes, however, are not uncommon in schizophreniform disorder, especially in the absence of vigorous follow-up treatment, leading to the diagnosis of schizophrenia. Such a pattern was seen in Myra Genain's breakdown, and she required several years of psychotherapy to ensure a lasting recovery. In some few instances, treatment efforts are unsuccessful, and the mixed symptoms of the early undifferentiated disorder slide into a more chronic phase, typically developing into the more specific symptoms of other types.

Catatonic Type   Though catatonic reactions often appear with dramatic suddenness, usually a patient has shown a background of eccentric behavior, often accompanied by some degree of withdrawal from reality. Though at one time common in Europe and North America, catatonic reactions have become less frequent in recent years.

The central feature of **schizophrenia, catatonic type** is the pronounced motor symptoms, either of an excited or a stuporous type, which sometimes make for difficulty in differentiating this condition from a psychotic mood disorder. As in the case of the Genains, all of whom had early diagnoses of catatonia, the clinical picture is often an early manifestation of a disorder that will become chronic and intractable unless the underlying process is somehow arrested.

Some catatonic patients alternate between periods of extreme stupor and extreme excitement, sometimes quite violent, but in most cases one reaction or the other is predominant. In a study of 250 people diagnosed as suffering from catatonic schizophrenia, Morrison (1973) found that 110 were predominantly withdrawn, 67 were predominantly excited, and 73 were considered "mixed." No significant differences were found between these groups with regard to age, sex, or education.

During a catatonic stupor, a person loses all animation and tends to remain motionless in a rigid, unchanging position—mute and staring into space—sometimes maintaining the same position for hours or even days, until the hands and feet become blue and swollen because of immobility. One patient felt that he had to hold his hand out flat because the forces of "good" and "evil" were waging a "war of the worlds" on his hand, and if he moved it, he might tilt the precarious balance in favor of the evil forces. Surprisingly, despite their seeming withdrawal and apparent lack of attention to their surroundings while in this condition, catatonic individuals may later relate in detail events that were going on around them.

Some of these patients are highly suggestible and will automatically obey commands or imitate the actions of others (*echopraxia*) or mimic their phrases (*echolalia*). If a patient's arm is raised to an awkward and uncomfortable position, he or she may keep it in that position for minutes or even hours. Ordinarily, patients in a catatonic stupor resist stubbornly any effort to change their position and may become mute, resist all attempts at feeding, and refuse to comply with even the slightest request. They pay no attention to bowel or bladder control and may drool. Their facial expression is typically vacant, and their skin appears waxy. Threats and painful stimuli have no effect, and they have to be dressed and washed.

Suddenly and without external provocation or warning, catatonic patients may pass from states of extreme stupor to great excitement, during which they seem to be under great "pressure of activity" and may become violent. They may talk or shout excitedly and incoherently, pace rapidly back and forth, openly indulge in sexual activities such as masturbation, attempt self-mutilation or even suicide, or impulsively attack and try to kill others. The suddenness and extreme frenzy of these attacks make such patients dangerous to both themselves and others. These excited states may last a few hours, days, or even weeks, if potent medication to sedate such patients is not administered. The following case illustrates some of the symptoms typical of catatonic reactions.

*T*odd Phillips, a 16-year-old high school student, was referred to a psychiatric hospital by his family physician. His family had been very upset by his increasingly strange behavior over the preceding eight months. They had consulted their family physician, who treated him with small doses of antipsychotic medication, without any improvement.

Although Todd has had many problems since he was a small child, there was a distinct change about eight months ago. He began spending more and more time in his room and seemed uninterested in doing many of his usual activities. His grades dropped. He started stuttering. He used to weigh about 215 pounds, but began to eat less, and lost 35 pounds. For no reason, he started drinking large quantities of water.

More recently, there was a change for the worse. A few months ago he began taking Tai Chi lessons and often stood for long periods in karatelike positions, oblivious to what was going on around him. He stopped doing his homework. He took an inordinately long time to get dressed, eat his meals, or bathe. Before getting dressed in the morning he would go through an elaborate ritual of arranging his clothes on the bed before putting them on. When his parents asked him a question, he repeated the question over and over and did not seem to hear or understand what was said.

At school he received demerits for the first time for being late to class. His family began to lose patience with him when he eventually refused to go to school. When his father tried to get him out of bed in the morning, he lay motionless, sometimes having wet the bed during the night. It was at this point that his parents, in desperation, consulted their family physician.

When first seen in the hospital, Todd was a disheveled looking, somewhat obese adolescent, standing motionless in the center of the room with his head flexed forward and his hands at his sides. He appeared perplexed, but was correctly oriented to time and place. He was able to do simple calculations, and his recent and remote memory were intact. He answered questions slowly and in a peculiar manner. An example of his speech follows:

Q: Why did you come to the hospital?

A: Why did I come? Why did I come to the hospital? I came to the hospital because of crazy things with my hands. Sometimes my hands jump up like that . . . wait a minute . . . I guess it's happening. . . . Well, yes, see it's been hap-

pening (making robotlike gestures with his hands).

Q: What thoughts go through your head?

A: What thoughts go through my head? What thoughts go through my head? Well, I think about things . . . like . . . yes, well . . . I think thoughts . . . I have thoughts. I think thoughts.

Q: What thoughts?

A: What thoughts? What kinds of thoughts? I think thoughts.

Q: Do you hear voices?

A: Do I hear voices? I hear voices. People talk. Do I hear voices? No. . . . People talk. I hear voices. I hear voices when people talk.

Q: Are you sick?

A: Am I sick? No I'm not sick . . . these fidgeting habits, these fidgeting habits. I have habits. I have fidgeting habits.

Throughout the examination he made repetitive chewing and biting motions. Occasionally, when questioned, he would smile enigmatically. He seemed unresponsive to much of what was going on around him. His infrequent movements were slow and jerky, and he often assumed the karatelike postures that his parents described, in which he would remain frozen. If the examiner placed the patient's hands in an awkward position the patient remained frozen in that position for several minutes. (Spitzer et al., 1983, pp. 139–140)

Although the matter is far from settled, some clinicians interpret a catatonic patient's immobility as a way of coping with the reduced filtering ability and increased vulnerability to stimulation: it seems to provide a feeling of some control over external sources of stimulation, though not necessarily over inner ones. Freeman has cited the explanation advanced by one patient: "I did not want to move, because if I did everything changed around me and upset me horribly so I remained still to hold onto a sense of permanence" (1960, p. 932).

Disorganized Type   Compared to the other subtypes of schizophrenia, **schizophrenia, disorganized type** usually occurs at an earlier age and represents a more severe disintegration of the personality. Fortunately, it is considerably less common than the other forms. In pre-DSM-III classifications, this type was called *hebephrenic schizophrenia*.

Typically, an affected individual has a history of oddness, overscrupulousness about trivial things, and preoccupation with religious and philosophical issues. Frequently, he or she broods over the dire results of masturbation or minor infractions of social conventions. While schoolmates are enjoying normal play and social activities, this person gradually becomes more seclusive and more preoccupied with fantasies.

As the disorder progresses, the individual becomes emotionally indifferent and infantile. A silly smile and inappropriate, shallow laughter after little or no provocation are common symptoms. If asked the reason for his or her laughter, the patient may state that he or she does not know or may volunteer some wholly irrelevant and unsatisfactory explanation. Speech becomes incoherent and may include considerable baby talk, childish giggling, a repetitious use of similar-sounding words, and a derailing of associated thoughts that may give a punlike quality to speech. In some instances, speech becomes completely incoherent, a "word salad."

Hallucinations, particularly auditory ones, are common. The voices heard by these patients may accuse them of immoral practices, "pour filth" into their minds, and call them vile names. Delusions are usually of a sexual, religious, hypochondriacal, or persecutory nature, and they are typically changeable, unsystematized, and fantastic. For example, one woman insisted not only that she was being followed by enemies but that she had already been killed a number of times. Another claimed that a long tube extended from the Kremlin directly to her uterus, through which she was being invaded by Russians.

In occasional cases, individuals become hostile and aggressive. They may exhibit peculiar mannerisms and other bizarre forms of behavior. These behaviors may take the form of word salad; facial grimaces; talking and gesturing to themselves; sudden, inexplicable laughter and weeping; and in some cases an abnormal interest in urine and feces, which they may smear on walls and even on themselves. Obscene behavior and the absence of any modesty or sense of shame are characteristic. Although they may exhibit outbursts of anger and temper tantrums in connection with fantasies, they are indifferent to real-life situations, no matter how horrifying or gruesome the latter may be. The clinical picture in disorganized schizophrenia is exemplified in the following interview:

The patient was a divorcée, 32 years of age, who had come to the hospital with bizarre delusions, hallucinations, and severe personality dis- *integration. She had a record of alcoholism, promiscuity, and possible incestuous relations with a brother. The following conversation shows typical hebephrenic responses to questioning.*
Doctor: *How do you feel today?*
Patient: *Fine.*
Doctor: *When did you come here?*
Patient: *1416, you remember, doctor (silly giggle).*
Doctor: *Do you know why you are here?*
Patient: *Well, in 1951 I changed into two men. President Truman was judge at my trial. I was convicted and hung (silly giggle). My brother and I were given back our normal bodies 5 years ago. I am a policewoman. I keep a dictaphone concealed on my person.*
Doctor: *Can you tell me the name of this place?*
Patient: *I have not been a drinker for 16 years. I am taking a mental rest after a "carter" assignment or "quill." You know, a "penwrap." I had contracts with Warner Brothers Studios and Eugene broke phonograph records but Mike protested. I have been with the police department for 35 years. I am made of flesh and blood—see doctor (pulling up her dress).*
Doctor: *Are you married?*
Patient: *No. I am not attracted to men (silly giggle). I have a companionship arrangement with my brother. I am a "looner" . . . a bachelor.*

The prognosis is poor if a person develops disorganized schizophrenia. As we have seen, Iris and Hester, the least functional of the Genain sisters, were also the only sisters to have been definitely diagnosed as hebephrenic, or disorganized, during the course of their disorders. To at least some extent, the disorganized variety of schizophrenia may be regarded as the "last stop" on a downward-coursing path of process schizophrenic psychosis. At this point, no form of treatment intervention yet discovered has a marked likelihood of effecting more than a modest recovery.

Paranoid Type   Formerly about one half of all schizophrenic first admissions to hospitals were diagnosed as **schizophrenia, paranoid type.** In recent years, however, the incidence of the paranoid type has shown a substantial decrease, while the undifferentiated type has shown a marked increase. The reasons for these changes are unknown.

Frequently, paranoid-type people show histories of increasing suspiciousness and of severe difficulties in interpersonal relationships. The eventual

A patient diagnosed as a paranoid schizophrenic was unable to respond at all when asked by a therapist to make an original drawing. Therefore, with the therapist's help, a picture (top left) was selected from a magazine for the patient to copy. One of his first attempts (top right) was a pencil drawing on manila paper showing great visual distortion, as well as an inability to use colors and difficulty in using letters of the alphabet. The evident visual distortion was a diagnostic aid for the therapist, who was able to learn from it that the patient, who was extremely fearful, saw things in this distorted way, aggravating his fear. In the picture at bottom left, the patient has shown obvious improvement, although it was not until a year after therapy began that he was able to execute a painting with the realism of the picture at bottom right.

symptom picture is dominated by absurd, illogical, and often changing delusions. Persecutory delusions are the most frequent and may involve a wide range of ideas and plots. An individual may become highly suspicious of relatives or associates and may complain of being watched, followed, poisoned, talked about, or influenced by various tormenting devices rigged up by "enemies."

In addition to persecutory themes, themes of grandeur are also common in paranoid-type delusions. Individuals with such delusions may, for example, claim to be the world's greatest economist or philosopher, or some prominent person of the past, such as Napoleon, the Virgin Mary, or even Jesus Christ. Rokeach (1964), in fact, has described a bizarre circumstance in which three Christs resided at the same hospital. These delusions are frequently accompanied by vivid auditory, visual, and other hallucinations. Patients may hear singing, or

God speaking, or the voices of their enemies, or they may see angels or feel damaging rays piercing their bodies at various points.

An individual's thinking and behavior become centered around the themes of persecution, grandeur, or both in a pathological "paranoid construction" that—for all its distortion of reality—provides a sense of identity and importance perhaps not otherwise attainable. There thus tends to be a higher level of adaptive coping and of cognitive integrative skills in a paranoid-type schizophrenic person than in other schizophrenic individuals. This relative preservation of intact cognitive functioning is undoubtedly one of the important bases for the paranoid-nonparanoid distinction noted earlier and increasingly employed by both clinicians and researchers.

Despite this seeming "advantage" that paranoid-type schizophrenic individuals enjoy, such people are far from easy to deal with. The weaving of delusions and hallucinations into a paranoid construction results in a loss of critical judgment and in erratic, unpredictable behavior. In response to a command from a "voice," such an individual may break furniture or commit other violent acts. Occasionally, paranoid schizophrenic patients can be dangerous, as when they attack people they are convinced have been persecuting them or otherwise causing harm. Somewhat paradoxically, such problems are exacerbated by the fact that such people show less bizarre behavior and less extreme withdrawal from the outside world than individuals with other types of schizophrenia; as a consequence, they are likely *not* to be confined in protective environments.

The following conversation is between a clinician and a man diagnosed as chronic paranoid schizophrenic. The case illustrates well the illogical, delusional symptom picture, together with continued attention to misinterpreted external data, that these individuals experience.

Doctor: What's your name?
Patient: Who are you?
Doctor: I'm a doctor. Who are you?
Patient: I can't tell you who I am.
Doctor: Why can't you tell me?
Patient: You wouldn't believe me.
Doctor: What are you doing here?
Patient: Well, I've been sent here to thwart the Russians. I'm the only one in the world who knows how to deal with them. They got their spies all around here though to get me, but I'm smarter than any of them.
Doctor: What are you going to do to thwart the Russians?
Patient: I'm organizing.
Doctor: Whom are you going to organize?
Patient: Everybody. I'm the only man in the world who can do that, but they're trying to get me. But I'm going to use my atomic bomb media to blow them up.
Doctor: You must be a terribly important person then.
Patient: Well, of course.
Doctor: What do you call yourself?
Patient: You used to know me as Franklin D. Roosevelt.
Doctor: Isn't he dead?
Patient: Sure he's dead, but I'm alive.
Doctor: But you're Franklin D. Roosevelt?
Patient: His spirit. He, God, and I figured this

out. And now I'm going to make a race of healthy people. My agents are lining them up. Say, who are you?
Doctor: I'm a doctor here.
Patient: You don't look like a doctor. You look like a Russian to me.
Doctor: How can you tell a Russian from one of your agents?
Patient: I read eyes. I get all my signs from eyes. I look into your eyes and get all my signs from them.
Doctor: Do you sometimes hear voices telling you someone is a Russian?
Patient: No, I just look into eyes. I got a mirror here to look into my own eyes. I know everything that's going on. I can tell by the color, by the way it's shaped.
Doctor: Did you have any trouble with people before you came here?
Patient: Well, only the Russians. They were trying to surround me in my neighborhood. One day they tried to drop a bomb on me from the fire escape.
Doctor: How could you tell it was a bomb?
Patient: I just knew.

Although it is true, as we have seen, that many paranoid schizophrenic individuals have histories of gradual onset and long-lasting difficulties in interpersonal relationships and productive functioning, it is also true that few of them show the true process pattern of schizophrenia (Ritzler, 1981). Sometimes, indeed, onset is quite rapid and occurs in individuals with entirely adequate, even distinguished, pasts. In fact, one of the most famous cases of paranoid schizophrenia involved a high-ranking German judge, Dr. Daniel Paul Schreber, who described his disorder at length in memoirs published after his partial recovery. Freud used these memoirs in developing his now largely discredited theory that paranoid thinking is due to repressed homosexuality.

Schreber's disorder began with the idea that he was to be transformed into a woman by some sort of conspiracy, and, once the transformation was accomplished, he was to be delivered over to a certain man for the purpose of sexual abuse. During the course of the disorder, the idea of conspiracy came gradually to be replaced by the idea that his "emasculation" and subsequent impregnation were inspired by a divine plan involving world redemption. In fact, he would be impregnated by divine rays so that a new race of humans might be created.

Schreber also felt that he was being persecuted by certain people, among them his former physician, and he heaped verbal abuse on these enemies. In turn, he heard voices that mocked him and jeered at him. At various times, he became convinced that he was dying of strange illnesses, such as "softening of the brain" and "the plague." At another point, he believed he was dead and his body, which was being handled by others in all sorts of revolting ways, was decomposing. He was tormented so much by such thoughts that he in fact attempted suicide on several occasions and demanded of the hospital staff that they provide him with the cyanide he was sure they were intending for him anyway. He felt he was "the plaything of the devils." As his thoughts turned more toward religion in the later phases of the disorder, he claimed to see "miraculous apparitions" and to hear "holy music." (Adapted from Spitzer et al., 1981)

In this case, we see clearly the deterioration from a previous level of functioning, the bizarre ideas, and the hallucinatory experiences so characteristic of schizophrenia generally. The paranoid type diagnosis is appropriate because of the prominent delusions of both persecution (being conspired against) and grandiosity (being selected by God to be impregnated and start a new race). Dr. Schreber regained sufficient control to secure his release from the hospital some nine years after the onset of his disorder; at the time, however, he was still considered delusional.

Other Schizophrenic Patterns   The remaining subcategories of schizophrenia contained in DSM-III-R, although not necessarily under the schizophrenia rubric, deserve mention. **Schizophrenia, residual type,** which is the fifth officially recognized type of schizophrenia, is a category used for people regarded as having recovered from schizophrenia but still manifesting some signs of their past disorder.

As was noted in the preceding chapter, the term **schizoaffective disorder** (manic or depressive or mixed) is applied to individuals who show features of both schizophrenia and severe affective disorder. In the DSM-III-R classification, this disorder is not listed as a formal category of schizophrenic disorder

but rather under *psychotic disorders not elsewhere classified.*

Also included in the latter category is **schizophreniform disorder,** a category reserved for schizophrenia-like psychoses of less than six months' duration. It may include any of the symptoms described in the preceding sections, but is probably most often seen in an undifferentiated form. At the present time, all new cases of schizophrenia first receive a diagnosis of schizophreniform disorder. Because of the possibility of an early and lasting remission in a first episode of schizophrenic breakdown, prognosis for schizophreniform disorder is better than for established forms of schizophrenia, and it appears likely that by keeping it out of the formal category of schizophrenic disorder, the potentially harmful effects of labeling may be minimized.

■ Biological Factors in Schizophrenia

Despite extensive research, the causal factors underlying the schizophrenias remain unclear. Primary responsibility has been attributed variously to (a) biological factors, including heredity and various biochemical, neurophysiological, and neuroanatomical processes; (b) psychosocial factors, including early psychic trauma, pathogenic interpersonal and family patterns, faulty learning, difficulties in social roles, and decompensation under excessive stress; and (c) sociocultural factors, especially as influences on the types and incidence of schizophrenic reactions. These three sets of factors are not mutually exclusive, of course, and it seems likely that each is involved in at least some cases. We will first discuss biological factors in the following sections.

Heredity   In view of the disproportionate incidence of schizophrenia in the family backgrounds of *index* schizophrenic patients (that is, the diagnosed group of people who provide the starting point for inquiry), genetic factors appear to play an important causal role in some instances of the disorder. Though the evidence seems persuasive, it remains circumstantial in that it is (a) entirely correlational in nature, and (b) extremely difficult to disentangle from possibly detrimental environmental factors. Much of this research is based on demonstrations of concordance rates among schizophrenic people and their close relatives. Let us examine some of these areas of research.

Twin studies.   The general strategy of twin studies was discussed in Chapter 4 and more specifically in relation to mood disorders in Chapter 11. As in the mood disorders, schizophrenia concordance rates for *identical* twins are routinely found to be significantly higher than those for *fraternal* twins or ordinary siblings. But again, it is difficult to separate hereditary from environmental influences using this method. Excellent technical critiques of perhaps the best of the twin data relating to schizophrenia come to essentially the same conclusion (Wagener & Cromwell, 1984).

Although the incidence of schizophrenia among twins is no greater than for the general population, study after study has shown a higher *concordance* for schizophrenia among identical (monozygotic) twins over people related in any other way, including fraternal (dizygotic) twins. Depending on a variety of factors, the degree of this inflation varies substantially from one study to another and tends to be inversely correlated with the methodological rigor of the study—that is, the more rigorous the methodology, the lower the concordance rate.

The results of two of the more methodologically rigorous twin studies in schizophrenia provide an interesting comparison. One of them, by Cohen et al. (1972), used a large but selected sample consisting of veterans of the American armed forces. Because the armed forces screen their "applicants," it may be assumed that individuals with obvious mental health problems were screened out, resulting in a relatively low incidence of mental disorder, including schizophrenia, among their dischargees. If absolute incidence is low, concordance figures will be correspondingly low. This assumption indeed seems to have been confirmed. In the study, the schizophrenia concordance rate was 23.5 percent for identical twins and 5.3 percent for fraternal twins, both figures being unusually low.

Using a sample more nearly representative of the general population, Gottesman and Shields (1972) arrived at overall schizophrenia concordance rates of 42 percent and 9 percent for identical and fraternal twins, respectively. The Gottesman and Shields figures are close to the medians for recent studies in this area and may be regarded as good estimates of the "true" values.

If schizophrenia were exclusively a genetic disorder, the concordance rate for identical twins would, of course, be 100 percent. In fact, however, there appear to be more *discordant* than *concordant* pairs, notwithstanding the remarkable example of the Genain sisters. On the other hand, some concordance clearly exists. What this means is that a person may have an enhanced risk of schizophrenia if his or her twin is schizophrenic. In other words, twin studies show us that *predisposition* for the

disorder is associated with genetic variables. It does not prove a *genetic* transmission of predisposition, however, because common environmental factors cannot be ruled out; as earlier noted, the environments, both prenatal and postnatal, of identical twins must inevitably be more similar on average than the environments of individuals sharing any other type of relationship. Moreover, because somewhat over half of the identical twins of schizophrenic patients do not develop the disorder, it means that there is a good chance the environment will be sufficiently benign to protect even an individual with a substantial predisposition, whatever its source.

A good example of the hazards of too readily accepting twin concordance data as necessarily addressing the question of genetic transmission of a schizophrenic diathesis is unexpectedly provided in studies of identical twins who are *discordant* for the diagnosis of schizophrenia. These are sets of twins in which one member of the pair meets diagnostic criteria for schizophrenia but the other does not and is in fact described as "normal." We will look at two such studies here.

The first study, an unaccountably neglected work by Pollin and Stabenau (1968; Pollin, Stabenau, & Tupin, 1965), involved a nationwide sample of 15 sets of twins who were studied thoroughly, along with their families. The essential results implicated some sort of prenatal biological compromise of the twin who was to become schizophrenic, one that began with a lower birth weight and continued in the form of a failure to match the "normal" twin in rate of progression through the various childhood developmental mileposts. As adults, the schizophrenic twins also showed a significantly greater number of "soft" neurological signs (such as reflex abnormalities), thus confirming the general picture of subtle biological deficit relative to the "normal" twins. These deficits were not, however, so subtle during childhood as to escape the notice of parents, who responded with differential parenting behavior in dealing with the "weak" versus the "strong" twin, apparently producing corresponding differences in emerging personality characteristics; the preschizophrenic twin was invariably described as more "submissive" than the other twin in each of the pairs, thus adding a potential psychosocial impediment to the extant biological one.

The companion study (Suddath et al., 1990) is much more recent and has received considerable notice in the popular media. Also involving 15 pairs of identical twins discordant for schizophrenia, the technique of *magnetic resonance imaging* (MRI) was used to examine the structural properties of the subjects' brains. The results, in brief, showed enlarged cerebral ventricles and reduction in size of a structure called the anterior hippocampus (both of these together indicating reduced brain mass) in the twins who had become schizophrenic. The anomaly cannot be ascribed directly to a genetic origin. The authors also correctly point out that the results do not in themselves permit a ruling out of causal factors that may have been *consequent* to the development of schizophrenia, such as long-term use of antipsychotic medication. As we will see, however, independent evidence suggests that brain abnormalities of the type seen here may make a causal contribution in some instances of schizophrenia.

In terms of hereditary factors in schizophrenia, the essential point made by these studies is that genetic identity does not guarantee biological identity. That is, differential prenatal (or postnatal) environmental factors can have significant biological effects apparently predictive for schizophrenia in cases where heredity is held constant. If this conclusion is accepted, however, it implies that some part of the concordance for schizophrenia in monozygotic twins is in all probability *not* genetically based, because intrauterine pathogenic influences are, overall, more likely to be shared by monozygotic than by dizygotic twins. We know, for example, that a majority of monozygotic twins share the same chorion tissue of the maternal placenta, whereas dizygotic twins never do.

The upshot, it seems to us, is that we can never be sure what, if anything, the classic twin studies of schizophrenia—of which there have been many going back many years—tell us about an alleged genetic contribution to the etiology of this form of disorder.

A seemingly much "cleaner" investigative strategy employing twins was pioneered by Fischer (1971, 1973). Reasoning that genetic influence, if present, would show up in the *offspring* of the nonschizophrenic twins of discordant pairs, she found exactly that outcome in a search of official records in Denmark. Gottesman and Bertelson (1989), in a follow-up of Fischer's subjects, have reported an age-corrected schizophrenia incidence rate (that is, a rate taking into account predicted breakdowns for subjects not yet beyond the age of risk) of 17.4 percent for the offspring of the nonschizophrenic monozygotic twins. This rate, which far exceeds normal expectancy, was not significantly different from that for offspring of the schizophrenic members of discordant pairs, or from that for offspring of schizophrenic dizygotic twins. Assuming that exposure to schizophrenic aunts and uncles would have, at most, limited etiologic significance, these results give impressive support to the genetic hypothesis. They also, as the authors note, indicate

that the implicated predisposition may remain "unexpressed" (as in the nonschizophrenic twins of discordant pairs) unless "released" by unknown environmental factors.

Adoption studies.   Several studies have attempted to overcome the shortcomings of the twin method in achieving a true and unassailable separation of hereditary from environmental influences by using what is called the *adoption strategy*. In this strategy, concordance rates of schizophrenia are compared for the biological and the adoptive relatives of individuals who have been adopted out of their biological families at an early age (preferably at birth) and have subsequently become schizophrenic. If rates of schizophrenia are greater among the patients' biological than adoptive relatives, a hereditary influence is strongly suggested; the reverse pattern would of course argue for environmental causation.

Heston (1966) was apparently the first to use one of several variants of this basic method. In a follow-up study of 47 people who had been born to schizophrenic mothers in a state mental hospital and placed with relatives or in foster homes shortly after birth, Heston found that 16.6 percent of these subjects were later diagnosed as schizophrenic. In contrast, none of the 50 control subjects selected from among residents of the same foster homes—whose mothers were not schizophrenic—later became schizophrenic. In addition to the greater probability of being labeled schizophrenic, Heston found that the offspring of schizophrenic mothers were more likely to be diagnosed as mentally retarded, neurotic, and psychopathic (that is, antisocial). They also had been involved more frequently in criminal activities and had spent more time in penal institutions.

Thus Heston concluded that children born to schizophrenic mothers, even when reared without contact with them, were more likely not only to become schizophrenic but also to suffer a wide spectrum of other difficulties. The diffuseness of these effects on offspring is actually something of an embarrassment for a theory that emphasizes a specific genetic risk for schizophrenia, and it invites speculation that variables other than the psychiatric diagnostic status of the mothers may have come into play. Conceivably, for example, the postnatal experience of these adoptees was in fact not independent of the psychiatric status of their mothers. Additionally, we now know that schizophrenic women, for some unknown reason, as a group have unusual difficulty bearing children, with consequent risk to the latter of subtle but possibly lasting nervous system impairment (Jacobsen & Kinney, 1980;

McNeil & Kaij, 1978). As we will see, such impairment, which is not genetically mediated, would in itself probably enhance the risk for schizophrenia, and possibly other diagnoses as well.

Independent of Heston's work, a large scale and multifaceted adoption study was undertaken in Denmark under the aegis of American investigators working in collaboration with Danish professionals (Kety, 1987; Kety et al., 1968, 1978; Rosenthal et al., 1968; Wender et al., 1974). The well-publicized results of these studies, purporting to establish the case for a genetic contribution to schizophrenia, have had an enormous impact on the field. They will not be reviewed here because their adequate discussion would consume too much space. A recent review of these studies, however, reveals serious shortcomings that preclude any unqualified judgment on the genetic transmission of schizophrenia (Carson & Sanislow, 1992). For example, an impressive incidence of schizophrenia among biological relatives of schizophrenic adoptees is on close examination limited to second-degree relatives (half-siblings, having 25 percent gene sharing) and disappears when only first-degree relatives (parents and full siblings, having 50 percent gene sharing) are considered (see also Benjamin, 1976). These results defy explanation in terms of any genetic transmission process of which we have knowledge, and in fact tend to disconfirm such an hypothesis.

The problems associated with a critical component of the Danish adoption studies were resolved by an independent reanalysis of its data—including the rediagnosis of all cases using DSM-III criteria and the use of other more advanced techniques to improve precision—conducted by Kendler and Gruenberg (1984). These investigators found convincing evidence of a modest genetic contribution to a certain class of disorders having schizophrenic-like features. They include, in addition to schizophrenia, schizotypal and paranoid personality disorders; the three together are said to constitute a "schizophrenia spectrum," a group of disorders believed to share a common, genetically determined diathesis. Thus, as Heston's early work had suggested, the vulnerability conveyed by genetic influences appears here not to be specific for schizophrenia per se but to involve a broader range of compromised functioning.

Regrettably, as now seems clear in retrospect, the Danish adoption studies did not include independent assessments of the child-rearing adequacy of the adoptive families into which index (those who became schizophrenic) and control (those who did not) youngsters had been placed. It remained for Tienari and his colleagues (Tienari et al., 1985, 1987) to remedy this oversight. Their study, still in progress, involves a follow-up of the adopted-away children of all women in Finland hospitalized for schizophrenia, beginning in 1960. Of the 271 index (children whose mothers were schizophrenic) and control (comparable children whose mothers were normal) adoptees evaluated as of the latest (1987) available report, there were *no* instances of "psychosis" among either index (n=51) or control (n=53) children who were raised in families independently considered "healthy." Of the adoptees raised in families considered moderately or severely disturbed, 9 of 73 index children and 2 of 94 controls had become psychotic. *HIGHLIGHT 12.4* tabulates the results of this study in greater detail. Supporting earlier work, these results show a moderate effect that might be considered genetic in origin—the differential breakdown rates of index versus control adoptees independent of family context. The magnitude of that effect, however, is actually exceeded by one associated with the variable of relative family disorganization which will be discussed more fully in a later section.

Parent-child studies.   Another line of research has focused on the incidence of schizophrenia among children reared by their schizophrenic parents. Rieder (1973) found a wide spectrum of psychopathology reported among the adult offspring of schizophrenic parents, ranging from schizophrenia to psychopathic personality disorders. The offspring of schizophrenic parents also showed a high incidence of psychological maladjustment as children—estimated at 20 percent—with two types being prominent: a withdrawn schizoid type and a hyperactive, antisocial, delinquent type. Thus Rieder concluded that the offspring of schizophrenic parents differ in important ways from the offspring of nonschizophrenic parents; such a study cannot of course address the question of hereditary versus environmental influence.

In the same vein, Kringlen (1978) showed that 28 percent of children born to parents who had both been diagnosed schizophrenic at some point in their adult lives were classifiable as psychotic or borderline psychotic; 20 percent of these children had developed clinical schizophrenia. Twenty-eight percent of the children of such unions, however, were diagnosed as entirely normal. That is, more than one quarter of these children escaped any form of psychopathology despite a presumably heavy genetic risk *and* the mental health hazards of being reared by two parents who were either psychotic or destined to become so. Evidently, having two schizophrenic (or preschizophrenic) parents increases the risk of poor mental health—but it need not always have ill effects.

Psychiatric Status of Adopted–Away Offspring of Schizophrenic (Index) and Normal (Control) Mothers as a Function of the Quality of Their Adoptive Families

The following table includes the numbers of index (n=124) and control (n=147) adoptees in each of four diagnostic groupings arrayed according to the degree of disturbance of the adoptive families. Note that in the "healthy" adoptive family context the "at-risk" and control adoptees are equally free of serious disorder, with no instances of psychosis in either group. The presumed vulnerability of the index adoptees becomes manifest only as the adoptive family dysfunction increases. A statistical model applied to these data shows a significant interaction between index and control status and level of family dysfunction.

Clinical Ratings of Adoptive Families

Offspring Diagnoses	Healthy		Moderately Disturbed		Severely Disturbed		TOTAL
	Index	Control	Index	Control	Index	Control	
No diagnosis	41	42	11	26	6	15	141
Neurotic	8	10	10	18	14	15	75
Personality disorder	2	1	5	7	18	11	44
Psychotic	0	0	3	0	6	2	11
TOTAL	51	53	29	51	44	43	271

From Tienari et al. (1987), p. 442.

Studies of high-risk children.   The research strategy of long-term monitoring of children known to be at high risk for schizophrenia (by virtue of having been born to a schizophrenic parent) is basically intended to identify the environmental factors that cause breakdown (or resistance to it) in predisposed people. As we have seen in Chapter 4, this strategy, pioneered by Mednick and Schulsinger (1968) and followed up by numerous additional research projects (for reviews see Garmezy, 1978a, 1978b; Neale & Oltmanns, 1980; Rieder, 1979; Watt et al., 1984), has thus far not paid off very well in terms of isolating specific environmental factors. In saying this, however, we must acknowledge both the enormous difficulties that attend long-term and complicated projects of this sort and our own admiration for those who undertake them.

The difficulties are nowhere better illustrated than in the first (and so far only) summary report of the Israeli-NIMH High-Risk Study (see *Schizophrenia Bulletin*, Vol. 11, No. 1, 1985). This project, begun in 1967 and surviving a war and much turmoil in its aftermath, compared the outcomes of an index group of high-risk Israeli youngsters who remained in towns with their biological families to those brought up in the surrogate-parent settlement communities known as *kibbutzim*, relative to closely matched control groups of low-risk youngsters. "High risk" was defined as having a schizophrenic mother.

Many behavioral differences were found between index and control children, almost always favoring the controls; few were found for the crosscutting variable of kibbutz versus normal rearing. Especially impressive was a high frequency of soft neurological signs observed in index children in two separate examinations five years apart. On the critical measure of psychopathological outcome at 15 years following project initiation (the average subject age was 25), rearing context proved apparently significant, although only in index cases and in an unexpected direction. Considering only schizophrenia and schizophrenia "spectrum" diagnoses, 9 of 46 index cases and 0 of 44 control cases had become disordered; 6 of the 9 casualties had been kibbutz-reared and hence to a considerable degree isolated from exposure to a psychotic parent. These trends are, if anything, strengthened when other diagnoses are included. Mirsky et al. (1985), who report these data, speculate that kibbutz living tends to evoke symptoms (although only in predisposed people) because it precludes privacy and "escape."

It may be noted in passing that, once again in this study, the children considered at risk on grounds that were at least implicitly genetic (their mothers being schizophrenic) were discovered as a group to be mildly neurologically compromised in childhood. We can by no means be certain that such compromise, which might itself be a causal factor in schizophrenic outcomes, was mediated by the inheritance of deficient genes—especially in view of the known obstetrical difficulties schizophrenic women tend to have in bearing children.

Although the available results of high-risk studies have generally proven difficult to interpret, they have added abundantly to the observation that having a schizophrenic parent is a good predictor of psychological disorder, including schizophrenia. Despite the complication of birthing difficulties just noted, it seems likely (although unproven) that some of this predictability comes about as a result of the genetic transmission of vulnerability to schizophrenia.

However, one additional problem with a genetic interpretation of such studies is that a child having a psychotic parent, or one whose parent is frequently missing because of required hospitalizations, is not quite comparable in environmental and experiential terms to the otherwise matched youngster whose parents are psychologically well-adjusted. In fact, parental separation seems to be the critical variable in accounting for the parent-to-child effect in many cases (Mednick et al., 1978).

Summing up, the question of genetic transmissibility of a predisposition to schizophrenia is not as easily answered as it may appear to be when first posed. Unfortunately, there is a tendency—even among professionals who should know better—to answer the question resoundingly in the affirmative. We think a more circumspect approach is appropriate, although we incline to the view that some genetic influence probably makes certain individuals vulnerable to schizophrenia. Many independent sources of information—though all of them may be imperfect and incomplete on an individual basis—when taken together point to a relatively strong case for genetic contribution. The data indicate that no such contribution is sufficient in itself to produce schizophrenia, and they provide no basis for concluding that such a contribution is a *necessary* condition for a schizophrenic outcome; indeed, most people who develop schizophrenia probably have no close relatives who are also known to have had the disorder.

We believe, too, that the classic methods of investigation in this field have been exhausted and that nothing definitive is likely to be confirmed by further use of these essentially pedigree-based techniques. It is frequently said that the next major advances in this area will likely come from molecular biology, from genetic linkage studies and gene mapping. As was earlier noted in discussing the mood disorders, however, the productive use of these techniques depends on precise diagnostic criteria that yield highly homogeneous patient groups (Carson & Sanislow, 1992). As we have seen, we are a long way from meeting this requirement in the area of schizophrenia.

Biochemical Factors   Research into the possibility of biochemical abnormalities in schizophrenic patients was given a boost in the 1950s when a connection was made between schizophrenic-like symptoms and the fact that the presence of some chemical agents in the bloodstream, even in minute amounts, can produce profound mental changes (Huxley, 1954). Lysergic acid diethylamide (LSD) and mescaline, for example, can lead to a temporary disorganization of thought processes and a variety of psychotic-like symptoms that have been referred to as "model psychoses." Such findings encouraged investigators to look for an *endogenous hallucinogen*—a chemical synthesized within the body, perhaps under stressful conditions—that might account for the hallucinations and disorganization of thought and affect in schizophrenia and other psychotic disorders. The states produced by the ingestion of these chemicals, however, only superficially resemble true psychotic disorders, and researchers have in any event not been able to find a good candidate for the natural hallucinogen role envisaged in this conception.

Instead, if schizophrenia turns out to be in part biochemically caused, it seems likely that it will involve some form of deficit in the quantitative regulation, or balance, of chemicals that occur naturally in the nervous system. At present, as in the case of the more severe mood disorders, the most widely accepted hypothesis is that a biochemical disturbance of synaptic transmission occurs in one or more important neural pathways in the brain. The most attractive of the specific ideas in this area has been the "dopamine hypothesis" of schizophrenia (Sacher et al., 1978; Snyder, 1978). *Dopamine* is a catecholamine neurotransmitter like norepinephrine, of which it is in fact a chemical precursor. It appears to be the main neurotransmitter for perhaps a half-dozen identified brain pathways.

According to the **dopamine hypothesis,** schizophrenia is the product of an excess of dopamine activity at certain synaptic sites. Variants of this view include hypotheses that a schizophrenic person has too many postsynaptic dopamine receptors or that these receptors have for some reason become supersensitive. The most important evidence for the hypothesis is that the effectiveness of the various established antipsychotic drugs, called *neuroleptics,* is highly correlated with the extent to which they block dopamine action at the receptor. Correlation does not, of course, establish a causal relationship, and in recent years the dopamine hypothesis has proven inadequate as a general formulation of etiology (Carlsson, 1988). Dopamine-blocking drugs, for instance, are therapeutically *nonspecific* for schizophrenia (that is, they are also used effectively to treat psychotic symptoms associated with various other disordered states, such as organic mental disorders, some manias, and even drug-induced "bad trips"). Additionally, the receptor-blocking effect is accomplished too quickly (within hours) to be consistent with the clinical picture of a gradual improvement (often over several weeks) following initiation of drug therapy in schizophrenia. In other words, if excess dopamine activity were the cause of schizophrenia, these drugs would have curative effects almost immediately; they do not. Moreover, their therapeutic activity is dependent on reducing dopaminergic activity to *abnormally* low levels. In light of these and other observations, Davis (1978) has suggested that some other (unspecified) factor causes schizophrenia, the symptoms of which are then amplified by dopaminergic neural transmission.

More recent research has provided no serious challenge to this view, although it has shown the dopaminergic systems within the brain to be far more complicated than was originally thought. For example, we now know that more than one type of dopamine receptor site exists on the dendrites of postsynaptic neurons, and that these are involved in differing biochemical processes. The dopamine hypothesis has also been dealt a serious blow by the emergence and recent authorization for routine use of the new antipsychotic drug *clozapine.* The side effects of this drug (which for some patients include a potentially fatal suppression of immune function) have a profile that is very different from that of the dopamine blockers, suggesting that its antipsychotic mode of action significantly differs from that of the neuroleptics. Clozapine has a potent antipsychotic effect for approximately 30 percent of those schizophrenic patients showing little or no response to standard neuroleptic medication (Kane et al., 1988), thus indicating a rather limited range of application.

The demise of the dopamine hypothesis in its etiologic aspect has been a serious disappointment, particularly for those researchers and clinicians sincerely believing that the answer to the schizophrenia puzzle must lie in the domain of biochemistry. To be sure, other biochemical theories of schizophrenia have been, and doubtless will continue to be, advanced, but to date no other such theory appears anywhere near as promising as had the dopamine theory in its prime. Ultimately, it seems extremely likely that a complete understanding of the biochemistry of schizophrenic disorders will have to include a sense of how other influences, including psychological ones, may interact with whatever biochemical aberrations are discovered regularly to accompany schizophrenic behavior.

Neurophysiological Factors   A good deal of research has focused on the role of neurophysiological disturbances in schizophrenia. These disturbances are thought to include an imbalance in excitatory and inhibitory processes and inappropriate autonomic arousal. We would expect such disordered physiology to disrupt the normal attentional and information-processing capabilities of an organism, and there seems to be a growing consensus that disturbances of this type underlie and are basic to the cognitive and perceptual distortions characteristic of individuals diagnosed as schizophrenic.

Consistently, schizophrenic people are found to be deficient in their ability to track visually a moving target (Levy et al., 1983), a deficiency attributed to a disorder of nonvoluntary attention. Some evidence even suggests that the close relatives of schizophrenics share this deficit (Kuechenmeister et al., 1977). Earlier work in this area has been well reviewed by Neale and Oltmanns (1980), and follow-up studies have continued to establish the reliability of the phenomenon (Holzman et al., 1988; Iacono, Tuason, & Johnson, 1981; Latham, et al., 1981). It appears that this visual tracking disability may be but one aspect of a more general performance deficit, widely shared among individuals diagnosed as schizophrenic, in the processing of sensory information (Woods, Kinney, & Yurgelun-Todd, 1986). Many researchers (e.g., George & Neufeld, 1985; Neale & Oltmanns, 1980) believe that a deeper and more fine-grained

In card-sort tests, such as the one shown here, in which subjects must sort cards in different ways to test abstract thought, many schizophrenic individuals fail, leading researchers to speculate that schizophrenic people are deficient in the ability to activate the prefrontal cortex, the brain region thought to be associated with abstract thought.

analysis of such deficits might enhance our understanding of hallucinations and other of the more gross and dramatic phenomena of schizophrenia.

Some findings that may well be related at a basic level indicate that individuals who are merely "at risk" for schizophrenia often experience difficulties in maintaining attention, in processing information, and in certain other indicators of cognitive functioning prior to schizophrenic breakdown (Buchsbaum et al., 1978; Erlenmeyer-Kimling & Cornblatt, 1978; J. Marcus et al., 1985b; Mednick, 1978; Silberman & Tassone, 1985; Spring & Zubin, 1978). Neurologic abnormalities, such as reflex hyperactivity, have also been found in the close relatives of schizophrenic individuals (Kinney, Woods, & Yurgelun-Todd, 1986). As yet, however, the role of these abnormalities in the development of schizophrenia is not clear. Conceivably, they only add another measure of compromised functioning in the adjustment struggles of those who, overburdened with many life problems, may eventually succumb to psychosis.

Considerable evidence suggests that schizophrenic people process information in a way that is both abnormal and relatively specific to schizophrenic disorders. In addition to the visual tracking difficulties already noted, reliable findings show a schizophreniform deficit in visual masking tasks (Balogh & Merritt, 1987) and attentional processes involved in reaction time (e.g., Rosenbaum, Shore, & Chapin, 1988). Magaro (1980, 1981) conceives these people as being unable to match the sensory data they receive with the preexisting schematic patterns normally used to interpret or decode such data; a schizophrenic person, according to this view,

accomplishes the task "automatically," unguided by preestablished cognitive processes. Applying this general approach, Magaro has been able to integrate and make sense of a multitude of findings showing that schizophrenic people perform deficiently on cognitive tasks. Whether or not Magaro is right remains to be seen.

Deficient performance on cognitive tasks is as well-documented as any finding extant on this group of people (Rabin, Doneson, & Jentons, 1979). However, as Sarbin and Mancuso (1980) have pointed out, such findings are virtually guaranteed in advance by the process of designating certain people to be schizophrenic. Moreover, a distressing number of the studies showing schizophrenic performance "deficits" readily conceived as neurophysiological in origin are as readily conceived in the far more simple terms of psychologically-based motivation and attention shortcomings. What if substantial numbers of these patients just don't care? This question is not facetious nor frivolous.

Abnormal neurophysiological processes in schizophrenia could be genetic in origin, but they could also be the product of faulty early conditioning or of biological deviations caused by other factors. For example, problems of this sort could as likely arise from mechanical difficulties in the birth process as from genetic predestination. The frequency of obstetrical complications in the histories of people who later become schizophrenic is, as already noted, markedly above that of the general population. Such observations have led to a resurgence of interest in an old question—that of the *anatomical* intactness of the schizophrenic brain—to which we now turn.

Neuroanatomical Factors Decisive research on the structural properties of the brain in given clinical groups, particularly among living subjects, was hampered by numerous difficulties until the development of modern computer-dependent technologies, such as computerized axial tomography (CAT) and magnetic resonance imaging (MRI). The use of these techniques in the study of schizophrenic people's brains has developed at an accelerating pace in recent years, with interesting results.

We have now accumulated a substantial amount of evidence indicating that in some cases of schizophrenia, particularly among those of chronic course, there is an abnormal enlargement of the brain's ventricles—the hollow areas filled with cerebrospinal fluid lying deep within the core (Andreasen et al., 1982a, 1982b; Boronow et al., 1985; Goetz & Van Kammen, 1986; Golden et al., 1982; Pearlson et al., 1989). In fact the same anomaly is sometimes found in the "normal" family members of schizophrenic patients (DeLisi et al., 1986) and in the high-risk offspring of schizophrenic mothers. In the latter instance, it appears to be associated with low birth weight and the possibility of fetal damage from some unknown agent, possibly infectious (Lyon et al., 1989; Silverton et al., 1985). Because the brain normally occupies fully the rigid enclosure of the skull, enlarged ventricles imply a decrement in brain tissue mass—that is, some type of atrophy or degeneration. Such decrements have in fact been reported by Andreasen et al. (1986), Pearlson et al. (1989), and others using the recently developed MRI technique, and by Bernhardt, Meertz, and Schonfeldt-Bausch (1985) and Brown et al. (1986) in postmortem studies of the brains of individuals who had been schizophrenic.

The findings of an organic brain anomaly associated with some cases of schizophrenia—largely limited to those in the process, chronic, or negative symptom ranges—is of enormous potential significance for at least these types of schizophrenia. There remains, however, the troubling possibility that at least some of this brain tissue loss is due to long-term use of antipsychotic medication, a possibility rendered more ominous by findings that implicate antianxiety drugs of the benzodiazepine class (such as Valium and Librium) in similar brain degeneration (Lader & Petursson, 1984; Schmauss & Krieg, 1987). Examination of the brain volume of schizophrenic people who have never taken therapeutic drugs—a rare class indeed—would be required to reassure us on this question, and some preliminary findings have already appeared to provide that reassurance (e.g., Weinberger et al., 1982).

Assuming that these basic observations of an organic brain anomaly are confirmed, which appears

likely, the discovery is important not only in its own right but also because it invites integration with certain other exciting research initiatives of recent years. In particular, this discovery relates to research on impaired neuropsychological test performances of schizophrenic people (Levin & Yurgelun-Todd, 1989) and to the already-noted subtle neurologic impairments of some children who are at risk for schizophrenia. Though some data suggest a connection between these early neurologic anomalies and ventricular enlargement in adult schizophrenics (Cannon, Mednick, & Parnas; 1989; Silverton et al., 1985), the case has not yet definitely been made.

It certainly cannot be ruled out that these subtle indicators of neurologic compromise in children at risk may be the early manifestations of some sort of progressively debilitating neurological process, possibly even a slowly degenerative one. We should also note the evidence that *some* individuals diagnosed as having a schizotypal personality pattern show behavioral deficit (such as poor perceptual-motor coordination or aberrant reaction-time performance) suggestive of neurological impairment (Rosenbaum, Shore, & Chapin, 1988; Siever, 1985). The relationship of schizotypal disorder (as presently defined) to schizophrenia, however, is less clear than it was once thought to be; that is, schizotypal disorder may not be predictive of schizophrenia (Gunderson & Siever, 1985).

Researchers have noted an overrepresentation in the late winter and early spring months of births of individuals who later become schizophrenic, estimated to be about an 8 percent deviation from norms (DeLisi, Crow, & Hirsch, 1986). This peculiar observation has given rise to a variety of hypotheses involving what has come to be called "the season of birth effect" in the epigenesis of schizophrenia. It now seems, however, that the observation is in all probability an artifact. Assuming that the whole construct of being at risk is a valid one, at-risk people born at an earlier time will have incidence rates in excess of those born at a later time over a considerable range of the at-risk period, simply because they will have been at risk longer. Aggregated data will therefore show a preponderance of births of schizophrenic people to have occurred in earlier rather than later months of the year. The fact that the season of birth effect is observed only among younger schizophrenic people is thus readily explained: few at-risk people remain in an older population.

Mark Lewis (1989a, 1989b, 1990; Lewis & Griffin, 1981), to whom we are indebted for this impressive analysis, and who has demonstrated that dying shows a similar month-of-birth distribution, likens the effect to the time function associated with the burning out of light bulbs; light bulbs become "at risk" when they are placed in electrical circuits, and in general those placed in earliest will be among the first to burn out.

At this point, it is likely that some of you will be committed to a biological *primary cause* interpretation of schizophrenia. Others, including many whose original bias was psychogenic, will be uncertain and perhaps confused. We suspect that few will remain entirely unimpressed with the biological case. We have treated this section in some detail because of our observation that many students tend to come to premature conclusions on either side of the biogenic-psychogenic controversy. We hope we have demonstrated that biological considerations in the etiology of schizophrenia cannot reasonably be dismissed in summary fashion. Nevertheless, comparably tantalizing data exist relating to psychosocial and sociocultural factors, as indeed has already been intimated. When we have a complete theory of the origins of schizophrenic breakdown, it will of necessity encompass biological as well as psychosocial and sociocultural factors. In the meantime, it is reasonable to take the view that *anything* that reduces the adaptive capacity of a person, including varied biological factors, may result in an increased probability of schizophrenic breakdown at some point in the life cycle.

■ Psychosocial Factors in Schizophrenia

Many behavioral scientists hold views that contrast sharply with those in which schizophrenia is held to be caused primarily by biological factors. Here schizophrenic individuals are seen as persons who escape from an unbearable world and seemingly unsolvable conflicts by altering their inner representations of reality. Although biological factors may contribute to and complicate the clinical picture, the origins of the disorder are held to be primarily psychosocial.

Unfortunately, research on psychosocial factors in the development of schizophrenia has been sparse in recent years, especially when compared with the huge research investment in biological correlates. This is the chief reason for the somewhat dated character of the research on which we will have to depend in the following discussion. Partly the problem seems due to normal cyclical variations in research focus, but it also doubtless reflects differences in the speed of technological advances in the two domains. Currently the field of neurobiology is in the throes of a technical revolution of astounding proportions, and there have been considerable—although sometimes grossly exaggerat-

ed—advances in our understanding of biological factors involved in psychopathology, notably including schizophrenia. By contrast, progress on the psychosocial front, lacking in comparable "high tech" investigative tools, has been slow and halting. Something of a self-fulfilling prophecy operates here, however. Funding agencies, notably the National Institute of Mental Health, provide miniscule funding to investigate psychosocial variables, presumably on the grounds of probable limited payoff; they thus ensure precisely that outcome.

Though some might question the validity of research conducted some 20 to 30 years ago, the nature of human behavior is, after all, quite enduring. Unless some critical variable has changed in the interim, we can assume that studies that were empirically sound then are still so today. Though we can hope for more research efforts on possible psychosocial causation, the older studies are as close as we can come to understanding psychosocial factors as they might contribute to schizophrenic outcomes.

In this section, we will deal with the psychosocial patterns that appear particularly relevant to the development of schizophrenia: (a) early psychic trauma and increased vulnerability; (b) pathogenic parent-child and family interactions; (c) faulty learning and coping; (d) social role problems; and (e) excessive stress and decompensation.

Early Psychic Trauma and Increased Vulnerability One of the more unsettling and tragic things we have learned in recent years, mostly through searching investigation of background experience in disorders other than schizophrenia, is the widespread occurrence of various forms of child abuse—as, for example, in multiple personality disorder (Chapter 6). Although we know of no convincing evidence that links the occurrence of such overt abuse to the emergence of schizophrenic behavior, it would not be entirely surprising to discover in future research that childhood abuse, particularly in its more subtle forms, is a contributory background factor in some instances of this type of disorder. In this connection, Karl Menninger has provided a vivid picture of the defenses—and special vulnerabilities—of adolescents and young adults who have suffered deep hurts and have as a result come to view the world as a dangerous and hostile place:

Children injured in this way are apt to develop certain defenses. They cover up, as the slang expression puts it. They deny the injury which they have experienced or the pain which they are suffering. They erect a facade or front, "All's well with me," they seem to say. "I am one of the fellows; I am just like everybody else. I am a normal person." And indeed they act like normal persons, as much as they can. . . . Often they are noticeable only for a certain reticence, shyness, perhaps slight eccentricity. Just as often, they are not conspicuous at all. . . .

What is underneath that front? . . . There is intense conflict and tension and anxiety and strong feelings of bitterness, resentment and hate toward those very people with whom the external relationships may be so perfectly normal. "I hate them! They don't treat me right. They will never love me and I will never love them. I hate them and I could kill them all! But I must not let them know all this. I must cover it up, because they might read my thoughts and then they wouldn't like me and wouldn't be nice to me."

All this is covered up as long as possible. . . . For the chief problem in the person who is going to develop what we call schizophrenia is, "How can I control the bitterness and hatred I feel because of the unendurable sorrow and disappointment that life has brought to me?" . . .

. . . the regimen under which they live has much to do with their successful adaptation. Given certain new stresses, the facade may break down and the underlying bitterness and conflict may break through. (1948, pp. 101–104)

Instead of withdrawing, children who have been traumatized may try to relate aggressively to other people, as we saw in the development of problematic peer relations in Chapter 4. Such children are highly vulnerable to hurt, however, and their existence is usually an anxious one. Often their lives are a series of crises, precipitated by minor setbacks and hurts that they magnify out of all proportion (Arieti, 1974; Dodge & Feldman, 1990). In other instances, a child manifests a pattern of somewhat disorganized paranoid thinking, often coupled with rebellious behavior involving pathological lying, episodes of unbridled aggression, and various types of delinquent behavior.

Although most children who undergo early psychic trauma show residual effects in later life, most do not become schizophrenic. Conversely, it is a virtual certainty that not all schizophrenic patients have undergone such traumatic childhood experiences; indeed, it is not uncommon to discover schizophrenic individuals having excessively overprotected backgrounds. Thus early psychic trauma appears to be, at most, only one among many interactional factors that may contribute to schizophrenia. A good example here is provided in the longitudinal follow-up of Danish "at-risk" children and control-group children of normal parents

who had also been institutionalized for one reason or another. The trauma of early childhood institutionalization appears to have had markedly deleterious effects on the psychological adjustment of *only* the "at-risk" children and not the normal ("low-risk") control cases (Parnas, Teasdale, & Schulsinger, 1985). Anthony (1978) has even suggested that early traumatic experiences may be less important than the overall context in which they occur:

The "headline" experiences—the attacks, the paranoid accusations, the incestuous approaches, the brutalities—seem easier for the child to endure than the constant confusions, mystifications, inconsistencies, and other seemingly minor problems of everyday living. It is not abnormality itself that proves so disturbing but the oscillations between normality and abnormality, and the wider these are, the more difficult it is for the child to sustain. (p. 481)

The absence of solid evidence pinpointing specific types of psychic insult or trauma differentiating the backgrounds of schizophrenic from nonschizophrenic people (e.g., Schofield & Balian, 1959) has prompted Meehl (1978, 1989) to suggest that emotionally significant events do not themselves launch a person on the path to schizophrenia; rather the particular patterns and sequences in which the events occur help bring on the disorder. A person who is to become schizophrenic has the "bad luck" to experience emotionally charged events in a temporal network that is, for the particular individual, pathogenic. If Meehl is right, the research task of discovering particular early life events that increase vulnerability to schizophrenia becomes formidable indeed, and perhaps even impossible.

The situation looks somewhat more hopeful when, as Anthony (1978) has recommended, we look at overall contextual features of an individual's development, as we do in the following section.

Pathogenic Parent-Child and Family Interactions   Studies of interactions in families having schizophrenic offspring have focused on such factors as (a) "schizophrenogenic" parents; (b) destructive marital interactions; (c) faulty communication; and (d) the undermining of personal authenticity. We should note that the focus of research has shifted in recent years from parent-child to total family interactions. Before we proceed, however, let us take a moment to gain some perspective on this sensitive topic.

In the early years of attention to family variables in schizophrenia, parents were routinely and uniquely assumed to have *caused* their children's disorders through hostility, deliberate rejection, or gross parental ineptitude. Many professionals engaged in high levels of blaming behavior, and their feedback to parents was often angry and insensitive, if not frankly brutal. We hope that nothing in the following discussion appears to condone such attitudes. Both authors know from experience that parenting is at best an inscrutable and hazardous responsibility, a veritable minefield, different for every child and none coming with a map. Most of the parents we have known, whether or not they experienced the "bad luck" of schizophrenia in a child, have done the best that could reasonably be expected, within the limits of their own situations, to foster their children's happiness and success. A few have been incredibly cruel and abusive, although as already noted there is no definitive evidence that such a pattern is especially associated with schizophrenic outcomes. Apart from the fact that it does not help and may indeed worsen matters, blame could only be based on an oversimplified notion of how people become schizophrenic.

"Schizophrenogenic" mothers and fathers. Many studies have been made of the parents of individuals who have developed schizophrenia—particularly the mothers of male patients. Termed **schizophrenogenic,** these mothers have typically been characterized as rejecting, domineering, cold, overprotective, and impervious to the feelings and needs of others (e.g., Fromm-Reichmann, 1948). While verbally such a mother may seem accepting, basically she is said to reject her child. At the same time, she depends on the child rather than the father for her emotional satisfactions and feelings of completeness as a woman. Perhaps for this reason, she tends to dominate, possessively overprotect, and smother the child—encouraging dependence on her.

Muddying the waters, the maternal characteristics attributed to the schizophrenogenic mother have also been alleged to be causally involved in many other types of offspring outcome—such as male homosexuality—so much so that the concept of the schizophrenogenic mother had been largely abandoned by the 1970s. It may have made a partial comeback, however, in the results of a well-designed retrospective study by Roff and Knight (1981). These researchers examined clinic records prepared many years prior to the subjects' schizophrenic breakdowns, thus eliminating the possibility of observer bias reactively affecting the results. They found that a mothering style involving the just-described characteristics did show up as a significant factor in the backgrounds of adult male schizophrenics experiencing unfavorable (that is, relatively chronic) outcomes. While these are impressive findings, they are also correlational in nature and so do not permit unqualified inferences about the etiologic significance of the schizophrenogenic mothering style. Still, we can say that the causal hypothesis remains somewhat tenable, albeit perhaps not specific for schizophrenia.

Often combined with this mothering pattern, observers have noted, are rigid, moralistic attitudes toward sex that cause such a mother to react with horror to any evidence of sexual impulses on her child's part. In many instances the mother is overtly seductive in physical contacts with her son, thus augmenting his sexual conflicts. In general, the mother-son relationship in schizophrenia appears to foster immaturity and anxiety in the youth—depriving him of a clear-cut sense of his own identity, distorting his views of himself and his world, and causing him to suffer from pervasive feelings of inadequacy and helplessness.

Nor are the daughters of such mothers likely to fare very well. In this connection, we refer your attention to the description of Mrs. Genain given at the beginning of this chapter.

Although mothers have been singled out for most of the attention in this area, fathers have not gone entirely unscathed. Roff and Knight (1981) also found that the mother-son relationship just described can be especially damaging if the father is passive and uninvolved in his relationship to his son. This finding is consistent with what has already been observed and reported about fathers and schizophrenia. Available studies (e.g., Lidz, Fleck, & Cornelison, 1965) have typically described a somewhat inadequate, indifferent, or passive father who appears detached and humorless—a father who rivals the mother in his insensitivity to others' feelings and needs. Often, too, he appears to be rejecting toward his son and seductive toward his daughter. At the same time, he is often highly contemptuous and derogatory toward his wife, thus making it clear that his daughter is more important to him. This treatment of the wife tends to force her into competition with her daughter, and it devalues her as a model for her daughter's development as a woman. In fact, the daughter may come to despise herself for any resemblance to her mother. Against this background, the daughter often moves into adolescence feeling an incestuous attachment to her father, which creates severe inner conflict and may eventually prove terrifying to her. The problems of the Genain sisters in attempting to cope with their seriously disturbed father, discussed earlier, are relevant here.

PET scans of the Genain quadruplets suggest a possible psychosocial impact resulting from the early matching of two pairs of co-twins. The scans indicate comparatively more severe brain impairment for Hester and Nora. The large areas of blue and yellow show that their brains consume lower levels of glucose, one indicator of lessened brain activity. The orange spots on the scans of Iris and Myra suggest more normal energy usage. Yet it is Iris, originally "matched" with Hester, who has had the poorer clinical outcome than either Nora or Myra.

As might be expected, studies have shown a high incidence of various emotional disturbances on the part of both mothers and fathers of schizophrenics. Kaufman et al. (1960) reported that both the mothers and fathers of 80 schizophrenic children and adolescents studied were emotionally disturbed: the mothers almost uniformly used psychotic-like defense patterns, and the fathers likewise used seriously maladaptive coping patterns. Other studies concerned with the mental health status of schizophrenics' parents, reviewed by Hirsch and Leff (1975), came to basically similar conclusions.

As was indicated in Chapter 4, however, we cannot reasonably assume that disturbance always passes from parent to offspring: it can work in the other direction as well. Aside from the original source of psychopathology, it appears that once it begins, the members of a family may stimulate each other to increased displays of pathological behavior. For example, studies by Mishler and Waxler (1968) and Liem (1974) both contain unequivocal evidence that parents' attempts to deal with the disturbed behavior of schizophrenic sons and daughters had pathological effects on their own behavior and communication patterns. In fact, the bidirectionality of effects may be the single most important thing we have learned from studying the families of schizophrenic people (Carson, 1984).

Destructive marital interactions.   Of particular interest here is the work of Lidz and his associates, which continued over some two decades. In an initial study of 14 families with schizophrenic offspring, Lidz et al. (1965) failed to find a single family that was reasonably well integrated. Eight of

the 14 couples lived in a state of severe chronic discord in which continuation of the marriage was constantly threatened—a condition the investigators called **marital schism.** Typical of this relationship was the chronic undermining of the worth of one marital partner by the other, which made it clear to the children that the parents did not respect or value each other. Each parent expressed fear that a child would resemble the other parent; a child's resemblance to one parent was a source of concern and rejection by the other parent.

The other six couples in this study had achieved a state of equilibrium in which the continuation of the marriage was not constantly threatened but in which the relationship was maintained at the expense of a basic distortion in family relationships; in these cases, family members entered into a "collusion" in which the maladaptive behavior of one or more family members was accepted as normal. This pattern was referred to as **marital skew.** The Genain family, for example, would be considered severely skewed because it was organized chiefly around the bizarre actions and ideas of Mr. Genain. Lidz (1978) proposed that a major effect of such severe family disturbance is the encouragement of "egocentric cognitive regression" in youngsters subjected to it, giving rise eventually to the distinctive cognitive derangements characteristic of the schizophrenic state. In these and other cases regarding parental influences, of course, both biological and psychological influences are likely to be involved. Interestingly, the Roff and Knight (1981) study found both types of marital interaction patterns described by Lidz and his colleagues to be predictive of later poor outcomes for schizophrenic offspring. An especially strong effect showed up for loss of a parent before age seven, and, as might be expected, many such losses were due to parental separation or divorce occasioned by marital disharmony.

Often, schizophrenic people have psychologically healthy siblings who were raised with them in the same families. How have these siblings escaped the presumed pathology of the family context? The answer appears to be that the subculture of a family is not constant, that every child raised within a family experiences a family pattern that is to a considerable extent distinctive for him or her. Stabenau and Pollin (1968; Stabenau et al., 1965), taking a direct approach to this issue, studied families in which siblings were discordant for schizophrenia and for juvenile delinquency. They found that 17 of their 19 "psychopathology siblings" (9 of 10 for schizophrenic siblings alone), as compared to only 2 of 29 controls, had encountered periods of maximum family crisis during their early childhoods. These crises, which were identified by the families themselves, included financial disasters, major parental strife, and depressive episodes in one or another parent, among other things.

Faulty communication.   Bateson (1959, 1960) was one of the first investigators to emphasize the conflicting and confusing nature of communications among members of schizophrenic families. He used the term **double-bind communication** to describe one such pattern. In this pattern the parent presents to the child ideas, feelings, and demands that are mutually incompatible. For example, a mother may be verbally loving and accepting but emotionally anxious and rejecting; or she may complain about her son's lack of affection but freeze up or punish him when he approaches her affectionately. The mother subtly but effectively prohibits comment on such paradoxes, and the father is too weak and ineffectual to intervene. In essence, such a son is continually placed in situations where he cannot win. He becomes increasingly anxious; presumably, such disorganized and contradictory communications in the family come to be reflected in his own thinking.

Singer and Wynne (1963, 1965a, 1965b) linked the thought disorders in schizophrenia to two styles of thinking and communication in the family —*amorphous* and *fragmented*. The amorphous pattern is characterized by a failure in differentiation; here, attention toward feelings, objects, or people is loosely organized, vague, and drifting. Fragmented thinking involves greater differentiation but lowered integration, with erratic and disruptive shifts in communication. Feinsilver (1970) found supporting evidence for such amorphous and fragmented

thinking in the impaired ability of schizophrenic family members to describe essential attributes of common household objects to each other. Bannister (1971) found that schizophrenic thinking tends to be even more "loose" and disordered when an individual is dealing with people and interpersonal relationships than when dealing with objects.

In their later work, Singer and Wynne (Singer, Wynne, & Toohey, 1978; Wynne, Toohey, & Doane, 1979) referred generally to "communication deviance" (or "transactional style deviance") as being at the heart of the purported negative effects parents have on their preschizophrenic children. Following up on this work, Goldstein and colleagues (Doane et al., 1981; Goldstein, 1985; Goldstein et al., 1978; Lewis et al., 1981), in a longitudinal study employing a variant of the "high-risk" strategy (that is, subjects who had been psychological clinic patients, but *not* schizophrenic, as adolescents were followed into adulthood), confirmed such an effect. Specifically, they found that high parental communication deviance, measured during their children's adolescence, did indeed predict the occurrence of adult schizophrenic spectrum disorders among these offspring. An atmosphere of negative affect appears to increase the likelihood of such outcomes. Even if interpreted cautiously, such findings, recently reviewed by Goldstein and Strachan (1987), show promise in enhancing our understanding of the origins of schizophrenia.

Undermining personal authenticity.   Philosopher Martin Buber (1957) pointed out that a confirmation of authenticity is essential to normal interpersonal relationships.

In human society at all its levels, persons confirm one another in a practical way, to some extent or other, in their personal qualities and capacities, and a society may be termed human in the measure to which its members confirm one another. . . . (p. 101)

Such confirmation apparently is often denied a person who later becomes schizophrenic. Several investigators (e.g., Wynne et al., 1958) have noted that the members of schizophrenic families consistently disqualify one or more members' statements and actions. In one family, for example, the father strongly approved of whatever the younger son did while he was to an equal extent disapproving of the older son's behavior. Thus the brothers might make similar statements about some matter, and the father would agree with one and find some basis for disqualifying or discrediting the other. Similarly, at

Christmas time, the younger son's present to his father was praised and appreciated, while that of the older son was criticized and found disappointing. The mother and younger sister went along with this differential treatment. Later, at the age of 27, the older son was hospitalized and diagnosed as a paranoid schizophrenic.

Such contradictory and disconfirming communications subtly and persistently mutilate the self-concepts of one or more of the family members, usually that of a particular child, as in the preceding example. The ultimate of this mutilation process occurs when

. . . no matter how [a person] feels or how he acts, no matter what meaning he gives his situation, his feelings are denuded of validity, his acts are stripped of their motives, intentions, and consequences, the situation is robbed of its meaning for him, so that he is totally mystified and alienated. (Laing & Esterson, 1964, pp. 135–136)

In the general context of faulty parent-child and family interactions, we may note that Lidz (1968, 1973) has characterized the parents of schizophrenic individuals as "deficient tutors": they create a family milieu inappropriate for training a child in the cognitive abilities essential for categorizing experience, thinking coherently, and communicating meaningfully. Coupled with feelings of inadequacy and other damage to the child's emerging self-concept, this may help explain the later cognitive distortions, communication failures, difficulties in interpersonal relationships, and identity confusions that commonly occur in schizophrenia.

Nevertheless, most of the children from families with persistently pathogenic characteristics do not become schizophrenic. Thus pathogenic family interactions that undermine personal authenticity cannot be the sole cause of schizophrenia.

Faulty Learning and Coping   It appears that faulty learning typically plays a key role in schizophrenia, as it does in most other forms of maladaptive behavior. From early traumatic experiences—both within the family and in the outer world—a child may learn conditioned fears and vulnerabilities that lead to perceiving the world as a dangerous and hostile place. Perhaps of even greater importance is faulty learning on a cognitive level, resulting from irrationalities in social interaction, attempts to meet inappropriate or impossible expectations and demands, and observations of pathological models.

Deficient self-structure.   Faulty learning in terms of deficient self-structure is typically reflected in (a) grossly inaccurate assumptions concerning reality, possibility, and value; (b) a confused sense of self-identity coupled with basic feelings of inadequacy, insecurity, and self-devaluation; (c) personal immaturity, often reflected in overdependence on others and overemphasis on being a "good boy" or a "good girl"; and (d) a lack of needed competencies coupled with ineffective coping patterns. These characteristics appear capable of paving the way for schizophrenic and other seriously maladaptive behaviors. If we consider the developmental problems of the Genain sisters in this light, we can see how difficult it must have been for them, as members of a tightly knit and socially isolated foursome, to gain the understandings and skills they needed.

The results of such faulty learning are often seen in such individuals' attempts to deal with inner impulses and establish satisfying interpersonal relationships. In the sexual sphere, schizophrenic individuals' problems are often complicated by rigidly moralistic attitudes toward sexual behavior. At the same time, they usually have had few, if any, meaningful sexual relationships. As a consequence, their sexual fantasies—like those of young adolescents—may be somewhat chaotic and encompass a wide range of sexual objects and behaviors. Such fantasies often lead to severe inner conflicts and to self-devaluation. Similarly, the hostility they may feel toward people important to them is apt to be particularly difficult for such "good" individuals to handle; they tend to view such hostility as both immoral and dangerous and do not know how to express it in socially acceptable ways. At the same time, they may be completely upset at being the object of hostility from those on whom they feel dependent.

This lack of competencies in dealing with sexual and hostile fantasies and impulses, combined with a general deficiency in social skills, usually leads to disappointment, hurt, and devaluation in intimate interpersonal relationships. As we will see, the stresses that commonly precipitate schizophrenic episodes typically center around the difficulties in such relationships. The inability of such individuals to establish and maintain satisfying interpersonal relationships does not void their needs for acceptance, approval, and love; it only reduces their chances for meeting these needs.

The exaggerated use of ego-defense mechanisms. Feeling inadequate and devalued and lacking an adequate frame of reference and needed competencies, such individuals, not surprisingly, learn to rely excessively on ego-defense mechanisms rather than on task-oriented coping patterns. These defense mechanisms often include psychophysiologic elements that have substantial secondary gain by "excusing" a person's withdrawal and nonperformance, particularly in early stages of the disorder. This was apparently the case with the Genain sisters, though somatic symptoms conceivably may also express an underlying biological defect. In any case, the development of a schizophrenic process does not preclude neurotic forms of coping.

The exaggerated use of many ego-defense mechanisms is common. Emotional insulation protects these individuals from the hurt of disappointment and frustration. Regression enables them to lower their level of aspiration and accept a position of dependence. Projection helps them maintain feelings of adequacy and worth by placing the blame for their failures on others and attributing their own unacceptable desires to someone else. Wish-fulfilling fantasies give them some compensation for their frustration and self-devaluation.

In particular, the excessive use of such defense mechanisms as projection and fantasy appears likely to predispose an individual to delusions and hallucinations, which not only represent the breakdown of organized perception and thought processes, but also—as part of a schizophrenic reorganization of reality—may have marked defensive value. Delusions of grandeur and persecution enable these individuals to project the blame for their own inadmissible thoughts and behaviors; hallucinations—such as voices that "pour filth into their minds" or keep them informed of what their "enemies" are up to—may serve a comparable defensive purpose. Delusions of grandeur and omnipotence may grow out of simple wishful thinking and enable them to counteract feelings of inferiority and inadequacy. Hallucinations, such as conversations in which they hear the voice of God confer great power on them and assign them the mission of saving the world, may likewise have comparable defensive value.

In acute schizophrenic episodes, the initial picture is somewhat different, as we have seen, and is dominated by massive disorganization of thought, with panic at the loss of control over thoughts and feelings and desperate attempts to understand the terrifying experience. As yet the individual has not developed defenses to cope with the situation, but no one can continue indefinitely in this state of panic and confusion. Either the acute

schizophrenic episode clears up eventually, or various extreme defenses, such as the ones mentioned earlier, are likely to develop.

Although extreme ego-defense mechanisms are commonly observed in schizophrenic patients, it is often unclear to what extent they are a causal factor, as opposed to a reaction to the frightening experience of disorganization. Here it may be emphasized that a schizophrenic breakdown often appears to represent a total defensive strategy. In essence, the individual seems to withdraw from the real world and evolve a defensive strategy that makes it possible to distort and "reshape" aversive experiences so that they can be assimilated without further self-devaluation. Even though this defensive system may be illogical and far from satisfactory, it relieves much of the inner tension and anxiety and protects the individual from complete psychological disintegration.

Social Role Problems   Social role behavior has been tied into the development and course of schizophrenic reactions in several different ways. A factor emphasized by Cameron and Margaret (1949, 1951) in their intensive studies of schizophrenic patients was the failure of such individuals to learn appropriate role-taking behavior. Inflexible in their own role behavior and uncomprehending of the role behavior of others, they do not know how to interact appropriately with other people.

Laing (1967, 1969, 1971), has carried this view of role behavior a step further, to seeing a schizophrenic person's creation of his or her own social role as protection from destructive social expectations and demands. Describing the so-called normal world as a place where all of us are "bemused and crazed creatures, strangers to our true selves, to one another, and to the spiritual and material world" (1967, p. 56), Laing maintains that a split arises between the false outer self and the true inner self. When the split reaches a point where it can no longer be tolerated, the result is a psychotic breakdown, which usually takes the form of schizophrenia. In this view, the "madness" labeled schizophrenia represents an individual's attempts to recover a sense of wholeness as a human being.

In essence, according to Laing, such an individual dons the "mask of insanity" as a social role and a barricade. Behind this "false self" and often turbulent facade, however, the real person—the "true inner self"—remains. In this hidden inner world, despite the outward role of madness, the schizophrenic individual's hopes and aspirations may remain intact. Accordingly, Laing thinks treatment

Joseph Rogers was diagnosed as a schizophrenic but later recovered and became chairman of the National Mental Health Consumers' Association. Until recent times the prognosis for schizophrenia was generally considered extremely unfavorable. The introduction of antipsychotic-drug therapy for schizophrenia in the 1950s has done much to relieve symptoms and to get schizophrenic individuals out of hospitals, but the long-range outlook for fully restoring personality and coherent thought is often still limited.

should focus less on removing "symptoms" than on finding a path to this remote and often inaccessible sanctuary and assisting the individual to regain wholeness as a person.

In any event, we do know that the occurrence of schizophrenic symptoms may depend to a considerable extent on the context in which an individual is being observed (Levy, 1976; Ritchie, 1975; Shimkunas, 1972). Such symptoms may come and go or be otherwise modified, depending on what demands are currently being placed on the patient. For example, a demand for intimate exchange appears to exacerbate schizophrenic symptoms. We also know that a certain subset of mental patients diagnosed as schizophrenic have demonstrated considerable skill in controlling both the diagnoses they receive and the likelihood of their discharge from the hospital (Braginsky, Braginsky, & Ring, 1969; Drake & Wallach, 1979). In some ways, these are deeply disconcerting findings that mock much of the research reported. They suggest the need for investigator caution in selecting "schizophrenic" patients for research—if only to weed out from studies those who are feigning their symptoms.

A related issue is the possibly fraudulent use of the insanity defense by people accused of serious crimes. Though this defense is infrequently employed, it tends to arise in dramatic cases in which the felonious act seems senseless, that is, unintelligible, to the average person. We can never be ultimately certain that such a plea is valid, or even that it has a viable meaning (Szasz, 1963). This is a problem with which our society will eventually have to come to grips.

Excessive Life Stress and Decompensation

Brown (1972) found a marked increase in the severity of life stress during the ten-week period prior to an actual schizophrenic breakdown. Problems typically centered around difficulties in intimate personal relationships. Similarly, Schwartz and Myers (1977) found interpersonal stressors to be significantly more common among schizophrenic people than among members of a matched control group. As yet, however, we have not come up with a truly adequate classification of the types of stressors that are likely to precipitate a schizophrenic episode (Dohrenwend & Egri, 1981). Forgus and DeWolfe (1974) found that schizophrenic patients seemed to have been defeated by their whole life situation and by difficulties in close personal relationships.

We do know that relapse into schizophrenia following remission is often associated with a certain type of negative communication, called **expressed emotion (EE),** directed at the patient by family members (Hooley, 1985; Miklowitz, Goldstein, & Falloon, 1983; Vaughn & Leff, 1976, 1981). Originally observed in Great Britain, the effect has also been demonstrated in the United States (Hooley, 1985; Vaughn et al., 1984). Two components appear critical in the pathogenic effects of EE: emotional overinvolvement with the patient, and excessive criticalness. Significantly, EE tends to be associated with familial communication deviance as previously described (Doane et al., 1985; Goldstein, 1985; Miklowitz et al., 1986). Parker, Johnston, and Hayward (1988) pointed out that EE is most likely to occur where a former patient is highly disturbed, a circumstance that might itself prompt rehospitalization. The force of this criticism is mitigated by findings that EE *predicts* schizophrenia prior to its initial onset (Goldstein, 1985). Finally, early results from intervention attempts to reduce EE and associated behaviors in family members have been most encouraging in terms of relapse prevention (Falloon et al., 1985; Hogarty et al., 1986).

As we noted, the course of decompensation (disorganization of thought and personality) in reactive (positive-symptom) schizophrenia tends to be sudden, while that in process (negative-symptom) schizophrenia tends to be gradual. The actual degree of decompensation may vary markedly, depending on the severity of stress and the makeup of the individual. The course of recovery or recompensation may also be relatively rapid or slow. Similarly, the degree of recovery may be complete, even leading to a better-adjusted person than before; it may be partial but sufficient for adequate adjustment; or it may be nonexistent, with the individual eventually receiving a diagnosis of chronic schizophrenia.

◼ Sociocultural Factors in Schizophrenia

While disorders of thought and emotion are common to schizophrenia the world over, cultural factors may influence the type, the symptom content, and even the incidence of schizophrenic disorders in different societies. For example, one of the more puzzling findings is that first admission rates for schizophrenia are very high for Irish Catholics in the Republic of Ireland (southern Ireland), especially in the western regions (Torrey et al., 1984), but not among Irish Catholics residing elsewhere (Murphy, 1978). One possibility is that different diagnostic criteria are used in the Republic of Ireland. This does not seem to be a wholly satisfactory explanation, however, because there are many areas around the world in which the incidence of schizophrenia has been clearly shown to be exceptionally high or exceptionally low when compared to the worldwide incidence rate of just under 1 percent. It appears that certain cultures, like certain families, are schizophrenogenic; conversely, others seem to protect their members from the ravages of the disorder, at least to a degree.

Systematic differences in the content and form of a schizophrenic disorder between cultures and even subcultures were documented by Carothers (1953, 1959) in his studies of different African groups. Carothers found the disorganized type of schizophrenia (known at that time as *hebephrenic schizophrenia*) to be most common among African tribal groups in remote areas. He attributed this finding to a lack of well-developed ego-defense mechanisms among the members of these groups, thus making a complete disorganization of personality more likely when schizophrenia did occur. Similarly, Field (1960) described the initial schizophrenic breakdown among natives in rural Ghana as typically involving a state of panic. In this case it was observed that when individuals were brought quickly to a shrine for treatment, they usually calmed down and in a few days appeared recovered. When there was considerable delay before reaching

the shrine, however, individuals often developed classic disorganized disorders.

In another study of schizophrenia among the aborigines of West Malaysia, Kinzie and Bolton (1973) found the acute type to be by far the most common manifestation; they also noted that symptom content often "had an obvious cultural overlay, for example, seeing a 'river ghost' or 'men-like spirits' or talking to one's 'soul'" (p. 773). However, the clinical picture seems to be changing as rural Africans and other people from developing nations are increasingly exposed to modern technology and social change (Copeland, 1968; Kinzie & Bolton, 1973; Torrey, 1973, 1979).

An important consideration in cross-cultural studies is that opinions concerning what is "normal" by professionals from another culture may not always correspond with the opinions held by members of the community in question. For example, in describing the schizophrenic disorders of members of the Hawaii-Japanese community, professional observers emphasized seclusiveness and shallow, blunted emotionality. Community members, on the other hand, were impressed by evidence of uncontrolled emotionality and distrust, behaviors that are strongly counter to the community's values (Katz et al., 1978).

Focusing on sociocultural factors within our own society, Murphy (1968) summarized the abundant evidence that the incidence of schizophrenia in the United States is inversely related to socioeconomic status: the lower the status, the higher the incidence of schizophrenia. Although the data on this point are not as clear as Murphy and others have indicated (Sanua, 1969), his conclusion would probably be accepted by most investigators. Interestingly, a reverse effect seems to exist in India; there, the upper classes (castes) experience higher rates of schizophrenia than the lower classes (Torrey, 1979).

In a sophisticated review of the evidence relating social class and the incidence of schizophrenia, Kohn (1973) suggested that the conditions of lower-class existence impair an individual's ability to deal resourcefully with varied life stressors. The correlation is decidedly imperfect, however, for we know that some lower-class people emerge from their backgrounds with superabundant resourcefulness. We should also emphasize that alleged ethnic differences in the incidence and clinical pictures of schizophrenia—for example, between African Americans, Hispanics, and Anglo-Americans—disappear when social class, education, and related socioeconomic conditions are equated.

In concluding our review of the causal factors in schizophrenia, it may be pointed out that research on the causation of human behavior is, as Shakow (1969) expressed it, "fiendishly complex," even with normal subjects.

Research with disturbed human beings is even more so, particularly with those with whom it is difficult to communicate, among them schizophrenics. The marked range of schizophrenia, the marked variance within the range and within the individual, the variety of shapes that the psychosis takes, and both the excessive and compensatory behaviors that characterize it, all reflect this special complexity. Recent years have seen the complication further enhanced by the use of a great variety of therapeutic devices, such as drugs, that alter both the physiological and psychological nature of the organism. Research with schizophrenics, therefore, calls for awareness not only of the factors creating variance in normal human beings, but also of the many additional sources of variance this form of psychosis introduces. (Shakow, 1969, p. 618)

Or as Bannister (1971) has pointed out, "We will eventually have to develop a theory of what makes all people march before we can say very much about why some people march to a different drummer" (p. 84).

In general, however, it appears that there is no one clinical entity or causal sequence in schizophrenia. Rather we seem to be dealing with several types of psychologically maladaptive processes resulting from an interaction of biological, psychosocial, and sociocultural factors; the role of these factors undoubtedly varies according to the given case and clinical picture. Often the interaction appears to involve a vicious spiral, in which life stress triggers metabolic changes that impair the functioning of a perhaps already compromised central nervous system, the latter, in turn, intensifying anxiety and panic as an individual realizes he or she is losing control. The spiral continues until more permanent reconstitutive patterns are established, treatment is undertaken, or the disorder has run its course. In severe instances, the "course" may be as long as 40 years or more. It is important to note that, although full recovery is rare after such a lengthy period of disorder, it does sometimes occur (M. Bleuler, 1978).

■ Treatments and Outcomes

Until recent times, the prognosis for schizophrenia was generally considered extremely unfavorable. Under the routine custodial treatment of large, institutionalized mental hospital settings, an approach that had persisted for a century prior to the 1950s, the rate of discharge approximated only 30 percent.

For most schizophrenic individuals, the outlook today is not nearly so bleak. Improvement in this situation came with dramatic suddenness when the phenothiazine class of drugs—then referred to as "major tranquilizers"—were introduced in the mid-1950s. *Pharmacotherapy* (treatment by drugs), especially when combined with other modern treatment methods, permits the majority of cases to be treated in outpatient clinics; a schizophrenic individual who enters a mental hospital or clinic as an inpatient for the first time has an 80 to 90 percent chance of being discharged within a matter of weeks or, at most, months. The rate of readmission, however, is still extremely high, although exact figures are difficult to calculate because the "careers" of individual patients are not readily tracked (Weinstein, 1983).

Overall, about one-third of schizophrenic patients recover, which means technically that they

Tom is a schizophrenic individual who is undergoing drug therapy. The contrast between Tom unmedicated (left) and medicated (right) is dramatic, underscoring the effectiveness of antipsychotic drugs in reducing symptoms of schizophrenia.

HIGHLIGHT 12.5

Conditions Associated with Favorable Outcomes in the Treatment of Schizophrenia

The following conditions often indicate a favorable outcome for a schizophrenic patient:

1. Reactive rather than process schizophrenia, in which the time from onset of full-blown symptoms is six months or less.
2. Clear-cut precipitating stressors.
3. Adequate heterosexual adjustment prior to the schizophrenic episode.
4. Good social and work adjustment prior to the schizophrenic episode.
5. Minimal incidence of schizophrenia and other pathological conditions in family background.
6. Involvement of depression or other schizoaffective pattern.
7. Favorable life situation to return to and adequate aftercare in the community.

In general, the opposite of the preceding conditions—including poor premorbid adjustment, slow onset, and relatives with schizophrenia—are indicative of an unfavorable prognosis.

We should note that in a five-year follow-up study of 61 schizophrenic individuals in the United States, Hawk, Carpenter, and Strauss (1975) failed to find any differences in long-range outcomes between acute and other subtypes of schizophrenia. (Data could be obtained on only 61 out of the original sample of 131 cases.) The study was part of an International Pilot Study of Schizophrenia (IPSS) designed to include transcultural data on over 1200 patients in 9 countries—Columbia, Czechoslovakia, Denmark, India, Nigeria, Taiwan, the U.S.S.R., the United Kingdom, and the United States.

remain symptom-free for five years; only some 10 percent now show the classical pattern of inexorable deterioration and permanent, profound disability. The remainder of people experiencing a first schizophrenic episode—some 60 percent of the total— show varying degrees of personality impoverishment and episodic psychotic behavior. Obviously, this is the group on whom our major treatment efforts should initially be concentrated, but evidence shows that in recent years this group, within our own society, has in fact been seriously neglected —as seen in the common "revolving door" pattern of endless cycles of discharge and brief rehospitalization for medication adjustment. Outcome ratios appear less favorable where the onset of symptoms occurs at an early point in the life cycle (Bender, 1973; Gross & Huber, 1973; Morrison, 1974; Roff, 1974). For an overview of conditions that suggest a favorable prognosis in schizophrenia, see *HIGHLIGHT 12.5.*

As we have done with respect to other disorders, we will postpone until later chapters a detailed discussion of the various kinds of treatment employed for schizophrenia. Here we note merely that, contrary to widespread belief, such treatment is— or should be—by no means limited to biological forms of intervention. It is our belief, in fact, that the pharmacologic approach has been grossly over-

sold. Consider in this regard the remarks of the distinguished Harvard social psychologist Roger Brown, who attended a meeting of Schizophrenics Anonymous in order to familiarize himself with the problems of these people:

[The group leader] began with an optimistic testimony about how things were going with him, designed in part to buck up the others. Some of them also spoke hopefully; others were silent and stared at the floor throughout. I gradually felt hope draining out of the group as they began to talk of their inability to hold jobs, of living on welfare, of finding themselves overwhelmed by simple demands. Nothing bizarre was said or done; there was rather a pervasive sense of inadequacy, of lives in which each day was a dreadful trial. Doughnuts and coffee were served, and then each one, still alone, trailed off into the Cambridge night.

What I saw a little of at that meeting of Schizophrenics Anonymous is simply that there is something about schizophrenia that the antipsychotic drugs do not cure or even always remit on a long-term basis. (Brown & Herrnstein, 1975, p. 641)

Unfortunately, Brown's assessment of the antipsychotic drugs is in our judgment painfully accurate; it may even be excessively generous. The devastating social deficits Brown describes are extremely common accompaniments of schizophrenic disorders and may indeed be far more disabling in their disruptive effects than an occasional eruption of psychotic symptoms. There is no evidence that long-term rates of *social* recovery from schizophrenia have been affected by the availability of these drugs (see, for example, Harding et al., 1987a, 1987b). Nor is it easy to see how drugs of any kind could be expected to provide these patients with the wherewithal, in terms of a social competence that many lacked before becoming actively schizophrenic, to lead reasonably successful and independent lives. We include in this assessment clozapine (Clozaril), mentioned earlier, the first of what will probably turn out to be a new generation of antipsychotics. It seems obvious to us that we are going to have to look elsewhere for a "cure" to this type of problem; the idea of finding a chemical that might do this job for us is, we think, unrealistic.

The tendency to think of the treatment of schizophrenia as being exclusively a matter of biological intervention has obscured some real progress that had been made in psychosocial approaches before this trend gained the force it now commands. In the large scale meta-analysis (see Chapter 18) of therapeutic outcomes conducted by Smith, Glass, and Miller (1980), the "average effect size" for all psychosocial treatments for schizophrenia was +0.68, a respectable figure; by contrast, the average effect size for drugs-alone treatment of schizophrenia was +0.51. Because the training, competence, and experience of the person or persons conducting the treatment are far less critical in drug than in psychosocial approaches (the active ingredients of the drug are the same no matter who writes the prescription), we suspect these figures *underestimate* the potential advantages of psychosocial forms of intervention. In any event, the combination drugs-plus-psychosocial intervention average effect size was as an impressive +.80, which suggests that systematic psychosocial treatment should always be part of the treatment offered in schizophrenia. Our experience suggests that at this time such treatment is actually rare.

Several forms of exclusively psychosocial intervention in schizophrenia have documented high rates of success. These interventions include a therapeutic community-based program having minimal professional oversight (Fairweather et al., 1969; Fairweather, 1980), a rigorous token economy program for chronic state hospital patients (Paul & Lentz, 1977), and specialized individual psychotherapy provided by therapists highly experienced with this group (Karon & Vandenbos, 1981).

DELUSIONAL (PARANOID) DISORDER

The term **paranoia** has been in use a long time. The ancient Greeks and Romans used it to refer more or less indiscriminately to any mental disorder. Our present, more limited use of the term stems from the work of Kraepelin, who reserved it for cases showing delusions and impaired contact with reality but without the severe personality disorganization characteristic of schizophrenia.

Currently two main types of psychoses are included under the DSM-III-R headings relating to (nonschizophrenic) paranoid disorders: **delusional disorder,** formerly called *paranoia* and *paranoid disorder,* and **induced psychotic disorder,** formerly *shared paranoid disorder,* in which two or more people develop persistent, interlocking delusional ideas. The latter of these conditions, historically known as *folie à deux,* is described briefly in *HIGHLIGHT 12.6.* Brief episodes of otherwise uncomplicated delusional thinking have been shifted in DSM-III-R to the "wastebasket" category *psychotic disorders not elsewhere classified.* Our focus in this section will be on delusional disorder. As will become apparent, there is a lack of recent literature on this disorder, and we will thus be forced to focus on a number of early but seemingly definitive studies. Because these earlier studies used the traditional terminology *paranoia* and *paranoid disorder,* we will use those terms and the newer *delusional disorder* classification interchangeably.

DSM-III-R requires that diagnoses of delusional disorder be specified by type, based on the predominant theme of the delusions present. These types are as follows:

- *Persecutory type.* The predominant delusional theme is that one (or someone to whom one is closely related) is being subjected to some kind of malevolent treatment. Legal actions of one sort or another are often instituted to redress the alleged injustice.

- *Jealous type.* The predominant theme is that one's sexual partner is being unfaithful.

- *Erotomanic type.* The predominant theme is that some other person of higher status, frequently someone of considerable prominence, is in love with one and wants to start a sexual liaison.

- *Somatic type.* The predominent theme is an unshakable belief in having some physical

HIGHLIGHT 12.6

Folie à Deux

A relatively neglected phenomenon in the functional psychoses is that of *folie à deux*—a form of psychological "contagion" in which one person copies and incorporates into his or her own personality structure the delusions and other psychotic patterns of another person. Familial relationships between individuals in 103 cases studied by Gralnick (1942) fell within one of the following four categories:

sister	⇄	sister	40 cases
husband	⇄	wife	28 cases
mother	⇄	child	24 cases
brother	⇄	brother	11 cases

Among the explanatory factors—all environmental—emphasized by Gralnick were (a) length of association, (b) dominance-submission, (c) type of familial relationship, and (d) prepsychotic personality. The high incidence in the husband-wife category is particularly striking because common heredity plays no part as an etiological factor in these cases.

In another study, Soni and Rockley (1974) reported on 8 cases of folie à deux seen at a European hospital. Their findings supported those of Gralnick and emphasized the role of pathological prepsychotic characteristics, such as increased suggestibility and submissive roles, as well as the type of relationship in explaining why these patients acquired their partner's delusions.

---

illness or disorder, often bizarre in nature, or in having some abnormality of appearance.

- *Grandiose type.* The predominant theme is that one is a person of extraordinary status, power, ability, talent, beauty, and so on.
- *Other.* This diagnosis is used when no single theme predominates.

Of these types, the persecutory is by far the most common, and our discussion will focus on this form of the disorder.

Although the formal diagnosis of delusional disorder is rare in clinic and mental hospital populations, this observation provides a somewhat misleading picture of its actual occurrence. Many exploited inventors, fanatical reformers, self-styled prophets, morbidly jealous spouses, persecuted teachers, business executives, or other professionals fall into this category. Unless they become a serious nuisance, these individuals are usually able to maintain themselves in the community and do not recognize their paranoid condition nor seek help to alleviate it.

In some instances, however, they are potentially dangerous, and in virtually all instances they are inveterate "injustice-detectors," inclined to undertake retributive actions of one sort or another.

■ The Clinical Picture in Delusional Disorder

A paranoid, or delusional, individual feels singled out and taken advantage of, mistreated, plotted against, stolen from, spied on, ignored, or otherwise mistreated by "enemies." The delusional system usually centers around one major theme, such as financial matters, a job, an invention, an unfaithful spouse, or another life affair. For example, a woman who is failing on the job may insist that her fellow workers and superiors have it in for her because they are jealous of her great ability and efficiency. As a result, she may quit her job and go to work elsewhere, only to find friction developing again and her new job in jeopardy. Now she may become convinced that the first company has written to her present employer and has turned everyone against her so that she has not been given a fair chance. With time, more and more of the environment is integrated into her delusional system as each additional experience is misconstrued and interpreted in the light of her delusional ideas. See *HIGHLIGHT 12.7* for a list of characteristics typical of paranoid thinking.

Although the evidence that paranoid people advance to justify their claims may be tenuous and inconclusive, they are unwilling to accept any other

Sequence of Events in a Paranoid Mode of Thinking

A number of investigators have concluded that the most useful perspective from which to view paranoia is in terms of a *mode of thinking*. The sequence of events that appears to characterize this mode of thinking may be summarized as follows:

1. *Suspiciousness*—the individual mistrusts the motives of others, fears he or she will be taken advantage of, and is constantly on the alert.
2. *Protective thinking*—the individual selectively perceives the actions of others to confirm suspicions and blames others for his or her failures.

3. *Hostility*—the individual responds to alleged injustices and mistreatment with anger and hostility and becomes increasingly suspicious.
4. *Paranoid Illumination*—the moment when everything "falls into place"; the individual finally understands the strange feelings and events being experienced.
5. *Delusions*—the individual has delusions of influence and persecution that may be based on "some grain of truth," presented in a logical and convincing way; often, the later

development of delusions of grandeur.

Over time, a paranoid individual may incorporate additional life areas, people, and events into the delusional system, creating a "pseudo-community" whose purpose is to carry out some action against him or her. Paranoid individuals who respond in this manner may come to feel that all the attention they are receiving from others is indicative of their unique abilities and importance, thus paving the way for delusions of grandeur.

Based in part on Meissner (1978) and Swanson, Bohnert, and Smith (1970).

---

possible explanation and are impervious to reason. A husband may be convinced of his spouse's unfaithfulness because on two separate occasions when he answered the phone the party at the other end hung up. Argument and logic are futile. In fact, any questioning of his delusions only convinces him that his interrogator has sold out to his enemies. The following case illustrates the sometimes tragic results of paranoid delusions:

*M*ilner *cited the case of a paranoid man, aged 33, who murdered his wife by battering her head with a hammer. Prior to the murder, he had become convinced that his wife was suffering from some strange disease and that she had purposely infected him because she wished him to die. He believed that this disease was due to a "cancer-consumption" germ. He attributed his conclusion in part to his wife's alleged sexual perversion and also gave the following reasons for his belief:*

1. His wife had insured him for a small sum immediately after marriage.

2. A young man who had been friendly with his wife before their marriage died suddenly.

3. A child who had lived in the same house as his wife's parents suffered from fits. (He also believed that his wife's parents were suffering from the same disease.)

4. For several months before the crime his food had had a queer taste, and for a few weeks before the crime he had suffered from a pain in the chest and an unpleasant taste in the mouth. (1949, p. 130)

Although ideas of persecution predominate, many paranoid individuals develop delusions of grandeur in which they endow themselves with superior or unique abilities. Such "exalted" ideas usually center around messianic missions, political or social reforms, or remarkable inventions. Paranoid people who are religious may consider themselves appointed by God to save the world and may spend most of their time "preaching" and "crusading." Threats of fire and brimstone, burning in hell, and similar persuasive devices are liberally employed. Many paranoid people become attached to extremist political movements and are tireless and fanatical crusaders, although they often do their cause more harm than good by their self-righteousness and their condemnation of others.

Some paranoid individuals develop remarkable inventions that they have endless trouble in patenting or selling. Gradually they become convinced that a plot is afoot to steal their invention, or that enemies of the United States are working against them to prevent the country from receiving the benefits of their remarkable talents. Hoffman cited the case of an individual who went to Washington to get presidential assistance in obtaining a patent for a flame thrower that, he claimed, could destroy all the enemies of the United States. He would patiently explain who he was: "There's God who is Number 1, and Jesus Christ who is Number 2, and me, I am Number 3" (1943, p. 574).

Aside from the delusional system, such an individual may appear perfectly normal in conversation, emotionality, and conduct. Hallucinations and the other obvious signs of psychopathology are rarely found. This normal appearance, together with the logical and coherent way in which the delusional ideas are presented, may make the individual most convincing. The following case is typical:

In one case an engineer developed detailed plans for eliminating the fog in San Francisco and other large cities by means of a system of reflectors that would heat the air by solar radiation and cause the fog to lift. The company for which he worked examined the plans and found them unsound. This rejection upset him greatly and he resigned his position, stating that the other engineers in the company were not qualified to pass judgment on any complex and advanced engineering projects like his. Instead of attempting to obtain other employment, he then devoted full time trying to find some other engineering firm that would have the vision and technical proficiency to see the great potential of his idea. He would present his plans convincingly but become highly suspicious and hostile when questions concerning their feasibility were raised. Eventually, he became convinced that there was a conspiracy among a large number of engineering firms to steal his plans and use them for their own profit. He reported his suspicions to the police, threatening to do something about the situation himself unless they took action. As a consequence, he was hospitalized for observation and diagnosed as suffering from paranoia.

The diagnosis of delusional disorder may be rendered difficult at times because of the unclarity of the term *delusion*. It is not always possible to determine the truth or falsity of an idea, and some ideas that are patently false are held with sincerity and conviction by many people. For this reason, formal definitions of "delusion" (as in DSM-III-R) usually specify that an idea must be held as preposterous by the majority of a person's own community. As the example of Columbus's fifteenth-century belief that the earth was round shows, however, this qualification does not always solve the problem. These and other difficulties surrounding the notion of delusional thinking have received a thorough airing recently in a book edited by Oltmanns and Maher (1988). A number of the chapters in this work, incidentally, suggest that delusional thinking is not so different from normal thinking as we would perhaps like to think. The problem also remains, of course, of differentiating delusional disorder from paranoid personality disorder (Chapter 8), which also involves a judgment call as to whether or not clearly eccentric and convoluted thinking merits the designation "delusional."

A patient's delusional system is apt to be particularly convincing if one accepts the basic premise or premises on which it is based. For example, where the delusional system develops around some actual injustice, it may be difficult to distinguish between fact and fancy. As a result, the individual's family and friends, as well as well-meaning public officials, may be convinced of the truth of the claims. However, the individual's inability to see the facts in any other light, typical lack of evidence for far-reaching conclusions, and hostile, suspicious, and uncommunicative attitude when the delusional ideas are questioned usually provide clues that something is wrong.

The following case history is a classic description of a mild paranoia. It reveals the development of a logically patterned delusional system and the pertinent selection of environmental evidence that involves more and more individuals in the supposed conspiracy. Despite this woman's delusional system, however, she was not severely out of touch with reality; many nonhospitalized cases in the community reveal similar symptomatology to a more serious degree.

The patient was a 31-year-old nurse who was commissioned a second lieutenant in the Army Nurse Corps shortly after the beginning of World War II. From the start she found it difficult to adjust to fellow nurses and to enlisted men under her supervision, the difficulty apparently arising from her overzealousness in carrying out ward regulations in the minutest detail. In any event, "No one could get along with her." After some two years of service, she was transferred to a new assignment.

. . . Initially she made an excellent impression, but soon showed herself to be a perfectionist, a hypercritical and domineering personality who insisted on the immediate, precise, exact and detailed execution of orders. Within a 14-week period she was transferred on three separate occasions from post to post, and at each new post her manner and her attitude, despite her precise and meticulous efficiency, constituted a virtual demand that nurses, wardmen, patients, and medical officers conform to her exceedingly rigid ideas about the management of ward and even departmental routines. . . .

During the course of her last assignment, she received every possible help. She requested additional responsibility and was, therefore, assigned, as charge nurse, to the Eye, Ear, Nose, and Throat Clinic. Within a week she lodged a complaint with the commanding officer of the hospital, accusing the enlisted men of conspiring against her, the nurses of lying about her, and the officer in charge of lack of cooperation. She was, therefore, transferred to one of the wards, where she expected wardmen, nurses and patients to execute her orders on the instant, in minute and exact detail, and where she violently berated them because of their inability to do so. A week later, the responsible medical officer requested that she be relieved from duty there. Instead, she discussed the problem with the chief nurse and promised to correct her attitude. Within four days, the patients as a group suggested her removal. Two weeks later, the ward officer repeated his request. She was, therefore, given a five-day leave, and during her absence all ward personnel were contacted in an attempt to help her adjust when she returned to duty.

During this period she became convinced that she was being persecuted. She grew tense and despondent, kept rigidly to herself, was unable to sleep in a room with a ticking clock, and frequently burst into tears. As she herself said, "Some of the nurses deliberately went out of their way to annoy and criticize me. They wanted to make me trouble. That's why I was so upset." On three separate occasions, she requested the appointment of a Board of Officers to investigate these alleged discriminatory acts. Finally she demanded that a Board of Officers be

convened to determine her efficiency as a nurse. Instead, she was ordered to report to our hospital for psychiatric observation.

On admission, few details of her military history were known. She seemed alert and cooperative, was well oriented in all three spheres [time, place, person], and was thought to be in complete contact. Extreme care, however, was necessary when addressing her. Even fellow patients would warn newcomers to the ward. "Be careful what you say when she's around. She won't mean it, but she'll twist your statements without changing your words, and give them some meaning you never intended." In addition, she was bitter about the unfair treatment she had received in the Army, wished to reform the Medical Department and the Army Nursing Corps, and indignantly repudiated the existence of any condition that could justify placing her under NP [neuropsychiatric] observation. . . .

The diagnosis of "paranoia, true type" was made, and she was returned to the United States, one month after admission to the hospital, a rigid and overzealous individual whose inelasticity had antagonized her associates and aroused severe emotional strain within herself, firmly convinced that she was being persecuted because of the necessary and badly needed work which she had much too efficiently performed. . . . She was received in the States as a patient in the very hospital to whose psychiatric section she had previously, for so brief a period of time, been assigned as ward nurse. (Rosen & Kiene, 1946, pp. 330–333)

Paranoid individuals are not always as dangerous as we have been led to believe by popular fiction and drama, but the chance always exists that they will decide to take matters into their own hands and deal with their enemies in the only way that seems effective. In one instance, a paranoid school principal became convinced that the school board was discriminating against him and shot and killed most of the board members. In another case, a paranoid man shot and killed a group of seven people he thought had been following him. The number of husbands and wives who have been killed or injured by suspicious, paranoid mates is undoubtedly large. As Swanson, Bohnert, and Smith (1970) have pointed out, such murderous violence is commonly associated with jealousy and the loss of self-esteem; the spouse feels that he or she has been deceived, taken advantage of, and humiliated. Paranoid people may also get involved in violent and subversive activities and in political assassinations.

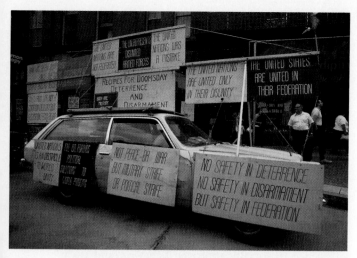

The insistent way the owner of this car has chosen to broadcast his or her ideas and the ideas themselves, which are hostile, suspicious, and a distortion of factual evidence, indicate delusional thinking.

■ Causal Factors in Delusional Disorder

Most of us on various occasions may wonder if we are not jinxed, when it seems as if everything we do goes wrong and the cards seem to be stacked against us. If we are generally somewhat suspicious and disposed to blame others for our difficulties, we may feel that most people are selfish and ruthless and that honest people, no matter what their abilities, do not have a fair chance. As a result, we may feel abused and become somewhat bitter and cynical. Many people go through life feeling underrated and frustrated, brooding over fancied and real injustices. Meissner (1978) regards such attitudes as a normal and essential phase of personality development, a necessary component in the achievement of personal identity and autonomy. Most people, according to this view, are able to grow beyond this phase, where a central feature is the need for an enemy. Some few are not, however, in which case they chronically entertain paranoid explanations of their problems.

As we have seen, recent thinking in this area has tended to view schizophrenic and paranoid processes as independent of one another, although sometimes occurring together in the same individual, in which case paranoid schizophrenia is the outcome (Magaro, 1980, 1981; Meissner, 1981). According to Magaro, schizophrenic and paranoid cognitions are of a different order and are related to two different stages of information processing. Whereas schizophrenia is seen as a disorder of *perception,* paranoia is regarded as a disorder of *conception.* A paranoid individual, in fact, is said to *overconceptual-*

ize his or her experience to the point of relative inattention to the actual data that are perceived. For example, a (nonparanoid) schizophrenic individual might perceive his or her thoughts as inspired by external sources; a paranoid individual might carry this one step farther and conclude that this experience is due to a systematic plot by his or her "enemies" to harass and punish him or her. As a result, meanings may be imposed on incoming information that have no or at most a minimal relationship to what has happened, at least as far as issues of great personal significance are concerned.

We have already noted that individuals with paranoid schizophrenia tend not to show the extensive cognitive disorganization seen in other forms of schizophrenia. We should also note that biological factors have rarely been implicated in the paranoid disorders, as they have been in schizophrenia—although we must acknowledge that little work has been done in this area. Most observers believe that psychosocial factors are sufficient to account for the development of most of the paranoid disorders.

It may also be noted that the maintenance of a severely paranoid "fix" on the world does indeed require drastic derangements of a person's basic cognitive equipment, although it does not require that such equipment be subject to virtual functional annihilation. If an individual were unable to function on a day-by-day basis, paranoia would be impossible as an effective coping strategy.

Faulty Learning and Development   Most paranoid individuals seem as children to have been aloof, suspicious, seclusive, secretive, stubborn, and resentful of punishment. When crossed, they became sullen and morose. Rarely do paranoid individuals show a history of normal play with other children or good socialization in terms of warm, affectionate relationships (Sarvis, 1962; Schwartz, 1963; Swanson et al., 1970).

Often such an individual's family background appears to have been authoritarian and excessively dominating, suppressive, and critical; frequently, some family members have practiced "mind reading" the thoughts of other family members. Such a family is often permeated with an air of superiority that is a cover-up for an underlying lack of self-acceptance and feelings of inferiority, creating for a child, in turn, the necessity of proving superiority. Inevitably, the family background of such individuals colors their feelings about people in general and their way of reacting to others. Inadequate socialization is likely to keep them from understanding others' motives and points of view and to lead them to suspicious misinterpretations of unintentional slights. Also, they tend to enter into social relationships with a hostile, dominating attitude that drives others away. Their inevitable social failures then further undermine their self-esteem and lead to deeper social isolation and mistrust.

In later personality development, these early trends merge into a picture of self-important, rigid, arrogant individuals. Such people long to dominate others and readily maintain their unrealistic self-picture by projecting the blame for difficulties onto others and seeking in others the weaknesses they cannot acknowledge in themselves. They are highly suspicious of the motives of other people and quick to sense insult or mistreatment. Such individuals lack a sense of humor—which is not surprising, since they view life as a deadly serious struggle—and are incapable of seeing things from any viewpoint but their own. Typically, they categorize people and ideas into "good" and "bad" and have difficulty in conceiving of something as having both good and bad qualities or shades of gray. Their goals and expectations are unrealistically high, and they refuse to make concessions in meeting life's problems by accepting more moderate goals. They expect to be praised and appreciated for even minor achievements, and when such praise is not forthcoming, they sulk and withdraw from normal contacts.

Many paranoid individuals' problems can be seen as problems of selfhood. A paranoid person may seem unable to achieve distance from deeply internalized struggles involving issues of aggression, victimization, power, weakness, and humiliation. Although such individuals may have broad interests and appear normal in general behavior, they are usually unable to relate closely to other people; they appear inaccessible, are overly aggressive, and maintain a somewhat superior air. Meissner (1978) views these personality traits largely as manifestations of a desperate attempt to maintain autonomy and a related fear of submission to the will of others, as though submission would constitute nothing less than total personality annihilation.

Failure and Inferiority   The lives of paranoid individuals are replete with failures in critical life situations—social, occupational, and marital—stemming from their rigidity, their unrealistic goals, and their inability to get along with other people. Such failures jeopardize their view of themselves as being adequate, significant, and important and also expose their easily wounded pride to what they interpret as the rejection, scorn, and ridicule of others.

These failures are made more difficult to cope with by paranoid individuals' utter inability to understand the causes. Why should their efforts to improve the efficiency of the company—which people approve in principle—lead to such negative reactions from others? Why should people dislike them when they are striving so hard to do the best possible job down to the very last detail? Unable to see themselves or the situation objectively, they simply cannot understand how they tend to alienate others and why they are rebuffed and rejected.

Although such people's feelings of inferiority are masked behind an air of superiority and self-importance, many aspects of their behavior give them away. Clues in profusion are found in their continual craving for praise and recognition, their hypersensitivity to criticism, their exact and formal adherence to socially approved behavior, and their overzealous performance of minute tasks.

In essence, then, a paranoid individual is confronted with experiences of failure that in effect say, "People don't like you," "Something is wrong with you," or "You are inferior." He or she is incapable, however, of dealing with the problem in a task-oriented way, instead tending to intensify the existing defenses, becoming more rigid, opinionated, and prone to blame others. This defensive pattern is a protection against having to face unbearable feelings of inferiority and worthlessness. In this connection, Meissner (1978) reports the case of a young man who was sexually seduced by his drunken mother. He lived in terror that his "sin" would be discovered, and in the process developed an elaborate paranoid system of thought.

Elaboration of Defenses and the "Pseudocommunity"   A rigid, self-important, humorless, and suspicious individual such as we have described becomes understandably unpopular with other people—in effect, an aversive stimulus. Thus, as Lemert (1962) has noted, a paranoid person frequently becomes in fact a target of actual discrimination and mistreatment. Ever alert to injustices, both imagined and real, such an individual finds abundant "proof" of persecution.

In this context, Grunebaum and Perlman (1973) have pointed to the naïveté of a "preparanoid" person in assessing the interpersonal world—in terms of who can be trusted and who cannot—as a fertile source of hurtful interactions. As they express it, "The ability to trust others realistically requires that the individual be able to tolerate minor and major violations of trust that are part of normal human relationships." (p. 32). The preparanoid individual is unprepared for the "facts of life," however, tending to both trust and mistrust inappropriately and to overreact when others are perceived, accurately or not, as betraying the trust.

Where delusional disorder develops, it usually does so gradually, as mounting failures and seeming betrayals force these individuals to an elaboration of their defensive structures. To avoid self-devaluation, they search for "logical" reasons for their lack of success. Why were they denied a much-deserved promotion? Why was it given to someone less experienced and obviously far less qualified? They become more vigilant, begin to scrutinize the environment, search for hidden meanings, and ask leading questions. They ponder like a detective over the "clues" they pick up, trying to fit them into some sort of meaningful picture.

Gradually the picture begins to crystallize—a process commonly referred to as "paranoid illumination." It becomes apparent that they are being singled out for some obscure reason, that other people are working against them, that they are being interfered with. In essence, they protect themselves against the intolerable assumption, "There is something wrong with me," with the projective defense, "They are doing something to me." They have failed not because of any inferiority or lack on their part, but because others are working against them. They are on the side of good and the progress of humankind, while their enemies are allied with the forces of evil. With this as their fundamental defensive premise, they proceed to distort and falsify the facts to fit it and gradually develop a logical, fixed, delusional system. Cameron (1959) has referred to this process as the building up of a paranoid "pseudo-community" in which an individual organizes surrounding people (both real and imaginary) into a structured group whose purpose is to carry out some action against him or her.

The role of highly selective information processing in the development of these delusional systems should be emphasized. Once these individuals begin to suspect that others are working against them, they start carefully noting the slightest signs pointing in the direction of their suspicions and ignore all evidence to the contrary (Swanson et al., 1970).

With this frame of reference, it is quite easy, in our highly competitive, somewhat ruthless world, for paranoid individuals to find ample evidence that others are working against them. This attitude itself leads to a vicious circle, for their suspiciousness, distrust, and criticism of others drive their friends and well-wishers away and keep them in continual friction with other people, generating new incidents for them to magnify. Often people do in fact have to conspire behind their backs in order to keep peace and cope with their eccentricities.

One additional factor often mentioned in connection with the development of delusional disorder is that of sexual maladjustment. Like schizophrenic patients, most paranoid individuals reveal sexual difficulties, typically centering around serious problems in interpersonal relationships in general, compounded by overwhelming feelings of inadequacy and inferiority.

Many early schizophrenic and paranoid patients make allusions to being "queer" or "gay," or to the thought that other people think they are. On investigation, it turns out that they typically have never engaged in homosexual behavior and show no indication of wishing to do so. It may be that they have finally hit on an "explanation" for the feeling of being so different from others, and for the slights and contempt they believe are emanating from others. An explanation of this sort may be better than no explanation at all as far as a troubled person is concerned. In brief, however, while underlying sexual conflicts, both heterosexual and homosexual, may be involved in the clinical picture, they do not appear to be of primary significance.

Treatments and Outcomes

In the early stages of delusional disorder, treatment with individual or group psychotherapy (or a combination of both) may prove effective, particularly if an individual voluntarily seeks professional assistance. Behavior therapy appears to show particular promise; for example, paranoid thinking may be altered by a combination of aversive conditioning, removal of the factors in a person's life that are reinforcing the maladaptive behavior, and development of more effective coping patterns.

Once a delusional system is well established, however, treatment is extremely difficult. It is usually impossible to communicate with such individuals in a rational way concerning their problems. In addition, they are not prone to seek treatment, but are more likely to seek justice for all the wrong done to them. Nor is hospitalization likely to help, for they are likely to see it as a form of punishment. They are apt to regard themselves as superior to other patients and will often complain that their families and the hospital staff have had them "put away" for no valid reason. Seeing nothing wrong with themselves, they refuse to cooperate or participate in treatment.

Eventually, however, they may realize that their failure to curb their actions and ideas will result in prolonged hospitalization. As a result, they may make a pretext of renouncing their delusions, admitting that they did hold such ideas but claiming that they now realize the ideas are absurd and are giving them up. After their release, they are often more reserved in expressing their ideas and in annoying other people, but they are far from recovered. Thus the prognosis for complete recovery from paranoia has traditionally been unfavorable.

UNRESOLVED ISSUES
on Schizophrenia

The unresolved issues concerning schizophrenia are so manifold that a truly adequate accounting of them would require the better part of an additional chapter. We will point up, therefore, only a few selected problems of the many we encounter in this realm of psychopathology. Issues of treatment, in particular, will be postponed to Chapters 17 and 18.

A major hurdle confronts us at the outset in trying to come to grips with the nature of this purported disorder. More than in any other recognized category of disorder, this one's conceptual boundaries are both murky and shifting. While we now have, in DSM-III and its revision, a set of defining criteria that when properly applied will permit us to say who is and who is not schizophrenic with a high degree of reliability, we remain to an extraordinary extent uncertain of the information contained in any such act of inclusion or exclusion. That is, it remains unusually difficult for most of us to arrive at a coherent picture of what schizophrenia is, one that goes beyond, so to speak, the defining criteria themselves. Considered in this light, the loss of some 50 percent of the category's members in moving from DSM-II to DSM-III is disconcerting. This is a *substantive,* not merely cosmetic, change. If the change is not the product of important conceptual advances (for which there seems little evidence), then to what may it be ascribed? Is this perhaps an example wherein considerations of enhanced reliability have pushed those pertaining to validity too far into the background? By all accounts, DSM-IV is to be installed in 1993 (Frances, Widiger, & Pincus, 1989). It is unreasonable to hope for a substantially improved set of diagnostic criteria for schizophrenia by that time; the extensive research effort that would be needed has not, as of this writing, even so much as begun (Carson, 1991).

In the meantime, we do not have a better definition to offer. Rather, we suspect that changing the definitional criteria for "schizophrenia" without having solid research data to support the change will never produce a satisfactory solution, and it is unclear that such data can be produced in the absence of fundamental redirections of approach.

What is needed is some sort of paradigm shift that enables us to view the pertinent behavioral phenomena in a new and more productive light. We feel reasonably certain that any such major conceptual advance will entail not one but many "schizophrenias." That is, it is likely that the class of people who merit this diagnosis is a heterogeneous one in terms of the nature, development, and sources of their aberrant behavior. An important implication is that there may be no single "core" condition. Another implication is that efforts at differentiation of basic subgroups should have a high research priority. Beyond that, the crystal ball is notably hazy.

Assuming eventual solution of the taxonomic problem, major difficulties will likely remain in respect to the observational, scientific, and philosophical status of certain of the major "symptoms" of schizophrenia, in particular hallucinations. In the assessment of such phenomena, we are wholly dependent on a patient's report of them because, unlike reports of most subjective symptoms in medical illness, we typically have no way of independently corroborating their presence or meaning within a network of more objective signs. While the typical schizophrenic patient would not likely be the observer we would choose to make critical appraisals of these subjective and often highly unusual phenomena, if only because of suspected psychosis, he or she is quite literally the only observer we have, the unique experiencer of essentially experiential data. It seems unwise to make such reports the centerpiece of the observational base we use in attempting to diagnose and understand the schizophrenias. Hopefully, we can find better ones more subject to direct public scrutiny.

Most of what we know about the schizophrenias points to the conclusion that their etiologies are extremely complex, involving myriad factors at many levels of organization from the molecular biological to the sociocultural (Carson & Sanislow, 1992). Few if any individual investigators are intellectually prepared to deal with more than limited portions of this matrix, suggesting a need for widespread, intensive collaboration among many different kinds of scientists in seeking solutions to what Gottesman and Shields (1982) have aptly termed the "epigenetic puzzle" of the schizophrenias. In fact such "teamwork" is extremely rare among researchers in this field. Most do not venture beyond their own scientific niche and may know or care little about what is going on in other niches. This sort of "tunnel vision" (Carson, in press-b) imparts to the whole enterprise a curious and insulated compartmentalization that discourages communication and integrative theory construction, and hence progress on the kind of broad front that appears needed. We may have reached the point where we can no longer afford the luxury of isolated research camps.

Finally, the delusional disorders are associated often enough with acts of violence that they confront us once again with difficult questions relating to jurisprudence, civil rights, and appropriate measures, if any, of containment and intervention. As in the case of suicide discussed in the previous chapter, the professional mental health community needs direction from the larger society on what level of homicidal (or other violent) risk is tolerable in light of the uncertainty in forcasting individual patients' behavior. It is *not,* in our judgment, realistic to anticipate that such uncertainty can be substantially eliminated at any time in the foreseeable future.

SUMMARY

The schizophrenic disorders especially, and the delusional (paranoid) disorders often associated with them, represent the major challenge facing the mental health professions—partly because virtually all of the psychopathological processes previously described come together in these classes of disorder.

One extraordinary case—that of the Genain quadruplets—sheds light on the sources and the complexity of schizophrenic disorders. All four of the Genain sisters became schizophrenic prior to the age of 25. After carefully tracking the progress of the Genains through the years, researchers have concluded that both biological and psychosocial factors contributed to their vulnerability to schizophrenia.

The schizophrenias are characterized by a loss in level of previous functioning, disturbances of communication, bizarre delusions and hallucinations, aberrations of perception and affect, and, in some instances, peculiarities of motor behavior. The last symptom is associated with the catatonic type of the disorder.

Other types of schizophrenia include undifferentiated (mixed symptoms not fitting into other categories or moving rapidly among them), disorganized (incoherent, silly, or inappropriate affect and behavior), and paranoid (persistent ideas or hallucinations regarding persecution or grandiosity, or other themes). Given these variations as well as other anomalies, some have questioned whether such a "thing" as schizophrenia exists. The credence of such questions is enhanced by the changing and somewhat arbitrary nature of the diagnostic criteria for schizophrenia.

Hardly anybody questions the existence of a cluster of behaviors, called schizophrenic, that are unintelligible to the average person. Such behaviors have been correlated with biological, psychosocial, and sociocultural variables. As yet, however, none of these broad sources of behavioral variation has been definitely established as *the* etiologic factor in schizophrenia. Several leads in each area are quite promising. The evidence suggests that the traditional pessimism with respect to understanding the sources of schizophrenic behavior and its therapeutic amelioration is to a large extent unjustified, although single approaches—as in the current emphasis on biology and drug treatment—seem to be hampering our efforts to move forward. In the area of treatment, the neglect of psychosocial approaches is inconsistent with their record of achievement.

The delusional (paranoid) disorders, in which schizophrenic disorganization seems not to be a significant factor, form a subgroup of psychoses that are even less well understood than the others. A paranoid individual harbors ideas of persecution, grandiosity, both, or more rarely of other patently false content. The person, however, is entirely functional—including, often, highly organized cognitive functioning—in areas that do not impinge on the delusional thought-structure (the paranoid construction) in which the person is centrally involved. These people can often function at a marginal level in society. Some of them, however, become dangerous, exposing problems at the interface between mental health professionals and society at large that continue unresolved. Treatment of chronically paranoid individuals is currently difficult, at best.

Key Terms

the schizophrenias (p. 428)
process schizophrenia (poor premorbid or chronic schizophrenia) (p. 432)
reactive schizophrenia (good premorbid or acute schizophrenia) (p. 433)
negative-symptom schizophrenia (p. 433)
positive-symptom schizophrenia (p. 433)
schizophrenia, undifferentiated type (p. 439)
schizophrenia, catatonic type (p. 441)
schizophrenia, disorganized type (p. 442)
schizophrenia, paranoid type (p. 443)

schizophrenia, residual type (p. 446)
schizoaffective disorder (p. 446)
schizophreniform disorder (p. 446)
dopamine hypothesis (p. 452)
schizophrenogenic (p. 457)
marital schism (p. 458)
marital skew (p. 458)
double-bind communication (p. 459)
expressed emotion (EE) (p. 462)
paranoia (p. 466)
delusional disorder (p. 466)
induced psychotic disorder (p. 466)

Chapter 13
Organic Mental Disorders

Franz Karl Bühler, *Untitled.* Bühler (1868–?), by trade a metalsmith, lost his job as a teacher in a trade school because of his erratic behavior. He was institutionalized in 1898 because of hallucinations and paranoia. He soon withdrew into an autistic existence that is reflected in his drawings and writings.

In contrast to most kinds of abnormal behavior, certain problems arise partly as a consequence of structural damage to the brain tissue. Such damage typically involves loss of nerve cells and can impair the brain's normal physiological functioning. As the brain is the organ of behavior, damage to it may disrupt effective thought, feeling, and action. The relationship of deficits associated with brain damage to abnormal behavior as we have defined it is complicated and often unclear. Accordingly, it seems wise at this point to digress slightly from the main task of clinical description to get a better understanding of brain damage and brain dysfunction. The next section provides this orientation.

BRAIN DAMAGE AND ABNORMAL BEHAVIOR

When structural defects in the brain occur before birth or at an early age, mental retardation may result, its severity depending to a large extent on the magnitude of the defect. In mental retardation, an individual fails to develop an optimal level of the various skills that underlie adequate and independent coping with environmental demands. Most mentally retarded people do not suffer from gross brain damage, but virtually all those individuals who can be described as *severely* retarded have some form of demonstrable organic pathology. The problem of mental retardation will be discussed in Chapter 14. Other people who sustain prenatal or perinatal (that is, during birth) brain damage may experience normal mental development in most aspects of behavior, but suffer from specific cognitive or motor deficits, such as dyslexia (Chapter 14) or spasticity (excessive muscle contraction that impairs motor performance).

Sometimes the intact brain sustains damage after it has completed all or most of its biological development. A wide variety of injuries, diseases, and toxic substances may result in the functional impairment or death of neurons (neural cells) or their connections, which may lead to obvious deficits in psychological functioning. In some instances such damage is associated with behavior that is not only impaired in various ways but also highly aberrant—even psychotic. People who sustain serious brain damage after they have mastered the basic tasks of life are in a very different situation from those who start life with a deficit of this kind. When brain injury occurs in an older child or adult, there is a *loss* in established functioning, and this loss—this deprivation of already-acquired and customary skills—can be painfully obvious to the victim, adding a psychological burden to the organic one. In other cases the impairment may extend to the capacity for realistic self-appraisal, leaving these patients relatively unaware of their losses and thus poorly motivated for rehabilitation. Many victims may also have to cope with the idea of little improvement, or worse, with a prognosis involving inexorable, progressive decline. The psychological impact in such cases can be devastating.

■ Brain Impairment and Adult Mental Disorder

In this chapter we will discuss those disorders that occur when the normal adolescent or adult brain has suffered significant organic impairment or damage. In the DSM system of classification these are called **organic mental disorders,** although neuroscientists usually refer to them as **neuropsychological disorders** or *neuropsychological conditions*. They may involve only limited behavioral deficits or a wide range of psychopathology, depending on (a) the nature, location, and extent of neural damage; (b) the premorbid (predisorder) personality of the individual; (c) the individual's total life situation; and (d) the amount of time passed since the first appearance of the condition. Although the degree of mental impairment is usually directly related to the extent of damage, in some cases involving relatively severe brain damage mental change is astonishingly slight; in other cases of apparently mild and limited damage there may be profoundly altered functioning.

As we shall see, some behavioral reactions to brain impairment, such as anxiety or depression, are clinically indistinguishable from disorders in which we have no reason to suspect organic brain involvement. This raises some rather subtle and complicated questions we will have to engage as we proceed. In general, however, we may suspect organic pathology as a contributing factor in a disorder when (a) the psychopathologic symptoms are especially severe, (b) they are accompanied by notable memory or other cognitive deficits, and (c) few other grounds exist for explaining the symptoms (Strayhorn, 1982). More specific suspect symptoms include prolonged catatonia or other movement disorders, anorexia, and a first psychotic episode or

notable personality change occurring after age 50 (Weinberger, 1984).

We reiterate here the important distinction, introduced in Chapter 3, between neurological disease or impairment and the aberrant mental and behavioral processes that constitute psychopathological symptoms. It is mere historical accident that some "mental" aspects of organic brain disease, such as personality change, became assigned to the medical specialty of psychiatry, whereas the "physical" ones, such as motor coordination disorders and certain cognitive disorders, often seen in association with physical deficits, became the purview of neurology. The fundamental disorders we are dealing with in this chapter are *always* in the strictest sense neurological ones, although they may have psychological elaborations associated with them.

Some "mental" symptoms in organic mental disorders are therefore the more or less direct product of the physical interruption of the established neural pathways along which the brain's messages travel. The bases of these symptoms are relatively well understood, and the symptoms themselves have relatively constant features among individuals sustaining comparable types of brain insult in terms of location and extent. For example, with mild to moderate *diffuse* (widespread) damage, such as might occur with moderate oxygen deprivation or the ingestion of toxic substances, attentional and self-monitoring impairments are quite common. An individual, for example, may complain of memory problems due to an inability to sustain focused retrieval efforts, while showing an intact ability to store new information. Severe diffuse damage results in *dementia,* described later.

In contrast to diffuse damage, *focal brain lesions* are circumscribed areas of abnormal change in brain structure, such as might occur with traumatic injury to a part of the head. With progressive brain disease, such as Alzheimer's disease or expanding brain tumors, one may see a gradual spreading over more and more focal sites, leading to permanent damage that is both diffuse and severe. Some consequences of organic brain disorders that have mainly focal origins but commonly appear in the context of progressively diffuse damage are as follows:

1. *Impairment of memory*—the individual has notable trouble remembering recent events and less trouble remembering events of the remote past, with a tendency in some patients to confabulate; that is, to "invent" memories to fill in gaps. In severe instances no new experience can be retained for more than a few minutes. It either fails entirely to be stored in long-term memory or is stored in a

way that provides no means for it to be readily retrieved at a later time.

2. *Impairment of orientation*—the individual is unable to locate himself or herself accurately, especially in time but also in space or in relation to the personal identities of self or others.

3. *Impairment of learning, comprehension, and judgment*—the individual displays ideation tending to be concrete and impoverished and is unable to think on higher conceptual levels or to plan with foresight.

4. *Impairment of emotional control or modulation*—the individual manifests emotional overreactivity and easy arousal to laughter, tears, rage, and other extreme emotions.

5. *Apathy or emotional blunting*—the individual shows little emotion, especially where deterioration is advanced.

6. *Impairment in the initiation of behavior*—the individual lacks "self-starting" capability and may have to be repeatedly reminded about what to do next, even where the behavior involved remains well within the person's range of competence.

7. *Impairment of controls over matters of propriety and ethical conduct*—the individual may manifest a marked lowering of personal standards in appearance, personal hygiene, sexuality, language, and so on.

8. *Impairment of receptive and expressive language*—the individual may be unable to comprehend written or spoken language, or may be unable to communicate thoughts orally or in writing.

Most individuals who have a neuropsychological disorder *do not* develop psychopathological symptoms, such as panic disorder or delusions, although many will show at least mild deficits in cognitive processing and self-regulation. The psychopathological symptoms that do sometimes accompany brain impairment are less predictable than those listed and more likely to show individual nuances consistent with the prior personality and the total psychological situation confronting a patient. We consider it important to maintain a sharp distinction between neurological and psychopathological types of "mental" symptoms.

This chapter is concerned with people who have both neurological disease and psychopathological disorder. Though the distinction between these differing types of disorders is reasonably clear in the abstract, it becomes murky in many cases as psychopathology and neuropathology can become inextricably enmeshed with one another. We emphasize that it is erroneous to assume that a behavioral disorder, for example, a serious depression accompanying deficits produced by neuropsychological insult, is necessarily and completely explained by reference to the patient's brain damage; it might better be explained in terms of the considerable psychological challenge presented by the patient's awareness of dramatically lessened competence.

The more variable effects of significant neurological impairment on individuals are explained by the fact that an individual is a functional unit and reacts as such to all stressors, whether they are organic or psychological. A well-integrated personality can usually withstand brain damage or any other stress better than a rigid, immature, or otherwise psychologically handicapped one—except where brain damage is so severe or its location so critical as to destroy the integrity of the personality. Similarly, an individual who has a favorable life situation is likely to have a better prognosis than one who does not. Because the brain is the center for the integration of behavior, however, there are limits to the amount of brain damage an individual can tolerate or compensate for without exhibiting behavior that is decidedly "abnormal."

◼ Hardware and Software

We generally believe it is somewhat hazardous to employ computer analogies in discussions of the brain and mental processes. However, such an analogy seems almost irresistibly appropriate in perhaps shedding additional light in the context of the present discussion of the relationship of brain impairment to behavioral abnormalities. Because the possibilities of such analogizing—for example, about differing kinds of "memory"—are both tantalizing and virtually limitless, we will strictly confine ourselves to only the most elementary and relevant points of contact.

When computers fail to behave adaptively in terms of what we want and expect them to do for us, our troubleshooting speculations normally begin with two possibilities: (a) a "hardware" problem—perhaps a "sticky" chip, a deficient power supply, or a defective resistor or capacitator; or (b) a "software" problem, such as having an inadequate program for the task at hand or a "bug" in the program we load into a machine that is in perfect working

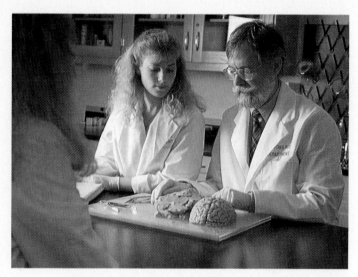

We may consider the intact human brain to be a highly programmable system of "hardware," and psychosocial experience to be functionally equivalent to "software." Organic mental disorders have hardware defects as their primary cause —there is a breakdown in one or several of the brain's components. The symptoms of such a breakdown show up in changes such as memory defects, impaired orientation, impaired learning, impaired language, impaired emotional control, and similar problems.

order. (The third alternative of a flawless machine and a flawless program that are incompatible has interesting possibilities as a model for certain abnormalities of behavior, but we will ignore this alternative here.) Note that the software programs we load into computers have an essentially symbolic, informational status that is prior to and independent of the physical characteristics of the machine itself, although the physical state of the machine is systematically transformed by the act of "loading" a program into it. The software information in a loaded machine *could,* in principle and with great difficulty, be completely and errorlessly reconstructed from a detailed description of the physical state of the machine. The two cannot for that reason be considered identical entities, however, nor is it reasonable to hold that the state of the machine is in any sense more "basic" than the information loaded into it, whose construction will usually in fact have preceded that of the machine.

We may thus consider the intact human brain to be a highly programmable system of "hardware," and psychosocial experience in both its developmental and current aspects to be functionally equivalent to "software." Such an analogy has widespread implications throughout the domain of abnormal psychology—as for example in posing a problem for exclusively biological interpretations of the "functional" (nonorganic) psychoses—but we

will focus on so-called organic mental disorders. Using our analogy, these disorders, by definition, have hardware defects as their primary cause. In other words, in such situations the brain cannot perform the physical operations called for in its "design" by virtue of a breakdown in one or another (or several) of its components. The *direct* "symptoms" of such a breakdown should be both limited in extent and, within reason, predictable from a knowledge of how these components "work." In fact they should be similar in general character to the symptoms, such as memory defects, listed in the preceding section.

A breakdown in the brain's hardware will necessarily have pervasive effects on the processing of software. Indeed, in the case of extensive hardware damage, much or perhaps most previously loaded information may be lost because the structural components in which it had been encoded are no longer operative; new information for the same reason fails to be adequately loaded. Such a condition is known clinically as *dementia.* With less extensive hardware damage we see effects that depend to a considerable extent on the particular characteristics of the software that constitutes the record of an individual's life experience, parts of which will be unique. We thus expect to see more variation in the "mental" symptoms manifested.

To use a somewhat trivial but obvious example, the delusion that one is Napoleon, rather common in the nineteenth century, would not have been seen in an eighteenth-century Alzheimer's or general paretic (syphilitic brain diseased) patient because the real Napoleon's more illustrious adventures had not yet occurred. Such symptoms are at most only *indirect* manifestations of organic hardware breakdown; their content is obviously a product of life experience, and they sometimes occur in the absence of any demonstrable hardware breakdown at all—in which case we must consider the possibility that they are due entirely to serious flaws in the individual's personality, or "software."

It is obvious that people vary a great deal in the adequacy, complexity, and resourcefulness of the software programs and "subroutines" their experiences have provided. Indeed, as we will see in Chapter 14, such variations are to a certain extent what IQ tests attempt to measure. It is equally obvious that few if any people have deployable programs ready to manage the contingency of *losing* basic competencies and skills that at an earlier time may well have become so automatized that their flawless performance required no deliberate attention or effort. Coping more or less adequately with such a disastrous turn of events thus seems to put a premium on the adaptive flexibility of a person's already extant software library. Failure to cope adequately, on the other hand, places an enormous additional load of stress and frustration on an already limited system, one that may be further compromised by newly acquired hardware defects. Such a "system," we suggest, is likely to develop indirect, secondary psychopathological symptoms, such as the delusional assumption of a new and more impressive personal identity.

Bearing in mind these fundamental and somewhat perplexing issues concerning relationships between the brain, mental events, and behavior, we move now to a consideration of the related clinical syndromes.

CLINICAL FEATURES OF ORGANIC MENTAL DISORDERS

The regenerative capacities of the central nervous system are limited. Cell bodies and neural pathways in the brain do not have the power of regeneration, which means that their destruction is permanent. Some functions lost as a result of brain damage may be relearned, however, typically at a compromised and less efficient level, or an individual may develop techniques to compensate for what is missing. The degree of improvement from disabilities following an irreversible brain lesion may be relatively complete or limited, and it may proceed rapidly or slowly. Because there are limits to both the plasticity and compensatory capacities of the brain, however, brain damage leads to more or less extensive permanent diminishment or loss of function over a wide range of physical and psychological abilities. In general, the greater the amount of tissue damage, the greater the impairment of function.

The damage's location may also play a significant role in determining a patient's ultimate neuropsychological status. The mammalian brain is highly specialized, each part—each cell in fact—making a unique contribution to the functional whole of an organism's activity (see *HIGHLIGHT 13.1*). Thus the two hemispheres, while interacting intimately at many levels, are involved in somewhat different types of mental processing. For example, functions that are dependent on serial processing of familiar information, such as language, take place mostly in the left hemisphere for nearly everyone. The right hemisphere is generally specialized for configurational or *gestalt* processing, which is best suited for grasping overall meanings in novel situations, reasoning on a nonverbal, intuitive level, and apprecia-

tion of spatial relations. Even within hemispheres, the various lobes and areas within lobes mediate somewhat specialized functions.

Although none of these relationships between brain location and behavior can be considered constant or universal, it is possible to make certain broad generalizations about the likely effects of damage to particular parts of the brain. Damage to the frontal areas, for example, is associated with either of two contrasting clinical pictures: (a) passivity, apathy, and an inability to give up a given stream of associations or initiate a new one (perseverative thought); or (b) impulsiveness, distractibility, and insufficient ethical restraint (Crockett, Clark, & Klonoff, 1981). Damage to specific areas of the right parietal lobe may produce distortions of body image, while certain aspects of language function can be impaired as a result of significant damage to the left parietal.

Damage to identified structures within the temporal lobes disrupts an early stage of memory storage, such that extensive bilateral temporal damage can produce a syndrome in which remote memory remains relatively intact but nothing new can be effectively stored for later retrieval. Damage to other structures within the temporal lobes is associated with disturbances of eating, sexuality, and the emotions, probably by way of disrupting the functioning of the adjacent limbic lobe. The latter is a deeper center that mediates these "primitive" functions in extensive interaction with frontal lobe structures. Occipital damage produces a variety of visual impairments and visual association deficits, the nature of the deficit depending on the particular site of the lesion; for example, a person may be unable to recognize familiar faces or to correctly visualize and understand symbolic stimuli (Filskov, Grimm, & Lewis, 1981). Unfortunately, many types of brain disease are general and diffuse in their destructive effects, thereby causing multiple and widespread interruptions of the brain's circuitry.

Traditionally, the organic mental disorders have been classified by disease entity or recognizable disorder, such as Huntington's chorea, general paresis, and so on. As we have seen, however, these are basically physical or neurological disorders that may have various kinds of associated psychopathology. In the DSM-III-R, physical disorders are coded on Axis III, and associated "mental" conditions on Axes I and II (psychiatric and personality disorders). Thus with the single (and as far as we can determine unaccountable) exception of the senile and presenile dementias such as Alzheimer's disease, the traditional organic mental disorders no longer appear as Axis I psychiatric categories. In-

Implications of Brain Damage

It is difficult to predict the effects of focal injuries to the brain. Because there is some localization of function (as indicated in this drawing of the right cerebral hemisphere), damage to a particular area may cause impairment of the behavioral functioning mediated by the site of the damage. For example, a significant lesion of the occipital lobe is likely to result in some impairment of vision or visual perception. However, the awesome complexity of the brain's organization ensures that virtually all behavior is in fact the product of neuronal activity in many parts of the brain, some in all probability quite distant from the site of primary mediation. A lesion in one of the frontal lobes, for example, might influence neuronal activity at a site in the subcortical limbic system, thus producing some type of emotional dysregulation for the person affected. The upshot is that brain-behavior relationships are never as simple as graphic brain localization charts (such as this one) make them appear to be.

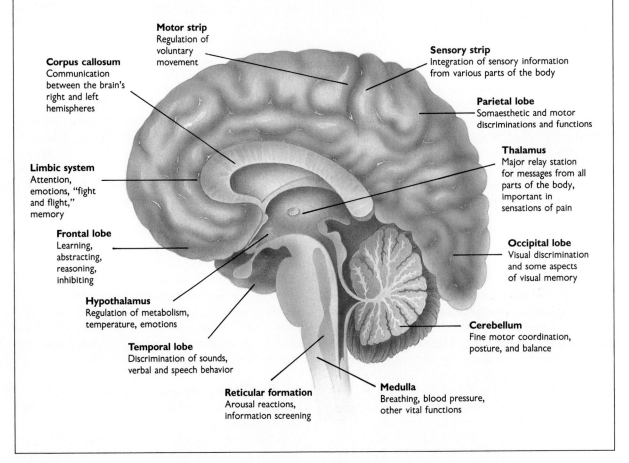

Motor strip
Regulation of voluntary movement

Corpus callosum
Communication between the brain's right and left hemispheres

Sensory strip
Integration of sensory information from various parts of the body

Parietal lobe
Somaesthetic and motor discriminations and functions

Limbic system
Attention, emotions, "fight and flight," memory

Thalamus
Major relay station for messages from all parts of the body, important in sensations of pain

Frontal lobe
Learning, abstracting, reasoning, inhibiting

Occipital lobe
Visual discrimination and some aspects of visual memory

Hypothalamus
Regulation of metabolism, temperature, emotions

Cerebellum
Fine motor coordination, posture, and balance

Temporal lobe
Discrimination of sounds, verbal and speech behavior

Reticular formation
Arousal reactions, information screening

Medulla
Breathing, blood pressure, other vital functions

stead, only particular clusters of symptoms presumptively based on brain damage and often seen in the various organic mental disorders are listed on Axis I. In our discussion, we will first describe these clusters of symptoms and then go on to describe the clinical picture, causal factors, and treatment approaches for four of the more common types of disorder associated with brain damage.

Organic Symptom Syndromes

A **syndrome** is a group of symptoms that tend to cluster together. The organic symptom syndromes include many symptoms similar to those that occur in the schizophrenias and the mood disorders, but in these syndromes the symptoms are *assumed* to reflect underlying brain pathology. The specific

Dramatic differences show up in these CAT scans of a normal brain (left) and the brain of a person afflicted with probable Alzheimer's dementia (right). The dark blue areas in both hemispheres of the diseased brain indicate an enlargement of the ventricles (the large, hollow spaces deep within the brain) due to the degeneration of the brain tissue.

brain pathology may vary; it may be due to some type of brain disease or as a result of the withdrawal of a chemical substance on which a person has become physiologically dependent. The most recently discovered etiological factor is infection with the HIV Type 1 (AIDS) virus, which, as we will see, leads in many cases to brain damage, sometimes of massive degree (Grant & Heaton, 1990). For our purposes, we will group these symptom syndromes into four categories: (a) delirium and dementia; (b) amnestic syndrome and hallucinosis; (c) organic delusional, mood, and anxiety syndromes; and (d) organic personality syndrome.

We should note that more than one syndrome may be present at a time in a given patient and that syndromes and patterns of syndromes may change over a particular disorder's course of development. As already noted, certain syndromes mimic at the behavioral level the types of disorders we have described in previous chapters. Although we suspect these often are basically the same types of (primarily psychogenic) disorders as those discussed earlier, clinicians need always to remain alert to the possibility of organic brain impairment having a *direct* causal role in the symptoms observed. Failure to do so could obviously result in serious diagnostic errors (Geschwind, 1975; Malamud, 1975; Weinberger, 1984).

Delirium and Dementia   The syndrome called **delirium** is characterized by a relatively rapid onset of widespread disorganization of the higher mental processes; it is caused by a generalized disturbance in brain metabolism. Information-processing capacities are more or less severely impaired, affecting such basic functions as attention, perception, memory, and thinking. Frequently, the syndrom includes abnormal psychomotor activity, such as wild thrashing about, and disturbance of the sleep cycle. Delirium reflects a breakdown in the functional integrity of the brain; in this respect, it may be seen as only one step above coma and, in fact, it may lead to coma. A delirious person is essentially unable to carry out purposeful mental activity of any kind; current experience appears to make no contact with the individual's previously acquired store of knowledge.

Delirious states tend to be acute conditions that rarely last more than a week, terminating in recovery or, less often, in death due to the underlying pathophysiologic state. They may result from several conditions, such as the following: head injury, toxic or metabolic disturbances, oxygen deprivation, insufficient delivery of blood to brain tissues, or precipitous withdrawal from alcohol or other drugs in an addicted person.

Dementia, already mentioned, has as its essential feature a progressive deterioration of brain functioning occurring after the completion of brain maturation (after, that is, about 15 years of age). Early in the course of the disease, an individual is alert and fairly well attuned to events in the environment. Episodic (memory for events), but not necessarily semantic (language and concept), mem-

Dementia in 417 Patients Fully Evaluated for Dementia

Diagnosis	Number	Percent
Alzheimer's disease or dementia of unknown cause	199	47.7
Alcoholic dementia	42	10.0
Multi-infarct dementia	39	9.4
Normal pressure hydrocephalus	25	6.0
Intracranial masses [tumors]	20	4.8
Huntington's chorea	12	2.9
Drug toxicity	10	2.4
Posttraumatic	7	1.7
Other identified dementing diseases[a]	28	6.7
Pseudodementias[b]	28	6.7
Dementia uncertain	7	1.7

[a]Including epilepsy, subarachnoid hemorrhage, encephalitis, amyotropic lateral sclerosis, Parkinson's disease, hyperthyroidism, syphilis, liver disease, and cerebral anoxia episode, all less than 1 percent incidence.
[b]Including depression (16), schizophrenia (5), mania (2), "hysteria" (1), and not demented (4).
Based on Wells (1979).

ory functioning is typically affected in the early stages, especially memory for recent events. Additionally, these patients display increasingly marked deficits in abstract thinking, the acquisition of new knowledge or skills, visuospatial comprehension, motor control, problem solving, and judgment. Personality deterioration and loss of "drive" accompany these other deficits.

Normally, dementia is also accompanied by an impairment in emotional control and in moral and ethical sensibilities. It may be progressive or static; occasionally it is even reversible. Its course depends to a large extent on the nature of the etiology.

Etiologic factors in dementia are many and varied. They include degenerative processes that affect some individuals—usually, but not always, older individuals. Repeated cerebrovascular accidents (strokes); certain infectious diseases, such as syphilis, meningitis, and HIV-1; intracranial tumors and abscesses; certain dietary deficiencies; severe or repeated head injury; anoxia; and the ingestion or inhalation of toxic substances have all been implicated in the etiology of dementias. As *HIGHLIGHT 13.2* makes clear, the most common cause of dementia is degenerative brain disease, particularly of the variety typified by Alzheimer's disease.

The Amnestic Syndrome and Hallucinosis

The essential feature of the **amnestic syndrome** is a striking deficit in the ability to recall ongoing events more than a few minutes after they have taken place. Immediate memory and, to a lesser extent, memory for events that occurred before the disorder's development remain largely intact, as does memory for words and concepts. An amnestic individual, then, is constrained to live for the most part only in the present or the remote past; the recent past is for most practical purposes unavailable. We should add here that the question of whether the recent past is unavailable in some absolute sense is subject to differing interpretations. Some evidence suggests that these individuals may recognize or even recollect events of the recent past if given sufficient cues, which would indicate that the information has been stored. Thus the difficulty may be in the *retrieval* mechanism (Hirst, 1982; Warrington & Weiskrantz, 1973).

In contrast to the dementia syndrome, overall cognitive functioning in the amnestic syndrome remains relatively intact. Theoretically, the disorder involves chiefly the relationship between the short-term and long-term memory systems; the contents of the former, always limited in scope and ephemeral in duration, are not stored in the latter in a way that permits ready accessibility or retrieval (Hirst, 1982).

In the most common forms of amnestic syndrome, those associated with alcohol or barbiturate addiction, the disorder may be irreversible. A wide range of other pathogenic factors may produce the amnestic syndrome. In these cases, depending on the nature and extent of damage to the affected neural structures and on the treatment undertaken, the syndrome may in time abate wholly, in part, or not at all.

The syndrome of **hallucinosis** has as its essential feature the persistent occurrence of hallucinations in the presence of known or suspected brain involvement; the term is not used where hallucinations are part of a more pervasive mental disorder such as schizophrenia. These false perceptions arise in a state of full wakefulness, when a person is alert and otherwise well oriented. The hallucinations most often involve the sense of hearing but may affect any sense; for example, visual hallucinations typically accompany psychedelic drug intoxication.

The course of the syndrome varies with the underlying pathology but rarely exceeds one month, assuming discontinuance of the causative agent. As in the case of the amnestic syndrome, the most common etiologic factor is severe or long-standing alcohol abuse.

Organic Delusional, Mood, and Anxiety Syndromes

In the **organic delusional syndrome,** false beliefs or belief systems arise in a setting of known or suspected brain damage and are considered a principal clinical manifestation of this damage. These delusions vary in content depending to some extent on the particular organic etiology. For example, a distinctly paranoid and suspicous delusional system is commonly seen with long-standing abuse of amphetamine drugs, whereas grandiose and expansive delusions are more characteristic of advanced syphilis (general paresis). In addition to infectious processes and the abuse of certain drugs, etiological factors in the organic delusional syndrome include head injury and intracranial tumors.

The **organic mood syndrome,** as the term implies, refers to manic or depressive states caused by the impairment of cerebral function. While the organic delusional syndrome may clinically mimic some forms of schizophrenic disorder, the organic mood syndrome closely resembles the symptoms seen in either depressive or manic mood disorders. Severe depressive syndromes, whether or not associated with organic pathology, may on superficial

This man has Parkinson's disease, which may be associated with organic mood syndrome, a cluster of symptoms that closely resembles those seen in either depressive or manic mood disorders.

examination appear as dementias, in which case the term *pseudodementia* is applied. The reaction may be minimal or severe, and the course of the disorder varies widely, depending on the nature of the organic pathology. Etiological factors include cerebrovascular accidents (strokes), Parkinson's disease, head injury, withdrawal of certain drugs, intracranial tumors or tumors of the hormone-secreting organs, and excessive use of steroids (adrenocortical hormones) or certain other medications. Of course, an awareness of lost function or a hopeless outlook might itself make a person depressed; in such instances the diagnosis of "organic" mood disorder may be at best a guess.

New to the DSM-III-R is the diagnosis **organic anxiety syndrome.** In this syndrome the clinical manifestation of anxiety is thought somehow to be the direct outcome of brain impairment. Although this disorder has to date received scant research attention, we suspect again that as a practical matter it often proves difficult to differentiate from the anxiety reaction a person would be expected to have on discovering impaired ability to perform in various ways.

Organic Personality Syndrome

The essential feature of the **organic personality syndrome** is a change in an individual's general personality style or traits following brain damage. Normally the change is in a socially negative direction; it may include impaired social judgment, lessened control of emotions and impulses, diminished concern about the consequences of one's behavior, and an inability to sustain goal-directed activity.

Many different etiologies are associated with the organic personality syndrome, and the course of the disorder depends on its etiology. Occasionally, as when it is induced by medication, it may be transitory. Often, however, it is the first sign of an impending deterioration, as when a kindly and gentle old man makes sexual advances toward a child or when a conservative executive suddenly begins to engage in unwise financial dealings. Some evidence indicates that a common feature in the organic personality syndrome may be damage to the frontal lobes (Blumer & Benson, 1975; Crockett, Clark, & Klonoff, 1981; Hecaen & Albert, 1975; Sherwin & Geschwind, 1978).

All of the organic symptom syndromes may appear singly or in combination in the various types of disorders associated with brain pathology. They are used as Axis I diagnoses where the assumed underlying organic brain impairment is either unknown or is coded as an additional diagnosis on Axis III (medical conditions)—already-noted exceptions being certain degenerative dementias included as separate Axis I disorders. In general, disorders involving the syndromes of delirium, dementia, amnesia, hallucinosis, or delusional thinking may be regarded as roughly equivalent to a psychotic level of functioning. Delirium is nearly always acute and short-lived, whereas disorders that have prominent elements of dementia, amnestic syndrome, or organic personality syndrome usually prove chronic—that is, they normally involve irreversible changes in the brain's anatomy.

The DSM-III-R classification lists about 50 different forms of mental disorder in which organic disturbance is present; many of these are related to drug use and involve only temporary physiological disruption (see Chapter 9). The disorders we will discuss in the rest of this section are longer-term disorders in which major, often permanent, brain pathology occurs but in which an individual's emotional, motivational, and behavioral reactions to the loss of function also play an important role. Indeed, as was earlier suggested, it is often impossible to distinguish between maladaptive behavior that is directly caused by neurological dysfunction and that which is basically part of an individual's psychological reaction to the deficits and disabilities experienced (Fabrega, 1981; Geschwind, 1975).

The four types of organic mental disorder we will discuss in greater detail are HIV-1 infection of the brain, disorders involving brain tumors, disorders involving traumatic head injury, and dementia of the Alzheimer type. Multi-infarct dementia will be addressed, chiefly as a contrast to Alzheimer's disease.

■ Organic Mental Disorder with HIV-1 Infection

Our discussion of mental disorders associated with the AIDS virus will necessarily be rather brief because the disorder is a newly recognized one. As we saw in Chapter 7, the devastating effects on the immune system produced by infection with the HIV Type 1 virus renders its victims "opportunistically" susceptible to a wide variety of other infectious agents. When organic brain syndromes were first observed among AIDS patients early in the last decade, it was assumed they were due to secondary infections of this sort or to the brain tumors also associated with immune system incompetence. Then, in 1983, Snider and colleagues published the first systematic evidence that the presence of the HIV-1 virus (or a mutant form of it) could itself result in the destruction of brain cells. Since then, two differing forms of such central nervous system pathology have been identified: aseptic meningitis (nonbacterial inflammation of the meninges), and the **AIDS dementia complex (ADC),** a more generalized degeneration of brain tissue. We will here focus on the AIDS dementia complex (ADC).

The neuropathology of ADC involves various changes in the brain, among them generalized atrophy, edema, inflammatory cells, and patches of demyelination (loss of the myelin sheath surrounding nerve fibers), as described by various investigators (Gabuzda & Hirsch, 1987; Gray, Gherardi, & Scaravilli, 1988; Price et al. 1988a). No brain area may be spared, but the damage appears concentrated in the central white matter, the matter surrounding the ventricles, and the gray matter at *subcortical* levels.

Clinical features, which tend to appear as a late phase of HIV infection (although often before the full development of AIDS itself), usually begin with psychomotor slowing, diminished concentration, mild memory difficulties, and perhaps slight motor clumsiness. Progression is typically rapid after this point, with clear-cut dementia appearing in many cases within one year, although considerably longer periods have been reported. The later phases of ADC can be quite grim and include behavioral regression, confusion, psychotic thinking, apathy, and marked withdrawal, leading before death to an incontinent, bedridden state (Navia, Jordan, & Price, 1986; Price et al., 1988a, 1988b).

As many as 80 percent of patients with full-blown AIDS have neuropathological findings at autopsy (Petito, 1988). Thirty-eight percent of 121 living AIDS patients studied by Navia et al. (1986) met DSM criteria for dementia. Patients with

AIDS-related complex (ARC), a pre-AIDS manifestation of HIV infection involving minor infections, various nonspecific symptoms (such as unexplained fever), and blood cell count abnormalities, may also experience cognitive difficulty, although it may be too subtle to be readily detected on clinical observation alone. In one study (Grant et al., 1987), 54 percent of ARC patients demonstrated definite impairment on a neuropsychological test battery. Other studies, reviewed by Grant and Heaton (1990), have shown inconsistent evidence of neuropsychological compromise in pre-ARC people who are merely seropositive for HIV-1. The evidence is thus compelling that infection with this virus poses a substantial threat to the functional integrity of the brain, quite apart from its other frightening characteristics. As of this writing, it is not known what protects the minority of AIDS patients who show no central nervous system involvement during the entire course of their illnesses.

The question of treatment for ADC is of course intimately tied to that involving control or eradication of the HIV-1 infection itself. To date, it is impossible to feel confident about our prospects because of the enormous and unprecedented challenges presented by the complex structure and life cycle of this viral entity (McCutchan, 1990). Thus preventing the infection is the only certain defensive strategy, a circumstance not unlike the problem posed by syphilis, another sexually transmitted and potentially dementing disease, in an earlier era. See *HIGHLIGHT 13.3* for a case description of brain involvement in the latter disorder. In general, humankind has not done well in controlling the spread of sexually transmitted diseases through cautious sexual behavior.

■ Disorders Involving Brain Tumors

In the writings of Felix Plater (1536–1614), we find the following rather remarkable account of "A Case of Stupor due to a Tumour in the Brain, Circular like a Gland":

Caspar Bone Curtius, a noble knight, began to show signs of mental alienation which continued through a period of two years until at last he became quite stupefied, did not act rationally, did not take food unless forced to do so, nor did he go to bed unless compelled, at a table he just lay on his arms and went to sleep, he did not speak when questioned even when admonished,

and if he did it was useless. Pituita dropped from his nose copiously and frequently: this condition continued for about six months, and finally he died. . . . At the postmortem when the skull was opened and the lobes of the brain separated, a remarkable globular tumor was found on the upper surface of the Corpus Callosum, resembling a gland fleshly, hard and funguslike, about the size of a medium sized apple, invested with its own membranes and having its own veins, lying free and without any connection with the brain itself. . . . This tumour, by its mass, produced pressure on the brain and its vessels, which caused stupor, torpor, and finally death. Some doctors who had seen this case earlier attributed it to sorcery, others just to the humors, but by opening the skull we made clear the abstruse and hidden cause. (1664)

A tumor is a *neoplasm,* or new growth, involving an abnormal proliferation of cells. Such growths are most apt to occur in the breast, the uterus, the prostate, the lungs, or the intestinal tract, although they are sometimes found in the central nervous system. In adults, brain tumors occur with the greatest frequency between the ages of 40 and 60.

Some brain tumors are malignant; they invade and destroy the brain tissue in which they arise. Others are benign; they are not destructive except by reason of the pressure they exert. Because the skull is a bony, unyielding container, a relatively small tumor in the brain may cause marked pressure and thus interfere seriously with normal brain functioning. Unlike their benign counterparts, malignant brain tumors usually originate in malignancies in other organs, typically the lungs; the cancer cells are transported to the brain by a process known as *metastasis.*

The Clinical Picture in Disorders Involving Brain Tumors   The clinical picture that develops in cases of brain tumor is extremely varied and its determined largely by (a) the location, size, and rapidity of a tumor's growth; and (b) the personality and stress tolerance of an affected individual. Brain tumors may lead to any or all of the recognized organic symptom syndromes discussed earlier.

A brain tumor itself may result in both localized and general symptoms. Damage to a particular part of the brain may result in localized disturbances of sensory or motor functions. General symptoms appear when the tumor becomes large enough to

Case Portrayal of General Paresis

General paresis is one of several forms of central nervous system invasion by the organism responsible for syphilitic infection, the spirochete *Treponema pallidum*. The mode of transmission is virtually always sexual. As we saw in Chapter 2, general paresis occupies an important place in the history of the mental health disciplines. Despite the availability of medical resources for total cure in its early stages, syphilis is still a significant medical problem. Unless properly treated, it eventually disables and then kills its victims.

The general paretic form of advanced syphilis is usually a late-stage development of the untreated infection, often making its appearance 10 to 15 years after primary infection and sometimes as many as 40 years later. For unknown reasons it develops in only 5 to 10 percent of those infected, and the large majority of these victims are men. The spirochete, which is present in the brains of affected people, somehow causes widespread and progressive destruction of cerebral tissue, eventuating in the familiar sequence of increasingly severe physical debility and dementia, vegetative delirium, coma, and death. The typical course duration after the initial appearance of symptoms is two to three years.

Although in many preterminal cases the mental symptoms are limited to the always-present dementia, other types of features—such as depression—may be displayed. A dramatic and frequent pattern in general paresis is expansive euphoria, in which a person manifests claims of great power, wealth, physical and sexual prowess, and so on, and also displays the emotional reactions of delight and pride consistent with these claims. The following case shows a fairly typical expansive pattern.

C. W. flew planes from the United States to North Africa. His route began in Florida, passed through Natal, Ascension Island, and terminated in Dakar. His earlier health record was excellent, save for some "difficulty" in his early twenties. Now, at 38, he was strong, well liked, and an expert pilot in the ferry command. He had completed a dozen or more trips.

As he flew his plane eastward on his last journey, C. W. was unusually happy, "It's a great world," he sang. "My rich aunt in Oklahoma is going to leave me $30,000,000."

During the periods of relief by his copilot, he talked loudly and became chummy with other members of the crew. As a matter of fact, he offered to loan the navigator $50,000. Landing safely in Dakar, his high spirits continued. Then his friends found him buying several "diamonds" from an Arab street merchant, spending most of his cash for this purpose.

"Boy," he exclaimed, "I got a swell bargain! Six diamonds for $100 cash now and $100 more on my next trip! I sure fooled that Arab; he's never going to collect the rest from me."

"How do you know the diamonds are genuine?" he was asked.

"I tested them," he boasted, "I struck one with a hammer and it proved hard; diamonds are hard."

Upon the return journey, C. W. continued the story of his expected wealth and the sum grew with the distance of travel.

"It's $40,000,000 I am getting and I expect to share some of it with you guys," he announced. When his copilot received this astounding information with doubt and anxiety, C. W. could not understand it. When the copilot asked him to rest, he assured him that his body was perfect, that he didn't need rest. Then he added that he could fly the plane without gas, which he tried to prove by doing some fancy maneuvers in the sky.

"Funny," he said later, "no one seemed to believe me. Even when I offered them a million each they weren't happy, but looked at each other in such a puzzled way. It made me laugh, how they begged me to rest and how worried they looked when I refused. I was the boss and I showed them."

When the plane landed in Brazil by a miracle, C. W. was examined by a physician, forced into another plane and brought to Florida. Upon examination he was talkative, eyes gleaming, exuberant with statements of wealth and power. "I am now one of the richest men in the world," he said. "I'll give you $5,000,000 to start a hospital. My eyes are jewels, diamonds, emeralds." (Fetterman, 1949, pp. 267–268) result in greatly increased intracranial pressure. Common early symptoms are persistent headaches, vomiting, memory impairment, listlessness, depression, convulsive seizures, and "choked disk"—a retinal anomaly characterized by swelling of the optic nerve caused when cerebrospinal fluid is forced into it by intracranial pressure.

As a tumor progresses and the intracranial pressure increases, there may be clouding of consciousness, disorientation for time and place, carelessness in personal habits, irritability, sensorimotor losses, hallucinations, apathy, and a general or specific impairment of intellectual functions. Terminal stages are usually similar to other types of severe brain damage; the patient is reduced to a vegetative stupor and eventually dies.

Some idea of the relative frequency of symptoms in brain tumor cases may be gleaned from an early study by Levin (1949), who analyzed 22 cases admitted to the Boston Psychopathic Hospital. These patients ranged in age from 22 to 65 years, the majority falling between the ages of 40 and 60 years. The study included 11 males and 11 females. Prior to hospitalization the range of symptoms shown by these patients included the following:

Memory impairment or confusion	13 cases
Depression	9 cases
Seizures	8 cases
Headaches	8 cases
Complaints of visual impairment	6 cases
Drowsiness	6 cases
Irritability	6 cases
Indifference	5 cases
Restlessness	4 cases
Generalized weakness	4 cases
Loss of sense of responsibility	3 cases
Paranoid ideas	2 cases
Tendency to be combative	2 cases
Euphoria	2 cases
Aphasia (communication disorder)	2 cases

The interval between the onset of the symptoms and hospitalization varied from 1 week to 6 years, with an average interval of 17 months. In most cases, symptoms were evident 6 months or more prior to admission to the hospital. In this connection, however, it has been pointed out that minor personality changes and depression often serve to mask the more definitive symptoms of a brain

Early detection of brain tumors is critical, and a number of new methods for detection have been developed in recent years. In this computer-generated image based on the CAT scan of a man who collapsed while gambling in Las Vegas, a tumor (vividly red) is visible. In this three-dimensional view, looking through the forehead, the skull's surface is shown as white and the brain's as yellow. Fortunately, surgeons were able to remove the tumor and the man recovered.

tumor—with the result that accurate diagnosis and appropriate treatment are often delayed (Schwab, 1970).

Patients' emotional reactions to the organic damage and to the resulting cognitive and other types of impairment vary. Initially, they may be overly irritable and mildly depressed. As their disorder progresses, however, those having some insight into the seriousness of their condition may become severely depressed, anxious, and apprehensive. Patients who have less insight into their condition may be relatively unaware of their failing functions. Those with lesions pressing on certain parts of the brain may actually become expansive and euphoric. These latter patients seem unconcerned about their illness and may joke and laugh, sometimes in a most unrestrained and hilarious manner. The intensity of these reactions seems the result of organic damage to the inhibitory control system; they may be most evident in advanced stages when considerable brain damage or intracranial pressure exists.

Tumors directly producing psychological complications usually involve the frontal, temporal, or parietal lobes. Frontal-lobe tumors often produce subtle peculiarities, such as an inability to concentrate, personal carelessness, loss of inhibitions, and absent-mindedness that later becomes a memory defect. An individual may become silly and prone to punning and general jocularity. In an analysis of 90 patients with frontal-lobe tumors, Dobrokhotova (1968) found three common forms of emotional disorder: (a) the absence of spontaneity; (b) disinhibition and lability of affect—often with euphoria; and (c) forced emotions, which were abruptly expressed and terminated.

Although personality change is so common in brain tumor cases that it is often attributed directly to the activity of a tumor, it must be understood that such symptoms are neither inevitable nor necessarily the result of the tumor alone. As we have noted, adjustive reactions are typically a function of both the stress situation (including biological, psychosocial, and sociocultural stressors) and the personal maturity, stability, and level of stress tolerance of the individual. As brain deterioration advances, however, personality contributions to the patient's general behavior diminish and finally disappear.

Treatments and Outcomes   Treatment of brain tumors is primarily a medical matter and thus is outside the scope of our present discussion. We should note, however, that the degree of improvement achieved in such cases depends both on the size and location of the growth and on the amount of brain tissue that must unavoidably be damaged in excising or neutralizing the tumor. In some cases, full function seems to return, while in others, a residue of symptoms remains, such as partial paralysis and a reduction in cognitive abilities. Where tumors are well-advanced and require extensive surgery, the mortality rate is high. German (1959) found that about 40 percent of all brain tumors were potentially curable, about 20 percent were capable of being arrested for periods of 5 years or more, and the remainder were fatal within a short period of time. Since then, newer methods of detecting and determining the precise location of brain tumors, together with more advanced treatment procedures, have resulted in a marked improvement in outcomes (Peterson, 1978).

■ Disorders Involving Head Injury

Since ancient times, traumatic brain injuries have provided a rich source of material for speculation about mental functions. Hippocrates pointed out that injuries to the head could cause sensory and motor disorders, and Galen included head injuries among the major causes of mental disorders.

Head injuries occur frequently, particularly as a result of falls, blows, and accidents. It has been estimated that well over a million people in the United States suffer head injuries each year in automobile and industrial accidents; a sizable number of cases are the result of bullets or other objects actually penetrating the cranium. Significant brain damage is sustained in some 300,000 of these instances (Chance, 1986). Relatively few people with head injuries find their way into mental hospitals because many head injuries do not involve appreciable damage to the brain, and even where they do psychopathological complications are often not observed.

The Clinical Picture in Disorders with Head Injuries   Head injuries usually give rise to immediate acute reactions, the severity of which depends on the degree and type of injury. These acute reactions may then clear up entirely or develop into chronic disorders.

Perhaps the most famous historical case is the celebrated American crowbar case reported by Dr. J. M. Harlow in 1868. Because it is of both historical and descriptive significance, it merits our including a few details:

The accident occurred in Cavendish, Vt., on the line of the Rutland and Burlington Railroad, at that time being built, on the 13th of September, 1848, and was occasioned by the premature explosions of a blast, when this iron, known to blasters as a tamping iron, and which I now show you, was shot through the face and head.

The subject of it was Phineas P. Gage, a perfectly healthy, strong and active young man, twenty-five years of age . . . Gage was foreman of a gang of men employed in excavating rock, for the road way. . . .

The missile entered by its pointed end, the left side of the face, immediately anterior to the angle of the lower jaw, and passing obliquely upwards, and obliquely backwards, emerged in the median line, at the back part of the frontal bone, near the coronal suture. . . . The iron which thus traversed the head, is round and rendered comparatively smooth by use, and is three feet seven inches in length, one and one fourth inches in its largest diameter, and weighs thirteen and one fourth pounds. . . .

The patient was thrown upon his back by the explosion, and gave a few convulsive motions of the extremities, but spoke in a few minutes. His men (with whom he was a great favorite) took him in their arms and carried him to the road, only a few rods distant, and put him into an ox cart, in which he rode, supported in a sitting posture, fully three quarters of a mile to his hotel. He got out of the cart himself, with a little assistance from his men, and an hour afterwards (with what I could aid him by taking hold of his left arm) walked up a long flight of stairs, and got upon the bed in the room where he was dressed. He seemed perfectly conscious, but was becoming exhausted from the hemorrhage, which by this time, was quite profuse, the blood pouring from the lacerated sinus in the top of his head, and also finding its way into the stomach, which ejected it as often as every fifteen or twenty minutes. He bore his sufferings with firmness, and directed my attention to the hole in his cheek, saying, "the iron entered there and passed through my head." (1868, pp. 330–332)

A cast of the head and the actual skull of Phineas Gage. Note the places in the skull pierced by the iron rod.

Some time later Dr. Harlow made the following report:

His physical health is good, and I am inclined to say that he has recovered. Has no pain in head, but says it has a queer feeling which he is not able to describe. Applied for his situation as foreman, but is undecided whether to work or travel. His contractors, who regarded him as the most efficient and capable foreman in their employ previous to his injury considered the change in his mind so marked that they could not give him his place again. The equilibrium or balance, so to speak, between his intellectual faculties and animal propensities, seems to have been destroyed. He is fitful, irreverent, indulging at times in the grossest profanity (which was not previously his custom), manifesting but little deference for his fellows, impatient of restraint or advice when it conflicts with his desires, at times pertinaciously obstinate, yet capricious and vacillating, devising many plans of future operations, which are no sooner arranged than they are abandoned in turn for others . . . his mind is radically changed, so decidedly that his friends and acquaintances said he was "no longer Gage." (1868, pp. 339–340)

It is evident from the above account that Gage acquired an organic personality syndrome from his encounter with the errant crowbar. This relatively dramatic syndrome, however, is not a particularly common sequel to head injury.

Fortunately, the brain is an extraordinarily well-protected organ; but even so, a hard blow on the head may result in a skull fracture in which portions of bone press on or are driven into the brain tissue. Even without a fracture, the force of the blow may result in small, pinpoint hemorrhages throughout the brain or in the rupturing of larger blood vessels in the brain.

A person rendered unconscious by a head injury usually passes through stages of stupor and confusion on the way to recovering clear consciousness. This recovery of consciousness may be complete in the course of minutes, or it may take hours or days. In rare cases an individual may live for extended periods of time without regaining consciousness. In such cases the prognosis for substantial improvement is poor. In some instances, significant cognitive or personality alterations following injury are observed even where a person experiences no loss of consciousness.

Specific symptoms, of course, depend largely on the nature of an injury. Normally, if a head injury is sufficiently severe to result in unconsciousness, the person experiences *retrograde amnesia,* or inability to recall events immediately preceding the injury. Apparently, such trauma interferes with the brain's capacity to consolidate into long-term storage the events that were being mentally processed at the time of the trauma.

Following a severe cerebral injury, a person's pulse, temperature, blood pressure, and important aspects of brain metabolism are all affected, and survival may be uncertain. The duration of the coma is generally related to the severity of the injury. If the patient survives, coma may be followed by delirium, in which acute excitement is manifested, with disorientation, hallucinations, and generally agitated, restless, and confused activity. Often the patient talks incessantly in a disconnected fashion, with no insight into the disturbed condition. Gradually the confusion clears up and the individual regains contact with reality. Again, the severity and duration of residual symptoms depends primarily on the nature and extent of the cerebral damage, the premorbid personality of the patient, and the life situation to which he or she will return. Even where an injury seems relatively mild with good return of function, recent research using highly refined and comprehensive neuropsychological assessments often demonstrates various types of subtle residual impairment.

Some degree of bleeding, or *intracerebral hemorrhage,* can occur with head injuries. In severe injuries, there may be gross bleeding or hemorrhaging at the site of the damage. Enough blood may accumulate within the rigid confines of the skull that disruptive pressure is exerted on neighboring regions of the brain; a common form of this problem is the *subdural hematoma,* which, if not relieved by aspiration of the excess blood, may endanger vital brain functions or produce permanent neuronal damage. When the hemorrhaging involves small spots of bleeding—often microscopic sleeves of red cells encircling tiny blood vessels—the condition is referred to as *petechial hemorrhages.* Some evidence shows tiny, scattered petechial hemorrhages in most brain injuries, but in fatal cases they are usually multiple or generalized throughout the brain. Brain swelling, or *cerebral edema,* occurs in many cases of severe damage, increasing the risk of significant mental impairment or death unless promptly treated.

Professional boxers are likely to suffer such petechial hemorrhaging from repeated blows to the head; they may develop a form of encephalopathy (characterized by an area or areas of permanently damaged brain tissue) from the accumulated damage of such injuries. Consequently, some former boxers suffer from impaired memory, slurred speech, inability to concentrate, involuntary movements, and other symptoms—a condition popularly referred to as being punch-drunk. Johnson (1969) found abnormal electroencephalograms in 10 of 17 retired boxers; Earl (1966) noted that two former welterweight champions suffered so much brain damage in their professional fights that they were confined in mental institutions before they reached the age of 30.

With one-time head injuries, resulting syndromes are usually limited to delirium and perhaps some features of the dementia, amnestic, and hallucinosis syndromes—all on a temporary basis. Where a trauma results in the permanent loss of neural tissue, however, all these syndromes may occur in their full-blown and irreversible forms; in addition to a variety of physical impairments and disabilities, the person may also experience personality disturbance, including delusional syndromes and serious depressive mood disorder.

Treatments and Outcomes   Treatment for brain damage due to head injury is primarily a medical matter. Prompt treatment may prevent further injury or damage—for example, when pooled blood under pressure must be removed from the skull. In severe cases, immediate medical treatment may have to be supplemented by a long-range program of reeducation and rehabilitation.

Although many head trauma patients show few residual effects from their injury, particularly if they have experienced only a brief loss of consciousness, other patients sustain definite and long-lasting impairment. Common aftereffects of moderate brain injury are chronic headaches, anxiety, irritability, dizziness, easy fatigability, and impaired memory and concentration. Where the brain damage is extensive, a patient's general intellectual level may be markedly reduced, especially if he or she has suffered severe temporal- or parietal-lobe lesions. In addition, various specific neurological and psychological defects may follow localized brain damage, as we have seen. Some 2 to 4 percent of head-injury cases develop posttraumatic epilepsy, usually within two years of the head injury but sometimes much later.

In a minority of brain-injury cases, personality changes occur, such as those described in the historic case of Phineas Gage. Other kinds of personality changes include passivity, loss of drive and spontaneity, agitation, anxiety, depression, and paranoid suspiciousness. Like cognitive changes, the kinds of personality changes that emerge in severely damaged people will depend, in large measure, on the site and extent of their injury.

The great majority of people suffering from mild concussions improve to a near normal status

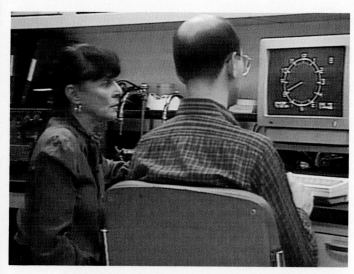

This man has suffered head trauma and his therapist is using a computer as a part of his treatment. Although many head-trauma patients show few residual effects from their injury, other patients sustain definite and long-lasting impairment.

within a short time. With moderate brain injuries, it takes longer for patients to reach their maximum level of improvement, and many suffer from headaches and other symptoms for prolonged periods. A few develop chronic, incapacitating symptoms.

In severe brain-injury cases, the prognosis is less favorable (Jennett et al., 1976). Many of these patients have to adjust to lower levels of occupational and social functioning, while others are so impaired intellectually that they require continuing supervision and, sometimes, institutionalization. Even in cases where considerable amounts of brain tissue have been destroyed, however, a minority of these patients are able to become socially independent. In many cases there is improvement with time, due largely to reeducation and to intact brain areas taking over new functions.

In general, the following factors indicate a favorable prognosis in cases of head injury: (a) a short period of unconsciousness or posttraumatic amnesia; (b) no focal brain lesion; (c) a well-integrated preinjury personality; (d) motivation to recover or make the most of residual capacities; (e) a favorable life situation to which to return; and (f) an appropriate program of retraining (Brooks, 1974; Diller & Gordon, 1981). The last factor, crucial for the future functioning of some individuals, is unfortunately far from generally available (Chance, 1986). Even where such treatment centers are conveniently located, they may be too expensive for many families to take advantage of them.

Other factors may also have a direct bearing on the outcomes of brain injuries. As we mentioned

earlier, the results of brain damage in infancy differ from those in adolescence and adulthood, although in both instances the results may range from death to any number of neurological disorders, including epilepsy and mental retardation. Moreover, the outlook for individuals who are also victims of alcoholism, drug dependence, or other organic conditions may be unfavorable. Alcoholics, in particular, are prone to head injuries and other accidents and do not have good improvement records. Severe emotional conflicts sometimes appear to predispose an individual to accidents and also may delay recovery. Although malingering is thought to be rare in brain-injury cases, the hope of receiving monetary compensation—for example, from an insurance settlement—may influence individuals to exaggerate and maintain symptoms.

■ Dementia of the Alzheimer Type

It is a commonplace observation that the organs of the body deteriorate with aging, a process, biologists tell us, that begins virtually at birth. The cause or causes of this deterioration, however, remain largely obscure; science has not yet solved the riddle of aging. Of course, the brain—truly the master organ—is not spared in the generalized aging process. As time goes on, it too wears out, or degenerates. Mental disorders that sometimes accompany this brain degeneration and occur in old age are traditionally called **senile dementias.** Unfortunately, a number of rare conditions result in degenerative changes in brain tissue earlier in life. Disorders associated with such earlier degeneration of the brain are known as **presenile dementias.**

Not only is the age of onset different in the presenile dementias, but they are also distinguished from the senile dementias by their different behavioral manifestations and tissue alterations (see *HIGHLIGHT 13.4*). One important exception is **Alzheimer's disease,** which is a typical and common senile disorder but which can, in certain individuals, occur well before old age. Alzheimer's disease is a characteristic dementia syndrome having an insidious onset and a usually slow but progressively deteriorating course terminating in death. The formal psychiatric diagnosis, *primary degenerative dementia of the Alzheimer type (DAT),* is normally given when all other potential causes of dementia are ruled out by case history, physical examination, and laboratory tests. The parallel medical diagnosis, *Alzheimer's disease,* is coded on Axis III (medical conditions) of the DSM-III-R, although as of this writing it is in fact usually not possible to establish definitely the presence of the distinctive Alzheimer

HIGHLIGHT 13.4

Presenile Dementias

In addition to early-occurring Alzheimer's disease, two other forms of presenile dementia occur with sufficient frequency to deserve mention: Pick's disease and Huntington's chorea.

Pick's Disease

Even rarer than early-onset Alzheimer's disease, Pick's disease (first described by Arnold Pick of Prague in 1892) is a degenerative disorder of the brain, usually having its onset in people between the ages of 45 and 50. Its cause is unknown. Women are apparently more subject to Pick's disease than men, at a ratio of about three to two. Onset is slow and insidious, involving difficulty in thinking, slight memory defects, easy fatigability, and, often, character changes with a lowering of many social inhibitions. At first there is a circumscribed atrophy of the frontal and temporal lobes; as the atrophy becomes more severe, the mental deterioration becomes progressively greater and includes apathy and disorientation as well as the impairment of judgment and other intellectual functions. The disease usually runs a fatal course within two to seven years.

Huntington's Chorea

Huntington's chorea is a genetically determined (autosomal dominant) degenerative disorder of the central nervous system. It was first described by the American neurologist George Huntington in 1872. With an incidence rate of about 5 cases per 100,000 people, the disease usually occurs in individuals between 30 and 50 years of age. Behavior deterioration often becomes apparent several years before there are any detectable neurological manifestations (Lyle & Gottesman, 1977). The disease itself is characterized by a chronic, progressive chorea (involuntary and irregular twitching, jerking movements) with mental deterioration leading to dementia and death within 10 to 20 years. Although Huntington's chorea cannot be cured or even arrested at the present time, it can be prevented, at least in theory, by genetic counseling, because its occurrence is a function of known genetic laws.

---

neuropathology (described later) in living patients. Brain imaging techniques, such as that of magnetic resonance imaging (MRI), may provide supportive evidence in showing enlarged ventricles or widening in the folds (sulci) of the cerebral cortex, indicative of brain atrophy. Nevertheless, the use of antemortem criteria for the diagnosis of dementia of the Alzheimer type (DAT) is somewhat imprecise (Carlsson, 1986) and may result in an overdiagnosis of the disorder as high as 30 percent (Hartford, 1986). DAT takes its name from Alois Alzheimer, a German neuropsychiatrist, who first described it in 1860.

When we try to envisage a "typical" Alzheimer patient—and most of us have had contact with such people—we imagine a person of advanced age. This picture is in fact true only in the statistical sense. Unfortunately, for some, DAT is a presenile dementia that begins in their 40s or 50s; in such cases the progress of the disease and its associated dementia is typically rapid. For example, in one study of early-onset DAT (Heyman et al., 1987) the five-year cumulative mortality rate was 2.5 times the expected rate, with the *younger* of these patients contributing disproportionately to the excess in deaths.

Considerable evidence suggests a substantial genetic contribution in early-onset DAT (Davies, 1986). These cases, occurring at the height of careers and in periods of maximum productivity and family responsibilities, portray the tragedy of Alzheimer's disease in an especially stark light.

In fact no way exists to portray the ravages of this disorder in other than an alarming fashion, even if we restrict attention to the more typical instance of onset after age 65. Survival to at least that point is becoming increasingly routine, and after the first decade of the twenty-first century, the first members of the enormous post–World War II baby boom generation will enter the age range of maximum risk. If we have not solved the problem of curing or preventing DAT by that time or shortly thereafter, the social and economic consequences will clearly be devastating (Fisher & Carstensen, 1990).

Nor is there any real assurance, despite our rapidly advancing knowledge about the disorder, that a solution will be found. Just as people do not die of old age per se but rather of failing organs, there is no cure or preventive measure for the aging of living organisms. Some investigators, for example, Selkoe (1986), suggest that Alzheimer's "disease" is merely the product of the aging process as manifested in a particular organ, the brain. Early onset is early brain aging, probably for the most part genetically determined. Prevention or cure, according to this view, would therefore approximate in its unlikelihood the discovery of the Fountain of Youth. Somewhat reassuringly, other researchers, Comfort (1984) and Glenner (1986), for example, reject this notion and hold that DAT is a specific disease process, hence in principle both preventable and curable. The final answer to this fascinating and important debate is nowhere in sight.

Whether or not we face an apocalyptic future in respect to overwhelming numbers of demented elderly people, the magnitude of the problem of DAT—often seriously underestimated—is even now straining societal and family resources, both economic and emotional. As shown in the table of *HIGHLIGHT 13.2*, the disorder accounts for nearly 50 percent of all cases of dementia of whatever cause. The ratio is doubtless considerably higher for people in older age ranges. It is estimated that one of every six people in the United States over age 65 is clinically demented, and one of every ten people in this age range suffers from DAT (Evans et al., 1989). By age 85 the prevalence rate of DAT is nearly 50 percent (Fisher & Carstensen, 1990). This figure translates to over one million victims in this country alone, and the number is increasing rapidly with the advancing average age of the population (Light & Lebowitz, 1989). Some 30 to 40 percent of nursing home residents are DAT patients (Kolata, 1981a). Some of these patients reside in mental hospitals or other types of institutional settings. The majority live in the community, typically with family members (Gurland & Cross, 1982), a circumstance that is often extremely stressful for caregivers (Brane, 1986; Fisher & Carstensen, 1990; Jenkins, Parham, & Jenkins, 1985; Mobily & Hoeft, 1985).

The Clinical Picture in Dementia of the Alzheimer Type   As already noted, the onset of Alzheimer's disease in older people is usually gradual, involving slow mental deterioration. In some cases a physical ailment or some other stressful event is a dividing point, but usually an individual passes into a demented state almost imperceptibly, so that it is impossible to date the onset of the disorder precisely. The clinical picture may vary markedly from one person to another, depending on the nature and extent of brain degeneration, the premorbid personality of the individual, the particular stressors that have been or are in operation, and the degree of environmental support.

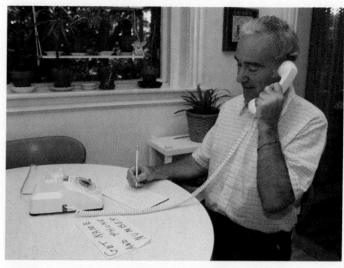

Written reminders can help Alzheimer's victims lead relatively normal lives. In the early stages, they can remember how to do things once they are reminded to do them. Later on, they may lose the ability to do even simple tasks.

Symptoms often begin with an individual's gradual withdrawal from active engagement with life. There is a narrowing of social and other interests, a lessening of mental alertness and adaptability, and a lowering of tolerance to new ideas and changes in routine. Often thoughts and activities become self-centered and childlike, including a preoccupation with the bodily functions of eating, digestion, and excretion. As these changes—typical in a lesser degree of many older people—become more severe, additional symptoms, such as impaired memory for recent events, "empty" speech (in which grammar and syntax remain intact but vague expressions replace meaningful nouns and verbs), messiness, impaired judgment, agitation, and periods of confusion, make their appearance. Specific symptoms may vary considerably from patient to patient and from day to day for the same patient; thus the clinical picture is by no means uniform until the terminal stages, when the patient is reduced to a vegetative level. There is also, of course, individual variation in the rapidity of the disorder's progression. In rare instances the symptoms may reverse and partial function may return, but in true DAT this reversal will prove temporary.

The end stages of Alzheimer's disease involve a depressingly similar pattern of reduction to a vegetative existence and ultimate death from some disease that overwhelms a person's limited defensive resources. Prior to this point, there is, as noted, some distinctiveness in patient behavior. Allowing for inevitable overlapping and individual changes in pattern as DAT develops, a given victim is likely to show one of the several dominant behavioral manifestations described in the following paragraphs.

Approximately half of all DAT patients display a course of *simple deterioration*. That is, they gradually lose various mental capacities, typically beginning with memory for recent events and progressing to disorientation, poor judgment, neglect of personal hygiene, and loss of contact with reality to an extent precluding independent functioning as adults. Distinctly psychopathological symptoms (such as delusions), if they occur at all, are likely to be transitory and inconsistent over time. The following case—involving an engineer who had retired some seven years prior to his hospitalization—is typical of simple deterioration resulting from DAT:

During the past five years, he had shown a progressive loss of interest in his surroundings and during the last year had become increasingly "childish." His wife and eldest son had brought him to the hospital because they felt they could no longer care for him in their home, particularly because of the grandchildren. They stated that he had become careless in his eating and other personal habits and was restless and prone to wandering about at night. He could not seem to remember anything that had happened during the day but was garrulous concerning events of his childhood and middle years.

After admission to the hospital, the patient seemed to deteriorate rapidly. He could rarely remember what had happened a few minutes before, although his memory for remote events of his childhood remained good. When he was visited by his wife and children, he mistook them for old friends, nor could he recall anything about the visit a few minutes after they had departed. The following brief conversation with the patient, which took place after he had been in the hospital for nine months and about three months before his death, shows his disorientation for time and person:

Doctor: *How are you today, Mr._____?*
Patient: *Oh . . . hello (looks at doctor in rather puzzled way as if trying to make out who he is).*
Doctor: *Do you know where you are now?*
Patient: *Why yes . . . I am at home. I must paint the house this summer. It has needed painting for a long time but it seems like I just keep putting it off.*
Doctor: *Can you tell me the day today?*
Patient: *Isn't today Sunday . . . why, yes, the children are coming over for dinner today.*

We always have dinner for the whole family on Sunday. My wife was here just a minute ago but I guess she has gone back into the kitchen.

In a less frequent but not uncommon manifestation of Alzheimer's disease, a person develops a decidedly *paranoid orientation* to the environment, becoming markedly suspicious and often convinced that others are engaged in various injurious plots and schemes. Uncooperativeness and verbal abuse are common accompaniments (Brink, 1983), making the task of caregiving significantly more stressful. In the early phases of this reaction pattern, the cognitive deficits characteristic of Alzheimer's disease (memory loss, disorientation) may not be prominent, perhaps enabling the individual to be quite observant and even logical in building the "case" for others' nefarious activities. Though themes of malevolent victimization predominate in this form of the disorder, also common is the so-called jealousy delusion in which the person persistently accuses his or her partner or spouse—who is often of advanced age and physically debilitated—of being sexually unfaithful. Family members may be the perpetrators of various foul deeds, such as poisoning the patient's food or plotting to steal the patient's funds. Fortunately, punitive retribution in the form of physical attacks on the "evildoers" are rare, but a combative pattern does occasionally occur, enormously complicating the patient's management. The following case is fairly typical of the paranoid reaction type:

A woman of 74 had been referred to a hospital after the death of her husband because she had become uncooperative and was convinced that her relatives were trying to steal the insurance money her husband had left her. In the hospital, she complained that the other patients had joined together against her and were trying to steal her belongings. She frequently refused to eat, on the grounds that the food tasted funny and had probably been poisoned. She grew increasingly irritable and disoriented for time and person. She avidly scanned magazines in the ward reading room but could not remember anything she had looked at. The following conversation reveals some of her symptoms:

Doctor: *Do you find that magazine interesting?*
Patient: *Why do you care? Can't you see I'm busy?*

> **Doctor:** *Would you mind telling me something about what you are reading?*
>
> **Patient:** *It's none of your business . . . I am reading about my relatives. They want me to die so that they can steal my money.*
>
> **Doctor:** *Do you have any evidence of this?*
>
> **Patient:** *Yes, plenty. They poison my food and they have turned the other women against me. They are all out to get my money. They even stole my sweater.*
>
> **Doctor:** *Can you tell me what you had for breakfast?*
>
> **Patient:** *. . . (Pause) I didn't eat breakfast . . . it was poisoned and I refused to eat it. They are all against me.*

Paranoid orientations tend to develop in individuals who have been sensitive and suspicious. Existing personality tendencies are apparently intensified by degenerative brain changes and the stress accompanying advancing age.

Other patterns seen in Alzheimer patients are comparatively infrequent. Some patients are confused but amiable, usually showing marked memory impairment and a tendency to engage in seemingly pointless activities, such as hoarding useless objects or repetitively performing household tasks in a ritualized manner. Other patients become severely agitated, with or without an accompanying "hand-wringing" depression. Depressed Alzheimer patients tend to develop extremely morbid preoccupations and delusions, such as hypochondriacal ideas about having various horrible diseases, often seen as just deserts for past sins. Suicide is a possibility in such cases should a patient be physically capable of carrying out the act.

In some cases, especially those with early onset, the disease progress is unusually rapid and a patient moves quickly into a state of incoherence verging on delirium. This mental clouding is frequently accompanied by marked agitation and unpredictable combativeness, severely trying the resources of caregivers. As we have seen, all Alzheimer patients who survive long enough eventually enter a stage of continuous delirium.

With appropriate treatment, which may include medication and the maintenance of a calm, reassuring, and unprovocative social milieu, many people with Alzheimer's disease show some symptom alleviation. In general, however, deterioration continues its downward course over a period of months or years. Eventually, patients become oblivious of their surroundings, bedridden, and reduced to vegetative existences. Resistance to disease is lowered, and

death usually results from pneumonia or some other infection.

Causal Factors in Dementia of the Alzheimer Type   The fundamental, invariant neuropathology of the Alzheimer brain has been known for some time. It has three elements: (a) the widespread appearance of "senile plaques," small areas of dark-colored matter that are in part the debris of damaged nerve terminals; (b) the tangling of the normally regular patterning of neurofibrils (strand-like protein filaments) within neuronal cell bodies; and (c) the abnormal appearance of small holes in neuronal tissue, called granulovacuoles, which derive from cell degeneration. Observation of these changes requires microscopic examination of brain tissue specimens, which is why unequivocal confirmation of the diagnosis can usually be accomplished only after a patient has died.

When sufficiently numerous, these microscopic alterations of the brain's substance lead to generalized brain atrophy, which, as already noted, may be visualized by imaging techniques. Unfortunately from the diagnostic standpoint, such atrophy may occur with other conditions as well. A more promising observation concerns the neurotransmitter acetylcholine, which is known to be important in the mediation of memory. While there is widespread destruction of neurons in DAT, evidence suggests that the most severely and perhaps earliest affected are a cluster of cell bodies located in the basal forebrain and involved in the release of acetylcholine (Coyle, Price, & DeLong, 1983; Whitehouse, et al., 1982). This observation and related ones (e.g., Wester et al., 1988) have given rise to the *acetylcholine (ACh) depletion theory* of DAT etiology. Although the evidence is still not conclusive (Perry, 1988), the theory does integrate an impressive array of research data, including the production of a temporary DAT-like syndrome in normal subjects given ACh-blocking drugs (Kopelman, 1986).

If we make the reasonable assumption that ACh depletion plays at least *some* role in the production of DAT symptoms, there is still the question of what place it occupies in the presumed causal chain. What, for example, causes the degeneration of ACh-releasing cells? No shortage of hypotheses purport to answer such questions, but many have proven to have serious flaws, and none has so far gained a dominating level of acceptance. For example, some investigators (e.g., Crapper McLachlan, 1986) have been impressed with the abnormal amounts of aluminum, known to have neurotoxic effects, found in the brains of some DAT patients. Others, however, have argued cogently that these abnormal accumulations of aluminum are

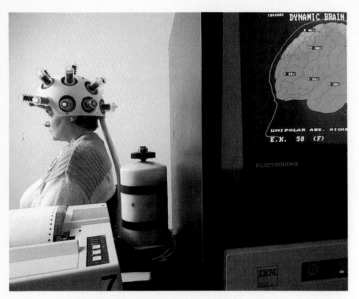

An electrode headset picks up signals from the brain of a 58-year-old woman, and a computer turns them into the brain map on the screen. Brain-mapping can detect the depletion of acetylcholine, which is thought to play a role in the production of Alzheimer's symptoms.

an effect, not a cause, of DAT brain degeneration (e.g., Alfrey, 1986; Wisniewski, Moretz, & Iqbal, 1986).

Some investigators have taken the more direct approach of trying to discover the sources of the primary DAT lesions such as neurofibrillary tangles and senile plaques. The search has yielded a considerable amount of information concerning, in particular, the composition of the latter. As stated earlier, these plaques contain cell debris, but their cores consist of a waxy amyloid protein substance, designated A4, that also occurs in abnormal abundance in other parts of DAT patients' brains (see, for example, Gajdusek, 1986; Hardy et al., 1986; Kang et al., 1987). This finding appears to be extremely important in leading to an understanding of DAT pathogenesis, and it also suggests an approach to the development of a much-needed diagnostic test of high sensitivity and selectivity for DAT that could be used with living patients. Though there have been no dramatic breakthroughs in these areas yet, the evidence suggests that their emergence is imminent.

We have already mentioned that early-onset DAT, in common with numerous other instances of early-onset disease, seems to have a significant genetic component in its etiology. In one particularly interesting study involving early onset, Nee (reported in Sargent, 1982b) traced the disease back eight generations in one family that immigrated to this continent in 1837. Of 531 family members, 53 were identified as suffering from the disease, even

though those who lived to 65 without symptoms were considered free of it. Collateral findings of this NIMH project showed that the mean interval between the onset of symptoms and death was 6 years (although in one case it was 24) and that the age at onset ranged between 44 and 64 years.

In fact, widespread evidence, none of it conclusive (Bird, 1986; Henderson, 1986; Reisberg, 1984), shows that a general vulnerability to the development of DAT may be inherited (Breitner, 1986; Davies, 1986). Much of this evidence points to a genetic connection with Down syndrome (see Chapter 14), which is due to a trisomy involving chromosome 21. Most Down syndrome individuals who survive beyond age 35 develop a DAT-like dementia (Bauer & Shea, 1986), with comparable neuropathological changes (Schapiro & Rapoport, 1987). Anomalies of chromosome 21 have also been implicated in DAT (e.g., Van Broeckhoven et al., 1987). Barnes (1987) reported evidence that the *same regions* of chromosome 21 are involved in both Down syndrome and DAT, and that one of the genes in this region produces the A4 amyloid protein that figures so prominently in the neuropathology of DAT. Finally, Hardy et al. (as reported by Marx, 1991) have recently identified a gene mutation on chromosome 21 in a DAT-prone family, one that could be implicated in the release of A4. The case for a connection between DAT and Down syndrome is thus quite strong. Beyond that, we may be on the verge of precisely identifying the genetic basis of one form of early-onset DAT.

One must still be cautious, however, about the general contribution of genetic variables to the pathogenesis of DAT, especially of the late-onset variety. While there is some evidence of genetic influence even for onsets as late as ages 80 to 90 (Mohs et al., 1987; Sturt, 1986), nongenetic variables are clearly involved in the etiology of DAT (Henderson, 1986). Indeed, both Nee et al. (1987) and Renvoize et al. (1986) described monozygotic twins discordant for DAT, a circumstance that can only be explained by some sort of critical environmental variation. A pedigree involving substantial incidence of apparent DAT does not therefore justify undue concern about risk. Unfortunately, we have essentially no reliable information about environmental risk factors; most hypotheses advanced in this area involve environmental toxins, including a (to us) somewhat fanciful theory suggesting entry through the nose (Roberts, 1986).

In considering the activity level and rate of progress in understanding DAT that we have briefly outlined, you may find reason to be impressed. We think it appropriate to echo that sentiment. Although there are still many loose ends to be tied together, and some that may remain resistant to our best efforts, the progress of the last decade in coming to grips with DAT has been nothing less than astonishing. These investigations are truly science of the highest order effectively directed at a human problem of enormous and increasing scope.

Treatments and Outcomes   There is to date no known treatment for DAT—medical, psychosocial, retraining-based, or rehabilitative, including attempts at replenishing brain ACh—that produces a sustained reversal or interruption of the deteriorating course. Until some means of accomplishing such an effect appears, we will have to content ourselves with palliative measures that diminish patient *and* caregiver distress and relieve as far as possible those complications of the disorder, such as combativeness, that increase the difficulties of management.

Concerning the latter objectives, Fisher and Carstensen (1990) recently reviewed the considerable literature on behavioral approaches used to control several of the more common problematic behaviors that are associated with DAT (and with other dementing disorders as well), such as wandering off, incontinence, inappropriate sexual behavior, and inadequate self-care skills. Because behavioral approaches need not be dependent on complex cognitive and communicational abilities, which are apt to be lacking in these patients, they may be particularly appropriate for therapeutic intervention with this group. In general, reports of results are at least moderately encouraging in terms of reducing unnecessary frustration and embarrassment for the patient and hassle for the caregiver.

Medication may be of some help for patients who experience difficulty in modulating their emotions and impulses. Some depressed DAT patients respond reasonably well to antidepressant or stimulant medication. Where medications are used, however, dosages must be carefully monitored because unanticipated effects are common and because the frequently debilitated state of these patients makes them susceptible to an exaggerated response.

Any comprehensive approach to therapeutic intervention must consider the extremely difficult situation of caregivers. They are, as a group, at extraordinarily high risk for depression (Cohen & Eisdorfer, 1988). They tend to consume high quantities of psychotropic medication themselves and to report numerous stress symptoms (George, 1984). Because the basic problem usually seems in fact to be one of high and sustained stress, we would anticipate that any measures found successful in the reduction and management of stress and the enhancement of coping resources could be effectively

used to ease caregivers' burdens. The available research literature on this problem confirms our assumption (Costa, Whitfield, & Stewart, 1989). Group support programs, for example, may produce measurable reductions in experienced stress and depression (e.g., Glosser & Wexler, 1985; Kahan et al., 1985).

Whether or not, or at what point, to institutionalize a DAT patient whose requirements for care threaten to engulf his or her spouse or other family members can be a vexing and emotional decision. It can also be one with significant financial implications because, on average, nursing home care is about twice as costly as home care (Hu, Huang, & Cartwright, 1986). As we have seen, most DAT patients are cared for at home, mostly for emotional reasons, such as continuing love, loyalty, and a sense of obligation for remembered good times with the now-stricken parent or partner. In one sense at least, the home care decision is a justifiable one; the move to an institution, particularly one lacking in social stimulation and support, may result in an abrupt worsening of symptoms and sometimes a markedly enhanced rate of deterioration—demonstrating once again the power of psychosocial influences even in this instance of widespread brain destruction. On the other hand, the emergence of marked confusion, gross and argumentative demeanor, stuporous depression, inappropriate sexual behavior, and disorientation for time, place, and person, not to mention possible combative violence, can put an intolerable strain on

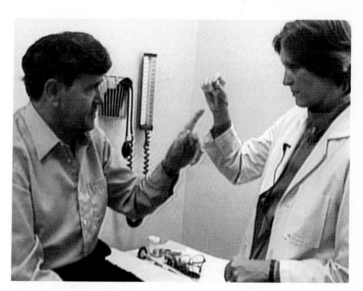

This Alzheimer's patient is being asked to identify keys held by a therapist. There is no known treatment for DAT that can reverse or interrupt the deteriorating course, although certain interventions have proven moderately helpful in controlling problematic behaviors and emotions.

caregivers to the point of psychological collapse. Because in all likelihood such conditions will *not* improve over time but in fact will worsen, wisdom dictates an early rather than a late removal to an institution, which in any event is where most DAT patients will have to spend their final weeks or months.

▪ A Note on Multi-Infarct Dementia

Multi-infarct dementia (MID), frequently confused with DAT because of its somewhat similar clinical picture and its increasing incidence and prevalence rates with advancing age, is actually an entirely different disease in terms of its underlying neuropathology. In this disorder, a series of cerebral infarcts—interruptions of the blood supply to parts of the brain because of arterial disease, commonly known as *strokes*—cumulatively destroy neurons over expanding brain regions. The affected regions become soft and may degenerate over time, leaving only cavities. The progressive loss of cells leads to brain atrophy and behavioral impairments that ultimately mimic those of DAT. The decline, however, is less smooth in course because of (a) the discrete character of infarct events and the processes they initiate, and (b) variations over time in the volume of blood delivered by a seriously clogged artery, producing variations in the functional adequacy of cells that have not yet succumbed to oxygen deprivation. Multi-infarct dementia is far less common than DAT, accounting for only some 10 percent of dementia cases. MID has a much shorter average course because of a patient's vulnerability to sudden death from a large infarct or one that affects vital centers. Occasionally, an unfortunate patient will be discovered to have *both* DAT and MID.

The medical treatment of MID, while hazardous and complicated, offers slightly more hope at this time than that of DAT. Unlike DAT, the basic problem of cerebral arteriosclerosis can be medically managed to some extent, perhaps decreasing the likelihood of further strokes.

The psychological and behavioral aspects of the dementia caused by DAT and MID are similar in many respects, and any management measure found useful in one is likely to be applicable in the other. Likewise, the maintenance of any gains achieved cannot be taken for granted because of the generally progressive nature of the underlying brain pathology. The daunting problems facing caregivers are also very much the same in the two conditions, indicating the appropriateness of support groups, stress reduction techniques, and the like.

UNRESOLVED ISSUES
on Organic Mental Disorders

There remains a great deal of unnecessary confusion concerning the definition and conceptualization of "organic mental disorders." Indeed, the term itself, taken as sincerely intended to be representative of actual clinical entities (as opposed to a mere nominal label for conditions that include both aberrant psychological phenomena and demonstrable brain impairment), poses certain baffling semantic and philosophical questions. One of the authors uses it as a ploy to enliven flagging conversations among colleagues by asking, "What does it *really* mean?"; or if that doesn't work by assertively declaring it to be an oxymoron, which almost always gets *something* going. More seriously, our efforts to differentiate between neurological "mental" symptoms and psychopathological ones, and our introduction of the computer hardware/software analogy early in the chapter, were inspired by an awareness of how difficult it must be for thoughtful students to find their way in the morass of imprecision and unstated assumption that confronts us in regard to this class of disorder. We hope we have not added to your confusion in engaging these issues, nor do we believe our efforts have entirely resolved them— not even for ourselves.

Regarding the dementias associated with aging, notably DAT and MID, our society is in something of a race with time, the stakes being sobering in magnitude. As we have learned how to prevent premature death, including that of infants, the proportion of our citizens living to advanced age has increased and continues to increase to unprecedented levels. This demographic trend carries with it a probably inescapable increase in the proportion of individuals at risk for spending some part of their lives in a demented condition. Indeed, a huge segment of the population is already reeling from the catastrophic monetary and emotional costs of providing adequate care for aging family members who, otherwise reasonably healthy, have lost the mental wherewithal to maintain themselves independently. In the absence of dramatic advances in the prevention of these disorders, no relief is in sight. On the contrary, as was noted, the age group that will put maximum strain on "the system," the baby boomers who were born in the years following World War II, are already among us, moving inexorably toward their generation's maximum-risk period. The impact will be both huge and sustained, the last of this bulging cohort *entering* the risk period (at age 65) in approximately the year 2030.

Clearly then, we must learn how to prevent or effectively arrest these degenerative brain diseases—especially DAT, in terms of numbers affected and life expectancy after onset—within the next two decades or we will face staggering problems of resource development and allocation. Fortunately, as we have seen, a considerable research effort with a record of solid accomplishment is already underway in recognition of the growing problem of dementia. Unfortunately, the ultimate success of the effort is by no means guaranteed within any predictable time frame. Given this uncertainty, we would feel a lot more comfortable about the problem if we detected signs of minimal preparation and contingency planning among government officials, particularly at the federal level. We do not.

SUMMARY

The organic mental disorders are those in which mental symptoms of a neurologic or psychopathologic sort (such as cognitive deterioration and delusions, respectively) are presumed to appear as a result of interference with the functioning of the brain's "hardware," typically involving the destruction of brain tissue. Many of the organic disorders are in some primary sense physical diseases and are accordingly coded on Axis III of DSM-III-R. Exceptions are the senile and presenile dementias (such as Alzheimer's disease); these disorders are accorded Axis I status. The current DSM recognizes certain *organic brain syndromes* that form a basis for an Axis I psychiatric diagnosis where the precise organic etiology is unknown or is implied in an accompanying Axis III disease; they are delirium, dementia, amnestic syndrome, hallucinosis, organic delusional syndrome, organic mood syndrome, organic anxiety syndrome, and organic personality syndrome. These syndromes are conceived as the primary behavioral indicators for organic brain disease. Some of them mimic disorders in which no gross brain pathology can be demonstrated, which may present problems in diagnosis.

Organic mental disorders may be acute and transitory; in this case, brain functioning is only temporarily compromised. Chronic organic mental disorders, on which we have focused, involve the permanent loss of neural cells. Psychosocial interventions are often helpful in minimizing psychopathologic reactions in the chronically disordered, although these people will remain neurologically disabled.

The primary causes of brain tissue destruction are many and varied; common ones include certain infectious diseases (such as the HIV virus), brain tumors, physical trauma, degenerative processes (as in Alzheimer's disease), and cerebrovascular arteriosclerosis, often manifested as multi-infarct dementia. The correlation between neurologic brain impairment and psychiatric disorder, however, is not an especially strong one: some people who have severe damage develop no severe mental symptoms, while others with slight damage have extreme reactions. Although such inconsistencies are not completely understood, it appears that an individual's premorbid personality and life situation are also important in determining his or her reactions to brain damage.

Elderly people are at particular risk for the development of chronic organic mental disorders, especially those related to brain degeneration caused by Alzheimer's disease. As at younger ages, the reaction to brain damage is determined by many nonbiological factors. With disproportionate increases in the numbers of elderly people in the population, and the upcoming wave of baby boomers who will become at risk beginning early in the twenty-first century, we face staggering social, emotional, and economic problems unless some way can be found to prevent or effectively treat Alzheimer's disease.

Key Terms

organic mental disorders (p. 478)

neuropsychological disorders (p. 478)

syndrome (p. 482)

delirium (p. 483)

dementia (p. 483)

amnestic syndrome (p. 484)

hallucinosis (p. 485)

organic delusional syndrome (p. 485)

organic mood syndrome (p. 485)

organic anxiety syndrome (p. 485)

organic personality syndrome (p. 485)

AIDS dementia complex (ADC) (p. 486)

AIDS-related complex (ARC) (p. 487)

senile dementias (p. 493)

presenile dementias (p. 493)

Alzheimer's disease (p. 493)

multi-infarct dementia (MID) (p. 500)

Chapter 14
Mental Retardation and Developmental Disorders

Simone Marye, *Personnage, Chien, et Oiseaux.*
Marye (1890–1961) had a successful, if rather
conventional, career as a sculptress in the 1920s. Her
popularity did not last long, however, and she was dogged by
poverty, poor health, and loneliness throughout her last 30
years. She was institutionalized at age 67 with the diagnosis
of Alzheimer's disease. Marye drew this strangely propor-
tioned, childlike design while hospitalized; by this time, she
was almost totally out of touch with reality, retaining little
but a professed devotion to Buddhism.

We begin here a two-chapter sequence on behavior disorders that usually make their first appearance in infancy, childhood, or adolescence. The present chapter focuses on developmental disorders, those childhood disorders that—like adult personality disorders—are currently coded on Axis II of the DSM-III-R. The following chapter (15) will discuss other common disorders of the early years that are considered Axis I disorders.

Various aspects of the distinction just noted have been and remain somewhat controversial, as we will see, and in fact the distinction itself is definitionally somewhat awkward and unclear. A **developmental disorder** can be defined as a problem that is somehow rooted in deviations in the developmental process itself, thus disrupting the acquisition of skills and adaptive behavior and often interfering with the transition to well-functioning adulthood. In general, neurological defects or dysfunctions are tacitly assumed to underlie these developmental anomalies (Kessler, 1988). However, with rare exceptions, such as organically based mental retardation, this assumption is also an issue of sometimes intense controversy.

In fact the entire matter of the classification of disorders appearing in childhood is controversial (Carson, 1990a). We will discuss this issue further in Chapter 15, by which point you will have gained a better appreciation of the problems needing attention. For now, we will concentrate on describing some particular types of early appearing disorders that are considered "developmental" and therefore Axis II in nature. These include mental retardation, the "pervasive developmental disorder" known as early infantile autism, and certain "specific developmental disorders" that involve persistent but circumscribed skill deficits, especially of an academic sort. We begin with mental retardation.

MENTAL RETARDATION

The American Association on Mental Deficiency (AAMD) has defined **mental retardation** as "significantly subaverage general intellectual functioning existing concurrently with deficits in adaptive behavior, and manifested during the developmental period" (AAMD, 1973, p. 11). Mental retardation is thus defined in terms of *level of behavioral performance*. The definition says nothing about causal factors—which may be primarily biological, psychosocial, sociocultural, or a combination of these.

The American Psychiatric Association has adopted the same definitional approach for its latest classification, DSM-III-R, listing mental retardation as an Axis II developmental disorder beginning before the age of 18. By definition, any functional equivalent of mental retardation that has its onset after age 17 must be considered a dementia rather than mental retardation. The distinction is an important one, because, as was pointed out in the previous chapter, the psychological situation of an individual who acquires a pronounced impairment of intellectual functioning after attaining maturity is vastly different from that of an individual whose intellectual resources were subnormal throughout all or most of his or her development. Some of the more important differences will become apparent in what follows.

Mental retardation is considered to be a specific disorder, but it may occur in combination with other disorders. In fact other psychiatric disorders, especially psychoses (Jacobson, 1990), occur at a markedly higher rate among retarded individuals than in the general population.

Mental retardation occurs among children throughout the world. In its most severe forms, it is a source of great hardship to parents as well as an economic and social burden on a community. The incidence of mental retardation in the United States is estimated to be about seven million people (see *HIGHLIGHT 14.1*). This figure is based on a cutoff point of about IQ 70, which is the cutoff point used by the AAMD. Most states have laws providing that individuals with IQs below 70 who show socially incompetent or disapproved behavior can be classified as mentally retarded and committed to an institution.

The incidence of mental retardation seems to increase markedly at ages 5 to 6, to peak at age 15, and to drop off sharply after that. For the most part, these changes in incidence reflect changes in life demands. During early childhood, individuals with only a mild degree of intellectual impairment, who constitute the vast majority of the mentally retarded, often appear to be relatively normal. Their subaverage intellectual functioning becomes apparent only when difficulties with schoolwork lead to a diagnostic evaluation. When adequate facilities are available for their education, children in this group can usually master essential school skills and achieve a satisfactory level of socially adaptive behavior (see *HIGHLIGHT 14.2*). Following the school years, they usually make a more or less acceptable adjustment in the community and thus lose the identity of being mentally retarded.

◼ Levels of Mental Retardation

It is important to remind ourselves once again that any classification system in the behavioral field will have strong features of both arbitrariness and pragmatism. In mental retardation, attempts to define varying levels of impairment have tended to rely increasingly on measurement—largely by means of standardized intelligence (IQ) tests (Robinson & Robinson, 1976). In the previously quoted AAMD definition, for example, the phrase "significantly subnormal general intellectual functioning" translates directly and officially into an IQ test score that is more than two standard deviations below the population mean. That mean, which represents the average test performance for children of a given age, is 100. The standard deviation of most IQ tests is about 15 points, and approximately two-thirds of the population score between plus and minus one standard deviation unit from the mean, that is, between 85 and 115. Thus a score of two standard deviations below the mean would be an IQ of approximately 70. About 2.5 percent of the population score in this range.

It is not improper to define mental retardation in this way, provided we keep in mind the implications of the definition. The original IQ tests were devised for the explicit purpose of predicting academic achievement among schoolchildren. Other IQ tests developed later were also validated largely on school performance and on the basis of how well they could predict scores on the original tests. Generally, then, what IQ tests measure is an individual's likely level of success in dealing with conventional academic materials, and in fact they do this very well when properly utilized. Thus when we speak of varying *levels* of mental retardation, we are to a great extent speaking of levels of ability to succeed at schoolwork.

Of course, this reliance on IQ scores is tempered somewhat by the other main part of the definition—the presence of concurrent "deficits in adaptive behavior." That is, the diagnosis of mental retardation is reserved for individuals who achieve low IQ test scores *and* demonstrate adaptational deficiencies, particularly in the areas of personal independence and social responsibility. The same dual criteria are involved in the officially recognized "levels" of retardation, although the IQ score often tends in practice to be the dominant consideration. This emphasis on the IQ score is reasonable at the lower end of the scale, because an individual with an

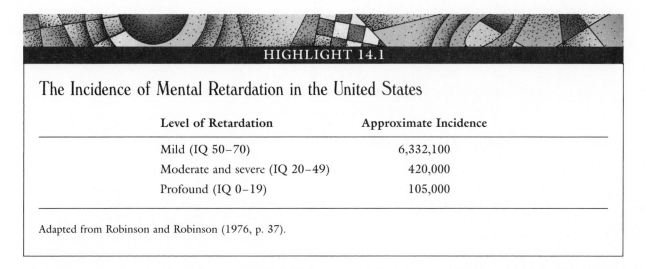

The Incidence of Mental Retardation in the United States

Level of Retardation	Approximate Incidence
Mild (IQ 50–70)	6,332,100
Moderate and severe (IQ 20–49)	420,000
Profound (IQ 0–19)	105,000

Adapted from Robinson and Robinson (1976, p. 37).

IQ of 50 or below will inevitably exhibit gross deficiencies in overall adaptive behavior as well. At the higher ranges of "retarded" IQ scores, however, behavioral adaptiveness and IQ score seem to be at least partially independent of one another.

Both the American Association on Mental Deficiency and the American Psychiatric Association classifications recognized four levels of retarded mental development, as follows:

1. *Mild mental retardation (IQ 52–67).* As shown in *HIGHLIGHT 14.1*, mildly retarded individuals constitute by far the largest number of those labeled mentally retarded. People in this group are considered *educable,* and their intellectual levels as adults are comparable with those of average 8- to 11-year-old children. Statements such as the latter, however, should not be taken too literally. A mildly retarded adult with a "mental age" of, say, 10 (that is, intelligence test performance is at the level of the average 10-year-old) may not in fact be comparable to the normal 10-year-old in information-processing ability (Weiss, Weisz, & Bromfield, 1986)— although some investigators (e.g., Hore & Tryon, 1989) dispute the notion of a basic difference in purely intellectual functioning.

In any event, the social adjustment of such people often approximates that of adolescents, although they tend to lack normal adolescents' imagination, inventiveness, and judgment. Ordinarily, they do not show signs of brain pathology or other physical anomalies, but often they require some measure of supervision because of their limited abilities to foresee the consequences of their actions. In fact, individuals at a somewhat higher, "borderline" IQ level (68–84) may also need special services to maximize their potentials (Zetlin & Murtaugh, 1990). With early diagnosis, parental assistance, and special educational programs, the great majority of borderline and mildly retarded individuals can adjust socially, master simple academic and occupational skills, and become self-supporting citizens (Schalock, Harper, & Carver, 1981).

2. *Moderate mental retardation (IQ 36–51).* Moderately retarded individuals are likely to fall in the educational category of *trainable,* which means that they are presumed able to master certain routine skills, such as cooking or minor janitorial work, if provided specialized instruction in these activities. In adult life, individuals classified as moderately retarded attain intellectual levels similar to those of average 4- to 7-year-old children. Although some can be taught to read and write a little and may manage to achieve a fair command of spoken lan-

Mildly retarded individuals constitute the largest number of those labeled mentally retarded. With help, a great majority of these individuals can adjust socially, master simple academic and occupational skills, and become self-supporting citizens.

Difficulties of Mentally Retarded People in Learning Basic Academic Skills

The basic learning processes of most mentally retarded children —aside from a minority with serious neurological defects—are not essentially different from those of normal children. Retarded children, however, learn at a slower rate than normal children and are less capable of mastering abstractions and complex concepts. These limitations are especially apparent in learning language and other skills requiring a high level of ability with symbols. The problems that retarded children typically encounter in learning basic academic skills may be summarized as follows:

1. *Difficulty in focusing attention.* Studies have shown that such children's poor learning is often due to the fact that their attention is focused on irrelevant aspects of learning situations. Once they know what stimulus dimensions are important—for example, attending to form because each letter's shape is important in learning the alphabet—they may

quickly master appropriate discrimination skills and show marked improvement in performance and learning.

2. *Deficiency in past learning.* Most formal learning requires prior learning. For example, a child who has not learned basic verbal, conceptual, and problem-solving skills will fall farther behind when he or she begins schooling. Thus a number of programs have been established to help disadvantaged children of preschool age develop basic skills requisite for learning in school.

3. *Expectancy of failure—a self-fulfilling prophecy.* Because of having experienced more failure in learning attempts than other children, a mentally retarded child tends to begin tasks with a greater expectancy of failure and to engage in avoidance behavior as well. Often such children feel that forces beyond their control determine the outcome of their actions. Thus, if they succeed in a task,

they may not perceive their success as due to their own efforts or abilities. They become passive, lose their initiative, and begin to rely too much on others. To counteract this tendency, learning experiences must be programmed into manageable components that can yield continuing experiences of success.

Special education classes should thus be directed at helping mentally retarded children discriminate relevant from irrelevant stimuli in learning and problem-solving situations; they should associate new learning with the children's present information, needs, and life situations; and they should structure learning tasks in a sequence of steps that can be readily mastered by the retarded and so provide experiences of success. Such measures, of course, are useful in all educational settings, but are particularly important in training mentally retarded children.

Based on Bijou (1966), Hagan and Huntsman (1971), Hyatt and Rolnick (1974), Karnes et al. (1970), Macmillan and Keogh (1971), Tarver and Hallahan (1974), and Robinson and Robinson (1976).

guage, their rate of learning is relatively slow, and their level of conceptualizing extremely limited. Physically, they usually appear clumsy and ungainly, and they suffer from bodily deformities and poor motor coordination. Some of these children are hostile and aggressive; more typically they present an affable and somewhat vacuous personality picture. In general, with early diagnosis, parental help, and adequate opportunities for training, most moderately retarded individuals can achieve partial independence in daily self-care, acceptable behavior, and economic usefulness in a family or other sheltered environment. Whether they require institutionali-

zation usually depends on their general level of adaptive behavior and the nature of their home situation.

3. *Severe mental retardation (IQ 20–35).* Severely retarded individuals are sometimes referred to as *dependent retarded.* Among these individuals, motor and speech development are severely retarded, and sensory defects and motor handicaps are common. They can develop limited levels of personal hygiene and self-help skills, which somewhat lessen their dependence, but they are always dependent on others for care, thus usually requiring institutionali-

zation. However, many profit to some extent from training and can perform simple occupational tasks under supervision.

4. *Profound Mental Retardation (IQ under 20).* The term *life support retarded* is sometimes used to refer to profoundly retarded individuals. Most of these people are severely deficient in adaptive behavior and unable to master any but the simplest tasks. Useful speech, if it develops at all, is rudimentary. Severe physical deformities, central nervous system pathology, and retarded growth are typical; convulsive seizures, mutism, deafness, and other physical anomalies are also common. These individuals must remain in custodial care all their lives. They tend, however, to have poor health and low resistance to disease and thus a short life expectancy.

Severe and profound cases of mental retardation can usually be readily diagnosed in infancy because of the presence of obvious physical malformations, grossly delayed habit training, and other obvious symptoms of abnormality. Although these individuals show a marked impairment of overall intellectual functioning, they may have considerably more ability in some areas than in others.

Indeed, in occasional cases, moderately retarded people may show an extraordinarily high level of skill in some specific aspect of behavior that does not depend on abstract reasoning; the French term *idiot savant* (learned idiot) is sometimes used to refer to these individuals. Thus, one seriously retarded individual was able to remember the serial number on every dollar bill he was shown or had ever seen; another was able to tell the day of the week of a given date in any year, without resorting to paper and pencil or even to making other numerical calculations. In other exceptional cases, a retarded person may show considerable talent in art or music. Viscott (1970) provided a detailed case study of a "musical idiot savant"; Hill (1975) cited the case of a mildly retarded individual with an IQ of 54 who could play 11 different musical instruments by ear and possessed outstanding skill in calculating dates. Similarly, Morishima (1975) cited the case of a famous Japanese painter whose assessed IQ was 47. Such unusual abilities among the retarded are rare, however.

Contrary to common understanding, the distribution of IQ scores in the United States does not precisely fit "normal curve" expectations, especially at the lower IQ ranges. These ranges tend to show a frequency bulge, with about 200,000 more cases than are expected (Robinson & Robinson, 1976). This finding suggests the operation of an intruding factor that tends to inflate beyond normal-curve

expectancy the numbers of cases at lower IQ ranges —probably the presence of major genetic abnormalities, brain injuries, or both that are not characteristic of mild retardation. The next section addresses these factors.

Organic Factors in Mental Retardation

Some instances of mental retardation—something on the order of 25 percent of the cases—occur with known organic brain pathology. In these cases, retardation is virtually always at least moderate, and it is often severe. Profound retardation, fortunately rare, always includes obvious organic impairment. Organically caused retardation is in essential respects similar to dementia as described in Chapter 13, except for a different history of prior functioning. In fact, in the past, a young person with organically caused retardation was referred to as *amented,* as distinct from a *demented* person.

In this section we will consider five biological conditions that may lead to mental retardation, noting some of the possible interrelations between them. Then we will review some of the major clinical types of mental retardation associated with these organic causes.

Genetic-Chromosomal Factors   Mental retardation tends to run in families. This tendency is particularly true of mild retardation. Poverty and sociocultural deprivation, however, also tend to run in families, and with early and continued exposure to such conditions, even the inheritance of average intellectual potential may not prevent subaverage intellectual functioning.

As we noted in Chapter 4, genetic and chromosomal factors play a much clearer role in the etiology of relatively rare types of mental retardation, such as Down syndrome or a condition known as *Fragile X,* a constriction or breaking off of the end portion of the long arm of the X sex chromosome. In such conditions specific chromosomal defects are responsible for metabolic alterations that adversely affect the brain's development. Genetic defects leading to metabolic alterations may, of course, involve many other developmental anomalies besides mental retardation. In general, the mental retardation most often associated with known genetic-chromosomal defects, that of Down syndrome, is moderate to severe in degree.

Infections and Toxic Agents   Mental retardation may be associated with a wide range of conditions due to infection. If a pregnant woman has syphilis or gets German measles, her child may suffer brain damage. Brain damage may also result from infections occurring after birth, such as viral encephalitis.

A number of toxic agents, such as carbon monoxide and lead, may cause brain damage during fetal development or after birth. In some instances, immunological agents, such as antitetanus serum or typhoid vaccine, may lead to brain damage. Similarly, certain drugs, including an excess of alcohol, taken by a pregnant woman may lead to congenital malformations; an overdose of drugs administered to an infant may result in toxicity and brain damage. In rare cases, brain damage results from incompatibility in blood types between mother and fetus—conditions known as Rh, or ABO, system incompatibility. Fortunately, early diagnosis and blood transfusions can now minimize the effects of such incompatibility.

Prematurity and Trauma (Physical Injury)

Follow-up studies of children born prematurely and weighing less than about 5 pounds at birth have revealed a high incidence of neurological disorders and often mental retardation. In fact, small premature babies are many times more likely to be mentally retarded than normal-size infants (MacDonald, 1964).

Physical injury at birth can also result in retardation. Isaacson (1970) has estimated that in 1 birth out of 1000 brain damage occurs that will prevent the child from reaching the intelligence level of an average 12-year-old. Although the fetus is normally well protected by its fluid-filled bag during gestation, and its skull appears designed to resist delivery stressors, accidents do happen during delivery and after birth. Difficulties in labor due to malposition of the fetus or other complications may irreparably damage the infant's brain. Bleeding within the brain is probably the most common result of such birth trauma. *Hypoxia*—lack of sufficient oxygen to the brain stemming from delayed breathing or other causes—is another type of birth trauma that may damage the brain. Hypoxia may also occur after birth as a result of cardiac arrest associated with operations, heart attacks, near drownings, or severe electrical shocks.

Ionizing Radiation

In recent years a good deal of scientific attention has been focused on the damaging effects of ionizing radiation on sex cells and other bodily cells and tissues. Radiation may act directly on the fertilized ovum or may produce gene mutations in the sex cells of either or both parents, which, in turn, may lead to defective offspring.

Sources of harmful radiation were once limited primarily to high-energy X rays used for diagnosis and therapy, but the list has grown to include nuclear weapons testing and leakages at nuclear power plants, among others.

Malnutrition and Other Biological Factors

As we noted in Chapter 4, deficiencies in protein and other essential nutrients during early development can result in irreversible physical and mental damage. Protein deficiencies in a mother's diet during pregnancy, as well as in a baby's diet after birth, have been pinpointed as particularly potent causes of lowered intelligence.

A limited number of cases of mental retardation are also associated with other biological agents, such as brain tumors, that either damage the brain tissue directly or lead to increased cranial pressure and concomitant brain damage. In some instances of mental retardation—particularly of the severe and profound types—the causes are uncertain or unknown, although extensive brain pathology is evident.

■ Organic Retardation Syndromes

Mental retardation stemming primarily from biological causes can be classified into several recognizable clinical types, of which four will be discussed here. *HIGHLIGHT 14.3* presents information on several other well-known forms.

Down Syndrome   First described by Langdon Down in 1866, **Down syndrome** is the most common of the clinical conditions associated with moderate and severe mental retardation. About 1 in every 600 babies born in the United States is diagnosed as having Down syndrome, a condition that "has life-long implications for physical appearance, intellectual achievement and general functioning" (Golden & Davis, 1974, p. 7). The availability of *amniocentesis* with elective abortion should the fetus prove chromosomally defective, while helpful for individual families, appears not to have affected substantially the overall incidence of the disorder. Because of demographic shifts, the majority of Down syndrome infants in recent decades were born to mothers under 35 years of age, not a group for whom amniocentesis is routinely recommended (Evans & Hamerton, 1985).

A number of physical features are often found among children with Down syndrome, but few of these children have all of the characteristics commonly thought of as typifying this group. In such children, the eyes appear almond-shaped, and the skin of the eyelids tends to be abnormally thick. The face and nose are often flat and broad, as is the back

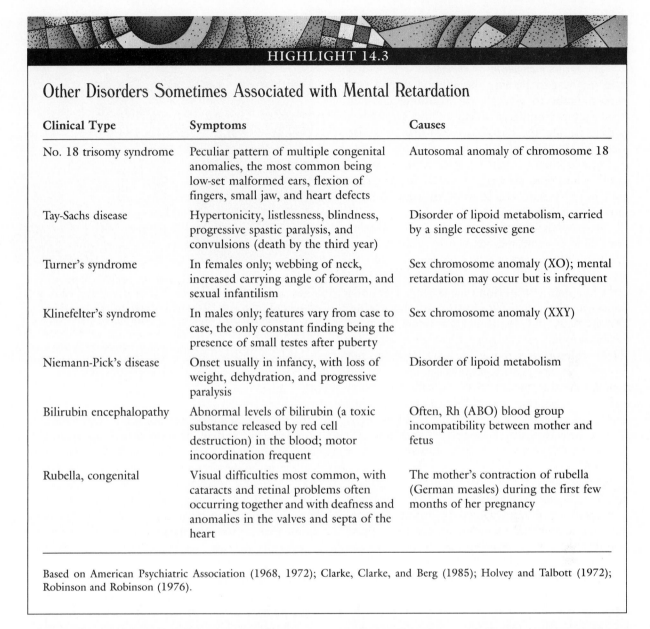

HIGHLIGHT 14.3

Other Disorders Sometimes Associated with Mental Retardation

Clinical Type	Symptoms	Causes
No. 18 trisomy syndrome	Peculiar pattern of multiple congenital anomalies, the most common being low-set malformed ears, flexion of fingers, small jaw, and heart defects	Autosomal anomaly of chromosome 18
Tay-Sachs disease	Hypertonicity, listlessness, blindness, progressive spastic paralysis, and convulsions (death by the third year)	Disorder of lipoid metabolism, carried by a single recessive gene
Turner's syndrome	In females only; webbing of neck, increased carrying angle of forearm, and sexual infantilism	Sex chromosome anomaly (XO); mental retardation may occur but is infrequent
Klinefelter's syndrome	In males only; features vary from case to case, the only constant finding being the presence of small testes after puberty	Sex chromosome anomaly (XXY)
Niemann-Pick's disease	Onset usually in infancy, with loss of weight, dehydration, and progressive paralysis	Disorder of lipoid metabolism
Bilirubin encephalopathy	Abnormal levels of bilirubin (a toxic substance released by red cell destruction) in the blood; motor incoordination frequent	Often, Rh (ABO) blood group incompatibility between mother and fetus
Rubella, congenital	Visual difficulties most common, with cataracts and retinal problems often occurring together and with deafness and anomalies in the valves and septa of the heart	The mother's contraction of rubella (German measles) during the first few months of her pregnancy

Based on American Psychiatric Association (1968, 1972); Clarke, Clarke, and Berg (1985); Holvey and Talbott (1972); Robinson and Robinson (1976).

of the head. The tongue, which seems too large for the mouth, may show deep fissures. The iris of the eye is frequently speckled. The neck is often short and broad, as are the hands, which tend to have creases across the palms. The fingers are stubby, and the little finger is often more noticeably curved than the other fingers. Although facial surgery is sometimes tried to correct the more stigmatizing features, its success is often limited (Dodd & Leahy, 1989; Katz & Kravetz, 1989).

Well over 50 percent of people with Down syndrome have cataracts, which are not congenital but tend to make their appearance when a child is about 7 or 8 (Falls, 1970). These cataracts aid in diagnosis, but fortunately they rarely become serious enough to warrant surgery. Interestingly, there appears to be little, if any, correlation between the number of physical symptoms and the degree of mental retardation in individuals with Down syndrome.

Death rates for children with Down syndrome have decreased dramatically in the past half century. In 1919, the life expectancy at birth for such children was about nine years; most of the deaths were due to gross physical anomalies, and a large proportion occurred in the first year. Today, thanks to antibiotics, surgical correction of lethal anatomical defects, and better general medical care, many more of these children are living to adulthood (Smith & Berg, 1976). In fact, overall, the mortality rate for this group is only 6 percent higher than that for the general population, though this figure remains higher in the early years and for those who live beyond 40 (Forseman & Akesson, 1965). At present, the average life expectancy for Down syndrome children at birth is about 16 years; by age 1, it increases to about 22 years (Smith & Berg, 1976).

The terms *mongolism* or *mongoloid* were widely used in the past because the almond-shaped eyes were thought to give Down syndrome children facial features similar to those of the Mongolian race. At times, the term *mongolian idiot* was also used. These terms are no longer acceptable, however, because they contain negative racial connotations. In addition, the term "idiot" is inappropriate both in itself and because most afflicted children show only moderate mental retardation.

Despite their limitations, children suffering from Down syndrome are usually able to learn self-help skills, acceptable social behavior, and routine manual skills that enable them to be of assistance in a family or institutional setting. The traditional view has been that Down syndrome youngsters are unusually placid and affectionate. Research has questioned the validity of this generalization. These children may indeed be very tractable, but probably in no greater proportion than normal youngsters; they may also be equally (or more) difficult in various areas (Bridges & Cicchetti, 1982). In general, the adequacy of a child's social relationships is positively correlated with both IQ level and a supportive home environment (Sloper et al., 1990).

Research has also suggested that the intellectual defect in Down syndrome may not be consistent across various abilities. Down syndrome children tend to remain relatively unimpaired in their appreciation of spatial relationships and in visual-motor coordination; they show their greatest deficits in verbal and language-related skills (Mahoney, Glover, & Finger, 1981; Silverstein et al., 1982). Inasmuch as spatial functions are known to be partially localized in the right cerebral hemisphere, and language-related functions in the left cerebral hemisphere, some investigators speculate that the syndrome is especially crippling to the left hemisphere.

Traditionally, the cause of Down syndrome was assumed to be faulty heredity. A number of early studies demonstrated, however, that more than a single case of Down syndrome in a family was unlikely, occurring in less than 1 family in 100 of those already affected. As a consequence of this finding, investigators turned to the study of metabolic factors and concluded that Down syndrome was probably due to some sort of glandular imbalance. Then, in 1959, the French scientists Lejeune, Turpin, and Gauthier found 47 chromosomes, instead of the usual 46, in several Down syndrome cases. A trisomy of chromosome 21 (an error of

Today many more Down syndrome children than in the past are living to adulthood and are able to learn self-help, social, and manual skills. It is not unusual for Down syndrome children to be mainstreamed to some extent with unimpaired children, such as this girl in a ballet class. Down syndrome children tend to remain relatively unimpaired in their appreciation of spatial relationships and visual-motor coordination; they show their greatest deficits in verbal and language-related skills.

zygosis in which chromosome 21 is represented in triplicate rather than the normal pair) has now been identified as a characteristic of Down syndrome children, being present in at least 94 percent of cases meeting strict Down syndrome criteria. As was noted in Chapter 13 (see page 498), it is possibly significant that this is the same chromosome that has been implicated in recent research on Alzheimer's disease, especially in light of the fact that surviving victims of Down syndrome are at extremely high risk for Alzheimer's as they get into and beyond their late 30s (Bauer & Shea, 1986; Reid, 1985).

Researchers have long believed that the "extra" chromosome in Down syndrome is in some way contributed by the mother. In 1973, however, it was learned that in certain instances it is in fact contributed by the father (Sasaki & Hara, 1973; Uchida, 1973). The reason for the trisomy of chromosome 21 is not clear, but the anomaly seems definitely related to parental age at conception.

It has been known for many years that the incidence of Down syndrome increases in regular fashion with the age of the mother. A woman in her 20s has about 1 chance in 2000 of conceiving a Down syndrome baby, whereas the risk for a woman in her 40s is 1 in 50 (Holvey & Talbot, 1972). As in the case of all birth defects, the risk of having a Down syndrome baby is high for young mothers whose reproductive systems have not yet fully ma-tured. The advanced maternal age correlation led naturally to the inference that an older woman's capacity to produce a chromosomally normal fetus was somehow impaired by the aging process. This observed effect obscured for many years a possible male contribution; older men tend, of course, to have older women partners.

More recent research has strongly indicated that the father's age at conception is also implicated in the occurrence of Down syndrome, particularly at higher ages (Hook, 1980; Stene et al., 1981). In one study involving 1279 cases of Down syndrome in Japan, Matsunaga and associates (1978) demonstrated an overall increase in incidence with advancing paternal age when maternal age was controlled. The risk for fathers aged 55 years and over was more than twice that for fathers in their early 20s. Curiously, these investigators noted that, in their sample, fathers in their early 40s had a lower risk factor than slightly younger as well as older men.

Thus it seems that advancing age in either parent increases the risk of the trisomy 21 anomaly, although the maternal age effect is the larger one. As yet we do not understand how aging produces this effect. A reasonable guess is that aging is related to cumulative exposure to varied environmental hazards, such as radiation, that might have adverse effects on the processes involved in zygote formation or development.

Whatever the cause of the chromosomal anomaly, the end result is the growth-process distortion characteristic of this syndrome. There is no known effective treatment. When parents have had a child with Down syndrome, they are usually quite concerned about having further children. In such cases, genetic counseling may provide some indication of the risk—which may be quite small—of abnormality in additional children. In recent years, amniocentesis, when used, has made it possible to diagnose most cases of Down's syndrome in utero, thus permitting parents to make a rational (although usually not easy) choice concerning termination of the pregnancy if the fetus is abnormal.

Phenylketonuria (PKU)   A rare metabolic disorder, **phenylketonuria (PKU)** occurs in about 1 in 20,000 births. Retarded individuals in institutions who suffer from PKU number about 1 in 100 (Holmes et al., 1972; Schild, 1972).

In PKU, a baby appears normal at birth but lacks a liver enzyme needed to break down phenylalanine, an amino acid found in many foods. The genetic error manifests itself in pathology only when significant quantities of phenylalanine are ingested, something that is virtually certain to occur if the child's condition remains undiagnosed. If the condition is undetected, the amount of phenylalanine in the blood increases and eventually produces brain damage.

The disorder usually becomes apparent between 6 and 12 months after birth, although such symptoms as vomiting, a peculiar odor, infantile eczema, and seizures may occur during the early weeks of life. Often the first symptoms noticed are signs of mental retardation, which may be moderate to severe depending on the degree to which the disease has progressed. Motor incoordination and other neurological manifestations relating to the severity of brain damage are also common, and often the eyes, skin, and hair of untreated PKU patients are very pale.

PKU was identified in 1934 when a Norwegian mother sought to learn the reason for her child's mental retardation and peculiar musty odor. She consulted with many physicians to no avail until Dr. Asbjorn Folling found phenylpyruvic acid in the child's urine and concluded that the child had a disorder of phenylalanine metabolism (Centerwall & Centerwall, 1961).

Most older PKU patients show severe to profound mental retardation, with the median IQ of untreated phenylketonuric adults being about 20. Curiously, however, a number of PKU individuals have PKU relatives with less severely affected intelligence. In addition, Perry (1970) reported the cases of two untreated PKU patients with superior intelligence. These findings have made PKU something of an enigma. It results from a liver enzyme deficiency involving one or more recessive genes, and 1 person in 70 is thought to be a carrier. There may be varying degrees of PKU, however, or another genetic factor may lessen the destructive potential of the enzyme defect (Burns, 1972).

The early detection of PKU by examining urine for the presence of phenylpyruvic acid is now routine in developed countries, and dietary treatment (such as the elimination of phenylalanine-containing foods) and related procedures can be used to prevent the disorder. With early detection and treatment—preferably before an infant is 6 months old—the deterioration process can usually be arrested so that levels of intellectual functioning may range from borderline to normal. A few children suffer mental retardation despite restricted phenylalanine intake and other measures, however.

For a baby to inherit PKU, it appears that both parents must carry the recessive genes. Thus when one child in a family is discovered to have PKU, it is important that other children in the family be screened as well.

Cretinism (Thyroid Deficiency)   Resulting from endocrine imbalance, **cretinism** produces a dramatic illustration of mental retardation. In this condition, the thyroid either has failed to develop properly or has undergone degeneration or injury; in either case, an infant suffers from a deficiency in thyroid secretion. Brain damage resulting from this insufficiency is most marked when the deficiency occurs during the prenatal and early postnatal periods of rapid growth.

In the valleys of central Switzerland and in other geographical areas where iodine is deficient in the soil (and therefore in the food grown in it), cretinism was once a common affliction. In such areas, infants often were born with defective thyroid glands that remained undeveloped or atrophied. Because in such areas cretinism was observed to run in families, it was thought to be a hereditary disorder. In 1891, however, Dr. George Murray published his discovery that the injection of thyroid gland extract was beneficial in cases of **myxedema**—a disorder resulting from thyroid deficiency in adult life and characterized by mental dullness. This discovery, in turn, led to the treatment of cretinism with thyroid gland extract and to the realization that this condition, too, was the result of thyroid deficiency.

Although most cases of cretinism result from lack of iodine in the diet, thyroid deficiency may also occur as a result of birth injuries (involving bleeding into the thyroid) or of infectious diseases such as measles, whooping cough, or diphtheria. Less frequently, it may be a result of a genetically determined enzyme defect. The resulting clinical picture depends on the age at which the thyroid deficiency occurs as well as on the degree and duration of the deficiency.

Typical descriptions of individuals with cretinism involve severe thyroid deficiency from an early age, often even before birth. Such an individual has a dwarflike, thick-set body and short, stubby extremities. Height is usually just a little over three feet, the shortness accentuated by slightly bent legs and a curvature of the spine. The individual walks with a shuffling gait that is easily recognizable and has a large head with abundant black, wiry hair. Thick eyelids give the person a sleepy appearance, and the skin is dry, thickened, and cold to the touch. Other pronounced physical symptoms include a broad, flat nose, large and floppy ears, a protruding abdomen, and a failure to mature sexually. The sufferer reveals a bland personality and sluggish thought processes. Most individuals with cretinism fall within the moderate and severe categories of mental retardation, depending on the extent of brain damage. In cases with less pronounced physical signs of cretinism, the degree of mental retardation is usually less severe.

Early treatment of cretinism with thyroid gland extract is considered essential; infants not treated until after the first year of life may have permanently impaired intelligence. In long-standing cases, thyroid treatment may have some ameliorating effects, but the damage to an individual's nervous system and general physical development is beyond repair.

Public health measures on both the national and international levels have concentrated on the use of iodized salt and the early detection and correction of thyroid deficiency. As a result, severe cases of cretinism have become practically nonexistent in the United States and in most, but not all, other countries.

Cranial Anomalies   Mental retardation is associated with a number of conditions that involve relatively gross alterations in head size and shape and for which the causal factors have not been definitely established (Wortis, 1973). In **macrocephaly** (large-headedness), for example, there is an increase in the size and weight of the brain, an enlargement of the skull, visual impairment, convulsions, and other neurological symptoms, resulting from the abnormal growth of glia cells that form the supporting structure for brain tissue. Other cranial anomalies include *microcephaly* and *hydrocephalus,* which we will discuss in more detail.

Microcephaly.   The term **microcephaly** means "small-headedness." It refers to a type of mental retardation resulting from impaired development of the brain and a consequent failure of the cranium to attain normal size. In an early study of postmortem examinations of microcephalic individual's brains, Greenfield and Wolfson (1935) reported that practically all cases examined showed development to have been arrested at the fourth or fifth month of fetal life. Fortunately, this condition is extremely rare.

The most obvious characteristic of microcephaly is the small head, the circumference of which rarely exceeds 17 inches, as compared with the normal size of approximately 22 inches. Penrose (1963) also described microcephalic youngsters as being invariably short in stature but having relatively normal musculature and sex organs. Beyond these characteristics, they differ considerably from one another in appearance, although there is a tendency for the skull to be cone-shaped, with a receding chin and forehead. Microcephalic children fall within the moderate, severe, and profound categories of mental retardation, but the majority show little language development and are extremely limited in mental capacity.

Microcephaly may result from a wide range of factors that impair brain development, including intrauterine infections and pelvic irradiation during the mother's early months of pregnancy (Koch, 1967). Miller (1970) noted a number of cases of microcephaly in Hiroshima and Nagasaki that apparently resulted from the atomic bomb explosions during World War II. The role of genetic factors is not as yet clear. Treatment is ineffective once faulty development has occurred; at present, preventive measures focus on the avoidance of infection and radiation during pregnancy.

Hydrocephalus.   **Hydrocephalus** is a relatively rare condition in which the accumulation of an abnormal amount of cerebrospinal fluid within the cranium causes damage to the brain tissues and enlargement of the skull.

In congenital cases of hydrocephalus, the head is either already enlarged at birth or begins to enlarge soon thereafter, presumably as a result of a disturbance in the formation, absorption, or circulation of the cerebrospinal fluid (Wortis, 1973). The disorder can also develop in infancy or early childhood, following the development of a brain tumor, subdural hematoma, meningitis, or other such conditions. In these cases the condition appears to result from a blockage of the cerebrospinal pathways and an accumulation of fluid in certain brain areas.

The clinical picture in hydrocephalus depends on the extent of neural damage, which, in turn, depends on the age at onset and the duration and severity of the disorder. In chronic cases, the chief symptom is the gradual enlargement of the upper part of the head out of all proportion to the face and the rest of the body. While the expansion of the skull helps minimize destructive pressure on the brain, serious brain damage occurs nonetheless. This damage leads to intellectual impairment and such other effects as convulsions and impairment or loss of sight and hearing. The degree of intellectual impairment varies, being severe or profound in advanced cases.

A good deal of attention has been directed to the surgical treatment of hydrocephalus. With early diagnosis and treatment, this condition can usually be arrested before severe brain damage has occurred (Geisz & Steinhausen, 1974).

■ Mental Retardation and Sociocultural Deprivation

Investigators formerly believed that all mental retardation was the result of faulty genes or of other causes of brain impairment. In recent years, however, it has become apparent that adverse sociocultural conditions, particularly those involving a deprivation of normal environmental stimulation, may play a primary role in the etiology of mental retardation.

Two subtypes of mental retardation fall in this general category: (a) mental retardation associated with extreme sensory and social deprivation, such as prolonged isolation during the developmental years, as may have happened in the case of the wild boy of Aveyron, discussed in *HIGHLIGHT 14.4*; and (b) **cultural-familial retardation,** in which a child is not subjected to extreme isolation but rather suffers from an inferior quality of interaction with the cultural environment and with other people. Because such sociocultural impoverishment may be associated with genetic deficiency in some cases, a child born to a family in such circumstances may be doubly jeopardized. In any event, it has proven all but impossible to assess adequately the differential influences of nature and nurture in these cases. The field is rife with controversy.

Because the great majority of all retarded individuals are of the cultural-familial type, our discussion will focus on this form of retardation.

Consider the following table depicting the average IQs of 586 Milwaukee children in differing age ranges. The children were separated according to whether or not the IQs of their mothers, all of whom dwelt in slum areas under deprived circumstances, fell below 80.

Note that the two groups of children did not differ in IQ at ages 1 through 2 and that both scored within the normal range. The children whose moth-

TABLE 14.1   Average IQs of 586 Milwaukee Children

Maternal IQ	Age of Children in Months						
	13–35	36–59	60–83	84–107	108–131	132–167	168+
80+ (n=48)	95	93	90	94	87.5	94	90
<80 (n=40)	95	76	84	80	75	70	67.5

(Garber, 1988. Constructed from Figure 2–1, p. 23.)

The "Wild Boy of Aveyron"

In 1800, long before the development of psychotherapy, Jean-Marc Itard attempted to inculcate normal human abilities in a "wild boy" who had been captured by peasants in the forests of Aveyron, France. The boy, who appeared to be between 10 and 12 years old, had been exhibited in a cage for about a year by his captors when Itard rescued him. By examining scars on the boy's body and by observing his personal habits, Itard concluded that he had been abandoned at the age of 2 or 3.

At first Victor (as Itard named the boy) seemed more animal than human. He was oblivious to other human beings, could not talk, and howled and ate off the ground on all fours like an animal. He evidenced unusual sensory reactions; for example, he did not react if a pistol was fired next to his ear, but he could hear the crack of a nut or the crackling of underbrush at a great distance.

No adverse reaction seemed to result from his going unclothed even in freezing weather. In fact, Victor had velvety skin, despite his years of exposure.

Victor exhibited animal-like behavior in many ways. He had an obstinate habit of smelling any object that was given to him— even objects we consider void of smell. He knew nothing of love and perceived other human beings only as obstacles—in other words, he was like the wild animals he had known in the forest. Victor was typically indifferent and uncomplaining but, occasionally, he showed a kind of frantic rage and became dangerous to those around him. If he had any sense of self-identity, it was apparently more that of an animal than a human.

Philippe Pinel, Itard's instructor, diagnosed Victor's condition as congenital idiocy—concluding that the boy was incapable

of profiting from training. Itard, however, although only 25 years old and inexperienced in comparison with Pinel, disagreed; in his view, Victor's savage behavior was the result of early and lengthy isolation from other humans. He believed that human contact and intensive training would enable the boy to become a normal person, and, ignoring Pinel's advice, he began his attempt to civilize "the wild boy of Aveyron."

No procedures had yet been formulated that Itard could use in treating Victor; thus he developed a program based on principles that included the following: (a) without contact with its own kind, a human infant—unlike a lower animal—cannot develop normally; (b) the instinct to imitate is the learning force by which our senses are educated, and this instinct is strongest in early childhood and decreases with age; and (c) in all human beings, from the

Based on Itard (1799; tr. Humphrey & Humphrey, 1932) and Silberstein and Irwin (1962).

---

ers had IQs of 80 or above continued to manifest average IQs in the normal range through age 14. However, children of mothers of IQ less than 80 showed, on average, a progressive (and, after age 5, nonreversing) decline with advancing age that approached the upper limits of the mental retardation range by age 14. Such a progressive loss is not easy to reconcile with a hereditary interpretation; it suggests, rather, the cumulative effects of a deficient environment, one well indexed by the mothers' IQ levels.

Garber (1988) in fact contends that the effect is due to the inadequacy of low IQ mothers in stimulating intellectual growth. Specifically, he maintains that the mothering person is normally responsible for creating the "microenvironment" determining a child's rate of cognitive development, and that a

low maternal IQ—which is associated with verbal and other skill deficits—tends to foster an environment that is deficient in its provision of cognitively enriching experience. Although this conclusion is consistent with most available evidence, it would be tragic to convert such evidence to an assignment of blame against these overburdened and sometimes overwhelmed women. They need compassion and help, not blame, and when they get this help, the IQs of their children may be dramatically elevated (Garber, 1988; Ramey & Haskins, 1981).

Whatever the specific etiology, children whose retardation is cultural-familial in origin are usually only mildly retarded; however, they make up the majority of people labeled as mentally retarded. These children show no identifiable brain pathology and are usually not diagnosed as mentally retard-most isolated to the most educated, a constant relationship exists between needs and ideas—the greater the needs, the greater the development of mental capacities to meet them.

In attempting to train Victor, Itard developed methods that have had considerable impact on the subsequent treatment of children with serious learning disabilities. Instructional materials were provided to broaden Victor's discrimination skills in touch, smell, and other sensory modalities, appropriate to his environment; language training was begun through the association of words with the objects Victor wanted; and modeling and imitation were used to reinforce Victor's learning of desired social behaviors.

Initial results were indeed promising. Victor learned to speak a number of words and could write in chalk to express his wants. He also developed affec-

tionate feelings toward his governess.

In June 1801, Itard reported to the Academy of Science in Paris on the rapid progress in the first nine months of training. In November 1806, however, he could only report that despite significant advances in several areas, Victor had not been made "normal" in the sense of becoming a self-directing and socially adjusted person. Being brought into the proximity of girls, for example, only upset the boy, leaving him restless and depressed, and Itard had to abandon his hope for a normal sexual response as a means of fostering Victor's motivation and socialization.

After devoting five and a half years to the task, Itard gave up the attempt to train "the wild boy of Aveyron." As for Victor, he lived to be 40, but never progressed appreciably beyond the achievements of that first year.

The story of Victor is of absorbing interest to both laypeople and scientists. A motion picture that portrays Itard's work with Victor—*The Wild Child*—was produced by François Truffaut. In scientific circles, the lack of conclusive answers will keep psychologists and others puzzling over the question of whether Victor was a congenital mental retardate, a brain-damaged individual, a psychotic, or simply a person who had been so deprived of human contact during early critical periods of development that the damage he had sustained could never be completely remedied.

ed until they enter school and have serious difficulties in their studies. As a large number of investigators have pointed out, most of these children come from economically deprived, unstable, and often disrupted family backgrounds characterized by a lack of intellectual stimulation, an inferior quality of interaction with others, and general environmental deprivation (e.g., Birns & Bridger, 1977; Braginsky & Braginsky, 1974; Feuerstein, 1977).

They are raised in homes with absent fathers and with physically or emotionally unavailable mothers. During infancy they are not exposed to the same quality and quantity of tactile and kinesthetic stimulations as other children. Often they are left unattended in a crib or on the floor of the dwelling.

Although there are noises, odors, and colors in the environment, the stimuli are not as organized as those found in middle-class and upper-class environments. For example, the number of words they hear is limited, with sentences brief and most commands carrying a negative connotation. (Tarjan & Eisenberg, 1972, p. 16)

Since a child's current level of intellectual functioning is based largely on previous learning—and since schoolwork requires complex skills, such as being able to control one's attention, follow instructions, and recognize the meaning of a considerable range of words—these children are at a disadvantage from the beginning because they have not had an opportunity to learn requisite background skills or to be motivated toward learning.

Thus with each succeeding year, unless remedial measures are undertaken, they tend to fall farther behind in school performance. They also fall farther behind in relative ratings on intelligence tests, which, as we have seen, are measures of ability for schoolwork. A report by the American Psychological Association (1970) noted the following:

Mental retardation is primarily a psychosocial and psychoeducational problem—a deficit in adaptation to the demands and expectations of society evidenced by the individual's relative difficulty in learning, problem solving, adapting to new situations, and abstract thinking. (p. 267)

This statement was not intended to minimize the possible role of adverse biological factors, including genetic deficiencies, in the total causal pattern. Certainly many of these children reveal histories of prematurity, inadequate diets, and little or no medical care. In the great majority of cases of cultural-familial mental retardation, however, no neurological or physical dysfunction has been demonstrated. Thus, efforts to understand mild mental retardation have focused increasingly on the role of environmental factors in impeding intellectual growth. The likelihood that many of these factors will prove preventable or reversible has given rise to new but as yet still largely unrealized hopes for effective, widespread intervention, as will be seen.

■ The Problem of Assessment

Because mental retardation is defined in terms of both intellectual (academic) and social competence, it is essential to assess both of these characteristics before labeling a person as mentally retarded.

Unfortunately, neither of the preceding tasks is easy. Errors in IQ assessment can stem from a variety of sources, including (a) errors in administering tests; (b) the personal characteristics of a child, such as a language problem or lack of motivation to do well on tests; and (c) limitations in the tests themselves. The latter point has been succinctly stated by Wortis (1972):

An IQ score, at best, can indicate where an individual stands in intellectual performance compared to others. What others? His nation? His social class? His ethnic group? No intelligence test that has ever been devised can surmount all of these complicating considerations and claim universal validity. (p. 22)

Wortis's point has been widely accepted and echoed by other observers.

Although the assessment of social competence may seem less complicated, especially if it is based on clinical observations and ratings, it is subject to many of the same errors as the measurement of intelligence. The criteria used by the person or persons doing the assessing are of particular importance. For example, if children are well-adapted socially to life in an urban ghetto but not to the demands of a formal school setting, should they be evaluated as having a high, intermediate, or low level of social competence? Competence for what? Again, Wortis's conclusions concerning the assessment of intelligence appear to apply.

To label a child as mentally retarded—as significantly subaverage in intellectual and adaptive capability—is an act likely to have profound effects on both the child's self-concept and the reactions of others, and thus on his or her entire future life. Most immediately, it may lead to institutionalization or to poor upbringing by discouraged, demoralized parents (Richardson, Koller, & Katz, 1985). Over the long term, such a label may become a self-fulfilling prophecy fueled by the tendency to behave in ways consistent with one's self-concept and with others' expectations. Obviously it is a label that has profound ethical and social implications and should never be affixed to anyone without the most careful and considered judgment.

■ Treatments, Outcomes, and Prevention

A number of programs have demonstrated that significant changes in adaptive capacity are possible through special education and other rehabilitative measures. The degree of change that can be expected is related, of course, to an individual's particular situation and level of mental retardation.

Treatment Facilities and Methods   One problem that often inflicts great anxiety on the parents of a mentally retarded child is whether or not to put their child in an institution. In general, the children who are institutionalized fall into two groups: (a) those who, in infancy and childhood, manifest severe mental retardation and associated physical impairment, and who enter an institution at an early age; and (b) those who have no physical impairments but show mild mental retardation and a failure to adjust socially in adolescence, eventually being institutionalized chiefly because of delinquency or other problem behavior. In these cases, social incompetence is the main factor in the decision. The families of those in the first group come from all socioeconomic levels, whereas a significantly higher percentage of the families of those in the second group come from lower educational and occupational strata.

Studies suggest that, in general, mentally retarded children are likely to show better emotional and mental development in a favorable home situation than in an institution (Golden & Davis, 1974). Thus, institutionalization is not generally recommended where a child is making a reasonably satisfactory adjustment at home and in school. Such a conclusion, however, must be tempered with the observation that most institutions for the retarded are decidedly substandard. In a classic study, Skeels (1966) demonstrated that an extraordinarily rich institutional environment can produce dramatic and lasting improvements in both IQ (an average gain of 28 points) and general adaptability among children originally diagnosed as mildly retarded.

The effect of being institutionalized in adolescence depends heavily, of course, on an institution's facilities as well as on individual factors. For the many retarded teenagers who do not have families in a position to take care of them, community-oriented residential care seems particularly promising (Alexander, Huganir, & Zigler, 1985; Landesman-Dwyer, 1981; Seidl, 1974; Thacher, 1978).

Fortunately, as we have seen, most retarded individuals do not need to be institutionalized. For those who do, however, state institutions for the mentally retarded are often desperately overcrowded and woefully inadequate in terms of the quality of care and special education programs offered (Robinson & Robinson, 1976; Tarjan et al., 1973). In 1970 the President's Committee on Mental Retardation reported that in many instances such facilities were no better than prisoner-of-war camps. Since then, some facilities have been greatly improved, but most lack the necessary funds and personnel to provide high-quality enhancement programs. Moreover, most private facilities—which are often, but not always, superior to public ones—are beyond the financial means of even the average family. With rare exceptions, they are hopelessly out of reach of the socioeconomic group most in need of them.

For the mentally retarded who do not require institutionalization, educational and training facilities have also been inadequate. In 1970 an estimated two million mentally retarded people who could have used job training and become self-supporting members of their communities were not getting this

In many more cases than had once been thought possible, institutionalized individuals have been able to get along in the community with adequate preparation and help, such as training in vocational and social skills. In the last 20 years there has been a rapid increase in alternate forms of care for the mentally retarded, and new techniques, materials, and specially trained teachers are producing encouraging results.

training (President's Committee on Mental Retardation, 1970). Although conditions may have since improved somewhat, it still appears that the majority of mentally retarded people in the United States are never reached by services appropriate to their specific needs (Tyor & Bell, 1984).

This neglect is especially tragic in view of what we now know about helping these individuals. For example, classes for the mildly retarded, which usually emphasize reading and other basic school subjects, budgeting and money matters, and the development of occupational skills, have succeeded in helping many people become independent, productive community members.

Classes for the moderately and severely retarded usually have more limited objectives, but they emphasize the development of self-care and other skills that enable individuals to function adequately and to be of assistance in either a family or institutional setting. Just mastering toilet training and learning to eat and dress properly may mean the difference between remaining at home and being placed elsewhere.

In many more cases than had once been thought possible, institutionalized individuals have been able to get along in the community with adequate preparation and help. For example, Clark, Kivitz, and Rosen (1969) reported on a special project undertaken at the Elwyn Institute in Pennsylvania.

The goal of this program was the successful discharge to independent living in the community of the institutionalized mentally retarded. The entire staff was oriented toward rehabilitation; emphasis was placed on the development of practical vocational skills; special programs provided remedial teaching and the learning of socialization skills; and counseling and assessment assured the individualization of training to meet each person's needs. As a result of this program, many mentally retarded persons who had been institutionalized for from 2 to 49 years were discharged and obtained skilled or semiskilled jobs in the community while coping successfully with everyday problems. Some married and had families; none had to be readmitted to the institutions. (p. 82)

Today about 70 percent of the approximately 150,000 individuals still in institutions for the retarded are severely or profoundly retarded. Even many of these individuals are being helped to be partly self-supporting in community programs (Brown, 1977; Landesman-Dwyer, 1981; Robinson & Robinson, 1976; Rodman & Collins, 1974; Sullivan & Batareh, 1973; Thacher, 1978; Zucker & Altman, 1973). These developments reflect both the new optimism that has come to prevail and also, in many instances, new laws and judicial decisions favorable to the rights of retarded individuals and their families. A notable example is Public Law 94-142, passed by Congress in 1975. This statute, termed the Education for All Handicapped Children Act, asserts the right of mentally retarded people to be educated at public expense in "the least restrictive environment" possible.

During the 1970s, there was a rapid increase in alternate forms of care for the mentally retarded (Tyor & Bell, 1984). These include, but are not limited to, the use of decentralized regional facilities for short-term evaluation and training; small private hospitals specializing in rehabilitative techniques; group homes or "halfway houses" integrated into the local community; nursing homes for the elderly retarded; the placement of severely retarded children in more "enriched" foster-home environments; and varied forms of support to the family for own-home care.

Many of these varied programs are still too new to permit comprehensive evaluation of their long-range effectiveness with different groups of retarded people and differing levels of retardation. At the least, however, it is clear that they provide a much expanded flexibility in considering the needs of any given retarded individual at any particular point in his or her development and rehabilitation (Clarke, Clarke, & Berg, 1985; Robinson & Robinson,

1976). Unfortunately, these gains tend to be distributed in a spotty and inconsistent manner throughout the nation. In addition, many programs still overuse potent medications such as neuroleptics (antipsychotics), whose therapeutic purpose in this area, apart from chemical straight-jacketing, is obscure (Breuning & Poling, 1982). In one study of this problem among a random sample of *noninstitutionalized* mentally retarded people, no fewer than 58 percent of them were found to be taking prescribed drugs of this sort (Davis, Cullari, & Breuning, 1982). In light of the sometimes serious side effects of these drugs, such prescribing verges, in our view, on medical malpractice.

Although much remains to be learned about the most effective educational and training procedures to use with the mentally retarded—particularly the moderate and severe types—new techniques, materials, and specially trained teachers have produced encouraging results. For example, computer-assisted instruction has been introduced in Canadian programs for the retarded and has been found to be more efficient as well as less expensive than traditional tutor-guided instruction (Brebner, Hallworth, & Brown, 1977; Hallworth, 1977). New uses for the computer in this field are developing at a rapid rate (Lovett, 1985). Operant conditioning methods are being used increasingly to teach a wide variety of skills (Kiernan, 1985). Specifically targeted independence training in various everyday functions shows great promise (Matson, 1981). A technique for teaching improved thinking skills, developed by Reuven Feuerstein in Israel, has been extensively evaluated and produces substantial, though not spectacular, improvements in cognitive functioning (e.g., Arbitman-Smith, Haywood, & Bransford, 1984).

Typically, educational and training procedures involve mapping out target areas of improvement, such as personal grooming, social behavior, basic academic skills, and simple occupational skills (for retarded adults). Within each area, specific skills are divided into simple components that can be learned and reinforced before more complex behaviors are required. Target areas are not selected arbitrarily, of course, but realistically reflect the requirements of an individual's life situation and his or her level of competence. Training that builds on step-by-step progression and is guided by such realistic considerations can bring retarded individuals repeated experiences of success and lead to substantial progress even by those previously regarded as uneducable.

For more mildly retarded youngsters, the question of what schooling is best is likely to vex both parents and school officials. For many years, organized parents' groups have fought an uphill battle to ensure the availability of special education classes for retarded children in the public schools, having learned that isolation from peers tends to compound the problem. Too often, however, success in getting a retarded child into a public school has meant that the child is treated as very special indeed and—along with other retarded students—becomes isolated *within* the school.

We have now learned that this type of "special" education may have serious limitations in terms of a child's social and educational development, and that many such children fare better by attending regular classes for at least much of the day. Of course, this type of approach—called **mainstreaming**—does require careful planning, a high level of teacher skill, and facilitative teacher attitudes (Birns & Bridger, 1977; Borg & Ascione, 1982; Budoff, 1977; Hanrahan et al., 1990).

Indeed, a great deal of research in recent years has led to the conclusion that mainstreaming is not the hoped-for panacea (Gottlieb, 1981). In terms of administration, such programs are difficult to launch and to maintain (Lieberman, 1982); their success (or lack of it) seems to depend largely on such change-resistant influences as teacher attitudes and overall classroom climate (Haywood, Meyers, & Switsky, 1982; Miller, 1989). Moreover, any educational gains may come at the expense of deficits in self-esteem suffered by handicapped children as they interact intensively with more cognitively advantaged peers (Haywood, Meyers, & Switsky, 1982). Gresham (1982) argues that such dangers may be decreased or eliminated if retarded children are given social skills training prior to their entry into a mainstream classroom. Recently, a variant of mainstreaming called the Parallel Alternate Curriculum program, which emphasizes specialized instruction in a regular classroom setting, has shown much promise. Even here, however, much attention must be given to teaching-staff development (Chandler, 1985; Smith & Smith, 1985).

A reasonable conclusion at this time is that school systems should not attempt mainstreaming without a great deal of advance planning and preparation. In other words, mere window-dressing to achieve an appearance of progressive educational practice is not enough; the system's leadership must be thoroughly committed to overcoming deeply entrenched attitudes and procedures within the education bureaucracy to ensure the success of the effort.

New Frontiers in Prevention   The problem of preventing mental retardation involves the need to control a wide range of biological and sociocul-

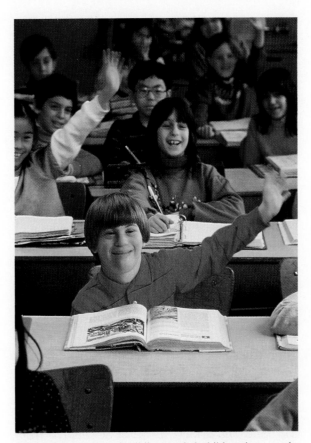

The mainstreaming of mildly retarded children into regular classes for much of the day requires careful planning and a high level of teacher skill and facilitative teacher attitudes.

tural conditions. Inevitably, it is a problem concerned with human development in general.

Until recently, the most hopeful preventive approaches have been through routine health measures for pregnant women and their newborns and the use of diagnostic measures to ensure the early detection and, if possible, correction of aberrant biological processes. In recent years, however, two new frontiers have opened up. The first involves work in genetics that has revealed the role of certain genetic defects in faulty development, as in Tay-Sachs disease. Investigators have devised tests to identify parents who have these faulty genes, thus making it possible to provide them with genetic counseling. Over 200 clinics now exist in the United States where such counseling is available.

The second frontier in prevention involves the alleviation of sociocultural conditions that deprive children of the stimulation, motivation, and opportunities necessary for normal learning and the full development of mental capacities. In this connection, Keniston (1977) said,

It is time to match the strong American tradition of healing individual parents and children with equal efforts to change the factors that make those parents and children need healing. To put it another way, it is time for Americans to start holding the social and economic institutions of our society just as accountable for their influence on family life as we traditionally have held parents. (p. 6)

Birns and Bridger (1977), in basic agreement, emphasized that social reforms will need to include a revamping of the educational system to serve better the varying needs of all children. This "new horizon" was well delineated by President John F. Kennedy:

Studies have demonstrated that large numbers of children in urban and rural slums, including preschool children, lack the stimulus necessary for proper development in their intelligence. Even when there is no organic impairment, prolonged neglect and a lack of stimulus and opportunity for learning can result in the failure of young minds to develop. Other studies have shown that, if proper opportunities for learning are provided early enough, many of these deprived children can and will learn and achieve as much as children from more favored neighborhoods. The self-perpetuating intellectual blight should not be allowed to continue. (1963, p. 286)

President Kennedy's report directed the attention of the nation to the tragic and costly problem of mental retardation. It was not until 1970, however—when the President's Committee on Mental Retardation, the American Psychological Association, and other concerned organizations stressed the necessity for a "broad spectrum" approach—that real impetus was given to implementing essential measures for the prevention of mental retardation. This broad spectrum approach focused on three ways of providing a more supportive sociocultural setting to prevent children from being harmed by adverse environmental conditions:

1. *Application of existing knowledge.* The first phase of this approach involved the provision of more adequate medical and general health care for mother and baby prior to, during, and after pregnancy—particularly for the socially disadvantaged and other high-risk groups.

2. *Community services.* Next, the approach focused on the provision of community-centered facilities that would provide a coordinated range of diagnostic, health, education, employment, rehabilitation, and related services. This phase of the program included the training of needed personnel.

A particularly important development in this area has involved efforts to reach high-risk children early with the intensive cognitive stimulation believed to underlie the sound development of mental ability. Project Head Start is a well-known example operating at the local community level, one whose effectiveness is difficult to measure and remains somewhat controversial (Gamble & Zigler, 1989). At the national level, a similar intention has been manifested in specialized television programming for children, such as "Sesame Street" and "Reading Rainbow." Rigorous assessment of the effectiveness of such efforts has never been completed, but they do appear to have positive effects on many children. Somewhat ironically, the children who seem to benefit most from these efforts are the children least in need of them—the children of relatively affluent families in which education is strongly valued and in which the parents are likely to encourage their children to watch enriching television programming.

Also somewhat sobering is the possibility that the educational performance of Head Start children increases primarily because of temporarily enhanced motivation rather than higher rates of cognitive development (Zigler et al., 1982). Where the environment continues to be debilitative over time, the gain for many youngsters exposed to short-term enrichment programs may be lost (Garber, 1988; Gray & Ramsey, 1982). Obviously, much remains to be learned and done in the area of maintaining early gains. Where notable and sustainable gains have been unequivocally demonstrated, as in the relatively lavish program described by Skeels (1966), the initial financial investment may be so great as to strain community resources—thus attracting the kind of short-sighted political opposition commonly directed at expensive "social" programs. The irony is that the money is spent anyway, usually at compounded rates of increase, on such things as ADC (welfare-based aid to dependent children), chronic institutionalization, correctional facilities, and the "war on drugs."

3. *Research.* Finally, emphasis was placed on the facilitation and acceleration of research on all phases of the problem: causality, educational procedures, social effects on the family, psychological effects on the individual, and the changing role and functions of state and community agencies.

Unfortunately, the federal initiatives begun by the Kennedy administration have eroded over the years. Demands on the federal budget for programs

Project Head Start is a well-known example of a community-centered effort to reach high-risk children with the intensive cognitive stimulation that is thought to be necessary for the sound development of mental ability.

seen as having greater national priority have increased, and the funds committed for helping the retarded have suffered devaluation through inflation. Beginning with the Nixon administration of the early 1970s, there were serious cutbacks in training and research in all of the mental health disciplines. The trend has become worse since that time as the national debt has increased to unprecedented levels and as many states have likewise experienced severe fiscal problems. As a result, we have not been able to capitalize fully on our increased understanding of how to reverse or prevent the deficits experienced by mentally retarded youngsters and adults.

PERVASIVE DEVELOPMENTAL DISORDER: AUTISM

The DSM-III-R category involving pervasive developmental disorders includes several severe psychological disorders marked by serious distortions in psychological functioning. These problems cover a wide range of behaviors, including deficits in language, perceptual, and motor development; defective reality testing; and an inability to function in social situations. The term **pervasive developmental disorder** was new with DSM-III, although the disorders included under this category have a long history under the names *symbiotic psychosis in children* and *early infantile autism*. The term *pervasive developmental disorders* was chosen over other possibilities because it focuses on the severe and extensive

developmental deficits present in children with these disorders (Gillberg, 1990). We will focus here on the pervasive developmental disorder that has received the greatest amount of attention from researchers—**autistic disorder**—whose central feature is a profound and unyielding imperviousness, or unresponsiveness, to the human environment. The following case illustrates some of the behaviors that may be seen in an autistic child:

The boy is five years old. When spoken to, he turns his head away. Sometimes he mumbles unintelligibly. He is neither toilet trained nor able to feed himself. He actively resists being touched. He dislikes sounds. He cannot relate to others and avoids looking anyone in the eye. He often engages in routine manipulative activities, such as dropping an object, picking it up, and dropping it again. While seated, he often rocks back and forth in a rhythmic motion for hours. Any change in routine is highly upsetting to him. He is in a school for severely disturbed children at UCLA. His diagnosis is childhood autism.

Autism in infancy and childhood was first described by Kanner (1943). It afflicts some 80,000 American children—about 4 children in 10,000—and occurs about four or five times more frequently among boys than girls (Schreibman & Koegel, 1975; Ritvo, Freeman, Pingree, et al., 1989; Steffenburg and Gillberg, 1986; Werry, 1979). It is usually identified before a child is 30 months of age (Rutter, 1978) and often is suspected in the early weeks of life. Autistic children come from all socio-economic levels, ethnic backgrounds, and family patterns. It was once believed that autism was more prevalent among families in upper socioeconomic levels; however, this finding may have been due to the particular sampling methods used in earlier studies (Wing, 1980). The recent epidemiological survey by Ritvo et al. (1989) has supported the view that autism is not associated with parental education, occupation, racial origin, or religion.

■ The Clinical Picture in Autistic Disorder

Autistic children form a heterogeneous population, with varying degrees of impairments and capabilities. In this section we will discuss some of the behaviors that may be evident in autism. A cardinal and typical sign is that a child seems apart or aloof from others, even in the earliest stages of life. Mothers often remember such babies as never being "cuddly," never reaching out when being picked up, never smiling or looking at them while being fed, and never appearing to notice the comings and goings of other people. Typically, autistic children do not show any need for affection or contact with anyone, usually not even seeming to know or care who their parents are.

The absence or severely restricted use of speech is characteristic of autistic children. If speech is present, it is almost never used to communicate except in the most rudimentary fashion, as by saying "yes" in answer to a question or by the use of **echolalia** (parrotlike repetition of a few words). Although the echoing of parents' verbal behavior is found to a small degree in normal children as they experiment with their ability to produce articulate speech, persistent echolalia is found in about 75 percent of autistic children (Prizant, 1983). Some research has focused on trying to understand if echolalia in autistic children is functional. Prizant and Duchan (1981) analyzed echolalic verbalizations—previously believed to be meaningless—according to tone, latency, and other speech characteristics. They concluded that, far from being meaningless, these verbalizations could aid clinicians or researchers in understanding the communicative and cognitive functioning of autistic children. Nevertheless, these utterances remain highly cryptic and are, of course, an inadequate substitute for true language functioning.

On the basis of their intensive study of 53 autistic children, Clancy and McBride (1969) suggested that the usual picture of an autistic child as lacking in language ability and being wholly with-

drawn is probably oversimplified. They found that at least some autistic children do comprehend language, even though they may not use it to express themselves. These investigators pointed to the occasional normal commencement of language development, followed by its disappearance as the autistic process becomes manifest. Perhaps even more significantly, they found evidence that the autistic children they studied were very much aware of—and actively involved with—their environments:

Autistic children actively seek to arrange the environment on their terms, and so as to exclude certain elements, e.g., intervention from other people and variety in any aspect of routine. (p. 243)

Often autistic children show an active aversion to auditory stimuli, crying even at the sound of a parent's voice. The pattern is not always consistent, however; autistic children "may at one moment be severely agitated or panicked by a very soft sound and at another time be totally oblivious to loud noise" (Ritvo & Ornitz, 1970, p. 6).

Self-stimulation is characteristic of these children, usually taking the form of such repetitive movements as head banging, spinning, and rocking, which may continue by the hour. Other bizarre as well as repetitive behavior is typical. Such behavior is well described by Gajzago and Prior (1974) in the case of a young autistic boy:

A was described as a screaming, severely disturbed child who ran around in circles making high-pitched sounds for hours. He also liked to sit in boxes, under mats, and [under] blankets. He habitually piled up all furniture and bedding in the center of the room. At times he was thought deaf—though he also showed extreme fear of loud noises. He refused all food except in a bottle, refused to wear clothes, chewed stones and paper, whirled himself, and spun objects. . . . He played repetitively with the same toys for months, lining things in rows, collected objects such as bottle tops, and insisted on having two of everything, one in each hand. He became extremely upset if interrupted and if the order or arrangement of things were altered. (p. 264)

In contrast to the behavior just described, some autistic children are skilled at fitting objects together. Thus their performance on puzzles or form boards may be average or above. Even in the manipulation of objects, however, difficulty with meaning is apparent. For example, when pictures are to be arranged in an order that tells a story, autistic children show a marked deficiency in performance.

Callum, at left, is thought to have autism, and Ryan, at right, is a normal child. Autism may be difficult to diagnose early, but some of the symptoms are apparent in these video sequences of Callum and Ryan. Autistic children are deficient in two-way communication and social interaction. Callum attends to the shaving cream, but only to the shaving cream, and is oblivious to his father's presence; Ryan, on the other hand, is also delighted with the shaving cream but brings everyone else around him into his play. He is skilled at communication even without words. Callum seemingly doesn't know how things happen or how to make them happen again. For him, each experience is a separate event, with no connection to anything or anyone else. The inability of a young child like Callum to interact with his parents in all the subtle ways that most babies do can result in a socially deficient individual.

Although some have regarded autistic children as potentially of normal intelligence, this view has been challenged by a number of investigators who consider many if not most of these children to be mentally retarded (Goodman, 1972). Prior and Wherry (1986) reported that about three-fourths of autistic children were mentally retarded. Some autistic children, however, show markedly discrepant abilities, such as astounding memory capabilities, as Dustin Hoffman depicted in the award-winning motion picture *Rain Man*. In this context, Goodman described the case of an "autistic-savant" who showed unusual ability at an early age in calendar calculating (rapidly determining the day of any calendar date in history) as well as in other areas, such as naming the capitals of most states and countries. Nevertheless, his language development was severely retarded, and he showed the indifference to others and related symptoms characteristic of autistic children.

Much has been learned recently about the cognitive deficits of autistic children (Wenar, 1990). When compared with other groups of children on cognitive or intellectual tasks, autistic children often show impairment (James & Barry, 1981; Ritvo & Freeman, 1978; Schopler, 1983). Boucher (1981), for example, found autistic children signifi-

cantly impaired on memory tasks when compared with both normal and retarded children. Whether this cognitive impairment is the result of actual organic brain damage or of motivational deficits has not been established. Koegel and Mentis (1985) have raised the possibility that the deficits result from motivational differences; they found that autistic children can learn and perform tasks at a higher level if motivation for a task is found and appropriate reinforcement is provided.

Many autistic children become preoccupied with and form strong attachments to unusual objects, such as rocks, light switches, film negatives, or keys. In some instances the object is so large or bizarre that merely carrying it around interferes with other activities. When their preoccupation with the object is disturbed—for example, by its removal or by attempts to substitute something in its place—or when anything familiar in their environment is altered even slightly, they may have a violent temper tantrum or a crying spell that continues until the familiar situation is restored. Thus autistic children are often said to be "obsessed with the maintenance of sameness." Furthermore, autistic children have been referred to as "negativistic" because they seemingly do not comply with requests. However, a study by Volkmar, Hoder, and

Cohen (1985) found that, under the carefully structured and reinforcing conditions in a clinic setting, autistic children were not negativistic and generally complied with requests made by staff.

In summary, autistic children typically show difficulties in relationships to other people, in perceptual-cognitive functioning, in language development, and in the development of a sense of identity (L. K. Wing, 1976). They also engage in bizarre and repetitive activities, demonstrate a fascination with unusual objects, and show an obsessive need to maintain environmental sameness. This is indeed a heavy set of handicaps.

Because the clinical picture in autism tends to blend almost imperceptibly with that in schizophrenia, a differential diagnosis is often difficult to make. The chief distinguishing feature appears to be the age of onset, with autism becoming evident very early and schizophrenia appearing more gradually and much later—typically not until adolescence or early adulthood—after several years of apparently normal development. As Bettelheim (1969) has put it, "While the schizophrenic child withdraws from the world, the autistic child fails to ever enter it" (p. 21).

■ Causal Factors in Autism

No brain pathology has been delineated in infant or childhood autism. Because it does not, in general, appear to run in families, it cannot be attributed directly to a hereditary defect. In a review of the genetic factors in autism and childhood schizophrenia, Smalley (1991) found no evidence for a genetic basis of autism. In a series of papers reviewing various types of evidence relating to both organic deficit and genetic factors in autism, Sanua (1986a, 1986b, 1987) concluded that no such contributions to the disorder have been unequivocally demonstrated. He points out, correctly in our judgment, that many investigators and commentators in this field have made uninformed and apparently biased assumptions about the true quality of the evidence tending to show an etiologic role for genetic or organic brain anomalies. On critical appraisal, the evidence is in fact quite weak.

The possibility remains, however, that defective genes or damage from radiation or other conditions during prenatal development may play a role in the etiologic picture. It seems likely at this point that the disorder we call autism involves both multiple kinds of deficit (Goodman, 1989) and multiple etiologic pathways (Gillberg, 1990). Thus we should perhaps not expect to find large risk factors accounting for autistic outcomes, nor even excep-

tional levels of consistency from one study to another where differing samples of autistic youngsters have been evaluated. For example, although Goldfine et al. (1985) failed to find the Fragile X chromosomal abnormality in a carefully selected group of 37 autistic children, such an anomaly could still make an etiologic contribution in given instances of the disorder (Bolton et al., 1989). Even subtler constitutional defects cannot of course be ruled out. In fact, most investigators believe that autism begins with some type of inborn defect that impairs an infant's perceptual-cognitive functioning—the ability to process incoming stimulation and to relate to the world. In support of possible genetic factors in autism (perhaps a familial subtype of the disorder), Ritvo et al. (1989) found that 9.7 percent of the affected families had more than one autistic offspring.

In his early studies of childhood autism, Kanner (1943) concluded that an innate disorder in a child is exacerbated by a cold and unresponsive mother, the first factor resulting in social withdrawal and the second tending to maintain this isolation. Most investigators, however, have failed to find the parents of autistic children to be "emotional refrigerators" (Schreibman & Koegel, 1975; Wolff & Morris, 1971). In a well-controlled study, McAdoo and De Myer (1978) found that the personality characteristics of parents of autistic children were not significantly different from those of parents of other types of disturbed children. They also discovered that the mothers of both autistic and disturbed children had significantly fewer psychological problems than did mothers who were being seen as patients in mental health settings.

As Harlow (1969) somewhat wryly pointed out, it is often extremely difficult to pinpoint cause and effect in studying relationships between mother and child:

Possibly . . . some children are rendered autistic by maternal neglect and insufficiency, but it is even more likely that many more mothers are rendered autistic because of an inborn inability of their infants to respond affectionately to them in any semblance of an adequate manner. (p. 29)

Tinbergen (1974) viewed autism as the result of an approach-avoidance conflict in which a child's natural tendency to explore and relate to the world is overbalanced by aversive experiences and fear. According to this view, instead of venturing forth into the world, such children withdraw into a world they create for themselves. This withdrawal, however, is not as haphazard or disorderly as it may seem; rather, it involves systematic avoidance of particular stimuli and events, including people. Some studies also indicate that metabolic processes in the brain are involved in autism (Rumsey et al., 1985).

Clearly, much remains to be learned about the etiology of childhood autism. It appears most reasonable to suppose, however, that this disorder normally begins with an inborn defect or defects in brain functioning, regardless of what other causal factors may subsequently become involved.

■ Treatments and Outcomes

Medical treatment of autistic children has often been tried but has not proven effective (Rutter, 1985). The drug most often used in the treatment of autism is Haloperidol, but the data on its effectiveness do not warrant use unless a child's behavior is unmanageable by other means (Sloman, 1991). We will thus direct our attention to a variety of psychological procedures that have been more successful in treating autistic children.

Bettelheim (1967, 1969, 1974), at the Orthogenic School of the University of Chicago, reported some success in treating autistic children with a program of warm, loving acceptance accompanied by reinforcement procedures, as can be seen in the case of Joey described in *HIGHLIGHT 14.5*. Similarly, Marchant and her associates (1974) in England have reported improvement using a method for introducing "graded change" into the environment of autistic children, thus tending to shift their behavior gradually from self-defeating to growth-oriented activities.

Another approach to treating autistic children is called **structural therapy.** In this approach the environment is structured to provide spontaneous physical and verbal stimulation in a playful and gamelike manner. The goal of this approach is to increase the amount and variety of stimuli for these children, gradually making them more aware of themselves and more related to their environment. The results of structural therapy have been encouraging, with 12 of 21 cases considered improved enough to be able to return home after the three-year treatment program (Ward, 1978). In another study involving social skills training, the majority of the treated children showed definite improvements in their peer relationships (Williams, 1989).

In an extensive study of autistic children who were mentally retarded, socially unresponsive, and behaviorally disturbed, Bartak and his colleagues at the Maudsley Hospital in England obtained significant results with educational procedures. Children who were assigned to a structured treatment unit focusing on formal schooling showed greater prog-

ress than those placed in units stressing play therapy, either free or structured (Bartak & Rutter, 1973; Russell, 1975). As a result of this work, Bartak (1978) suggested a "qualified optimism" for the educational progress of autistic children. The best predictor of a positive outcome in the treatment of autism, according to Bartak and Rutter (1976), is intelligence.

Behavior therapy in an institutional setting has been used successfully in the elimination of self-injurious behavior, the mastery of the fundamentals of social behavior, and the development of some language skills (Lovaas, 1977; Lovaas, Schaeffer, & Simmons, 1974; Williams, Koegel, & Egel, 1981). Lovaas (1987) reported highly positive results from a long-term experimental treatment program of autistic children. Of the treated children, 47 percent achieved normal intellectual functioning and another 40 percent attained the mildly retarded level. In comparison, only 2 percent of the untreated, control children achieved normal functioning and 45 percent attained mildly retarded functioning. These remarkable results did, however, require a considerable staffing effort, with well-qualified therapists working 40 hours per week for two years. Interestingly, studies on the effectiveness of behavior therapy with institutionalized children have found that children who were discharged to their parents continued to improve, whereas those who remained in an institution tended to lose much of what they had gained (Lovaas, 1977; Schreibman & Koegel, 1975).

Wesley is moderately to severely autistic and, because he could not communicate in any meaningful way, was thought to be retarded. When introduced to an electronic keyboard that displays typed messages, however, Wesley began, over a period of time, to type coherent messages to his mother and others, without ever having been taught to read or write. This remarkable feat raises questions about the role of mental retardation in autism: Are autistic individuals lacking in intelligence or are they simply unable to communicate in understandable ways?

HIGHLIGHT 14.5

Joey: A "Mechanical Boy"

These four pictures were drawn by Joey, an autistic boy who entered the Sonia Shankman Orthogenic School of the University of Chicago at the age of 9. His unusual case history has been reported by Bettelheim (1959).

Joey presumably denied his own emotions because they were unbearably painful. Apparently not daring to be human in a world that he felt had rejected him, Joey withdrew into a world of fantasy and perceived himself as a machine that "functioned as if by remote control." This idea is brought out in drawing 1—a self-portrait in which Joey depicts himself as an electrical robot. Bettelheim interpreted this portrait as symbolizing Joey's rejection of human feelings.

So elaborately constructed and acted out was Joey's mechanical character that "entering the dining room, for example, he would string an imaginary wire from his 'energy source'—an imaginary electrical outlet—to the table. There he 'insulated' himself with paper napkins and finally plugged himself in. Only then could Joey eat, for he firmly believed that the 'current' ran his ingestive apparatus" (p. 117).

Joey's performance was convincing—so much so that others found themselves responding to him as a mechanical boy rather than as a human being: ". . . one had to look twice to be sure there was neither wire nor outlet nor plug. Children and members of our staff . . . avoided stepping on the 'wires' for fear of interrupting what seemed the source of his very life." When his machinery was idle, Joey "would sit so quietly that he would disappear from the focus of the most conscientious observation. Yet in the next moment he might be 'working' and the center of our captivated attention" (p. 117).

In his report on Joey, Bettelheim alluded to the painfully slow process by which Joey was eventually able to establish true relations with other human beings. Three of the drawings depict part of the process. In the earliest of the three (drawing 2), Joey portrays himself "as an electrical 'papoose,' completely enclosed, suspended in empty space and operated by wire-

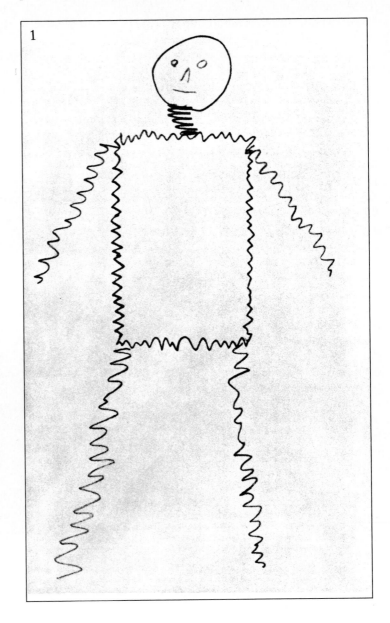

1

less signals." In the next one (drawing 3), he apparently demonstrates increasing self-esteem, for although he is still operated by wireless signals, he is much larger in stature. In the final drawing (drawing 4), Joey depicts "the machine which controls him," but in this one, unlike the previous drawings, "he has acquired hands with which he can manipulate his immediate environment" (p. 119).

When Joey was 12—three years after he had entered the school—". . . he made a float for our Memorial Day parade. It carried the slogan: 'Feelings are more important than anything under the sun.' Feelings, Joey had learned, are what make for humanity; their absence, for a mechanical existence. With this knowledge Joey entered the human condition" (p. 127).

Some of the most impressive results with autistic children have been obtained in projects that involve parents, with treatment in the home preferable to hospital-based therapy (Rutter, 1985; Schopler, Mesibov, & Baker, 1982). Treatment "contracts" with parents specify the desired behavior changes in their child and spell out the explicit techniques for bringing about these changes. Such contracting acknowledges the value of the parents as potential change agents—in contrast with the previously held belief that the parents were somehow to blame for their child's disorder (Schopler, 1978). Perhaps the most favorable results are those of Schreibman and Koegel (1975), who reported successful outcomes in the treatment of 10 of 16 autistic children. These investigators relied heavily on the use of parents as therapists to reinforce normal behavior in their children. They concluded that autism is potentially a "defeatable horror."

It is too early to evaluate the long-term effectiveness of these newer treatment methods or the degree of improvement they actually bring about. The prognosis for autistic children, particularly for children showing symptoms before the age of 2, is poor (Hoshino et al., 1980). Traditionally, the long-term results of autism treatments have been unfavorable. A great deal of attention has been given recently to high-functioning autistic children (children who meet the criteria for autism yet develop functional speech). Ritvo et al. (1988) studied 11 parents whom they believed met diagnostic criteria for autism (they were identified through having had children who were autistic). These individuals had been able to make modest adjustments to life, hold down jobs, and get married. The outcome in autism is often problematic, however. Clarke et al. (1989) followed up five high-functioning autistic children and found that four of them later developed symptoms of psychosis.

One important factor limiting treatment success is the problems autistic children experience in generalizing behavior outside the treatment context (Handleman, Gill, & Alessandri, 1988). Children with severe developmental disabilities do not transfer skills across situations very well. Consequently, learned behavior in one situation does not appear to help them meet challenges in others. This important component needs to be addressed if training or treatment programs are to be successful. Even with intensive long-term care in a clinical facility, where gratifying improvements may be brought about in specific behaviors, children are a long way from becoming "normal." Gillberg and Schaumann (1981) have noted that some autistic children make substantial improvement during childhood, only to deteriorate, showing symptom aggravation, at the onset of puberty. Less than one-fourth of the autistic children who receive treatment appear to attain even marginal adjustment in later life.

SPECIFIC DEVELOPMENTAL DISORDERS: LEARNING DISABILITIES

In contrast to pervasive developmental disorders such as autism, **specific developmental disorders** have a circumscribed character and may occur in children who are otherwise normal or even gifted in their overall functioning. The inadequate development may be manifested in academic, language, speech, or motor skills areas, and it is not due to any demonstrable physical or neurological defect. The diagnosis is restricted to those cases in which there is clear impairment in school performance or (if the person is not a student) in daily living activities, not due to mental retardation or a pervasive developmental disorder. By implication, skill deficits due to attention-deficit hyperactivity disorder, described in Chapter 15, are coded under that diagnosis. This coding presents another diagnostic dilemma because some investigators hold that an attentional deficit is basic to many learning disorders. In any event, we will focus in this section on specific developmental disorders involving academic skills, also known as **specific learning disabilities,** or—in DSM-III-R terms—academic skills disorders. Children with these disorders are more generally said to be **learning disabled (LD).** Significantly more boys than girls are diagnosed as learning disabled, but proportional estimates of this gender discrepancy have varied widely from study to study.

■ The Clinical Picture in Learning Disabilities

LD children are identified as such because of a disparity between their expected academic achievement level and their actual academic performance in one or more of the traditional school subjects, such as math, spelling, writing, or reading. (Reading problems are commonly known as **dyslexia.**) Typically, these children have full-scale IQs, family backgrounds, and exposure to cultural norms and symbols that are consistent with at least average achievement in school. They do not have obvious crippling emotional problems, nor do they seem to be lacking in motivation, cooperativeness, or eagerness to please their teachers and parents—at least not at the outset of their formal education. Nevertheless, they fail, often abysmally and usually with a stubborn, puzzling persistence. Why? As we will see, satisfactory answers are hard to come by.

Frustration for teachers, school officials, parents, professional helpers, and perhaps most notably for the victims themselves (although the last may go unnoticed in the general turmoil) is virtually guaranteed in this scenario, and it is likely to complicate efforts to find a solution. Wenar (1990) poignantly depicts the problem:

You are a child clinical psychologist. It has been a rough day. The climax was a phone call to the principal of Wykwyre Junior High School. It is the kind of suburban school in which children from two-swimming-pool families do not speak to children from one-swimming-pool families. The call had been about Jon Hastings, a 16-year-old with a long history of school failures. The intelligence test showed him to be bright enough to do college work, and yet he is only in the eighth grade. He is articulate, has a talent for making miniature rockets and speedboats, and a real flair for drawing cartoons. Yet the written word is Jon's nemesis. He reads laboriously one word at a time, while his writing is even more painfully slow. Because of repeated failures and because he is now a social misfit with peers, he has begun cutting up in class and talking back to the teacher.

You had phoned the principal to suggest ways of bypassing Jon's reading disability. Since he is sufficiently bright to absorb most of the lecture material, could he be given oral examinations every now and then? If he were taught to type, could he type instead of writing his examinations? Would the principal consider introducing special classes for all the learning-disabled children?

The principal was suave and ingratiating and a compendium of the resistances you have run up against in the past. He "understood your concern" but asked that you "look at the situation from my point of view." The school had "tried everything possible to no avail," "the boy is incorrigible," "you can't help a child unless the child wants help," and finally—you could feel this one coming, since you had heard it so often—"I can't give one student a favor without giving a favor to all of them. I'd have half the mothers in my office next day demanding something extra to pull their child's grades up." You had always doubted the validity of this "special-

favor" objection but had never found an effective way of countering it. Stalling for time you asked if you could come in and talk with the principal. He was most gracious. He would be happy to tell you about the school and have a student show you around—which was not at all what you had in mind.

A few years back an insightful but poorly educated mother had remarked, "When I get frustrations I come here and bring them to you. When you get frustrations, where do you put them?" The question comes back at times like these. (p. 197)

It is unfortunately the case that LD, despite its having been recognized as a distinct and rather common type of disorder for more than 30 years, and despite its having generated voluminous research literature, still fails to be accorded the status it deserves in many school jurisdictions. Instead, as in the preceding example, the familiar diversion of blaming the victim and of attributing the affected child's problems to various character deficiencies is still routinely employed by many classroom teachers and school administrators, whether in public or private settings. Where lockstep uniformity is the rule, as it is in most public and many "alternative" educational systems, a youngster who learns academic skills slowly or in a different way is treated as a troublesome pariah, as a threat to the prevailing theory of education. The consequences of these encounters between LD children and rigidly doctrinaire or regimented school systems can be disastrous to a child's self-esteem and general psychological well-being, and research indicates that these effects do not necessarily dissipate after secondary schooling ends (Bruck, 1987; Cato & Rice, 1982; Saracoglu, Minden, & Wilchesky, 1989). Thus even where LD difficulties are no longer a significant impediment, an individual may bear the scars of many painful school-related episodes into maturity and beyond.

■ Causal Factors in Learning Disabilities

Probably the most generally held view of the cause of specific learning disabilities is that they are the products of subtle central nervous system disorders. In particular, these disabilities are thought to result from some sort of immaturity, defect, or dysregulation limited to those brain areas supposedly mediating, for normal children, the behaviors that LD children cannot efficiently acquire. A few years back the term *minimal brain dysfunction (MBD)* was in

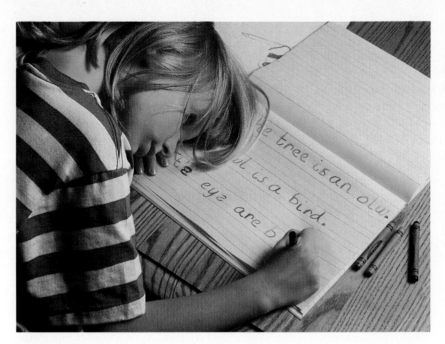

Dyslexia is a learning disability that interferes with the ability to read and write. This dyslexic student is transposing letters and writing other letters backward. Learning-disabled children, frustrated by their academic failures, may become social failures as well. If undiagnosed, these children may be seen by school authorities as troublesome and intractable, thus compounding their problems and further damaging their self-esteem. The long-term academic, social, and personal adjustment for those who grew up with undiagnosed dyslexia is generally discouraging, but there are important exceptions.

popular use to refer to such presumed organic malfunction—until it was generally recognized that nobody had the slightest idea what the term really meant. While some LD children show definite or highly suggestive evidence of brain disease, such as cerebral palsy, epilepsy, or a history of severe head trauma (e.g., Yule & Rutter, 1985), the large majority do not. In others, there may be subtle indications, "soft signs," of neurological compromise, but again such findings are by no means routine. Overall, no convincing evidence shows a specific dysfunction of the central nervous system among LD children generally (Schwartz & Johnson, 1985). The search for such factors has lessened in recent years, possibly because investigators have become discouraged by the meager available findings.

A variant of the central nervous system dysfunction hypothesis proposes some type of defect or imbalance in the brain's normal laterality—that is, in the tendency for specific functions to be localized to a large extent in either the right or the left side of the brain. Studies in this area, mainly concerned with dyslexia, have failed to produce a consistent or coherent set of findings (Kessler, 1988). They have also been plagued with many methodological shortcomings (Hynd & Semrud-Clikeman, 1989).

By this point you are unlikely to be surprised that some investigators believe the various forms of LD, or vulnerability to develop them, may be genetically transmitted. This issue seems not to have been studied with the same intensity or methodologic rigor as in other disorders. Two family pedigree

studies, those of Hallgren (1950) and Finucci et al. (1976), showed evidence of familial concordance for "reading disorders" (dyslexia), and Owen (1978) cites a twin study in which monozygosity was associated with 100 percent concordance for reading disorders. As we have seen in other contexts, the methods employed here do not permit a true separation of hereditary from environmental influences, but the magnitude of the concordances reported in all three studies is fairly impressive. The hypothesis of a genetic contribution to at least the dyslexic form of LD therefore remains tenable.

Summing up, biological or organic hypotheses concerning the etiology of LD, though widely held, tend to be rather vague on mechanisms and do not have an exceptionally strong record of evidence supporting them. They continue to have a sort of intuitive appeal that is at least as great as alternative psychosocial theories of causation.

Psychosocially based hypotheses about the origins of LD generally derive from psychodynamic, learning, or cognitive perspectives, or a combination of them. To date, none of them has sufficient empirical support to warrant extended discussion. The apparent complexity of the psychological processes involved in LD (see, for example, Ceci & Baker, 1987) evidently makes it difficult to do rigorous and definitive studies on potential causal factors. Thus the research that is available, most of it again directed to the problem of dyslexia, tends to be riddled with problems of subject selection, inappropriate controls, and other serious methodological flaws (Vellutino, 1987).

Despite what appears to be a multitude of seemingly differing factors involved in LD, there may yet be some common elements. This is the position taken by Worden (1986), who argues that we should study what is characteristic in the approaches taken by good learners to be able to identify the areas of significant weakness from which LD children suffer. He offers the following list as a beginning in this direction:

1. What *memory strategies* are used by normal or good learners, and in what manner do these differ from those employed by LD children?

2. How do normal or good learners *monitor* their ongoing performances? For example, how do good learners use performance information to gauge where they are being successful and where not, and to introduce corrective action as needed?

3. What *metastrategy information* is used by good learners and not by LD children? For example, do LD children understand the advantage of having a strategy at all, as in dealing with the time constraints of many school tasks?

4. What *motivates* good learners, and how does this differ from the motivation of poor learners? Is a learner's orientation one of seeking success or of avoiding failure? To what is success or failure attributed: oneself, task difficulty, chance, or some other factor?

Worden's approach to analyzing the complex issues involved in academic skill acquisition strikes us as a potentially useful beginning. However, even precise information on the manner in which LD children's learning approaches differ from those of normal children would still leave us with unanswered questions about the sources of these differences. Nevertheless, pursuit of this idea might produce a set of rational, fine-tuned strategies for intervening to correct LD children's inefficient modes of learning. We are not aware of any follow-up studies along this line.

■ Treatments and Outcomes

Because we obviously do not as yet have a confident grasp on what is "wrong" with the average LD child, we have not been too successful in treating these children. While many informal and single-case reports claim success for various treatment approaches, there are few well-designed and well-

executed outcome studies on specific treatments for LD problems. Focusing on reading disorders, where most of the effort appears to have been concentrated, Gittelman's (1983) review contains little evidence of impressive results. Moreover, any short-term gains that are made tend in many cases to diminish or even disappear over time (Yule & Rutter, 1985).

We have only limited data on the long-term, adult adjustments of people who grew up with the academic and social problems LD entails. Two recent studies of college students having LD (Gregg & Hoy, 1989; Saracoglu, Minden, & Wilchesky, 1989) suggested that as a group they continue to have problems—academic, personal, and social—into the postsecondary education years. Cato and Rice (1982) extracted from the available literature a lengthy list of somewhat discouraging problems experienced by the typical LD adult. These include—in addition to expected difficulties with self-confidence—continuing problems with deficits in the ordinary skills, such as math, that these people originally encountered as children. The authors did note, however, that there are considerable individual differences in these outcomes, thus reminding us that some adults with LD are able to manage very well.

UNRESOLVED ISSUES
on Cultural–Familial Retardation

The problem of cultural-familial mental retardation continues to be a baffling and frustrating one—complicated in no small measure by sensitive issues of race relations and imputed ethnic differences in native abilities. No scientifically respectable evidence in fact suggests that the quality of brain tissue is in any degree correlated with race or ethnicity. A great deal of evidence, on the other hand, shows that different ethnic groups, on average, vary considerably in performance on standardized tests designed to predict academic achievement. Unfortunately, we have long been encouraged to regard such tests as more or less directly measuring "intelligence," which they do not—unless one is willing to accept school grades as the primary defining element of that construct. IQ tests are and have always been validated primarily on their ability to predict school performance.

Schools may reasonably be viewed as having the principal function of transmitting a culture's approved products from earlier to later generations; approved products are those deemed valuable by a cultural elite. So-called intelligence tests, then, are designed to measure the facility with which a child may be expected to acquire and adequately process what the school offers in this respect. It does not seem farfetched to suggest that a child's performance in school will be determined to a considerable extent by the amount of prior and continuing extracurricular exposure he or she has to the products of the dominant culture that the school almost necessarily represents. Indeed, we have a fair amount of empirical evidence showing that this is so. We also have a fair amount of empirical evidence, only a fraction of it reviewed here, suggesting that a person's IQ ("intelligence" quotient) rises significantly with enhanced exposure to these cultural products. It is therefore more than a mere possibility that what IQ tests mostly measure is prior exposure to approved cultural products. Considered from this perspective, the notion of a "culture-free" IQ test that would also do well at predicting school grades is a practical impossibility.

The fact that African Americans in the United States are to a marked degree disproportionately represented among those labeled "retarded" is clearly related to the prominence of the IQ measure in the definition of retardation. African Americans have a persistent 15-point deficit, on average, relative to whites on this type of test. However interpreted—whether in terms of "test bias" or in terms of a "real" difference (and from the preceding argument we suggest that these are the same things)—one implication seems clear. Namely, African Americans *as a group* are seriously disadvantaged in engagements with the standard educational system. Relative success in such engagements, as already noted, is mostly what IQ tests are designed to predict, and for the most part they do so effectively. If, as is often said (we have our own small doubts), conventional academic success leads to such happiness and riches as are attainable in our larger culture, then enormously disproportionate numbers of African Americans will continue to be excluded from the good life unless some remedy can be found and put in place.

As we have seen, serious and broad-based efforts to find a remedy to this problem were begun in the 1960s, Project Head Start being a notable example. Much was learned in the programs that were launched during that era, one of the most important lessons being that genuine and sustained advance was costly and difficult. For example, we learned that the gains in academic skill acquired in an enriched preschool experience, as in Head Start, were not lasting without a more general environmental enrichment. However, subsequent changes in national priorities and in the political atmosphere, particularly at the federal level, precluded a vigorous follow-up of these initiatives. We have not regained momentum in this area, nor does it appear likely, as of this writing, that we soon will. If progress in laying to rest the cold war and in the achievement of "the new world order" were happily to continue, however, sufficient funds and energies might be liberated to contemplate seriously a new *national* order, one in which all of our children might truly be granted equal opportunity. It is a cruel deception, in our judgment, to suggest that they have it now.

SUMMARY

Developmental disorders are those disorders of the early years that are rooted in the developmental process. They are thought to be due to defects or delays in normal development itself, thus manifesting themselves in failures to attain expected levels of mastery, competence, or skill in various areas. Investigators commonly assume that some defect or developmental retardation exists at the organic (brain) level in regard to these disorders, although often without sound empirical support. This chapter is concerned with mental retardation, the pervasive developmental disorder of autism, and specific developmental disorders involving learning disabilities, all of which are coded as DSM-III-R Axis II disorders of childhood.

Certain cases of mental retardation, approximately 25 percent of the total incidence, are related to gross structural defects in the brain. They are distinguished from organic brain syndromes by age-related criteria; that is, the structural defects are either congenital or are acquired before the brain has completed its development. An affected individual is prevented from acquiring certain forms of knowledge and cognitive skills and thus is considered *amented* as opposed to *demented*. In these cases, retardation is likely to be severe or profound and to be accompanied by obvious physical anomalies of one sort or another. Down syndrome and phenylketonuria (PKU) are examples of this type of disorder.

The large majority—some 75 percent—of mental retardation cases are unrelated to obvious physical defects and are considered cultural-familial in origin, a term that acknowledges our inability to disentangle genetic and environmental influences in the disorder. Caution is warranted in applying the label "mentally retarded" because of our heavy reliance on IQ test scores in its definition. The IQ test is—and always has been—a measure of *academic* skill, not of ability to survive and perhaps even prosper in other areas of life. A variety of evidence points to the conclusion that cultural-familial retardation may be treatable and even preventable, provided we can find the means of providing the necessary cognitive stimulation to socially and economically deprived children.

Some of the most severe and inexplicable childhood disorders are the pervasive developmental disorders, the most prominent example of which is infantile autism. In these disorders, extreme maladaptive behavior occurs during the early years and prevents affected children from developing psychologically. Autistic children, for example, seem to remain aloof from others, never responding to or seemingly not caring about what goes on around them. Many never learn to speak. These disorders likely have a biological basis, although definite proof of such a basis has proven elusive. Neither medical nor psychological treatment has been notably successful in fully normalizing the behavior of autistic children, but newer instructional and behavior-modification techniques have sometimes scored significant gains in improving their ability to function. In general, the long-term prognosis in autism appears discouraging.

Specific developmental disorders are those in which failure of mastery is limited to circumscribed areas, chiefly involving academic skills such as reading; general cognitive ability may be normal or superior. Affected children are commonly described as learning disabled (LD). Here again some localized defect in brain development is usually considered the primary cause, although independent corroboration of an organic cause is the exception rather than the rule. These disorders create great turmoil and frustration in victims, their families, schools, and professional helpers. Various remedies, most involving training regimens of one sort or another, are tried and apparently are sometimes successful. However, solid outcome research in the area of intervention techniques is seriously lacking. The long-term prognosis for LD, overall, is not encouraging.

■ Key Terms

developmental disorder (p. 503)

mental retardation (p. 503)

Down syndrome (p. 508)

phenylketonuria (PKU) (p. 511)

cretinism (p. 512)

myxedema (p. 512)

macrocephaly (p. 512)

microcephaly (p. 512)

hydrocephalus (p. 513)

cultural-familial retardation (p. 513)

mainstreaming (p. 519)

pervasive developmental disorder (p. 521)

autistic disorder (p. 521)

echolalia (p. 522)

structural therapy (p. 525)

specific developmental disorders (p. 528)

specific learning disabilities (p. 528)

learning disabled (LD) (p. 528)

dyslexia (p. 528)

Chapter 15
Behavior Disorders of Childhood and Adolescence

Aloïs Wey, *Maisons* (1977). Wey (1894–?) attended for a short time a primary school where he developed an interest in art and drawing. At the age of 14, Wey quit school and entered upon a difficult life complicated by bouts with alcoholism and by exacting toil, first as a helper in his father's roofing business, later as a master roofer, a factory worker, an electrician, a miner, and a cook. At the age of 80, in retirement and living in a rest home, Wey resumed drawing. Many of his works take as their subjects exotic architectural structures, quite often resembling the architecture of foreign countries (though Wey's travels in other lands were, in fact, quite limited).

During the nineteenth century, little account was taken of the special characteristics of psychopathology in children; maladaptive patterns that are considered relatively specific to childhood, such as hyperactivity, received virtually no attention at all. Since the turn of the twentieth century, with the advent of the mental health movement and the availability of child guidance facilities, marked strides have been made in assessing, treating, and understanding the maladaptive behavior patterns of children and youth. This progress has, however, lagged behind efforts to deal with adult psychopathology. In fact, as we will see, early efforts at classifying problems of childhood were simply extensions of adult-oriented diagnostic systems.

These early conceptualizations seemed to reflect a prevailing view of children as "miniature adults" and failed to take into account special problems, such as those associated with the developmental changes that normally take place in a child or adolescent. Only recently have we come to realize that we cannot fully understand childhood disorders without taking into account these developmental processes; in fact, the field is often referred to as **developmental psychopathology.** Today, even though great progress has been made in providing treatment for disturbed children, our facilities are woefully inadequate in relation to the magnitude of the task, and the majority of problem children do not receive psychological attention (Links, Boyle, & Offord, 1989). The numbers of children affected by psychological problems are considerable. For example, the Office of Technology Assessment (OTA, 1986) places the percentage of American children with psychological disorders at 12 to 15 percent. In a cross-cultural study, Wunsch-Hitzig, Gould, and Dohrenwend (1980) found the incidence of childhood maladjustment to be similar for the United States (11.8 percent) and for Great Britain (13.2 percent). In both countries, maladjustment among boys significantly exceeded that among girls. In a more recent survey of psychological disorder in children, Anderson et al. (1987) found that an overall prevalence of 17.6 percent of 11-year-old children had one or more disorders. Boys were diagnosed more frequently than girls at 1.7 to 1. The most prevalent disorders were attention-deficit hyperactivity disorder and separation anxiety disorders.

In the first section of this chapter we will note some general characteristics of maladaptive behavior in children as compared with adult disorders. Next we will examine the issues surrounding the diagnostic classification of children's disorders. Then we will look at a number of important disorders of childhood and adolescence. In the final section we will give detailed consideration to some of the special factors involved in both the treatment and prevention of children's problems.

MALADAPTIVE BEHAVIOR IN DIFFERENT LIFE PERIODS

Because personality differentiation, developmental tasks, and typical stressors differ for childhood, adolescence, and adulthood, we would expect to find some differences in maladaptive behavior in these different periods. The special characteristics of childhood disorders are discussed here.

■ Varying Clinical Pictures

The clinical picture in childhood disorders tends to be different from those of other life periods. Although some disorders, such as attention-deficit hyperactivity disorder, are primarily problems of childhood, even the disorders that occur at all life periods reflect the developmental level of the individual experiencing them. For example, the suicidal impulses commonly found in adolescent and adult depression are fairly rare in childhood depression (Kovacs & Beck, 1977). In childhood schizophrenia, although there is the characteristic schizophrenic withdrawal and inability to relate to others, delusions and hallucinations are less common; when they do occur, they are more transient and less well systematized (Elkind & Weiner, 1978). In fact, some of the emotional disturbances of childhood may be relatively short-lived, undifferentiated, and changeable compared with those of later life periods (Lewis et al., 1988). It should be kept in mind, however, that some childhood disorders severely affect future development. Kuperman, Black, and Burns (1988) reported that individuals who had been hospitalized as child psychiatric patients (between the ages of 5 and 17) showed excess mortality in unnatural deaths (about twice the rate of the general population) when followed up from 4 to 15 years later. Suicide accounted for the majority of these deaths, and the suicide rate was significantly greater than in the general population.

■ Special Vulnerabilities of Young Children

Young children do not have as clear-cut a view of themselves and their world as they will have at a later age. They have less self-understanding and have not yet developed a stable sense of identity and an adequate frame of reference regarding reality, possibility, and value. Immediately perceived threats are tempered less by considerations of the past or future and thus tend to be seen as disproportionately important. As a result, children often have more difficulty in coping with stressful events than do adults.

Children's limited perspectives, as might be expected, lead them to use childlike concepts to explain what is happening. For example, in the comparatively rare case of child suicide, a child may be trying to rejoin a dead parent, sibling, or pet. For young children, suicide—or violence against another person—may be undertaken without any real understanding that death is final.

Children also are more dependent on other people than are adults. Though in some ways this dependency serves as a buffer against other dangers, it also makes them highly vulnerable to experiences of rejection, disappointment, and failure. On the other hand, although their inexperience and lack of self-sufficiency make them easily upset by problems that seem minor to the average adult, children typically recover more quickly from their hurts.

It's easy to spot the one child in this group who seems especially vulnerable to the stress of classroom competition. While others have their hands raised or otherwise look alert, her head is down and her demeanor is withdrawn. Children's inexperience and lack of self-sufficiency make them easily upset by problems that may seem minor to the average adult, and they often have more difficulty in coping with stressful events than they will have when they are older.

Moreover, it is important to view a child's behavior in reference to normal childhood development. One cannot understand or consider as "abnormal" a child's behavior without considering whether the behavior in question is appropriate for the child's age. Behavior such as temper tantrums or eating inedible objects might be viewed as symptoms of abnormal behavior at age 10 but not at age 2. Despite these somewhat distinctive characteristics of childhood disturbances, there is no sharp line of demarcation between the maladaptive behavior patterns of childhood and those of adolescence, nor between those of adolescence and those of adulthood. Thus, although our focus in this chapter will be on the behavior disorders of children and adolescents, we will find some inevitable overlapping with those of later life periods. In this context, it is useful to emphasize the basic continuity of an individual's behavior over time as he or she attempts to cope with the problems of living.

THE CLASSIFICATION OF CHILDHOOD AND ADOLESCENT DISORDERS

Diagnosis of the psychological disorders of childhood has traditionally been a rather confused practice, and until recently no formal, specific system was available for classifying the emotional problems of children and adolescents. Kraepelin's (1883) classic textbook on the classification of mental disorders did not include childhood disorders. Not until 1952, when the first formal psychiatric nomenclature (DSM-I) was published, was a classification system for childhood disorders made available. The DSM-I system, however, was quite limited and included only two childhood emotional disorders: *childhood schizophrenia* and *adjustment reaction of childhood.* Although several additional categories were added to the 1968 revision (DSM-II), a growing concern remained, both among clinicians attempting to diagnose and treat childhood problems and among researchers attempting to broaden our understanding of childhood psychopathology, that the then-current ways of viewing psychological disorders in children and adolescents were inappropriate and inaccurate.

Several reasons can be found for the early inadequacies of these diagnostic systems. First, the greatest problem stemmed from the fact that the same classification system that had been developed for adult problems was used for childhood problems. No allowance was made for the special considerations that enter into childhood conditions, such as an often mixed symptom pattern. Second, the early systems ignored the fact that in childhood disorders, environmental factors play an important part in the expression of symptoms; that is, symptom manifestations are highly influenced by a family's acceptance or rejection of the behavior. For example, either extreme tolerance of deviant behavior or total rejection and neglect could lead a child to accept his or her extreme behavior as "normal." Third, the symptoms were often incorporated without regard to a child's developmental level. In other words, the troubling behaviors might simply be behaviors a child will grow out of in time.

Over the years, discontent with the classification system for childhood behavior problems has led to considerable rethinking, discussion, and empirical investigation of the issues related to diagnosis. You may recall that in Chapter 1 we discussed various methods of classification. In the classification of childhood disorders, two of these methods —the categorical and the dimensional—have both been prominent. The first approach, a *categorical strategy,* is typically used by clinicians and has evolved from previous diagnostic classification systems. DSM-III-R is an example of a categorical strategy. In this strategy, a clinician—or, in the case of DSM-III-R, a group of clinicians—arrives at a descriptive class or category by examining, through clinical study, the behaviors that appear to define that class of children. For example, the similar behaviors that appear in children who are judged to fit the diagnostic class *attention-deficit hyperactivity disorder* are used as the defining criteria of that class.

The second approach—which is rarely used by clinicians but which is favored by many empirical researchers in psychopathology—is a *dimensional strategy.* This approach involves the application of sophisticated statistical methods to provide clear behavior clusters or "dimensions" for the widely observed symptoms manifested by children. A researcher gathers his or her symptomatic information through teachers', parents', or clinicians' observations or through a child's *presenting symptoms*—that is, the behaviors characteristic of the clinical picture at the time the child is first seen by professional personnel. The researcher then allows the statistical method—for example, factor analysis—to determine the various behavior dimensions evidenced by an individual child. For example, the Child Behavior Checklist (CBCL) is the most widely researched and used dimensional strategy for assessing childhood behavior problems. Achenbach (1985) and his colleagues (Achenbach & Edelbrock, 1983: Achenbach & McConaughy, 1985; Achenbach & Weisz,

1975) rated the symptoms of problem children based on two broad dimensions: *internalizing* and *externalizing,* which describe the differing tendencies to deal with problems through internal processes or through external actions against the environment. Thus symptoms on the internalizing dimension might include depression, social withdrawal, and anxiety, while symptoms on the externalizing dimension might include hyperactivity, aggression, and delinquent behavior.

Both systems are based on observation of an individual's behavior, and both result in classifying the person according to the presence or absence of symptoms. There are marked differences between the systems, however. The categorical approach generally requires the presence of relatively few symptoms to arrive at a diagnosis. The dimensional approach, on the other hand, usually requires the presence of a number of related symptoms before a case is included on a dimension. As a result, a categorical system will tend to have many categories defined by few, sometimes quite rare, behaviors, while dimensional approaches typically involve a small number of general classes covering numerous related behaviors.

Broadly, the categorical approach follows the disease model of psychopathology and attempts to organize or classify the aberrant behavior observed in problem children into meaningful classes of mental diseases to provide useful prognoses and treatments. The dimensional approach is based on the idea that these behaviors are continuous and are found even among many "normals"; it attempts to provide an objective classification scheme for assessing the relative frequency of these behavioral problems in an individual or group. It is possible to see benefits and problems in both these approaches to classification. Because this textbook focuses on the clinical manifestation of disorders, including infrequent symptoms that would be minimized in a dimensional approach, we will, for practical purposes, follow the DSM-III-R classification system of childhood and adolescent disorders. Keep in mind, however, that the approach taken here is only one possible way of viewing disorders.

DISORDERS OF CHILDHOOD

In this section we will discuss several disorders of childhood with a focus on describing the clinical picture of each syndrome, surveying the possible causal factors, and outlining treatment approaches that have proved effective. A broader discussion of treatment methods can be found in Chapters 17 and 18.

The disorders that will be covered are attention-deficit hyperactivity disorder, conduct disorder (including juvenile delinquency), anxiety disorders of childhood, depressive disorders, and several other special symptom disorders. These disorders are less stable than most of the abnormal behavior patterns discussed in earlier chapters and also perhaps more amenable to treatment. If treatment is not received, childhood developmental problems sometimes merge almost imperceptibly into more serious and chronic disorders as the child passes into adulthood, or they manifest themselves later as different disorders (Gelfand, Jenson, & Drew, 1988).

Attention–Deficit Hyperactivity Disorder

The **attention-deficit hyperactivity disorder (ADHD),** often referred to as **hyperactivity,** is characterized by difficulties that interfere with effective task-oriented behavior in children—particularly impulsivity, excessive motor activity, and an inability to attend. The presenting symptoms in attention-deficit hyperactivity disorder are relatively common among children seen at child guidance centers. In fact, hyperactive children are the most frequent psychological referrals to mental health and pediatric facilities, and it is estimated that between 3 and 5 percent of elementary-school-aged children manifest the symptoms (Ross & Pelham, 1981). Attention-deficit hyperactivity disorder is the most frequent disorder among preadolescent boys, with a 6.7 percent prevalence (Anderson et al., 1987). The disorder, which is six to nine times more prevalent among boys (DSM-III-R, 1987), occurs with the greatest frequency before age 8 and tends to become less frequent and with briefer episodes thereafter. As we will see, some residual effects, such as attention difficulties, may persist into adolescence or the adult years. Few well-controlled, prospective, longitudinal studies have focused on hyperactivity, so most of our understanding is based on clinical reports.

The Clinical Picture in Attention-Deficit Hyperactivity Disorder As the term implies, attention-deficit hyperactive children show excessive or exaggerated muscular activity—for example, aimless or haphazard running or fidgeting. Difficulty in sustaining attention is another central feature of the disorder. Hyperactive children are highly distractible and do not follow instructions or respond to demands placed on them. Impulsive behavior and a low frustration tolerance are also characteristic.

Hyperactive children do not typically show deficits in intelligence, but they tend to talk incessantly and to be socially uninhibited and immature. Barkley and Cunningham (1979) reported that hyperactive children usually have great difficulties in getting along with their parents, usually because they do not obey rules. King and Young (1981) found that hyperactive children are viewed negatively by their peers. In general, however, hyperactive children do not appear to be anxious, although their overactivity, restlessness, and distractibility are often interpreted as indications of anxiety. Usually they do poorly in school, commonly showing specific learning disabilities, such as difficulties in reading or in learning other basic school subjects. Hyperactive children also pose behavior problems in the elementary grades. The following case, involving an eight-year-old girl, reveals a typical clinical picture:

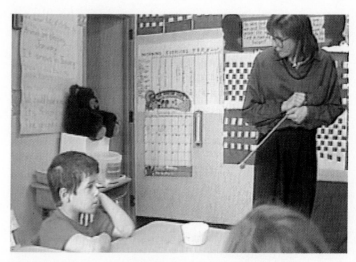

The special education teacher shown here works with children who have behavioral problems, such as attention-deficit hyperactivity disorder. Unrecognized and left untreated, a child with ADHD runs the risk of a multitude of problems with schoolwork, teachers, and other students. In her classroom, this teacher constantly reminds her students about behaviors they are working on, and reinforces positive behaviors with poker chips that may be cashed in for treats, toys, or privileges.

The subject was referred to a community clinic because of overactive, inattentive, and disruptive behavior. She was a problem to her teacher and to other students because of her hyperactivity and her uninhibited behavior. She would impulsively hit other children, knock things off their desks, erase material on the blackboard, and damage books and other school property. She seemed to be in perpetual motion —talking, moving about, and darting from one area of the classroom to another. She demanded an inordinate amount of attention from her parents and her teacher, and she was intensely jealous of other children, including her own brother and sister. Despite her hyperactive behavior, inferior school performance, and other problems, she was considerably above average in intelligence. Nevertheless, she felt "stupid" and had a seriously devaluated self-image. Neurological tests revealed no significant organic brain disorder.

In spite of the frequency with which the diagnosis is made, there is some disagreement about whether a "hyperactive syndrome" really exists. Quay (1979) argued that the research data on objective symptom classification did not support the existence of the hyperactive disorder separate from conduct disorders. This view has received some support from the research literature. In one study, Prinz, Connor, and Wilson (1981) found that hyperactive and aggressive behaviors were often confused with one

another and were in fact highly related rather than distinct disorders. In another study, Sanson (1980) found virtually no difference between hyperactivity and conduct disorders and concluded that hyperactivity, as a diagnostic category, appeared to have little meaning with respect to etiology or treatment.

Ross and Pelham (1981) concluded that before substantial progress could be made in the understanding of hyperactivity as a diagnostic category, the criteria for defining the disorder would need to be refined. This process would need to include the development of clear normative data on children's behavior, which would make it possible to determine where a hyperactive child actually deviates from normal development. Meanwhile, the symptoms described earlier remain the usual basis for a diagnosis of hyperactivity.

Causal Factors in Attention-Deficit Hyperactivity Disorder   The lack of clarity in diagnosing hyperactivity makes it difficult for researchess to evaluate the possibility that underlying biological conditions might cause the disorder. Rapoport and Ferguson (1981) reviewed the research on possible biological causes for hyperactivity; they found that the correlations between biological data and hyperactivity were weak and that there was no compelling evidence for a biological basis.

One viewpoint (Feingold, 1977) that received a great deal of public attention suggested that hyperactivity in children may be produced by dietary factors—particularly food coloring. Feingold even proposed a dietary treatment for hyperactive children; however, the food-additive theory of hyperactivity has generally been discredited (Mattes & Gittelman, 1981; Stare, Whelan, & Sheridan, 1980). A current variation of the food additive theory was recently published by Marshall (1989). This researcher reviewed the evidence for allergic reactions to certain additives or dyes in foods and concluded that evidence warrants further research into the possibility that allergic reactions could stimulate the nervous system, resulting in hyperactivity in some children. Firm conclusions as to the potential biological basis for ADHD must await further research.

The search for psychological causes of hyperactivity has had similarly inconclusive results. Investigators have not clearly established any psychological causes for the disorder, although they have emphasized both temperament and learning factors. Some evidence shows that the home environment is influential in the development of the disorder (Paternite & Loney, 1980). One study suggested that family pathology, particularly parental personality problems, leads to hyperactivity in children. Morrison (1980) found that many parents of hyperactive children had psychological problems; for example, a large number of them were found to have clinical diagnoses of personality disorder or hysteria. Currently, ADHD is considered to have multiple causes and effects (Campbell & Wherry, 1986).

Treatments and Outcomes   Although the hyperactive syndrome was first described more than 100 years ago, disagreement remains over the most effective methods of treatment, especially regarding the use of drugs to calm a hyperactive child. As with other problem behaviors, variations in treatment procedures may be required to meet the needs of individual hyperactive children.

Interestingly—although some data contradict the findings (Lou, Heinriken, & Bruhn, 1984)—research has shown that cerebral stimulants, such as amphetamines, have a quieting effect on hyperactive children—just the opposite of what we would expect from their effects on adults (Green & Warshauer, 1981). In addition, research has shown that amphetamines have similar calming effects on non-hyperactive children (Zahn, Rapoport, & Thompson, 1980). Such medication decreases hyperactive children's overactivity and distractibility and at the same time increases their attention and ability to concentrate. As a result they are often able to function much better at school (Henker & Whalen, 1989). In fact, many hyperactive children who have

not been acceptable in regular classes can function and progress in a relatively normal manner when they use such drugs. The medication does not appear to affect their intelligence, but rather seems to help them use their basic capacities more effectively (NIMH, 1971). Although the drugs do not "cure" hyperactivity, they have reduced the behavioral symptoms in about half to two-thirds of the cases in which medication appears warranted.

While the short-term pharmacologic effect of stimulants on the symptoms of hyperactive children is apparently well established, their long-term effects are not well-known (Weiss, 1981). Some concern has been expressed about the effects of the drugs, particularly when used in heavy dosages over time. Safer and Allen (1973) concluded from a longitudinal study of 63 hyperactive children—49 of whom were on medication and 14 of whom were used as controls—that Ritalin, the most commonly used drug, can suppress normal growth in height and weight. In a carefully controlled study, however, Beck and colleagues (1975) failed to find such effects. Nevertheless, the use of such drugs should be carefully monitored to avoid harmful side effects and addiction. Some questions that have been raised concerning the use of these drugs are discussed in *HIGHLIGHT 15.1*. The use of drug therapy with children will be taken up again in Chapter 17.

Another effective approach to treating hyperactive children involves behavior therapy techniques featuring positive reinforcement and the structuring of learning materials and tasks in a way that minimizes error and maximizes immediate feedback and success. The use of behavioral treatment methods (see Chapter 18) for hyperactivity has reportedly been quite successful, at least for short-term gains. Robinson, Newby, and Ganzell (1981), using a token economy system, were able to increase the number of completed school tasks for hyperactive children up to the average number of tasks completed by other children in the school. In another approach, Dunn and Howell (1982) successfully used relaxation training to reduce hyperactivity in a group of boys.

Several investigators have reported that impulsive behavior in children can be successfully modified by the use of cognitive-behavioral techniques in which rewards for desired behavior are combined with training in the use of verbal self-instructions (Kendall, 1981; Meichenbaum, 1977; Meichenbaum & Goodman, 1971). The focus of cognitive-behavioral treatment is to help hyperactive children learn to shift attention less frequently and to behave reflectively rather than impulsively. The following case, reported by Kendall and Finch (1976), shows some aspects of cognitive-behavioral treatment:

HIGHLIGHT 15.1

Drug Therapy with Children

A number of important questions have been raised concerning the increasing use of drugs in the treatment of certain behavior disorders of children. The principal questions include:

1. *Who is being selected for treatment?* Few investigators question the usefulness of amphetamines or related drugs for treating many cases of hyperactivity, but many question the adequacy of the assessment procedures used in identifying children who actually need medication. For example, a clearcut distinction is not always made between children who appear to need drug therapy because of hyperactivity and children whose inattention and restlessness may be the result of hunger, crowded classrooms, irrelevant curriculum content, or anxiety and depression stemming from a pathogenic home situation.

2. *Are drugs sometimes being used simply to "keep peace in the classroom"?* Those who raise this question point to the possibility that children who manifest bewilderment, anger, restlessness, or lethargy at school may only be showing a normal reaction to edu-cational procedures that fail to spark their interest or meet their needs. These investigators maintain that to label such children as "sick"—as evidencing hyperactivity or some other behavior disorder—and to treat them through medication is to sidestep the difficult and expensive alternative of providing better educational programs. Possibly such an approach also reinforces the notion—all too prevalent in our culture—that if things are not going well, all a person has to do is take some type of drug.

3. *Do the drugs have harmful side effects?* Even in the small dosages usually prescribed for children, drugs sometimes have undesirable side effects. Symptoms including decreased appetite, dizziness, headaches, and insomnia have been reported in some cases to accompany the use of stimulants, such as methylphenidate-hydro-chloride (Ritalin); recently these drugs have been implicated in suspected growth retardation. Minor tranquilizers also may have adverse side effects, including lethargy. Even with drugs that seem to produce minimal side effects, the possibility of adverse long-range effects resulting from sustained usage during early growth and development is still being assessed.

The consensus among investigators seems to be that drug therapy for children should be used with extreme caution, and only with those children for whom other alternatives simply do not work, such as a hyperactive child who cannot control his or her behavior without drug therapy. It is also important that drug therapy be undertaken only with the informed consent of the parent, as well as the child if he or she is old enough, and that the child not be given the sole responsibility for taking the medication—a procedure that can lead to drug abuse. At the same time, there is a need to avoid exaggerated public attitudes against the use of drug therapy for children who genuinely need it. Finally, children who do benefit from drug therapy also need other therapeutic measures for dealing with coexisting problems, such as learning deficiencies and psychological, interpersonal, and family difficulties.

Based on Beck et al. (1975), Cole (1975), Eisenberg (1971), Hayes, Panitch, and Barker (1975), Martin and Zaug (1975), Whalen and Henker (1976), and Winsberg et al. (1975).

A nine-year-old boy was referred to a psychiatric facility because of problems at school. The teacher had described him as hyperactive, impulsive, and oversensitive to criticism. After only a month in fourth grade, he had been demoted to third grade because of his inability to adjust.

During the initial interview, the child was constantly moving about. He climbed into and out of chairs, talked rapidly about many topics, and changed the direction and purpose of his behavior without apparent reason. Test data also suggested overactivity and impulsivity to be the central problems.

Therapy sessions started with the therapist working on a maze and talking aloud as he thought through each step he was performing—defining the problem, indicating the focus of his attention and the approach he was using, and including coping statements (after making an intentional error) such as, "I should have gone slower and thought and been more careful.". After the therapist finished the maze, the boy worked it, instructing himself aloud in the same way.

Several other mazes were solved in this way, except that the self-instructions were whispered. Then, the use of self-instructions for target behaviors was rehearsed. For example, to learn not to switch topics during a conversation, the boy practiced the following self-instructions: "What should I remember? I'm to finish talking about what I start to talk about. O.K. I should think before I talk and remember not to switch. If I complete what I'm talking about before I start another topic, I get to keep my dimes. I can look at this card [cue] to remind me" (p. 854).

The boy was given several coins, one of which was subject to forfeit each time he switched to some other topic in the middle of what he was saying. Whatever he had left at the end of the session he could keep.

It was hoped that this verbal rehearsal and reinforcement for success would help the boy develop control over his own behavior, and, in fact, it did. The boy's in-therapy behavior became less hyperactive, his test performance improved, and the teacher noted improvements in the classroom.

From the above case, it appears that one way to deal with the problems associated with hyperactivity is to teach children to stop and think before undertaking a behavior so that they can then guide their own performance by deliberate self-instruction. The extent to which such gains made in cognitive-behavioral therapy generalize to other settings, such as the home and play situations, must be further researched.

The continued use of psychological therapy with medication in a total treatment program has reportedly shown good success. Pelham and associates (1980) found that the combination of behavioral intervention and psychostimulant medication was more effective than either treatment alone in modifying the behavior of hyperactive children. Satterfield, Satterfield, and Cantwell (1981) reported that individualized treatment of various types in conjunction with the use of medication resulted in favorable treatment outcomes in a three-year follow-up.

It should be kept in mind, however, that even though behavioral interventions and medication have reportedly enjoyed short-term successes, there has been insufficient critical evaluation of the long-term effects of either treatment method (O'Leary, 1980). One follow-up study of the drug treatment of 75 children over a 10- to 12-year period reported that young adults who had been hyperactive children had less education than control subjects and had a history of more auto accidents and more geographical moves. The authors found, however, that only a minority of the formerly hyperactive subjects continued their antisocial behavior into adulthood or developed severe psychopathology (Weiss et al., 1979). Glow (1981) cautioned against drug treatment for hyperactivity on grounds that, while it may curb the symptoms, it does not cure the disorder. Similarly, Glow claimed that behavioral interventions require a great deal of effort, are not free from hazard, and have not been demonstrated to have long-range effects.

It is clear from an evaluation of the literature on the treatment of hyperactivity that, in addition to a general disagreement about the nature of hyperactivity, an equal degree of controversy exists about the most effective treatment approach.

Even without treatment, hyperactive behavior tends to diminish by the time children reach their middle teens. Research has demonstrated, however, that many hyperactive children go on to have other psychological problems in their late teens and early adulthood. Hechtman, Weiss, and Perlman (1980), for example, found that hyperactive children had significantly more problems than control subjects when they reached young adulthood. The hyperactive subjects had poor social skills and low self-esteem as young adults. This group also may have a higher-than-average incidence of delinquency and other maladaptive behavior during adolescence and beyond (Solomon, 1972). A recent, longitudinal study of ADHD was conducted by Gittleman et al. (1985). These investigators evaluated and followed up a group of 101 boys aged 6 through 12 who showed hyperactivity, contrasting their later adjustment, at 16 to 23 years of age, with a control sample of 100 nonhyperactive boys. They found that the majority of the boys who had been diagnosed as hyperactive showed diminished symptom patterns in later adolescence and early adulthood. However, the full attention deficit disorder persisted in 31 percent of the hyperactive boys, while only 3 percent of the control sample showed hyperactive symptoms at follow-up. The authors also found that the hyperactive boys showed a greater likelihood of developing psychiatric problems than the control boys. Their "most striking finding is the degree to which the syndrome consisting of impulsivity, inattention, and hyperactivity persisted" (p. 943), and boys in which the hyperactivity persisted had a greater likelihood of developing conduct disorders. Hyperactive boys who did not receive a DSM-III-R diagnosis at follow-up showed no differences from the control boys (Mannuzza et al., 1988).

◼ Conduct Disorders

The next group of disorders emphasizes a child's or an adolescent's relationship to social norms and rules of conduct. In **conduct disorders,** aggressive or antisocial behavior is the focus. With these disorders, it is important to distinguish between persistent antisocial acts, in which the rights of others are violated, and the less serious pranks often carried out by "normal" children and adolescents. We should point out, too, that conduct disorders involve misdeeds that may or may not be against the law; *juvenile delinquency*—to be discussed in the next section—is the legal term used to refer to violations of the law committed by minors.

The behavior to be described in the following sections may appear to be similar to the early stages in the development of personality disorders, discussed in Chapter 8. Indeed, the personality characteristics and causal considerations are much the same. It is difficult, if not impossible, to distinguish among a conduct disorder, a "predelinquent" pattern of behavior, and the early stages in the development of an antisocial personality. Behaviorally, the patterns are alike and may simply represent three ways of describing or accounting for the same behavior. Many adult antisocial personalities, as children, showed the aggressive behavior and rule violations that often are labeled conduct disorders, and many came into contact with the authorities as a result of this delinquent behavior. Fortunately, not all children who are described as having conduct disorders or who engage in delinquent behavior grow up to become antisocial personalities or commit themselves to lives of crime. As we will see, although these disorders of conduct are quite serious and rather complex to treat, there are effective ways of working with disordered individuals to help them become accepted and productive members of society.

The Clinical Picture in Conduct Disorders
The essential symptomatic behavior in the conduct disorders involves a persistent, repetitive violation of rules and a disregard for the rights of others. Stewart and associates (1980) found conduct-disordered children to be characterized by fighting, disobedience, destructiveness, meanness, and precocious sexual behavior. Behar and Stewart (1982) reported that conduct disorder began at a much earlier age than other disorders of childhood (excluding autism and organic syndromes). Approximately 9 percent of males and 2 percent of females have conduct disorder problems (DSM-III-R, 1987). The following case is typical of children with conduct disorder and illustrates many of the features commonly found:

Craig, an 8-year-old boy, had already established himself as a social outcast by the time he entered first grade. Previously, he had been expelled from kindergarten two times in two years for being unmanageable. His mother brought him to a mental health center at the insistence of the school when she attempted to enroll him in the first grade. Within the first week of school, Craig's quarrelsome and defiant behavior had tried the special education teacher, who was reputedly "excellent" with problem children like him, to the point where she recommended his suspension from school. His classmates likewise were completely unsympathetic to Craig, whom they viewed as a bully. At even the slightest sign of movement on his part, the other children would tell the teacher that Craig was "being bad again."

At home, Craig was uncontrollable. His mother and six other children lived with his domineering grandmother. Craig's mother was ineffective at disciplining or managing her children. She worked long hours as a domestic maid and "did not feel like hassling with those kids" when she got home. Her present husband, the father of the three youngest children (including Craig), had deserted the family.

In general, children who are seen as conduct disordered manifest such characteristics as overt or covert hostility, disobedience, physical and verbal aggressiveness, quarrelsomeness, vengefulness, and destructiveness. Lying, solitary stealing, and temper tantrums are common. Such children tend to be sexually uninhibited and inclined toward sexual aggressiveness. Some may engage in firesetting (see *HIGHLIGHT 15.2*), vandalism, and even homicidal acts.

HIGHLIGHT 15.2

Fire Setting: An Extreme Conduct Disorder?

Fire setting in children is a potentially dangerous and difficult to understand problem. Estimates of the prevalence of fire setting by children have been as high as 8 percent of all recorded fires (Fire Statistics UK, 1980). Fire setting is more common among boys by about five to one. What motivates children to set fires? Early studies (Lewis & Yarnel, 1951) concluded that fire setters are typically of low intelligence and from disrupted homes. Early clinical theorists placed the cause of fire setting in personality develop-

ment and considered the problem to co-occur with problems of sexual maladjustment and enuresis (Hellman & Blackmun, 1966; Schmid, 1914). A number of investigators (Jacobson, 1985a; Kuhnley, Hendron, & Quinlan, 1982) report a strong association between fire setting and the presence of conduct disorders. Recent studies, however, report more diagnostic heterogeneity and do not find a consistent association with conduct disorder (Jacobson, 1985b; Kolko, Kazdin, & Meyer, 1985).

Even though the general diagnosis may vary among fire setters, several problems appear to be consistently observed in the children who set fires. They tend to be extremely aggressive and fight a great deal, and they tend to have psychosocial disturbances and poor social skills. It should be noted, however, that the great majority of conduct-disordered, aggressive, and socially unskilled children do not engage in fire setting. Why some disturbed children do is not clearly known.

In DSM-III-R, the broad category *conduct disorder* contains three subtypes. These subtypes are as follows:

- *Group type.* The conduct problems occur in group activity with peers.
- *Solitary aggressive type.* The youngster engages in aggressive behavior against both adults and peers.
- *Undifferentiated type.* Features of both the group type and the solitary aggressive type are present.

Causal Factors in Conduct Disorders   Investigators seem generally to agree that the family setting of a conduct-disordered child is typically characterized by ineffective parenting, rejection, harsh and inconsistent discipline, and often parental neglect (Patterson, DeBarsyshe, & Ramsey, 1989). Frequently, the parents have an unstable marital relationship, are emotionally disturbed or sociopathic, and do not provide the child with consistent guidance, acceptance, or affection. Family discord, such as the conflict and disharmony accompanying divorce (Chess & Thomas, 1984), is instrumental in the development of conduct disorders. In a disproportionate number of cases, the child lives in a home broken by divorce or separation, may have a stepparent, or may have had a series of stepparents. Regardless of whether a home is

broken or not, a child in a conflict-charged home feels overtly rejected. Rutter and Quinton (1984), for example, concluded that family discord and hostility were "the chief mediating variables" in the association between disturbed parents and disturbed children, particularly with regard to the development of conduct disorders in children and adolescents.

Treatments and Outcomes   Therapy for a conduct-disordered child is likely to be ineffective unless some means can be found for modifying the child's environment. This task is difficult when the parents are maladjusted and in conflict with each other. Often an overburdened parent who is separated or divorced and working simply does not have the time or inclination to learn and practice a more adequate parental role. In some cases, the circumstances may call for a child to be removed from the home and placed in a foster home or institution, with the expectation of a later return to the home if intervening therapy with the parents appears to justify it.

Unfortunately, children who are removed to new environments often interpret this removal as further rejection—not only by their parents but by society as well. Unless the changed environment offers a warm, kindly, and accepting—yet consistent and firm—setting, such children are likely to make little progress. Even then, treatment may have

Family discord and hostility have been found to play a role in the development of conduct disorders, but removing a child from the home may be interpreted by the child as further rejection. One program that attempts to involve both parents and children is the Oregon Social Learning Center's foster care program. A child in this program lives with specially trained foster parents for up to six months, and during this time the natural parents meet with a therapist once a week (as shown here) to learn better parenting skills. Through individual and family therapy, the program tries to develop a family pattern that is stable, accepting, consistent, and affectionate.

only a temporary effect. Faretra (1981) followed up 66 aggressive and disturbed adolescents who had been admitted to an inpatient unit. She found that antisocial and criminal behavior persisted into adulthood with a lessening of psychiatric involvement. The most antisocial children were from homes with histories of antisocial problems, one-parent homes, or minority or deprived environments. Zeitlin (1986) studied psychiatric patients who were treated as both children and adults, finding that many conduct-disordered children go on to have personality disorders as adults. Rutter (1988) concluded that "most (but not all) forms of adult personality disorder (and not just the antisocial or sociopathic variety) have been preceded by conduct disorders in children" (p. 490).

Aggressiveness at an early age has been found to be related to adult criminal behavior. Stattin and Magnusson (1989) conducted a study of 1027 boys and girls between late childhood and early adolescence using teacher ratings made at ages 10 and 13. An evaluation of the recorded behavior problems of the boys through age 26 found that high ratings of childhood aggressiveness were characteristic of subjects who later committed violent crimes and damage to public property. The relationship between early aggressiveness and later crime was not associated for girls.

By and large, our society tends to take a punitive, rather than rehabilitative, attitude toward an antisocial, aggressive youth. Thus, the emphasis is on punishment and on "teaching the child a lesson." Such "treatment," however, appears to intensify rather than correct the behavior. Where treatment is unsuccessful, the end product is likely to be an antisocial personality with aggressive behavior. Several studies have shown the long-range negative consequences of unchecked aggressiveness. In one longitudinal study of antisocial, aggressive behavior in childhood, Robins (1970) evaluated aggressive behavior in young adolescent boys and then followed them up in later adolescence and young adulthood. Early aggressive behavior was found to be highly predictive of sociopathic actions in later adolescence and adulthood; similar findings have been reported by Wolkind (1974).

The advent of behavior therapy techniques has, however, made the outlook brighter for children who manifest conduct disorders. Teaching control techniques to the parents of such children is particularly important, so that they function as therapists in reinforcing desirable behavior and modifying the environmental conditions that have been reinforcing maladaptive behavior. The changes brought about when they consistently accept and reward their child's positive behavior and stop focusing attention on the negative behavior may finally change their perception of and feelings toward the child, leading to the basic acceptance that the child has so badly needed.

Though effective techniques for behavioral management can be taught to parents (Fleishman, 1981), often they have difficulty carrying out treatment plans. If this is the case, other techniques, such as family therapy or parental counseling, can be employed to ensure that the parent or person responsible for the child's discipline is sufficiently assertive to follow through on the program. Shoemaker and Paulson (1976) described a program of assertiveness training for mothers in which women who had children with aggressive behavior problems were taught more effective skills in self-expression and verbal discipline. Ratings of their children's behavior showed improvement following the assertiveness training.

■ Delinquent Behavior

In this section we will examine one of the most troublesome and extensive problems in childhood and adolescence: delinquent behavior. This behavior includes such acts as destruction of property, violence against other people, and various behaviors contrary to the needs and rights of others and in violation of society's laws. As noted earlier, the term

juvenile delinquency is a legal one; it refers to illegal acts committed by individuals under the age of 16, 17, or 18 (depending on state law). Children under 8 who commit such acts are not considered delinquents, because it is assumed that they are too immature to understand the significance and consequences of their actions. Delinquency is generally regarded as calling for some punishment or corrective action.

The Incidence and Severity of Delinquent Acts The actual incidence of juvenile delinquency is difficult to determine because many delinquent acts are not reported. Of the two million young people who go through the juvenile courts each year in the United States, about half are there for actions, such as running away, that are not considered crimes for adults. These actions are referred to as status offenses (see *HIGHLIGHT 15.3*). In 1988, arrests of people under 18 years of age accounted for 28 percent of all crime (Uniform Crime Reports, 1989). Juveniles accounted for over 1 out of every 3 arrests for robbery, 1 out of 3 arrests for crimes against property, 1 out of 6 arrests for rape, and 1 out of 11 arrests for murder. Although most of the juvenile crime was committed by males, the rate has also risen for females. About 1 teenager out of every 15 in the nation was arrested. Well over half of the juveniles who are arrested each year have prior police records (Uniform Crime Reports, 1989). Female delinquents are commonly apprehended for drug usage, sexual offenses, running away from home, and "incorrigibility," but crimes against property, such as stealing, have markedly increased among this group. Male delinquents are commonly arrested for drug usage and crimes against property; to a lesser extent, they are arrested for armed robbery, aggravated assault, and other crimes against people.

Fear of violent juvenile crime has created in many people the idea that juvenile criminals as a group are uncontrollable and antisocial personalities. The extent of dangerous and violent behavior among delinquents has been questioned, however. Dinitz and Conrad (1980) reported that, of a sample of 811 juveniles arrested for violent crimes, only about 2 percent had been involved in repeated aggressive or violent acts; even the acts of this 2 percent were mostly "clumsy and inadvertent" (p. 145).

In general, it is assumed that both the incidence and the severity of delinquent behavior are disproportionately high for slum and lower-class youth. This view has been supported by findings of the President's Commission on Law Enforcement and Administration of Justice (1967) as well as by later reports (Zimring, 1979). Other investigators, however, have found no evidence that delinquency is predominately a lower-class phenomenon. In a study of 433 teenagers who had committed almost 2500 delinquent acts, Haney and Gold (1973) reported "no strong relationship between social status and delinquent behavior" (p. 52). Similar findings have been described by Krohn et al. (1980). It may also be noted that the delinquency rate for socially disadvantaged youths appears about equal for whites and nonwhites (Uniform Crime Reports, 1989). In summary, although much juvenile crime is committed by lower class youth, some problems have been noted in all social strata (Elliott, Dunford, & Huizinga, 1987).

Causal Factors in Delinquency Various conditions, singly and in combination, may be involved in the development of delinquent behavior. In general, however, several key variables seem to play a part: personal pathology, pathogenic family patterns, undesirable peer relationships, general sociocultural factors, and special stress.

Personal pathology. A number of investigators have attempted to "type" delinquents in terms of pervasive patterns and sources of personal pathology.

1. *Genetic determinants.* Although the research on genetic determinants of antisocial behavior is far from conclusive, some evidence indicates possible hereditary contributions to criminality. Schulsinger (1980) identified 57 sociopathic adoptees from psychiatric and police files in Denmark and matched them with 57 nonsociopathic control adoptees on the basis of age, sex, social class, geographic region, and age at adoption. He found that natural parents of the adopted sociopaths, particularly fathers, were more likely to have sociopathic characteristics than the natural parents of the controls. Because these natural parents had little contact with their offspring, thus reducing the possibility of environmental influence, the results are interpreted as reflecting the possibility of some genetic transmission of a predisposition to antisocial behavior.

2. *Brain damage and mental retardation.* In a distinct minority of delinquency cases—an estimated 1 percent or less—brain pathology results in lowered inhibitory controls and a tendency toward episodes of violent behavior (Caputo & Mandell, 1970). Such youths are often hyperactive, impulsive, emotionally unstable, and unable to inhibit themselves when strongly stimulated. Fortunately,

HIGHLIGHT 15.3

Problems That Lead Children to Run Away

Of serious concern in the United States is the problem of youngsters who run away from home—an estimated one million or more each year. Although the average age is about 15, an increasing number are in the 11- to 14-year-old age bracket. Many of these runaways are from the suburbs, and at least half are girls. The following case illustrates this problem:

Joan, an attractive girl who looked older than her 12 years, came to the attention of juvenile authorities when her parents reported her as a runaway. Twice before she had run away from home, but no report had been filed. In the first instance, she had gone to the home of a girlfriend and returned two days later; in the second, she had hitchhiked to another city with an older boy and returned home about a week later. Investigation revealed that the girl was having difficulty in school and was living in a family situation torn by bickering and dissension. In explaining why she ran away from home, she stated simply that she "just couldn't take it anymore—all that quarreling and criticism, and no one really cared anyway."

Why do children and adolescents run away? English (1973) concluded that reasons for running away from home tend to fall into three categories: (a) getting out of a destructive family situation, as in the case of a girl who runs away to avoid sexual advances by her father or stepfather; (b) running away in an effort to better the family situation; and (c) having a secret, unsharable problem, such as, for girls, being pregnant.

In a study of runaway girls, Homer (1974) distinguished between "run from's," who had usually fought with their parents and run away because they were unable to resolve the situation or their anger, and "run to's," who were seeking something outside the home. The "run to's" were typically seeking pleasure—sex, drugs, liquor, escape from school, or a peer group with similar interests. Usually they stayed with friends or at other "peer-established" facilities. The "run from's" usually ran away from home only once, while the "run to's" were more likely to be repetitive runaways.

An increasing number of children are "run from's" who are trying to get away from intolerable home situations. In many in-

stances, for economic or other reasons, they are actually encouraged to leave—and their parents do not want them back. Most do not feel that they can return to their parents but instead want a foster home where they will be treated well and respected.

The majority of runaways are not reported. Of those who are, about 90 percent or more are located by law enforcement officers and, when feasible, returned home. Beginning in 1974, a toll-free hotline was established that informs runaways where the nearest temporary shelter is located and enables them to send messages to their parents if they wish.[1] Treatment for runaways is similar to that for individuals who manifest other emotional problems during childhood and adolescence. Often family therapy is an essential part of the treatment program. In some instances—as in those involving parental abuse, unconcern, or lack of cooperation—juvenile authorities may place a child in a foster home. Parents, however, are by no means always the primary reason for their child's running away, and a "what-have-we-done-wrong" attitude may lead to unnecessary feelings of guilt.

[1]One of the toll-free numbers is 1-800-621-4000. This hotline does not operate in either Alaska or Hawaii.

their inner controls appear to improve during later adolescence and young adulthood. The actual role intellectual factors, particularly learning disabilities, play in causing juvenile delinquency is still being debated. In a recent review of the evidence, Lombardo and Lombardo (1991) concluded that there is no empirical evidence linking learning disabilities with delinquency.

3. *Psychological disorders.* A small percentage of delinquent acts appear to be directly associated with behavior disorders, such as hyperactivity. In some cases, delinquent acts take the form of a behavior such as "peeping" or stealing things that are not needed. This behavior often seems related to deviant sexual gratification in overinhibited adolescents who have been indoctrinated in the belief that masturbation and other overt forms of sexual release are evil and sinful. Often such individuals fight their inner impulses before committing a delinquent act and then feel guilty afterward.

Delinquent acts associated with psychotic behavior often involve a pattern of prolonged emotional hurt and turmoil, culminating, after long frustration, in an outburst of violent behavior (Bandura, 1973). In the case of psychologically disturbed delinquents, the delinquent act is a byproduct of severe personality maladjustment rather than a reflection of antisocial attitudes.

4. *Antisocial traits.* A sizable number of habitual delinquents appear to share the traits typical of antisocial personalities—they are impulsive, defiant, resentful, devoid of feelings of remorse or guilt, incapable of establishing and maintaining close interpersonal ties, and seemingly unable to profit from experience. Because they lack needed reality and ethical controls, they often engage in seemingly senseless acts that are not planned but occur on the spur of the moment. They may steal a small sum of money they do not need, or they may steal a car, drive it a few blocks, and abandon it. In some instances, they engage in impulsive acts of violence that are not committed for personal gain but rather reflect underlying resentment and hostility toward the world. In essence, these individuals are "unsocialized."

Although research has focused primarily on male delinquents, several investigators have also emphasized the high incidence of antisocial personalities among females in state correctional institutions (Cloninger & Guze, 1970; Konopka, 1964, 1967).

5. *Drug abuse.* A sizable number of delinquent acts—particularly theft, prostitution, and assault— are directly associated with alcohol or drug use. Most adolescents who abuse hard drugs, such as heroin, are forced to steal to maintain their habit, which can be very expensive. In the case of female addicts, theft may be combined with or replaced by prostitution as a means of obtaining money.

Pathogenic family patterns. In evaluating the role of pathogenic family patterns in delinquency, it should be emphasized that a given pattern is only one of many interacting factors. Of the various patterns that have been emphasized in the research on juvenile delinquency, the following appear to be the most important:

Teen prostitution is often directly associated with alcohol or drug use. For female addicts, prostitution is a means of obtaining money.

1. *Broken homes.* The term "broken home" is a catchall to describe the absence of one or both parents due to a variety of conditions, including desertion, separation, death, or imprisonment. Several investigators have pointed to the high incidence of broken homes and multiple or missing parental figures in the backgrounds of delinquent youths (Lefkowitz et al., 1977). In general, delinquency appears to be much more common among youths coming from homes broken by parental separation or divorce than from homes broken by the death of a parent, suggesting that parental conflict may be a key element in causing delinquency.

As we have seen, however, the effects of broken homes vary greatly. Even when the disruption is due to parental separation or divorce, children in such families may be less adversely affected than children raised in homes torn by parental conflict and dissension. Homes may be "broken" at different times and under varying circumstances; thus these disruptions have differing influences, depending on the individual involved ane his or her total life situation. Consequently, the effects of a given family pattern can be assessed adequately only in relation to an individual's total situation.

2. *Parental rejection and faulty discipline.* In many cases, one or both parents reject a child. When the father is the rejecting parent, it is difficult for a boy to identify with him and use him as a model for his own development. In an early study of 26 aggressively delinquent boys, Bandura and Walters (1963) delineated a pattern in which rejection by the father was combined with inconsistent handling of the boy by both parents. To complicate the pathogenic picture, the father typically used physically punitive methods of discipline, thus modeling aggressive behavior and augmenting the hostility that the boy already felt toward him. The end result of such a pattern was a hostile, defiant, inadequately socialized youth who lacked normal inner controls and tended to act out his aggressive impulses in antisocial behavior.

The detrimental effects of parental rejection and inconsistent discipline are by no means attributable only to fathers. Researchers have found that such behavior by either parent is associated with aggression, lying, stealing, running away from home, and a wide range of other difficulties (Langner et al., 1974; Lefkowitz et al., 1977; Pemberton & Benady, 1973). Often, too, inconsistent discipline may involve more complex family interactions, as when a mother imposes severe restrictions on a youth's behavior and then leaves "policing" to a timid or uncaring father who fails to follow through. In general, parental supervision has been found to be inversely related to delinquency—higher rates of delinquency are found in families that provide less supervision for their children (Morton & Ewald, 1987).

3. *Antisocial parental models.* Several investigators have found a high incidence of antisocial traits in the parents of delinquents—particularly but not exclusively in the father (Bandura, 1973; Glueck & Glueck, 1969). These traits included alcoholism, brutality, antisocial attitudes, failure to provide, frequent unnecessary absences from home, and other characteristics that made the father an inadequate and unacceptable model. Elkind (1967), for example, cited the case of a

father who encouraged his 17-year-old son to drink, frequent prostitutes, and generally "raise hell." This particular father was awakened late one night by the police who had caught his son in a raid on a so-called "massage" parlor. The father's reaction was, "Why aren't you guys out catching crooks?" This same father would boast to his coworkers that his son was "all boy" and "a chip off the old block." (p. 313)

Sociopathic fathers—and mothers—may contribute in various ways to the delinquent behavior of girls as well. Covert encouragement of sexual pro-

miscuity is fairly common, and in some instances there is actual incest with the daughter. In a study of 30 delinquent girls, Scharfman and Clark (1967) found evidence of serious psychopathology in one or both parents of 22 of the girls, including three cases of incest and many other types of early sexual experience. These investigators also reported a high incidence of broken homes (only 11 of the 30 girls lived with both parents) and harsh, irrational, and inconsistent discipline:

Any form of consistent discipline or rational setting of limits was unknown to the girls in their homes. Rather, there was an almost regular pattern of indifference to the activities or whereabouts of these girls, often with the mother overtly or indirectly suggesting delinquent behavior by her own actions. This would alternate with unpredictable, irrational, and violent punishment." (p. 443)

4. *Limited parental relationships outside the family.* Some research suggests that the parents' interpersonal relationships outside the family may contribute to their children's behavioral problems (Griest & Wells, 1983). Wahler (1980) found that the children's oppositional behavior was inversely related to the amount of friendly contacts that parents had outside the home. Wahler et al. (1981) reported that mothers who are isolated or who have negative community interactions are less likely to "track" or control their children's behavior in the community than parents who have friendly relationships outside the family.

Undesirable peer relationships. Delinquency tends to be a shared experience. In their study of delinquents in the Flint, Michigan, area, Haney and Gold (1973) found that about two-thirds of delinquent acts were committed in association with one or two other people, and most of the remainder involved three or four other people. Usually the offender and the companion or companions were of the same sex. Interestingly, girls were more likely than boys to have a constant friend or companion in delinquency. The role of gang membership in delinquency is discussed in the next section.

General sociocultural factors. Broad social conditions may also tend to produce or support delinquency. Interrelated factors that appear to be of key importance include alienation and rebellion, social rejection, and the psychological support afforded by membership in a delinquent gang.

1. *Alienation and rebellion.* Feelings of alienation and rebellion are common to many teenagers from all socioeconomic levels. Alienated teenagers may outwardly submit passively to their elders' demands, or they may openly disobey parental and other adult authority and create no end of problems for themselves and their families. In either event, alienation from family and from the broader society exposes them to becoming captives of their peers, to whom they may turn for guidance and approval. Thus they are vulnerable to pressures to identify with and join peer groups that engage in the use of illegal drugs or other behavior considered delinquent.

2. *The "social rejects."* Our society has become increasingly aware of young people who lack the motivation or ability to do well in school and who drop out as soon as they can (Schwartz & Johnson, 1985). With increasing automation and the demand for occupational skills—whether in the trades or in managerial or professional fields—there are few jobs for which they can qualify. Augmenting this group of youngsters are students who graduate from high school but whose training does not qualify them for available occupational opportunities.

Whether these young people come from upper-, middle-, or lower-income homes, and whether they drop out or continue through high school, they have one crucial problem in common—they discover that they are not needed in our society. They are victims of social progress—"social rejects." While some are able to obtain training in specific job areas, others appear unable to find or hold jobs, and still others drift aimlessly from one unsatisfactory job to another.

3. *Delinquent gang cultures.* With gangs, we are dealing not so much with personal psychopathology as with organized group pathology involving rebellion against the norms of society. As Jenkins (1969) has expressed it:

The socialized delinquent represents not a failure of socialization but a limitation of loyalty to a more or less predatory peer group. The basic capacity for social relations has been achieved. What is lacking is an effective integration with the larger society as a contributing member. (p. 73)

Although the problem of delinquent gangs is most prevalent in lower socioeconomic areas, it is by no means restricted to them. Fusther, delinquent gangs are not a male province—in recent years, females have also formed gangs. Nor does the problem of juvenile delinquent gangs occur only in particular racial, ethnic, or social groups. It is pervasive, most particularly in inner-city areas. Though there are many reasons for joining delinquent gangs—including fear of personal injury from gang members if one does not join—most members appear to feel inadequate in and rejected by the larger society.

Gang membership gives members a sense of belonging and a means of gaining some measure of status and approval. It may also represent a means of committing robberies and other illegal acts for financial gain—acts that an individual could not successfully perform alone (Feldman & Weisfeld, 1973).

We should emphasize that the majority of delinquents do not belong to delinquent gangs, though gang membership may be increasing because young people appear to be joining groups for protection. Not all delinquent gangs are highly organized, cohesive groups. Recently, however, there seems to be an increase in both the organization and cohesiveness of delinquent gangs and in the violence of their activities.

Dealing with Delinquency   If they have adequate facilities and personnel, juvenile institutions and training schools can be of great help to youths who need to be removed from aversive environments. These institutions can give youths a chance to learn about themselves and their world, to further their education and develop needed skills, and to find purpose and meaning in their lives. In such settings, youths may have the opportunity to receive psychological counseling and group therapy. In these situations it is of key importance that peer group pressures be channeled in the direction of resocialization, rather than toward repetitive delinquent behavior. Behavior therapy techniques—based on the assumption that delinquent behavior is learned, maintained, and changed according to the same principles as other learned behavior—have shown marked promise in the rehabilitation of juvenile offenders who require institutionalization. Counseling with parents and related environmental changes are generally of vital importance in a total rehabilitation program.

Probation is widely used with juvenile offenders and may be granted either in lieu of or after a period of institutionalization. Many delinquents can be guided into constructive behavior without being removed from their family or community.

The recidivism rate for delinquents—the most commonly used measure for assessing rehabilitation programs—depends heavily on the type of offenders being dealt with and on the particular facility or

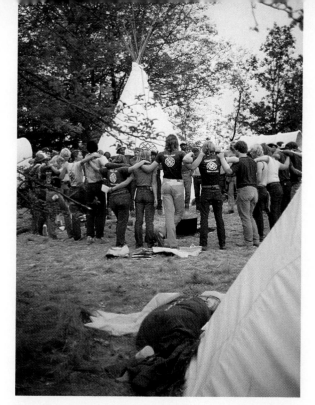

Institutionalizing troubled youths may only aggravate behavior problems. Vision Quest is a social rehabilitative program for troubled teens that offers an alternative to institutionalization by providing positive group experiences with the goal of resocialization.

procedures used. The overall recidivism rate for delinquents sent to training schools has been estimated to be high (Uniform Crime Reports, 1989). Because many crimes are committed by juveniles who have been recently released from custody or who were not incarcerated after being arrested, a number of state officials have become advocates of stiffer penalties for some types of juvenile crime. Individuals who commit crimes of violence or armed assault, or who have a long history of arrests, are often being given harsher penalties than they once would have been (Fersch, 1980).

Institutionalization seems particularly questionable in the case of juvenile status offenders, those youths whose offenses involve acts (such as running away from home or engaging in sexual relations) that would not be considered criminal if committed by an adult. In such instances, institutionalization may aggravate behavior problems rather than correct them. Mixing status offenders with delinquents or adults who have committed violent and antisocial offenses may simply provide them with an unfortunate education in how to become seriously delinquent.

On the other hand, failure to institutionalize youths who have committed serious offenses, such as robbery, assault, and murder, may be a disservice to both the delinquents and the public. In a provocative review of the limitations of programs aimed at reducing juvenile crime by psychological therapies,

Clarke (1985) maintained that past efforts aimed at alterations of personality "dispositions" have fallen well short of success. He described a long history of psychological treatment programs in England aimed at promoting better psychological adjustment in convicted delinquents, thereby reducing recidivism and theoretically preventing juvenile crime. All these efforts to remediate delinquents through medical and psychological means had similar and generally disappointing results. Consequently, in Britain delinquency is viewed as a "rational" act and one that should be dealt with through environmental means rather than through psychological treatment. Situational measures that are aimed at eliminating the "opportunity for crime" are viewed as more effective at reducing crime among juveniles than attempts to "treat" individual delinquents. Such measures include

flat fare and "no change" systems on public transport, cheque guarantee cards, the control of alcohol sales at football matches, supervision of children's play on public housing estates, vandal-resistant materials and design, defensible space architecture, improved lighting, closed circuit television surveillance, the routine screening of airline passengers and baggage, and the employment of doormen in offices, caretakers in blocks of flats and more shop assistants. (p. 517)

These environmental modifications are coupled with the continued use of incarceration to suppress involvement with delinquency among individuals who persist in committing criminal acts.

◼ Anxiety Disorders of Childhood and Adolescence

In modern society, no one is totally insulated from anxiety-producing events or situations. Most children are vulnerable to fears and uncertainties as a part of growing up, and most children encounter many normal developmental steps and environmental demands that challenge their adaptation skills.

Children with anxiety disorders appear to share the following characteristics: oversensitivity, unrealistic fears, shyness and timidity, pervasive feelings of inadequacy, sleep disturbances, and fear of school. Children diagnosed as suffering from an anxiety disorder typically attempt to cope with their fears by becoming overly dependent on others for support and help. Symptoms of anxiety disorder are apparently quite common in the general population. Kashani and Orvaschel (1988) reported that

8.7 percent of their community-based school sample clearly met DSM-III-R criteria for an anxiety diagnosis based on a diagnostic interview.

In the DSM-III-R, anxiety disorders of childhood and adolescence are covered in two subclassifications: *separation anxiety disorder* and *overanxious disorder*. Both syndromes are more common among boys than among girls. We will briefly describe the clinical picture of each of these syndromes, then deal with causal factors and treatment considerations.

Separation Anxiety Disorder   Children who have **separation anxiety disorder** are characterized by unrealistic fears, oversensitivity, self-consciousness, nightmares, and chronic anxiety. These children lack self-confidence, are apprehensive in new situations, and tend to be immature for their age. Such children often are described by their parents as shy, sensitive, nervous, submissive, easily discouraged, worried, and frequently moved to tears. Typically, they are overly dependent, particularly on their parents. The essential feature of this disorder's clinical picture involves excessive anxiety about separation from major attachment figures, such as mother, and from familiar home surroundings. In most cases a clear psychosocial stressor can be identified, such as the death of a relative or a pet. The following case illustrates the clinical picture in this disorder:

*J*ohnny was a highly sensitive six-year-old boy who suffered from numerous fears, nightmares, and chronic anxiety. He was terrified of being separated from his mother, even for a brief period. When his mother tried to enroll him in kindergarten, he became so upset when she left the room that the principal arranged for her to remain in the classroom. After two weeks, however, this arrangement had to be discontinued, and Johnny had to be withdrawn from kindergarten because his mother could not leave him even for a few minutes. Later, when his mother attempted to enroll him in the first grade, Johnny manifested the same intense anxiety and unwillingness to be separated from her. At the suggestion of the school counselor, Johnny's mother brought him to a community clinic for assistance with the problem. The therapist who initially saw Johnny and his mother was wearing a white clinic jacket, which led to a severe panic reaction on Johnny's part. His mother had to hold him to keep him from running away, and he did not settle down until the therapist removed his

jacket. Johnny's mother explained that "he is terrified of doctors, and it is almost impossible to get him to a physician even when he is sick."

When children with separation anxiety disorder are actually separated from their significant others, they typically become preoccupied with morbid fears, such as the worry that their parents are going to become ill or die. They cling helplessly to attachment figures, have difficulty sleeping, and become intensely demanding.

Overanxious Disorder   Children with **overanxious disorder** are characterized by excessive worry and persistent fear; however, their fears are usually not specific and are not due to a recent stressful event. Such a child appears generally anxious and may worry a great deal about future events. He or she is preoccupied with trivial problems. His or her anxiety may also be expressed in somatic ways—stomach distress, shortness of breath, dizziness, headaches, and the like (see *HIGHLIGHT 15.4*). Sleeping problems, especially difficulty in falling asleep, are common. Many children showing overanxious disorder appear to have personality characteristics such as perfectionistic ideas and obsessional self-doubt. The disorder is illustrated in the following case:

*C*indy, an overweight eleven-year-old girl, was taken to the emergency room following an "attack" of dizziness, faintness, and shortness of breath. She believed she was having a heart attack because of the discomfort she was experiencing in her chest. Cindy had a long history of health problems and concerns and was a frequent visitor to doctors. She had missed, on the average, three days of school a week since school had begun four months before.

Cindy was viewed by her mother as a "very good girl" but "sickly." Cindy was good about helping around the house and with her two younger sisters. She seemed conscientious and concerned about doing things right but seemed to lack self-confidence. She always checked out things with her mother, sometimes several times. She was particularly concerned about safety and would, for example, ask her mother frequently if the kitchen stove was turned off correctly.

Cindy would become extremely fearful at times, often for no external reason. For example, on one clear summer day a few months before,

HIGHLIGHT 15.4

Do Children Develop Psychologically Based Somatic Disorders?

The idea that children may develop somatic symptoms to avoid unpleasant tasks, such as schoolwork, or interpersonal conflict, such as parental discord, is well rooted in clinical observation. The extent to which somatization comprises a distinct disorder in children is not as well understood.

A study by Ernst, Routh, and Harper (1984) established the likelihood of the occurrence of somatization disorder in children. They studied a group of children with functional somatic complaints. They reported that the symptom patterns shown by these children differed from those of children with known organic-medical conditions in terms of duration of illness, body systems affected, and susceptibility to additional symptoms over time.

In an effort to evaluate the possibility of parental influence on the development of somatization disorders in children, Routh and Ernst (1984) employed a clinical-diagnostic interview to evaluate mothers of children with organic physical disease and children with likely somatization disorder. They found that a significantly higher percentage of children with functional abdominal pain had relatives with psychopathology, such as alcoholism, antisocial personality disorder, and somatization disorder. Moreover, they found that 10 of the 20 children with somatization disorder had 1 or more relatives with somatization disorders, while only 1 child with organic disorder had a relative with a somatization disorder. This study raises the possibility that somatization disorders, or the development and expression of functional pain, is influenced by parental personality or psychopathology.

she had become panicked over the possibility that a tornado might strike and had insisted that her family take shelter for several hours in the basement.

Causal Factors in Anxiety Disorders   A number of causal factors have been emphasized in explanations of the childhood anxiety disorders. The more important of them appear to be the following:

1. An unusual constitutional sensitivity, an easy conditionability by aversive stimuli, and a buildup and generalization of "surplus fear reactions."

2. The undermining of feelings of adequacy and security by early illnesses, accidents, or losses that involved pain and discomfort. The traumatic effect of such experiences is often due partly to such children finding themselves in unfamiliar situations, as during hospitalization. The traumatic nature of certain life changes, such as moving away from friends and into a new situation, can have an intensely negative effect on a child's adjustment. Kashani and associates (1981a) found that the most common recent life event for children receiving psychiatric care was moving to a new school district.

3. The "modeling" effect of an overanxious and protective parent who sensitizes a child to the dangers and threats of the outside world. Often the parent's overprotectiveness communicates a lack of confidence in the child's ability to cope, thus reinforcing the child's feelings of inadequacy.

4. The failure of an indifferent or detached parent to provide adequate guidance for a child's development. Although the child is not necessarily rejected, neither is he or she adequately supported in mastering essential competencies and in gaining a positive self-concept. Repeated experiences of failure, stemming from poor learning skills, may lead to subsequent patterns of anxiety or withdrawal in the face of "threatening" situations.

Sometimes children are made to feel that they must earn their parents' love and respect through outstanding achievement, especially in school. Such children tend to be overcritical of themselves and to feel intensely anxious and devaluated when they perceive themselves as failing. These children are perfectionists who may actually do well but are left with a feeling of failure because they are sure they should have done better.

The various causal factors we have been discussing in relation to childhood anxiety disorders can obviously occur in differing degrees and combinations. All of them, however, are consistent with the view that these disorders essentially result from maladaptive learning.

Treatments and Outcomes   The anxiety disorders of childhood may continue into adolescence and young adulthood—first leading to maladaptive avoidance behavior and later to increasingly idiosyncratic thinking and behavior. Typically, however, this is not the case. As affected children grow and have wider interactions in school and in peer-group activities, they are likely to benefit from such corrective experiences as making friends and succeeding at given tasks. Teachers have become more and more aware of the needs of both overanxious and shy, withdrawn children—and of ways to help them—and thus they are often able to ensure successful experiences for such children and to foster constructive interpersonal relationships.

Behavior therapy procedures, used in structured group experiences within educational settings, can often help speed up and ensure favorable outcomes. Such procedures include assertiveness training, help with mastering essential competencies, and desensitization. This last procedure may be limited in its application to young children, however, for a number of reasons, including the inability of young children to relax while imagining emotionally charged stimuli (Hatzenbuehler & Schroeder, 1978). With children, desensitization

procedures must be explicitly tailored to a particular problem, and in vivo methods (using graded real-life situations) may be more effective than the use of imagined situations. For example, Montenegro (1968) described the successful treatment of a six-year-old boy, Romeo, who showed pathological anxiety when he was separated from his mother. The treatment included the following procedures:

1. Exposure of the child to a graded series of situations involving the actual fear-arousing stimulus—that is, separation from the mother for increasingly longer intervals.

2. Use of food during these separations as an anxiety inhibitor—which might involve taking the child to the hospital cafeteria for something to eat.

3. Instruction of the parents on how to reduce the child's excessive dependence on the mother—for example, through letting him learn to do things for himself.

After ten consecutive sessions, Romeo's separation anxiety was reduced to the point that he could stay home with a competent babysitter for an hour and then for increasingly longer periods. During the summer, he was enrolled in a vacation church school, which he enjoyed; when the new semester began at public school, he entered the first grade and made an adequate adjustment. It should be emphasized that the cooperation of the parents—particularly the mother—was a key factor in the treatment. For a look at two other therapies that are often successful with children experiencing anxiety, see *HIGHLIGHT 15.5*

■ Childhood Depression

Clinicians working with children in mental health settings have long noted a pattern of symptoms that seemed indicative of depression. Spitz (1946) first described the problem, which he called *anaclitic depression,* as a behavior pattern, similar to adult depression, that occurred in children experiencing prolonged separation from their mothers. This specific childhood depression syndrome included slowed development and such symptomatic behavior as weepiness, sadness, immobility, and apathy.

The Clinical Picture in Childhood Depression   Childhood depression has been recognized as a diagnostic problem by a number of investigators (Herzog & Rathbun, 1982; Kashani et al., 1981b; Ryan et al., 1987). It includes behaviors such as withdrawal, crying, avoidance of eye con-

Amanda has separation anxiety disorder and has been in therapy for three years. Amanda's anxiety over being separated from her mother was severe and interfered with going to school, restaurants, movies, friends' houses, and all manner of situations that are common to a child of her age. Her therapist sees both Amanda and her mother in family therapy and also treats Amanda using exposure therapy, which involves a step-by-step process of encouraging the child to confront the situations that create anxiety for her. Amanda is improving and is now able to enjoy activities such as sleepovers at friends' houses.

tact, physical complaints, poor appetite, and even aggressive behavior. Moreover, Kovacs (1989) recently noted that there is "compelling evidence from a variety of sources that affective disorders among children and adolescents are more persistent than hitherto thought" (p. 209). Some clinicians have reported that depressive disorders in children are quite commonplace (Costello, 1980). Estimates of the frequency of depressive symptoms in children have ranged from 13 percent (Kashani et al., 1982) to 23 percent (Kashani, Venzke, & Millar, 1981). Lefkowitz and Tesiny (1985), in a large scale study of "normal" children in an elementary school system, found the overall prevalence rate of depression symptoms to be 5.2 percent. Rutter, Izard, and Read (1986) reported that depressive disorders show an increase in incidence over the age span. A marked rise in depression symptoms occurs during teenage years (Fleming, Offord, & Boyle, 1989).

Some investigators have questioned the existence of a separate syndrome of childhood depression (Lefkowitz & Burton, 1978; Schulterbrandt & Raskin, 1977). For one thing, the symptoms listed as central to the syndrome are common in many normal children (MacFarlane, Allen, & Honzik, 1954; Werry & Quay, 1971). Another argument against a special depressive disorder for children is that cross-cultural studies of depression have not supported the idea of a childhood depression (Marsella, 1980). One investigator, Makita (1973), noted that out of 3000 cases of disturbed children in Japan, not one was diagnosed with childhood depression.

Currently, childhood depression is classified using the mood disorder categories in the DSM-III-R adult diagnostic system. This use of adult diagnostic depressive categories with children is considered to be appropriate by many. Lobovits and Handel (1985), for example, found that DSM-III adult diagnostic categories could reliably be used with children. They reported a depression prevalence rate of 35 percent for boys and 31 percent for girls who were being seen for various school-related problems in an outpatient clinic. Lobovits and Handel conclude that the use of DSM-III adult criteria with children "offers a useful starting point for untangling the confusion surrounding the diagnosis and prevalence rate of childhood disorder" (p. 52).

The advisory committee of the American Psychiatric Association chose not to incorporate a special diagnostic disorder for childhood depression in DSM-III-R. Instead, it recommends the use of adult-oriented diagnoses of depression, even though a number of people were lobbying for a special class of depression within the childhood disorders section. It appears that further research will be needed to document more clearly the "uniqueness" in childhood depression before a separate diagnostic category will be devised.

Causal Factors in Childhood Depression

The causal factors described in the childhood anxiety disorders are pertinent to the depressive disorders as well. Maladaptive learning appears to be central in childhood depressive disorders. Children who are exposed to negative parental behavior or negative emotional states may develop depressed affect themselves.

One important area of recent research is focusing on the mother-child interaction in the transmission of depressed affect. Specifically, investigators have been evaluating the possibility that mothers who are depressed, through their interactions with their infants, transfer their low mood to them. Depression among mothers is not uncommon, and can result from several sources. Of course, many women who are clinically depressed have children. Some women, however, become depressed during pregnancy or following the delivery of their child. Several investigators have reported that marital distress, delivery complications, and difficulties with the infant are associated with depression in the mothers (Campbell et al., 1990; Sameroff, Seifer, & Zax, 1982).

Extensive research supports the view that the patterns of mother-infant behavior are critical to the development of attachment in a child (Egeland & Farber, 1984). Negative (depressed) affect and constricted mood on the part of a mother, manifested in unresponsive facial expressions and irritable behavior, can produce similar responses in her infant (Cohn & Tronick, 1983; Tronick & Cohn, 1989). Cohn and Campbell (in press) have shown that "infants respond in specific and characteristic ways to depressed maternal affect, and that these effects carry over to situations in which mothers no longer behave in a depressed way."

Cohn and his colleagues (Cohn & Tronick, 1983; Cohn & Campbell, in press) have shown that when mothers interact with their depressed infants the children respond by turning away from them. Even nondepressed mothers, when trained to simulate a constricted-depressed interaction with their child, produce similar infant coping responses. Moreover, these infant coping responses persist even after the mother has stopped interacting with a "depressive" interaction style (Cohn & Tronick, 1983).

The extent to which an infant's negative response to a mother's depressed, constricted mood results in later childhood depression has not been

Family Therapy and Play Therapy with Children

For a number of reasons, therapeutic intervention with children experiencing psychological problems is often a more complicated process than providing psychotherapy for adults. First, the source of a child's problem and the means for changing are often not within the child's power but instead are imbedded in the context of complex family interaction patterns. To remedy the child's problems, it is often necessary to alter those pathological family interaction patterns that produce or maintain the child's behavior. Second, even if the child's problems are viewed as primary and in need of specific therapeutic intervention, he or she may not be motivated for therapy or sufficiently verbal to gain understanding through psychotherapeutic methods that work with adults. Consequently, effective psychological treatment with children may involve using more indirect methods, such as treating an entire family in *family therapy* or providing individual psychological therapy for children in a less intrusive and more familiar way—through the activity of play in *play therapy*. We will examine these two approaches in more detail.

Family therapy. An important means of treating psychological problems in disturbed children is through family therapy. Several family therapy approaches have been developed (Bowen, 1978; Fisch, Weakland, & Segal, 1982; Minuchin, 1974; Patterson, 1971). These approaches differ in some important ways, for example, in terms of how the family is defined (whether to include extended family members, such as grandparents, cousins, and so on); what the treatment process will focus on (for example, whether communications between the family members or the "aberrant behavior" of the problem family members is the focus); what procedures are used in the treatment process (for example, analyzing and interpreting hidden messages in the family communications or focusing on altering the reward and punishment contingencies through behavioral assessment and reinforcement). Regardless of their differences, all family therapies view a child's problems, at least in part, as an outgrowth of pathological interaction patterns within his or her family, and they attempt to bring about positive change in the family members

through analysis and modification of the deviant family patterns.

How effective is family therapy at improving disruptive family relationships and promoting a more positive atmosphere for children? This is, of course, a difficult question to answer through research because treatment processes and outcomes are often difficult to measure. Nevertheless, Hazelrigg, Cooper, and Borduin (1987), after comparing the research to date on family therapy, concluded that family therapy had positive effects when contrasted with no-treatment control samples or with alternative treatment approaches, such as individual therapy. Research has shown that negative interaction patterns can be effectively changed by family therapy (Johnson & Maloney, 1979). Moreover, a number of studies have also shown that positive changes in a child's behavior can be brought about more effectively with family therapy than with alternative treatment methods (Christensen et al., 1980).

Play therapy. As a treatment technique, play therapy emerged out of efforts to apply psychodynamic therapy to children. A number of factors limit the application of tra-

---

fully determined. This research is highly suggestive, however, and may eventually lead to a fuller understanding of the possible link between a mother's mood and her child's behavior.

Treatments and Outcomes   The psychological treatment of depressed children and adolescents generally follows the intervention strategies used with children suffering anxiety-based disorders. An important facet of psychological therapy with children involves providing a supportive emotional

environment for them to learn more adaptive coping strategies and effective emotional expression. Older children and adolescents can often benefit from a positive therapeutic relationship in which they can discuss their feelings openly. Younger children or those with lower verbal skills may benefit from play therapy when they can, through play activities, experience a more full, positive range of emotions.

In many respects, the treatment of childhood depression has followed the treatment intervenditional psychodynamic therapy methods to children. Children do not voluntarily seek treatment and their motivation for self-change is different than for many troubled adults. They tend to be oriented to the present and lack the capability for insight and self-scrutiny that psychodynamic therapy requires. Their perceptions of their therapist differ from those of adult patients, and they may have an unrealistic view that the therapist can magically change their environment (Wenar, 1990).

Through their play, children often express their feelings, fears, and emotions in a direct and un-censored fashion, providing a clinician with a considerable means of understanding a child's problems and feelings. The activity of play has become a valuable source of obtaining personality and problem information about children. Psychodynamic techniques have been adapted for children by using play activity (in lieu of free association, used with adults) to enable a therapist to infer emotional conflicts, inappropriate affects, and excessive emotions a child might be experiencing. Play therapy sessions are usually centered around doll or puppet play

to give a child a vehicle for expressing feelings. Other activities, particularly construction with different materials, such as play dough, crayons, and paper, are also used to encourage free expression.

In a play therapy session, the therapist usually needs to provide some structure or to guide play activities so that pertinent feelings and emotions are allowed to be expressed. This might mean that the therapist asks direct questions of the child during the play session, such as: "Is the doll happy now?" or "What makes the doll cry?"

In addition to using play activity as a means of understanding a troubled child's problems, it also provides a medium for bringing about change in the child's behavior. A central process in play therapy is that the therapist, through interpretation, providing emotional support, and clarification of feelings (often by labeling them for the child), provides the child with a corrective emotional experience. That is, the therapist provides the child with an accepting and trusting relationship that promotes healthier personality and relationship development.

The play therapy situation enables the child to reexpesience conflict or problems in the safety of the therapy room, thereby providing a chance to conquer fears, to acclimate to necessary life changes, or to gain a feeling of security to replace the anxiety and uncertainty that had troubled him or her.

How effective is play therapy in reducing a child's problems and promoting better adjustment? When compared with adult treatment studies, play therapy compares quite favorably. Casey and Berman (1985) conducted a careful study of treatment research with children and concluded that such treatment "appears to match the efficacy of psychotherapy with adults" (p. 395). Play therapy was found to be as effective as other types of treatment, such as behavior therapy.

tions found successful with adults experiencing depression, with both psychological approaches and medications receiving prominence. Moreau (1990), for example, recommended that a combination of individual psychotherapy and tricyclic medication be used in the treatment of childhood depression to provide both a mood elevation and the opportunity for the child to discuss his or her feelings.

An important aspect in the treatment of depression in young people is the necessity of a suicide appraisal, as illustrated by the following case:

Jack was admitted to a child psychiatric hospital unit after he attempted to stab himself in the stomach with a medium sized kitchen knife. The suicide attempt was foiled by his mother, who pulled the knife away from her son. This suicide attempt occurred immediately after Jack had an argument with his father. Jack felt that his "father hates me" and that "I would be better off dead." A variety of factors made Jack vulnerable to suicidal tendencies. Jack grew up in an atmos-

phere in which there was intense disagreement between his parents. His father drank heavily and when drunk would physically assault his mother. Jack's mother was chronically depressed and often said that "life is not worth living." However, she loved her son and felt that because he needed her, she must continue to work and manage the home. Jack has a serious learning disability, and he struggled to maintain his school grades. He had a private tutor who helped him overcome his sad feelings and shame. Often, when teased by his classmates, he thought about ending his life. (Pfeffer, 1985, pp. 218–219)

Depressed mood has come to be viewed as an important risk factor in suicide among children and adolescents (Posener, Le Haye, & Cheifetz, 1989; Rubenstein et al., 1989; Slap et al., 1989; Velez & Cohen, 1987). In fact, over 5000 American adolescents kill themselves each year (Youth Suicide in the United States, 1986), and suicide has tripled for individuals between the ages of 15 and 24 during the 1980s (Blumenthal, 1990).

■ Other Symptom Disorders

The behavior disorders we will deal with in this section—elimination disorders (enuresis and encopresis), sleepwalking, and tics—typically involve a single outstanding symptom rather than a pervasive maladaptive pattern.

Functional Enuresis   The term **enuresis** refers to the habitual involuntary discharge of urine, usually at night, after the age of expected continence (age 5). In DSM-III-R, *functional enuresis* refers to bed-wetting that is not organically caused. Children who have *primary functional enuresis* have never been continent; children who have *secondary functional enuresis* have been continent for at least a year, but have regressed.

Enuresis may vary in frequency, from nightly occurrence to occasional instances when an individual is under considerable stress or is unduly tired. The actual incidence of enuresis is unknown, but it has been estimated that some four to five million children and adolescents in the United States suffer from the inconvenience and embarrassment of this disorder (Turner & Taylor, 1974). Estimates of the prevalence of enuresis reported in DSM-III-R are 7 percent for boys and 3 percent for girls at age 5; 3 percent for boys and 2 percent for girls at age 10; and 1 percent for boys and almost nonexistent for girls at age 18. Research has shown that there are

clear sex differences in enuresis as well as age differences. In a recent epidemiological study of enuresis in Holland, Verhulst et al. (1985) determined that between the ages of 5 and 8, the percentages of enuresis problems for boys is about two to three times that for girls. The percentages for boys also diminish at a slower rate; the decline for girls between ages 4 and 6 is about 71 percent, while the declioe for boys is only 16 percent. The authors recommend that the age criteria for boys' enuresis be extended to age 8 because it is at about age 9 that approximately the same percentage of boys as girls reach "dryness," that is, wetting the bed less than once a month.

Although enuresis may result from a variety of organic conditions, such as disturbed cerebral control of the bladder (Kaada & Retvedt, 1981), most investigators have pointed to a number of other possible causal factors: (a) faulty learning, resulting in the failure to acquire a needed adaptive response—that is, inhibition of reflex bladder emptying; (b) personal immaturity, associated with or stemming from emotional problems; and (c) disturbed family interactions, particularly those that lead to sustained anxiety, hostility, or both. In some instances, a child may regress to bed-wetting when a new baby enters the family and becomes the center of attention. Children also may resort to bed-wetting when they feel hostile toward their parents and want to get even, realizing that such behavior is annoying and upsetting to adults. In adolescence and adulthood, enuresis is often associated with other psychological problems. Research evidence supports a multiplicity of possible causes for enuresis, with many cases being explained by either environmental factors or maturational lags (Christie, 1981).

Conditioning procedures have proven effective in the treatment of enuresis (Doleys, 1979). Maurer and Maurer (1938) introduced a procedure in which a child may sleep on a pad that is wired to a battery-operated bell. At the first few drops of urine, the bell is set off, thus awakening the child. Through conditioning, the child comes to associate bladder tension with awakening. Fortunately, with or without treatment, the incidence of enuresis tends to decrease significantly with age. Nevertheless, many experts believe that enuresis should be treated in childhood because no way currently exists to identify which children will remain enuretic into adulthood.

Functional Encopresis   The term **encopresis** describes children who have not learned appropriate toileting for bowel movements after age 4. This condition is less common than enuresis. However, about 2.3 percent of 8-year-old boys and 0.7 percent of 8-year-old girls are encopretic (Bellman, 1966). The following list of characteristics was provided by Levine (1976) from a study of 102 cases of encopretic children:

- The average age was 7, with a range from ages 4 to 13.
- About one-third of encopretic children were also enuretic.
- A large sex difference was found, with about six times more boys than girls in the sample.
- Many of the children soiled their clothing when they were under stress. A common time was in the late afternoon after school. Few children actually had this problem at school.
- Most of the children reported that they did not know when they needed to have a bowel movement.

Many encopretic children suffer from constipation; thus an important element in the diagnosis of the disorder involves a physical examination to determine whether physiological factors are contributing to the disorder. The treatment of encopresis usually involves both medical and psychological aspects. Levine and Bakow (1975) found that, of the encopretic children they studied who were treated by medical and behavioral procedures, more than half were cured—that is, no additional incidents occurred within six months following treatment. An additional 25 percent were improved.

Sleepwalking (Somnambulism)   Though the onset of **sleepwalking disorder** is usually between the ages of 6 and 12, the disorder is classified broadly under sleep disorders in DSM-III-R rather than under disorders of infancy, childhood, and adolescence. The symptoms of sleepwalking disorder involve repeated episodes in which a person leaves his or her bed and walks around without being conscious of the experience or remembering it later.

Statistics are meager, but it is estimated that 1 to 6 percent of children experience regular or periodic sleepwalking episodes. Children subject to this problem usually go to sleep in a normal manner but arise during the second or third hour of sleep. They may walk to another room of the house or even outside, and they may engage in complex activities. Finally they return to bed and in the morning remember nothing that has taken place.

While moving about, sleepwalkers' eyes are partially or fully open; they avoid obstacles, listen when spoken to, and ordinarily respond to commands, such as to return to bed. Shaking them will usually awaken sleepwalkers, and they will be surprised and perplexed at finding themselves in an unexpected place. Sleepwalking episodes usually last from 15 to 30 minutes. The risk of injury during sleepwalking is illustrated by the following case study:

14-year-old Donald Elliot got up from his bunk in his sleep, looked in the refrigerator, then, still asleep, walked out the back door. It would have been just another sleepwalking episode except that Donald was in a camper-pickup truck traveling 50 miles an hour on the San Diego freeway. Miraculously, he escaped with cuts and bruises. But his experience, and that of many other sleepwalkers, disproves one of the myths about somnambulism: that people who walk in their sleep don't hurt themselves. (Taves, 1969, p. 41)

The causes of sleepwalking are not fully understood. Kales and associates (1966) have shown that sleepwalking takes place during NREM (non–rapid eye movement) sleep, but its relationship to dreaming remains unclear. In general, it appears that sleepwalking is related to some anxiety-arousing situation that has just occurred or is expected to occur in the near future.

Little attention has been given to the treatment of sleepwalking. Clement (1970), however, has reported on the treatment of a 7-year-old boy through behavior therapy, as described in *HIGHLIGHT 15.6*. Nagaraja (1974) has reported the successful treatment of an 8-year-old boy and a 9-year-old girl with a combination of tranquilizers and psychotherapy. Nevertheless, a good deal of additional research is needed before we can determine the most effective treatment procedures for sleepwalking.

Tics   A **tic** is a persistent, intermittent muscle twitch or spasm, usually limited to a localized muscle group. The term is used broadly to include blinking the eye, twitching the mouth, licking the lips, shrugging the shoulders, twisting the neck, clearing the throat, blowing the nose, and grimacing, among other actions. Tics occur most frequently between the ages of 6 and 14 (Schowalter, 1980). In some instances, as in clearing the throat, an individual may be aware of the tic when it occurs; but usually he or she performs the act habitually and does not notice it. In fact, many individuals do not even realize they have a tic unless someone brings it to their attention. The psychological impact tics can

HIGHLIGHT 15.6

The Treatment of Sleepwalking Utilizing Conditioning Procedures

Bobby, a 7-year-old boy, walked in his sleep an average of four times a week. His mother kept a record indicating that Bobby's sleepwalking episodes were associated with nightmares, perspiring, and talking in his sleep. During the actual sleepwalking, Bobby usually was glassy-eyed and unsteady on his feet. On one occasion, he started out the front door. The sleepwalking had commenced about six weeks before the boy was brought for therapy. Usually an episode would begin about 45 to 90 minutes after he had gone to bed.

During treatment, the therapist learned that just before each sleepwalking episode Bobby usually had a nightmare about being chased by "a big black bug." In his dream, Bobby thought "the bug would eat off his legs if it caught him" (Clement, 1970, p. 23).

Bobby's sleepwalking episodes usually showed the following sequence: after his nightmare began, he perspired freely, moaned and talked in his sleep, tossed and turned, and finally got up and walked through the house. He did not remember the sleepwalking episode when he awoke the next morning.

Assessment data revealed no neurological or other medical problems and indicated that Bobby was of normal intelligence. He was, however, found to be "a very anxious, guilt-ridden little boy who avoided performing assertive and aggressive behaviors appropriate to his age and sex" (p. 23). Assertiveness training and related measures were used but were not effective. The therapist then focused treatment on having Bobby's mother awaken the boy each

time he showed signs of an impending episode. After washing Bobby's face with cold water and making sure he was fully awake, the mother would return him to bed, where he was "to hit and tear up a picture of the big black bug." (At the start of the treatment program, Bobby had made up several of these drawings.)

Eventually, the nightmare was associated with awakening, and Bobby learned to wake up on most occasions when he was having a bad dream. Clement considered the basic behavior therapy model in this case to follow that used in the conditioning treatment for enuresis, where a waking response is elicited by an intense stimulus just as urination is beginning and becomes associated with, and eventually prevents, nocturnal bed-wetting.

---

have on an adolescent is exemplified in the following case:

> *An adolescent who had wanted very much to be a teacher told the school counselor that he was thinking of giving up his plans. When asked the reason, he explained that several friends had told him that he had a persistent twitching of the mouth muscles when he answered questions in class. He had been unaware of this muscle twitch and even after being told about it could not tell when it took place. However, he became acutely self-conscious and was reluctant to answer questions or enter into class discussions. As a result, his general level of tension increased, and so did the frequency of the tic, which now became apparent even when he was talking to his friends. Thus a vicious circle had been established. Fortunately, it proved amenable to treatment by conditioning and assertiveness training.*

An extreme tic disorder involving multiple motor and vocal patterns is **Tourette's syndrome.** This disorder typically involves uncontrollable head movements with accompanying sounds, such as grunts, clicks, yelps, sniffs, or words. About one-third of individuals with Tourette's syndrome manifest *coprolalia,* which is a complex vocal tic involving the uttering of obscenities. The average age of onset for Tourette's syndrome is age 7, and most cases have an onset before age 14. The disorder is about three times more frequent among males. Although the exact cause of Tourette's syndrome is undetermined, some evidence suggests an organic basis for the syndrome.

Most tics, however, do not have an organic basis but usually stem from psychological causes, such as self-consciousness or tension in social situations. As in the case of the adolescent boy previously described, an individual's awareness of the tic often increases the tension—and the tic. Tics have been successfully treated by means of drugs, psychotherapy, and conditioning techniques. Ollendick

(1981) reported success in treating tics by using behavioral techniques of self-monitoring and over-correction.

PLANNING BETTER PROGRAMS TO HELP CHILDREN AND YOUTH

In our discussion of several problems of childhood and adolescence, we have noted the wide range of treatment procedures available, as well as the marked differences in outcomes. In concluding the chapter, we will discuss certain special factors associated with the treatment of children, the problem of child abuse, and the new emphasis on child advocacy and the rights of children, which involves a social commitment to provide conditions conducive to their optimal development.

Special Factors Associated with Treatment for Children

A number of special factors must be considered in relation to treatment for children.

1. *The child's inability to seek assistance.* The great majority of emotionally disturbed children who need assistance are not in a position to ask for it themselves or to transport themselves to and from child guidance clinics. Thus, unlike an adult or an adolescent, who usually can seek help during crisis periods, a child is dependent, primarily on his or her parents. Adults should realize when a child needs professional help and take the initiative in obtaining it. Sometimes, however, adults neglect this responsibility. Plotkin (1981) pointed out:

Parents have traditionally had the right to consent to health services for their children. In situations where the interest of the parents and children differ the rule has had unfortunate consequences and has left treatment professionals in a quandary. (p. 121)

The law identifies four areas in which treatment without parental consent is permitted: (a) in the case of mature minors (those considered to be capable of making decisions about themselves); (b) in the case of emancipated minors (those living independently—away from their parents); (c) in emergency situations; and (d) in situations in which

a court orders treatment. Many children, of course, come to the attention of treatment agencies as a consequence of school referrals, delinquent acts, or parental abuse.

2. *The double deprivation of children from pathogenic homes.* Many families provide an undesirable environment for their growing children. In fact, studies have shown that up to a fourth of American children may be living in inadequate homes (Joint Commission on the Mental Health of Children, 1968; Office of Technology Assessment, 1986). Child care, however, is traditionally the responsibility of parents, and local and state agencies intervene only in extreme cases—usually those involving physical abuse. This means that children growing up in pathogenic homes are at a double disadvantage. Not only are they deprived from the standpoint of environmental influence on their personality development, but they also lack parents who will perceive their need for help and actively seek and participate in treatment programs.

3. *The need for treatment of the parents as well as the child.* Because most of the behavior disorders specific to childhood appear to grow out of pathogenic family interactions, it is usually essential for the parents, as well as their child, to receive treatment. In some instances, in fact, the treatment program may focus on the parents entirely, as in the case of child abuse.

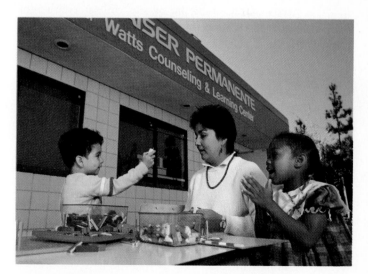

It is important that adults realize when a child needs professional help and take the initiative in obtaining it. For some parents, however, the effort involved in finding appropriate help, not to mention the economic factors of paying for treatment and of taking time away from work to take their child to therapy sessions, are very real deterrents to seeking help.

Increasingly, then, the treatment of children has come to mean family therapy, in which one or both parents, along with the child and siblings, may participate in all phases of the program. For working parents, however, and for parents who basically reject the affected child, such treatment may be difficult to arrange, especially in the case of poorer families who lack transportation and money. Thus, both parental and economic factors help determine which emotionally disturbed children will receive assistance.

4. *The possibility of using parents as change agents.* A recent trend, as we have seen, has been to teach parents to be change agents. In essence, the parents are trained in techniques that enable them to help their child. Typically, such training focuses on helping the parents understand the child's behavior disorder and learn to reinforce adaptive behavior while withholding reinforcement for undesirable behavior. Encouraging results have been obtained with parents who care about their children and want to help (Arnold, 1978; Atkeson & Forehand, 1978; Forehand et al., 1981; Johnson & Katz, 1973; Lexow & Aronson, 1975; Mash et al., 1976; O'Dell, 1974).

5. *The problem of placing the child outside the family.* Most communities have juvenile facilities that, day or night, will provide protective care and custody for young victims of unfit homes, abandonment, abuse, neglect, and related conditions. Depending on the home situation and the special needs of the child, he or she will later either be returned to his or her parents or placed elsewhere. In the latter instance, four types of facilities are commonly relied on: foster homes, private institutions for the care of children, county or state institutions, or the homes of relatives. At any one time, over half a million children are living in foster-care facilities.

The quality of a child's new home, of course, is a crucial determinant of whether the child's problems will be alleviated or made worse. Although efforts are made to screen the placement facilities and maintain contact with the situation through follow-up visits, there have been too many reported cases of mistreatment. Perhaps the most dramatic example of unintended harm from the placement of children in foster homes was the large number of children who were forced to commit suicide by the Reverend Jim Jones in the 1978 Jonestown murder-suicide. Jones was a cult leader who persuaded his followers to leave the United States to live in a jungle compound in Jonestown, Guyana. He received large amounts of money for the foster children in his care.

In cases of child abuse, child abandonment, or a serious childhood behavior problem that parents cannot control, it has often been assumed that the only feasible action was to take the child out of the home and find a temporary substitute. With such a child's own home so obviously inadequate, the hope has been that a more stable outside placement would be better. But when children are taken from their own homes and placed in an impersonal institution (which promptly tries to change them) or in a series of foster homes (where they obviously do not really belong), they are likely to feel rejected by their own parents, unwanted by their new caretakers, rootless, constantly insecure—and lonely and bitter.

Accordingly, the trend today is toward *permanent planning*. First, every effort is made to hold a family together and to give the parents the support and guidance they need for adequate childrearing. If this is impossible, then efforts are made to free the child legally for adoption and to find an adoptive home as soon as possible. This, of course, means that the public agencies need specially trained staffs with reasonable caseloads and access to resources that they and their clients may need.

6. *The importance of intervening early, before problems become acute.* Over the last 20 years, a primary concern of many researchers and clinicians has been to identify and provide early help for children who are at special risk. Rather than wait until these children develop acute psychological problems that may require therapy or major changes in living arrangements, psychologists are attempting to identify conditions in such children's lives that seem likely to bring about or maintain behavior problems and, where such conditions exist, to intervene before a child's development has been seriously distorted. An example of this approach is provided in the work of Wallerstein and Kelly (1980):

These researchers identified children who were at risk for psychological disturbance as a result of their parents going through a divorce. Each of the 66 participating families was seen by a clinician, and the children were seen separately for several sessions. The goals of the counseling sessions were to provide the children with a means of expressing their worries and frustrations and to strengthen their resources for dealing with them.

In addition to the counseling sessions, there were several follow-up sessions after the divorce to examine the psychological changes in the children and the changes in the family structure over time. The interventions were judged to be successful in lowering the tension levels in the family situations and in enhancing the children's adjustment to their new living arrangements.

Such early intervention has the double goal of reducing the stressors in a child's life and strengthening the child's coping mechanisms. If successful, it can effectively reduce the number and intensity of later problems, thus averting much grief for both the individuals concerned and the broader society. It is apparent that children's needs can be met only if adequate preventive and treatment facilities for children exist and are available to the children who need assistance. In the next section, we will look at the specific issue of child abuse, which is of growing concern to researchers and practitioners who want to know what causes it and how it can be prevented. In our final section, we will look at the leadership that government agencies have been providing in spotlighting the special needs of children and youth, and we will also discuss our society's responsibility to meet those needs.

■ Child Abuse

Child abuse is a growing concern in the United States. A Department of Health and Human Services Report (House of Representatives, 1990) indicated that the numbers of children reported as abused and neglected rose 64 percent from 1980 to 1988, for an astounding total of 2.2 million cases of childhood maltreatment reported in 1988.

In child abuse cases, 20 to 40 percent of the children have been seriously injured. Although children and adolescents of all ages are physically abused, the most frequent cases involve children under 3 years of age. Some evidence suggests that boys are more often abused than girls. It is usually clear that many children brought to the attention of legal agencies for abuse have been abused before (Kempe & Kempe, 1979; President's Commission on Mental Health, 1978).

In a survey of family violence, Gelles (1978) reported that violence well beyond ordinary physi-

cal punishment is a widespread phenomenon in parent-child relationships. Milder forms of punishment, Gelles found, were common among respondents; for example, 71 percent of parents reported having slapped or spanked their children, 46 percent reported pushing and shoving incidents, and around 10 percent reported having thrown something at their children. Gelles extrapolated estimates of serious violence from his survey to the general population and concluded that 46 percent of American children had suffered serious abuse, such as being kicked, bitten, or punched by parents.

The seriousness of the child abuse problem in our society was not realized until the 1960s, when researchers began to report case after case like the following two:

The mother of a 29-month-old boy claimed he was a behavior problem, beat him with a stick and screwdriver handle, dropped him on the floor, beat his head on the wall or threw him against it, choked him to force his mouth open to eat, and burned him on the face and hands. After she had severely beaten him, the mother found the child dead.

Because her 2½-year-old daughter did not respond readily enough to toilet training the mother became indignant and in a fit of temper over the child's inability to control a bowel movement gave her an enema with near scalding water. To save the child's life a doctor was forced to perform a colostomy. (Earl, 1965)

Many abused children show impaired cognitive ability and memory when compared with control children (Friedrich, Einbender, & Luecke, 1983). In addition, abused children are likely to show problems in social adjustment and are particularly likely to feel that the outcomes of events are determined by external factors beyond their own control (Barahal, Waterman, & Martin, 1981). They are also more likely to experience depressive symptoms (Kazdin et al., 1985). Abused children are dramatically less likely to assume personal responsibility, and they generally demonstrate less interpersonal sensitivity than control children. Abused children also tend to show more self-destructive behavior than nonabused control subjects (Green, 1978).

When the abuse involves a sexual component, such as incest or rape, the long-range consequences can be very marked. Harter, Alexander, and Nei-meyer (1988) found that victims of sexual abuse often suffered interpersonal adjustment difficulties for years following the incident. Jackson and colleagues (1990) found that women who had experienced intrafamily sexual abuse had significantly poorer social adjustment, especially in dating relationships. The women also reported significantly lower sexual satisfaction, more sexual dysfunctions, and lower self-esteem than control women.

The role of sexual abuse in the experience of psychological problems has recently been the subject of several longitudinal studies. A number of investigators have followed up sexually abused children to study the long-term effects of abuse on a victim's behavior. A large percentage of sexually abused children experience intense psychological symptoms following the incident (for example, 74 percent reported by Bentovim, Boston, & Van Elburg, 1987). At follow-up, however, the improvement often seems dramatic. Gomes-Schwartz, Horowitz, and Cardarelli (1990) found that 55 percent of victims had substantially improved at follow-up 18 months later, particularly in terms of sleeping problems, fears of uhe offender, and anxiety. However, 28 percent of the victims showed worsening behavior, such as family conflict and inappropriate attention seeking. Similarly, several other studies have reported substantial improvement of sexually abused victims at follow-up (Bentovim et al., 1987; Conte, Berliner, & Schuerman, 1986).

Although many children experience improvement in the months following the incident, some victims do not actually show problems until buried memories begin to surface during later psychological treatment for other reasons (Courtois & Sprei, 1988). In a recent study of psychiatric outpatients being treated at a university hospital, Jacobson (1989) reported that 68 percent of the women studied had experienced major sexual assault.

Several investigators have conceptualized the residual symptoms of sexual abuse as a type of posttraumatic stress disorder (PTSD) because the symptoms experienced are similar; for example, nightmares, flashbacks, sleep problems, and feelings of estrangement (Donaldson & Gardner, 1985; Frederick, 1986). However, other investigators (e.g., Finkelhor, 1990) object to this explanation on grounds that viewing these symptoms as an example of PTSD will "lead us to miss some of [the] most serious effects" of the sexual abuse experience such as prolonged depression or anxiety (p. 329).

Causal Factors in Child Abuse   Since the 1960s, a great deal of research has been aimed at finding out which parents abuse their children and why, in the hope that ultimately these parents can be stopped, or better yet, prevented, from abusing their children. We now know that parents who physically abuse their children tend to be young, with the majority under 30. In most reported cases, they come from the lower socioeconomic levels (Egeland & Erickson, 1990). An important common factor among families with abusing parents is a higher-than-average degree of frustration; many stressors are present in their lives, including marital discord, high unemployment, and alcohol abuse (Egeland, Cicchetti, & Taraldson, 1976). Many incidents of physical abuse occur as parental reactions to a child's misbehavior in areas such as fighting, sexual behavior, aggression, and so on (Herrenkohl, Herrenkohl, & Egolf, 1983). Although no clear and consistent personality pattern emerges as typical of child-abusing parents, they seem to show a higher-than-average rate of psychological disturbance (Serrano et al., 1979). Some evidence from personality testing shows that they tend to be aggressive, nonconforming, selfish, and lacking in appropriate impulse control (Lund, 1975).

Knowledge about causal factors in child abuse is limited and incomplete because most studies have involved retrospective analyses of cases identified through legal agencies. However, one study (Egeland & Brunnquell, 1979) identified 275 families in a population generally at risk for child abuse *before* the birth of a child. From this group, the investigators then identified the 25 mothers at highest risk for child abuse and the 25 mothers most likely not to be child abusers. These two groups have now been followed over several years. Eight of the highest-risk mothers have actually abused their children; none of the other group has done so. There are many striking differences between the two groups. The mothers in the group identified as at lowest risk tend to be older, to show more understanding of the psychological complexity of their children, to have better caretaking skills, and to show more positive feeling for their children. The other mothers, in general, live more chaotic lives. Over twice as many are single (74 percent as compared with 32 percent). They are also more involved in disrupted relationships, physical fights, and heavy drinking in the immediate family. A recent study found that antisocial personality features were common among the women in the sample (Egeland et al., 1990). Another study by Egeland and his colleagues showed a clear intergenerational pattern of child abuse; that is, 70 percent of the mothers who were identified as having been abused as children also mistreated their children (Egeland, Jacobvitz, & Papatola, 1987).

The Prevention of Child Abuse   Practitioners and child protection agencies have begun an extensive effort to reduce the amount and impact of child abuse. Their efforts include the following:

- Community education programs have been developed to increase public awareness of the problem. Television advertisements have been especially effective here.

- Child protection teams have been organized by many state and county welfare departments to investigate and intervene in reported cases of child abuse.

- Teams of mental health specialists in many community mental health centers are working to evaluate and provide psychological treatment for!both abused children and their parents.

- Parent support groups, often made up of former child abusers, are forming that can offer abusing parents or those at risk for child abuse alternative ways of behaving toward their children.

- Many communities are making it a legal requirement for physicians and other professionals to report cases of child abuse that come to their attention.

Research designed to enable early intervention with parents identified as likely to abuse their children has been promising. Wolfe and colleagues (1988) identified women who were at high risk for maltreatment of their children. They randomly assigned mothers to either a treatment or control group. The treatment consisted of behaviorally oriented parent training which provided child management skills; instruction in child care; modeling; rehearsal instructions to give clear, concise demands; and the use of "time out" as a punishment. The study showed that this early parent intervention reduced the risk for child abuse among the mothers provided the treatment. Through such efforts on many levels it is hoped that children will be spared abuse and that abusive or potentially abusive parents will be helped to be more effective and nurturant.

Unfortunately, child abuse all too frequently produces maladaptive social behavior in its victims. The treatment of abused children needs to address the problems of social adjustment, depression, and poor interpersonal skills that these children exhibit. An interesting treatment approach to reducing the negative consequences of child abuse is the use of peers to help modify abused children's tendency to withdraw and their poor social skills. Fantuzzo and colleagues (1988) trained peer confederates to make play overtures to abused children. They found that peer-initiated efforts were more effective at increasing the social!interaction of withdrawn children than adult-initiaued treatment efforts. Further work on rehabilitative efforts is needed to assist these unfortunate children in overcoming the psychologically disabling effects of being abused.

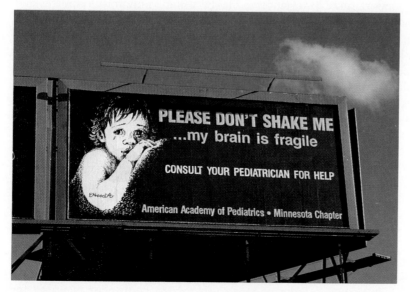

Community education programs to increase public awareness of the problem of child abuse are but one of the current efforts to reduce the amount and impact of child abuse.

■ Child Advocacy Programs

Today there are nearly 68 million people under age 18 in the United States (Spencer, 1989). This figure indicates that a massive social commitment is needed not only to provide adequate treatment facilities for children with problems but also to ensure the physical and social conditions that will foster the optimal development of all children.

Unfortunately, however, both treatment and preventive programs in our society have been—and remain—inadequate. In 1970 the National Institute of Mental Health pointed out that fewer than 1 percent of the disturbed children in our society were receiving any kind of treatment, and less than half of those children were getting adequaue help. In the same year, in its final report, *Crisis in Child Mental Health: Challenge for the 1970s,* the Joint Commission on the Mental Health of Children (1970) referred to our lack of commitment to our children and youth as a "national tragedy." The commission's report concluded:

Either we permit a fifth of the nation's children to go down the drain—with all that this implies for public disorder and intolerable inhumanity—or we decide, once and for all, that the needs of children have first priority on the nation's resources. (p. 408)

Unfortunately, eight years later, the President's Commission on Mental Health (1978) was still calling attention to the fact that children and adolescents were not receiving mental health services commensurate with their needs. The commission's report recommended again that greater efforts and financial resources be expended to serve the mental health needs of children and youth. It appears, however- that the needed financial support and redirected program focuses have not materialized in the years since the report was issued.

One approach to meeting mental health needs, known as **advocacy,** has been prominent in recent years. Advocacy attempts to help children or others receive services that they need but often are unable to obtain for themselves. In some cases, advocacy seeks to better conditions for underserved populations by changing the system (Biklen, 1976; Meyers & Parsons, 1987; Roberts & Peterson, 1984).

Twice in recent years the federal government has established a National Center for Child Advocacy to coordinate the many kinds of work for children's welfare performed by different government agencies. Both times the new agency proved ineffective and was given up after a year or so. Currently, the physical welfare of children is the responsibility of the Children's Bureau of the Labor Department, and the mental health needs of children are the responsibility of the Alcoholism, Drug Abuse, and Mental Health Administration of the Public Health Service. Delinquents are dealt with by the Justice Department. This fragmentation in children's services means that different agencies serve different needs; no government agency is charged with considering the whole child and planning comprehensively for children who need help.

Outside the federal government, until recently, advocacy efforts for children have been supported largely by legal and special-interest citizens' groups, such as the Children's Defense Fund, a public-interest organization based in Washington, D.C. Mental health professionals have typically not been involved. Today, however, there is greater interdisciplinary involvement in attempts to provide effective advocacy programs for children (Hermalin & Morell, 1986).

Unfortunately, although such programs have made important local gains toward bettering conditions for mentally disabled children, a great deal of confusion, inconsistency, and uncertainty still exists in the advocacy movement as a whole (Biklen, 1976; Levine & Perkins, 1987). In addition, the mood at both federal and state levels has for some time been to cut back on funds for social services.

In her presidential address to the Society of Pediatric Psychology, Magrab (1982) warned that economic cutbacks in child-oriented programs and the fragmented nature of existing programs represent a challenge "to the very survival" of psychological services to children. She encouraged mental health and health care professionals working in child advocacy not to become disheartened with the recent and continuing erosion of services but to exert a unified commitment to broadening advocacy programs by using community resources and by working with parents. Clearly, there is a great threat to existing children's programs and the coming years will require substantial effort on the part of professionals, parent groups, and enlightened elected officials to maintain past gains and to expand services to other needed areas. Tuma (1989), in a more recent examination of the problem, called for a better integration of scattered services to provide more effective help to the over 63 million children and adolescents in need of attention.

Clearly, the challenge issued in 1970 by the Joint Commission on the Mental Health of Children has not been adequately answered. Some important beginning steps, however, have been taken in the work toward child advocacy, the new efforts to identify and help high-risk children, and the present push toward permanent planning for

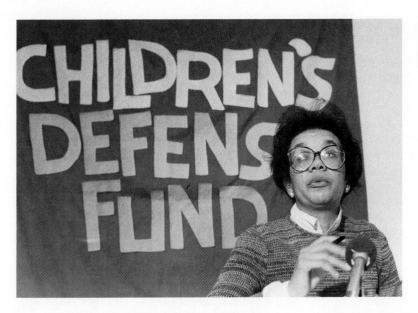

Marion Wright Edelman, leader of the Children's Defense Fund, a child-advocacy public-interest organization based in Washington, D.C.

children formerly sent to institutions or foster homes. If the direction and momentum of these efforts can be maintained and if sufficient financial support for them can be procured, the psychological environment for children could substantially improve.

 UNRESOLVED ISSUES
on Parental Pathology and Childhood Disorders

A great deal of research effort is being devoted to the question of whether parents' emotional problems are associated with the development of behavior problems in children and adolescents. Research has shown that parents who have children being seen in clinics for emotional problems tend to have more psychological problems than people in general. Furthermore, some recent research has suggested that parents of specific groups of severely disturbed children, such as conduct-disordered children, showed more deviant personality characteristics than parents of attention-deficit hyperactive children (Lahey et al., 1989). The question as to whether specific emotional problems among parents are associated with specific pathology in children and adolescents has not been clearly determined.

Are parents who are experiencing emotional problems transmitting their problems to their chil-

dren in some way? The evidence seems to be clear that children of disturbed parents are more vulnerable to developing psychological problems themselves than children of parents without emotional problems. For example, children of parents who were clinically depressed have been found to show a reduced level of psychological functioning and an increased preponderance of psychological disorders, including major depression, substance abuse, or internalization problems (Laroche et al., 1987; Weissman et al., 1987; Gotlib & Colby, 1987). Other emotional disorders in parents have also been found to be associated with emotional problems in children. Turner, Beidel, and Costello (1987) reported that children of parents diagnosed with an anxiety disorder showed more fears and more mood disturbance than children of control (community) parents. Dumas, Gibson, and Albin (1989) found that parental pathology was related to more conduct disorders in children.

The actual mechanisms for the transmission of pathology from parent to child remain unclear. Hammen et al. (1987), however, caution that it is not specific diagnoses among parents that result in specific disorders in children, but it is the stress and symptoms that parents experience that influence the child's behavior. Some research suggests that the mechanisms for instilling behavior problems in children are to be found in learning processes. For example, Gelfand and Teti (1990) concluded that maternal depression was associated with undesirable parenting practices, such as unresponsiveness, inattention, intrusiveness, inept discipline, and negative perceptions of children. Other researchers have pointed to family problems that create unfavorable emotional states; for example, tensions evolving from such incidents as parental divorce (Kornberg & Caplan, 1980) may produce psychological problems and achievement problems (Bisnaire, Firestone, & Rynard, 1990) in youngsters.

Although emotionally upsetting events, such as divorce, have been traced to childhood pathology, relationships between these and specific childhood psychopathology have not been clearly determined. Recent evidence suggests that it is not divorce per se that produces disorder in a child—it is parental pathology. Lahey and colleagues (1988) found that parental divorce alone did not account for increased conduct disorder among boys. Rather, antisocial personality characteristics among parents were associated with conduct problems, suggesting that parental identification may be involved. Other researchers have attributed some types of psychopathology in children to genetic factors (Rosenthal et al., 1975).

One extensive effort to understand the relationships between parental pathology and problems in children has been the Rochester longitudinal risk study (Sameroff et al., 1987). These investigators have followed up a sample of chronically ill schizophrenic women and their offspring to determine what, if any, impact their psychological problems and other possible risk factors (such as socioeconomic status, race, and family size) have on the development of behavior problems in their children. The women were initially assessed during their pregnancy and followed periodically since then. Their children have been evaluated over several periods since their birth. Sameroff et al. found that specific maternal diagnoses had the least impact on the development of behavior problems in the children. They reported that both socioeconomic status and the severity of the mother's illness had a greater impact on the child's developing problems. Children with multiple risk factors had much worse outcomes than children with fewer risk factors. The Rochester Adaptive Behavior Inventory (RABI) was used to obtain objective ratings of social-emotional competence on the children at the 4-year follow-up. The risk variables studied were chronicity of illness, anxiety, parental education and occupation, parental perspectives, interaction skill, minority status, family support, family size, and the presence of stressful life events. The graph in *HIGHLIGHT 15.7* shows that multiple risk factors are associated with low social and emotional competence ratings in children. The investigators also reported that although children of schizophrenic mothers are in-

deed at high risk for developing emotional problems, so too were children of severely ill mothers and those from poor and minority backgrounds.

Whether the transmission of psychopathology from parent to child is due to faulty learning processes, genetic transmission, or some combination of these and other factors, it seems clear that at least some childhood and adolescent disorders are related to parental psychopathology. The precise mechanism or mechanisms for the transmission itself remains for future research to untangle.

SUMMARY

Traditionally, diagnosing behavior problems of children and adolescents has been a rather confused practice, in part because children have sometimes been viewed as "miniature" adults. It was not until the second half of the twentieth century that a diagnostic classification system focused clearly on the special problems of children.

Two broad approaches to the classification of childhood and adolescent behavior problems have been undertaken: a categorical approach, reflected most extensively in the DSM-III-R, and a dimensional approach. Both classification approaches involve organized classes of symptoms that are based on observations of behavior. In the categorical approach, symptoms of behavior problems are grouped together as syndromes based on clinical observations. In the dimensional approach, a broad range of symptoms and observations on cases are submitted to multivariate statistical techniques; the symptoms that group together make up the diagnostic classes referred to as "dimensions."

In this chapter, the DSM-III-R classification system is followed in order to provide clinical descriptions of a wide range of childhood behavior problems. Attention-deficit hyperactivity disorder is one of the more frequent behavior problems of childhood. In this disorder, the child shows impulsive, overactive behavior that interferes with his or her ability to accomplish tasks. There is some controversy over the explicit criteria used to distinguish hyperactive children from "normal" children or from children who exhibit other behavior disorders, such as conduct disorders. This lack of clarity in defining hyperactivity increases the difficulty of determining causal factors for the disorder. The major approaches to treating hyperactive children

HIGHLIGHT 15.7

The Effect of Multiple Risk Factors on Social–Emotional Competence in Children

The relationship between the number of family risk factors and social-emotional competence in 4- year-old children is shown in the following graph. Children who receive the lowest ratings on social and emotional competency tend to have the greatest risk for developing emotional problems.

Sameroff et al. (1987).

Number of Risk Factors

RABI Global Rating

have been medication and behavior therapy. Using medications, such as amphetamines, with children is somewhat controversial. Behavior therapy, particularly cognitive-behavioral methods, has shown a great deal of promise in modifying the behavior of hyperactive children.

Another common behavior problem among children is that of conduct disorder. In this disorder, a child engages in persistent aggressive or antisocial acts. In cases where the child's misdeeds involve illegal activities, the terms *delinquent* or *juvenile delinquent* may be applied. A number of potential causes of conduct disorder or delinquent behavior have been determined, ranging from bio-

logical factors to personal pathology to social conditions. Treatment of conduct disorders and delinquent behavior is often frustrating and difficult; treatment is likely to be ineffective unless some means can be found for modifying a child's environment.

Another group of disorders, the childhood anxiety disorders, are quite different from the conduct disorders. Children who suffer from these disorders typically do not cause difficulty for others through their aggressive conduct. Rather they are fearful, shy, withdrawn, insecure, and have difficulty adapting to outside demands. The anxiety disorders may be characterized by extreme anxiety, withdrawal, or avoidance behavior. A likely cause for these disorders is early family relationships that generate anxiety and prevent the child from developing more adaptive coping skills. Behavior therapy approaches—such as assertiveness training and desensitization—may be helpful in treating this kind of disorder.

Several other disorders of childhood involve behavior problems centering around a single outstanding symptom rather than pervasive maladaptive patterns. The symptoms may involve enuresis, encopresis, sleepwalking, or tics. In these disorders, treatment is generally more successful than in the other disorders just described.

A number of potential causal factors were considered for the disorders of childhood and adolescence. Although genetic predisposition appears to be important in several disorders, parental psychopathology, family disruption, and stressful circumstances, such as parental death or desertion and child abuse, can have an important causal influence. Recent research has underscored the importance of multiple risk factors in the development of psychopathology.

There are special problems, and special opportunities, involved in treating childhood disorders. The need for preventive and treatment programs for children is always growing, and in recent years the concept of child advocacy has become a reality in some states. Child abuse is a serious problem that has and continues to foster both research and clinical efforts into finding causes and devising preventive measures and treatment. Unfortunately, financial and other resources necessary for such services are not always readily available, and the future of programs for improving psychological environments for children remains uncertain.

■ Key Terms

developmental psychopathology (p. 535)
attention-deficit hyperactivity disorder (ADHD) (p. 538)
hyperactivity (p. 538)
conduct disorders (p. 543)
juvenile delinquency (p. 546)
separation anxiety disorder (p. 552)

overanxious disorder (p. 552)
enuresis (p. 558)
encopresis (p. 558)
sleepwalking disorder (p. 559)
tic (p. 559)
Tourette's syndrome (p. 560)
advocacy (p. 566)

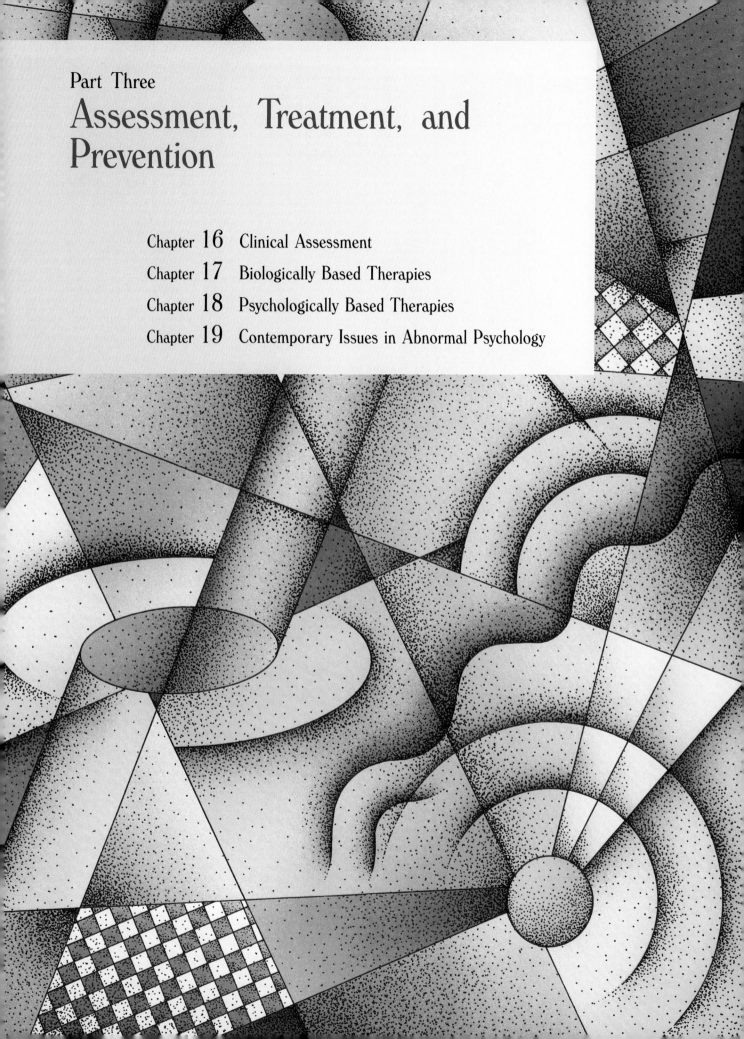

Part Three
Assessment, Treatment, and Prevention

Chapter 16
Clinical Assessment

Robert "Scottie" Wilson, *The City Among Flowers*.
Wilson (1890–?) grew up in a poor family in
Glasgow, Scotland. An itinerant merchant by trade, he
traveled extensively, making his home at various times in
Scotland, London, and Canada. In his early forties, while
living in Toronto, Wilson suddenly began to make complex
sketches in ink on various surfaces. His stylized self–
portraits and symbolic designs reveal Wilson's originality
and inward–looking vision.

A patient's "presenting complaint" to a clinician always initiates a process of *assessment,* whereby the clinician attempts to understand the nature and extent of the problem for which help is being sought. At times this process of inquiry is extremely convoluted and challenging, reminiscent of a Sherlock Holmes exercise in inductive and deductive logic. On other occasions assessment is a relatively straightforward matter in which the clinician may, with a high probability of being correct, come to a rapid conclusion about the basis for the complaint and the proper disposition of the case. Pediatricians whose practices tend to be confined to a local clientele, for example, quickly discern what childhood infections are "going around" at a given time. A child who is brought to the office with complaints that mimic the characteristic symptom profile for a then-common infection will likely be found to have that disease. Even so, the conscientious pediatrician will usually want to confirm the initial diagnostic impression with lab studies that identify, as far as possible, the infectious organism involved before initiating specifically targeted treatment.

Such confirming of diagnostic impressions is thus a matter of good practice even in the most routine clinical situations. For the mental health practitioner, few if any clinical situations are as routine as our pediatric example, and adequate techniques for confirming initial impressions may prove far more elusive. With rare exception, the precisely quantified "lab work" essential to much medical assessment is irrelevant in this domain. Psychological disorders do not as a rule have identifying biological characteristics. Furthermore, they are always interlaced with the personalities of the individuals suffering them and usually with the entire surrounding social fabric. Every instance is to that extent unique and is likely to be the product of a complex organization of contributing factors, many of which may not be apparent on brief or cursory examination, or sometimes even after many months of intense scrutiny in the course of psychotherapy. As this last statement implies, psychological assessment or diagnosis can actually be an ongoing process that proceeds apace with, rather than only preceding, treatment efforts.

In addition, as we have seen in earlier chapters, even where a specific *diagnosis* may be confidently determined it will normally clarify little of direct clinical significance beyond summarizing in descriptive terms the behavioral observations that the clinician has been able to make. It will not reveal, as do most diagnoses of medical conditions, the underlying pathologic processes producing the phenomena (for example, fever) that are observed. For these reasons the assessment process in the domain of mental disorders is usually more difficult, more uncertain, and more protracted than in the case of physical diseases. In the opinions of most mental health practitioners, however, it is no less critically important. No rational, specific treatment plan may be instituted in the absence of at least some general notion of what problems need to be addressed, and ongoing treatment decisions are typically made on the basis of the accumulating evidence pertaining to increasingly refined assessment hypotheses as treatment proceeds.

We will focus in this chapter on assessment procedures especially appropriate to the initial phase of the clinical process, where an attempt is made to circumscribe and identify the main dimensions of a client's problem or problems and to predict the likely course of events under various exigencies. Although a responsible and competent clinician will engage in assessment throughout the course of any treatment undertaken, it is at this initial stage where some of the most crucial decisions have to be made—such as what if any treatment approach is to be offered, whether or not the problem will require hospitalization, to what extent family members will need to be included as co-clients, and so on. Sometimes decisions such as these must be made within a constrained time frame, including emergency conditions, and without recourse to critical information that would probably (but not necessarily) become available with unlimited client contact in a more leisurely clinical context. As will be seen, various special psychological measurement instruments are frequently employed to maximize assessment efficiency in this type of pretreatment examination process.

A variant of this pretreatment type of assessment is the use of psychological assessment instruments in *screening* candidates for various roles and occupations. Here the effort is basically one of identifying individuals who appear to be psychologically unfit (or, alternatively, highly suited) for the particular type of assignment or work sought. For example, a police recruit who appears to have uncertain control of anger and aggressive impulses may need to be counseled about possibly adopting another occupational goal, or about seeking therapy to remedy a lack of control that could be dangerous in an occupation involving both great stress and constant access to lethal weapons.

A less obvious but equally important function of pretreatment assessment is that of establishing baselines for various psychological functions in order to measure with relative precision the effects produced by any treatment offered. In some treatment contexts, criteria based on these measurements are established as part of the treatment plan, such that the therapy is considered successful and is terminated only when client performance meets these predetermined criteria. Also, as will be seen in Chapters 17 and 18, comparison of posttreatment with pretreatment assessment results is an essential feature of many research projects specifically designed to evaluate the efficacy of various therapies for different types of disorder.

In this chapter, we will review some of the more commonly used assessment procedures and show how the data obtained can be integrated into a coherent clinical picture for use in making decisions about referral and treatment. Our survey will include a discussion of neuropsychological assessment, the clinical interview, behavioral observation, and personality assessment through the use of projective and objective psychological tests.

Let us look first at what, exactly, a clinician is trying to learn during psychological assessment of a client.

THE INFORMATION SOUGHT IN ASSESSMENT

What does a clinician need to know? First, of course, *the problem must be identified.* Is it a situational problem precipitated by some environmental stressor, a manifestation of a more pervasive and long-term disorder, or is it perhaps some combination of the two? Is there any evidence of recent deterioration in cognitive functioning? What is the duration of the current complaint and how is the individual dealing with the problem? What if any prior help has been sought? Are there indications of self-defeating behavior and personality deterioration, or is the individual using available personal and environmental resources in a good effort to cope? How pervasively has the problem affected the person's performance of important social roles? Does the individual's symptomatic behavior fit any of the diagnostic patterns in the current edition of the DSM?

As we have seen, there has been a trend against overdependence on diagnostic labeling because of its intrinsic limitations and the potential damage that labels can do in setting up self-fulfilling prophecies for the individual, blinding members of the therapeutic staff to other relevant behavior on the individual's part. On the other hand, it is often important to have an adequate classification of the presenting problem for a number of reasons. In many cases, a formal diagnosis is necessary before insurance claims can be filed. Clinically, knowledge of an individual's type of disorder can help in planning and managing the most appropriate treatment procedures. Administratively, it is essential to know the range of diagnostic problems that are represented among the patient or client population and for which treatment facilities need to be available. If the majority of patients at a facility have been diagnosed as having personality disorders, for example, then the staffing, physical environment, and treatment facilities should be arranged accordingly. Thus, the nature of the difficulty needs to be understood as clearly as possible, including a categorization if appropriate.

For most clinical purposes, a formal diagnostic classification per se is much less important than having *a basic understanding of the individual's history, intellectual functioning, personality characteristics, and environmental pressures and resources.* That is, an adequate assessment includes much more than the diagnostic label. For example, it should include an objective description of the individual's behavior. How does the individual characteristically respond to other people? Are there *excesses* in behavior, such as eating or drinking too much? Are there notable *deficits,* as, for example, in social skills? How *appropriate* is the individual's behavior? Is the individual manifesting behavior that would be acceptable in some contexts but is often displayed where it is plainly unresponsive to the situation or to reasonable social expectations? Excesses, deficits, and appropriateness are key dimensions to be noted if the clinician is to understand the particular disorder that has brought the individual to the clinic or hospital.

In addition, assessment needs to include *a description of any relevant long-term personality characteristics.* Has the individual typically responded in deviant ways to particular kinds of situations, for example, ones requiring submission to legitimate authority? Do there seem to be personality traits or behavior patterns that predispose the individual to behave in maladaptive ways across a broad range of circumstances? Does the person tend to become enmeshed with others to the point of losing his or her identity, or is he or she so self-contained that intimate exchange is routinely aborted? Is the person able to accept help from others? Is the person capable of genuine affection, or of accepting appropriate responsibility for others' welfare? Such questions are necessarily at the heart of many assessment efforts.

It is also important to assess *the social context in which the individual operates.* What kinds of environmental demands are typically placed on the individual, and what supports or special stressors exist in the individual's life situation? For example, being the primary caretaker for a spouse suffering from Alzheimer's disease is sufficiently challenging that relatively few can manage the task without significant psychological impairment, especially where outside supports are lacking. As we have seen, the DSM-III-R classification includes guidelines for rating both the severity of the stressors in an individual's current environment and the level of an individual's overall adjustment in meeting the demands of a complex social environment.

The diverse and often conflicting bits of information about the individual's personality traits, behavior patterns, environmental demands, and so on must then be integrated into a consistent and meaningful picture. Some clinicians refer to this picture as a **dynamic formulation,** because it not only describes the current situation but includes hypotheses about what is driving the person to behave in maladaptive ways. At this point in the assessment, the clinician should have a plausible explanation, for example, for why a normally passive and mild-mannered man suddenly flew into a rage and started breaking up furniture; or why the breakup of a relationship with a clearly unsuitable partner should initiate a stubbornly persistent major depression.

The formulation should *allow the clinician to develop hypotheses about the client's future behavior* as well. What is the likelihood of improvement or deterioration if the individual's problems are left untreated? Which behaviors should be the initial focus of change, and what treatment methods are likely to be most efficient in producing this change? How much change might reasonably be expected from a particular type of treatment?

Where feasible, decisions about treatment are made collaboratively with the consent and approval of the individual. In cases of severe disorder, however, they may have to be made without the patient's participation or in rare instances even without consulting responsible kin. As has already been indicated, a knowledge of the patient's strengths and resources is important; in short, what qualities does the patient bring to the treatment program that can enhance the prognosis?

VARYING TYPES OF ASSESSMENT DATA

Because a wide range of factors can play important roles in causing and maintaining maladaptive behavior, assessment may involve the coordinated use of physical, psychological, and environmental assessment procedures. As we have indicated, however, the nature and comprehensiveness of clinical assessments vary depending on the problem and the treatment agency's facilities. Assessment by phone in a suicide prevention center, for example, is quite different from assessment aimed at determining whether a particular hospitalized patient is sufficiently intelligent, verbal, and psychologically minded to be likely to profit significantly from individual psychotherapy.

Furthermore, exactly how a clinician goes about the assessment process often depends on his or her basic orientation. For example, a biologically oriented clinician, typically a psychiatrist or other medical practitioner, will likely focus on biological assessment methods aimed at determining any underlying organic malfunctioning that may be causing the maladaptive behavior. A psychoanalytically oriented clinician will likely use unstructured personality assessment techniques, such as the Rorschach inkblots or the Thematic Apperception Test (TAT), to identify latent intrapsychic conflicts. A behaviorally oriented clinician, in an effort to determine the functional relationships between environmental events or reinforcements and the abnormal behavior, will rely on such techniques as behavioral observation and systematic self-monitoring to identify maladaptive learned patterns; for a cognitively oriented behaviorist, the focus would shift to the dysfunctional thoughts supposedly mediating those patterns. A humanistically oriented clinician might use interview techniques to uncover blocked or distorted personal growth, and an interpersonally oriented clinician will use such techniques as personal confrontations to pinpoint difficulties in interpersonal relationships.

The preceding examples represent general trends and are in no way meant to imply that clinicians of a particular orientation limit themselves to a particular assessment method or that each assessment technique is limited to a particular theoretical orientation. Such trends are instead a matter of emphasis and point up the fact that certain types of assessments are more conducive than others to uncovering particular causal factors, or for eliciting information about symptomatic behavior central to understanding and treating the disorder within a given conceptual framework.

In what follows, we will discuss the way in which both physical and psychosocial data are collected. Then we will examine an actual psychological study that has drawn on a variety of assessment data.

ASSESSMENT OF THE PHYSICAL ORGANISM

In some situations or with certain psychological problems, a medical evaluation is necessary to rule out physical abnormalities that may be contributing to the problem. The medical evaluation may include both general physical and special examinations aimed at assessing the structural (anatomical) and functional (physiological) integrity of the brain as a behaviorally significant physical system.

■ The General Physical Examination

A physical examination consists of the kinds of procedures most of us have experienced in getting a "medical checkup." Typically, a medical history is obtained and the major systems of the body are checked. This part of the assessment procedure is of obvious import for disorders that focus on physical problems, such as psychogenically induced disease, and somatoform, addictive, and organic brain syndromes. In addition, a variety of nonobvious, systemic organic conditions, including various hormonal irregularities, can produce in some individuals behavioral symptoms that closely mimic those of certain mental disorders usually considered to have predominantly psychosocial origins. A case in point is the problem of male erectile dysfunction. A diagnostic error in this type of situation could prove costly; hence, in equivocal cases most clinicians insist on a medical clearance before initiating psychosocially based interventions.

■ The Neurological Examination

Because brain pathology is involved in some mental disorders, a specialized neurological examination is frequently given in addition to the general medical examination. This may involve getting an **electroencephalogram (EEG)** to assess brain-wave patterns in awake and sleeping states. An EEG is a graphic record of the brain's electrical activity. It is obtained noninvasively by placing electrodes on the scalp and by amplifying the minute brain-wave impulses from various brain areas; these amplified impulses drive oscillating pens whose deviations are traced on fanfold paper moving at a constant speed. Much is known about the normal pattern of these impulses in waking and sleeping states and under various conditions of sensory stimulation. Significant divergences from the normal pattern can thus reflect abnormalities of brain function, such as might be caused by a brain tumor or other lesion. Where EEGs reveal such **dysrythmias** in the brain's electrical activity, other specialized techniques may then be used in an attempt to arrive at a more precise diagnosis of the nature and extent of the problem.

Radiological technology, such as **computerized axial tomography,** known in brief as the **CAT scan,** is one of these specialized techniques. Through the use of X rays, a CAT scan reveals images of parts of the brain that might be diseased. This procedure has revolutionized neurological study in recent years by providing rapid access, without surgery, to accurate information about the localization and extent of anomalies in the brain's structural characteristics. The procedure involves the use of computer analysis applied to X-ray beams across sections of a patient's brain to produce images that a neurologist can then interpret.

A newer scanning technique is **positron emission tomography,** the **PET scan.** Though a CAT scan is limited to distinguishing anatomical features, such as the shape of a particular internal structure, a PET scan allows for an appraisal of how an organ is functioning by measuring metabolic processes. The PET scan provides metabolic portraits through tracking natural compounds, like glucose, as they are metabolized by the brain or other organs. By revealing areas of differential metabolic activity, the PET scan enables a medical specialist to obtain more clear-cut diagnoses of brain pathology by, for example, pinpointing sites responsible for epileptic seizures, trauma from head damage or stroke, and brain tumors. Thus the PET scan may be able to reveal problems that are not immediately apparent anatomically. Moreover, the use of PET scans in research on brain pathology occurring in abnormal conditions, such as schizophrenia, depression, and alcoholism, has the potential of leading to important discoveries about the organic processes underlying these disorders, thus providing clues to more effective treatment. To date, unfortunately, progress on this front has not, in our judgment, proven very illuminating.

The newest of these internal scanning techniques is **nuclear magnetic resonance imaging (MRI).** Like a CAT scan, this procedure allows visualization of the anatomical features of internal organs, including the brain. Unlike a CAT scan, protracted x-radiation of the site of interest is not required, and yet the images achieved are often of decidedly higher quality in terms of resolution and clarity. Essentially, MRI involves the precise measurement of variations in magnetic fields that are caused by the varying amounts of water (hydrogen) content of various organs and parts of organs. In this manner the anatomical structure of a "cut" at any given plane through an organ, say the brain, can be computed and graphically depicted with astonishing structural differentiation and clarity.

In fact, MRI technology will likely render obsolete the CAT scan, which was considered at the cutting edge of medical technology only a few years ago. MRI thus makes possible, by noninvasive means, visualization of all but the most minute

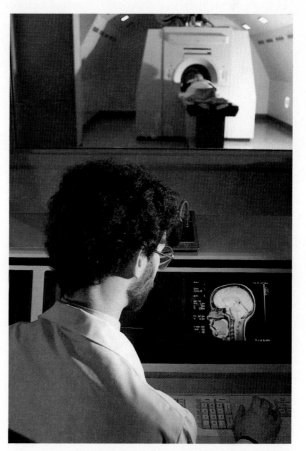

Nuclear magnetic resonance imaging (MRI) allows visualization of the anatomical features of the brain without protracted x-radiation, as in CAT scans. In MRI an anatomical structure can be computed and graphically depicted with astonishing differentiation and clarity.

abnormalities of brain structure. It has been particularly useful in confirming degenerative brain processes, as manifested, for example, in enlarged cerebrospinal fluid spaces within the brain. Again here, MRI studies have considerable potential to illuminate the contribution of brain anomalies to "nonorganic" psychoses, such as schizophrenia, and some progress in this area has in fact been made, as noted in Chapter 12. No genuine "breakthroughs," however, are as yet on the horizon.

■ The Neuropsychological Examination

The techniques so far described are fairly accurate in identifying abnormalities in the brain's physical properties. Usually, although by no means always, such abnormalities are accompanied by gross impairments in behavior and varied psychological deficits, although the particular nature of the latter may not be accurately predicted even after precisely localizing these physical abnormalities. Also, behavioral and psychological impairments due to organic brain abnormalities may become manifest before any organic brain lesion is detectable by scanning or other means. Needed in these instances are reliable techniques for precisely measuring any alteration in behavioral or psychological functioning that has occurred in consequence of the organic brain pathology. This need is met by a growing cadre of clinical psychologists specializing in the field of **neuropsychological assessment,** which involves the use of an expanding array of testing devices to measure a person's cognitive, perceptual, and motor performance as aids in determining the extent and location of brain damage.

In many instances of known or suspected organic brain involvement, a clinical neuropsychologist will administer a test battery to a patient. The purpose of such testing is to describe the behavioral functioning of the individual in terms of brain-behavior relationships. By means of a battery of tests, the individual's performance on various standardized tasks, particularly perceptual-motor ones, can give valuable clues about that person's cognitive and intellectual impairment following brain damage (Boll, 1978; Filskov & Locklear, 1982; Heaton & Pendleton, 1981). Such testing can even provide clues as to the probable location of the brain damage, though PET scans, MRIs, and other physical tests are still more effective in determining the exact location of the injury.

Many neuropsychologists prefer to select a highly individualized array of tests to administer, depending on a patient's case history and other available information. Others opt for a battery consisting of a standard set of tests that have been preselected so as to sample in a systematic and comprehensive manner a broad range of psychological competencies known to be adversely affected by various types of brain insult. The use of a constant set of tests has many research and clinical advantages, although it may compromise flexibility. One such standard battery, widely used, is the Halstead-Reitan, whose components are described in *HIGHLIGHT 16.1*

Typically taking about six hours to administer, the Halstead-Reitan can be a problem in some clinical settings where time and funding is limited. Understandably, examinee fatigue may also be a limiting factor, particularly where a patient is in a debilitated condition. In the last decade, the Luria-Nebraska battery (Golden, 1978), which takes only about two-and-a-half hours to administer, has been receiving much attention as an alternative to the Halstead-Reitan. Both these batteries, as well as others of similar purpose and construction, provide their information without the risks attendant to more invasive neurological examination procedures (Filskov & Goldstein, 1974). Still, however, the Halstead-Reitan battery continues to grow in use because it yields a great deal of useful information —more than the Luria-Nebraska—about an individual's cognitive and motor processes (Boll, 1980; Filskov & Locklear, 1982; Hartlage, Asken, & Hornsby, 1987).

In summary, the medical and neuropsychological sciences are developing many new procedures to assess brain functioning and behavioral manifestations of organic disorder. Medical procedures to assess organic brain damage include EEGs, and CAT, PET, and MRI scans. The new technology holds a great deal of promise for detecting and evaluating organic brain dysfunction and for providing increased understanding of brain functioning through graphic mapping of the brain. Neuropsychological testing provides a clinician with important behavioral information on how organic brain damage is affecting an individual's present functioning.

PSYCHOSOCIAL ASSESSMENT

Psychosocial assessment attempts to provide a realistic picture of an individual in interaction with the environment. This picture includes relevant information concerning the individual's personality makeup and present level of functioning, as well as information about the stressors and resources in his

HIGHLIGHT 16.1

Neuropsychological Examinations: Determining Brain–Behavior Relationships

The Halstead-Reitan battery is a neuropsychological examination composed of several tests and variables from which an "index of impairment" can be computed (Boll, 1978, 1980). In addition, it provides specific information about a subject's functioning in several skill areas. Though it typically takes four to six hours to complete and requires substantial administrative time, it is being used increasingly in neurological evaluations because it yields a great deal of useful information about an individual's cognitive and motor processes (Filskov & Boll, 1986; Filskov & Goldstein, 1974; Filskov & Locklear, 1982). Moreover, the Halstead-Reitan battery provides valid information without the risk of injury or death that is so great with more invasive procedures. The Halstead-Reitan battery for adults is made up of the following tests:

1. *The Halstead Category Test* measures a subject's ability to learn and remember material and can provide clues as to his or her judgment and impulsivity. The subject is presented with a stimulus (on a screen) that suggests a number between one and four. The subject presses a button indicating which number is "correct."

A correct choice is followed by the sound of a pleasant doorbell and an incorrect choice by a loud buzzer. The person is required to determine from the pattern of buzzers and bells what the underlying principle of the correct choice is.

2. *The Tactual Performance Test* measures a subject's motor speed, response to the unfamiliar, and ability to learn and use tactile and kinesthetic cues. The test consists of a board that has spaces for ten blocks of varied shapes. The subject is blindfolded (never actually seeing the board) and asked to place the blocks into the correct grooves in the board. Later, the subject is asked to draw the blocks and the board from tactile memory.

3. *The Rhythm Test* is an auditory perception task used to measure attention and sustained concentration. It is a subtest of Seashore's Test of musical talent and includes 30 pairs of rhythmic beats that are presented on a tape recorder. On this test, a subject is required to determine if the pairs are the same or different.

4. *The Speech Sounds Perception Test* is a test to determine if an

individual can identify spoken words. Nonsense words are presented on a tape recorder, and the subject is asked to identify the presented word from a list of four printed words. This task measures the subject's concentration, attention, and comprehension.

5. *The Finger Oscillation Task* measures the speed at which an individual can, with the index finger, depress a lever. Several trials are given with each hand.

In addition to the Halstead-Reitan battery, other tests, referred to as *allied procedures,* may be used in a neuropsychology laboratory. For example, Boll (1980) recommends the use of the modified Halstead-Wepman Aphasia Screening Test for obtaining information about a subject's language ability and about his or her abilities to identify numbers and body parts, to follow directions, to spell, and to pantomime simple actions.

or her life situation. For example, early in the process, clinicians may act like puzzle solvers, absorbing as much information about the client as possible—present feelings, attitudes, memories, demographic facts, and so on—and trying to fit the pieces together into a meaningful pattern. They typically formulate hypotheses and discard or confirm them as they proceed. Starting usually with a global technique, such as a clinical interview, clinicians may later select more specific assessment tasks

or tests. The following are some of the psychosocial procedures that may be used.

■ Assessment Interviews

An assessment interview, often considered the central element of the assessment process, usually involves a face-to-face interaction conducted in such a way that a clinician obtains information about various aspects of a patient's situation, behavior, and personality makeup. The interview may vary from a simple set of questions or prompts, as in the *mental status exam* used chiefly by psychiatrists and other physicians, to a more extended and detailed format. It may be relatively "free-wheeling" in character, with an interviewer making moment-to-moment selections about his or her next probe based on responses to prior ones, or it may be more tightly controlled and structured so as to ensure that a particular set of questions and probes is introduced. In the latter case, the interviewer may choose from a number of highly structured, standardized interview formats whose reliability has been established in prior research. As used here, *reliability* means simply that two interviewers assessing the same client will generate highly similar conclusions about the client, a type of consensus that research shows can by no means be taken for granted.

Although we know of few clinicians who express enthusiasm for the more controlled and structured type of assessment interview, the research data are clear in showing it to yield far more reliable results, in general, than the more flexible format. This appears to be an instance of a widespread overconfidence among clinicians in the accuracy of their own methods and judgments (Garb, 1989; Kleinmuntz, 1990). On the other hand, every rule has its exceptions, and we have seen brilliantly conducted assessment interviews where each probe was fashioned on the spur of the moment. The upshot seems to be that in most instances an assessor would be wise to conduct an interview that is carefully structured in terms of goals, comprehensive symptom review, other content to be explored, and the type of relationship the interviewer attempts to establish with the subject. Such an approach is likely to minimize error over the long course, although we acknowledge that a more creative and spontaneous interview format may be more productive in particular clinical situations.

The reliability of the assessment interview may also be enhanced by the use of rating scales that help focus inquiry and quantify the interview data. For example, a subject may be rated on a three-, five-, or seven-point scale with respect to self-esteem, anxiety, and various other characteristics. Such a structured and preselected format is particularly effective in giving a comprehensive impression or "profile" of the subject and his or her life situation, and in revealing specific problems or crises—such as marital difficulties, drug dependence, or suicidal fantasies—that may require immediate therapeutic intervention (Matarazzo, 1983).

As already suggested, clinical interviews are subject to error and have been criticized as an unreliable source of information on which to base important clinical decisions. Evidence of this unreliability includes the fact that, on the basis of the interview data they elicit for a particular patient, different clinicians have often arrived at different formal diagnoses. It is chiefly for this reason, in fact, that recent versions of the DSM (that is, III and III-R) have emphasized an "operational" assessment approach, one that specifies observable criteria for diagnosis and provides specific guidelines for making diagnostic judgments. A clinician who is seeking to render a formal diagnosis is thus essentially forced to incorporate at least minimal structure into the interview or risk coming up empty-handed in regard to eliciting data essential to such a diagnosis. "Winging it" has thus become a somewhat maladaptive strategy in this type of assessment process. Although the available data on the improved reliability of psychiatric diagnoses have shown the operational approach to have decided advantages, there has also doubtless been some cost in reducing interviewer flexibility and in encouraging undue preoccupation with observable "signs" at the expense of overall understanding of patient functioning (Simons, 1987).

As was suggested in Chapter 1, the developments just described can be characterized as favoring the removal of the diagnostician, as a subjective judge, from the diagnostic process; to the degree possible, diagnosis is rendered "automatic." But if a human judge is unnecessary—perhaps even a troublesome source of error—then why not take the extra step of computerizing the diagnostic process? Computers, after all, are superb at remembering and following explicitly stated rules for decision making. Where clinically feasible, they can even be used on-line to ask the same sorts of questions, and elicit the same sorts of answers, as would a human interviewer; that is, a patient can be "interviewed" by a computer terminal or console.

In fact, efforts of this sort have already been developed to a relatively advanced stage (Erdman, Klein, & Greist, 1985). Computer programs with highly sophisticated branching subroutines are available to "tailor-make" a diagnostic interview for a patient. Stein (1987), for example, designed a program called the Computerized Diagnostic Interview for Children that can conduct a standard psychiatric interview. Several more specific clinical assessment tasks have been adapted for computer administration. For example, Fowler et al. (1987) have designed a Clinical Problem Checklist that can provide a therapist with an overview of a client's presenting symptoms. Allen and Skinner (1987) have designed a computer program that takes down a client's alcohol- and drug-abuse history, and Giannetti (1987) has a computer program that records a client's social history. All these are fairly easy-to-administer programs that can provide a clinician with a wealth of reliable data that can be useful during the assessment process.

Despite the considerable progress made in reducing subjective factors by computerizing or otherwise making various aspects of the assessment process relatively automatic, it is important to understand that excessive reliance on such techniques can also introduce error. The complexity of human behavior is bound to produce many exceptions to any "rule." In the final analysis, therefore, there is probably no adequate substitute for expert clinical judgment (Carson, 1990b). Where such judgment is available as a backstop, these techniques can substantially improve assessment efficiency while minimizing the risks of mindless decision making.

■ The Clinical Observation of Behavior

Direct observation of an individual's characteristic behavior has long been considered important for adequate psychosocial assessment. The main purpose of direct observation is to find out more about the person's psychological makeup and level of functioning through the objective description of appearance and behavior in various contexts. Though such observations would ideally occur within the individual's natural environment, they are typically confined to clinic or hospital settings. For example, a brief description is usually made of a subject's behavior on hospital admission, and more detailed observations are made periodically on the ward. These descriptions include concise notations of relevant information about the subject's personal hygiene, emotional behavior, delusions or hallucinations, anxiety, sexual behavior, aggressive or suicidal tendencies, and so on.

In addition to making their own observations, many clinicians enlist their patients' help in this endeavor by providing instruction in self-observation and objective reporting of behavior, thoughts, and feeling states as they occur in various natural settings. Such **self-monitoring** can be a valuable aid in determining the kinds of situations, possibly previously unrecognized, in which maladaptive behavior is likely to be evoked, and numerous studies also show it to have therapeutic benefits in its own right. Alternatively, a patient may be asked to fill out a more or less formal *self-report* or a checklist concerning problematic reactions experienced in various situations. Numerous such instruments have been published in the professional literature and are commercially available to clinicians. These

approaches recognize that individuals are excellent sources of information about themselves. Assuming that the right questions are asked and that people are willing to disclose information about themselves, the results can have a crucial bearing on treatment planning—for example, by providing essential information for structuring a behavioral treatment intervention.

As in the case of interviews, the use of **rating scales** in clinical observation and in self-reports helps not only to organize information but also to encourage reliability and objectivity. That is, the formal structure of a scale is likely to keep unwarranted observer inferences to a minimum. Rating scales commonly used are those that enable a rater to indicate not only the presence or absence of a trait or behavior but also its prominence. The following is an example of such a rating-scale item; the observer would check the most appropriate alternative.

Sexual behavior:

_____ 1. Sexually assaultive: aggressively approaches males or females with sexual intent.

_____ 2. Sexually soliciting: exposes genitals with sexual intent, makes overt sexual advances to other patients or staff, masturbates openly.

_____ 3. No overt sexual behavior: not preoccupied with discussion or sexual matters.

_____ 4. Avoids sex topics: made uneasy by discussion of sex, becomes disturbed if approached sexually by others.

_____ 5. Excessive prudishness about sex: considers sex filthy, condemns sexual behavior in others, becomes panic-stricken if approached sexually.

Obviously, these sorts of observations may be made not only to fill in the original picture but also to check on the course or outcome of treatment procedures.

One of the rating scales most widely used for recording observations in clinical practice and in psychiatric research is the *Brief Psychiatric Rating Scale (BPRS)*. The BPRS provides a structured and quantifiable format for rating clinical symptoms, such as somatic concern, anxiety, emotional withdrawal, guilt feelings, hostility, suspiciousness, and unusual thought patterns. It contains 18 scales that are scored from ratings made by a clinician following an interview with a patient. The distinct patterns of behavior reflected in the BPRS ratings enable clinicians to make a standardized comparison of their patients' symptoms with the behavior of other psychiatric patients (Overall & Hollister,

1982). The BPRS has been found to be an extremely useful instrument in clinical research, especially for the purpose of assigning patients to treatment groups on the basis of similarity in symptoms. A similar but more specifically targeted instrument, the *Hamilton Rating Scale for Depression (HRSD),* has become almost the standard in this respect for selecting clinically depressed research subjects, and also for assessing the response of such subjects to various treatment interventions.

Observations made in clinical settings by trained observers can provide behavioral data useful in ongoing clinical management. Paul and his colleagues (Lichy, 1982; Mariotto, 1979; Paul, 1982; Paul & Lentz, 1977; Rich, Paul, & Mariotto, 1988), for example, have developed a comprehensive behavioral assessment program that they have implemented experimentally in a number of hospitals. The program includes evaluating the behavior of chronic patients and monitoring the activities of staff members working with them. Through the use of observational rating systems, they have been able to measure staff behavior in the daily management of patients and ongoing patient behavior on the ward. The behavioral ratings can be used to pinpoint specific behaviors to be changed on the part of members of either group.

Recently, a good deal of attention has focused on observing a subject's behavior in his or her natural surroundings. For example, children who have been showing behavior problems may be observed at school, in their peer groups, and in their homes. Here the purpose is to obtain a sampling of their behavior in ordinary situations to understand

It can be helpful to both a practitioner and a client to observe and assess the client's behavior in an everyday setting, such as his or her home, where there is the opportunity to talk with family members and to discern the stressors and resources in the client's life situation.

the problems they are facing, the coping patterns they are using, and the environmental conditions that may be reinforcing their maladaptive behavior.

The procedures described above focus on a subjects overt behavior, omitting the often equally important consideration of concurrent mental events—that is, the individual's own ongoing thoughts. In an attempt to get a sampling of naturally occurring thoughts, psychologists are experimenting with having individuals carry small electronic beepers that produce a signal, such as a soft tone, at unexpected intervals. At each signal, these individuals are to write down or electronically record whatever thoughts the signal interrupted. These "thought reports" can then be analyzed in various ways, and can be used for some kinds of personality assessment and diagnosis as well as for monitoring progress in psychological therapy.

In situations where it is not feasible to observe a subject's behavior in everyday settings—as when he or she is institutionalized—an entire family may be asked to meet together in the clinic or hospital where their interactions and difficulties can be observed and studied. In other cases, a social worker may obtain relevant data by visiting a subject's home, talking with family members and others who are important to the subject, and observing the stressors and resources in the subject's life situation. In addition to providing important assessment data, this procedure incorporates the "observers" into the therapy program, thereby enhancing the therapy.

Where the object of study is a child, Jones, Reid, and Patterson (1975) have developed a method for coding and quantifying the observations of the child's behavior at school and at home. Concrete instances of behavior and interaction can be observed, recorded, and coded, either by trained observers or by the parents themselves. This method provides the clinician with information about the stimuli that are controlling the child's interactions, which in turn makes it possible for the clinician to evaluate the quality of the child's interactions and to identify the situations that result in behavior problems.

In still other situations where observation in a natural setting is not possible, a clinician may construct or contrive observational opportunities that can provide information about an individual's response to particular circumstances. For example, an individual who has a phobia for snakes might be placed in a situation where snakelike objects and pictures are presented.

An often-used procedure that enables a clinician to observe a client's behavior directly is **role playing.** The client is instructed to play a part—for example, someone standing up for his or her rights. Role playing a situation like this not only can provide assessment information for the clinician but also can serve as a vehicle for new learning for the client.

Extending the use of observational data a bit further, a clinician may analyze situations with which a subject is likely to be confronted in the future. For example, a patient with little education and a history of chronic unemployment might improve sufficiently to leave an institution but be little better off than before, an unfortunately common occurrence, unless treatment has included training in job skills. Thus, knowledge of a troubled individual's life situation not only helps in understanding present maladaptive behavior, but is often essential for planning a treatment program that will enable him or her to meet future challenges in more adaptive ways.

■ Psychological Tests

Interviews and behavioral observation are relatively *direct* attempts to determine an individual's beliefs, attitudes, and problems. Psychological tests, on the other hand, are a more *indirect* means of assessing psychological characteristics. Scientifically developed psychological tests (as opposed to the recreational ones sometimes appearing in newspapers and magazines) are standardized sets of procedures or tasks for obtaining samples of behavior; a subject's responses to the standardized stimuli are compared with those of other people having comparable demographic characteristics, usually through established test norms or test score distributions. From these comparisons, a clinician can then draw inferences about the extent to which the person's individual psychological qualities differ from those of a reference group, typically a psychologically normal one. Among the characteristics these tests can ascertain are coping patterns, motive patterns, personality characteristics, role behaviors, values, levels of depression or anxiety and intellectual functioning. Impressive advances in the technology of test development have in fact made it possible to develop instruments of acceptable reliability and validity to measure almost any conceivable psychological characteristic in which people vary.

Though more precise and often more reliable than interviews or less standardized observational techniques, psychological tests are far from perfect tools. Often, if not always, their value depends on the competence of the clinician who interprets their outcomes (Carson, 1990b). In general, they are useful diagnostic tools for psychologists in much

the same way that blood tests, X-ray films, or MRI scans are useful to physicians competent in interpreting the outputs from those procedures. In all these cases, pathology may be revealed in people who appear on the surface to be quite normal, or a general impression of "something wrong" can be checked against more precise information.

Two general categories of psychological tests for use in clinical practice are *intelligence tests* and *personality tests.* We discuss each in the following sections.

Intelligence Tests   A clinician can choose from a wide range of intelligence tests. The Wechsler Intelligence Scale for Children-Revised (WISC-R) and the current revision of the prototypal Stanford-Binet Intelligence Scale are widely used in clinical settings for measuring the intellectual abilities of children. Probably the most commonly used test for measuring adult intelligence is the Wechsler Adult Intelligence Scale-Revised (WAIS-R). It includes both verbal and performance material and consists of 11 subtests. A brief description of two of the subtests—one verbal and one performance—will serve to illustrate the type of functions the WAIS-R measures:

General information (verbal). This subtest consists of questions designed to tap the individual's range of information on material that is ordinarily encountered. For example, the individual is asked to do such things as tell how many weeks there are in a year, name the colors of the American flag, and tell who Martin Luther King was.

Picture completion (performance). This subtest consists of 20 cards showing pictures, each with a part missing. The task for the subject is to indicate what is missing. This test is designed to measure the individual's ability to discriminate between essential and nonessential elements in a situation. (Wechsler, 1981)

An analysis of scores on the various subtests reveals an individual's present level of intellectual functioning. In addition, the subject's behavior in the test situation may reveal much relevant information. For example, he or she may be apprehensive about not doing well, may vacillate in responses, may seek continual reassurance from the clinician, or may be so disturbed that concentration on the tasks presented is difficult. These observed behaviors may tell the clinician as much as the actual test scores.

Individually administered intelligence tests—such as the WISC-R, WAIS-R, and the Stanford-

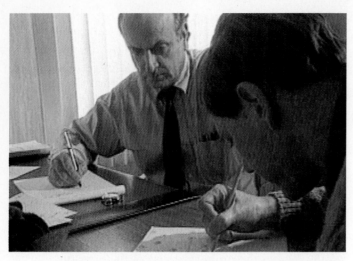

Here a psychologist administers part of the WAIS-R, an intelligence test that provides information about how well an individual performs on a variety of cognitive challenges. An individually administered test such as this can require considerable time—often two to three hours—to give, score, and interpret; as such, it is appropriate to use these types of tests primarily when intelligence testing is considered critical to the diagnosis.

Binet—typically require two to three hours to administer, score, and interpret. In many clinical situations, there is not sufficient time or funding to use these tests in every assessment situation. In cases where intellectual impairment or organic brain damage is suspected to be central to a patient's problem, intelligence testing may be the most crucial diagnostic procedure to include in the test battery. Yet in many clinical settings and for many clinical cases, gaining a thorough understanding of a client's problems and initiating a treatment program do not require knowing the kind of detailed information about intellectual functioning these instruments provide. In these cases, intelligence testing would not be recommended.

Personality Tests   There are a great many tests designed to measure personal characteristics other than intellectual facility. It is customary to group these personality tests into *projective* and *objective* tests.

Projective tests.   **Projective tests** are unstructured in that they rely on various ambiguous stimuli, such as inkblots or pictures, rather than explicit verbal questions, and subjects' responses are not constrained by a preselected format of the "true," "false," or "cannot say" variety. Through their interpretations of these ambiguous materials, individuals reveal a good deal about their personal preoccupations, conflicts, motives, coping techniques, and other personality characteristics. An

assumption underlying the use of projective techniques is that in trying to make sense out of vague, unstructured stimuli, individuals "project" their own problems, motives, and wishes into the situation, inasmuch as they have little else on which to rely in formulating their responses to these materials. Such responses are akin to the childhood pastime of detecting familiar scenes in cloud formations, with the important exception that the stimuli are in this case fixed and largely the same for all subjects. It is the latter circumstance that permits determination of the normative range of responses to the test materials, which in turn can be used to identify objectively deviant responding. Thus projective tests are aimed at discovering the ways in which an individual's past learning and self-structure may lead him or her to organize and perceive ambiguous information from the environment. Prominent among the several projective tests in common use are the Rorschach Test, the Thematic Apperception Test (TAT), and sentence-completion tests.

The **Rorschach Test** is named after the Swiss psychiatrist Hermann Rorschach, who initiated experimental use of inkblots in personality assessment in 1911. The test uses ten inkblot pictures to which a subject responds in succession after being instructed somewhat as follows (Klopfer & Davidson, 1962):

People may see many different things in these inkblot pictures; now tell me what you see, what it makes you think of, what it means to you.

A facsimile of a Rorschach inkblot is shown here. The following excerpts are taken from the responses of a subject to one of the actual blots:

"This looks like two men with genital organs exposed. They have had a terrible fight and blood has splashed up against the wall. They have knives or sharp instruments in their hands and have just cut up a body. They have already taken out the lungs and other organs. The body is dismembered . . . nothing remains but a shell . . . the pelvic region. They were fighting as to who will complete the final dismemberment . . . like two vultures swooping down. . . ."

The extremely gory, violent content of this response was not very common for the particular blot, nor for any other blot in the series. While no responsible examiner would base conclusions on a single instance, such content was consistent with other data from this subject, who was diagnosed as an antisocial personality with strong hostility.

For several reasons, use of the Rorschach test has decreased over the past 20 years (Polyson, Peterson, & Marshall, 1986). Although methods of administering the test vary, some approaches can take several hours and hence must compete for time with other essential clinical services. Furthermore, the results of the Rorschach can be unreliable because of the subjective nature of test data interpretations and thus the high premium placed on the somewhat esoteric skills required of an examiner. In addition, the types of clinical treatments used in the majority of today's mental health facilities generally require more specific behavioral descriptions rather than descriptions of deep-seated personality dynamics, such as those that typically result from Rorschach Test interpretation.

The Rorschach has been criticized, to some extent unfairly, as an instrument with low or negligible validity. In fact, like the stethoscope in medicine, the validity of the "instrument" depends on who is using it (Carson, 1990b). In the hands of a skilled interpreter, the Rorschach has been shown to be quite useful in uncovering certain psychodynamic issues, such as the impact of unconscious motivations on current perceptions of others. Furthermore, there have been attempts to move beyond the original discursive and free-wheeling approaches and to objectify Rorschach interpretations by clearly specifying test variables and empirically exploring their relationship to external criteria, such as clinical diagnosis (Viglione & Exner, 1983). These efforts, indeed, typify and affirm the historic scientist-practitioner tradition of the clinical psychology profession.

The Rorschach, although generally touted as an open-ended, subjective instrument aimed at studying an individual's personality as a uniquely organized system ("idiographically"), has recently been adapted for computer interpretation. Exner (1987) has developed a computer-based interpretation system for the Rorschach that, after scored responses are input, provides scoring summaries and a listing of likely personality descriptions and references about an individual's adjustment. The Exner Comprehensive Rorschach System (an example of which can be found in the case study of Esteban in *HIGHLIGHT 16.3* on page 596) may answer the criticism that Rorschach interpretation is unreliable because the computer output provides a reliable and invariant set of descriptors for any given set of Rorschach scores. Assuming that clinicians agree on the scoring of particular responses, the computer outputs, that is, the interpretations, will be the same.

The **Thematic Apperception** introduced in 1935 by its coauth/ Murray of the Harvard Psycholog a series of simple pictures, some tional and others quite "abstract, subject is instructed to make up stories. The of the pictures, much of it depicting people in various contexts, is highly ambiguous as to actions and motives, so that subjects tend to project their own conflicts and worries into it (Bellak, 1975).

Several scoring and interpretation systems have been developed to focus on different aspects of a subject's stories, such as expressions of needs (Atkinson, 1958; Winter, 1973), the individual's perception of reality (Arnold, 1962), and the individual's fantasies (Klinger, 1979). Generally these systems are cumbersome and time-consuming, and little evidence shows that they make a clinically significant contribution. Hence, most often a clinician simply makes a qualitative and subjective determination of how the story content reflects an individual's underlying traits, motives, and preoccupations. Such interpretations often depend as much on "art" as on "science," and there is much room for error in such an informal procedure.

An example of the way an individual's problems may be reflected in TAT stories is shown in the following story based on Card 1 (a picture of a boy staring at a violin on a table in front of him). The client, David, was a 15-year-old male who had been referred to the clinic by his parents because of their concern about his withdrawal behavior and his poor work at school.

*D*avid was generally cooperative during the testing although he remained rather unemotional and unenthusiastic throughout. When he was given Card 1 of the TAT, he paused for over a minute, carefully scrutinizing the card.

"I think this is a . . . uh . . . machine gun . . . yeah, it's a machine gun. The guy is staring at it. Maybe he got it for his birthday or stole it or something." (Pause. The examiner reminded him that he was to make up a story about the picture.)

"OK. This boy, I'll call him Karl, found this machine gun . . . a Browning automatic rifle . . . in his garage. He kept it in his room for protection. One day he decided to take it to school to quiet down the jocks that lord it over everyone. When he walked into the locker hall, he cut loose on the top jock, Amos, and wasted him. Nobody bothered him after that because they knew he kept the BAR in his locker."

It was inferred from this story that David was experiencing a high level of frustration and anger in his life. The extent of this anger was reflected in his perception of the violin in the picture as a machine gun—a potential instrument of violence. The clinician concluded that David was feeling threatened not only by people at school but even in his own home where he needed "protection." This example shows how stories based on TAT cards may provide a clinician with information about an individual's conflicts and worries, as well as clues as to how the individual is handling these problems.

The TAT has been criticized on several grounds in recent years. There is a "dated" quality to the test stimuli: the pictures, developed in the 1930s, appear quaint to many contemporary subjects who have difficulty identifying with the characters in the pictures. Subjects will often preface their stories with, "This is something from a movie I saw on the Late Show." Additionally, the TAT can require a great deal of time to administer and interpret. Interpretation of responses to the TAT is generally subjective and limits the reliability and validity of the test. Again, however, we must note that some examiners, notably among those who have accumulated vast experience in the instrument's use, are capable of astonishingly accurate interpretations with TAT stories. Typically, they have difficulty in teaching these skills to others. On reflection, such an observation should not be unduly surprising, but it does point up the essentially "artistic" element involved at this skill level.

Another projective procedure that has proven useful in personality assessment is the **sentence-completion test.** There are a number of such tests designed for children, adolescents, and adults. Such tests consist of the beginnings of sentences that a subject is asked to complete, as in these examples:

1. I wish _____
2. My mother _____
3. Sex _____
4. I hate _____
5. People _____

Sentence-completion tests are somewhat more structured than the Rorschach and most other projective tests. They help examiners pinpoint important clues to an individual's problems, attitudes, and symptoms through the content of his or her responses. Interpretation of the item responses, however, is generally subjective and unreliable. Despite the fact that the test stimuli (the sentence stems) are standard, interpretation is usually done in an ad hoc manner and without benefit of norms.

In sum, projective tests have an important place in many clinical settings, particularly those that attempt to obtain a comprehensive picture of an individual's psychodynamic functioning and have the necessary trained staff to conduct extensive individual psychological evaluations. The great strengths of projective techniques—their unstructured nature and their focus on the unique aspects of personality—are at the same time their weaknesses because they make interpretation subjective, unreliable, and difficult to validate. Moreover, projective tests typically require a great deal of time to administer and advanced skill to interpret—both scarce quantities in many clinical settings.

Objective tests.   **Objective tests** are structured—that is, they typically use questionnaires, self-inventories, or rating scales in which questions or items are carefully phrased and alternative responses are specified as choices. They therefore involve a far more controlled format than projective devices and thus are more amenable to objectively based quantification. One virtue of such quantification is that of precision, which in turn enhances the reliability of test outcomes.

One of the major structured inventories for personality assessment is the **Minnesota Multiphasic Personality Inventory (MMPI).** We focus on it here because in many ways it is the prototype and the standard of this class of instruments. By gaining an understanding of "how it works," you should acquire considerable sophistication about more general issues in psychological measurement.

Several years in development, the MMPI was introduced for general use in 1943 by Hathaway

The Thematic Apperception Test, or TAT, asks a patient to make up stories based on a series of drawings. Here a psychologist administers the TAT to John, a psychiatric patient. Like other psychological tests, the TAT's purpose is to give a greater in-depth view of an individual. The interpreter is trained to assess personality characteristics based on the individual's responses.

and McKinley; it is today the most widely used personality test for both clinical assessment and psychopathologic research in the United States (Lubin et al., 1984, 1985). Moreover, translated versions of the inventory are widely used internationally. In all, the MMPI has been translated into more than 115 languages, and it is used in over 46 countries (Butcher, 1984).

The inventory, a kind of self-report technique, consists of 550 items covering topics ranging from physical condition and psychological states to moral and social attitudes. Normally, subjects are encouraged to answer all 550 items either *true* or *false*. Some sample items follow:

I sometimes keep on at a thing until others lose their patience with me.   T F
Bad words, often terrible words, come into my mind and I cannot get rid of them.   T F
I often feel as if things were not real.   T F
Someone has it in for me.   T F
(Hathaway & McKinley, 1951, p. 28)

The pool of items for the MMPI was originally administered to a large group of normal individuals (affectionately called the "Minnesota normals") and several quite homogeneous groups of patients having particular psychiatric diagnoses. Answers to all the items were then item-analyzed to see which ones differentiated the various groups. On the basis of the findings, ten clinical scales were constructed, each consisting of the items that were answered by one of the patient groups in the direction opposite to the predominant response of the normal group. This rather ingenious method of scorable item selection, known as *empirical keying,* was original to the MMPI and doubtless accounts for much of the instrument's power. Note that it involves no subjective prejudgment about the "meaning" of a true or false answer to any item; that meaning resides entirely in whether or not the answer is the same as that deviantly given by patients of varying diagnoses. Most examiners do not even review the actual responses made because doing so encourages speculative hypotheses that have a distressingly high likelihood of being wrong. Should an examinee's *pattern* of true/false responses closely approximate that of a particular pathological group, it is a reasonable inference that he or she shares other psychiatrically significant characteristics with that group—and may in fact "psychologically" be a *member* of that group.

Each of these ten "clinical" scales, then, measures tendencies to respond in psychologically deviant ways. Raw scores on these scales are compared with the corresponding scores of the normal population, many of whom did (and do) answer a few items in the critical direction, and the results are plotted on the standard MMPI profile form. By drawing a line connecting the scores for the different scales, a clinician can construct a profile that shows how far from normal a patient's performance is on each of the scales. The *Schizophrenia scale,* for example (and to reiterate the basic strategy), is made up of the items that schizophrenic patients consistently answered in a way that differentiated them from normal individuals. People who score high (relative to norms) on this scale, though not necessarily schizophrenic, often show propensities typical of the schizophrenic population. For example, high scorers on this scale may be socially inept, withdrawn, and have peculiar thought processes; they may have diminished contact with reality and in severe cases may have delusions and hallucinations.

The MMPI also includes four validity scales to detect whether a patient has answered the questions in a straightforward, honest manner. Extreme endorsement of the items on any of these scales may invalidate the test, while lesser endorsements frequently contribute important interpretive insights. In addition to the validity scales and the ten clinical scales, hundreds of "special" scales have been devised, four of which have become so widely used for both clinical and research purposes that they are now listed on the MMPI profile form. There is in principle no limit to the number of additional scales that *could* be generated from the MMPI item pool and available item norms. All the scales listed on the standard original MMPI profile form are given in *HIGHLIGHT 16.2.*

Clinically, the MMPI is used in several ways to evaluate a patient's personality characteristics and clinical problems. Perhaps the most typical use of the MMPI is as a *diagnostic standard.* That is, the individual's profile pattern is compared with profiles of known patient groups. If the profile fits a particular group, then the diagnostic information that has been collected on typical patients in this group can be used as a broad *descriptive diagnosis* of likely behavior, symptoms, and so on, for the patient under study. Another approach to MMPI interpretation, *content interpretation,* is used to supplement the empirical correlates provided in the just-described approach. Here, a clinician focuses on the objective content themes, although not usually individual items, in a person's response to the inventory; such content groups in the MMPI item pool have been identified and can be scaled in the same manner as already described. For example, if an individual endorses an unusually large number of items about fears, a clinician might well conclude that the individual is preoccupied with fear, or

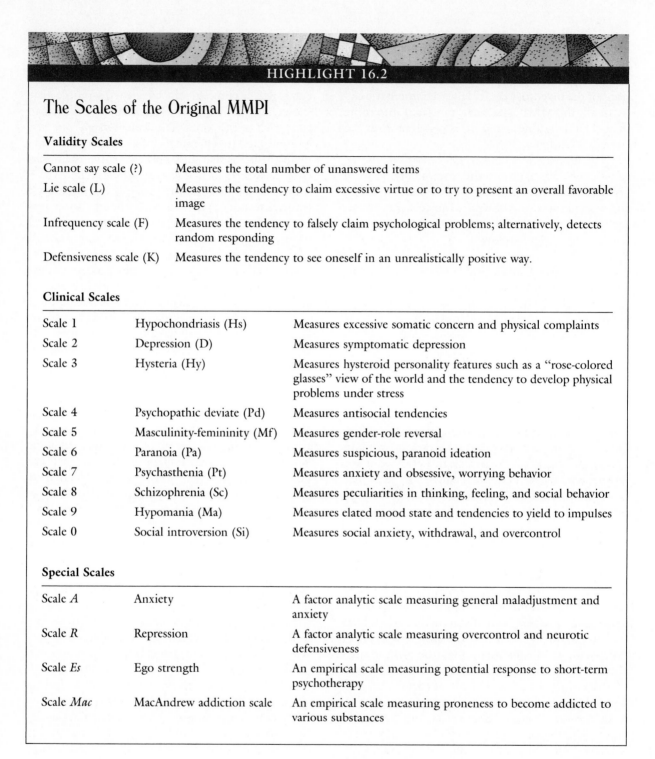

HIGHLIGHT 16.2

The Scales of the Original MMPI

Validity Scales

Cannot say scale (?)	Measures the total number of unanswered items
Lie scale (L)	Measures the tendency to claim excessive virtue or to try to present an overall favorable image
Infrequency scale (F)	Measures the tendency to falsely claim psychological problems; alternatively, detects random responding
Defensiveness scale (K)	Measures the tendency to see oneself in an unrealistically positive way.

Clinical Scales

Scale 1	Hypochondriasis (Hs)	Measures excessive somatic concern and physical complaints
Scale 2	Depression (D)	Measures symptomatic depression
Scale 3	Hysteria (Hy)	Measures hysteroid personality features such as a "rose-colored glasses" view of the world and the tendency to develop physical problems under stress
Scale 4	Psychopathic deviate (Pd)	Measures antisocial tendencies
Scale 5	Masculinity-femininity (Mf)	Measures gender-role reversal
Scale 6	Paranoia (Pa)	Measures suspicious, paranoid ideation
Scale 7	Psychasthenia (Pt)	Measures anxiety and obsessive, worrying behavior
Scale 8	Schizophrenia (Sc)	Measures peculiarities in thinking, feeling, and social behavior
Scale 9	Hypomania (Ma)	Measures elated mood state and tendencies to yield to impulses
Scale 0	Social introversion (Si)	Measures social anxiety, withdrawal, and overcontrol

Special Scales

Scale *A*	Anxiety	A factor analytic scale measuring general maladjustment and anxiety
Scale *R*	Repression	A factor analytic scale measuring overcontrol and neurotic defensiveness
Scale *Es*	Ego strength	An empirical scale measuring potential response to short-term psychotherapy
Scale *Mac*	MacAndrew addiction scale	An empirical scale measuring proneness to become addicted to various substances

minimally that this is a message the individual wishes for some reason to convey to the clinician.

In spite of its extensive use, the MMPI has not been without its critics. Many psychodynamically oriented clinicians feel that the MMPI (like other structured, objective tests) is superficial and does not adequately reflect the complexities of an individual taking the test. Some behaviorally oriented critics, on the other hand, criticize the MMPI, and in fact the entire genre of personality tests, as being too oriented toward measuring unobservable "mentalistic" constructs, such as traits.

A more specific criticism had been leveled at the datedness of the MMPI, including in particular its anachronistic norms and item pool. The original MMPI had been in use since the early 1940s, and even though much of the MMPI interpretive research is much more recent, the item pool and the basic scaling of raw response data had remained unchanged. In response to these criticisms, the publisher of the MMPI contracted to underwrite a revision of the instrument. This revised MMPI, designated MMPI-2 (Butcher et al., 1989), became available for general professional use in mid-1989. Perhaps inevitably, in light of the distinction of its forebear and the strong loyalties this instrument has engendered among clinicians over many years, the introduction of MMPI-2 has not been greeted with unanimous enthusiasm, despite what most acknowledge to be its psychometrically improved character. We will attempt here to outline the changes that have been made and to address briefly some misunderstandings that have arisen concerning MMPI-2.

The most important changes introduced with MMPI-2 were directed at overcoming the deficiencies already noted—namely (a) the outmoded idioms and sometimes prejudicial language of some of the items in the pool, and (b) the outdated and demographically unrepresentative character of the normal standardization sample, most of whose members came from 1930s-vintage rural Minnesota. A third major alteration, too technical for detailed discussion here, involves the scaling method used to convert raw scale scores to standardized ones having common parameters (that is, means and standard deviations).

Changes made in the original MMPI item pool can be summarized as follows:

- The original item pool was edited and modernized to eliminate expressions that were out of date (about 14 percent of the items required alteration).

- Additional items were written to address additional problem areas, such as treatment compliance, Type A behavior, suicide, and personality problems.

- Two separate item pools were established: an adult form and an adolescent form, designated MMPI-A.

The new adult normative sample for MMPI-2—2600 subjects randomly sampled from eight communities across the United States—is considerably more representative of the American population than was that for the original MMPI. Efforts were made to include representative groups from different racial and ethnic backgrounds, age groups, and social classes. Concern has been expressed that the education level of this standardization sample —averaging 14.7 years of schooling—exceeds that of the general U.S. population, which in fact it does by about two years. Available data indicate, however, that the education level of the people who will be examined with the MMPI-2 more closely approximates that of the new than of the original standardization group. In any event, there is no reason to believe that MMPI results are markedly or pervasively affected by modest variations in the educational levels of subjects. Being able to read and comprehend the items (which are at about a sixth-grade level) has of course always been a requirement of MMPI administration.

The adolescent form of the MMPI (MMPI-A) was standardized on 815 girls and 805 boys who were students in public and private schools in seven regions of the United States. Designed for use with youngsters aged 14 through 17, it contains a number of new scales. Its basic clinical scales, as in the case of MMPI-2, are the same as for the original MMPI.

The MMPI-2 has been validated in several clinical studies to date (Butcher & Graham, 1989). The clinical scales, which have been retained in their original form apart from minimal item deletion or rewording, seem, as expected, to measure the same properties of personality organization and functioning as they always have. A comparable stability of meaning is observed for the (also essentially unchanged) standard validity scales, which have been reinforced with three additional scales to detect tendencies to respond untruthfully to some items. The essential psychometric comparability of the main scales of the two adult versions has been empirically demonstrated by Ben-Porath and Butcher (1989). The basic MMPI-2 profile form is reproduced in *HIGHLIGHT 16.3* (page 596), in the case study of Esteban.

Overall, then, the authors of MMPI-2 have retained the central elements of the original instrument, but have added a number of features and refinements to it, including provision for systematic "content" profile analysis. As was their intent, the scales of MMPI-2 correlate highly with those of the original. MMPI. Some interpretive adjustments need to be made, however, in respect to *relative* scale elevations because the new normative base may have altered slightly the meaning to be assigned to interscale relationships. Experience with the new version to date indicates that practitioners are able, with little change in their interpretive approaches, to use it in the same manner as they were accustomed to using the original instrument. Recent research (Graham et al., in press) has shown that the two versions produce different results in approximately 1 percent of cases, and that where such discrepancies occur the MMPI-2 profile is typically more valid. Meanwhile, ongoing clinical research with MMPI-2 will doubtless teach us how to get the most out of the instrument, as it did with the original.

Another kind of objective self-report personality inventory uses the statistical procedure of **factor analysis,** a method for reducing a large array of intercorrelated measures to the minimum number of "factors" necessary to account for the observed overlap or associations among them. Because their scales are a product of such a refinement process, tests of this type are considered to measure purportedly basic and relatively independent personality traits. The goal is to measure one trait at a time with maximum precision and selectivity; a personality profile can then be drawn showing the degree to which several such methodologically rarefied traits are characteristic of an individual, as well as the overall pattern of the traits. McCrae and Costa (1986) have in fact recommended the adoption for clinical use of a factor-derived profile consisting of five purportedly "basic" trait dimensions: Introversion-Extraversion, Friendly Compliance-Hostile Noncompliance, Conscientiousness, Neuroticism, and Openness to Experience.

Self-report inventories, such as the MMPI, have a number of advantages over other types of personality tests. They are cost-effective, highly reliable, and objective; they also can be scored and interpreted, or if desired even administered, by computer. A number of general criticisms, however, have been leveled against the use of self-report inventories. As we have seen, some clinicians consider them to be too mechanistic to accurately portray the complexity of human beings and their problems. Also, because these tests require an individual to read, comprehend, and answer verbal material, patients who are illiterate or confused will not be able to take the test. Furthermore, the individual's cooperation is required in self-report inventories, and it is possible that the subject may distort his or her answers to create a particular impression. The validity scales of the MMPI and MMPI-2 are a direct attempt to deal with this last criticism.

Computer Interpretation of Objective Personality Tests   Scientifically constructed objective personality inventories, because of their scoring formats and emphasis on test validation, lend themselves particularly well to computer scoring and interpretation. The earliest practical applications of computer technology to test scoring and interpretation involved the MMPI. Over 30 years ago, psychologists at the Mayo Clinic programmed a computer to score and interpret clinical profiles. A number of other highly sophisticated MMPI and MMPI-2 interpretation systems have subsequently been developed (Butcher, 1979; Fowler, 1987).

Computer-based MMPI interpretation systems typically employ, insofar as possible, demonstrably powerful **actuarial procedures.** In such systems, descriptions of the actual behavior or other systematically established characteristics of numerous individuals with particular patterns of test scores have been stored in the computer. Whenever an individual turns up with one of these test score patterns, the appropriate description is printed out in the computer's evaluation. Such descriptions have been written and stored for a number of different test score patterns, most of them based on MMPI scores.

The accumulation of precise actuarial data for an instrument like the MMPI is difficult, time-consuming, and expensive. A large part of this problem is due to the complexity of the instrument itself, because the potential number of significantly different MMPI profile patterns is legion. The result is that the profiles of many subjects to whom the test is administered do not "fit" the criterial specifications of profile types for which adequate actuarial data are available. Problems of actuarial data acquisition also arise at the other end, the events or states of affair to be detected or predicted by the instrument. Many conditions that are of vital clinical importance are relatively rare in occurrence (for example, suicide) or are psychologically complex (for example, possible psychogenic components in a patient's physical illness), thus making it difficult to accumulate a sufficient number of cases to serve as an adequate actuarial data base. In these situations, then, the interpretive program writer is forced to fall back on general clinical lore and wisdom to formulate clinical descriptions appropriate to the types of profiles actually obtained. Hence, the best programs are written by expert clinicians who, in addition, have long experience with the particular instrument *and* keep up with its continuously developing research base (Carson, 1990b).

Examples of computer-generated descriptions appear in the evaluations reprinted in *HIGHLIGHT 16.3* (page 596). Sometimes the different paragraphs generated by the computer will have elements that seem inconsistent. These inconsistencies result from the fact that different parts of an individual's test pattern call up different paragraphs from the computer. The computer simply prints out blindly what has been found to be typical for individuals making similar scores on the various clinical scales. The computer cannot *integrate* the descriptions it picks up, however. At this point the human element comes in: in the clinical use of computers, it is *always* essential that a trained professional further interpret and monitor the assessment data (American Psychological Association, 1986).

Computerized personality assessment is no longer a novelty, but an important, dependable adjunct to clinical assessment. Computerized psychological evaluations are a quick and efficient means of providing a clinician with needed information early in the decision-making process. Some lingering controversies surrounding computerized psychological assessment are discussed in the Unresolved Issues section at the end of this chapter.

■ The Use of Psychological Tests in Personnel Screening

Many people who are experiencing personal problems or extreme psychological distress are able to function well enough in their job to get by. Some occupations, however, including those of airline flight crews, police officers, fire fighters, air-traffic controllers, nuclear power plant workers, and certain military specialties require a consistently higher level of psychological performance or greater emotional stability than others; these jobs allow for less personal variation in performance. Emotional problems in such employees can be extremely dangerous to other employees and to society as a whole. For example, an individual who holds a key position in a nuclear power plant control room and who is experiencing symptoms of severe depression can have his or her ability to function significantly impaired, possibly resulting in a failure to recognize problems requiring prompt and decisive counteraction.

The potential impact that mistakes in some occupations can have on the lives and safety of others makes the selection of employees and the monitoring of their mental health particularly critical. The psychological disorders that prompted a small group of Los Angeles police officers to repeatedly strike with their nightsticks a prone and helpless motorist in March of 1991, as recorded on videotape, is not simply an internal police matter; it is also a significant issue of concern for all of us. The potential for job failure or for becoming psychologically maladjusted under stress is so great for individuals in some high-stress occupations that measures need to be taken in the preemployment hiring process to evaluate applicants for emotional adjustment and to determine their capability of performing the job.

Psychological Screening of Emotional Problems
The use of personality tests in personnel

The emotional problems of employees in sensitive or high-stress occupations have potentially dangerous consequences for the lives and safety of others. For example, a small group of Los Angeles police officers physically abused a prone and helpless motorist in March of 1991, as recorded on videotape. Personnel screening for applicants' emotional stability can be an effective tool for determining a person's ability to perform a high-stress job.

screening has a long tradition. In fact, the first formal use of a standardized personality scale, the *Woodworth Personal Data Sheet*, was implemented to screen out World War I draftees who were psychologically unfit for military service (Woodworth, 1920). Today, psychological tests are widely used for personnel screening in occupations that require a high degree of emotional stability or great public trust. A recent controversial extension of this work is the attempt by some private corporations to assess potential employees for "honesty."

An important distinction needs to be made between *personnel selection* and *personnel screening* or, phrased differently, between "screening in" versus "screening out" job candidates. In situations where certain personality characteristics are desired for a particular job, a psychologist would choose instruments that directly assess those qualities, such as the 16 PF or the California Psychological Inventory, which measure "normal" range personality characteristics, such as dominance or sociability.

Personnel screening for emotional stability, on the other hand, requires a somewhat different set of assumptions. An important assumption is that personality or emotional problems, such as poor reality contact, impulsivity, or low self-esteem, would adversely impact on the way in which an individual would function in a critical job. In this situation, a psychologist could choose an instrument to assess the presence of psychopathology or maladjustment, such as the MMPI, to detect personality problems or symptoms that would affect personal or interpersonal functioning. To extend an earlier example, in police officer selection, an applicant with an MMPI profile pattern reflecting tendencies toward extreme aggressiveness, making hasty generalizations about others, and impulsivity would be eliminated from consideration or would undergo further evaluation to determine if these personality factors had resulted in negative job behaviors in the past.

Issues in Personality Test Job Screening

Before implementing a psychological assessment program of preemployment screening, an ethically responsible psychologist needs to consider a number of issues to determine both the relevance and appropriateness of the procedures to be used. The following questions need to be addressed:

1. *How should the preemployment test be used or how much weight should be given to a particular test in preemployment decisions?* Psychological tests should not be the sole means of determining whether a person should be hired. Instruments like the MMPI should be used in conjunction with evaluations based on an employment interview, a background check, evaluation of previous work record, and so on. Psychological tests provide useful hypotheses concerning an individual's adjustment, but they have not been developed to be or validated as the sole criteria of employment decisions.

2. *Is the use of a psychological test an unwarranted invasion of privacy?* Undeniably, many (and perhaps in a certain sense all) psychological tests, especially clinical tests like the MMPI, invade an individual's privacy by asking many personal questions concerning symptoms, attitudes, and life-styles. Concerns over invasion of privacy have long been expressed and the question of the appropriateness of these tests in employment selection has been the subject of congressional hearings (see Brayfield et al., 1965). Subsequently, the appropriateness of personality testing in employment decisions has been tested in court (*McKenna* v. *Fargo*, 1978), where their use in screening for some occupations was found to be appropriate. Therefore, the question becomes one of determining whether a particular test used in personnel screening is a warranted invasion of privacy—that is, determining whether the particular placement decisions being made are consistent with the greater interests of society. For some occupations, such decisions are deemed justifiable; it is considered within the criterion of "pub-

lic good" that individuals being placed in positions of high responsibility are emotionally stable according to our best information available.

3. *Are the procedures fair to all candidates, including members of ethnic minorities?* The question of the fairness of psychological tests in personnel screening is an important one. In order for a psychological test to be considered appropriate (both ethically and legally) for use in personnel selection situations, it must be demonstrated that the test does not unfairly portray or discriminate against ethnic minorities. This question needs to be addressed for each psychological test or personnel procedure used. The psychological tests being used must have a demonstrated validity for the particular test application. In the case of the MMPI, which is the most widely used clinical test in personnel screening, minority group performance has been widely studied (Butcher, 1979; Dahlstrom, Lachar, & Dahlstrom, 1986; King, Carroll, & Fuller, 1977; Wennerholm & Lopez-Roig, 1983). Assuming that an individual can read the items (for example, his or her reading level is sufficient or the appropriate language version, such as Spanish, is administered), the MMPI does not portray or discriminate against various ethnic minority subjects in an unfair manner. Given the more representative normative sample for MMPI-2, it is even less likely than its predecessor to present a problem in this respect.

■ A Psychological Case Study: Esteban

In this section, we will illustrate psychological assessment through an extensive diagnostic case study of a young man who presented a complicated clinical picture that was substantially clarified through psychological and neuropsychological assessment. This is an unusual case in several respects: the young man's problems were quite severe and involved both psychological and organic elements; the case involved cross-cultural considerations—the young man was from South America and assessment was done in both English and Spanish (the latter only as necessary); and a number of psychological specialists participated in the assessment study, including a neuropsychologist, a behaviorally oriented clinical psychologist, a Hispanic clinical psychologist, and a psychiatrist.

Esteban, a 21-year-old student from Colombia, South America, had been enrolled in an English language program at a small college in the United States. He had become disruptive in school, evidencing loud, obnoxious behavior in class and quarreling with his roommates (whom he accused of stealing his wallet). After a period of time during which his behavior did not improve, he was expelled from the program. The director of the program indicated that he felt Esteban needed psychological help for his problems, which included not only the behavioral problems but also, reportedly, severe headaches and confused thinking. The director added that Esteban would be considered for readmission only if he showed significant improvement in therapy.

On hearing of his expulsion, Esteban's parents, who were well-to-do international banking entrepreneurs, flew in from South America and arranged for a complete physical examination for him at a well-known medical center in New York. After an extensive medical and neurological examination to determine the source of his headaches and confusion, Esteban was diagnosed as having some "diffuse" brain impairment, but he was found to be otherwise in good health. His parents then sought a further, more definitive neurological examination. The neurologist at the second hospital recommended a psychological and neuropsychological examination because he suspected that Esteban's mild neurological condition would not account for his extreme psychological and behavioral symptoms. He referred the family to a psychologist for assessment and treatment. Because Esteban was experiencing a number of pressing situational problems —for example, his behavior problems continued, he appeared anxious to find a new English program, and, as we will see, he had some hard issues to face about his career aspirations to become a physician —the psychologist decided to begin with therapy immediately, concurrent with the additional assessment evaluation.

Interviews and Behavior Observations

Esteban was seen in the initial session with his parents. The interview was conducted in English with some translation into Spanish (mostly by Esteban) because the parents knew little English. Throughout the session, Esteban was disorganized and distractible. He had difficulty keeping to the topic being discussed and periodically interrupted his own conversation with seemingly random impulses to show the interviewer papers, books, pamphlets, and the like from his knapsack. He talked incessantly, often loudly. He was not at all defensive about his problems but talked freely about his symptoms and attitudes. His behavior resembled that of a hyperactive child—he was excitable, impulsive, and immature. He did not appear to be psychotic; he reported no hallucinations or delusions and was in contact with reality. He related well with the interviewer, seemed to enjoy the

session, and expressed an interest in having additional sessions.

During subsequent interviews, Esteban expressed frequent physical complaints, such as headaches, tension, and sleeping problems. He reported that he had a great deal of difficulty concentrating on his studies. He could not study because he always found other things to do—particularly talking about religion. He was seemingly outgoing and sociable and had no difficulty initiating conversations with other people. He tended, however, to say socially inappropriate things or become frustrated and lose his temper easily. For example, during one family interview, he became enraged and kicked his mother.

Family History   Esteban's father was a Spanish-Colombian banker in his mid-sixties. He was well-dressed, somewhat passive, though visibly quite warm toward his son. He had had his share of difficulties in recent years; severe business problems coupled with two heart attacks had brought on a depressive episode that had left him ineffective in dealing with his business. His wife and her brother, an attorney from Madrid, had had to straighten out the business problems. She reported that her husband had had several depressive episodes in the past and that Esteban's moods resembled her husband's in his earlier years.

Esteban's mother was a tense, worried, and somewhat hypochondriacal woman who appeared to be rather domineering. Prior to the first and second interviews, she handed the therapist, in secret, written "explanations" of her son's problems. Her own history revealed that she was unhappy in her marriage and that she lived only for her children, on whom she doted.

Esteban's brother, Juan, was an engineering student at an American university and apparently was doing well academically and socially. He was one year older than Esteban.

Esteban's childhood had been marked with problems. His mother reported that although he had been a good baby—noting that he had been pretty and happy as a small child—he had changed after age 2½. At about that time, he had fallen on his head and was unconscious for a while; he was not hospitalized. Beginning in the preschool years, he exhibited behavioral problems, including temper tantrums, negativism, and an inability to get along with peers. These problems continued when he began school. He frequently refused to go to school, had periods of aggressive behavior, and appeared in general to be "hyperactive." It appeared that he was probably overprotected and "infantilized" by his mother.

Esteban was quite close to his brother Juan, with whom he reported having had extensive homosexual relations when they were growing up. The "darkest day" in Esteban's life was reportedly when Juan broke off the homosexual relationship with him at age 16 and told him to "go and find men." Although he later carried on a platonic relationship with a woman in Colombia, it was never a serious one. Esteban had strong homosexual urges of which he was consciously aware and attempted to control through a growing preoccupation with religion.

Esteban had been in psychotherapy on several occasions since he was 11 years old. After he graduated from high school, he attended law school in Colombia for a quarter, but dropped out because he "wanted to become a doctor instead." (In Colombia, professional schools are combined with college.) He left school, according to his parents' report, because he could not adapt. He worked for a time in the family business but had difficulty getting along with other employees and was encouraged to try other work. When that failed, his parents sent him to the United States to study English, rationalizing that Colombia was not as good an environment for him as the United States.

Intelligence Testing   Esteban underwent psychological testing to evaluate further the possibility of neurological deficits and to determine if he had the intellectual capabilities to proceed with a demanding academic career. He scored in the borderline to average range of intelligence on the WAIS-R (English version) and on the WAIS (Spanish version). He was particularly deficient in tasks involving practical judgment, common sense, concentration, visual-motor coordination, and concept formation. In addition, on memory tests, he showed a below average memory ability, such as a poor immediate recall of ideas from paragraphs read aloud (in both English and Spanish). Under most circumstances, individuals showing similar intellectual or neurological deficits are able to live comfortable, fulfilling lives in careers whose formal intellectual demands are relatively modest. It was clear from the test data and Esteban's behavior during testing that his stated career aspirations—seemingly nurtured by his parents—exceeded his abilities and might well be a factor in much of his frustration.

Personality Testing   Esteban was given both the Rorschach Test and the MMPI. Both tests have been used extensively with Hispanic subjects. The Rorschach is believed by some to be particularly well-suited for cases like Esteban's because the test stimuli are relatively unstructured and not culture-bound. Esteban's performance on the Rorschach revealed tension, anxiety, and a preoccupation with morbid topics. He appeared to be overly concerned about his health, prone to depression, indecisive and yet at other times impulsive and careless. His responses were often immature and he showed a strong and persistent ambivalence toward females. In some responses, he viewed females in highly aggressive ways—often a fusion of sexual and aggressive images was evident. In general, he demonstrated aloofness and an inability to relate well to other people. Although his Rorschach responses suggested that he could view the world in conventional ways and was probably not psychotic, at times he had difficulty controlling his impulses. Esteban's Rorschach protocol was computer analyzed using the Exner Comprehensive Rorschach System.

Esteban took the original version of the MMPI in both English and Spanish. His MMPI profile was virtually identical in both languages. It has been converted to MMPI-2 format and is reproduced in *HIGHLIGHT 16.3* (page 596) along with the original and the MMPI-2-based computer interpretations of his test scores.

Summary of the Psychological Assessment
Esteban showed mild neurological deficits on neuropsychological testing and a borderline to average level of intellectual ability. He clearly did not have the academic ability to pursue a demanding medical career. Difficult or demanding intellectual tasks placed a great deal of stress on him and resulted in a high degree of frustration. Furthermore, his poor memory made learning complex material very difficult.

The MMPI interpretation indicated that Esteban's disorganized behavior and symptomatic patterns reflected a serious psychological disorder. Although he was not currently psychotic, both his past behavior and his test performance suggested that he was functioning marginally and that he showed the potential for personality deterioration in some situations.

Esteban's most salient psychological problems concerned his tendency to become frustrated and his ready loss of impulse control. He was volatile and became upset easily. Additionally, it appeared that Esteban's relative isolation during his early years (due in part to his overprotective mother) did not prepare him to function adequately in many social situations. Another important problem area for Esteban was in psychosexual adjustment. The psychological test results and his personal history clearly indicated a gender-identity confusion.

Within the parameters of DSM-III-R, Esteban would receive an Axis I diagnosis of *organic personality syndrome* and an Axis II diagnosis of *borderline personality disorder*. Furthermore, it was recommended that he undertake social-skills training and that—rather than a career in medicine—he be encouraged to pursue occupational goals more in keeping with his abilities. Psychotropic medication (Lithium and Mellaril) were prescribed for his emotional control problems.

A Follow-up Note   Esteban was seen in psychological therapy twice a week and was kept on medication. He was also seen in a social-skills training program for ten sessions. Through the help of his therapist, he was admitted to a less-demanding English program, which seemed more appropriate for his abilities.

For the first six months, Esteban made considerable progress, especially after his behavior became somewhat stabilized, largely, it appeared, as a result of the medications. He became less impulsive and more in control of his anger. He successfully completed the English classes in which he was enrolled. During this period, he lived with his mother, who had taken up a temporary residence near the college. She then returned to Colombia, and Esteban moved into an apartment with a roommate, with whom, however, he had increasing difficulty.

Several weeks after his mother left, Esteban quit going to therapy and quit taking his medication. He began to frequent local gay bars, at first out of curiosity but later to seek male lovers. At the same time, his preoccupation with religion increased and he moved into a house near campus that was operated by a fundamentalist religious cult. His parents, quite concerned by his overt homosexual behavior (which he described in detail over the phone, adding the suggestion that they visit the gay bar with him), returned to the United States. Realizing that they could not stay permanently to supervise Esteban, they then sought a residential treatment program that would provide him with a more structured living arrangement. All assessment and therapy records were forwarded to those in charge of the residential program.

THE INTEGRATION OF ASSESSMENT DATA

As assessment data are collected, their significance must be interpreted so that they can be integrated into a coherent working model for use in planning or changing treatment. Clinicians in individual private practice normally assume this often arduous task on their own.

In a clinic or hospital setting, assessment data are usually evaluated in a staff conference attended by members of an interdisciplinary team (perhaps a clinical psychologist, a psychiatrist, a social worker, and other mental health personnel) who are concerned with the decisions to be made regarding treatment. By putting together all the information they have gathered, they can see whether the findings complement each other and form a definitive clinical picture or whether gaps or discrepancies exist that necessitate further investigation.

At the time of an original assessment, integration of all the data may lead to agreement on a tentative diagnostic classification for a patient—such as *paranoid schizophrenia*. In any case, the findings of each member of the team, as well as the recommendations for treatment, are entered in the case record, so that it will always be possible to check back and see why a certain course of therapy was undertaken, how accurate the clinical assessment was, and how valid the treatment decision turned out to be.

New assessment data collected during the course of therapy provide feedback on its effective-

In a clinic or hospital setting, assessment data are usually evaluated in a staff conference attended by members of an interdisciplinary team, including, for example, a clinical psychologist, a psychiatrist, a social worker, and a psychiatric nurse. Sharing findings may lead to a diagnostic classification for a patient and a course of treatment. Staff decisions can have far-reaching consequences for patients; as such, it is important that clinicians be aware of the limitations of assessment.

Esteban's Rescored MMPI-2 Profile and His Original and MMPI-2 Computer-based Reports

Esteban was originally tested with the original MMPI. His responses from that testing were converted to the MMPI-2 format by J. N. Butcher. The computer-based reports for both editions of the test are provided below.

On the facing page is the converted MMPI-2 profile chart compiled for Esteban. The validity scales are shown in the column at left (the column in which the word MALE appears). The clinical scales are to the right. The special scales are not included in this version of the profile. *(HIGH-LIGHT 16.2* on page 588 describes each of these scales.) Based on the scores originally obtained and those you see displayed in the chart, a computer produced the narrative descriptions given below. On pages 598–599 are hypotheses about the psychological functioning of Esteban from a computer-generated report of his Rorschach protocol performed by the Exner Comprehensive Rorschach System.

Computer-based Report: The Original MMPI

Profile validity. This MMPI profile should be interpreted with caution. There is some possibility that the clinical report is an exaggerated picture of the client's present situation and problems. He is presenting an unusual number of psychological symptoms. This extreme response set could result from poor reading ability, confusion, disorientation, stress, or a need to seek attention for his problems.

His test-taking attitudes should be evaluated for the possibility that he has produced an invalid profile. He may be showing a lack of cooperation with the testing or he may be "malingering" by attempting to present a false claim of mental illness. Determining the sources of his confusion, whether conscious distortion or personality deterioration, is important since immediate attention may be required. Clinical patients with this profile are often confused, distractible, and show memory problems. Evidence of delusions and thought disorder may be present. He may be showing a high degree of distress and personality deterioration.

Symptomatic pattern. He is presenting with a mixed pattern of psychological symptoms. This profile shows a pattern of chronic depression and alienation. The client tends to feel quite withdrawn, tense, and anxious. He is having problems concentrating, feels agitated, and is functioning at a very low level of psychological efficiency. He feels apathetic and indifferent and like a passive participant in life. He also feels that he has little energy left over from mere survival to expend on any pleasure in life.

He may be showing signs of serious psychopathology—delusions, problems in thinking, and inappropriate affect. His long-standing lack of achievement and his work behavior have caused him many problems, and he may have serious plans for suicide.

He experiences some conflicts concerning his sex-role identity, appearing somewhat passive and effeminate in his orientation toward life. He may appear somewhat insecure in the masculine role, and he may be uncomfortable in relationships with women. His interests, in general, are more characteristic of women than of men. He tends to be quite passive and submissive in interpersonal relationships, and he tends to make concessions in an effort to avoid confrontation. In addition, he may have low heterosexual drive.

His response content indicates that he is preoccupied with feeling guilty and unworthy, and feels that he deserves to be punished for wrongs he has committed. He feels regretful and unhappy about life, complains about having no zest for life, and seems plagued by anxiety and worry about the future. According to his response content, there is strong possibility that he has seriously contemplated suicide. A careful evaluation of this possibility is suggested. He views his physical health as failing and reports numerous somatic concerns. He feels that life is no longer worthwhile and that he is losing control of his thought processes. He reports in his response content that he is high-strung and believes that he feels things more, or more intensely, than others do. He feels

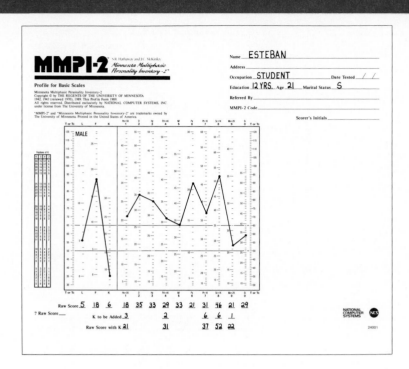

NATIONAL COMPUTER SYSTEMS   NCS

24001

lonely and misunderstood at times. The content of his responses indicates that he feels as though he is losing his mind, and that he does not understand things going on around him. The items he endorsed included content suggesting that his thinking is confused and bizarre. He feels that others do not understand him and are trying to control him. He is also tending toward withdrawal into a world of fantasy.

Interpersonal relations. He has great problems with alienation and social relationships. He feels vulnerable to interpersonal hurt, lacks trust, and may never form close satisfying relationships. He feels very insecure in relationships and may be preoccupied with guilt and self-defeating behavior.

He appears somewhat shy, with some social concerns and inhibitions. He is a bit hypersensitive about what others think of him and is occasionally concerned over his relationship with others. He appears to be somewhat overcontrolled and submissive in personal relationships and social situations, and may have some difficulty expressing his feelings toward others.

The content of the client's MMPI responses suggests the following additional information concerning his interpersonal relations. He views his home situation as unpleasant and lacking in love and understanding. He feels like leaving home to escape a quarrelsome, critical situation, and to be free of family domination.

Behavioral Stability. Individuals with this profile type often lead stormy, chaotic lives and never seem to develop satisfying relationships.

Diagnostic Considerations. Individuals with this profile tend to have features of both an affective disorder and a thought disorder. In addition, there seems to be a long-standing pattern of maladjustment that is characteristic of people with severe personality disorders. He is likely to be diagnosed as having a Schizophrenic or Major Affective Disorder.

The content of his responses to the MMPI items suggests symptoms (convulsions, paralysis, clumsiness, and double vision) that are associated with neurological disorder. Vague pain symptoms, nausea, etc., that are found in neurotic conditions are also present, however. Further neurological evaluation would be needed to make a clear differentiation.

Treatment Considerations. Multiple-problem life situations and difficulties forming interpersonal relationships make patients with this profile type poor candidates for relationship-based psychotherapy. Their basic lack of trust and withdrawal would also make psychotherapy difficult. Some outpatients with this profile type seem to benefit from minimal contact treatment, such as brief periodic visits with a directive, supportive therapist. Many need psychotropic medication to control their bizarre thinking or to elevate their mood.

Computer-based Report: The MMPI-2

Profile validity. This MMPI-2 profile should be interpreted with caution. There is some possibility that the clinical report is an exaggerated picture of his present situ-

SUBJECT NAME:ESTEBAN.MMPI   AGE:21   SEX:M   RACE:W   MS:Sin   ED:14

SEMANTIC INTERPRETATION OF THE RORSCHACH
PROTOCOL UTILIZING THE COMPREHENSIVE SYSTEM
(COPYRIGHT 1976, 1985 BY JOHN E. EXNER, JR.)

THE FOLLOWING COMPUTER-BASED INTERPRETATION IS DERIVED ** EXCLUSIVELY **
FROM THE STRUCTURAL DATA OF THE RECORD AND DOES NOT INCLUDE CONSIDERATION OF
THE SEQUENCE OF SCORES OR THE VERBAL MATERIAL. IT IS INTENDED AS A GUIDE FROM
WHICH THE INTERPRETER OF THE TOTAL PROTOCOL CAN PROCEED TO STUDY AND REFINE
THE HYPOTHESES GENERATED FROM THESE ACTUARIAL FINDINGS.

* * * * *

1. THE RECORD APPEARS TO BE VALID AND INTERPRETIVELY USEFUL.

2. THIS IS THE TYPE OF PERSON WHO IS PRONE TO TRY TO OVERSIMPLIFY STIMULI
    IN ORDER TO MAKE THE WORLD LESS THREATENING AND/OR DEMANDING. THIS
    BASIC COPING STYLE TENDS TO BE PERVASIVE WHEN NEW SITUATIONS AND/OR
    STRESSES OCCUR. WHEN DONE TO EXCESS, AS APPEARS TO BE THE CASE HERE,
    THE SUBJECT IS LIKELY TO EXPERIENCE FREQUENT SOCIAL DIFFICULTIES
    BECAUSE THE STYLE PROMOTES A NEGLECT OF THE DEMANDS AND/OR
    EXPECTATIONS OF THE ENVIRONMENT.

3. THIS SUBJECT USUALLY HAS ENOUGH RESOURCE ACCESSABLE TO PARTICIPATE
    MEANINGFULLY IN THE FORMULATION AND DIRECTION OF RESPONSES. TOLERANCE
    FOR STRESS IS LIKE THAT OF MOST PEOPLE, THAT IS, CONTROLS USUALLY WILL
    NOT FALTER UNLESS THE STRESS IS UNEXPECTED AND INTENSE AND PROLONGED
    UNREASONABLY.

4. THERE IS EVIDENCE INDICATING THE PRESENCE OF CONSIDERABLE SUBJECTIVELY
    FELT DISTRESS.

5. THIS SUBJECT TENDS TO INTERNALIZE FEELINGS MUCH MORE THAN IS CUSTOMARY
    AND THIS OFTEN RESULTS IN SUBSTANTIAL DISCOMFORT THAT CAN TAKE THE
    FORM OF TENSION AND/OR ANXIETY.

6. THIS IS THE TYPE OF PERSON WHO PREFERS TO DELAY MAKING RESPONSES IN
    COPING SITUATIONS UNTIL TIME HAS BEEN ALLOWED TO CONSIDER RESPONSE
    POSSIBILITIES AND THEIR POTENTIAL CONSEQUENCES. SUCH PEOPLE LIKE TO
    KEEP THEIR EMOTIONS ASIDE UNDER THESE CONDITIONS.

7. THIS PERSON TENDS TO USE DELIBERATE THINKING MORE FOR THE PURPOSE OF
    CREATING FANTASY THROUGH WHICH TO IGNORE THE WORLD THAN TO CONFRONT
    PROBLEMS DIRECTLY. THIS IS A SERIOUS PROBLEM BECAUSE THE BASIC COPING
    STYLE IS BEING USED MORE FOR FLIGHT THAN TO ADAPT TO THE EXTERNAL
    WORLD.

8. THIS TYPE OF PERSON IS NOT VERY FLEXIBLE IN THINKING, VALUES, OR
    ATTITUDES. IN EFFECT, PEOPLE SUCH AS THIS HAVE SOME DIFFICULTY IN
    SHIFTING PERSPECTIVES OR VIEWPOINTS.

(c)1976, 1985 by John E. Exner, Jr.

SUBJECT NAME:ESTEBAN.MMPI   AGE:21   SEX:M   RACE:W   MS:Sin   ED:14
PAGE -2-

9. THERE IS A STRONG POSSIBILITY THAT THIS IS A PERSON WHO PREFERS TO
    AVOID INITIATING BEHAVIORS, AND INSTEAD, TENDS TOWARDS A MORE PASSIVE
    ROLE IN PROBLEM SOLVING AND INTERPERSONAL RELATIONSHIPS.

10. THIS SUBJECT DOES NOT MODULATE EMOTIONAL DISPLAYS AS MUCH AS MOST
    ADULTS AND, BECAUSE OF THIS, IS PRONE TO BECOME VERY INFLUENCED BY
    FEELINGS IN MOST THINKING, DECISIONS, AND BEHAVIORS.

11. THIS IS A PERSON WHO IS VERY ATTRACTED TO BEING AROUND EMOTIONAL
    STIMULI. THIS MAY POSE A SIGNIFICANT PROBLEM IN ADAPTATION BECAUSE OF
    PROBLEMS IN CONTROL. THAT IS, THE MORE EMOTIONAL STIMULI BEING
    PROCESSED, THE GREATER THE DEMAND FOR EMOTIONAL EXCHANGE. IF THAT
    EXCHANGE IS NOT WELL CONTROLLED, PROBLEMS CAN EASILY OCCUR.

12. THIS IS AN INDIVIDUAL WHO DOES NOT EXPERIENCE NEEDS FOR CLOSENESS IN
    WAYS THAT ARE COMMON TO MOST PEOPLE. AS A RESULT, THEY ARE TYPICALLY
    LESS COMFORTABLE IN INTERPERSONAL SITUATIONS, HAVE SOME DIFFICULTIES
    IN CREATING AND SUSTAINING DEEP RELATIONSHIPS, ARE MORE CONCERNED WITH
    ISSUES OF PERSONAL SPACE, AND MAY APPEAR MUCH MORE GUARDED AND/OR
    DISTANT TO OTHERS.

13. THIS SUBJECT HAS AS MUCH INTEREST IN OTHERS AS DO MOST ADULTS AND
    CHILDREN. HOWEVER, THE SUBJECT DOES NOT APPEAR TO HAVE A VERY
    REALISTIC UNDERSTANDING OF PEOPLE. INSTEAD, CONCEPTIONS OF OTHERS
    TEND TO BE DERIVED MORE FROM IMAGINATION THAN FROM REAL EXPERIENCE.

14. THIS SUBJECT APPEARS TO HAVE AN UNUSUAL BODY PREOCCUPATION.

15. THIS SUBJECT APPEARS TO HAVE A MARKED SEXUAL PREOCCUPATION.

16. THIS SUBJECT IS VERY PRONE TO INTERPRET STIMULUS CUES IN A UNIQUE AND
    OVERPERSONALIZED MANNER. PEOPLE SUCH AS THIS OFTEN VIEW THEIR WORLD
    WITH THEIR OWN SPECIAL SET OF BIASES AND ARE LESS CONCERNED WITH BEING
    CONVENTIONAL AND/OR ACCEPTABLE TO OTHERS.

17. IN SPITE OF THE ABOVE MENTIONED TENDENCY TO MISINTERPRET OR OVERPERSON-
    ALIZE THE INTERPRETATION OF STIMULUS CUES, THE SUBJECT DOES TEND TO
    RESPOND IN CONVENTIONAL WAYS TO SITUATIONS IN WHICH CONVENTIONAL OR
    EXPECTED RESPONSES ARE OBVIOUS AND EASILY IDENTIFIED.

18. MUCH OF THE COGNITIVE ACTIVITY OF THIS SUBJECT IS LESS SOPHISTICATED
    OR LESS MATURE THAN IS EXPECTED. THIS MAY BE A FUNCTION OF A
    DEVELOPMENTAL LAG, DISORGANIZATION, OR MAY SIMPLY REFLECT A RELUCTANCE
    TO COMMIT RESOURCES TO A TASK.

19. THIS SUBJECT TENDS TO SCAN A STIMULUS FIELD HASTILY AND NOT
    METHODICALLY. THESE KINDS OF PEOPLE OFTEN COME TO DECISIONS
    PREMATURELY AND ERRONEOUSLY SIMPLY BECAUSE THEY HAVE NOT PROCESSED ALL
    AVAILABLE INFORMATION ADEQUATELY. THIS SHOULD NOT BE CONFUSED WITH

(c)1976, 1985 by John E. Exner, Jr.

---

ation. He presented an unusual number of psychological problems and symptoms. His test-taking attitudes should be evaluated to determine if his response pattern is a valid approach to the testing. This extreme response set could result from poor reading ability, confusion, disorientation, stress, or a need to seek attention for his problems. Clinical patients with this profile are often confused, distractible, and show memory problems. Evidence of delusions and thought disorder may be present.

Symptomatic pattern. His MMPI-2 profile reflects a high degree of psychological distress at this time. The client is presenting with a mixed pattern of psychological symptoms. He appears to be tense, apathetic, and withdrawn, and is experiencing some

personality deterioration. He seems to be quite confused and disorganized, and probably secretly broods about unusual beliefs and suspicions. Autistic behavior and inappropriate affect are characteristic features of individuals with this profile. Some evidence of an active psychotic process is apparent. He may have delusions and occult preoccupations, and may feel that others are against him because of his beliefs. In interviews, he is likely to be vague, circumstantial, and tangential, and may be quite preoccupied with abstract ideas.

He is having problems concentrating, feels agitated, and is functioning at a very low level of psychological efficiency. He feels apathetic, indifferent, and like a passive participant in life. He also feels that he has little energy left over from mere survival to expend

on any pleasure in life. He may be showing signs of serious psychopathology such as delusions, problems in thinking, and inappropriate affect. His long-standing lack of achievement and his work behavior have caused him many problems.

Many individuals with this profile consider committing suicide and he may actually have serious plans for self-destruction.

He experiences some conflicts concerning his sex-role identity, appearing somewhat passive and effeminate in his orientation toward life. He may appear somewhat insecure in the masculine role and may be uncomfortable in his relationships with women.

His response content indicates that he is preoccupied with feeling guilty and unworthy, and feels that he deserves to be punished for wrongs he has commit-

```
SUBJECT NAME:ESTEBAN.MMPI        AGE:21  SEX:M  RACE:W  MS:Sin  ED:14

    PAGE -3-

=================================================================
    IMPULSIVENESS ALTHOUGH SOME DECISIONS AND BEHAVIORS THAT RESULT MAY
    HAVE THAT FEATURE.  IT IS A CONSEQUENCE OF NEGLECT IN SCANNING AND
    ORGANIZING TACTICS WHICH MAY BE THE PRODUCT OF A PERCEPTUAL DEFICIT,
    PSYCHOLOGICAL HABITS DEVELOPED EARLY IN LIFE, OR CAN BE A FUNCTION OF
    COGNITIVE DISARRAY PROVOKED BY NEUROLOGICALLY RELATED OR
    PSYCHOPATHOLOGICAL PROBLEMS.  IT SHOULD ALSO BE NOTED FOR THIS SUBJECT
    THAT THE COMPOSITE OF HASTY SCANNING OF STIMULUS FIELDS PLUS LIMITED
    EMOTIONAL CONTROLS IS ONE IMPORTANT FACTOR THAT LEADS TO IMPULSIVE
    LIKE BEHAVIORS.

20. THIS PERSON USUALLY SEEKS AN ECONOMICAL APPROACH TO PROBLEM SOLVING OR
    COPING BY FOCUSING MORE ON THE EASILY MANAGED ASPECTS OF A SITUATION
    AND TENDING TO NEGLECT BROADER ISSUES THAT MAY BE PRESENT.  THIS IS
    TYPICAL OF MANY PEOPLE AND CAN BE AN ASSET.  HOWEVER, IT CAN ALSO
    BECOME A LIABILITY IN MORE COMPLEX AND DEMANDING SITUATIONS THAT
    REQUIRE HIGHER LEVELS OF MOTIVATION AND EFFORT TO ACHIEVE EFFECTIVE
    RESULTS.

21. THIS PERSON IS SOMEWHAT CONSERVATIVE IN SETTING GOALS.  USUALLY PEOPLE
    LIKE THIS WANT TO COMMIT THEMSELVES ONLY TO OBJECTIVES WHICH OFFER A
    SIGNIFICANT PROBABILITY OF SUCCESS.

22. THIS PERSON TENDS TO USE INTELLECTUALIZATION AS A BASIC TACTIC TO
    CONTEND WITH EMOTIONAL THREATS AND STRESSES. PEOPLE LIKE THIS ARE
    OFTEN VERY RESISTIVE DURING EARLY PHASES OF INTERVENTION AS THIS
    TENDENCY TOWARD DENIAL CAUSES THEM TO AVOID ANY AFFECTIVE
    CONFRONTATIONS.

                    * * *  END OF REPORT  * * *




=================================================================
(c)1976, 1985 by John E. Exner, Jr.
```

ted. He feels regretful and unhappy about life, complains about having no zest for life, and seems plagued by anxiety and worry about the future. According to his response content there is a strong possibility that he has contemplated suicide. A careful evaluation of this possibility is suggested. He views his physical health as failing and reports numerous somatic complaints. He feels that life is no longer worthwhile and that he is losing control of his thought processes. He reports in his response content that he feels things more, or more intensely, than others do.

Interpersonal relations. Disturbed interpersonal relationships are characteristic of individuals with this profile type. He feels vulnerable to interpersonal hurt, lacks trust, and may never form close, satisfying interpersonal ties. He feels very insecure in relationships and may be preoccupied with guilt and self-defeating behavior. Many individuals with this profile are so self-preoccupied and unskilled in sex-role behavior that they never develop rewarding heterosexual relationships. Some never marry.

Behavioral Stability. Individuals with this profile type often lead chronically stormy, chaotic lives.

Diagnostic Considerations. The most likely diagnosis for individuals with this MMPI-2 profile type is Schizophrenia, possibly Paranoid type, or Paranoid Disorder. Similar clients tend to also have features of an affective disorder. In addition, there seems to be a long-standing pattern of maladjustment that is characteristic of people with severe personality disorders.

Because this behavioral pattern may also be associated with Organic Brain Syndrome or Substance-Induced Organic Mental Disorder, these possibilities should be evaluated.

Treatment Considerations. Individuals with this profile may be experiencing considerable personality deterioration, which may require hospitalization if they are considered dangerous to themselves or others.

Psychotropic medication may reduce their thinking disturbance and mood disorder. Outpatient treatment may be complicated by their regressed or disorganized behavior. Multiple-problem life situations and difficulties forming interpersonal relationships make patients with this profile poor candidates for relationship-based psychotherapy. Day treatment programs or other such structured settings may be helpful in providing a stabilizing treatment environment. Long-term adjustment is a problem. Frequent, brief "management" therapy contacts may be helpful in structuring his activities. Insight-oriented or relationship therapies tend not to be helpful for individuals with these severe problems and may actually exacerbate the symptoms. He probably would have difficulty establishing a trusting working relationship with a therapist.

ness and serve as a basis for making needed modifications in an ongoing treatment program. As we have noted, clinical assessment data are also commonly used in evaluating the final outcome of therapy and in comparing the effectiveness of different therapeutic and preventive approaches. Summers (1979), among others, has pointed out the importance of assessing a patient's level of functioning prior to hospital discharge. Too often, individuals who cannot function well outside a mental hospital are released into the community with little or no provision for continuing mental health care.

The decisions made on the basis of assessment data may have far-reaching implications for the people under study. A staff decision may determine whether a depressed person will be hospitalized or remain with his or her family; whether divorce will be accepted as a solution to an unhappy marriage or a further attempt will be made to salvage the relationship; or whether an accused person will be declared competent to stand trial. Thus a valid decision, based on accurate assessment data, is of far more than theoretical importance. Because of the impact that assessment can have on the lives of others, it is important that those involved keep in mind factors that may limit the accuracy of assessment. Some of these factors are noted in *HIGH-LIGHT 16.4*

UNRESOLVED ISSUES
on the Use of Computerized Assessment

Perhaps the most dramatic innovation in clinical assessment during the last 25 years has been the increasing sophistication and use of computers in individual assessment. As we have seen, computers are used in assessment both to gather information directly from an individual and to put together and evaluate all the information that has been gathered previously through interviews, tests, and other assessment procedures. By comparing the incoming information with data previously stored in its memory banks, a computer can perform a wide range of assessment tasks. It can supply a probable diagnosis, indicate the likelihood of certain kinds of behavior, suggest the most appropriate form of treatment, predict the outcome, and print out a summary report concerning the subject. In many of these functions, a computer is actually superior to an individual clinician because it is more efficient and accurate in recalling stored material.

With the increased efficiency and reliability accompanying the use of computers in clinical practice, one might expect a near unanimous welcoming of computers into the clinic. This is not the case, however. There is controversy over computerized assessment and a reluctance on the part of some practitioners to use computer-based tests in their practice. We will discuss these general issues in turn.

Concerns have been raised by some psychologists that the widespread use of computer-based assessment procedures is not sufficiently supported by pertinent research (Matarazzo, 1986). In addition, some believe that unvalidated measures have been "oversold" to the point that external professional sanctions or even laws might be required to ensure compliance with standards of good practice (Lanyon, 1984; Matarazzo, 1986). Matarazzo, particularly, feels that reliance on present-day computer-based assessment procedures is problematic because it will result in an increase in the cost of health care—with the ready availability of such procedures, clinicians will be tempted to "overtest."

In a rejoinder to Matarazzo's critique, Fowler and Butcher (1986) questioned Matarazzo's position that there are such serious problems with computerized psychological assessment that external controls or legislation are required. Although acknowledging that some largely unvalidated software programs and weak test measures are commercially available, and that practitioners need to exercise care in using computer-based tests, they considered the substantial progress in computer-based psychological testing over the past 25 years to justify further development. According to Fowler and Butcher, many of the problems addressed by Matarazzo have already been resolved and are reflected in the APA guidelines for computer-based assessment (American Psychological Association, 1986). Matarazzo's concern that professionals would "overtest" and increase health care costs was considered by Fowler and Butcher to be overstated. Research has shown that the use of computers in psychological testing can actually *reduce* the cost of services. Available surveys in fact point to an overall lessening of psychodiagnostic testing recently among clinicians (Moreland & Dahlstrom, 1983).

Another of Matarazzo's concerns, in which he called for viewing computerized psychological reports as tools rather than ends in themselves, is an important but not a new concern. The recommended policy for computerized tests, that they be considered as working hypotheses and not as final recommendations, has been a policy since the earli-

HIGHLIGHT 16.4

The Limitations of Psychosocial Assessment

Despite the need for assessment to understand an individual's problems and to plan appropriate treatment, the assessment process has several limitations and possible risks. These are summarized in what follows:

1. *Cultural bias of the instrument or the clinician.* There is the possibility that psychological tests may not elicit valid information from a patient from a minority group (Gynther, 1979), or a clinician from one sociocultural background may have trouble assessing objectively the behavior of an individual from another background, such as a Southeast Asian refugee. It is important to assure, as Dahlstrom, Lachar, and Dahlstrom (1986) have done with the MMPI, that the instrument can be confidently used with individuals from minority group backgrounds.

2. *Theoretical orientation of the clinician.* Assessment is inevitably influenced by a clinician's assumptions, perceptions, and theoretical orientation. For example, a psychoanalyst and a behaviorist might assess the same behaviors quite differently. If the differing assessments should lead to treatment recommendations of significantly differing efficacy for a client's problems, these biases could have serious repercussions.

3. *Overemphasis on internal traits.* Many clinicians overemphasize personality traits as the cause of patients' problems without due attention to the possible role of stressors or other circumstances in their life situations. An undue focus on a patient's personality, which may be encouraged by some assessment techniques, can divert attention from potentially critical environmental factors.

4. *Insufficient validation.* Many psychological assessment procedures have not been sufficiently validated. For example, unlike many of the personality scales, widely used procedures for behavioral observation and behavioral self-report have not been subjected to strict psychometric validation. The tendency on the part of clinicians to accept the results of these procedures at face value has recently been giving way to a broader recognition of the need for more explicit validation.

5. *Inaccurate data or premature evaluation.* There is always the possibility that some assessment data—and any diagnostic label or treatment based on them—may be inaccurate. For example, some risk is always involved in making predictions for an individual on the basis of group data or averages; while "schizophrenic" symptoms normatively imply a difficult treatment course, some people having them recover quickly even without treatment and never experience another episode. Inaccurate data or premature conclusions not only may lead to a misunderstanding of a patient's problem but may close off attempts to get further information, with possibly grave consequences for the patient.

est days of computer assessment and is a central assumption of the American Psychological Association's (1986) most recent guidelines on computer-based assessment. Practitioners should not employ computer-based interpretations as the ultimate criterion. The final responsibility in a diagnostic study rests with a human clinician—it is she or he who must decide the relevance and utility to the particular case of the various (and, as we have seen, sometimes contradictory) elements of a computer narrative printout.

The second issue raised here is the reluctance of some clinicians to use computer-based test interpretations in spite of their demonstrated utility and low cost. Even though many clinics and independent practitioners acquire microcomputers for record-keeping and billing purposes, a minority actually incorporate computer-based clinical assessment procedures into their practice. Possible reasons for the underutilization of computer-based assessment procedures include the following:

• Practitioners trained prior to the microcomputer age, like many in other types of work, may have hesitancy about "new-fangled gadgets" and do not feel comfortable with or "have time" to become acquainted with them.

- Many practitioners limit their practice to psychological treatment and do not do extensive pretreatment assessments of their cases. Many also have little interest in, or time for, the systematic evaluation of treatment efficacy that periodic formal assessments would facilitate.

- To some clinicians the impersonal and mechanized look of the booklets and answer sheets common to much computerized assessment is contrary to the image and style of warm and personal engagement they hope to convey to clients.

- Some clinicians view computer-based assessment as a threat to their own functioning. Some are concerned, as suggested in Matarazzo's (1986) critique, that computer-assessment specialists seek to replace human diagnostic functioning with automated reports. Others are concerned that unqualified practitioners may gain access to such reports and "set up shop" as competitors.

Some of these concerns are not unlike those expressed by many craftspersons or production personnel in industry when computers and robots come to the workplace. Are human practitioners in danger of being replaced by computers? Not at all. Computers in psychological assessment have intrinsic limitations consigning them to an accessory role in the process; they would not be useful, in fact quite the contrary, if employed as the sole means of evaluation. It is the clinician who must assume the major organizing role and accept the responsibility for an assessment. An unqualified person wholly dependent on computerized reports for carrying on a practice would quickly be identified as incompetent by discerning referral sources, and probably by most self-referred clients; a thriving practice would not be a likely outcome. On the other hand, judicious use of computerized assessment can free up much time for doing those things that can *only* be accomplished by the personal application of high levels of clinical skill and wisdom (Carson, 1990b).

SUMMARY

Clinical assessment is one of the most important and complex activities facing mental health professionals. The extent to which a person's problems are understood and appropriately treated depend, largely, on the adequacy of the psychological assessment. The goals of psychological assessment include identifying and describing the individual's symptoms; determining the chronicity and severity of the problem; evaluating the potential causal factors in the person's background; and exploring the individual's personal resources, which might be assets in his or her treatment program.

Interdisciplinary sources of assessment data include both physical evaluation methods and psychosocial assessment techniques. Because many psychological problems have physical components, either as underlying causal factors or as symptom patterns, it is often important to include a medical examination in the psychological assessment. In cases where organic brain damage is suspected, it is important to have neurological tests—such as an EEG or a CAT, PET, or MRI scan—to aid in determining the site and extent of organic brain disorder. In addition, it may be important to have the person take a battery of neuropsychological tests to determine if or in what manner the underlying brain disorder is affecting his or her mental and behavioral capabilities.

Psychosocial assessment methods are techniques for gathering relevant psychological information for clinical decisions about patients. The most widely used and most flexible psychosocial assessment methods are the clinical interview and behavior observation. These methods provide a wealth of clinical information. They may be subject, however, to extraneous influences that make them somewhat unreliable, and structured interview formats and objective behavior rating scales have been developed to improve their reliability.

Whereas interviews and behavior observations attempt to assess an individual's beliefs, attitudes, and symptoms directly, psychological tests attempt to measure these aspects of personality indirectly. Psychological tests include standardized stimuli for collecting behavior samples that can be compared with other individuals through test norms. Two different personality testing approaches have been developed: (a) projective tests, such as the Rorschach, in which unstructured stimuli are presented to a subject, who then "projects" meaning or structure on to the stimulus, thereby revealing "hidden" motives, feelings, and so on; and (b) objective tests, or personality inventories, in which a subject is required to read and respond to itemized statements or questions. Objective personality tests provide a cost-effective means of collecting a great deal of personality information rapidly. The MMPI, the most widely used and validated objective personality inventory, and MMPI-2, its recently revised offspring, provide a number of clinically relevant scales for describing abnormal behavior.

Possibly the most dramatic recent innovation in clinical assessment involves the widespread use of computers in the administration, scoring, and interpretation of psychological tests. It is now possible to obtain immediate interpretation of psychological test results, either through a direct computer interactive approach or through modem to a mainframe computer that interprets tests. In the past few years, rapid developments have been taking place in the computer assessment area. It is conceivable that, within the next few years, most clinical assessments will involve computers in some capacity, either for administration, scoring, and interpretation or for completing an entire test battery. Of course, mental health professionals will still play a major role in determining the appropriateness and adequacy of the computer's diagnostic output.

■ Key Terms

dynamic formulation (p. 575)
electroencephalogram (EEG) (p. 576)
dysrythmias (p. 577)
computerized axial tomography (CAT scan) (p. 577)
positron emission tomography (PET scan) (p. 577)
nuclear magnetic resonance imaging (MRI) (p. 577)
neuropsychological assessment (p. 578)
self-monitoring (p. 581)

rating scales (p. 581)
role playing (p. 582)
projective tests (p. 584)
Rorschach Test (p. 584)
Thematic Apperception Test (TAT) (p. 585)
sentence-completion test (p. 586)
objective tests (p. 586)
Minnesota Multiphasic Personality Inventory (MMPI) (p. 586)
factor analysis (p. 590)
actuarial procedures (p. 590)

Chapter 17
Biologically Based Therapies

Raymond Oui, *Monsieur Oui Oui* (1948?). Having always suffered from severe psychological impairment, Raymond Oui (b. 1915?) was admitted to a psychiatric institution in Lot–et–Garonne, France, in about 1948. During ordinary conversation, Oui continually interjects the word *oui*. He also includes the word repeatedly in his artwork.

Therapy is directed toward modifying maladaptive behavior and fostering adaptive behavior. The concept of therapy is not new. Throughout recorded history, human beings have tried to help each other with life's problems—including mental disorders—in both informal and formal ways. In Chapter 2 we noted the wide range of procedures that have, throughout history, been advocated for helping the mentally disturbed—from exorcism to incarceration and torture, from understanding and kindness to the most extreme cruelty.

Today both biological and psychological procedures are used in attempts to help individuals overcome psychopathology. In this chapter we will focus on biological methods that have evolved for the treatment of mental disorders, such as the schizophrenias, mood disorders, and disorders in which severe anxiety is central. In the next chapter we will focus on psychological approaches.

EARLY ATTEMPTS AT BIOLOGICAL INTERVENTION

The idea that a disordered mind might be set straight by treatment directed at the body goes back, as we have seen, to ancient times. Beginning with those early "medicine men" who trephined skulls, through to Hippocrates and Kraepelin, and on to modern psychiatrists, there have always been those who believed that, ultimately, the cure of mental aberration would be through alteration of an organism's biological state. Today we still have no reliable knowledge of point-to-point correspondence between certain behaviors and particular events in the brain at cellular or subcellular levels. Nonetheless, the dictum "no twisted thought without a twisted molecule," while philosophically and scientifically naive in certain respects, has been deeply internalized by many workers in the mental health field. For them, it is but a small step to conclude that the search for treatment methods should concentrate on finding effective means of rearranging or reconstituting aberrant molecules—of changing the presumed physical substrate of abnormal mentality.

The history of psychiatry reflects interesting, though by today's standards often extreme and primitive, methods of treating mental illness by altering bodily processes. Some have been widely used in several periods of history. For example, ridding the body of unwanted substances by purging (with laxatives and emetics) was a typical treatment in ancient Rome, during the medieval period, and during the eighteenth century (Agnew, 1985). In fact, purging was so widespread during some periods, particularly the eighteenth century, that it was considered a common practice in medicine and among people in general. Other seemingly more barbaric techniques, such as bleeding, have been widely used as treatments of the mentally disordered just as they have been used for a broad range of physical diseases. The use of bleeding was apparently consistent and acceptable to the views of medical science in the eighteenth century. Interestingly, many medical procedures were derived from or paralleled research and development in other sciences. For example, after the discovery of electricity, many efforts to use electrical stimulation to alter mental states ensued. Early electrical devices were used to stimulate patients' nerves, muscles, and organs as a treatment for a variety of illnesses. The rationale behind early somatic efforts to "treat" mental patients was often unclear, although frightening patients out of their madness or punishing the demons within may have been as much a reason as was any belief that an individual's bodily processes were being restored.

In general, as more has been learned in the various subfields of medicine, treatment measures have become more benign and less risky. As re-searchers come to understand scientifically the nature of a disorder, they typically are then able to develop biological treatments that are more precisely designed to meet the specific problem. The specificity of these new treatments typically means that they have fewer potentially damaging side effects.

The human brain and mind have yielded their secrets grudgingly. As a result, relative to other medical subdisciplines, psychiatry has had a slow and often uncertain development. It should not be surprising, therefore, to find that it has contributed its own array of dubious treatment techniques in the comparatively short history of its recognition as a medical subspecialty. In fact, by 1917, with the discovery of Wagner-Jauregg that general paresis, or neurosyphilis, could be curbed by intentionally infecting a patient with malaria (the consequent fevers were lethal to the spirochete), the stage was set for the development of extraordinarily bold and often hazardous ventures in the treatment arena. Wagner-Jauregg later received the Nobel Prize for this discovery. We will look now at two treatments that emerged during this period: the convulsive therapies and psychosurgery.

■ Coma and Convulsive Therapies

Insulin coma therapy, rarely used today, was initially used as a treatment for morphine withdrawal. It was introduced by Sakel in 1932 as a physiologi-

Some of the stranger instruments used for the treatment of the mentally ill in the eighteenth and nineteenth centuries are shown here: at left, glass cups and scarificators—which make cuts in the skin—that were used for bleeding patients; at right, an electrostatic generator that was used to shock patients.

cal treatment for schizophrenia. The technique involves administration of increasing amounts of insulin (a hormone that regulates sugar metabolism in the body) on a daily basis until a patient goes into "shock"—actually a hypoglycemic coma caused by an acute deficiency of glucose (sugar) in the blood. Coma-inducing doses of insulin are administered daily thereafter until the patient has experienced approximately 50 comas, each an hour or more in duration. The comas are terminated by administering glucose. This treatment causes profound biological and physiological stress, especially to the cardiovascular and nervous systems. The patient must be closely monitored both during and after the comatose state because of a variety of medical complications that may ensue, including some that are fatal.

The results of insulin coma therapy have been generally disappointing. Where patients have shown improvement, it has been difficult to determine whether it was due to the experience of the comas or to some other feature associated with the treatment, such as the markedly increased attention of the medical staff. Moreover, patients who do show some improvement tend to be those who would improve readily under other treatment regimens as well; severe, chronic schizophrenic patients remain for the most part unimproved. Finally, the relapse rate for those who improve has been high. With such a record—and in the face of marked medical risks—it is hardly surprising that the use of insulin coma as a therapeutic method has largely disappeared (Kalinowski & Hippius, 1969).

Shortly after the discovery of electricity, electrical stimulation came to be used in the treatment of mental disorders. As early as 1849 the physician Bucknill, working with asylum patients, used galvanic electrical stimulation and potassium oxide to successfully treat patients with melancholia (Beveridge & Renvoize, 1988). During the latter part of the nineteenth century, the therapeutic use of electrical stimulation was fairly widespread. Toward the end of the century, however, great concern over its safety resulted in a diminished use of electricity for treatment.

The potential value of electrostimulation therapy was reconsidered after the Hungarian physician Von Meduna speculated—erroneously, as it turned out—that schizophrenia rarely occurred in individuals with epilepsy. This observation led to the inference that schizophrenia and epilepsy were somehow incompatible, and that thus one might be able to cure schizophrenia by inducing convulsions. Various methods of convulsion induction, including Metrazol, which produced violent convulsions, were attempted. In 1938 two Italian physicians,

Cerletti and Bini, after visiting a slaughterhouse and seeing animals rendered unconscious by electric shock, tried the simplest method of all—that of passing an electric current through a patient's head. The method, which became known as **electroconvulsive therapy (ECT),** is much more widely used today than insulin therapy, mostly because of its effectiveness in alleviating depressive episodes. There are two types of ECT—*bilateral* and *unilateral*. The latter is a more recent introduction and is considered, by some, less intrusive. We will review both here.

Despite modest variations in the placement of electrodes and the introduction of safeguards, the standard form of *bilateral ECT* (involving both hemispheres of the brain) remains basically as Cerletti and Bini developed it: an electric current of approximately 150 volts is passed from one side of a patient's head to the other for up to about one and one-half seconds. The patient immediately loses consciousness and undergoes a marked tonic (extensor) seizure of the muscles, followed by a lengthy series of clonic (contractile) ones of lesser amplitude. Typically, sedative and muscle-relaxant premedication is used to prevent violent contractions. In the days before such medication was available, the initial seizure was sometimes so violent as to fracture vertebrae, one of several potential complications of this therapy.

After awakening several minutes later, the patient has amnesia for the period immediately preceding the therapy, and is usually somewhat confused for the next hour or so. With repeated treatments, usually administered three times weekly, the patient gradually becomes disoriented, a state that clears after termination of the treatments. Memory impairment, however, can remain for months (Squire, Slater, & Chase, 1975), or, in some instances, even years (Breggin, 1979).

Normally, a treatment series consists of less than a dozen sessions, although in times past there was widespread overuse of the technique as a means of controlling excited or violent behavior. Today one can still find chronic patients in the "back wards" of mental hospitals whose treatment history includes the inducement of literally hundreds of seizures. The damage created by these excesses is difficult to estimate in precise terms, but it could well be substantial (Breggin, 1979; Palmer, 1981). It is possible that each electroconvulsive treatment administered to a person destroys a varying number of central nervous system neurons.

At present, the use of ECT is still considered controversial. Some support its use as the only effective way of dealing with some severely depressed and suicidal patients. Others within the profession deplore the lack of objective appraisals of this treatment. These contrary views would have been more easy to dismiss in the 1940s, because little else of proven efficacy was then available. Today it is more difficult to defend the widespread use of the technique because effective alternative approaches—such as antidepressant medication—are abundant. These issues have been discussed at length by Breggin (1979) in a comprehensive review of available evidence concerning the potentially damaging effects of ECT.

Although Breggin's treatise has been criticized for its somewhat biased language and style (e.g., Weiner, 1982), there exists no wholly effective counterargument to his expert review of the evidence. For example, demonstrable brain damage has been found in animals sacrificed immediately after ECT treatment. In short, while there is little doubt about the effectiveness of ECT in alleviating certain disorders—chiefly within the psychotic depressive range (although Breggin disputed even this conclusion)—a cautious appraisal of the technique requires that it be considered potentially brain damaging. The appropriate use of the treatment, therefore, should be preceded by a careful assessment of its potential costs and benefits in light of the circumstances attending a particular case. Unfortunately, Breggin noted that such a review is not necessarily routine; this is especially the case, at present, in private psychiatric hospitals, where ECT is often used.

Responding to these sorts of concerns, the citizens of Berkeley, California, in November 1982, voted overwhelmingly to ban the use of ECT treatment within that city (*Science News,* November 13, 1982), an action that was later judicially overturned. Though the wisdom of holding public elections on such issues may be seriously questioned, the event demonstrates increased citizen awareness and concern about the treatment mental patients receive.

In 1985 the National Institute of Mental Health sponsored a Consensus Development Conference on electroconvulsive therapy to evaluate the issues surrounding the use of ECT (NIMH, 1985a). A panel of experts in psychiatry, psychology, neurology, psychopharmacology, epidemiology, and law, along with several laypersons, considered evidence as to (a) the effectiveness of ECT for patients with various disorders; (b) the risks of ECT; (c) the indications for administration of ECT; and (d) the best ways to implement ECT with patients.

The panel recognized a number of potential risks associated with the use of ECT, including such medical problems as limb fractures, circulatory insufficiency, tooth damage, and skin burns. With the present techniques used, however, these risks have been virtually eliminated. Mortality following ECT, a significant problem in the early days of the treatment, has also been significantly reduced to about 2.9 deaths per 10,000 patients. The injury and mortality rates are considered comparable to other somatic treatments, such as barbiturate anesthetics. The panel reached a number of conclusions as to which disorders responded best to ECT. They agreed that the effect of ECT was well established for some types of depression, particularly delusional depression and "endogenous" depression. They also concluded that ECT can be effectively used with some types of manic disorders, particularly acute mania. On the other hand, they found that ECT was not particularly effective with some depressions, such as dysthymic disorder. Although ECT is sometimes used with certain types of schizophrenia, the evidence for effectiveness is not convincing.

Scott (1989) reviewed the literature and found that many depressed patients do not respond to ECT. When therapeutic benefits do result from the use of ECT, they sometimes prove to be short-lived, with a patient relapsing into the previous disorder. The NIMH consensus panel concluded that relapse rates following ECT were high unless the treatment was followed by maintenance doses of antidepressant medication. As has been true with some other techniques, the mechanism by which therapeutic effects are brought about has never been adequately explained. Some researchers believe that the therapeutic effect is mediated by induced changes in the biochemistry of brain synapses (Fink, 1979; Fink et al., 1974).

Despite all the questions and controversy, the therapeutic efficacy of ECT, at least for some depressions and acute mania, is well established in the research literature (Abrams, 1988; Fink, 1979; Scovern & Kilman, 1980) and in personal testimonials from those who have been helped by it (Endler, 1990). The comparatively low mortality rate among depressive individuals, a group considered to be at high risk for early mortality, has been attributed to ECT (Avery & Winoker, 1976; Martin et al., 1985).

A dramatic example of the unprecedented early success of ECT that sometimes occurred following its introduction is provided in the autobiographical account of Lenore McCall (1947), who suffered a severe depressive disorder in her middle years.

A patient administered electroconvulsive therapy (ECT) today (left) is given sedative and muscle-relaxant premedication to prevent violent contractions. In the days before such medication was available (right), the initial seizure was sometimes so violent as to fracture vertebrae.

Ms. McCall, a well-educated woman of affluent circumstances and the mother of three children, noticed a feeling of persistent fatigue as the first sign of her impending descent into depression. Too fearful to seek help, she at first attempted to fight off her increasingly profound apathy by engaging in excessive activity, a defensive strategy that accomplished little but the depletion of her remaining strength and emotional reserves.

In due course, she noticed that her mental processes seemed to be deteriorating—her memory appeared impaired and she could concentrate only with great difficulty. Emotionally, she felt an enormous loneliness, bleakness of experience, and increasingly intense fear about what was happening to her mind. She came to view her past small errors of commission and omission as the most heinous of crimes and increasingly withdrew from contact with her husband and children. Eventually, at her husband's and her physician's insistence, she was hospitalized despite her own vigorous resistance. She felt betrayed, and shortly thereafter attempted suicide by shattering a drinking glass and ingesting its fragments; to her great disappointment, she survived.

Ms. McCall thereafter spent nearly four years continuously in two separate mental hospitals,

during which time she deteriorated further. She was silent and withdrawn, behaved in a mechanical fashion, lost an alarming amount of weight, and underwent a seemingly premature aging process. She felt that she emitted an offensive odor. At this time, ECT was introduced into the therapeutic procedures in use at her hospital.

A series of ECT treatments was given to Ms. McCall over about a three-month period. Then, one day, she woke up in the morning with a totally changed outlook: "I sat up suddenly, my heart pounding. I looked around the room and a sweep of wonder surged over me. God in heaven, I'm well. I'm myself. . . ." After a brief period of convalescence, she went home to her husband and children to try to pick up the threads of their painfully severed lives. She did so, and then wrote the engrossing and informative book from which this history is taken.

Some years ago, a modification in the standard method of administering ECT was introduced. Instead of placing the electrodes on each side of the head in the temple region, thereby causing a transverse flow of current through both cerebral hemispheres, the new procedure involves limiting current flow through only one side of the brain, typically the nondominant (right, for most people) side. This procedure is called *unilateral ECT,* and strong evidence shows that it lessens distressing side effects (such as memory impairment) without decreasing therapeutic effectiveness (Daniel & Crovitz, 1983b; Squire, 1977; Squire & Slater, 1978). Unfortunately, it has been estimated that some 75 percent of psychiatrists who employ ECT still use the original bilateral method exclusively (American Psychiatric Association, 1978; NIMH, 1985b). Though this trend may now be changing in favor of unilateral ECT, we must await further data for confirmation. Evidence also suggests that the use of a lower-energy, pulsating electrical stimulus may produce less mental impairment than the standard treatment (Daniel & Crovitz, 1983a). The extent of this modification's effective use is not known, however.

■ Psychosurgery

Brain surgery used in the treatment of functional or central nervous system disorders is called **psychosurgery.** In 1935 in Portugal, Moniz introduced a psychosurgical procedure in which the frontal lobes of the brain were severed from the deeper centers underlying them. This technique eventually evolved into an operation known as **prefrontal lobotomy.** This operation stands as a dubious tribute to the levels to which professionals have sometimes been driven in their search for effective treatments for the psychoses. In retrospect, it seems somewhat surprising that this procedure—which results in permanent brain damage to the patient— won for its originator the Nobel Prize in Medicine for the year 1949.

In the two decades between 1935 and 1955 (after which the new antipsychotic drugs became widely available), tens of thousands of mental patients in this country and abroad were subjected to prefrontal lobotomy and related neurosurgical procedures. In fact, in some settings, as many as 50 patients were treated in a single day (Freeman, 1959). As is often the case with newly developed techniques of therapy, initial reports of results tended to be enthusiastic, downplaying complications (including a 1 to 4 percent death rate) and undesirable side effects. It was eventually recognized, however, that the "side effects" of psychosurgery could be very undesirable indeed. In some instances they included a permanent inability to inhibit impulses; in others, an unnatural "tranquility," with undesirable shallowness or absence of feeling. By 1951 the Soviet Union had banned all such operations; though rarely performed, they are still permitted by law in the United States and in

many other countries. See *HIGHLIGHT 17.1* for an illustration of the sometimes tragic outcome of lobotomy.

The advent of the major antipsychotic drugs caused an immediate decrease in the widespread use of psychosurgical procedures. Such operations are extremely rare today and are used only as a last resort for the intractable psychoses, severely and chronically debilitating obsessive-compulsive disorders, and occasionally for the control of severe pain in cases of terminal illness.

On the rare occasion when it is employed today, psychosurgery is unquestionably a much more circumspect procedure than in the heyday of lobotomies. Today the permanent damage to the brain has been substantially minimized and thus fewer detrimental side effects follow. The surgical technique involves the selective destruction of minute areas; for example, in the "cingulotomy" procedure— which seems to relieve the subjective experience of pain, including "psychic" pain—a small bundle of nerve fibers connecting the frontal lobes with a deeper structure known as the limbic system is interrupted with virtually pinpoint precision.

Despite these advances, continuing concern has been voiced about such operations, and in the mid-1970s the Congress of the United States called a special national commission to evaluate their effects. The report of that commission indicated some surprisingly beneficial effects that had been achieved with modern psychosurgery—for example, the alleviation of chronic depression—but it also warned that such benefits were often achieved at the expense of the loss of certain cognitive capacities. The commission recommended that cautious exploration of these techniques be continued with selected patients (Culliton, 1976).

The debate about psychosurgery has recently received a thorough airing in two fascinating books by Elliot Valenstein (1980; 1986). Valenstein scrutinized the procedures of psychosurgery—and by implication other "brain-disabling" therapies—in relation to the psychiatric, ethical, legal, and social issues they necessarily raise. In the 1986 book, entitled *Great and Desperate Cures,* Valenstein examined the historical basis of psychosurgery and explained how an unproven and potentially life-threatening treatment could emerge in a field devoted to scientific explanation and become an accepted treatment method with little empirical justification. Factors underlying this premature and "desperate" acceptance of psychosurgery included psychiatry's need to "gain respectability" as a medical science by having an organic-surgical treatment method; the professional rivalry between psychia-

The Accomplishments and Subsequent Tragedy of Rosemary Kennedy

One of the tragic victims of the zeal to perform prefrontal lobotomies to alleviate behavior problems was Rosemary Kennedy, the sister of President John F. Kennedy and Senators Robert and Edward Kennedy. Rosemary was the third child of Joseph and Rose Kennedy, born during the height of the flu epidemic of 1918. She was a beautiful baby, with a sweet temperament, but as she grew, her mother became more and more concerned about her developmental delays compared to her brothers and sisters. When the family finally concluded that Rosemary likely was retarded since birth from unknown causes, the best experts in the country at the time could offer no guidance: "We went from doctor to doctor. . . . From all, we heard the same answer: 'I'm sorry, but we can do nothing.' For my husband and me it was nerve-racking and incomprehensible" (Goodwin, 1988, p. 416).

Rose Kennedy and the family rebelled against the suggestion that Rosemary be institutionalized. Instead, she was kept at home with the benefit of a special governess and many private tutors. She participated fully in the Kennedy's family activities, and she made considerable progress. Doris Kearns Goodwin (1988), a biographer of the Fitzgerald and Kennedy families, described an arithmetic paper that the 9-year-old Rosemary completed on February 21, 1927. She correctly answered several multiplication (428 times 32) and division (3924 divided by 6) problems. By the age of 18 years, Rosemary had obtained a fifth-grade level in English and remained at the fourth-grade level in math that she had obtained by age 9.

Because of the considerable stigma associated with mental retardation at the time, Rosemary's parents kept her condition hidden from those outside the family, a major task given the scrutiny of the family by the press. Although her parents and siblings were always nearby to protect her, Rosemary developed the social skills needed to be presented successfully as a debutante and later to the King and Queen of England at Buckingham Palace. The British press complimented Rose Kennedy for her beautiful daughters, never even noticing Rosemary's mental retardation.

Unfortunately, Rosemary's behavior deteriorated around the beginning of World War II when the family returned to the United States from England, where Joseph Kennedy had been ambassador. There are several possible explanations for this deterioration, including her increasing frustration about not being able to do all the things her siblings were able to do and having to leave the school in England where she had felt successful. The 21-year-old Rosemary became quite violent and frequently ran away from home or her convent school. There was considerable concern for her safety, and Joseph Kennedy—without Rose's knowledge—turned to the medical experts of the time, searching for a solution.

These experts convinced Joe that the miracle treatment lay in prefrontal lobotomy. Rosemary Kennedy became one of the thousands submitted to that "desperate" cure. In Rosemary's case, the surgery was a tragic failure—all her previous accomplishments were wiped out, leaving little of her former personality and adaptive ability intact:

"They knew right away that it wasn't successful. You could see by looking at her that something was wrong, for her head was tilted and her capacity to speak was almost entirely gone. There was no question now that she could no longer take care of herself and that the only answer was an institution." (Ann Gargan King, a cousin, as reported by Goodwin, 1988, p. 744)

try, neurology, and neurosurgery; and the need to provide a cost-effective treatment and maintain control over mental hospitals.

Valenstein (1980) further discussed important ethical and philosophical issues underlying the use of psychosurgery. For example, what meaning can be assigned to the concept of *informed consent* if a patient is so disabled that this radical form of intervention is seriously considered? When, if ever, is it justifiable to employ surgical means to alter human personality? It appears we are finally reaching a level of public awareness and surveillance that will make it increasingly unlikely for these extreme measures to be employed without due considera-

Shown here is a demonstration of a transorbital lobotomy, which was used extensively in this country from the 1940s until the late 1950s. First, a doctor administers ECT to anesthetize the patient (left). Immediately following ECT, another doctor performs the actual lobotomy (right). It is estimated that tens of thousands of patients were subjected to such procedures, resulting in permanent brain damage (which was, after all, the actual intent of the procedure) and sometimes death.

tion—in a context of full disclosure—of the risks as well as the benefits potentially entailed.

THE EMERGENCE OF PHARMACOLOGICAL METHODS OF TREATMENT

A long-term goal of medicine has been to discover drugs that can effectively combat the ravages of mental disorder. This goal, one of the pursuits of **pharmacology,** the science of drugs, has until fairly recently remained elusive. Early efforts in this direction were limited largely to a search for chemical compounds or drugs that would have soothing, calming, or sleep-inducing effects. Such drugs, if they could be found, would make it easier to manage distraught, excited, and sometimes violent patients. Little thought was given to the possibility that the status and course of the disorder itself might actually be brought under control by appropriate medication; the focus was on rendering a patient's overt behavior more manageable and thereby making restraints, such as straitjackets, unnecessary.

As the field of psychopharmacology developed, many such compounds were introduced and tried in the mental hospital setting. Almost without exception, however, those that produced the desired calming effects proved to have serious shortcomings. At effective dosage levels, they often produced severe drowsiness if not outright sleep, and many of them were dangerously addicting. On the whole, little real progress was made in this field until the mid-1950s, at which point, as we will see, a genuine revolution in the treatment of the more severe disorders occurred. This breakthrough was followed shortly by the discovery of drugs helpful in the treatment of the less severe anxiety-based disorders, and eventually by recognition of the therapeutic benefits of antidepressants and lithium salts for the mood disorders.

■ Types of Drugs Used in Therapy

In this section we will trace the discovery of the four types of chemical agents now commonly used in therapy for mental disorders—antipsychotic drugs, antidepressant drugs, antianxiety drugs (minor tranquilizers), and lithium. These drugs are sometimes referred to as *psychotropic drugs,* in that their main effect is on an individual's mental life. As we examine drugs used in therapy, it is important to remember that individuals differ in how rapidly they metabolize drugs—that is, in how quickly their bodies break down the drugs once ingested.

What this means is that individuals differ, too, in what dosage of a drug they may need to experience the desired therapeutic effect. Determining correct dosage is a critical factor of drug therapy because too much or too little of a drug can be ineffective and (in the case of too much) even life-threatening, depending on the individual.

Antipsychotic Drugs   The **antipsychotic drugs** as a group are sometimes called *major tranquilizers,* but this term is somewhat misleading. They are used with the major disorders, such as the schizophrenias, but they do more than tranquilize. Though they do indeed produce a calming effect on many patients, their unique quality is that of somehow alleviating or reducing the intensity of psychotic symptoms, such as delusions and hallucinations. In some cases, in fact, a patient who is already excessively "tranquil" (for example, withdrawn or immobile) becomes active and responsive to the environment under treatment by these drugs. In contrast, the antianxiety drugs, to be described shortly, are effective in reducing tension without in any way affecting psychotic symptoms.

Although the benefits of the antipsychotic drugs have often been exaggerated, it is difficult to convey the truly enormous influence they have had in altering the environment of the typical mental hospital. One of the authors, as part of his training, worked several months in the maximum security ward of one such hospital just before the introduction of this type of medication in 1955. The ward patients fulfilled the common stereotypes of individuals "gone mad." Bizarreness, nudity, wild screaming, and an ever-present threat of violence pervaded the atmosphere. Fearfulness and a near-total preoccupation with the maintenance of control characterized the staff's attitude. Such an attitude was not unrealistic in terms of the frequency of serious physical assaults by patients, but it was hardly conducive to the development or maintenance of an effective therapeutic program.

Then, quite suddenly—within a period of perhaps a month—all of this dramatically changed. The patients began receiving antipsychotic medication. The ward became a place in which one could get to know one's patients on a personal level and perhaps even initiate programs of "milieu therapy," a form of psychosocial therapy in which the entire facility is regarded as a therapeutic community, and the emphasis is on developing a meaningful and constructive environment in which the patients participate in the regulation of their own activities. Promising reports of changes in hospital environments began to appear in the professional literature. A new era in hospital treatment had arrived, aided enormously and in many instances actually made possible by the development of these extraordinary drugs.

The beginnings of this development were quite commonplace. For centuries, the root of the plant *rauwolfia* (snakeroot) had been used in India for the treatment of mental disorders. In 1943 the *Indian Medical Gazette* reported improvements in manic reactions, schizophrenia, and other types of psychopathology following the use of *reserpine,* a drug derived from rauwolfia. Reserpine was first used in the United States in the early 1950s, after it was found to have a "calming" effect on mental patients (Kline, 1954). Early enthusiasm for the drug was tempered, however, by the finding that it also might produce low blood pressure, nasal congestion, and, perhaps most seriously, severe depression. Reanalysis of this latter finding suggested that the danger of serious depression was mainly for patients with a prior history of depression (Mendels & Frazer, 1974). Reserpine is now used mainly for the control of hypertension.

Meanwhile, the first of the phenothiazine family of drugs, *chlorpromazine* (Thorazine), was being synthesized in the early 1950s by one of the major pharmaceutical houses. It was first marketed at about the same time that reserpine was introduced, and it quickly proved to have virtually the same benefits but fewer undesirable side effects. It soon became the treatment of choice for schizophrenia.

The remarkable early successes reported with chlorpromazine led quickly to a bandwagon effect among other pharmaceutical companies, who began to manufacture and market their own variants of the basic phenothiazine compound. Some of the best known variants are trifluoperazine (Stelazine), promazine (Sparine), prochlorperazine (Compazine), thioridazine (Mellaril), perphenazine (Trilafon), and fluphenazine (Prolixin). Currently, too, there are at least six classes of nonphenothiazine antipsychotic drugs available in the United States (Carson, 1984), of which the best known is haloperidol (Haldol). This diversity becomes less bewildering when it is remembered that virtually all of the antipsychotics accomplish a common biochemical effect, namely the blocking of dopamine receptors, as was noted in Chapter 12.

With persistent use or at high dosage, however, all of these preparations have varying degrees of troublesome side effects, such as dryness of the mouth and throat, muscular stiffness, jaundice, and a Parkinson-like syndrome involving tremors of the extremities and immobility of the facial muscles. Which side effects develop appears to depend on the particular compound used in relation to the particular vulnerabilities of the treated patient. Many of

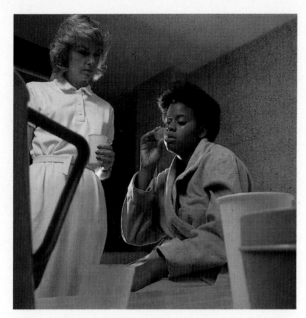

The introduction of antipsychotic drugs in hospital treatment of the mentally ill was a major breakthrough in altering the environment of the typical mental hospital.

these side effects are temporary and may be relieved by substituting another drug of the same class, by switching to a different class of drug, or by reducing the dosage. We should also note that some schizophrenic individuals, particularly those with negative symptoms or chronic schizophrenia, do not respond to antipsychotic drug therapy and may indeed be made worse by it (Buckley, 1982).

For certain patients, a particularly troublesome side effect of long-term antipsychotic drug treatment is the development of a disfiguring disturbance of motor control, particularly of the facial muscles, known as **tardive dyskinesia.** Symptoms of tardive dyskinesia, which often seem to disappear when a patient is asleep, are both dramatic to an observer and disabling to the patient. The symptoms involve involuntary movements of the tongue, lips, jaw, and extremities. An individual with tardive dyskinesia may show involuntary limb movement and usually shows characteristic chewing movements, lip smacking, and sucking of the mouth. There is some indication that the more severe the facial and other symptoms of tardive dyskinesia, the more severe the cognitive deficit (DeWolfe, Ryan, & Wolf, 1988). The disturbance is believed to be due to an imbalance in dopamine and acetylcholine activity in the brain, secondary to alterations in receptor sensitivity by antipsychotics and other drugs commonly used in combination to control their side effects. Side effects of tardive dyskinesia can occur months to years after the antipsychotic drug treatment is initiated and after

the treatment has been stopped or the drug reduced in dosage.

Tardive dyskinesia has increased in recent years due to the extensive use of antipsychotic medication with severely schizophrenic individuals (Kane & Smith, 1982), although the manifestation of the disturbance appears to fluctuate in patients over time (Bergen et al., 1989). The use of antipsychotic medications in treatment is usually discontinued if a patient shows symptoms of tardive dyskinesia. Although there are medications that control the symptoms of tardive dyskinesia, drug therapy is generally not recommended (AMA, 1986). In some cases where the patient continues to display psychotic symptoms, the use of antipsychotic medication treatment may be resumed; however, discontinuation of the treatment is recommended if any symptoms of tardive dyskinesia reappear. To reduce the chances of this disturbance during the drug treatment of chronic schizophrenics, clinicians are more frequently using what is called "target dosing" (Rosen, 1986), which entails administering a drug when symptoms appear or are likely to appear rather than giving continuous dosages, as commonly practiced in the past.

A recent trend in the treatment of schizophrenia involves the application of lower doses of standard drugs to reduce negative side effects. Hogarty et al. (1988) have shown that low-dose-treated schizophrenics actually showed more improvement than normal-dose-treated patients in terms of many observable behaviors. Moreover, relapse rates were found to be comparable to patients treated with higher doses.

The range of effects achieved by the antipsychotic drugs may be illustrated by two brief case histories of patients who served as subjects in a clinical research project designed to evaluate differing treatment approaches to the schizophrenias (Grinspoon, Ewalt, & Shader, 1972).

*M*s. W. was a 19-year-old, white, married woman who was admitted to the treatment unit as a result of gradually increasing agitation and hallucinations over a three-month period. Her symptoms had markedly intensified during the four days prior to admission, partly as a result of a homosexual seduction she had undergone while under the influence of marijuana. She had had a deprived childhood, but had managed to function reasonably well until breakdown.

At the outset of her hospitalization, Ms. W. continued to have auditory and visual hallucinations and appeared frightened, angry, and confused. She believed that she had a unique relationship with God or the devil. Her thought content displayed loosening of associations, and her affect was inappropriate to this content. Her condition continued to deteriorate for more than two weeks, at which point medication was begun.

Ms. W. was assigned to a treatment group in which the patients were receiving thioridazine (Mellaril). She responded dramatically during the first week of treatment. Her behavior became, for the most part, quiet and appropriate, and she made some attempts at socialization. She continued to improve, but by the fourth week of treatment began to show signs of mild depression. Her medication was increased, and she resumed her favorable course. By the sixth week she was dealing with various reality issues in her life in a reasonably effective manner, and by the ninth week she was spending considerable time at home, returning to the hospital in a pleasant and cheerful mood. She was discharged exactly 100 days after her admission, being then completely free of symptoms.

*M*r. S., the eldest of three sons in a fairly religious Jewish family, was admitted to the hospital after developing marked paranoid ideation and hallucinations during his first weeks of college. He had looked forward to going to college, an elite New England school, but his insecurity once on campus caused him to become unduly boastful about his prowess with drinking and women. He stayed up late at night to engage in "bull sessions" and neglected his studies and other responsibilities. Within ten days he panicked about his ability to keep up and tried frantically to rearrange his course schedule and his life, to no avail.

His sense of incompetence was transformed over time into the idea that others—including all the students in his dormitory—were against him, and that fellow male students were perhaps flirting homosexually with him. By the time of his referral to the college infirmary, he was convinced that the college was a fraud he would have to expose, that the CIA was plotting against him, and that someone was going to kill him. He heard voices and smelled strange odors. He also showed a marked loosening of associations and flat, inappropriate affect. At the time of his transfer to the hospital, he was diagnosed as an acute paranoid schizophrenic.

Mr. S. was assigned to a treatment group receiving haloperidol (Haldol). His initial response to treatment was rapid and favorable, but observers noted that his behavior remained immature. Then suddenly during the fifth week of treatment, he became tense, negativistic, and hostile. Thereafter, he gradually became less defiant and angry, and he responded well to a day-care program prescribed by his therapist, although he was nervous and apprehensive about being outside the hospital. He was discharged as improved ten weeks after the initiation of his drug therapy.

Three months later Mr. S. was readmitted to the hospital. Although he had done well at first, he had begun to deteriorate concurrently with his doctor-monitored withdrawal from haloperidol. His behavior showed increasing signs of a lack of effective control. He began to set random fires and was described by the investigators as "sociopathic." Two days after his readmission, he signed himself out of the hospital "against medical advice." His parents immediately arranged for his confinement in another hospital, and the investigators subsequently lost contact with him.

Recent research with treatment-resistant schizophrenics has focused on possible alternative drugs. One such compound that differs from the phenothiazines, Clozapine (a dibenzodiazepine), has produced promising results. Kane et al. (1988) studied the therapeutic effects of clozapine with a large group of treatment-resistant schizophrenics and found the treatment effects modestly encouraging. Thirty percent of the treatment-resistant patients improved under the regimen and no negative side effects were noted. Further research on the side effects of this drug is indicated, however, because some studies have found that many patients taking the drug develop an immune deficiency that is life-threatening and that has resulted in the death of several patients. Even though this medication has been heralded as the most effective treatment for schizophrenia, it appears that few patients will actually receive its benefits. A 30 percent response rate is not a panacea. Also, the potentially lethal characteristic of the drug prompted the drug company to develop and market a highly structured blood-monitoring system along with the medication to guard against its misuse. Unfortunately, the cost of the drug in combination with this monitoring system makes the treatment expensive and drastically limits its availability for most patients needing the drug (Winslow, 1990).

Antidepressant Drugs   The **antidepressant drugs** made their appearance shortly after the introduction of reserpine and chlorpromazine. There are two basic classes of these compounds: the monoamine oxidase (MAO) inhibitors and the tricyclics. Many variants of the latter class, including some that are not, strictly speaking, "tricyclic" in their chemical formulation, have appeared in the past few years. Although they differ considerably in their chemical makeup, it is currently believed that they accomplish a common biochemical result—namely, that of increasing the concentrations of the neurotransmitters serotonin and norepinephrine at pertinent synaptic sites in the brain (Berger, 1978; see *HIGHLIGHT 3.1* on p. 61). In fact, there has been speculation that measurably different types of depression may correlate with differing functional levels of these and possibly other neurotransmitters, and that it may be possible to discover how to use antidepressant drugs in a selective manner, depending on which neurotransmitter systems they maximally affect (Akiskal, 1979; Maugh, 1981).

Unfortunately, the *etiological* significance of these ideas is complicated by problems similar to those relating excess dopamine activity to schizophrenia. For example, the effect of these drugs on neurotransmitter synaptic concentrations occurs promptly, whereas the *clinical* effects of the drugs on modifying depressive affect and behavior are often agonizingly delayed. Hence it seems unlikely that depressive phenomena are directly and uniquely caused by the neurotransmitter anomalies purportedly corrected by these substances.

Of the two main classes of antidepressants, the tricyclics and their variants are by far the more often used. This is largely because the MAO inhibitors are more toxic and require troublesome dietary restrictions; in addition, they are widely believed to have less potent therapeutic effects. Nevertheless, some patients who do not respond favorably to tricyclics will subsequently do well on an MAO inhibitor. A minority of severely depressed patients respond to neither type of antidepressant compound, in which case alternative modes of intervention, such as electroconvulsive therapy, may be tried. Commonly used tricyclics are imipramine (Tofranil), amitriptyline (Elavil), and nortriptyline (Aventyl). MAO inhibitors include isocarboxazid (Marplan), phenelzine (Nardil), and tranylcypromine (Parnate).

Antidepressant drugs, particularly tricyclics, continue to be developed, tested, and marketed at a high rate. Among the more recent entrants to the field are amoxapine (Asendin), maprotiline (Ludiomil), and trazodone (Desyrel). Amoxapine is a tricyclic related to certain of the antipsychotic drugs and thus may prove to have a special role in the treatment of schizoaffective disorder. Maprotiline and trazodone are technically not tricyclics at all, but rather tetracyclics; the chemical addition of an extra benzene ring is in each case claimed to reduce problematic side effects. Trazodone, in particular, appeared on introduction to be a very promising drug (Moore, 1982). One study reported, however, that permanent impotence can result from extensive use (Lansky & Selzer, 1984).

A "second generation" antidepressant, chemically unrelated to other antidepressant medications, that has become the preferred antidepressant drug in the 1990s, is *fluoxetine,* better known by the trade name *Prozac.* This drug acts to inhibit the reuptake of serotonin and norepinephrine, thus increasing their availability. Prozac is thought to be a relatively "safe" drug in that it is not considered physiologically addicting and is not found to be fatal in overdose. Clinical trials with fluoxetine have reported that patients tend to improve after about three weeks of treatment with the drug. Several adverse side effects of Prozac have been reported, particularly nausea, nervousness, and insomnia (Cole & Bodkin, 1990; Tacke, 1990). In addition, after a few weeks on the drug, some patients have experienced increased blood pressure levels and others have reported suicidal urges and agitation (Cole & Bodkin, 1990; Papp & Gorman, 1990). Notably, some depressed patients who had not previously been suicidal have reported suicidal thoughts.

Pharmacological treatment for depression often produces dramatic results. Improvement in response to antidepressant medication is in sharp contrast to the effects of antipsychotic medications, which apparently only suppress schizophrenic symptoms. This statement, however, must be tempered with the observation that individuals suffering from severe depression, unlike people with schizophrenia, often respond to any treatment or even no treatment at all.

Over the past ten years, a great deal of research has been undertaken to determine how drugs operate to alleviate depression (McNeal & Cimbolic, 1986), and which treatment or combination of treatments is appropriate for patients who are depressed (Hollon & Beck, 1986). To date, however, little progress has been made in identifying patient characteristics or other clinical factors that relate to success by a given treatment method. In one nationwide study on psychological and pharmacological treatment for depression, Keller et al. (1986) found that there were no consistent patient characteristics related to whether a person received psychotherapy or medications for depression.

HIGHLIGHT 17.2

Chemically Induced Sleep: Is It Worth the Risks?

Prescriptions for the benzo-diazepine class of antianxiety drugs currently exceed 70 million per year in the United States. Of these, a huge proportion are written for the ostensible purpose of enabling people to sleep better at night. The most common benzodiazepine prescribed specifically for this purpose is fluraz-epam (Dalmane). Some 8 million individuals use this general class of drug sometime during any one year, and up to 2 million people take these pills nightly for more than two months at a time. It is prescribed for many patients hospitalized for physical disease.

Reacting to this overuse, the Institute of Medicine (IOM) of the National Academy of Sciences issued a report outlining the hazards of this remedy for sleeping difficulties—difficulties that in any case they found to be severely overestimated on a routine basis by the people allegedly suffering from them. Noting that the barbiturates justly deserve their reputation as dangerous drugs, the IOM report indicated that the benzodiazepines may be just as risky, and in some cases more so. For example, flurazepam, while not quite as addicting as the barbiturates, remains in the body in the form of metabolites far longer than do the barbiturates, resulting in a build-up of toxic substances in the body that may reach a critical level within a week of regular ingestion. Although flurazepam overdose is usually not in itself lethal, it may interact with other drugs, such as alcohol, to produce lethal effects. Because of these readily misunderstood characteristics, the IOM concluded that, overall, flurazepam does not diminish the number of deaths attributable to sleeping pill medication, relative to earlier types of "hypnotic" drugs, such as the barbiturates.

A particularly worrisome aspect of this problem is the fact that a certain amount of benign "insomnia" naturally accompanies advancing age. Nevertheless, elderly people receive some 39 percent of all sleeping pill prescriptions. For these individuals there is a real danger that the side effects of these drugs, such as daytime lethargy and clouding of consciousness, may be considered indicators of senile deterioration by family members and even by professional caretakers.

Considering the risks involved in taking these drugs, it seems appropriate to keep in mind an observation of one of the IOM members: losing some sleep now and then is *not* a life-threatening problem (Smith, 1979).

Overall, the use of antidepressant medication in the treatment of depressive episodes has shown considerable short-term effectiveness in spite of our lack of specific understanding of how it works and with what type of patient particular treatments are best suited.

Antianxiety Drugs   If it is true, as some have observed, that ours is the age of anxiety, it is certainly no less true that ours is also the age of the search for anxiety reducers. At the present time, literally millions of physician-prescribed pills alleged to contain anxiety- and tension-relieving substances are consumed daily by the American public. In addition, Americans employ manifold alternative methods to reduce their anxiety—ranging from biofeedback to the practice of ancient Eastern religious rituals—that promise to relieve "uptight" feelings. The nonprescription drug market, which includes alcoholic beverages, marijuana, and decidedly more problematic substances, has had an unprecedented growth rate since the 1960s —much of it presumably due to the same widespread wish to be somehow relieved of hassle.

Besides the *barbiturates* (see Chapter 9), which are seldom used in treatment today because they have high addictive potential and a low margin of dosage safety, two additional classes of prescription **antianxiety drugs** (minor tranquilizers) have gained widespread acceptance in recent years. One of these, the propanediols (mostly meprobamate compounds), seems to operate mainly through the reduction of muscular tension, which in turn is experienced by a patient as calming and emotionally soothing. Meprobamate drugs are marketed under the trade names Miltown and Equanil.

The other class of antianxiety drugs is the *benzodiazepines,* whose use as sleeping pills is discussed in *HIGHLIGHT 17.2.* Up until recently, their use in this country was increasing at an alarming rate; however, thanks to effective public warnings about the addictive potential of these drugs, this trend is now leveling off. Under this rubric are included chlordiazepoxide (Librium), diazepam (Valium), oxazepam (Serax), clorazepate (Tranxene), flurazepam (Dalmane), and alprazolam (Xanax). In experimental studies on animals, the most striking effect of these drugs has been the recurrence of behavior previously inhibited by conditioned fears, without serious impairment in overall behavioral efficiency. Benzodiazepines, in other words, somehow selectively diminish generalized fear (or anxiety) yet leave adaptive behaviors largely intact. They are thus far superior to many other types of anxiety-reducing chemicals, which tend to produce widespread negative effects on adaptive functioning.

Nevertheless, all of the antianxiety drugs have a basically sedative effect on an organism, and many patients treated with them complain of drowsiness and lethargy. This has been a particular problem among schoolchildren treated with these drugs. We must also emphasize that all of these drugs have the potential of inducing dependence when used unwisely or in excess (Bassuk, Schoonover, & Gelenberg, 1983; Levenson, 1981).

Anxiety drugs' range of application is quite broad. They are used in all manner of conditions in which tension and anxiety may be significant components, including anxiety-based and psychophysiologic disorders. They are also used as supplementary treatment in certain neurological disorders to control such symptoms as convulsive seizures, but they have little place in the treatment of the psychoses. They are now the most widely prescribed of all the drugs available to physicians, a fact that has caused concern among some leaders in the medical and psychiatric fields.

Continuing research on benzodiazepines and related compounds is turning up promising leads that will almost certainly result in important future advances in the treatment of anxiety and other conditions. It is now known that the benzodiazepines produce their effects by chemically binding to specific receptors at neuronal synapses, blocking normal transmission; this finding suggests that these receptors are implicated in mediating the experience of anxiety. Additionally, because these compounds also have sedative, muscle relaxant, and anticonvulsive properties, it might be possible to differentiate specific receptors for each, and to discover variant compounds that will selectively bind to them. In fact, researchers at one of the larger pharmaceutical companies have already discovered a chemical that appears to counteract anxiety and convulsions without being a muscle relaxant or

sedative. Work in this area has important implications for our basic understanding of brain processes, in addition to its obvious clinical import.

Lithium for the Bipolar Mood Disorders

Lithium is the lightest of the metals. Its simple salts, such as lithium carbonate, were discovered—as early as 1949 by J. Cade in Australia—to be effective in treating manic disorders. Some 20 years passed before this treatment was introduced in the United States. This delay may have been, in part, for two reasons. First, if not used at the proper dosage, lithium can be toxic, causing numerous side effects, such as delirium, convulsions, and even death. At the same time, if lithium is to have any notable therapeutic effect, it must be used in quantities within the range of potential dangerousness, which varies among different individuals. Thus, at the outset of lithium treatment, a patient's blood levels of lithium must be monitored carefully in relation to observable behavioral effects so that the minimum effective dosage can be established. For each individual, there is a relatively narrow range of effectiveness for the drug. Too little of the drug and the therapeutic effect will be negligible; too much of the drug and the effect could be lethal.

A second possible reason for the delay in widespread lithium usage in the United States may have been the simple fact that researchers were skeptical that it was the lithium itself that was producing the beneficial results; the lithium compounds used in treatment are simple inorganic salts that have no known physiological function (Berger, 1978). Lithium, then, is a somewhat peculiar drug.

Its curious qualities notwithstanding, there can be no doubt at this point concerning lithium's remarkable effectiveness in promptly resolving about 70 to 80 percent of clearly defined manic states, particularly cases in which other psychiatric disorders are not also present (Black et al., 1988). In addition, as we saw in Chapter 11, lithium is sometimes successful in relieving depressions, although possibly only in those patients who are subject to both manic and depressive episodes—that is, who are bipolar in type (Bassuk, Schoonover, & Gelenberg, 1983; Berger, 1978; Segal, Yager, & Sullivan, 1976). More recent research, however, suggests that there may be a subclass of unipolar depressive patients who benefit from lithium treatment (Coppen, Metcalfe, & Wood, 1982).

The drug has been a boon, especially to those people who heretofore have experienced repeated bouts with mania, depression, or both throughout their adult lives. For many, these cycles can now be

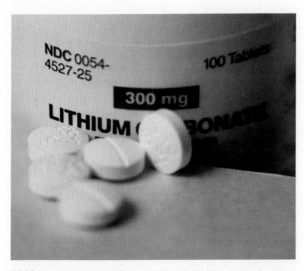

Lithium treatment requires careful monitoring of the dosage—too much can be lethal and too little is ineffective. There is no doubt, however, that the drug has been a boon to those people who have experienced repeated bouts with mania, depression, or both throughout their adult lives.

modulated or even prevented by regular maintenance doses of lithium—for example, by taking a single tablet each morning and evening. Psychiatry may thus have achieved its first essentially preventive treatment method—although, for some patients maintained on the drug for lengthy periods, there may be serious complications, including kidney damage (Bassuk, Schoonover, & Gelenberg, 1983) and memory and motor speed problems (Shaw et al., 1987). There is also some recent evidence that the prevention of further attacks of mania by lithium maintenance treatment may be less reliable than was once thought. In one study, 40 percent of such patients relapsed within 1.7 years following hospital discharge (Harrow et al., 1990).

One of Cade's (1949) own cases will serve well as an illustration of the effects of lithium treatment:

*M*r. W. B. was a 51-year-old man who had been in a state of chronic manic excitement for five years. So obnoxious and destructive was his behavior that he had long been regarded as the most difficult patient on his ward in the hospital.

He was started on treatment with a lithium compound, and within three weeks his behavior had improved to the point that transfer to the convalescent ward was deemed appropriate. He remained in the hospital for another two months, during which his behavior continued to be essentially normal. Prior to discharge, he was switched to another form of lithium salts because the one he had been taking had caused stomach upset.

He was soon back at his job and living a happy and productive life. In fact, he felt so well that, contrary to instructions, he stopped taking his lithium. Thereafter he steadily became more irritable and erratic; some six months following his discharge, he had to cease work. In another five weeks he was back at the hospital in an acute manic state.

Lithium therapy was immediately reestablished, with prompt positive results. In another month Mr. W. B. was pronounced ready to return to home and work, provided he would continue taking a prescribed dosage of lithium.

The biochemical basis of lithium's therapeutic effect is unknown. One well-received hypothesis is that it achieves its effect by limiting the availability of norepinephrine and serotonin, which function as neurotransmitters or modulators at certain synapses in the brain. This effect is opposite that of antidepressant drugs and presumably reduces an individual's ability to process the amount of input typical during a manic state. Of course, this still leaves unexplained the fact that lithium can also alleviate some depressions. An alternative hypothesis is that lithium, being a mineral salt, may have an effect on electrolyte balances, which may also alter the properties of neurotransmission within the brain. So far, however, this connection remains largely speculative. Clearly, the riddle of exactly what occurs will be solved only by more and better research.

Recently another drug has been used with considerable success to treat bipolar disorders. The drug *carbamazepine* (Tegretol), used extensively as an anticonvulsant agent to control grand mal seizures, has been found effective in controlling rapidly cycling mood and reducing aggressivity in bipolar disorders (Ballenger, 1988). Its use has been somewhat disappointing for the treatment of acute mania (Lusznat, Murphy, & Nunn, 1988), which suggests that carbamazepine's usefulness may be more as a prophylactic. Carbamazepine has been associated with significant side effects, especially neurotoxic problems, such as an awkward gait, increased reflexes, and ataxia (Birkhimer, Curtis, & Jann, 1985). As such, careful monitoring of carbamezipine treatment, as with lithium use, is required.

Drug Therapy for Children

Our discussion of the use of drugs in treating maladaptive behavior would be incomplete without some reiteration of their role in the management of childhood disturbances and disorders. We have already addressed this matter to some extent in Chapter 15. Although our society has often been too quick to label as deviant (and thus to "treat") various annoying or inconvenient behaviors in which children sometimes indulge, it is nevertheless true that *some* children do evidence more or less serious behavior disorders. It is also true that some of them may be helped by the judicious use of medication.

Antianxiety, antipsychotic, and antidepressant medications have all been used effectively with children who are, respectively, excessively anxious or "nervous," psychotic, or depressed. Considerable caution must be exercised in the use of these powerful drugs with children, however, to be certain that dosage levels are within tolerable limits for a small and as yet biologically immature organism. Not only are excessive blood levels of these drugs physically dangerous, but in some instances they may produce paradoxical reversal effects—that is, a child's problem may become more severe (Bassuk, Schoonover, & Gelenberg, 1983).

We have already mentioned the apparently widespread problem of excessively tranquilized elementary school pupils. Though the diagnostic terms *hyperactivity, hyperkinesis,* and *specific learning disability* have been used somewhat haphazardly in recent years, there appears to be a subset of highly distractable youngsters of normal but unevenly developed cognitive ability who benefit dramatically, and paradoxically, from drugs that stimulate the central nervous system. As we saw in Chapter 15, the most widely used of these stimulants are the amphetamines; a closely related compound known as methylphenidate (Ritalin) is also used. Recently, Whalen et al. (1989) found that hyperactive children treated with Ritalin were viewed more positively by other children. In certain instances, these drugs promptly terminate hyperactivity, which typically results in an increased attention span and an ability to do schoolwork (Sprague, Barnes, & Werry, 1970; Weiss & Hechtman, 1979; Wender, Reimherr, & Wood, 1981). Normally, a child thus helped is kept on the drug until he or she reaches adolescence, when hyperactivity tends to diminish by an as yet unknown natural process (Bassuk, Schoonover, & Gelenberg, 1983).

The danger, of course, is that restless, overactive children will be summarily diagnosed as "hyperkinetic" or "hyperactive" and treated with drugs *whether or not the problem is essentially a physical one.* If such is the case, the option to use less extreme but potentially effective psychological approaches in treating these children may be forgotten (see Chapter 15).

A Biopsychosocial Perspective on Pharmacological Therapy

Modern psychopharmacology has brought a reduction in the severity and chronicity of many types of psychopathology, particularly the psychoses. It has helped many individuals who would otherwise require hospitalization to function in their family and community settings; it has led to the earlier discharge of those who do require hospitalization and to the greater effectiveness of aftercare programs; and it has made restraints and locked wards largely obsolete. All in all, pharmacological therapy not only has outmoded more drastic forms of treatment but has led to a much more favorable hospital climate for patients and staff alike (see *HIGHLIGHT 17.3* for a summary of the drugs used in psychopharmacological therapy).

Nevertheless, a number of complications and limitations arise in the use of psychotropic drugs. Aside from possible undesirable side effects, the problem of matching drug and dosage to the needs of a given individual is often a difficult one, and it is sometimes necessary to change medication in the course of treatment. In addition, the use of medications in isolation from other treatment methods is usually inappropriate and ineffective because drugs themselves do not cure disorders. As many investigators have pointed out, drugs tend to alleviate symptoms by inducing biochemical changes rather than bring an individual to grips with personal or situational factors that may be reinforcing maladaptive behaviors. Although the reduction in anxiety, disturbed thinking, and other symptoms may tempt therapists to regard a patient as "recovered," it seems important to include psychotherapy in the total program if such gains are to be maintained or improved on.

On the other hand, the failure to incorporate medication into a psychotherapeutic treatment program can lead to serious problems. A recent court case, *Osherhoff* v. *Chestnut Lodge,* raised a number of issues concerning the importance of clinical diagnosis, the effectiveness of medication, and appropriate treatment intervention (Klerman, 1990). Osherhoff, a physician, was severely depressed and functioning so ineffectively that his family hospitalized him at Chestnut Lodge, an exclusively psychoanalytic treatment facility. He was treated with intensive psychoanalytic treatment, without medication, four times a week. After several months, his family became concerned over his lack of progress; he had lost 40 pounds, was experiencing severe sleep disturbance, had marked psychomotor agitation to the point that his pacing caused his feet to become swollen and blistered. The family sought a reevaluation of his case. The staff, in a case conference, decided to continue the treatment program that had been initiated. Dr. Osherhoff's condition worsened and his family had him discharged and admitted into another facility where he was treated with a combination of phenothiazines and tricyclic antidepressants. He improved markedly and was discharged in three months. Later he filed a suit claiming that Chestnut Lodge had not administered the proper treatment—drug therapy—which had caused him to lose a year of employment in his medical practice. Preliminary court arbitration indicated an initial award of damages to Dr. Osherhoff; however, the case was settled out of court before a final judgment was rendered. A number of complicated issues were involved in the case, but the finding that therapists may be liable for failing to provide medication to patients is an important and potentially disruptive new development in the field.

Thus the combination of chemical and psychological forms of therapy is fast becoming the major thrust of current research and treatment for severe psychopathology (Kahn, 1990). This integrative approach involves the use of psychotropic medication and psychosocial approaches, such as behavior therapy or psychoanalysis (Carpenter & Keith, 1986). It has been shown to be valuable with both adults (Liberman & Evans, 1985; Rosen, 1986) and children (Sprague & Brown, 1981). The combined therapeutic approach appears to be especially useful with treatment-resistant disorders in which major mental disorders and persistent personality disorders are involved. Marcus and Bradley (1990), for example, found this approach to be effective in about two-thirds of such treatment-resistant cases. The most effective uses of drugs in the treatment of psychological disorders involve drug administrations that are embedded in the context of other treatment approaches; for example, the use of antidepressant medication along with cognitive-behav-

ioral treatment for depression (Hollon & Beck, 1986). Overall, there is much reason to be optimistic about the combined use of drugs and psychosocial approaches, especially in the more severe disorders, such as schizophrenia (Smith, Glass, & Miller, 1980), and the major mood disorders (Beckham & Leber, 1985a; Klerman & Schechter, 1982).

UNRESOLVED ISSUES
on Drug Treatment and Psychiatry's Future

For about a quarter-century following World War II, the medical specialty of psychiatry—its leadership, its professional and research literature, and its residency training programs—was dominated by Freudian and other related psychodynamic viewpoints. (Alternative psychosocial approaches were still largely undiscovered at the time.) The rejection of all things "organic," "biological," and (narrowly) "medical," although not universal in the discipline, was widespread. In some centers, even the emergence of the new psychotropic drugs was greeted with decided ambivalence, sometimes with contempt and scorn, and occasionally with assertions that they were useless or worse. This was an extreme position, so much so that it contained the seeds of its own demise.

The professional tables began to turn as increasingly sophisticated research demonstrated old-line psychodynamic treatment approaches to be relatively ineffective and the newer drug treatments to have considerable, sometimes even astonishing, benefits. Concurrently, some newer psychosocial approaches, notably the behaviorally based therapies, began also to show extraordinary promise. For the most part, however, these latter therapies were developed outside of the purview of psychiatry—chiefly within the increasingly surgent discipline of clinical psychology. Few psychiatrists had the background training necessary for understanding or contributing to the development of these newer and noninvasive psychosocial approaches. The parallel but unfortunately insular developments of these two trends—drug treatment (in psychiatry) on the one hand and newer psychosocial treatments (in psychology) on the other—made interdisciplinary conflict and competition almost inevitable.

We do not intend to suggest that this competition was the only source of the "remedicalization"

Frequently Used Drugs in the Treatment of Mental and Behavioral Disorders

Class	Generic Name	Trade Name	Used to Treat	Effects
Antipsychotic				
(a) phenothiazines	chlorpromazine	Thorazine	Psychotic (especially schizophrenia) symptoms, such as extreme agitation, delusions, and hallucinations; aggressive or violent behavior	Somewhat variable in achieving intended purpose of suppression of psychotic symptoms. Side effects, such as dry mouth, are often uncomfortable. In long-term use may produce motor disturbances, such as Parkinsonism and tardive dyskinesia.
	thioridazine	Mellaril		
	promazine	Sparine		
	trifluoperazine	Stelazine		
	prochlorperazine	Compazine		
	perphenazine	Trilafon		
	fluphenazine	Prolixin		
	triflupromazine	Temaril		
(b) butyrophenone	haloperidol	Haldol		
(c) thioxanthenes	thiothixine	Navane		
	chlorprothixene	Taractan		
(d) dibenzodiazepine	clozapine	Clozaril		
Antidepressant				
(a) tricyclics	imipramine	Tofranil	Relatively severe depressive symptoms, especially of psychotic severity and unipolar in type	Somewhat variable in alleviating depressive symptoms, and noticeable effects may be delayed up to three weeks. Multiple side effects—some of them dangerous. Use of MAO inhibitors requires dietary restrictions.
	amitriptyline	Elavil		
	nortriptyline	Aventyl		
	protriptyline	Vivactil		
	doxepin	Sinequan		
	trimipramine maleate	Surmontil		
(b) monoamine oxidase (MAO) inhibitors	isocarboxazid	Marplan		
	phenelzine	Nardil		
	tranylcypromine	Parnate		
(c) norepinephrine/ serotonin reuptake inhibitor	fluoxetine	Prozac	Depressive symptoms	Fluoxetine is effective in reducing depressive symptoms. Effects take about 3 weeks. Safety is considered high; overdose unlikely. Side effect profile is favorable, though some nausea, insomnia, and even suicidal tendencies have been reported.
Antimanic (biopolar)	lithium carbonate	Eskalith Lithane Lithonate Lithotabs Phi-Lithium	Manic episodes and some severe depressions, particularly recurrent ones or those alternating with mania	Usually effective in resolving manic episodes, but highly variable in effects on depression, probably because the latter is a less homogeneous

Class	Generic Name	Trade Name	Used to Treat	Effects
				grouping. Multiple side effects unless carefully monitored; high toxicity potential.
	carbamazepine	Tegretol	Manic episodes	Highly effective in treating bipolar disorders (especially acute mania); treatment of depression is less effective. Neurotoxic side effects have been noted, including unsteady gait, tremor, ataxia, and increased restlessness.
Antianxiety (minor tranquilizers)				
(a) propanediols	meprobamate	Equanil Miltown	Nonpsychotic personality problems in which anxiety and tension are prominent features; also used as anticonvulsants and as sleep-inducers (especially flurazepam)	Somewhat variable in achieving intended purpose of tension reduction. Side effects include drowsiness and lethargy. Dependence and toxicity are dangers.
(b) benzodiazepines	diazepam chlordiazepoxide flurazepam oxazepam clorazepate alprazolam prazepam	Valium Librium Dalmane Serax Tranxene Xanax Centrax		
Stimulant	dextroamphetamine amphetamine methylphenidate	Dexedrine Benzedrine Ritalin	Hyperactivity, distractability, specific learning disabilities, and, occasionally, extreme hypoactivity	Rather unpredictable. When maximally effective, can enable otherwise uneducable children to attend regular schools. Side effects often troublesome, including recently discovered retardation of growth.

Based on data from Goodman, et al. (1985); Tacke (1989).

of psychiatry in recent years. Many other pressures —the political and economic climates, the disappointing levels of new trainees for psychiatry, and so on—were building on the discipline during the period under consideration (roughly the early 1970s to present), prompting one distinguished psychiatrist, early on, to refer to "the death of psychiatry" (Torrey, 1974). This concern has been echoed more recently by many others (e.g., Dietz, 1977; Lehmann, 1986; Talbott, 1985b).

The upshot was to cause psychiatry as both a profession and a scientific discipline to veer even more sharply toward what has been called the "neo-Kraepelinian" revolution (Andreasen, 1984), whose fundamental tenet is the reductionistic one that most of the more significant disorders of behavior we see are in fact disorders (organic diseases) of the brain. Many leading psychiatrists see most behavior disorders, in other words, as *medical* conditions requiring *medical* treatments, by (of course) *medical* doctors. This trend excludes nonmedical practitioners, who in the interim have become numerous and politically powerful in their own right. The downside of this position, for psychiatry, is the fact that nonpsychiatric physicians can and do provide a great deal of such treatment themselves, which is yet another source of anxiety about the profession's survival. If any medical doctor can prescribe psychoactive drugs, and if psychiatrists know little about psychosocial treatment, what is the essential function of psychiatry?

It is unfortunate that this sort of "turf" warfare has driven a deep wedge between the biological and psychosocial camps. We also regret what has clearly become an excessive reliance on drugs in attempts to solve human problems. At least equally distressing, however, is the deleterious effect these tactics have had on the rational search for improved treatment programs. We refer here to the large-scale campaign seemingly led by the biological forces in psychiatry (in conjunction with pharmaceutical companies) to convince the public that biological treatment, chiefly drugs, is exclusively the treatment of choice for nearly the entire realm of abnormal behavior. No objective reading of the evidence, of which there is a great deal (much of it reported in this text), supports such a conclusion. The inevitable long-range consequence, in our judgment, will be a failure of psychiatry, once again, to deliver on its promissory note of a better life for all, this time through chemistry.

When the pendulum once again swings back (which it undoubtedly will) toward a general recognition of the importance of psychosocial and sociocultural factors in the management and treatment of mental disorders, including the most severe ones, we hope that it will not again overcorrect and encourage neglect of the biological route of intervention. We also hope that psychiatry will survive its period of peril; we will need good, solidly trained psychiatrists to bridge the biopsychosocial gap and to make discriminating use of drug therapy in the more limited arena in which we expect it will have a vital role.

SUMMARY

Except for the development of electroconvulsive therapy (ECT) beginning in 1938, the biological approach to the treatment of mental disorders, at least on this continent and in Europe, had made little headway until about 1955. Indeed, some of the early biological treatments, such as insulin coma therapy and lobotomy, probably did more harm than good, as did many early medical treatments for purely physical diseases.

The mode of therapeutic action of ECT, which continues to be widely used, is not yet understood. There is little doubt, however, of its efficacy for certain patients, especially those suffering from severe depression. Appropriate premedication together with other modifications in technique (for example, unilateral placement of electrodes) have made this treatment relatively safe and, for the most part, have checked the serious or long-term side effects. Nevertheless, controversy about this method of treatment persists, and there is evidence that it can produce permanent brain damage. Obviously, ECT should be used with caution and circumspection, and preferably only after less dramatic methods have been tried and have failed.

The antipsychotic compound chlorpromazine (Thorazine) became widely available in the mid-1950s. It was followed shortly by numerous other related (that is, phenothiazine class) and nonrelated antipsychotic drugs of proven effectiveness in diminishing psychotic (especially schizophrenic) symptoms. Thus was initiated a true revolution in the treatment of severe mental disorders—one that, among other things, permanently altered the environment and the function of mental hospitals. Within a short period, too, the antidepressant medications became available to help patients with severe depressions, making it possible in many instances to avoid the use of ECT. Finally, in the late 1960s (after an unaccountable delay in its introduction in this country), the antimanic drug lithium was recognized as having major therapeutic significance. With the availability of these three types of drugs, the major psychoses—for the first time in history—now came to be seen as generally and effectively treatable.

Meanwhile, antianxiety drugs (mild tranquilizers) had been developed that circumvented many of the problems of the barbiturates used earlier in combating excessive tension and anxiety. This development extended the benefit of effective drug treatment to many people who were struggling with neurotic problems or with high-stress life circumstances. The meprobamates (for example, Equanil) were the first of these new antianxiety drugs but were largely superseded by the more potent benzodiazepines (such as Valium) for general use.

New biological treatments for mental disorders will doubtless continue to be proposed, but, as in the case of psychosurgery, many will prove undeserving of a high degree of confidence. A measure of caution is recommended concerning claims made by the proponents of newly introduced therapies.

Finally, the admittedly impressive gains in biological treatment methods may cause us to lose sight of important psychological processes that may be intrinsic to any mental disorder. In fact, some evidence shows that combinations of biologically and psychologically based approaches may be more successful than either alone, at least with some of the more severe disorders.

■ Key Terms

insulin coma therapy (p. 606)
electroconvulsive therapy
  (ECT) (p. 607)
psychosurgery (p. 610)
prefrontal lobotomy (p. 610)

pharmacology (p. 612)
antipsychotic drugs (p. 613)
tardive dyskinesia (p. 614)
antidepressant drugs (p. 616)
antianxiety drugs (p. 617)

Chapter 18
Psychologically Based Therapies

Adolf Wölfli, *Saint Adolf Portant des Lunettes, Entre les Deux Villes Geantes Niess et Mia.* Wölfli (1864–1930), born in Bern, Switzerland, was abandoned by his father in early childhood and at the age of 8 was removed from the care of his mother—occurrences that marked the beginning of violent, erratic behaviors that finally culminated in schizophrenic breakdown. In his paintings, Wölfli typically returns to an idealized childhood, in which as "Saint Adolf," a child divinity, he journeys through the universe, often accompanied by assorted gods and goddesses.

Most of us have experienced a time or situation when we were dramatically helped by "talking things over" with a relative or friend. Or perhaps we made a drastic change in our life-style after a particular event led to new understanding. As the noted psychoanalyst Franz Alexander (1946) pointed out long ago, formal psychotherapy as practiced by a mental health professional shares many aspects in common with this type of familiar experience. Most therapists, like all good listeners, rely on a common repertoire of receptiveness, warmth, empathy, and a nonjudgmental approach to the problems their clients present. Most, however, also introduce into the relationship certain psychological interventions that are designed to promote new understandings, behaviors, or both on the client's part. The fact that these interventions are deliberately planned and guided by certain theoretical preconceptions (of the kind discussed in Chapter 3) is what distinguishes professional **psychotherapy,** the treatment of mental disorders by psychological methods, from more informal helping relationships. As we will see, it is the varying nature of these theoretical preconceptions that largely distinguishes a given type of psychotherapy from the others available.

Psychotherapy is based on the assumption that, even in cases where physical pathology is present, an individual's perceptions, evaluations, expectations, and coping strategies also play a role in the development of the disorder and will probably need to be changed if maximum benefit is to be realized. The belief that individuals with psychological problems can change—can learn more adaptive ways of perceiving, evaluating, and behaving—is the conviction underlying all psychotherapy. The goal of psychotherapy, then, is to make this belief a reality.

To achieve this goal, a psychotherapist may attempt to (a) change maladaptive behavior patterns; (b) minimize or eliminate environmental conditions that may be causing or maintaining such behavior; (c) improve interpersonal and other competencies; (d) resolve handicapping or disabling conflicts among motives; (e) modify individuals' cognitions, their dysfunctional beliefs about themselves and their world; (f) reduce or remove discomforting or disabling emotional reactions; and (g) foster a clear-cut sense of self-identity. All these strategies can open pathways to a more meaningful and fulfilling existence.

Achieving these changes is by no means easy. Sometimes an individual's distorted view of the world and unhealthy self-concept are the end products of faulty parent-child relationships reinforced by many years of life experiences. In other instances, inadequate occupational, marital, or social adjustment requires major changes in a person's life situation, in addition to psychotherapy. Magnifying such difficulties is the fact that it is often easier to hold to one's present problematic but familiar course than to risk change and the unpredictability it entails. It would be too much to expect that a psychotherapist, even a highly skilled and experienced one, could in a short time undo an individual's entire past history and prepare him or her to cope with a difficult life situation in a fully adequate manner. Psychotherapists can offer no magical transformations of either selfhood or the realities in which people live their lives. Nevertheless, a well-formulated and -executed plan of psychotherapy holds promise in even the most severe of the mental disorders, and indeed for certain of them may provide the only realistic hope for significant and lasting change.

It has been estimated that several hundred "therapeutic approaches" exist, ranging from psychoanalysis to Zen meditation. Indeed, the last few decades have witnessed a stream of "new therapies" —each winning avid proponents and followers for a time. The faddism in the popular literature on self-change might give the casual reader the idea that the entire field of psychotherapy is in constant flux. In reality, the professional field of psychotherapy has shown both considerable stability over time and coherence around a few basic orientations, albeit ones that vary appreciably in the "visions" they embody of the world and of human nature (Andrews, 1989a). This chapter will explore the most widely used and accepted of these formal psychological treatment approaches.

AN OVERVIEW OF PSYCHOLOGICAL TREATMENT

Before we turn our attention to the specific psychological intervention techniques, we will attempt to gain perspective by considering more closely the individuals involved in therapy and their relationship.

■ Who Receives Psychotherapy?

People who receive psychotherapy vary widely in their problems and their motivations to solve them. Perhaps the most obvious candidates for psychological treatment are individuals experiencing sudden and highly stressful situations, people who feel so overwhelmed by the crisis conditions in which they find themselves that they cannot manage on their own. These individuals typically feel quite vulnerable and tend to be open to psychological treatment because they are motivated to alter their present intolerable mental states. They often respond well to short-term, directive, crisis-oriented treatment (to be discussed in Chapter 19). In such situations, clients may gain considerably, in a brief time, from the outside perspective provided by their therapist.

Some individuals enter psychological therapy somewhat as a surprise to themselves. Perhaps they had consulted a physician for their headache or stomach pain, only to be told that there was nothing physically wrong with them. Such individuals, referred to a therapist, may at first resist the idea that their physical symptoms are emotionally based, especially if the referring physician has been brusque or unclear as to the rationale for his or her judgment. The resistant attitudes often encountered following this type of referral underscore the fact that motivation to enter treatment differs widely among psychotherapy clients. Reluctant clients may come from many sources—for example, an alcoholic whose spouse threatens "either therapy or divorce," or a suspected felon whose attorney advises that things will go better at trial if it can be announced that the suspect has "entered therapy." A substantial number of angry parents bring their children to therapists with demands that their "uncontrollable" behavior, viewed as independent of the family context, be "fixed."

Many people entering therapy have experienced long-term psychological distress and have had lengthy histories of maladjustment. They may have been experiencing interpersonal problems for some time or may have felt susceptible to low moods that are difficult for them to dispel. Chronic unhappiness and inability to feel confident and secure may finally prompt them to seek outside help. These individuals seek psychological assistance out of dissatisfaction and despair. They may enter treatment with a high degree of motivation but, as therapy proceeds, their persistent patterns of maladaptive behavior may become resistant forces with which a therapist must contend. For example, a narcissistic client who anticipates therapist praise and admiration may become disenchanted and hostile when these are not forthcoming.

A number of people who enter therapy have problems that would be considered relatively normal. That is, they appear to have achieved success, have financial stability, have generally accepting and loving families, and have accomplished many of their life goals. They enter therapy not out of personal despair or impossible interpersonal involvements, but out of a sense that they have not lived up to their own expectations and realized their own potential. These individuals, partly because their problems are more manageable than the problems of others, may make substantial gains in personal growth. Much of these therapeutic gains can be attributed to their high degree of motivation and personal resources. Individuals who seem to have the best prognosis for personality change, according to repeated research outcomes, have been described in terms of the so-called YAVIS pattern (Schofield, 1964)—they are Young, Attractive, Verbal, Intelligent, and Successful. Ironically, those who tend to do best in psychotherapy are those who seem objectively to need it least.

Psychotherapy, however, is not just for individuals who have clearly defined problems, high levels of motivation, and an ability to gain ready insight into their behavior. Psychotherapeutic interventions have been applied to a wide variety of chronic problems. Even a severely disturbed psychotic client may profit from a therapeutic relationship that takes into account his or her level of functioning and maintains therapeutic subgoals that are within the client's present capabilities. Contrary to common understanding (and to frequently biased media reports), the success record for psychological treatment in major psychoses, such as schizophrenia, is very respectable (Carson & Sanislow, 1992).

It should be clear from this brief description of individuals in psychological therapy that there is indeed no "typical" client, nor, as we will see, is there a "model" therapy. No currently extant form of therapy is applicable to all types of clients, and it appears that all of the standard therapies can document success with some types of individuals. Most authorities agree that client variables, such as the extent of the problem and client motivation, are exceedingly important to the outcome of therapy (Bergin & Lambert, 1978; Garfield, 1986; Rounsaville, Weissman, & Prusoff, 1981). As we will see, the various therapies have relatively greater success when a therapist takes the characteristics of a particular client into account in determining the treatment of choice.

In psychological therapy, there is no "typical" client, nor is there a "model" therapy. Client variables, such as the extent of the problem and client motivation, are important to the outcome of therapy, and the therapist who takes these factors into account in determining treatment will likely have greater success.

■ Who Provides Psychotherapeutic Services?

Members of many different professions have traditionally provided advice and counsel to individuals in emotional distress. Physicians have, in addition to their role of providing care for their clients' physical problems, often become trusted advisers in emotional matters as well. In past eras, before the advent of large health maintenance organizations and highly differentiated medical specialists, the family physicians was called on for virtually all health questions. Even today, the medical practitioner—although he or she may have little psychological background and limited time to spend with individual clients—may be asked to give consultation in psychological matters. Most physicians are trained to recognize psychological problems that are beyond their expertise and to refer individuals to psychological specialists.

Another professional group that deals extensively with people's emotional problems is the clergy. Members of the clergy are usually in intimate contact with the emotional needs and problems of their congregations. A minister, priest, or rabbi may be the first professional to encounter an individual experiencing emotional crisis. Some clergy actively acquire counseling training and supervised experience in dealing with psychological problems and go on to obtain mental health professional credentials, including pastoral counseling degrees.

Personnel in Psychotherapy

Professional

Clinical psychologist. Ph.D. in psychology with both research and clinical skill specialization. One-year internship in a psychiatric hospital or mental health center. *Or,* Psy.D. in psychology (a professional degree with more clinical than research specialization) plus one-year internship in a psychiatric hospital or mental health center.

Counseling psychologist. Ph.D. in psychology plus internship in a marital- or student-counseling setting; normally, a counseling psychologist deals with adjustment problems not involving mental disorder.

School psychologist. Ideally a person having doctoral training in child-clinical psychology, with additional training and experience in academic and learning problems. At present, many school systems lack the resources to maintain an adequate school psychology program.

Psychiatrist. M.D. degree with residency training (usually three years) in a psychiatric hospital or mental health facility.

Psychoanalyst. M.D. or Ph.D. degree plus intensive training in the theory and practice of psychoanalysis.

Psychiatric social worker. B.A., M.S.W., or Ph.D. degree with specialized clinical training in mental health settings.

Psychiatric nurse. R.N. degree plus specialized training in the care and treatment of psychiatric clients. Nurses can attain M.A. and Ph.D. degrees in psychiatric nursing.

Occupational therapist. B.S. in occupational therapy plus internship training with physically or psychologically handicapped individuals, helping them make the most of their resources.

Pastoral counselor. Ministerial background plus training in psychology. Internship in mental health facility as a chaplain.

Paraprofessional

Community mental health worker. Capable person with limited professional training who works under professional direction (especially crisis intervention).

Alcohol- or drug-abuse counselor. Limited professional training but trained in the evaluation and management of alcohol- and drug-addicted people.

In both mental health clinics and hospitals, personnel from several fields may function as an interdisciplinary team—for example, a psychiatrist, a clinical psychologist, a social worker, a psychiatric nurse, and an occupational therapist may work together.

Most limit their counseling to religious matters and spiritual support and do not attempt to provide psychotherapy. Rather, they are trained to recognize problems that require professional management and refer troubled individuals to mental health specialists.

Beyond physicians and clergy, the professionals of primary interest to us in this context are those formally trained to identify and treat mental disorders. The three types of mental health professionals found most often in mental health settings are clinical psychologists, psychiatrists, and psychiatric social workers (see *HIGHLIGHT 18.1*). The **clinical psychologist** typically has training at the undergraduate level in psychology and has a Ph.D. or Psy.D. degree in clinical psychology, with specialization in personality theory, abnormal psychology,

psychological assessment, and psychotherapy. Most clinical psychologists receive broad clinical experience in assessment and psychotherapy in addition to their mental health research training. The **psychiatrist** is an M.D. who has had further training—minimally a three-year residency—in dealing with clients in a mental health setting. The medical training of psychiatrists qualifies them for administering somatic therapies, such as electroconvulsive therapy and psychotropic medication. In addition, during residency, psychiatric residents receive supervision in psychotherapy. **Psychiatric social workers** are usually trained in social science at the bachelor's level and may hold an M.A. or Ph.D. from a school of social work. Their graduate training usually involves courses in family evaluation, psychotherapy, and supervised field experiences.

In any given therapy program, a wide range of medical, psychological, and social work procedures may be used. Such procedures range from the use of drugs to individual or group psychotherapy and to home, school, or job visits aimed at modifying adverse conditions in a client's life. Often the latter—as in helping a teacher become more understanding and supportive of a child client's needs—is as important as treatment directed toward modifying the client's personality makeup, behavior, or both.

This willingness to use a variety of procedures is reflected in the frequent use of a *team approach* to assessment and treatment, particularly in institutional settings. This approach involves the coordinated efforts of medical, psychological, social work, and other mental health personnel working together as the needs of each case warrant. Also of key importance is the current practice of providing treatment facilities in the community. Instead of considering maladjustment as an individual's private misery, which in the past often required confinement in a distant mental hospital, this approach integrates family and community resources in the treatment.

■ The Therapeutic Relationship

The therapeutic relationship is formed out of what both a careseeker and a caregiver bring to the therapeutic situation. The client's major contribution is his or her motivation. The humanistic tenet —that all humans are at base far more like each other than different and possess an inner drive toward mental and physical health—makes effective psychotherapy possible. Just as physical medicine, properly used, essentially frees and cooperates with the body's own healing mechanisms, an important ally for a psychotherapist is an individual's own drive toward wholeness and toward the development of unrealized potentialities. Although this inner drive is often obscured in severely disturbed clients, the majority of anxious and confused people are sufficiently discouraged with their situation to be eager to cooperate in any program that holds hope for improvement.

Motivation to change is probably the most crucial element in determining the success or failure of psychotherapy, and a wise therapist is, of course, appropriately cautious about accepting therapeutic responsibility where client motivation may be suspect. Not all prospective clients, regardless of an objective need for treatment, are ready at the time of referral to undertake seriously the often uncomfortable experiences that effective therapy entails. Even the motivation of self-referred clients may dissipate

in the face of the painful confrontations good therapy may require.

Almost as important is a client's *expectation* of receiving help. This expectancy is often sufficient in itself to bring about some improvement (Frank, 1978). Just as a placebo pill often lessens pain for an individual who believes it will do so, an individual who expects to be helped by psychotherapy is likely to be helped, almost regardless of the particular methods used by a therapist. The downside of this fact is that a therapist who appears inept, bumbling, or unconfident may compromise potential benefits even where the treatment plan is entirely appropriate for the presenting problem. Those in the helping professions are usually the first to admit that their "art" is inexact and dependent on what a client and therapist bring to the experience of treatment.

To the art of therapy, a therapist brings a variety of professional skills and methods intended to help individuals see themselves and their situations more objectively—that is, to gain a different perspective. Insight and new perspective, however, are only a start and not usually enough alone to bring about the necessary changes in behavior. Besides helping an individual toward a new perspective, most therapy situations also provide a protected setting in which he or she is helped to practice new ways of feeling and acting, gradually developing both the courage and the ability to take responsibility for acting in more effective and satisfying ways.

To bring about such changes, an effective psychotherapist must interact with a client in a such a manner as to discourage old and dysfunctional behavior patterns and induce new and more functional ones in their place. Because differing clients will present varying challenges in this regard, the therapist must be sufficiently flexible to deploy a variety of interactive styles. For example, a therapist who inadvertently but unfailingly takes charge in finding solutions for clients' problems will have considerable difficulty in working with people presenting serious difficulties in the area of inhibited autonomy, as in dependent personality disorder. To at least some extent, effective therapy depends on a good match between client and therapist (Talley, Strupp, & Morey, 1990). Hence, a therapist's own personality is necessarily a factor of some importance in determining therapeutic outcomes, quite aside from his or her background and training or the particular formal treatment plan adopted (Lambert, 1989).

Despite general agreement among psychotherapists on these aspects of the client-therapist relationship, professionals can and do differ in their diagnoses and treatments of psychological disorders. This statement should not be too surprising, of course.

Even in the treatment of physical disorders, we sometimes find that physicians disagree. In psychopathology, such disagreements are even more often the case. The differing viewpoints on human motivation and behavior outlined in Chapter 3 lead, as might be expected, to quite different diagnoses of what "the problem" is and how an individual should be helped to overcome it. The next section provides a brief perspective on the several types of therapy available and on how they are able to coexist and complement one another, despite their evident differences.

▪ A Perspective on Therapeutic Pluralism

Gaining an overall mastery of the sometimes bewildering array of available therapeutic techniques is difficult at best. One way to do so is to reduce the domain to four general types or classes of therapy interventions according to the principal client subsystem targeted for therapeutic attention: affect, behavior, cognition, or environment (ABCE). The ABCE framework (a graphic of which is in *HIGHLIGHT 18.2*) is our own attempt to summarize this complex domain; we hope it will be of value to you by providing a convenient orienting framework.

According to this scheme, biological therapies, reviewed in the preceding chapter, would mainly be considered Type A therapies because they are by and large directed toward altering a client's affects, or emotions, including anxiety. Operant conditioning therapies, on the other hand, would practically always be of Type B because of their focus on bringing about direct changes in maladaptive behavior through the manipulation of reinforcement contingencies.

As we will see, and indeed as might be anticipated, not all therapies fit neatly into one or another of the types; usually, however, a *dominant* therapeutic target is discernible that makes such classification feasible, although not necessarily exhaustive in terms of subsidiary therapeutic strategies used. Of course, such a classification scheme becomes irrelevant for truly comprehensive programs of therapy, such as the so-called multimodal, but these seem (unfortunately, we think) still the exception rather than the rule in clinical practice. Although most therapists describe themselves as "eclectic" in orientation, most in fact strongly favor particular approaches, and some (e.g., Patterson, 1989) doubt even the possibility of "integration." We will point out in the following sections what seem to be the dominant type memberships (either A, B, C, or E) of the several types of psychotherapy to be described.

Before proceeding, one other aspect of *HIGHLIGHT 18.2* deserves mention—namely, its form as a *continuous loop* having neither beginning nor end. We think this form reflects the reality of the relationships among (a) the client, conceived as a system of integrated cognitions and affects; (b) his or her abnormal behavioral output, assumed to be a product of (a); and (c) the reactions of the individual's environment and surroundings to that output, in turn "feeding back" to the person's cognition and affect system some information that, in the typical instance, tends to confirm the "contents" of the system. This aspect of our model is neither idiosyncratic nor new, and explicit developments of certain of its facets now commonly appear in contemporary professional literature (e.g., Andrews, 1989b; Safran, 1990a, 1990b).

The model has two important and related implications for therapy. First, the question of *causal primacy*, of how it (the abnormal behavior) all got started, is not in this context especially relevant; once in operation, the loop, theoretically, is self-sustaining. Second, it should be possible to effect a positive overall outcome by fostering adaptive change in *any* pertinent component of the loop, whether cognitions, affects, overt behaviors, or even the reacting environment. That is, effective therapy, reduced to its most basic operations, consists of interrupting this pathology-sustaining loop. In our view then, most competing types of therapy can realistically claim their share of successes (Smith, Glass, & Miller, 1980) *precisely because* they normally induce adaptive change in one or another of these critical system components, thereby (perhaps in a sense unwittingly) positively affecting the whole (see, for example, Stiles et al., 1986).

Maintaining this overview as a backdrop, we now will consider several forms of psychotherapy that have evolved over the century since Sigmund Freud's first such effort. In fact, we will begin with that tradition.

▪ PSYCHODYNAMIC THERAPY

Psychodynamic therapy is a psychological treatment approach that focuses on individual personality dynamics from a psychoanalytic perspective. Also called *psychoanalytically oriented therapy* or *psychoanalysis* (see Chapter 3), the therapists who practice it are often referred to as *psychoanalysts* or, simply, *analysts*. As developed by Freud and his immediate followers, psychoanalytic therapy is an intensive, long-term procedure for uncovering repressed

HIGHLIGHT 18.2

Classes of Therapeutic Strategies According to the Primary Target for Change

The following figure depicts in schematic fashion the situation of a typical psychotherapy client, who is conceived here as a conglomerate of mutually influencing cognitions and affects. A principal output of this conglomerate system is overt behavior, some of which is maladaptive or abnormal. The impact of this abnormal behavior on the environment (chiefly the social or interpersonal environment) generates information-laden reactions that are in turn registered by the client's cogni-tive-affect system. (The reverse direction arrow from behavior to client acknowledges the scattered evidence that this type of influence also occurs.) In the case of persisting behavioral abnormality, we assume that much of the information gleaned from the reacting environment is such as to "confirm," or at least not disconfirm, client cognitions and affects; were it otherwise, we would anticipate a restructuring of the system and, typically, a reasonably prompt termination of the abnormal behav-ior. Therapy is thus a matter of interrupting the self-sustaining loop supporting the behavioral abnormality. Seen in this light, therapy might conceivably be effective by inducing positive change in *any one* of the component nodes of the loop. Differing types of therapy, here organized into Types A (affect), B (behavior), C (cognitions), and E (environment), do in fact tend to focus efforts at therapeutic change on one or another of these nodes, as further described in the text.

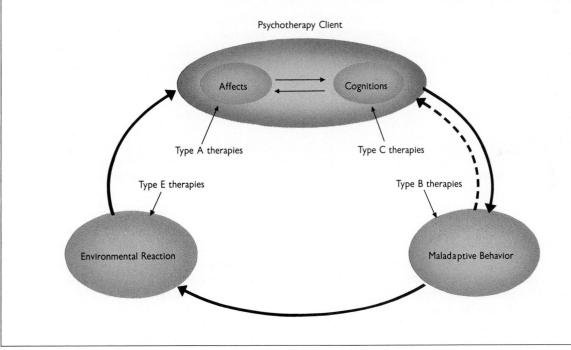

memories, thoughts, fears, and conflicts—presumably stemming from problems in early psychosexual development—and helping individuals come to terms with them in the light of adult reality. It is thought that gaining insight into such repressed material frees individuals from the need to keep squandering their energies on repression and other defense mechanisms. Instead, they can bring their personality resources to bear on consciously resolving the anxieties that prompted the repression in the first place. Freed from this load of threatening material and from the effort of keeping it out of consciousness, they can turn their energies to better personality integration and more effective living.

Other psychodynamic treatment approaches do not rigidly adhere to orthodox Freudian theory yet are, in part, based on psychoanalytic concepts. We will examine first Freud's original treatment methods, in part because of their historical significance and enormous influence; then we will look briefly at some of the contemporary modifications of psychoanalytic therapy.

The Use of Hypnosis in Therapy

Hypnosis was known among the ancient Egyptians and other early peoples, but its modern use in psychotherapy dates only from the time of Mesmer, as we saw in Chapter 3. Since that time, there have been periodic fluctuations in the popularity of hypnosis in psychotherapy, and differing viewpoints have arisen concerning the exact nature of hypnotic phenomena. In general, hypnosis may be defined as an altered state of consciousness involving extreme suggestibility. Hypnotic induction procedures are designed to bring about a heightened state of selective attention in which a subject "tunes out" irrelevant stimuli and concentrates solely on the hypnotist's suggestions. The induction of hypnosis and its therapeutic uses are briefly outlined here.

1. *Induction of hypnosis.* Hypnosis may be induced by a variety of techniques, most of which involve the following factors: (a) enlist-ing a subject's cooperation and allaying any fears of hypnosis; (b) having the subject assume a comfortable position and relax completely; (c) narrowing and focusing the subject's attention, perhaps by having him or her gaze on some bright object; and (d) directing the subject's activities by means of suggestions. The latter often involves establishing the assumption that normal bodily reactions have in fact come about at the direction of the hypnotist. For example, a subject may be directed to gaze upward toward an object and then be told, "your eyelids are starting to feel heavy." This is a normal reaction to the strain of looking upward, but the subject thinks it is caused by the hypnotist; thus the way is paved to accept further suggestions.

2. *Recall of buried memories.* Traumatic experiences that have been repressed from consciousness may be recovered under hyp-nosis. This technique was used in treating combat-exhaustion cases during World War II. Under hypnosis, an amnesic soldier could relive his battle experience, thus discharging the emotional tensions associated with it and permitting the experience to be assimilated into his self-structure. Civilian reactions involving amnesia may be similarly handled.

3. *Age regression.* Closely related to memory recall is hypnotic age regression. A hypnotized woman, for example, may be told that she is now a 6-year-old child again and will subsequently act, talk, and think much as she did at the age of 6. Regression to the age just preceding the onset of phobias often brings to light the traumatic experiences that precipitated them. Here again, reliving the traumatic experience may desensitize a subject to it. Age regression *below* the point at which an individual acquired verbally mediated memory

■ Freudian Psychoanalysis

Psychoanalysis is a system of therapy that evolved over a period of years during Freud's long career. It is not an easy system of therapy to describe, and the problem is complicated by the fact that most people have some more or less inaccurate conceptions of it based on cartoons and other forms of caricature. The best way to begin our discussion is to describe the four basic techniques of this form of therapy: free association, analysis of dreams, analysis of resistance, and analysis of transference. Then we will note some of the most important changes that have taken place in psychoanalytic therapy since Freud's time.

Free Association   As we saw in Chapter 3, Freud used hypnosis in his early work to free repressed thoughts from his clients' unconscious

(see *HIGHLIGHT 18.3*). Later, he stopped using hypnosis in favor of a more direct method of gaining access to an individual's hidden thoughts and fears—**free association.**

The basic rule of free association is that an individual must say whatever comes into his or her mind, regardless of how personal, painful, or seemingly irrelevant it may be. Usually a client sits comfortably in a chair or lies in a relaxed position on a couch and gives a running account of all the thoughts, feelings, and desires that come to mind as one idea leads to another. The therapist usually takes a position behind the client so as not to in any way distract or disrupt the free flow of associations.

Although such a running account of whatever comes into one's head may seem random, Freud did not view it as such; rather, he believed that associations are determined like other events. As we have is not possible. Contrary to what some claim, age regression to "past lives" is also not possible.

4. *Dream induction.* Dreams can be induced through hypnosis, although some investigators consider hypnotic dreams to more nearly resemble fantasies than nocturnal dreams. In any event, hypnotic dreams may be used to explore intrapsychic conflicts along the lines of dream analysis worked out by Freud. Perhaps the particular value of such dreams is that a therapist can suggest the theme about which the hypnotic dream should center, using it much like a projective technique in exploring an individual's inner conflicts.

5. *Posthypnotic suggestion.* One of the hypnotic phenomena most widely used in psychotherapy is posthypnotic suggestion. In this technique, a therapist makes suggestions to a subject during the hypnotic state for behavior to be carried out later in the waking state, with the subject remaining unaware of the source of the behavior. For example, a subject may be told that he or she will no longer have a desire to smoke upon coming out of the hypnotic state. Although such suggestions do carry over into the waking state, their duration is usually short. That is, the individual may again experience a desire to smoke in a few hours or a few days. This time factor can be partially compensated for, however, by regular reinforcement of the posthypnotic suggestion in booster sessions.

Some investigators attribute the altered state of consciousness in hypnosis to the subject's strong motivation to meet the demand characteristics of the situation. Barber (1969) has shown that many of the behaviors induced under hypnosis can be replicated in nonhypnotized subjects simply by giving instructions which they are strongly motivated to follow. The preponderance of research evidence, however, indicates that behavior induced in hypnotized subjects does differ significantly from that evidenced during simulated hypnosis or role enactment (Diamond, 1974; Fromm & Shor, 1972; Hilgard, 1973, 1974; Miller & Springer, 1974; Nace, Orne, & Hammer, 1974). For example, a number of investigators have offered dramatic evidence that the pain response can be brought almost completely under hypnotic control in many subjects, permitting a degree of pain reduction well beyond that produced in nonhypnotized subjects.

Such drugs as sodium pentothal can be used to produce phenomena similar to those manifested in a hypnotic trance. This form of biological therapy is referred to as *narcoanalysis* or *narcosynthesis*. Sodium pentothal has been used to treat severe cases of combat exhaustion involving amnesia.

seen, he also thought that the conscious represents a relatively small part of the mind, while the preconscious and unconscious are the much larger portions. The purpose of free association is to explore thoroughly the contents of the preconscious, that part of mind considered subject to conscious attention but largely ignored. The preconscious contents, it is thought, contain derivatives of repressed unconscious material, which if properly "interpreted" can lead to an uncovering of the latter. Analytic interpretation involves a therapist's tying together a client's often disconnected ideas, beliefs, actions, and so forth into a meaningful explanation to help the client gain insight into the relationship between his or her maladaptive behavior and the repressed (unconscious) events and fantasies that drive it.

Analysis of Dreams   Another important, related procedure for uncovering unconscious material is dream analysis. When a person is asleep, repressive defenses are lowered and forbidden desires and feelings may find an outlet in dreams. For this reason, dreams have been referred to as the "royal road to the unconscious." Some motives, however, are so unacceptable to an individual that even in dreams they are not revealed openly but are expressed in disguised or symbolic form. Thus a dream has two kinds of content: **manifest content,** which is the dream as it appears to the dreamer, and **latent content,** composed of the actual motives that are seeking expression but are so painful or unacceptable that they are disguised.

It is a therapist's task to uncover these disguised meanings by studying the images that appear in the manifest content of a client's dream and his or her preconscious associations to them. For example, a client's dream of being engulfed in a tidal wave may be interpreted by a therapist as indicating that the client feels in danger of being overwhelmed by inadequately repressed fears and hostilities.

Analysis of Resistance   During the process of free association or of associating to dreams, an individual may evidence **resistance**—an unwillingness or inability to talk about certain thoughts, motives, or experiences (Strean, 1985). For example, a client may be talking about an important childhood experience and then suddenly switch topics, perhaps stating that "It really isn't that important," or that "It is too absurd to discuss." Resistance may also be evidenced by the client's giving a too-glib interpretation of some association, or coming late to an appointment, or even "forgetting" an appointment altogether. Because resistance prevents painful and threatening material from entering awareness, its sources must be sought if an individual is to face the problem and learn to deal with it in a realistic manner.

Analysis of Transference   As client and therapist interact, the relationship between them may become complex and emotionally involved. Often people carry over and apply to their therapist attitudes and feelings that they had in their relations with a parent or other person close to them in the past, a process known as **transference.** Thus clients may react to their analyst as they did to that earlier person and feel the same hostility and rejection that they felt long ago.

By recognizing the transference relationship, a therapist may provide an individual with insight as to the inappropriateness of his or her reactions in the present context, and may also introduce a corrective emotional experience by behaving in a manner, classically an extraordinarily passive and "impersonal" one, that is distinctly inconsistent with the attitudes and feelings that have been falsely attributed. In this manner it may be possible for the individual to work through the conflict in feelings about the real parent or perhaps to overcome feelings of hostility and self-devaluation that stemmed from the earlier parental rejection. In essence, the pathogenic effects of an undesirable early relationship are counteracted by working through a similar emotional conflict in a therapeutic setting. Because a person's reliving of a pathogenic past relationship in a sense recreates the neurosis in real life, this experience is often referred to as a *transference neurosis.*

It is not possible here to consider at length the complexities of transference relationships, but it may be stressed that a client's attitudes toward his or her therapist usually do not follow such simple patterns as our example suggests. Often the client is ambivalent—distrusting the therapist and feeling hostile toward him or her as a symbol of authority, but at the same time seeking acceptance and love. In addition, the problems of transference are by no means confined to the client, for the therapist may also have a mixture of feelings toward the client. This phenomenon is known as **counter-transference** and must be recognized and handled properly by the therapist in question. For this reason, it is considered important that therapists have a thorough understanding of their own motives, conflicts, and "weak spots"; in fact, all psychoanalysts themselves undergo psychoanalysis before they begin independent practice. The resolution of the transference neurosis is said to be the key element in effecting a psychoanalytic "cure." Such resolution can only occur if an analyst successfully avoids the pitfalls of counter-transference. That is, the analyst must focus on control of the "environmental" (i.e., his or her own) reaction to a client's behavior. Accordingly, we consider psychoanalytically oriented therapy to be primarily Type E in character.

◼ Psychodynamic Therapy Since Freud

Although some psychoanalysts still adhere to standard long-term psychoanalysis—which may take years—most analysts have worked out modifications in procedure designed to shorten the time and expense required. Mann (1973), for example, described what he refers to as "time-limited" psychotherapy. This approach, which focuses on providing symptom relief, follows psychodynamic methods but is confined to a 12-session treatment course. Probably the most extensive program of short-term psychodynamic therapy, and one which involves a strong research/evaluation component, is that of Strupp and his colleagues (Strupp, 1981; Strupp & Binder, 1984). This therapy, known as *time-limited dynamic psychotherapy,* goes beyond the symptom relief of Mann's program; it aims for lasting modification of an individual's personality by applying modified psychodynamic principles in therapy that lasts for 25 to 30 sessions. The modifications introduced here have a substantial *interpersonal* focus, in keeping with a clear trend of contemporary psychodynamic thinking.

The interpersonal focus of much modern psychodynamic therapy, sometimes called *object-relations therapy* (Cashdan, 1988), has roots in England as well as the United States. (As was seen in Chapter

3, a major American figure in this development was Harry Stack Sullivan.) Most generally these procedures make central and build on one of Freud's most brilliant insights—that is, that a person's current relationship to the social environment is determined significantly by precedents laid down in his or her earliest relationships with significant others. While the classical analysts have tended to see these precedents as played out mainly under the special circumstances of transference in psychoanalytic treatment, interpersonal therapists hold that these precedents are in fact *always* operative in a person's relationship to all others, not just to his or her therapist.

Often these precedents, schemas about what people are like and what one may expect from them, are not only erroneous in terms of present circumstances but also quite destructive in their effects on current interpersonal functioning. Sometimes they lead to repeating the same mistakes and the same poor choices in relationships time and time again, and to the maintenance of highly dysfunctional self-fulfilling prophecies (Carson, 1982). Interpersonal and object-relations therapists tend to ignore the sorts of libidinal drives and psychic structures Freudians emphasize and tend to focus their efforts on correcting their clients' distorted views of the interpersonal environment. In this respect the approach is indistinguishable from certain aspects of cognitive therapy, although interpersonalists tend more to use their own relationship to clients as the laboratory for the latter's acquisition of new and more functional cognitive schemas.

An important variant of interpersonally based psychotherapy, Interpersonal Psychotherapy (IPT) for depression, has been developed in recent years by a group of therapist-researchers from Harvard and Yale Universities. It was featured prominently in a national study comparing various treatments for depression (see *HIGHLIGHT 18.8*, page 665).

Other differences in contemporary psychodynamic treatment have also evolved. For example, today's analytic therapists tend to place more emphasis on current ego functioning and see the ego as a developing and controlling agent in an individual's life, not merely an uncertain regulator of uncompromising drives. Thus an individual is seen as more capable of being in control and less dominated by early repressed sexuality than in traditional analysis. Although childhood events are still viewed as important formative experiences, most modern analysts also place more emphasis on clients' current life situations and less on their childhood experiences. Many of the more important of these

contemporary situations are, of course, ones involving other people, thus making for a certain rapprochement with other trends already noted.

■ Evaluation of Psychodynamic Therapy

Despite such modifications, psychodynamic therapy is still commonly criticized for being relatively time-consuming and expensive; for being based on a questionable, stultified, and cultlike theory of human nature; for neglecting a client's immediate problems in the search for unconscious conflicts in the remote past; and for inadequate proof of general effectiveness. Concerning the last of these, we actually have relatively little solid research data on the efficacy of the newer variants of psychodynamic therapy, as these tend to blend with other approaches and are difficult to disentangle from them; there is certainly no good basis for believing them to be *less* effective than other approaches.

The criticisms noted above have been mostly directed at classical psychoanalysis, and in our judgment are merited to a degree. With a few notable exceptions, analysts have been less than enthusiastic to subject their treatment outcomes to rigorous scrutiny, and when they have (see, e.g., Smith, Glass, & Miller, 1980; Wallerstein, 1989) the results have not been especially impressive, at least when considered in relation to the usually optimistic goals and considerable investments involved. Because it expects an individual to achieve insight and major personality change, psychoanalysis is also limited in its applicability. For example, it appears best suited for people who are average or above in intelligence and economically well off, and who do not suffer from severe psychopathology. In the present era of concern for "cost-effectiveness" and "accountability" in the mental therapy field, classical psychoanalysis appears increasingly to be a therapy for the elite.

Nevertheless, many individuals do feel that they have profited from psychoanalytic therapy—particularly in terms of greater self-understanding, relief from inner conflict and anxiety, and improved interpersonal relationships. Psychoanalytically oriented psychotherapy remains the treatment of choice for many individuals who are seeking extensive self-evaluation or insight into themselves. Even many behavior therapists, when they seek treatment for themselves, select this approach over behavioral methods (Gochman, Allgood, & Geer, 1982), which surely says *something* about the value they place on it.

BEHAVIOR THERAPY

Although the use of conditioning techniques in therapy has a long history, it was not until the 1960s that **behavior therapy,** the use (as originally formulated) of therapeutic procedures based on the principles of respondent and operant conditioning, really came into its own. The major reason for the long delay was the dominant position of psychoanalysis in the field. In recent years, however, the therapeutic potentialities of behavior therapy techniques have been strikingly demonstrated in dealing with a wide variety of maladaptive behaviors, and literally thousands of research publications have dealt with the systematic application of behavior-change principles to modify maladaptive behavior.

In the behavioristic perspective, as we saw in Chapter 3, a maladjusted person (unless suffering from brain pathology) is seen as differing from other people only in (a) having failed to acquire competencies needed for coping with the problems of living, (b) having learned faulty reactions or coping patterns that are being maintained by some kind of reinforcement, or (c) both. Thus a behavior therapist specifies in advance the precise maladaptive behaviors to be modified and the adaptive behaviors to be achieved, as well as the specific learning principles or procedures to be used.

Instead of exploring past traumatic events or inner conflicts to bring about personality change, behavior therapists attempt to modify behavior directly by extinguishing or counter-conditioning maladaptive reactions, such as anxiety, or by manipulating environmental contingencies—that is, by the use of reward, suspension of reward, or, occasionally, punishment to shape overt actions. Indeed, for the strict behaviorist, "personality" does not exist except in the form of a collection of modifiable habits. Behavior therapy techniques seem especially effective in altering maladaptive behavior when a reinforcement is administered contiguous with a desired response, and when a person knows what is expected and why the reinforcement is given. The ultimate goal, of course, is not only to achieve the desired responses but to bring them under the control and self-monitoring of the individual.

We have cited many examples of the application of behavior therapy in earlier chapters. In this section, we will elaborate briefly on the key techniques of behavior therapy.

■ Extinction

Because learned behavior patterns tend to weaken and disappear over time if they are not reinforced, often the simplest way to eliminate a maladaptive pattern is to remove the reinforcement for it. This is especially true in situations where maladaptive behavior has been reinforced unknowingly by others, an extremely common occurrence.

Billy, a 6-year-old first grader, was brought to a psychological clinic by his parents because he "hated school" and his teacher had told them that his showing-off behavior was disrupting the class and making him unpopular. It became apparent in observing Billy and his parents during the initial interview that both his mother and father were noncritical and approving of everything he did. After further assessment, a three-phase program of therapy was undertaken: (a) the parents were helped to discriminate between showing-off behavior and appropriate behavior on Billy's part; (b) the parents were instructed to show a loss of interest and attention when Billy engaged in showing-off behavior while continuing to show their approval of appropriate behavior; and (c) Billy's teacher was instructed to ignore Billy, insofar as it was feasible, when he engaged in showing-off behavior, and to devote her attention at those times to children who were behaving more appropriately.

Although Billy's showing-off behavior in class increased during the first few days of this behavior therapy program, it diminished markedly thereafter when it was no longer reinforced by his parents and teacher. As his maladaptive behavior diminished, he was better accepted by his classmates, which, in turn, helped reinforce more appropriate behavior patterns and changed his negative attitude toward school.

Billy's therapy, thus, was basically of the Type B sort (direct modification of abnormal behavior), as mediated by a Type E strategy—changing the environmental reaction (of his parents and teacher) to the behavior.

Two techniques that rely on the principle of extinction are *implosive therapy* and *flooding.* Both focus on extinguishing the conditioned avoidance of anxiety-arousing stimuli and can thus be used to treat anxiety disorders. Accordingly, they are primarily Type A therapies in focusing on the modification of affect. The techniques are roughly similar, except that implosive therapy involves having a client *imagine* anxiety-arousing situations, usually with much coaching and dramaturgical hype provided by a therapist; flooding, on the other hand, involves inducing a client to undergo repeated exposures to his or her *real-life* anxiety-arousing situations.

In **implosion,** clients are asked to imagine and relive aversive scenes associated with their anxiety. However, instead of trying to banish anxiety from the treatment sessions, as in the older technique of *systematic desensitization,* a therapist deliberately attempts to elicit a massive "implosion" of anxiety. This is somewhat reminiscent of psychodynamic approaches because it often deals with past trauma and with an internal conceptualization of anxiety, though most traditional analysts would doubtless strongly disapprove of the procedure. With repeated exposure in a "safe" setting, the stimulus loses its power to elicit anxiety and the neurotic avoidance behavior is extinguished. Hypnosis or drugs may be used to enhance suggestibility under implosive therapy.

In a report of an actual case, Stampfl (1975) described a young woman who could not swim and was terrified of water—particularly of sinking under the water. Although she knew it was irrational, she was so terrified of water "that she wore a life preserver when she took a bath" (p. 66). She was instructed by the therapist to imagine in minute detail taking a bath without a life preserver in a "bottomless" tub, and slipping under the water. Initially, the client showed intense anxiety, and the scene was repeated over and over. In addition, she was given a "homework" assignment in which she was asked to imagine herself drowning. Eventually, after imagining the worst and finding that nothing happened, her anxiety diminished. After the fourteenth therapy session, she was able to take baths without feelings of anxiety; the maladaptive behavior had been effectively extinguished. Implosion techniques are sometimes referred to as *in vitro* desensitization.

Flooding, or *in vivo* procedures, which involve placing an individual in a real-life situation as opposed to a therapeutic setting, may be used with individuals who do not imagine scenes realistically. For example, a client with a phobia of heights may be taken to the top of a tall building or bridge. This is another means of exposing the client to the anxiety-eliciting stimulus and demonstrating that the feared consequences do not occur. In a study of clients with agoraphobia (fear of open spaces),

Flooding is a technique that involves placing an individual in a real-life, anxiety-arousing situation with the goal of extinguishing the conditioned avoidance of an anxiety-provoking stimulus. For example, a client with a fear of heights may be taken to the top of a tall building to demonstrate that the feared consequences do not occur.

Emmelkamp and Wessels (1975) concluded that prolonged exposure *in vivo* plainly proved superior to simple reliance on the imagination, and in the past few years the flooding procedure seems to have gained a definite ascendancy over that of implosion (Barlow, 1988).

Reports on the effectiveness of implosive therapy and flooding have generally been favorable, and they may be considered the treatments of choice for simple phobias (Foa & Kozak, 1985). Some investigators, however, have reported unfavorable as well as favorable results (Emmelkamp & Wessels, 1975; Mealiea, 1967; Wolpe, 1969b). These mixed results appear to be particularly true of flooding *in vivo.* For example, Emmelkamp and Wessels (1975) found that flooding *in vivo* was terrifying for some clients. In one case, the agoraphobic client "hid in a cellar out of fear of being sent into the street for 90 minutes by the therapist" (p. 14). On the other hand, the flooding procedure can be made relatively bearable without diminished effectiveness for even a severely fearful client by increasing therapist support and active guidance during exposure, as was recently demonstrated by Williams and Zane

(1989) in a study also involving the treatment of agoraphobia.

In general, it appears that while many clients respond favorably to implosion or flooding, some do not respond, and a few suffer an exacerbation of their phobias. This finding suggests a need for caution in the use of these techniques, particularly because they involve experiences that may be highly traumatic.

A modified form of flooding that involves repeated exposure to the somatic cues—"false alarms" (Barlow, 1988)—usually preceding panic (for example, heart palpitations), rather than to traumatizing situations themselves, may provide a key to circumventing undesirable reactions to exposure treatment. Accumulating evidence shows that it is these sorts of cues that in fact trigger full-blown anxiety attacks, and Barlow and associates (e.g., Barlow et al., 1989) have developed effective procedures for extinguishing this type of chain reaction, for example, by teaching clients to self-induce their false alarm symptoms repeatedly. In a recent important study in which the exposure to anticipatory cues procedure was a centerpiece in a treatment package for panic disorder, effectiveness was demonstrated to be far superior to drug treatment with alprazolam (Xanax), a benzodiazepine compound touted as having strong antipanic properties (Klosko et al., 1990).

■ Systematic Desensitization

The process of extinction can be applied to behavior that is positively reinforced or negatively reinforced. Of the two, behavior that is *negatively* reinforced—reinforced by the successful *avoidance* of a painful situation—is harder to deal with. Because an individual with negatively reinforced maladaptive behavior becomes anxious and withdraws at the first sign of the painful situation, he or she never gets a chance to find out whether the expected aversive consequences do in fact come about. In addition, the avoidance is anxiety-reducing and hence is itself reinforced.

One technique that has proven especially useful in extinguishing negatively reinforced behavior involves eliciting an antagonistic or competing response. Because it is difficult if not impossible to feel both pleasant and anxious at the same time, the method of **systematic desensitization** is aimed at teaching an individual to relax or behave in some other way that is inconsistent with anxiety while in the presence (real or imagined) of the anxiety-producing stimulus. The term *systematic* refers to the carefully graduated manner in which the person

is exposed to the feared stimulus, the procedural opposite of implosion and flooding. It should be pointed out that systematic desensitization is not used *exclusively* to deal with avoidance behaviors brought about by negative reinforcement—that is, by successfully avoiding aversive experience. It can be used for other kinds of behavioral problems as well. In general, however, it is a Type A therapeutic procedure aimed at anxiety reduction.

The prototype of this approach is the classic experiment of Jones (1924), in which she successfully eliminated a small boy's conditioned fears of a white rabbit and other furry animals. First she brought the rabbit just inside the door at the far end of the room while the boy, Peter, was eating. On successive days, the rabbit was gradually brought closer until Peter could pat it with one hand while eating with the other.

Wolpe (1958; Rachman & Hodgson, 1980) elaborated on the procedure developed by Jones and devised the term *systematic desensitization* to refer to it. On the assumption that most anxiety-based patterns are, fundamentally, conditioned responses, Wolpe worked out a way to train a client to remain calm and relaxed in situations that formerly produced anxiety. Wolpe's approach is elegant in its simplicity, and his method is equally straightforward.

Because more direct techniques of guided exposure, such as implosion and flooding, appear in recent years to have supplanted systematic desensitization to a large extent, our description of the latter procedure can be brief. A client is first taught to induce a state of relaxation, typically by progressive concentration on the relaxing of various muscle groups. Meanwhile, in collaboration with the therapist, an "anxiety hierarchy" is constructed consisting of imagined scenes graded as to their capacity to elicit anxiety. For example, were the problem one of disabling sexual anxiety, a low-anxiety scene might be a candlelight dinner with the prospective partner, while a high-anxiety scene might be imagining the penis actually entering the vagina.

Following these preliminaries, active therapy sessions consist of repeatedly imagining the scenes in the hierarchy under conditions of deep relaxation, beginning with the minimum anxiety items and gradually working toward those rated in the more extreme ranges. A session is terminated at any point where the client reports experiencing significant anxiety, the next session resuming at a lower point in the hierarchy. Treatment continues until all items in the hierarchy can be tolerated without notable discomfort, by which point the client's real-life difficulties will typically have shown substantial improvement. The usual duration of a

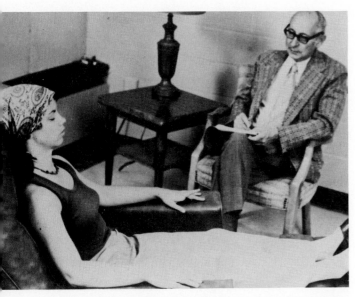

Joseph Wolpe is shown here conducting systematic desensitization therapy to reduce a client's anxiety. The client, in a relaxed state, is told to imagine the weakest anxiety on her list of anxiety-producing stimuli. If she feels anxious, she is instructed to stop imagining and relax again.

desensitization session is about 30 minutes, and the sessions are often given two to three times per week. The overall therapy program may, of course, take a number of weeks or even months. Kennedy and Kimura (1974) have shown, however, that even clients who have progressed only 25 to 50 percent of the way through their anxiety hierarchy show significant therapeutic gains, as evidenced by a marked reduction in specific avoidance behaviors when compared with their pretreatment levels.

Several variants of systematic desensitization have been devised. One variation involves the use of a tape recorder to enable a client to carry out the desensitization process at home. Another utilizes group desensitization procedures—as in "marathon" desensitization groups, in which the entire program is compressed into a few days of intensive treatment. One of the present authors routinely employs hypnosis to induce relaxation (the standard relaxation training can be quite tedious) and to achieve vividness in the imagining of hierarchy scenes. Perhaps the most important variation is *in vivo* desensitization, which is essentially similar to flooding but typically involves graduated exposure to the feared situations after a state of relaxation has been attained.

You will probably have concluded by this point that the truly essential element in the behavioral treatment of anxiety is repeated *exposure* of a client to the stimuli, even if only imaginarily, that elicit the fear response, regardless of the methods em-

ployed in achieving that end. Despite some continued wrangling among proponents of one or another specific procedure, that conclusion appears to be fair and accurate. Where a therapist has a choice—that is, depending on client cooperation and tolerance—*in vivo* procedures seem to have an edge in efficiency and possibly in ultimate efficacy over those employing imagery as the mode of confrontation. Overall, the outcome record for exposure treatments is impressive (Emmelkamp, 1986).

■ Aversion Therapy

Aversion therapy involves modifying undesirable behavior by the old-fashioned method of punishment. Punishment may involve either the removal of desired reinforcers or the use of aversive stimuli, but the basic idea is to reduce the "temptation value" of stimuli that elicit undesirable behavior. The most commonly used aversive stimulus is electric shock, although drugs may also be used. As we will see, however, punishment is rarely employed as the sole method of treatment.

Apparently the first formal use of aversion therapy was made by Kantorovich (1930), who administered electric shocks to alcoholics in association with the sight, smell, and taste of alcohol, an early version of the Antabuse drug treatment in use today. Since that time, aversion therapy has been used in the treatment of a wide range of maladaptive behaviors, including smoking, drinking, overeating, drug dependence, gambling, sexual variants, and bizarre psychotic behavior. As normally employed, it is a Type B therapeutic procedure. Because we have described the use of aversion therapy in the course of our discussion of abnormal behavior patterns, we will restrict ourselves here to a review of a few brief examples and principles.

Lovaas (1977) found punishment by electric shock to be effective in extreme cases of severely disturbed autistic children. In one case, a 7-year-old autistic boy, diagnosed as severely retarded, had to be kept in restraints 24 hours a day because he would continually beat his head with his fists or bang it against the walls of his crib, inflicting serious injuries. Though it may seem paradoxical to employ punishment to reduce the frequency of self-destructive behavior, electric shock following this behavior was nevertheless effective, bringing about complete inhibition of the maladaptive behavior pattern in a relatively short time (Bucher & Lovaas, 1967).

The use of electric shock as an aversive stimulus, however, has generally diminished in recent years because of the ethical and "image" problems involved in its use and because the new behaviors induced by it do not automatically generalize to other settings (Harris & Ersner-Hershfield, 1978). Also, less dangerous and more effective procedures have been found. The method of choice today is probably differential reinforcement of other responses (DOR), in which behaviors incompatible with the undesired behavior are positively reinforced. For example, for a child who indulges in antisocial, destructive behavior, positive reinforcement might be used for every sign of constructive play. At the same time, any reinforcement that has been maintaining maladaptive behavior is removed. Lovaas and his colleagues, who reported the successful use of electric shock with autistic children, have themselves recommended the use of nonpunitive treatment for self-injurious behavior (Russo, Carr, & Lovaas, 1980).

Aversion therapy is primarily a way—often a very effective one—of stopping maladaptive responses for a period of time. With this interruption, an opportunity exists for substituting new behavior or for changing a life-style by encouraging more adaptive alternative patterns that will prove reinforcing in themselves. This point is particularly important because otherwise a client may simply refrain from maladaptive responses in "unsafe" therapy situations, where such behavior leads to immediate aversive results, but keep making them in "safe" real-life situations, where there is no fear of immediate discomfort. Also, there is little likelihood that a previously gratifying but maladaptive behavior pattern will be permanently relinquished unless alternative forms of gratification are learned during the aversion therapy. A therapist who believes it possible to "take away" something without "giving something back" is likely to be disappointed. This is an important point in regard to the treatment of addictions and paraphilias, one often not appreciated in otherwise well-designed treatment programs.

◼ Modeling

As Bandura (1977b) has pointed out,

Learning would be exceedingly laborious, not to mention hazardous, if people had to rely solely on the effects of their own actions to inform them what to do. Fortunately, most human behavior is learned observationally through modeling: from observing others one forms an idea of how new behaviors are performed, and on later occasions this coded information serves as a guide for action. Because people can learn from example what to do, at least in

approximate form, before performing any behavior, they are spared needless error. (p. 22)

Although reinforcement of modeled behavior can influence whether an observer-learner attends to a model's actions and strengthens the response imitated, observational learning does not seem to require extrinsic reinforcement. Rather, according to Bandura, reinforcement functions as a facilitative condition to learning. Anticipation of a reinforcement may also make an individual more likely to perform a behavior.

As the name implies, **modeling** involves the learning of skills through imitating another person, such as a parent or therapist who perform the behavior; as such, it is a Type B procedure. A client may be exposed to behaviors or roles in peers or therapists and encouraged to imitate the desired new behaviors. For example, modeling may be used to promote the learning of simple skills, such as self-feeding in a profoundly mentally retarded child, or more complex ones, such as being more effective in social situations for a shy, withdrawn adolescent.

As we have noted, modeling and imitation are used in various forms of behavior therapy. Bandura (1964) found that live modeling of fearlessness combined with instruction and guided participation is the most effective desensitization treatment, resulting in the elimination of snake phobias in over 90 percent of the cases treated.

◼ Systematic Use of Reinforcement

Systematic programs involving the use of reinforcement to elicit and maintain effective behavior (Type B therapy) have achieved notable success, particularly in institutional settings. Response shaping, token economies, and behavioral contracting are among the most widely used of such techniques.

Response Shaping   Positive reinforcement is often used in **response shaping;** that is, in establishing by gradual approximation a response that is not initially in an individual's behavior repertoire. This technique has been used extensively in working with children's behavior problems. The following case reported by Wolf, Risley, and Mees (1964) is illustrative:

> *A 3-year-old autistic boy lacked nominal verbal and social behavior. He did not eat properly, engaged in self-destructive behavior, such as*

banging his head and scratching his face, and manifested ungovernable tantrums. He had recently had a cataract operation, and required glasses for the development of normal vision. He refused to wear his glasses, however, and broke pair after pair.

The technique of shaping was decided on to counteract the problem with his glasses. Initially, the boy was trained to expect a bit of candy or fruit at the sound of a toy noisemaker. Then training was begun with empty eyeglass frames. First the boy was reinforced with the candy or fruit for picking them up, then for holding them, then for carrying them around, then for bringing the frames closer to the eyes, and then for putting the empty frames on his head at any angle. Through successive approximations, the boy finally learned to wear his glasses up to twelve hours a day.

Token Economies   Approval and other intangible reinforcers may be ineffective in behavior therapy programs, especially those dealing with severely maladaptive behavior. In such instances, appropriate behaviors maybe rewarded with tangible reinforcers in the form of tokens that can later be exchanged for desired objects or privileges (Kazdin, 1980). In working with hospitalized schizophrenic clients, for example, Ayllon and Azrin (1968) found that using the commissary, listening to records, and going to movies were considered highly desirable activities by most clients. Consequently, these activities were chosen as reinforcers for socially appropriate behavior. To participate in any of them, a client had to earn a number of tokens by demonstrating appropriate ward behavior. In Chapter 19, we will describe another token economy program, an extraordinarily successful one, with chronic hospitalized clients who had been considered resistant to treatment (Paul, 1982; Paul & Lentz, 1977).

Token economies have been used to establish adaptive behaviors ranging from elementary responses, such as eating and making one's bed, to the daily performance of responsible hospital jobs. In the latter instance, the token economy resembles the outside world where an individual is paid for his or her work in tokens (money) that can later be exchanged for desired objects and activities. The use of tokens as reinforcers for appropriate behavior has a number of distinct advantages: (a) the number of tokens earned depends directly on the amount of desirable behavior shown; (b) tokens, like money in the outside world, may be made a general medium of currency in terms of what they will "purchase"; hence they are not readily subject to satiation and tend to maintain their incentive value; (c) tokens can reduce the delay that often occurs between appropriate performance and reinforcement; (d) the number of tokens earned and the way in which they are "spent" are largely up to the client; and (e) tokens tend to bridge the gap between the institutional environment and the demands and system of payment that will be encountered in the outside world.

The ultimate goal in token economies, as in other programs of extrinsic reinforcement, is not only to achieve desired responses but to bring such responses to a level where their adaptive consequences will be reinforcing in their own right—thus enabling natural rather than artificial rewards to maintain the desired behavior. For example, extrinsic reinforcers may be used initially to help children overcome reading difficulties, but once a child becomes proficient in reading, this skill will presumably provide intrinsic reinforcement as the child comes to enjoy reading for its own sake.

Although their effectiveness has been clearly demonstrated with chronic schizophrenic clients, mentally retarded residents in institutional settings, and children, the use of token economies has declined in recent years. In part, this decline is a result of budget-inspired reductions in trained hospital treatment staffs, which are required for the effective management of such programs. Ironically, the corollary excessive reliance on medication, which in our judgment has little likelihood of enhancing independent living skills, is probably far more expensive in the long run. Token economies are also poorly understood by lay persons, many of whom see them as inhumane or crassly manipulative. If these people are "sick," so the thought goes, they should have medicine and not be expected to "perform" for simple amenities. Unfortunately, such thinking makes for chronic social disability.

Behavioral Contracting   A technique called **behavioral contracting** is used in some types of psychotherapy and behavior therapy to identify and agree on the behaviors that are to be changed and to maximize the probability that these changes will occur and be maintained (Nelson & Mowry, 1976). By definition, a contract is an agreement between two or more parties—such as a therapist and a client, a parent and a teenager, or a husband and a wife—that governs the nature of an exchange. The agreement, often in writing, specifies a client's obligations to change as well as the responsibilities

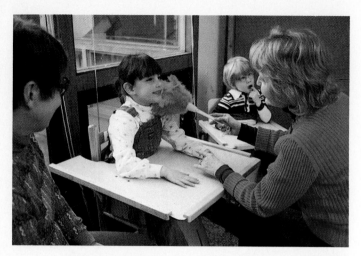

Positive reinforcement is an effective technique for managing behavior problems, with food or other treats or privileges often used as reinforcers. This autistic child is being reinforced for some positive behavior by being stroked with a feather tickler.

of the other party to provide something the client wants in return, such as tangible rewards, privileges, or therapeutic attention. Behavior therapists frequently make behavioral contracting an explicit focus of treatment, thus helping establish the treatment as a joint enterprise for which both parties have responsibility.

Behavioral contracting can facilitate therapy in several ways: (a) the structuring of the treatment relationship can be explicitly stated, giving the client a clear idea of each person's role in the treatment; (b) the actual responsibilities of the client are outlined and a system of rewards is built in for changed behavior; (c) the limitations of the treatment, in terms of the length and focus of the sessions, are specified; (d) by agreement, some behaviors (for example, the client's sexual orientation) may be eliminated from the treatment focus, thereby establishing the "appropriate content" of the treatment sessions; (e) clear treatment goals can be defined; and (f) criteria for determining success or failure in achieving these goals can be built in to the program.

Sometimes a contract is negotiated between a disruptive child and a teacher, according to which the child will maintain or receive certain privileges as long as he or she behaves in accordance with the contract. Usually the school principal is also a party to such a contract to ensure the enforcement of certain conditions that the teacher may not be in a position to enforce, such as removing the child from the classroom for engaging in certain types of misbehavior.

■ Assertiveness Therapy

Assertiveness therapy or training has been used as an alternative to relaxation in the desensitization procedure and as a means of developing more effective coping techniques. It appears particularly useful in helping individuals who have difficulties in interpersonal interactions because of anxiety responses that may prevent them from speaking up, claiming their rights, or even from showing appropriate affection. Such inhibition may lead to continual inner turmoil, particularly if an individual feels strongly about a situation. Assertiveness therapy may also be indicated in cases where individuals consistently allow others to take advantage of them or maneuver them into uncomfortable situations.

Assertiveness is viewed as the open and appropriate expression of thoughts and feelings, with due regard to the rights of others. Assertiveness training programs typically follow stages in which the desired assertive behaviors are first practiced in a therapy setting. Then, guided by the therapist, the individual is encouraged to practice the new, more appropriately assertive behaviors in real-life situations. Often attention is focused on developing more effective interpersonal skills. For example, a client may learn to ask the other person such questions as "Is anything wrong? You don't seem to be your usual self today." Such questions put the focus on the other person without suggesting an aggressive or hostile intent on the part of the speaker. Each act of intentional assertion is believed to inhibit the anxiety associated with the situation and therefore to weaken the maladaptive anxiety-response pattern. At the same time, it tends to foster more adaptive interpersonal behaviors. Assertiveness therapy is a Type B procedure.

Although assertiveness therapy is a highly useful procedure in certain types of situations, it does have limitations. For example, Wolpe (1969b) has pointed out that it is largely irrelevant for phobias involving nonpersonal stimuli. It may also be of little use in some types of interpersonal situations; for instance, if an individual has in fact been rejected by someone, assertive behavior may tend to aggravate rather than resolve the problem. However, in interpersonal situations where maladaptive anxiety can be traced to lack of self-assertiveness, this type of therapy appears particularly effective.

■ Biofeedback Treatment

For many years it was generally believed that voluntary control over physiological processes, such as heart rate, galvanic skin response, and blood pressure, was not possible. In the early 1960s, however, this view began to change. A number of investigators, aided by the development of sensitive electronic instruments that could accurately measure physiological responses, demonstrated that many of the processes formerly thought to be "involuntary" were modifiable by learning procedures—operant learning and classical conditioning. Kimmel (1974) demonstrated, for example, that the galvanic skin response could be conditioned by operant learning techniques.

The importance of the autonomic nervous system in the development of abnormal behavior has long been recognized. For example, autonomic arousal is an important factor in anxiety states. Thus many researchers have applied techniques developed in the autonomic conditioning studies in an attempt to modify the internal environment of troubled individuals to bring about more adaptive behavior—for instance, to modify heart rates in clients with irregular heartbeats (Weiss & Engel, 1971), to treat stuttering by feeding back information on the electric potential of muscles in the speech apparatus (Lanyon, Barrington, & Newman, 1976), and to reduce lower-back pain (Wolf, Nacht, & Kelly, 1982) and chronic headaches (Blanchard et al., 1983).

This treatment approach—in which a person is taught to influence his or her own physiological processes—is referred to as **biofeedback.** Several steps are typical in the process of biofeedback treatment: (a) monitoring the physiological response that is to be modified (perhaps blood pressure or skin temperature); (b) converting the information to a visual or auditory signal; and (c) providing a means of prompt feedback—indicating to a subject as rapidly as possible when the desired change is taking place (Blanchard & Epstein, 1978). Given this feedback, the subject may then seek to reduce his or her emotionality, as by lowering the skin temperature. For the most part, biofeedback is oriented to reducing the reactivity of some organ system innervated by the autonomic nervous system—specifically, a physiological component of the anxiety response. Hence we consider biofeedback to be principally a Type A therapy.

Biofeedback treatment is a popular treatment approach that requires the investment of capital to purchase complicated equipment and, in larger centers, a cadre of semiprofessional biofeedback technicians to perform the treatment. Whether its effectiveness justifies this expense is not an easily answered question. Although there is general agreement that many physiological processes can be regulated to some extent by learning, the application of biofeedback procedures to alter abnormal behavior has produced equivocal results. Demonstrations of clinical biofeedback applications abound, but carefully controlled research has not sufficiently supported earlier impressions of clinically significant improvement.

Blanchard and Young (1973, 1974) pointed out that the effects of biofeedback procedures are generally small and often do not generalize to situations outside the laboratory, where the biofeedback devices are not present. Two well-controlled studies have failed to show a treatment effect for biofeedback with migraine clients (Kewman & Roberts, 1979) and Raynaud's disease clients (Gugliemi, 1979). In addition, biofeedback has not been shown to be any more effective than relaxation training, leading to the suggestion that biofeedback may simply be a more elaborate (and usually more costly) means of teaching clients relaxation (Blanchard & Epstein, 1978; Blanchard et al., 1980; Tarler-Benliolo, 1978). As with almost any treatment procedure, however, a small percentage of clients may show an unusually good response with biofeedback.

■ Evaluation of Behavior Therapy

As compared with psychoanalytic and other psychotherapies, behavior therapy appears to have three distinct advantages. First, the treatment approach is precise. The target behaviors to be modified are specified, the methods to be used are clearly delineated, and the results can be readily evaluated (Marks, 1982). Second, the use of explicit learning principles is a sound basis for effective interventions as a result of their demonstrated scientific validity (Kazdin & Wilson, 1978). Third, the economy of time and costs is quite good. Not surprisingly, then, the overall outcomes achieved with behavior therapy compare favorably with those of other approaches (Smith, Glass, & Miller, 1980). Behavior therapy usually achieves results in a short period of time because it is generally directed to specific symptoms, leading to faster relief of an individual's distress and to lower financial costs. In addition, more people can be treated by a given therapist.

As with other approaches, the range of effectiveness of behavior therapy is not unlimited, and it works better with certain kinds of problems than with others. Generally speaking, the more pervasive and vaguely defined the client problem, the less likely is behavior therapy to be useful. For example, it appears to be only rarely employed to treat Axis II personality disorders, where specific symptoms are rare. On the other hand, behavioral techniques are the backbone of modern approaches to treating sexual dysfunctions, as discussed in Chapter 10. The meta-analysis of therapeutic outcomes confirms the expectation that behavior therapy has a particular place in the treatment of "neurotic" disorders, particularly where anxiety is a manifest feature, and therefore where the powerful Type A exposure techniques of behavior therapy can be brought to bear (Andrews & Harvey, 1981; Smith, Glass, & Miller, 1980). Smith et al.'s (1980) analysis in fact reveals the less expected finding of a relatively good outcome record with the psychoses. Thus, although behavior therapy is not a cureall, it has earned in a relatively brief period a highly respected place among the available psychosocial treatment approaches.

COGNITIVE–BEHAVIORAL THERAPY

Early behavior therapists focused on observable behavior. They regarded the inner thoughts of their clients at best as not really part of the causal chain, and in their zeal to be objective they focused on the relationship between observable behaviors and observable reinforcing conditions. Thus they were often viewed as mechanistic technicians who simply manipulated their subjects without considering them as people. More recently, however, a number of behavior therapists have reappraised the importance of "private events"—thoughts, perceptions, evaluations, and self-statements—seeing them as processes that mediate the effects of objective stimulus conditions and thus help determine behavior (Borkovec, 1985; Mahoney & Arnkoff, 1978).

Homme (1965), a student of Skinner, began this exodus from strict behaviorism in a paper arguing that these private events were behaviors that could be objectively analyzed. He proposed, as had Dollard and Miller (1950) earlier, that thoughts be regarded as emitted internal events comparable to emitted external behaviors, and that a technology be developed for modifying thoughts by using the same learning principles that were proving so effective in changing outer behavior. These internal, private events he called *coverants,* considering them to be operants of the mind. Following Homme's "coverant behaviorism," many investigators began

to apply conditioning principles to covert events, such as thoughts and assumptions.

Cognitive-behavioral therapy, as the term suggests, stems from both cognitive psychology, with its emphasis on the effects of thoughts on behavior, and behaviorism, with its rigorous methodology and performance-oriented focus. At the present time, there is no single method of operation in cognitive-behavioral therapy: numerous methods are being developed with varying foci. Two main themes seem to characterize them all, however: (a) the conviction that cognitive processes influence both motivation and behavior, and (b) the use of behavior-change techniques in a pragmatic (hypothesis-testing) manner. That is, the therapy sessions are analogous to experiments in which a therapist and a client apply learning principles to alter the client's cognitions, continuously evaluating the effects that the changes in cognitions have on both thoughts and outer behavior.

The exact nature of the relationship between thought and behavior, a venerable problem whose philosophical roots go back to the distant past, is far from clear even today. Can it be, for example, that thoughts, by some accounts ephemeral and imma-

Here an actor using a case history of a real person (for purposes of telecourse instruction) plays Tom, seeking help from a professional psychotherapist because he is having serious problems at work dealing with his boss. The therapist uses a cognitive-behavioral model in working with Tom. She views his complaints as stemming from faulty thinking and attempts to help Tom develop new thought patterns that will lead to more productive behavior. The therapist and Tom role-play new behavior and new ways of communicating that will help Tom cope with his boss and blame himself less when there are problems. With a more realistic picture of his situation, Tom will be able to realize that he is not a failure because his supervisor devalues his work and that he may have to change jobs to be appreciated.

terial in nature, *cause* behavior? Any serious discussion of such an issue would take us far afield indeed, but it is important to understand that the intellectual status of cognitive therapy fuels some controversy. Beck (Beck & Weishaar, 1989), an important leader in the field, acknowledges that disordered cognitions are not a *cause* of abnormal behavior, but rather are an intrinsic (yet alterable) *element* of such behavior. If the critical cognitive components of the behavior can be changed, according to this view, then the behavior will change. Because altering cognitions is central in these therapies, we consider them to be Type C approaches. In our discussion, we will focus on three approaches to cognitive-behavioral therapy: the rational-emotive therapy of Ellis, the cognitive therapy of Beck, and the stress-inoculation training illustrated by the work of Meichenbaum.

■ Rational–Emotive Therapy (RET)

One of the earliest behaviorally oriented cognitive therapies was the **rational-emotive therapy (RET)** of Ellis (1958, 1973, 1975, 1989). RET attempts to change a client's basic maladaptive thought processes, on which maladaptive emotional responses and thus behavior are presumed to depend. In its infancy, RET was viewed skeptically by many professionals who doubted its effectiveness, but it has now become one of the most widely used therapeutic approaches (Ellis, 1989).

Ellis posited that a well-functioning individual behaves rationally and in tune with empirical reality. For Ellis, thoughts do have causal primacy in behavior, notably *emotional* behavior. Unfortunately, many of us have learned unrealistic beliefs and perfectionistic values that cause us to expect too much of ourselves, leading us to behave irrationally and then to feel unnecessarily that we are worthless failures. For example, a person may continually think, "I should be able to win everyone's love and approval" or "I should be thoroughly adequate and competent in everything I do." Such unrealistic assumptions and self-demands inevitably lead to ineffective and self-defeating behavior in the real world, which reacts accordingly, and then to the recognition of failure and the emotional response of self-devaluation. This emotional response is thus the necessary consequence not of "reality," but of an individual's faulty expectations, interpretations, and self-demands.

As a more specific example, consider a man who has an intense emotional reaction of despair with deep feelings of worthlessness, unlovability, and self-devaluation when he is jilted by his fiancée. With a stronger self-concept and a more realistic picture of both himself and his fiancée, as well as of their actual relationship, his emotional reaction might have been one of relief. It is his interpretation of the situation and of himself, rather than the objective situation, that has led to his intense emotional reaction.

Ellis (1970) believed that one or more of the following core irrational beliefs are at the root of most psychological maladjustment:

- One should be loved by everyone for everything one does.
- Certain acts are awful or wicked, and people who perform them should be severely punished.
- It is horrible when things are not the way we would like them to be.
- Human misery is produced by external causes, or outside people, or events, rather than by the view that one takes of these conditions.
- If something may be dangerous or fearsome, one should be terribly upset about it.
- It is better to avoid life problems if possible than to face them.
- One needs something stronger or more powerful than oneself to rely on.
- One should be thoroughly competent, intelligent, and achieving in all respects.
- Because something once affected one's life, it will indefinitely affect it.
- One must have certain and perfect self-control.
- Happiness can be achieved by inertia and inaction.
- We have virtually no control over our emotions and cannot help having certain feelings.

Irrationality can, however, be viewed in different ways. Arnkoff and Glass (1982) cautioned against an overly simplistic view of irrational behavior as the mere holding of irrational beliefs. Rather, they contended that irrationality may also involve faulty thought processes reflecting a "closed-mindedness" that is more resistant to change than Ellis's view suggests.

The task of rational-emotive therapy is to restructure an individual's belief system and self-evaluation, especially with respect to the irrational "shoulds," "oughts," and "musts" that are preventing a more positive sense of self-worth and a creative, emotionally satisfying, and fulfilling life. Several methods are used.

One method is to *dispute* a person's false beliefs through rational confrontation. For example, a therapist dealing with the jilted young man previously discussed might ask, "Why should your fiancée's changing her mind mean that *you* are worthless?" Here the therapist would teach the client to identify and dispute the beliefs that were producing the negative emotional consequences.

A rational-emotive therapist also uses behaviorally oriented techniques to bring about changed thoughts and behaviors. Sometimes, for example, homework assignments are given to encourage clients to have new experiences and break negative chains of behavior. For example, clients might be instructed to reward themselves by an external reinforcer, such as a food treat, after working 15 minutes at disputing their beliefs. Another method of self-reinforcement might be through covert statements such as "You are doing a really good job."

In some ways, rational-emotive therapy can be viewed as a *humanistic* therapy (to be discussed in a later section) because it takes a clear stand on personal worth and human values. Rational-emotive therapy aims at increasing an individual's feelings of self-worth and clearing the way for self-actualization by removing the false beliefs that have been stumbling blocks to personal growth.

■ Cognitive–Behavioral Therapy for Depression

Beck's cognitive-behavioral therapy was developed for the treatment of depression (Beck et al., 1979; Hollon & Beck, 1978) and was later extended to anxiety disorders and phobias (Beck, 1985; Beck & Emery, 1985). One basic assumption underlying this approach is that problems like depression result from clients' illogical thinking about themselves, the world they live in, and the future. These illogical ideas are maintained even in the face of contradictory evidence because the individuals typically engage in self-defeating and self-fulfilling behaviors in which they (a) *selectively perceive* the world as harmful while ignoring evidence to the contrary; (b) *overgeneralize* on the basis of limited examples—for example, seeing themselves as totally worthless because they were laid off at work; (c) *magnify* the significance of undesirable events—for example, seeing the job loss as the end of the world for them; and (d) *engage in absolutistic thinking*—for example, exaggerating the importance of someone's mildly

critical comment and perceiving it as proof of their instant descent from goodness to worthlessness.

In Beck's cognitive-behavioral therapy, however, clients are not persuaded to change their beliefs by debate and persuasion as in rational-emotive therapy; rather, they are encouraged to gather information about themselves through unbiased experiments that allow them to discomfirm their false beliefs. Together, a therapist and an individual identify the individual's assumptions, beliefs, and expectations and formulate them as hypotheses to be tested. They then design ways in which the individual can check out these hypotheses in the world. These behavior-disconfirmation experiments are planned to give the individual successful experiences, thereby interrupting the destructive loop previously described. They are arranged according to difficulty, so that the least difficult tasks will be accomplished successfully before the more difficult ones are attempted (see *HIGHLIGHT 18.4*).

Sometimes a client and a therapist schedule the client's daily activities on an hour-by-hour basis. Such activity scheduling is an important part of therapy with depressed individuals because by reducing such clients' inactivity, it interrupts their tendencies to ruminate about themselves. An important part of the arrangement is the scheduling of pleasurable events because many depressed clients have lost the capacity for gaining pleasure from their own activities. Both the scheduled pleasurable activities and the rewarding experiences from carrying out the behavioral experiments tend to increase an individual's satisfaction and positive mood.

Besides planning the behavioral assignments, evaluating the results in subsequent sessions, and planning further disconfirmation experiments, such therapy sessions include several other cognitive foci. For example, an individual is encouraged to discover underlying assumptions and "automatic thoughts" that may be leading to self-defeating tendencies. With this background, the individual is taught to self-monitor his or her thought content and to keep challenging its validity.

■ Stress-Inoculation Therapy

A third cognitive-behavioral approach to treatment is **stress-inoculation therapy**—a type of self-instructional training focused on altering self-statements that an individual is routinely making in order to restructure his or her characteristic approach to stress-producing situations (Meichenbaum & Cameron, 1982). Like other cognitive-behavioral therapies, stress-inoculation therapy as-

Cognitive–Behavioral Therapy for a Case of Depression

Rush, Khatami, and Beck (1975) have reported several cases of successful treatment using cognitive clarification and behavioral assignments for clients with recurring chronic depression. The following case illustrates their approach:

A 53-year-old white male engineer's initial depressive episode 15 years ago necessitated several months' absence from work. Following medication and psychotherapy, he was asymptomatic up to four years ago. At that time, sadness, pessimism, loss of appetite and weight, and heavy use of alcohol returned.

Two years later, he was hospitalized for six weeks and treated with lithium and imipramine. He had three subsequent hospitalizations with adequate trials of several different tricyclics. During his last hospitalization, two weeks prior to initiating cognitive-behavioral therapy, he was treated with 10 sessions of ECT. His symptoms were only partially relieved with these various treatments.

When the client started cognitive-behavioral therapy, he showed moderate psychomotor retardation. He was anxious, sad, tearful, and pessimistic. He was self-depreciating and self-reproachful without any interest in life. He reported decreased appetite, early morning awakening, lack of sexual interest, and worries about his physical health. Initially he was treated with weekly sessions for 3 months, then biweekly for 2 months. Treatment, termi-

nated after 5 months, consisted of 20 sessions. He was evaluated 12 months after the conclusion of therapy.

Therapist and client set an initial goal of his becoming physically active (i.e., doing more things no matter how small or trivial). The client and his wife kept a separate list of his activities. The list included raking leaves, having dinner, and assisting his wife in apartment sales, etc. His cognitive distortions were identified by comparing his assessment of each activity with that of his wife. Alternative ways of interpreting his experiences were then considered.

In comparing his wife's resume of his past experiences, he became aware that he had (1) undervalued his past by failing to mention many previous accomplishments, (2) regarded himself as far more responsible for his "failures" than she did, and (3) concluded that he was worthless since he had not succeeded in attaining certain goals in the past. When the two accounts were contrasted he could discern many of his cognitive distortions. In subsequent sessions, his wife continued to serve as an "objectifier."

In midtherapy, the client compiled a list of new attitudes that he had acquired since initiating therapy.

These included:

(1) I am starting at a lower level of functioning at my job, but it will improve if I persist.

(2) I know that once I get

going in the morning, everything will run all right for the rest of the day.

(3) I can't achieve everything at once.

(4) I have my periods of ups and downs, but in the long run I feel better.

(5) My expectations from my job and life should be scaled down to a realistic level.

(6) Giving in to avoidance never helps and only leads to further avoidance.

He was instructed to re-read this list daily for several weeks even though he already knew the content. The log was continued, and subsequent assumptions reflected in the log were compared to the assumptions listed above.

As the client became gradually less depressed, he returned to his job for the first time in 2 years. He undertook new activities (e.g., camping, going out of town) as he continued his log. (pp. 400–401)

The focus of the therapy was on encouraging the client to restructure his thought content—to reduce the negative self-judgments and to evaluate his actual achievements more realistically. Making and reviewing the list of new attitudes gave the client more perspective on his life situation, which resulted in an improved mood, less self-blame, and more willingness to risk alternative behavior.

sumes that an individual's problems result from maladaptive beliefs that are leading to negative emotional states and maladaptive behavior, familiar elements in the loop we have posited.

Stress-inoculation therapy usually involves three stages. In the initial phase, *cognitive preparation,* client and therapist together explore the client's beliefs and attitudes about the problem situation and the self-statements to which they are leading. The focus is on how the individual's self-talk can influence later performance and behavior. Together, the therapist and the client agree on new self-statements that would be more adaptive. Then the second phase of the stress inoculation, *skill acquisition and rehearsal,* is begun. In this phase, more adaptive self-statements are learned and practiced. For example, an individual undergoing stress-inoculation therapy for coping with the "feeling of being overwhelmed" would rehearse self-statements such as,

When fear comes, just pause.
Keep the focus on the present; what is it you have to do?
Label your fear from 0 to 10 and watch it change. You should expect your fear to rise.
Don't try to eliminate fear totally; just keep it manageable.
You can convince yourself to do it. You can reason fear away.
It will be over shortly.
It's not the worst thing that can happen.
Just think about something else.
Do something that will prevent you from thinking about fear.
Describe what is around you. That way you won't think about worrying. (Meichenbaum, 1974, p. 16)

The third phase of stress-inoculation therapy, *application and practice,* involves applying the new coping strategies in actual situations. This practice is graduated in such a way that an individual is placed in easier situations first and is only gradually introduced to more stressful situations as he or she feels confident of mastering them.

Stress-inoculation therapy has been successfully used with a number of clinical problems, especially anxiety (Meichenbaum, 1975), pain (Turk, 1974), and Type A behavior (Jenni & Wollersheim, 1979). This approach is particularly suited to increasing the adaptive capabilities of individuals who have shown a vulnerability to developing problems in certain stressful situations. In addition to its value as a therapeutic technique for identified problems,

stress-inoculation therapy may be a viable method for preventing behavior disorders. Although the preventive value of this and other cognitive-behavioral therapy procedures has not been demonstrated by empirical study, many believe that the incidence of maladjustment might be reduced if more individuals' general coping skills were improved (Meichenbaum & Jaremko, 1983).

Evaluation of Cognitive–Behavioral Therapy

A review of research evaluating cognitive-behavioral treatment methods suggests that these approaches to intervention are extremely effective in alleviating some behavioral problems (e.g., Hollon & Beck, 1986). Several empirical studies have compared cognitive-behavioral methods with other treatment approaches. Data from these evaluation studies—on Beck's cognitive-behavioral therapy for individuals experiencing depression (see the reviews by Hollon & Garber, 1990; and Robinson, Berman, & Neimeyer, 1990); on rational-emotive therapy (Lipsky, Kassinove, & Miller, 1980; Smith, Glass, & Miller, 1980); and on stress-inoculation procedures (Denicola & Sandler, 1980; Holcomb, 1979; Klepac et al., 1981)—indicate that cognitive-behavioral methods are strongly associated with positive treatment outcomes.

In the case of depression, in fact, considerable evidence, reviewed in Chapter 11, suggests that cognitive-behavioral therapy is superior to drug treatment in all but the most severe cases (and perhaps even in these cases; see *HIGHLIGHT 18.8,* page 665, and our later discussion on The Evaluation of Success in Psychotherapy). In a study by Simons et al. (1986), for example, relapse in the posttreatment year was less likely if a client had been treated with cognitive therapy, *whether or not* there was also treatment with antidepressant drugs.

The combining of cognitive and behavior therapy approaches in practice is growing rapidly. In the next few years, we can expect to see many more studies evaluating the effectiveness of cognitive-behavioral methods as approaches to therapeutic change. There remains disagreement about whether some approaches are "truly" behavioral or "truly" cognitive, and whether or how cognitive change can bring about lasting behavior change (e.g., Hollon, DeRubeis, & Evans, 1987). In light of the present ferment in the field, we anticipate that the cognitive-behavioral viewpoint will undergo a great deal of further theoretical development in the foreseeable future.

HUMANISTIC-EXPERIENTIAL THERAPIES

The **humanistic-experiential therapies** have emerged as significant treatment approaches during the last four decades. To a large extent, they developed in reaction to the psychodynamic and behavioristic perspectives, which many feel do not accurately take into account either the existential problems or the full potentialities of human beings. In a society dominated by self-interest, mechanization, computerization, mass deception, and "mindless" bureaucracy, proponents of the humanistic-experiential therapies see psychopathology as stemming in many cases from problems of alienation, depersonalization, loneliness, and a failure to find meaning and genuine fulfillment. Problems of this sort, it is held, are not likely to be solved either by delving into forgotten memories or by correcting specific responses.

The humanistic-experiential therapies follow some variant of the general humanistic and existential perspectives spelled out in Chapter 3. They are based on the assumption that we have both the freedom and the responsibility to control our own behavior—that we can reflect on our problems, make choices, and take positive action. Whereas some behavior therapists see themselves as "behavior engineers," responsible for changing specific behaviors *they* deem problematic by appropriate modifications in an individual's environment, humanistic-experiential therapists feel that a client must take most of the responsibility for the directions and success of therapy, with a therapist merely serving as counselor, guide, and facilitator. These therapies may be carried out with individual clients or with groups of clients (see *HIGHLIGHT 18.5*). Although differing among themselves in details, the central focus of humanistic-experiential therapies is always that of expanding a client's "awareness"; accordingly, we consider them Type C (cognition-oriented) approaches.

Client-centered Therapy

The **client-centered (person-centered) therapy** of Carl Rogers (1951, 1961, 1966) actually antedated the strong movement toward behavior therapy that began in the 1950s and the "humanistic revolution" of the 1960s. It was developed in the 1940s as a truly innovative alternative to psychoanalysis, the only major psychotherapy of the time.

Rogers rejected both Freud's view of the primacy of irrational instinct and of the therapist's role as prober, interpreter, and director of the therapeutic process. Instead, believing in the natural power of an organism to heal itself, he saw psychotherapy as a process of removing the constraints and hobbling restrictions that often prevent this process from operating. These constraints, he believed, grow out of unrealistic demands that people tend to place on themselves when they believe they should not have certain kinds of feelings, such as hostility. By denying that they do in fact have such feelings, they become unaware of their actual "gut" reactions. As they lose touch with their own genuine experience, the result is lowered integration, impaired personal relationships, and various forms of maladjustment.

The primary objective of Rogerian therapy is to resolve this incongruence—to help clients become able to accept and *be* themselves. To this end, client-centered therapists establish a psychological climate in which clients can feel unconditionally accepted, understood, and valued as people. In this climate they can begin to feel free for perhaps the first time to explore their real feelings and thoughts and to accept hates and angers and "ugly feelings" as parts of themselves. As their self-concept becomes more congruent with their actual experiencing, they become more self-accepting and more open to new experience and new perspectives; in short, they become better-integrated people.

In client-centered therapy, also called *nondirective therapy,* it is not the therapist's task to direct the course of therapy. Thus a therapist does not give answers or interpret what a client says or probe for unconscious conflicts or even steer the client onto certain topics. Rather he or she simply listens attentively and acceptingly to what the client wants to talk about, interrupting only to restate in other words what the client is saying. Such restatements, without any judgment or interpretation by the therapist, help the client clarify further the feelings and ideas that he or she is exploring—really to look at them and acknowledge them. The following excerpt from a counselor's second interview with a young woman will serve to illustrate these techniques of reflection and clarification:

Alice: *I was thinking about this business of standards. I somehow developed a sort of a knack, I guess, of—well—habit—of trying to make people feel at ease around me, or to make things go along smoothly. . . .*
Counselor: *In other words, what you did*

HIGHLIGHT 18.5

Group Therapy

The treatment of clients in groups first received impetus in the military during World War II, when psychotherapists were in short supply. Group therapy was found to be effective in dealing with a variety of problems, and it rapidly became an important therapeutic approach in civilian life. In fact, all the major systematic approaches to psychotherapy that we have discussed—psychoanalysis, behavior therapy, and so on—have been applied in group as well as individual settings.

Group therapy has traditionally involved a relatively small group of clients in a clinic or hospital setting, using a variety of procedures depending on the age, needs, and potentialities of the clients and the orientation of the therapists. The degree of structure and of client participation in

the group process varies in different types of groups.

Most often, groups are informal, and many follow the format of encounter groups. Occasionally, however, more or less formal lectures and visual materials are presented to clients as a group. For example, a group of alcoholic clients may be shown a film depicting the detrimental effects of excessive drinking on the human body, with a group discussion afterward. Although this approach by itself has not proven effective in combating alcoholism, it is often a useful adjunct to other forms of group therapy.

An interesting form of group therapy is psychodrama, based on role-playing techniques. A client, assisted by staff members or other clients, is encouraged to act out problem situations in a theater-

like setting. This technique frees the individual to express anxieties and hostilities or relive traumatic experiences in a situation that simulates real life but is more sheltered. The goal is to help the client achieve emotional catharsis, increased understanding, and improved interpersonal competencies. This form of therapy, developed initially by Moreno (1959), has proved beneficial for the clients who make up the "audience" as well as for those who participate on the "stage" (Sundberg & Tyler, 1962; Yablonsky, 1975).

Group therapy may also be almost completely unstructured, as in activity groups where children with emotional problems are allowed to act out their aggressions in the safety and control of the group setting.

---

was always in the direction of trying to keep things smooth and to make other people feel better and to smooth the situation.

Alice: *Yes. I think that's what it was. Now the reason why I did it probably was—I mean, not that I was a good little Samaritan going around making other people happy, but that was probably the role that felt easiest for me to play. I'd been doing it around home so much. I just didn't stand up for my own convictions, until I don't know whether I have any convictions to stand up for.*

Counselor: *You feel that for a long time you've been playing the role of kind of smoothing out the frictions or differences or what not. . . .*

Alice: *M-hm.*

Counselor: *Rather than having any opinion or reaction of your own in the situation. Is that it?*

Alice: *That's it. Or that I haven't been really honestly being myself, or actually knowing what my real self is, and that I've been just playing a sort of a false role. Whatever role no one else was playing, and that needed to be played at the time, I'd try to fill it in.* (Rogers, 1951, pp. 152–153)

In a survey of trends in psychotherapy and counseling, Rogers was rated one of the most influential psychotherapists among clinical practitioners (Smith, 1982). In addition to his influence in clinical settings, Rogers was a pioneer in attempting to carry out empirical research on psychotherapy. Using recordings of therapy sessions, he was able to make objective analyses later of what was said, of the client-counselor relationships, and of many aspects of the ongoing processes in these therapy sessions. He was also able to compare a client's behavior and attitudes at different stages of therapy. These comparisons revealed a typical sequence that clients tended to go through. Early sessions were dominated by negative feelings and discouragement. Then, after a time, tentative statements of hope and greater self-acceptance began to appear. Eventually, positive feelings, a reaching out toward others, greater self-confidence, and interest in future plans appeared. This characteristic sequence gave support to Rogers's hypothesis that, once freed to do so, individuals have the capacity to lead themselves to psychological health.

Pure client-centered psychotherapy, as originally practiced, is rarely used today. It did, however, open the way for a variety of humanistically oriented therapies in which the focus is a client's present conscious problems and in which it is assumed that the client is the primary actor in the curative process, with the therapist essentially being just the facilitator. The newer humanistic therapies thus accept Rogers's concept of an active self, capable of sound value choices; they also emphasize the importance of a high degree of empathy, genuine warmth, and unconditional positive regard on the part of a therapist. They differ from original client-centered therapy in having found various shortcuts by which the therapist, going beyond simple reflection and clarification, can hasten and help focus the client's search for wholeness. Such a therapist might, for example, directly confront a client's deceitful mode of self-presentation. It is still the client's search and the client's insights that are seen as central in therapy, however.

■ Existential Therapy

Several important concepts underlie **existential psychotherapy.** The existentialist perspective emphasizes the importance of the human situation as experienced by an individual. Existentialists are deeply concerned about the predicament of humankind, the breakdown of traditional faith, the alienation and depersonalization of individuals in contemporary society, and the lack of meaning in individuals' lives. They see individuals, however, as having a high degree of freedom and thus as capable both of doing something about their predicament and of being responsible for doing the best they can. The unique ability of human beings to be aware of their mortality and to reflect on and question their existence confronts them with the responsibility for *being*—for deciding what kind of person to become within the constraint of a single lifetime, for establishing their own values, and for actualizing their potentialities.

The application of existential thought to understanding human problems and to helping individuals alter their lives has been recognized over the years by several psychological theorists, including Binswanger (1942) and May, Angel, and Ellenberger (1958). Binswanger, a psychoanalyst, applied the existential frame of reference to his psychoanalytic work and developed a method he referred to as *Daseinanalyse,* or existential analysis. May et al. followed later with what has become a classic work detailing existential analysis. Existential analysts do not limit themselves to an investigation of conscious and subconscious states, as do traditional analysts; rather, they attempt to assist an individual to reconstruct his or her inner world by focusing on the surrounding external reality. Most existential therapists do not strictly follow the methods of *Daseinanalyse,* but nevertheless accept an existential framework to challenge a client to experience his or her human feelings.

Existential therapists do not follow any rigidly prescribed procedures, but emphasize the uniqueness of each individual and his or her "way of being in the world." They stress the importance of being aware of one's own existence—challenging an individual directly with questions concerning the meaning and purpose of existence—and of the therapeutic encounter—the complex relationship established between two interacting human beings in the therapeutic situation as they both try to be open and "authentic." In contrast to both psychoanalysis and behavior therapy, existential therapy calls for therapists to share themselves—their feelings, their values, and their own existence.

Besides being authentic themselves, it is the task of existential therapists to keep a client responding authentically to the present reality (Havens, 1974; May, 1969). For example, if a client says, "I hate you just like I hated my father," a therapist might respond by saying, "I am not your father, I am me, and you have to deal with me as Dr. S., not as your father." The focus is on the here and now—on what an individual is choosing to do, and therefore to be, at this moment. This sense of immediacy, of the urgency of experience, is the touchstone of existential therapy and sets the stage for the individual to clarify and choose between alternative ways of being.

With what types of clients and which clinical problems does existential therapy work best? Like classical psychoanalytic therapy, existential psychotherapy is probably for the few. It is directed primarily toward intelligent and verbal individuals who appear to be having existential crises. The existential treatment approach is believed to work best with individuals who have anxiety-based disorders or personality disorders rather than psychoses. The following case illustrates the type of problem situation that would lend itself to treatment in the existential framework:

> *A 42-year-old business executive seeks therapy because he feels that life has lost its meaning—he no longer feels that family matters are important to him (his wife is busy starting her career and his only child recently got married and moved to Alaska). Additionally, his work, at which he has had extraordinary success—earning him both financial security and respect—no longer holds meaning for him. He views his days as "wasted and worthless"—he feels both "bored and panicked"—and he goes through the motions of the business day feeling "numb," as though he isn't even there. At times, he feels fearful and overwhelmed with a sense of dread that this is all that life has left for him.*

■ Gestalt Therapy

The term *gestalt* means "whole," and gestalt therapy emphasizes the unity of mind and body—placing strong emphasis on the need to integrate thought, feeling, and action. **Gestalt therapy** was developed by Frederick (Fritz) Perls (1967, 1969) as a means of teaching clients to recognize the bodily processes and emotional modalities they had been blocking off from awareness. The main goal of gestalt therapy is to increase an individual's self-awareness and self-acceptance.

Although gestalt therapy is commonly used in a group setting, the emphasis is on one individual at a time with whom a therapist works intensively, attempting to help identify aspects of the individual's self or world that are not being acknowledged in awareness. The individual may be asked to act out fantasies concerning feelings and conflicts, or to "be" one part of a conflict while sitting in one chair and then switch chairs to take the part of the "adversary." Often the therapist or other group members will ask questions like, "What are you aware of in your body now?" or "What does it feel like in your gut when you think of that?"

In Perls's approach to therapy, a good deal of emphasis is also placed on dreams:

> *. . . all the different parts of the dream are fragments of our personalities. Since our aim is to make every one of us a wholesome person, which means a unified person, without conflicts, what we have to*

do is put the different fragments of the dream together. We have to re-own these projected, fragmented parts of our personality, and re-own the hidden potential that appears in the dream. (1967, p. 67)

In the following dialogue, taken from the transcript of a "dreamwork seminar," Perls (Fritz) helps a young woman (Linda) discover the meaning of her dream:

> **Linda:** *I dreamed that I watch . . . a lake . . . drying up, and there is a small island in the middle of the lake, and a circle of . . . porpoises—they're like porpoises except that they can stand up, so they're like porpoises that are like people, and they're in a circle, sort of like a religious ceremony, and it's very sad—I feel very sad because they can breathe, they are sort of dancing around the circle, but the water, their element, is drying up. So it's like a dying—like watching a race of people, or a race of creatures, dying. And they are mostly females, but a few of them have a small male organ, so there are a few males there, but they won't live long enough to reproduce, and their element is drying up. And there is one that is sitting over here near me and I'm talking to this porpoise and he has prickles on his tummy, sort of like a porcupine, and they don't seem to be a part of him. And I think that there's one good point about the water drying up, I think—well, at least at the bottom, when all the water dries up, there will probably be some sort of treasure there, because at the bottom of the lake there should be things that have fallen in, like coins or something, but I look carefully and all that I can find is an old license plate. . . . That's the dream.*
> **Fritz:** *Will you please play the license plate?*
> L: *I am an old license plate, thrown in the bottom of a lake. I have no use because I'm no value—although I'm not rusted—I'm outdated, so I can't be used as a license plate . . . and I'm just thrown on the rubbish heap. That's what I did with a license plate, I threw it on a rubbish heap.*
> F: *Well, how do you feel about this?*
> L: *(quietly) I don't like it. I don't like being a license plate—useless.*
> F: *Could you talk about this? That was such a long dream until you come to find the license plate, I'm sure this must be of great importance.*
> L: *(sighs) Useless. Outdated. . . . The use of a license plate is to allow—give a car permission*

to go . . . and I can't give anyone permission to do anything because I'm outdated. . . . In California, they just paste a little—you buy a sticker—and stick it on the car on the old license plate (faint attempt at humor). So maybe someone could put me on their car and stick this sticker on me, I don't know . . .

F: Okay, now play the lake.

L: I'm a lake . . . I'm drying up, and disappearing, soaking into the earth . . . (with a touch of surprise) dying. . . . But when I soak into the earth, I become a part of the earth—so maybe I water the surrounding area, so . . . even in the lake, even in my bed, flowers can grow (sighs). . . . New life can grow . . . from me (cries) . . .

F: You get the existential message?

L: Yes. (sadly, but with conviction) I can paint—I can create—I can create beauty. I can no longer reproduce. I'm like the porpoise . . . but I . . . I'm . . . I . . . keep wanting to say I'm food . . . I . . . as water becomes . . . I water the earth, and give life-growing things, the water—they need both the earth and water, and the . . . and the air and the sun, but as the water from the lake, I can play a part in something, and producing—feeding.

F: You see the contrast: On the surface, you find something, some artifact—the license plate, the artificial you—but then when you go deeper, you find the apparent death of the lake is actually fertility . . .

L: And I don't need a license plate, or a permission, a license in order to . . .

F: (gently) Nature doesn't need a license plate to grow. You don't have to be useless, if you are organismically creative, which means if you are involved.

L: And I don't need permission to be creative . . . Thank you. (Perls, 1969, pp. 81–82)

In gestalt therapy sessions, the focus is on the more obvious elements of a person's behavior. Such sessions are often called "gestalt awareness training" because the therapeutic results of the experience stem from the process of becoming more aware of one's total self and environment. The technique of working through unresolved conflicts is called "taking care of unfinished business." We all go through life, according to Perls, with unfinished or unresolved traumas and conflicts. We carry the excess baggage of these unfinished situations into new relationships and tend to reenact them in our relations with other people. If we are able to complete our past unfinished business, we then have

less psychological tension to cope with and can be more realistically aware of ourselves and our world.

Expressing themselves in front of the group, perhaps taking the part of first one and then another fragment of a scene, and denied the use of their usual techniques for avoiding self-awareness, individuals are brought to an "impasse," at which point they must confront their feelings and conflicts. According to Perls, "In the safe emergency of the therapeutic situation, the neurotic discovers that the world does not fall to pieces if he or she gets angry, sexy, joyous, mournful" (1967, p. 331). Thus individuals find that they can, after all, get beyond impasses on their own.

■ Evaluation of the Humanistic–Experiential Therapies

The humanistic-experiential therapies have been criticized for their lack of highly systematized models of human behavior and its specific aberrations, their lack of agreed-upon therapeutic procedures, and their vagueness about what is supposed to happen between client and therapist. These very features, however, are seen by many proponents of this general approach as contributing to its strength and vitality. Systematized theories can reduce individuals to abstractions, which can diminish their perceived worth and deny their uniqueness as individuals. Because people are so different, we should expect that different techniques are appropriate for different cases. Rigorous research on the outcomes produced by the humanistic-existential therapies is rare, but some has been carried out on the gestalt variety. This technique has a respectable, though unspectacular, record (Smith, Glass, & Miller, 1980).

In any event, many of the humanistic-experiential concepts—the uniqueness of each individual, the satisfaction that comes from developing and using one's potentials, the importance of the search for meaning and fulfillment, and the human power for choice and self-direction—have had a major impact on our contemporary views of both human nature and psychotherapy.

THERAPY FOR INTERPERSONAL RELATIONSHIPS

In Chapter 3, we noted the interpersonal perspective's emphasis on the role of faulty communications, interactions, and relationships in maladaptive behavior. This viewpoint has had an important impact on approaches to therapy—particularly, as we have seen, on contemporary psychodynamic therapy, but also to a considerable extent on the behavioristic and humanistic-existential therapies. For example, in behavior therapy we have seen a notable rise in concern with the client-therapist relationship and a growing emphasis on modifying social reinforcements that may be maintaining maladaptive responses; in humanistic-existential therapies we have seen the focus on such problems as lack of acceptance, relatedness, and love in an individual's life.

Although the interpersonal perspective is increasingly seen as essential to fully understanding many types of "individual" disorder, numerous problems brought to practitioners are explictly relationship problems. That is, the presenting complaint is not so much one of dissatisfaction with self or one's own behavior as one of inability to achieve satisfactory accords with people who are close enough that one's relationship with them could not readily be given up. A common example is marital distress. The maladaptive behavior is in these instances shared among the members of the relationship; it is, to use the contemporary term, "systemic" (Gurman, Kniskern, & Pinsof, 1986). Such problems require therapeutic techniques that focus on relationships as much as or more than on individuals. As was seen in Chapter 10, many problems presenting as individual sexual dysfunctions turn out to be systemic in character. In this section, we will explore the growing fields of couples and family therapy as examples of this type of multiple-client intervention. In general, these therapies, when placed (as they often are) in the context of helping *individuals* to change, focus on altering the *reactions* of the interpersonal environment to the behavior of each of the involved people. To this extent, they may be considered chiefly Type E approaches.

It is important to note that couples and family therapies can be and are conducted from any of the perspectives discussed in this chapter and in Chapter 3. Thus behavioral marital therapy, often utilizing a contracting approach, is one of several widely available variations on the theme.

■ Couples Counseling (Marital Therapy)

The large numbers of couples seeking assistance with relationship problems have made couples counseling a growing field of therapy. Typically the partners are seen together, and therapy focuses on clarifying and improving their interactions and relationships. Therapy for only one of the partners

has proved less effective for resolving such problems (Gurman & Kniskern, 1978), although it is common at the start of couples therapy for each partner secretly to harbor the wish that only the other will have to do the changing. It is almost always necessary, however, that *both* partners alter their reactions to the other.

Couples counseling, or **marital therapy,** includes a wide range of concepts and procedures. Most therapists emphasize mutual need gratification, social role expectations, communication patterns, and similar interpersonal factors. Not surprisingly, happily married couples tend to differ from unhappily married couples in that they remain good friends, talk more to each other, keep channels of communication open, make more use of nonverbal communication, and show more sensitivity to each other's feelings and needs. For example, in a study comparing distressed versus nondistressed couples, Margolin and Wampold (1981) found that nondistressed couples showed more problem-solving behavior than distressed couples, a result found often in studies of this sort. The extremely common scenario, "He never talks to me, he withdraws" versus "All she does is bitch and complain, so who needs to talk," is one whose resolution obviously calls for considerable problem-solving skill, not to mention a degree of maturity and patience in employing it. Not all people who decide to share their lives are at the time abundantly equipped in these respects.

Faulty role expectations often play havoc with marital adjustment. For example, Paul (1971) cited the case of a couple who came for marital therapy when the 39-year-old husband was about to divorce his wife to marry a much younger woman. During therapy, he broke into sobs of grief as he recalled the death of his Aunt Anna, who had always accepted him as he was and created an atmosphere of peace and contentment. In reviewing this incident, the husband realized that his girlfriend represented his lifelong search for another Aunt Anna. This led to a reconciliation with his wife, who was now more understanding of his needs, feelings, and role expectations and thus altered her behavior toward her husband accordingly.

One of the difficulties in couples therapy is the intense emotional involvement of the partners, which makes it difficult for them to perceive and accept the realities of their relationship. Often wives can see clearly what is "wrong" with their husbands but not what attitudes and behaviors of their own are contributing to the relationship, while husbands tend to have remarkable "insight" into their wives' flaws but not their own. To help correct this problem, videotape recordings have been used increas-

Here two actors using case histories of real people (for purposes of telecourse instruction) role-play a couple in marital therapy. In this session, they argue about the fact that Wanda did not make pork chops for Harry the way he likes them made. The therapist must assume that this disagreement reflects a hidden agenda and try to get at the real issues. A couple in distress may have faulty expectations of their spouse's role in the marriage, may be too emotionally involved to see the realities of the relationship, and may be unskilled at communicating needs and feelings as well as expressing affection and approval. The therapist must focus not only on the relationship, but on the partners' personal limitations, which may be affecting how they react to each other.

ingly to recapture crucial moments of intense interaction between the partners. By watching playbacks of these tapes after immediate tensions have diminished, the partners can gain a fuller awareness of the nature of their interactions. Thus a husband may realize for the first time that he tries to dominate rather than listen to his wife and consider her needs and expectations, or a wife may realize that she is continually undermining her husband's feelings of worth and esteem. The following statement was made by a young wife after viewing a videotape playback of the couple's first therapy session:

"See! There it is—loud and clear! As usual you didn't let me express my feelings or opinions, you just interrupted me with your own. You're always telling me what I think without asking me what I think. And I can see what I have been doing in response—withdrawing into silence. I feel like, what's the use of talking."

This insight was shared with the husband, and the couple was able to work out a much more satisfactory marital relationship within a few months.

Other relatively new and innovative approaches to couples therapy include training the partners to use Rogerian nondirective techniques in listening to each other and helping each other clarify and verbalize their feelings and reactions. A mutual readiness to really listen and try to understand what the other one is experiencing—and an acceptance of whatever comes out in this process—can be both therapeutic for the individuals and productive of a more open and honest relationship in the future.

Eisler et al. (1974) used an interesting combination of videotape playbacks and assertiveness therapy, as illustrated in the following instance:

In one case, a 45-year-old high school teacher was responding passively and ineffectively to his highly critical wife at the beginning of therapy. By watching videotapes of their interactions, they both received feedback on their roles in the interactions. The husband received assertiveness training and practiced being more assertive, continuing to watch videotapes of the gradually changing interactions between him and his wife.

In contrast to the videotapes made at the beginning of therapy, those made at the end showed such positive results as improved communication, more expressions of affection and approval, and a marked increase in the amount of smiling during their interactions. Both spouses stated that their posttreatment marital adjustment seemed more satisfying.

Behavior therapy has also been used to bring about desired changes in marital relationships. Here the spouses are taught to reinforce instances of desired behavior while withdrawing reinforcement for undesired behavior (see *HIGHLIGHT 18.6*). In a recent study comparing behavioral with insight-oriented psychodynamic marital therapy, neither proved superior to the other, but both significantly outperformed a waiting-list control condition (Snyder & Wills, 1989).

How effective in general are marital therapies at resolving marital crises and promoting more effective marriages or intimate partnerships? One study involved a five-year follow-up of 320 former marital therapy clients and compared their divorce rates with those of the general population (Cookerly, 1980). In cases in which both partners underwent therapy together, 56.4 percent had remained married for the five-year period; in cases in which other types of therapy were used, 29 percent had remained married. All forms of therapy were associ-

Structured Behavior Therapy for Couples

Margolin, Christensen, and Weiss (1975) developed a brief, highly structured form of couples therapy organized around six topics, or modules. The sequence takes about ten weeks.

1. *Pinpointing contingencies.* In an intensive period, the partners' problem behaviors and the conditions maintaining them are identified.

2. *Training in communication skills.* Several techniques to improve communication, such as paraphrasing and reflecting the partners' feelings, are taught through modeling by the therapist, behavioral rehearsal, and video feedback.

3. *Training in conflict resolution.* Partners view videotapes of other couples illustrating good and bad ways to deal with conflicts. Sometimes a poor method, such as sidetracking or name-calling, is followed by a constructive approach.

4. *Formation of utility matrices.* Here the partners identify rewards and penalties that they can use in contracts with each other about what they will and will not do.

5. *Negotiating and "contingency contracting."* This is one of the most important phases. Practicing their new communication skills, the couple negotiates agreements on behavioral contracts that will provide a more rewarding and less punishing relationship for both of them.

6. *Termination and maintenance.* Once the agreements go into effect, the therapist helps promptly with any problems that arise to ensure that the learned skills are being practiced and the improved relationship maintained. In fact, throughout the course of the therapy sequence, evening phone contacts supplement the laboratory sessions for obtaining information on the partners' interactions, problems, and use of new skills.

Treatment is ended gradually as the spouses assume their new roles.

Follow-up is an important part of this therapy. The therapist may make weekly telephone contacts for the first weeks following termination. Booster sessions may be scheduled after termination, if they are needed.

This form of behavioral marital therapy has been shown to be one of the most effective approaches to improving marriage relationships (Gurman, Kniskern, & Pinsof, 1986; Jacobson & Martin, 1976). Moreover, its relatively well-structured modules can be precisely applied and taught readily to beginning therapists. The relatively specific interventions also lend themselves to empirical verification more easily than other, nonbehavioral methods; thus research into marital therapy, a previously neglected area, may now be encouraged.

ated with significantly better results in resolving marital crises and keeping marriages together than was the use of no therapy at all. This conclusion is also supported in Gurman, Kniskern, and Pinsof's (1986) more recent review of numerous outcome studies. Finally, couples therapy has been successfully used as an adjunct in the treatment of individual problems, such as depression, agoraphobia, and alcohol abuse (Jacobson, Holtzworth-Monroe, & Schmaling, 1989).

Of course, a motivational factor in outcome assessments of this sort makes interpretation somewhat difficult. People strongly motivated to stay in their relationships are more likely to give couples therapy a serious try than their less motivated counterparts. Such motivation may itself, irrespective of therapy, make for partnership longevity or, perhaps, tolerance of partner abnormality. On the

other hand, as we have seen, strong motivation is a key element in the likely success of *any* psychological therapy, so the research on outcomes of couples therapy has a certain face validity even acknowledging some unclarity about the role of motivational variations.

■ Family Therapy

Therapy for a family group overlaps with marital therapy but has somewhat different roots. Whereas marital therapy developed in response to the large number of clients who came for assistance with marital problems, family therapy began with the finding that many people who had shown marked improvement in individual therapy—often in institutional settings—had a relapse on their return home. It soon became apparent that many of these people came from disturbed family settings that required modification if they were to maintain their gains. A pioneer in the field of family therapy has described the problem as follows:

Psychopathology in the individual is a product of the way he deals with his intimate relations, the way they deal with him, and the way other family members involve him in their relations with each other. Further, the appearance of symptomatic behavior in an individual is necessary for the continued function of a particular family system. Therefore, changes in the individual can occur only if the family system changes. . . . (Haley, 1962, p. 70)

This viewpoint led to an important concept in the field of psychotherapy, namely, that the problem or disorder shown by an "identified client" is often only a symptom of a larger family problem. A careful study of the family of a disturbed child, for example, may reveal that the child is merely reflecting the pathology of the family unit. As a result, most family therapists share the view that the family —not simply the designated "client"—must be directly involved in therapy if lasting improvement is to be achieved. This is a conclusion also implied in our pathogenic loop model described earlier. Its application is increasingly seen in attempts to understand relapse after recovery from even severe disorder, as in the work on expressed emotion (EE) in mood disorders and schizophrenia (see Chapters 11 and 12).

Perhaps the most widely used approach to family therapy is the "conjoint family therapy" of Satir (1967). Her emphasis is on improving faulty communications, interactions, and relationships among family members and on fostering a family system that better meets the needs of each member. The following example shows Satir's emphasis on the problem of faulty communication:

Husband: *She never comes up to me and kisses me. I am always the one to make the overtures.*

Therapist: *Is this the way you see yourself behaving with your husband?*

Wife: *Yes, I would say he is the demonstrative one. I didn't know he wanted me to make the overtures.*

Th: *Have you told your wife that you would like this from her—more open demonstration of affection?*

H: *Well, no you'd think she'd know.*

W: *No, how would I know? You always said you didn't like aggressive women.*

H: *I don't, I don't like dominating women.*

W: *Well, I thought you meant women who make the overtures. How am I to know what you want?*

Th: *You'd have a better idea if he had been able to tell you. (Satir, 1967, pp. 72–73)*

Another encouraging approach to resolving family disturbances is called **structural family therapy** (Minuchin, 1974). This approach, based on "systems theory," assumes that a family system itself is more influential than individual personality or intrapsychic conflicts in producing abnormal behavior. It assumes that the family system has contributed to the characteristic behaviors that individual family members have developed; if the family context changes, then the individual members will have altered experiences in the family and will behave differently in accordance with the changed requirements of the new family context. Thus an important goal of structural family therapy is to change the organization of the family in such a way that the family members will behave more positively and supportively toward each other.

Structural family therapy is focused on present interactions and requires an active but not directive approach on the part of a therapist. Initially, the therapist gathers information about the family—a "structural map" of the typical family interaction patterns—by acting like one of the family and participating in the family interactions as an insider. In this way, the therapist discovers whether the family system has rigid or flexible boundaries, who dominates the power structure, who gets blamed when things go wrong, and so on.

Armed with this understanding, the therapist then uses himself or herself as a change medium for altering the interaction among the members. For example, Aponte and Hoffman (1973) reported the successful use of structural family therapy in treating an anorexic 14-year-old girl:

*A*nalyzing the communications in the family, the therapists saw a competitive struggle for the father's attention and observed that the girl, Laura, was able to succeed in this competition and get "cuddly" attention from her father by not eating. To bring the hidden dynamics out into the open, they worked at getting the family members to express their desires more directly— in words instead of through cryptic behavioral *messages. In time, Laura became much more able to verbalize her wishes for affection and gave up the unacceptable and dangerous method of not eating.*

Similarly, Schwartz, Barrett, and Saba (1983) reported successful treatment of bulimia with structural family therapy. Minuchin et al. (1975) conducted a study in which structural family therapy was used successfully with families in which children had developed psychophysiologic illnesses. Stanton and Todd (1976) also related dramatic improvement rates with its use in several families in which one member was an identified heroin addict.

As with couples problems, maladaptive family relationships have also been successfully overcome by behavioristically oriented therapies. With this type of therapy, Huff (1969) has suggested that the therapist's task is to reduce the aversive value of the family for the identified client as well as that of the client for other family members. "The therapist does this by actively manipulating the *relationship* between members so that the relationship changes to a more positively reinforcing and reciprocal one" (p. 26).

N. Hurwitz (1974) has elaborated on the role of the family therapist as an intermediary whose functions include "interpreter, clarifier, emissary, go-between, messenger, catalyst, mediator, arbitrator, negotiator, and referee" (p. 145). As virtually anyone who has ever done family therapy will testify, these role demands are most exacting and emotionally draining; hence they are commonly shared by cotherapists, one male and one female.

After reviewing family therapy approaches, Gurman and Kniskern (1978) concluded that structural family therapy had had more impressive results than most other experientially- and analytically-oriented approaches they had reviewed. In a more recent update (Gurman, Kniskern, & Pinsof, 1986) that included additional work that had been published in the interim on behavioral approaches, the results have tended to favor behavioral intervention.

In addition, many clinicians working with severely disturbed individuals have concluded that family therapy is effective at reducing family tensions and promoting more adaptive functioning of all family members. As was seen in Chapter 12, the work on reducing family expressed emotion (EE) in preventing schizophrenic relapse looks very promising. However, the relative success of family intervention methods versus individual methods of therapy is an exceedingly difficult area of research. Wellisch and Trock (1980) found, at a three-year

follow-up, that the previously superior effects of family therapy for severe disorder had deteriorated; 57 percent of the clients had had to be rehospitalized, as compared with 20 percent of the individual therapy cases. We can only speculate about the reasons for this relatively poor showing for family therapy. If these results suggest anything, it is perhaps that, for chronic problems with a pattern of recurrent exacerbation, the more focused impact of individual psychotherapy may in the long run be more beneficial.

THE INTEGRATION OF THERAPY APPROACHES

Although an integration of psychoanalysis and learning theory was attempted as early as 1950 by Dollard and Miller in their *Personality and Psychotherapy,* the two treatment approaches diverged significantly in the 1960s and 1970s. Recently, a great deal has been written about the possibility of gaining a rapprochement between behavior therapy and other schools of therapy, particularly psychodynamic therapy (Arkowitz & Messer, 1984; Goldfried, Greenberg, & Marmar, 1990; Marmor & Woods, 1980; Wachtel, 1977, 1982). At first, this trend may seem surprising, given the generally competitive atmosphere and the critical struggles that have traditionally existed between psychoanalysts and behavior therapists. Early behaviorists were adamant in their criticism of psychoanalysis as inefficient and mystical. The analysts reacted with strong counterarguments, partly in their own defense but also in keeping with their beliefs that behavioral therapies were superficial and treated only symptoms, while psychoanalytic treatments sought "deeper" and more permanent cures.

Over the years, however, behavioral and psychoanalytic proponents have had time to become accustomed (or perhaps "desensitized") to each other's criticisms. With the wide dissemination and practice of behavioral methods, it has become apparent to some psychodynamically oriented therapists that behavioral methods are quite effective in the treatment of many disorders. Similarly, many behaviorally oriented therapists have concluded that it is not simply the application of a *technique* that brings about change in a client. They acknowledge that "relationship" factors are exceedingly important—even when rigorous behavior modification procedures are being used (Lazarus, 1981, 1985). In addition, research comparing both treatment methods has generally shown that neither approach has been demonstrated consistently to be superior to the other (Sloane et al., 1975), although, overall, there seems to be a small advantage for behavior and cognitive-behavioral methods (Lambert, Shapiro, & Bergin, 1986; Smith, Glass, & Miller, 1980).

Kendall (1982b) has concisely summarized the reasons for the current interest in integrating behavior therapy with other methods. He noted that (a) some behaviorists have concluded that the human organism is multifaceted and that focusing only on "behavior" is not sufficient as a treatment goal; (b) the "less than perfect" success of available therapy methods justifies combining the most successful treatment strategies from all approaches; (c) integrating diverse therapies might inspire a new enthusiasm and promote novel applications of varied treatment methods and perhaps promote new formulations of old problems; and (d) integrating diverse therapy schools would require members of a given school to begin to question the assumptions underlying their treatment approaches and would promote a broad reappraisal from different perspectives. Our own "loop" model is, of course, completely in accord with this perspective.

According to Kendall, however, inherent problems face the integrationist position. First, no common language unites the various therapy schools. Second, it is much easier for a trainee to learn a single therapeutic approach than to learn elements of various approaches. Finally, basic conceptual differences exist that would preclude a fully satisfactory merger between behavior therapy and psychodynamic therapy, such as their different emphases on etiological factors, treatment goals, and tactical methods.

Further examination of therapeutic methods from the vantage point of alternative views may, in time, lead to interestingly amalgamated psychosocial therapies. It does not appear at this point, however, that many of the advocates of the various positions will be able to put aside their long identification with particular schools and easily assimilate alien notions and practices, notwithstanding a common self-description among therapists as "eclectic."

Meanwhile, an equally if not more vexing problem concerns the integration of psychosocial and biological forms of treatment. As shown in earlier chapters, combined treatment of this sort, where it has been tried, has often proved to be more effective than either alone. In this area we confront not only philosophical differences but interdisciplinary political and economic ones as well. Although there is a developing movement among a segment of clinical psychologists, endorsed to a degree by the American Psychological Association, to seek prescription-writing privileges that would permit them to ad-

In group therapy, the relationship among the group members is as important as the relationship between client and therapist in individual therapy. In this unique setting, the therapy may be of various therapeutic orientations, with the therapist using a combination of psychoanalytic, behavioral, and other approaches.

minister psychoactive drugs (strongly opposed by organized medicine and psychiatry), as of this writing the overwhelming majority of nonmedical therapists may not legally do so. Even among clinical psychologists, many are opposed to this trend, mostly out of concern that easy access to drug treatment will corrupt the further and much needed development of even more powerful forms of psychosocial intervention. In our judgment, the latter concern is not specious; too frequently, we have seen the clinical process distorted by an excessively hasty and exclusive recourse to what is usually, at best, palliative medication. Still, judicious combined treatment surely has much to recommend it for certain types of disorder. It will be interesting to see how this issue is played out by the mental health professions over the next decade.

THE EVALUATION OF SUCCESS IN PSYCHOTHERAPY

Competition between individual therapies has tended to obscure the actual success of therapy. Four decades ago, Eysenck (1952), a well-known British psychologist, shook the field of psychological intervention by concluding in his review of evidence on treatment outcomes that people who were untreated or simply placed on a waiting list for psychotherapy improved about as much as those who actually received therapy. This pronouncement prompted a flurry of research activity and a thorough reanalysis of the existing data. Reevaluation of therapy-outcome research accomplished prior to Eysenck's review, as well as a great deal done since, has painted a different and more positive picture of the overall effectiveness of psychotherapy (Lambert, Shapiro, & Bergin, 1986). In particular, the development of meta-analysis techniques for evaluating therapeutic outcomes, described in *HIGHLIGHT 18.7*, has had an enormous and positive impact in revitalizing a sense of purpose among evaluation researchers.

■ Problems of Evaluation

Evaluating the effectiveness of psychological treatment is a difficult enterprise for several reasons. At best, it is an inexact process, dependent on inexact and inevitably somewhat subjective data. For example, attempts at evaluation generally depend on one or more of the following sources of information: (a) a therapist's impression of changes that have occurred, (b) a client's reports of change, (c) reports from the client's family or friends, (d) comparison of pretreatment and posttreatment personality test scores, and (e) measures of change in selected overt behaviors.

Unfortunately, each of these sources has serious limitations. A therapist may not be the best judge of a client's progress, since any therapist is likely to be biased in favor of seeing himself or herself as competent and successful. Furthermore, therapists can inflate improvement averages by consciously or unconsciously encouraging difficult clients to discontinue therapy. The problem of how to manage "dropouts" complicates most therapy outcome studies (for example, are they to be counted as "failures" when in fact they receive little or none of the therapy being evaluated?). It has also been somewhat facetiously remarked that a therapist often thinks a client is getting better because he or she is getting accustomed to the client's symptoms.

A client, also, is an unreliable source concerning the outcomes of therapy. Clients may not only want to think that they are getting better for personal reasons, but they may report that they are being helped in an attempt to please the therapist. In addition, because therapy often requires a considerable investment of time, money, and sometimes emotional distress, the idea that it is useless is a dissonant one. Family and relatives may also be inclined to "see" the improvement they had hoped for, although they often seem to be more realistic than either the therapist or the client in their long-term evaluations.

Outside clinical ratings by an independent observer are sometimes used in psychotherapy outcome research to evaluate the progress of a client;

these may be more objective than ratings by those directly involved in the therapy. Another widely used objective measure of client change is performance on psychological tests. A client evaluated in this way takes a battery of tests before and after therapy and the differences in scores are assumed to reflect progress or deterioration. Although such tests may indeed show changes, they are, however, likely to focus on the particular measures in which the therapist or researcher is interested. They are not necessarily valid predictors of how the client will behave in real life, nor can they give any indication of whether the changes that have occurred are likely to be enduring. Of interest here, however, is some strong evidence that the effects of psychotherapy in general, as variously measured, are decidedly not ephemeral or temporary (Nicholson & Berman, 1983).

Changes in selected and specifically denoted behaviors appear to be the safest measures of outcome, especially where the occurrence of these outside of the therapy situation itself is systematically monitored. Such techniques, including client self-monitoring, have been widely and effectively used, especially by behavior therapists. Generalized terms such as *recovery, marked improvement,* and *moderate improvement,* as applied to initially problematic behavior and often used in outcome research, are of course open to considerable differences in interpretation. In addition, even under the best of outcome measurement circumstances there is always the possibility that improvement will be attributed to the particular form of treatment used, when it is in fact a product of other events in a client's life or even of "spontaneous" change.

In spite of these difficulties, however, it is to at least some extent possible to study the effectiveness of various treatment approaches separately—determining what procedures work best with various types of individuals (Kendall & Norton-Ford, 1982; Smith, Glass, & Miller, 1980). In the course of our discussion of abnormal behavior patterns, we have mentioned a number of such studies, most of which have demonstrated positive outcomes from psychotherapy.

In this context, it is relevant to ask what happens to people who do not obtain formal treatment. In view of the many ways that people can help each other, it is not surprising that often considerable improvement occurs without therapeutic intervention. Some forms of psychopathology, such as manic and depressive episodes and some instances of schizophrenia, appear to run a fairly brief course with or without treatment, and there are many other instances in which disturbed people improve over time for reasons that are not apparent.

Meta–Analysis in the Evaluation of Therapy Outcomes

Systematic outcome studies on the effects of various forms of psychotherapy for various kinds of disorder have been done for decades, and recently there has been a phenomenal increase in their rate of appearance in the professional literature. Although this is doubtless a healthy sign indicating the vitality of the field and its sense of scientific responsibility, the sheer volume and diversity of the work undertaken and published have made it difficult for researchers and clinicians to answer any specific questions they may have—such as what types of therapy produce the best outcomes for a specific type of disorder, or indeed if any do have measurable benefits. Narrative-based summary reviews of portions of this literature, often containing "box scores" of results from different studies, are published from time to time. These can be helpful but are often limited by the difficulties of comparing studies whose essential characteristics, such as the therapy outcome measures used, vary enormously.

The technique of *meta-analysis* was invented as a means of summarizing the results of large and varied data sets of this sort by recasting them into a standard metric format whose meaning, at least statistically, is immediately apparent. As applied in the case of therapeutic outcomes in psychopathology, the technique is quite straightforward, although so mathematically tedious as to require electronic computation.

In the simplest case, three items of information are needed for every outcome measure used in every study in the analysis. These are the means of the outcome measure or measures for both (a) the treated and (b) the untreated (control) sample of patient-subjects, and (c) the standard deviation for the untreated sample. These three figures are usually reported directly by the original investigator, but even where they are not they are frequently recoverable from data that are reported. The basic statistic known as an *effect size* (ES) is computed from these quantities according to the following formula:

$$ES = \frac{M_{Therapy} - M_{Control}}{SD_{Control}}$$

where:

$M_{Therapy}$ is the mean score for the psychotherapy group on the outcome measure;

$M_{Control}$ is the mean score for the control group; and

$SD_{Control}$ is the control group standard deviation. (Note: some investigators prefer to use a pooled standard deviation calculated from the scores of both the treated and control groups.)

Readers familiar with elementary statistics will recognize this as a variant of the formula for the z-score, one that expresses the deviation of the treatment group's mean from that of the control group in (control group or pooled) standard deviation units. In other words, the ES locates the treated group's mean on a distribution of standard ("z") scores whose mean is the mean of the control group for the particular outcome measure being considered; in z-score units, that mean would be zero. An ES of, let us say, +1.0 would indicate an out-come for the treated group that is one standard deviation above the mean of the control group on that outcome measure. By assuming that the outcome measure for the untreated group is "normally distributed" (that is, approximates the bell-shaped normal probability curve), we could infer from normal curve statistical properties that the treated group's mean performance or level on this measure is at the eighty-fourth percentile of that of the control group; or, to put it another way, we could say that 84 percent of untreated people fall below the mean level of the treated group.

Notice that the ES statistic gives us a powerful means of reducing all manner of quantified outcome data to the same metric or scale, thus allowing for direct comparisons among them. In particular, we can pool the results of many studies having the same or similar independent variables (such as the nature of treatment, the type of disorder treated, and so on) and dependent variables (the outcomes of treatment) to arrive at an overall ES estimate, usually the mean or average of all the ESs obtained. This is then reported as the *Average Effect Size,* or $\overline{ES}$, for the particular type of treatment or diagnostic group being considered.

In several instances in this text we have used data from meta-analytic studies to estimate the effectiveness of various therapies with various populations of clients. Particular attention has been given in this regard to the original and massive meta-analytic work on mental disorder therapies undertaken by Smith, Glass, and Miller (1980).

Nevertheless, even if many emotionally disturbed individuals tend to improve over time without psychotherapy, it seems clear that psychotherapy can often accelerate improvement or ensure desired behavior change that might not otherwise occur (Lambert, Shapiro, & Bergin, 1986; Telch, 1981). Most researchers today would agree that psychotherapy is more effective than no treatment. The rate of individuals experiencing significant improvement across studies of therapy outcome, regardless of approach, averages about 80 percent; if there is such a thing as "spontaneous" improvement, a doubtful occurrence, it would not in all likelihood exceed 15 percent. Furthermore, improvement seems a function of the number of therapy sessions undertaken—with the largest gains achieved early (that is, within six months) in the therapeutic relationship (Howard et al., 1986). Very long-term psychotherapy is actually quite rare, but such cases tend to create the impression, even among professionals, that disordered behavior is more intractable than for the most part it actually is. In one study of this problem (Howard et al., 1989), 56 percent of the total therapy sessions offered by a clinic were "consumed" by only 16 percent of the clients.

Nonetheless, the issue of treatment evaluation remains a vital one—both ethically and practically—if psychologists and other mental health personnel are to be justified in intervening in other people's lives. The issue becomes especially vital in light of evidence that some clients are *harmed* in their encounters with psychotherapists (Lambert, Shapiro, & Bergin, 1986; Mays & Franks, 1985; Strupp, Hadley, & Gomes-Schwartz, 1977). This problem of negative effects, which many therapists acknowledge when directly queried (see, e.g., Appendix C, pp. 223–343, of the Strupp et al., 1977, volume for interesting first-person accounts), is addressed further in the Unresolved Issues section.

Finally, we must note some problems in the growing trend for varied psychological treatments to be directly compared, within the same study, with the outcomes of biological treatments, usually drug therapies. Although such studies have frequently reported the "superiority" of one or the other of these therapy types in the treatment of various disorders, we remain skeptical that a truly definitive comparison of the outcomes of the two forms of therapy is ultimately possible. In fact, it is not clear that a completely valid outcome study can be done with psychosocial treatment when the design of the study adheres to established modes of evaluating the efficacy of drugs, as most by custom do. As Stiles and Shaprio (1989) have pointed out in a detailed examination of the issues involved,

psychotherapy and drug therapy differ on many dimensions of critical importance in deciding on, and in interpreting, issues both of study design and the outcome measures used.

Take, for example, a therapist himself or herself as a variable, including such attributes as experience in treating the particular disorder, interpersonal skill, familiarity with the subcultural background of a client, faith in the treatment, and perhaps even personal attractiveness or charisma as experienced by the client. We have solid reason, based on available research findings, to believe that such things may be of crucial significance in determining the outcome of any psychosocial treatment effort. Now contrast this with the typical situation for drug treatment. Here, the "active ingredient" of the treatment is pretty much the same no matter who writes the prescription, and a therapist's personal attributes or his or her experience in treating the disorder (with the possible exception of a nonspecific placebo component) are largely irrelevant. With such important differences that vary in uncontrolled (and probably uncontrollable) ways in psychotherapy versus drug comparison studies, it is not easy to see how any *general* and *unequivocal* conclusions regarding differential effectiveness could be made, almost regardless of the quantitative results obtained.

Precisely this sort of difficulty, in fact, attends the NIMH multisite "model" study of the treatment of depression described in *HIGHLIGHT 18.8*, where the preliminary results so far reported show a rather disconcerting effect that might, however, have been predicted from the considerations just discussed. Even during their project-specific pretraining, the psychotherapists recruited for this study showed significantly varying aptitudes (and eventual clinical results) in applying the techniques that were to be used for the interpersonal psychosocial treatment (IPT) aspect of the study (O'Malley et al., 1988). When we turn to the short-term outcomes reported for the main project, we observe that they include significant statistical interactions involving the *sites* at which psychosocial treatment took place (Elkin et al., 1989).

In other words, the psychotherapists at some sites had significantly better immediate outcomes than those at others—even though all were supposedly doing the same types of psychosocial interventions. Although it was not possible to rule out, in preliminary analyses, unexpected but conceivable intersite differences in the characteristics of the patients treated, this seems an unlikely alternative explanation because the site interaction effect was apparent mainly among the most severely disordered patients (Elkin et al., 1989). One way of

Anatomy of a Controlled Field Trial of Therapeutic Outcome

The long-awaited initial results of an NIMH-supported clinical field trial competitively evaluating a cognitive-behavioral therapy (CBT), an interpersonal psychotherapy (IPT), and an antidepressant drug (imipramine) therapy plus clinical management (IMI-CM) in the treatment of unipolar depression became available in late 1989 (Elkin et al., 1989). The design of this study, widely regarded to be state of the art, and its preliminary findings are analyzed here in some detail to give you an appreciation of the choices, the internal logic, and the inference network typically involved in research on therapeutic processes and outcomes in the mental health field.

Subjects. Following prescreening to rule out clearly ineligible patients, 560 purportedly depressed people were seen by a clinical evaluator who used a well-known structured diagnostic interview for establishing a clinical diagnosis. Only patients who met criteria for a current episode of major depressive disorder, and who in addition attained a score of at least 14 on a 17-item version of the Hamilton Rating Scale for Depression (HRSD), were considered eligible for inclusion in the study. The HRSD is a widely used clinician checklist for depressive symptomatology whose validity has been well established. Various exclusion criteria were also applied, chiefly to rule out people having other concurrent mental disorders. Patients who passed this clinical screening were given a complete medical evaluation and then put on a 7- to 14-day waiting and drug-washout period. They were then rescreened by the initial clinical evaluator before final admission to the program. Two hundred fifty people survived the screening procedures and were offered entry into the program as research patient-subjects; 239 actually entered treatment. Of this treated group, only 36 percent had experienced no previous major depressive disorder, and 15 percent had had previous episodes requiring hospitalization. Seventy percent had received some form of previous treatment for depression.

Research sites. Three widely dispersed university psychiatric centers had been chosen as the actual sites in which the clinical trials would be conducted, each recruiting, by the standard means already described, its own group of research subjects. Two of the sites each began with 84 screened subjects, and the third with 82. At each of the sites, patients were assigned at random to one of the three treatments already noted or to a control condition involving administration of a placebo pill plus clinical management (PLA-CM condition). The clinical management component, identical for both imipramine and placebo conditions, involved general encouragement and support, but no specific psychotherapeutic intervention. (The investigators concluded that it was not possible to devise a specifically *psychotherapeutic* control condition.)

Therapists. At each site a different group of experienced therapists (with an overall mean age of 41.5 years and mean experience of 11.4 years) conducted treatment in each of the study conditions, with the exception that the same therapists ("pharmacotherapists") administered either imipramine or placebo, but were blind as to which they were giving in respect to any particular pharmacotherapy-assigned patient-subject. A total of 28 therapists (10 psychologists and 18 psychiatrists) took part. They were given further training in their "specialty" therapies during a training-pilot phase of the study, and they met competence criteria in conducting this therapy prior to assignment to project patient-subjects. Their actual treatment sessions were carried out according to a detailed manual describing the interventions appropriate to the respective specialty therapies, and these sessions were continuously monitored via audiotaping by project staff.

Experimental treatment conditions. All treatments were designed to be 16 weeks in length, but there were 77 early termination cases where the average number of sessions completed was only 6.2. Overall, project patients, of whom there were 162 having at least 15 weeks of treatment, completed an average of 13.0 sessions. Unfortunately, termination evaluations could not be done on 7 of these 162 patients, reducing the number of "completers" to 155. The rates of dropout were not significantly different for the four treatment conditions. The con-

Continued

tent of the various therapies is described as follows:

CBT—*Cognitive behavior therapy was conducted as described by Beck and colleagues [see page 648]. . . . The cognitive therapist uses strategies and techniques designed to help depressed patients correct their negative, distorted views about themselves, the world, and the future, and the underlying maladaptive beliefs that give rise to these cognitions.*

IPT—*Interpersonal psychotherapy was conducted as described by Klerman et al. [see page 637]. . . . The IPT therapist seeks to help the patient to identify and better understand his or her interpersonal problems and conflicts and to develop more adaptive ways of relating to others.*

Imipramine-CM—*The pharmacotherapy conditions were [those considered standard]. Medication was administered double blind within the context of a CM [clinical management] session. . . . The average dosage for imipramine hydrochloride completers, averaged over all weeks after the first 2 weeks of treatment, was 185 mg., with 95% of the patients receiving at least 150 mg. . . .*

PLA-CM—*The pill-placebo condition was administered double blind, within the context of a CM session. . . . Although specific psychotherapeutic interventions were proscribed (especially those that might overlap with the two*

psychotherapies), the CM component approximated a "minimal supportive therapy" condition. (Elkin et al., 1989, p. 973)

Results. Though therapy outcomes are reported separately for all patients entering treatment (n=239), for those completing at least 3.5 weeks of treatment (n=204), and for those completing at least 15 weeks of treatment (n=155), we will concentrate here on results for this last, full-exposure group.

Principal outcome measures were the Hamilton Rating Scale (HRSD), the Beck Depression Inventory (BDI—a self-administered questionnaire commonly used to measure level of depression), a version of the Hopkins Symptom Checklist (HSCL-90T—a more general questionnaire measuring various symptoms of distress), and the Global Assessment Scale (GAS—a clinician's rating form for general level of functioning). Because all of these measures had been administered pretreatment, it was possible to control for initial levels (none of which varied significantly among the four treatment groups) in analyzing treatment outcomes.

Briefly summarizing a rather complicated set of outcome data, these are the main findings:

1. Compared to their pretreatment scores, all four treatment groups on all four outcome measures showed significant improvement.

2. At treatment end, there was an overall statistically significant variation among the four treatment groups on only the two self-administered outcome measures, the BDI and the HSCL-90T. For the BDI, the highest (most pathological) average score was obtained by the PLA-CM group and the lowest by the IMI-CM group, with the IPT group close on its heels. On the HSCL-90T measure, IMI-CM patients had clearly superior, and PLA-CM patients clearly inferior, outcomes—with the two psychotherapy groups falling between and having virtually identical mean scores.

3. In terms of a predefined level of clinical "recovery" (that is, a score of 6 or less on the HRSD, a score of 9 or less on the BDI, or both) only the HRSD measure showed an overall significant difference among treatment groups. Specifically, IMI-CM, IPT, and CBT patients had HRSD-measured termination recovery rates, respectively, of 57 percent, 55 percent, and 51 percent, which are not significantly different from each other in statistical or probability terms. These contrast with a PLA-CM recovery rate of only 29 percent, marginally significantly different in pair-wise comparison from both IMI-CM and IPT.

4. In secondary analyses, pretreatment HRSD and GAS criteria were separately employed to divide the total patient groups into

viewing the latter finding is that differential psychotherapist efficacy was revealed only in work with more severely disturbed patients—that group of patients for whom antidepressant drug treatment showed its only superiority.

The implication is that some psychotherapists having certain as yet undetermined characteristics might do as well or even better than drugs in working with severe major depressive disorder. If that were the case, the unqualified conclusion that more- and less-severely depressed subgroups. The data were then reanalyzed according to this breakdown. This split resulted in a substantially enhanced differentiation of the outcomes of the treatment groups that was largely limited to the more severely disturbed patients. Both measures of pretreatment severity yielded the same ordinal arrangement of outcome HRSD and GAS scores for these more disturbed patients. The IMI-CM treatment produced the best results, followed in order by the IPT and CBT treatment conditions; PLA-CM came in last. These differences, overall, were statistically significant on the HRSD measure for both the severity criteria; for the GAS severity criterion, they were also significant on the HSCL-90T outcome measure. The general pattern was somewhat different with "recovery" rates as the outcome criterion. Here, the two psychotherapy conditions tended to outperform (but nonsignificantly) IMI-CM and PLA-CM with the less-severely disturbed patients. Among more disturbed patients, IPT and IMI-CM were associated with essentially similar recovery rates, both of them being significantly superior to PLA-CM, with CBT falling in between.

5. Also reported, but not analyzed in detail, was a finding of significant interactions between treatments and sites showing up especially in outcomes for the more disturbed patient subsample. Such patients receiving CBT at one site did extremely well and were comparable on outcome measures to IMI-CM patients. The same was true for IPT patients at another site. These residual findings strike us as quite important conceptually (and possibly practically), and are further discussed in the text.

Discussion. In many ways the most impressive result reported here is the performance of the control condition, PLA-CM. "Recovery" rates of 35 to 40 percent among less-disturbed patients and 15 to 20 percent among the more disturbed for a treatment consisting of pharmacologically inert pills and general support, encouragement, and advice speak to the power of reassurance and suggestion as nonspecific treatment factors presumably inherent in all serious efforts at intervention for major depressive disorder.

Overall, the "active" treatments investigated—antidepressant medication and cognitive-behavioral and interpersonal psychotherapies—all add something to this nonspecific baseline effect. Although the antidepressant drug treatment appeared, on average, to fare somewhat better than the others (although only marginally so than the interpersonal therapy) with those patients having more severe symptoms, outcome differences among the active therapies were in absolute terms rather small. Given the site interaction effects noted, it appears that site (that is, therapist) variation is a more important determinant of outcome in the psychotherapies than drug treatment, which on reflection makes a great deal of sense. A standard dose of imipramine is the same no matter who administers it, whereas this would hardly be true in the case of the two psychotherapies—as the results indeed confirm. The fact that both cognitive and interpersonal psychotherapists at particular sites were as effective as medication in the treatment of the severest cases is a finding of considerable theoretical and practical import.

Finally, it must be emphasized that, as of this writing, we have access only to outcomes measured at the termination of therapy. Other studies, mentioned in Chapter 11, have shown cognitive-behavioral therapy to have superior long-term effects.

drugs work better when a major depression is severe would be unwarranted, or at least potentially misleading. Again, the main point to be made here is that psychotherapy—even psychotherapy bearing a specific label—unlike a particular drug cannot realistically be treated as though it were a uniform and invariant therapeutic input. Plainly, it is not.

Given the few but consistent findings of better *long-term* outcomes with psychosocial, as opposed to drug, treatment of depression (reviewed in Chapter 11), we take it as by no means established that drug therapy is the treatment of choice for severe major depression. The present evidence indicates this to be a valid conclusion only for situations in which maximally competent psychotherapy is unavailable, with the further constraint that it addresses only outcomes measured at treatment end but not in long-term follow-up. "Competence" here, by the way, is probably best assessed by a therapist's outcome record in treating clients of this sort.

■ Social Values and Psychotherapy

The criticism has been raised—from both inside and outside the mental health professions—that psychotherapy can be viewed as an attempt to get people adjusted to a "sick" society rather than to encourage them to work toward its improvement. As a consequence, psychotherapy has often been considered the guardian of the status quo. This issue is perhaps easier for us to place in perspective by looking at other cultures. For example, there have been frequent allegations that psychiatry was until recently used as a means of political control in the Soviet Union, an abuse that, with *glasnost,* has now been officially acknowledged (see *Schizophrenia Bulletin,* 1990, v. 16, no. 4). It is encouraging to note that these practices had been all but universally condemned by the international mental health community. Although few people make the claim that psychiatry in the Western world is used to gain control over social critics, there is nevertheless the possibility that therapists are, in some ways, placed in the roles of "gatekeepers" of social values. Such charges, of course, bring us back to the question we raised in Chapter 1: What do we mean by *abnormal?* Our answer to that question can only be made in the light of our values.

In a broader perspective, of course, we are concerned with the complex and controversial issue of the role of values in science. Psychotherapy is not, or at least *should* not be, a system of ethics; it is a set of tools to be used at the discretion of a therapist in pursuit of a client's welfare. Thus mental health professionals are confronted with the same kinds of questions that confront scientists in general. Should a physical scientist who helps develop thermonuclear weapons be morally concerned about how they are used? Similarly, should a psychologist or behavioral scientist who develops powerful techniques of behavior control be concerned about how they are used?

Many psychologists and other scientists try to sidestep this issue by insisting that science is value-free—that it is concerned only with gathering "facts," not with how they are applied. Each time therapists decide that one behavior should be eliminated or substituted for another, however, they are making a value choice. The increasing social awareness of today's mental health professionals has brought into sharp focus ethical questions concerning their roles as therapists and value models, as well as their roles as agents for maintaining the status quo or fostering social change. For example, is a therapist to *assume* the depression of a young homemaker-mother who is abused by a drunken husband to be an internally based disorder requiring "treatment"—as once would have been routine—or does the therapist perhaps not have a larger responsibility to look beyond this individual-pathology viewpoint and confront the abnormality implicit in some of our more sacrosanct cultural expectations? Therapy takes place in a context that involves the values of the therapist, the client, and the society in which they live. There are strong pressures on a therapist—from parents, schools, courts, and other social institutions—to help people adjust to "the world as it is." At the same time, there are many counterpressures, particularly from young people who are seeking support in their attempts to become authentic people rather than blind conformists.

The dilemma in which contemporary therapists may find themselves is illustrated by the following case:

> *A* 15-year-old high school sophomore is sent to a therapist because her parents have discovered that she has been having sexual intercourse with her boyfriend. The girl tells the therapist that she thoroughly enjoys such relations and feels no guilt or remorse over her behavior, even though her parents strongly disapprove. In addition, she reports that she is quite aware of the danger of becoming pregnant and is careful to take contraceptive measures.

What is the role of the therapist in such a case? Should the girl be encouraged to conform to her parents' mores and postpone sexual activity until she is older and more mature? Or should the parents be helped to adjust to the pattern of sexual behavior she has chosen? What should be the therapist's goal? As was noted earlier, it is not unusual to find some individuals being referred for psychological treatment because their behavior, not particularly destructive or disturbing, has caused concern among family members who wish the therapist to "fix" them.

It is apparent that there are diametrically opposed ways of dealing with problems in therapy. Society must enforce conformity to certain norms if it is to maintain its organization and survive. But how does one distinguish between norms that are vital for the common good and those that are irrelevant, outmoded, or arbitrarily imposed by thoughtless devotion to a particular subgroup's notion of revealed truth? It is often up to individual therapists to decide what path to take, and this requires value decisions on their part concerning what is best for an individual and for the larger society. Thus a mental health professional is confronted with the problem of "who (or what) controls the controller"; that is, of developing ethical standards and societal safeguards to prevent misuse of the techniques they have developed for modifying individual and group behavior (Lakin, 1991).

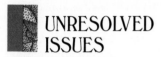

UNRESOLVED ISSUES
in Psychotherapy

Probably no treatment procedure in general medicine or surgery is without risk in the sense of potentially harmful or even fatal effects on a client. Generally speaking, moreover, the more potent the treatment in terms of potential dramatic benefit, the more risky the procedure. The situation appears to be no different in respect to psychotherapy. As we have noted, the outcomes of psychotherapy do not range, as was once thought, from neutral (no effect) to positive, but rather seem to encompass a significant negative or deteriorative effect. One extreme here is client suicide, although we certainly do not suggest that all such outcomes could be avoided with more skillful psychotherapy. In any event, some client-psychotherapist relationships, approaching perhaps 10 percent in frequency (Lambert, Shapiro, & Bergin, 1986), apparently result in the client's being worse off than if psychotherapy had never been undertaken.

Our judgment about the gravity of this situation would be less severe if it were taken more seriously among professional psychotherapists than our experience suggests, and if we knew more about how to prevent it from happening. Regarding the latter point, we do have some guidelines about factors that should be considered, based in part on reviews of the entire issue in books offered by Mays and Franks (1985) and Strupp, Hadley, and Gomes-Schwartz (1977). By and large, there are few surprises in these works. We know that clients with certain types of disorders that are notoriously difficult to treat (such as borderline personality disorder) are more likely than others to deteriorate in treatment. We have also known for some time that an overly aggressive, intrusive, abruptly defense-challenging therapeutic style can be dangerous to client functioning, particularly where it is unmodulated by therapist warmth and empathy. Similarly, the concurrent occurrence of uncontrollable negative events (such as divorce) in a client's "extra-therapeutic" life can obviously impact negatively on therapeutic progress.

These more obvious therapeutic impasses account for only a portion of the failures. In other instances we find a bewildering network of interactive factors that, operating together and idiosyncratically in an individual case (for example, the "match" of therapist and client characteristics), produce deteriorating outcomes. Our impression, supported by some evidence reviewed by Lambert (1989), is that certain therapists, probably for reasons of personality, just do not do well with certain types of client problems. In light of these intangible factors, we take it as every therapist's responsibility to monitor their work with various types of clients to discover any such deficiencies in therapeutic range, and to refer promptly to other therapists those individuals with whom one may be ill-equipped, for whatever reason, to work.

A special case of therapeutic misadventure is the problem of therapist-client sexual entanglements, typically seduction of a client (or "former" client) by a therapist, which is considered unethical conduct. Given the frequently intense and intimate quality of therapeutic relationships, we should perhaps not be surprised that the issue of sexual attraction arises. What is astonishing is the apparent frequency with which it is manifested in an unethical and unprofessional behavior on the part of therapists—all the more so in light of the fact that virtually all authorities agree that such liaisons are *nearly always* destructive of client functioning in the long run.

A variety of evidence, including anonymous admissions of therapists in various surveys over the years, suggests that this source of client exploitation and likely negative outcome is by no means rare. According to one recent report, (Ethics Committee, American Psychological Association, 1990) 23 of 89 professional ethics cases (26 percent) opened in a recent year involved sexual improprieties. In a recently completed national survey of psychologists (Pope & Vetter, in press), *half* of the respondents reported assessing or treating at least one client who had been sexually intimate with a prior therapist, a total of 958 separate instances; 90 percent of these encounters were judged to have been of harm to the client, with an 11 percent subsequent hospitalization rate and a 14 percent rate of attempted suicide. Most of the victims (87 percent) were female, and three of them were children.

Even these chilling statistics, however, do not do justice to the magnitude of the problem in terms of already vulnerable lives being further undermined, nor do they speak to the difficulties victims often have in seeking redress for their psychic injury. That gap has been partially filled with the publication of a remarkable and courageous book by Bates and Brodsky (1989) that deals informatively with these subjects. In it, Bates renders a compelling account of her own sexual vicitimization by a therapist, one who, incredibly, has given a prominent address on "the problem" before a national professional audience. Her "second victimization," involving painful and humiliating experiences, occurred when she instituted legal means to discourage this man from further violations of professional trust. The book, thoroughly researched, offers little encouragement that an offender in this area can be reliably rehabilitated, and yet it has proven extremely difficult to achieve prevention through delicensing or other professional or legal sanction.

Even allowing for the likelihood of occasional fraudulent or frivolous client complaints in this area—the Pope and Vetter data suggest a frequency of 4 percent—the well-established occurrence of this type of event indicates an appalling level of misconduct, and probable client injury, among people holding themselves out to be "psychotherapists," which incidentally is not in most jurisdictions a legally regulated term. A prospective client seeking therapy needs to be sufficiently wary to spare no effort in determining that the therapist chosen is one of the large majority committed to high ethical and professional standards.

Unfortunately, there are otherwise few guidelines a prospective client can reliably employ in choosing a therapist. Reputation in the community and among professional colleagues and quality of background training and experience are obvious things to consider. We think that a "trial" interview or brief series of them is a good idea as a means of assessing one's "fit" and comfort with a given therapist's style. In the end, however, we do not have the data to predict with even reasonable assurance the outcome or likely benefit of any particular therapist-client relationship. This is a knowledge gap on which research is badly needed.

Finally, we should comment briefly on the seeming disarray of the field of therapy with its many competing variations. One aspect of the competition, already noted, involves a currently intense struggle, fueled by interprofessional rivalries, concerning the place of biological therapies in the mental health field. In this chapter we focus on the several varieties of psychosocial approach. We have already indicated our judgment that probably most of these are "right," at least in the limited sense that they have fashioned intervention techniques having a high probability, when sensitively applied, of helping people overcome their problems. The obvious question, then, is this: Why doesn't the typical therapist employ a multifaceted, multitargeted approach to every client with whom treatment is undertaken, instead of doing his or her "own thing," be it psychoanalysis, behavioral, gestalt, or some other therapy? Wouldn't this approach maximize treatment efficiency? We suspect so, and we have no entirely satisfactory answer to the first part of our query. Ideological commitment has historically been very strong in this field—in large part because virtually nobody had solid research data with which to back their claims. That situation is changing rapidly, but the commitment tends to remain despite the change and despite sincere efforts (e.g., Goldfried, Greenberg, & Marmar, 1990; Goldfried & Safran, 1986) to enhance communication across the many intersecting barriers. As every therapist knows, dysfunctional habits are often hard to break.

SUMMARY

Psychotherapy is aimed at the reduction of abnormal behavior in individuals through psychological means. The goals of psychotherapy include changing maladaptive behavior, minimizing or eliminating stressful environmental conditions, reducing negative affect, improving interpersonal competencies, resolving personal conflicts, modifying an individual's inaccurate assumptions about himself or herself, and fostering a more positive self-image. Although these goals are by no means easy to achieve, psychological treatment methods have been shown to be generally effective in promoting adaptive psychological functioning in many troubled individuals.

Numerous approaches to psychological treatment ("schools of psychotherapy") have been developed to treat individuals with psychological disorders. We have organized these approaches into a scheme that focuses attention on the primary target selected for intervention. Type A therapies are directed at a client's affects or emotions; Type B at client behaviors; Type C at problematic aspects of cognition; and Type E at reactions in a client's environment. It is argued that, because these elements are organized in an unending loop, positive change in any one of them will produce a good therapeutic effect overall.

Nevertheless, this chapter is developed in accord with the traditional breakdown of "schools" of therapy. One of the oldest approaches to psychological treatment, psychoanalysis, or psychodynamic therapy, was originated nearly a century ago by Sigmund Freud. Although complicated systems of psychodynamic treatment have evolved since Freud's time, many features of "orthodox" psychoanalysis today closely resemble Freud's original system. Several other schools of therapy have developed out of the psychoanalytic tradition. These approaches accept some elements of Freudian theory but diverge on key points, such as the length of time to be devoted to therapy or the role of the ego in personality dynamics. By and large, we consider them Type E therapies because of the attention they give to the management of "transference."

A second major approach to psychological intervention is behavior therapy. Originating over 50 years ago, behavior therapy has come to be used extensively in treating clinical problems. Behavior therapy approaches make use of a number of techniques, such as systematic desensitization and biofeedback (which are Type A therapies). Other behavior therapy techniques include aversion therapy, modeling, reinforcement approaches, and assertiveness therapy (all Type B therapies). Recently, behavior therapy methods have been applied to internal processes—that is, thought or cognitions (Type C)—with a great deal of success. Known as cognitive-behavioral therapy, this approach attempts to modify an individual's self-statements to change his or her behavior. Cognitive-behavioral methods have been used for a wide variety of clinical problems—from depression to anger control—and with a range of clinical populations.

Several other psychological treatment methods have been referred to as humanistic-experiential therapies (which we regard as primarily Type C, owing to their focus on "awareness"). One of the earliest of these approaches is the client-centered, or person-centered, therapy of Carl Rogers. This treatment approach, originating in the 1940s, has received broad acceptance and has provided a valuable conceptualization of the client-therapist interaction as well as specific techniques for generating personal change or personal growth in motivated clients.

In addition to individual treatment approaches, some psychological treatment methods are applied in group settings, such as group therapy and marital or family therapy. These approaches typically assume that an individual's problems lie partly in his or her interactions with others. Consequently, the focus of treatment is to change ways of interacting among individuals in the social or family context (a Type E approach).

In recent years an attempt has been made to integrate behavior therapy methods with other psychological treatment approaches, particularly psychodynamic therapy. This effort is a result of the recognition that elements from both approaches can be used to increase our understanding of troubled clients and to bring about desired behavior changes. These integration issues are actually part of a broader problem of therapists largely doing their "own thing," addressed in the chapter's Unresolved Issues section.

Evaluation of the success of psychotherapy in producing desired behavior changes in clients is difficult. Research in psychotherapy, however, has shown that most treatment approaches are more effective than no treatment at all. Beyond the question of evaluating the success of psychotherapy lies other, larger questions involving the ethical dilemmas posed by therapy. Does psychotherapy encourage conformity to the status quo? Should it do this? These constitute some of the difficult moral and social issues that daily confront mental health professionals.

Other unresolved issues include the often perplexing occurrence of negative or deteriorative outcomes in psychotherapy. One likely source of such outcomes, by no means the only or necessarily most common, is sexual misconduct on the part of a therapist.

■ Key Terms

psychotherapy (p. 627)
clinical psychologist (p. 630)
psychiatrist (p. 630)
psychiatric social workers
   (p. 630)
psychodynamic therapy
   (p. 632)
free association (p. 634)
manifest content (p. 635)
latent content (p. 635)
resistance (p. 636)
transference (p. 636)
counter-transference (p. 636)
behavior therapy (p. 638)
implosion (p. 639)
flooding (p. 639)
systematic desensitization
   (p. 640)
aversion therapy (p. 641)
modeling (p. 642)
response shaping (p. 642)
token economies (p. 643)

behavioral contracting
   (p. 643)
assertiveness therapy (p. 644)
biofeedback (p. 645)
cognitive-behavioral therapy
   (p. 646)
rational-emotive therapy
   (RET) (p. 647)
stress-inoculation therapy
   (p. 648)
humanistic-experiential
   therapies (p. 651)
client-centered
   (person-centered) therapy
   (p. 651)
existential psychotherapy
   (p. 653)
gestalt therapy (p. 654)
couples counseling (marital
   therapy) (p. 656)
structural family therapy
   (p. 659)

Chapter 19
Contemporary Issues in Abnormal Psychology

Guillaume Pujolle, *Le Provence—Dessin Animé*.
Pujolle (1893–?) was born in the Haute-Garonne
area in France. A joiner by trade, he was torn by emotional
conflicts and was eventually admitted to a hospital in
Toulouse. He began to draw in 1935. His pictures have a
dreamlike, fluid appearance, composed as they are of a
mosaic of broad, undulating strips of color.

Over the years, most efforts toward mental health have been largely restorative, geared toward helping people only after they have already developed serious problems. Prior to the 1960s, mental health professionals typically did not become involved until after an individual had suffered a breakdown; then they often sent such individuals for treatment far away from their home communities, often compounding their distress and disrupting their lives.

Seemingly, a more effective strategy would be to try to catch problems *before* they become severe, or better yet, to establish conditions in which psychological disorders will not occur. Specific causal backgrounds for many mental disorders, however, are not sufficiently understood to enable practitioners to initiate explicit preventive programs. Efforts toward prevention in the mental health field are still based largely on hypotheses about what works rather than on substantial empirical research. Nonetheless, many professionals in the field believe that preventive mental health efforts are worthwhile.

Of course, preventive efforts, like treatment programs, cost money. During periods of economic decline, federal, state, and local governments typically reduce their support for such programs. Unfortunately, programs aimed at prevention, because of their long-range scope and their often indirect focus, are perhaps more difficult to justify because they appear less cost-effective than other programs with more direct and explicit outcome criteria. The irony, of course, is that prevention can be in the long run far less costly (Lorion, 1990).

Where preventive efforts fail and a serious mental health problem develops, today's professionals place more emphasis on the importance of prompt treatment. It is considered preferable, too, that the treatment be in the individual's own community so that clinicians can use available family and other familiar supports and reduce the disruption to the individual's life pattern. If hospitalization becomes necessary, every effort is taken to prevent the disorder from becoming chronic and to return the individual to the community as soon as possible, with whatever aftercare and continued support that may be needed.

In this last chapter, we will examine the kinds of measures that are being taken to prevent maladaptive behavior or limit its seriousness. Our discussion will begin with a review of preventive strategies. Next, we will explore some factors related to the care and hospitalization of individuals with severe psychological problems: commitment, deinstitutionalization, and assessment of dangerousness. Closely related to these factors are the matters of (a) a therapist's duty to warn others if a client threatens violence and (b) the use—and some think abuse—of the insanity defense as a plea in capital crimes. Next, we will briefly survey the scope of organized efforts for mental health both in the United States and throughout the world. Finally, we will conclude the chapter by considering what each of us can do to foster mental health.

PERSPECTIVES ON PREVENTION

In our present discussion we will use the concepts of primary, secondary, and tertiary prevention, which are widely used in public health medicine to describe general strategies of disease prevention. **Primary prevention** is aimed at reducing the possibility of disease and fostering positive health. **Secondary prevention** is typically emergency or crisis intervention, and involves efforts to reduce the impact, duration, or spread of a problem that has already developed—if possible, catching it before it has become serious. **Tertiary prevention** seeks to reduce the long-term consequences of disorders or serious problems. These preventive strategies, although primarily devised for understanding and controlling infectious physical diseases, provide a useful perspective in the mental health field as well.

It is important to note here that this tripartite view of mental health prevention efforts may be creating some problems. Long (1986), for example, feels that the term *prevention* should only be used to refer to *primary* prevention efforts; secondary prevention, such as emergency psychotherapy, and tertiary prevention, such as hospital rehabilitation programs, should be considered, respectively, as *treatment* and *rehabilitation*. Though some may feel that this problem is just a matter of semantics, Long is concerned that it is negatively affecting the funding of primary prevention programs. By being grouped together with treatment and rehabilitative efforts, she argues, primary prevention efforts are not receiving the financial support required to make an impact on reducing mental health problems in society, in large part because the other mental health efforts with which they are grouped seem more urgent and typically get more of the already

limited resources. Clearly, funding at all three levels is critical to the future of mental health.

Primary Prevention

In primary prevention, we are concerned with two key tasks: altering conditions that can cause or contribute to mental disorders and establishing conditions that foster positive mental health. In primary prevention, epidemiological studies are particularly important because they help investigators obtain information about the incidence and distribution of various maladaptive behaviors needing prevention efforts (Dohrenwend & Dohrenwend, 1982). These findings can then be used to suggest what preventive efforts might be most appropriate. For example, various epidemiological studies have shown that certain groups of individuals are at high risk for mental disorders, including recently divorced people (Bloom, Asher, & White, 1978), the physically disabled (Freemen, Malkin, & Hastings, 1975), elderly people living alone (Neugarten, 1977) and individuals who have been uprooted from their homes (Westermeyer, Williams, & Nguyen, 1991). Although findings such as these may be the basis for immediate secondary prevention, they may also aid later in primary prevention by telling us what to look for and where to look—in essence by focusing our efforts in the right direction. Primary prevention includes biological, psychosocial, and sociocultural efforts. As Kessler and Albee (1975) have noted, "Everything aimed at improving the human condition, at making life more fulfilling and meaningful, may be considered to be part of primary prevention of mental or emotional disturbance" (p. 557).

Biological Measures   Biologically based primary prevention begins with help in family planning and includes both prenatal and postnatal care. A good deal of current emphasis is being placed on guidance in family planning—how many children to have, when to have them in relation to marital and other family conditions, and even whether to have children at all. Such guidance may include genetic counseling, in which tests for diagnosing genetic defects may be administered to potential parents to assess their risk of having children with birth defects that can result in mental disorders.

Breakthroughs in genetic research have also made it possible to detect and often alleviate genetic defects before a baby is born; when in utero treatment is not feasible, such information provides the parents with the choice of having an abortion rather than going on to bear a baby with serious defects. Continued progress in genetic research may make it possible to identify genetic disorders early or even to correct faulty genes, thus providing humankind with fantastic new power to prevent hereditary pathology.

Many of the goals of health psychology can also be viewed as primary prevention. Efforts geared toward improving one's diet, establishing a routine of physical exercise, and overall good health patterns can do much to improve one's physical well-being. To the extent that physical illness always produces some sort of psychological stress that can eventuate in such problems as depression, good health is primary prevention in respect to good mental health.

Psychosocial Measures   In regarding normality as optimal development and functioning rather than as the mere absence of pathology, we imply that an individual requires opportunities to learn needed competencies—physical, intellectual, emotional, and social. The first requirement of psychosocial "health" is that an individual develop the skills needed for effective problem solving, for handling emotions constructively, and for establishing satisfying interpersonal relationships; failure to develop these skills places the individual at a serious disadvantage in coping with life problems and at risk for developing mental health problems.

The second requirement for psychosocial health is that an individual acquire an accurate frame of reference on which to build self-identity. We have seen repeatedly that when people's assumptions about themselves or their world are inaccurate, their behavior is likely to be maladaptive. Likewise, an inability to find satisfying values that foster a meaningful and fulfilling life constitutes a fertile source of maladjustment and mental disorders.

Third, psychosocial well-being also requires preparation for the types of problems an individual is likely to encounter during given life stages. For example, pregnancy and childbirth usually have a great deal of emotional significance for both parents and may disturb family equilibrium or exacerbate an already disturbed marital situation. Young people who want to marry and have children must be prepared for the tasks of building a mutually satisfying relationship and helping children develop their potentialities. Similarly, an individual needs to be prepared adequately for other developmental tasks characteristic of given life periods, including retirement and old age.

In recent years, psychosocial measures aimed at ensuring primary prevention have received a great

Parents can be helped to be more effective in their relationships with their children. Diane, shown here with one of her children, is enhancing her parenting skills through the Avance *Program in San Antonio, Texas—a program for low-income Mexican-American families that attempts to prevent child neglect and abuse by helping parents, many of whom were emotionally deprived as children, learn to give appropriate emotional support to their children.*

deal of attention. The field of behavioral medicine has had substantial influence here. As we saw in Chapter 7, efforts are being made to change the psychological factors underlying life-style patterns —especially in terms of high-risk habits, such as smoking, excessive drinking, and poor eating, that may be contributing to the development of both physical and psychological problems.

Sociocultural Measures   The relationship between an individual and his or her community is a reciprocal one, a fact we sometimes forget in our prizing of individualism. We need autonomy and freedom to be ourselves, but we also need to belong and contribute to a community. Without a supportive community, individual development is stifled. At the same time, without responsible, psychologically healthy individuals, the community will not thrive and, in turn, cannot be supportive. Sociocultural efforts toward primary prevention are focused on making the community as nourishing as possible for the individuals within it.

With our growing realization of the importance of pathological social conditions in producing maladaptive behavior, increased attention must be devoted to creating social conditions that will foster healthy development and functioning in individuals. Efforts to create these conditions are seen in a broad spectrum of social measures ranging from public education and Social Security to economic planning and social legislation directed at ensuring adequate health care for all citizens. Such measures, of course, must take into account the stressors and health problems we are likely to encounter as our rapidly changing society moves into the future.

Primary prevention through social change in the community is difficult. Although the whole psychological climate can ultimately be changed by a social movement, such as the civil rights movement of the 1960s, the payoff of such efforts is generally far in the future and may be difficult or impossible to measure.

An Illustration of Primary Prevention Strategies.

Though difficult to formulate and even more difficult to mobilize and carry out, primary prevention efforts can bring about major improvements if successful. We will look in this section at the mobilization of primary prevention resources aimed at curtailing or reducing the problem of teenage alcohol and drug abuse.

Although drug use among most adolescent groups has declined in recent times (Oetting & Beauvais, 1990), teenage drug and alcohol use is still viewed as one of today's most significant psychological and community problems. Mental health professionals and political figures alike have called for a more concerted effort to deal with this enormous social problem. It is clear that traditional health or psychological intervention models, aimed at remediation only *after* a youngster has become addicted to narcotics or alcohol, have not substantially addressed the problem of drug and alcohol abuse among teenagers. Tragically, these traditional treatment approaches are implemented after the child has damaged his or her life through substance use.

Many contemporary researchers and theorists have taken a more proactive position with regard to solving the problems of teenage drug and alcohol use. They have attempted to establish programs that prevent the development of abuse disorders *before* individuals become so involved with drugs or alcohol that their lives are altered to the point that future adjustment becomes difficult, if not impossible. These recent prevention strategies have taken several diverse and hopeful directions, addressing somewhat different aspects of teenagers' lives. We will examine several that show promise and then discuss the limitations to these prevention approaches.

Education programs.   Drug and alcohol education programs represent a prevention strategy aimed at providing information about the damaging effects of these substances. Many are school-based and focus on increasing the youngsters' resistance to drugs and alcohol through education. These

programs are usually premised on the idea that if children are made aware of the dangers of ingesting dangerous drugs and alcohol, they will choose not to begin using them. Englander-Golden et al. (1986), for example, provided "Say it straight" training to sixth through eighth graders in which they taught them both the dangers of drug and alcohol abuse and how to be assertive enough to resist drugs and alcohol in spite of peer pressure. In a follow-up evaluation, these investigators reported that youngsters who were trained in the program had a lower rate of drug- and alcohol-related suspensions from school than did children who received no training.

Intervention programs for high-risk teens.   Intervention programs involve identifying high-risk teenagers and providing special approaches to circumvent their further use of alcohol or potentially dangerous drugs. Programs such as these are often school-based efforts and are not strictly prevention programs; rather, they are treatment programs that provide early intervention for high-risk teens who are vulnerable to drug or alcohol use, in order to reduce the likelihood of their becoming further involved with these substances. Newman et al. (1988–1989) described a procedure for the early identification of young people who are having school-related difficulties because of drug and alcohol use. The developers of this program train school teachers and administrators to effectively identify and manage alcohol- and drug-use problems. Critical to this school intervention is a fair and consistently enforced drug and alcohol policy in the schools.

Parent education and family-based intervention programs.   Because parents typically underestimate their own children's drug and alcohol use (Silverman & Silverman, 1987), several programs have been aimed at increasing parent's awareness of the extent of this problem among teens and at teaching them possible ways to deal with drug and alcohol use in the family context. These programs teach parents how to recognize drug- or alcohol-abuse problems so that youngsters can be diverted away from negative and self-destructive behaviors. One such program by Grady, Gersick, and Boratynski (1985) worked with parents whose children were about to become teenagers. They first assessed the parents with regard to their skill in dealing with drug-related issues; then they trained them to understand and respond empathically to youngsters who might be exposed to drugs during their adolescent years. They were then taught to respond to their children's questions and stated concerns and to help them consider alternative, more adaptive behavior.

Other family-oriented programs have been aimed at strengthening the family bonds and providing more positive family relationships to insulate a child from external negative influences. For example, DeMarsh and Kumpfer (1985) developed a program that focused on involving parents or a family in the positive socialization of a child by increasing the communications within the family and enhancing the parents' child-management skills to aid them in appropriate disciplining of their children.

When there is a drug or alcohol problem, assuring family cooperation in the treatment program can be problematic, and many programs have reported low rates of participation. In an effort to increase the participation rate and lower resistance to treatment, Szapocznik et al. (1988) used family-systems therapeutic techniques to reduce the resistance of families to drug treatment. They reported that 77 percent of the families completed the treatment program compared with only 25 percent in a control condition.

Peer group influence programs. Clearly, peers exert a powerful influence on teenagers in every aspect of their lives, including drug and alcohol abuse. Programs designed to help youngsters overcome negative pressures from peers focus on teaching social skills and assertiveness. Of course, peer pressure can be positive as well—in this case, influencing a teen *not* to use drugs or alcohol—and many programs focus on the positive aspects of peer pressure. In fact, Swadi and Zeitlin (1988) advocated the positive use of peer influence because, for teenagers, such influence seems much more powerful than the influence of others, including teachers and even parents.

Programs to increase self-esteem. Programs designed to increase a sense of self-worth attempt to ensure that individuals will be able to fend for themselves more assuredly and not fall into dependent, negative relationships with stronger and more dominant peers. Pentz (1983) designed one such program by providing teenagers with social skills training and the modeling of appropriate behaviors to reduce drug use and other related negative behaviors, such as truancy. In another program, Botvin (1983) relied on cognitive-behavioral intervention techniques to enhance teenagers' feelings of competency in basic life skills and improving their problem-solving skills. This approach was thought to be effective in reducing the impact of tobacco, alcohol, and marijuana use (Botvin, et al., 1990).

Mass media and modeling programs. Most youngsters are bombarded with drug- or alcohol-related stimuli in TV commercials, movies, and other visual blitzes. Airing such TV commercials or programs at times that children may view them serves to glamorize alcohol or drug use by giving youngsters messages such as "Drink Bud" or "Switch to wine coolers" during television programs they view and like. Several recent efforts have been aimed at deglamorizing or counteracting these messages by showing commercials that graphically depict the negative aspects of alcohol and drug use (Coombs, Paulson, & Palley, 1988; Schilling & McAlister, 1990).

The various prevention strategies discussed here are by no means mutually exclusive. Most programs do not rely on a single intervention strategy but actually incorporate one or more of them (Forman & Linney, 1988; Perry & Murray, 1985). For example, Botvin and Tortu (1988) described an extensive five-stage program involving both didactic and peer interaction interventions designed to enhance youngsters' self-esteem and enable them to function effectively in social contexts to resist negative peer influences. In the first component of this program, several sessions are devoted to biofeedback demonstrations of the effects of cigarettes, marijuana, and alcohol on heart rate. In the second component, several sessions are aimed at teaching them how to make effective decisions. In the third component, sessions focus on aiding the youngsters in understanding their self-image and improving their self-esteem. In the

The students shown here are participating in the New Haven Social Development Project, a preventive program designed to teach children the critical thinking skills they need to deal more effectively with stressors and problem solving—skills that will help these children enhance their self-esteem and better handle difficult social situations and pressures.

fourth component, teenagers are taught to deal with anxiety, particularly social anxiety. Finally, the fifth component of the program involves training the teens in both social communication and assertiveness, thus ensuring a more effective peer group interaction.

How successful are primary prevention programs at reducing the overall impact of adolescent drug and alcohol use? It is difficult to say. Some researchers have concluded that drug and alcohol education programs have only limited success (Tobler, 1986). Conducting rigorous research in primary prevention is often problematic because the interventions may be only remotely connected to the behavior being targeted for change. Moreover, it is typically impossible to exert experimental control over all of the relevant variables influencing drug and alcohol use. Clearly, it is difficult to provide a powerful enough intervention to offset the motivation to use or sell drugs many youngsters experience. For many individuals living in abject poverty, the only way they can tolerate or possibly get out of the ghetto is through using or selling drugs. The recent decline in drug use among teenagers does not include minorities living in ghettos, barrios, or American Indian reservations, where drug use continues to grow at record levels (Oetting & Beauvais, 1990).

Some critics of drug and alcohol prevention programs consider the source of drug and alcohol problems in adolescence to be the result of early socialization processes—and not amenable to superficial reeducation efforts occurring so late in a youngster's life. Shedler and Block (1990), in a well-controlled longitudinal study in which subjects were carefully studied from about age 5 to age 18, found clear precursors to frequent drug use in the youngsters' early personality development. They found that teenagers developing drug-abuse patterns in their late teens had clear psychological maladjustment in early childhood, well before they were exposed to drugs; these psychological problems predisposed the adolescents to drug abuse. As such, Shedler and Block considered the "peer-centered" or environmental influence explanations to be flawed and inadequate to explain the behavior. They thus argued that many of the drug education program efforts are inadequate to address the true source of the problem: the personality syndrome that appears to underlie drug abuse.

Unfortunately, many of the recent programs that have been initiated in response to the drug crisis are seen as "too little, too late." The lackluster performance or outright failure of some drug pre-

vention efforts may hinder future research. Because of the lack of clear research findings and an ambiguous demonstration of the effectiveness of prevention programs, it is difficult to convince lawmakers or funding agencies that more extensive financial support for such programs is needed or worth the effort. Policymakers may take such unproductive results as an indication that primary prevention efforts are not effective in reducing the problem behavior being addressed. Thus more substantial, better-designed, and longer-range programs that could be powerful enough to bring about major changes may not be supported.

■ Secondary Prevention

Secondary prevention emphasizes the early detection and prompt treatment of maladaptive behavior in an individual's family and community setting. In some cases—for example, in a crisis or a disaster—secondary prevention involves immediate and relatively brief intervention to prevent any long-term behavioral consequences. In other cases, secondary prevention is aimed at longer-term consulting and educational services to reduce the consequences of some identified maladaptive behavior or problem. We will look briefly at both types of secondary prevention and then follow with an in-depth examination of secondary prevention efforts after an airplane crash.

Crisis Intervention   Crisis intervention has emerged in response to a widespread need for immediate help for individuals and families confronted with especially stressful situations—be they disasters or family situations that have become intolerable (Auerbach & Stolberg, 1986; Butcher & Dunn, 1989; Butcher, Stelmachers, & Maudal, 1983; Gist & Lubin, 1989; Mitchell & Resnik, 1981; Taylor, 1989). Often, people in crisis are in a state of acute turmoil and feel overwhelmed and incapable of dealing with the stress by themselves. They do not have time to wait for the customary initial therapy appointment, nor are they usually in a position to continue therapy over a sustained period of time. They need immediate assistance.

To meet this need, two modes of therapeutic intervention have been developed: (a) short-term crisis therapy involving face-to-face discussion, and (b) the telephone hot line. These forms of crisis intervention are usually handled either by professional mental health personnel or by paraprofessionals—lay people who have been trained for this work.

Short-term crisis therapy.   **Short-term crisis therapy,** as the name implies, is of brief duration and focuses on the immediate problem with which an individual or family is having difficulty. Although medical problems may also require emergency treatment, we are concerned here with personal or family problems of an emotional nature. In such crisis situations, a therapist is usually very active, helping to clarify the problem, suggesting plans of action, providing reassurance, and otherwise giving needed information and support. In essence, the therapist tries to provide as much help as the individual or family will accept.

If the problem involves psychological disturbance in one of the family members, emphasis is usually placed on mobilizing the support of other family members. Often this enables the person to avoid hospitalization and a disruption of family life. Crisis intervention may also involve bringing other mental health or medical personnel into the treatment picture. Most individuals and families who come for short-term crisis therapy do not continue in treatment for more than one to six sessions. An example of crisis intervention as a secondary preventive effort is given in *HIGHLIGHT 19.1.*

The telephone hot line.   As we noted in Chapter 11, the Los Angeles Suicide Prevention Center opened up a whole new approach to dealing with people undergoing crises—the telephone hot line. Today all major cities in the United States and most smaller ones have developed some form of telephone hot line to help individuals undergoing periods of deep stress. Although the threat of suicide is the most dramatic example, the range of problems that people call about is virtually unlimited—from breaking up with someone to being on a bad drug trip. In addition, there are specific hot lines in various communities for rape victims and for runaways who need assistance.

As with other crisis intervention, a person handling hot-line calls is confronted with the problem of rapidly assessing what is wrong and how bad it is. Even if an accurate assessment is possible and the hot-line therapist does everything within his or her power to help the individual—within the confines imposed by the telephone—a distraught caller may hang up without leaving any name, telephone number, or address. This can be a deeply disturbing experience for the therapist—particularly if, for example, the caller has announced that he or she has just swallowed a lethal dose of sleeping pills. Even in less severe cases, of course, the hot-line therapist may never learn whether the caller's problem has

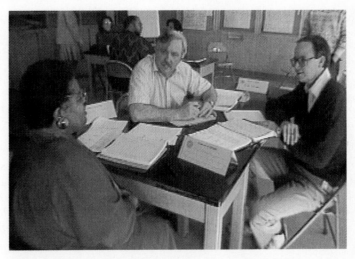

The Jobs Project in Michigan is designed to help recently unemployed workers through the initial stress of unemployment in order to prevent disorders from occurring. For five consecutive mornings, participants attend workshops that enhance both self-esteem and job-hunting skills. Joanna, shown here, is role-playing for a job interview as a factory foreman.

been solved. In other instances, however, the caller may be induced to come in for counseling, making more personal contact possible.

For a therapist, crisis intervention is probably the most discouraging of any treatment approach that we have discussed. The urgency of the intervention and the frequent inability to provide any therapeutic closure or follow-up are probably key factors in this discouragement. Free clinics and crisis centers have reported that their counselors—many of whom are volunteers—tend to burn out after a short period of time. Despite the high frustration level of this work, however, crisis-intervention therapists fill a crucial need in the mental health field, particularly for the young people who make up the majority of their clients. This need is recognized by the many community mental health centers and general hospitals that provide emergency psychological services, either through hot lines or walk-in services. For the thousands of individuals in desperate trouble, an invaluable social support is provided by the fact that there is somewhere they can go for immediate help or someone they can call who will listen to their problems and try to help them. Thus the continuing need for crisis intervention services and telephone hot lines is evident.

Consultation and Education of Intermediaries   Often, community mental health professionals, such as psychologists and psychiatrists, are able to reach a larger group of individuals in need of secondary prevention efforts by working through

Crisis Intervention in Troubled Families

Smith (1938) humorously referred to families as "that dear octopus from whose tentacles we never quite escape, nor, in our innermost hearts, ever quite wish to" (p. 120). Though extremely important to us all, families clearly go awry at times. Family crises involve a disruption in the normal pattern of relationships and aspirations, and such crises produce increased tension in family members by threatening them with unmanageable internal or external forces. Family crises can result from many sources; for example, a family may lose its home through economic emergency, or a family member may die or become severely ill, or one of the family members may become psychotic, or, as in the following case, one of the family members may attempt suicide:

A 17-year-old girl, Leah, was brought into the emergency department of a general hospital by her mother, father, and maternal grandmother. She had walked into her parents' bedroom earlier in the morning and announced that she had swallowed all her mother's pills. The parents had brought their daughter for emer-

gency medical treatment and were enraged when a psychiatrist was called. The history was obtained from mother, since Leah said little, and mother answered every question. During the interview, father paced in and out of the room, repeatedly declaring that he was taking his daughter home. He aggressively asked each person who entered the room "What do you want?" but each time left before a response was possible. Grandmother sat in the room, announcing from time to time, "That girl always makes trouble."

Leah was the oldest of three children. None of them attended school. According to mother, she tutored them at home. Mother also worked outside of the home and complained about how much she had to do. Leah "won't even go to the store alone, so I must accompany her everywhere." Mother said that her husband had told her not to bother with Leah, who would only get married and leave them anyway. But she (mother) had to "bother" because Leah could not go out alone in their neighborhood.

When asked about the suicide attempt, Leah said she would "do it again" if she went home. She

wanted to talk to someone about the fights with mother that made her so angry she wanted to die. Mother said it was father's fault. He worked erratically, drank heavily, and made them live in a bad house in a poor neighborhood. They had terrible neighbors who were "nosey" and bothered them.

Since Leah had indicated she still had suicidal intentions and the family conflict continued unabated, hospitalization was recommended. In response, Leah immediately announced she was better and would go home. She said she would not stay in the hospital. Her mother said she could never persuade her to stay and the family gathered itself up to leave (Kress, 1984, p. 419–420).

The family crisis in this case brought to light several difficult problems due, in part, to the psychopathology of the individuals in the family—adjustment problems that threatened the integrity of the family organization. While Leah appeared to be the most disturbed, other family members, particularly the father, seemed to have significant psychological

---

primary care professionals, such as teachers, social workers, and police personnel (Iscoe, Bloom, & Spielberger, 1977; Levine & Perkins, 1987; Mann, 1978). For such programs, mental health professionals identify a population at risk for the development of psychological disorder and then work with the personnel in community institutions who have frequent contact with members of this population. For example, police officers might be trained to

direct individuals involved in domestic quarrels to seek mental health services rather than to settle their differences through violence.

Mental health professionals had originally intended that *consultation and education* (C & E) be included among the services offered by all community mental health centers. This would have meant that the impact of these centers would have been more indirect—helping individuals experiencing problems that directly affected the family strife as well. The suicide attempt, like many other crises a family is unprepared to resolve, required outside intervention. Not only was an immediate solution needed for the present emergency, but psychological intervention for the longer-term problem of the family's inability to resolve conflict was recommended. However, the closed, almost reclusive, nature of the family suggested that treatment for the individuals involved and for the disturbed family relationships, though needed, was not likely to be accepted at that point. Neither Leah nor her father appeared open to examining their problems or to changing their behavior. Unfortunately, we have no follow-up on the case of Leah. This is often the situation in crisis therapy, where the intervention efforts are limited to what can be accomplished only during the immediate crisis, that is, many such clients never return for more therapy, no matter how adamant the crisis worker's recommendation that they do so.

As is by now obvious, crisis intervention therapy with families is usually different and more limited in scope than family therapy as described in Chapter 18. The goals of family crisis intervention do not involve changing the basic family functioning, as in family therapy, but are usually aimed at returning a disrupted family to precrisis functioning (Umana, Gross, & McConville, 1980). For example, the mental health practitioner's task in the case of Leah involved resolving the immediate emergency and helping ease her life-threatening state of mind while, hopefully, engaging her family in future family or individual treatment to resolve the pressing problems that appeared to have caused the immediate crisis.

Family-oriented crisis intervention is aimed at restoring family equilibrium through resolution of the current situational stressors acting on a family (Auerbach & Stolberg, 1986). It is important for a practitioner to assess clearly the crucial issues underlying the family distress, the family dynamics, and the possible role that individual psychopathology plays in the family relationships. The therapist needs to determine and reinforce those family members who possess strengths that can be enlisted in the change process—that is, to bring about the necessary crisis resolution. The primary role of the therapist in the emergency intervention is to determine how the family resources can be mobilized to solve the immediate problem that prompted the crisis.

The task of resolving individual psychological problems or reorganizing the family structure and dynamics are deferred until after the immediate crisis situation is resolved. If the family can be brought into family or individual therapy later, it will be the task of the therapist to determine what family resources can be engaged to move the family toward the constructive development of more effective problem-solving techniques. In the Leah case, a major goal for later therapy would be determining how the family could be encouraged to become involved in a longer-term solution to their problems. Individual therapy might also be required for some family members to enable them to deal with the ensuing family changes that might occur.

problems by increasing the skill and sensitivity of those who come into contact with them in the community and are in a position to make their lives either more stressful or less so. Currently, however, most community mental health centers provide little such indirect service; only about 4 percent of their total effort is devoted to consultation with and education of primary care professionals. Typically, half or more of this consultation and education involves working with the schools or with other juvenile services; less than a tenth of this effort is spent with police and correctional personnel (NIMH, 1978b).

An Illustration of Secondary Prevention

In many ways, airline disasters are terrifying and unthinkable events. Nevertheless, it is difficult today to deny their reality, considering how many communities have experienced the aftermath of such a disaster. The immediate consequences of an air crash are devastating. Survivors of air crashes typically have traumatic responses to the accident that impair their immediate functioning and place great demands on their psychological adjustment for weeks after the disaster. Family members of air crash victims often experience extensive psychological trauma following the accident; they may need to make extensive changes during their loved one's lengthy recovery period or, more likely, they will need to make major life changes to adjust to their loved one's death. Even various rescue personnel who are caught up in dealing with the aftermath of an airline disaster may suffer from posttraumatic stress disorder.

In many respects the emotional responses of and adjustive demands placed on air crash victims are similar to those of victims of natural disasters, such as hurricanes, floods, and volcanic eruptions (Manglesdorff, 1985). A number of special considerations, however, influence the intensity of the problems seen following airplane crashes: typically airplane crashes are sudden and unexpected; they are usually quite chaotic in terms of their destruction; and air disasters usually occur away from one's familiar settings and with individuals who are strangers. Consequently, the sense of community that characterizes many disasters is lacking. In addition, the impact of an air disaster has a strong emotional *irradiation effect;* that is, it impacts to a greater or lesser degree a larger number of individuals than those immediately affected by the accident itself. Air disasters differ from natural disasters in another important respect—they usually involve considerable blame and anger that can aggravate or intensify the emotional reactions of survivors even months after the crash.

Most airports, particularly those involved in air carrier operations, are required to have a disaster plan that includes fire-rescue and medical evacuation procedures to deal with an airplane crash. Recently, some airport disaster plans have incorporated a psychological support program to provide emergency mental health services to survivors and the family members of crash victims as well as to rescue workers (Butcher, 1980; Butcher & Dunn, 1989). These programs are viewed as secondary prevention efforts in that they are aimed at providing emergency psychological services to prevent the development of psychological disorders or to reduce the severity of such problems if they occur.

Three types of secondary prevention services have been shown to be effective in dealing with the psychological problems related to air disasters: immediate crisis intervention services to crash survivors and surviving family members; crisis telephone hot-line services to provide information and referrals to victims who do not have crisis intervention services available; and postdisaster debriefing sessions for secondary victims, such as rescue personnel, affected by the disaster. We will look at each of these services briefly.

Postdisaster crisis therapy.   Timing is critical to crisis intervention, which, when applied in the immediate aftermath of a disaster, can reduce the emotional distress experienced and can result in a more effective future psychological adjustment (Butcher & Hatcher, 1988; Williams, Solomon, & Bartone, 1988). Crisis intervention treatment involves providing a victim with a supportive, understanding crisis intervention specialist to enable the victim to express his or her intense feelings about the incident.

Fewer situations are more intimidating for a mental health professional than to be suddenly cast into a treatment session with grieved individuals— especially those who only recently suffered a sudden loss, such as in a disaster. In these times human beings, regardless of previous level of adjustment, need a great deal more emotional support than traditional mental health roles provide. How do trained crisis counselors help disaster victims manage their emotional distress in the aftermath of a disaster?

Foremost, a crisis counselor *provides objective emotional support.* The mental health professional must maintain an objective perspective when faced with the intense grief and confusion that accompanies tragedy. It is indeed human for individuals working with trauma victims to become affected by the traumatic events as much as others are. Even hardened rescue personnel, such as police officers and fire fighters, may become immediately engrossed in and severely affected by the intense loss in an air disaster. The traditionally distant roles of mental health providers are swept away in situations involving loss through disaster. The crisis worker must strive to maintain a balanced perspective to help those involved in the disaster who will be more intensely affected and will have a more diminished perspective. The mental health professional tries to provide a long-term perspective—to allow victims to see that there is hope of surviving psychologically.

A crisis counselor also *serves as a source of information and a buffer against misinformation* coming from ever-present rumor. Disasters are always followed by periods of confusion, misinformation, and negative emotional states. One important role of the mental health professional in disaster response efforts is to obtain, decipher, and clearly communicate to victims the most accurate picture of the situation obtainable at the moment. The crisis intervention specialist is an information link with the most accurate sources and should maintain an up-to-date picture of the situation. The mental health professional must be knowledgeable about disaster victims' options to provide the information they need for personal decisions.

Finally, a crisis counselor *provides directive, effective suggestions to promote adaptation.* An important facet of the mental health professional's role in dealing with disaster victims is to guide them through the difficult times by providing a perspective on the problems being faced and by offering valuable guidance for alleviating those problems.

Crisis telephone hot-line counseling services.   In the aftermath of an air disaster, great confusion prevails. Airplane disasters always involve considerable psychological turmoil and may produce psychological problems among passengers and crew members. Inaccurate information and anxiety-producing doubts can create a tension state that results in demoralization and negative behavior, such as absenteeism from work, excessive drinking, and morale problems. An effective way to deal with this psychological uncertainty and reduce the negative atmosphere following an air disaster is to provide telephone counseling services—an informational hot line of sorts—for all those who feel the need to discuss their concerns, be they airline employees or passenger families. For example, a 24-hour crisis telephone hot-line counseling service was established shortly after the crash of an airliner in Detroit, Michigan, in 1987 in which 156 people died; it continued in operation for four weeks. This service was staffed by qualified psychologists in crisis counseling who provided counseling, information, and referral services.

Postdisaster debriefing sessions.   One goal of a disaster response program is to provide aftercare psychological services to passenger-victims, surviving family members, and rescue personnel. Those who appear to function well at the disaster site may experience difficulties after the immediate crisis has subsided and they have returned to family and normal duties. Even hardened disaster workers who are well trained and effective at the site can be affected later by the pressures and problems experienced during the disaster.

The desire to "unwind" in a psychologically safe environment and to share one's experience of the disaster are universal needs of people following a traumatic situation. Debriefing sessions are de-

signed to provide those who might be directly affected by the accident an opportunity to relate their experiences and to express their feelings and concerns about the disaster. Mitchell (1985) and Keating (1987), for example, have explored the use of debriefing sessions in dealing with emergency workers and found this approach to be effective in reducing the emotional reactions of emergency workers to traumatic events.

Immediate crisis intervention, telephone hot-line counseling, and debriefing programs have become standard efforts following major disasters to help victims and emergency workers return more quickly and effectively to normal functioning. By reducing the harsh impact of a tragedy, these programs prevent the development of more severe psychological disorders.

■ Tertiary Prevention

Tertiary prevention involves efforts aimed at reducing the impact of a disorder and restoring an individual to functioning once the mental health problem has been identified. Mental health rehabilitative efforts are important aspects of tertiary prevention and will be discussed in the following sections.

The Mental Hospital as a Therapeutic Community   Most of the traditional forms of therapy that we discussed in Chapters 17 and 18 may, of course, be used in a hospital setting to promote tertiary prevention. In addition, in more and more mental hospitals these techniques are being supplemented by efforts to make the hospital environment itself a "therapeutic community" (Gunderson, 1980; Jones, 1953; Paul & Lentz, 1977). That is, all the ongoing activities of the hospital are brought into the total treatment program, and the environment, or *milieu*, is a crucial aspect of the therapy. This approach is thus often referred to as **milieu therapy.**

Three general therapeutic principles guide the milieu approach to treatment:

1. Staff expectations are clearly communicated to patients. Both positive and negative feedback are used to encourage appropriate verbalizations and actions on the part of patients.
2. Patients are encouraged to become involved in all decisions made and all actions taken concerning them. A do-it-yourself attitude prevails.
3. All patients belong to social groups on the ward. The experience of group cohesiveness

gives the patients support and encouragement, and the related process of group pressure helps exert control over their behavior.

In a therapeutic community, as few restraints as possible are placed on the patients' freedom, and the orientation is toward encouraging patients to take responsibility for their behavior and to participate actively in their treatment programs. Open wards permit patients to use the grounds and premises. Self-government programs give patients responsibility for managing their own affairs and those of the ward. All hospital personnel are expected to treat the patients as human beings who merit consideration and courtesy. Research has shown that intensive milieu programs significantly benefit nonchronic patients (Gunderson, 1980).

The interaction among patients—whether in group therapy sessions, social events, or other activities—is planned in such a way as to be of therapeutic benefit. In fact, it is becoming apparent that often the most beneficial aspect of a therapeutic community is the interaction among the patients themselves. Differences in social roles and backgrounds may make empathy between staff and patients difficult, but fellow patients have been there—they have had similar problems and breakdowns and have experienced the anxiety and humiliation of being labeled mentally ill and hospitalized. Thus, constructive relationships frequently develop among patients in a warm, encouraging milieu.

Another highly successful method for helping patients take increased responsibility for their own behavior is the use of **social-learning programs.** These programs use learning principles and techniques, such as token economies, to shape more socially acceptable behavior (Paul, 1979; Paul & Lentz, 1977; Rhoades, 1981).

A persistent concern with hospitalization is that the mental hospital may become a permanent refuge from the world, either because it offers total escape from the demands of everyday living or because it encourages patients to settle into a chronic sick role with a permanent excuse for letting other people take care of them (see *HIGHLIGHT 19.2.*) To keep the focus on returning patients to the community and on preventing a return to the institution, hospital staffs try to establish close ties with patients' families and communities and to maintain a recovery-expectant attitude. Between 70 and 90 percent of patients labeled as psychotic and admitted to mental hospitals can now be discharged within a few weeks, or at most a few months. Current estimates suggest that there are about 2 to 3 million chronically mentally ill individuals in America, of whom about half reside in mental hospitals

and the other half live in nursing homes or in the community (Talbott, 1985).

Even where disorders have become chronic, effective treatment methods have been developed. In one of the most extensive and well-controlled studies of chronic hospitalized patients, Paul and Lentz (1977) compared the relative effectiveness of three treatment approaches:

1. *Milieu therapy*, focused on structuring a patient's environment to provide clear communications of expectations, and to get the patient involved in the treatment and participating in the therapeutic community through the group process.
2. *A social-learning treatment program*, organized around learning principles and using a token economy system, with ward staff as reinforcing agents. Undesirable behavior was not reinforced.
3. *Traditional mental hospital treatments*, including pharmacotherapy, occupational therapy, recreational therapy, activity therapy, and individual or group therapy. No systematic application of milieu therapy or the social-learning program was given to this group.

The treatment project covered a period of six years, with an initial phase of staff training, patient assessment, and baseline recording; a treatment phase; an aftercare phase; and a long (year and a half) follow-up. The changes targeted included resocialization, the learning of new roles, and the reduction or elimination of bizarre behavior. There were 28 chronic schizophrenic patients in each treatment group, matched for age, sex, socioeconomic level, symptoms, and duration of hospitalization.

The results of the study were impressive. Both milieu therapy and the social-learning program produced significant improvement in overall functioning and resulted in more successful hospital releases than the traditional hospital care. The behaviorally based social learning program, however, was clearly superior to the more diffuse program of milieu therapy, as evidenced by the fact that over 90 percent of the released patients from the social-learning program remained continuously in the community as compared with 70 percent of the released patients who had had milieu therapy. The figure for the traditional treatment program was less than 50 percent.

Aftercare Programs   Even where hospitalization has successfully modified maladaptive behavior and a patient has learned needed occupational and

The Hospitalization Syndrome

Although individuals differ markedly in their response to hospitalization, some who reside in large mental hospitals over long periods of time tend to adopt a passive role, losing the self-confidence and motivation required for reentering the outside world. In fact, a sizable number of chronic patients become adept at manipulating their symptoms and making themselves appear "sicker" than they are to avoid the possibility of discharge from the sheltered hospital environment. This pattern is not ordinarily considered to be the result of hospitalization alone, but rather is attributed to an interaction between the patient and the hospital milieu. The following are some of the steps that have been delineated in the development of this hospitalization syndrome or, as it is also called, *social breakdown syndrome:*

1. *Deficiency in self-concept.* A precondition for the development of the social breakdown syndrome is the presence of severe self-devaluation and inner confusion concerning social roles and responsibilities.

2. *Social labeling.* During an acute crisis period in the person's life, he or she has probably been labeled psychotic and perhaps even dangerous, has been sent involuntarily to a mental hospital, and has been legally certified as incompetent and lacking in self-control.

3. *Induction into the "sick" role.* Admission procedures, diagnostic labeling, and treatment by staff members and other patients all too often initiate the individual into the role of a "sick" person— helpless, passive, and requiring care and external control.

4. *Atrophy of work and social skills.* In institutions that serve primarily as "storage bins" for the emotionally disturbed, basic work and social skills may atrophy through disuse. During prolonged hospitalization, technological changes in the outside world may contribute to the obsolescence of the individual's work skills.

5. *Development of the chronic sick role.* Eventually the confused and devaluated patient becomes a full member of the sick community in which passive dependence and "crazy" behavior are not only common, but expected.

The staffs of large mental hospitals today are more aware of the pitfalls of chronicity than in the past, and they are introducing various corrective procedures for remotivation and resocialization as well as stressing a recovery-expectant attitude.

interpersonal skills, readjustment in the community following release may still be difficult. Many studies have shown that in the past up to 45 percent of schizophrenic patients have been readmitted within the first year after their discharge. This is where tertiary prevention can play a major role, especially in terms of providing former clients and patients with supportive services that will help them toward long-term psychological well-being.

Today, aftercare programs are helping smooth the transition from institutional to community life and are markedly reducing the number of relapses. Glasscote (1978) found that only 16 percent of patients who received adequate aftercare were readmitted within the first six months as compared with 37 percent for patients not receiving aftercare. By the end of 5 years, more of both groups had been readmitted, but 47 percent of the aftercare group were still in the community, as compared with only 30 percent of the group who had not received aftercare.

Aftercare is the responsibility of community mental health facilities and personnel, the community as a whole, and, of course, the person's family. Its goal is to ensure that released patients will be helped to make an adequate readjustment and return to full participation in their home and community with a minimum of delay and difficulty.

Sometimes aftercare includes a "halfway" period in which a released patient has a gradual return to the outside world in what were formerly termed *halfway houses.* Community-based treatment programs, now referred to as *aftercare programs,* are live-in facilities that serve as a home base for former patients as they make the transition back to adequate functioning in the community. Typically, community-based facilities are run not by profes-

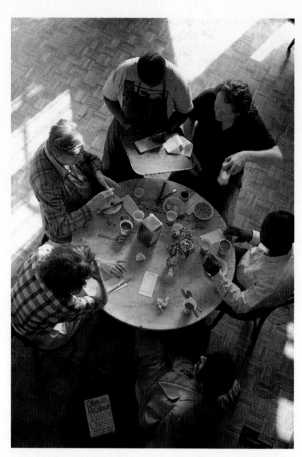

In addition to providing prompt and intense inpatient therapy for patients who need it, tertiary prevention also involves provisions for aftercare, such as this halfway house, to smooth the transition from institutional to community life.

sional mental health personnel but by the residents themselves.

There is even some evidence that community-based living is preferable to hospital confinement for patients who are still actively psychotic. In a pilot program with a group of seriously disturbed mental patients, Fairweather and his colleagues (1969) demonstrated that these patients could function in the community, living in a patient-run facility. Initially, a member of the research staff coordinated the daily operations of the "lodge," but he was shortly replaced by a layperson. The patients were given full responsibility for operating the lodge, for regulating each other's behavior, for earning money, and for purchasing and preparing food.

Forty months after their discharge, a comparison was made of these former patients and a comparable group of 75 patients who had been discharged at the same time but had not had the lodge experience. Whereas most members of the

lodge facility were able to hold income-producing jobs, to manage their daily lives, and to adjust in the outside world, the majority of those who had not had the community group-living experience were unable to adjust to life on the outside and required rehospitalization.

Day hospital facilities in community mental health centers may also be used as alternatives to hospitalization. For example, Penk, Charles, and Van Hoose (1978) showed that partial hospitalization in a day treatment setting resulted in as much improvement (at a lower cost) as full inpatient psychiatric treatment in a group of patients they studied.

Similar community-based treatment facilities have been established for alcoholics, drug addicts, and other people attempting to make an adjustment into the community after institutionalization. Such facilities may be said to be specialized in the sense that all residents share similar backgrounds and problems, and this seems to contribute to the facilities' effectiveness.

One of the chief problems of community-based treatment facilities is that of gaining the acceptance and support of community residents. As Dennes (1974) pointed out in the early years of the growth of community-based treatment, this requires educational and other social measures directed toward increasing community understanding, acceptance, and tolerance of troubled people who may differ somewhat from community norms. The viability of such an approach, however, is demonstrated in the example of Geel, Belgium—"the town that cares"—which we discussed in Chapter 2 (Aring, 1975a).

CONTROVERSIAL ISSUES AND THE MENTALLY ILL

A number of important issues arise related to the legal status of the mentally ill. These issues comprise the subject matter of a field referred to as **forensic psychology,** or **forensic psychiatry,** and they center around the rights of mental patients and the rights of members of society to be protected from disturbed individuals. For a survey of some of the legal rights that have been gained for the mentally ill over the years, see *HIGHLIGHT 19.3.*

The issues we will cover in this section are those that have been the center of controversy for many years. We will first review the procedures involved in involuntarily committing disturbed and dangerous individuals to psychiatric institutions. Next, we

Patient Advocacy: Important Court Decisions in Establishing Patient Rights

Several important court decisions in recent years have helped establish certain basic rights for individuals suffering from mental disorders.

Right to treatment. In 1972, a U.S. District Court in Alabama made a landmark decision in the case of *Wyatt* v. *Stickney.* The ruling held that a mentally ill or mentally retarded individual had a right to receive treatment. Since the decision, the State of Alabama has increased its budget for the treatment of mental health and mental retardation by 300 percent.

Freedom from custodial confinement. In 1975, the U.S. Supreme Court upheld the principle that patients have a right to freedom from custodial confinement if they are not dangerous to themselves or others and if they can safely survive outside of custody. In the *Donaldson* v. *O'Connor* decision, the defendants were re-

quired to pay Donaldson $10,000 for having kept him in custody without providing treatment.

Right to compensation for work. In 1973, a U.S. District Court ruled in the case of *Souder* v. *Brennan* (the secretary of labor) that a patient in a nonfederal mental institution who performed work must be paid according to the Fair Labor Standards Act. Although a 1978 Supreme Court ruling nullified the part of the lower court's decision dealing with state hospitals, the ruling still applied to mentally ill and mentally retarded patients in private facilities.

Right to legal counsel at commitment hearings. The State Supreme Court in Wisconsin decided in 1976, in the case of *Memmel* v. *Mundy,* that an individual had the right to legal counsel during the commitment process.

Right to live in a community. In 1974, the U.S. District Court decided, in the case of *Staff* v. *Mill-*

er, that released state mental hospital patients had a right to live in "adult homes" in the community.

Right to refuse treatment. Several court decisions have provided rulings and some states have enacted legislation permitting patients to refuse certain treatments, such as electroconvulsive therapy and psychosurgery.

Right to less restrictive treatment. In 1975, a U.S. District Court issued a landmark decision in the case of *Dixon* v. *Weinberger.* The ruling establishes the right of individuals to receive treatment in less restrictive facilities than mental institutions.

The need for confinement must be shown by clear, convincing evidence. In 1979, the Supreme Court ruled, in the case of *Addington* v. *Texas,* that a person's need to be kept in an institution must be based on demonstrable evidence.

Based on Bernard (1979), National Association for Mental Health (1979), and Mental Health Law Project (1987).

will turn to the assessment of dangerousness in disturbed individuals; we will also discuss a related issue, which has become of key concern to psychotherapists—the court decision that psychotherapists have a duty to warn potential victims of any threatened violence by their patients. In addition, we will examine the controversial insanity defense for capital crimes as well as the issue of deinstitutionalization, or what some have called the premature "dumping" of mental patients into the community. Finally, in the Unresolved Issues section we will discuss the possibility that contemporary society promotes a trend toward the "criminalization of the mentally ill," that is, incarcerating mentally ill individuals for crimes they commit rather than

treating them for the psychological problems that underlie their crimes.

■ The Commitment Process

Individuals with psychological problems or behaviors that are so extreme and severe as to pose a threat to themselves or others may require protective confinement. Those who commit crimes, whether or not they have a psychological disorder, are dealt with primarily through the judicial system—police arrest, court trial, and, if convicted, possible confinement in a penal institution. Individuals who are judged to be potentially dangerous because of their psychological state may, after civil commitment procedures, be confined in a mental institution.

The steps in the commitment process vary slightly depending on the state law,[1] the available community mental health resources, and the nature of the problem—for example, commitment procedures for a mentally retarded individual will be different from those for a person with an alcohol-abuse problem. A distinction should be made here between voluntary hospitalization and involuntary commitment. In most cases, individuals are placed in mental institutions without court order; that is, they accept voluntary commitment or hospitalization. In these cases, they can, with sufficient notice, leave the hospital if they wish. In cases where an individual is believed to be dangerous or unable to provide for his or her own care, the need for involuntary commitment may arise.

Being mentally ill is not sufficient grounds for placing an individual in a mental institution against his or her will. Although procedures vary somewhat from state to state, several conditions beyond mental illness usually must be met before formal commitment can occur (Schwitzgebel & Schwitzgebel, 1980). In brief, the person must be judged to be

- dangerous to himself or herself;
- incapable of providing for his or her basic physical needs;
- unable to make responsible decisions about hospitalization; and
- in need of treatment or care in a hospital.

Typically, filing a petition for a commitment hearing is the first step in the process of committing an individual involuntarily. This petition is usually filed by a concerned person, such as a relative, physician, or mental health professional. When a petition is filed, a judge appoints two examiners to evaluate the "proposed patient." In Minnesota, for example, one examiner must be a physician (not necessarily a psychiatrist); the other can be a psychiatrist or a psychologist. The patient is asked to voluntarily appear for psychiatric examination prior to the commitment hearing. The hearing must be held within 14 days, which can be extended for 30 more days if good cause for the extension can be shown. The law requires that the court-appointed examiners interview the patient before the hearing.

If an individual is committed to a mental hospital for treatment, the hospital must report to the court within 60 days as to whether the person needs to be confined even longer. If no report is given by the hospital, the patient must be set free. If the hospital indicates that the individual needs further treatment, then the commitment period becomes indeterminate, subject to periodic reevaluations.

Because the decision to commit an individual is based on the judgments of others about the individual's capabilities and his or her potential for dangerous behavior, the civil commitment process leaves open the possibility of the unwarranted violation of a person's civil rights. As a consequence, most states have stringent safeguards in the procedures to assure that any individual who is the subject of a petition for commitment is granted due process, including rights to formal hearings with representation by legal counsel. If there is not time to get a court order for commitment or if there is imminent danger, however, the law allows emergency hospitalization without a formal commitment hearing. In such cases, a physician must sign a statement saying that an imminent danger exists. The patient can then be picked up (usually by the police) and detained under a "hold order," usually not to exceed 72 hours, unless a petition for commitment is filed within that period.

Involuntary commitment in a psychiatric facility is, in large part, contingent on a determination that an individual is dangerous and needs to be confined out of a need to protect himself or herself or society. We will now turn to the important question of evaluating patients in terms of their potential dangerousness.

■ The Assessment of "Dangerousness"

As we have seen, though the majority of psychiatric patients are not considered dangerous and need no special safety precautions, a minority of individuals are violent and require close supervision—perhaps confinement until their "dangerousness" is no longer a problem. Few psychiatric patients are assaultive at or prior to their admission to psychiatric facilities. Rates of assaultiveness vary from setting to setting, though in all reported studies the number of assaultive patients is relatively low. Tardiff (1984), for example, reported that 10 percent of patients admitted to private psychiatric hospitals were considered to be assaultive at the time of admission. Tardiff and Sweillam (1982) found that 7 percent of chronic patients residing in state hospitals were assaultive, and Tardiff and Koenigsberg (1985) found that only 3 percent of outpatients at two psychiatric clinics had been assaultive toward others. The possibility that an individual is

---

[1] The examples of the legal procedures for commitment cited in this section are based on Minnesota state law.

dangerous or likely to commit violent acts is, indeed, one of the primary reasons why some individuals are committed to mental institutions—to protect themselves from harm and society from unwanted violence. Rubin (1972) pointed out that approximately 50,000 people a year are kept in preventive confinement, such as maximum security hospitals, and over 400,000 inmates are kept in maximum security prisons because they are believed to be dangerous to society. McNeil and Binder (1986) reviewed the rates of violence preceding psychiatric hospitalization in one psychiatric facility for the ten-year period 1973 through 1983. They found that while the rate of violence among patients did not increase significantly, the use of "dangerousness" as grounds for civil commitment did.

The determination that a patient is potentially dangerous is a difficult one to make (Litwack & Schlesinger, 1987). A 43-year-old homeless Cuban refugee, for example, who had only a few days earlier undergone a psychiatric evaluation and been released, stabbed two tourists to death on the Staten Island ferry because "God told him to kill" (*Time*, July 21, 1986). Obviously, determining potential dangerousness is a crucial judgment for mental health professionals to make—not only from a therapeutic standpoint, to assure that the most

appropriate treatment is conducted, but also from a legal point of view, as we will see later. A clinician has a clear responsibility in attempting to protect the public from potential violence from the uncontrolled behavior of dangerous patients. A dramatic incident of a failure to assess the extent of a patient's dangerousness was reported by Gorin (1980, 1982) on the television news program "60 Minutes":

In December, 1979, Mrs. Eva B. was brutally stabbed to death by her former husband while a police dispatcher listened to her terrified screams over the telephone. Only hours before the stabbing incident occurred, Mr. B., who had attacked Mrs. B. eight times in the past, had been judged by two staff psychiatrists not to be dangerous. He had then been released, as part of his treatment, on a temporary pass from the Pilgrim State Hospital in New York. The hospital staff had released Mr. B. from confinement at this time despite the fact that both the judge and the prosecuting attorney who had been involved in his trial (for attempting to kill his wife) had independently written the New York State Department of Mental Health recommending that Mr. B. be held in the strictest confinement because of his persistent threats against Mrs. B. (Indeed, on two previous occasions, Mr. B. had escaped from the hospital and attempted to kill her.) The judge and attorney had also recommended that Mrs. B. should be warned if Mr. B. was released. Ironically, six hours after she had been murdered, a telegram from the hospital was delivered to Mrs. B.'s home warning her that her husband had not returned from his pass.

Looking beyond what appears to be some failure to follow through on the court's recommendations, this case illustrates a number of difficult yet critical dilemmas involved in trying to identify or predict dangerousness in psychiatric patients:

- First, it emphasizes the fact that some individuals are capable of uncontrolled violent behavior and hence are potentially dangerous if left unsupervised in the community.

- It also reflects the dilemma faced by mental health professionals who, attempting to rehabilitate disturbed patients by gradually easing them back into society, must exhibit some degree of trust in these individuals.

- Finally, and critically, it illustrates the fact that it is very difficult—for professionals

Juan Gonzalez stabbed and killed two people and injured nine others on the Staten Island Ferry. A few days before the incident, Gonzalez had undergone psychiatric evaluation after making wild death threats on the street. Though doctors concluded that he had a psychotic paranoid disorder, Gonzalez was released after two days because there was not enough space at the facility and he could not be involuntarily committed to a mental institution.

and laypersons alike—to accurately appraise "dangerousness" in some individuals.

Attempts to Predict "Dangerousness"   It is usually an easy matter to determine, after the fact, that an individual has committed a violent act or acts and has demonstrated "dangerous behavior." The difficulty comes when one attempts to determine, in advance, if the individual is going to commit a particular violent act. Assessing a general state of "dangerousness" is not the same thing as predicting whether a violent act will occur.

How well do mental health professionals do in predicting "dangerousness"? The definition of what is "dangerous" is itself unclear. It depends, in large part, on who is asked. Some individuals have a limited or restrictive definition of what behaviors are dangerous and are willing to tolerate more aggressive behavior than others who view a broader range of behaviors as potentially dangerous. There is greater consensus about the dangerousness of extreme behaviors, such as murder, rape, and assault, for example. From the standpoint of society, these kinds of behaviors are condemned as dangerous and viewed as requiring restraint.

Violent acts are particularly difficult to predict because they are apparently determined as much by situational circumstances as they are by an individual's personality traits or violent predispositions. It is, of course, impossible to predict what environmental circumstances are going to occur or if particular circumstances will provoke or instigate aggression on the part of the person. At the individual level, one obvious risk factor is a history of violence (Noble & Rodger, 1989). Some types of patients, particularly schizophrenic and manic individuals (Binder & McNiel, 1988) or patients with well-entrenched delusions (de Pauw & Szulecka, 1988), are more likely to commit violent acts.

Mental health professionals typically err on the conservative side when assessing "violence proneness" in a patient; that is, they overpredict violence. They consider some individuals more dangerous than they actually are and, in general, predict a greater percentage of clients to be dangerous, requiring protective confinement, than actually become involved in violent acts (Megargee, 1970; Monahan, 1981). Gordon (1977) pointed out that the mental health professional's tendency to overpredict dangerousness places him or her in a "no-lose" situation: if the person commits a violent act, he or she can say, "I told you so," and if the patient does not commit a violent act, it's because the patient is locked up—"It is just lucky that no one has triggered this person's dangerousness yet" (p. 234).

Methods for Assessing Potential for "Dangerousness"   Evaluating an individual's potential for committing violent acts is difficult because only part of the equation is available for study:

$$\frac{\begin{array}{c} \text{predisposing personality} \\ + \text{ environmental instigation} \end{array}}{= \text{aggressive act}}$$

As we have noted, psychologists and psychiatrists usually do not know enough about the environmental circumstances the individual will encounter to evaluate what the instigation to aggression will be. Predictions of dangerousness focus, then, primarily on aspects of the individual's personality. The two major sources of personality information are data from personality tests and the individual's previous history. Personality testing can reveal whether the individual shows personality traits of hostility, aggressiveness, impulsiveness, poor judgment, and so on. Nevertheless, many individuals with such characteristics never act on them. Still, as noted, practitioners tend to overpredict the likelihood of aggressive acts. The use of previous history —such as having committed prior aggression, having verbalized threats of aggression, having an available means of committing violence (such as possession of a gun), and so on—are useful predictors (Monahan, 1981). Like personality testing, however, these data only focus on the individual factors and do not account for the situational forces that impinge on the person.

The prediction of violence is even more difficult in the case of an overcontrolled person who does not have a history of aggressive behavior. Megargee (1970) studied extensively the "overcontrolled hostile" person who is the epitome of well-controlled behavior but who, on one occasion, loses control and kills another person. Examples of this type of murder are dramatic: the high school honor student, reportedly civic-minded and fond of helping sick and old people, who is arrested for torturing and killing a 3-year-old girl in his neighborhood; or the mild, passive father of four who loses his temper over being cheated by a car dealer and beats the man to death with a tire iron. These examples illustrate the most difficult type of aggressive behavior to predict—the sudden, violent, impulsive act of a seemingly well-controlled and "normal" individual.

A general pessimism has prevailed in recent years about our ability to predict dangerousness. Several studies in violence prediction, however, have attempted to improve prediction by identifying individuals at risk for violence. Using demographic data on family background, history of violence, friendships, and substance use, Klassen and

O'Connor (1988) were able to identify 76 percent of the people who later became violent. They concluded that predictive assessments could be improved even more so if the context in which violence occurs is taken into consideration.

The Duty to Warn: Implications of the Tarasoff Decision

What should a therapist do on learning that one of his or her patients is planning to harm another person? Can the therapist violate the confidence of the therapy and take action to prevent the patient from committing the act? In many states, the therapist not only can violate the confidentiality but is required by law to do so— that is, to warn the endangered person of the threat against him or her. The duty-to-warn doctrine was given a great deal of impetus in a California court ruling in the case of *Tarasoff* v. *The Regents of the University of California et al.* (Cal. Reptr. 14, 551 P., 2d 334, 1976). In this case, Prosenjit Poddar was being seen in outpatient psychotherapy by a psychologist at the university mental health facility. During the treatment, Mr. Poddar indicated that he intended to kill his former girlfriend, Tatiana Tarasoff, when she returned from vacation. The psychologist, concerned about the threat, discussed the case with his supervisors, and they agreed that Mr. Poddar was dangerous and should be committed for further observation and treatment. They informed the campus police, who picked up Mr. Poddar for questioning. The police judged Mr. Poddar to be rational and released him after he promised to leave Ms. Tarasoff alone. Mr. Poddar terminated treatment with the psychologist. About two months later, he killed Ms. Tarasoff. Her parents later sued the University of California and its staff involved in the case for their failure to hospitalize Mr. Poddar and their failure to warn Ms. Tarasoff about the threat to her life.

The court did not find the defendants liable for failing to hospitalize Mr. Poddar; it did, however, find them liable for their failure to warn the victim. In a later analysis of the case, Knapp (1980) said that the court

ruled that difficulty in determining dangerousness does not exempt a psychotherapist from attempting to protect others when a determination of dangerousness exists. The court acknowledged that confidentiality was important to the psychotherapeutic relationship but stated that the protective privilege ends where the public peril begins. (p. 610)

The duty-to-warn ruling in the Tarasoff case, while spelling out a therapist's responsibility in situations where there has been an explicit threat on another's life, left other areas of application unclear. For example, does this ruling apply in cases where a patient threatens to commit suicide? Or when the object of violence is not clearly named, such as when global threats are made? Or would the duty-to-warn ruling hold up in other states?

Knapp and Vandecreek (1982) pointed out in a follow-up review that subsequent court decisions have not extended the duty to protect to suicidal cases. Furthermore, if a patient does not specifically name an intended victim, then the duty-to-warn ruling does not apply. Regarding the application of the Tarasoff precedent in other states, four out of five of those states having related court cases have upheld the Tarasoff decision and required a duty to warn. Interestingly, a Maryland Court decision (*Shaw* v. *Glickman*, 415 A. 2d. 625, MD. Ct. Spec. App. 1980) found that, in Maryland, laws pertaining to privileged communications did not allow a therapist to warn a potential victim—even if a death threat was involved. Thus a psychotherapist must be aware of state laws and judicial precedents in addition to making a determination of potential dangerousness on the part of a patient. The final form of the duty-to-warn doctrine has not fully evolved in the courts; future court decisions will, no doubt, further define a practitioner's responsibility. In the meantime, clinicians are encouraged to follow closely the guidelines for staged responses to such threats and to carefully document and substantiate their decisions for actions taken (Gross et al., 1987).

In response to the ambiguities concerning the actual application of the duty-to-warn doctrine in clinical settings, Appelbaum (1985) discussed practical problems that clinicians face in dealing with this obligation. He pointed out that the most detrimental mistake that clinicians make in applying this legal obligation is to neglect the "basic principles of clinical care when a legal issue arises." A clinician should not lose track of the need to help an individual making a threat while fulfilling the obligation to warn the endangered person.

■ The Insanity Defense

In recent years, the use of **the insanity defense**— "innocent by reason of insanity"—in capital crime trials has been surrounded by considerable controversy, largely resulting from concerns that criminals may use this plea to avoid criminal responsibility. Actually, the insanity defense has been used in less than 2 percent of cases over time (Fersch, 1980). Studies have confirmed the fact, however, that individuals acquitted of crimes by reason of insanity spend less time, on the whole, in a psychiatric hospital than individuals who are actually convicted of crimes spend in prison (Kahn & Raifman, 1981; Pasewark, Pantle, & Steadman, 1982).

Although historically the insanity defense has been used infrequently, its use has apparently increased over the past 25 years as the definition of "insanity" has been broadened in the courts. Moreover, much of the controversy over the insanity defense has arisen because it has been used in many highly visible trials. For example, following the assassination attempt on President Reagan and the subsequent ruling that the alleged assassin (John Hinckley) was "insane" at the time, there was a great public outcry over the misuse of the insanity defense. Judging from the media coverage, many people apparently doubt the veracity of the insanity defense, believing instead that it may be contrived to escape justice.

The established precedents defining the insanity defense are as follows:

1. *The M'Naghten Rule (1843).* Under this ruling, people are believed to be sane unless it can be proved that, at the time of committing the act, they were laboring under such a defect of reason (from a disease of the mind) that they did not know the nature and quality of the act they were doing—or, if they did know they were committing the act, they did not know that what they were doing was wrong.

2. *The irresistible impulse (1887).* A second precedent in the insanity defense is the doctrine of the "irresistible impulse." This view holds that accused individuals might not be responsible for their acts, even if they knew that what they were doing was wrong (according to the M'Naghten Rule), if they had lost the power to choose between right and wrong. That is, they could not avoid doing the act in question because they were compelled beyond their will to commit the act (Fersch, 1980).

3. *The Durham Rule.* In 1954, Judge David Bazelon, in a decision of the United States Court of Appeals, broadened the insanity defense further. Bazelon did not believe that the previous precedents allowed for a sufficient application of established scientific knowledge of mental illness and proposed a test that would be based on this knowledge. Under this rule, the accused is "not criminally responsible if his or her unlawful act was the product of mental disease or mental defect." As we have seen, with the expansion of the diagnostic classification of mental disorder, a broad range of behaviors can be defined as mental disease or defect. Which mental diseases serve to excuse a defendant from criminal responsibility? Generally, under

The use of the insanity defense in highly publicized cases, such as John Hinckley's assassination attempt on President Reagan in 1981, has led to controversy over whether it legitimately protects a mentally ill offender's rights or is a contrivance to avoid criminal responsibility.

M'Naghten, psychotic disorders were the basis of the insanity defense; but under the Durham Rule, other conditions (such as personality disorder or dissociative disorder) might also apply. How, then, is guilt or innocence determined? Many authorities believe that the Durham Rule has broadened the insanity defense in such a way as to require of the courts an impossible task—to determine guilt or innocence by reason of insanity on the basis of psychiatric testimony. In many cases, this has involved conflicting testimony because both the prosecution and the defense have "their" psychiatric witnesses who are in complete disagreement (Fersch, 1980; Marvit, 1981).

4. *Diminished capacity.* An additional insanity test has been proposed by the New York State Department of Mental Hygiene (1978): "Evidence of abnormal mental condition would be admissible to affect the degree of crime for which an accused could be convicted. Specifically, those offenses requiring intent or knowledge could be reduced to lesser included offenses requiring only reckless or criminal neglect." In this insanity defense, the accused would not be declared innocent by reason of insanity, but would be found guilty of a lesser charge, such as criminal negligence instead of murder.

The controversy over the insanity defense has led to much discussion about its reform by professionals in both the mental health and legal fields (Clark, 1987; Simon & Aaronson, 1988). Some individuals would like to do away with the insanity defense altogether, while others would prefer a modification of the defense to allow criminal responsibility to be established before an individual's sanity is considered in a case. Several states have revised the insanity defense to "guilty but mentally ill." In these cases, a defendant may be sentenced but placed in a treatment facility rather than in a prison. This two-part judgment serves to prevent the type of situation where an individual commits a murder, is found not guilty by reason of insanity, is turned over to a mental health facility, is found to be rational and in no further need of treatment by the hospital staff, and is released to the community after only two months of confinement. Under the two-part decision, such an individual would ultimately remain in the custody of the correctional department. Marvit (1981) suggested that this approach might "realistically balance the interest of the mentally ill offender's rights and the community's need to control criminal behavior" (p. 23).

■ Deinstitutionalization

As we learned in Chapter 2, asylums or mental hospitals were originally viewed as the most humane settings for dealing with chronic patients. The people who founded the institutions and the society that supported them saw these facilities as havens for retarded or disturbed individuals who could not survive in the world on their own. Ironically, though, as hospitals became overcrowded and hospital staffs overworked, patient care deteriorated. Mental hospitals, founded out of a concern for human welfare, came to be viewed as horrid places where humane care was more a philosophy than a practical reality. Bassuk and Gerson (1978) noted that

the reform movement, having seen its original objectives apparently accomplished, had ceased to be a significant influence. By early in this century the network of state mental hospitals, once the proud tribute to an era of reform, had largely turned into a bureaucratic morass within which patients were interned, often neglected and sometimes abused. (p. 47)

Beginning in the 1960s, widespread disenchantment grew with the large, state mental hospitals designed to treat chronic psychiatric patients. Many authorities concluded that these institutions served primarily as "warehouses" for the insane and that they dehumanized individuals rather than helped them resolve their problems and return to society. Mental hospital reformers saw the move-

ment as an opportunity to rid society of an unwelcome evil; hospital administrators and staff members initially viewed this movement as a way of lowering the hospital population to manageable numbers; and state governments viewed the movement with favor because it allowed legislatures (ever concerned about budgets) to reduce state spending. Many reformers recommended that some state mental hospitals be permanently closed and their residents returned either to more humane facilities or to their families and community (Bachrach, 1976). In fact, in a number of cases, the courts decided to close some hospitals.

Paralleling these recommendations was the effort, on the part of many concerned people, to develop expanded community resources to provide chronic patients with continued psychiatric care in their local community. Supporters of this effort believed then—and now—that society should be able to integrate these individuals back into the community and treat patients with the least restrictive alternative. This movement, referred to as **deinstitutionalization,** has become a focus of controversy in the mental health field today. Some authorities consider the emptying of the mental hospitals to be a positive expression of society's desire to confer freedom on previously confined individuals, while others speak of the "abandonment" of chronic patients to a cruel and harsh existence.

There has indeed been a significant reduction in hospital populations: from over 524,878 in 1970 to around 267,638 in 1986 (U.S. Department of Health, 1989). A number of factors have interacted to alter the pattern of mental hospital admissions and discharges over the past 20 years. As has been noted in previous chapters, the introduction of the antipsychotic drugs made it possible for many patients who would formerly have required confinement to be released into the community. The availability of these drugs led many to believe (falsely) that all mental health problems could be managed with medication. In addition, the changing treatment philosophy and the desire to eliminate mental institutions was accompanied by the belief that society wanted and could financially afford to provide better community-based care for chronic patients outside of large mental hospitals.

In theory, the movement to close the mental hospitals seemed workable. Many community-based mental health centers would be opened and would provide continuing care to the residents of hospitals after discharge. Residents would be given welfare funds (supposedly costing the government less than it takes to maintain large mental hospitals) and would be administered medication to keep them stabilized until they could obtain continuing care. Many patients would be discharged to home and family, while others would be placed in smaller, homelike board-and-care facilities or nursing homes.

Many unforeseen problems arose, however. Many residents of mental institutions had no families or homes to go to; board-and-care facilities were often substandard; the community mental health centers were ill-prepared to provide needed services for chronic patients, particularly on an outpatient basis; many patients had not been carefully selected for discharge and were not ready for community living; and many of those who were discharged were not followed up sufficiently or with enough regularity to ensure their successful adaptation outside the hospital. Indeed, countless individuals were discharged to fates that were far more dehumanizing than the conditions in any of the hospitals (Westermeyer, 1987). The following case illustrates the situation:

Dave B., age 49, had been hospitalized for 25 years in a state mental hospital. When the hospital was scheduled for phaseout, many of the patients, particularly those who were regressed or aggressive, were transferred to another state hospital. Dave was a borderline mentally retarded man who had periodic episodes of psychosis. At the time of hospital closing, however, he was not hallucinating and was "reasonably intact." Dave was considered to be one of the "less disturbed" residents because his psychotic behavior was less pronounced and he presented no dangerous problems.

He was discharged to a board-and-care facility (actually an old hotel whose clientele consisted mostly of former inpatients). At first, Dave seemed to fit in well at the facility; mostly he sat in his room or in the outside hallway, and he caused no trouble for the caretakers. Two weeks after he arrived, he wandered off the hotel grounds and was missing for several days. The police eventually found him living in the city dump. He had apparently quit taking his medication and when he was discovered he was regressed and catatonic. He was readmitted to a state hospital.

Concern over the increasing number of vagrants in New York City prompted the *New York Post* to conclude in an article on psychiatric hospi-

tals that "warehousing" of mental patients no longer took place in state institutions but in "New York streets, transport terminals, flophouses, and shelters for the homeless" (May 10, 1982). The increase in "bag ladies" in major cities was attributed to the premature or inappropriate discharging of patients from psychiatric hospitals. The *Post* article reported that the New York state hospitals, which once had held 93,000 patients, in 1982 held only 21,000. It was estimated that 40 percent of the street crime in New York City could be attributed to former psychiatric patients released from hospitals. This situation is, unfortunately, quite common, as Westermeyer (1982a) noted:

Patients are returned to the community, armed with drugs to control their illness. The worst aspects of their illnesses may be under control. But many of the patients are not ready to function in society. They need a gradual reintroduction—facilities where someone else can see that they take their drugs, see their psychiatrists, get food, clothing and shelter. Such care is too often more than families can provide and such services are not generally available in a community. As a result, the numbers of bag ladies and men, vagrants and mentally disabled people, living in lonely hotels and dangerous streets, have burgeoned. (p. 2)

The extent of problems created by deinstitutionalization is not fully known. The ambiguity

The extent of problems created by deinstitutionalization is not fully known, but some evidence suggests that the emptying of mental hospitals has contributed to the number of homeless people. Deinstitutionalization is not likely to be successful unless continuing care is available and adequate in the community, and unless it allows for readmission to the hospital for short periods if necessary.

comes, in part, from the scarcity of rigorous follow-up data on patients who have been discharged from mental hospitals. There have not been a sufficient number of adequate research studies in this area. Moreover, the research investigations have tended to be difficult to conduct because the patients are transient and are hard to keep track of over time.

Many individuals, once discharged from state hospitals, do join the ranks of what contemporary writers have called "the homeless" and become vulnerable to victimization (French, 1987). Certainly not all homeless people are former mental patients, but evidence suggests that deinstitutionalization has contributed to the number of homeless people (Jones, 1983; Lamb, 1984). Researchers have also demonstrated that a greater percentage of homeless people have significant psychopathology, as reflected in higher rates of hospitalization and felony convictions, than people who have homes. Fischer and colleagues (1986) conducted an epidemiological study of a random sample of homeless people (94 percent men) from four missions in the Baltimore area. These homeless people were interviewed when they came to the transient housing for a room for the night. They were administered the instruments used in the NIMH epidemiological survey (see Regier et al., 1984), the General Health Questionnaire, and the Diagnostic Interview Schedule; their responses were compared with a control sample of subjects from the Baltimore Catchment Area Study of the NIMH study. The results of the study confirmed expectations that homeless people would manifest poorer psychological adjustment: 33 percent of the homeless people had been hospitalized for psychiatric problems while only 5 percent of the control sample had been hospitalized; 58 percent had been arrested versus 24 percent of the control sample; 16 percent had had felony convictions versus 5 percent of controls; and about 35 percent had General Health Questionnaire scores in the impaired-functioning range, which was about three times the number of control subjects. More recently, Rossi (1990) estimated that 33 percent of homeless individuals suffer from chronic mental disorder and about 33 percent have severe addiction problems.

In spite of the problems just described, some data on patient discharge and outcome status support the deinstitutionalization process. Braun et al. (1981), for example, concluded:

The most satisfactory studies allow the qualified conclusion that selected patients managed outside the hospital in experimental programs do no worse and by some criteria have psychiatric outcomes superior to those of hospitalized control patients. (p. 747)

These same researchers, however, also concluded that deinstitutionalization is likely to be unsuccessful in continuing care in the community is not available or if it is inadequate.

After Deinstitutionalization   Goering and colleagues (1984) found serious deficiencies in discharge planning and aftercare services. They followed up 505 discharged patients over a two-year period and found that psychological symptoms and distress levels were high. The high readmission rates of these patients (32 to 38 percent within six months and 56 to 67 percent in two years) was considered to result, in part, from the lack of community resources to facilitate the patients' reentry into society.

One of the most significant problems in the maintenance of discharged patients outside of hospitals involves preventing an individual from developing what has been referred to as the "chronic social breakdown syndrome" (Archer & Gruenberg, 1982). This pattern of maladaptive behavior involves the individual's failing to maintain his or her self-care and social functioning skills at the level he or she attained prior to discharge from the hospital. Although maintenance on psychoactive drugs can help such individuals to cope, it is important that assistance be provided to help maintain or attain an adequate social adjustment. This assistance or continuing care in the community can provide a patient with needed structure while he or she is learning new responsibilities and roles that are required in the new living situation.

Some successful programs designed to reintegrate chronic patients into the community were described by Bachrach (1980). All these programs, despite their differences, are based on the following principles:

- *Targeting of chronic patients.* The most successful model programs are targeted toward patients who have been persistently and chronically ill.
- *Linkage with other services.* The most successful programs incorporate "full-spectrum" planning, including treatment and social services.
- *Functional integrity.* Successful programs generally provide for their patients a full range of services that are usually associated with institutional care.

- *Individually tailored treatment.* Treatment programs should allow for social work case management and crisis-intervention services on a 24-hour basis, if needed.
- *Cultural- or ethnic-group relevance.* Successful programs include a consideration of the ethnic or racial characteristics of the population served.
- *Specifically trained staff.* Successful programs employ staff members who are apprised of the problems of chronic mental patients living in community settings.
- *Hospital liaison.* Because some patients may require readmission to a hospital for brief periods, successful modern programs maintain a relationship with a local hospital and coordinate readmissions, if necessary.
- *Internal evaluation.* Successful programs usually maintain an ongoing self-review program to monitor their functioning on a continuous basis.

Successful community care, according to Bachrach, involves the prospect of readmission to a hospital for short periods if necessary. The importance of short-term hospitalization has been noted by other investigators as well (Archer & Gruenberg, 1982). The underlying premise here is that each day that a patient can spend in the real world is better than none. If short-term rehospitalization is necessary to provide the patient with real-world experiences, then it is a valuable treatment approach. Furthermore, the availability of short-term readmission to a hospital can limit the feeling of abandonment that some mental patients may have when they are released into the community. As such, this general pattern of hospital readmission is prevalent today.

The ease with which former mental patients readjust to living in the real world depends, in large part, on the character of the residential surroundings and the social milieu they encounter in their return to the community (Sommers, 1988). To improve the readjustment of former mental patients to society, a new case-management approach has been initiated over the past few years. This novel approach involves assigning a patient to a case manager, usually not a mental health professional, who attempts to improve the quality of the patient's life and reduce readmissions to the hospital by serving as a link or go-between for the patient and the services available in the community. The effectiveness of this approach was recently studied by Franklin et al. (1987). They explored the efficiency and effectiveness of case management by following up a group of patients being served by this approach and comparing them to a group of similarly discharged patients who had community services available but were not case-managed. Unfortunately, the results at 12-month follow-up showed that the case-management approach was no more effective at reducing readmissions to hospitals than the no-case-management condition. Moreover, the patients in the case-management group did not report an improved quality of life. The only difference between the two conditions was that the case-management approach was less cost-effective.

The various approaches that have been implemented to circumvent patient failures to readjust to the community have not been particularly successful at reducing hospital readmissions and at further reducing the census in state hospitals. Nevertheless, advocates for deinstitutionalization continue to maintain that this is the most desirable approach to treating the chronically mental ill. The controversy over deinstitutionalization is likely to continue over the next few years, with advocates on both sides of

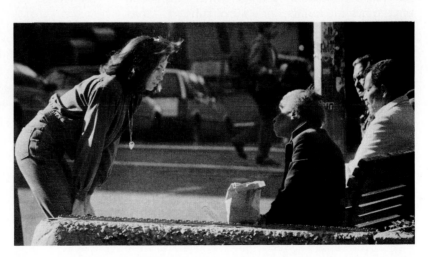

Project Reachout in New York City tries to help mentally ill street people. The workers try to get confused, scared, and disoriented people into the office (they usually gain their trust by giving them food), where they can be helped in many ways, from simply getting a cup of coffee or a shower to obtaining a room and psychiatric care.

the issue laying claim to the correctness of their views until more definitive research is conducted.

It is of interest to note one recent trend in mental health care—privatization. The mental health system appears to be undergoing considerable evolution in recent years, due in large part to changes in funding for mental health care. More and more emotionally disturbed individuals are being admitted to large private institutions. This phenomenon, referred to as the "privatization" of the mental health system (Dorwart et al., 1989), has developed because funding for public treatment facilities has waned and private insurance companies are willing to cover the cost of inpatient mental health services. Several large private hospital corporations have filled the treatment void left by the mental hospital closings and are providing inpatient psychiatric care for a growing number of patients.

Another related development in the care of chronic mental patients is the growth and expansion of private nursing home facilities. Since the deinstitutionalization movement spurred the discharge of psychiatric patients into the community, alternative care facilities have expanded to fill the need for continued care (Morlock, 1989). This expansion of facilities has been made possible through financial incentives provided by Medicare to fund treatment. Nursing homes have become the largest single setting to care for the chronic mentally ill. Mentally ill individuals (a total of 668,000 are currently in nursing homes) make up over 51 percent of the nursing home population at present (Goldman, Feder, & Scanlon, 1986).

ORGANIZED EFFORTS FOR MENTAL HEALTH

Public awareness of the magnitude and severity of our contemporary mental health problem and the interest of government, professional, and lay organizations have prompted programs directed at better understanding, more effective treatment, and long-range prevention. Efforts to improve mental health are apparent not only in our society, but also in many other countries; and international as well as national and local organizations and approaches are involved.

U.S. Efforts for Mental Health

In the United States, the primary responsibility for dealing with mental disorders fell initially to state and local agencies. During World War II, however, the extent of mental disorders in the United States was brought to public attention when a large number of young men—two out of every seven recruits—were rejected for military service for psychiatric reasons. This discovery led to a variety of organized measures for coping with the nation's mental health problem.

The Government and Mental Health   In 1946, aware of the need for more research, training, and services in the field of mental health, Congress passed its first comprehensive mental health bill, the National Mental Health Act, which laid the basis for the federal government's programs in the 1950s and 1960s.

The 1946 bill provided for the establishment of a National Institute of Mental Health (NIMH) in or near Washington, D.C., to serve as a central research and training center and as headquarters for the administration of a grant-in-aid program. The grant-in-aid feature was designed to foster research and training elsewhere in the nation and to help state and local communities expand and improve their own mental health services. New powers were conferred on the NIMH in 1956, when Congress, under Title v of the Health Amendments Act, authorized the institute to provide "mental health project grants" for experimental studies, pilot projects, surveys, and general research having to do with the understanding, assessment, treatment, and aftercare of mental disorders.

As a result of organizational changes since then, the NIMH is now one of the three institutes under the Alcoholism, Drug Abuse, and Mental Health Administration, a division of the Public Health Service. The NIMH (a) conducts and supports research on the biological, psychosocial, and sociocultural aspects of mental disorders; (b) supports the training of professional and paraprofessional personnel in the mental health field; (c) assists communities in planning, establishing, and maintaining more effective mental health programs; and (d) provides information on mental health to the public and to the scientific community. Its two companion institutes—the National Institute on Alcohol Abuse and Alcoholism (NIAAA) and the National Institute on Drug Abuse (NIDA)—perform comparable functions in their respective fields (Office of the Federal Registry, 1982).

Although the federal government provides leadership and financial aid, the states and localities actually plan and run most NIMH programs. In addition, the states establish, maintain, and supervise their own mental hospitals and clinics. A number of states have also pioneered, through their legislation, in the development of community mental health centers; rehabilitation services in the community for former patients; and facilities for dealing with alcoholism, drug abuse, and other special mental health problems. In the 1980s, federal support for mental health programs diminished considerably. Most state and local governments, which were expected to assume much of the support of mental health activities, have not been able to fund programs and facilities at 1960s and 1970s levels. As a result, many programs devoted to mental health training, research, and service have been greatly reduced or even abandoned. As to the future, there is widespread uncertainty about continued financial support for mental health activities.

Professional Organizations and Mental Health

A number of professional organizations exist in the mental health field. Some of the most influential of these are listed in *HIGHLIGHT 19.4.*

One of the most important functions of these organizations is to set and maintain high professional and ethical standards within their special areas. This function may include (a) establishing and reviewing training qualifications for professional and paraprofessional personnel; (b) setting standards and procedures for the accreditation of undergraduate and graduate training programs; (c) setting standards for the accreditation of clinics, hospitals, or other service operations and carrying out inspections to see that the standards are followed; and (d) investigating reported cases of unethical or unprofessional conduct and taking disciplinary action when necessary.

A second key function of these professional organizations involves communication and information exchange within their areas via meetings, symposia, workshops, refresher courses, the publication of professional and scientific journals, and related activities. In addition, all such organizations sponsor programs of public education as a means of advancing the interests of their professions, drawing attention to mental health needs, and attracting students to careers in their areas.

A third key function of professional organizations, one that is receiving increasing attention, is the application of insights and methods to contemporary social problems, for example, in lobbying national and local government agencies to provide more services for homeless people. Composed as they are of qualified personnel, professional mental health organizations are in a unique position to serve as consultants on mental health problems and

programs not only on the national level but also on the state and local levels.

The Role of Voluntary Mental Health Organizations and Agencies

Although professional mental health personnel and organizations can give expert technical advice in regard to mental health needs and programs, real progress in helping plan and implement these programs must come from an informed and concerned citizenry. In fact, it has been repeatedly stated that it has been nonprofessionals who have blazed the trails in the mental health field.

Prominent among the many voluntary mental health agencies is the National Association for Mental Health (NAMH). This organization was founded in 1950 by the merger of the National Committee for Mental Hygiene, the National Mental Health Foundation, and the Psychiatric Foundation; it was further expanded in 1962 by merging with the National Organization for Mentally Ill Children. Through its national governing body and some 1000 local affiliates, the NAMH works for the improvement of services in community clinics and mental hospitals; it helps recruit, train, and place volunteers for service in treatment and aftercare programs; and it works for enlightened mental health legislation and for the provision of needed facilities and personnel. It also carries on special educational programs aimed at fostering positive mental health and helping people understand mental disorders.

In addition, the National Association for Mental Health has been actively involved in many court decisions affecting patient rights (NAMH, 1979). In several cases the NAMH has sponsored litigation or served as amicus curiae (friend of the court) in efforts to establish the rights of mental patients to treatment, to freedom from custodial confinement, to freedom to live in the community, and to protection of their confidentiality.

With a program and organization similar to that of the NAMH, the National Association for Retarded Citizens (NARC) works to reduce the incidence of mental retardation, to seek community and residential treatment centers and services for the retarded, and to carry on a program of education aimed at better public understanding of retarded individuals and greater support for legislation on their behalf. The NARC also fosters scientific research into mental retardation, the recruitment and training of volunteer workers, and programs of community action.

These and other voluntary health organizations, such as Alcoholics Anonymous, need the backing of a wide constituency of knowledgeable and involved citizens in order to succeed.

Mental Health Resources in Private Industry

Personal problems—such as marital distress or other family problems, alcohol or drug abuse, financial difficulties, or job-related stress—can adversely affect employee morale and performance. Psychological difficulties among employees may result in numerous types of problems, such as absenteeism, accident proneness, poor productivity, and high job turnover. Many corporations have long recognized this fact, and yet it has been a relatively recent phenomenon to see them act on this knowledge. Today many companies have expanded their "obligations" to employees to include numerous psychological services. Often referred to as employee-assistance programs, these are the means through which corporations can actively provide mental health services to employees and their family members.

One corporation that has pioneered in the development of employee-assistance programs is Control Data Corporation of Minneapolis, Minnesota. Following the implementation of a successful alcoholism treatment program in 1974, Control Data's management founded its employee-assistance program, the Employee Advisory Resource (known as EAR). This program was initiated to assist employees and their family members in solving personal or job-related problems. The program —modeled after the telephone hot-line programs —provides a 24-hour telephone counseling service staffed by approximately 40 EAR counselors. In addition, a counselor is on duty at all times in the event that an employee wishes a personal consultation. All counselors have been trained to identify problems and to refer troubled employees to internal counseling resources or to community agencies. Callers may remain anonymous and the contact is completely confidential. The service is provided at no cost to employees.

Control Data's EAR program has proven to be of help to many employees. During the first five years of operation, over 19,000 employee contacts were recorded. The number of counseling contacts has increased to about 5,000 a year at present. Though individuals seek help for a range of problems, the majority of contacts are for legal difficulties, financial problems, alcoholism, and marital stress.

The EAR program provides a number of employee services in addition to personal counseling and referral. These include employee education, providing information on the prevention of future

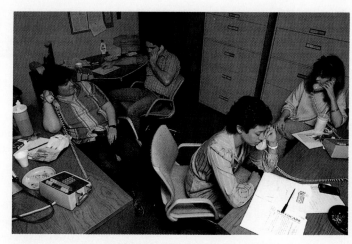

Employee assistance programs are a relatively recent phenomenon that recognizes the link between psychological difficulties and job problems. Corporations are increasingly providing personal counseling and referral programs for employees having legal, financial, marital, and substance-abuse problems. Shown here is one such employee program that provides drug-rehabilitation telephone counseling.

problems, employee relations consultation, and employee input into policy-making decisions. The success of the EAR program is reflected in the fact that since 1976 Control Data has assisted numerous other companies in setting up similar employee-assistance programs.

■ International Efforts for Mental Health

Mental health is a major problem not only in the United States but in the rest of the world as well. Indeed, many of the unfavorable conditions in this country with regard to the causes and treatment of mental disorders are greatly magnified in poorer countries and countries with repressive governments. According to the World Health Organization (WHO, 1978a), 40 million people in the world suffer from severe mental illness; more than 80 million suffer from alcohol and drug addiction, mental retardation, and organic brain disorders; and another 80 million suffer from other mental disorders, such as the neuroses. The severity of the world mental health problem is shown in WHO's estimates that mental disorders affect more than 200 million people worldwide.

It was the knowledge of this great problem that served to bring about the formation of several international organizations at the end of World War

Professional Organizations Concerned with Mental Health

American Psychological Association (APA). An association of professionally trained psychologists. Its purpose is to advance psychology as a science, as a profession, and as a means of promoting human welfare. It has over 30 divisions concerned with various special areas within psychology, and it establishes and monitors standards for the training and practice of psychologists in mental health work.

American Psychological Society (APS). An association of academically oriented psychologists whose purpose is to advance psychology as a science and as a means of promoting human welfare.

American Psychiatric Association (APA). An association of physicians with training in psychiatry. Its purpose is to further the study of the nature, treatment, and prevention of mental disorders; to help set, improve, and maintain standards of practice and service in mental hospitals, clinics, general hospital psychiatric units, and institutions for the mentally retarded; to further psychiatric research and education; and to fos-

ter enlightened views with regard to the social and legal aspects of psychopathology and the role of psychiatry in fostering human welfare.

American Medical Association (AMA). An association of physicians who are members of constituent state medical associations. In addition to its myriad other functions, it is concerned with mental disorder as a general health problem and with fostering research, education, and legislation to advance comprehensive health efforts in the United States.

American Psychoanalytic Association (APA). An association of analytically trained psychiatrists. It sets standards for the training of psychoanalysts.

Association for Advancement of Behavior Therapy (AABT). An association of behaviorally oriented psychologists interested in promoting the research and application of behavioral techniques in the treatment of mental disorders.

American Sociological Association (ASA). An association of sociologists, social scientists, and other professional people interest-

ed in research, teaching, and applications of sociology. Its sections on social psychology, medical sociology, and criminology have special pertinence to mental health.

National Association of Social Workers (NASW). An association of professionally trained social workers, organized to promote the quality and effectiveness of social work and to foster mental health. It establishes and monitors standards for training and practice, encourages research, and interprets the role of social work in the community.

American Nurses Association (ANA). An association of registered nurses concerned with high standards of professional practice. Two of its clinical committee groups (one on psychiatric nursing practice and one on maternal and child health nursing) have special mental health concerns.

American Occupational Therapy Association (AOTA). A society of registered occupational therapists administering medically supervised activities to physically or mentally ill people. It maintains standards of education and train-

---

II. We will briefly discuss here the World Health Organization and the World Federation for Mental Health.

The World Health Organization (WHO)

The World Health Organization defines health as not simply the absence of disease, but as a positive state of physical, mental, and social well-being. From the first, it has been keenly aware of the close interrelationships between physical, psychosocial, and sociocultural factors—such as the influence of

rapid change and social disruption on both physical and mental health; the impossibility of major progress toward mental health in societies where a large proportion of the population suffer from malnutrition, parasites, and disease; and the frequent psychological and cultural barriers to successful programs in family planning and public health.

Formed after World War II as part of the UN system, WHO's earliest focus was on physical diseases; through its efforts dramatic progress has been made toward the conquest of ancient scourges like ing, makes surveys and recommendations on request, and works with its state associations in the preparation and certification of occupational therapy volunteer assistants.

National Rehabilitation Association (NRA). An association of physicians, counselors, therapists, and others (including organizations) concerned with the rehabilitation of the physically and mentally handicapped. It reviews existing services and makes recommendations for improved rehabilitation programs.

American Orthopsychiatric Association (AOA). An organization of psychiatrists, psychologists, social workers, sociologists, and members of other disciplines working in a collaborative approach to the study and treatment of human behavior, primarily in clinical settings. Its focus is on the problems of children. The AOA encourages research and is directly concerned with fostering human welfare.

National Council for Family Relations (NCFR). Composed primarily of and directed toward practitioners serving couples and

families through counseling, therapy, education, and community service. The NCFR fosters research and the application of its findings to practice.

American Association on Mental Deficiency (AAMD). An interdisciplinary association of physicians, educators, administrators, social workers, psychologists, psychiatrists, and others interested in assisting the mentally retarded. It works with the American Psychiatric Association in setting standards for hospitals and schools for the mentally retarded.

Council for Exceptional Children (CEC). Made up largely of professional workers in fields dealing with mentally retarded, physically handicapped, and emotionally disturbed children. It fosters research and its applications, education, and social legislation relating to exceptional children.

American Association for the Advancement of Science (AAAS). Composed of scientists from many disciplines. Its objectives include furthering the work and mutual cooperation of scientists, improving the effectiveness of science and its contribution to hu-

man welfare, and increasing understanding and appreciation of the importance and promise of scientific methods in human progress.

Society for Research in Child Development (SRCD). An association of psychologists whose aim is to study normal processes of child development. Members are concerned with issues related to improving the welfare of children as well as with encouraging scientific research on developmental processes.

Most of these organizations sponsor national conventions, workshops, symposia, and public educational programs, and many publish journals in their respective areas. They are also concerned with broad social problems as well as with the special problems in their professional areas.

smallpox and malaria. Over the years, mental health, too, became an increasing concern among the member countries. In response, WHO's present program now integrates mental health concerns with the broad problems of overall health and socioeconomic development that must be faced by member countries (WHO, 1978a). For example, WHO's program includes strategies to both prevent and control mental disorders. Furthermore, it includes efforts to ensure healthy psychosocial development, to protect traditional cultural values and

family relationships in the face of rapid industrialization, and to foster community participation in public health programs.

WHO has headquarters in Geneva and regional offices for Africa, the Americas, Southeast Asia, Europe, the Eastern Mediterranean, and the Western Pacific. Hence its activities extend into areas with diverse physical environments, types of social organization, and mental health facilities. It enters a country only on invitation, helping identify the basic health needs of each country and working with the local authorities to plan and carry out the most useful and appropriate programs. Where possible, it strives to make its services available over a period of several years to ensure continuity and success for the programs that are undertaken.

Another important contribution of WHO has been its International Classification of Diseases, which enables clinicians and researchers in different countries to use a uniform set of diagnostic categories (WHO, 1978b). The American Psychiatric Association's DSM-IV classification is being coordinated with the WHO classification (ICD-10).

The World Federation for Mental Health

The World Federation for Mental Health was established in 1948 as an international congress of nongovernmental organizations and individuals concerned with mental health. Its purpose is to promote cooperation at the international level between governmental and nongovernmental mental health agencies, and its membership now extends to more than 50 countries. The federation has been granted consultative status by WHO and it assists the UN agencies by collecting information on mental health conditions all over the world.

We have now seen something of the maze of local, national, and international measures that are being undertaken in the mental health field. We can expect these efforts to continue. Furthermore, we can expect to see more and more mental health problems unraveled to reveal discoverable causes and to respond to treatment and prevention by scientific means. The 1990s have already witnessed an amazing openness and a diminishing of previously impassable borders. Along with this increased interchange of ideas and cooperation, we expect to see a broader interchange of mental health collaboration. Reductions in international tensions and a greater international cooperation in the sciences and health planning will likely promote more sharing of information and views on mental health.

CHALLENGES FOR THE FUTURE

We have a long way to go before our dreams of a better world are realized. Many question whether the United States or any other technologically advanced nation can achieve mental health for the majority of its citizens in our time. Racism, poverty, the uprooting of third world populations, and other social problems that contribute to mental disorder sometimes seem insurmountable.

Events in the rest of the world affect us also, both directly and indirectly. Worldwide economic instability and shortages and the possibility of the destruction of our planet's life support system breed widespread anxiety about the future. The vast resources we have spent on military programs over the past 45 years to protect against perceived threats have absorbed funds and energy that otherwise might have been turned to meeting human and social needs here and elsewhere in the world. The limited resources we are now willing to apply to solving mental health problems prevent the solution of major problems resulting from cocaine abuse, homelessness, broken families, and squalid living conditions for many families.

The Need for Planning

It seems imperative that more effective planning be done at community, national, and international levels if mental health problems are going to be reduced or eliminated. Many challenges must be met if we are to create a better world for ourselves and future generations. Without slackening our efforts to meet needs at home, we will probably find it increasingly essential to participate more broadly in international measures toward reducing group tensions and promoting mental health and a better world for people everywhere. At the same time, we can expect that measures undertaken to reduce international conflict and improve the general condition of humankind will make their contribution to our own nation's social progress and mental health. Both kinds of measures will require understanding and moral commitment from concerned citizens.

The Individual's Contribution

Each man can make a difference,
and each man should try.
John F. Kennedy

The history of abnormal psychology provides clear examples of individuals whose efforts were instrumental in changing thinking about problems. Recall that Pinel took off the chains, Dorothea Dix initiated an incredible movement to improve the conditions of asylums, and Clifford Beers inspired the modern mental health movement with his autobiographical account of his own experience with mental illness. Who may lead the next revolution in mental health is anyone's guess. What is clear is that a great deal can be accomplished by individual effort.

When students become aware of the tremendous scope of the mental health problem both nationally and internationally and the woefully inadequate facilities for coping with it, they often ask, "What can I do?" This is not an idle question, for much of the progress that has been achieved in the treatment of mental disorders has resulted from the work of concerned citizens. Thus it seems appropriate to suggest a few of the lines of action interested students can profitably take.

Many opportunities in mental health work are open to trained personnel, both professional and paraprofessional. Social work, clinical psychology, psychiatry, and other mental health occupations are rewarding in terms of personal fulfillment. In addition, many occupations, ranging from law enforcement to teaching and the ministry, can and do play key roles in the mental health and well-being of many people. Training in all these fields usually offers individuals opportunities to work in community clinics and related facilities, to gain experience in understanding the needs and problems of people in distress, and to become familiar with community resources.

Citizens can find many ways to be of direct service if they are familiar with national and international resources and programs, and if they invest the effort necessary to learn about their community's special needs and problems. Whatever their roles in life—student, teacher, police officer, lawyer, homemaker, business executive, or trade unionist—their interests are directly at stake. For although the mental health of a nation may be manifested in many ways—in its purposes, courage, moral responsibility, scientific and cultural achievements, and quality of daily life—its health and resources derive ultimately from the individuals within it. In a participatory democracy, it is they who plan and implement the nation's goals.

Besides accepting some measure of responsibility for the mental health of others through the quality of one's own interpersonal relationships, there are several other constructive courses of action open to each citizen, including (a) serving as a volunteer in a mental hospital, community mental health center, or service organization; (b) supporting realistic measures for ensuring comprehensive health services for all age groups; and (c) working toward improved public education, responsible government, the alleviation of group prejudice, and the establishment of a more sane and harmonious world.

All of us are concerned with mental health for personal as well as altruistic reasons, for we want to overcome the harassing problems of contemporary living and find our share of happiness in a meaningful and fulfilling life. To do so, we may sometimes need the courage to admit that our problems are too

In Austin, Texas, the Austin Groups for the Elderly (AGE) represents a broad-based preventive effort of more than 15 agencies that provide activities and services to the elderly, thus promoting better mental health either directly or indirectly. Shown here is one of the programs available—Elderhaven, a unique day-care center for elderly adults.

much for us. When existence seems futile or the going becomes too difficult, it may help to remind ourselves of the following basic facts, which have been emphasized throughout this text:

- From time to time, each of us has serious difficulties in coping with the problems of living.
- During such crisis periods, we may need psychological and related assistance.
- Such difficulties are not a disgrace; they can happen to anyone if the stress is sufficiently severe.
- The early detection and correction of maladaptive behavior is of great importance in preventing the development of more severe or chronic conditions.
- Preventive measures—primary, secondary, and tertiary—are the most effective long-range approach to the solution of both individual and group mental health problems.

Recognizing these facts is essential because statistics show that almost all of us will at some time in our lives have to deal with severely maladaptive behavior or mental disorder either in ourselves or in someone close to us. Our interdependence and the loss to us all, individually and collectively, when any one of us fails to achieve his or her potential are eloquently expressed in the famous lines of John Donne (1624):

No man is an island, entire of itself; every man is a piece of the continent, a part of the main. If a clod be washed away by the sea, Europe is less, as well as if a promontory were, as well as if a manor of thy friends or of thine own were: any man's death diminishes me, because I am involved in mankind, and therefore never send to know for whom the bell tolls; it tolls for thee.

UNRESOLVED ISSUES
on the Mentally Disordered in the Prison System

Teplin (1990a) reported that the rates of schizophrenia, major depression, and mania were two to three times higher in jails than in the general population. These findings reaffirm the view that many individuals with severe mental disorders are in jails or prisons in the United States rather than in mental health facilities. The incarceration of mentally disabled individuals in prison or jail may result from people being mentally disordered when they commit crimes or, once incarcerated for a crime, becoming mentally disordered in reaction to the imprisonment.

Some investigators have recently argued that the greater prevalence of severe mental disorders in prison inmates than in the general population supports the view that jails, rather than mental hospitals, have become the repository for the chronically mentally disordered. This scenario is thought to be the result of numerous inpatients being released from psychiatric hospitals and being left to fend for themselves. Failing to function in the community, they resort to committing crimes, which results in their eventual imprisonment. This view has been referred to as the *criminalization hypothesis*. Some authorities believe that prisons have also become the dumping grounds for individuals with other problems, such as drug abuse, or for homeless people in winter, when living on the streets becomes difficult (Adler, 1987; Pogrebin & Poole, 1987; Shenson, Dubler, & Michaels, 1990).

Can the fact that there are many psychologically disturbed individuals in prison support the criminalization hypothesis? This view would be more tenable if, for example, the prisons became more filled with former psychiatric patients after deinstitutionalization became fashionable. Teplin (1990a) pointed out, however, that there appears *not* to have been a substantial increase of the mentally disordered in jails over previous estimates of similar studies, which have traditionally been higher than the population at large (Bolton, 1976). That is, the census of mentally disordered individuals in prison appears to have been relatively constant over the years, albeit higher than the general population. Thus the problem is not new and it is not simply a result of deinstitutionalization and the shifting of people from psychiatric facilities to prisons.

Whatever the source, the problem nevertheless exists. Many individuals whose primary problem is mental illness, rather than or in addition to criminality, are institutionalized in facilities where understanding and treatment of mental health problems are sorely lacking. In an extensive study of 486 admissions to Philadelphia prisons using a battery of psychological tests, Guy and colleagues (1985) reported that 34 percent of the inmates were identified as having substantial psychological problems and 11 percent were deemed as in clear need of psychiatric hospitalization.

Mental health resources, however, have traditionally not been available or only minimally available in correctional facilities. It appears that our society has taken the view, at least as far as our past actions reflect, that prisons are places of retention rather than treatment or rehabilitation. Teplin's study (1990b) confirmed this view—when the mentally disordered are incarcerated, few receive attention for their psychological problems. She found that, while somatic illnesses were discovered 91.7 percent of the time for individuals experiencing problems, mental health problems were detected in less than 33 percent of the severely mentally disordered detainees. Symptoms of depression among detainees were frequently overlooked, being detected in only 7.1 percent of the cases. This is a particularly tragic oversight in correctional programs because suicide is the second most frequent cause of death among jail detainees—a total of 39 percent of all inmate deaths (U.S. Justice Department, 1987). Teplin (1990b) found that, of those detainees meeting criteria for severe mental disorder, only about 33 percent were provided treatment within a week of detention. She concluded that "once arrested, treatment is unlikely to be forthcoming. Clearly, society must provide liaison between the criminal justice and mental health systems, as well as improve screening techniques to ensure that mentally disordered detainees receive needed treatment" (p. 236).

Whether these mentally disordered inmates are incarcerated as a result of their disorders or whether their severe psychological disorders resulted from their imprisonment is not important. What is more pertinent is that their problems be recognized and treated. Clearly, many people in prison are suffering from severe psychological disorders and need more attention for their problems than they currently receive.

SUMMARY

Increasingly today, professionals are trying not only to cure mental health problems but also to prevent them, or at least reduce their effects. Prevention can be viewed as focusing on three levels. Primary prevention is aimed at reducing the possibility of disorder and fostering positive mental health efforts. Secondary prevention attempts to reduce the impact or duration of a problem that has already occurred. Tertiary prevention attempts to reduce the long-term consequences of having had a disorder.

In recent years, several legal issues concerning the treatment of mental patients have surfaced. The commitment process and procedures for committing individuals for inpatient care have been reconsidered. Being "mentally ill" is not considered sufficient grounds for commitment. There must be, in addition, evidence that the individual is either dangerous to himself or herself or represents a danger to society. It is not an easy matter, even for trained professionals, to determine in advance if an individual is "dangerous" and likely to cause harm to others. Nevertheless, professionals must, at times, make such judgments. Recent court rulings have found professionals liable when patients they were treating caused harm to others. The Tarasoff decision held that a therapist has a duty to warn potential victims if his or her patient has threatened to kill them.

Another important issue of forensic psychology involves the insanity plea for capital crimes. Many mental health and legal professionals, journalists, and laypersons have questioned the present use of the insanity defense. The original legal precedent, the M'Naghten Rule, held that, at the time of committing the act, the accused must have been laboring under such a defect of reason as to not know the nature and quality of the act or to not know that what he or she was doing was wrong. The more recent broadening of the insanity plea, under the Durham Rule, has placed more credibility on scientific knowledge in that the accused is not "criminally responsible if his or her unlawful act was the produce of mental disease or mental defect." This broadening of the insanity plea has led to its use in more and more cases, and decisions often involve conflicting psychiatric testimony. Many people have been questioning the appropriateness of the insanity plea, and some experts are recommending changes in it, asking that an accused individual's guilt or innocence be established separately from a determination of sanity.

There has been a great deal of legal controversy recently over the release of patients from mental hospitals, called deinstitutionalization, and the failure to provide adequate follow-up of these patients in the community. In their zeal to close large psychiatric institutions, many administrators underestimated the amount of care that would be needed after discharge, and overestimated communities' abilities to deal with patients with chronic problems. The result was that some chronic patients were placed in circumstances that required more adaptive abilities than they possessed. Recent work in the area of aftercare for former mental patients has provided clearer guidelines for discharge and therapeutic follow-up.

A large number of organizations are concerned and involved with establishing organized efforts for mental health. Several government agencies have mental health as their primary mission. For example, federal agencies such as the National Institute of Mental Health (NIMH), the National Institute on Drug Abuse (NIDA), and the National Institute on Alcohol Abuse and Alcoholism (NIAAA) are devoted to promoting varied research, training, and service. State and county government agencies may focus their efforts on the delivery of mental health services to residents on an inpatient or outpatient basis.

Mental health programming in the United States is also the concern of several professional and mental health organizations, many corporations, and a number of voluntary mental health organizations. In addition, international organization, such as the World Health Organization (WHO) and the World Federation for Mental Health, have contributed to mental health programs worldwide.

Key Terms

primary prevention (p. 674)
secondary prevention (p. 674)
tertiary prevention (p. 674)
short-term crisis therapy (p. 679)
milieu therapy (p. 683)

social-learning programs (p. 684)
forensic psychology (forensic psychiatry) (p. 686)
the insanity defense (p. 691)
deinstitutionalization (p. 693)

Glossary

Many of the key terms that appear in the glossary appear in boldface when first introduced in the text discussion. A number of other terms commonly encountered in this or other psychology texts are also included; you are encouraged to make use of this glossary both as a general reference tool and as a study aid for the course in abnormal psychology.

Abnormal behavior. Maladaptive behavior deterimental to an individual and/or a group.

Abnormal psychology. Field of psychology concerned with the study, assessment, treatment, and prevention of abnormal behavior.

Abstinence. Refraining altogether from the use of a particular addictive substance.

Accommodation. Cognitive process whereby new information causes a reorganization of previously existing cognitive maps or structures.

Activation (arousal). Energy mobilization required for an organism to pursue its goals and meet its needs.

Actuarial approach. Application of probability statistics to human behavior, as in insurance.

Actuarial interpretation. Application of interpretations developed from a reference group with test scores similar to those of a subject to evaluate the subject's test performance.

Acute (disorder). Term used to describe a disorder of sudden onset and relatively short duration, usually with intense symptoms.

Acute alcoholic hallucinosis. State of alcoholic intoxication characterized by hallucinations.

Acute posttraumatic stress disorder. Disorder in which symptoms develop within six months of extremely traumatic experience instead of entering recovery stage.

Acute schizophrenia. See **Reactive schizophrenia**.

Addictive behavior. Behavior based on the pathological need for a substance or activity; it may involve the abuse of substances, such as alcohol or cocaine, or the excessive ingestion of high-caloric food, resulting in extreme obesity.

Adjustive behavior. Behavior by which an individual attempts to deal with stress and meet his or her needs, including efforts to maintain harmonious relationships with the environment.

Adjustment. Outcome of an individual's efforts to deal with stress and meet his or her needs.

Adjustment disorders. Category of disorders in which an individual has difficulty adjusting to a common stressor.

Adjustment disorder with depressed mood. Moderately severe mood disorder behaviorally identical to dysthymic disorder or depressed phase of cyclothymic disorder but having an identifiable, though not severe, psychosocial stressor occurring within three months prior to the onset of depression.

Adrenal cortex. Outer layer of the adrenal glands; secretes the adrenal steroids and other hormones.

Adrenal glands. Endocrine glands located at the upper end of the kidneys; consist of inner adrenal medulla and outer adrenal cortex.

Adrenaline. Hormone secreted by the adrenal medulla during strong emotion; causes such bodily changes as an increase in blood sugar and a rise in blood pressure. Also called *epinephrine*.

Advocacy. Approach to meeting mental health needs in which advocates, often an interested group of volunteers, attempt to help children or others receive services that they need but often are unable to obtain for themselves.

Advocacy programs. Programs aimed at helping people in underserved populations to obtain aid with which to improve their situations.

Affect. Experience of emotion or feeling.

Aftercare. Follow-up therapy after release from a hospital.

Aggression. Behavior aimed at hurting or destroying someone or something.

Agitation. Marked restlessness and psychomotor excitement.

Agoraphobia. Morbid fear of large, open places.

AIDS-dementia complex (ADC). Generalized degeneration of brain tissue as a result of HIV-1 infection.

AIDS-related complex (ARC). Pre-AIDS manifestation of HIV infection involving minor infections, various nonspecific symptoms (such as unexplained fever), and blood cell count abnormalities.

Alarm and mobilization reaction. First state of the general adaptation syndrome, characterized by the mobilization of defenses to cope with a stressful situation.

Alcoholic. Individual with serious drinking problems, whose drinking impairs life adjustment in terms of health, personal relationships, and/or occupational functioning.

Alcoholic deterioration. Personality deterioration, including impaired judgment, associated with alcoholism.

Alcoholic intoxication. State reached when alcohol content of blood is 0.1 percent or above.

Alcoholism. Dependence on alcohol to the extent that it seriously interferes with life adjustment.

Algophobia. Irrational fear of pain.

Alienation. Lack or loss of relationships to others.

Alpha waves. Brain waves having a frequency of 8 to 12 cycles per second and accompanied by a state of wakeful relaxation.

Alzheimer's disease. Most common form of senile disorder; in some cases, Alzheimer's disease may occur well before old age.

Amnesia. Total or partial loss of memory.

Amnestic syndrome. Inability to remember events more than a few minutes after they have occurred coupled with the ability to recall the recent and remote past.

Amniocentesis. Technique that involves drawing fluid from the amniotic sac of a pregnant woman so that the sloughed-off fetal cells can be examined for chromosomal irregularities, including that of Down syndrome.

Amphetamine. One type of drug that produces a psychologically stimulating and energizing effect.

Analgesia. Insensitivity to pain without loss of consciousness.

Analogue studies. Studies in which a researcher attempts to simulate the conditions under investigation.

Anal stage. In psychoanalytic theory, stage of psychosexual development in which behavior is presumably focused on anal pleasure and activities.

Analytic psychology. School or system of psychology developed by Carl Jung.

Androgen. Hormone associated with the development and maintenance of male characteristics.

Androgyny. Theoretically, psychologically ideal combination of masculine and feminine traits.

Anesthesia. Loss or impairment of sensitivity (usually to touch but often applied to sensitivity to pain and other senses as well).

Anhedonia. Inability to experience pleasure or joy; believed by some to be a basic characteristic of schizophrenic individuals.

Anorexia nervosa. Loss or severe diminishment of appetite, apparently of psychogenic origin.

Anoxia. Lack of sufficient oxygen.

Antabuse. Drug used in the treatment of alcoholism.

Anterograde amnesia. Loss of memory for events *following* trauma or shock.

Antianxiety drugs. Drugs that are used primarily for alleviating anxiety.

Antibody. Circulating blood substance coded for detection of and binding to a particular antigen.

Antidepressant drugs. Drugs that are used primarily to elevate mood and relieve depression.

Antigen. Substance detected as "foreign" by the body's immune defenses, giving rise to the immune reaction.

Antipsychotic drugs. Group of drugs, sometimes called *major tranquilizers,* that produce a calming effect on many patients as well as alleviate or reduce the intensity of psychotic symptoms, such as delusions and hallucinations.

Antisocial personality disorder. Personality disorder involving a marked lack of ethical or moral development; also commonly referred to as *psychopathic* or *sociopathic personality.*

Anxiety. Generalized feelings of fear and apprehension.

Anxiety attack. Acute episode of intense anxiety.

Anxiety disorder. DSM-III-R category characterized by chronic anxiety and apprehension. Includes generalized anxiety disorder, panic disorder, obsessive-compulsive disorder, posttraumatic disorder, and phobic disorder.

Anxiety hierarchy. Ranking of anxiety-eliciting situations utilized in systematic desensitization therapy.

Anxiety-response pattern. Model of the genesis of anxiety as involving biological, psychological, and environmental events that become a self-sustaining feedback system.

Aphasia. Loss or impairment of ability to communicate and understand language symbols—involving loss of power of expression by speech, writing, or signs, or loss of ability to comprehend written or spoken language—resulting from brain injury or disease.

Aphonia. Inability to speak above a whisper; a conversion disorder.

Approach-avoidance conflict. Type of stress situation involving both positive and negative features.

Apraxia. Loss of ability to perform purposeful movements.

Arousal. See **Activation.**

Arteriosclerosis. Degenerative thickening and hardening of the walls of the arteries, occurring usually in old age.

Assertiveness training. Behavior therapy technique for helping individuals become more self-assertive in interpersonal relationships.

Assimilation. Cognitive process whereby new information is fitted into previously existing cognitive maps or structures.

Astasia-abasia. Inability to stand or walk without the legs wobbling about and collapsing, although a person has normal control of legs while sitting or lying down; no associated organic pathology.

Asylums. Institutions established soley for the care of the mentally ill.

Ataxia. Muscular incoordination, particularly of the arms and legs. See also **Locomotor ataxia.**

At risk. Condition of being considered vulnerable to the development of certain abnormal behaviors.

Atrophy. Wasting away or shrinking of a bodily organ, particularly muscle tissue.

Attention-deficit hyperactivity disorder (ADHD). Disorder of childhood characterized by difficulties—e.g., impulsivity, excessive motor activity, and an inability to focus attention for appropriate periods of time—that interfere with effective task-oriented behavior; also known as *hyperactivity.*

Attribution theory. Theory by which causes in the behavior of others are interpreted, based on unseen or unrecognized qualities in ourselves.

Autistic disorder. Pervasive developmental disorder whose central feature is a profound and unyielding unresponsiveness to the human environment. The disorder begins in infancy and is characterized by an inability to relate to the environment, to others, or to form a normal self-concept.

Automated assessment. Psychological test interpretation by electronic computer or some other mechanical means.

Autonomic nervous system. Section of the nervous system that regulates the internal organs; consists primarily of ganglia connected with the brain stem and spinal cord and may be subdivided into the sympathetic and parasympathetic systems.

Autonomic reactivity. Individual's characteristic degree of emotional reactivity to stress.

Autonomy. Self-reliance; the sense of being an individual in one's own right.

Autosome. Any chromosome other than those determining sex.

Aversion therapy. Form of behavior therapy in which punishment or aversive stimulation is used to eliminate undesired responses.

Aversive conditioning. Use of noxious stimuli to suppress unwanted behavior.

Aversive stimulus. Stimulus that elicits psychic or physical pain.

Avoidance conditioning. Form of conditioning in which a subject learns to behave in a certain way in order to avoid an unpleasant stimulus.

Avoidant personality disorder. Personality disorder characterized by hypersensitivity to rejection, limited social relationships, and low self-esteem.

"Bad trip." Unpleasant or traumatic experience while under the influence of a hallucinogenic drug, such as LSD.

Barbiturate. Type of synthetic sedative drug.

Baseline. In behavior therapy, the initial level of responses emitted by an individual.

B-cell. Variety of lymphocyte (white blood cell) capable of producing specific antibodies to an antigen. Principal element of "humoral" immune functioning.

Bedlam. Popular contraction of the name of the early London asylum of St. Mary of Bethlehem.

Behavioral assessment. Technique to determine the functional relationships between an individual's behavior and environmental stimuli.

Behavioral contracting. Positive reinforcement technique using a contract, often between family members, stipulating privileges and responsibilities.

Behavioral medicine. Broad interdisciplinary field concerned with relations between physical health and the psychological aspects of individuals who have, or are at risk for, physical disease.

Behavioral sciences. Various interrelated disciplines, including psychology, sociology, and anthropology, that focus on human behavior.

Behavior control. Shaping and manipulation of behavior by drugs, persuasion, and other techniques.

Behavior disorder. Synonym for psychological problem.

Behaviorism. School of psychology that formerly restricted itself primarily to study of overt behavior.

Behavioristic perspective. Approach to understanding maladaptive behavior that is organized around the role of learning in human behavior.

Behavior modification. Techniques used to change specific behaviors.

Behavior sample. Assessment data that presumably provide an accurate reflection of a subject's typical behavior.

Behavior therapy. Therapeutic procedures based primarily on principles of respondent and operant conditioning.

Benign. Of a mild, self-limiting nature; not malignant.

Beta waves. Brain waves having a frequency of 18 to 30 cycles per second or associated with problem solving and feelings of tension.

Biochemical disorders. Disorders involving disturbances in internal chemical regulation.

Biofeedback. Treatment technique by which individuals are taught to change and control internal bodily processes formerly thought to be involuntary (e.g., blood pressure and skin temperature); involves giving an individual immediate feedback about the bodily changes as they occur.

Biogenic amines. Chemicals that serve as neurotransmitters or modulators.

Biological clocks. The 24-hour rhythmic fluctuations in metabolic processes of plants and animals. See also **Circadian rhythms.**

Biological viewpoint. Approach to mental disorders emphasizing biological causation.

Bipolar disorder. Manic or depressive episode of mood disorder believed to be a manifestation of an underlying condition predisposing an individual to severe mood swings; has largely replaced the term *manic-depressive psychosis.*

Bisexuality. Sexual attraction to both females and males.

Blocking. Involuntary inhibition of recall, ideation, or communication (including sudden stoppage of speech).

Borderline personality disorder. Personality disorder characterized by instability and drastic mood shifts; such individuals are impulsive and at times may appear psychotic.

Brain pathology. Diseased or disordered condition of the brain.

Brainwashing. Extreme form of thought modification and control.

Brain waves. Minute oscillations of electrical potential given off by neurons in the cerebral cortex and measured by the electroencephalograph.

Brief Psychiatric Rating Scale (BPRS). Objective method of rating clinical symptoms that provides scores on eighteen variables (e.g., somatic concern, anxiety, withdrawal, hostility, and bizarre thinking).

Brief psychotherapy. Short-term therapy, usually 8 to 10 sessions, focused on restoring an individual's functioning and offering emotional support.

Bulimia nervosa. Recurring episodes of seemingly uncontrollable binge eating, accompanied by extreme efforts to disgorge.

Caffeine. Chemical compound found in many commonly available drinks and foods and whose negative effects can include intoxication, restlessness, nervousness, excitement, insomnia, muscle twitching, and gastrointestinal complaints.

Cardiovascular. Pertaining to the heart and blood vessels.

Case study. Assessment information on a specific individual.

Castrating. Refers to any source of injury to or deprivation of the genitals, or more broadly, to a threat to the masculinity or femininity of an individual.

Castration anxiety. As postulated by Freud, the anxiety a young boy experiences when he has incestuous cravings for his mother while at the same time viewing his father as a rival and fearing that his father may harm him by removing his penis; this anxiety forces the boy to repress his sexual desire for his mother and his hostility toward his father.

Catalepsy. Condition in which the muscles are waxy and semirigid, tending to maintain the limbs in any position in which they are placed.

Catecholamine. Class of amines sharing a similar chemical structure and involved chiefly in neural transmission.

Categorical approach. Approach to classifying abnormal behavior that assumes that (a) all human behavior can be sharply divided into the categories *normal* and *abnormal,* and (b) there exist discrete, non-overlapping classes or types of abnormal behavior, often referred to as "mental" illnesses or diseases.

Catharsis. Discharge of emotional tension associated with repressed traumatic material, e.g., by "talking it out."

CAT scan. See **Computerized axial tomography.**

Causal pattern. In a cause-and-effect relationship, the situation where more than one causal factor is involved.

Causation. Relationship in which the preceding variable causes the other(s).

Central nervous system (CNS). The brain and spinal cord.

Cerebral arteriosclerosis. Hardening of the arteries in the brain.

Cerebral concussion. Mild head injury that disrupts brain functions.

Cerebral contusion. Brain damage resulting from head injury severe enough to shift brain and compress it against skull.

Cerebral cortex. Surface layers of the cerebrum.

Cerebral hemorrhage. Bleeding into brain tissue from a ruptured blood vessel.

Cerebral laceration. Tearing of brain tissue associated with severe head injury.

Cerebral syphilis. Syphilitic infection of the brain.

Cerebral thrombosis. Formation of a clot or thrombus in the vascular system of the brain.

Cerebrovascular accident (CVA). Blockage or rupture of large blood vessel in brain leading to both focal and generalized impairment of brain function. Also called *stroke.*

Cerebrum. Main part of brain; divided into left and right hemispheres.

Character disorders. See **Personality disorders.**

Character traits. See **Temperament traits.**

Chemotherapy. Use of drugs to treat mental disorders.

Child abuse. Infliction of physical damage on a child by parents or other adults.

Child advocacy. Movement concerned with protecting rights and ensuring well-being of children.

Childhood depression. Mood disorder occurring in children often in a masked form, e.g., as acting-out behavior.

Chlorpromazine. One of the major antipsychotic drugs.

Chorea. Pathological condition characterized by jerky, irregular, involuntary movements. See also **Huntington's chorea.**

Chromosomal anomalies. Inherited defects or vulnerabilities caused by irregularities in chromosomes.

Chromosomes. Chainlike structures within cell nucleus that contain genes.

Chronic (disorder). Term used to describe a disorder that is a relatively permanent maladaptive pattern or condition.

Chronic schizophrenia. See **Process schizophrenia.**

Circadian rhythms. Regular biological cycle of sleep and activity characteristic of each species.

Civil commitment. Procedure whereby an individual certified as mentally disordered can be hospitalized, either voluntarily or against his or her will.

Classical (respondent) conditioning. Basic form of learning in which a previously neutral stimulus comes to elicit a given response.

Claustrophobia. Irrational fear of small enclosed places.

Client-centered (person-centered) psychotherapy. Nondirective approach to psychotherapy developed chiefly by Carl Rogers and based on his personality theory.

Climacteric. Life period associated with the menopause in women and related glandular and bodily changes in men.

Clinical picture. Diagnostic picture formed by observation of patient's behavior or by all available assessment data.

Clinical problem checklist. Computer-administered psychological assessment procedure for surveying the range of psychological problems a patient is experiencing.

Clinical psychologist. Mental health professional with Ph.D. degree or Psy.D. degree in clinical psychology and clinical experience in assessment and psychotherapy.

Clinical psychology. Field of psychology concerned with the understanding, assessment, treatment, and prevention of maladaptive behavior.

Cocaine. Stimulating and pain-reducing psychoactive drug.

Cognition. Act, process, or product of knowing or perceiving.

Cognitive-behavioral therapy. Treatment approach in which behavioral methods or learning principles are applied to thought processes (cognitions).

Cognitive derailment ("slippage"). Tendency for thoughts and associations not to follow one another in logical order; believed to be a basic characteristic of schizophrenic disorders.

Cognitive dissonance. Condition existing when new information is contradictory to one's assumptions.

Cognitive map. Network of assumptions that form an individual's "frame of reference" for interpreting and coping with his or her world.

Cognitive mediation. Thought processes in an individual that occur between the stimulus and the response.

Cognitive processes (cognition). Mental processes, including perception, memory, and reasoning, by which one acquires knowledge, solves problems, and makes plans.

Cognitive restructuring therapy. Cognitive-behavioral therapy that aims to alter an individual's false or maladaptive frame of reference.

Collective unconscious. Term used by Carl Jung to refer to that portion of the unconscious that he considered common to all humanity.

Coma. Profound stupor with unconsciousness.

Community mental health. Application of psychosocial and sociocultural principles to the improvement of given environments.

Community psychology. Use of community resources in dealing with maladaptive behavior; tends to be more concerned with community intervention rather than with personal or individual change.

Complex. Group of emotionally toned attitudes, desires, or memories which are partially or totally repressed.

Compulsion. Irrational and repetitive impulse to perform some act.

Compulsive gambling. See **Pathological gambling.**

Compulsive personality. Personality disorder characterized by excessive concern with rules, order, efficiency, and work.

Computer assessment. Use of computers to obtain or interpret assessment data.

Computer model. Use of computer to simulate psychological functioning.

Computerized axial tomography (CAT scan). Radiological technique used to locate and assess the extent of organic damage without surgery.

Computerized diagnostic interview for children. Computer-administered and scored diagnostic interview that provides a DSM-III-R diagnosis.

Concordance rates. Rates at which a diagnosis or a trait of one person is predictive of the same diagnosis or trait in relatives.

Concussion. See **Cerebral concussion.**

Conditioned reinforcer. Reinforcer that derives its value from basic unconditioned reinforcers.

Conditioning. Simple form of learning involving stimulus and response. See also **Classical conditioning** and **Operant conditioning.**

Conduct disorders. Childhood disorders marked by persistent acts of aggressive or antisocial behavior that may or may not be against the law.

Confabulation. Filling in of memory gaps with false and often irrelevant details.

Confidentiality. Commitment on part of a professional person to keep information he or she obtains from a client confidential.

Conflict. Simultaneous arousal of opposing impulses, desires, or motives.

Congenital. Existing at birth or before birth but not necessarily hereditary.

Congenital defect. Genetic defect or environmental condition occurring prior to birth and causing a child to develop a physical or psychological anomaly.

Conscience. Functioning of an individual's system of moral values in the approval or disapproval of his or her own thoughts and actions. Roughly equivalent to the Freudian concept of superego.

Consciousness. Awareness of inner and/or outer environment.

Constitution. Relatively constant biological makeup of an individual, resulting from the interaction of heredity and environment.

Constitutional liability. Any detrimental characteristic that is either innate or acquired so early and in such strength that it is functionally similar to a genetic characteristic.

Consultation. Community intervention approach that aims at helping individuals at risk for disorder by working indirectly through caretaker institutions (e.g., police and teachers).

Contingency. Relationship, usually causal, between two events in which one is usually followed by the other.

Continuous reinforcement. Reward or reinforcement given regularly after each correct response.

Control group. Group of subjects compared with an experimental group in assessing the effects of independent variables.

Controlled drinking therapy. Behavioral treatment approach aimed at reducing an individual's drinking by self-control methods.

Conversion disorder. Type of somatoform disorder in which symptoms of organic illness appear in the absence of any related organic pathology; previously called *hysteria.*

Convulsion. Pathological, involuntary muscular contractions.

Coping strategies. Efforts used to deal with stress.

Coprolalia. Verbal tic in which an individual utters obscenities aloud.

Coronary heart disease (CHD). Potentially lethal blockage of the arteries supplying blood to the heart muscle, or myocardium.

Corpus callosum. Nerve fibers that connect the two hemispheres of the brain.

Correlation. Relationship of variables to one another suggesting, but not establishing, a causal context.

Corticovisceral control mechanisms. Brain mechanisms that regulate autonomic and other bodily functions.

Counseling psychology. Field of psychology that focuses on helping people with problems pertaining to education, marriage, or occupation.

Counterconditioning. Relearning by using a particular stimulus to establish a new (and generally more adaptive) response.

Counter-transference. Arousal by a client of inappropriate feelings of transference on the part of an analyst during the course of psychoanalytic therapy.

Couples counseling. Treatment for disordered interpersonal relationships involving sessions with both members of the relationship present; also known as *marital therapy.*

Coverants. Internal, private events, such as thoughts and assumptions, to which conditioning principles are applied in cognitive-behavioral therapy.

Covert. Concealed, disguised, not directly observable.

Covert sensitization. Behavioral treatment method for extinguishing undesirable behavior by associating noxious mental images with that behavior.

Cretinism. Condition arising from thyroid deficiency in early life and marked by mental retardation and distinctive physical characteristics.

Criminal responsibility. Legal question of whether an individual should be permitted to use insanity as a defense after having committed some criminal act.

Crisis. Stress situation which approaches or exceeds adaptive capacities of an individual or group.

Crisis intervention. Various methods for rendering therapeutic assistance to an individual or group during a period of crisis.

Criterion group. Group of subjects who exhibit the variable or disorder under study.

Critical period. Period of development during which an

organism most needs certain inputs or is most ready for acquisition of a given response.

Cultural-familial retardation.   Mental retardation as a result of an inferior quality of interaction with the cultural environment and with other people, with no evidence of brain pathology.

Cultural lag.   Tendency for formal conceptions of reality and "appropriate" behavior within a given culture to change more slowly than the actual thinking and actions of a society's members.

Cultural relativism.   Position that one cannot apply universal standards of normality or abnormality to all societies.

Cushing's syndrome.   Endocrine disorder resulting from oversecretion of *cortisone* and marked by mood swings, irritability, and other mental symptoms.

Cyclothymia.   Mild mood disorder characterized by extreme mood swings of nonpsychotic intensity.

Day hospital.   Community-based mental hospital where the patients are treated during the day, returning to their homes at night.

Decompensation.   Ego or personality disorganization under excessive stress.

Defense mechanism.   See **Ego-defense mechanism.**

Defense-oriented response.   Reaction involving one's feelings of adequacy and worth rather than objective handling of the stress situation.

Deficiency motivation.   Motivation directed primarily toward maintaining or restoring physiological or psychological equilibrium rather than toward personal growth.

Deinstitutionalization.   Movement to provide chronic patients with continued psychiatric care in the local community rather than committing them to institutions.

Delinquency.   Antisocial or illegal behavior by a minor.

Delirium.   State of mental confusion characterized by clouding of consciousness, disorientation, restlessness, excitement, and often hallucinations.

Delirium tremens.   Acute delirium associated with prolonged alcoholism; characterized by intense anxiety, tremors, and hallucinations.

Delusion.   Firm belief opposed to reality but maintained in spite of strong evidence to the contrary.

Delusional disorder.   Type of psychosis characterized by a systematized delusional system; formerly called *paranoia* and *paranoid disorder.*

Delusional system.   Internally coherent, systematized pattern of delusions.

Delusion of persecution.   False belief that one is being mistreated or interfered with by one's enemies. Often found in schizophrenia.

Dementia.   Severe mental disorder involving impairment of mental ability; not congenital.

Dementia praecox.   Older term for schizophrenia.

Demonology.   Viewpoint emphasizing supernatural causation of mental disorder, especially "possession" by evil spirits or forces.

Denial of reality.   Ego-defense mechanism by means of which an individual protects himself or herself from unpleasant aspects of reality by refusing to acknowledge them.

Dependency.   Tendency to rely overly on others.

Dependent personality disorder.   Personality disorder marked by lack of self-confidence and feelings of acute panic or discomfort at having to be alone.

Dependent variable.   In an experiment, the factor that the hypothesis predicts will change with changes in the independent variable.

Depersonalization.   Loss of sense of personal identity, often with a feeling of being something or someone else.

Depersonalization disorder.   Dissociative disorder, usually occurring in adolescence, in which individuals lose their sense of self and feel unreal or displaced to a different location.

Depression.   Emotional state characterized by extreme sadness, gloomy ruminations, feelings of worthlessness, loss of hope, and often apprehension.

Depressive neurosis (now called *dysthymia*).   Depression of intermediate severity with little or no evidence of personality breakdown or loss of contact with reality.

Depressive stupor.   Extreme degree of depression characterized by marked psychomotor underactivity.

Desensitization.   Therapeutic process by means of which reactions to traumatic experiences are reduced in intensity by repeatedly exposing an individual to them in mild form, either in reality or in fantasy.

Deterrence.   Premise that punishment for criminal offenses will deter that criminal and others from future criminal acts.

Detox.   Center or facility for receiving and detoxifying alcohol-or drug-intoxicated individuals.

Detoxification.   Treatment directed toward ridding the body of alcohol or other drugs.

Developmental disorder.   Problem that is rooted in deviations in the development process itself, thus disrupting the acquisition of skills and adaptive behavior and often interfering with the transition to well-functioning adulthood.

Developmental psychopathology.   Field of psychology that studies disorders of childhood within the context of developmental processes.

Deviant behavior.   Behavior which deviates markedly from the average or norm.

Dexedrine.   Amphetamine drug; a stimulant used to curb appetite or elevate mood.

Diagnosis.   Determination of the nature and extent of a specific disorder.

Diathesis.   Predisposition or vulnerability toward developing a given disorder.

Diathesis-stress model.   View of abnormal behavior as the result of stress operating on an individual with a biological, psychosocial, or sociocultural predisposition toward developing a specific disorder.

Differential reinforcement of other behavior (DOR).   Behavior modification technique for extinguishing undesirable behavior by reinforcing incompatible behaviors.

Dilantin.   Anticonvulsant medication often used in controlling epileptic seizures.

Dimensional approach.   Approach to classifying abnormal behavior that assumes that a person's typical behavior is the product of differing strengths or intensities of behavior along several definable dimensions, such as mood, emotional stability, aggressiveness, gender, identity, anxiousness, interpersonal trust, clarity of thinking and communication, social introversion, and so on.

Directive therapy.   Type of therapeutic approach in which a therapist supplies direct answers to problems and takes much of the responsibility for the progression of therapy.

Disaster syndrome.   Response pattern that appears to characterize the initial and long-lasting reactions of many victims of catastrophes.

Discordant family.   Family in which one or both of the parents is not gaining satisfaction from the relationship and one spouse may express frustration and disillusionment in hostile ways, such as nagging, belittling, and purposely doing things to annoy the other person.

Discrimination.   Learning to interpret and respond differently to two or more similar stimuli.

Diseases of adaptation.   Stomach ulcers and other disease conditions resulting from the stresses of life.

Disintegration.   Loss of organization or integration in any organized system.

Disorganization.   Severely impaired integration.

Disorientation.   Mental confusion with respect to time, place, or person.

Displacement.   Ego-defense mechanism in which an emotional attitude or symbolic meaning is transferred from one object or concept to another.

Disrupted family.   Family that is incomplete as a result of death, divorce, separation, or some other circumstance.

Dissociation.   Separation or "isolation" of mental processes in such a way that they become split off from the main personality or lose their normal thought-affect relationships.

Dissociative disorders.   Disorder in which a person avoids stress by dissociating—in essence by escaping—from his or her own personal identity through behavior patterns such as amnesia, fugue, somnambulism, or multiple personality.

Distress. Negative stress.

Disturbed family. Family in which one or both parents behave in grossly eccentric or abnormal ways and may keep the home in constant emotional turmoil.

Dizygotic (fraternal) twins. Twins that develop from two separate eggs.

DNA. Deoxyribonucleic acid, principal component of genes.

Dominant gene. A gene whose hereditary characteristics prevail in the offspring.

Dopamine. Catecholamine neural transmitter substance.

Dopamine hypothesis. Hypothesis that schizophrenia is the product of an excess of dopamine activity at certain synaptic sites.

Double-approach conflict. Type of conflict in which an individual is confronted with choosing between two or more desirable alternatives.

Double-avoidant conflict. Type of conflict in which an individual is confronted with choosing between two or more aversive alternatives.

Double-bind. Situation in which an individual will be disapproved for performing a given act and equally disapproved if he or she does not perform it.

Double-bind communication. Type of faulty communication in which the one person (e.g., a parent) presents to another (e.g., a child) ideas, feelings, and demands that are mutually incompatible.

Down syndrome. Form of mental retardation associated with chromosomal anomalies.

Dramatization. Defense against anxiety in which an individual engages in attention-getting behavior and self-dramatization.

Dream analysis. Psychotherapeutic technique involving the interpretation of a patient's dreams.

Drive. Internal conditions directing an organism toward a specific goal, usually involving biological rather than psychological motives.

Drug abuse. Use of a drug to the extent that it interferes with health and/or occupational or social adjustment.

Drug addiction (dependence). Physiological and/or psychological dependence on a drug.

Drug therapy. See **Chemotherapy** and **Pharmacotherapy.**

DSM-III-R. Current diagnostic manual of the American Psychiatric Association.

Dwarfism. Condition of arrested growth and very short stature.

Dyad. Two-person group.

Dynamic formulation. Integrated evaluation of a client's traits, attitudes, conflicts, and symptoms that attempts to explain his or her problem.

Dysfunction. Impairment or disturbance in the functioning of an organ or in behavior.

Dyslexia. Impairment of the ability to read.

Dyspareunia. Painful coitus in a male or a female.

Dysrhythmias. Abnormal brain-wave patterns.

Dysthymia. Moderately severe mood disorder characterized by extended periods of nonpsychotic depression and brief periods of normal moods. Also called *depressive neurosis.*

Echolalia. Meaningless repetition of words by an individual, usually of whatever has been said to that person.

Echopraxia. Repetition of another person's actions or gestures.

Ecology. Relation or interaction between organisms and their physical environment.

EEG. See **Electroencephalogram.**

Ego. In psychoanalytic theory, the rational subsystem of the personality which mediates between id and superego demands and reality. More generally, an individual's self-concept.

Egocentric. Preoccupied with one's own concerns and relatively insensitive to the concerns of others.

Ego-defense mechanism (reaction). Type of reaction designed to maintain an individual's feelings of adequacy and worth rather than to cope directly with the stress situation; usually unconscious and reality distorting.

Ego-dystonic homosexuality. Category of "mental disorder" in which an individual wishes to change his or her homosexual orientation.

Ego-ideal (self-ideal). Person or "self" an individual thinks he or she could and should be.

Ego involvement. Perception of a situation in terms of its importance to oneself.

Ejaculatory incompetence. Male's inability to ejaculate.

Electra complex. In psychoanalytic theory, an excessive emotional attachment (love) of a daughter for her father.

Electroconvulsive therapy (ECT). Use of electricity to produce convulsions and unconsciousness; also called *electroshock therapy.*

Electroencephalogram (EEG). Graphic record of the brain's electrical activity, obtained by placing electrodes on the scalp and measuring the brain-wave impulses from various brain areas.

Electrotherapy. Methods of therapy which involve the influence of electric current on the central nervous system.

Embolism. Lodgment of a blood clot in a blood vessel too small to permit its passage.

Emotion. Strong feeling accompanied by physiological changes.

Emotional disturbance. Psychological disorder.

Emotional inoculation. Therapeutic procedures designed to prepare people who face stressful situations, such as surgery, by providing such people with adaptive techniques.

Emotional insulation. Ego-defense mechanism in which an individual reduces the tensions of need and anxiety by withdrawing into a shell of passivity.

Empathy. Ability to understand and to some extent share the state of mind of another person.

Encephalitis. Inflammation of the brain.

Encopresis. Disorder defined by having bowel movements in one's clothing after the age of 3.

Encounter. Term applied to the interaction between client and therapist (in existential therapy) or between clients (in encounter-group therapy).

Encounter group. Small group designed to provide an intensive interpersonal experience focusing on feelings and group interactions; used in therapy or to promote personal growth.

Endocrine glands. Ductless glands that secrete hormones directly into the lymph or bloodstream.

Endogenous factors. Factors originating within an organism that affect behavior.

Endorphins. Opium-like substances produced in the brain and pituitary gland in response to stimulation; thought to play a role in an organism's reaction to pain.

Energizer. Drug that has a stimulating effect.

Engram. Hypothesized physiological change in nervous system; thought to be responsible for memory.

Enuresis. Bed-wetting; involuntary discharge of urine.

Environmental psychology. Field of psychology focusing on the effects of an environmental setting on an individual's feelings and behavior.

Enzyme. Catalyst regulating metabolic activities.

Epidemiology. Study of the distribution of physical or mental disorders in a population.

Epilepsy. Group of disorders varying from momentary lapses of consciousness to generalized convulsions.

Epinephrine. Hormone secreted by the adrenal medulla; also called *adrenaline.*

Episodic (disorder). Term to describe a disorder that tends to abate and to recur.

Equilibrium. Steady state; balance.

Erectile insufficiency. Inability of a male to achieve erection.

Erotic. Pertaining to sexual stimulation and gratification.

Escape learning. Conditioned response in which a subject learns to terminate or escape an aversive stimulus.

Essential hypertension. High blood pressure, presumably of a psychological or emotional origin.

Estrogens. Female hormones produced by the ovaries.

Ethnic group.   Group of people who are treated as distinctive in terms of culture and group patterns.

Ethnocentrism.   Belief that one's own country and race are superior to other countries and races.

Etiology.   Causation; the systematic study of the causes of disorders.

Eugenics.   Application of methods of selective breeding of human beings with the intent of improving the species.

Euphoria.   Exaggerated feeling of well-being and contentment.

Eustress.   Positive stress.

Exacerbate.   Intensify.

Excitation.   Process whereby activity is elicited in a nerve.

Exhaustion and disintegration.   Third and final stage in the general adaptation syndrome, in which an organism is no longer able to resist continuing stress; at the biological level may result in death.

Exhibitionism.   Public display or exposure of genitals for the conscious or unconscious purpose of sexual excitement and pleasure.

Existential anxiety.   Anxiety concerning one's ability to find a satisfying and fulfilling way of life.

Existentialism.   View of human beings that emphasizes an individual's responsibility for becoming the kind of person he or she should be.

Existential neurosis.   Disorder characterized by feelings of alienation, meaninglessness, and apathy.

Existential psychotherapy.   Type of therapy that is based on existential thought and focuses on individual uniqueness and authenticity on the part of both client and therapist.

Exner Comprehensive Rorschach System.   Procedure for scoring and objectively interpreting the Rorschach inkblot test.

Exogenous.   Originating from or due to external causes.

Exorcism.   Religiously inspired treatment procedure designed to drive out evil spirits or forces from a "possessed" person.

Expanded consciousness.   Sensation caused by psychedelic drugs or meditation in which an individual feels his or her mind is opened to new types of experience.

Experimental group.   Group of subjects used to assess the effects of independent variables.

Experimental method.   Rigorous scientific procedure by which hypotheses are tested.

Experimental neurosis.   Neurotic behavior produced in animals by inescapable conflicts and other types of stress.

Expressed emotion (EE).   Type of negative communication involving excessive criticalness and emotional overinvolvement directed at a patient by family members.

Extinction.   Gradual disappearance of a conditioned response when it is no longer reinforced.

Extrapunitive.   Characterized by a tendency to evaluate the source of frustrations as external and to direct hostility outward.

Extraversion.   Personality type oriented toward the outer world of people and things rather than concepts and intellectual concerns.

Fabrication.   Relating imaginary events as if they were true without intent to deceive; confabulation.

Factor analysis.   Statistical technique used in identifying and measuring the relative importance of the underlying variables, or factors, which contribute to a complex ability, trait, or form of behavior.

Fading.   Technique whereby a stimulus causing some reaction is gradually replaced by a previously neutral stimulus, such that the latter acquires the property of producing the reaction in question.

Familial.   Pertaining to characteristics which tend to run in families and have a higher incidence in certain families than in the general population.

Family therapy.   Form of interpersonal therapy focusing on relationships within a family.

Fantasy.   Daydream; also, an ego-defense mechanism by means of which an individual escapes from the world of reality and gratifies his desires in fantasy achievements.

Faulty genes.   Genes containing information that is inimical to healthy development or functioning.

Feedback.   Explicit information pertaining to internal physiological processes or to the social consequences of one's overt behavior.

Female sexual arousal disorder.   Dysfunction accompanied by complaints of an absence of sexual arousal feelings and of being unresponsive to most or all forms of erotic stimulation.

Fetal alcohol syndrome.   Observed pattern in infants of alcoholic mothers in which there is a characteristic facial or limb irregularity, low body weight, and behavioral abnormality.

Fetishism.   Maladaptive sexual deviation in which an individual achieves sexual gratification by means of some inanimate object or nonsexual part of the body.

Fetus.   Embryo after the sixth week following conception.

Field properties.   Characteristics of the environment surrounding a living system.

Fixation.   Unreasonable or exaggerated attachment to some person or arresting of emotional development on a childhood or adolescent level.

Fixed-interval schedule.   Schedule of reinforcement based on fixed period of time after previous reinforced response.

Fixed-ratio schedule.   Schedule of reinforcement based on reinforcement after fixed number of nonreinforced responses.

Flashback.   Recurrence of a drug experience, usually in a negative manner, without further ingestion of the drug.

Flooding.   Anxiety-eliciting technique involving placing a client in a real-life, anxiety-arousing situation.

Folie à deux.   Psychotic interpersonal relationship involving two people; e.g., husband and wife both become psychotic with similar or complementary symptomatology.

Follow-up study.   Research procedure in which individuals are studied over a period of time or are recontacted at a later time after initial study.

Forcible rape.   Act of violence in which sexual relations are forced on an unwilling partner who is over the age of 18.

Forensic psychology and psychiatry.   Branches of psychology and psychiatry dealing with legal problems relating to mental disorders.

Fraternal twins.   Dizygotic twins; fertilized by separate germ cells, thus not having same genetic inheritance. May be of the same or opposite sex.

Free association.   Psychoanalytic procedure for probing the unconscious in which an individual gives a running account of every thought and feeling.

Free-floating anxiety.   Anxiety not referable to any specific situation or cause.

Frigidity.   Inability to experience sexual pleasure or orgasm on the part of a female. Now called *inhibited arousal* or *orgasmic dysfunction*.

Frontal lobe.   Portion of the brain active in reasoning and other higher thought processes.

Frustration.   Thwarting of a need or desire.

Frustration tolerance.   See **Stress tolerance.**

Fugue state.   Neurotic dissociative disorder; entails loss of memory accompanied by actual physical flight from one's present life situation to a new environment or less threatening former one.

Functional psychoses.   Severe mental disorders for which a specific organic pathology has not been demonstrated.

Future shock.   Condition brought about when social change proceeds so rapidly that an individual cannot cope with it adequately.

Gambling.   Wagering on games or events in which chance largely determines the outcome.

Gay.   Synonym for *homosexual.*

Gender identity.   Individual's identification as being male or female.

Gender identity disorder (transsexualism). Identification of oneself with members of the opposite sex, as opposed to acceptance of one's anatomical sexual identity.

General adaptation syndrome (GAS). Reaction of an individual to excessive stress; consists of the alarm reaction, the stage of resistance, and exhaustion.

Generalization. Tendency of a response that has been conditioned to one stimulus to become associated with other similar stimuli.

Generalized anxiety disorder. Chronic diffuse anxiety and apprehension, possibly punctuated by acute anxiety attacks, stemming from no specific, identifiable threat.

Generalized reinforcer. Reinforcer, such as money, which may influence a wide range of stimuli and behaviors.

General paresis. Mental disorder associated with syphilis of the brain.

General systems theory. Comprehensive theoretical model embracing all living systems.

Genes. Ultramicroscopic areas of DNA that are responsible for the transmission of hereditary traits.

Genetic code. Means by which DNA controls the sequence and structure of proteins manufactured within each cell and also makes exact duplicates of itself.

Genetic counseling. Counseling prospective parents concerning the probability of their having defective offspring as a result of genetic defects.

Genetic inheritance. Potential for development and behavior determined at conception by egg and sperm cells.

Genetics. Science of heredity.

Genitalia. Organs of reproduction, especially the external organs.

Genital stage. In psychoanalytic theory, the final stage of psychosexual development involving shift from autoeroticism to heterosexual interest.

Genotype. Genetic characteristics inherited by an individual.

Geriatrics. Science of the diseases and treatment of the aged.

Germ cells. Reproductive cells (female ovum and male sperm) which unite to produce a new individual.

Gerontology. Science dealing with the study of old age.

Gestalt psychology. School of psychology which emphasizes patterns rather than elements or connections; taking the view that the whole is more than the sum of its parts.

Gestalt therapy. Type of psychotherapy emphasizing wholeness of the person and integration of thought, feeling, and action.

Gigantism. Abnormally tall stature resulting from hyperfunctioning of the pituitary.

Glucocorticoids. Adrenocortical hormones involved in sugar metabolism but also having widespread effects on injury-repair mechanisms and resistance to disease; they include hydrocortisone, corticosterone, and cortisone.

Gonads. Sex glands.

Good premorbid schizophrenia. See **Reactive schizophrenia.**

Grand mal epilepsy. Type of epilepsy characterized by generalized convulsive seizures.

Grief work. Necessary period of mourning for an individual to assimilate personal loss into the self-structure and view it as an event of the past.

Group therapy. Psychotherapy with two or more individuals at the same time.

Guilt. Feelings of culpability arising from behavior or desires contrary to one's ethical principles. Involves both self-devaluation and apprehension growing out of fears of punishment.

Habit. Any product of learning, whether it is a customary or transitory mode of response.

Habituation. Process whereby an individual's response to the same stimulus lessens with repeated presentations.

Halfway house. Facility which provides aftercare following institutionalization, seeking to ease an individual's adjustment to the community.

Hallucination. Sense perception for which there is no appropriate external stimulus.

Hallucinogens. Drugs or chemicals capable of producing hallucinations.

Hallucinosis. Persistent hallucinations in the presence of known or suspected organic brain pathology.

Halo effect. Tendency when rating a specific trait to be influenced by another trait, such as appearance, or by one's overall impression.

Halstead-Reitan battery. Neuropsychological test aimed at providing information as to a patient's cognitive ability or intellectual impairment.

Hashish. Strongest drug derived from the hemp plant; a relative of marijuana.

Health psychology. Subspecialty within the behavioral-medicine approach that deals with psychology's contributions to diagnosis, treatment, and prevention of behaviorally caused physical illnesses.

Hebephrenic schizophrenia. See **Schizophrenia, disorganized type.**

Hemiplegia. Paralysis of one lateral half of the body.

Hemophobia. Pathological fear of blood. Also called *hematophobia.*

Heredity. Genetic transmission of characteristics from parents to their children.

Hermaphroditism. Anatomical sexual abnormality in which an individual has sex organs of both sexes.

Heroin. Powerful psychoactive substance, chemically derived from morphine, that relieves pain but is even more intense and addictive than morphine.

Heterosexuality. Sexual interest in a member of the opposite sex.

Hierarchy of needs. Concept that needs arrange themselves in a hierarchy in terms of importance or "prepotence," from the most basic biological needs to those psychological needs concerned with self-actualization.

High-risk. Individuals showing great vulnerability to physical or mental disorders.

Histrionic personality disorder. A personality disorder characterized by excitability, emotional instability, and self-dramatization.

Holistic. Systematic approach to science involving the study of the whole or total configuration; the view of human beings as unified psychobiological organisms inextricably immersed in a physical and sociocultural environment.

Homeostasis. Tendency of organisms to maintain conditions making possible a constant level of physiological functioning.

Homosexuality. Sexual preference for a member of one's own sex.

Hormones. Chemicals released by the endocrine glands that regulate development of and activity in various bodily organs.

Hostility. Emotional reaction or drive toward the destruction or damage of an object interpreted as a source of frustration or threat.

Humanistic-existential therapy. Type of psychotherapy emphasizing personal growth and self-direction.

Humanistic perspective. Approach to understanding abnormal behavior that emphasizes growth and self-actualization rather than the curing of diseases or serious disorders.

Human potential movement. Movement concerned with enrichment of experience, increased sensory awareness, and fulfillment of human potentials.

Huntington's chorea. Incurable disease of hereditary origin, which is manifested in jerking, twitching movements and mental deterioration.

Hydrocephalus. Relatively rare condition in which the accumulation of an abnormal amount of cerebrospinal fluid within the cranium causes damage to the brain tissues and enlargement of the skull.

Hydrotherapy. Use of hot or cold baths, ice packs, etc., in treatment.

Hyper-. Prefix meaning *increased* or *excessive.*

Hyperactivity. See **Attention-deficit-hyperactivity disorder.**

Hyperkinetic (hyperactive) reaction. Disorder of childhood characterized by overactivity, restlessness, and distractibility.

Hyperobesity. Extreme overweight; more than 100 pounds over ideal body weight.

Hypertension. High blood pressure.

Hyperventilation. Rapid breathing associated with intense anxiety.

Hypesthesia. Partial loss of sensitivity.

Hypnosis. Trancelike mental state induced in a cooperative subject by suggestion.

Hypnotherapy. Use of hypnosis in psychotherapy.

Hypnotic regression. Process by which a subject is brought to relive, under hypnosis, early forgotten or repressed experiences.

Hypo-. Prefix meaning *decreased* or *insufficient*.

Hypoactive sexual desire disorder. Sexual desire disorder in which either a man or a woman shows little or no sexual drive or interest.

Hypochondriacal delusions. Delusions concerning various horrible disease conditions, such as the belief that one's brain is turning to dust.

Hypochondriasis. Condition dominated by preoccupation with bodily processes and fear of presumed diseases.

Hypomania. Mild form of manic reaction, characterized by moderate psychomotor activity.

Hypothalamus. Key structure at the base of the brain; important in emotion and motivation.

Hypothesis. Statement or proposition, usually based on observation, which is tested in an experiment; may be denied or supported by experimental results but never conclusively proved.

Hypoxia. Insufficient delivery of oxygen to an organ, especially the brain.

Hysteria. Older term used to include conversion disorders; involves the appearance of symptoms of organic illness in the absence of any related organic pathology.

Hysterical disorder. Disorder characterized by involuntary psychogenic dysfunction of motor, sensory, or visceral processes.

ICD-9. See **International Classification of Diseases.**

Id. In psychoanalytic terminology, the reservoir of instinctual drives; the most inaccessible and primitive stratum of the mind.

Identical twins. Monozygotic twins; developed from a single fertilized egg.

Identification. Ego-defense mechanism in which an individual identifies himself or herself with some person or institution, usually of an illustrious nature.

Ideology. System of beliefs.

Idiot. Older term referring to severe and profound degrees of mental retardation (IQ below 25).

Idiot savant. Mentally retarded person who can perform unusual mental feats, usually involving music or manipulation of numbers.

Illusion. Misinterpretation of sensory data; false perception.

Imipramine. Antidepressant medication.

Immaturity. Pattern of childhood maladaptive behaviors suggesting lack of adaptive skills.

Immune reaction. Complex defensive reaction initiated on detection of an antigen invading the body.

Immune system. Intricately organized bodily apparatus involved in the detection and destruction of antigens.

Immunoglobulin. Naturally occurring substance essential in the formation of antibodies.

Implosion. Therapeutic technique in which clients are asked to imagine and relive aversive scenes associated with the anxiety; the assumption here is that, with repeated exposure in a "safe" setting, the aversive stimulus will lose its power to elicit anxiety.

Implosive therapy. Type of behavior therapy in which desen-

sitization is achieved by eliciting, through the imagination, a massive implosion of anxiety.

Impotence. Inability of a male to achieve erection.

Incentive. External inducement to behave in a certain way.

Incest. Sexual relations between close relatives, such as father and daughter or brother and sister.

Incidence. Occurrence rate of a given disorder in a given population.

Independent variable. Factor whose effects are being examined in an experiment; it is manipulated in some way while the other variables are held constant.

Index case. In a genetic study, an individual who evidences the trait in which the investigator is interested. Same as *proband*.

Induced psychotic disorder. Type of psychosis in which two or more people develop persistant interlocking delusional ideas; formerly called *shared paranoid disorder*.

Infantile autism. Disorder manifested at birth and characterized by the inability of a child to relate to others or to form a normal relationship to reality.

Inferiority complex. Strong feelings of inadequacy and insecurity which color an individual's entire adjustive efforts.

Inhibited female orgasm. Dysfunction in which a female experiences difficulty in achieving orgasm, whether manually or through intercourse.

Inhibited male orgasm. Dysfunction in which a male is unable to ejaculate during intercourse (also known as *retarded ejaculation*).

Inhibition. Restraint of impulse or desire.

Innate. Inborn.

Inner controls. Reality, value, and possibility assumptions that serve to inhibit dangerous or undesirable behavior; could also apply to conditioned avoidance reactions.

Inpatient. Hospitalized patient.

Insanity. Legal term for mental disorder, implying lack of responsibility for one's acts and inability to manage one's affairs.

Insanity defense. "Innocent by reason of insanity" plea used as a legal defense in criminal trials.

Insight. Clinically, an individual's understanding of his or her illness or of the motivations underlying a behavior pattern; in general psychology, the sudden grasp or understanding of meaningful relationships in a situation.

Insight therapy. Type of psychotherapy focusing on helping a client achieve greater self-understanding with respect to his or her motives, values, coping patterns, and so on.

Insomnia. Difficulty in sleeping.

Inspectionalism. See **Voyeurism.**

Instinct. Inborn tendency to particular behavior patterns under certain conditions in absence of learning; characteristic of species.

Instrumental (operant) conditioning. Type of conditioning in which a subject is reinforced for making a predetermined response, such as pressing a lever.

Insulin coma therapy. Biological treatment that involves administration of increasing amounts of insulin until a patient goes into "shock"; the treatment is extremely dangerous and rarely used today.

Integrative properties. Tendency of living systems to maintain their organization and functional integrity.

Intellectualization. Ego-defense mechanism by which an individual achieves some measure of insulation from emotional hurt by cutting off or distorting the emotional charge which normally accompanies hurtful situations.

Intelligence. Pertaining to the ability to learn, reason, and adapt.

Intelligence quotient (IQ). Measurement of "intelligence" expressed as a number or position on a scale. Comparable to term *intellectual level*.

Intelligence test. Test used in establishing a subject's level of intellectual capability.

Interdisciplinary (multidisciplinary) approach. Integration of various scientific disciplines in understanding, assessing, treating, and preventing mental disorders.

Intermittent reinforcement. Reinforcement given intermittently rather than after every response.

International Classification of Diseases (ICD-9). System of classification of disorders published by the World Health Organization.

Interpersonal accommodation. Reciprocal process of give and take meant to promote satisfactory interpersonal relationships.

Interpersonal perspective. Approach to understanding abnormal behavior that views much of psychopathology as rooted in maladaptive behavior we have learned while dealing with our interpersonal environments; it thus focuses on our relationships, past and present, with other people.

Intrapsychic conflict. Psychoanalytic concept referring to conflict between the id, ego, and superego.

Introjection. Incorporation of qualities or values of another person or group into one's own ego structure with a tendency to identify with them and to be affected by what happens to them.

Intromission. Insertion of the penis into the vagina or anus.

Intropunitive. Responding to frustration by tending to blame oneself.

Introspection. Observing (and often reporting on) one's inner experiencing.

Introversion. Direction of interest toward one's inner world of experience and toward concepts rather than external events and objects.

Invasion of privacy. Concerns that an individual's right to privacy has been violated.

In vivo. Taking place in a real-life situation as opposed to the therapeutic or laboratory setting.

Ionizing radiation. Form of radiation; major cause of gene mutations.

Isolation. Ego-defense mechanism by means of which contradictory attitudes or feelings that normally accompany particular attitudes are kept apart, thus preventing conflict or hurt.

Jejunal bypass operation. Surgical treatment for extreme obesity that involves disconnecting and bypassing a large portion of the small intestine.

Juvenile delinquency. Legal term used to refer to illegal acts committed by individuals under the age of 16, 17, or 18 (depending on state law).

Juvenile paresis. General paresis in children, usually of congenital origin.

Klinefelter's syndrome. Type of mental retardation associated with sex chromosome anomaly.

Korsakoff's psychosis. Psychosis usually associated with chronic alcoholism and characterized by disorientation, gross memory defects, and confabulation.

Labeling. Assigning an individual to a particular diagnostic category, such as schizophrenia.

Lability. Instability, particularly with regard to affect.

Latency stage. In psychoanalytic theory, a stage of psychosexual development during which sexual motivations recede in importance and a child is preoccupied with developing skills and other activities.

Latent. Inactive or dormant.

Latent content. In psychoanalytic theory, repressed wishes indirectly expressed in the manifest content of dreams.

Latent learning. Learning that becomes evident only after an incentive is introduced.

Law of effect. Principle that responses that have rewarding consequences are strengthened and those that have aversive consequences are weakened or eliminated.

Learning. Modification of behavior as a consequence of experience.

Learning disabled (LD). Term used to describe children who exhibit deficits in academic skills.

Lesbian. Female homosexual.

Lesion. Anatomically localized area of tissue pathology in an organ.

Lethality scale. Criteria used to assess the likelihood of an individual's committing suicide.

Level of aspiration. Standard by which an individual judges success or failure of his or her behavior.

Libido. In general psychoanalytic terminology, the instinctual drives of the id. In a narrow sense, the drive for sexual gratification.

Life crisis. Stress situation that approaches or exceeds an individual's adjustive capacity.

Life history method. Technique of psychological observation in which the development of particular forms of behavior is traced by means of records of a subject's past or present behavior.

Life-style. General pattern of assumptions, motives, cognitive styles, and coping techniques that characterize the behavior of a given individual and give it consistency.

Lobotomy. Drastic form of psychosurgery rarely used at present. It involves cutting the nerve fibers that connect the frontal lobes to the limbic system.

Locomotor ataxia. Muscular incoordination usually resulting from syphilitic damage to the spinal-cord pathways.

Logic-tight compartments. Form of intellectualization in which contradictory desires or attitudes are "sealed off" in separate areas of consciousness.

Lovemap. Pattern of an individual's own erotic attachments and preferences, his or her idealized scenario for the achievement of sexual fulfillment.

LSD (lysergic acid diethylamide). Potent, chemically synthesized hallucinogen that is odorless, colorless, and tasteless and that can produce intoxication with an amount smaller than a grain of salt.

Lunacy. Old term roughly synonymous with *insanity*.

Lycanthropy. Delusion of being a wolf.

Lymphocyte. Generalized term for white blood cells involved in immune protection.

Lymphokines. Chemical substances produced by T-cells that facilitate the immune reaction.

Macrocephaly. Type of mental retardation characterized by an increase in the size and weight of the brain as a result of abnormal growth of glial cells in the brain.

Macrophage. Literally, "big eater." A white blood cell that destroys antigens by engulfment.

Madness. Nontechnical synonym for severe mental disorder.

Mainstreaming. Placement of mentally retarded children in regular school classrooms to avoid certain negative effects of "special education."

Maintaining cause. Environmental reinforcers or contingencies that tend to maintain maladaptive behavior.

Major depression (unipolar disorder). Severe mood disorder in which only depressive episodes occur.

Major tranquilizers. Antipsychotic drugs, such as the phenothiazines.

Maladaptive (abnormal) behavior. Behavior that is detrimental to the well-being of an individual and/or group.

Maladjustment. More or less enduring failure of adjustment; lack of harmony with self or environment.

Male erectile disorder. Dysfunction in which a male is unable to achieve or maintain an erection sufficient for successful sexual intercourse.

Malingering. Faking illness or disability symptoms consciously.

Malleus Malleficarum. Infamous handbook prepared by two monks dealing with the "diagnosis" and "treatment" of witches and witchcraft.

Mania. Emotional state characterized by intense and unrealistic feelings of excitement and euphoria. Often used as a suffix, *-mania*, denoting a compulsive or morbid preoccupation with some impulse or activity; e.g., compulsive stealing is called *kleptomania*.

Manic-depressive psychoses. Older term denoting a group of psychotic disorders characterized by prolonged periods of excitement and overactivity (mania) or by periods of depression and underactivity (depression) or by alternation of the two.

Manifest content. In psychoanalytic theory, the apparent meaning of a dream; masks the latent content.

Marathon encounter group. Intensive group experience lasting for two or more days with only brief breaks for sleep.

Marijuana. Drug derived from the plant *cannabis indica;* often used in cigarettes called reefers or joints.

Marital schism. Marriage characterized by severe chronic discord that threatens continuation of the marital relationship.

Marital skew. Marriage maintained at the expense of a distorted relationship.

Marital therapy. See **Couples counseling.**

Masked deprivation. Rejection of a child by a mother; does not involve separation.

Masked disorder. "Masking" of underlying depression or other emotional disturbance by delinquent behavior or other patterns seemingly unrelated to the basic disturbance.

Masochism. Sexual variant in which an individual obtains sexual gratification through the infliction of pain.

Mass hysteria. Group outbreak of hysterical reactions.

Masturbation. Self-stimulation of genitals for sexual gratification.

Maternal deprivation. Lack of adequate care and stimulation by the mother or mother surrogate.

Maturation. Process of development and body change resulting from heredity rather than learning.

Medical model. View of disordered behavior as a symptom of a more basic process, rather than a pattern representing faulty learning. Also associated with approaches to disorder that involve medical ideology, procedures, and rituals—such as the "white coat."

Megalomania. Delusions of grandeur.

Melancholia. Subset of major depression marked by several symptoms; formerly, a mental disorder characterized by severe depression.

Meninges. Membranes that envelop the brain and spinal cord.

Mental age (MA). Scale unit indicating level of intelligence in relation to chronological age.

Mental deficiency. Synonym for *mental retardation;* the latter term is now preferred.

Mental disorder. Entire range of abnormal behavior patterns.

Mental hygiene movement. Movement that, as a method of treatment for the mentally ill, focused almost exclusively on the physical well-being of hospitalized mental patients.

Mental illness. Once used synonymously with mental disorder but now ordinarily restricted to psychoses.

Mental retardation. Significantly subaverage general intellectual functioning that includes deficits in adaptive behavior and is obvious during the developmental period.

Mescaline. Hallucinogenic drug derived from the peyote cactus.

Mesmerism. Theories of "animal magnetism" (hypnosis) formulated by Anton Mesmer.

Methadone hydrochloride. Orally administered synthetic narcotic that replaces the craving for heroin and weans an individual from heroin addiction.

Microcephaly. Form of mental retardation characterized by an abnormally small cranium and retarded development of the brain.

Micturate, micturition. Pertaining to urination.

Migraine headache. Intensely painful, recurrent headache that typically involves only one side of the head and is associated with emotional tension and a change in the flow of blood to the brain.

Mild (disorder). Disorder of a low order of severity.

Milieu. Immediate environment, physical or social or both; sometimes used to include the internal state of an organism.

Milieu therapy. General approach to therapy for hospitalized patients that focuses on making the hospital environment itself a part of the treatment program.

Minimal brain dysfunction (MBD). Controversial term referring to various "soft" neurological signs presumably indicative of malfunctioning of the brain.

Minnesota Multiphasic Personality Inventory-2 (MMPI-2). Widely used and empirically validated personality scale.

Minor tranquilizers. Antianxiety drugs, such as the meprobamates and benzodiazepines.

Model. Analogy that helps a scientist order findings and see important relationships among them.

Modeling. Form of learning in which an individual learns by watching someone else (a model) perform a desired response.

Model psychoses. Psychotic-like states produced by various hallucinogenic drugs, such as LSD.

Moderate (disorder). Disorder of an intermediate order of severity.

Modus operandi. Manner or mode of behavior; a criminal's typical pattern of performing crimes.

Mongolism. See **Down syndrome.**

Monozygotic twins. Identical twins, developed from one fertilized egg.

Mood-congruent thinking. Thinking that is consistent with an individual's predominant mood.

Mood disorders. Psychoses and related disturbances characterized by severe disturbances of feeling or affect.

Moral management. Wide-ranging method of treatment for the mentally ill that focuses on a patient's social, individual, and occupational needs.

Moral therapy. Therapy based on provision of kindness, understanding, and favorable environment; prevalent during early part of the nineteenth century.

Morbid. Unhealthy, pathological.

Morita therapy. Treatment of neuroses involving the deprivation of external stimulation and other procedures.

Moron. Term formerly used to refer to mild degrees of mental retardation.

Morphine. Addictive opiate drug.

Motivation. Often used as a synonym for *drive* or *activation;* implies that an organism's actions are partly determined in direction and strength by its own inner nature.

Motivational selectivity. Influence of motives on perception and other cognitive processes.

Motive. Internal condition that directs action toward some goal; term usually used to include both the drive and the goal to which it is directed.

Motive pattern. Relatively consistent cluster of motives centered around particular strivings and goals.

Multi-infarct dementia. Organic disorder in which a series of cerebral infarcts, commonly known as "strokes," destroy brain cells over expanding brain regions, resulting in brain atrophy and behavioral impairments.

Multiple personality disorder. Type of dissociative disorder characterized by the development of two or more relatively independent personality systems in the same individual.

Mutant gene. Gene that has undergone some change in structure.

Mutation. Change in the composition of a gene, usually causing harmful or abnormal characteristics to appear in the offspring.

Mutism. Refusal or inability to speak.

Myxedema. Disorder due to thyroid deficiency in adult life, characterized by mental dullness.

Nancy School, The. Group of physicians in the nineteenth century who accepted the view that hysteria was a sort of self-hypnosis.

Narcissism. Self-love.

Narcissistic personality disorder. Personality disorder characterized by grandiosity, an exaggerated sense of self-importance, arrogance, and exploitation of others.

Narcolepsy. Disorder characterized by transient, compulsive states of sleepiness.

Narcotherapy (narcoanalysis, narcosynthesis). Psychotherapy carried on while a patient is in a sleeplike state of relaxation induced by a drug, such as sodium pentothal.

Narcotic drugs. Drugs, such as morphine, that lead to physiological dependence and increased tolerance.

Natural killer cell. White blood cell that destroys antigens by chemical dissolution.

Need. Biological or psychological condition whose gratification is necessary for the maintenance of homeostasis or for self-actualization.

Negative-symptom schizophrenia. Schizophrenic disorders characterized by an *absence* of normal or desirable behaviors, such as emotional reactivity.

Negativism. Form of aggressive withdrawal that involves refusing to cooperate or obey commands, or doing the exact opposite of what has been requested.

Neologism. New word; commonly coined by people labeled as schizophrenic.

Neonate. Newborn infant.

Neoplasm. Tumor.

Nervous breakdown. Refers broadly to lowered integration and inability to deal adequately with one's life situation.

Neurasthenic neurosis. Term formerly used to refer to a neurotic disorder characterized by complaints of chronic weakness, easy fatigability, and lack of enthusiasm.

Neurodermatitis. Skin eruption frequently accompanied by intense itching and often considered to be psychosomatically caused.

Neurological examination. Examination to determine the presence and extent of organic damage to the nervous system.

Neurology. Field concerned with the study of the brain and nervous system and disorders thereof.

Neuron. Individual nerve cell.

Neurophysiology. Branch of biology concerned with the functioning of nervous tissue and the nervous system.

Neuropsychological assessment. Use of psychological tests that measure a subject's cognitive, perceptual, and motor performance to determine the extent and locus of brain damage.

Neuropsychological disorders. Disorders that occur when there has been significant organic impairment or damage to a normal adolescent or adult brain.

Neurosis. Nonpsychotic emotional disturbance characterized by the exaggerated use of avoidance behavior and defense mechanisms against anxiety.

Neurosyphilis. Syphilis affecting the central nervous system.

Neurotic behavior. Anxiety-driven, exaggerated use of avoidance behaviors and defense mechanisms.

Neurotic nucleus. Basic personality characteristics underlying neurotic disorders.

Neurotic paradox. Failure of neurotic patterns to extinguish despite their self-defeating nature.

Neurotic style. General personality disposition toward inhibiting certain anxiety-causing behaviors; distinguishable from anxiety, somatoform, and dissociative disorders in that neurotic styles do not manifest themselves in specific, disabling neurotic symptoms.

Neurotransmitters. Chemical substances that transmit nerve impulses from one neuron to another.

Nicotine. Addictive akaloid that is the chief active ingredient in tobacco.

Night hospital. Mental hospital in which an individual may receive treatment during all or part of the night while carrying on his or her usual occupation in the daytime.

Nihilistic delusion. Fixed belief that everything is unreal.

Nomadism. Withdrawal reaction in which an individual continually attempts to escape frustration by moving from place to place or job to job.

Nondirective therapy. Approach to psychotherapy in which a therapist refrains from advice or direction of the therapy. See also **Client-centered psychotherapy.**

Norepinephrine. Catecholamine neurotransmitter substance.

Norm. Standard based on the measurement of a large group of people; used for comparing the scores of an individual with those of others in a defined group.

Normal. Conforming to the usual or norm; healthy.

Normal distribution. Tendency for most members of a population to cluster around a central point or average with respect to a given trait, with the rest spreading out to the two extremes.

NREM sleep. Stages of sleep not characterized by the rapid eye movements that accompany dreaming.

Nuclear magnetic resonance imaging (MRI). Internal scanning technique involving measurement of variations in magnetic fields that allows visualization of the anatomical features of internal organs, including the brain.

Objective tests. Structured personality test—such as a questionnaire, self-inventory, or rating scale—used in psychological assessment that allows for more objectively based quantification.

Object-relations. In psychoanalytic theory, a viewpoint that emphasizes interpersonal relationships by focusing on internalized "objects" that can have varying conflicting properties.

Observational method. Systematic technique by which observers are trained to watch and record behavior without bias.

Obsession. Persistent idea or thought that an individual recognizes as irrational but cannot get rid of.

Obsessive-compulsive disorder. Disorder characterized by the persistent intrusion of unwanted desires, thoughts, or actions.

Obsessive-compulsive personality disorder. Personality disorder characterized by excessive concern with conformity and adherence to ethical values.

Occipital lobe. Portion of cerebrum concerned chiefly with visual function.

Occupational therapy. Use of occupational training or activity in psychotherapy.

Oedipus complex. Desire for sexual relations with parent of opposite sex, specifically that of a boy for his mother.

Olfactory hallucinations. Hallucinations involving the sense of smell, as of poison gas.

Operant conditioning. Form of learning in which a particular response is reinforced and becomes more likely to occur.

Operational definition. Defining a concept on the basis of a set of operations that can be observed and measured.

Opium. Narcotic drug that leads to physiological dependence and the building up of tolerance; derivatives are morphine, heroin, paregoric, and codeine.

Oral stage. First stage of psychosexual development in Freudian theory, in which mouth or oral activities are primary source of pleasure.

Organic anxiety syndrome. Disorder in which the clinical manifestation of anxiety is thought somehow to be the direct outcome of brain impairment.

Organic brain syndromes. Mental disorders associated with organic brain pathology.

Organic delusional syndrome. Delusions or false beliefs caused by known or suspected brain damage.

Organic mental disorders. Mental disorders that occur secondary to damage to the normal brain; also referred to as *neuropsychological disorders.*

Organic mood syndrome. Manic or depressive states caused by brain damage.

Organic personality syndrome. Change in an individual's general personality style or traits caused by brain damage.

Organic viewpoint. Concept that all mental disorders have an organic basis. See also **Biological viewpoint.**

Orgasm. Peak sexual tension followed by relaxation.

Outcome research. Studies of effectiveness of treatment.

Outpatient. Ambulatory client who visits a hospital or clinic for examination and treatment, as distinct from a hospitalized client.

Ovaries. Female gonads.

Overanxious disorder. Disorder of childhood characterized by excessive worry and persistent fears unrelated to any specific event; often includes somatic and sleeping problems.

Overcompensation. Type of ego-defense mechanism in which an undesirable trait is covered up by exaggerating a desirable trait.

Overloading. Subjecting an organism to excessive stress, e.g., forcing the organism to handle or "process" an excessive amount of information.

Overprotection. Shielding a child to the extent that he or she becomes too dependent on the parent.

Overt behavior. Activities which can be observed by an outsider.

Ovum. Female gamete or germ cell.

Pain cocktail. Concoction of all the medication a pain patient is taking in a single liquid that can be systematically controlled and reduced in strength.

Panic. Severe personality disorganization involving intense anxiety and usually either paralyzed immobility or blind flight.

Panic disorder. Type of anxiety disorder involving recurring periods of acute panic or anxiety.

Paradigm. Model or pattern; in research, a basic design specifying concepts considered legitimate and procedures to be used in the collection and interpretation of data.

Paranoia. Symptoms of delusions and impaired contact with reality but without the severe personality disorganization characteristic of schizophrenia.

Paranoid personality disorder. Personality disorder characterized by projection (as a defense mechanism), suspiciousness, envy, extreme jealousy, and stubbornness.

Paranoid state. Transient psychotic disorder in which the main element is a delusion, usually persecutory or grandiose in nature.

Paraphasia. Garbled speech.

Paraphilias. Sexual variant in which unusual objects, rituals, or situations are required for full sexual satisfaction to occur.

Paraprofessional. Individual who has been trained in mental health services, but not at the professional level.

Parasympathetic nervous system. Division of the autonomic nervous system that controls most of the basic metabolic functions essential for life.

Paresis. See **General paresis.**

Paresthesia. Exceptional sensations, such as tingling.

Parkinson's disease (paralysis agitans). Progressive disease characterized by a masklike, expressionless face and various neurological symptoms, such as tremors.

Partial reinforcement. Intermittent reinforcement of a response.

Passive-aggressive personality disorder. Personality disorder characterized by passively expressed aggressiveness.

Path analysis. Statistical technique that takes into account how variables are related to one another through time and how they predict one another.

Pathogenic. Pertaining to conditions that lead to pathology.

Pathological gambling. Addictive disorder in which gambling behavior disrupts an individual's life.

Pathological intoxication. Severe cerebral and behavioral disturbance in an individual whose tolerance to alcohol is extremely low.

Pathology. Abnormal physical or mental condition.

PCP. Phencyclidine; developed as a tranquilizer but not marketed because of its unpredictability. Known on the streets as "angel dust," this drug produces stuporous conditions and, at times, prolonged comas or psychoses.

Pederasty. Sexual intercourse between males via the anus.

Pedophilia. Sexual variant in which an adult engages in or desires sexual relations with a child.

Peptic ulcers. Ulcerations of the stomach or upper intestine as a result of an excessive flow of the stomach's acid-containing digestive juices, which eat away the lining of the stomach or duodenum, leaving a craterlike wound.

Perception. Interpretation of sensory input.

Perceptual defense. Process in which threatening stimuli are filtered out and not perceived by an organism.

Perceptual filtering. Processes involved in selective attention to aspects of the great mass of incoming stimuli that continually impinge on an organism.

Performance test. Test in which perceptual-motor rather than verbal content is emphasized.

Peripheral nervous system. Nerve fibers passing between the central nervous system and the sense organs, muscles, and glands.

Perseveration. Persistent continuation of a line of thought or activity once it is under way. Clinically inappropriate repetition.

Personal constructs. According to Kelly, the uniquely individual ways of perceiving other people and events that people use to interpret events around them.

Personality. Unique pattern of traits that characterizes an individual.

Personality (character) disorders. Group of maladaptive behavior syndromes characterized by immature and distorted personality patterns, which result in persistently maladaptive ways of perceiving, thinking about, and relating to the world.

Personality profile. Graphic summary from several tests or subtests of the same test battery or scale that shows the personality configuration of an individual or group of individuals.

Person-centered therapy. See **Client-centered therapy.**

Pervasive developmental disorder. Severe disorder of childhood marked by deficits in language, perceptual, and motor development; defective reality testing; and inability to function in social situations.

Perversion. Deviation from normal.

Petit mal. Relatively mild form of epilepsy involving a temporary partial lapse of consciousness.

PET scan. See **Positron emission tomography.**

Phagocyte. Circulating white blood cell that binds to antigens and partially destroys them by engulfment.

Phallic stage. In psychoanalytic theory, the stage of psychosexual development during which genital exploration and manipulation occur.

Phallic symbol. Any object that resembles the erect male sex organ.

Pharmacology. Science of drugs.

Pharmacotherapy. Treatment by means of drugs.

Phenomenological. Referring to the immediate perceiving and experiencing of an individual.

Phenylketonuria (PKU). Type of mental retardation resulting from a metabolic deficiency.

Phobia. Persistent and disproportionate fear of some specific object or situation that presents little or no actual danger to a person.

Phobic disorder. Type of anxiety disorder characterized by intense fear of an object or situation which an individual consciously realizes poses no real danger.

Physiological dependence. Type of drug dependence involving withdrawal symptoms when drug is discontinued.

Pick's disease. Form of presenile dementia.

Pineal gland. Small gland at the base of the brain which helps regulate the body's biological clock and may also pace sexual development.

Pituitary gland. Endocrine gland associated with many regulatory functions.

Placebo effect. Positive effect experienced after an inactive treatment is administered in such a way that an individual thinks he or she is receiving an active treatment.

Play therapy. Use of play activities in psychotherapy with children.

Pleasure principle. In psychoanalysis, the demand that an instinctual need be immediately gratified, regardless of reality.

Polygenic. Action of many genes together in an additive or interactive fashion.

Poor premorbid schizophrenia. See **Process schizophrenia.**

Positive reinforcer. Reinforcer that increases the probability of recurrence of a given response.

Positive-symptom schizophrenia. Schizophrenic disorders characterized by elements *added* to normal behavior, such as delusions and hallucinations.

Positron emission tomography (PET scan). Scanning technique that measures the level of metabolic activity in particular regions of the body.

Posthypnotic amnesia. Subject's lack of memory for the period during which he or she was hypnotized.

Posthypnotic suggestion. Suggestion given during hypnosis to be carried out by a subject after he or she is brought out of hypnosis.

Postpartum disturbances. Emotional disturbances associated with childbirth.

Posttraumatic disorders. Residual symptoms following a traumatic experience.

Posttraumatic stress disorder (PTSD). Disorder in which a stressor is severe and residual symptoms occur following the traumatic experience and last for at least one month.

Precipitating cause. Particular stress that triggers a disorder.

Predisposing cause. Factor that lowers an individual's stress tolerance and paves the way for the appearance of a disorder.

Predisposition. Likelihood that an individual will develop certain symptoms under given stress conditions.

Prefrontal lobotomy. Surgical procedure used before the advent of antipsychotic drugs in which frontal lobes of the brain were severed from the deeper centers underlying them, resulting in permanent brain damage.

Prejudice. Emotionally toned conception favorable or unfavorable to some person, group, or idea—typically in the absence of sound evidence.

Premature ejaculation. Inability of a male to inhibit ejaculation long enough to satisfy his partner.

Prematurity. Birth of an infant before the end of a normal period of pregnancy.

Premorbid. Existing prior to the onset of mental disorder.

Prenatal. Before birth.

Presenile dementia. Senile brain deterioration occurring at an early age and accompanied by mental disorder.

Pressure. Demand made on an organism.

Prevalence. Term that refers to the rate of active cases of something under study (in this case, a disorder) that can be identified at a given period in time.

Primary cause. Cause without which a disorder would not have occurred.

Primary erectile insufficiency. Dysfunction in which a male has never been able to sustain an erection long enough to have successful intercourse.

Primary orgasmic dysfunction. Inability on the part of a woman to have an orgasm.

Primary prevention. Preventive efforts aimed at establishing conditions designed to prevent the occurrence of mental disorders.

Primary process. Gratification of an instinctual id demand by means of imagery or fantasy; a psychoanalytic concept.

Primary reaction tendencies. Constitutional tendencies apparent in infancy, such as sensitivity and activity level.

Privileged communication. Freedom from the obligation to report to the authorities information concerning legal guilt revealed by a client or patient.

Proband. In a genetic study, the original individual who evidences the trait in which the investigator is interested. Same as *index case*.

Problem checklist. Inventory used in behavioral assessment to determine an individual's fears, moods, and other problems.

Problem drinker. Behavioral term referring to one who has serious problems associated with drinking. Term is currently preferable to *alcoholic*.

Process schizophrenia. Schizophrenic pattern—marked by seclusiveness, gradual lack of interest in the surrounding world, diminished emotional responsivity, and mildly inappropriate responses—that develops gradually and tends to be long-lasting; alternatively known as *poor premorbid schizophrenia* and *chronic schizophrenia*.

Prognosis. Prediction as to the probable course and outcome of a disorder.

Programmed learning. Method of instruction or learning in which a student is guided through the subject matter step-by-step.

Projection. Ego-defense mechanism in which an individual attributes unacceptable desires and impulses to others.

Projective test. Technique using neutral or ambiguous stimuli that a subject is encouraged to interpret and from which the subject's personality characteristics can be analyzed.

Prospective research. Research that focuses, before the fact, on individuals who have a higher-than-average likelihood of becoming psychologically disordered, following them over time.

Prototypal approach. Approach to classifying abnormal behavior that assumes the existence of prototypes of behavior disorders that, rather than being mutually exclusive, may blend into others with which they share many characteristics.

Pseudocommunity. Delusional social environment developed by a paranoid individual.

Pseudomutuality. Relationship among family members that appears to be mutual, understanding, and open, but in fact is not.

Psilocybin. Hallucinogenic drug derived from a mushroom.

Psychedelic drugs. "Mind expanding" drugs, such as LSD, which often result in hallucinations.

Psychiatric nursing. Field of nursing primarily concerned with mental disorders.

Psychiatric social worker. Professional having graduate training in social work with psychiatric specialization, typically involving a master's degree.

Psychiatrist. Medical doctor who specializes in the diagnosis and treatment of mental disorders.

Psychiatry. Field of medicine concerned with understanding, assessing, treating, and preventing mental disorders.

Psychic pain. Synonym for *anxiety*.

Psychic trauma. Stressful psychological experience of a severely traumatic nature.

Psychoactive drugs. Any drug that primarily affects mental functioning.

Psychoactive substance abuse. Pathological use of a substance resulting in potentially hazardous behavior or in continued use despite a persistent social, psychological, occupational, or health problem.

Psychoactive substance dependence. Use of a psychoactive substance to the point that one has a physiological need for it.

Psychoanalysis. Theoretical model and therapeutic approach developed by Freud.

Psychoanalytic perspective. Theory of psychopathology, initially developed by Freud, that emphasizes the inner dynamics of unconscious motives.

Psychodrama. Psychotherapeutic technique in which the acting of various roles is a cardinal part.

Psychodynamic perspective. Term in psychoanalytic theory referring to the psychic forces and processes developed through an individual's childhood experiences and that influence adult thinking and behavior.

Psychodynamic therapy. Treatment focusing on individual personality dynamics from a psychoanalytic perspective.

Psychogenic. Of psychological origin: originating in the psychological functioning of an individual.

Psychogenic amnesia. Amnesia of psychological origin, common in initial reactions to intolerable traumatic experiences.

Psychogenic illness. Psychologically induced or maintained disease.

Psychogenic pain disorder. Neurotic disorder in which pain is the predominant complaint.

Psychological autopsy. Analytical procedure used to determine whether or not death was self-inflicted.

Psychological need.   Need emerging out of environmental interactions, e.g., the need for social approval.

Psychological screening.   Use of psychological procedures or tests to detect psychological problems among applicants in preemployment evaluations.

Psychological test.   Standardized procedure designed to measure a subject's performance on a specified task.

Psychomotor.   Involving both psychological and physical activity.

Psychomotor epilepsy.   State of disturbed consciousness in which an individual may perform various actions, sometimes of a homicidal nature, for which he or she is later amnesic.

Psychomotor retardation.   Slowing down of psychological and motor functions.

Psychoneuroimmunology.   Developing new field whose focus is on understanding the psychological influences affecting immune functioning.

Psychopathic personality.   See **antisocial personality disorder.**

Psychopathology.   Abnormal behavior.

Psychopharmacological drugs.   Drugs used in treatment of mental disorders.

Psychophysiologic (psychosomatic) disorders.   Physical disorders in which psychological factors play a major causative role.

Psychosexual development.   Freudian view of development as involving a succession of stages, each characterized by a dominant mode of achieving libidinal pleasure.

Psychosexual stages of development.   According to Freudian theory, there are five stages of psychosexual development, each characterized by a dominant mode of achieving sexual pleasure: the oral stage, the anal stage, the phallic stage, the latency stage, and the genital stage.

Psychosis.   See **psychotic behavior.**

Psychosocial deprivation.   Lack of needed stimulation and interaction during early life.

Psychosocial viewpoints.   Approaches to understanding behavior disorders that emphasize the importance of early experience and an awareness of social influences and psychological processes within an individual.

Psychosomatic disorders.   See **Psychophysiologic disorders.**

Psychosurgery.   Brain surgery used in the treatment of functional mental disorders or occasionally to relieve pain.

Psychotherapy.   Treatment of mental disorders by psychological methods.

Psychotic behavior.   Behavior that represents a loss of contact with reality to the extent that delusional beliefs are harbored or bizarre perceptions (hallucinations) are reported. Also called *psychosis.*

Psychotropic drugs.   Drugs whose main effects are mental or behavioral in nature.

Q-sort.   Personality inventory in which a subject, or a clinician, sorts a number of statements into piles according to their applicability to the subject.

Racism.   Prejudice and discrimination directed toward individuals or groups because of their racial background.

Random sample.   Sample drawn in such a way that each member of a population has an equal chance of being selected; hopefully representative of the population from which drawn.

Rape.   Act of violence in which sexual relations are forced on another person.

Rapport.   Interpersonal relationship characterized by a spirit of cooperation, confidence, and harmony.

Rating scale.   Device for evaluating oneself or someone else in regard to specific traits.

Rational-emotive therapy.   Form of psychotherapy focusing on cognitive and emotional restructuring to foster adaptive behavior.

Rationalization.   Ego-defense mechanism in which an individual thinks up "good" reasons to justify his or her actions.

Reaction formation.   Ego-defense mechanism in which an individual's conscious attitudes and overt behavior are opposite to repressed unconscious wishes.

Reactive schizophrenia.   Schizophrenia pattern—marked by confusion and intense emotional turmoil—that normally develops suddenly and has identifiable precipitating stressors; alternatively known as *good premorbid schizophrenia* and *acute schizophrenia.*

Reality principle.   Awareness of the demands of the environment and adjustment of behavior to meet these demands.

Reality testing.   Behavior aimed at testing or exploring the nature of an individual's social and physical environment; often used more specifically to refer to the testing of the limits of permissiveness of social environment.

Reality therapy.   Form of therapy based on the assumption that emotional difficulties arise when an individual violates his or her basic sense of right and wrong.

Recessive gene.   Gene which is effective only when paired with an identical gene.

Recidivism.   Shift back to one's original behavior (often delinquent or criminal) after a period of treatment or rehabilitation.

Reciprocal inhibition.   Technique of desensitization used in behavior therapy in which responses antagonistic to anxiety are paired with anxiety-eliciting stimuli.

Recompensation.   Increase in integration or inner organization. Opposite of *decompensation.*

Reentry.   Return from the openness of an encounter group to the real world, which is presumably less open and honest.

Referral.   Sending or recommending an individual and/or family for psychological assessment and/or treatment.

Regression.   Ego-defense mechanism in which an individual retreats to the use of less mature responses in attempting to cope with stress and maintain ego integrity.

Rehabilitation.   Use of reeducation rather than punishment to overcome behavioral deficits.

Reinforcement.   In classical conditioning, the process of following the conditioned stimulus with the unconditioned stimulus; in operant conditioning, the rewarding of desired responses.

Reinforcing cause.   Circumstance tending to maintain behavior that is ultimately maladaptive, as in *secondary gain.*

Rejection.   Lack of acceptance of another person, usually referring to such treatment of a child by the parents.

Reliability.   Degree to which a test or measuring device produces the same result each time it is used to measure the same thing.

Remission.   Marked improvement or recovery appearing in the course of a mental illness; may or may not be permanent.

REM sleep.   Stage of sleep involving rapid eye movements (REM), associated with dreaming.

Renaud's disease.   Potentially serious constriction of the small blood vessels of the extremities, cutting off adequate blood flow to them; sometimes considered psychosomatic.

Representative sample.   Small group selected in such a way as to be representative of the larger group from which it is drawn.

Repression.   Ego-defense mechanism by means of which dangerous desires and intolerable memories are kept out of consciousness.

Reserpine.   One of the early antipsychotic drugs, now largely supplanted by newer drugs.

Resistance.   Tendency to maintain symptoms and resist treatment or uncovering of repressed material.

Resistance to extinction.   Tendency of a conditioned response to persist despite lack of reinforcement.

Respondent conditioning.   See **Classical conditioning.**

Response shaping.   Positive reinforcement technique used in therapy to establish a response not initially in an individual's behavioral repertoire.

Reticular activating system (RAS).   Fibers going from the reticular formation to higher brain centers and presumably functioning as a general arousal system.

Reticular formation.   Neural nuclei and fibers in the brain stem that apparently play an important role in arousing and alerting an organism and in controlling attention.

Retrograde amnesia. Loss of memory for events during a circumscribed period prior to brain injury or damage.

Retrospective research. Research that looks backward from the present.

Retrospective study. Research approach that attempts to retrace earlier events in the life of a subject.

Rigid control. Coping patterns involving reliance on inner restraints, such as inhibition, suppression, repression, and reaction formation.

Rigidity. Tendency to follow established coping patterns, with failure to see alternatives or extreme difficulty in changing one's established patterns.

Ritalin. Central nervous system stimulant often used to treat hyperactivity in children.

Role distortion. Violation of expected role behavior in an undesirable way.

Role obsolescence. Condition occurring when the ascribed social role of a given individual is no longer of importance to the social group.

Role playing. Form of assessment or psychotherapy in which an individual acts out a social role other than his or her own or tries out a new role.

Rorschach test. Series of inkblots to which a subject responds with associations that come to mind. Analysis of these productions enables a clinician to infer personality characteristics.

Sadism. Sexual variant in which sexual gratification is obtained by the infliction of pain on others.

Sadistic personality disorder. Proposed diagnostic category of personality disorder that is characterized by a pervasive pattern of cruel, demeaning, and aggressive behavior toward other people.

Sample. Group on which measurements are taken; should normally be representative of the population about which an inference is to be made.

Scapegoating. Displacement of aggression onto some object, person, or group other than the source of frustration.

Schedule of reinforcement. Program of rewards for requisite behavior.

Schizoaffective disorder. Disorder in which a person experiences severe but highly episodic disturbances of psychological functioning, such as mood-incongruent delusions and hallucinations.

Schizoid personality disorder. Personality disorder characterized by shyness, oversensitivity, seclusiveness, and eccentricity.

Schizophrenia. Psychosis characterized by the breakdown of integrated personality functioning, withdrawal from reality, emotional blunting and distortion, and disturbances in thought and behavior.

Schizophrenia, catatonic type. Type of schizophrenia in which the central feature is pronounced motor symptoms, either of an excited or stuporous type, which sometimes make it difficult to differentiate this condition from a psychotic mood disorder.

Schizophrenia, disorganized type. Type of schizophrenia that usually begins at an earlier age and represents a more severe disintegration of the personality than in the other types of schizophrenia.

Schizophrenia, paranoid type. Type of schizophrenia in which an individual is increasingly suspicious, has severe difficulties in interpersonal relationships, and experiences absurd, illogical, and often changing delusions.

Schizophrenia, residual type. Diagnostic category used for people regarded as having recovered from schizophrenia but still manifesting some signs of their past disorder.

Schizophrenia, undifferentiated type. Type of schizophrenia in which an individual meets the usual criteria for being schizophrenic—including (in varying combinations) delusions, hallucinations, thought disorder, and bizarre behavior—but does not clearly fit into one of the other types because of a mixed symptom picture.

Schizophreniform disorder. Category of schizophrenic disorder, usually in an undifferentiated form, of less than six months duration.

Schizophrenogenic (parents). Qualities in parents that appear to be associated with the development of schizophrenia in offspring; often applied to rejecting, cold, domineering, overprotective mothers or passive, uninvolved fathers.

Schizotypal personality disorder. Personality disorder in which egocentricity, avoidance of others, and eccentricity of thought and perception are distinguishing traits.

Scotophilia. See **Voyeurism.**

Secondary cause. Factor which contributes to a mental illness but which in and of itself would not have produced it, as distinct from the *primary* cause.

Secondary drives. Motives for approval, achievement, etc., as distinguished from basic biological needs.

Secondary erectile insufficiency. Condition in which a male has been capable of successful intercourse but is currently dysfunctional.

Secondary gain. Indirect benefit from neurotic or other symptoms.

Secondary prevention. Prevention techniques that typically involve emergency or crisis intervention, with efforts focused on reducing the impact, duration, or spread of a problem.

Secondary process. Reality-oriented rational processes of the ego.

Secondary reinforcer. Reinforcement provided by a stimulus that has gained reward value by being associated with a primary reinforcing stimulus.

Sedative. Drug used to reduce tension and induce relaxation and sleep.

Selective vigilance. Tuning of attentional and perceptual processes toward stimuli relevant or central to goal-directed behavior, with decreased sensitivity to stimuli irrelevant or peripheral to this purpose.

Self (ego). Integrating core of a personality that mediates between needs and reality.

Self-acceptance. Being satisfied with one's attributes and qualities while remaining aware of one's limitations.

Self-actualization. Fulfillment of one's potentialities as a human being.

Self-concept. Individual's sense of his or her own identity, worth, capabilities, and limitations.

Self-defeating personality disorder. Proposed diagnostic category of personality disorder, often called masochistic personality disorder, which is characterized by an individual's avoidance of pleasurable experiences and persistent involvement in disappointing relationships.

Self-differentiation. Degree to which an individual achieves a sense of unique identity apart from a group.

Self-direction. Basing one's behavior on inner assumptions rather than external contingencies.

Self-esteem. Feeling of personal worth.

Self-evaluation. Way in which an individual views the self, in terms of worth, adequacy, etc.

Self-ideal (ego-ideal). Person or "self" an individual thinks he or she could and should be.

Self-identity. Individual's delineation and awareness of his or her continuing identity as a person.

Self-instructional training. Cognitive-behavioral method aimed at teaching an individual to alter his or her covert behavior.

Self-monitoring. Observing and recording one's own behavior.

Self-reinforcement. Reward of self for desired or appropriate behavior.

Self-report inventory. Procedure in which a subject is asked to respond to statements in terms of their applicability to him or her.

Self-statements. Implicit "verbalizations" of what a person is experiencing.

Self-system. According to Sullivan's interpersonal theory, a system that protects an individual from anxiety by controlling awareness—the individual simply does not attend to elements of experience that cause anxiety and may even block out of consciousness especially severe anxiety-arousing experiences.

Self-theory. Personality theory that utilizes the self-concept as the integrating core of personality organization and functioning.

Senile. Pertaining to old age.

Senile dementia. Deteriorative brain changes due to aging.

Sensate focus learning. Training to derive pleasure from touching one's partner and being touched by him or her; used in sexual therapy to enhance sexual feelings and help overcome sexual dysfunction.

Sensitivity training group (T-group). One type of small group designed to provide intensive group experience and foster self-understanding and personal growth.

Sensory awareness. Openness to new ways of experiencing and feeling.

Sensory deprivation. Restriction of sensory stimulation below the level required for normal functioning of the central nervous system.

Sentence-completion test. Form of projective technique utilizing incomplete sentences that a subject is to complete, analysis of which enables a clinician to infer personality dynamics.

Separation anxiety disorder. Childhood disorder characterized by unrealistic fears, oversensitivity, self-consciousness, nightmares, chronic anxiety, and, typically, overdependency.

Separation-individuation. According to Mahler, a developmental phase in which a child gains an internal representation of self as distinct from representations of other objects.

Sequelae. Symptoms remaining as the aftermath of a disorder.

Severe (disorder). Disorder of a high degree of severity.

Sex chromosomes. Pair of chromosomes inherited by an individual that determines sex and certain other characteristics.

Sexual aversion disorder. Sexual desire disorder in which an individual views sexual intercourse as psychologically aversive.

Sexual deviate. Individual who manifests nonconforming sexual behavior, often of a pathological nature.

Sexual dysfunction. Inability or impaired ability to experience or give sexual gratification.

Shaping. Form of instrumental conditioning; at first, all responses resembling the desired one are reinforced, then only the closest approximations, until finally the desired response is attained.

Sheltered workshops. Workshops where mentally retarded or otherwise handicapped individuals can engage in constructive work in the community.

Short-term crisis therapy. Therapy that is of brief duration and that focuses on the immediate problem—personal or family problems of an emotional nature—with which an individual or family is having difficulty.

Siblings. Offspring of the same parents.

Sick role. Protected role provided by society via medical model for individual suffering from severe physical or mental disorder.

Significant others. In interpersonal theory, parents or others on whom an infant is dependent for meeting all physical and psychological needs.

Simple phobia. See **phobia.**

Simple tension headaches. Commonplace headache in which stress leads to contractions of the muscles surrounding the skull; these contractions, in turn, result in vascular constrictions that cause headache pain.

Situational test. Test that measures performance in a simulated life situation.

Sleepwalking disorder. Disorder of childhood that involves repeated episodes in which a child leaves his or her bed and walks around without being conscious of the experience or remembering it later.

Social exchange. Model of interpersonal relationships based on the premise that such relationships are formed for mutual need gratification.

Social introversion. Trait characterized by shy, withdrawn, and inhibited behavior.

Socialization. Process by which a child acquires the values and impulse controls deemed appropriate by his or her culture.

Socialized-aggressive disorder. Pattern of childhood maladaptive behaviors involving social maladaptation, such as stealing, truancy, gang membership.

Social-learning programs. Behavioral treatment techniques using learning principles, especially token economies, to help chronic patients assume more responsibility for their own behavior.

Social norms. Group standards concerning behaviors viewed as acceptable or unacceptable.

Social pathology. Abnormal patterns of social organization, attitudes, or behavior; undesirable social conditions that tend to produce individual pathology.

Social phobia. Fear of one or more situations in which one is exposed to focused scrutiny by others, and the corollary fear that one may do something or act in such a manner as to risk humiliation or embarrassment.

Social role. Behavior expected of an individual occupying given position in group.

"Social" self. Facade an individual displays to others as contrasted with the private self.

Social work. Applied offshoot of sociology concerned with the analysis of social environments and providing services which assist the adjustment of a client in both family and community settings.

Social worker. Person in a mental health field with a master's degree in social work (MSW) plus supervised training in clinical or social service agencies.

Sociocultural viewpoint. Pertaining to broad social conditions that influence the development and/or behavior of individuals and groups.

Socioeconomic status. Position on social and economic scale in community; determined largely by income and occupational level.

Sociogenic. Having its roots in sociocultural conditions.

Sociopathic personality. See **antisocial personality disorder.**

Sociotherapy. Treatment of interpersonal aspects of an individual's life situation.

Sodium pentothal. Barbiturate drug sometimes used in psychotherapy to produce a state of relaxation and suggestibility.

Sodomy. Sexual intercourse via the anus.

Somatic. Pertaining to the body.

Somatic weakness. Special vulnerability of given organ systems to stress.

Somatization disorder. Type of somatoform disorder beginning before age thirty and continuing for many years, characterized by multiple complaints of physical ailments not necessarily involving organic pathology.

Somatoform disorder. Anxiety-based pattern in which an individual complains of bodily symptoms that suggest the presence of a physical problem, but for which no organic basis can be found.

Somatoform pain disorder. Somatoform disorder characterized by the report of severe and lasting pain for which no physical basis is apparent, or the reaction is greatly in excess of what would be expected from the physical pathology.

Somatotype. Physique or build of a person, as assessed by various theories relating temperament to physical characteristics.

Somnambulism. Sleepwalking.

Spasm. Intense, involuntary, usually painful contraction of a muscle or group of muscles.

Spasticity. Marked hypertonicity or continual overcontraction of muscles, causing stiffness, awkwardness, and motor incoordination.

Specific developmental disorders. Disorders of childhood that reflect inadequate development in academic, language, speech, or motor skills that may occur in children who are otherwise normal or even gifted in their overall functioning.

Specific learning disabilities. Developmental disorders involving deficits in specific academic skills.

Sperm. Male gamete or germ cell.

Split-brain research. Research associated with split-brain surgery, which cuts off the transmission of information from one cerebral hemisphere to the other.

Spontaneous recovery (remission). Recovery of a mental patient without treatment or with minimal treatment.

Stage of exhaustion. Third and final stage in the general adaptation syndrome, in which an organism is no longer able to resist continuing stress; may result in death.

Stage of resistance. Second stage of the general adaptation syndrome.

Standardization. Procedure for establishing the expected performance range on a test.

Stanford-Binet. Standardized intelligence test for children.

Startle reaction. Sudden involuntary motor reaction to intense unexpected stimuli; may result from mild stimuli if a person is hypersensitive.

Statutory rape. Sexual intercourse with a minor.

Steady states (homeostasis). Tendency of an organism to maintain conditions making possible a constant level of physiological functioning.

Stereotype. Generalized notion of how people of a given race, religion, or other group will appear, think, feel, or act.

Stereotypy. Persistent and inappropriate repetition of phrases, gestures, or acts.

Stimulants. Drugs that tend to increase feelings of alertness, reduce feelings of fatigue, and enable an individual to stay awake over sustained periods of time.

Stimulus generalization. Spread of a conditioned response to some stimulus similar to, but not identical with, the conditioned stimulus.

Stress. Internal responses caused by the application of a stressor.

Stress-decompensation model. View of abnormal behavior that emphasizes progressive disorganization of behavior under excessive stress.

Stress-inoculation therapy. Type of self-instructional training focused on altering self-statements that an individual is routinely making in order to restructure his or her characteristic approach to stress-producing situations.

Stress interview. Interview of a subject in which stressors are introduced.

Stressor. Any adjustive demand that requires coping behavior on the part of an individual or group.

Stress tolerance (frustration tolerance). Nature, degree, and duration of stress which an individual can tolerate without undergoing serious personality decompensation.

Stroke. See **Cerebrovascular accident.**

Structural family therapy. Treatment of an entire family by analysis of communication between family members.

Structural therapy. Treatment of autistic children in which the environment is structured to provide spontaneous physical and verbal stimulation.

Stupor. Condition of lethargy and unresponsiveness, with partial or complete unconsciousness.

Stuttering. Speech disorder characterized by a blocking or repetition of initial sounds of words.

St. Vitus's dance. Hysterical chorea of common occurrence during the Middle Ages.

Sublimation. Ego-defense mechanism by means of which frustrated sexual energy is partially channeled into substitutive activities.

Substance-abuse disorders. Pathological use of a substance for at least a month, resulting in self-injurious behavior.

Substance-dependence disorders. Severe form of substance-abuse disorder involving physiological dependence on the substance.

Substance-induced organic disorder. Category of disorders based on organic impairment resulting from toxicity or physiologic changes in the brain.

Substance-use disorder. Patterns of maladaptive behavior centered around the regular use of the substance involved.

Substitution. Acceptance of substitute goals or satisfactions in place of those originally sought after or desired.

Successive approximation. See **Shaping.**

Suicide. Taking one's own life.

Suicidology. Study of the causes and prevention of suicide.

Superego. Conscience; ethical or moral dimensions (attitudes) of personality.

Suppression. Conscious forcing of desires or thoughts out of consciousness; conscious inhibition of desires or impulses.

Surrogate. Substitute parent, child, or mate.

Symbol. Image, word, object, or activity that is used to represent something else.

Symbolism. Representation of one idea or object by another.

Sympathetic division. Division of the autonomic nervous system that is active in emergency conditions of extreme cold, violent effort, and emotions.

Symptom. Observable manifestation of a physical or mental disorder.

Syncope. Temporary loss of consciousness resulting from cerebral anoxia.

Syndrome. Group or pattern of symptoms that occur together in a disorder and represent the typical picture of the disorder.

Syphilophobia. Morbid fear of syphilis.

System. Assemblage of interdependent parts, living or nonliving.

Systematic desensitization. Behavior therapy technique for eliminating maladaptive anxiety responses by teaching an individual to relax or behave in some other way that is inconsistent with anxiety while in the presence of the anxiety-producing stimulus.

Tachycardia. Rapid heartbeat.

Tactual hallucinations. Hallucinations involving the sense of touch, such as feeling cockroaches crawling over one's body.

Tarantism. Dancing mania that occurred in Italy and later spread to Germany and the rest of Europe, where it was known as *St. Vitus's dance.*

Tardive dyskinesia. Neurological disorder resulting from excessive use of phenothiazines. The drug side effects can occur months to years after treatment has been initiated or has stopped. The symptoms involve involuntary movements of the tongue, lips, jaw, and extremities. An affected person usually shows characteristic "chewing movements."

Task-oriented response. Realistic rather than ego-defensive approach to stressors.

Tay-Sachs disease. Genetic disorder of lipoid metabolism usually resulting in death by age 3.

T-cell. Generic type of lymphocyte crucial in "cellular" (nonantibody, or "humoral") immune functioning and having several subtypes that support and regulate the entire immune reaction.

Telepathy. Communication from one person to another without use of any known sense organs.

Teleprocessing. Computer-based data processing procedure by which psychological tests are processed, scored, and interpreted through telephone link-up with a central processing center.

Temperament (character) traits. Personality characteristics that are considered to be primarily hereditary or constitutional.

Temporal lobe. Portion of cerebrum located in front of the occipital lobe and separated from frontal and parietal lobes by the fissure of Sylvius.

Tension. Condition arising out of the mobilization of psychobiological resources to meet a threat; physically, involves an increase in muscle tonus and other emergency changes; psychologically, is characterized by feelings of strain, uneasiness, and anxiety.

Tertiary prevention. Preventive techniques focusing on reducing long-term consequences of disorders or problems by means of short-term hospitalization and intensive aftercare when an emotional breakdown has occurred, with aim of returning an individual to his or her family and community setting as soon as possible.

Testes. Male reproductive glands or gonads.

Testosterone. Male sex hormone.

Test reliability. Consistency with which a test measures a given trait on repeated administrations of the test to given subjects.

Test validity. Degree to which a test actually measures what it was designed to measure.

Thematic Apperception Test (TAT). Psychological test composed of a series of pictures based on which a subject makes up a story. Analysis of the story gives a clinician clues about the individual's conflicts, traits, personality dynamics, and so on.

Therapeutic. Pertaining to treatment or healing.

Therapeutic community. Hospital environment used for therapeutic purposes.

Therapy. Treatment; application of various treatment techniques.

Thermistors. Extremely sensitive small thermometers taped to a subject's skin to provide feedback during biofeedback training.

Theta wave. Brain wave having a frequency of only 5 to 7 cycles per second.

Thyroids. Endocrine glands located in the neck that influence body metabolism, rate of physical growth, and development of intelligence.

Thyroxin. Hormone secreted by the thyroid glands.

Tic. Intermittent twitching or jerking, usually of facial muscles.

Token economy. Reinforcement technique often used in hospital or institutional settings in which individuals are rewarded for socially constructive behavior with tokens that can then be exchanged for desired objects or activities.

Tolerance. Physiological condition in which an increased dosage of an addictive drug is needed to obtain effects previously produced by a smaller dose.

Tonic. Pertaining to muscle tension or contraction; muscle tone.

Tourette's syndrome. Extreme tic disorder in which an individual has extensive uncontrollable motor and verbal mannerisms.

Toxic. Poisonous.

Toxic deliria (psychoses). Severe disturbances in cerebral functions resulting from toxins.

Toxicity. Poisonous nature of a substance.

Trait. Characteristic of an individual that can be observed or measured.

Trance. Sleeplike state in which the range of consciousness is limited and voluntary activities are suspended; a deep hypnotic state.

Tranquilizers. Drugs used for antipsychotic purposes and/or reduction of anxiety and tension. See also **Major tranquilizers** and **Minor tranquilizers.**

Transactional analysis. Form of interpersonal therapy based on interaction of "Child," "Adult," and "Parent" ego states.

Transference. Process whereby a client projects attitudes and emotions applicable to another significant person onto the therapist; emphasized in psychoanalytic therapy.

Transsexualism. Identification of oneself with members of the opposite sex, as opposed to acceptance of one's anatomical sexual identity.

Transvestic fetishism. Achievement of sexual arousal and satisfaction by dressing as a member of the opposite sex.

Transvestism. Persistent desire to dress in clothing of the opposite sex, often accompanied by sexual excitement.

Trauma. Severe psychological or physiological stressor.

Traumatic. Pertaining to a wound or injury, or to psychic shock.

Treatment contract. Explicit arrangement between a therapist and a client designed to bring about specific behavioral changes.

Tremor. Repeated fine spastic movement.

Trephining. Early operation to treat abnormal behavior that consisted of chipping away a circular area of the skull until it was cut through, in the hopes of allowing the evil spirit that was causing the disordered behavior to escape.

Trichotillomania. Nervous habit involving the pulling out of hair.

Turner's syndrome. Form of mental retardation associated with sex chromosome anomaly.

Type-A behavior pattern. Complex set of behaviors—involving excessive competitive drive in the absence of well-defined goals, impatience or time urgency, and hostility—that may be observed in certain individuals under appropriately stressful or challenging circumstances.

Unconscious. As used by Freud, psychological material that has been repressed. Also, loss of consciousness; lack of awareness.

Underarousal. Inadequate physiological response to a given stimulus.

Undoing. Ego-defense mechanism by means of which an individual performs activities designed to atone for his or her misdeeds, thereby, in a sense, "undoing" them.

Unipolar disorder. Severe mood disorder in which only depressive episodes occur, as opposed to *bipolar disorder* in which both manic and depressive processes are assumed to occur.

Unsocialized disturbance of conduct. Childhood disorder in which a child is disobedient, hostile, and highly aggressive.

Vaginismus. Involuntary muscle spasm at the entrance to the vagina that prevents penetration and sexual intercourse.

Validity. Extent to which a measuring instrument actually measures what it purports to measure.

Variable. Characteristic or property that may assume any one of a set of different qualities or quantities.

Vasomotor. Pertaining to the walls of the blood vessels.

Vegetative. Withdrawn or deteriorated to the point where an individual leads a passive, vegetable-like existence.

Verbal test. Test in which a subject's ability to understand and use words and concepts is important in making the required responses.

Vertigo. Dizziness.

Virilism. Accentuation of masculine secondary sex characteristics, especially in a woman or young boy, caused by hormonal imbalance.

Viscera. Internal organs.

Voyeurism. Achievement of sexual pleasure through clandestine "peeping," usually watching other people disrobe and/or engage in sexual activities. Also known as *scotophilia* and *inspectionalism.*

Vulnerabilities. Factors rendering an individual susceptible to behaving abnormally.

Wechsler Intelligence Scale for Children (WISC). Standardized intelligence scale for children.

Withdrawal. Intellectual, emotional, or physical retreat.

Withdrawal disturbance. Disorder of childhood in which a child becomes aloof and detached from a world he or she sees as dangerous.

Withdrawal symptoms. Wide range of symptoms evidenced by addicts when the drug on which they are physiologically dependent is not available.

Word salad. Jumbled or incoherent use of words by psychotic or disoriented individuals.

X chromosome. Sex-determining chromosome: all female gametes contain X chromosomes, and if the fertilized ovum has also received an X chromosome from its father it will be female.

XYY syndrome. Chromosomal anomaly in males (presence of an extra Y chromosome) possibly related to impulsive behavior.

Y chromosome. Sex-determining chromosome found in half of the total number of male gametes; uniting with X chromosome always provided by female produces a male offspring.

Zygote. Fertilized egg cell formed by the union of male and female gametes.

References

JOURNAL ABBREVIATIONS
Acta Psychiatr. Scandin.—*Acta Psychiatrica Scandinavica*
Amer. J. Med. Sci.—*American Journal of the Medical Sciences*
Amer. J. Ment. Def.—*American Journal of Mental Deficiency*
Amer. J. Ment. Retard—*American Journal of Mental Retardation*
Amer. J. Nurs.—*American Journal of Nursing*
Amer. J. Orthopsychiat.—*American Journal of Orthopsychiatry*
Amer. J. Psychiat.—*American Journal of Psychiatry*
Amer. J. Psychother.—*American Journal of Psychotherapy*
Amer. J. Pub. Hlth.—*American Journal of Public Health*
Amer. Psychol.—*American Psychologist*
Ann. Int. Med.—*Annals of Internal Medicine*
Annu. Rev. Psychol.—*Annual Review of Psychology*
Arch. Gen. Psychiat.—*Archives of General Psychiatry*
Arch. Int. Med.—*Archives of Internal Medicine*
Arch. Sex. Behav.—*Archives of Sexual Behavior*
Behav. Res. Ther.—*Behavior Research and Therapy*
Behav. Ther.—*Behavior Therapy*
Behav. Today—*Behavior Today*
Brit. J. Psychiat.—*British Journal of Psychiatry*
Brit. Med. J.—*British Medical Journal*
Bull. Menninger Clin.—*Bulletin of the Menninger Clinic*
Canad. J. Psychiat.—*Canadian Journal of Psychiatry*
Child Develop.—*Child Development*
Clin. Psychol.—*The Clinical Psychologist*
Clin. Psychol. Rev.—*Clinical Psychology Review*
Cog. Ther. Res.—*Cognitive Therapy and Research*
Comm. Ment. Hlth. J.—*Community Mental Health Journal*
Compr. Psychiat.—*Comprehensive Psychiatry*
Contemp. Psychol.—*Contemporary Psychology*
Crim. Just. Behav.—*Criminal Justice and Behavior*
Develop. Med. Child Neurol.—*Developmental Medicine & Child Neurology*
Develop. Psychol.—*Developmental Psychology*
Dis. Nerv. Sys.—*Diseases of the Nervous System*
Fam. Hlth.—*Family Health*
Hosp. Comm. Psychiat.—*Hospital and Community Psychiatry*
Human Behav.—*Human Behavior*
Human Develop.—*Human Development*
Human Genet.—*Human Genetics*
Integr. Psychiat.—*Integrative Psychiatry*
Inter. J. Addictions—*International Journal of Addictions*
Inter. J. Psychiat.—*International Journal of Psychiatry*
Inter. J. Psychoanal.—*International Journal of Psychoanalysis*
Inter. J. Soc. Psychiat.—*International Journal of Social Psychiatry*
J. Abnorm. Child Psychol.—*Journal of Abnormal Child Psychology*
J. Abnorm. Psychol.—*Journal of Abnormal Psychology*
J. Abnorm. Soc. Psychol.—*Journal of Abnormal and Social Psychology*
JAMA—*Journal of the American Medical Association*
J. Amer. Acad. Child Psychiat.—*Journal of the American Academy of Child Psychiatry*
J. Amer. Geriat. Soc.—*Journal of the American Geriatrics Society*
J. Appl. Beh. Anal.—*Journal of Applied Behavior Analysis*
J. Autism Devel. Dis.—*Journal of Autism and Developmental Disorders*
J. Behav. Assess.—*Journal of Behavioral Assessment*
J. Behav. Med.—*Journal of Behavioral Medicine*
J. Chem. Depen. Treat.—*Journal of Chemical Dependency Treatment*
J. Child Psychol. Psychiat.—*Journal of Child Psychology and Psychiatry*
J. Clin. Psychiat.—*Journal of Clinical Psychiatry*
J. Clin. Psychopharm.—*Journal of Clinical Psychopharmacology*
J. Clin. Psychol.—*Journal of Clinical Psychology*
J. Cons. Clin. Psychol.—*Journal of Consulting and Clinical Psychology*
J. Couns. Psychol.—*Journal of Counseling Psychology*
J. Exper. Psychol.—*Journal of Experimental Psychology*
J. Gen. Psychol.—*Journal of General Psychology*

J. Learn. Dis.—*Journal of Learning Disabilities*
J. Ment. Sci.—*Journal of Mental Science*
J. Nerv. Ment. Dis.—*Journal of Nervous and Mental Diseases*
J. Pediat. Psychol.—*Journal of Pediatric Psychology*
J. Personal.—*Journal of Personality*
J. Pers. Assess.—*Journal of Personality Assessment*
J. Pers. Soc. Psychol.—*Journal of Personality and Social Psychology*
J. Psychosom. Res.—*Journal of Psychosomatic Research*
J. Speech Hear. Dis.—*Journal of Speech and Hearing Disorders*
J. Stud. Alcoh.—*Journal of Studies on Alcohol*
Ment. Hlth. Dig.—*Mental Health Digest*
Monogr. Soc. Res. Child Develop.—*Monographs of the Society for Research in Child Development*
New Engl. J. Med.—*New England Journal of Medicine*
Profess. Psychol.—*Professional Psychology*
Psychiat. Clin. N. Amer.—*Psychiatric Clinics of North America*
Psychiat. News—*Psychiatric News*
Psychiat. Res.—*Psychiatric Research*
Psychol. Bull.—*Psychological Bulletin*
Psychol. Med.—*Psychological Medicine*
Psychol. Rep.—*Psychological Reports*
Psychol. Rev.—*Psychological Review*
Psych. Today—*Psychology Today*
Psychosom. Med.—*Psychosomatic Medicine*
Schizo. Bull.—*Schizophrenia Bulletin*
Scientif. Amer.—*Scientific American*
Sci. News—*Science News*
Soc. Psychiat.—*Social Psychiatry*

Abel, G. G., Blanchard, E. B., Becker, J. V., & Djenderejian, A. (1978). Differentiating sexual aggressives with penile measures. *Crim. Just. Behav., 5,* 315–32.
Abel, G. G., & Rouleau, J.-L. (1990). The nature and extent of sexual assault. In W. L. Marshall, D. R. Laws, & H. E. Barbaree (Eds.), *Handbook of sexual assault* (pp. 9–22). New York: Plenum.
Abraham, H. D., & Wolf, E. (1988). Visual function in past users of LSD: Psychophysical findings. *J. Abnorm. Psychol., 97,* 443–47.
Abrahamson, D. J., Barlow, D. H., & Abrahamson, L. S. (1989). Differential effects of performance demand and distraction on sexually functional and dysfunctional males. *J. Abnorm. Psychol., 98,* 241–47.
Abramowitz, S. I. (1986). Psychosocial outcomes of sex reassignment surgery. *J. Cons. Clin. Psychol., 54,* 183–89.
Abrams, D. B., Emmons, K. M., Niaura, R. S., Goldstein, M. G., & Sherman, C. B. (in press). Tobacco dependence. In P. E. Nathan, J. W. Langenbucher, B. S. McCrady, and W. Frankenstein (Eds.), *The Annual Review of Addictions: Treatment and Research* (Vol. 1).
Abrams, R. (1988). *Electroconvulsive treatment: It apparently works, but how and at what risks are not yet clear.* New York: Oxford University Press.
Abrams, R., & Essman, W. B. (1982). *Electroconvulsive therapy: Biological foundations and clinical applications.* Jamaica, NY: Sp Medical and Scientific Books.
Abramson, L. Y., Seligman, M. E. P., & Teasdale, J. D. (1978). Learned helplessness in humans: Critique and reformulation. *J. Abnorm. Psychol., 87,* 49–74.
Achenbach, T. M. (1985). *Assessment and taxonomy of child and adolescent psychopathology.* Beverly Hills, CA: Sage.
Achenbach, T. M., & Edelbrock, C. S. (1983). *Manual for the child behavior checklist and revised child behavior profile.* Burlington, VT: University of Vermont.
Achenbach, T. M., & McConaughy, S. H. (1985). *Child interview checklist self—report form; Child interview checklist-observation form.* Burlington, VT: University of Vermont.

Achenbach, T. M., & Weisz, J. R. (1975). Impulsivity-reflectivity and cognitive development in preschoolers: A longitudinal analysis of developmental and trait variance. *Develop. Psychol., 11,* 413–14.

Adams, H. E., & Chiodo, J. (1984). Sexual deviations. In H. E. Adams & P. B. Sutker (Eds.), *Comprehensive handbook of psychopathology.* New York: Plenum.

Adams, H. E., & Sturgis, E. T. (1977). Status of behavioral reorientation techniques in the modification of homosexuality: A review. *Psychol. Bull., 841,* 1171–88.

Adams, M. S., & Neel, J. V. (1967). Children of incest. *Pediatrics, 40,* 55–62.

Ader, R., & Cohen, N. (1984). Behavior and the immune system. In W. D. Gentry (Ed.), *Handbook of behavioral medicine* (pp. 117–73). New York: Guilford.

Adler, A. (1943). Neuropsychiatric complications in victims of Boston's Coconut Grove disaster. *JAMA, 123,* 1098–1101.

Adler, F. (1987). Jails as a repository for former mental patients. *International Journal of Offender Therapy and Comparative Criminology, 30,* 225–36.

Agnew, J. (1985). Man's purgative passion. *Amer. J. Psychother., 39*(2), 236–46.

Agras, W. S. (1982). Behavioral medicine in the 1980's: Non-random connections. *J. Cons. Clin. Psychol., 50*(6), 820–40.

Agras, W. S., Schneider, J. A., Arnow, B., Raeburn, S. D., et al. (1989). Cognitive-behavioral and response-prevention treatments for bulimia nervosa. *J. Cons. Clin. Psychol., 57,* 215–21.

Akhtar, S. (1989). Narcissistic personality disorder: Descriptive features and differential diagnosis. *Psychiat. Clin. N. Amer., 12,* 505–30.

Akhtar, S., & Thompson, J. A. (1982). Overview: Narcissistic personality disorder. *Amer. J. Psychiat., 140,* 1013–16.

Akil, H., Watson, S. J., Sullivan, S., & Barchas, J. D. (1978). Enkephalin-like material in normal human cerebrospinal fluid: Measurement and levels. *Life Sciences, 23,* 121–26.

Akiskal, H. S. (1979). A biobehavioral approach to depression. In R. A. Depue (Ed.), *The psychobiology of depressive disorders: Implications for the effects of stress.* New York: Academic Press.

Akiskal, H. S., & Simmons, R. C. (1985). Chronic and refractory depressions: Evaluation and management. In E. E. Becham & W. R. Leber (Eds.), *Handbook of depression: Treatment, assessment, and research* (pp. 587–605). Homewood, IL: Dorsey Press.

Al-Issa, I. (1982). Does culture make a difference in psychopathology? In I. Al-Issa (Ed.), *Culture and psychopathology.* Baltimore: University Park Press.

Alander, R., & Campbell, T. (1975, Spring). An evaluation of an alcohol and drug recovery program: A case study of the Oldsmobile experience. *Human Resource Management,* 14–18.

Albertson's Inc. vs. Worker's Compensation Board of the State of California, 131, Cal App 3d, 182 Cal Reptr 304, 1982.

Alcohol, Drug Abuse, and Mental Health Administration. (1982). DHHS Pub. No. (ADM) 82–1190. Washington, DC: U.S. Government Printing Office.

Alden, L. (1989). Short-term structured treatment for avoidant personality disorder. *J. Cons. Clin. Psychol., 57,* 756–64.

Alden, L., & Capp, R. (1988). Characteristics predicting social functioning and treatment response in clients impaired by extreme shyness: Age of onset and the public/private shyness distinction. *Canadian Journal of Behavioural Science, 20,* 40–49.

Aldwin, C., & Revenson, T. A. (1986). Vulnerability to economic stress. *American Journal of Community Psychology, 14,* 161–75.

Alexander, A. B. (1977). Chronic asthma. In R. B. Williams, Jr., & W. D. Gentry (Eds.), *Behavioral approaches to medical treatment* (pp. 7–24). Cambridge, MA: Ballinger.

Alexander, B. (1981). Behavioral approaches to the treatment of bronchial asthma. In C. K. Prokop & L. A. Bradley (Eds.), *Medical psychology: Contributions to behavioral medicine.* New York: Academic Press.

Alexander, B. K., & Hadaway, P. F. (1982). Opiate addiction: The case for an adaptive orientation. *Psychol. Bull., 92*(2), 367–81.

Alexander, F. (1946). Individual psychotherapy. *Psychosom. Med., 8,* 110–15.

Alexander, F. (1948). *Fundamentals of psychoanalysis.* New York: Norton.

Alexander, F. (1950). *Psychosomatic medicine.* New York: Norton.

Alexander, K., Huganir, L. S., & Zigler, E. (1985). Effects of different living settings on the performance of mentally retarded individuals. *Amer. J. Ment. Def., 90,* 9–17.

Alfrey, A. C. (1986). Systemic toxicity of aluminum in man. *Neurobiology of Aging, 7,* 543–45.

Allebeck, P., & Wistedt, B. (1986). Mortality in schizophrenia: A ten-year follow-up based on the Stockholm County Inpatient register. *Arch. Gen. Psychiat., 43,* 650–53.

Allen, B., & Skinner, H. (1987). Lifestyle assessment using microcomputers. In J. N. Butcher (Ed.), *Computerized psychological assessment: A practitioner's guide.* New York: Basic Books.

Allerton, W. S. (1970). Psychiatric casualties in Vietnam. *Roche Medical Image and Commentary, 12*(8), 27.

Alterman, A. I. (1988). Patterns of familial alcoholism, alcoholism severity, and psychopathology. *J. Nerv. Ment. Dis., 176,* 167–75.

Alterman, A. I., Searles, J. S., & Hall, J. G. (1989). Failure to find differences in drinking behavior as a function of familial risk for alcoholism: A replication. *J. Cons. Clin. Psychol., 98,* 50–53.

Altshuler, K. Z. (1984). On the question of bisexuality. *Amer. J. Psychother., 38,* 484–93.

Amcoff, S. (1980). The impact of malnutrition on the learning situation. In H. M. Sinclair & G. R. Howat (Eds.), *World nutrition and nutrition education.* New York: Oxford University Press.

Amenson, C. S., & Lewinsohn, P. M. (1981). An investigation into the observed sex difference in prevalence of unipolar depression. *J. Abnorm. Psychol., 90,* 1–13.

American Association on Mental Deficiency (AAMD). (1973). *Manual on terminology and classification in mental retardation* (rev. ed.). H. J. Grossman (Ed.). Special Publication Series No. 2, 11+. Washington, DC.

American Medical Association. (1982, June 30). *The alcoholism report, 10*(17).

American Medical Association. (1986). *Drug evaluation.* 6th Edition. Chicago: Author.

American Medical Association, Department of Mental Health. (1968a). The crutch that cripples: Drug dependence, Part 1. *Today's Health, 46*(9), 11–12, 70–72.

American Psychiatric Association. (1968). *Diagnostic and statistical manual of mental disorders* (2nd ed.). Washington, DC: Author.

American Psychiatric Association. (1972). Classification of mental retardation. Supplement to the *Amer. J. Psychiat., 128*(11), 1–45.

American Psychiatric Association. (1978). Task Force on Electroconvulsive Therapy. *Report: Electroconvulsive therapy.* Washington, DC: Author.

American Psychiatric Association. (1980). *Diagnostic and statistical manual of mental disorders* (3rd ed.). Washington, DC: Author.

American Psychiatric Association. (1987). *Diagnostic and statistical manual of mental disorders* (3rd ed.—rev.). Washington, DC: Author.

American Psychological Association. (1970). Psychology and mental retardation. *Amer. Psychol., 25,* 267–68.

American Psychological Association. (1986). *Guidelines for computer-based tests and interpretations.* Washington, DC: Author.

American Psychological Association. (1990). Ethical principles for psychologists (amended June 2, 1989). *Amer. Psychol., 45,* 390–95.

Anchin, J. C., & Kiesler, D. J. (Eds.). (1982). *Handbook of interpersonal psychotherapy.* New York: Pergamon.

Andersen, B. L. (1983). Primary orgasmic dysfunction: Diagnostic considerations and review of treatment. *Psychol. Bull., 93,* 105–36.

Anderson, J. C., Williams, S., McGee, R., & Silva, P. A. (1987). DSM III disorders in preadolescent children. *Arch. Gen. Psychiat., 44,* 69–80.

Anderson, N. B., & Jackson, J. S. (1987). Race, ethnicity, and health psychology: The example of essential hypertension. In G. C. Stone (Ed.), *Health psychology: A discipline and a profession* (pp. 265–84). Chicago: University of Chicago Press.

Andrasik, F., Blanchard, E. B., Arena, J. G., Teders, S. J., Teevan, R. C., & Rodichok, L. D. (1982). Psychological functioning in headache sufferers. *Psychosom. Med., 44,* 171–82.

Andrasik, F., Holroyd, K. A., & Abell, T. (1979). Prevalence of headache within a college student population: A preliminary analysis. *Headache, 20,* 384–87.

Andreasen, N. C. (1982). Concepts, diagnosis and classification. In E. S. Paykel (Ed.), *Handbook of affective disorders.* New York: Guilford Press.

Andreasen, N. C. (1984). *The broken brain: The biological revolution in psychiatry.* New York: Harper & Row.

Andreasen, N. C. (1985). Positive vs. negative schizophrenia: A critical evaluation. *Schizophrenia, 11,* 380–89.

Andreasen, N. C., Flaum, M., Swayze, V. W., Tyrrell, G., & Arndt, S. (1990). Positive and negative symptoms in schizophrenia: A critical reappraisal. *Arch. Gen. Psychiat., 47,* 615–21.

Andreasen, N. C., Nasrallah, H. A., Dunn, V., Olson, S. C., Grove, W. M. (1986). Structural abnormalities in the frontal system in schizophrenia: A magnetic resonance imaging study. *Arch. Gen. Psychiat. 43,* 136–44.

Andreasen, N. C., Olsen, S. A., Dennert, J. W., & Smith, M. R. (1982a). Ventricular enlargement in schizophrenia: Definition and prevalence. *Amer. J. Psychiat., 139,* 292–96.

Andreasen, N. C., Olsen, S. A., Dennert, J. W., & Smith, M. R. (1982b). Ventricular enlargement in schizophrenia: Relationship to positive and negative symptoms. *Amer. J. Psychiat., 139,* 297–302.

Andrews, G., & Harvey, R. (1981). Does psychotherapy benefit neurotic patients? A reanalysis of the Smith, Glass, and Miller data. *Arch. Gen. Psychiat., 38,* 1203–8.

Andrews, J. D. W. (1989a). Integrating visions of reality: Interpersonal diagnosis and the existential vision. *Amer. Psychol., 44,* 803–17.

Andrews, J. D. W. (1989b). Psychotherapy of depression: A self-confirmation model. *Psychol. Rev., 96,* 576–607.

Angst, J. (1980). Clinical typology of bipolar illness. In R. H. Belmaker & H. M. van Praag (Eds.), *Mania: An evolving concept.* New York: Spectrum.

Anthony, E. J. (1978). Concluding comments on treatment implications. In L. C. Wynne, R. L. Cromwell, & S. Matthysse (Eds.), *The nature of schizophrenia: New approaches to research and treatment* (pp. 481–84). New York: Wiley.

Antoni, M. H., Schneiderman, N., Fletcher, M. A., & Goldstein, D. A. (1990). Psychoneuroimmunology and HIV-1. *J. Cons. Clin. Psychol., 58,* 38–49.

Apfelbaum, B. (1989). Retarded ejaculation: A much-misunderstood syndrome. In S. R. Leiblum & R. C. Rosen (Eds.), *Principles and practice of sex therapy* (2nd ed., pp. 168–206). New York: Guilford.

Apfelberg, B., Sugar, C., & Pfeffer, A. Z. (1944). A psychiatric study of 250 sex offenders. *Amer. J. Psychiat., 100,* 762–70.

Aponte, H., & Hoffman, L. (1973). The open door. A structural approach to a family with an anorectic child. *Family Process, 12,* 144.

Appelbaum, P. S. (1985). Tarasoff and the clinician: Problems in fulfilling the duty to protect. *Amer. J. Psychiat., 142*(4), 425–29.

Arana, G. W., Baldessarini, R. J., & Ornsteen, M. (1985). The dexamethasone suppression test for diagnosis and prognosis in psychiatry: Commentary and review. *Arch. Gen. Psychiat. 42,* 1193–1204.

Arbitman-Smith, R., Haywood, H. C., & Bransford, J. D. (1984). Assessing cognitive change. In P. Brooks, C. M. Sperber, & R. McCauley (Eds.), *Learning and cognition in the mentally retarded* (pp. 433–72). Hillsdale, NJ: Erlbaum.

Archer, J. and Gruenberg, E. (1982). The chronically mentally disabled and "deinstitutionalized." *Annual Review of Public Health, 3,* 445–68.

Archibald, H. C., & Tuddenham, R. D. (1965). Persistent stress reaction after combat. *Arch. Gen Psychiat., 12*(5), 475–81.

Arieti, S. (1974). An overview of schizophrenia from a predominantly psychological approach. *Amer. J. Psychiat., 131*(3), 241–49.

Arieti, S. (1982). Individual psychotherapy. In E. S. Paykel (Ed.), *Handbook of affective disorders.* New York: Guilford Press.

Arieti, S., & Bemporad, J. R. (1980). The psychological organization of depression. *Amer. J. Psychiat., 237,* 1360–65.

Aring, C. D. (1974). The Gheel experience: Eternal spirit of the chainless mind! *JAMA, 230*(7), 998–1001.

Aring, C. D., (1975a). Gheel: The town that cares. *Fam. Hlth., 7*(4), 54–55, 58, 60.

Aring, C. D., (1975b). Science and the citizen. *Scientif. Amer., 232*(1), 48–49; 52–53.

Arkowitz, H., & Messer, S. B. (Eds.) (1984). *Psychoanalytic and behavior therapy. Is integration possible?* New York: Plenum.

Arnkoff, D. B., & Glass, C. R. (1982). Clinical cognitive constructs: Examination, evaluation, and elaboration. In P. C. Kendall (Ed.), *Advances in cognitive-behavioral research and therapy* (Vol. 1, pp. 2–30). New York: Academic Press.

Arnold, L. E. (1978). *Helping parents help their children.* New York: Brunner/Mazel.

Arnold, M. B. (1962). *Story sequence analysis: A new method of measuring motivation and predicting achievement.* New York: Columbia University Press.

Aronoff, B. (1987). *Needs assessments: What have we learned. Experiences from Refugee Assistance Programs in Hawaii.* Paper given at the Refugee Assistance Program: Mental Health Workgroup Meeting, UCLA, February 12–13.

Atkeson, B. M., Calhoun, K. S., Resick, P. A., & Ellis, E. M. (1982). Victims of rape: Repeated assessment of depressive symptoms. *J. Cons. Clin. Psychol., 50,* 96–102.

Atkeson, B. M., & Forehand, R. (1978). Parent behavior training for problem children: An examination of studies using multiple outcome measures. *J. Abnorm. Child Psychol., 6,* 449–60.

Atkinson, J. W. (Ed.). (1958). *Motives in fantasy, action, and society.* Princeton, NJ: Van Nostrand.

Auerbach, S. M., & Stolberg, A. L. (1986). *Crisis intervention with children and families.* New York: Hemisphere Press.

Averill, J. R. (1973). Personal control over aversive stimuli and its relationship to stress. *Psychol. Bull., 80*(4), 286–303.

Avery, D., & Winoker, G. (1976). Mortality in depressed patients treated with electroconvulsive therapy and antidepressants. *Arch. Gen. Psychiat., 33,* 1619–37.

Ayllon, T., & Azrin, N. H. (1968). *The token economy: A motivational system for therapy and rehabilitation.* New York: Appleton-Century-Crofts.

Bachrach, L. L. (1976). *Deinstitutionalization: An analytic review and sociological perspective.* U.S. Department of Health, Education, and Welfare. National Institute of Mental Health, Washington, DC: U.S. Government Printing Office.

Bachrach, L. L. (1980). Overview: Model programs for chronic patients. *Amer. J. Psychiat., 132,* 1023–31.

Bagley, C. (1969). Incest behavior and incest taboo. *Social Problems, 16*(4), 505–19.

Bagley, C. (1973). Occupational class and symptoms of depression. *Social Science and Medicine, 7*(5), 327–40.

Baker, L., & Lyen, K. R. (1982). Anorexia nervosa. In M. Winick (Ed.), *Adolescent nutrition.* New York: Oxford University Press.

Baker, L. A., & Daniels, D. (1990). Nonshared environmental influences and personality differences in adult twins. *J. Pers. Soc. Psychol., 58,* 103–10.

Bales, R. F. (1946). Cultural differences in rates of alcoholism. *Quarterly Journal of Studies in Alcoholism, 6,* 480–99.

Ballenger, J. C. (1988). The clinical use of carbamazepine in affective disorders. *J. Clin. Psychiat., 49,* 13–19.

Balogh, D. W., & Merritt, R. D. (1987). Visual masking and the schizophrenia spectrum: Interfacing clinical and experimental methods. *Schizo. Bull., 13,* 679–98.

Bandura, A. (1964). *Principles of behavior modification.* New York: Holt, Rinehart & Winston.

Bandura, A. (1969). *Principles of behavior modification.* New York: Holt, Rinehart & Winston.

Bandura, A. (1973). *Aggression: A social learning analysis.* Englewood Cliffs, NJ: Prentice-Hall.

Bandura, A. (1974). Behavior theory and the models of man. *Amer. Psychol., 29*(12), 859–69.

Bandura, A. (1977a). Self-efficacy: Toward a unifying theory of behavioral change. *Psychol. Rev., 84*(2), 191–215.

Bandura, A. (1977b). *Social learning theory.* Englewood Cliffs, NJ: Prentice-Hall.

Bandura, A., & Walters, R. H. (1963). *Social learning and personality development.* New York: Holt, Rinehart & Winston.

Bannister, D. (1971). Schizophrenia: Carnival mirror of coherence. *Psych. Today, 4*(8), 66–69, 84.

Bannister, G., Jr. (1975). Cognitive and behavior therapy in a case of compulsive gambling. *Cog. Ther. Res., 1,* 223–27.

Barahal, R. M., Waterman, J., & Martin, H. P. (1981). The social cognitive development of abused children. *J. Cons. Clin. Psychol., 49*(4), 508–16.

Barbaree, H. E. (1990). Stimulus control of sexual arousal: Its role in sexual assault. In W. L. Marshall, D. R. Laws, & H. E. Barbaree (Eds.), *Handbook of sexual assault* (pp. 115–42). New York: Plenum.

Barber, T. X. (1969). *Hypnosis: A scientific approach.* New York: Van Nostrand Reinhold.

Barchas, J., Akil, H., Elliott, G., Holman, R., & Watson, S. (1978, May 26). Behavioral neurochemistry: Neuroregulators and behavioral states. *Science, 200,* 964–73.

Barkley, R. A., & Cunningham, C. E. (1979). The effects of methylphenidate on the mother-child interaction of hyperactive children. *Arch. Gen. Psychiat., 36,* 201–11.

Barlow, D. H. (1974). The treatment of sexual deviation:

Toward a comprehensive behavioral approach. In K. S. Calhoun, H. E. Adams, & K. M. Mitchell (Eds.), *Innovative treatment methods in psychopathology.* New York: Wiley Interscience Series.

Barlow, D. H. (1986). Causes of sexual dysfunction: The role of anxiety and cognitive interference. *J. Cons. Clin. Psychol., 54,* 140–48.

Barlow, D. H. (1988). *Anxiety and its disorders: The nature and treatment of anxiety and panic.* New York: Guilford.

Barlow, D. H., & Abel, G. G. (1976). Sexual deviation. In W. E. Craighead, A. E. Kazdin, & M. J. Mahoney (Eds.), *Behavior modification: Principles, issues, and applications.* Boston: Houghton Mifflin.

Barlow, D. H., & Cerny, J. A. (1988). *Psychological treatment of panic.* New York: Guilford.

Barlow, D. H., Craske, M. G., Cerny, J. A., & Klosko, J. S. (1989). Behavioral treatment of panic disorder. *Behav. Ther., 20,* 261–82.

Barlow, D. H., Vermilyea, J., Blanchard, E. B., Vermilyea, B. B., & Di Nardo, P. A. (1985). The phenomenon of panic. *J. Abnorm. Psychol., 94,* 320–28.

Barlow, D. H., & Waddell, M. T. (1985). Agoraphobia. In D. H. Barlow (Ed.), *Clinical handbook of psychological disorders* (pp. 1–68). New York: Guilford.

Barnes, D. M. (1987). Defect of Alzheimer's is on chromosome 21. *Science, 253,* 846–47.

Barnes, G. E., & Prosen, H. (1985). Parental death and depression. *J. Abnorm. Psychol., 94,* 64–69.

Barry, H., III. (1982). Cultural variations in alcohol abuse. In I. Al-Issa (Ed.), *Culture and psychopathology.* Baltimore: University Park Press.

Bartak, L. (1978). Educational approaches. In M. Rutter & E. Schopler (Eds.), *Autism: A reappraisal of concepts and treatment.* New York: Plenum.

Bartak, L., & Rutter, M. (1973). Special education treatment of autistic children: A comparative study, I. *J. Child Psychol. Psychiat., 14,* 161–79.

Bartak, L., & Rutter, M. (1976). Differences between mentally retarded and normally intelligent autistic children. *Journal of Autism and Childhood Schizophrenia, 6,* 109–20.

Bartone, P. T., Ursano, R. J., Wright, K. M., & Ingraham, L. H. (1989). The impact of air disaster on the health of assistance workers. *J. Nerv. Ment. Dis., 177,* 317–27.

Bassuk, E. L., & Gerson, S. (1978). Deinstitutionalization and mental health services. *Scientif. Amer., 238*(2), 46–53.

Bassuk, E. L., Schoonover, S. C., & Gelenberg, A. J. (1983). *The practitioner's guide to psychiatric drugs* (2nd ed.). New York: Plenum.

Bates, C. M., & Brodsky, A. M. (1989). *Sex in the therapy hour: A case of professional incest.* New York: Guilford.

Bateson, G. (1959). Cultural problems posed by a study of schizophrenic process. In A. Auerback (Ed.), *Schizophrenia: An integrated approach.* New York: Ronald Press.

Bateson, G. (1960). Minimal requirements for a theory of schizophrenia. *Arch. Gen. Psychiat., 2,* 477–91.

Baucom, D. H. (1983). Sex role identity and the decision to regain control among women: A learned helplessness investigation. *J. Pers. Soc. Psychol., 44,* 334–43.

Bauer, A. M., & Shea, T. M. (1986). Alzheimer's disease and Down syndrome: A review and implications for adult services. *Education and Training of the Mentally Retarded, 21,* 144–50.

Baum, A., Gatchel, R. J., & Schaeffer, M. A. (1983). Emotional, behavioral, and physiological effects of chronic stress at Three Mile Island. *J. Cons. Clin. Psychol., 51,* 565–72.

Baumeister, R. F. (1990). Suicide as escape from self. *Psychol. Rev., 97,* 90–113.

Baumrind, D. (1971). Current patterns of parental authority. *Develop. Psychol., 4*(1), 1–103.

Baumrind, D. (1975). *Early socialization and the discipline controversy.* Morristown, NJ: General Learning Press.

Baxter, L. R., Jr., Phelps, M. E., Mazziotta, J. C., Schwartz, J. M., & Gerner, R. H. (1985). Cerebral metabolic rates for glucose in mood disorders: Studies with positron emission tomography and fluorodeoxyglucose F18. *Arch. Gen. Psychiat., 42,* 441–47.

Bayer, R., & Spitzer, R. L. (1985). Neurosis, psychodynamics, and DSM-III: A history of the controversy. *Arch. Gen. Psychiat., 42,* 187–96.

Bazell, R. J. (1973, Feb. 23). Drug abuse: Methadone becomes the solution and the problem. *Science, 179*(4975), 772–75.

Beardslee, W. R., Bemporad, J., Keller, M. B., & Klerman, G. L. (1983). Children of parents with major affective disorder: A review. *Amer. J. Psychiat., 140,* 825–32.

Beck, A. T. (1967). *Depression: Causes and treatment.* Philadelphia: University of Pennsylvania Press.

Beck, A. T. (1985). Theoretical perspectives on clinical anxiety. In A. H. Tuma & J. D. Maser (Eds.), *Anxiety and the anxiety disorders* (pp. 183–98). Hillsdale, NJ: Lawrence Erlbaum Press.

Beck, A. T., Beck, R., & Kovacs, M. (1975). Classification of suicidal behaviors: I. Qualifying intent and medical lethality. *Amer. J. Psychiat., 132*(3), 285–87.

Beck, A. T., Brown, G., & Steer, R. A. (1989). Prediction of eventual suicide in psychiatric inpatients by clinical ratings of hopelessness. *J. Cons. Clin. Psychol., 57,* 309–10.

Beck, A. T., & Emery, G., (with) Greenberg, R. L. (1985). *Anxiety disorders and phobias: A cognitive perspective.* New York: Basic Books.

Beck, A. T., Hollon, S. D., Young, J. E., Bedrosian, R. C., & Budenz, D. (1985). Treatment of depression with cognitive therapy and amitriptyline. *Arch. Gen. Psychiat., 42,* 142–48.

Beck, A. T., Laude, R., & Bohnert, M. (1974). Ideational components of anxiety neurosis. *Arch. Gen. Psychiat., 31*(3), 319–25.

Beck, A. T., Rush, A. J., Shaw, B., & Emery, G. (1979). *Cognitive therapy of depression: A treatment manual.* New York: Guilford Press.

Beck, A. T., & Weishaar, M. (1989). Cognitive therapy. In A. Freeman, K. M. Simon, L. E. Beutler, & H. Arkowitz (Eds.), *Comprehensive handbook of cognitive therapy* (pp. 21–36). New York: Plenum.

Beck, J. G., & Barlow, D. H. (1984). Current conceptualizations of sexual dysfunction: A review and an alternative perspective. *Clin. Psychol. Rev., 4,* 363–78.

Beck, L., Langford, W. S., Mackay, M., & Sum, G. (1975). Childhood chemotherapy and later drug abuse and growth curve: A follow-up study of 30 adolescents. *Amer. J. Psychiat., 132*(4), 436–38.

Becker, J. V., Hunter, J. A., Jr., Stein, R. M., & Kaplan, M. S. (1989). Factors associated with erection in adolescent sex offenders. *Journal of Psychopathology and Behavioral Assessment, 11,* 353–64.

Becker, W. C. (1964). Consequences of different kinds of parental discipline. In M. L. Hoffman & L. W. Hoffman (Eds.), *Review of child development research* (Vol. 1). New York: Russell Sage Foundation.

Beckham, E. E., & Leber, W. R. (1985a). The comparative efficacy of psychotherapy and pharmacotherapy for depression. In E. E. Beckham & W. R. Leber (Eds.), *Handbook of depression: Treatment, assessment, and research* (pp. 316–42). Homewood, IL: Dorsey.

Beckham, E. E., & Leber, W. R. (Eds.). (1985b). *Handbook of depression: Treatment, assessment, and research.* Homewood, IL: Dorsey Press.

Beech, H. R., Burns, L. E., & Sheffield, B. F. (1982). *A behavioral approach to the management of stress.* New York: John Wiley & Sons.

Beers, C. (1970). *A mind that found itself* (rev. ed.) New York: Doubleday.

Behar, D., & Stewart, M. A. (1982). Aggressive conduct disorder of children. *Acta Psychiatr. Scandin., 65*(3), 210–20.

Belgian Consulate. (1990). Washington, DC. Personal communication.

Bell, A. O. (1974). Homosexualities: Their range and character. In J. K. Cole & E. Dienstbier (Eds.), *Nebraska symposium on motivation, 1973* (pp. 1–26). Lincoln, NE: University of Nebraska Press.

Bell, A. P., & Weinberg, M. S. (1978). *Homosexualities: A study of diversity among men and women.* New York: Simon & Schuster.

Bell, A. P., Weinberg, M. S., & Hammersmith, S. K. (1981). *Sexual preference: Its development in men and women.* Bloomington, IN: Indiana University Press.

Bell, E., Jr. (1958). The basis of effective military psychiatry. *Dis. Nerv. Sys., 19,* 283–88.

Bellak, L. (1975). *The Thematic Apperception Test, the Children's Apperception Test, and the Senior Apperception Technique in clinical use* (3rd ed.). New York: Grune & Stratton.

Bellak, L. (1979). Introduction: An idiosyncratic overview. In L. Bellak (Ed.), *Disorders of the schizophrenic syndrome.* New York: Basic Books.

Bellman, M. (1966). Studies on encopresis. *Acta Paediatrica Scandanovica Suppl., 170,* 121.

Belsky, J., & Steinberg, L. D. (1978). The effects of day care: A critical review. *Child Develop., 49,* 929–49.

Bem, D. J. (1972). Self-perception theory. In L. Berkowitz (Ed.), *Advances in experimental social psychology* (Vol. 6). New

York: Academic Press.

Bemis, K. M. (1978). Current approaches to the etiology and treatment of anorexia nervosa. *Psychol. Bull., 85,* 593–617.

Ben-Porath, Y. S., & Butcher, J. N. (1989). The comparability of MMPI and MMPI-2 scales and profiles. *Psychological Assessment: A Journal of Consulting and Clinical Psychology, 1,* 345–47.

Bender, L. (1973). The life course of children with schizophrenia. *Amer. J. Psychiat., 130*(7), 783–86.

Benedict, R. (1934). Anthropology and the abnormal. *J. Gen. Psychol., 10,* 59–82.

Bengelsdorf, I. S. (1970, Mar. 5). Alcohol, morphine addictions believed chemically similar. *Los Angeles Times,* II, 7.

Benjamin, H. (1966). *The transsexual phenomenon.* New York: Julian Press.

Benjamin, L. S. (1974). Structural analysis of social behavior. *Psychol. Rev., 81,* 392–425.

Benjamin, L. S. (1976). A reconsideration of the Kety and associates study of genetic factors in the transmission of schizophrenia. *Amer. J. Psychiat., 133,* 1129–33.

Benjamin, L. S. (1982). Use of structural analysis of social behavior (SASB) to guide intervention in psychotherapy. In J. C. Anchin & D. L. Kiesler (Eds.), *Handbook of interpersonal psychotherapy.* New York: Pergamon.

Benkelfat, C., Murphy, D. L., Zohar, J., Hill, J. L., Grover, G., & Insel, T. R. (1989). Clomipramine in obsessive-compulsive disorder: Further evidence for a serotonergic mechanism of action. *Arch. Gen. Psychiat., 46,* 23–28.

Bennett, A. E. (1947). Mad doctors. *J. Nerv. Ment. Dis., 106,* 11–18.

Bentler, P. M., & Prince, C. (1969). Personality characteristics of male transvestites. III. *J. Abnorm. Psychol., 74*(2), 140–43.

Bentler, P. M., & Prince, C. (1970). Psychiatric symptomology in transvestites. *J. Clin. Psychol., 26*(4), 434–35.

Bentler, P. M., Shearman, R. W., & Prince, C. (1970). Personality characteristics of male transvestites. *J. Clin. Psychol., 126*(3), 287–91.

Bentovim, A., Boston, P., & Van Elburg, A. (1987). Child sexual abuse—children and families referred to a treatment project and the effects of intervention. *Brit. Med. J., 295,* 1453–57.

Beres, D., & Obers, S. J. (1950). The effects of extreme deprivation in infancy on psychic structure in adolescence. In R. S. Eissler et al. (Eds.), *The psychoanalytic study of the child* (Vol. 5). New York: International Universities Press.

Berg, A. (1954). *The sadist* (O. Illner & G. Godwin, Trans.). New York: Medical Press of New York.

Bergen, J. A., Eyland, E. A., Campbell, J. A., Jenkins, P., Kellehear, K., Richards, A., & Beumont, P.J.V. (1989). The course of tardive dyskinesia in patients on long-term neuroleptics. *Brit. J. Psychiat., 154,* 523–28.

Berger, P. A. (1978). Medical treatment of mental illness. *Science, 200,* 974–81.

Berger, R. J. (1970). Morpheus descending. *Psych. Today, 4*(1), 33–36.

Bergin, A. E., & Lambert, M. J. (1978). The evaluation of therapeutic outcomes. In S. L. Garfield & A. E. Bergin (Eds.), *Handbook of psychotherapy and behavior change* (2nd ed.). New York: Wiley.

Bergler, E. (1947). Analysis of an unusual case of fetishism. *Bull. Menninger Clin. 2,* 67–75.

Bergsma, D. (Ed.). (1974). *Medical genetics today* (National Foundation Series). Baltimore: Johns Hopkins University Press.

Bernard, J. L. (1979). Reply to Siegal. *Amer. Psychol., 34*(3), 280–82.

Bernhardt, B., Meertz, E., & Schonfeldt-Bausch, P. (1985). Basal ganglia and limbic system pathology in schizophrenia: A morphometric study of brain volume and shrinkage. *Arch. Gen. Psychiat., 42,* 784–91.

Bettelheim, B. (1959, Mar.). Joey: A "mechanical boy." *Scientif. Amer., 200,* 116–27.

Bettelheim, B. (1967). *The empty fortress.* New York: Free Press.

Bettelheim, B. (1969). Laurie. *Psych. Today, 2*(12), 24–25, 60.

Bettelheim, B. (1974). *A home for the heart.* New York: Alfred A. Knopf.

Beveridge, A. W., & Renvoize, E. B. (1988). Electricity: A history of its use in the treatment of mental illness in Britain during the second half of the 19th Century. *Brit. J. Psychiat., 153,* 157–62.

Bibring, E. (1953). The mechanism of depression. In P. Greenacre (Ed.), *Affective disorders.* New York: International Universities Press.

Bijou, S. W. (1966). A functional analysis of retarded development. In N. R. Ellis (Ed.), *International review of research in mental retardation* (Vol. 1). New York: Academic Press.

Biklen, D. (1976). Advocacy comes of age. *Exceptional Children, 42,* 308–13.

Billings, A. G., Cronkite, R. C., & Moos, R. H. (1983). Social-environmental factors in unipolar depression: Comparisons of depressed patients and nondepressed controls. *J. Abnorm. Psychol., 92,* 119–33.

Binder, R. L. & McNiel, D. E. (1988). Effects of diagnosis and context of dangerousness. *Amer. J. Psychiat., 145,* 788–92.

Binswanger, L. (1942). *Grundformen und Erkenntnis Menschlichen Daseing.* Zurich: Max Nichans.

Bird, T. D. (1986). Problems and limitations in studying a genetic component of Alzheimer's disease. *Neurobiology of Aging, 7,* 477–78.

Birkhimer, L. J., Curtis, J. L., & Jann, M. W. (1985). Use of carbamazepine in psychiatric disorders. *Clinical Pharmacy, 4,* 425–34.

Birns, B., & Bridger, W. (1977). Cognitive development and social class. In J. Wortis (Ed.), *Mental retardation and developmental disabilities* (Vol. 9, pp. 203–33). New York: Brunner/Mazel.

Bisnaire, L. M., Firestone, P., & Rynard, D. (1990). Factors associated with academic achievement in children following parental separation. *Amer. J. Orthopsychiat., 60,* 67–76.

Black, D. W., Warrack, G., & Winokur, G. (1985). The Iowa Record-Linkage Study: I. Suicides and accidental deaths among psychiatric patients. *Arch. Gen. Psychiat., 42,* 71–75.

Black, D. W., Winoker, G., Bell, S., Nasrallah, A., & Hulbert, J. (1988). Complicated mania: Comorbidity and immediate outcome in the treatment of mania. *Arch. Gen. Psychiat., 45,* 232–36.

Black, D. W., Yates, W., Petty, F., Noyes, R., & Brown, K. (1986). Suicidal behavior in alcoholic males. *Compr. Psychiat., 27*(3), 227–33.

Blackburn, I. M., Bishop, S., Glen, A. I. M., Whalley, L. J., & Christie, J. E. (1981). The efficacy of cognitive therapy in depression: A treatment trial using cognitive therapy and pharmacotherapy, each alone and in combination. *Brit. J. Psychiat., 139,* 181–89.

Blair, C. D., & Lanyon, R. I. (1981). Exhibitionism: Etiology and treatment. *Psychol. Bull., 89,* 439–63.

Blanchard, E. B., & Andrasik, F. (1982). Psychological assessment and treatment of headache: Recent developments and emerging issues. *J. Cons. Clin. Psychol., 50*(6), 859–79.

Blanchard, E. B., Andrasik, F., Ahles, T. A., Teders, S. J., & O'Keefe, D. (1980). Migraine and tension headache: A metaanalytic review. *Behav. Ther., 11,* 613–31.

Blanchard, E. B., Andrasik, F., Neff, D. F., Saunders, N. L., Arena, J. G., Pallmeyer, T. P., Teders, S. J., & Jurish, S. G. (1983). Four process studies in the behavioral treatment of chronic headache. *Behav. Res. Ther., 21,* 209–20.

Blanchard, E. B., Andrasik, F., Neff, D. F., Teders, S. J., Pallmeyer, T. P., Arena, J. G., Jurish, S. E., Saunders, N. L., & Rodichok, L. D. (1983). Sequential comparisons of relaxation training and biofeedback in the treatment of three kinds of chronic headache or, The machines may be necessary some of the time. *Behav. Res. Ther.*

Blanchard, E. B., Appelbaum, K. A., Radnitz, C. L., Michultka, D., Morrill, B., Kirsch, C., Hillhouse, J., Evans, D. D., Guarnieri, P., Attanasio, V., & Andrasik, F. et al. (1990a). Placebo-controlled evaluation of abbreviated progressive muscle relaxation and of relaxation combined with cognitive therapy in the treatment of tension headache. *J. Cons. Clin. Psychol., 58,* 210–15.

Blanchard, E. B., Appelbaum, K. A., Radnitz, C. L. et al. (1990b). A controlled evaluation of thermal biofeedback and thermal biofeedback combined with cognitive therapy in the treatment of vascular headache. *J. Cons. Clin. Psychol., 58,* 216–24.

Blanchard, E. B., & Epstein, L. H. (1978). *A biofeedback primer.* Reading, MA: Addison-Wesley.

Blanchard, E. B., Miller, S. T., Abel G. G., Haynes, M. R., & Wicker, R. (1979). Evaluation of biofeedback in treatment of borderline essential hypertension. *J. Appl. Beh. Anal., 12,* 99–109.

Blanchard, E. B., & Young, L. D. (1973). Self-control of cardiac functioning: A promise as yet unfulfilled. *Psychol. Bull., 79,* 145–63.

Blanchard, E. B., & Young, L. D. (1974). Clinical applications of biofeedback training: A review of evidence. *Arch. Gen. Psychiat., 30,* 573–89.

Blanchard, R., Steiner, B. W., & Clemmensen, L. H. (1985).

Gender dysphoria, gender reorientation, and the clinical management of transsexualism. *J. Cons. Clin. Psychol., 53,* 295–304.

Blashfield, R. K., & Breen, M. J. (1989). Face validity of the DSM III-R personality disorders. *Amer. J. Psychiat., 146,* 1575–79.

Blaszczynski, A., McConaghy, N., & Frankova, A. (1989). Crime, antisocial personality and pathological gambling. *Journal of Gambling Behavior, 5,* 137–52.

Blatt, S. J., D'Afflitti, J. P., & Quinlan, D. M. (1976). Experiences of depression in normal young adults. *J. Abnorm. Psychol., 85,* 383–89.

Blatt, S. J., Quinlan, D. M., Chevron, E. S., McDonald, C., & Zuroff, D. (1982). Dependency and self-criticism: Psychological dimensions of depression. *J. Cons. Clin. Psychol., 50,* 113–24.

Blau, A., Slaff, B., Easton, K., Welkowitz, J., Springarn, J., & Cohen, J. (1963). The psychogenic etiology of premature births. *Psychosom. Med., 25,* 201–11.

Blazer, D., Crowell, B. A., & George, L. K. (1987). Alcohol abuse and dependence in the rural south. *Arch. Gen. Psychiat., 44,* 736–40.

Blazer, D., George, L. K., Landerman, R., Pennybacker, M., & Melville, M. L. (1985). Psychiatric disorders: A rural/urban comparison. *Arch. Gen. Psychiat., 42,* 651–56.

Bleeker, E. (1968). Many asthma attacks psychological. *Sci. News, 93*(17), 406.

Blehar, M. C., & Rosenthal, N. E. (1989). Seasonal affective disorders and phototherapy: Report of a National Institute of Mental Health-sponsored workshop. *Arch. Gen. Psychiat., 46,* 469–74.

Bleuler, E. (1950). *Dementia praecox or the group of schizophrenias.* New York: International Universities Press. (Originally published in 1911.)

Bleuler, M. (1978). The long-term course of schizophrenic psychoses. In L. C. Wynne, R. L. Cromwell, & S. Matthysse (Eds.), *The nature of schizophrenia: New approaches to research and treatment* (pp. 631–36). New York: Wiley.

Bloch, H. S. (1969). Army clinical psychiatry in the combat zone—1967–1968. *Amer. J. Psychiat., 126,* 289.

Bloom, B. L., Asher, S. J., & White, S. W. (1978). Marital disruption as a stressor: A review and analysis. *Psychol. Bull., 85,* 867–94.

Bloom, F. E. (1983). Endogeneous opioids: Histochemistry, neurophysiology, and pharmacology, *Psychiat. Clin. N. Amer., 9,* 365–76.

The Bloomington Sun Current (1986, June 16). TV news anchor tells story of recovery from alcoholism.

Blount, R. L., Dahlquist, L. M., Baer, R. A., & Wuori, D. (1984). A brief, effective method for teaching children to swallow pills. *Behav. Ther., 15,* 381–87.

Blum, R. (1969). *Society and drugs* (Vol. 1). San Francisco: Jossey-Bass.

Blumenthal, S. J. (1990). Youth suicide: Risk factors, assessment, and treatment of adolescent and young adult suicidal patients. *Psychiat. Clin. N. Amer., 13,* 511–56.

Blumer, D., & Benson, D. F. (1975). Personality changes with frontal and temporal lobe lesions. In D. F. Benson & D. Blumer (Eds.), *Psychiatric aspects of neurological disease* (pp. 151–70). New York: Grune & Stratton.

Bockhoven, J. S. (1972). *Moral treatment in community mental health.* New York: Springer.

Boehm, G. (1968). At last—a nonaddicting substitute for morphine? *Today's Health, 46*(4), 69–72.

Bolen, D. W., & Boyd, W. H. (1968). Gambling and the gambler. *Arch. Gen. Psychiatr., 18*(5), 617–30.

Bolen, D. W., Caldwell, A. B., & Boyd, W. H. (1975, June). *Personality traits of pathological gamblers.* Paper presented at the Second Annual Conference on Gambling, Lake Tahoe, NV.

Bolger, N. (1990). Coping as a personality process: A prospective study. *J. Pers. Soc. Psychol., 59,* 525–37.

Boll, T. J. (1978). Diagnosing brain impairment. In B. B. Wolman, (Ed.), *Clinical diagnosis of mental disorders: A handbook.* New York: Plenum.

Boll, T. J. (1980). The Halstead-Reitan neuropsychological battery. In S. B. Filskov & T. J. Boll (Eds.), *Handbook of neurophysiology.* New York: Wiley Interscience Series.

Bolls, R. C., & Fanselow, M. S. (1982). Endorphins and behavior. *Annu. Rev. Psychol., 33,* 87–101.

Bolton, A. (1976). *A study of the need for and availability of mental health services for mentally disordered jail inmates and juveniles in detention facilities.* Boston: Arthur Bolton Associates.

Bolton, P., Rutter, M., Butler, L., & Summers, D. (1989). Females with autism and the fragile X. *J. Autism Devel. Dis., 19,* 473–76.

Booth-Kewley, S., & Friedman, H. S. (1987). Psychological predictors of heart disease: A quantitative review. *Psychol. Bull., 101,* 343–62.

Borg, W. R., & Ascione, F. R. (1982). Classroom management in elementary mainstreaming classrooms. *J. Educ. Psychol., 74,* 84–95.

Borkovec, T. D. (1970). Autonomic reactivity to sensory stimulation in psychopathic, neurotic, and normal juvenile delinquents. *J. Cons. Clin. Psychol., 35,* 217–22.

Borkovec, T. D. (1985). The role of cognitive and somatic cues in anxiety and anxiety disorders: Worry and relation-induced anxiety. In A. H. Tuma & J. D. Maser (Eds.), *Anxiety and the anxiety disorders* (pp. 463–78). Hillsdale, NJ: Lawrence Erlbaum.

Boronow, J., Pickar, D., Ninan, P. T., Roy, A., & Hommer, D. (1985). Atrophy limited to the third ventricle in chronic schizophrenic patients: Report of a controlled series. *Arch. Gen. Psychiat., 42,* 266–71.

Borus, J. F. (1974). Incidence maladjustment in Vietnam returnees. *Arch. Gen. Psychiat., 30*(4), 554–57.

Boskind-White, M., & White, W. C. (1983). *Bulimarexia: The binge-purge cycle.* New York: W. W. Norton.

Boskind-White, M., & White, W. C. (1986). Bulimarexia: A historical-sociocultural perspective. In K. D. Brownell & J. P. Foreyt (Eds.), *Handbook of eating disorders* (pp. 353–66). New York: Basic Books.

Botvin, G. J. (1983). Prevention of adolescent substance abuse through the development of personal and social competence. *National Institute on Drug Abuse Research Monograph Series, 47,* 115–40.

Botvin, G. J., Baker, E., Dusenbury, L., Tortu, S., & Botvin, E. M. (1990). Preventing adolescent drug abuse through a multimodal cognitive-behavioral approach: Results of a 3 year study. *J. Cons. Clin. Psychol., 58,* 437–57.

Botvin, G. J., & Tortu, S. (1988). Preventing substance abuse through life skills training. In R. H. Price, E. L. Cowen, R. P. Lorion, & J. Ramos-McKay (Eds.), *14 ounces of prevention.* Washington, DC: American Psychological Association.

Bouchard, T. J., Lykken, D. T., McGue, M., Segal, N., & Tellegen, A. (1990). Sources of human psychological differences: The Minnesota Study of Twins Reared Apart. *Science, 250,* 223–28.

Boucher, J. (1981). Memory for recent events in autistic children. *J. Autism Devel. Dis., 11*(3), 293–301.

Bourne, P. G. (1970). Military psychiatry and the Vietnam experience. *Amer. J. Psychiat., 127*(4), 481–88.

Bowen, M. (1978). *Family therapy in clinical practice.* New York: Aronson.

Bowlby, J. (1960). Separation anxiety. *Inter. J. Psychoanal., 41,* 89–93.

Bowlby, J. (1973). Separation: Anxiety and anger. *Psychology of attachment and loss series* (Vol. 3). New York: Basic Books.

Boyd, J. H., & Weissman, M. M. (1982). Epidemiology. In E. S. Paykel (Ed.), *Handbook of affective disorders.* New York: Guilford Press.

Boyd, W. H., & Bolen, D. W. (1970). The compulsive gambler and spouse in group psychotherapy. *International Journal of Group Psychotherapy, 20,* 77–90.

Bradley, L. A., & Prokop, C. K. (1981). The relationship between medical psychology and behavioral medicine. In C. K. Prokop & L. A. Bradley (Eds.), *Medical psychology: Contributions to behavioral medicine.* New York: Academic Press.

Bradley, L. A., & Prokop, C. K. (1982). Research methods in contemporary medical psychology. In P. C. Kendall & J. N. Butcher (Eds.), *Handbook of research methods in clinical psychology.* New York: Wiley Interscience.

Braff, D. L., Silverton, L., Sacuzzo, D. P., & Janowsky, D. S. (1981). Impaired speed of visual information processing in marijuana intoxication. *Amer. J. Psychiat., 138*(5), 613–17.

Bradley, B. M., & Braginsky, D. D. (1974). The mentally retarded: Society's Hansels and Gretels. *Psych. Today, 7*(10), 18, 20–21, 24, 26, 28–30.

Braginsky, B. M., Braginsky, D. D., & Ring, K. (1969). *Methods of madness: The mental hospital as a last resort.* New York: Holt, Rinehart & Winston.

Brandel, S. K. (1980). Refugees: New dimensions to an old problem. *Communique.* Washington, DC: Overseas Development Council.

Brandsma, J. M., Maultsby, M. C., & Welsh, R. J. (1980).

Outpatient treatment of alcoholism: A review and comparative study. Baltimore: University Park Press.

Brane, G. (1986). Normal aging and dementia disorders: Coping and crisis in the family. *Progress in Neuro-Psychopharmacology & Biological Psychiatry, 10,* 287–95.

Brantley, P., & Sutker, P. B. (1984). Antisocial personalities. In P. Sutker & H. Adams (Eds.), *Comprehensive handbook of psychopathology.* New York: Plenum.

Braun, P., Kochansky, R., Shapiro, R., Greenberg, S., Gudeman, J. E., Johnson, S., & Shore, M. (1981). Overview: Deinstitutionalization of psychiatric patients, a critical review of outcome studies. *Amer. J. Psychiat., 138*(6), 736–49.

Brayfield, A. H. et al. (1965). Special Issue: Testing and public policy. *Amer. Psychol., 20,* 857–1005.

Brebner, A., Hallworth, H. J., & Brown, R. I. (1977). Computer-assisted instruction programs and terminals for the mentally retarded. In P. Mittler (Ed.), *Research to practice in mental retardation* (Vol. 2, pp. 421–26). Baltimore: University Park Press.

Brecksville V. A. Medical Center. (1981). *Annual report for 1981: Gambling treatment program.* Cleveland, OH.

Breggin, P. R. (1979). *Electroshock: Its brain-disabling effects.* New York: Springer.

Breier, A., Charney, D. S., & Heninger, G. R. (1984). Major depression in patients with agoraphobia and panic disorder. *Arch. Gen. Psychiat. 41,* 1129–35.

Breitner, J. C. (1986). On methodology and appropriate inference regarding possible genetic factors in typical, late-onset AD. *Neurobiology of Aging, 7,* 476–77.

Brennan, J. H., & Hemsley, D. R. (1984). Illusory correlations in paranoid and nonparanoid schizophrenia. *British Journal of Clinical Psychology, 23,* 225–26.

Brenner, M. H. (1973). *Mental illness and the economy.* Cambridge, MA: Harvard University Press.

Breslau, N. (1990). Does brain dysfunction increase children's vulnerability to environmental stress? *Arch. Gen. Psychiat., 47,* 15–20.

Brett, E. A., Spitzer, R. L., & Williams, J. B. (1988). DSM III-R criteria for posttraumatic stress disorder. *Amer. J. Psychiat., 145,* 1232–36.

Breuning, S. E., & Poling, A. D. (1982). Pharmacotherapy. In J. L. Matson & R. P. Barrett (Eds.), *Psychopathology in the mentally retarded* (pp. 195–251). New York: Grune & Stratton.

Bridges, F. A., & Cicchetti, D. (1982). Mothers' ratings of the temperament characteristics of Down's Syndrome infants. *Develop. Psychol., 18,* 238–44.

Brink, T. L. (1983). Paranoia in Alzheimer's patients: Prevalence and impact on caretakers. *International Journal of Behavioral Geriatrics, 1,* 53–55.

Brom, D., Kleber, R. J., & Defares, P. B. (1989). Brief psychotherapy for posttraumatic stress disorders. *J. Cons. Clin. Psychol., 57,* 607–12.

Brooks, D. N. (1974). Recognition, memory, and head injury. *Journal of Neurology, Neurosurgery, & Psychiatry, 37*(7), 794–801.

Brown, B. (1974). Depression roundup. *Behav. Today, 5*(17), 117.

Brown, G. W. (1972). Life-events and psychiatric illness: Some thoughts on methodology and causality. *J. Psychosom. Res., 16,* 311–20.

Brown, G. W., & Harris, T. (1978). *Social origins of depression.* London: Tavistock Publications.

Brown, J. D., & McGill, K. L. (1989). The cost of good fortune: When positive life events produce negative health consequences. *J. Pers. Soc. Psychol., 57,* 1103–10.

Brown, J. F., & Menninger, K. A. (1940). *Psychodynamics of abnormal behavior.* New York: McGraw-Hill.

Brown, R., Colter, N., Corsellis, J. A. N., Crow, T. J., & Frith, C. D. (1986). Postmortem evidence of structural brain changes in schizophrenia: Differences in brain weight, temporal horn area, and parahippocampal gyrus compared with average data. *Arch. Gen. Psychiat., 43,* 36–42.

Brown, R., & Herrnstein, R. J. (1977). *Psychology.* Boston: Little, Brown.

Brown, R. I. (1977). An integrated program for the mentally handicapped. In P. Mittler (Ed.), *Research to practice in mental retardation* (Vol. 2, pp. 387–88). Baltimore: University Park Press.

Browne, A., & Finkelhor, D. (1986). Impact of child sexual abuse: A review of the research. *Psychol. Bull., 99,* 66–77.

Browne, E. G. (1921). *Arabian Medicine.* New York: Macmillan.

Brozek, J., & Schurch, B. (1984). *Malnutrition and behavior: Critical assessment of key issues.* Lausanne, Switzerland: Nestle Foundation.

Bruch, H. (1973). *Eating disorders: Obesity, anorexia nervosa and the person within.* New York: Basic Books.

Bruch, H. (1988). *Conversations with anorexics.* New York: Basic Books.

Bruch, R. (1986). Anorexia nervosa: The therapeutic task. In K. D. Brownell & J. P. Foreyt (Eds.), *Handbook of eating disorders* (pp. 328–32). New York: Basic Books.

Bruck, M. (1987). Social and emotional adjustments of learning-disabled children. In S. J. Ceci (Ed.), *Handbook of cognitive, social, and neuropsychological aspects of learning disabilities* (Vol. 1, pp. 361–80). Hillsdale, NJ: Erlbaum.

Bry, B. H., McKeon, P., & Pandina, R. J. (1982). The extent of drug use as a function of number of risk factors. *J. Abnorm. Psychol., 91*(4), 273–79.

Buber, M. (1957). Distance and relation. *Psychiatry, 20,* 97–104.

Bucher, B., & Lovaas, O. I. (1967). Use of aversive stimulation in behavior modification. In M. R. Jones (Ed.), *Miami symposium on the prediction of behavior 1967: Aversive stimulation* (pp. 77–145). Coral Gables, FL: University of Miami Press.

Buchsbaum, M. S., Murphy, D. L., Coursey, R. D., Lake, C. R., & Zeigler, M. G. (1978). Platelet monoamine oxidase, plasma dopamine betahydroxylase and attention in a "biochemical high-risk" sample. In L. C. Wynne, R. L. Cromwell, & S. Matthysse (Eds.), *The nature of schizophrenia: New approaches to research and treatment* (pp. 387–96). New York: Wiley.

Buckley, P. (1982). Identifying schizophrenic patients who should not receive medication. *Schizo. Bull., 8,* 429–32.

Buckner, H. T. (1970). The transvestic career path. *Psychiatry, 3*(3), 381–89.

Budoff, M. (1977). The mentally retarded child in the mainstream of the public school: His relation to the school administration, his teachers, and his age-mates. In P. Mittler (Ed.), *Research to practice in mental retardation* (Vol. 2, pp. 307–13). Baltimore: University Park Press.

Bullard, D. M., Glaser, H. H., Heagarty, M. C., & Pivcheck, E. C. (1967). Failure to thrive in the neglected child. *Amer. J. Orthopsychiat., 37,* 680–90.

Bumbalo, J. H., & Young, D. E. (1973). The self-help phenomenon. *Amer. J. Nurs., 73,* 1588–91.

Burgess, A. W., & Holmstrom, L. (1974). Rape trauma syndrome. *Amer. J. Psychiat., 131,* 981–86.

Burgess, A. W., & Holmstrom, L. (1976). Coping behavior of the rape victim. *Amer. J. Psychiat., 133,* 413–18.

Burns, G. W. (1972). *The science of genetics.* New York: Macmillan.

Burnstein, M. H. (1981). Child abandonment: Historical, sociological, and psychological perspectives. *Child Psychiatry and Human Development, 11,* 213–21.

Burros, W. M. (1974). The growing burden of impotence. *Fam. Hlth., 6*(5), 18–21.

Burstein, A. (1985). How common is delayed posttraumatic stress disorder? *Amer. J. Psychiat., 142*(7), 887.

Buss, A., & Plomin, R. (1975). *A temperament theory of personality development.* New York: Wiley.

Buss, A. H. (1966). *Psychopathology.* New York: Wiley.

Butcher, J. N. (1979). Use of the MMPI in industry. In J. N. Butcher (Ed.), *New developments in the use of the MMPI.* Minneapolis: University of Minnesota Press.

Butcher, J. N. (1980, Nov.). The role of crisis intervention in an airport disaster plan. *Aviation, Space and Environmental Medicine,* 1260–62.

Butcher, J. N. (1984). Current developments in MMPI use: An international perspective. In J. N. Butcher & C. D. Spielberger (Eds.), *Advances in personality assessment* (Vol. 4). Hillsdale, NJ: Lawrence Erlbaum Press.

Butcher, J. N., Dahlstrom, W. G., Graham, J. R., Tellegen, A., & Kaemmer, B. (1989). *Minnesota Multiphasic Personality Inventory: MMPI-2: Manual for administration and scoring.* Minneapolis: University of Minnesota Press.

Butcher, J. N., & Dunn, L. (1989). Human responses and treatment needs in airline disasters. In R. Gist and B. Lubin (Eds.), *Psychosocial aspects of disaster.* New York: John Wiley & Sons.

Butcher, J. N., & Graham, J. R. (Eds.), (1989). *Topics in MMPI-2 interpretation.* Minneapolis: MMPI-2 Workshops and Symposia.

Butcher, J. N., & Hatcher, C. (1988). The neglected entity in air disaster planning: Psychological services. *Amer. Psychol., 43,* 724–29.

Butcher, J. N., & Pancheri, P. (1976). *Handbook of international MMPI research.* Minneapolis: University of Minnesota Press.

Butcher, J. N., Stelmachers, Z., & Maudal, G. R. (1983). Crisis intervention and emergency psychotherapy. In I. Weiner (Ed.), *Handbook of clinical methods* (2nd ed.). New York: Wiley.

Byassee, J. E. (1977). Essential hypertension. In R. B. Williams, Jr. & W. D. Gentry (Eds.), *Behavioral approaches to Medical treatment* (pp. 113–37). Cambridge, MA: Ballinger.

Bychowski, G. (1950). On neurotic obesity. *Psychoanalytic Review, 37,* 301–19.

Cade, J. F. J. (1949). Lithium salts in the treatment of psychotic excitement. *Medical Journal of Australia, 36* (part II): 349–52.

Cadoret, R. J., O'Gorman, T. W., Troughton, E., & Heywood, E. (1985). Alcoholism and antisocial personality: Interrelationships and environmental factors. *Arch. Gen. Psychiat., 42,* 161–67.

Cameron, N. (1959). Paranoid conditions and paranoia. In S. Arieti (Ed.), *American handbook of psychiatry.* New York: Basic Books.

Cameron, N., & Margaret, A. (1949). Experimental studies in thinking. I. Scattered speech in the responses of normal subjects to incomplete sentences. *J. Exper. Psychol., 39*(5), 617–27.

Cameron, N., & Margaret, A. (1951). *Behavior pathology.* Boston: Houghton Mifflin.

Campbell, D. (1926). *Arabian medicine and its influence on the Middle Ages.* New York: Dutton.

Campbell, S.B., Cohn, J.F., Ross, S., Elmore, M., & Popper, S. (April, 1990). *Postpartum adaptation and postpartum depression in primiparous women.* International Conference of Infant Studies, Montreal.

Campbell, S. B., & Wherry, J.S. (1986). Attention deficit disorder (hyperactivity). In H. C. Quay (Ed.), *Psychological disorders of childhood* (3rd ed., p. 111–55). New York: Wiley.

Cannon, T. D., Mednick, S. A., & Parnas, J. (1989). Genetic and perinatal determinants of structural brain deficits in schizophrenia. *Arch. Gen. Psychiat., 46,* 883–89.

Cannon, W. B. (1929). *Bodily changes in pain, hunger, fear and rage.* New York: Appleton.

Caputo, D. V., & Mandell, W. (1970). Consequences of low birth weight. *Develop. Psychol., 3*(3), 363–83.

Carlson, G., & Goodwin, F. K. (1973). The stages of mania: A longitudinal analysis of the manic episode. *Arch. Gen. Psychiat., 28*(2), 221–28.

Carlsson, A. (1986). Searching for antemortem markers premature. *Neurobiology of Aging, 7,* 400–401.

Carlsson, A. (1988). The current status of the dopamine hypothesis of schizophrenia. *Neuropsychopharmacology, 1,* 179–86.

Carothers, J. C. (1947). A study of mental derangement in Africans, and an attempt to explain its peculiarities more especially in relation to the African attitude of life. *J. Ment. Sci., 93,* 548–97.

Carothers, J. C. (1951). Frontal lobe function and the African. *J. Ment. Sci., 97,* 12–48.

Carothers, J. C. (1953). The African mind in health and disease. In *A study of ethnopsychiatry.* Geneva: World Health Organization, No. 17.

Carothers, J. C. (1959). Culture, psychiatry, and the written word. *Psychiatry, 22,* 307–20.

Carpenter, W. T., & Keith, S. J. (1986). Integrative treatments in schizophrenia. *Psychiat. Clin. N. Amer., 9,* 153–64.

Carpenter, W. T., & Strauss, J. S. (1979). Diagnostic issues in schizophrenia. In L. Bellak (Ed.), *Disorders of the schizophrenic syndrome.* New York: Basic Books.

Carr, A. T. (1971). Compulsive neurosis: Two psychophysiological studies. *Bulletin of the British Psychological Society, 24,* 256–57.

Carroll, B. J. (1982). The dexamethasone suppression test for melancholia. *Brit. J. Psychiat. 140,* 292–304.

Carruthers, M., (1980). Hazardous occupations and the heart. In C. L. Cooper & R. Payne (Eds.), *Current concerns in occupational stress.* New York: Wiley.

Carson, R. C. (1969). *Interaction concepts of personality.* Chicago: Aldine.

Carson, R. C. (1979). Personality and exchange in developing relationships. In R. L. Burgess & T. L. Huston (Eds.), *Social exchange in developing relationships.* New York: Academic Press.

Carson, R. C. (1982). Self-fulfilling prophecy, maladaptive behavior, and psychotherapy. In J. C. Anchin & D. J. Kiesler

(Eds.), *Handbook of interpersonal psychotherapy* (pp. 64–77). New York: Pergamon.

Carson, R. C. (1983). The social-interactional viewpoint. In M. Hersen, A. E. Kazdin, & A. S. Bellack (Eds.), *The clinical psychology handbook* (pp. 143–54). New York: Pergamon.

Carson, R. C. (1984). The schizophrenias. In H. E. Adams & P. B. Sutker (Eds.), *Comprehensive handbook of psychopathology.* New York: Plenum.

Carson, R. C. (1989). Personality. *Annu. Rev. Psychol.* (Vol. 40, pp. 227–48). Palo Alto, CA: Annual Reviews.

Carson, R. C. (1990a). Needed: A new beginning. *Contemp. Psychol., 35,* 11–12.

Carson, R. C. (1990b). Assessment: What role the assessor? *J. Pers. Assess., 54,* 435–45.

Carson, R. C. (1991). Discussion: Dilemmas in the pathway of DSM-IV. *J. Abnorm. Psychol., 100.*

Carson, R. C. (in press-a). The social-interactional viewpoint. In M. Hersen, A. E. Kazdin, & A. S. Bellack (Eds.), *The clinical psychology handbook* (2nd ed.). Elmsford, NY: Pergamon.

Carson, R. C. (in press-b). Discussion: Tunnel vision and schizophrenia. In W. Flack, D. R. Miller, & M. Wiener (Eds.), *What is schizophrenia?* New York: Springer-Verlag.

Carson, R. C., & Sanislow, C. A., III. (1992). The schizophrenias. In H. E. Adams & P. B. Sutker (Eds.), *Comprehensive handbook of psychopathology* (2nd ed.). New York: Plenum.

Carson, T. P., & Adams, H. E. (1981). Affective disorders: Behavioral perspectives. In S. M. Turner, K. S. Calhoun, & H. E. Adams (Eds.), *Handbook of clinical behavior therapy.* New York: Wiley.

Carson, T. P., & Carson, R. C. (1984). The affective disorders. In H. E. Adams & P. B. Sutker (Eds.), *Comprehensive handbook of psychopathology.* New York: Plenum.

Casey, R. J., & Berman, J. S. (1985). The outcome of psychotherapy with children. *Psychol. Bull., 98,* 388–400.

Cashdan, S. (1988). *Object relations therapy:* Using the relationship. New York: Norton.

Castiglioni, A. (1946). *Adventures of the mind.* New York: Knopf.

Cato, C., & Rice, B. D. (1982). *Report from the study group on rehabilitation of clients with specific learning disabilities.* St. Louis: National Institute of Handicapped Research.

Cautela, J. R. (1967). Covert sensitization. *Psychol. Rep., 20,* 459–68.

Cavillin, H. (1966). Incestuous fathers: A clinical report. *Amer. J. Psychiat., 122*(10), 1132–38.

Ceci, S. J., & Baker, J. C. (1987). How shall we conceptualize the language problems of learning-disabled children?, In S. J. Ceci (Ed.), *Handbook of cognitive, social, and neuropsychological aspects of learning disabilities* (Vol. 2, pp. 103–14). Hillsdale, NJ: Erlbaum.

Celentano, D. D., & McQueen, D. V. (1978). Comparison of alcoholism prevalence rates obtained by survey and indirect estimators. *J. Stud. Alcoh., 39,* 420–34.

Centerwall, W. R., & Centerwall, S. A. (1961). Phenylketonuria (Folling's disease): The story of its discovery. *Journal of the History of Medicine, 16,* 292–96.

Chambers, R. E. (1952). Discussion of "Survival factors . . ." *Amer. J. Psychiat., 109,* 247–48.

Chance, P. (1986, Oct.). Life after head injury. *Psych. Today, 20,* 62–69.

Chandler, H. N. (1985). The kids-in-between: Some solutions. *J. Learn. Dis. 18,* 368.

Charney, F. L. (1979). Inpatient treatment programs. In W. H. Reid (Ed.), *The psychopath: A comprehensive study of antisocial disorders and behaviors.* New York: Brunner/Mazel.

Chase, T., The Troops for (1990). *When rabbit howls.* New York: Jove.

Chesno, F. A., & Kilmann, P. R. (1975). Effects of stimulation on sociopathic avoidance learning. *J. Abnorm. Psychol., 84*(2), 144–50.

Chess, S., & Thomas, A. (1984). *Origins and evolution of behavior disorders: From infancy to early adult life.* New York: Brunner/Mazel.

Chess, S., Thomas, A., & Birch, H. G. (1965). *Your child is a person.* New York: Viking.

Chesser, E. (1971). *Strange loves: The human aspects of sexual deviation.* New York: William Morrow.

Cheung, F. M., & Song, W. Z. (1989). A review on the clinical applications of the Chinese MMPI. *Psychological Assessment: A Journal of Consulting and Clinical Psychology, 1,* 230–38.

Christensen, A., Johnson, S., Phillips, S., & Glasgow, R.

(1980). Cost effectiveness in behavioral family therapy. *Behav. Ther., 11*, 208–26.

Christensen, D., & Rosenthal, R. (1982). Gender and nonverbal decoding skill as determinants of interpersonal expectancy effects. *J. Pers. Soc. Psychol., 42*, 75–87.

Christenson, R. M., Walker, J. I., Ross, D. R., & Maultbie, A. A. (1981). Reactivation of traumatic conflicts. *Amer. J. Psychiat., 138*, 984–85.

Christie, B. L. (1981). Childhood enuresis: Current thoughts on causes and cures. *Social Work Health Care, 6*(3), 77–90.

Claeson, L. E., & Malm, U. (1973). Electro-aversion therapy of chronic alcoholism. *Behav. Res. Ther., 11*(4), 663–65.

Clancy, H., & McBride, G. (1969). The autistic process and its treatment. *J. Child Psychol. Psychiat., 10*(4), 233–44.

Clark, C. R. (1987). Specific intent and diminished capacity. In A. Hess and I. Weiner (Eds.), *Handbook of forensic psychology.* New York: John Wiley & Sons.

Clark, D. A., Beck, A. T., & Stewart, B. (1990). Cognitive specificity and positive-negative affectivity: Complementary or contradictory views on anxiety and depression. *J. Abnorm. Psychol., 99*, 148–55.

Clark, G. R., Kivitz, M. S., & Rosen, N. (1969). Program for mentally retarded. *Sci. News, 96*, 82.

Clark, L. A. (1987). The mutual relevance of mainstream and cross-cultural psychology. *J. Cons. Clin. Psychol., 55*, 461–70.

Clarke, A. M., Clarke, A. D. B., & Berg, J. M. (Eds.). (1985). *Mental deficiency: The changing outlook,* (4th ed.). London: Methuen & Co.

Clarke, D. J., Littlejohns, C. S., Corbett, J. A., & Joseph, S. (1989). Pervasive developmental disorders and psychoses in adult life. *Brit. J. Psychiat., 155*, 692–99.

Clarke, R. V. G. (1985). Jack Tizard Memorial Lecture: Delinquency, environment and intervention. *J. Child Psychol. Psychiat., 26*(4), 505–23.

Clayton, P. J. (1982). Bereavement. In E. S. Paykel (Ed.), *Handbook of affective disorders.* New York: Guilford Press.

Clement, P. (1970). Elimination of sleepwalking in a seven-year-old boy. *J. Cons. Clin. Psychol., 34*(1), 22–26.

Cloninger, C. R. (1987). A systematic method for clinical description and classification of personality invariants. *Arch. Gen. Psychiat., 44*, 161–67.

Cloninger, C. R., & Guze, S. (1970). Psychiatric illness and female criminality: The role of sociopathy and hysteria in the antisocial woman. *Amer. J. Psychiat., 127*(3), 303–11.

Cloninger, C. R., Reich, T., Sigvardsson, S., von Knorring, A. L., & Bohman, M. (1986). The effects of changes in alcohol use between generations on the inheritance of alcohol abuse. In *Alcoholism: A medical disorder.* Proceedings of the 76th Annual Meeting of the American Psychopathological Association.

Coates, T. J., Perry, C., Killen, J., & Slinkard, L. A. (1981). Primary prevention of cardiovascular disease in children and adolescents. In C. K. Prokop & L. A. Bradley (Eds.), *Medical psychology: Contributions to behavioral medicine.* New York: Academic Press.

Cochran, S. D., & Hammen, C. L. (1985). Perceptions of stressful life events and depression: A test of attributional models. *J. Pers. Soc. Psychol. 48*, 1562–71.

Cockayne, T. O. (1864–1866). *Leechdoms, wort cunning, and star craft of early England.* London: Longman, Green, Longman, Roberts & Green.

Cockerham, W. (1981). *Sociology of mental disorder.* Englewood Cliffs, NJ: Prentice-Hall.

Cohen, D., & Eisdorfer, C. (1988). Depression in family members caring for a relative with Alzheimer's disease. *J. Amer. Geriat. Soc., 36*, 885–89.

Cohen, D. B. (1974). On the etiology of neurosis. *J. Abnorm. Psychol., 83*, 473–79.

Cohen, J., & Hansel, M. (1956). *Risk and gambling: A study of subjective probability.* New York: Philosophical Library.

Cohen, S. L., & Fiedler, J. E. (1974). Content analysis of multiple messages in suicide notes. *Life-Threatening Behavior, 4*(2), 75–95.

Cohen, S. M., Allen, M. G., Pollin, W., & Hrubec, Z. (1972). Relationship of schizo-affective psychosis to manic depressive psychosis and schizophrenia. *Arch. Gen. Psychiat., 26*(6), 539–46.

Cohn, J. F., & Campbell, S. B. (in press). Influence of maternal depression on infant affect regulation. In D. Cicchetti & S. Toth (Eds.), *Rochester Symposium on Developmental Psychopathology: Vol. 4. A developmental approach to affective disorders.*

Cohn, J.F., & Tronick, E.Z. (1983). Three months infant's reaction to simulated maternal depression. *Child Develop. 54*, 185–93.

Cohn, J.F., & Tronick, E.Z. (1987). Mother-infant interaction: The sequence of dyadic states at 3, 6, and 9 months. *Develop. Psychol., 23*, 68–77.

Coie, J. D. (1990). Toward a theory of peer rejection. In S. R. Asher & J. D. Coie (Eds.), *Peer rejection in childhood* (pp. 365–402). New York: Cambridge University Press.

Coie, J. D., & Dodge, K. A. (1983). Continuity and changes in children's sociometric status: A five-year longitudinal study. *Merrill-Palmer Quarterly, 29*, 261–82.

Coie, J. D., & Kupersmidt, J. B. (1983). A behavioral analysis of emerging social status in boys' groups. *Child Develop., 54*, 1400–16.

Cole, D. A. (1989). Psychopathology of adolescent suicide: Hopelessness, coping beliefs, and depression. *J. Abnorm. Psychol., 98*, 248–55.

Cole, J. O., & Bodkin, J. A. (1990). Antidepressant drug side effects. *J. Clin. Psychiat., 51*, 21–26.

Cole, S. O. (1975). Hyperkinetic children: The use of stimulant drugs evaluated. *Amer. J. Orthopsychiat., 45*(1), 28–37.

Comfort, A. (1984). Alzheimer's disease or Alzheimerism? *Psychiatric Annals, 14*, 130–32.

Conquest, R. (1986). *The harvest of sorrow: Soviet collectivization and the terror-famine.* New York: Oxford University Press.

Conte, H. R., Plutchik, R., Wild, K. V., & Karasu, T. B. (1986). Combined psychotherapy and pharmacotherapy for depression: A systematic analysis of the evidence. *Arch. Gen. Psychiat., 43*, 471–79.

Conte, J., Berliner, L., & Schuerman, J. (1986). *The impact of sexual abuse on children* (Final Report No. MH 37133). Rockville, MD: National Institute of Mental Health.

Cook, E. W., III, Hodes, R. L., & Lang, P. J. (1986). Preparedness and phobia: Effects of stimulus content on human visceral conditioning. *J. Abnorm. Psychol., 95*, 195–207.

Cookerly, J. R. (1980). Does marital therapy do any lasting good? *Journal of Marital and Family Therapy, 6*(4), 393–97.

Coombs, R. H., Paulson, M. J., & Palley, R. (1988). The institutionalization of drug use in America: Hazardous adolescence, challenging parenthood. *J. Chem. Depen. Treat., 1*(2), 9–37.

Cooper, A. J. (1969). A clinical study of "coital anxiety" in male potency disorders. *J. Psychosom. Res., 13*(2), 143–47.

Cooper, J. E., Kendell, R. E., Gurland, B. J., Sharpe, L., Copeland, J. R. M., & Simon, R. (1972). *Psychiatric diagnosis in New York and London.* London: Oxford University Press.

Coopersmith, S. (1967). *The antecedents of self-esteem.* San Francisco: Freeman.

Coovert, D. L., Kinder, B. N., & Thompson, J. K. (1989). The psychosexual aspects of anorexia nervosa and bulimia: A review of the literature. *Clin. Psychol. Rev., 9*, 169–80.

Copeland, J. (1968). Aspects of mental illness in West African students. *Soc. Psychiat., 3*(1), 7–13.

Coppen, A., Metcalfe, M., & Wood, K. (1982). Lithium. In E. S. Paykel (Ed.), *Handbook of affective disorders.* New York: Guilford Press.

Coryell, W., Keller, M., Lavori, P., & Endicott, J. (1990a). Affective syndromes, psychotic features, and prognosis: I. Depression. *Arch. Gen. Psychiat., 47*, 651–57.

Coryell, W., Keller, M., Lavori, P., & Endicott, J. (1990b). Affective syndromes, psychotic features, and prognosis: II. Mania. *Arch. Gen. Psychiat., 47*, 658–62.

Coryell, W., & Winokur, G. (1982). Course and outcome. In E. S. Paykel (Ed.), *Handbook of affective disorders.* New York: Guilford Press.

Cosby, B. (1986). *Fatherhood.* Garden City, NY: Doubleday.

Costa, P. T., Jr., Whitfield, J. R., & Stewart, D. (Eds.). (1989). *Alzheimer's disease: Abstracts of the psychological and behavioral literature.* Washington, DC: American Psychological Association.

Costello, C. G. (1980). Childhood depression: Three basic but questionable assumptions in the Lefkowitz and Burton critique. *Psychol. Bull. 87*, 187–90.

Cotler, S. B. (1971). The use of different behavioral techniques in treating a case of compulsive gambling. *Behav. Ther., 2*, 579–81.

Cotton, N. S. (1979). The familiar incidence of alcoholism. *J. Stud. Alcoh., 40*, 89–116.

Courtois, C., & Sprei, J. (1988). Retrospective incest therapy for women. In L.E.A. Walker (Ed.), *Handbook on sexual abuse of children* (pp 270–308). New York: Springer.

Covi, L., Lipman, R. S., Derogatis, L. R., Smith, J. E., III, & Pattison, J. H. (1974). Drugs and group psychotherapy in neurotic depression. *Amer. J. Psychiat., 13*(2), 191–97.

Cowdry, R. W., & Gardner, D. L. (1988). Pharmacotherapy of borderline personality disorder. *Arch. Gen. Psychiat., 45,* 111–19.

Cox, D. J., Freundlich, A., & Meyer, R. G. (1975). Differential effectiveness of electromyographic feedback, verbal relaxation instructions, and medication placebo with tension headaches. *J. Cons. Clin. Psychol., 43,* 892–98.

Cox, W. M., & Klinger, E. (1988). A motivational model of alcohol use. *J. Abnorm. Psychol., 97,* 168–80.

Coyle, J. T., Price, D. L., & DeLong, M. R. (1983). Alzheimer's disease: A disorder of cortical cholinergic innervation. *Science, 219,* 1184–90.

Coyne, J. C. (1976). Depression and the response of others. *J. Abnorm. Psychol., 55*(2), 186–93.

Crapper McLachlan, D. R. (1986). Aluminum and Alzheimer's disease. *Neurobiology of Aging, 7,* 525–32.

Cravioto, J., & de Licardie, E. R. (1975). Environmental and nutritional deprivation in children with learning disabilities. In W. M. Cruickshank & D. P. Hallahan (Eds.), *Perceptual and learning disabilities in children: Vol. 2. Research and theory.* Syracuse, NY: Syracuse University Press.

Creasy, M. R., & Crolla, J. A. (1974, Mar. 23). Prenatal mortality of trisomy 21 (Down's syndrome). *Lancet, 1*(7856), 473–74.

Crisp, A. H., Douglas, J. W. B., Ross, J. M., & Stonehill, E. (1970). Some developmental aspects of disorders of weight. *J. Psychosom. Res., 14,* 313–20.

Crittenden, P. M. (1985). Maltreated infants: Vulnerability and resilience. *J. Child Psychol. Psychiat., 26,* 85–96.

Crockett, D., Clark, C., & Klonoff, H. (1987). Introduction—an overview of neuropsychology. In S. B. Filskov & T. J. Boll (Eds.), *Handbook of clinical neuropsychology.* New York: Wiley.

Crook, T., & Eliot, J. (1980). Parental death during childhood and adult depression: A critical review of the literature. *Psychol. Bull., 87,* 252–59.

Culliton, B. J. (1970, Jan. 24). Pot facing stringent scientific examination. *Sci. News, 97*(4), 102–5.

Culliton, B. J. (1976). Psychosurgery: National Commission issues surprisingly favorable report. *Science, 194,* 299–301.

Cummings, C., Gordon, J. R., & Marlatt, G. A. (1980). Relapse: Prevention and prediction. In W. R. Miller (Ed.), *The addictive behaviors.* New York: Pergamon Press.

Curlee, J. (1969). Alcoholism and the "empty nest." *Bull. Menninger Clin., 33*(3), 165–71.

Custer, R. L. (1982). An overview of compulsive gambling. In P. A. Carone, S. F. Yolies, S. N. Kieffer, & L. W. Krinsky (Eds.), *Addictive disorders update.* New York: Human Sciences.

Dahlstrom, W. G., Lachar, D., & Dahlstrom, L. E. (1986). *MMPI patterns of American minorities.* Minneapolis: University of Minnesota Press.

Dain, N. (1964). *Concepts of insanity in the United States: 1789–1865.* New Brunswick, NJ: Rutgers University Press.

Daniel, W. F., & Crovitz, H. F. (1983a). Acute memory impairment following electroconvulsive therapy: 1. Effects of electrical stimulus and number of treatments. *Acta Psychiatr. Scandin., 67,* 1–7.

Daniel, W. F., & Crovitz, H. F. (1983b). Acute memory impairment following electroconvulsive therapy: 2. Effects of electrode placement. *Acta Psychiatr. Scandin., 67,* 57–68.

Danto, B. L. (1990). Stress experienced by robbery victims, hostages, kidnapping victims, and prisoners of war. In J.D. Noshpitz & R. D. Coddington (Eds.), *Stressors and the adjustment disorders.* New York: Wiley Intersciences.

Darbonne, A. R. (1969). Suicide and age: A suicide note analysis. *J. Cons. Clin. Psychol., 33,* 46–50.

Darke, J. L. (1990). Sexual aggression: Achieving power through humiliation. In W. L. Marshall, D. R. Laws, & H. E. Barbaree (Eds.), *Handbook of sexual assault* (pp. 55–72). New York: Plenum.

Davidson, A. D. (1979a, Spring). Coping with stress reactions in rescue workers: A program that worked. *Police Stress.*

Davidson, A. D. (1979b). Personal communication.

Davidson, L. M., & Baum, A. (1986). Chronic stress and posttraumatic stress disorders. *J. Cons. Clin. Psychol., 54,* 303–8.

Davidson, W.S. (1974). Studies of aversive conditioning for alcoholics: A critical review of theory and research methodology. *Psychol. Bull., 81*(9), 571–81.

Davies, P. (1986). The genetics of Alzheimer's disease: A review and discussion of the implications. *Neurobiology of Aging, 7,* 459–66.

Davis, J. M. (1978). Dopamine theory of schizophrenia: A two-factor theory. In L. C. Wynne, R. L. Cromwell, & S. Matthysse (Eds.), *The nature of schizophrenia: New approaches to research and treatment* (pp. 105–15). New York: Wiley.

Davis, V. J., Cullari, S., & Breuning, S. E. (1982). Drug use in community foster homes. In S. E. Breuning & A. D. Poling (Eds.), *Drugs and mental retardation.* Springfield, IL: Thomas.

Davison, G. C. (1976). Homosexuality: The ethical challenge. *J. Cons. Clin. Psychol., 44*(2), 157–62.

Davison, G. C. (1978). Not can but ought: The treatment of homosexuality. *J. Cons. Clin. Psychol., 46*(1), 170–2.

Day, G. (1951, May 12). The psychosomatic approach to pulmonary tuberculosis. *Lancet, 6663.*

de Pauw, K. W., & Szulecka, T. K. (1988). Dangerous delusions: Violence and misidentification syndromes. *Brit. J. Psychiat., 152,* 91–96.

De Young, M. (1982). Innocent seducer and innocently seduced? The role of the child incest victim. *J. Clin. Child Psychol., 11,* 56–60.

DeFazio, V. J., Rustin, S., & Diamond, A. (1975). Symptom development in Vietnam era veterans. *Amer. J. Orthopsychiat., 45*(1), 158–63.

DeFrancis, V. (1969). *Protecting the child victim of sex crimes committed by adults.* Denver: Children's Division, American Humane Association.

DeLisi, L. E., Crow, T. J., & Hirsch, S. R. (1986). The third biannual winter workshops on schizophrenia. *Arch. Gen. Psychiat. 43,* 706–11.

DeLisi, L. E., Goldin, L. R., Hamovit, J. R., Maxwell, E., & Kuritz, D. (1986). A family study of the association of increased ventricular size with schizophrenia. *Arch. Gen. Psychiat., 43,* 148–53.

DeLisi, L. E., Mirsky, A.F., Buchsbaum, M.S., van Kammen, D.P., Berman, K.F., Phelps, B. H., Karoum, F., Ko, G. N., Korpi, E. R., et al. (1984). The Genain quadruplets 25 years later: A diagnostic and biochemical followup. *Psychiat. Res., 13,* 59–76.

DeMarsh, J., & Kumpfer, K. L. (1985). Family-oriented interventions for the prevention of chemical dependency in children and adolescents. Special Issue: Childhood and Chemical Abuse: Prevention and Intervention. *Journal of Children in Contemporary Society, 18*(1–2), 117–51.

Denicola, J., & Sandler, J. (1980). Training abusive parents in child management and self-control skills. *Behav. Ther., 11,* 263–70.

Dennes, B. (1974). Returning madness to an accepting community. *Comm. Ment. Hlth. J., 10*(2), 163–72.

Department of Labor. (1991, Feb.). *Employment and earnings.* Bureau of Labor Statistics. U.S. Government Printing Office.

Depue, R. A., & Monroe, S. M. (1978). The unipolar-bipolar distinction in the depressive disorders. *Psychol. Bull., 85,* 1001–29.

Depue, R. A., & Monroe, S. M. (1986). Conceptualization and measurement of human disorder in life stress research: The problem of chronic disturbance. *Psychol. Bull., 99*(1), 36–51.

Depue, R. A., Slater, J. F., Wolfstetter-Kausch, H., Klein, D., Goplerud, E., & Farr, D. (1981). A behavioral paradigm for identifying persons at risk for bipolar disorder: A conceptual framework. *J. Abnorm. Psychol., 90,* 381–437.

DeRubeis, R. J. (1983, Dec.). *The cognitive-pharmacotherapy project: Study design, outcome, and clinical followup.* Paper presented at American Association of Behavior Therapy. Washington, DC.

Detels, R., English, P., Visscher, B., Kigsley, L., Chmiel, J., Dudley, J., Eldred, L. J., & Ginzburg, H. (1988, June). *Sexual activity, condom use, and HIV-1 seroconversion.* Paper presented at the Fourth International Conference on AIDS, Stockholm, Sweden.

Detera-Wadleigh, S. D., Berrettini, W. H., Goldin, L. R., Boorman, D., Anderson, S., & Gershon, E. S. (1987) Close linkage of c-harvey-ras-1 and the insulin gene to affective disorders is ruled out in three North American pedigrees. *Nature, 325,* 806–9.

Deur, J. I., & Parke, R. D. (1970). Effects of inconsistent punishment on aggression in children. *Develop. Psychol., 2,* 403–11.

DeWolfe, A. S., Ryan, J. J., & Wolf, M. E. (1988). Cognitive sequelae of tardive dyskinesia. *J. Nerv. Ment. Dis., 176,* 270–74.

Diamond, M. C. (1988). *Enriching heredity: The impact of the environment on the anatomy of the brain.* New York: Free Press.

Diamond, M. J. (1974). Modification of hypnotizability: A review: Psychol. Bull., 81(3), 180–98.

Dietz, P. E. (1977). Social discrediting of psychiatry: The protasis of legal disfranchisement. Amer. J. Psychiat., 134, 1356–60.

Diller, L., & Gordon, W. A. (1981). Interventions for cognitive deficits in brain-injured adults. J. Cons. Clin. Psychol., 49, 822–34.

Dinitz, S., & Conrad, J. P. (1980). The dangerous two percent. In D. Shichor & D. H. Kelly (Eds.), Critical issues in juvenile delinquency. Lexington, MA: Lexington Books.

Dixen, J., & Jenkins, J. O. (1981). Incestuous child sexual abuse: A review of treatment strategies. Clin. Psychol. Rev., 1, 211–22.

Doane, J. A., Falloon, I. R. H., Goldstein, M. J., & Mintz, J. (1985). Parental affective style and the treatment of schizophrenia: Predicting course of illness and social functioning. Arch. Gen. Psychiat., 42, 34–42.

Doane, J., West, K., Goldstein, M. J., Rodnick, E., & Jones, J. (1981). Parental communication deviance and affective style as predictors of subsequent schizophrenia spectrum disorders in vulnerable adolescents. Arch. Gen. Psychiat., 38, 679–85.

Dobrokhotova, T. A. (1968). On the pathology of the emotional sphere in tumorous lesion of the frontal lobes of the brain. Zhurnal Neuropatologii i Psikhiartrii, 68(3), 418–22.

Dobson, K. S. (1989). A meta-analysis of the efficacy of cognitive therapy for depression. J. Cons. Clin. Psychol., 57, 414–19.

Dodd, B., & Leahy, J. (1989). Facial prejudice. Amer. J. Ment. Retard., 94, 111.

Dodge, K. A. (1980). Social cognition and children's aggressive behavior. Child Develop., 51, 162–70.

Dodge, K. A. (1983). Behavioral antecedents of peer social status. Child Develop., 54, 1386–99.

Dodge, K. A., Coie, J. D., & Brakke, N. P. (1982). Behavioral patterns of socially rejected and neglected preadolescents: The roles of social approach and aggression. J. Abnorm. Child. Psychol. 10, 389–410.

Dodge, K. A., & Feldman, E. (1990). Issues in social cognition and sociometric status. In S. R. Asher & J. D. Coie (Eds.), Peer rejection in childhood, (pp. 119–55). New York: Cambridge University Press.

Dodge, K. A., & Frame, C. L. (1982). Social cognition biases and deficits in aggressive boys. Child Develop., 53, 620–35.

Dodge, K. A., Murphy, R. R., & Buchsbaum, K. (1984). The assessment of intention-cue detection skills in children: Implications for developmental psychopathology. Child Develop., 55, 163–73.

Dodge, K. A., Newman, J. P. (1981). Biased decision-making processes in aggressive boys. J. Abnorm. Psychol., 90, 375–79.

Dohrenwend, B. P., & Dohrenwend, B. S. (1982). Perspectives on the past and future of psychiatric epidemiology: The 1981 Rena Lapouse Lecture. Amer. J. Pub. Hlth., 72(1), 1271–79.

Dohrenwend, B. P., Dohrenwend, B. S., Gould, M. S., Link, B., Neugebauer, R., & Wunsch-Hitzig, R. (1980). Mental illness in the United States: Epidemiological estimates. New York: Praeger.

Dohrenwend, B. P., & Egri, G. (1981). Recent stressful life events and episodes of schizophrenia. Schizo. Bull., 7, 12–23.

Dole, V. P., & Nyswander, M. (1967). The miracle of methadone in the narcotics jungle. Roche Report, 4(11), 1–2, 8, 11.

Dole, V. P., Nyswander, M., & Warner, A. (1968). Successful treatment of 750 criminal addicts. JAMA, 206, 2709–11.

Doleys, D. M. (1979). Assessment and treatment of childhood enuresis. In R. J. Finch & P. C. Kendall (Eds.), Clinical treatment and research in child psychopathology. New York: Spectrum Publications.

Dollard, J., & Miller, N. E. (1950). Personality and psychotherapy. New York: McGraw-Hill.

Donaldson, M. A., & Gardner, R. Jr., (1985). Diagnosis and treatment of traumatic stress among women after childhood incest. In C. R. Filley (Ed.), Trauma and its wake: The study and treatment of post-traumatic stress disorder (pp. 356–77). Newbury Park, CA: Sage.

Donne, J. (1624). Meditation XVII. Devotions upon emergent occasions. London.

Dooley, D., & Catalano, R. (1980). Economic change as a cause of behavioral disorder. Psychol. Bull. 87, 450–68.

Dorfman, D. D. (1978). The Cyril Burt question: New findings. Science, 201, 1177–86.

Dorwart, R. A., Schlesinger, M., Horgan, C., & Davidson, H. (1989). The privatization of mental health care and directions for mental health services research. In C. A. Taube, D.

Mechanic, & A. A. Hohmann (Eds.), The future of mental health services research (pp. 139–54). Washington, DC: U. S. Department of Health and Human Services. US Government Printing Office.

Downey, G., & Coyne, J. C. (1990). Children of depressed parents: An integrative review. Psychol. Bull., 108, 50–76.

Downing, R. W., & Rickels, K. (1974) Mixed anxiety-depression: Fact or myth? Arch. Gen. Psychiat., 30(3), 312–17.

Draguns, J. G. (1979). Culture and personality. In A. J. Marsella, R. Tharp, & T. Cibowrowski (Eds.), Perspectives in cross-cultural psychology. New York: Academic Press.

Drake, R. E., & Wallach, M. A. (1979). Will mental patients stay in the community: A social psychological perspective. J. Cons. Clin. Psychol., 42(2), 285–94.

Drug Enforcement Administration, Department of Justice. (1979). Controlled Substance Inventory List. Washington, DC.

Dumas, J.E., Gibson, J.A., & Albin, J. B. (1989). Behavioral correlates of maternal depressive symptomatology in conduct-disorder children. J. Cons. Clin. Psychol., 57, 516–21.

Dunbar, F., (1943). Psychosomatic diagnosis. New York: Harper & Row.

Dunbar, P. (1954). Emotions and bodily changes (4th ed.). New York: Columbia University Press.

Dunn, F. M., & Howell, R. J. (1982). Relaxation training and its relationship to hyperactivity in boys. J. Clin. Psychol., 38(1), 92–100.

Dunner, D. L., & Hall, K. S. (1980). Social adjustment and psychological precipitants in mania. In R. H. Belmaker & H.M. van Praag (Eds.), Mania: An evolving concept. New York: Spectrum.

Dura, J. R., & Bornstein, R. A. (1989). Differences between IQ and school achievement in anorexia nervosa. J. Clin. Psychol., 45, 433–35.

Durkheim, E. (1951). Suicide: A study in sociology (J.A. Spaulding & G. Simpson, Trans., G. Simpson, Ed.). New York: Free Press. (Originally published 1897.)

Earl, H. G. (1965). 10,000 children battered and starved: Hundreds die. Today's Health, 43(9), 24–31.

Earl, H. G. (1966). Head injury: The big killer. Today's Health, 44(12), 19–21.

Earlywine, M., & Finn, P. R. (1990, March). Personality, drinking habits, and responses to cues for alcohol. Paper presented at the 5th Congress of the International Society for Biomedical Research on Alcoholism and the Research Society on Alcoholism, Toronto, Canada.

East, W. N. (1946). Sexual offenders. J. Nerv. Ment. Dis., 103, 626–66.

Edwards, C. C. (1973). What you can do to combat high blood pressure. Fam. Hlth., 5(11), 24–26.

Egbert, L., Battit, G., Welch, C., & Bartlett, M. (1964). Reduction of postoperative pain by encouragement and instruction of patients. New Engl. J. Med., 270, 825–27.

Egeland vs. City of Minneapolis, 344 N.W. 2nd 597. (1984).

Egeland, B., & Brunnquell, D. (1979). An at-risk approach to the study of child abuse: Some preliminary findings. J. Amer. Acad. Child Psychiat., 18, 219–35.

Egeland, B., Cicchetti, D., & Taraldson, B. (1976, Apr. 26). Child abuse: A family affair. Proceedings of the N. P. Masse Research Seminar on Child Abuse, 28–52. Paper presented Paris, France.

Egeland, B., & Erickson, M. F. (1990). Rising above the past: Strategies for helping new mothers to break the cycle of abuse and neglect. Zero to Three, 11, 29–35.

Egeland, B., Erickson, M., Butcher, J. N., & Ben-Porath, Y. S. (1990). MMPI-2 profiles of women at risk for child abuse. J. Pers. Assess.

Egeland, B., & Farber, E.A. (1984). Infant-mother attachment: Factors related to its development and change over time. Child Develop., 55, 753–71.

Egeland, B., Jacobvitz, D., & Papatola, K. (1987). Intergenerational continuity of abuse. In R. Gelles & J. Lancaster (Eds.), Child abuse and neglect: Biosocial aspects (pp. 255–76). New York: Aldine de Gruyter.

Egeland, J. A., Gerhard, D. S., Pauls, D. L., Sussex, J. N., Kidd, K. K., Allen, C. R., Hostetter, A. M., & Housman, D. E. (1987). Bipolar affective disorders linked to DNA markers on chromosome 11. Nature, 325, 783–87.

Egendorf, A. (1986). Healing from the war. Boston: Houghton Mifflin.

Ehrhardt, A.A., & Meyer-Bahlburg, H. F. L. (1981). Effects of prenatal sex hormones on gender-related behavior. Science, 211, 1312–18.

Eisenberg, L. (1971). Principles of drug therapy in child psychiatry with special reference to stimulant drugs. *Amer. J. Orthopsychiat., 4*(3). 371–79.

Eisenberg, H. M. (1990). Behavioral changes after closed head injury in children. *J. Cons. Clin. Psychol., 58,* 93–98.

Eisler, R. M., Miller, P. M., Hersen, M., & Alford, H. (1974). Effects of assertive training on marital interaction. *Arch. Gen. Psychiat., 30*(5), 643–49.

Eitinger, L. (1964). *Concentration camp survivors in Norway and Israel.* New York: Humanities Press.

Eitinger, L. (1969). Psychosomatic problems in concentration camp survivors. *J. Psychosom. Res., 13,* 183–90.

Eitinger, L. (1973, Sept.). A follow-up study of the Norwegian concentration camp survivors: Mortality and morbidity. *Israel Annals of Psychiatry and Related Disciplines, 11,* 199–210.

Elkin, I., Shea, M. T., Watkins, J. T., Imber, S. D., Sotsky, S. M., Collins, J. F., Glass, D. R., Pilkonis, P. A., Leber, W. R., Docherty, J. P., Fiester, S. J., & Parloff, M. B. (1989). National Institute of Mental Health Treatment of Depression Collaborative Research Program: General effectiveness of treatments. *Arch. Gen. Psychiat., 46,* 971–82.

Elkind, D. (1967). Middle-class delinquency. *Mental Hygiene, 51,* 80–84.

Elkind, D., & Weiner, I. B. (1978). *Development of the child.* New York: Wiley.

Ellinwood, E. H. (1971). Assault and homicide associated with amphetamine abuse. *Amer. J. Psychiat., 127*(9), 90–95.

Elliott, D. S., Dunford, F. W., & Huizinga, D. (1987). The identification and prediction of career offenders utilizing self-reported and official data. In J. D. Burchard & S. N. Burchard (Eds.), *Prevention of delinquent behavior* (pp. 90–121). Newbury Park, CA: Sage.

Elliott, G. (1989). Stress and illness. In S. Cheren (Ed.), *Psychosomatic medicine: Theory, physiology, and practice* (Vol. 1, pp. 45–90). Madison, CT: International Universities Press.

Ellis, A. (1958). Rational psychotherapy. *J. Gen. Psychol., 59,* 35–49.

Ellis, A. (1970). *Reason and emotion in psychotherapy.* New York: Lyle Stuart.

Ellis, A. (1973). Rational-emotive therapy. In R. J. Corsini (Ed.), *Current psychotherapies.* Itasca, IL: Peacock Publishers.

Ellis, A. (1975). Creative job and happiness: The humanistic way. *The Humanist, 35*(1), 11–13.

Ellis, A. (1977). The treatment of a psychopath with rational therapy. In S. J. Morse & R. I. Watson (Eds.), *Psychotherapies: A comparative casebook.* New York: Holt, Rinehart & Winston.

Ellis, A. (1989). The history of cognition in psychotherapy. In A. Freeman, K. M. Simon, L. E. Beutler, & H. Arkowitz (Eds.), *Comprehensive handbook of cognitive therapy* (pp. 5–19). New York: Plenum.

Ellis, E. M., Atkeson, B. M., & Calhoun, K. S. (1982). An examination of differences between multiple- and single-incident victims of sexual assault. *J. Abnorm. Psychol., 91,* 221–24.

Ellison, K. (1977). Personal communication.

Emmelkamp, P. M. G. (1986). Behavior therapy with adults. In S. L. Garfield & A. E. Bergin (Eds.) *Handbook of psychotherapy and behavior change* (3rd ed., pp. 385–442). New York: Wiley.

Emmelkamp, P. M. G., & Wessels, H. (1975). Flooding in imagination vs. flooding in vivo: A comparison with agoraphobics. *Behav. Res. Ther., 13*(1), 7–15.

Endicott, J., Nee, J., Cohen, J., Fleiss, J. L., & Simon, R. (1986). Diagnosis of schizophrenia: Prediction of short-term outcome. *Arch. Gen. Psychiat., 43,* 13–19.

Endicott, N. A. (1989). Psychosocial and behavioral factors in myocardial infarction and sudden cardiac death. In S. Cheren (Ed.), *Psychosomatic Medicine: Theory, physiology, and practice* (Vol. 2, pp. 611–60). Madison, CT: International Universities Press.

Endler, N. (1990). *Holiday of darkness: A psychologist's journey out of his depression* (rev. ed.). Toronto: Wall & Thompson.

Engel, G. L. (1977). The need for a new medical model: A challenge for biomedicine. *Science, 196,* 129–36.

Engelhardt, D. M. (1974). Pharmacologic basis for use of psychotropic drugs: An overview. *New York State Journal of Medicine, 74*(2), 360–66.

Englander-Golden, P., Elconin, J., Miller, K. J., & Schwarzkopf, A. B., (1986). Brief SAY IT STRAIGHT training and follow-up in adolescent substance abuse prevention. *Journal of Primary Prevention, 6*(4), 219–30.

English, C. J. (1973). Leaving home: A typology of runaways. *Society, 10*(5), 22–24.

Epstein, H. (1979). *Children of the holocaust: Conversations with sons and daughters of survivors.* New York: Putnam.

Epstein, S., & Fenz, W. D. (1962). Theory and experiment on the measurement of approach-avoidance conflict. *J. Abnorm. Soc. Psychol., 64*(1), 97–112.

Epstein, S., & Fenz, W. D. (1965). Steepness of approach and avoidance gradients in humans as a function of experience: Theory and experiment. *J. Exper. Psychol., 70*(1), 1–12.

Erdman, H. P., Klein, M., & Greist, J. H. (1985). Direct patient computer interviewing. *J. Cons. Clin. Psychol., 53*(6), 760–73.

Erlenmeyer-Kimling, L., & Cornblatt, B. (1978). Attentional measures in a study of children at high risk for schizophrenia. In L. C. Wynne, R. L. Cromwell, & S. Matthysse (Eds.), *The nature of schizophrenia: New approaches to research and treatment* (pp. 359–65). New York: Wiley.

Ernst, A. R., Routh, D. K., & Harper, D. C. (1984). Abdominal pain in children and symptoms of somatization disorder. *J. Pediat. Psychol., 9*(1), 77–85.

Eron, L. D., Huesmann, L. R., Lefkowitz, M. M., & Walder, L. O. (1974). How Teaming conditions in early childhood—including mass media—relate to aggression in late adolescence. *Amer. J. Orthopsychiat., 44*(3), 412–23.

Eron, L. D., & Peterson, R. A. (1982). Abnormal behavior: Social approaches. In M. R. Rosenzweig & L. W. Porter (Eds.), *Annu. Rev. Psychol. 33,* 231–65.

Esler, M., Julius, S., Zweifler, A., Randall, O., Harburgh, E., Gardiner, H., & DeQuattro, V. (1977). Mild high-renin essential hypertension: Neurogenic human hypertension? *New Engl. J. Med., 296,* 405–11.

Ethics Committee, American Psychological Association. (1990). Report of the Ethics Committee: 1988. *Amer. Psychol., 45,* 873–74.

Evans, D. A., Funkerstein, H., Albert, M. S., Scherr, P. A., Cook, N. R., Chown, M. J., Hebert, L. E., Hennekens, C. H., & Taylor, J. O. (1989). Prevalence of Alzheimer's disease in a community population of older persons. *JAMA, 262,* 2551–56.

Evans, J. A., & Hamerton, J. L. (1985). Chromosomal anomalies. In A. M. Clarke, A. D. B. Clarke, & J. M. Berg (Eds.). *Mental deficiency: The changing outlook* (4th ed., pp. 213–66). London: Methuen.

Exner, J. E. (1987). Computer assistance in Rorschach interpretation. In J. N. Butcher (Ed.) *Computerized psychological assessment: A practitioner's guide.* NY: Basic Books.

Eysenck, H. J. (1952). The effects of psychotherapy: An evaluation. *Journal of Consulting Psychology, 16,* 319–24.

Eysenck, H. J. (1960). *Behaviour therapy and the neuroses.* London: Pergamon Press.

Eysenck, H. J. (1976). The learning theory model of neurosis: A new approach. *Behav. Res. Ther., 14,* 251–67.

Fabrega, H. (1981). Cultural programming of brain-behavior relationships. In J. R. Merikangas (Ed.), *Brain-behavior relationships.* Lexington, MA: D. C. Heath.

Fabrega, H. (1989). Cultural relativism and psychiatric illness. *J. Nerv. Ment. Dis., 177,* 415–24.

Fairweather, G. W. (Ed.) (1980). *The Fairweather Lodge: A twenty-five year retrospective.* San Francisco: Jossey-Bass.

Fairweather, G. W., Sanders, D. H., Maynard, H., & Cressler, D. L. (1969). *Community life for the mentally ill: An alternative to institutional care.* Chicago: Aldine.

Fallon, A. E., & Rozin, P. (1985). Sex differences in perceptions of desirable body shape. *J. Abnorm. Psychol., 94,* 102–5.

Falloon, I. R. H., Boyd, J. L., McGill, C. W., Williamson, M., & Razani, J. (1985). Family management in the prevention of morbidity of schizophrenia: Clinical outcome of a two-year longitudinal study. *Arch. Gen. Psychiat., 42,* 887–96.

Falls, H. F. (1970). Ocular changes in Down's syndrome help in diagnosis. *Roche Report, 7*(16), 5.

Fantuzzo, J. W., Jurecic, L., Stovall, A., Hightower, A. D., Goins, C., & Schachtel, D. (1988). Effects of adult and peer social initiations on the social behavior of withdrawn, maltreated, preschool children. *J. Cons. Clin. Psychol., 56,* 40–47.

Faraone, S. V., Kremen, W. S., & Tsuang, M. T. (1990). Genetic transmission of major affective disorders: Quantitative models and linkage analysis. *Psychol. Bull., 108,* 109–27.

Faraone, S. V., & Tsuang, M. T. (1985). Quantitative models of the genetic transmission of schizophrenia. *Psychol. Bull., 98,* 41–66.

Farberow, N. L. (1974). *Suicide.* Morristown, NJ: General Learning Press.

Farberow, N. L. (1975). Cultural history of suicide. In N. L. Farberow (Ed.), *Suicide in different cultures* (pp. 1–15). Baltimore: University Park Press.

Farberow, N. L., & Litman, R. E. (1970). A comprehensive suicide prevention program. Suicide Prevention Center of Los Angeles, 1958–1969. Unpublished final report DHEW NIMH Grants No. MH 14946 & MH 00128. Los Angeles.

Farberow, N. L., Shneidman, E. S., & Leonard, C. (1963). Suicide among general medical and surgical hospital patients with malignant neoplasms. Veterans Administration, Dept. of Medicine and Surgery. *Medical Bulletin* MB-9, Feb. 25, 1963, 1–11.

Farberow, N. L., & Simon, M. D. (1975). Suicide in Los Angeles and Vienna. In N. L. Farberow (Ed.), *Suicide in different cultures* (pp. 185–204). Baltimore: University Park Press.

Faretra, G. (1981). A profile of aggression from adolescence to adulthood: An 18-year follow-up of psychiatrically disturbed and violent adolescents. *Amer. J. Orthopsychiat., 51,* 439–53.

Farina, A., Burns, G. L., Austad, C., Bugglin, C., & Fischer, E. H. (1986). The role of physical attractiveness in the readjustment of discharged psychiatric patients. *J. Abnorm. Psychol., 95,* 139–43.

Faris, R. E. L., & Dunham, H. W. (1939). *Mental disorders in urban areas.* Chicago: University of Chicago Press. (Reprinted, 1965.)

Farley, F. H., & Farley, S. V. (1972). Stimulus seeking motivation and delinquent motivation among institutionalized delinquent girls. *J. Cons. Clin. Psychol., 39,* 94–97.

Feingold, B. F. (1977). Behavioral disturbances linked to the ingestion of food additives. *Delaware Medical Journal, 49,* 89–94.

Feinsilver, D. (1970). Communication in families of schizophrenic patients. *Arch. Gen. Psychiat., 22*(2), 143–48.

Feldman, R., & Weisfeld, G. (1973). An interdisciplinary study of crime. *Crime and Delinquency. 19*(2), 150–62.

Fenna, D. et al. (1971). Ethanol metabolism in various racial groups. *Canadian Medical Association Journal, 105,* 472–75.

Fenz, W. D. (1971). Heart rate responses to a stressor: A comparison between primary and secondary psychopaths and normal controls. *Journal of Experimental Research in Personality, 5*(1), 7–13.

Fersch, E. A., Jr., (1980). *Psychology and psychiatry in courts and corrections.* New York: Wiley.

Ferster, C. B. (1973). A functional analysis of depression. *Amer. Psychol., 28*(10), 857–70.

Fetterman, J. L. (1949). *Practical lessons in psychiatry.* Springfield, IL: Charles C. Thomas.

Feuerstein, R. (1977). Mediated learning experience: A theoretical basis for cognitive modifiability during adolescence. In P. Mittler (Ed.), *Research to practice in mental retardation* (Vol. 2, pp. 105–16). Baltimore: University Park Press.

Field, M. J. (1960). *Search for security: An ethnopsychiatric study of rural Ghana.* Evanston, IL: Northwestern University Press.

Filskov, S. B., & Boll, T. J. (1986). *Handbook of clinical neuropsychology* (2nd ed.). New York: Wiley.

Filskov, S. B., & Goldstein, S. G. (1974). Diagnostic validity of the Halstead-Reitan Neuropsychology battery., *J. Cons. Clin. Psychol., 42,* 383–88.

Filskov, S. B., Grimm, B. H., & Lewis, J. A. (1981). Brain-behavior relationships. In S. B. Filskov & T. J. Boll (Eds.), *Handbook of clinical neuropsychology.* New York: Wiley.

Filskov, S. B., & Locklear, E. (1982). A multidimensional perspective on clinical neuropsychology research. In P. C. Kendall & J. M. Butcher (Eds.), *Handbook of research methods in clinical psychology.* New York: Wiley.

Fine, M. A., & Sansone, R. A. (1990). Dilemmas in the management of suicidal behavior in individuals with borderline disorder. *Amer. J. Psychother., 44,* 160–71.

Fine, R. (1979). *A history of psychoanalysis.* New York: Columbia University Press.

Fink, M. (1979). *Convulsive therapy: Theory and practice.* New York: Raven Press.

Fink, M., Kety, S., McGaugh, I., & Williams, T. A. (Eds.). (1974). *Psychobiology of convulsive therapy.* New York: Wiley.

Finkelhor, D. (1990). Early and long term effects of child sexual abuse: An update. *Professional Psychology: Research and Practice, 21,* 325–30.

Finn, P. R. (1990, March). Dysfunction in stimulus-response modulation in men at high risk for alcoholism. Paper presented at a symposium on the *Genetics of Alcoholism: Recent Advances.* Satellite Symposium of the Annual Meeting of the Research Society on Alcoholism, Montreal, Canada.

Finn, P. R., & Pihl, R.O. (1987). Men at high risk for alcoholism: The effect of alcohol on cardiovascular response to unavoidable shock. *J. Abnorm. Psychol., 96,* 230–36.

Finn, P. R., Zeitouni, N., & Pihl, R. (1990). Effects of alcohol on psychophysiological hyperactivity to nonaversive and aversive stimuli in men at high risk for alcoholism. *J. Abnorm. Psychol., 99,* 79–85.

Finucci, J. M., Guthrie, T., Childs, A. L., Abbey, H., & Childs, B. (1976). The genetics of specific reading disability. *Annals of Human Genetics, 40,* 1–23.

Fire Statistics U.K. (1980). London: Home Office.

Fisch, R., Weakland, J. H., & Segal, L. (1982). *The tactics of change: Doing therapy briefly.* San Francisco: Jossey-Bass.

Fischer, M. (1971). Psychoses in the offspring of schizophrenic monozygotic twins and their normal co-twins. *Brit. J. Psychiat., 118,* 43–52.

Fischer, M. (1973). Genetic and environmental factors in schizophrenia: A study of schizophrenic twins and their families. *Acta Psychiatr. Scandin.,* Suppl. No. 238.

Fischer, P. J., Shapiro, S., Breakey, W. R., Anthony, J. C., & Kramer, M. (1986). Mental health and social characteristics of the homeless: A survey of mission users. *Amer. J. Pub. Hlth. 76*(5), 519–24.

Fischl, M. A., Dickinson, G. M., Scott, G. B., Klimas, N., Fletcher, M. A., & Parks, W. (1987). Evaluation of heterosexual partners, children, and household contacts of adults with AIDS. *JAMA, 257,* 640–44.

Fischman, J. (1987, Feb.). Type A on trial. *Psych. Today, 21,* 42–50.

Fischman, M. W., & Schuster, C. R. (1982). Cocaine self-administration in humans. *Federal Proc. 41,* 241–46.

Fish, B. (1975). Biologic antecedents of psychosis in children. In D. X. Freedman (Ed.), *Biology of the major psychoses.* New York: Raven.

Fisher, J. E., & Carstensen, L. L. (1990). Behavior management for the dementias. *Clin. Psychol. Rev., 10,* 611–30.

Fisher, K. (1986). DSM-III-R protest: Critics say psychiatry has been stonewalling. *Monitor, 17*(7), 4–6.

Fleishman, M. J. (1981). A replication of Patterson's "Intervention for boys with conduct problems." *J. Cons. Clin. Psychol., 49*(3), 342–51.

Fleming, J. E., Offord, D. R., & Boyle, M. H. (1989). Prevalence of childhood and adolescent depression in the community: Ontario Health Study. *Brit. J. Psychiat., 155,* 647–54.

Foa, E. B., & Kozak, M. J. (1985). Treatment of anxiety disorders: Implications for psychopathology. In A. H. Tuma & J. D. Maser (Eds.), *Anxiety and the anxiety disorders* (pp. 421–52). Hillsdale, NJ: Lawrence Erlbaum and Associates.

Foa, E. B., Steketee, G., & Young, M. C. (1984). Agoraphobia: Phenomenological aspects, associated characteristics, and theoretical considerations. *Clin. Psychol. Rev., 4,* 431–57.

Fontana, A. F., & Dowds, B. N. (1975). Assessing treatment outcomes. *J. Nerv. Ment. Dis., 161,* 221–30.

Forehand, R., Rogers, T., McMahon, R. J., Wells, K. C., & Griest, D. L. (1981). Teaching parents to modify child behavior problems: An examination of some follow-up data. *J. Pediat. Psychol., 6*(3), 313–32.

Foreyt, J. P. (1986). Treating the diseases of the 1980s: Eating disorders. *Contemp. Psychol., 31,* 658–60.

Forgac, G. E., & Michaels, E. J. (1982). Personality characteristics of two types of male exhibitionists. *J. Abnorm. Psychol., 91,* 287–93.

Forgus, R. H., & DeWolfe, A. S. (1974). Coding of cognitive input in delusional patients. *J. Abnorm. Psychol., 83*(3), 278–84.

Forman, S. G., & Linney, J. A. (1988). School-based prevention of adolescent substance abuse: Programs, implementation and future directions. *School Psychology Review, 17*(4), 550–58.

Forseman, H., & Akesson, H. O. (1965). Mortality in patients with Down's syndrome. *Journal of Mental Deficiency Research, 9,* 146–61.

Fowler, R. C., Rich, C. L., & Young, D. (1986). San Diego suicide study: Substance abuse in young cases. *Arch. Gen. Psychiat., 43,* 962–65.

Fowler, R. D. (1987). Developing a computer based test interpretation system. In J. N. Butcher (Ed.), *Computerized psychological assessment: A practitioner's guide.* New York: Basic Books.

Fowler, R. D., & Butcher, J. N. (1986). Critique of Matarazzo's view of computerized testing: All sigma and no meaning. *Amer. Psychol., 41,* 94–96.

Fowler, R. D., Finkelstein, A., Penk, W., Bell, W., & Itzig, B.

(1987). An automated problem-rating interview: The DPRI. In J. N. Butcher (Ed.), *Computerized psychological assessment: A practitioner's guide.* New York: Basic Books.

Fox, R. E. (1976). Family therapy. In I. Weiner (Ed.), *Clinical methods in psychology.* New York: Wiley.

Frances, A. (1980). The DSM-III personality disorders section: A commentary. *Amer. J. Psychiat., 137*(9), 1050–54.

Frances, A. J., Widiger, T. A., & Pincus, A. (1989). The development of DSM-IV. *Arch. Gen. Psychiat., 46,* 373–75.

Frank, J. D. (1978). *Persuasion and Healing* (2nd ed.). Baltimore: Johns Hopkins University Press.

Franklin, J. L., Solovitz, B., Mason, M., Clemons, J. R., & Miller, G. E. (1987). An evaluation of case management. *Amer. J. Pub. Hlth., 77*(6), 674–78.

Frederick, C. J. (1985). An introduction and overview of youth suicide. In M. L. Peck, N. L. Farberow, & R. E. Litman (Eds.), *Youth Suicide* (pp. 1–16). New York: Springer.

Frederick, C. J. (1986). Post-traumatic stress disorder and child-molestation. In A. Burgess & C. Hartman (Eds.), *Sexual exploitation of parents by health professionals* (pp. 133–42). New York: Praeger.

Free, M. L., & Oei, T. P. S. (1989). Biological and psychological processes in the treatment and maintenance of depression. *Clin. Psychol. Rev., 9,* 653–88.

Freedman, A. M., Kaplan, H. I., & Sadock, B. J. (1976). *Modern synopsis of comprehensive textbook of psychiatry* (2nd ed.). Baltimore: Williams & Wilkins.

Freedman, B., & Chapman, L. J. (1973). Early subjective experience in schizophrenic episodes. *J. Abnorm. Psychol., 82*(1), 46–54.

Freedman, M. (1975). Homosexuals may be healthier than straights. *Psych. Today, 8*(10), 28–32.

Freeman, R. D., Malkin, S. F., & Hastings, J. O. (1975). Psychosocial problems of deaf children and their families: A comparative study. *American Annals of the Deaf, 120,* 391–405.

Freeman, T. (1960). On the psychopathology of schizophrenia. *J. Ment. Sci., 106,* 925–37.

Freeman, W. (1959). Psychosurgery. In S. Arieti (Ed.), *American handbook of psychiatry* (Vol. 2, pp. 1521–40). New York: Basic Books.

Fremouw, W. J., de Perczel, M., & Ellis, T. E. (1990). *Suicide risk: Assessment and response guidelines.* Elmsford, NY: Pergamon.

French, L. (1987, Nov.–Dec.). Victimization of the mentally ill: An unintended consequence of deinstitutionalization. *Social Work,* 502–5.

Freud, A. (1946). *Ego and the mechanisms of defense.* New York: International Universities Press.

Friedman, H. S., & Booth-Kewley, S. (1987a). Personality, Type A behavior, and coronary heart disease: The role of emotional expression. *J. Pers. Soc. Psychol., 53,* 783–92.

Friedman, H. S., & Booth-Kewley, S. (1987b). The "disease-prone" personality: A meta-analytic view of the construct. *Amer. Psychol., 42,* 539–55.

Friedman, J. H., (1974). Woman's role in male impotence. *Medical Aspects of Human Sexuality, 8*(6), 8–23.

Friedman, M., Manwaring, J. H., Rosenman, R. H., Donlon, G., & Ortega, P. (1973). Instantaneous and sudden death: Clinical and pathological differentiation in coronary artery disease. *JAMA, 225,* 1319–28.

Friedman, M., & Rosenman, R. H. (1959). Association of specific overt behavior pattern with blood and cardiovascular findings. *JAMA, 169,* 1286.

Friedman, M., & Ulmer, D. (1984). *Treating Type A behavior and your heart.* New York: Knopf.

Friedman, P., & Linn, L. (1957). Some psychiatric notes on the Andrea Doria disaster. *Amer. J. Psychiat., 114,* 426–32.

Friedman, R., & Iwai, J. (1976). Genetic predisposition and stress-induced hypertension. *Science, 193,* 161–92.

Friedrich, W., Einbender, A. J., & Luecke, W. J. (1983). Cognitive and behavioral characteristics of physically abused children. *J. Cons. Clin. Psychol., 51*(2), 313–14.

Fromm, E., & Shor, R. E. (1972). *Hypnosis: Research developments and perspectives.* Chicago: Aldine.

Fromm-Reichmann, F. (1948). Notes on the development of treatment of schizophrenics by psychoanalytic psychotherapy. *Psychiatry, 11,* 263–73.

Fry, P. S. (1984). Development of a geriatric scale of hopelessness: Implications for counseling and intervention with the depressed elderly. *J. Couns. Psychol. 31,* 322–31.

Fuller, A. K., & Blashfield, R. K. (1989). Masochistic personality disorder, a prototype analysis of diagnosis and sex bias. *J. Nerv. Ment. Dis., 177,* 168–72.

Fulmer, R. H., & Lapidus, L. B. (1980). A study of professed reasons for beginning and continuing heroin use. *Inter. J. Addictions, 15,* 631–45.

Furby, L., Weinrott, M. R., & Blackshaw, L. (1989). Sex offender recidivism: A review. *Psychol. Bull., 105,* 3–30.

Furlong, W. B. (1971). How "speed" kills athletic careers. *Today's Health, 49*(2), 30–33, 62, 64, 66.

Gabuzda, D. H., & Hirsch, M. S. (1987). Neurologic manifestations of infection with human immunodeficiency virus: Clinical features and pathogenesis. *Ann. Int. Med., 107,* 383–91.

Gager, N., & Schurr, C., (1976). *Sexual assault: Confronting rape in America.* New York: Grosset & Dunlap.

Gajdusek, D. C. (1986). On the uniform source of amyloid in plaques, tangles, and vascular deposits. *Neurobiology of Aging, 7,* 453–54.

Gajzago, C., & Prior, M. (1974). Two cases of "recovery" in Kanner syndrome. *Arch. Gen. Psychiat., 31*(2), 264–68.

Gamble, T. J., & Zigler, E. (1989). The head start synthesis project: A critique. *Journal of Applied Developmental Psychology, 10,* 267–74.

Ganju, V., & Quan, H. (1987). Mental health service needs of refugees in Texas. Paper given at the *Refugee Assistance Program: Mental Health Workgroup Meeting,* UCLA, February 12–13.

Garb, H. N. (1989). Clinical judgment, clinical training, and professional experience. *Psychol. Bull., 105,* 387–96.

Garb, J. R., & Stunkard, A. J. (1974). Effectiveness of a self-help group in obesity control: A further assessment. *Arch. Int. Med., 134,* 716–20.

Garber, H. L. (1988). *The Milwaukee Project: Preventing mental retardation in children at risk.* Washington, DC: American Association on Mental Retardation.

Garfield, S. L. (1986). Research on client variables in psychotherapy. In S. L. Garfield & A. E. Bergin (Eds.), *Handbook of psychotherapy and behavior change* (3rd ed., pp. 213–56). New York: Wiley.

Garmezy, N. (1978a). Current status of other high-risk research programs. In L. C. Wynne, R. L. Cromwell, & S. Matthysse (Eds.), *The nature of schizophrenia: New approaches to research and treatment.* New York: Wiley.

Garmezy, N. (1978b). Observations of high-risk research and premorbid development in schizophrenia. In L. C. Wynne, R. L. Cromwell, & S. Matthysse (Eds.), *The nature of schizophrenia: New approaches to research and treatment.* New York: Wiley.

Garner, D. M. (1986). Cognitive-behavioral therapy for eating disorders. *Clin. Psychol., 39*(2), 36–39.

Garner, D. M. (1986). Cognitive therapy for anorexia nervosa. In K. D. Brownell & J. P. Foreyt (Eds.), *Handbook of eating disorders* (pp. 301–27). New York: Basic Books.

Gartner, A., & Riessman, F. (1974). Is there a new work ethic? *Amer. J. Orthopsychiat., 44*(4), 563–67.

Gawin, F. H., & Kleber, H. D. (1986). Abstinence symptomatology and psychiatric diagnosis in cocaine abusers. *Arch. Gen. Psychiat., 43,* 107–13.

Gebhard, P. H. (1965). Situational factors affecting human sexual behavior. In F. Beach (Ed.), *Sex and behavior.* New York: Wiley.

Gebhard, P. H., Gagnon, J. H., Pomeroy, W. B., & Christenson, C. V. (1965). *Sex offenders: An analysis of types.* New York: Harper & Row.

Geiser, D. S. (1989). Psychosocial influences on human immunity. *Clin. Psychol. Rev., 9,* 689–715.

Geisz, D., & Steinhausen, H. (1974). On the "psychological development of children with hydrocephalus." (German) *Praxis der Kinderpsychologie und Kinderpsychiatrie, 23*(4), 113–18.

Gelfand, D. M., Jenson, W. R., & Drew, C. J. (1988). *Understanding child behavior disorders* (2nd ed.). New York: Holt, Rinehart & Winston.

Gelfand, D. M., & Teti, D. M. (1990). The effects of maternal depression on children. *Clin. Psychol. Rev., 10,* 329–53.

Gelles, R. J. (1978). Violence toward children in the United States. *Amer. J. Orthopsychiat., 48,* 580–90.

Gentry, W. D. (1984a). Behavioral medicine: A new research paradigm. In W. D. Gentry (Ed.), *Handbook of behavioral medicine* (pp. 1–12). New York: Guilford Press.

Gentry, W. D. (Ed.). (1984b). *Handbook of behavioral medicine.* New York: Guilford.

Gentry, W. D., Chesney, A. P., Gary, H. G., Hall, R. P., &

Harburg, E. (1982). Habitual anger-coping styles: I. Effect of mean blood pressure and risk for essential hypertension. *Psychosom. Med., 44*, 195–202.

George, L., & Neufeld, R. W. J. (1985). Cognition and symptomatology in schizophrenia. *Schizo. Bull., 11*, 264–85.

George, L. K. (1984). The burden of caregiving. *Center Reports of Advances in Research.* Durham, NC: Duke University Center for the Study of Aging and Human Development.

German, W. J. (1959). Initial symptomatology in brain turners. *Connecticut Medicine, 23*, 636–37.

Geschwind, N. (1975). The borderland of neurology and psychiatry: Some common misconceptions. In D. F. Benson & D. Blumer (Eds.), *Psychiatric aspects of neurological disease* (pp. 1–9). New York: Grune & Stratton.

Giannetti, R. A. (1987). The GOLPH Psychosocial History: Response contingent data acquisition and reporting. In J. N. Butcher (Ed.), *Computerized psychological assessment: A practitioners guide.* New York: Basic Books.

Gilbert, J. G., & Lombardi, D. N. (1967). Personality characteristics of young male narcotic addicts. *J. Couns. Psychol., 31*, 536–38.

Gillberg, C., & Schaumann, H. (1981). Infantile autism and puberty. *J. Autism Develop. Dis., 11*(4), 365–71.

Gillberg, C. U. (1990). Autism and pervasive developmental disorders. *Journal of Child Psychology & Psychiatry & Allied Disciplines, 31*, 99–119.

Ginsberg, G. L., Frosch, W. A., & Shapiro, T. (1972). The new impotence. *Arch. Gen. Psychiat., 26*(3), 218–20.

Gist, R., & Lubin, B. (Eds.) (1989). *Psychosocial aspects of disaster.* New York: Wiley.

Gittelman, R. (1983). Treatment of reading disorders. In M. Rutter (Ed.), *Developmental neuropsychiatry* (pp. 520–39). New York: Guilford.

Gittelman, R., Mannuzza, S., Shenker, R., & Bonagura, N. (1985). Hyperactive boys almost grown up. *Arch. Gen. Psychiat., 42*, 937–47.

Glaser, R., Kiecolt-Glaser, J. K., Speicher, C. E., & Holliday, J. E. (1985). Stress, loneliness, and changes in herpes virus latency. *J. Behav. Med., 8*, 249–60.

Glaser, R., Rice, J., Sheridan, J., Fertel, R., Stout, J., Speicher, C., Pinsky, R., Kotur, M., Post, A., Beck, M., & Kiecolt-Glaser, J. (1987). Stress-related immune suppression: Health implications. *Brain, Behavior, and Immunity, 1*, 7–20.

Glaser, R., Rice, J., Speicher, C. E., Stout, J. C., & Kiecolt-Glaser, J. K. (in press). Stress depresses interferon production by lymphocytes and natural killer cell activity in humans. *Behavioral Neuroscience.*

Glasner, P. D., & Kaslow, R. A. (1990). The epidemiology of human immunodeficiency virus infection. *J. Cons. Clin. Psychol., 58*, 13–21.

Glasscote, R. (1978). What programs work and what programs do not work for chronic mental patients? In J. A. Talbott (Ed.), *The chronic mental patient: Problems, solutions and recommendations for a public policy.* Washington, DC: American Psychiatric Association.

Glenner, G. C. (1986). Marching backwards into the future. *Neurobiology of Aging, 7*, 439–41.

Gleser, G., & Sacks, M. (1973). Ego defenses and reaction to stress: A validation study of the Defense Mechanisms Inventory. *J. Cons. Clin. Psychol., 40*(2), 181–87.

Glosser, G., & Wexler, D. (1985). Participants' evaluation of education/support groups for families of patients with Alzheimer's disease and other dementias. *Gerontologist, 25*, 232–36.

Glow, R. A. (1981). Treatment alternatives for hyperactive children—a comment on "problem children" and stimulant drug therapy. *Australian Journal of Psychiatry, 15*(2), 123–28.

Glueck, S., & Glueck, E. (1968). *Non-delinquents in perspective.* Cambridge, MA: Harvard University Press.

Glueck, S., & Glueck, E. T. (1969). Delinquency prediction method reported highly accurate. *Roche Reports, 6*(15), 3.

Gochman, S. I., Allgood, B. A., & Geer, C. R. (1982). A look at today's behavior therapists. *Profess. Psychol., 13*(5), 605–9.

Goering, P., Wasylenki, D., Lancee, W., & Freeman, S. J. (1984). From hospital to community: Six month and two-year outcomes for 505 patients. *J. Nerv. Ment. Dis., 17*(11), 667–73.

Goetz, K. L., & Van Kammen, D. P. (1986). Computerized axial tomography scans and subtypes of schizophrenia: A review of the literature. *J. Nerv. Ment. Dis., 174*, 31–41.

Gold, E. R. (1986). Long-term effects of sexual victimization in

childhood: An attributional approach. *J. Cons. Clin. Psychol., 54*, 471–75.

Gold, M. S., & Rea, W. S. (1983). The role of endorphins in opiate addiction, withdrawal, and recovery. *Psychiat. Clin. N. Amer., 6*, 489–520.

Goldberg, J., True, W. R., Eisen, S. A., & Henderson, W. G. (1990). A twin study of the effects of the Vietnam War on posttraumatic stress disorder. *JAMA, 263*, 1227–32.

Goldberg, S., Schultz, C., Schultz, P., et al. (1986). Borderline and schizotypal personality disorders treated with low-dose thiothixene vs. placebo. *Arch. Gen. Psychiat., 43*, 680–86.

Golden, C. J. (1978). *Diagnosis and rehabilitation in clinical neuropsychology.* Springfield, IL: Charles C. Thomas.

Golden, C. J., Graber, B., Blose, I., Berg, P., Coffman, J., & Bloch, S. (1981). Differences in brain densities between chronic alcoholic and normal control patients. *Science, 211*(30), 508–10.

Golden, C. J., MacInnes, W. D., Ariel R. N., Ruedrich, S. L., Chu C-C., Coffman, J. A., Graber, B., & Bloch, S. (1982). Cross-validation of the ability of the Luria-Nebraska Neuropsychological Battery to differentiate chronic schizophrenics with and without ventricular enlargement. *J. Cons. Clin. Psychol., 50*, 87–95.

Golden, D. A., & Davis, J. G. (1974). Counseling parents after the birth of an infant with Down's syndrome. *Children Today, 3*(2), 7–11.

Goldfried, M. R. (1980). Toward the delineation of therapeutic change principles. *Amer. Psychol., 35*, 991–99.

Goldfried, M. R., Greenberg, L. S., & Marmar, C. (1990). Individual psychotherapy: Process and outcome. *Annu. Rev. Psychol.* (Vol. 41, pp. 659–88). Palo Alto, CA: Annual Reviews, Inc.

Goldfried, M. R., Linehan, M. M., & Smith, J. L. (1978). Reduction of test anxiety through cognitive restructuring. *J. Cons. Clin. Psychol., 46*(1), 32–39.

Goldfried, M. R., & Merbaum, M. (Eds.). (1973). *Behavior change through self control.* New York: Holt, Rinehart & Winston.

Goldfried, M. R., & Safran, J. D. (1986). Future directions in psychotherapy integration. In J. C. Norcross (Ed.), *Handbook of eclectic psychotherapy* (pp. 463–83). New York: Brunner/Mazel.

Goldman, H.H., Feder, J., & Scanlon, W. (1986). Chronic mental patients in nursing homes: Reexamining data from the national nursing home survey. *Hosp. Comm. Psychiat., 37*, 269–72.

Goldman, M. S., Williams, D. L., & Klisz, D. K. (1983). Recoverability of psychological functioning following alcohol abuse: Prolonged spatial-visual dysfunction in older alcoholics. *J. Cons. Clin. Psychol., 51*(3), 370–78.

Goldsmith, W., & Cretekos, C. (1969). Unhappy odysseys: Psychiatric hospitalization among Vietnam returnees. *Amer. J. Psychiat., 20*, 78–83.

Goldstein, A., et al. (1974, Mar. 4). Researchers isolate opiate receptor. *Behav. Today, 5*(9), 1.

Goldstein, M. J. (1985). Family factors that antedate the onset of schizophrenia and related disorders: The results of a fifteen year prospective longitudinal study. *Acta Psychiatr. Scandin.* (Suppl. No. 319), *71*, 7–18.

Goldstein, M. J., Rodnick, E. H., Jones, J. E., McPherson, S. R., & West, K. L. (1978). Family precursors of schizophrenia spectrum disorders. In L. C. Wynne, R. L. Cromwell, & S. Matthysse (Eds.), *The nature of schizophrenia: New approaches to research and treatment.* New York: Wiley Medical.

Goldstein, M. J., & Strachan, A. M. (1987). The family and schizophrenia. In T. Jacob (Ed.), *Family interaction and psychopathology: Theories, methods, and findings* (pp. 481–508). New York: Plenum.

Goldstein, W. N. (1983). DSM-III and the diagnosis of schizophrenia. *Amer. J. Psychother., 37*, 168–81.

Gomberg, E. S. (1989). Suicide rates among women with alcohol problems. *Amer. J. Pub. Hlth., 79*, 1363–65.

Gomes-Schwartz, B., Horowitz, J., & Cardarelli, A. (1990). *Child sexual abuse: The initial effects.* Newbury Park, CA: Sage.

Gonzales, L. R., Lewinsohn, P. M., & Clarke, G. N. (1985). Longitudinal follow-up of unipolar depressives: An investigation of predictors of relapse. *J. Cons. Clin. Psychol., 53*, 461–69.

Goodman, J. (1972). A case study of an "autistic-savant": Mental function in the psychotic child with markedly discrepant abilities. *J. Child Psychol. Psychiat., 13*(4), 267–78.

Goodman, R. (1989). Infantile autism: A syndrome of multiple primary deficits? *J. Autism Devel. Dis., 19*, 409–24.

Goodman, R. A., Mercy, J. A., Loya, F., Rosenberg, M.,

Smith, J. C., Allen, N. H., Vargas, L., & Kolts, R. (1986). Alcohol use and interpersonal violence: Alcohol detected in homicide victims. *Amer. J. Pub. Hlth., 76*(2), 144–49.

Goodwin, D. K. (1988). *The Fitzgeralds and the Kennedys: An American saga.* New York: St. Martin's Press.

Goodwin, D. W., Schulsinger, F., Hermansen, L., Guze, S. B., & Winokur, G. (1973). Alcohol problems in adoptees raised apart from alcoholic biological parents. *Arch. Gen. Psychiat., 28*(2), 238–43.

Goodwin, D. W., Schulsinger, F., Moller, N., Hermansen, L., Winokur, G., & Guze, S. B. (1974). Drinking problems in adopted and nonadopted sons of alcoholics. *Arch. Gen. Psychiat., 31*(2), 164–69.

Goplerud, E., & Depue, R. A. (1985). Behavioral response to naturally occurring stress in cyclothymia and dysthymia. *J. Abnorm. Psychol., 94,* 128–39.

Gordon, R. (1977). A critique of the evaluation of Patuxent Institution, with particular attention to the issues of dangerousness and recidivism. *Bulletin of the American Academy of Psychiatry and the Law, 5,* 210–55.

Gorenstein, E. E. (1982). Frontal lobe functions in psychopaths. *J. Abnorm. Psychol., 91,* 368–79.

Gorenstein, E. E. (1987). Cognitive-perceptual deficit in an alcoholism spectrum disorder. *J. Stud. Alcoh., 48,* 310–18.

Gorin, N. (1980). Looking out for Mrs. Berwid. *Sixty Minutes.* (Narrated by Morley Safer.) New York: CBS Television News.

Gorin, N. (1982). It didn't have to happen. *Sixty Minutes.* (Narrated by Morley Safer.) New York: CBS Television News.

Gorman, J. M., Battista, D., Goetz, R. R., Dillon, D. J., Liebowitz, M. R., Fyer, A. J., Kahn, J. P., Sandberg, D., & Klein, D. F. (1989). A comparison of sodium bicarbonate and sodium lactate infusion in the induction of panic attacks. *Arch. Gen. Psychiat., 46,* 145–50.

Gorton, G., & Akhtar, S. (1990). The literature on personality disorders, 1985–1988: Trends, issues, and controversies. *Hosp. Comm. Psychiat., 41,* 39–51.

Gosslin, C. C., & Eysenck, S. B. G. (1980). The transvestite "double image": A preliminary report. *Personality and Individual Differences, 1,* 172–73.

Gotlib, I. H., & Colby, C. A. (1987). *Treatment of depression: An interpersonal systems approach.* New York: Pergamon.

Gottesman, I. I., & Bertelson, A. (1989). Confirming unexpressed genotypes for schizophrenia: Risks in the offspring of Fischer's Danish identical and fraternal discordant twins. *Arch. Gen. Psychiat., 46,* 867–72.

Gottesman, I. I., & Shields, J. (1972). *Schizophrenia and genetics.* New York: Academic Press.

Gottesman, I. I., & Shields, J. (1982). *Schizophrenia: The epigenetic puzzle.* Cambridge, UK: Cambridge University Press.

Gottheil, E., Thornton, C. C., Skoloda, T. E., & Alterman, A. I. (1982). Follow-up of abstinent and non-abstinent alcoholics. *Amer. J. Psychiat., 139*(5), 560–65.

Gottlieb, J. (1981). Mainstreaming: Fulfilling the promise? *Amer. J. Ment. Def., 86,* 115–26.

Gottschalk, L. A., Haer, J. L., & Bates, D. E. (1972). Effect of sensory overload on psychological state: Changes in social alienation—personal disorganization and cognitive-intellectual impairment. *Arch. Gen. Psychiat., 27*(4), 451–56.

Grady, K., Gersick, K.E., & Boratynski, M. (1985). Preparing parents for teenagers: A step in the prevention of adolescent substance abuse. *Family Relations Journal of Applied Family and Child Studies, 34*(4), 541–49.

Graham, J. R. (1978a). *MMPI characteristics of alcoholics, drug abusers and pathological gamblers.* Paper presented at the 13th Annual Symposium on Recent Developments in the Use of the MMPI. Puebla, Mexico, March, 1978.

Graham, J. R. (1978b). The Minnesota Multiphasic Personality Inventory. In B. B. Wolman (Ed.), *Clinical diagnosis of mental disorders: A handbook.* New York: Plenum.

Graham, J. R., Timbrook, R., Ben-Porath, Y. S., & Butcher, J. N. (in press). Code-type congruence between MMPI and MMPI-2: Separting fact from artifact. *J. Pers. Assess.*

Gralnick, A. (1942). Folie a deux—The psychosis of association: A review of 103 cases and the entire English literature, with case presentations. *Psychiatric Quarterly, 14,* 230–63.

Grand, T. P., et al. (1984). Association among alcoholism, drug abuse, and antisocial personality: A Review of the literature. *Psych. Rep., 55,* 455–74.

Grant, I., Atkinson, J. H., Hesselink, J. R., Kennedy, C. J., Richman, D. D., Spector, S. A., & McCutchan, J. A. (1987). Evidence for early central nervous system involvement in the acquired immunodeficiency syndrome (AIDS) and other human immunodeficiency virus (HIV) infections. *Ann. Int. Med., 107,* 828–36.

Grant, I., & Heaton, R. K. (1990). Human immunodeficiency virus-Type 1 (HIV-1) and the brain. *J. Cons. Clin. Psychol., 58,* 22–30.

Grant, L., Sweetland, H. L., Yager, J., & Gerst, M. (1981). Quality of life events in relation to psychiatric symptoms. *Arch. Gen. Psychiat., 38*(3), 335–39.

Grant, V. W. (1953). A case study of fetishism. *J. Abnorm. Soc. Psychol., 48,* 142–49.

Gray, W. W., & Ramsey, B. K. (1982). The early training project: A life-span view. *Human Develop., 25,* 48–57.

Gray, F., Gherardi, R., & Scaravilli, F. (1988). The neuropathology of the acquired immune deficiency syndrome (AIDS). *Brain, 111,* 245–66.

Green, A. (1978). Self-destructive behavior in battered children. *Amer. J. Psychiat., 135,* 579–82.

Green, L., & Warshauer, D. (1981). Note on the "paradoxical" effect of stimulant drugs on hyperactivity with reference to the rate-dependency effect. *J. Nerv. Ment. Dis., 169*(3), 196–98.

Green, R. (1974). *Sexual identity conflict in children and adults.* New York: Basic Books.

Green, R. (1985). Gender identity in childhood and later sexual orientation: Follow-up of 78 males. *Amer. J. Psychiat., 142,* 339–41.

Greenacre, P. (1945). Conscience in the psychopath. *Amer. J. Orthopsychiat., 15,* 495–509.

Greene, M. H., & Dupont, R. L. (1974). Heroin addiction trends. *Amer. J. Psychiat., 131*(5), 545–50.

Greenfield, J. C., & Wolfson, J. M. (1935). Microcephalia vera. *Archives of Neurology and Psychiatry, 33,* 1296–1316.

Greer, S. (1964). Study of parental loss in neurotics and sociopaths. *Arch. Gen. Psychiat., 11*(2), 177–80.

Gregory, I., & Rosen, E. (1965). *Abnormal psychology.* Philadelphia: W. B. Saunders.

Gregg, C., & Hoy, C. (1989). Coherence: The comprehension and production abilities of college writers who are normally achieving, learning disabled, and underprepared. *J. Learn. Dis., 22,* 370–72.

Gresham, F. M. (1982). Misguided mainstreaming: The case for social skills training with handicapped children. *Exceptional Children, 48,* 422–33.

Griest, D. L., & Wells, K. C. (1983). Behavioral family therapy with conduct disorders in children. *Behav. Ther., 14,* 37–53.

Griest, J. H., Gustafson, D. H., Stauss, F. F., Rowse, G. L., Laughren, T. P., & Chiles, J. A. (1974). Suicide risk prediction: A new approach. *Life-Threatening Behavior, 4*(4), 212–23.

Grinker, R. R. (1969). An essay on schizophrenia and science. *Arch. Gen. Psychiat., 20,* 1–24.

Grinspoon, L., Ewalt, J. R., & Shader, R. I. (1972). *Schizophrenia: Pharmacotherapy and psychotherapy.* Baltimore: Williams & Wilkins.

Grob, C. S. (1985). Female exhibitionism. *J. Nerv. Ment. Dis., 173,* 253–56.

Gross, B. H., Southard, M. J., Lamb, H. R., & Weinberger, L. (1987). Assessing dangerousness and responding appropriately: Hedland expands the clinician's liability established by Tarasoff. *J. Clin. Psychiat., 48,* 9–12.

Gross, G., & Huber, G. (1973). Zur prognose der schizophenier. *Psychiatria Clinica, 6*(1), 1–16.

Groth, A. N., Burgess, A. W., & Holmstrom, L. L. (1977). Rape: Power, anger, and sexuality. *Amer. J. Psychiat., 134,* 1239–43.

Grunebaum, H., & Perlman, M. S. (1973). Paranoia and naivete. *Arch. Gen. Psychiat., 28*(1), 30–32.

Guelfi, G. P., Faustman, W. O., & Csernansky, J. G. (1989). Independence of positive and negative symptoms in a population of schizophrenic patients. *J. Nerv. Ment. Dis., 177,* 285–90.

Guerra, F. (1971). *The pre-Columbian mind.* New York: Seminar Press.

Gugliemi, R. S. (1979). *A double-blind study of the effectiveness of skin temperature biofeedback as a treatment for Raynaud's disease.* Unpublished doctoral dissertation, University of Minnesota.

Gunderson, J. G. (1980). A reevaluation of milieu therapy for nonchronic schizophrenic patients. *Schizo. Bull., 6*(1), 64–69.

Gunderson, J. G., & Siever, L. J. (1985). Relatedness of schizotypal to schizophrenic disorders. *Schizo. Bull., 11,* 532–37.

Gunderson, J. G., & Singer, M. T. (1986). Defining borderline patients: An overview. In M. H. Stone (Ed.), *Essential papers on borderline disorders* (pp. 453–74). New York: New York University Press.

Gurland, B. J., & Cross, P. S. (1982). Epidemiology of psychopathology in old age. In L. F. Jarvik & G. W. Small (Eds.), *Psychiat. Clin. N. Amer.* Philadelphia: Saunders.

Gurman, A. S., & Kniskern, D. P. (1978). Research on marital and family therapy: Progress, perspective and prospect. In S. L. Garfield & A. E. Bergin (Eds.), *Handbook of psychotherapy and behavior change.* New York: Wiley.

Gurman, A. S., Kniskern, D. P., & Pinsof, W. M. (1986). Research on marital and family therapies. In S. L. Garfield & A. E. Bergin (Eds.), *Handbook of psychotherapy and behavior change* (pp. 565–626). New York: Wiley.

Gurtman, M. B. (1986). Depression and the response of others: Reevaluating the reevaluation. *J. Abnorm. Psychol., 95,* 99–101.

Guy, E., Platt, J. J., Zwerling, I., & Bullock, S. (1985). Mental health status of prisoners in an urban jail. *Crim. Just. Behav., 12,* 29–53.

Gynther, M. D. (1979). Ethnicity and personality. In J. N. Butcher (Ed.), *New directions in MMPI research.* Minneapolis: University of Minnesota Press.

Hafner, R. J. (1984). Predicting the effects on husbands of behavior therapy for wives' agoraphobia. *Behav. Res. Ther., 22,* 227–42.

Hagan, J. W., & Huntsman, N. J. (1971). Selective attention in mental retardation. *Develop. Psychol., 5*(1), 151–60.

Halberstam, M. (1972). Can you make yourself sick? A doctor's report on psychosomatic illness. *Today's Health, 50*(12), 24–29.

Haley, J. (1959). The family of the schizophrenic: A model system. *J. Nerv. Ment. Dis., 129,* 357–74.

Haley, J. (1962). Whither family therapy. *Family Process, 1,* 69–100.

Haley, S. A. (1978). Treatment implications of post-combat stress response syndromes for mental health professionals. In C. R. Figley (Ed.), *Stress disorders among Vietnam veterans.* New York: Brunner/Mazel.

Hall, J. C., Bliss, M., Smith, K., & Bradley, A. (1970, July 1). Suicide gestures, attempts found high among poor. *Psychiat. News,* p. 20.

Hallgren, B. (1950). Specific dyslexia ("congenital word-blindness"). *Acta Psychiatrica Neurologica Scandinavica,* Suppl., 65, 1–287.

Hallworth, H. J. (1977). Computer-assisted instruction for the mentally retarded. In P. Milder (Ed.), *Research to practice in mental retardation* (Vol. 2, pp. 419–20). Baltimore: University Park Press.

Halmi, K. A., Falk, J. R., & Schwartz, E. (1981). Binge-eating and vomiting: A survey of a college population. *Psychol. Med., 11,* 697–706.

Hammen, C., Adrian, C., Gordon, D., Burge, D., Jaenicke, C., & Hiroto, D. (1987). Children of depressed mothers: Maternal strain and symptom predictors of dysfunction. *J. Abnorm. Psychol., 96,* 190–98.

Hammen, C., Ellicott, A., Gitlin, M., & Jamison, K. R. (1989). Sociotropy/autonomy and vulnerability to specific life events in patients with unipolar depression and bipolar disorders. *J. Abnorm. Psychol., 98,* 154–60.

Hammen, C., Marks, T., Mayol, A., & DeMayo, R. (1985). Depressive self-schemas, life stress, and vulnerability to depression. *J. Abnorm. Psychol., 94,* 308–19.

Hammen, C. L., & Peters, S. D. (1977). Differential responses to male and female depressive reactions. *J. Cons. Clin. Psychol., 45,* 994–1001.

Hammen, C. L., & Peters, S. D. (1978). Interpersonal consequences of depression: Responses to men and women enacting a depressed role. *J. Abnorm. Psychol., 87*(3), 322–32.

Handleman, J. S., Gill, M. J., & Alessandri, M. (1988). Generalization by severely developmentally disabled children: Issues, advances, and future directions. *The Behavior Therapist, 11,* 221–23.

Hanerton, J. L., Canning, N., Ray, M., & Smith, S. (1975). A cytogenetic survey of 14,069 newborn infants: Incidence of chromosome abnormalities. *Clinical Genetics, 8,* 223–43.

Haney, B., & Gold, M. (1973). The juvenile delinquent nobody knows. *Psychol. Today, 7*(4), 48–52, 55.

Hanrahan, J., Goodman, W., & Rapagna, S. (1990). Preparing mentally retarded students for mainstreaming: Priorities of regular class and special school teachers. *Amer. J. Ment. Retard., 94,* 470–74.

Hanson, D. R., Gottesman, I. I., & Meehl, P. E. (1977). Generic theories and the validation of psychiatric diagnoses: Implications for the study of children of schizophrenics. *J. Abnorm. Psychol., 86*(6), 575–88.

Harburgh, E., Erfurt, J. C., Hauenstein, L. S., Chape, C., Schull, W. J., & Schork, M. A. (1973). Socioecological stress, suppressed hostility, skin color, and black-white male blood pressure: Detroit. *Psychosom. Med., 35,* 276–96.

Harder, D. W., Strauss, J. S., Greenwald, D. F., Kokes, R. F., et al. (1989). Life events and psychopathology severity: Comparisons between psychiatric inpatients and outpatients. *J. Clin. Psychol., 45,* 202–9.

Harding, C. M., Brooks, G. W., Ashikaga, T., Strauss, J. S., & Breier, A. (1987a). The Vermont longitudinal study of persons with severe mental illness, I: Methodology, study sample, and overall status 32 years later. *Amer. J. Psychiat., 144,* 718–26.

Harding, C. M., Brooks, G. W., Ashikaga, T., Strauss, J. S., & Breier, A. (1987b). The Vermont longitudinal study of persons with severe mental illness, II: Long-term outcome of subjects who retrospectively met DSM-III criteria for schizophrenia. *Amer. J. Psychiat., 144,* 727–35.

Harding, W. M., Zinberg, N. E., Stelmack, S. M., & Barry, M. (1980). Formerly-addicted-noncontrolled opiate users. *Inter. J. Addictions, 15,* 47–60.

Hardy, J. A., Mann, D. M., Wester, P., & Winblad, B. (1986). An integrative hypothesis concerning the pathogenesis and progression of Alzheimer's disease. *Neurobiology of Aging, 7,* 489–502.

Hare, R. D. (1968). Psychopathy, autonomic functioning and the orienting response. *J. Abnorm. Psychol., 73,* (Monograph Suppl. 3, part 2), 1–24.

Hare, R. D. (1970). *Psychopathy: Theory and research.* New York: Wiley.

Hare, R. D. (1984). Performance of psychopaths on cognitive tasks related to frontal lobe function. *J. Abnorm. Psychol., 93*(2), 133–40.

Hare, R. D., McPherson, L.M., & Forth, A. E. (1988). Male psychopaths and their criminal careers. *J. Cons. Clin. Psychol., 56,* 710–14.

Harlow, H. (1969). A brief look at autistic children. *Psychiatry and Social Science Review, 3*(1), 27–29.

Harlow, J. M. (1868). Recovery from the passage of an iron bar through the head. *Publication of the Massachusetts Medical Society, 2,* 327.

Harris, S. L., & Ersner-Hershfield, R. (1978). Behavioral suppression of seriously disruptive behavior in psychotic and retarded patients: A review of punishment and its alternatives. *Psychol. Bull., 85,* 1352–75.

Harrow, M., Carone, B. J., & Westermeyer, J. F. (1985). The course of psychosis in early phases of schizophrenia. *Amer. J. Psychiat., 142,* 702–7.

Harrow, M., Goldberg, J. F., Grossman, L. S., & Meltzer, H. Y. (1990). Outcome in manic disorders: A naturalistic follow-up study. *Arch. Gen. Psychiat., 47,* 665–71.

Harter, S., Alexander, P.C., & Neimeyer, R. A. (1988). Long term effects of incestuous child abuse in college women: Social adjustment, social cognition, and family characteristics. *J. Cons. Clin. Psychol., 56,* 5–8.

Hartford, J. T. (1986). A review of antemortem markers of Alzheimer's disease. *Neurobiology of Aging, 7,* 401–2.

Hartlage, L., Asken, M., & Hornsby, J. (1987). *Essentials of neuropsychological assessment.* New York: Springer.

Hartmann, E. (1968). Longitudinal studies of sleep and dream patterns in manic-depressive patients. *Arch. Gen. Psychiat., 19,* 312–29.

Hartmann, E., Milofsky, E., Vaillant, G., Oldfield, M., & Falke, R. (1984). Vulnerability to schizophrenia: Predormation. *Arch. Gen. Psychiat., 41,* 1050–56.

Hartup, W. W. (1983). Peer relations. In P. H. Mussen (Ed.), *Handbook of child psychology* (Vol. 4, pp. 274–385). New York: Wiley.

Hathaway, S. R., & McKinley, J. C. (1951). *The Minnesota multiphasic personality inventory* (rev. ed.). New York: Psychological Corporation.

Hatzenbuehler, L. C., & Schroeder, H. E. (1978). Desensitization procedures in the treatment of childhood disorders. *Psychol. Bull., 85,* 831–44.

Havens, L. L. (1974). The existential use of the self. *Amer. J. Psychiat., 131*(1), 1–10.

Hawk, A. B., Carpenter, W. T., & Strauss, J. S. (1975). Diagnostic criteria and five-year outcome in schizophrenia. *Arch. Gen. Psychiat., 32*(3), 343–47.

Hayes, T. A., Panitch, M. L., & Barker, E. (1975). Imipramine dosage in children: A comment on "Imipramine and electrocardiographic abnormalities in hyperactive children." *Amer. J. Psychiat., 132*(5), 546–47.

Haynes, S. G., Feinleib, M., & Kannel, W. B. (1980). The relationship of psychosocial factors to coronary heart disease in the Framingham study: III. Eight-year incidence of coronary heart disease. *American Journal of Epidemiology, 111,* 37–58.

Haywood, H. C., Meyers, C. E., & Switsky, H. N. (1982). Mental retardation. In M. R. Rosenzweig & L. W. Porter (Eds.), *Annu. Rev. Psychol., 33.*

Hazelrigg, M., Cooper, H., & Borduin, C. (1987). Evaluating the effectiveness of family therapies: An integrative review and analysis. *Psychol. Bull., 101,* 428–42.

Hazlett, B. (1971, Mar. 2). Two who played with death—and lost the game. *Los Angeles Times,* II, 1, 5.

Hearn, M. D., Murray, D. M., & Luepker, R. V. (1989). Hostility, coronary heart disease, and total mortality: A 33-year follow-up study of university students. *J. Behav. Med., 12,* 105–21.

Heaton, R. K., & Pendleton, M. G. (1981). Use of neuropsychological tests to predict adult patient's everyday functioning. *J. Cons. Clin. Psychol., 49*(6), 807–21.

Heaver, W. L. (1943). A study of forty male psychopathic personalities before, during and after hospitalization. *Amer. J. Psychiat., 100,* 342–46.

Hecaen, H., & Albert, M. L. (1975). Disorders of mental functioning related to frontal lobe pathology. In D. F. Benson & D. Blumer (Eds.), *Psychiatric aspects of neurological disease* (pp. 137–49). New York: Grune & Stratton.

Hechtman, L., Weiss, G., & Perlman, T. (1980). Hyperactives as young adults: Self-esteem and social skills. *Canad. J. Psychiat., 25*(6), 478–83.

Heckler, M. M. (1983). Fifth special report to the U.S. Congress on Alcohol and Health. U.S. Department of Health and Human Services (NIAAA). Washington, DC: U.S. Government Printing Office.

Hefez, A. (1985). The role of the press and the medical community in the epidemic of "mysterious gas poisoning" in the Jordan West Bank. *Amer. J. Psychiat., 142,* 833–37.

Heider, F. (1958). *The psychology of interpersonal relations.* New York: Wiley.

Heiman, J. R., & Grafton-Becker, V. (1989). Orgasmic disorders in women. In S. R. Leiblum & R. C. Rosen (Eds.), *Principles and practice of sex therapy* (2nd ed. pp. 51–88). New York: Guilford.

Hekimian, L. J., & Gershon, S. (1968). Characteristics of drug abusers admitted to a psychiatric hospital. *JAMA, 205*(3), 125–30.

Heller, K., Sher, K. J., & Benson, C. S. (1982). Problems associated with risk of overprediction in studies of offspring of alcoholics: Implications for prevention. *Clin. Psychol. Rev., 2,* 183–200.

Hellman, D. S., & Blackmun, N. (1966). Enuresis, firesetting, and cruelty to animals: a triad predictive of adult crime. *Amer. J. Psychiat., 122,* 1431–35.

Henderson, V. W. (1986). Non-genetic factors in Alzheimer's disease pathogenesis. *Neurobiology of Aging, 7,* 585–87.

Hendin, H. (1975). Student suicide: Death as a life-style. *J. Nerv. Ment. Dis., 160*(3), 204–19.

Hendin, H. (1985). Suicide among the young: Psychodynamics and demography. In M. L. Peck, N. L. Farberow, & R. E. Litman (Eds.), *Youth suicide* (pp. 19–38). New York: Springer.

Henker, B. & Whalen, C. K. (1989). Hyperactivity and attention deficits. *Amer. Psychol., 44,* 216–23.

Herd, J. A. (1984). Cardiovascular disease and hypertension. In W. D. Gentry (Ed.), *Handbook of behavioral medicine* (pp. 222–81). New York: Guilford.

Hermalin, J., & Morell, J. A. (Eds.). (1986). *Prevention planning in mental health.* Beverly Hills, CA: Sage.

Herman, J. L. (1981). *Father-daughter incest.* Cambridge, MA: Harvard University Press.

Herman, J. L. (1986). Histories of violence in an outpatient population: An exploratory study. *Amer. J. Orthopsychiat., 56*(1), 137–41.

Herman, J. L. (1990). Sex offenders: A feminist perspective. In W. L. Marshall, D. R. Laws, & H. E. Barbaree (Eds.), *Handbook of sexual assault* (pp. 177–94). New York: Plenum.

Herrenkohl, R. C., Herrenkohl, E. C., & Egolf, B. P. (1983). Circumstances surrounding the occurrence of child maltreatment. *J. Cons. Clin. Psychol., 51*(3), 424–31.

Herzog, D. B., & Rathbun, J. M. (1982). Childhood depression: Developmental considerations. *American Journal of Disorders in Children, 136*(2), 15–20.

Heston, L. (1966). Psychiatric disorders in foster home reared children of schizophrenic mothers. *Brit. J. Psychiat., 112,* 819–25.

Hetherington, E. M. (1973). Girls without fathers. *Psych. Today, 6*(9), 47, 49–52.

Hetherington, E. M., Cox, M., & Cox, R. (1978, May). *Family interaction and the social, emotional and cognitive development of children following divorce.* Symposium on the family: Setting priorities, Institute for Pediatric Service, Johnson & Johnson Baby Food Company. Washington, DC.

Heyman, A., Wilkinson, W. E., Hurwitz, B. J., Helms, M. J., et al. (1987). Early-onset Alzheimer's disease: Clinical predictors of institutionalization and death. *Neurology, 37,* 980–84.

Hilgard, E. R. (1973). The domain of hypnosis: With some comments on alternative paradigms. *Amer. Psychol., 28*(11), 972–82.

Hilgard, E. R. (1974). Weapon against pain: Hypnosis is no mirage. *Psych. Today, 8*(6), 120–22, 126, 128.

Hill, A. L. (1975). Investigation of calendar calculating by an idiot savant. *Amer. J. Psychiat., 132*(5), 557–59.

Hine, F. R. (1971). *Introduction to psychodynamics: A conflict-adaptational approach.* Durham, NC: Duke University Press.

Hine, F. R., Carson, R. C., Maddox, G. L., Thompson, R. J., & Williams, R. B. (1983). *Introduction to behavioral science in medicine.* New York: Springer-Verlag.

Hine, F. R., Pfeiffer, E., Maddox, G. L., Hein, P. L., & Friedel, R. O. (1972). *Behavioral science: A selective view.* Boston: Little, Brown.

Hintzman, D. L. (1990). Human learning and memory: Connections and dissociations. *Ann. Rev. Psychol., 41.* Palo Alto, CA: Annual Reviews, Inc.

Hiroto, D. S., & Seligman, M. E. P. (1975). Generality of learned helplessness in man. *J. Pers. Soc. Psychol., 31*(2), 311–27.

Hirsch, S. R., & Leff, J. P. (1975). *Abnormalities in parents of schizophrenics.* London: Oxford University Press.

Hirschfeld, R. M. A., Klerman, G. L., Andreasen, N. C., Clayton, P. J., & Keller, M. B. (1985). Situational major depressive disorder. *Arch. Gen. Psychiat., 42,* 1109–14.

Hirschfeld, R. M. A., Klerman, G. L., Lavori, P., Keller, M. B., Griffith, P., & Coryell, W. (1989). Premorbid personality assessments of first onset of major depression. *Arch. Gen. Psychiat., 46,* 345–50.

Hirst, W. (1982). The amnesic syndrome: Descriptions and explanations. *Psychol. Bull., 91,* 435–60.

Hoberman, H. M., & Lewinsohn, P. M. (1985). The behavioral treatment of depression. In E. E. Beckham, & W. R. Leber (Eds.), *Handbook of depression: Treatment, assessment, and research* (pp. 39–81). Homewood, IL: Dorsey Press.

Hodgson, R. J., & Rachman, S. (1972). The effects of contamination and washing in obsessional patients. *Behav. Res. Ther., 10*(2), 111–17.

Hodkinson, S., Sherrington, R., Gurling, H., Marchbanks, R., Reeders, S., Mallet, J., McInnis, M., Petursson, H., & Brynjolfsson, J. (1987). Molecular evidence for heterogeneity in manic depression. *Nature, 325,* 805–6.

Hoffman, A. (1971). LSD discoverer disputes "chance" factor in finding. *Psychiat. News, 6*(8), 23–26.

Hoffman, J. L. (1943). Psychotic visitors to government offices in the national capital. *Amer. J. Psychiat., 99,* 571–75.

Hogarty, G. E., Anderson, C. M., Reiss, D. J., Kornblith, S. J., & Greenwald, D. P. (1986). Family psychoeducation, social skills training, and maintenance chemotherapy in the aftercare treatment of schizophrenia: 1. One-year effects of a controlled study. *Arch. Gen. Psychiat., 43,* 633–42.

Hogarty, G. E., McEvoy, J.P., Munetz, M., DiBarry, L., Bartone, P., Cather, R., Cooley, S. J., Ulrich, R. F., Carter, M., & Madonia, M.J. (1988). Dose of Fluphanazine, familial expressed emotion, and outcome in schizophrenia. *Arch. Gen. Psychiat., 45,* 797–805.

Hokanson, J. E., & Burgess, M. (1962). The effects of three types of aggression on vascular process. *J. Abnorm. Soc. Psychol., 64,* 446–49.

Hokanson, J. E., Rubert, M. P., Welker, R. A., Hollander, G. R., et al. (1989). Interpersonal concomitants and antecedents of depression among college students. *J. Abnorm. Psychol., 98,* 209–17.

Hokanson, J. E., Sacco, W. P., Blumberg, S. R., & Landrum, G. C. (1980). Interpersonal behavior of depressed individuals in a mixed-motive game. *J. Abnorm. Psychol.*, 89, 320–33.

Holcomb, W. (1979). *Coping with severe stress: A clinical application of stress-inoculation therapy.* Unpublished doctoral dissertation, University of Missouri-Columbia.

Holden, R. R., Medonca, J. D., & Serin, R. C. (1989). Suicide, hopelessness, and social desirability: A test of an interactive model. *J. Cons. Clin. Psychol.*, 57, 500–4.

Hollander, E., Liebowitz, M. R., Gorman, J. M., Cohen, B., Fyer, A., & Klein, D. F. (1989). Cortisol and sodium lactate-induced panic. *Arch. Gen. Psychiat.*, 46, 135–40.

Hollon, S., & Beck, A. T. (1978). Psychotherapy and drug therapy: Comparisons and combinations. In S. L. Garfield & A. E. Bergin (Eds.), *Handbook of psychotherapy and behavior change* (pp. 437–90). New York: Wiley.

Hollon, S., & Beck, A. T. (1986). Research on cognitive therapies. In S. L. Garfield & A. E. Bergin (Eds.), *Handbook of psychotherapy and behavior change* (3rd ed., pp. 443–82). New York: Wiley.

Hollon, S. D., DeRubeis, R. J., & Evans, M. D. (1987). Causal mediation of change in treatment for depression: Discriminating between nonspecificity and noncausality. *Psychol. Bull.*, 102, 139–49.

Hollon, S. D., & Garber, J. (1990). Cognitive therapy for depression: A social cognitive perspective. *Personality and Social Psychology Bulletin*, 16, 58–73.

Hollt, V., Dum, J., Blasig, J., Schubert, J. P., & Herz, A. (1975). Comparison of in vivo and in vitro parameters of opiate receptor binding in naive and tolerant dependent rodents. *Life Sciences*, 16, 1823–28.

Holmes, L. B., Moser, H. W., Halldorsson, S., Mack, C., Pant, S., & Matzilevich, B. (1972). *Mental retardation: An atlas of diseases with associated physical abnormalities.* New York: Macmillan.

Holmes, T. H., & Rahe, R. H. (1967). The social readjustment rating scale. *J. Psychosom. Res.*, 11(2), 213–18.

Holmes, T. S., & Holmes, T. H. (1970). Short-term intrusions into the life style routine. *J. Psychosom. Res.*, 14(2), 121–32.

Holmstrom, L., & Burgess, A. W. (1975). Assessing trauma in the rape victim. *Amer. J. Nurs.*, 75, 1288.

Holroyd, K. A., & Andrasik, F. (1978). Coping and the self-control of chronic tension headache. *J. Cons. Clin. Psychol.*, 46, 1036–45.

Holroyd, K. A., Andrasik, F., & Westbrook, T. (1977). Cognitive control of tension headache. *Cog. Ther. Res.*, 1, 121–33.

Holvey, D. N., & Talbott, J. H. (Eds.). (1972). *The Merck manual of diagnosis and therapy* (12th ed.). Rahway, NJ: Merck, Sharp, & Dohme Research Laboratories.

Holzman, P. S., Kringlen, E., Matthysse, S., Flanagan, S. D., Lipton, R. B., Cramer, G., Levin, S., Lange, K., & Levy, D. L. (1988). A single dominant gene can account for eye tracking dysfunctions and schizophrenia in offspring of discordant twins. *Arch. Gen. Psychiat.*, 45, 641–47.

Homans, G. C. (1961). *Social behavior: Its elementary forms.* New York: Harcourt Brace Jovanovich.

Homer, L. E. (1974). The anatomy of a runaway. *Human Behav.*, 3(4), 37.

Homme, L. E. (1965). Perspectives in psychology: Control of coverants, the operants of the mind (Vol. 24). *Psychological Record*, 15, 501–11.

Hook, E. B. (1980). Genetic counseling dilemmas: Down's syndrome, paternal age, and recurrence risk after remarriage. *American Journal of Medical Genetics*, 5, 145–51.

Hooker, E. (1957). The adjustment of the male overt homosexual. *Journal of Projective Techniques*, 21, 18–31.

Hooker, E. (1962). The homosexual community. In *Proceedings of the XIV International Congress of Applied Psychology* (Vol. II). *Personality research.* Copenhagen: Munksgaard.

Hooley, J. M. (1985). Expressed emotion: A review of the critical literature. *Clin. Psychol. Rev.*, 5, 119–39.

Hooley, J. M. (1986). Expressed emotion and depression: Interactions between patients and high- versus low-expressed-emotion spouses. *J. Abnorm. Psychol.*, 95, 237–46.

Hooley, J. M., Orley, J., & Teasdale, J. D. (1986). Levels of expressed emotion and relapse in depressed patients. *Brit. J. Psychiat.*, 148, 642–47.

Hooley, J. M., & Teasdale, J. D. (1989). Predictors of relapse in unipolar depressives: Expressed emotion, marital distress, and perceived criticism. *J. Abnorm. Psychol.*, 98, 229–35.

Hore, A. P., & Tryon, W. W. (1989). Study of the similar

structure hypothesis with mentally retarded adults and nonretarded children of comparable mental age. *Amer. J. Ment. Retard.*, 94, 182–88.

Horowitz, M., Marmar, C., Krupnick, J., Wilner, N., & Kaltreider, N. (1984). *Personality styles and brief psychotherapy.* New York: Basic Books.

Horowitz, M. J. (1969a). Flashbacks: Recurrent intrusive images after the use of LSD. *Amer. J. Psychiat.*, 126(4), 147–51.

Horowitz, M. J. (1969b). Psychic trauma. *Amer. Gen. Psychiat.*, 20, 552–59.

Horowitz, M. J., & Solomon, G. F. (1978). Delayed stress response syndromes in Vietnam veterans. In C. R. Figley (Ed.), *Stress disorders among Vietnam veterans: Theory, research, and treatment.* New York: Brunner/Mazel.

Horowitz, M. J., Wilner, N., & Alvarez, W. (1979). Impact of Events Scale: A measure of subjective stress. *Psychosom. Med.*, 41, 209–18.

Horton, D. (1943). The functions of alcohol in primitive societies: A cross-cultural study. *Quarterly Journal of Studies in Alcoholism*, 4, 199–320.

Horton, P. C., Louy, J. W., & Coppolillo, H. P. (1974). Personality disorder and transitional relatedness. *Arch. Gen. Psychiat.*, 30(5), 618–22.

Hoshino, Y., et al. (1980). Early symptoms of autism in children and their diagnostic significance, *Japanese Journal of Child and Adolescent Psychiatry*, 21(5), 284–99.

House of Representatives. (1990). No place to call home: Discarded children in America. A report of the Select Committee on Children, Youth, and Families. Washington, DC: U. S. Government Printing Office.

Householder, J., Hatcher, R., Burns, W., & Chasnoff, I. (1982). Infants born to narcotic addicted mothers. *Psychol. Bull.*, 92(2), 453–68.

Howard, K. I., Davidson, C.V., O'Mahoney, M.T., & Orlinsky, D. E. (1989). Patterns of psychotherapy utilization. *Amer. J. Psychiat.*, 146, 775–78.

Howard, K. I., Kopta, S. M., Krause, M. S., & Orlinsky, D. E. (1986). The dose-effect relationship in psychotherapy. *Amer. Psychol.*, 41, 159–64.

Howes, M. J., & Hokanson, J. E. (1979). Conversational and social responses to depressive interpersonal behavior. *J. Abnorm. Psychol.*, 88, 625–34.

Howes, M. J., Hokanson, J. E., & Loewenstein, D. A. (1985). Induction of depressive affect after prolonged exposure to a mildly depressed individual. *J. Pers. Soc. Psychol.*, 49, 1110–13.

Hsu, L. K. G. (1989). The gender gap in eating disorders: Why are the eating disorders more common among women? *Clin. Psychol. Rev.*, 9, 393–407.

Hu, T. -W., Huang, L. -F., & Cartwright, W. (1986). Evaluation of the costs of caring for the senile demented elderly: A pilot study. *Gerontologist*, 26, 158–63.

Huff, F. W. (1969). A learning theory approach to family therapy. *The Family Coordinator*, 18(1), 22–26.

Hughes, J. R., Higgins, S. T., & Hatsukami, D. K. (1990). Effects of abstinence from tobacco: A critical review. In L. T. Kozlowski, H. Annis, & H. D. Cappell, et al. (Eds.), *Recent advances in alcohol and drug problems* (Vol. 10, pp. 317–97).

Hughes, P. L., Wells, L. A., Cunningham, C. J., & Ilstrup, D. M. (1986). Treating bulimia with desipramine: A double-blind, placebo-controlled study. *Arch. Gen. Psychiat.*, 43, 182–86.

Humphrey, L. L. (1989). Observed family interactions among subtypes of eating disorders using Structural Analysis of Social Behavior. *J. Cons. Clin. Psychol.*, 57, 206–14.

Hunter, E. J. (1976). The prisoner of war: Coping with the stress of isolation. In R. H. Moos (Ed.), *Human adaptation: Coping with life crises.* Lexington MA: D.C. Heath.

Hunter, E. J. (1978). The Vietnam POW veteran: Immediate and long-term effects. In C. R. Figley (Ed.), *Stress disorders among Vietnam veterans.* New York: Brunner/Mazel.

Hunter, E. J. (1981). *Wartime stress: Family adjustment to loss* (USIU Report No. TR-USIU-81-07). San Diego, CA: United States International University.

Hurley, J. R. (1965). Parental acceptance-rejection and children's intelligence. *Merrill-Palmer Quarterly*, 11(1), 19–32.

Hurwitz, N. (1974). The family therapist as intermediary. *The Family Coordinator*, 23(2), 145–58.

Hurwitz, T. D. (1974). Electroconvulsive therapy: A review. *Compr. Psychiat.*, 15(4), 303–14.

Huxley, A. (1954). *The doors of perception.* New York: Harper & Row.

Huxley, A. (1965). Human potentialities. In R. E. Farson (Ed.),

Science and human affairs. Palo Alto, CA: Science and Behavior Books.

Hyatt, R., & Rolnick, N. (Eds.). (1974). *Teaching the mentally handicapped child.* New York: Behavioral Publications.

Hymel, S., & Rubin, K. H. (1985). Children with peer relationships and social skills problems: Conceptual, methodological, and developmental issues. *Annals of child development* (Vol. 2). Greenwich, CT: JAI Press.

Hynd, G. W., & Semrud-Clikeman, M. (1989). Dyslexia and brain morphology. *Psychol. Bull., 106,* 447–82.

Iacono, W. G., Tuason, V. B., & Johnson, R. A. (1981). Dissociation of smooth-pursuit and saccadic eye tracking in remitted schizophrenics: An ocular reaction time task that schizophrenics perform well. *Arch. Gen. Psychiat., 38,* 991–96.

Ikemi, Y., Ago, Y., Nakagawa, S., Mori S., Takahashi, N., Suematsu, H., Sugita, M., & Matsubara, H. (1974). Psychosomatic mechanism under social changes in Japan. *J. Psychosom. Res., 18*(1), 15–24.

Imber, S. D., Glanz, L. M., Elkin, I., Sotsky, S. M., & Boyer, J. L. (1986). Ethical issues in psychotherapy research: Problems in a collaborative clinical trials study. *Amer. Psychol., 41,* 137–46.

Ironside, R., & Batchelor, I. R. C. (1945). The ocular manifestations of hysteria in relation to flying. *British Journal of Ophthalmology, 29,* 88–98.

Isaacson, R. L. (1970). When brains are damaged. *Psych. Today, 3*(4), 38–42.

Iscoe, I., Bloom, B. L., & Spielberger, C. D. (Eds.). (1977). *Community psychology in transition.* Washington, DC: Hemisphere.

Itard, J. (1932). *The wild boy of Aveyron* (G. Humphrey & M. Humphrey, Trans.). New York: Century. (Original work published in Paris, 1799).

Jackson, J. L., Calhoun, K., Amick, A. E., Maddever, H. M., & Habif, V. (1990). Young adult women who experienced childhood intrafamilial sexual abuse: Subsequent adjustment. *Arch. Sex. Behav., 19,* 211–21.

Jaco, E. G. (1960). *The social epidemiology of mental disorders.* New York: Russell Sage Foundation.

Jacobsen, B., & Kinney, D. K. (1980). Perinatal complications in adopted and nonadopted schizophrenics and their controls. *Acta Psychiatr. Scandin.* (Suppl. No. 285), *61,* 337–46.

Jacobson, A. (1989). Physical and sexual assault histories among psychiatric outpatients. *Amer. J. Psychiat., 146,* 755–58.

Jacobson, J. W. (1990). Do some mental disorders occur less frequently among persons with mental retardation? *Amer. J. Ment. Retard., 94,* 596–602.

Jacobson, N. S., Holtzworth-Monroe, A., & Schmaling, K. B. (1989). Marital therapy and spouse involvement in the treatment of depression, agoraphobia, and alcoholism. *J. Cons. Clin. Psychol., 57,* 5–10.

Jacobson, N. S., & Martin, B. (1976). Behavioral marriage therapy: Current status. *Psychol. Bull., 83,* 540–56.

Jacobson, R. R. (1985a). Child firesetters: A clinical investigation. *J. Child Psychol. Psychiat., 26*(5), 759–68.

Jacobson, R. R. (1985b). The subclassification of child firesetters. *J. Child Psychol. Psychiat., 26*(5), 769–75.

James, A. L., & Barry, R. J. (1981). General maturational lag as an essential correlate of early onset psychosis. *J. Autism Devel. Dis., 11*(3), 271–83.

James, S. P., Wehr, T. A., Sack, D. A., Parry, B. L., & Rosenthal, N. E. (1985). Treatment of seasonal affective disorder with light in the evening. *Brit. J. Psychiat., 147,* 424–28.

Janis, I. L. (1958). *Psychological stress: Psychoanalytic and behavioral studies of surgical patients.* New York: Wiley.

Janis, I. L., & Leventhal H. (1965). Psychological aspects of physical illness and hospital care. In B. B. Wolman (Ed.), *Handbook of clinical psychology* (pp. 1360–77). New York: McGraw-Hill.

Janis, I. L., Mahl, G. F., Kagan, J., & Holt, R. R. (1969). *From personality: Dynamics, development, and assessment.* New York: Harcourt Brace Jovanovich.

Janowsky, D. S., El-Yousef, M. K., & Davis, J. M. (1974). Interpersonal maneuvers of manic patients. *Amer. J. Psychiat., 131*(3), 250–55.

Janowsky, D. S., Leff, M., & Epstein, R. (1970). Playing the manic game. *Arch. Gen. Psychiat., 22,* 252–61.

Jarvik, M. E. (1967). The psychopharmacological revolution. *Psych. Today, 1*(1), 51–58.

Jeffrey, R. W., Wing, R. R., & Stunkard, A. J. (1978). Behavioral treatment of obesity: The state of the art, 1978. *Behav. Ther., 9,* 189–99.

Jemmott, J. B., III, & Locke, S. E. (1984). Psychosocial factors, immunologic mediation, and human susceptibility to infectious diseases: How much do we know? *Psychol. Bull., 95,* 78–108.

Jenkins, C. D., Zyzansky, S. J., & Rosenman, R. H. (1971). Progress toward validation of a computer-scored test for the Type A coronary-prone behavior pattern. *Psychosom. Med., 33,* 193–202.

Jenkins, C. D., Zyzanski, S. J., & Rosenman, R. H. (1976). Risk of new myocardial infarction in middle-age men with manifest coronary heart disease. *Circulation, 53,* 342–47.

Jenkins, R. L. (1968). The varieties of children's behavioral problems and family dynamics. *Amer. J. Psychiat., 124*(10), 134–39.

Jenkins, R. L. (1969). Classification of behavior problems of children. *Amer. J. Psychiat., 125*(8), 68–75.

Jenkins, T. S., Parham, I. A., & Jenkins, L. R. (1985). Alzheimer's disease: Caregivers' perceptions of burden. *Journal of Applied Gerontology, 4,* 40–57.

Jennet, B., et al. (1976). Predicting outcome in individual patients after severe head injury. *Lancet, 1,* 1031.

Jenni, M. A., & Wollersheim, J. P. (1979). Cognitive therapy, stress-management training and the type A behavior pattern. *Cog. Ther. Res., 3*(1), 61–73.

Johnson, C. A., & Katz, R. C. (1973). Using parents as change agents for their children: A review. *J. Child Psychol. Psychiat., 14*(3), 181–200.

Johnson, J. (1969). The EEG in the traumatic encephalography of boxers. *Psychiatrica Clinica, 2*(4), 204–11.

Johnson, T., & Maloney, H. (1979). Effects of short-term family therapy on patterns of verbal interchange in disturbed families. *Family Therapy, 4,* 207–13.

Joint Commission on the Mental Health of Children. (1968). Position statement: Statement of the American Orthopsychiatric Association on the work of the Joint Commission on the Mental Health of Children. *Amer. J. Orthopsychiat., 38*(3), 402–9.

Joint Commission on the Mental Health of Children. (1970). *Crisis in child mental health: Challenge for the 1970's.* New York: Harper & Row.

Jones, E. E. (1990). *Interpersonal perception.* New York: W. H. Freeman.

Jones, E. E., Farina, A., Hastorf, A. H., Markus, H., & Miller, D. T. (1984). *Social stigma: The psychology of marked relationships.* New York: W. H. Freeman.

Jones, K. L., & Smith, B. W. (1975). The fetal alcohol syndrome. *Teratology, 12,* 1–10.

Jones, K. L., Smith, B. W., & Hansen, J. W. (1976). Fetal alcohol syndrome: A clinical delineation. *Annals of the New York Academy of Science, 273,* 130–37.

Jones, M. (1953). *The therapeutic community.* New York: Basic Books.

Jones, M. C. (1924). A laboratory study of fear: The case of Peter. *Pedagogical Seminary, 31,* 308–15.

Jones, R. (1984). *The pharmacology of cocaine.* National Institute on Drug Abuse Research Monograph Series 50. Washington, DC: National Institute on Drug Abuse.

Jones, R. A. (1977). *Self-fulfilling prophecies: Social, psychological, and physiological effects of expectancies.* Hillsdale, NJ: Erlbaum Associates.

Jones, R. E. (1983). Street people and psychiatry: an introduction. *Hosp. Comm. Psychiat., 34,* 807–11.

Jones, R. R., Reid, J. B., & Patterson, G. R. (1975). Naturalistic observation in clinical assessment. In P. M. Reynolds (Ed.), *Advances in psychological assessment* (Vol. 3). San Francisco: Jossey-Bass.

Jordan, H.A., & Levitz, L. S. (1975). Behavior modification in a self-help group. *Journal of the American Dietetic Association, 62,* 27–29.

Kaada, B., & Retvedt, A. (1981). Enuresis and hyperventilation response in the EEG. *Develop. Med. Child Neurol., 23*(5), 591–99.

Kagan, J. (1973). In B. Pratt (Ed.), Kagan counters Freud, Piaget theories on early childhood deprivation effects. *APA Monitor, 4*(2), 1–7.

Kagan, J., Kearsley, R. B., & Zelazo, P. R. (1976, February). *The effects of infant day-care on psychological development.* Symposium on the effect of early experience on child development, American Association for the Advancement of Science. Boston.

Kagan, J., Reznick, J.S., & Snidman, N. (1988). Biological bases of childhood shyness. *Science, 240,* 167–171.

Kagan, J., Reznick, R. J., Clarke, C., Snidman, N., & Garcia-Coll, C. (1984). Behavioral inhibition and the unfamiliar. *Child Develop., 55,* 2212–25.

Kahan, J., Kemp, B., Staples, F. R., & Brummel-Smith, K. (1985). Decreasing the burden in families caring for a relative with a dementing illness: A controlled study. *J. Amer. Geriat. Soc., 33,* 664–70.

Kahana, B., Harel, Z., & Kahana, E. (1988). Predictors of psychological well-being among survivors of the Holocaust. In J. P. Wilson, Z. Harel, & B. Kahana (Eds.), *Human adaptation to extreme stress: From the Holocaust to Vietnam* (pp. 171–92). New York: Plenum Press.

Kahn, D. (1990). The dichotomy of drugs and psychotherapy. *Psychiat. Clin. N. Amer., 13,* 197–207.

Kahn, M. W., & Raifman, L. (1981). Hospitalization versus imprisonment and the insanity plea. *Crim. Just. Behav., 8*(4), 483–90.

Kahn, R. L. (1969). Stress: from 9 to 5. *Psych. Today, 3*(4), 34–38.

Kaiser Foundation Health Plan, Inc. (1970). *Planning for Health.* Summer, 1–2.

Kales, A., Paulson, M. J., Jacobson, A., & Kales, J. (1966). Somnambulism: Psychophysiological correlates. *Arch. Gen. Psychiat., 14*(6), 595–604.

Kalin, N. H., Risch, S. C., Janowsky, D. S., & Murphy, D. L. (1981). Use of the dexamethasone suppression test in clinical psychiatry. *J. Clin. Psychopharm., 1,* 64–69.

Kalinowski, L. B., & Hippius, H. (1969). *Pharmacological, convulsive and other somatic treatments in psychiatry.* New York: Grune & Stratton.

Kallmann, F. J. (1958). The use of genetics in psychiatry. *J. Ment. Sci., 104,* 542–49.

Kandel, D. B., Davies, M., Karus, D., & Yamaguchi, K. (1986). The consequences in young adulthood of adolescent drug involvement. *Arch. Gen. Psychiat., 43,* 746–54.

Kandel, E., Mednick, S. A., Kirkegaard-Sorensen, L., Hutchings, B., Knop, J., Rosenberg, R., & Schulsinger, F. (1988). IQ as a protective factor for subjects at high risk for antisocial behavior. *J. Cons. Clin. Psychol., 56,* 224–26.

Kane, J., Honigfeld, G., Singer, J., & Meltzer, H. (1988). Clozapine for the treatment-resistant schizophrenic. *Arch. Gen. Psychiat., 45,* 789–96.

Kane, J., Honigfeld, G., Singer, J., Meltzer, H., & Clozapine Collaborative Study Group. (1988). Clozapine for the treatment-resistant schizophrenic: A double-blind comparison with chlorpromazine. *Arch. Gen. Psychiat., 45,* 789–96.

Kane, J. M., & Smith, J. M. (1982). Tardive dyskinesia: Prevalence and risk factors, 1959–79. *Arch. Gen. Psychiat., 39,* 473–81.

Kang, J., Lemaire, H.-G., Unterbeck, A., Salbaum, J. M., et al. (1987). The precursor of Alzheimer's disease amyloid A4 protein resembles a cell surface receptor. *Nature, 325,* 733–36.

Kanin, E. J. (1985). Date rapists: Differential sexual socialization and relative deprivation. *Arch. Sex. Behav., 14,* 219–31.

Kanner, L., (1943). Autistic disturbances of effective content. *Nervous Child, 2,* 217–40.

Kantorovich, F. (1930). An attempt at associative reflex therapy in alcoholism. *Psychological Abstracts,* 4282.

Kaplan, H. S. (1974). *The new sex therapy.* New York: Brunner/Mazel.

Kaplan, H. S. (1975). *The illustrated manual of sex therapy.* New York: Quadrangle/The New York Times Book Company.

Kaplan, H. S. (1987). *The illustrated manual of sex therapy* (2nd ed.). New York: Brunner/Mazel.

Kaplun, D., & Reich, R. (1976). The murdered child and his killers. *Amer. J. Psychiat., 133*(7), 809–13.

Karnes, M. B., Teska, J. A., & Hodgins, A. S. (1970). The effects of four programs of classroom intervention on the intellectual and language development of 4-year-old disadvantaged children. *Amer. J. Orthopsychiat., 40,* 58–76.

Karnesh, L. J. (with collaboration of Zucker, E. M.). (1945). *Handbook of psychiatry.* St. Louis: C. V. Mosby

Karno, M., Golding, J. M., Sorenson, S. B., & Burnam, M. A. (1988). The epidemiology of obsessive-compulsive disorder in five US communities. *Arch. Gen. Psychiat., 45,* 1094–99.

Karon, B. P., & Vandenbos, G. R. (1981) *Psychotherapy of schizophrenia: Treatment of choice.* New York: Jason Aronson.

Kashani, J. H., Cantwell, D. P., Shekim, W. O., & Reid, J. C. (1982). Major depressive disorder in children admitted to an inpatient community mental health center. *Amer. J. Psychiat., 139*(6), 671–72.

Kashani, J. H., Hodges, K. K., Simonds, J. F., & Hilderbrand, E. (1981a). Life events and hospitalization in children: A comparison with a general population. *Brit. J. Psychiat., 139,* 221–25.

Kashani, J. H., Husain, A., Shekim, W. O., Hodges, K. K., Cytryn, L., McKnew, D. H. (1981b). Current perspectives on childhood depression: An overview. *Amer. J. Psychiat., 138*(2), 143–53.

Kashani, J. H., & Orvaschel, H. (1988). Anxiety disorders in mid-adolescence: A community sample. *Amer. J. Psychiat., 145,* 960–64.

Kashani, J. H., Venzke, R., & Millar, E. A. (1981). Depression in children admitted to hospital for orthopaedic procedures. *Brit. J. Psychiat., 138,* 21–25.

Kasper, S., Wehr, T. A., Bartko, J. J., Gaist, P. A., & Rosenthal, N. E. (1989). Epidemiological findings of seasonal changes in mood and behavior. *Arch. Gen. Psychiat., 46,* 823–33.

Kass, F., Spitzer, R. L., Williams, J. B., & Widiger, T. (1989). Self-defeating personality disorder and DSM III-R: Development of diagnostic criteria. *Amer. J. Psychiat., 146,* 1022–26.

Katon, W., Egan, K., & Miller, D. (1985). Chronic pain: Lifetime psychiatric diagnoses and family history. *Amer. J. Psychiat. 142,* 1156–60.

Katz, M. M., Sanborn, K. O., Lowery, H. A., & Ching, J. (1978). Ethnic studies in Hawaii: On psychopathology and social deviance. In L. C. Wynne, R. L. Cromwell, & S. Matthysse (Eds.), *The nature of schizophrenia: New approaches to research and treatment* (pp. 572–85). New York: Wiley.

Katz, S., & Kravetz, S. (1989). Facial plastic surgery for persons with Down syndrome: Research findings and their professional and social implications. *Amer. J. Ment. Retard., 94,* 101–10.

Kaufman, I., Frank, T., Heims, L., Herrick, J., Reiser, D., & Willer, L. (1960). Treatment implications of a new classification of parents of schizophrenic children. *Amer. J. Psychiat., 116,* 920–24.

Kaufmann, W. (1973). *Without guilt and justice: From decidophobia to autonomy.* New York: Peter H. Wyden.

Kay, S. R., & Singh, M. M. (1989). The positive-negative distinction in drug-free schizophrenic patients. *Arch. Gen. Psychiat., 46,* 711–18.

Kazdin, A. E. (1980). *Behavior modification in applied settings* (2nd ed.). Homewood, IL: Dorsey.

Kazdin, A. E., Moser, J., Colbus, D. & Bell, R. (1985). Depressive symptoms among physically abused and psychiatrically disturbed children. *J. Cons. Clin. Psychol., 94*(3), 298–307.

Kazdin, A. E., & Wilson, G. T. (1978). *Evaluation of behavior therapy: Issues, evidence and research strategies.* Cambridge, MA: Ballinger.

Keating, J.P. (1987, Aug.). *An overview of research on human response during disasters: Major fires, earthquakes, tornadoes, and airplane accidents since 1980.* Paper presented at the American Psychological Association, New York.

Keefe, F. J., & Williams, D. A. (1989). New directions in pain assessment and treatment. *Clin. Psychol. Rev., 9,* 549–68.

Keller, M. B., & Shapiro, R. W. (1982). "Double Depression": Superimposition of acute depressive episodes on chronic depressive disorders. *Amer. J. Psychiat., 139,* 438–42.

Keller, M. B., et al. (1983). "Double Depression": Two-year follow-up. *Amer. J. Psychiat., 140,* 689–94.

Kellner, R. (1985). Functional somatic symptoms and hypochondriasis: A survey of empirical studies. *Arch. Gen. Psychiat., 42,* 821–33.

Kelly, J. A., St. Lawrence, J. S., Brasfield, T. L., Lemke, A., Amidei, T., Roffman, R. E., Hood, H. V., Smith, J. E., Kilgore, H., & McNeill, C., Jr. (1990). Psychological factors that predict AIDS high-risk versus AIDS precautionary behavior. *J. Cons. Clin. Psychol., 58,* 117–20.

Kempe, R., & Kempe, H. (1979). *Child Abuse.* London: Fontana/Open Books.

Kendall, P. C. (1981). Cognitive-behavioral interventions with children. In B. Lahey & A. E. Kazdin (Eds.), *Advances in clinical child psychology* (Vol. 4). New York: Plenum.

Kendall, P. C. (1982a). Cognitive processes and procedures in behavior therapy. In C. M. Franks, G. T. Wilson, P. C. Kendall, & K. D. Brownell, (Eds.), *Annual Review of Behavior Therapy* (Vol. 8). New York: Guilford Press.

Kendall, P. C. (1982b). Integration: Behavior therapy and other schools of thought. *Behav. Ther., 13,* 559-71.

Kendall, P. C., & Braswell, L. (1985). *Cognitive behavioral therapy for impulsive children.* New York: Guilford Press.

Kendall, P. C., & Finch, A. J. (1976). A cognitive-behavioral treatment for impulse control: A case study. *J. Cons. Clin. Psychol., 44,* 852-57.

Kendall, P. C., & Norton-Ford, J. D. (1982). Therapy outcome research methods. In P. C. Kendall & J. N. Butcher (Eds.), *Handbook of research methods in clinical psychology.* New York: Wiley.

Kendler, K. S., & Davis, K. L. (1981). The genetics and biochemistry of paranoid schizophrenia and other paranoid psychoses. *Schizo. Bull., 7,* 689-709.

Kendler, K. S., & Gruenberg, A. M. (1982). Genetic relationship between paranoid personality disorder and the "schizophrenic" spectrum disorders. *Amer. J. Psychiat., 139*(9), 1185-86.

Kendler, K. S., & Gruenberg, A. M. (1984). An independent analysis of the Danish adoption study of schizophrenia: VI. The relationship between psychiatric disorders as defined by DSM-III in the relatives and adoptees. *Arch. Gen. Psychiat., 41,* 555-64.

Kendler, K. S., & Tsuang, M. T. (1981). Nosology of paranoid schizophrenia and other paranoid psychoses. *Schizo. Bull., 7,* 594-610.

Keniston, K. (1977, Nov. 28). Meeting the needs of children: I, The necessity of politics. *Christianity and Crisis.*

Kennedy, J. F. (1963). Message from the President of the United States relative to mental illness and mental retardation. *Amer. Psychol., 18,* 280-89.

Kennedy, T. D., & Kimura, H. K. (1974). Transfer, behavioral improvement, and anxiety reduction in systematic desensitization. *J. Cons. Clin. Psychol., 42*(5), 720-28.

Kernberg, O. F. (1984). *Severe personality disorders.* New Haven, CT: Yale University Press.

Kernberg, O. F. (1989). An ego-psychology-object relations theory of the structure and treatment of pathologic narcissism. *Psychiat. Clin. N. Amer., 10,* 723-31.

Kessler, J. W. (1988). *Psychopathology of childhood* (2nd ed.). Englewood Cliffs, NJ: Prentice Hall.

Kessler, M., & Albee, G.W. (1975). Primary prevention. *Annu. Rev. Psychol., 26,* 557-91.

Kety, S. S. (1987). The significance of genetic factors in the etiology of schizophrenia. *Journal of Psychiatric Research, 21,* 423-29.

Kety, S. S., Rosenthal, D., Wender, P. H., & Schulsinger, F. (1968). The types and prevalence of mental illness in the biological and adoptive families of adopted schizophrenics. In D. Rosenthal & S. S. Kety (Eds.), *The transmission of schizophrenia.* Elmsford, NY: Pergamon.

Kety, S. S., Rosenthal, D., Wender, P. H., Schulsinger, F., & Jacobsen, B. (1975). Mental illness in the biological and adoptive families of adopted individuals who have become schizophrenics: A preliminary report based on psychiatric interviews. In R. Fieve, P. Rosenthal, & H. Brill (Eds.), *Genetic research in psychiatry.* Baltimore: Johns Hopkins University Press.

Kety, S. S., Rosenthal, D., Wender, P. H., Schulsinger, F., & Jacobsen, B. (1978). The biologic and adoptive families of adopted individuals who became schizophrenic: Prevalence of mental illness and other characteristics. In L. C. Wynne, R. L. Cromwell, & S. Matthyse (Eds.), *The nature of schizophrenia: New approaches to research and treatment* (pp. 25-37). New York: Wiley.

Kewman, D., & Roberts, A. H. (1979). Skin temperature biofeedback and migraine headaches. Paper presented at the *Annual Conference of the Biofeedback Society of America,* San Diego.

Keys, A., Brozek, J., Henschel, A., Mickelson, O., & Taylor, H. L. (1950). *The biology of human starvation.* Minneapolis: University of Minnesota Press.

Khantzian, E. J., & Treece, C. (1985). DSM-III psychiatric diagnosis of narcotic addicts: Recent findings. *Arch. Gen. Psychiat., 42*(11), 1067-71.

Kidd, K. K., & Morton, L. A. (1989). The genetics of psychosomatic disorders. In S. Cheren (Ed.), *Psychosomatic medicine: Theory, physiology, and practice* (Vol. 1, pp. 385-424). Madison, CT: International Universities Press.

Kidson, M., & Jones, I. (1968). Psychiatric disorders among aborigines of the Australian Western Desert. *Arch. Gen. Psychiat., 19,* 413-22.

Kidson, M. A. (1973). Personality and hypertension. *J. Psychosom. Res., 17*(1), 35-41.

Kiecolt-Glaser, J., & Glaser, R. (1988). Psychological influences in immunity: Implications for AIDS. *Amer. Psychol., 43,* 892-98.

Kiernan, C. (1985). Behaviour modification. In A. M. Clarke, A. D. B. Clarke, & J. M. Berg (Eds.), *Mental deficiency: The changing outlook* (4th ed., pp. 465-511). London: Methuen.

Kiersch, T. A. (1962). Amnesia: A clinical study of ninety-eight cases. *Amer. J. Psychiat., 119,* 57-60.

Kiesler, C. A. (1983). Social psychologic issues in studying consumer satisfaction with behavior therapy. *Behav. Ther., 14,* 226-36.

Kiev, A. (1972). *Transcultural psychiatry.* New York: Free Press.

Kilpatrick, D. G., Sutker, P. B., Roitch, J. C., & Miller, W. C. (1976). Personality correlates of polydrug users. *Psychol. Rep., 38,* 311-17.

Kimmel, H. D. (1974). Instrumental conditioning of autonomically mediated responses. *Amer. Psychol., 29,* 325-35.

King, C. A., & Young, R. D. (1981). Peer popularity and peer communication patterns: Hyperactivity versus active but normal boys. *J. Abnorm. Child Psychol., 9*(4), 464-82.

King, H. F., Carroll, J. L., & Fuller, G. B. (1977). Comparison of nonpsychiatric blacks and whites on the MMPI. *J. Clin. Psychol., 33,* 725-28.

Kingsley, R. G., & Wilson, G. T. (1977). Behavior therapy for obesity: A comparative investigation of long-term efficacy. *J. Cons. Clin. Psychol., 45,* 288-98.

Kinney, D. K., Woods, B. T., & Yurgelun-Todd, D. (1986). Neurologic abnormalities in schizophrenic patients and their families: II. Neurologic and psychiatric findings in relatives. *Arch. Gen. Psychiat., 43,* 665-68.

Kinsey, A. C., Pomeroy, W. B., & Martin, C. E. (1948). *Sexual behavior in the human male.* Philadelphia: W. B. Saunders.

Kinsey, A. C., Pomeroy, W. B., & Martin, C. E. (1953). *Sexual behavior in the human female.* Philadelphia: W. B. Saunders.

Kinzie, J. D., & Bolton, J. M. (1973). Psychiatry with the aborigines of West Malaysia. *Amer. J. Psychiat., 130*(7), 769-73.

Kirmayer, L. J. (1991). The place of culture in psychiatric nosology: Taijin Kyofusho and DSM III-R. *J. Nerv. Ment. Dis., 179,* 19-28.

Kirsch, E. S. (1974). Narcotics overdosage. *Hospital Medicine, 10,* 8-10, 12, 17-24.

Kirstein, L., Prusoff, B., Weissman, M., & Dressler, D. M. (1975). Utilization review of treatment for suicide attempters. *Amer. J. Psychiat., 132*(1), 22-27.

Klagsbrun, F. (1976). *Too young to die: Youth and suicide.* Boston: Houghton Mifflin.

Klassen, D., & O'Connor, W. A. (1988). A prospective study of predictors of violence in adult male mental health admissions. *Law and Human Behavior, 12,* 143-58.

Klein, D. N., & Depue, R. A. (1984). Continued impairment in persons at risk for bipolar affective disorder: Results of a 19-month follow-up study. *J. Abnorm. Psychol., 93,* 345-47.

Klein, D. N., & Depue, R. A. (1985). Obsessional personality traits and risk for bipolar affective disorder: An offspring study. *J. Abnorm. Psychol., 94,* 291-397.

Klein, D. N., Depue, R. A., & Slater, J. F. (1985). Cyclothymia in the adolescent offspring of parents with bipolar affective disorder. *J. Abnorm. Psychol., 94,* 115-27.

Klein, D. N., Depue, R. A., & Slater, J. F. (1986). Inventory identification of cyclothymia: IX. Validations in offspring of bipolar I patients. *Arch. Gen. Psychiat., 43,* 441-45.

Kleinman, A. (1986). *Social origins of distress and disease: Depression, neurasthenia and pain in modern China.* New Haven, CT: Yale University Press.

Kleinman, A., & Good, B. (1985). *Culture and depression.* Berkeley, CA: University of California Press.

Kleinman, P. H., Miller, A. B., Millman, R. B., Woody, G. E., Todd, T., Kemp, J., & Lipton, D. S. (1990). Psychopathology among cocaine abusers entering treatment. *J. Nerv. Ment. Dis., 178,* 442-47.

Kleinmuntz, B. (1990). Why we still use our heads instead of formulas: Toward an integrative approach. *Psychol. Bull., 107,* 296-310.

Klepac, R. K., Hauge, G., Dowling, J., & McDonald, M. (1981). Direct and generalized effects of three components of stress-inoculation for increased pain tolerance. *Behav. Ther., 12,* 417-24.

Klerman, G. L. (1982). Practical issues in the treatment of depression and mania. In E. S. Paykel (Ed.), *Handbook of affective disorders.* New York: Guilford Press.

Klerman, G. L. (1990). The psychiatric patient's right to effective treatment: Implications of Osheroff v. Chestnut Lodge. *Amer. J. Psychiat., 147,* 409–18.

Klerman, G. L., & Schechter, G. (1982). Drugs and psychotherapy. In E. S. Paykel (Ed.), *Handbook of affective disorders.* New York: Guilford Press.

Klerman, G. L., Weissman, M. M., Rounsaville, B. J., & Chevron, E. S. (1984). *Interpersonal psychotherapy of depression.* New York: Basic.

Kline, N. S. (1954). Use of *Rauwolfia serpentina* in neuropsychiatric conditions. *Annals of the New York Academy of Science, 54,* 107–32.

Klinger, E. (1979). Modes of normal conscious flow. In K. S. Pope & J. L. Singer (Eds.), *The stream of consciousness: Scientific investigations into the flow of human experience.* New York: Plenum.

Klopfer, B., & Davidson, H. (1962). *The Rorschach technique: An introductory manual.* New York: Harcourt Brace Jovanovich.

Klosko, J. S., Barlow, D. H., Tassinari, R., & Cerny, J. A. (1990). A comparison of alprazolam and behavior therapy in the treatment of panic disorder. *J. Cons. Clin. Psychol., 58,* 77–84.

Knapp, P. H. (1989). Psychosomatic aspects of bronchial asthma: A review. In S. Cheren (Ed.), *Psychosomatic medicine: Theory, physiology, and practice* (Vol. 2, pp. 503–64). Madison, CT: International Universities Press.

Knapp, S. (1980). A primer on malpractice for psychologists. *Profess. Psychol., 11*(4), 606–12.

Knapp, S., & Vandecreek, L. (1982). Tarasoff: Five years later. *Profess. Psychol., 13*(4), 511–16.

Knight, R. A., Carter, D. L., & Prentky, R. A. (1989). A system for the classification of child molesters: Reliability and application. *Journal of Interpersonal Violence, 4,* 3–23.

Knight, R. A., & Prentky, R. A. (1990). Classifying sexual offenders: The development and corroboration of taxonomic models. In W. L. Marshall, D. R. Laws, & H. E. Barbaree (Eds.), *Handbook of sexual assault* (pp. 23–52). New York: Plenum.

Knittle, J. L., Timmers, K. I., & Katz, D. P. (1982). Adolescent obesity. In M. Winick (Ed.), *Adolescent nutrition.* New York: Oxford University Press.

Knowles, J. H. (1977). Editorial. *Science, 198,* 1103–4.

Kobasa, S. C. (1979). Stressful life events, personality, and health: An inquiry into hardiness. *J. Pers. Soc. Psychol., 37*(1), 1–11.

Kobasa, S. C. O. (1985). Personality and health: Specifying and strengthening the conceptual fill. In P. Shaver (Ed.), *Self situations and social behavior* (pp. 291–311). Beverly Hills, CA: Sage.

Koch, R. (1967). The multidisciplinary approach to mental retardation. In A. A. Baumeister (Ed.), *Mental retardation: Appraisal, education, and rehabilitation.* Chicago: Aldine.

Koegel, R. L., & Mentis, M. (1985). Motivation in childhood autism: Can they or won't they? *J. Child Psychol. Psychiat., 26*(2), 185–91.

Kog, E., & Vandereycken, W. (1985). Family characteristics of anorexia nervosa and bulimia: A review of the research literature. *Clin. Psychol. Rev., 5,* 159–80.

Kohn, M. L. (1973). Social class and schizophrenia: A critical review and a reformulation. *Schizo. Bull., 7,* 60–79.

Kohut, H., & Wolff, E. (1978). The disorders of the self and their treatment: An outline. *Inter. J. Psychoanal., 59,* 413–26.

Kolata, G. B. (1981a). Clues to the cause of senile dementia: Patients with Alzheimer's disease seem to be deficient in a brain neurotransmitter. *Science, 211,* 1032–33.

Kolata, G. B. (1981b). Fetal alcohol advisory debated. *Science, 214,* 642–46.

Kolko, J. D., Kazdin, A. E., & Meyer, E. C. (1985). Aggression and psychopathology in childhood firesetters: Parent and child reports. *J. Cons. Clin. Psychol., 53*(3), 377–85.

Konopka, G. (1964). Adolescent delinquent girls. *Children, 11*(1), 21–26.

Konopka, G. (1967). Rehabilitation of the delinquent girl. *Adolescence, 2*(5), 69–82.

Kopelman, M. D. (1986). The cholinergic neurotransmitter system in human memory and dementia: A review. *Quarterly Journal of Experimental Psychology: Human Experimental Psychology, 38,* 535–73.

Koranyi, E. K. (1989). Physiology of stress reviewed. In S. Cheren (Ed.), *Psychosomatic medicine: Theory, physiology, and practice* (Vol. 1, pp. 241–78). Madison, CT: International Universities Press.

Kornberg, M. S., & Caplan, G. (1980). Risk factors and preventive intervention in child psychopathology: A review. *Journal of Prevention, 1,* 71–133.

Koscheyev, V. S. (October, 1990). Psychological functioning of Chernobyl workers in the period after the nuclear accident. Invited address. University of Minnesota.

Koss, M. P. (1983). The scope of rape: Implications for the clinical treatment of victims. *Clin. Psychol., 36,* 88–91.

Koss, M. P., & Dinero, T. E. (1989). Discriminant analysis of risk factors for sexual victimization among a national sample of college women. *J. Cons. Clin. Psychol., 57,* 242–50.

Koss, M. P., Gidycz, C., & Wisniewski, N. (1987). The scope of rape: Incidence and prevalence of sexual aggression in a national sample of higher education students. *J. Cons. Clin. Psychol., 55,* 162–70.

Koss, M. P., & Oros, C. J. (1982). Sexual experiences survey: A research instrument investigating sexual aggression and victimization. *J. Cons. Clin. Psychol., 50,* 455–57.

Kosten, T. R. (1989). Pharmacotherapeutic interventions for cocaine abuse. Matching patients to treatments. *J. Nerv. Ment. Dis., 177,* 379–89.

Kosten, T. R., & Rounsaville, B.J. (1986). Psychopathology in opioid addicts. *Psychiat. Clin. N. Amer., 9,* 515–32.

Kosten, T. R., Rounsaville, B.J., & Kleber, H. D. (1988). Antecedents and consequences of cocaine abuse among opioid addicts. A 2.5 year follow-up. *J. Nerv. Ment. Dis., 176,* 176–81.

Kovacs, M. (1989). Affective disorders in children and adolescents. *Amer. Psychol., 44,* 209–15.

Kovacs, M., & Beck, A. T. (1977). An empirical clinical approach towards a definition of childhood depression. In J. G. Schulterbrand & A. Raskin (Eds.), *Depression in children: Diagnosis, treatment and conceptual models.* New York: Raven Press.

Kovacs, M., Gatsonis, C., Paulauskas, S. L., & Richards, C. (1989). Depressive disorders in childhood: IV. A longitudinal study of comorbidity with and risk for anxiety disorders. *Arch. Gen. Psychiat., 46,* 776–82.

Kraepelin, E. (1883). *Compendium der psychiatrie.* Leipzig: Abel.

Krafft-Ebing, R. V. (1950). *Psychopathica sexualis.* New York: Pioneer Publications.

Kraines, S. H. (1948). *The therapy of the neuroses and psychoses* (3rd ed.). Philadelphia: Lea & Febiger.

Kramlinger, K. G., & Post, R. M. (1989). The addition of lithium to carbamezine: Antidepressant efficacy in treatment-resistant depression. *Arch. Gen. Psychiat., 46,* 794–800.

Krantz, D. S., & Glass, D. C. (1984). Personality, behavior patterns, and physical illness: Conceptual and methodological issues. In W. D. Gentry (Ed.), *Handbook of behavioral medicine* (pp. 38–86). New York: Guilford.

Krech, D. (1966). *Environment, heredity, brain, and intelligence.* Paper presented at the Southwestern Psychological Association, Arlington, TX.

Krech, D., Rosenzweig, M. R., & Bennett, E. L. (1962). Relations between brain chemistry and problem-solving among rats raised in enriched and impoverished environments. *Journal of Comparative and Physiological Psychology, 55,* 801–7.

Kress, H. W. (1984). Role of family and networks in emergency psychotherapy. Chapter in E. L. Bassuk & A. Birk (Eds.), *Emergency Psychiatry.* New York: Plenum Press.

Kringlen, E. (1978). Adult offspring of two psychotic parents, with special reference to schizophrenia. In L. C. Wynne, R. L. Cromwell, & S. Matthysse (Eds.), *The nature of schizophrenia: New approaches to research and treatment* (pp. 9–24). New York: Wiley.

Krohn, M. D., Akers, R. L., Radosevich, M. J., & Lanza-Kaduce, L. (1980). Social status and deviance. *Criminology, 18*(3), 303–18.

Kroll, J., & Bachrach, B. (1984). Sin and mental illness in the Middle Ages. *Psychol. Med., 14,* 507–14.

Krystal, H. (1968). *Massive psychic trauma.* New York: International Universities Press.

Kuechenmeister, C. A., Linton, P. H., Mueller, T. V., & White, H. B. (1977). Eye tracking in relation to age, sex, and illness. *Arch. Gen. Psychiat., 34,* 578–79.

Kuhn, T. S. (1962). *The structure of scientific revolutions.* Chicago: University of Chicago Press.

Kuhnley, E. J., Hendron, R. L., & Quinlin D. M. (1982). Firesetting by children. *J. Amer. Acad. Child Psychiat., 21,* 560–63.

Kuperman, S., Black, D. W., & Burns, T.L. (1988). Excess mortality among formerly hospitalized child psychiatric patients. *Arch. Gen. Psychiat., 45,* 277–82.

Kupersmidt, J. B., Coie, J. D., & Dodge, K. A. (1990). The role of poor peer relationships in the development of disorder. In S. R. Asher & J. D. Coie (Eds.), *Peer rejection in childhood* (pp. 274–308). New York: Cambridge University Press.

Kurdeck, L. A., Blisk, D., & Siesky, A.E. (1981). Correlates of children's long-term adjustment to their parents' divorce. *Develop. Psychol., 17,* 565–79.

Kurland, H. D. (1967). Extreme obesity: A psychophysiological disorder. *Psychosomatics, 8,* 108–11.

Kushner, M. (1968). The operant control of intractable sneezing. In C. D. Spielberger (Ed.), *Contributions to general psychology: Selected readings for introductory psychology.* New York: Ronald Press.

Ladd, G. W. (1983). Social networks of popular, average, and rejected children in school settings. *Merrill-Palmer Quarterly, 29,* 283–308.

Lader, M. H., & Petursson, H. (1984). Computed axial brain tomography in long-term benzodiazepine users. *Psychol. Med., 14,* 203–6.

Lahey, B. B., Hartdagen, S. E., Frick, P.J., McBurnett, K., Connor, R., & Hynd, G. W. (1988). Conduct disorder: Parsing the confounded relation to parental divorce and antisocial personality. *J. Abnorm. Psychol., 97,* 334–37.

Lahey, B. B., Russo, M.F., Walker, J. L., & Piacentini, J.C. (1989). Personality characteristics of the mothers of children with disruptive behavior disorders. *J. Cons. Clin. Psychol., 57,* 512–15.

Laing, R. D. (1967, Feb. 3). Schizophrenic split. *Time,* 56.

Laing, R. D. (1969). *The divided self.* New York: Pantheon.

Laing, R. D. (1971). Quoted in J. S. Gordon, *Who is mad? Who is sane? R. D. Laing: In search of a new psychiatry. Atlantic, 227*(1), 50–66.

Laing, R. D., & Esterson, A. (1964). *Sanity, madness, and the family.* London: Tavistock.

Lakin, M. (1991). *Coping with ethical dilemmas in psychotherapy.* Elmsford, NY: Pergamon.

Lamb, H. R. (1984). Deinstitutionalization and the homeless mentally ill. *Hosp. Comm. Psychiat., 35,* 899–907.

Lambert, M. J. (1989). The individual therapist's contribution to psychotherapy process and outcome. *Clin. Psychol. Rev., 9,* 469–85.

Lambert, M. J., Shapiro, D. A., & Bergin, A. E. (1986). The effectiveness of psychotherapy. In S. L. Garfield & A. E. Bergin (Eds.), *Handbook of psychotherapy and behavior change* (3rd ed., pp. 157–212). New York: Wiley.

Lamson, B. (1980). *Sexual arousal of heterosexual, homosexual, and bisexual women.* Unpublished master's thesis, University of Georgia.

Landesman-Dwyer, S. (1981). Living in the community. *Amer. J. Ment. Def., 86,* 223–34.

Lando, H. (in press). Formal quit smoking treatments. In C. T. Orleans and J. Slade (Eds.), *Nicotine addiction: Principles & management.*

Lang, A. R., & Kidorf, M. (1990). Problem drinking: Cognitive behavioral strategies for self control. In M. E. Thase, B. A. Edelstein, & M. Hersen (Eds.), *Handbook of outpatient treatment of adults* (pp. 413–42). New York: Plenum.

Lang, A. R., & Marlatt, G. A. (1983). Problem drinking: A social learning perspective. In R. J. Gatchel, A. Baum, & J. E. Singer, (Eds.), *Handbook of psychology and health* (Vol. 1, pp. 121–69). Hillsdale, NJ: Lawrence Erlbaum Associates.

Lang, P. (1970). Autonomic control. *Psych. Today, 4*(5), 37–41.

Langevin, R., Handy, L., Day, D., & Russon, A. (1985). Are incestuous fathers pedophilic, aggressive, and alcoholic? In R. Langevin (Ed.), *Erotic preference, gender identity, and aggression* (pp. 161–80). Hillsdale, NJ: Erlbaum.

Langner, T. S., Gersten, J. C., Greene, E. L., Eisenberg, J. G., Herson, J. H., & McCarthy, E. D. (1974). Treatment of psychological disorders among urban children. *J. Cons. Clin. Psychol. 42*(2), 70–79.

Lansky, M. R., & Selzer, J. (1984). Priapism associated with trazodone therapy: Case report. *J. Clin. Psychiat., 45,* 232–33.

Lanyon, R. (1984). Personality assessment. *Annu. Rev. Psychol. 35,* 689–701.

Lanyon, R. I. (1986). Theory and treatment in child molestation. *J. Cons. Clin. Psychol., 54,* 176–82.

Lanyon, R. I., Barrington, C. C., & Newman, A. C. (1976). Modification of stuttering through EMG biofeedback: A preliminary study. *Behav. Ther., 7,* 96–103.

Laroche, C., Sheiner, R., Lester, E., Benierakis, C., Marrache, M., Engelsmann, F., & Cheifetz, P. (1987). Children of parents with manic-depressive illness: A follow-up study. *Canad. J. Psychiat., 32,* 563–69.

Latham, C., Holzman, P. S., Manschreck, T. C., & Tole, J. (1981). Optokinetic nystagmus and pursuit eye movements in schizophrenia. *Arch. Gen. Psychiat., 38,* 997–1003.

Laufer, R. S., Brett, E., & Gallops, M. S. (1985). Dimensions of posttraumatic stress disorder among Vietnam veterans. *J. Nerv. Ment. Dis., 173*(9), 538–45.

Laws, D. R., & Marshall, W. L. (1990). A conditioning theory of the etiology and maintenance of deviant sexual preference and behavior. In W. L. Marshall, D. R. Laws, & H. E. Barbaree (Eds.), *Handbook of sexual assault* (pp. 209–30). New York: Plenum.

Lazarus, A. A. (1981). *The practice of multimodal therapy.* New York: McGraw-Hill.

Lazarus, A. A. (Ed.). (1985). *Casebook of multimodal therapy.* New York: Guilford.

Lazarus, A. A. (1989). Dyspareunia: A multimodal psychotherapeutic perspective. In S. R. Leiblum & R. C. Rosen (Eds.), *Principles and practice of sex therapy* (2nd ed., pp. 89–112). New York: Guilford.

Lazarus, A. P. (1968). Learning theory in the treatment of depression. *Behav. Res. Ther., 8,* 83–89.

Leary, T. (1957). *Interpersonal diagnosis.* New York: Ronald.

Lebedev, B. A. (1967). Corticovisceral psychosomatics. *Inter. J. Psychiat., 4*(3), 241–46.

Lebergott, S. (1964). *Manpower in economic growth: The American record since 1800.* New York: McGraw-Hill.

Lebra, W. (Ed.). (1976). Culture-bound syndromes, ethnopsychiatry and alternate therapies. In *Mental health research in Asia and the Pacific* (Vol. 4). Honolulu: University Press of Hawaii.

Lee, J. R., & Goodwin, M. E. (1987). Deinstitutionalization: A new scenario. *Journal of Mental Health Administration, 14,* 40–45.

Leeman, C. P., & Mulvey, C. H. (1974). Brief psychotherapy of the dependent personality: Specific techniques. *Psychonometrics, 25,* 36–42.

Leff, M. J., Roatch, J. F., & Bunney, W. E., Jr. (1970). Environmental factors preceding the onset of severe depressions. *Psychiatry, 33*(3), 298–311.

Lefkowitz, M. M., & Burton, N. (1978). Childhood depression: A critique of the concept. *Psychol. Bull., 85,* 716–26.

Lefkowitz, M. M., Eron, L. D., Walder, L. O., & Huesmann, L. R. (1977). *Growing up to be violent: A longitudinal study of the development of aggression.* New York: Pergamon Press.

Lefkowitz, M. M., Huesmann, L. R., Walder, L. O., & Eron, L. D. (1973). Developing and predicting aggression. *Sci. News, 103*(3), 40.

Lefkowitz, M. M., & Tesiny, E. P. (1985). Depression in children: Prevalence and correlates. *J. Cons. Clin. Psychol., 53,* 647–56.

Lehmann, H. E. (1967). Psychiatric disorders not in standard nomenclature. In A. M. Freedman, H. I. Kaplan, & H. S. Kaplan (Eds.), *Comprehensive textbook of psychiatry.* Baltimore: Williams & Wilkins.

Lehmann, H. E. (1986). The future of psychiatry: Progress-mutation or self-destruct. *Canad. J. Psychiat., 31,* 362–67.

Lehmann, L. (1985). The relationship of depression to other DSM-III Axis I disorders. In E. E. Beckham & W. R. Leber (Eds.), *Handbook of depression: Treatment, assessment, and research* (pp. 669–99). Homewood, IL: Dorsey Press.

Leiblum, S. R., & Pervin, L. A. (1980). *Principles and practice of sex therapy.* New York: Guilford Press.

Leiblum, S. R., Pervin, L. A., & Campbell, E. H. (1989). The treatment of vaginismus: Success and failure. In S. R. Leiblum & R. C. Rosen (Eds.), *Principles and practice of sex therapy* (2nd ed., pp. 113–40). New York: Guilford.

Leiblum, S. R., & Rosen, R. C. (Eds.) (1989a). *Principles and practice of sex therapy,* 2nd ed. New York: Guilford.

Leiblum, S. R., & Rosen, R. C. (1989b). Introduction: Sex therapy in the age of AIDS. In S. R. Leiblum & R. C. Rosen (Eds.), *Principles and practice of sex therapy,* (2nd ed., pp. 1–18). New York: Guilford.

Leiderman, P. H., & Leiderman, G. F. (1974). Affective and cognitive consequences of polymatric infant care in the East African highlands. In A. Pick (Ed.), *Minnesota symposium on child development* (Vol. 8). Minneapolis: University of Minnesota Press.

Lelliott, P., Marks, I., McNamee, G., & Tobena, A. (1989). Onset of panic disorder with agoraphobia. *Arch. Gen. Psychiat., 46,* 1000–1004.

Lemert, E. M. (1962). Paranoia and the dynamics of exclusion. *Sociometry, 25,* 2–25.

Leon, G. (1976). Current directions in the treatment of obesity. *Psychol. Bull., 83,* 557–78.

Leon, G. L. (1983). *Treating eating disorders: Obesity, anorexia nervosa and bulimia.* Lexington, MA: Lewis.

Leon, G. L., Butcher, J. N., Kleinman, M., Goldberg, A., Almagor, M. (1981). Survivors of the holocaust and their children: Current status and adjustment. *J. Pers. Soc. Psychol., 41*(3), 503–16.

Leon, G. R., & Chamberlain, K. (1973). Emotional arousal, eating patterns, and body image as differential factors associated with varying success in maintaining a weight loss. *J. Cons. Clin. Psychol., 40,* 474–80.

Leon, G. R., Eckert, E. D., Teed, D., & Buckwald, H. (1978). Changes in body image and other psychological factors after intestinal bypass surgery for massive obesity. *J. Behav. Med., 2,* 39–59.

Leon, G. R., & Roth, L. (1977). Obesity: Psychological causes, correlations and speculations. *Psychol. Bull., 84,* 117–39.

Leonard, C. V. (1974). Depression and suicidality. *J. Cons. Clin. Psychol., 42*(1), 98–104.

Levenson, A. J. (1981). *Basic psychopharmacology.* New York: Springer.

Levenson, R.W., Sher, K. J., Grossman, L. M., Newman, J., & Newlin, D. B. (1980). Alcohol and stress response dampening: Pharmacological effects, expectancy and tension reduction. *J. Abnorm. Psychol., 89*(4), 528–38.

Levin, S. (1949). Brain tumors in mental hospital patients. *Amer. J. Psychiat., 105,* 897–900.

Levin, S., & Yurgelun-Todd, D. (1989). Contributions of clinical neuropsychology to the study of schizophrenia. *J. Abnorm. Psychol., 98,* 341–56.

Levine, M., & Perkins, D. V. (1987). *Principles of community psychology: Perspectives and applications.* New York: Oxford University Press.

Levine, M. D. (1976). Children with encopresis: A descriptive analysis. *Pediatrics, 56,* 412.

Levine, M. D., & Bakow, H. (1975). Children with encopresis: A study of treatment outcomes. *Pediatrics, 58,* 845.

Levine, S., & Koenig, J. (Eds.). (1980). *Why men rape: Interviews with convicted rapists.* Toronto: Macmillan.

Levitan, H. (1989). Onset situation in three psychosomatic illnesses. In S. Cheren (Ed.), *Psychosomatic medicine: Theory, physiology, and practice* (Vol 1., pp. 119–34). Madison, CT: International Universities Press.

Levitt, L. P. (1974, Apr. 1). *Illinois State Plan for the Prevention, Treatment, and Control of Alcohol Abuse and Alcoholism (Vol. 1): Objectives—Plan of Action—Basic Data.* Department of Mental Health and Developmental Disabilities, State of Illinois.

Levor, R. M., Cohen, M. J., Naliboff, B. D., & McArthur, D. (1986). Psychosocial precursors and correlates of migraine headache. *J. Cons. Clin. Psychol., 54,* 347–53.

Levy, D. L., Yasillo, N. J., Dorcus, E., Shaughnessy, R. Gibbons, R. D., Peterson, J., Janicak, P.G., Gaviria, M., & Davis, J. M. (1983). Relatives of unipolar and bipolar patients have normal pursuit. *Psychiat. Res., 10,* 285–93.

Levy, S. M. (1976). Schizophrenic symptomatology: Reaction or strategy? A study of contextual antecedents. *J. Abnorm. Psychol., 85,* 435–45.

Lewinsohn, P. M. (1974). A behavioral approach to depression. In R. J. Friedman & M. M. Katz (Eds.), *The psychology of depression: Contemporary theory and research.* New York: Halstead Press.

Lewinsohn, P. M., Zeiss, A. M., & Duncan, E. M. (1989). Probability of relapse after recovery from an episode of depression. *J. Abnorm. Psychol., 98,* 107–16.

Lewinson, T. S. (1940). Dynamic disturbances in the handwriting of psychotics; with reference to schizophrenic, paranoid, and manic-depressive psychoses. *Amer. J. Psychiat., 97,* 102–35.

Lewis, C. E., Cloninger, C. R., & Pais, J. (1983). Alcoholism, anti-social personality, and drug use in a criminal population. *Alcohol and Alcoholism, 18,* 53–60.

Lewis, C. E., Robins, L., & Rice, J. (1985). Association of alcoholism with antisocial personality in urban men. *J. Nerv. Ment. Dis., 173*(3), 166–74.

Lewis, J. M., Rodnick, E. H., & Goldstein, M. J. (1981). Intrafamilial interactive behavior, communication deviance, and risk for schizophrenia. *J. Abnorm. Psychol., 90,* 448–57.

Lewis, M. S. (1989a). Age incidence and schizophrenia: Part I. The season of birth controversy. *Schizo. Bull., 15,* 59–73.

Lewis, M. S. (1989b). Age incidence and schizophrenia: Part II. Beyond age incidence. *Schizo. Bull., 15,* 75–80.

Lewis, M. S. (1990). Res ipsa loquitur: The author replies. *Schizo. Bull., 16,* 17–28.

Lewis, M. S., & Griffin, P. A. (1981). An explanation for the season of birth effect in schizophrenia and certain other diseases. *Psychol. Bull., 89,* 589–96.

Lewis, N. D., & Yarnell, H. (1951). Pathological fire setting (pyromania). *Nervous and Mental Disease Monograph,* No. 82.

Lewis, N. D. C. (1941). *A short history of psychiatric achievement.* New York: Norton.

Lewis, R. J., Dlugokinski, E. L., Caputo, L. M., & Griffin, R. B. (1988). Children at risk for emotional disorders: Risk and resource dimensions. *Clin. Psychol. Rev., 8,* 417–40.

Lewis, W. C. (1974). Hysteria: The consultant's dilemma. *Arch. Gen. Psychiat., 30*(2), 145–51.

Lexow, G. A., & Aronson, S. S. (1975). Health advocacy: A need, a concept, a model. *Children Today, 4*(1), 2–6, 36.

Li, T. K., Lumeng, L., McBride, L., & Murphy, J.M. (1987). Rodent lines selected for factors affecting alcohol consumption. *Alcohol and Alcoholism,* Suppl. 1, 91–96.

Liberman, R. P., & Evans, C. C. (1985). Behavioral rehabilitation for chronic mental patients. *J. Clin. Psychopharm., 5,* 8S–14S.

Liberman, R. P., Mueser, K. T., & DeRisi, W. J. (1989). *Social skills training for psychiatric patients.* Elmsford, NY: Pergamon Press.

Liberman, R. P., & Raskin, D. E. (1971). Depression: A behavioral formulation. *Arch. Gen. Psychiat., 24*(6), 515–23.

Lichy, M. H. (1982). Assessment of client functioning in residential settings. In M. Miraba (Ed.), *The chronically mentally ill; Research and services.* New York: SP Medical and Scientific Books.

Lidz, T. (1968). The family, language, and the transmission of schizophrenia. In D. Rosenthal & S. S. Kety (Eds.), *The transmission of schizophrenia* (pp. 175–84). Elmsford, NY: Pergamon Press.

Lidz, T. (1973). *The origin and treatment of schizophrenoid disorders.* New York: Basic Books.

Lidz, T. (1978). Egocentric cognitive regression and the family setting of schizophrenic disorders. In L. C. Wynne, R. L. Cromwell, & S. Matthysse (Eds.), *The nature of schizophrenia: New approaches to research and treatment* (pp. 526–33). New York: Wiley.

Lidz, T., Fleck, S., & Cornelison, A. R. (1965). *Schizophrenia and the family.* New York: International Universities Press.

Lieberman, L. M. (1982). The nightmare of scheduling. *J. Learn. Dis., 15,* 57–58.

Liebowitz, M. R., Fyer, A. J., Gorman, J. M., Dillon, D., Appleby, I. L., Levy, G., Anderson, S., Palij, M., Davies, S. O., & Klein, D. F. (1984). Lactate provocation of panic. *Arch. Gen. Psychiat., 41,* 764–70.

Liebowitz, M. R., Gorman, J. M., Fyer, A. J., Levitt, M., Dillon, D., Levy, P., Appleby, I. L., Anderson, S., Palij, M., Davis, S. O., & Klein, D. F. (1985). Lactate provocation of panic attacks: II. Biochemical and physiological findings. *Arch. Gen. Psychiat., 42,* 709–19.

Liem, J. H. (1974). Effects of verbal communications of parents and children: A comparison of normal and schizophrenic families. *J. Cons. Clin. Psychol., 42,* 438–50.

Liem, J. H. (1980). Family studies of schizophrenia: An update and commentary. *Schizo. Bull., 6,* 429–55.

Lifton, R. J. (1972). The "Gook syndrome" and "numbed warfare," *Saturday Review, 55*(47), 66–72.

Light, E., & Lebowitz, B. D. (1989). Introduction. *Alzheimer's disease treatment and family stress: Directions for research* (pp. vii–viii). Rockville, MD: U.S. Department of Human Services.

Liljefors, I., & Rahe, R. H. (1970). An identical twin study of psychosocial factors in coronary heart disease in Sweden. *Psychosom. Med., 32*(5), 523–42.

Link, B. G., Cullen, F. T., Frank, J., & Wozniak, J.F. (1987). The social rejection of former mental patients: Understanding why labels matter. *American Journal of Sociology, 92,* 1461–1500.

Links, P. S., Boyle, M. H., & Offord, D. R. (1989). The prevalence of emotional disorder in children. *J. Nerv. Ment. Dis., 177,* 85–91.

Lipsky, M. J., Kassinove, H., & Miller, N. J. (1980). Effects of rational-emotive therapy, rational role reversal and rational-emotive imagery on the emotional adjustment of community mental health center patients. *J. Cons. Clin. Psychol., 48,* 366–74.

Lipton, E. L., Steinschneider, A., & Richmond, J. B. (1966). Psychophysiologic disorders in children. In L. W. Hoffman & M. L. Hoffman (Eds.), *Review of child development research* (pp. 169–220). Russell Sage Foundation.

Lisak, D., & Roth, S. (1988). Motivational factors in nonincarcerated sexually aggressive men. *J. Pers. Soc. Psychol., 55*, 795–802.

Lishman, W. A. (1990). Alcohol and the brain. *Brit. J. Psychiat., 156*, 635–44.

Lishman, W. A., Jacobson, R. R., & Acker, C. (1987). Brain damage in alcoholism: Current concepts. *Acta Medica Scandinavica*, (suppl. 717), 5–17.

Litwack, T. R., & Schlesinger, L. B. (1987). Assessing and predicting violence: Research, law, and applications. In A. Hess & I. Weiner (Eds.), *Handbook of forensic psychology*. New York: John Wiley & Sons.

Livesley, W. J., West, M., & Tanney, A. (1985). Historical comment on the DSM III schizoid and avoidant personality disorders. *Amer. J. Psychiat., 142*, 1344–47.

Livingston, J. (1974, Mar.). Compulsive gamblers: A culture of losers. *Psych. Today*, 51–55.

Lloyd, R. W., Jr., & Salzberg, H. C. (1975). Controlled social drinking: An alternative to abstinence as a treatment goal for some alcohol abusers. *Psychol. Bull., 82*, 815–42.

Lobitz, W. C., & Lobitz, G. K. (1978). Clinical assessment in the treatment of sexual dysfunctions. In J. LoPiccolo & L. LoPiccolo (Eds.), *Handbook of sex therapy* (pp. 85–102). New York: Plenum.

Lobovits, D. A., & Handel, P. (1985). Childhood depression: Prevalence using DSM III criteria and validity of parent and child depression scales. *J. Pediat. Psychol., 10*(1), 45–54.

Locke, B. Z., & Regier, D. A. (1985). Prevalence of selected mental disorders. *Mental Health, United States, 1985* (pp. 1–6). Washington, DC: U. S. Government Printing Office.

Lombardo, V.S., & Lombardo, E.F. (1991). The link between learning disabilities and juvenile delinquency: Fact or fiction? *The Correctional Psychologist, 23*, 1–3.

Long, B. (1986). The view from the top: National prevention policy. In M. Kessler and S. E. Goldston (Eds.), *A decade of progress* (pp. 346–62). Hanover, NH: University Press of New England.

LoPiccolo, J. (1978). Direct treatment of sexual dysfunction. In J. LoPiccolo & L. LoPiccolo (Eds.), *Handbook of sex therapy* (pp. 1–17). New York: Plenum.

LoPiccolo, J., & LoPiccolo, L. (Eds.). (1978). *Handbook of sex therapy*. New York: Plenum.

LoPiccolo, J., & Stock, W. E. (1986). Treatment of sexual dysfunction. *J. Cons. Clin. Psychol., 54*, 158–67.

Loranger, A. W., Oldham, J. M., & Tulis, E. H. (1982). Familial transmission of DSM-III borderline personality disorder. *Arch. Gen. Psychol., 39*(7), 795–99.

Lorenz, V. C., & Shuttlesworth, D. E. (1983). The impact of pathological gambling on the spouse of the gambler. *Journal of Community Psychology, 11*, 67–76.

Lorion, R. P. (1990). *Protecting the children: Strategies for optimizing emotional and behavioral development*. New York: Haworth.

Lorr, M., & Klett, C. J. (1968). Cross-cultural comparison of psychotic syndromes. *J. Abnorm. Psychol., 74*(4), 531–43.

Los Angeles Times. (1973, Sept. 30). A transvestite's plea for understanding and tolerance. IV, 7.

Lothstein, L. M. (1982). Sex reassignment surgery: Historical, bioethical, and theoretical issues. *Amer. J. Psychiat., 139*, 417–26.

Lothstein, L. M. (1983). *Female-to-male transsexualism: Historical, ethical, and theoretical issues*. Boston: Routledge & Kegan Paul.

Lou, H. C., Heinriken, L., & Bruhn, P. (1984). Focal cerebral hypoperfusion in children with dysphasia and/or attention deficit disorder. *Archives of Neurology, 14*, 825–29.

Lovaas, O. I. (1977). *The autistic child: Language development through behavior modification*. New York: Holsted Press.

Lovaas, O. I., Schaeffer, B., & Simmons, J. Q. (1974). In O. I. Lovaas & B. D. Bucker (Eds.), *Perspectives in behavior modification with deviant children*. Englewood Cliffs, NJ: Prentice-Hall.

Lovaas, O. I. (1987). Behavioral treatment of normal educational and intellectual functioning in young autistic children. *J. Cons. Clin. Psychol., 44*, 3–9.

Lovett, S. (1985). Microelectronic and computer-based technology. In A. M. Clarke, A. D. B. Clarke, & J. M. Berg (Eds.), *Mental deficiency: The changing outlook* (4th ed., pp. 549–83). London: Methuen.

Lovibond, S. H., & Caddy, G. R. (1970). Discriminated aversive control in the moderation of alcoholics' drinking behavior. *Behav. Ther. 1*, 437–44.

Lubin, B. (1976). Group therapy. In I. Weiner (Ed.), *Clinical methods in psychology*. New York: Wiley.

Lubin, B., Larsen, R. M., & Matarazzo, J. (1984). Patterns of psychological test usage in the United States, 1935–1982. *Amer. Psychol., 39*, 451–54.

Lubin, B., Larsen, R. M., Matarazzo, J. D., & Seever, M. F. (1985). Psychological test usage patterns in five professional settings. *Amer. Psychol., 40*, 857–61.

Lucas, A. R., Duncan J. W., & Piens, V. (1976). The treatment for anorexia nervosa. *Amer. J. Psychiat., 133*, 1034–38.

Lukas, C., & Seiden, H. M. (1990). *Silent grief: Living in the wake of suicide*. New York: Bantam Books.

Lund, S. N. (1975). *Personality and personal history factors of child abusing parents*. Unpublished doctoral dissertation, University of Minnesota.

Lusznat, R. M., Murphy, D. P., & Nunn, C.M. H. (1988). Carbamazepine vs. lithium in the treatment and prophylaxis of mania. *Brit. J. Psychiat., 153*, 198–204.

Lutz, D. J., & Snow, P. A. (1985). Understanding the role of depression in the alcoholic. *Clin. Psychol. Rev., 5*, 535–51.

Lykken, D. T. (1957). A study of anxiety in the sociopathic personality. *J. Abnorm. Soc. Psychol., 55*(1), 6–10.

Lynch, J. J. (1977). *The broken heart*. New York: Basic Books.

Lyon, M., Barr, C. E., Cannon, T. D., Mednick, S. A., & Shore, D. (1989). Fetal neural development and schzophrenia. *Schizo. Bull., 15*, 149–61.

MacDonald, A. D. (1964). Intelligence in children of very low birth weight. *British Journal of Preventive Social Medicine, 18*, 59–75.

MacDonald, M. R., & Kuiper, N. A. (1983). Cognitive-behavioral preparations for surgery: Some theoretical and methodological concerns. *Clin. Psychol. Rev., 3*, 27–39.

MacFarlane, J. W., Allen, L., & Honzik, M. P. (1954). *A developmental study of the behavior problems of normal children between 21 months and 14 years*. Berkeley, CA: University of California Press.

MacLusky, N. J., & Naftolin, F. (1981). Sexual differentiation of the central nervous system. *Science, 211*, 1294–1303.

MacMillan, D. L., & Keogh, B. K. (1971). Normal and retarded children's expectancy for failure. *Develop. Psychol., 4*(3), 343–48.

MacMillan, J., & Kofoed, L. (1984). Sociobiology and antisocial personality: An alternative perspective. *J. Ment. Dis., 172*(12), 701–6.

Maddi, S. R., Bartone, P. T., & Puccetti, M. C. (1987). Stressful events are indeed a factor in physical illness: Reply to Schroeder and Costa. *J. Pers. Soc. Psychol., 52*, 833–43.

Magaro, P. A. (1980) *Cognition in schizophrenia and paranoia*. Hillsdale, NJ: Laurence Erlbaum Associates.

Magaro, P. A. (1981). The paranoid and the schizophrenic: The case for distinct cognitive style. *Schizo. Bull., 7*, 632–61.

Magrab, P. R. (1982). Services for children: Challenge for the 1980's. *J. Pediat. Psychol., 7*(2), 105–10.

Mahler, M. (1976). *On Human symbiosis and the vicissitudes of individuation*. New York: Library of Human Behavior.

Mahoney, G., Glover, A., & Finger, I. (1981). Relationship between language and sensorimotor development of Down's syndrome and nonretarded children. *Amer. J. Ment. Def., 86*, 21–27.

Mahoney, M., & Arnkoff, D. (1978). Cognitive and self-control therapies. In S. Garfield & A. Bergin (Eds.), *Handbook of psychotherapy and behavior change: An empirical analysis*. New York: Wiley.

Mahoney, M. J. (1974). Cognition and behavior modification. Cambridge, MA: Ballinger.

Maida, C. A., Gordon, N. S., & Farberow, N. L. (1989). *The crisis of competence*. New York: Bruner/Mazel.

Maisch, H. (1972). *Incest*. New York: Stein & Day.

Makita, K. (1973). The rarity of "depression" in childhood. *Acta Psychiatrica, 40*, 37–44.

Malamud, N. (1975). Organic brain disease mistaken for psychiatric disorder: A clinicopathologic study. In D. F. Benson & D. Blumer (Eds.), *Psychiatric aspects of neurological disease* (pp. 287–307). New York: Grune & Stratton.

Malamuth, N. M. (1986). Predictors of naturalistic sexual aggression. *J. Pers. Soc. Psychol., 50*, 953–62.

Malatesta, V. J., Sutker, P. B., & Treiber, F. A. (1981).

Sensation seeking and chronic public drunkenness. *J. Cons. Clin. Psychol.*, *49*, 292–94.

Malinowski, B. (1927). *Sex and repression in savage society.* New York: Humanities.

Manderscheid, R. W., Witkin, M. J., Rosenstein, M. J., Milazzo-Sayre, L. J., Bethel, H. E., & MacAskill, R. L. (1985). In C. A. Taube & S. A. Barrett (Eds.), *Mental Health, United States, 1985.* Washington, DC: National Institute of Mental Health, U.S. Government Printing Office.

Manglesdorff, D. (1985). Lessons learned and forgotten: The need for prevention and mental health interventions in disaster preparedness. *Journal of Community Psychology, 13,* 239–57.

Mann, J. (1973). *Time-dated psychotherapy.* Cambridge, MA: Harvard University Press.

Mann, L. M., Chassin, L., & Sher, K. J. (1987). Alcohol expectancies and risk for alcoholics. *J. Cons. Clin. Psychol., 55,* 411–17.

Mann, P. A. (1978). *Community psychology: Concepts and applications.* New York: The Free Press.

Mannuzza, S., Gittelman, R., Bonagura, N., Konig, P. H., & Shenker, R. (1988). Hyperactive boys almost grown up. *Arch. Gen. Psychiat., 45,* 13–18.

Marchant, R., Howlin, P., Yule, W., & Rutter, M. (1974). Graded change in the treatment of the behavior of autistic children. *J. Child Psychol. Psychiat., 15*(3), 221–27.

Marcus, E. R., & Bradley, S. S. (1990). Combination psychotherapy and psychopharmacotherapy with treatment-resistent inpatients with dual disorder. *Psychiat. Clin. N. Amer., 13,* 209–14.

Marcus, J., Hans, S. L., Lewow, E., Wilkinson, L., & Burack, C. M. (1985). Neurological findings in high-risk children: Childhood assessment and 5-year followup. *Schizo. Bull., 11,* 85–100.

Marcus, J., Hans, S. L., Mednick, S. A., Schulsinger, F., & Michelson, N. (1985). Neurological dysfunctioning in offspring of schizophrenics in Israel and Denmark: A replication analysis. *Arch. Gen. Psychiat., 42,* 753–61.

Margolin, G., Christensen, A., & Weiss, R. L. (1975). Contracts, cognition, and change: A behavioral approach to marriage therapy. *The Counseling Psychologist, 5*(3), 15–26.

Margolin, G., & Wampold, B. E. (1981). Sequential analysis of conflict and accord in distressed and non-distressed marital partners. *J. Cons. Clin. Psychol., 49*(4), 554–67.

Mariotto, M. J. (1979). Observational assessment systems use for basic and applied research. *J. Behav. Assess., 1*(3), 239–50.

Marks, I. (1978). Behavioral psychotherapy of adult neurotics. In S. L. Garfield & A. E. Bergin (Eds.), *Handbook of psychotherapy and behavior change: An empirical analysis.* New York: Wiley.

Marks, I. M. (1982). Toward an empirical clinical science: Behavioral psychotherapy in the 1980's. *Behav. Ther., 13,* 63–81.

Marlatt, G. A. (1985). Cognitive assessment and intervention procedures for relapse prevention. In G. A. Marlatt & J. R. Gordon (Eds.), *Relapse prevention.* New York: Guilford Press.

Marlatt, G. A., & Gordon, J. R. (1980). Determinants of relapse: Implications for the maintenance of behavior change. In P. Davidson & S. Davidson (Eds.), *Behavioral medicine: Changing health lifestyles.* New York: Brunner/Mazel.

Marmor, J., & Woods, S. M. (Eds.), (1980). *The interface between psychodynamic and behavior therapies.* New York: Plenum.

Marsella, A. J. (1980). Depressive experience and disorder across cultures. In H. C. Triandis, & J. Draguns (Eds.), *Handbook of cross-cultural psychology* (Vol. 6). Boston: Allyn & Bacon.

Marsella, A. J., Sartorius, N., Jablensky, A., & Fenton, F. R. (1985). Cross-cultural studies of depressive disorders: An overview. In A. Kleinman & B. Good (Eds.), *Culture and depression.* Berkeley, CA: University of California Press.

Marshall, P. (1989). Attention deficit disorder and allergy: A neurochemical model of the relation between the illnesses. *Psychol. Bull., 106,* 434–46.

Marshall, W. L. (1974). A combined treatment approach to the reduction of multiple fetish-related behaviors. *J. Cons. Clin. Psychol., 42*(4), 613–16.

Marshall, W. L., & Barbaree, H. E. (1990). An integrated theory of the etiology of sexual offending. In W. L. Marshall, D. R. Laws, & H. E. Barbaree (Eds.), *Handbook of sexual assault* (pp. 257–69). New York: Plenum.

Marshall, W. L., Laws, D. R., & Barbaree, H. E. (Eds.). (1990a). *Handbook of sexual assault.* New York: Plenum.

Marshall, W. L., Laws, D. R., & Barbaree, H. E. (1990b). Present status and future directions. In W. L. Marshall, D. R.

Laws, & H. E. Barbaree (Eds.), *Handbook of sexual assault* (pp. 389–95). New York: Plenum.

Martin, G. I., & Zaug, P. J. (1975). Electrocardiographic monitoring of enuretic children receiving therapeutic doses of imipramine. *Amer. J. Psychiat., 132*(5), 540–42.

Martin, R. L., Cloninger, R., Guze, S. B., & Clayton, P. J. (1985). Mortality in a follow-up of 500 psychiatric outpatients: I. Total mortality. *Arch. Gen. Psychiat., 42,* 47–54.

Marvit, R. C. (1981). Guilty but mentally ill—an old approach to an old problem. *Clin. Psychol., 34*(4), 22–23.

Marx, J. (1991). Mutation identified as possible cause of Alzheimer's disease. *Science, 251,* 876–77.

Mash, E. J., Handy, L. C., & Hamerlynck, L. A. (1976). *Behavior modification approaches to parenting.* New York: Brunner/Mazel.

Maslow, A. H. (1962). *Toward a psychology of being.* New York: Van Nostrand.

Maslow, A. H. (1969). Toward a humanistic biology. *Amer. Psychol., 24*(8), 734–35.

Masserman, J. H. (1961). *Principles of dynamic psychiatry* (2nd ed.). Philadelphia: W. B. Saunders.

Masters, W. H., & Johnson, V. E. (1966). *Human sexual response.* Boston: Little, Brown.

Masters, W. H., & Johnson, V. E. (1970). *Human sexual inadequacy.* Boston: Little, Brown.

Masters, W. H., & Johnson, V. E. (1975). *The pleasure bond: A new look at sexuality and commitment.* Boston: Little, Brown.

Matarazzo, J. D. (1983). The reliability of psychiatric and psychological diagnosis. *Clin. Psychol. Rev., 3,* 103–45.

Matarazzo, J. D. (1986). Computerized clinical psychological test interpretations: Unvalidated plus all mean and no sigma. *Amer. Psychol., 41,* 14–24.

Matson, J. L. (1981). Use of independence training to teach shopping skills to mildly mentally retarded adults. *Amer. J. Ment. Def., 86,* 178–83.

Matsunaga, E., Tonomura, A., Hidetsune, O., & Yasumoto, K. (1978). Reexamination of paternal age effect in Down's syndrome. *Human Genet., 40,* 259–68.

Mattes, J. A., & Gittelman, R., (1981). Effects of artificial food colorings in children with hyperactive symptoms: A critical review and results of a controlled study. *Arch. Gen. Psychiat., 38*(6), 714–18.

Mattick, R. P., Peters, L., & Clarke, J. C. (1989). Exposure and cognitive restructuring for social phobia: A controlled study. *Behav. Ther., 20,* 3–23.

Maugh, T. M. (1981). Biochemical markers identify mental states. *Science, 214,* 39–41.

Maurer, R., Cadoret, R. J., & Cain, C. (1980). Cluster analysis of childhood temperament data on adoptees. *Amer. J. Orthopsychiat., 50,* 522–34.

Maurer, O. H., & Maurer, W. M. (1938). Enuresis: A method for its study and treatment. *Amer. J. Orthopsychiat., 8,* 436–59.

Mavissakalian, M. R., & Perel, J. M. (1989). Imipramine dose-response relationship in panic disorder with agoraphobia. *Arch. Gen. Psychiat., 46,* 127–31.

May, R. (1969). *Love and will.* New York: Norton.

May, R., Angel, E., & Ellenberger, H. S. (Eds.). (1958). *Existence: A new dimension in psychiatry and psychology.* New York: Basic Books.

Mays, D. T., & Franks, C. M. (Eds.). (1985). *Negative outcome in psychotherapy and what to do about it.* New York: Springer.

Mays, J. A. (1974, Jan. 16). High blood pressure, soul food. *Los Angeles Times,* II, 7.

Maziade, M., Caron, C., Cote, R., Boutin, P., & Thivierge, J. (1990). Extreme temperament and diagnosis: A study in a psychiatric sample of consecutive children. *Arch. Gen. Psychiat., 47,* 477–84.

McAdoo, W. G., & DeMyer, M. K. (1978). Personality characteristics of parents. In M. Rutter & E. Schopler (Eds.), *Autism: A reappraisal of concepts and treatment.* New York: Plenum.

McAlister, A., Puska, P., Koskela, K., Pallonen, U., & Maccoby, N. (1980). Mass communication and community organization for public health education. *Amer. Psychol., 35,* 375–79.

McCall, L. (1961). *Between us and the dark* (originally published in 1947). Summary in W. C. Alvarez, *Minds that came back.*

McCann, I. L., Sakheim, D. K., & Abrahamson, D. J. (1988). Trauma and victimization: A model of psychological adaptation. *Counseling Psychologist, 16,* 531–94.

McCarthy, B. W. (1989). Cognitive-behavioral strategies and techniques in the treatment of early ejaculation. In S. R. Leiblum & R. C. Rosen (Eds.), *Principles and practice of sex therapy* (2nd ed., pp. 141–67). New York: Guilford.

McClelland, D. C. (1979). Inhibited power motivation and high blood pressure in men. *J. Abnorm. Psychol., 88*(2), 182–90.

McCombie, S. L. (1976). Characteristics of rape victims seen in crisis intervention. *Smith College Studies in Social Work, 46,* 137–58.

McCord, W., & McCord, J. (1964). *The psychopath: An essay on the criminal mind.* New York: Van Nostrand Reinhold.

McCrae, R. R., & Costa, P. T. (1986). Clinical assessment can benefit from recent advances in personality psychology. *Amer. Psychol., 41,* 1001–2.

McCutchan, J. A. (1990). Virology, immunology, and clinical course of HIV infection. *J. Cons. Clin. Psychol., 58,* 5–12.

McEwen, B. S. (1981). Neural gonadal steroid actions. *Science, 211,* 1303–11.

McFall, R. M. (1990). The enhancement of social skills: An information-processing analysis. In W. L. Marshall, D. R. Laws, & H. E. Barbaree (Eds.), *Handbook of sexual assault* (pp. 311–30). New York: Plenum.

McFarlane, A. C. (1986). Posttraumatic morbidity of a disaster: A study of cases presenting for psychiatric treatment. *J. Nerv. Ment. Dis., 174*(1), 4–14.

McFarlane, A. C. (1988). The longitudinal course of posttraumatic morbidity: The range of outcomes and their predictors. *J. Nerv. Ment. Dis., 176,* 30–39.

McGlashan, T. H. (1986). The Chestnut Lodge follow-up study: Long-term outcome of borderline personalities. *Arch. Gen. Psychiat., 43,* 20–30.

McLemore, C. W., & Benjamin, L. S. (1979). Whatever happened to interpersonal diagnosis: A psychological alternative to DSM III. *Amer. Psychol., 34,* 17–34.

McNeal, E. T., & Cimbolic, P. (1986). Antidepressants and biochemical theories of depression. *Psychol. Bull., 99*(3), 361–74.

McNeil, D. E., & Binder, R. L. (1986). Violence, civil commitment, and hospitalization. *J. Nerv. Ment. Dis., 174*(2), 107–11.

McNeil, T. F., & Kaij, L. (1978). Obstetrical factors in the development of schizophrenia: Complications in the births of preschizophrenics and in reproduction by schizophrenic parents. In L. C. Wynne, R. L. Cromwell, & S. Matthysse (Eds.), *The nature of schizophrenia: New approaches to research and treatment.* New York: Wiley.

Mead, M. (1949). *Male and female.* New York: Morrow.

Mealiea, W. L., Jr. (1967). *The comparative effectiveness of systematic desensitization and implosive therapy in the elimination of snake phobia.* Unpublished doctoral dissertation, University of Missouri.

Mechanic, D. (1962). *Students under stress.* New York: Free Press.

Medea, A., & Thompson, K. (1974). *Against rape.* New York: Farrar, Straus & Giroux.

Mednick, S. A. (1978). Berkson's fallacy and high-risk research. In L. C. Wynne, R. L. Cromwell, & S. Matthysse (Eds.), *The nature of schizophrenia: New approaches to research and treatment* (pp. 442–52). New York: Wiley.

Mednick, S. A., & Schulsinger, F. (1968). Some premorbid characteristics related to breakdown in children with schizophrenic mothers. In D. Rosenthal & S. S. Kety (Eds.), *The transmission of schizophrenia* (pp. 267–91). Oxford: Pergamon.

Mednick, S. A., Schulsinger, F., Teasdale, T. W., Schulsinger, H., Venables, P., & Rock, D. (1978). Schizophrenia in high risk children: Sex differences in predisposing factors. In G. Serban (Ed.), *Cognitive defects in the development of mental illness.* New York: Brunner/Mazel.

Mednick, S. A., Schulsinger, H., & Schulsinger, F. (1975). Schizophrenia in children of schizophrenic mothers. In A. Davis (Ed.), *Child personality and psychopathology: Current topics* (Vol. 2). New York: Wiley.

Meehl, P. E. (1962). Schizotaxia, schizotypy, schizophrenia. *Amer. Psychol., 17,* 827–38.

Meehl, P. E. (1978). Theoretical risks and tabular asterisks: Sir Karl, Sir Ronald, and the slow progress of soft psychology. *J. Cons. Clin. Psychol., 46,* 806–34.

Meehl, P. E. (1989). Schizotaxia revisited. *Arch. Gen. Psychiat., 46,* 935–44.

Megargee, E. I. (1966). Undercontrolled and overcontrolled personality types in extreme antisocial aggression. *Psychological Monographs, 80* (Whole No. 611).

Megargee, E. I. (1970). The prediction of violence with psychological tests. In C. D. Spielberger (Ed.), *Current topics in clinical and community psychology* (Vol. 2). New York: Academic Press.

Mehrabian, A., & Weinstein, L. (1985). Temperament characteristics of suicide attempters. *J. Cons. Clin. Psychol., 53,* 544–46.

Meichenbaum, D. (1974). *Cognitive behavior modification.* General Learning Corporation, 16.

Meichenbaum, D. (1975). A self-instructional approach to stress management: A proposal for stress-inoculation training. In C. Spielberger & I. Sarason (Eds.), *Stress and anxiety* (Vol. 2). New York: Wiley.

Meichenbaum, D. (1977). *Cognitive-behavior modification.* New York: Plenum.

Meichenbaum, D., & Cameron, R. (1982). Cognitive behavior therapy. In G. T. Wilson & C. M. Franks (Eds.), *Contemporary behavior therapy: Conceptual and empirical foundations.* New York: Guilford.

Meichenbaum, D., & Cameron, R. (1983). Stress inoculation training: Toward a general paradigm for training coping skills. In D. Meichenbaum & M. E. Jaremko (Eds.), *Stress reduction and prevention* (pp. 115–54). New York: Plenum.

Meichenbaum, D., & Goodman, J. (1971). Training impulsive children to talk to themselves: A means of developing self-control. *J. Abnorm. Psychol., 77,* 115–26.

Meichenbaum, D., & Jaremko, M. E. (1983). *Stress reduction and prevention.* New York: Plenum.

Meiselman, K. C. (1978). *Incest.* San Francisco: Jossey-Bass.

Meissner, W. W. (1978). *The paranoid process.* New York: Jason Aronson.

Meissner, W. W. (1981). The schizophrenic and the paranoid process. *Schizo. Bull., 7,* 611–31.

Melges, F. T., & Bowlby, J. (1969). Types of hopelessness in psychopathological process. *Arch. Gen. Psychiat., 20,* 690–99.

Melville, K. (1973). Changing the family game. *The Sciences, 13,* 17–19.

Mendels, J., & Frazer, A. (1974). Brain biogenic amine depletion and mood. *Arch. Gen. Psychiat., 30,* 447–51.

Mendlewicz, J. (1980). X-linkage of bipolar illness and the question of schizoaffective illness. In R. H. Belmaker & H. M. van Praag (Eds.), *Mania: An evolving concept.* New York: Spectrum.

Mendlewicz, J. (1985). Genetic research in depressive disorders. In E. E. Beckham & W. R. Leber (Eds.), *Handbook of depression: Treatment, assessment and research* (pp. 795–815). Homewood, IL: Dorsey Press.

Menninger, K. (1938). *Man against himself.* New York: Harcourt, Brace.

Menninger, K. (1945). *The human mind* (3rd ed.). New York: Knopf.

Menninger, K. (1948). Diagnosis and treatment of schizophrenia. *Bull. Menninger Clin., 12,* 101–4.

Mental Health Law Project. (October, 1987). Court decisions concerning mentally disabled people confined in institutions. *MHLP Newsletter.* Washington, DC.

Merbaum, M. (1977). Some personality characteristics of soldiers exposed to extreme war stress: A follow-up study of post-hospital adjustment. *J. Clin. Psychol., 33,* 558–62.

Merbaum, M., & Hefez, A. (1976). Some personality characteristics of soldiers exposed to extreme war stress. *J. Cons. Clin. Psychol., 44*(1), 1–6.

Merikangas, K. R., Spence, M. A., & Kupfer, D. J. (1989). Linkage studies of bipolar disorder: Methodologic and analytic issues. *Arch. Gen. Psychiat., 46,* 1137–41.

Meyer, C. B., & Taylor, S. E. (1986). Adjustment to rape. *J. Pers. Soc. Psychol., 50,* 1226–34.

Meyer, R. E., & Mirin, S. M. (1979). *The heroin stimulus: Implications for a theory of addiction.* New York: Plenum.

Meyers, J., & Parsons, R. D. (1987). Prevention planning in the school system. In J. Hermalin & J. A. Morell (Eds.), *Prevention planning in mental health.* Beverly Hills, CA: Sage.

Mezey, G. C., & Taylor, P. J. (1988). Psychological reactions of women who have been raped: A descriptive and comparative study. *Brit. J. Psychiat., 152,* 330–39.

Miklowitz, D. J., Goldstein, M. J., & Falloon, I. R. (1983). Premorbid and symptomatic characteristics of schizophrenics from families with high and low levels of expressed emotion. *J. Abnorm. Psychol. 92,* 359–67.

Miklowitz, D. J., Strachan, A. M., Goldstein, M. J., Doane, J. A., & Snyder, K. S. (1986). Expressed emotion and communication deviance in families of schizophrenics. *J. Abnorm. Psychol., 95,* 60–66.

Milby, J. B. (1988). Methadone maintenance to abstinency: How many make it? *J. Nerv. Ment. Dis., 176,* 409–22.

Miles, C. (1977). Conditions predisposing to suicide: A review. *J. Nerv. Ment. Dis., 164,* 232–46.

Miller, J. P. (1975, Spring). Suicide and adolescence. *Adolescence, 10*(37), 11–24.

Miller, K. A. (1989). Enhancing early childhood mainstreaming through cooperative learning: A brief literature review. *Child Study Journal, 19,* 285–92.

Miller, M. L., Chiles, J. A., & Barnes, V. B. (1982). Suicide attempts within a delinquent population. *J. Cons. Clin. Psychol., 50,* 491–98.

Miller, R. (1970). Does Down's syndrome predispose children to leukemia? *Roche Report, 7*(16), 5.

Miller, R. R., & Springer, A. D. (1974). Implications of recovery from experimental amnesia. *Psychol. Rev., 81*(5), 470–73.

Miller, W. R. (1978). Behavioral treatment of problem drinkers: A comparative outcome study of three controlled drinking therapies. *J. Cons. Clin. Psychol., 46,* 74–86.

Miller, W. R. (1979). Problem drinking and substance abuse: Behavioral perspectives. In N. Krasnegar (Ed.), *Behavioral approaches to analysis and treatment of substance abuse.*

Miller, W. R., & Caddy, G. R. (1977). Abstinence and controlled drinking in the treatment of problem drinking. *J. Stud. Alcoh., 38,* 986–1003.

Miller, W. R., & Hester, R. K. (1986). Inpatient alcoholism treatment: Who benefits? *Amer. Psychol., 41,* 794–805.

Miller, W. R., Leckman, A. L., Tinkcom, M., & Rubenstein, J. (1986). Long-term follow-up of controlled drinking therapies. Paper given at the Ninety-fourth Annual Meeting of the American Psychological Association, Washington, DC.

Miller, W. R., & Muñoz, R. F. (1976). *How to control your drinking.* Englewood Cliffs, NJ: Prentice-Hall.

Millon, T. (1981). *Disorders of personality: DSM III, Axis II.* New York: Wiley.

Millon, T. (1986). On the past and future of the DSM-III: Personal recollections and projections. In T. Millon & G. L. Klerman (Eds.), *Contemporary directions in psychopathology: Toward the DSM-IV* (pp. 29–70). New York: Guilford.

Millon, T. (in press). Classification in psychopathology: Rationale, alternatives, standards. *J. Abnorm. Psychol.*

Milner, K. O. (1949). The environment as a factor in the aetiology of criminal paranoia. *J. Ment. Sci., 95,* 124–32.

Milns, R. D. (1986). Squibb academic lecture: Attitudes towards mental illness in antiquity. *Australian and New Zealand J. of Psychiat., 20,* 454–62.

Mindham, R. H. S. (1982). Tricyclic antidepressants and amine precursors. In E. S. Paykel (Ed.), *Handbook of affective disorders.* New York: Guilford Press.

Minuchin, S. (1974). *Families and family therapy.* Cambridge, MA: Harvard University Press.

Minuchin, S., Baker, L., Rosman, B., Liebman, R., Milman, L., & Todd, T. (1975). A conceptual model pf psychosomatic illness in children. *Arch. Gen. Psychiat., 32,* 1031–38.

Mirsky, A. F., DeLisi, L. E., Buchsbaum, M. S., Quinn, O. W., Schwerdt, P., Siever, L. J., Mann, L., Weingartner, H., Zec, R., et al. (1984). The Genain quadruplets: Psychological studies. *Psychiat. Res., 13,* 77–93.

Mirsky, A. F., Silberman, E. K., Latz, A., & Nagler, S. (1985). Adult outcomes of high-risk children. *Schizo. Bull., 11,* 150–54.

Mischel, W. (1973). Toward a cognitive social learning reconceptualization of personality. *Psychol. Rev., 80*(4), 252–83.

Mishler, E. G., & Waxler, N. E. (1968). *Interaction in families: An experimental study of family processes and schizophrenia.* New York: Wiley.

Mitchell, J. (1985). Healing the helper. In National Institute of Mental Health (Ed.), *Role stressors and supports for emergency workers* (pp. 105–18), DHHS Publication No. ADM 85–1408). Washington, DC: U.S. Government Printing Office.

Mitchell, J. E., Pyle, R. L., Eckert, E. D., Hatsukami, D., Pomeroy, C., & Zimmerman, R. (1990). A comparison study of antidepressants and structured intensive group psychotherapy in the treatment of bulimia nervosa. *Arch. Gen. Psychiat., 47,* 149–57.

Mitchell, J. T., & Resnik, H. L. P. (1981). *Emergency response to crisis.* Bowie, MD: Robert J. Brady.

Mobily, K. E., & Hoeft, T. M. (1985). The family's dilemma: Alzheimer's disease. *Activities, Adaptation, and Aging, 6,* 63–71.

Mohr, D. C., & Beutler, L. E. (1990). Erectile dysfunction: A review of diagnostic and treatment procedures. *Clin. Psychol. Rev., 10,* 123–50.

Mohs, R. C., Breitner, J. C., Siverman, J. M., & Davis, K. L. (1987). Alzheimer's disease: Morbid risk among first-degree

relatives approximates 50% by 90 years of age. *Arch. Gen. Psychiat., 44,* 405–8.

Monahan, J. (1981). *Predicting violent behavior: An assessment of clinical techniques.* Beverly Hills, CA: Sage.

Money, J. (1974). Prenatal hormones and postnatal socialization in gender identity differentiation. In J. K. Cole & R. Dienstbier (Eds.), *Nebraska symposium on motivation, 1973* (pp. 221–95). Lincoln, NE: University of Nebraska Press.

Money, J. (1980). *Love and love sickness: The science of sex, gender difference, and pair-bonding.* Baltimore: Johns Hopkins University Press.

Money, J. (1986). *Lovemaps: Clinical concepts of sexual/erotic health and pathology, paraphilia, and gender transposition.* New York: Irvington.

Money, J., & Alexander, D. (1969). Psychosexual development and absence of homosexuality in males with precocious puberty. *J. Nerv. Ment. Dis., 148*(2), 111–23.

Money, J., & Ehrhardt, A. A. (1972). *Man & woman, boy & girl: Differentiation and dimorphism of gender identity.* Baltimore: Johns Hopkins University Press.

Money, J., & Lamacz, M. (1989). *Vandalized lovemaps.* Buffalo, NY: Prometheus.

Monnelly, E. P., Woodruff, R. A., & Robins, L. N. (1974). Manic depressive illness and social achievement in a public hospital sample. *Acta Psychiatr. Scandin., 50,* 318–25.

Monroe, S. M., & Steiner, S. C. (1986). Social support and psychopathology: Interrelations with preexisting disorder, stress, and personality. *J. Abnorm. Psychol., 95,* 29–39.

Montenegro, H. (1968). Severe separation anxiety in two preschool children: Successfully treated by reciprocal inhibition. *J. Child Psychol. Psychiat., 9*(2), 93–103.

Moore, D. F. (Ed.). (1982, Aug.). New antidepressants. *Psychopharmacology Update, 3.* Asheville, NC: Appalachian Hall.

Mora, G. (1967). Paracelsus' psychiatry. *Amer. J. Psychiat., 124,* 803–11.

Moreau, D. L. (1990). Major depression in childhood and adolescence. *Psychiat. Clin. N. Amer., 13,* 355–68.

Moreland, K., & Dahlstrom, W. G. (1983). Professional training with and use of the MMPI. *Profess. Psychol., 14,* 218–23.

Moreno, J. L. (1959). Psychodrama. In S. Arieti et al. (Eds.), *American handbook of psychiatry* (Vol. 2). New York: Basic Books.

Morey, L. C., Skinner, H. A., & Blashfield, R. K. (1984). A typology of alcohol abusers: Correlates and implications. *J. Abnorm. Psychol., 93,* 408–17.

Morishima, A. (1975). His spirit raises the ante for retardates. *Psych. Today, 9*(1), 72–73.

Morlock, L.L. (1989). Recognition and treatment of mental health problems in the general health care sector. In C. A. Taube, D. Mechanic, & A. A. Hohmann (Eds.), *The future of mental health services research* (pp. 39–62). Washington, DC: U.S. Department of Health and Human Services. U.S. Government Printing Office.

Morrison, J. (1980). Adult psychiatric disorders in parents of hyperactive children. *Amer. J. Psychiat., 137*(7), 825–27.

Morrison, J. R. (1973). Catatonia: Retarded and excited types. *Arch. Gen. Psychiat., 28*(1), 39–41.

Morrison, J. R. (1974). Catatonia: Prediction of outcome. *Compr. Psychiat., 15*(4), 317–24.

Morrow, J., & Nolen-Hoeksema, S. (1990). Effects of responses to depression on the remediation of depressive affect. *J. Pers. Soc. Psychol., 58,* 519–27.

Morton, T. L., & Ewald, L. S. (1987). Family-based interventions for crime and delinquency. In E. K. Morris & C. J. Braukmann (Eds.), *Behavioral approaches to crime and delinquency: A handbook of application, research, and concepts* (pp. 271–94). New York: Plenum.

Mott, F. W. (1919). *War neuroses and shell shock.* Oxford: Oxford Medical Publications.

Mucha, T. F., & Reinhardt, R. F. (1970). Conversion reactions in student aviators. *Amer. J. Psychiat., 127,* 493–97.

Munro, J. F., & Duncan, L. J. P. (1972). Fasting in the treatment of obesity. *The Practitioner, 208,* 493–98.

Murphy, G. (1988). Suicide and substance abuse. *Arch. Gen. Psychiat., 45,* 593–94.

Murphy, G. E., Simons, A. D., Wetzel, R. D., & Lustman, P. J. (1984). Cognitive therapy and pharmacotherapy: Singly and together in the treatment of depression. *Arch. Gen. Psychiat., 41,* 33–41.

Murphy, G. E., & Wetzel, R. D. (1990). The lifetime risk of suicide in alcoholism. *Arch. Gen. Psychiat., 47,* 383–92.

Murphy, H. B. (1968). Cultural factors in the genesis of

schizophrenia. In D. Rosenthal & S. S. Kety (Eds.), *The transmission of schizophrenia* (pp. 137-52). Elmsford, NY: Pergamon Press.

Murphy, H. B. (1978). Cultural influences on incidence, course, and treatment response. In L. C. Wynne, R. L. Cromwell, & S. Matthysse (Eds.), *The nature of schizophrenia: New approaches to research and treatment* (pp. 586-94). New York: Wiley.

Murphy, H. B. M. (1982). Culture and schizophrenia. In I. Al-Issa (Ed.), *Culture and psychopathology.* Baltimore: University Park Press.

Murphy, J. M. (1976). Psychiatric labeling in cross-cultural perspective. *Science, 191,* (4231), 1019-28.

Murray, D. C. (1973). Suicidal and depressive feelings among college students. *Psychol. Rep., 33*(1), 175-81.

Murray, H. A. (1938). *Exploration in personality.* New York: Oxford University Press.

Murrin, M. R., & Laws, D. R. (1990). The influence of pornography on sex crimes. In W. L. Marshall, R. D. Laws, & H. E. Barbaree (Eds.), *Handbook of sexual assault* (pp. 73-92). New York: Plenum.

Myers, J. K., Weissman, M. M., Tischler, G. L., Holzer, C. E., Leaf, P. J., & Stoltzman, R. (1984). Six-month prevalence of psychiatric disorders in three communities: 1980 to 1982. *Arch. Gen. Psychiat., 41,* 959-67.

Myers, M. B., Templer, D. I., & Brown, R. (1985). Reply to Wieder on rape victims. Vulnerability does not imply responsibility. *J. Cons. Clin. Psychol., 53,* 431.

Nace, E. P., Orne, M. T., & Hammer, A. G. (1974). Posthypnotic amnesia as an active psychic process. *Arch. Gen. Psychiat., 31*(2), 257-60.

Nagaraja, J. (1974). Somnambulism in children: Clinical communication. *Child Psychiatry Quarterly. 7*(1), 18-19.

Napoleon, N., Chassin, L., & Young, R. D. (1980). A replication and extension of "Physical attractiveness and mental illness." *J. Abnorm. Psychol., 89,* 250-53.

Narby, J. (1982). The evolution of attitudes towards mental illness in pre-industrial England. *Orthomolecular Psychiatry, 11,* 103-10.

Nation's Health. (1986, Aug. 5). Prevention of Wernicke-Korsakoff Syndrome.

National Academy of Sciences. (1990, Mar.). Expanded community role, comprehensive treatment programs urged for alcohol problems. *News from the Institute of Medicine.*

National Association for Mental Health. (1979, Mar. 23). Bulletin No. 103.

National Center for Health Statistics. (1982). Washington, DC: U.S. Government Printing Office.

National Institute of Drug Abuse. (1981). *Trend report: January 1978-September 1980.* Data from Client Oriented Data Acquisition Program (CODAP) (Series E, No. 24). Washington, DC: U.S. Department of Health and Human Services.

National Institute of Drug Abuse. (1990). Washington, DC: U.S. Department of Health and Human Services.

National Institute of Mental Health. (1971). Amphetamines approved for children. *Sci. News, 99*(4), 240.

National Institute of Mental Health. (1976, Apr. 20). Rising suicide rate linked to economy. *Los Angeles Times,* VIII, 2, 5.

National Institute of Mental Health. (1978a, Oct.). *Third report on alcohol and health.* Washington, DC: U.S. Government Printing Office.

National Institute of Mental Health. (1978b). *Indirect services* (Statistical Note No. 147). Washington, DC: U.S. Government Printing Office.

National Institute of Mental Health. (1985a). *Electroconvulsive therapy Consensus Development Conference statement.* Bethesda, MD: U.S. Department of Health and Human Services.

National Institute of Mental Health. (1985b). *Mental Health, United States, 1985.* Washington, DC: U.S. Government Printing Office.

Navia, B. A., Jordan, B. D., & Price, R. W. (1986). The AIDS dementia complex: I. Clinical features. *Annals of Neurology, 19,* 517-24.

Neale, J. M., & Oltmanns, T. F. (1980). *Schizophrenia.* New York: Wiley.

Nee, L. F., Eldridge, R., Sunderland, T., Thomas, C. B., et al. (1987). Dementia of the Alzheimer type: Clinical and family study of 22 twin pairs. *Neurology, 37,* 359-63.

Nelson, F. L. (1984). Suicide: Issues of prevention, intervention, and facilitation. *J. Clin. Psychol., 40,* 1328-33.

Nelson, H. (1969, Oct. 6). Study compares drug dangers. *Los Angeles Times,* 1, 3, 25.

Nelson, H. (1971, Jan. 26). County suicide rate up sharply among young. *Los Angeles Times, II,* 1.

Nelson, H. (1973, Mar. 27). High blood pressure found in third of adults in survey. *Los Angeles Times,* II, 1, 3.

Nelson, H. (1974, Apr. 29). How to be successfully fired. *Behav. Today, 5*(17), 118-19.

Nelson, Z. P., & Mowry, D. D. (1976). Contracting in crisis intervention. *Comm. Ment. Hlth. J., 12,* 37-43.

Nemiah, J. C. (1961). The case of Mary S. *Foundations of psychopathology.* Cambridge: Oxford University Press.

Nemiah, J. C. (1967). Obsessive-compulsive reaction. In A. M. Freedman & H. I. Kaplan (Eds.), *Comprehensive text book of psychiatry.* Baltimore: Williams & Wilkins.

Neufeld, R. W. (1990). Coping with stress, coping without stress, and stress with coping: In inter-construct redundencies. *Stress Medicine, 6,* 117-25.

Neugarten, B. L. (1977). Personality and aging. In J. E. Birren & K. W. Schaie (Eds.), *Handbook of the psychology of aging.* New York: Van Nostrand.

New York Post (1982, May 10). City streets now "warehouse" the mentally ill.

New York State Department of Mental Hygiene. (1978). *The insanity defense in New York.* New York: The New York Department of Mental Hygiene.

Newman, B., Selby, J. V., Quesenberry, C. P., King, M., Friedman, G. D., & Fabsitz, R. P. (1990). Nongenetic influences of obesity on other cardiovascular disease risk factors: An analysis of identical twins. *Amer. J. Pub. Hlth., 80,* 675-78.

Newman, L., Henry, P. B., DiRenzo, P., & Stecher, T. (1988-89). Intervention and student assistance: The Pennsylvania model. Special Issue: Practical approaches in treating adolescent chemical dependency: A guide to clinical assessment and intervention. *J. Chem. Depen. Treat., 2*(1), 145-62.

Newman, L. E. & Stoller, R. J. (1974). Nontranssexual men who seek sex reassignment. *Amer. J. Psychiat., 131*(4), 437-41.

Newman, M. G., & Cates, M. S. (1977). *Methadone treatment in narcotic addiction.* New York: Academic Press.

Nicholson, R. A., & Berman, J. S. (1983). Is follow-up necessary in evaluating psychotherapy? *Psychol. Bull., 93,* 261-78.

Niederland, W. G. (1968). Clinical observations of the survivor syndrome. *Inter. J. Psychoanal., 49,* 313-16.

Nietzel, M. T., & Harris, M. J. (1990). Relationship of dependency and achievement/autonomy to depression. *Clin. Psychol. Rev., 10,* 279-97.

NIMH Psychopharmacology Service Center Collaborative Study Group (1964). Phenothiazine treatment in acute schizophrenia: Effectiveness. *Arch. Gen. Psychiat., 10,* 246-61.

Noble, E. P. (Ed.). (1979). Alcohol and health: Technical support document. Third special report to the U.S. Congress (DHEW Publication No. ADM79-832). Washington, DC: U.S. Government Printing Office.

Noble, P., & Rodger, S. (1989). Violence by psychiatric inpatients. *Brit. J. Psychiat., 155,* 384-90.

Nolen-Hoeksma, S. (1987). Sex differences in unipolar depression: Evidence and theory. *Psychol. Bull., 101,* 259-82.

Noles, S. W., Cash, T. F., & Winstead, B. A. (1985). Body image, physical attractiveness, and depression. *J. Cons. Clin. Psychol., 53,* 88-94.

Noll, K. M., Davis, J. M., & DeLeon-Jones, F. (1985). Medication and somatic therapies in the treatment of depression. In E. E. Beckham & W. R. Leber (Eds.), *Handbook of depression: Treatment, assessment, and research* (pp. 220-315). Homewood, IL: Dorsey Press.

Notman, N. T., & Nadelson, C. C. (1976). The rape victim: Psychodynamic considerations. *Amer. J. Psychiat., 133*(4), 408-13.

Novaco, R. W. (1977). Stress inoculation: A cognitive therapy for anger and its application to a case of depression. *J. Cons. Clin. Psychol., 45,* 600-608.

Noyes, R., Jr., Crowe, R. R., Harris, E. L., Hamra, B. J., & McChesney, C. M. (1986). Relationship between panic disorder and agoraphobia: A family study. *Arch. Gen. Psychiat., 43,* 227-32.

Nurnberger, J., Roose, S. P., Dunner, D. S., & Fieve, R. R. (1979). Unipolar mania: A distinct clinical entity? *Amer. J. Psychiat., 136,* 1420-23.

Nurnberger, J. I., & Gershon, E. S. (1982). Genetics. In E. S. Paykel (Ed.), *Handbook of affective disorders.* New York: Guilford Press.

O'Brien, D. (1979, Mar.). Mental anguish: An occupational hazard. *Emergency, 61–64.*

O'Connell, M., Cooper, S., Perry, J. C., & Hoke, L. (1989). The relationship between thought disorder and psychotic symptoms in borderline personality disorder. *J. Nerv. Ment. Dis., 177,* 273–78.

O'Connell, P. (1976, Nov.). Trends in psychological adjustment: Observations made during successive psychiatric follow-up interviews of returned Navy–Marine Corps POWs. In R. Spaulding (Ed.), *Proceedings of the 3rd annual Joint meeting concerning POW/MIA matters* (pp. 16–22). San Diego.

O'Dell, S. (1974). Training parents in behavior modification: A review. *Psychol. Bull., 81*(7), 418–33.

O'Leary, A. (1985). Self-efficacy and health. *Behav. Res. Ther., 23,* 437–51.

O'Leary, K. D. (1980). Pills or skills for hyperactive children. *J. Appl. Beh. Anal., 13*(1), 191–204.

O'Malley, S. S., Foley, S. H., Rounsaville, B. J., Watkins, J. T., Sotsky, S. M., Imber, S. D., & Elkin, I. (1988). Therapist competence and patient outcome in interpersonal psychotherapy of depression. *J. Cons. Clin. Psychol., 56,* 496–501.

O'Neill, M., & Kempler, B. (1969). Approach and avoidance responses of the hysterical personality to sexual stimuli. *J. Abnorm. Psychol., 74,* 300–305.

Oetting, E. R., & Beauvais, F. (1990). Adolescent drug use: Findings of national and local surveys. *J. Cons. Clin. Psychol., 58,* 385–94.

Office of the Federal Registry. (1982). *The United States Government Manual 1982/1983.* National Archives and Records Service. Washington, DC: U.S. Government Printing Office.

Office of Technology Assessment, U.S. Congress. (1986, Dec.) *Children's mental health: Problems and services.* (OTA Publication No. OTA–BP–H–33). Washington, DC: U.S. Government Printing Office.

Offit, A. K. (1981). *Night thoughts: Reflections of a sex therapist.* New York: Congdon & Lattés.

Ogata, S. N., Silk, K. R., Goodrich, S., Lohr, N. E., & Hill, E. M. (1990). Childhood sexual and physical abuse in adult patients with borderline personality. *Amer. J. Psychiat., 147,* 1008–13.

Okura, K. P. (1975). Mobilizing in response to a major disaster. *Community Health Journal, 2*(2), 136–44.

Oldenburg, B., Perkins, R. J., & Andrews, G. (1985). Controlled trial of psychological intervention in myocardial infarction. *J. Cons. Clin. Psychol., 53,* 852–59.

Olds, S. (1970). Say it with a stomach ache. *Today's Health, 48*(11), 41–43, 88.

Ollendick, T. H. (1981). Self-monitoring and self-administered overcorrection.: The modification of nervous tics in children. *Behavior Modification, 5*(1), 75–84.

Oltmanns, T. F., & Maher, B. A. (Eds.). (1988). *Delusional beliefs.* New York: Wiley.

Opler, M. K., & Singer, J. L. (1959). Ethnic differences in behavior and psychopathology. *Inter. J. Soc. Psychiat., 2,* 11–23.

Orford, J. (1985). *Excessive appetites: A psychological view of addiction.* New York: John Wiley & Sons.

Orlofsky, J. L., & O'Heron, C. A. (1987). Stereotypic and nonstereotypic sex role trait and behavior orientations: Implications for personal adjustment. *J. Pers. Soc. Psychol., 52,* 1034–42.

Orne, M. T., Dinges, D. F., & Orne, E. C. (1984). On the differential diagnosis of multiple personality in the forensic context. *International Journal of Clinical and Experimental Hypnosis, 32,* 118–69.

Oros, C. J., & Koss, M. P. (1978, Aug.). *Women as rape victims.* Paper presented at the American Psychological Association Annual Meeting, Toronto.

Osler, W. (1892). Lectures on angina pectoris and allied states. New York: Appleton-Century-Crofts.

Ost, L-G, & Hugdahl, K. (1981). Acquisition of phobias and anxiety response patterns in clinical patients. *Behav. Res. Ther., 19,* 439–47.

Ostfeld, A. M., & D'Atri, D. A. (1977). Rapid sociocultural change and high blood pressure. In S. Kasl & F. Reichsman (Eds.), *Advances in psychosomatic medicine: Vol. 9, Epidemiologic studies in psychosomatic medicine* (pp. 20–37). Basel, Switzerland, S. Karger.

Overall, J. E., & Hollister, L. E. (1982). Decision rules for phenomenological classification of psychiatric patients. *J. Cons. Clin. Psychol., 50*(4), 535–45.

Overholser, J. C., & Beck, S. (1986). Multimethod assessment of rapists, child molesters, and 3 control groups on behavioral and psychological measures. *J. Cons. Clin. Psychol., 54,* 682–87.

Owen, F. W. (1978). Dyslexia—genetic aspects. In A. L. Benton & D. Pearl (Eds.), *Dyslexia: In appraisal of current knowledge.* (pp. 267–84). New York: Oxford University Press.

Owens, T. H. (1984). Personality traits of female psychotherapy patients with a history of incest. *J. Pers. Assess., 48,* 606–8.

Palmer, R. L. (Ed.). (1981). *Electroconvulsive therapy: An appraisal.* New York: Oxford University Press.

Papp, L., & Gorman, J. M. (1990). Suicidal preoccupation during fluoxetine treatment. *Amer. J. Psychiat., 147,* 1380.

Parker, G., Johnston, P., & Hayward, L. (1988). Parental "expressed emotion" as a predictor of schizophrenic relapse. *Arch. Gen. Psychiat., 45,* 806–13.

Parkes, C. M., Benjamin, B., & Fitzgerald, R. G. (1969). Broken heart: A statistical study of increased mortality among widowers. *Brit. Med. J., 1,* 740–43.

Parkin, M. (1974). Suicide and culture in Fairbanks: A comparison of three cultural groups in a small city of interior Alaska. *Psychiatry, 37*(1), 60–67.

Parnas, J., Teasdale, T. W., & Schulsinger, H. (1985). Institutional rearing and diagnostic outcome in children of schizophrenic mothers. *Arch. Gen. Psychiat., 42,* 762–69.

Pasewark, R. A., Pantle, M. L., & Steadman, H. J. (1982). Detention and rearrest rates of persons found not guilty by reason of insanity and convicted felons. *Amer. J. Psychiat., 139*(7), 892–97.

Paternite, C. E., & Loney, J. (1980). Childhood hyperkinesis: Relationships between symptomatology and home environment. In C. K. Whelan & B. Henker (Eds.), *Hyperactive children: The social ecology of identification and treatment.* New York: Academic Press.

Paterson, R. J., & Neufeld, R. W. (1987). Clear danger: Situational determinants of the appraisal of threat. *Psychol. Bull., 101,* 404–16.

Patterson, C. H. (1989). Eclecticism in psychotherapy: Is integration possible? *Psychotherapy, 26,* 157–61.

Patterson, G. (1971). *Families: Applications of social learning to family life.* Champaign, IL: Research Press.

Patterson, G. R. (1979). Treatment for children with conduct problems: A review of outcome studies. In S. Feshbach & A. Fraczek (Eds.), *Aggression and behavior change: Biological and social processes.* New York: Praeger.

Patterson, G. R., DeBarsyshe, B. D., & Ramsey, E. (1989). A developmental perspective on antisocial behavior. *Amer. Psychol., 44,* 329–35.

Paul, G. L. (1979). New assessment systems for residential treatment, management, research and evaluation: A symposium. *J. Behav. Assess., 1*(3), 181–84.

Paul, G. L. (1982). The development of a "transportable" system of behavioral assessment for chronic patients. Invited address. University of Minnesota, Minneapolis.

Paul, G. L., & Lentz, R. J. (1977). *Psychosocial treatment of chronic mental patients: Milieu versus social-learning programs.* Cambridge, MA: Harvard University Press.

Paul, N. (1971, May 31). The family as patient. *Time,* 60.

Pauly, I. B. (1968). The current status of the change of sex operation. *J. Nerv. Ment. Dis., 147*(5), 460–71.

Pausnau, R. O., & Russell, A. T. (1975). Psychiatric resident suicide. An analysis of five cases. *Amer. J. Psychiat., 132*(4), 402–6.

Paykel, E. S. (1973). Life events and acute depression. In J. P. Scott & E. C. Senay (Eds.), *Separation and depression,* (pp. 215–36.). Washington, DC: American Association for the Advancement of Science.

Paykel, E. S. (Ed.). (1982a). *Handbook of affective disorders.* New York: Guilford Press.

Paykel, E. S. (1982b). Life events and early environment. In E. S. Paykel (Ed.), *Handbook of affective disorders.* New York: Guilford Press.

Paykel, E. S., Hallowell, C., Dressler, D. M., Shapiro, D. L., & Weissman, M. M. (1974). Treatment of suicide attempters. *Arch. Gen. Psychiat., 31*(4), 487–91.

Paykel, E. S., Prusoff, B. A., & Myers, J. K. (1975). Suicide attempts and recent life events. *Arch. Gen. Psychiat., 32*(3), 327–33.

Payne, R. L. (1975). Recent life changes and the reporting of psychological states. *J. Psychosom. Res., 19*(1), 99–103.

Pearlson, G. D., Kim, W. S., Kubos, K. L., Moberg, P. J., Jayaram, G., Bascom, M. J., Chase, G. A., Goldfinger, A. G., & Tune, L. E. (1989). Ventricle-brain ratio, computed tomographic density, and brain area in 50 schizophrenics. *Arch. Gen. Psychiat., 46,* 690–97.

Peck, M. A., & Schrut, A. (1971). Suicidal behavior among college students. *HSMHA Health Reports, 86*(2), 149–56.

Peck, M. L., Farberow, N. L., & Litman, R. E. (Eds.). (1985). *Youth suicide.* New York: Springer.

Pelham, W. E., Schnedler, R. W., Bologna, N. C., & Contreras, J. A. (1980). Behavioral and stimulant treatment of hyperactive children. A therapy study with methylphenidate probes in a within subject design. *J. Appl. Beh. Anal., 13*(2), 221–36.

Pemberton, D. A., & Benady, D. R. (1973). Consciously rejected children. *Brit. J. Psychiat., 123*(576), 575–78.

Penk, W. E., Charles, H. L., & Van Hoose, T. A. (1978). Comparative effectiveness of day hospital and inpatient psychiatric treatment. *J. Cons. Clin. Psychol., 46,* 94–101.

Penna, M. W. (1986). Classification of personality disorders. In J. R. Lion (Ed.), *Personality disorders: Diagnosis and management,* (pp. 10–31). Malabar, FL: Robert F. Kreiger Publishing.

Penrose, L. S. (1963). *Biology of mental defect* (3rd ed.). New York: Grune & Stratton.

Pentz, M. A. (1983). Prevention of adolescent substance abuse through social skill development. *National Institute on Drug Abuse Research Monograph Series, 47,* 195–232.

Perlberg, M. (1979, Apr.). Adapted from Trauma at Tenerife: The psychic aftershocks of a jet disaster. *Human Behav.,* 49–50.

Perls, F. S. (1967). Group vs. individual therapy. *ETC: A review of general semantics, 34,* 306–12.

Perls, F. S. (1969). *Gestalt therapy verbatim.* Lafayette, CA: Real People Press.

Perris, C. (1979). Recent perspectives in the genetics of affective disorders. In J. Mendlewicz & B. Shopsin (Eds.), *Genetic aspects of affective illness.* New York: SP Medical & Scientific Books.

Perris, C. (1982). The distinction between bipolar and unipolar affective disorders. In E. S. Paykel (Ed.), *Handbook of affective disorders.* New York: Guilford Press.

Perry, C. L., & Murray, D. M. (1985). The prevention of adolescent drug abuse: Implications from etiological, developmental, behavioral, and environmental models. *Journal of Primary Prevention, 6*(1), 31–52.

Perry, E. (1988). Acetylcholine and Alzheimer's disease. *Brit. J. Psychiat., 152,* 737–40.

Perry, T. (1970). The enigma of PKU. *The Sciences, 10*(8), 12–16.

Pert, C. B., & Snyder, S. H. (1973, Mar. 9). Opiate receptor: Demonstration in nervous tissue. *Science, 179*(4077), 1011–14.

Pervin, L. A. (1978). *Current controversies and issues in personality.* New York: Wiley.

Peters, J. J. (1976). Children who are victims of sexual assault and the psychology of offenders. *Amer. J. Psychother., 30,* 398–421.

Peterson, C., & Seligman, M. E. P. (1987). Explanatory style and illness. *J.Personal., 55,* 237–265.

Peterson, C., Villanova, P., & Raps, C. S. (1985). Depression and attributions: Factors responsible for inconsistent results in the published literature. *J. Abnorm. Psychol., 94,* 165–68.

Peterson, G. C. (1978). Organic brain syndrome: Differential diagnosis and investigative procedures. *Psychiat. Clin. N. Amer., 1,* 21–36.

Petito, C. K. (1988). Review of central nervous system pathology in human immunodeficiency virus infection. *Annals of Neurology, Suppl., 23,* 54–57.

Pfeffer, C. R. (1981). The family system of suicidal children. *Amer. J. Psychother., 35,* 330–41.

Pfeffer, C. R. (1981). Self-destructive behavior in children and adolescents, *Psychiat. Clin. N. Amer., 8,* 215–26.

Phifer, J. F., & Murrell, S. A. (1986). Etiologic factors in the onset of depressive symptoms in older adults. *J. Abnorm. Psychol., 95,* 282–91.

Pithers, W. D. (1990). Relapse prevention with sexual aggressors: A method for maintaining therapeutic gain and enhancing external supervision. In W. L. Marshall, D. R. Laws, & H. E. Barbaree (Eds.), *Handbook of sexual assault* (pp. 343–62). New York: Plenum.

Pitt, B. (1982). Depression and childbirth. In E. S. Paykel (Ed.), *Handbook of affective disorders.* New York: Guilford Press.

Plater, F. (1664). *Praxeos medical Tomi tres.* (Basil 1656), *Histories and Observations.* London: Culpeper and Cole.

Plato, (n.d.). *The laws* (Vol. 5). (G. Burges, Trans.). London: George Bell & Sons.

Pliner, P. L., & Cappell, H. D. (1974). Modification of affective consequences of alcohol: A comparison of social and solitary drinking. *J. Abnorm. Psychol., 83*(4), 418–25.

Plotkin, R. (1981). When rights collide: Parents, children and consent to treatment. *J. Pediat. Psychol., 6*(2), 121–30.

Plummer, K. J. (1980). Self-help groups for sexual minorities: The case of the pedophile. In D. J. West (Ed.), *Sexual offenders in the criminal justice system* (pp. 72–90). Cambridge, UK: Cambridge University Press.

Pogrebin, M. R., & Poole, E. D. (1987). Deinstitutionalization and increased arrest rates among the mentally disordered. *Journal of Psychiatry & Law,* Spring, 117–27.

Pogue-Guile, M. F., & Rose, R. J. (1985). Developmental genetic studies of adult personality. *Develop. Psychol., 21*(3), 547–57.

Poland, B. J., & Lowry, R. B. (1974). The use of spontaneous abortuses and stillbirths in genetic counseling. *American Journal of Obstetrics and Gynecology, 118,* 322–26.

Polich, J. M., Armor, D. J., & Braiker, H. B. (1981). *The course of alcoholism: Four years after treatment.* New York: Wiley Interscience.

Pollack, J. H. (1968). Five frequent mistakes of parents. *Today's Health, 46*(5), 14–15, 26–29.

Pollack, J. M. (1979). Obsessive-compulsive personality: A review. *Psychol. Bull. 86*(2), 225–41.

Pollard, C. A., Pollard, H. J., & Corn, K. J. (1989). Panic onset and major events in the lives of agoraphobics: A test of contiguity. *J. Abnorm. Psychol., 98,* 318–21.

Pollin, W., Allen, M. G., Hoffer, A., Stabenau, J. R., & Hrubec, Z. (1969). Psychopathology in 15,909 pairs of veteran twins. *Amer. J. Psychiat., 126,* 597–609.

Pollin, W., Stabenau, J. & Tupin, J. (1965). Family studies with identical twins discordant for schizophrenia. *Psychiatry, 28,* 60–78.

Polner, M. (1968). Vietnam War stories. *Transaction, 6*(1), 8–20.

Polvan, N. (1969). Historical aspects of mental ills in Middle East discussed. *Roche Reports, 6*(12), 3.

Polyson, J., Peterson, R., & Marshall, C. (1986). MMPI and Rorschach: Three decades of research. *Profess. Psychol. 17*(5), 476–78.

Pope, K. S., & Vetter, V. A. (in press). Prior therapist-patient sexual involvement among patients seen by psychologists. *Psychotherapy.*

Posener, J. A., Le Haye, A., & Cheifetz, P. N. (1989). Suicide notes in adolescence. *Canad. J. Psychiat., 34,* 171–76.

Post, R. M. (1975). Cocaine psychoses: A continuum model. *Amer. J. Psychiat., 132*(3), 225–31.

Poznanski, E., & Zrull, J. P. (1970). Childhood depression. *Arch. Gen. Psychiat., 23*(1), 8–15.

Poznanski, E. O. (1973). Children with excessive fears. *Amer. J. Orthopsychiat., 43*(3), 428–38.

President's Commission on Law Enforcement and Adminstration of Justice. (1967). Katzenbach, N. D. (Chairman), *The challenge of crime in a free society.* Washington, DC: U.S. Government Printing Office.

President's Commission on Mental Health. (1978). *Report to the President.* Washington, DC: U.S. Government Printing Office.

President's Committee on Mental Retardation. (1970). The *decisive decade.* Washington, DC: U.S. Government Printing Office.

Price, R. W., Brew, B., Sidtis, J., Rosenblum, M., Scheck, A. C., & Cleary, P. (1988a). The brain in AIDS: Central nervous system HIV-1 infection and the AIDS dementia complex. *Science, 239,* 586–92.

Price, R. W., Sidtis, J., & Rosenblum, M. (1988b). The AIDS dementia complex: Some current questions. *Annals of Neurology, Suppl., 23,* 27–33.

Pringle, M. L. K. (1965). *Deprivation and education.* New York: Humanities Press.

Prinz, R. J., Connor, P. A., & Wilson, C. C. (1981). Hyperactive and aggressive behaviors in childhood: Intertwined dimensions. *J. Abnorm. Child Psychol., 9*(2), 191–202.

Prior, M., & Wherry, J. S. (1986). Autism, schizophrenia, and allied disorders. In H. C. Quay and J. S. Wherry (Eds.), *Psychopathological disorders of childhood* (3rd ed., pp. 156–210). New York: Wiley.

Prizant, B. M. (1983). Language acquisition and communicative behavior in autism: Toward an understanding of the "whole" of it. *J. Speech Hear. Dis., 46,* 241–49.

Prizant, B. M., & Duchan, J. F. (1981). The functions of

immediate echolalia in autistic children. *J. Speech Hear. Dis.*, *465*(3), 241–49.

Project DAWN Drug Enforcement Agency (1988). Drug Abuse Warning Newtwork: Project DAWN.

Provence, S., & Lipton, R. C. (1962). *Infants in institutions.* New York: International Universities Press.

Prusoff, B., & Klerman, G. L. (1974). Differentiating depressed from anxious neurotic outpatients. *Arch. Gen. Psychiat.*, *30*(3), 302–9.

Puig-Antich, J., Goetz, D., Davies, M., Kaplan, T., Davies, S., Ostrow, L., Asnis, L., Twomey, J., Iyengar, S., & Ryan, N. D. (1989). A controlled family history study of prepubertal major depressive disorder. *Arch. Gen. Psychiat.*, *46*, 406–18.

Puig-Antich, J., Lukens, D., Davies, M., Goetz, D., & Brennan-Quattrock, J. (1985). Psychosocial functioning in prepubertal major depressive disorders: I. Interpersonal relationships during the depressive episode. *Arch. Gen. Psychiat.*, *42*, 500–57.

Puska, P. (1983, Feb./Mar.). Television can save lives. *World Health.* Geneva, Switzerland: Magazine of the World Health Organization, 8–11.

Puska, P., Tuomíehto, J., Salonen, J., Neittaanmäki, L., Maki, J., Virtamo, J., Nissinen, A., Koskela, K., & Takalo, T. (1979). Changes in coronary risk factors during a comprehensive five-year community programme to control cardiovascular diseases (North Karelia Project). *Brit. Med. J.*, *2*, 1173–78.

Putallaz, M., & Gottman, J. M. (1983). Social relationship problems in children: An approach to intervention. In B. B. Lahey & A. E. Kazdin (Eds.), *Advances in clinical child psychology* (Vol. 6). New York: Plenum.

Putnam, F. W., Guroff, J. J., Silberman, E. K., Barban, L., & Post, R. M. (1986). The clinical phenomenology of multiple personality disorder: Review of 100 recent cases. *J. Clin . Psychiat.*, *47*, 285–93.

Pynoos, R. S., Frederick, C., Nader, K., Arroyo, W., Steinberg, A., Eth, S., Nunez, F., & Fairbanks, L. (1987). Life threat and posttraumatic stress in school-age children. *Arch. Gen. Psychiat.*, *44*, 1057–63.

Quay, H. C. (1965). Psychopathic personality as pathological stimulation seeking. *Amer. J. Psychiat.*, *122*(2), 180–83.

Quay, H. C. (1979). Classification. In H. C. Quay & J. S. Wherry (Eds.), *Psychopathological disorders of childhood.* New York: Wiley.

Quinsey, V. L., Chaplin, T. C., & Upfold, D. (1984). Sexual arousal to nonsexual violence and sadomasochistic themes among rapists and non-sex offenders. *J. Cons. Clin. Psychol.*, *52*, 651–57.

Rabin, A. I., Doneson, S. L., & Jentons, R. L. (1979). Studies of psychological functions in schizophrenia. In L. Bellak (Ed.), *The schizophrenic syndrome.* New York: Basic Books.

Rabkin, J. (1972). Public attitudes about mental illness: A review of the literature. *Schizo. Bull.*, *10*, 9–33.

Rachman, J. G., & Hodgson, R. (1980). *Obsessions and compulsions.* Englewood Cliffs, NJ: Prentice-Hall.

Rachman, S. J. (1978). *Fear and courage.* San Francisco, CA: Freeman.

Rado, S. (1956). *Psychoanalysis and behavior.* New York: Grune & Stratton.

Ragland, D. R., & Brand, R. J. (1988). Type A behavior and mortality from coronary heart disease. *New Engl. J. Med.*, *318*, 65–69.

Rahe, R. H. (1974). Life changes and subsequent illness reports. In K. E. Gunderson & R. H. Rahe (Eds.), *Life stress and illness.* Springfield, IL: Thomas.

Rahe, R. H., & Arthur, R. J. (1978). Life changes and illness studies: Past history and future directions. *Journal of Human Stress*, *4*, 3–15.

Ramey, C. T., & Haskins, R. (1981). The causes and treatment of school failure: Insights from the Carolina Abecedarian Project. In M. J. Begab, H. C. Haywood, & H. L. Garber (Eds.), *Psychosocial influences in retarded performance*, Vol. II. Baltimore: University Park Press.

Rao, A. V. (1970). A study of depression as prevalent in South India. *Transcultural Psychiat. Research Review*, *7*, 116–20.

Rapaport, K., & Burkhart, B. R. (1984). Personality and attitudinal characteristics of sexually coercive college males. *J. Abnorm. Psychol.*, *93*, 216–21.

Rapoport, J. L., & Ferguson, H. B. (1981). Biological

validiation of the hyperkinetic syndrome. *Dev. Med. Child Neurol.*, *23*(5), 667–82.

Reed, S. D., Katkin, E. S., & Goldband, S. (1986). Biofeedback and behavioral medicine. In F. H. Kanfer & A. P. Goldstein (Eds.), *Helping people change: A textbook of methods* (3rd ed.). Elmsford, NY: Pergamon.

Rees, T. P. (1957). Back to moral treatment and community care. *J. Ment. Sci.*, *103*, 303–13. In H. B. Adams "Mental illness" or interpersonal behavior? *Amer. Psychologist*, 1964, 19, 191–97.

Regier, D. A., Boyd, J. H., Burke, J. D., Rae, D. S., Myers, J. K., Kramer, M., Robins, L. N., George, L. K., Karno, M., & Locke, B. Z. (1988). One-month prevalence of mental disorders in the United States. *Arch. Gen. Psychiat.*, *45*, 877–986.

Regier, D. A., Myers, J. K., Kramer, M., Robins, L. N., Blazer, D. G., Hough, R. L., Eaton, W. W., & Locke, B. Z. (1984). The NIMH epidemiologic catchment area program. *Arch. Gen. Psychiat.*, *41*, 934–48.

Reice, S. (1974). Editorial. *Fam. Hlth.*, *6*(4), 4.

Reich, J. (1989). Validity of criteria for DSM III self-defeating personality disorder. *Psychiat. Res.*, *30*, 145–53.

Reich, J., Yates, W., Nduaguba, M. (1989). Prevalence of DSM III personality disorders in the community. *Social Psychiatry and Psychiatric Epidemiology*, *24*, 12–16.

Reid, A. H. (1985). Psychiatric disorders. In A. M. Clarke, A. B. D. Clarke, & J. M. Berg (Eds.), *Mental deficiency: The changing outlook*, (4th ed., pp. 291–325). London: Methuen.

Reisberg, B. (1984). "Is Alzheimer's disease inherited? A methodologic review": Commentary. *Integr. Psychiat.*, *2*, 171–73.

Rentzel, L. (1972). *When all the laughter died in sorrow.* New York: Saturday Review Press.

Renvoize, E. B., Mindham, R. H., Stewart, M., McDonald, R., et al. (1986). Identical twins discordant for presenile dementia of the Alzheimer type. *Brit. J. Psychiat.*, *149*, 509–12.

Retterstøl, N. (1975). Suicide in Norway. In N. L. Farberow (Ed.), *Suicide in different cultures* (pp. 77–94). Baltimore: University Park Press.

Revitch, E., & Weiss, R. G. (1962). The pedophiliac offender. *Dis. Nerv. Sys.*, *23*, 73–78.

Reynolds, D. K., & Farberow, N. L. (1976). *Suicide: Inside and out.* Berkeley, CA: University of California Press.

Reynolds, W. M., & Coats, K. I. (1986). A comparison of cognitive-behavioral therapy and relaxation training for the treatment of depression in adolescents. *J. Cons. Clin. Psychol.*, *54*, 653–60.

Rhoades, L. J. (1981). *Treating and assessing the chronically mentally ill: The pioneering research of Gordon L. Paul.* U.S. Department of Health and Human Services. Public Health Service. (Library of Congress Catalog #81–600097). Washington, DC: U.S. Government Printing Office.

Ribble, M. A. (1944). Infantile experience in relation to personality development. In J. McV. Hunt (Ed.), *Personality and the behavior disorders* (Vol. 2, pp. 621–51). New York: Ronald.

Ribble, M. A. (1945). Anxiety in infants and its disorganizing effects. In N. D. C. Lewis & B. L. Pacella (Eds.), *Modern trends in child psychiatry*. New York: International Universities Press.

Rice, R. D. (1977). Neurophysiological development in premature infants following stimulation. *Develop. Psychol.*, *13*, 69–76.

Rich, B. E., Paul, G. L., & Mariotto, M. J. (1988). Judgmental relativism as a validity threat to standardized psychiatric relating scales. *Journal of Psychopathology and Behavioral Assessment*, *10*, 241–57.

Rich, C. L., Fowler, R. C., Fogarty, L. A., & Young, D. (1988). San Diego suicide study: III. Relationships between diagnoses and stressors. *Arch. Gen. Psychiat.*, *45*, 589–92.

Rich, C. L., Young, D., & Fowler, R. C. (1986). San Diego suicide study: I. Young vs. old subjects. *Arch. Gen. Psychiat.*, *43*, 577–82.

Richardson, S. A., Koller, H., & Katz, M. (1985). Relationship of upbringing to later behavior disturbance of mildly mentally retarded young people. *Amer. J. Ment. Def.*, *90*, 18.

Rieder, R. O. (1973). The offspring of schizophrenic parents: A review. *J. Nerv. Ment. Dis.*, *157*(3), 179–90.

Rieder, R. O. (1979). Children at risk. In L. Bellak (Ed.), *The schizophrenic syndrome*. New York: Basic Books.

Rimm, D. C., & Lefebvre, R. C. (1981). Phobic disorders. In S. M. Turner, K. S. Calhoun, & H. E. Adams (Eds.), *Handbook of clinical behavior therapy*. New York: Wiley.

Rinear, E. E. (1988). Psychosocial aspects of parental response patterns to the death of a child by homicide. *Journal of Traumatic Stress, 1*, 305–22.

Ritchie, J. C., Carroll, B. J., Olton, P. R., Shively, V., & Feinberg, M. (1985). Plasma cortisol determination for the dexamethasone suppression test: Comparison of competitive protein-binding and commercial radioimmunoassay methods. *Arch. Gen. Psych., 42*, 493–97.

Ritchie, P. L. (1975). *The effect of the interviewer's presentation on some schizophrenic symptomatology*. Unpublished doctoral dissertation, Duke University.

Ritvo, E., Brothers, A. M., Freeman, B. J., & Pingree, J. C. (1988). Eleven possibly autistic parents. *J. Autism Devel. Dis., 18*, 139–43.

Ritvo, E., & Ornitz, E. (1970). A new look at childhood autism points to CNS disease. *Roche Report, 7*(18), 6–8.

Ritvo, E. R., & Freeman, B. J. (1978). Current research on the syndrome of autism. *J. Amer. Acad. Child Psychiat., 17*, 565–75.

Ritvo, E. R., Freeman, B. J., Pingree, C., Mason-Brothers, A., Jorde, L., Jenson, W. R., McMahon, W. M., Peterson, P. B., Mo, A., & Ritvo, A. (1989). The UCLA-University of Utah epidemiologic survey of autism: Prevalence. *Amer. J. Psychiat., 146*, 194–99.

Ritzler, B. A. (1981). Paranoia-prognosis and treatment: A review. *Schizo. Bull., 7*, 710–28.

Roberts, E. (1986). Alzheimer's disease may begin in the nose and may be caused by aluminosilicates. *Neurobiology of Aging, 7*, 561–67.

Roberts, M. C., & Peterson, L. (1984). *Prevention of problems in childhood*. New York: Wiley Interscience.

Robins, L. N. (1970). The adult development of the antisocial child. *Seminars in Psychiatry, 2*(4), 420–34.

Robins, L. N., & Helzer, J. E. (1986). Diagnosis and clinical assessment: The current state of psychiatric diagnosis. In M. R. Rosenzweig & L. W. Porter (Eds.), *Annu. Rev. Psychol.*, (Vol. 37, pp. 409–32). Palo Alto, CA: Annual Reviews.

Robins, L. N., Helzer, J. E., Weissman, M. M., Orvaschel, H., Gruenberg, E., Burke, J. D., & Regier, D. (1984). Lifetime prevalence of specific psychiatric disorders in three sites. *Arch. Gen. Psych., 41*, 949–58.

Robinson, L. A., Berman, J. S., & Neimeyer, R. A. (1990). Psychotherapy for the treatment of depression: A comprehensive review of controlled outcome research. *Psychol. Bull., 108*, 30–49.

Robinson, N. M., & Robinson, H. B. (1976). *The mentally retarded child* (2nd ed.). New York: McGraw-Hill.

Robinson, P. W., Newby, T. J., & Ganzell, S. L. (1981). A token system for a class of underachieving, hyperactive children, *J. Appl. Beh. Anal., 14*(3), 307–15.

Robinson, S., & Winick, H. Z. (1973). Severe psychotic disturbances following crash diet weight loss. *Arch. Gen. Psychiat., 29*(4), 559–62.

Rodin, J. (1974, Apr.). *Obesity and external responsiveness*. Paper presented at the meeting of the Eastern Psychological Association, Philadelphia.

Rodman, D. H., & Collins, M. J. (1974). A community residence program: An alternative to institutional living for the mentally retarded. *Training School Bulletin, 71*(1), 41–48.

Roff, J. D. (1974). Adolescent schizophrenia: Variables related to differences in long-term adult outcome. *J. Cons. Clin. Psychol., 42*(2), 180–83.

Roff, J. D., & Knight R. (1981). Family characteristics, childhood symptoms, and adult outcome in schizophrenia. *J. Abnorm. Psychol., 90*, 510–20.

Roff, J. D., & Wirt, R. D. (1984). Childhood social adjustment, adolescent status, and young adult mental health. *Amer. J. Orthopsychiat., 54*, 595–602.

Roff, M. (1960). Relations between certain preservice factors and psychoneurosis during military duty. *Armed Forces Medical Journal, 11*, 152–60.

Roff, M. (1963). Childhood social interactions and young adult psychosis. *J. Clin. Psychol., 19*, 152–57.

Rogers, C. R. (1951). *Client-centered therapy*. Boston: Houghton Mifflin.

Rogers, C. R. (1959). A theory of therapy personality, and interpersonal relationships as developed in the client-centered framework. In S. Koch (Ed.), *Psychology: A study of a science*, (Vol. 3, pp. 184–256). New York: McGraw-Hill.

Rogers, C. R. (1961). *On becoming a person: A client's view of psychotherapy*. Boston: Houghton Mifflin.

Rogers, C. R. (1966). Client-centered therapy. In S. Arieti et al. (Eds.), *American handbook of psychiatry* (Vol. 3). New York: Basic Books.

Rogers, M. P. (1989). The interaction between brain behavior and immunity. In S. Cheren (Ed.), *Psychosomatic Medicine: Theory, physiology, and practice*, (Vol. 1, pp. 279–330). Madison, CT: International Universities Press.

Rokeach, M. (1964). *The three Christs of Ypsilanti*. New York: Knopf.

Rolfs, R. T., Goldberg, M., & Sharrar, R. G. (1990). Risk factors for syphilis: Cocaine use and prostitution. *Amer. J. Pub. Hlth., 80*, 853–57.

Rolider, A., & Houten, R. V. (1985). Suppressing tantrum behavior in public places through the use of delayed punishment mediated by audio recordings. *Behav. Ther., 16*, 181–94.

Ronningstam, E. & Gunderson, J. (1989). Descriptive studies on narcissistic personality disorder. *Psychiat. Clin. N. Amer., 12*, 585–601.

Rooth, G. (1974). Exhibitionists around the world. *Human Behav., 3*(5), 61.

Rorvik, D. M. (1970, Apr. 7). Do drugs lead to violence? *Look*, 58–61.

Rosen, A. J. (1986). Schizophrenic and affective disorders: Rationale for a biopsychosocial treatment odel. *Integr. Psychiat., 4*, 173–85.

Rosen, D. H. (1970). The serious suicide attempt: Epidemiological and follow-up study of 886 patients. *Amer. J. Psychiat., 127*(6), 64–70.

Rosen, H., & Kiene, H. E. (1946). Paranoia and paranoiac reaction types. *Dis. Nerv. Sys., 7*, 330–37.

Rosen, R. C., & Leiblum, S. R. (1989). Assessment and treatment of desire disorders. In S. R. Leiblum & R. C. Rosen (Eds.), *Principles and practice of sex therapy*, (2nd ed., pp. 19–50). New York: Guilford.

Rosenbaum, G., Shore, D. L., & Chapin, K. (1988). Attention deficit and schizotypy: Marker versus symptom variables. *J. Abnorm. Psychol., 97*, 41–47.

Rosenblatt, A. (1984). Concepts of the asylum in the care of the mentally ill. *Hosp. Comm. Psychiat., 35*, 244–50.

Rosenman, R. H. (1978). The interview method of assessment of the coronary-prone behavior pattern. In T. P. Dembroski, S. M. Weiss, J. L. Shields, S. G. Haynes, & M. Feinleib (Eds.), *Coronary-prone behavior*. New York: Springer-Verlag.

Rosenman, R. H., Brand, R. J., Jenkins, C. D., Friedman, M., & Straus, R. (1975). Coronary heart disease in the Western Collaborative Group Study: Final follow-up experience of 8½ years. *JAMA, 233*, 872–77.

Rosenstein, M. J., Milazzo-Sayre, L. J., & Manderscheid, R. W. (1989). Care of persons with schizophrenia: A statistical profile. *Schizo. Bull., 15*, 45–58.

Rosenthal, D. (Ed.). (1963). *The Genain quadruplets*. New York: Basic Books.

Rosenthal, D., Wender, P. H., Kety, S. S., Schulsinger, F., Welner, J., & Ostergaard, L. (1968). Schizophrenics' offspring reared in adoptive homes. In D. Rosenthal & S. S. Kety (Eds.), *The transmission of schizophrenia* (pp. 377–92). New York: Pergamon.

Rosenthal, D., Wender, P. H., Kety, S. S., Schulsinger, F., Welner, J., & Reider, R. O. (1975). Parent-child relationships and psychopathological disorder in the child. *Arch. Gen. Psychiat., 32*, 466–76.

Rosenthal, N. E., Carpenter, C. J., James, S. P., Parry, B. L., Rogers, S. L. B., & Wehr, T. A. (1986). Seasonal affective disorder in children and adolescents. *Amer. J. Psychiat., 143*, 356–58.

Rosenthal, N. E., Sack, D. A., Gillin, J. C., Lewry, A. J., Goodwin, F. K., Davenport, Y., Mueller, P. S., Newsome, D. A., & Wehr, T. A. (1984). Seasonal affective disorder: A description of the syndrome and preliminary findings with light therapy. *Arch. Gen. Psychiat., 41*, 72–80.

Rosenzweig, M. R., Krech, D., Bennett, E. L., & Diamond, M. C. (1968). Modifying brain chemistry and anatomy by enrichment or impoverishment of experience. In G. Newton & S. Levine (Eds.), *Early experience and behavior*. Springfield, IL: Charles C. Thomas.

Ross, A. O., & Pelham, W. E. (1981). Child psychopathology. *Annu. Rev. Psychol., 32*, 243–78.

Ross, C. A. (1989). *Multiple personality disorder: Diagnosis, clinical features, and treatment*. New York: Wiley.

Ross, C. A., Norton, G. R., & Wozney, K. (1989). Multiple personality disorder: An analysis of 236 cases. *Canad. J. Psychiat., 34,* 413–18.

Ross, M. (1974). This doctor will self-destruct. . . . *Human Behav., 3*(2), 54.

Ross, M. (1975). Suicide among physicians. *Tufts Medical Alumni Bulletin, 34,* (3).

Rossi, P. H. (1990). The old homeless and the new homelessness in historical perspective. *Amer. Psychol., 45,* 954–59.

Rosten, R. A. (1961). Some personality characteristics of compulsive gamblers. Unpublished dissertation, UCLA.

Roth, M., & Mountjoy, C. Q. (1982). The distinction between anxiety states and depressive disorders. In E. S. Paykel (Ed.), *Handbook of affective disorders.* New York: Guilford Press.

Roth, S., & Cohen, L. J. (1986). Approach, avoidance, and coping with stress. *Amer. Psychol., 41,* 813–19.

Roth, S., & Lebowitz, L. (1988). The experience of sexual trauma. *Journal of Traumatic Stress, 1,* 79–107.

Rothbart, M. K. (1981). Measurement of temperament in infancy. *Child Develop., 52,* 569–78.

Rotter, J. I., Jones, J. Q., Samloff, I. M., Richardson, C. T., Gursky, J. M., Walsh, J. H., & Rimoin, D. L. (1979). Duodenal-ulcer disease associated with elevated serum pepsinogen I: An inherited autosomal dominant disease. *New Engl. J. Med., 300,* 63–66.

Rounsaville, B. J., Dolinsky, Z. S., Babor, T. F., & Meyer, R. E. (1987). Psychopathology as a predictor of treatment outcome in alcoholics. *Arch. Gen. Psychiat., 44,* 505–13.

Rounsaville, B. J., Kosten, T. R., Weissman, M. M., & Kleber, H. D. (1986). A 2.5 year follow-up of short-term interpersonal psychotherapy in methadone-maintained opiate addicts. *Compr. Psychiat., 27*(3), 201–10.

Rounsaville, B. J., Weissman, M. M., & Prusoff, B. A. (1981). Psychotherapy with depressed outpatients: Patient and process variables as predictors of outcome. *Amer. J. Psychiat., 138,* 67–74.

Routh, D. K., & Ernst, A. R. (1984). Somalization disorder in relatives of children and adolescents with functional abdominal pain. *J. Pediat. Psychol., 9*(4), 427–37.

Rovner, S. (1990, Nov.). Dramatic overlap of addiction, mental illness. *Washington Post Health,* 14–15.

Roy, A. (1985). Early parental separation and adult depression. *Arch. Gen. Psychiat., 42,* 987–91.

Rubenstein, J. L., Heeren, T., Houseman, D., Rubin, C., & Stechler, G. (1989). Suicidal behavior in "normal" adolescents: Risk and protective factors. *Amer. J. Orthopsychiat., 59,* 59–71.

Rubin, B. (1972). Prediction of dangerousness in mentally ill criminals. *Arch. Gen. Psychiat., 25,* 392–407.

Rubin, R. T., Reinisch, J. M., & Haskett, R. F. (1981). Postnatal gonadal steroid effects on human behavior. *Science, 211,* 1318–24.

Rudestam, K. E. (1971). Stockholm and Los Angeles: A cross-cultural study of the communication of suicidal intent. *J. Cons. Clin. Psychol., 36,*(1), 82–90.

Rumsey, J. M., Duara, R., Grady, C., Rapoport, J., Margolin, R. A., Rapoport, S. I., & Cutler, N. R. (1985). Brain metabolism in autism. *Arch. Gen. Psychiat., 42,* 48–55.

Runcie, J., & Thompson, T. J. (1970), Prolonged starvation—A dangerous procedure? *Brit. Med. J., 3,* 432–35.

Rush, A. J., Beck, A. T., Kovacs, M., & Hollon, S. (1977). The comparative efficacy of cognitive therapy and imipramine in the treatment of depressed out-patients. *Cog. Ther. Res., 1*(1), 17–37.

Rush, A. J., Beck, A. T., Kovacs, M., Weissenburger, J., & Hollon, S. D. (1982). Comparison of the effects of cognitive therapy and pharmacotherapy on hopelessness and self-concept. *Amer. J. Psychiat., 139,* 862–66.

Rush, A. J., Khatami, M., & Beck, A. T. (1975). Cognitive and behavior therapy in chronic depression. *Behav. Ther., 6,* 398–404.

Russell, S. (1975). The development and training of autistic children in separate training centres and in centres for retarded children. *Special Publication No. 6.* Victoria: Mental Health Authority.

Russo, D. C., Carr, E. G., & Lovaas, O. I. (1980). Self-injury in pediatric populations. In J. Ferguson & C. R. Taylor (Eds.), *Comprehensive handbook of behavioral medicine. Vol. 3: Extended applications and issues.* Holliswood, NY: Spectrum Publications.

Rutter, M. (1971). Parent-child separation: Psychological effects on the children. *J. Child Psychol. Psychiat., 12,* 233–60.

Rutter, M. (1972). Maternal deprivation reconsidered. *J. Psychosom. Res., 16*(4), 241–50.

Rutter, M. (1978). Diagnosis and definition. In M. Ruter & E. Schopler (Eds.), *Autism: A reappraisal of concepts and treatment.* New York: Plenum.

Rutter, M. (1979). Maternal deprivations. 1972–1978: New findings, new concepts, new approachs. *Child Develop., 50,* 283–305.

Rutter, M. (1985). The treatment of autistic children. *Journal of Child Psychiatry, 26*(2), 193–214.

Rutter, M. (1988). Epidemiological approaches to developmental psychopathology. *Arch. Gen. Psychiat., 45,* 486–500.

Rutter, M., Izard, C., & Read, P. (Eds.) (1986). *Depression in young people: Developmental perspectives.* New York: Guilford Press.

Rutter, M., & Quinton, D. (1984). Parental psychiatric disorder: Effects on children. *Psychol. Med., 14,* 853–80.

Rutter, M., Tizard, J., & Whitmore, K. (1970). *Education, health and behavior: Psychologicl and medical study of childhood development.* New York: Wiley.

Ryan, N. D., Puig-Antich, J., Ambrosini, P., Rabinovich, H., Robinson, D., Nelson, B., Iyengar, S. & Twomey, J. (1987). The clinical picture of major depression in children and adolescents. *Arch. Gen. Psychiat., 44,* 854–61.

Ryle, A. (1969). *Student Casualties.* London: Penguin.

Sachar, E. J., Gruen, P. H., Altman, N., Langer, G., & Halpern, F. S. (1978). Neuroendocrine studies of brain dopamine blockade in humans. In L. C. Wynne, R. L. Cromwell, & S. Matthysse (Eds.), *The nature of schizophrenia: New approaches to research and treatment,* (pp. 95–104.). New York: Wiley.

Sack, R. L., Lewry, A. J., White, D. M., Singer, C. M., Fireman, M. J., & Vandiver, R. (1990). Morning vs. evening light treatment for winter depression: Evidence that the therapeutic effects of light are mediated by circadian phase shifts. *Arch. Gen. Psychiat., 47,* 343–51.

Sack, R. L., & Miller, W. (1975). Masochism: A clinical and theoretical overview. *Psychiatry, 38*(3), 244–57.

Safer, D. J., & Allen, R. P. (1973). Stimulant drugs said to suppress height, weight. *Psychiat. News, 8*(9), 9.

Safran, J. D. (1990a). Towards a refinement of cognitive therapy in light of interpersonal theory: I. Theory. *Clin. Psychol. Rev., 10,* 87–105.

Safran, J. D. (1990b). Towards a refinement of cognitive therapy in light of interpersonal theory: II. Practice. *Clin. Psychol. Rev., 10,* 107–21.

Salkovskis, P. M., & Westbrook, D. (1989). Cognitive-behavioral treatment of depressed inpatients. *Behav. Res. Ther., 27,* 149–60.

Salter, A. (1949). *Condition reflex therapy.* New York: Creative Age Press.

Salzman, L. (1968). Obsessions and phobias. *Inter. J. Psychiat., 6,* 451–68.

Sameroff, A., Seifer, R., & Zax, M. (1982). Early development of children at risk for emotional disorders. *Monographs of the Society for Research in Child Development, 47,* (7 No. 199).

Sameroff, A., Seifer, R., Zax, M., & Barocas, R. (1987). Early indicators of developmental risk: Rochester longitudinal study. *Schizo. Bull., 13,* 383–94.

Sanderson, W. C., Rapee, R. M., & Barlow, D. H. (1989). The influence of an illusion of control on panic attacks induced via inhalation of 5.5%-carbon dioxide-enriched air. *Arch. Gen. Psychiat., 46,* 157–62.

Sandhu, H. S., & Cohen, L. M. (1989). Endocrine disorders. In S. Cheren (Ed.), *Psychosomatic Medicine: Theory, physiology, and practice,* (Vol. 2, pp. 661–706). Madison, CT: International Universities Press.

Sanson, A. V. (1980). Classification of hyperactive symptoms. *Medical Journal of Australia, 1*(8), 375–76.

Santiago, J. M., McCall-Perez, F., Gorcey, M., & Beigel, A. (1985). Long-term psychological effects of rape in 35 rape victims. *Amer. J. Psychiat., 142,* 1338–40.

Sanua, V. (1986a). The organic etiology of infantile autism: A critical review of the literature. *International Journal of Neuroscience, 30,* 195–225.

Sanua, V. (1986b). A comparative study of opinions of U.S.A. and European professionals on the etiology of infantile autism. *Inter. J. Soc. Psychiat., 32,* 16–30.

Sanua, V. D. (1969). Sociocultural aspects. In L. Bellak & L. Loeb (Eds.), *The schizophrenic syndrome.* New York: Grune & Stratton.

Sanua, V. D. (1987). Standing against an established ideology: Infantile autism, a case in point. *Clin. Psychol.*, 4, 96–10.

Sapolsky, R. M. (1989). Hypercortisolism among socially subordinate wild baboons originates at the CNS level. *Arch. Gen. Psychiat.*, 46, 1047–51.

Saracoglu, B., Minden, H., & Wilchesky, M. (1989). The adjustment of students with learning disabilities to university and its relationship to self-esteem and self-efficacy. *J. Learn. Dis.*, 22, 590–92.

Sarbin, T. R., (in press). The social construction of schizophrenia. In W. Flack, D. R. Miller, & M. Wiener (Eds.), *What is schizophrenia.* New York: Springer-Verlag.

Sarbin, T. R., & Juhasz, J. B. (1967). The historical background of the concept of hallucination. *Journal of the History of the Behavioral Sciences*, 3, 339–58.

Sarbin, T. R., & Mancuso, J. C. (1970). Failure of a moral enterprise: Attitudes of the public toward mental illness. *J. Cons. Clin. Psychol.*, 35, 159–73.

Sarbin, T. R., & Mancuso, J. C. (1980). *Schizophrenia: Medical diagnosis or moral verdict.* New York: Pergamon.

Sargeant, J. K., Bruce, M. L., Florio, L. P., & Weissman, M. M. (1990). Factors associated with 1-year outcome of major depression in the community. *Arch. Gen. Psychiat.*, 47, 519–26.

Sargent, M. (1982a, Jul. 16). Schizophrenic quads not identically ill, studies show. *ADAMHA News*, 8(13), 4–5.

Sargent, M. (1982b, Dec. 3), Researcher traces Alzheimer's disease eight generations back in one family. *ADAMHA News*, 8(23), 3.

Sarvis, M. A. (1962). Paranoid reactions: Perceptual distortion as an etiological agent. *Arch. Gen. Psychiat.*, 6, 157–62.

Sasaki, M., & Hara, Y. (1973). Paternal origin of the extra chromosome in Down's syndrome. *Lancet*, 2(7840), 1257–58.

Satir, V. (1967). *Conjoint family therapy* (rev. ed.). Palo Alto, CA: Science and Behavior Books.

Satterfield, J. H., Satterfield, B. T., & Cantwell, D. P. (1981). Three year multimodal treatment study of 100 hyperactive boys. *Journal of Pediatrics*, 98,(4), 650–55.

Savasir, I., & Erol, N. (1990). The Turkish MMPI: Translation, standardization, and validation. In J. N. Butcher & C. D. Spielberger (Eds.), *Advances in personality assessment*, (Vol. 8). Hillsdale, NJ: Lawrence Erlbaum Press.

Sawyer, J. B., Sudak, H. S., & Hall, S. R. (1972, Winter). A follow-up study of 53 suicides known to a suicide prevention center. *Life-Threatening Behavior*, 2(4), 227–38.

Scalf-McIver, L., & Thompson, K. J. (1989). Family correlates of bulimic characteristics in college females. *J. Clin. Psychol.*, 45, 467–72.

Scarr, S. (1984). *Mother care, other care.* New York: Basic Books.

Schaar, K. (1974). Suicide rate high among women psychologists. *APA Monitor*, 5(7), 1, 10.

Schaefer, J. M. (1977, Aug. 30). Firewater myths revisited: Towards a second generation of ethanol metabolism studies. Paper presented at Cross-cultural Approaches to Alcoholism. Physiological variation: Invited Symposium. NATO Conference, Bergen, Norway.

Schaefer, J. M. (1978). Alcohol metabolism reactions among the Reddis of South India. *Alcoholism: Clinical and experimental research*, 2(1), 61–69.

Schalock, R. L., Harper, R. S., & Carver, G. (1981). Independent living placement: Five years later. *Amer. J. Ment. Def.*, 86, 170–77.

Schapiro, M. B., & Rapoport, S. I. (1987). "Pathological similarities between Alzheimer's disease and Down's syndrome: Is there a genetic link?": Commentary. *Integr. Psychiat.*, 5, 167–69.

Scharfman, M., & Clark, R. W. (1967). Delinquent adolescent girls: Residential treatment in a municipal hospital setting. *Arch. Gen. Psychiat.*, 17(4), 441–47.

Scheff, T. J. (1984). *Being mentally ill: A sociological theory* (2nd ed.). New York: Aldine.

Scheier, M. F., & Carver, C. S. (1987). Dispositional optimism and physical well-being: The influence of generalized outcome expectancies on health. *J. Personal.*, 55, 169–210.

Schild, S. (1972). Parents of children with PKU. *Children Today*, 1(4), 20–22.

Schilling, R. F., & McAlister, A. L. (1990). Preventing drug use in adolescents through media interventions. *J. Cons. Clin. Psychol.*, 58, 416–24.

Schleifer, S. J., Keller, S. E., & Stein, M. (1985). Central nervous system mechanisms and immunity: Implications for tumor responses. In S. M. Levy, *Behavior and cancer*, (pp. 120–33). San Francisco: Jossey-Bass.

Schleifer, S. J., Keller, S. E., Bond, R. M., Cohen, J., & Stein, M., (1989). Major depressive disorder and immunity: Role of age, sex, severity, and hospitalization. *Arch. Gen. Psychiat.*, 46, 81–87.

Schmauk, F. J. (1970). Punishment, arousal, and avoidance learning in sociopaths. *J. Abnorm. Psychol.*, 76(3), 325–35.

Schmauss, C., & Krieg, J. C. (1987). Enlargement of cerebrospinal fluid spaces in benzodiazepine abusers. *Psychol. Med.*, 17, 869–73.

Schmid, H. (1914). Zur Psychologie der Brandstifter. *Psychologische Abhandlungen, Band*, 1, 80–179.

Schneider, S. (1978). Attitudes toward death in adolescent offspring of holocaust survivors. *Amer. J. Orthopsychiat.*, 13, 575–83.

Schneidman, E. S. (1973). Suicide notes reconsidered. *Psychiatry*, 36, 379–94.

Schoeneman, T. J. (1984). The mentally ill witch in textbooks of abnormal psychology: Current status and implications of a fallacy. *Profess. Psychol.*, 15(3), 299–314.

Schofield, W. (1964). *Psychotherapy: The purchase of friendship.* Englewood Cliffs, NJ: Prentice-Hall.

Schofield, W., & Balian, L. (1959). A comparative study of the personal histories of schizophrenic and nonpsychiatric patients. *J. Abnorm. Soc. Psychol.*, 59, 216–25.

Schopler, E. (1978). Changing parental involvement in behavioral treatment. In M. Rutter & Schopler (Eds.), *Autism: A reappraisal of concepts and treatment.* New York: Plenum Press.

Schopler, E. (1983). New developments in the definition and diagnosis of autism. In B. B. Lahey & A. E. Kazdin (Eds.), *Advances in clinical child psychology* (Vol. 6, pp. 93–127). New York: Plenum Press.

Schopler, E., Mesibov, G., & Baker, A. (1982). Evaluation of treatment for autistic children and their parents. *J. Amer. Acad. Child Psychiat.*, 21, 262–67.

Schowalter, J. E. (1980). Tics. *Pediatrics in Review*, 2, 55–57.

Schreiber, F. R. (1973). *Sybil.* New York: Warner Paperback.

Schreibman, L., & Koegel, R. L. (1975). Autism: A defeatable horror. *Psych. Today*, 8(10), 61–67.

Schuckit, M. A., & Gould, R. O. (1988). A simultaneous evaluation of multiple markers of ethanol/placebo challenges in sons of alcoholics and controls. *Arch. Gen. Psychiat.*, 45, 211–16.

Schulsinger, F. (1980). Biological psychopathology. *Annu. Rev. Psychol.*, 31, 583–606.

Schulsinger, F., Knop, J., Goodwin, D. W., Teasdale, T. W., & Mikkelsen, U. (1986). A prospective study of young men at high risk for alcoholism. *Arch. Gen. Psychiat.*, 43, 755–60.

Schulterbrandt, J. D., & Raskin, A. (Eds.). (1977). *Depression in children: Diagnosis, treatment and conceptual models.* New York: Raven Press.

Schwab, J. J. (1970). Comprehensive medicine and the concurrence of physical and mental illness. *Psychosomatics*, 11(6), 591–95.

Schwartz, C. C., & Myers, J. K. (1977). Life events and schizophrenia: I. Comparison of schizophrenics with a community sample. *Arch. Gen. Psychiat.*, 34, 1238–41.

Schwartz, D. A. (1963). A review of the "paranoid" concept. *Arch. Gen. Psychiat.*, 8, 349–61.

Schwartz, G. E. (1978). Psychobiological foundations of psychotherapy and behavior change. In S. L. Garfield & A. E. Bergin (Eds.), *Handbook of psychotherapy and behavior change* (2nd ed., pp. 63–99). New York: Wiley.

Schwartz, G. E. (1989). Disregulation theory and disease: Toward a general model for psychosomatic medicine. In S. Cheren (Ed.), *Psychosomatic medicine: Theory, physiology, and practice*, (Vol. 1, pp. 91–118). Madison, CT: International Universities Press.

Schwartz, J. L., (1987). *Review and evaluation of smoking cessation methods: The United States and Canada 1978–1985.* US Department of Health and Human Services, NIH Publication No. 87–2940.

Schwartz, R. C., Barrett, M. J., & Saba, G. (1983, Oct.). *Family therapy for bulimia.* Paper presented at American Association for Marriage and Family Therapy, Washington, DC.

Schwartz, S., & Johnson, J. H. (1985). *Psychopathology of childhood: A clinical-experimental approach*, (2nd ed.). New York: Pergamon.

Schwartzman, J. (1974). The individual, incest, and exogamy. *Psychiatry*, 37, 171–80.

Schwitzgebel, R. L., & Schwitzgebel, R. K. (1980). *Law and psychological practice.* New York: Wiley.

Scott, A. I. F. (1989). Which depressed patients will respond to electroconvulsive therapy? The search for biological predictors of recovery. *Brit. J. Psychiat.,* 154, 8–17.

Scovern, A. W., & Kilmann, P. R. (1980). Status of electroconvulsive therapy: A review of the outcome literature. *Psychol. Bull.,* 87, 260–303.

Searles, J. S. (1988). The role of genetics in the pathogenesis of alcoholism. *J. Abnorm. Psychol.,* 97, 153–67.

Sears, R. R. (1961). Relation of early socialization experiences to aggression in middle childhood. *J. Abnorm. Soc. Psychol.,* 63, 466–92.

Sears, R. R., Maccoby, E. E., & Levin, H. (1957). *Patterns of child rearing.* New York: Harper & Row.

Sedvall, G., Farde, L., Persson, A., & Wiesel, F. A. (1986). Imaging of neurotransmitter receptors in the living human brain. *Arch. Gen. Psychiat.,* 43, 995–1005.

Segal, D. S., Yager, J., & Sullivan, J. L. (1976). *Foundations of biochemical psychiatry.* Boston: Butterworth.

Segal, S. (1978). Attitudes toward the mentally ill: A review. *Social Work,* 23, 211–17.

Segal, Z. V., & Marshall, W. M. (1985). Heterosexual social skills in a population of rapists and child molesters. *J. Cons. Clin. Psychol.,* 53, 55–63.

Segal, Z. V., & Stermac, L. E. (1990). The role of cognition in sexual assault. In W. L. Marshall, D. R. Laws, & H. E. Barbaree (Eds.), *Handbook of sexual assault* (pp. 161–75). New York: Plenum.

Seiden, R. H. (1974). Suicide: preventable death. *Public Affairs Report,* 15(4), 1–5.

Seidl, F. W. (1974). Community oriented residential care: The state of the art. *Child Care Quarterly,* 3(3), 150–63.

Seixas, F. A. & Cadoret, R. (1974, Apr. 15). What is the alcoholic man? *New York Academy of Sciences,* 223, 13–14.

Seligman, M. E. P. (1973). Fall into hopelessness. *Psych.Today,* 7(1), 43–47, 48.

Seligman, M. E. P. (1975). *Helplessness: On depression, development, and death.* San Francisco: W. H. Freeman.

Seligman, M. E. P., & Hager, M. (Eds.). (1972). *Biological boundaries of learning.* New York: Appleton-Century-Crofts.

Selkin, J. (1975). Rape. *Psych. Today,* 8(8), 70–72.

Selkin, J., & Loya, F. (1979). Issues in the psychological autopsy of controversial public figures. *Profess. Psychol.,* 10(1), 87–93.

Selkoe, D. J. (1986). Altered structural protein in plaques and tangles: What do they tell us about the biology of Alzheimer's disease? *Neurobiology of Aging,* 7, 425–32.

Selling, L. S. (1943). *Men against madness.* New York: Garden City Books.

Selye, H. (1956). *The stress of life.* New York: McGraw-Hill.

Selye, H. (1976a). *Stress in health and disease.* Woburn, MA: Butterworth.

Selye, H. (1976b). *The stress of life* (2nd ed.). New York: McGraw-Hill.

Senay, E. C., & Redlich, F. C. (1968). Cultural and social factors in neuroses and psychosomatic illnesses. *Soc. Psychiat.,* 3(3), 89–97.

Sergovich, F., Valentine, G. H., Chen, A. T., Kinch, R., & Smout, M. (1969). Chromosomal aberrations in 2159 consecutive newborn babies, *New Engl. J. Med.,* 280(16), 851–54.

Serrano, A. C., Zuelzer, M. B., Howe, D. D., & Reposa, R. E. (1979). Ecology of abusive and nonabusive families, *J. Amer. Acad. Child Psychiat.,* 18, 167–75.

Sgroi, S. M. (1977). Sexual molestation of children: The last frontier in child abuse. In S. Chess & A. Thomas (Eds.), *Annual progress in child psychiatry and child development: 1976.* New York: Brunner/Mazel.

Shakow, D. (1969). On doing research in schizophrenia. *Arch. Gen. Psychiat.,* 20(6), 618–42.

Shanfield, S. B., & Swain, B. J. (1984). Death of adult children in traffic accidents. *J. Nerv. Ment. Dis.,* 172(9), 533–38.

Shapiro, A. K., & Morris, L. A. (1978). The placebo effect in medical and psychological therapies. In S. L. Garfield & A. E. Bergin (Eds.), *Handbook of psychotherapy and behavior change* (2nd ed., pp. 369–410). New York: Wiley.

Shapiro, D. (1965). *Neurotic styles.* New York: Basic Books.

Shapiro, S. (1968). Maturation of the neuroendocrine response to stress in the rat. In G. Newton & S. Levine (Eds.), *Early experience and behavior.* Springfield, IL: Charles S. Thomas.

Shatan, C. F. (1978). Stress disorders among Vietnam veterans: The emotional content of combat continues. In C. R. Figley (Ed.), *Stress disorders among Vietnam veterans: Theory, research and treatment.* New York: Brunner/Mazel.

Shaw, E. D., Stokes, P. E., Mann, J. J., & Manevitz, A. Z. A.
(1987). Effects of lithium carbonate on the memory and motor speed of bipolar outpatients. *J. Abnorm. Psychol.,* 96, 64–69.

Shaw, J. A. (1990). Stress engendered by military action on military and civilian populations. In J. D. Noshpitz & R. D. Coddington (Eds.), *Stressors and the adjustment disorders.* New York: Wiley Intersciences.

Shedler, J. & Block, J. (1990). Adolescent drug use and psychological health: A longitudinal inquiry. *Amer. Psychol.,* 45, 612–30.

Sheldon, W. H. (with the collaboration of C. W. Dupertuis & E. McDermott). (1954). *Atlas of men.* New York: Harper & Row.

Shenson, D., Dubler, N., & Michaels, D. (1990). Jails and prisons: The new asylums? *Amer. J. Pub. Hlth.,* 80, 655–56.

Sherrod, B. (1968). *Dallas Times Herald* (n.d.). Quoted in D. Bolen & W. H. Boyd, Gambling and the gambler. *Arch. Gen. Psychiat.,* 18(5), 617–30.

Sherwin, I., & Geschwind, N. (1978). Neural substrates of behavior. In A. M. Nicholi (Ed.), *The Harvard guide to modern psychiatry* (pp. 59–80). Cambridge, MA: Harvard University Press.

Shimkunas, A. M. (1972). Demand for intimate self-disclosure and pathological verbalizations in schizophrenia. *J. Abnorm. Psychol.,* 80, 197–205.

Shneidman, E. S. (1969). Fifty-eight years. In E. S. Shneidman (Ed.), *On the nature of suicide* (pp. 1–30). San Francisco: Jossey-Bass.

Shneidman, E. S., & Farberow, N. L. (Eds.). (1957). *Clues to suicide.* New York: McGraw-Hill.

Shneidman, E. S., Parker, E., & Funkhouser, G. R. (1970). You and death. *Psych. Today,* 4(3), 67–72.

Shoemaker, M. E., & Paulson, T. L. (1976). Group assertion training for mothers: A family intervention strategy. In E. J. Mash, L. C. Handy, & L. A. Hamerlynck (Eds.), *Behavior modification approaches to parenting.* New York: Brunner/Mazel.

Shore, J. H., Tatum, E. L., & Vollmer, W. M., (1986). Evaluation of mental health effects of disaster. *Amer. J. Pub. Hlth.,* 76(Suppl.), 76–83.

Shore, J. H., Vollmer, W. M., & Tatum, E. L. (1989). Community patterns of posttraumatic stress disorders. *J. Nerv. Ment. Dis.,* 177, 681–85.

Shrout, P. E., Link, B. G., Dohrenwend, B. P., Skodol, A. E., Stueve, A., & Mirotznik, J. (1989). Characterizing life events as risk factors for depression: The role of fateful loss events. *J. Abnorm. Psychol.,* 89, 460–67.

Siegel, J. M., & Kuykendall, D. H. (1990). Loss, widowhood, and psychological distress among the elderly. *J. Cons. Clin. Psychol.* 58, 519–24.

Siegel, R. K. (1984). Hostage hallucinations: Visual imagery induced by isolation and life-threatening stress. *J. Nerv. Ment. Dis.,* 172(5), 264–72.

Siever, L. J. (1985). Biological markers in schizotypal personality disorder. *Schizo. Bull. 11,* 564–75.

Siever, L. J. (1986). Schizoid and schizotypal personality disorders. In J. R. Lion (Ed.), *Personality disorders: Diagnosis and management.* (pp. 32–64). Malabar, Fl.: Robert F. Kreiger Publishing.

Sigal J. J., Silver, D., Rakoff, V., & Ellin, B. (1973, Apr.). Some second-generation effects of survival of the Nazi persecution. *Amer. J. Orthopsychiat.,* 43(3), 320–27.

Sigerist, H. E. (1943). *Civilization and disease.* Ithaca, NY: Cornell University Press.

Silberman, E. K., & Tassone, E. P. (1985). The Israeli high-risk study: Statistical overview and discussion. *Schizo. Bull. 11,* 138–45.

Silberstein, R. M., & Irwin, H. (1962). Jean-Marc-Gaspard Itard and the savage of Aveyron: An unsolved diagnostic problem in child psychiatry. *J. Amer. Acad. Child Psychiat.,* 1(2), 314–22.

Silverman, W. H., & Silverman, M. M. (1987). Comparison of key informants, parents, and teenagers for planning adolescent substance abuse prevention programs. *Psychology of Addictive Behaviors,* 1(1), 30–37.

Silverstein, A. B., Legutki, G., Friedman, S. L., & Takayama, D. L. (1982). Performance of Down's syndrome individuals on the Stanford-Binet Intelligence Scale. *Amer. J. Ment. Def.,* 86, 548–5.

Silverton, L., Finello, K. M., Schulsinger, F., & Mednick, S. A. (1985). Low birth weight and ventricular enlargement in a high-risk sample. *J. Abnorm. Psychol.,* 94, 405–9

Simon, R. J., & Aaronson, D. E. (1988). *The insanity defense: A critical assessment of law and policy in the post-Hinckley era.* New York: Praeger.

Simon, W. (1975). Male sexuality: The secret of satisfaction. *Today's Health, 53*(4), 32–34, 50–52.

Simons, A. D., Murphy, G. E., Levine, J. L., & Wetzel, R. D. (1986). Cognitive therapy and pharmacotherapy for depression: Sustained improvement over one year. *Arch. Gen. Psychiat., 43,* 43–48.

Simons, R. C. (1987). Applicability of the DSM-III to psychiatric education. In G. L. Tischler (Ed.), *Diagnosis and classification in psychiatry: A critical appraisal of DSM-III* (pp. 510–29). New York: Cambridge University Press.

Simons, R. C., & Hughes, C. C. (Eds.). (1985). *The culture bound syndromes.* Boston: Reidel.

Singer, J., & Singer, I. (1978). Types of female orgasm. In J. LoPiccolo & L. LoPiccolo (Eds.), *Handbook of sex therapy* (pp. 175–86). New York: Plenum Press.

Singer, J. E. (1980). Traditions of stress research: Integrative comments. In I. G. Sarason & C. D. Spielberger (Eds.), *Stress and anxiety* (Vol. 7, pp. 3–10). Washington, DC: Hemisphere.

Singer, M., & Wynne, L. C. (1963). Differentiating characteristics of the parents of childhood schizophrenics, childhood neurotics and young adult schizophrenics. *Amer. J. Psychiat., 120,* 234–43.

Singer, M., & Wynne, L. C. (1965a). Thought disorder and family relations of schizophrenics. III. Methodology using projective techniques. *Arch. Gen. Psychiat., 12,* 182–200.

Singer, M., & Wynne, L. C. (1965b). Thought disorder and family relations of schizophrenics. IV. Results and implications. *Arch. Gen. Psychiat., 12,* 201-12.

Singer, M. T., Wynne, L. C., & Toohey, M. L. (1978). Communication disorders and the families of schizophrenics. In L. C. Wynne, R. L. Cromwell, & S. Matthysse (Eds.), *The nature of schizophrenia: New approaches to research and treatment* (pp. 499–511). New York: Wiley.

Skeels, H. M. (1966). Adult status of children with contrasting early life experiences: A follow-up study. *Monographs of the Society for Research in Child Development* (Serial No. 105), *31.*

Skinner, B. F. (1948). *Walden two.* New York: Macmillan.

Skinner, B. F. (1971). *Beyond freedom and dignity.* New York: Knopf.

Skinner, B. F. (1974). *About behaviorism.* New York: Knopf.

Skinner, B. F. (1990). Can psychology be a science of mind? *Amer. Psychol. 45,* 1206–10.

Skolnick, A. S. (1986). *The psychology of human development.* Harcourt Brace Jovanovich.

Slap, G. B., Vorters, D. F., Chaudhuri, S., & Centor, R. (1989). Risk factors for attempted suicide during adolescence. *Pediatrics, 84,* 762–72.

Slater, E., with the assistance of J. Shields. (1953). Psychotic and neurotic illness in twins. Special Report Series No. 278. Medical Research Council (Great Britain).

Slater, E. T. O. (1944). Genetics in psychiatry. *J. Ment. Sci., 90,* 17–35.

Slater, J., & Depue, R. A. (1981). The contribution of environmental events and social support to serious suicide attempts in primary depressive disorder. *J. Abnorm. Psychol., 90,* 275–85.

Sloane, R. B., Staples, F. R., Cristol, A. H., Yorkston, N. J., & Whipple, K. (1975). *Psychotherapy versus behavior therapy.* Cambridge, MA: Harvard University Press.

Sloman, L. (1991). Use of medication in pervasive developmental disorders. *Psychiat. Clin. N. Amer. 14,* 165–82.

Sloper, P., Turner, S., Knussen, C., & Cunningham, C. C. (1990). Social life of school children with Down's syndrome. *Child: Care, health, and development, 16,* 235–51.

Smalley, S. L. (1991). Genetic influences in autism. *Psychiat. Clin. N. Amer., 14,* 125–39.

Smith, D. (1938). *Dear octopus: A comedy in three acts.* Great Britain: Windmill Press.

Smith, D. (1982). Trends in counseling and psychotherapy. *Amer. Psychol., 37*(7), 802–9.

Smith, G., & Smith, D. (1985). A mainstreaming program that really works. *J. Learn. Dis., 18,* 369–72.

Smith, G. F., & Berg, J. M. (1976). *Down's anomaly.* New York: Churchill Livingstone (Distributed by Longman, Inc.).

Smith, M. L., Glass, G. V., & Miller, T. I. (1980). *The benefits of psychotherapy.* Baltimore: Johns Hopkins University Press.

Smith, R. J. (1978). *The psychopath in society.* New York: Academic Press.

Smith, R. J. (1979). Study finds sleeping pills overprescribed. *Science, 204,* 287–88.

Smith, W. (1989). *A profile of health and disease in America.* New York: Facts on File.

Snider, W. D., Simpson, D. M., Nielsen, S., Gold, J. W., Metroka, C. E., & Posner, J. B. (1983). Neurological complications of acquired immune deficiency syndrome: Analysis of 50 patients. *Annals of Neurology, 14,* 403–18.

Snyder, D. K., & Wills, R. M. (1989). Behavioral versus insight-oriented marital therapy: Effects on individual and interspousal functioning. *J. Cons. Clin. Psychol. 57,* 39–46.

Snyder, M., Tanke, E. D., & Berschied, E. (1977). Social perception and interpersonal behavior. On the self-fulfilling nature of social stereotypes. *J. Pers. Soc. Psychol., 35*(9), 656–66.

Snyder, S. H. (1978). Dopamine and schizophrenia. In L. C. Wynne, R. L. Cromwell & S. Matthysse (Eds.), *The nature of schizophrenia: New approaches to research and treatment* (pp. 87–94). New York: Wiley.

Solomon, J. (1972). Why gamble? A psychological profile of pathology. *The Sciences, 12*(6), 20–21.

Solomon, Z. (1989). Psychological sequelae of war. A 3-year prospective study of Israeli combat stress reaction casualties. *J. Nerv. Ment. Dis., 177,* 342–46.

Sommers, I. (1988). The influence of environmental factors on the community adjustment of the mentally ill. *J. Nerv. Ment. Dis., 176,* 221–26.

Soni, S. D., & Rockley, G. J. (1974). Socio-cultural substrates of folie à deux. *Brit. J. Psychiat., 125*(9), 230–35.

Sonnenberg, S. M. (1988). Victims of violence and post-traumatic stress disorder. *Psychiat. Clin. N. Amer., 11,* 581–90.

Sontag, L. W., Steele, W. G., & Lewis, M. (1969). The fetal and maternal cardiac response to environmental stress. *Human Develop., 12,* 1–9.

Spanos, N. P., Weekes, J. R., & Bertrand, L. D. (1985). Multiple personality: A social psychological perspective. *J. Abnorm. Psychol., 94,* 362–76.

Speed, N., Engdahl, B., Schwartz, J., & Eberly, R. (1989). Posttraumatic stress disorder as a consequence of the POW experience. *J. Nerv. Ment. Dis. 177,* 147–53.

Spence, J. T., & Helmreich, R. L. (1978). *Masculinity and femininity: Their psychological dimensions, correlates, & antecedents.* Austin, TX: University of Texas Press.

Spencer, G. (1989). *Projections of the population of the United States, by age, sex, and race: 1988–2080.* U.S. Department of Commerce, Bureau of Census. U. S. Government Printing Office.

Spielberger, C. D., Johnson, E. H., Russell, S. F., Crane, R. J., & Worden, T. J. (1985). The experience and expression of anger. In M. A. Chesney & R. H. Rosenman (Eds.), *Anger and hostility in cardiovascular and behavioral disorders.* New York: Hemisphere.

Spiess, W. F. J., Geer, J. H., & O'Donohue, W. T. (1984). Premature ejaculation: Investigation of factors in ejaculatory latency. *J. Abnorm. Psychol., 93,* 242–45.

Spirito, A., Brown, L., Overholser, J., & Fritz, G. (1989). Attempted suicide in adolescence: A review and critique of the literature. *Clin. Psychol. Rev. 9,* 335–63.

Spitz, R. A. (1945). Hospitalization: An inquiry into the genesis of psychiatric conditions of early childhood. In R. S. Eissler, A. Freud, H. Hartman, & E. Kris (Eds.), *The psychoanalytic study of the child* (Vol. 1). New York: International Universities Press.

Spitz, R. A. (1946). Anaclitic depression. In *Psychoanalytic study of the child* (Vol. 2). New York: International Universities Press.

Spitzer, R. L., Gibbon, M., Skodol, A. E., Williams, J. B. W. & First, M. B. (1989). *DSM-III-R casebook.* Washington, DC: American Psychiatric Press.

Spitzer, R. L., Skodol, A. E., Gibbon, M., & Williams, J. B. W. (1981). *DSM-III case book.* Washington, DC: American Psychiatric Association.

Spitzer, R. L., Skodol, A. E., Gibbon, M., & Williams, J. B. W. (1983). *Psychopathology: A case book.* New York: McGraw-Hill.

Spitzer, R. L., & Williams, J. B. (1988). Having a dream: A research strategy for DSM-IV. *Arch. Gen. Psychiat., 45,* 871–74.

Sprague, R. L., Barnes, K. R., & Werry, J. S. (1970). Methylphenidate and thioridazine: Learning reaction time, activity, and classroom behavior in disturbed children. *Amer. J. Orthopsychiat., 40,* 615–28.

Sprague, R. L., & Brown, T. (1981). Behavioral pharmacology research with children. In T. Thompson and P. B. Dews (Eds.), *Advances in behavioral pharmacology* (Vol. 3). New York: Academic Press.

Spring, B. J., & Zubin, J. (1978). Attention and

information-processing as indicators of vulnerability to schizophrenic episodes. In L. C. Wynne, R. L. Cromwell & S. Matthysse (Eds.), *The nature of schizophrenia: New approaches to research and treatment* (pp. 366–175). New York: Wiley.

Squire, L. R. (1977). ECT and memory loss. *Amer. J. Psychiat., 134,* 997–1001.

Squire, L. R., & Slater, P. C. (1978). Bilateral and unilateral ECT: Effects on verbal and nonverbal memory. *Amer. J. Psychiat., 135,* 1316–20.

Squire, L. R., Slater, P. C., & Chase, P. M. (1975). Retrograde amnesia: Temporal gradient in very long-term memory following electroconvulsive therapy. *Science, 187,* 77–79.

Stabenau, J., & Pollin, W. (1968). Comparative life history differences of families of schizophrenics, delinquents and "normals." *Amer. J. Psychiat. 124,* 1526–34.

Stabenau, J. R. (1984). Implications of family history of alcoholism, antisocial personality, and sex differences in alcohol dependence. *Amer. J. Psychiat., 141*(10), 1178–82.

Stabenau, J. R., Tupin, J., Werner, M., & Pollin, W. (1965). A comparative study of families of schizophrenics, delinquents, and normals. *Psychiatry, 28,* 45–59.

Stampfl, T. G., (1975). Implosive therapy: Staring down your nightmares. *Psych. Today, 8*(9), 66–68, 72–73.

Stanley, E. J., & Barter, J. T. (1970). Adolescent suicidal behavior. *Amer. J. Orthopsychiat., 40*(1), 87–96.

Stanton, M. D., & Todd, T. C. (1976, June). *Structural family therapy with heroin addicts: Some outcome data.* Paper presented at the Society for Psychotherapy Research. San Diego.

Stare, F. J., Whelan, E. M., & Sheridan, M. (1980). Diet and hyperactivity: Is there a relationship?, *Pediatrics, 6*(4), 521–25.

Stattin, H., & Magnusson, D. (1989). The role of early aggressive behavior in the frequency, seriousness, and types of later crimes. *J. Cons. Clin. Psychol., 57,* 710–18.

Steffenberg, S., & Gillberg, C. (1986). Autism and autistic-like conditions in Swedish rural and urban areas: A population study. *Brit. J. Psychiat. 149,* 81–87.

Stein, J. (1970). *Neurosis in contemporary society: Process and treatment.* Belmont, CA: Brooks/Cole.

Stein, S. (1987). Computer-assisted diagnosis for children and adolescents. In J. N. Butcher (Ed.), *Computerized psychological assessment: A practitioner's guide.* New York: Basic Books.

Steinmann, A., & Fox, D. J. (1974). *The male dilemma: How to survive the sexual revolution.* New York: Jason Aronson.

Steketee, G., & Foa, E. B. (1985). Obsessive-compulsive disorder. In D. H. Barlow (Ed.), *Clinical handbook of psychological disorders.* (pp. 69–144) New York: Guilford.

Stene, J., Stene, E., Stengel-Rutkowski, S., & Murken, J. D. (1981). Paternal age and Down's syndrome, data from prenatal diagnoses (DFG). *Human Genet. 59,* 119–24.

Stephens, R., & Cottrell, E. (1972). A follow-up study of 200 narcotic addicts committed for treatment under the narcotic addiction rehabilitation act. *British Journal of Addiction, 67,* 45–53.

Stephens, R. S., Hokanson, J. E., & Welker, R. (1987). Responses to depressed interpersonal behavior: Mixed reactions in a helping role. *J. Pers. Soc. Psychol., 52,* 1274–82.

Stermac, L. E., Segal, Z. V., & Gillis, R. (1990). Social and cultural factors in sexual assault. In W. L. Marshall, D. R. Laws, & H. E. Barbaree (Eds.), *Handbook of sexual assault* (pp. 143–60). New York: Plenum.

Stern, R. L. (1947). Diary of a war neurosis. *J. Nerv. Ment. Dis., 106,* 583–86.

Stern, R. S., Lisedge, M. S., & Marks, I. M. (1973). Obsessive ruminations: A controlled trial of thought-stopping technique. *Behav. Res. Ther., 11*(4), 659–62.

Stewart, A. L., & Brook, R. H. (1983). Effects of being overweight. *Amer. J. Pub. Hlth., 73*(2), 171–78.

Stewart, J. W., McGrath, P. J., Liebowitz, M. R., Harrison, W., & Quitkin, F. (1985). Treatment outcome validation of DSM-III depressive subtypes: Clinical usefulness in outpatients with mild to moderate depression. *Arch. Gen. Psychiat., 42,* 1148–53.

Stewart, M. A., Deblois, C. S., Meardon, J., & Cummings, C. (1980). Aggressive conduct disorder of children. The clinical picture. *J. Nerv. Ment. Dis., 168*(10), 604–10.

Stewart, S. H., Finn, P. R., & Pihl, R. O. (1990, Mar.). The effects of alcohol on the cardiovascular stress response in men at high risk for alcoholism: A dose response study. Paper presented at the annual meeting of the Canadian Psychological Association, Ottawa.

Stierlin, H. (1973). A family perspective on adolescent runaways. *Men. Hlth. Dig., 5*(10), 1–4.

Stiles, W. B., & Shapiro, D. A., (1989). Abuse of the drug metaphor in psychotherapy process-outcome research. *Clin. Psychol. Rev., 9,* 521–43.

Stiles, W. B., Shapiro, D. A., & Elliott, R. (1986). "Are all psychotherapies equivalent?" *Amer. Psychol., 41,* 165–80.

Stokes, P. E., & Sikes, C. R. (1987). Hypothalamic-pituitary-adrenal axis in affective disorders. In H. Y. Meltzer (Ed.), *Psychopharmacology: A third generation of progress.* (pp. 589–607) New York: Raven Press.

Stoller, R. J. (1974). *Sex and gender (Vol. 1): The development of masculinity and femininity.* New York: Jason Aronson.

Stone, A. A., Cox, D. S., Valdimarsdottir, H., Jandorf, N., & Neale, J. M. (1987). Evidence that secretory IgA antibody is associated with daily mood. *J. Pers. Soc. Psychol. 52,* 988–93.

Stone, G. C., Weiss, S. M., Matarazzo, J. D., Miller, N. E., Rodin, J., Belar, C. D., Follick, M. J., & Singer, J. E. (Eds.), (1987). *Health psychology: A discipline and a profession.* Chicago: University of Chicago Press.

Stone, L. J., & Hokanson, J. E. (1969). Arousal reduction via self-punitive behavior. *J. Pers. Soc. Psychol., 12,* 72–79.

Stone, M. H. (1990). Treatment of borderline patients: A pragmatic approach. *Psychiat. Clin. N. Amer., 13,* 265–82.

Stone, S. (1937). Psychiatry through the ages. *J. Abnorm. Soc. Psychol., 32,* 131–60.

Strack, S., & Coyne, J. C. (1983). Social confirmation of dysphoria: Shared and private reactions to depression. *J. Pers. Soc. Psychol., 44,* 798–806.

Strang, J. P. (1989). Gastrointestinal disorders. In S. Cheren (Ed.), *Psychosomatic medicine: Theory, physiology, and practice* (Vol. 2, pp. 427–502). Madison, CT: International Universities Press.

Strange, R. E., & Brown, D. E., Jr. (1970). Home from the wars. *Amer. J. Psychiat., 127,*(4), 488–92.

Strauss, T. S. (1979). Social and cultural influences on psychopathology. *Annu. Rev. Psychol., 30*(4), 397–415.

Stravynski, A., Lesage, A., Marcouiller, M., & Elie, R. (1989). A test of the therapeutic mechanism in social skills training with avoidant personality disorder. *J. Nerv. Ment. Dis., 177,* 739–44.

Strayer, R., & Ellenhorn, L. (1975). Vietnam veterans: A study exploring adjustment patterns and attitudes. *Journal of Social Issues, 31,* 81–93.

Strayhorn, J. M. (1982). *Foundations of clinical psychiatry.* Chicago: Year Book Medical Publishers.

Strean, H. S. (1985). *Resolving resistances in psychotherapy.* New York: Wiley Interscience.

Streissguth, A. P. (1976). Maternal alcoholism and the outcome of pregnancy: A review of the fetal alcohol syndrome. In M. Greenblatt & M. A. Schuckit (Eds.), *Alcoholism: Problems in women and children.* New York: Grune & Stratton.

Strine, G. (1971, Mar. 30). Compulsive gamblers pursue elusive dollar forever. *Los Angeles Times,* III, 1–6.

Strober, M. (1986). Anorexia nervosa: history and psychological concepts. In K. D. Brownell & J. P. Foreyt (Eds.), *Handbook of eating disorders* (pp. 231–46). New York: Basic.

Stroebe, M. S., & Stroebe, W. (1983). Who suffers more? Sex differences in health risks of the widowed. *Psychol. Bull., 93*(2), 279–301.

Strupp, H. H. (1981). Toward a refinement of time-limited dynamic psychotherapy. In S. H. Budman (Ed.), *Forms of brief therapy.* New York: Guilford Press.

Strupp, H. H., & Binder, J. L. (1984). *Psychotherapy in a new key: A guide to time-limited dynamic psychotherapy.* New York: Basic Books.

Strupp, H. H., Hadley, S. W., & Gomes-Schwartz, B. (1977). *Psychotherapy for better or worse: An analysis of the problem of negative effects.* New York: Jason Aronson.

Stuart, R. B. (1967). Behavioral control of overeating. *Beh. Res. Ther., 5,* 357–65.

Stuart, R. B. (1971a). Behavioral contracting within the families of delinquents. *Journal of Behavior Therapy and Experimental Psychiatry, 2,* 1–11.

Stuart, R. B. (1971b). A three-dimensional program for the treatment of obesity. *Beh. Res. Ther., 9,* 177–86.

Stunkard, A., D'Aquili, E., Fox, S., & Filion, R. D. L. (1972). Influence of social class on obesity and thinness in children. *JAMA, 221,* 579–84.

Sturgis, E. T., & Adams, H. E. (1978). The right to treatment: Issues in the treatment of homosexuality. *J. Cons. Clin. Psychol., 46*(1), 165–69.

Sturgis, E. T., & Meyer, V. (1981). Obsessive-compulsive

disorders. In S. M. Turner, K. S. Calhoun, & H. E. Adams (Eds.), *Handbook of clinical behavior therapy.* New York: Wiley.

Sturt, E. (1986). Application of survival analysis to the inception of dementia. *Psychol. Med., 16,* 583–93.

Su, C. V., Lin, S., Wang, Y. T., Li, C. H. Hung, L. H., Lin, C. S., & Lin, B. C. (1978). Effects of B-endorphin on narcotic abstinence syndrome in man. *Taiwan I Hoven Hui Tsa Chih, 77,* 133–41.

Suddath, R. L., Christison, G. W., Torrey, E. F., Casanova, M. F., & Weinberger, D. R. (1990). Anatomical abnormalities in the brains of monozygotic twins discordant for schizophrenia. *New Engl. J. Med., 322,* 789–94.

Sue, D., & Sue, S. (1987). Cultural factors in the clinical assessment of Asian Americans. *J. Cons. Clin. Psychol., 55,* 479–87.

Sulkunen, P. (1976). Drinking patterns and the level of alcohol consumption: An international overview. In R. I. Gibbons et al. (Eds.), *Research advances in alcohol and drug problems* (Vol. 3). New York: Wiley.

Sullivan, H. S. (1953). In H. S. Perry & M. L. Gawel (Eds.), *The interpersonal theory of psychiatry.* New York: Norton.

Sullivan, H. S. (1956). *Clinical studies in psychiatry.* New York: Norton.

Sullivan, J. P., & Batareh, G. J. (1973). Educational therapy with the severely retarded. *The Training School Bulletin, 70*(1), 5–9.

Summers, F. (1979). Characteristics of new patient admissions to aftercare. *Hosp. Comm. Psychiat., 30*(3), 199–202.

Summit, R., & Kryso, J. (1978). Sexual abuse of children: A clinical spectrum. *Amer. J. Orthopsychiat., 48,* 237–51.

Sundberg, N. D., & Tyler, L. E. (1962). *Clinical psychology.* New York: Appleton-Century-Crofts.

Surwit, R. S., Shapiro, D., & Good, M. L. (1978). Comparison of cardiovascular biofeedback, neuromuscular biofeedback, and meditation in the treatment of borderline essential hypertension. *J. Cons. Clin. Psychol., 46,* 252–53.

Suter, B. (1976). Suicide and women. In B. B. Wolman & H. H. Krauss (Eds.), *Between survival and suicide* (pp. 129–61). New York: Gardner.

Sutker, P. B., Archer, R. P., & Kilpatrick, D. G. (1979). Sociopathy and antisocial behavior: Theory and treatment. In S. M. Turner, K. S. Calhoun, & H. E. Adams (Eds.), *Handbook of clinical behavior therapy.* New York: Wiley.

Sutker, P. B., Galina, H., & West, J. A. (1990). Trauma-induced weight loss and cognitive deficits among former prisoners of war. *J. Cons. Clin. Psychol., 58,* 323–328.

Svanum, S., & Schladenhauffen, J. (1986). Lifetime and recent alcohol consumption among male alcoholics. *J. Nerv. Ment. Dis., 174*(4), 214–20.

Svrakic, D. M. (1990). The functional dynamics of the narcissistic personality. *Amer. J. Psychother., 44,* 189–203.

Swadi, H., & Zeitlin, H. (1988). Peer influence and adolescent substance abuse: A promising side? *Brit. J. Addiction, 83*(2), 153–57.

Swanson, D. W. (1968). Adult sexual abuse of children: The man and circumstances. *Dis. Nerv. Sys., 29*(10), 677–83.

Swanson, D. W., Bohnert, P. J., & Smith, J. A. (1970). *The paranoid.* Boston: Little, Brown.

Swedo, S. E., Rapoport, J. L., Leonard, H., Lenane, M., & Cheslow, D. (1989). Obsessive-compulsive disorder in children and adolescents: Clinical phenomenology of 70 consecutive cases. *Arch. Gen. Psychiat., 46,* 335–41.

Swenson, C. R., & Wood, M. J. (1990). Issues involved in combining drugs with psychotherapy for the borderline patient. *Psychiat. Clin. N. Amer. 13,* 297–306.

Switzer, E. (1974). Female sexuality. *Fam. Hlth., 6*(3), 34–36, 38.

Symonds, M. (1976). The rape victim. Psychological patterns of response. *American Journal of Psychoanalysis, 36*(1), 27–34.

Szapocznik, J., Perez-Vidal, A., Brickman, A. L., Foote, F. H., Santisteban, D., Hervis, O., & Kurtines, W. M. (1988). Engaging adolescent drug abusers and their families in treatment: A strategic structural systems approach. *J. Cons. Clin. Psychol., 56,* 552–57.

Szasz, T. S. (1961). *The myth of mental illness.* New York: Harper & Row.

Szasz, T. S. (1963). *Law, liberty, and psychiatry.* New York: Macmillan.

Szasz, T. S. (1970). *The manufacture of madness.* New York: Harper & Row.

Szasz, T. S. (1976). The ethics of suicide. In B. B. Wolman & H. H. Krauss (Eds.), *Between survival and suicide* (pp. 163–85). New York: Gardner.

Szmukler, G. I., & Russell, G. F. M. (1986). Outcome and prognosis of anorexia nervosa. In K. D. Brownell & J. P. Foreyt (Eds.), *Handbook of eating disorders* (pp. 283–300). New York: Basic.

Tacke, U. (1990). Fluoxetine: An alternative to the tricyclics in the treatment of major depression. *Amer. J. Med. Sci., 298,* 126–29.

Talbott, J. A. (1985a). Community care for the chronically mentally ill. *Psychiat. Clin. N. Amer., 8,* 437–48.

Talbott, J. A. (1985b, Apr 19.) Psychiatrists must unify to survive. *Psychiat. News, 14.*

Talley, P. F., Strupp, H. H., & Morey, L. C. (1990). Matchmaking in psychotherapy: Patient-therapist dimensions and their impact on outcome. *J. Cons. Clin. Psychol., 58,* 182–88.

Tardiff, K. (1984). Characteristics of assaultive patients in private psychiatric hospitals. *Amer. J. Psychiat., 141,* 1232–35.

Tardiff, K., & Koenigsberg, H. W. (1985). Assaultive behavior among psychiatric outpatients. *Amer. J. Psychiat., 142*(8), 960–63.

Tardiff, K., & Sweillam, A. (1982). Assaultive behavior among chronic inpatients. *Amer. J. Psychiat., 139,* 212–15.

Tarjan, G., & Eisenberg, L. (1972). Some thought on the classification of mental retardation in the United States of America. *Amer. J. Psychiat.,* Suppl., *128*(11), 14–18.

Tarjan, G., Wright, S. W., Eyman, R. K., & Keeran, C. V. (1973). Natural history of mental retardation: Some aspects of epidemiology. *Amer. J. Ment. Def., 77*(4), 369–79.

Tarler-Beniolo, L. (1978). The role of relaxation in biofeedback training: A critical review of the literature. *Psychol. Bull., 85*(4), 727–55.

Tarter, R. E. (1988). Are there inherited behavioral traits that predispose to substance abuse? *J. Cons. Clin. Psychol., 56,* 189–196.

Tarver, S. G., & Hallahan, D. P. (1974). Attention deficits in children with teaming disabilities: A review. *J. Learn. Dis., 7*(9), 560–69.

Tasto, D. L., & Hinkle, J. E. (1973). Muscle relaxation treatment for tension headaches. *Beh. Res. Ther., 11,* 347–50.

Tavel, M. E. (1962). A new look at an old syndrome: Delirium tremens. *Arch. Int. Med., 109,* 129–34.

Taves, I. (1969). Is there a sleepwalker in the house? *Today's Health, 47*(5), 41, 76.

Taylor, A. J. W. (1989). *Disasters and disaster stress.* New York: AMS Press.

Telch, M. J. (1981). The present status of outcome studies: A reply to Frank. *J. Cons. Clin. Psychol., 49*(3), 472–75.

Teplin, L.A. (1990a). The prevalence of severe mental disorder among male urban jail detainees: A comparison with the epidemiologic catchment area program. *Amer. J. Pub. Hlth., 80,* 663–69.

Teplin, L. A. (1990b). Detecting disorder: The treatment of mental illness among jail detainees. *J. Cons. Clin. Psychol., 58,* 233–36.

Thacher, M. (1978, Apr.). First steps for the retarded. *Human Behav.*

Thase, M. E., Frank, E., & Kupfer, D. J. (1985). Biological processes in major depression. In E. E. Beckham & W. R. Leber (Eds.), *Handbook of depression: Treatment, assessment, and research* (pp. 816–913). Homewood, IL: Dorsey Press.

Theodor, L. H., & Mandelcorn, M. S. (1973). Hysterical blindness: A case report and study using a modern psychophysical technique. *J. Abnorm. Psychol., 82*(3), 552–53.

Thibaut, J. W., & Kelley, H. H. (1959). *The social psychology of groups.* New York: Wiley.

Thomas, A., & Chess, S. (1977). *Temperament and development.* New York: Brunner/Mazel.

Thomas, A., Chess, S., & Birch, H. G. (1968). *Temperament and behavior disorders in children.* New York: New York University Press.

Thompson, J. C. (1982). The role of surgery in peptic ulcer. *New Engl. J. Med., 307,* 550–51.

Thompson, N. L., Jr., & McCandless, B. R., & Strickland, B. R. (1971). Personal adjustment of male and female homosexuals and heterosexuals. *J. Abnorm. Psychol., 78*(2), 237–40.

Tiefer, L., & Melman, A. (1989). Comprehensive evaluation of erectile dysfunction and medical treatments. In S. R. Leiblum & R. C. Rosen (Eds.), *Principles and practice of sex therapy* (2nd ed., pp. 207–36). New York: Guilford.

Tien, A. Y., & Anthony, J. C. (1990). Epidemiological analysis of alcohol and drug use as risk factors for psychotic experiences. *J. Nerv. Ment. Dis., 178*, 473–80.

Tienari, P., Lahti, I., Sorri, A., Naarala, M., Moring, J., Wahlberg, K.–E., & Wynne, L. C. (1987). The Finnish adoptive family study of schizophrenia. *Journal of Psychiatric Research, 21*, 437–45.

Tienari, P., Sorri, A., Lahti, I., Naarala, M., Wahlberg, K.–E., Pohjola, J., & Moring, J. (1985). Interaction of genetic and psychosocial factors in schizophrenia. *Acta Psychiatr. Scandin.* (Suppl. No. 319), *71*, 19–30.

Time. (1966, June 17). From shocks to stop sneezes, p. 72.

Time. (1974, Apr. 22). Alcoholism: New victims, new treatment. *103*(16), pp. 75–81.

Time. (1981, May 4). Stomping and whomping galore, pp. 73–74.

Time. (1983, Apr. 18). Ailing schoolgirls. *121*(16), p. 52.

Tinbergen, N. (1974). Ethology and stress disease. *Science, 185*(4145), 20–27.

Tizard, B., & Rees, J. (1975). The effect of early institutional rearing on the behavior problems and affectional relationships of four-year-old children. *J. Child Psychol. Psychiat., 16*(1), 61–73.

Tobler, N. S. (1986). Meta-analysis of 143 adolescent drug prevention programs: Quantitative outcome results of program participation compared to a control or comparison group. *Journal of Drug Issues, 16*, 537–68.

Toffler, A. (1970). *Future shock.* New York: Random House.

Tollison, C. D., & Adams, H. E. (1979). *Sexual disorders.* New York: Gardner Press.

Tollison, C. D., Adams, H. E., & Tollison, J. W. (1979). Cognitive and physiological measurement of sexual arousal in homosexual, bisexual, and heterosexual males. *J. Behav. Assess., 1*, 305–14.

Tomarken, A. J., Mineka, S., & Cook, M. (1989). Fear-relevant selective associations and covariation bias. *J. Abnorm. Psychol., 98*, 381–94.

Torrey, E. F. (1973). Is schizophrenia universal? An open question. *Schizo. Bull., 7*, 53–59.

Torrey, E. F. (1974). *The death of psychiatry.* New York: Penguin Books.

Torrey, E. F. (1979). Epidemiology. In L. Bellak (Ed.), *Disorders of the schizophrenic syndrome.* New York: Basic Books.

Torrey, E. F., et al. (1984). Endemic psychosis in western Ireland. *Amer. J. Psychiat., 141*, 966–70.

Tripp, C. A. (1975). *The homosexual matrix.* New York: McGraw-Hill.

Tronick, E. Z., & Cohn, J. F. (1989). Infant-mother face-to-face interaction: Age and gender differences in coordination and miscoordination. *Child Develop., 59*, 85–92.

Trull, T. J., Widiger, T. A., & Frances, A. (1987). Covariation of criteria sets for avoidant, schizoid, and dependent personality disorders. *Amer. J. Psychiat., 144*, 767–71.

Tseng, W. S. (1973). The development of psychiatric concepts in traditional Chinese medicine. *Arch. Gen. Psychiat., 29*(4), 569–75.

Tuckman, J., Kleiner, R., & Lavell, M. (1959). Emotional content of suicide notes. *Amer. J. Psychiat. 116*, 59–63.

Tuma, J. (1989). Mental health services for children: The state of the art. *Amer. Psychol., 44*, 188–99.

Turk, D. (1974). *Cognitive control of pain: A skills training approach.* Unpublished manuscript, University of Waterloo, Ontario, Canada.

Turner, R. K., & Taylor, P. D. (1974). Conditioning treatment of nocturnal enuresis in adults: Preliminary findings. *Behav. Res. Ther., 12*, 41–52.

Turner, S. M., Beidel, D. C., & Costello, A. (1987). Psychopathology in the offspring of anxiety disorder patients. *J. Cons. Clin. Psychol., 55*, 229–35.

Turner, S. M., Beidel, D. C., & Nathan, R. S. (1985). Biological factors in obsessive-compulsive disorders. *Psychol. Bull.* 97, 430–50.

Tyor, P. L., & Bell, L. V. (1984). *Caring for the retarded in America: A history.* Westport, CT: Greenwood Press.

Tyrer, P. (1988). What's wrong with DSM III personality disorders? *Journal of Personality Disorders, 2*, 281–91.

U.S. Committee for Refugees. (1990). *Refugee Reports,* Vol. XI, No. 12. Washington, DC.

U.S. Department of Health and Human Services. (1988). *The Health Consequences of Smoking: Nicotine addiction.* Public Health Service, Office on Smoking and Health, Maryland.

U.S. Department of Health and Human Services. (1989).

Health United States 1988. National Center for Health Statistics, Washington, DC: U.S. Government Printing Office.

U.S. Department of Health and Human Services. (1989). *Reducing the Consequences of Smoking: 25 years of Progress.* Public Health Service, Office on Smoking and Health, Maryland.

U.S. Department of Health, Education, and Welfare. (1974). *Alcohol and health.* Morris E. Chafetz, Chairman of the Task Force. Washington, DC: U.S. Government Printing Office.

U.S. Department of Health, Education and Welfare. (1978). *The alcoholism report: The authoritative newsletter for professionals.* Washington, DC: U.S. Government Printing Office, 7(3), 2.

U.S. Department of Justice. (1987). *Jail inmates 1986.* Bureau of Justice Statistics, Washington, DC: U.S. Government Printing Office.

Uchida, I. A. (1973). Paternal origin of the extra chromosome in Down's syndrome. *Lancet, 2*(7840), 1258.

Uhde, T. W., Bierer, L. M., & Post, R. M. (1985). Caffeine-induced escape from dexamethasone suppression. *Arch. Gen. Psychiat., 42*, 737.

Uhlenhuth, E. (1973, Feb. 7). Free therapy said to be helpful to Chicago train wreck victim. *Psychiat. News, 8*(3), 1, 27.

Ullmann, L. P., & Krasner, L. (1975). *Psychological approach to abnormal behavior* (2nd ed.). Englewood Cliffs, NJ: Prentice-Hall.

Umana, R. F., Gross, S. J., & McConville, M. T. (1980). *Crisis in the family.* New York: Gardner Press.

Uniform Crime Reports. (1989). *Federal Bureau of Investigation, U. S. Department of Justice.* U. S. Government Printing Office.

United Press International. (1982, Oct. 24). "Tylenol hysteria" hits 200 at football game. *Chicago Tribune*, Sec. 1, p. 4.

Ursano, R.J., Boydstun, J. A., & Wheatley, R. D., (1981). Psychiatric illness in U.S. Air Force Vietnam prisoners of war: A five-year follow-up. *Amer. J. Psychiat.* 138(3), 310–14.

Vaillant, G. E. (1975). Sociopathy as a human process: A viewpoint. *Arch. Gen. Psychiat., 32*(2), 178–83.

Vaillant, G. E., & Schnurr, P. (1988). What is a case? *Arch. Gen. Psychiat., 45*, 313–19.

Valenstein, E. S. (Ed.). (1980). *The psychosurgery debate: Scientific, legal, and ethical perspectives.* San Francisco: W. H. Freeman.

Valenstein, E. S. (1986). *Great and desperate cures.* New York: Basic Books.

Vallacher, R. R., Wegner, D. M., & Hoine, H. (1980). A postscript on application. In D. Megner & R. R. Vallacher (Eds.), *The sell in social psychology.* New York: Oxford University Press.

Van Broeckhoven, C., Genthe, A. M., Vandenberghe, A., Horsthemke, B. et al. (1987). Failure of familial Alzheimer's disease to segregate with the A4-amyloid gene in several European families. *Nature, 329*, 153–55.

VandenBos, G. R. (1986). Psychotherapy research: A special issue. *Amer. Psychol., 41*, 111–12.

Vandereycken, W. (1982). Paradoxical strategies in a blocked sex therapy. *Amer. J. Psychother., 36*, 103–8.

Vasiljeva, O. A., Kornetov, N. A., Zhankov, A. I., & Reshetnikov, V. I. (1989). Immune function in psychogenic depression. *Amer. J. Psychiat., 146*, 284–85.

Vaughn, C. E., & Leff, J. P. (1976). The influence of family and social factors on the course of psychiatric illness: A comparison of schizophrenic and depressed neurotic patients. *Brit. J. Psychiat., 129*, 125–37.

Vaughn, C.E., Snyder, K. S., Jones, S., Freeman, W. B., & Falloon, I. R H. (9184). Family factors in schizophrenic relapse: Replication in California of British research on expressed emotion. *Arch. Gen. Psychiat., 41*, 1169–77.

Vega, W. A., & Rumbaut, R. G. (1991). Reasons of the heart: Ethnic minorities and mental health. *Annual Review of Sociology, 17*.

Velez, C. N. & Cohen, P. (1987). Suicidal behavior and ideation in a community sample of children: Maternal and youth reports. *Journal of the American Academia of Child and Adolescent Psychiatry, 27*, 349–56.

Vellutino, F. R. (1987). Linguistic and cognitive correlates of learning disability: Review of three reviews. In S. J. Ceci (Ed.), *Handbook of cognitive, social and neuropsychological aspects of learning disabilities* (Vol. 1, pp. 317–35). Hillsdale, NJ: Erlbaum.

Verhulst, J. H., Van Der Lee, J. H., Akkerhuis, G. W., Sanders-Woudstra, J. A. R., Timmer, F. C., & Donkhorst, I. D. (1985). The prevalence of nocturnal enuresis: Do

DSM–III criteria need to be changed: A brief research report. *J. Child Psychol. Psychiat.*, 26(6), 983–93.

Viglione, D. J., & Exner, J. E. (1983). Current research on the Comprehensive Rorschach System. In J. N. Butcher & C. D. Spielberger (Eds.), *Advances in personality assessment* (Vol. 4). New York: Lawrence Erlbaum and Associates.

Viney, W., & Bartsch, K. (1984). Dorthea Lynde Dix: Positive or negative influence on the development of treatment for the mentally ill. *Social Science Journal, 21,* 71–82.

Viscott, D. S. (1970). A musical idiot savant. *Psychiatry, 33*(4), 494–515.

Volkmar, F. R., Hoder, E. L., & Cohen, D. J. (1985). Compliance, "negativism," and the effects of treatment structure in autism: A naturalistic behavioral study. *J. Child Psychol. Psychiat.*, 26(6), 865–77.

Wachtel, P. L. (1977). *Psychoanalysis and behavior therapy: Toward an integration.* New York: Basic Books.

Wachtel, P. L. (1982). What can dynamic therapies contribute to behavior therapy? *Behav. Ther., 13,* 594–609.

Wadden, T. A., Luborsky, L., Greer, S., & Crits-Christopher, P. (1985). The behavioral treatment of essential hypertension: An update and comparison with pharamacological treatment. *Clin. Psychol. Rev., 4,* 403–29.

Wagener, D. K., & Cromwell, R. L. (1984). Schizophrenia: A right and just war. (Review of *Schizophrenia: The epigenetic puzzle,* by I. I. Gottesman & J. Shields.) *Contemp. Psychol., 29,* 110–15.

Wagner, G. (1981). Methods for differential diagnosis of psychogenic and organic erectile failure. In G. Wagner, & R. Green (Eds.), *Impotence: Physiological, psychological, surgical diagnosis and treatment.* New York: Plenum.

Wagner, G., & Green, R. (Eds.). (1981). *Impotence: Physiological, psychological, surgical diagnosis and treatment.* New York: Plenum.

Wahler, R. G. (1980). The insular mother: Her problems in parent-child treatment. *J. Appl. Beh. Anal., 13,* 207–19.

Wahler, R. G., Hughey, J. B., & Gordon, J. S. (1981). Chronic patterns of mother-child coercion: Some differences between insular and noninsular families. *Analysis and Intervention in Developmental Disorders, 1,* 145–56.

Walinder, J. (1968). Transsexualism: Definition, prevalence, and sex distribution. *Acta Psychiatr. Scandin., 203,* 255–58.

Wallerstein, J. S. (1984). Children of divorce: Preliminary report of a ten-year follow-up of young children. *Amer. J. Orthopsychiat., 54,* 444–58.

Wallerstein, J. S., & Kelly, J. B. (1980). Surviving the breakup: How children and parents cope with divorce. New York: Basic Books.

Wallerstein, R. S. (1989). The psychotherapy research project of the Menninger Foundation: An overview. *J. Cons. Clin. Psychol., 57,* 195–205.

Walsh, T. B. (1980). The endocrinology of anorexia nervosa. *Psychiat. Clin. N. Amer., 3*(2), 299–312.

Ward, A. J. (1978). Early childhood autism and structural therapy: Outcome after 3 years. *J. Cons. Clin. Psychol., 46,* 586–87.

Warnes, H. (1973). The traumatic syndrome. *Ment. Hlth. Dig., 5*(3), 33–34.

Warrington, E. K., & Weiskrantz, L. (1973). An analysis of short-term and long-term memory defects in man. In J. A. Deutsch (Ed.), *The psychological basis of memory.* New York: Academic Press.

Watkins, C., Gilbert, J. E., & Bass, W. (1969). The persistent suicidal patient. *Amer. J. Psychiat., 125,* 1590–93.

Watson, S., & Akil, H. (1979). Endorphins: Clinical issues. In R. Pickens & L. Heston (Eds.), *Psychiatric factors in drug abuse.* New York: Grune & Stratton.

Watt, N. F., Anthony, E. J., Wynne, L. C., & Rolf, J. E. (Eds.). (1984). *Children at risk for schizophrenia: A longitudinal perspective.* Cambridge: Cambridge University Press.

Weary, G., & Mirels, H. L. (1982). *Integrations of clinical and social psychology.* New York: Oxford University Press.

Wechsler, D. (1981). *Manual for the Wechsler Adult Intelligence Scale.* New York: Psychological Corporation.

Wehr, T. A., & Rosenthal, N. E. (1989). Seasonality and affective illness. *Amer. J. Psychiat., 146,* 829–39.

Wehr, T. A., Jacobsen, F. M., Sack, D. A., Arendt, J., Tamarkin, L., & Rosenthal, N. E. (1986). Phototherapy of seasonal affective disorder. *Arch. Gen. Psychiat., 43,* 870–75.

Weinberg, M., & Williams, C. J. (1974). *Male homosexuals: Their problems and adaptations in three societies.* New York: Oxford University Press.

Weinberger, D. R. (1984). Brain disease and psychiatric illness: When should a psychiatrist order a CAT scan? *Amer. J. Psychiat., 141,* 1521–27.

Weinberger, D. R., DeLisi, L. E., Perman, G. P., Targum, S., & Wyatt, R. J. (1982). Computed tomography in schizophreniform disorder and other acute psychiatric disorders. *Arch. Gen. Psychiat., 39,* 778–83.

Weiner, H. (1977). *Psychobiology and human disease.* New York: Elsevier.

Weiner, H., & Fawzy, F. I. (1989). An integrative model of health, disease, and illness. In S. Cheren (Ed.), *Psychosomatic medicine: Theory, physiology, and practice* (Vol. 1, pp. 9–44). Madison, CT: International Universities Press.

Weiner, H. F., Thaler, M., Reiser, M. F., & Mirsky, I. A. (1957). Etiology of duodenal ulcer: I. Relation of specific psychological characteristics to rate of gastric secretion (Serum pepsenogen). *Psychosom. Med., 19,* 1–10.

Weiner, R. (1982). Another look at an old controversy. *Contemporary Psychiatry, 1,* 61–62.

Weinstein, A. S. (1983). The mythical readmissions explosion. *Amer. J. Psychiat., 140*(3), 332–35.

Weintraub, M., & Frankel, J. (1977). Sex differences in parent-infant interaction during free play, departure, and separation. *Child Develop., 48,* 1240–48.

Weisenberg, M. (1977). Pain and pain control. *Psychol. Bull., 84,* 1008–44.

Weiss, B., Weisz, J. R., & Bromfield, R. (1986). Performance of retarded and nonretarded persons on information-processing tasks: Further tests of the similar structure hypothesis. *Psychol. Bull., 100,* 157–75.

Weiss, G. (1981). Controversial issues of the pharmacotherapy of the hyperactive child. *Canad. J. Psychiat., 26*(6), 385–92.

Weiss, G., & Hechtman, L. (1979). The hyperactive child syndrome. *Science, 205,* 1348–54.

Weiss, G., Hechtman, L., Perlman, T., Hopkins, J., & Wener, A. (1979). Hyperactives as young adults: A controlled prospective ten-year follow-up of 75 children. *Arch. Gen. Psychiat., 36,* 675–81.

Weiss, J. M. (1974). Cited in Depressing situations. *Sci. News, 105*(14), 224.

Weiss, J. M. (1984). Behavioral and psychological influences on gastrointestinal pathology: Experimental techniques and findings. In W. D. Gentry (Ed.), *Handbook of behavioral medicine,* (pp. 174–221). New York: Guilford.

Weiss, S. M., Herd, J. A., & Fox, B. H. (1981). *Perspectives on behavioral medicine.* New York: Academic Press.

Weiss, T., & Engel, B. T. (1971). Operant conditioning of heart rate in patients with premature ventricular contractions. *Psychosom. Med., 33,* 301–21.

Weissman, M. M., Fox, K., & Klerman, G. L. (1973). Hostility and depression associated with suicide attempts. *Amer. J. Psychiat., 130*(4), 450–55.

Weissman, M. M., Gammon, D., John, K., Merikangas, K. R., Warner, V., Prusoff, B. A., & Sholomskas, D. (1987). Children of depressed parents. *Arch. Gen. Psychiat., 44,* 847–53.

Weissman, M. M., Leckman, J. F., Merikangas, K. R., Gammon, G. D., & Prusoff, B. A. (1984). Depression and anxiety disorders in parents and children: Results from the Yale family study. *Arch. Gen. Psychiat., 41,* 845–52.

Weissman, M. M., Pottenger, M., Kleber, H., Ruben, H. L., Williams, D., & Thompson, D. (1977). Symptom pattern in primary and secondary depression. *Arch. Gen. Psychiat., 34,* 854–62.

Wekstein, L. (1979). *Handbook of suicidology: Principles, problems, and practice.* New York: Brunner/Mazel.

Wellisch, D. K., & Trock, G. K., (1980). A three-year follow-up of family therapy. *International Journal of Family Therapy, 2*(3), 169–75.

Wells, C. E. (1979). Diagnosis of dementia. *Psychosomatics, 20,* 517–12.

Wells, C. F., & Stuart, I. R. (Eds.). (1981). *Self-destructive behavior in children and adolescents.* New York: Van Nostrand Reinhold.

Wenar, C. (1990). *Developmental psychopathology: From infancy through adolescence* (2nd ed.). New York: McGraw-Hill.

Wender, P. H., Kety, S. S., Rosenthal, D., Schulsinger, F., & Ortmann, J. (1986). Psychiatric disorders in the biological and adoptive families of adopted individuals with affective disorders. *Arch. Gen. Psychiat., 43,* 923–29.

Wender, P. H., Reimherr, F. W., & Wood, D. R. (1981). Attention deficit disorder (minimal brain dysfunction) in adults. *Arch. Gen. Psychiat., 38,* 449–56.

Wender, P. H., Rosenthal, D., Kety, S. S., Schulsinger, F., & Weiner, J. (1974). Cross-fostering: A research strategy for clarifying the role of genetic and experimental factors in the etiology of schizophrenia. *Arch. Gen. Psychiat., 30*(1), 121–28.

Wennerholm, M., & Lopez-Roig, L. (1983). Use of the MMPI with executives in Puerto Rico. Paper given at the *Eighth Annual Conference on Personality Assessment,* Copenhagen, Denmark.

Werry, J. S. (1979). The childhood psychosis. In H. C. Quay & J. S. Werry (Eds.), *Psychopathological disorders of childhood.* New York: Wiley.

Werry, J. S., & Quay, H. C. (1971). The prevalence of behavior symptoms in younger elementary school children. *Amer. J. Orthopsychiat., 41,* 136–43.

Wertham, F. (1949). *The show of violence.* New York: Doubleday.

West, J. (1976). *The woman said yes: Encounters with life and death.* New York: Harcourt Brace Jovanovich.

Wester, P., Eriksson, S., Forsell, A., Puu, G., & Adolfsson, R. (1988). Monoamine metabolite concentrations and cholinesterase activities in cerebrospinal fluid of progressive dementia patients: Relation to clinical parameters. *Acta Neurologica Scandinavica, 77,* 12–21.

Westermeyer, J. (1982a). Bag ladies in isolated cultures, too. *Behav. Today, 13*(21), 1–2.

Westermeyer, J. (1982b). *Poppies, pipes and people: Opium and its use in Laos.* Berkeley, CA: University of California Press.

Westermeyer, J., (1987). Public health and chronic mental illness. *Amer. J. Pub. Hlth., 77*(6), 667–68.

Westermeyer, J., Neider, J., & Callies, A. (1989). Psychosocial adjustment of Hmong refugees during their first decade in the United States. A longitudinal study. *J. Nerv. Ment. Dis., 177,* 132–39.

Westermeyer, J., Williams, C. L., & Nguyen, N. (Eds.). (1991). *Mental health and social adjustment: A guide to clinical and prevention services.* Washington, DC: U. S. Government Printing Office.

Whalen, C. K., & Henker, B. (1976). Psychostimulants and children: A review and analysis. *Psychol. Bull., 83,* 1113–30.

Whalen, C. K., Henker, B., Buhrmester, D., Hinshaw, S. P., Huber, A., & Laski, K. (1989). Does stimulant medication improve the peer status of hyperactive children? *J. Cons. Clin. Psychol., 57,* 545–49.

Whiffen, V. E., & Gotlib, I. H. (1989). Infants of postpartum depressed mothers: Temperament and cognitive status. *J. Abnorm. Psychol., 98,* 274–79.

White, A. D. (1986). *A history of the warfare of science with theology in Christendom.* New York: Appleton.

Whitehead, W. E., Winget, C., Fedoravicius, A. S., Wooley, S., & Blackwell, B. (1982). Learned illness behavior in patients with irritable bowel syndrome and peptic ulcers. *Digestive Diseases and Sciences, 27,* 202–08.

Whitehouse, P. J., et al. (1982). Alzheimer's disease and senile dementia: Loss of neurons in the basal forebrain. *Science, 215,* 1237–39.

Widiger, T. A., & Frances, A. (1985). Axis II personality disorders: Diagnostic and treatment issues. *Hosp. Comm. Psychiat., 36,* 619–27.

Widiger, T. A., Frances, A., & Trull, T. J. (1987). A psychometric analysis of social-interpersonal and cognitive-perceptual items for the schizotypal personality disorder. *Arch. Gen. Psychiat., 44,* 741–45.

Widiger, T. A., Frances, A., Warner, L., & Bloom, C. (1986). Diagnostic criteria for the Borderline and Schizotypal Personality Disorders. *J. Abnorm. Psychol., 95*(1), 43–51.

Widom, C. S. (1977). A methodology for studying noninstitutionalized psychopaths. *J. Cons. Clin. Psychol., 45,* 674–83.

Wiggins, J. S. (1982). Circumplex models of interpersonal behavior in clinical psychology. In P. C. Kendall & J. N. Butcher (Eds.), *Handbook of research methods in clinical psychology.* New York: Wiley Interscience.

Wilbur, R. S. (1973, June 2). In S. Auerbach (Ed.), POWs found to be much sicker than they looked upon release. *Los Angeles Times,* Part I, p. 4.

Williams, C. L., & Westermeyer, J. (1986). *Refugee mental health in resettlement countries.* New York: Hemisphere Press.

Williams, C. L., Solomon, S. D., & Bartone, P. (1988). Primary prevention in aircraft disasters: Integrating research and practice. *Amer. Psychol., 43,* 724–39.

Williams, J. A., Koegel, R. L., & Egel, A. L. (1981). Response-reinforcer relationships and improved learning in autistic children. *J. Appl. Beh. Anal., 14*(1), 53–60.

Williams, L. M., & Finkelhor, D., (1990). The characteristics of incestuous fathers: A review of recent studies. In W. L. Marshall, D. R. Laws, & H. E. Barbaree (Eds.), *Handbook of sexual assault* (pp. 231–56). New York: Plenum.

Williams, R. B., Jr. (1977). Headache. In R. B. Williams, Jr. & W. D. Gentry (Eds.), *Behavioral approaches to medical treatment* (pp. 41–53). Cambridge, MA: Ballinger.

Williams, R. B., Jr., Barefoot, J. C., & Shekelle, R. B. (1985). The health consequences of hostility. In Chesney, M. A., Goldston, S. E., & Rosenman, R. H. (Eds.), *Anger, hostility, and behavioral medicine* (pp. 173–85). New York: Hemisphere/McGraw-Hill.

Williams, R. B., Jr., & Gentry, W. D. (Eds.), (1977). *Behavioral approaches to medical treatment.* Cambridge, MA: Ballinger.

Williams, R. B., Jr., Haney, T. L., Lee, K. L., Kong, V., & Blumenthal, J. A. (1980). Type A behavior, hostility, and coronary atherosclerosis. *Psychosom. Med., 42,* 529–38.

Williams, S. L., Turner, S. M., & Peer, D. F. (1985). Guided mastery and performance desensitization treatments for severe acrophobia. *J. Cons. Clin. Psychol., 53,* 237–47.

Williams, S. L., & Zane, G. (1989). Guided mastery and stimulus exposure treatments for severe performance anxiety in agoraphobics. *Behav. Res. Ther., 27,* 237–45.

Williams, T. I. (1989). A social skills group for autistic children. *J. Autism Devel. Dis., 19,* 143–55.

Wing, J. K., & Bebbington, P. (1985). Epidemiology of depression. In E. E. Beckham & W. R. Leber (Eds.), *Handbook of depression: treatment, assessment, and research* (pp. 765–94). Homewood, IL: Dorsey Press.

Wing, L. (1980). Childhood autism and social class: A question of selection. *Brit. J. Psychiat., 137,* 410–17.

Wing, L. K., (1976). Diagnosis, clinical description and prognosis. In L. Wing (Ed.), *Early childhood autism.* London: Pergamon Press.

Wing, S., & Manton, K. G. (1983). The contribution of hypertension to mortality in the U.S.: 1968, 1977. *Amer. J. Pub. Hlth., 73*(2), 140–44.

Winick, M. (Ed.). (1976). *Malnutrition and brain development.* New York: Oxford University Press.

Winick, M., & Rosso, P. (1973). Effects of malnutrition on brain development. *Biology of Brain Dysfunction, 1,* 301–17.

Winokur, G. (1985). The validity of neurotic-reactive depression: New data and reappraisal. *Arch. Gen. Psychiat., 42,* 1116–22.

Winokur, G., Clayton, P. J., & Reich, T. (1969). *Manic depressive illness.* St. Louis: Mosby.

Winokur, G., & Pitts, F. N. (1964). Affective disorder: Is reactive depression an entity? *J. Nerv. Ment. Dis., 138,* 541–47.

Winsberg, B. G., Goldstein, S., Yepes, L. E., & Perel, J. M. (1975). Imipramine and electrocardiographic abnormalities in hyperactive children. *Amer. J. Psychiat., 132*(5), 542–45.

Winslow, R. (1990, May 14). Sandoz Corps Clozaril treats schizophrenia but can kill patients. *Wall Street Journal,* p. 1.

Winter, D. G. (1973). *The power motive.* New York: Free Press.

Winters, K. C., Weintraub, S., & Neale, J. M. (1981). Validity of MMPI code types in identifying DSM-III schizophrenics, unipolars, and bipolars. *J. Cons. Clin. Psychol., 49,* 486–87.

Wisniewski, H. M., Moretz, R. C., & Igbal, K. (1986). No evidence for aluminum in etiology and pathogenesis of Alzheimer's disease. *Neurobiology of Aging, 7,* 532–35.

Witzig, J. S. (1968). The group treatment of male exhibitionists. *Amer. J. Psychiat. 125,* 75–81.

Wolf, M., Risley, T., & Mees, H. (1964). Application of operant conditioning procedures to the behavior problems of an autistic child. *Behav. Res. Ther., 1,* 305–12.

Wolf, S. L., Nacht, M., & Kelly, J. L. (1982). EMG feedback training during dynamic movement for low back pain patients. *Behav. Ther., 13,* 395–406.

Wolfe, D. A. (1985). Child-abusive parents: An empirical review and analysis. *Psychol. Bull., 97,* 462–82.

Wolfe, D. A., Edwards, B., Manion, I., & Koverola, C. (1988). Early intervention for parents at risk of child abuse and neglect: A preliminary investigation. *J. Cons. Clin. Psychol., 56,* 34–39.

Wolfe, V. V., Gentile, C., & Wolfe, D. A. (1989). The impact of sexual abuse on children: A PTSD formulation. *Behav. Ther., 20,* 215–28.

Wolff, H. G. (1950). Life stress and cardiovascular disorders. *Circulation, 1,* 187–203.

Wolff, H. G. (1960). Stressors as a cause of disease in man. In J. M. Tanner (Ed.), *Stress and psychiatric disorder.* London: Oxford University Press.

Wolff, P. H. (1972). Ethnic differences in alcohol sensitivity. *Science, 175,* 449–50.

Wolff, W. M., & Morris, L. A. (1971). Intellectual personality characteristics of parents of autistic children. *J. Abnorm. Psychol., 77*(2), 155–61.

Wolkind, S. N. (1974). The components of "affectionless psychopathy" in institutionalized children. *J. Child Psychol. Psychiat., 15*(3), 215–20.

Wolpe, J. (1958). *Psychotherapy by reciprocal inhibition.* Stanford, CA: Stanford University Press.

Wolpe, J. (1969a). For phobia: A hair of the hound. *Psych. Today, 3*(1), 34–37.

Wolpe, J. (1969b). *The practice of behavior therapy.* New York: Pergamon.

Wood, C. (1986). The hostile heart. *Psych. Today, 20,* 10–12.

Wood, W., Rhodes, N., & Whelan, M. (1989). Sex differences in positive well-being: A consideration of emotional style and marital status. *Psychol. Bull., 106,* 249–64.

Woodruff, R. A., Guze, S. B., Clayton, P. J., & Carr, D. (1973). Alcoholism and depression. *Arch. Gen. Psychiat., 28*(1), 97–100.

Woods, B. T., Kinney, D. K., & Yurgelun-Todd, D. (1986). Neurologic abnormalities in schizophrenic patients and their families: I. Comparison of schizophrenic, bipolar, and substance abuse patients and normal controls. *Arch. Gen. Psychiat., 43,* 657–63.

Woods, S. W., Charney, D. S., Goodman, W. K., & Heninger, G. R. (1987). Carbon dioxide-induced anxiety: Behavioral, physiologic, and biochemical effects of 5% CO_2 in panic disorder patients and 5 and 7.5% CO_2 in healthy subjects. *Arch. Gen. Psychiat., 44,* 365–75.

Woodworth, R. S. (1920). *The Personal Data Sheet.* Chicago, IL: Stoelting Press.

Woody, G. E., McLellan, A. T., Luborsky, L., & O'Brien, C. P. (1985). Sociopathy and psychotherapy outcome. *Arch. Gen. Psychiat., 42,* 1081–86.

Worden, P. E. (1986). Prose comprehension and recall in disabled learners. In S. J. Ceci (Ed.), *Handbook of cognitive, social and neuropsychological aspects of learning disabilities,* (Vol. 1, pp. 241–62). Hillsdale, NJ: Erlbaum.

World Health Organization. (1974, Oct. 25). In W. Tuohy, World health agency zeroes in on suicide. *Los Angeles Times,* VI, 1–3.

World Health Organization. (1975). *Schizophrenia: A multinational study.* Geneva: Author.

World Health Organization. (1978a, Apr.). *Report of the director-general.* Geneva: Author.

World Health Organization. (1978b). *Mental disorders: Glossary and guide to their classification in accordance with the ninth revision of the International Classification of Diseases.* Geneva: Author.

World Health Organization. (1979). *International classification of diseases,* (9th ed.) (ICD-9). Geneva: Author.

World Health Organization. (1982). *EURO reports and studies.* Geneva: Author.

Worthington, E. R. (1978). Demographic and pre-service variables as predictors of post-military adjustment. In C. R. Figley (Ed.), *Stress disorders among Vietnam veterans.* New York: Brunner/Mazel.

Wortis, J. (1972). Comments on the ICD classification of mental retardation. *Amer. J. Psychiat., Suppl., 128*(11), 21–24.

Wortis, J. (Ed.). (1973). *Mental retardation and developmental disabilities: An annual review* (Vol. 5). New York: Brunner/Mazel.

Wortman, C. B., & Silver, R. C. (1989). The myths of coping with loss. *J. Cons. Clin. Psychol., 57,* 349–57.

Wright, L., Schaefer, A. B., & Solomons, G. (1979). *Encyclopedia of pediatric psychology.* Baltimore: University Park Press.

Wunsch-Hitzig, R. Gould, M. S., & Dohrenwend, B. P. (1980). Hypotheses about the prevalence of clinical maladjustment in children in the United States. In S. Salzinger, J. Antrobus, & J. Glick (Eds.), *The ecosystem of the "sick" child: Implications for classification and intervention for disturbed and mentally retarded children.* New York: Academic Press.

Wynne, L. C., Ryckoff, I. M., Day, J., & Hirsh, S. I. (1958). Pseudomutuality in the family relations of schizophrenics. *Psychiatry, 21,* 205–20.

Wynne, L. C., Toohey, M. L., & Doane, J. (1979). Family studies. In L. Bellak (Ed.), The *schizophrenic syndrome.* New York: Basic Books.

Yablonsky, L. (1975). Psychodrama lives. *Human Behav., 4,* 24–29.

Yager, J., Grant, I., & Bolus, R. (1984). Interaction of life events and symptoms in psychiatric patient and nonpatient married couples. *J. Nerv. Ment. Dis., 171*(1), 21–25.

Yap, P. M. (1951). Mental diseases peculiar to certain cultures: A survey of comparative psychiatry. *J. Ment. Sci., 97*(3), 313.

Yates, A. (1981). Narcissistic traits in certain abused children. *Amer. J. Orthopsychiat., 51,* 55–62.

Yates, E. P., Barbaree, H. E., & Marshall, W. L. (1984). Anger and deviant sexual arousal. *Behav. Ther., 15,* 287–94.

Yolles, S. F. (1967, Apr.). Quote from "Unraveling the mystery of schizophrenia." *Today's Health.*

Youth Suicide in the United States, 1970–1980. (1986). Centers for disease control. Atlanta, GA.

Yule, W., & Rutter, M. (1985). Reading and other learning difficulties. In M. Rutter & L. Hersov (Eds.), *Child and adolescent psychiatry: Modern approaches* (2nd ed., pp. 444–64). Oxford, UK: Blackwell.

Zahn, T. P., Rapoport, J. L., & Thompson, C. L. (1980). Autonomic and behavioral effects of dextroamphetamine and placebo in normal and hyperactive boys. *J. Abnorm. Child Psychol., 8*(2), 145–60.

Zeitlin, H. (1986). *The natural history of psychiatric disorder in childhood.* New York: Oxford University Press.

Zetlin, A., & Murtaugh, M. (1990). Whatever happened to those with borderline IQs? *Amer. J. Ment. Retard., 94,* 463–69.

Zigler, E., Abelson, W. D., Trickett, P. K., & Seitz, V. (1982). Is an intervention program necessary in order to improve economically disadvantaged children's IQ scores? *Child Develop., 53,* 340–48.

Zilberg, N. J., Weiss, D. S., & Horowitz, M. (1982). Impact of events scale: A cross validation study and some empirical evidence supporting a conceptual model of stress response syndromes. *J. Cons. Clin. Psychol., 50*(3), 407–14.

Zilbergeld, B., & Evans, M. (1980, Jan.). The inadequacy of Masters and Johnson. *Psych. Today,* 29–43.

Zilbergeld, B., & Kilmann, P. R. (1984). The scope and effectiveness of sex therapy. *Psychotherapy, 21,* 319–26.

Zilboorg, G., & Henry, G. W. (1941). *A history of medical psychology.* New York: Norton.

Zimbardo, P. G., Haney, C., Banks, W. C., & Jaffe, D. (1975). The psychology of imprisonment. Privation, power and pathology. In D. Rosenhan & P. London (Eds.), *Theory and research in abnormal psychology* (2nd ed., pp. 270–87). New York: Holt, Rinehart & Winston.

Zimmerman, M. (1983). Methodological issues in the assessment of life events: A review of issues and research. *Clin. Psychol. Rev., 3,* 339–70.

Zimmerman, M., Coryell, W., & Pfohl, B. (1986). The validity of the dexamethasone suppression test as a marker for endogenous depression. *Arch. Gen. Psychiat., 43,* 347–55.

Zimring, F. (1979). *American Youth Violence.* Chicago: University of Chicago Press.

Zinberg, N. E. (1980). The social setting as a control mechanism in intoxicant use. In D. J. Lettieri, M. Sayers, & H. W. Pearson (Eds.), *Theories on drug abuse: Selected contemporary perspectives.* Rockville, MD: National Institute on Drug Abuse.

Zis, A. P., & Goodwin, F. K. (1982). The amine hypothesis. In E. S. Paykel (Ed.), *Handbook of affective disorders.* New York: Guilford Press.

Zola, I. K. (1966). Culture and symptoms—An analysis of patients' presenting complaints. *American Sociological Review, 31,* 615–30.

Zucker, S. H., & Altman, R. (1973). An on-the-job training program for adolescent trainable retardates. *The School Bulletin, 70*(2), 106–10.

Zuckerman, M. (1972). *Manual and research report for the Sensation Seeking Scale (SSS).* Newark, DE: University of Delaware.

Zuckerman, M. (1978). Sensation seeking and psychopathy. In R. D. Hare and D. Schalling (Eds.), *Psychopathic behavior: Approaches to research.* New York: Wiley.

Zung, W. W. K. (1969). A cross-cultural survey of symptoms in depression. *Amer. J. Psychiat., 126*(1), 116–21.

Zung, W. W. K., & Green, R. L., Jr. (1974). Seasonal variations of suicide and depression. *Arch. Gen. Psychiat., 30*(1), 89–91.

Zwelling, S. S. (1985). *Quest for a cure.* Williamsburg, VA: The Colonial Williamsburg Foundation.

Acknowledgments

Photo Credits

Unless otherwise acknowledged, all photographs are the property of ScottForesman.

Front cover: (t) Hill Gallery, Birmingham, Michigan; (c) Collection de l'Art Brut, Lausanne; (b) Collection de la'Art Brut, Lausanne; **Back cover and spine:** Collection de l'Art Brut, Lausanne.

Chapter 1: 2, v Collection de l'Art Brut, Lausanne; **3** Dan McCoy/Rainbow; **5(t)** The Tate Gallery, London; **5(b)** Film Stills Archieve/The Museum of Modern Art, New York; **7** Rick Smolan; **8** Courtesy American Heritage Publishing; **9** Will & Deni McIntyre/Photo Researchers; **12** Bob Adelman; **15(t)** AP/Wide World; **15(b)** Bob Daemmrich/The Image Works; **16** Brad Bower/Picture Group; **18** M. Siluk/The Image Works; **20** Robert Brenner/Photo Edit; **22** Hank Morgan/Rainbow; **25** Dan McCoy/Rainbow. **Chapter 2: 28** Collection de l'Art Brut, Lausanne; **30** The Granger Collection, New York; **32** The Granger Collection, New York; **33** The Granger Collection, New York; **34** The Granger Collection, New York; **36(t)** *Removal of the Stone of Folly* by Brueghel/Giraudon/Art Resource, NY; **36 (b)** The Granger Collection, New York; **37** Sven Nackstrand/Gamma-Liaison; **38** The Granger Collection, New York; **39** The Bettmann Archive; **40(t)** Historical Pictures Service, Chicago; **40(b)** Mary Evans Picture Library; **42** The Trustees of Sir John Soane's Museum; **43** Ets J. E. Bulloz; **44** The Granger Collection, New York; **45(all)** Historical Pictures Service, Chicago; **46** Courtesy of the Psychiatric Museum, Saint Joseph Hospital; **47** Historical Pictures Service, Chicago; **48** Brown Brothers; **50** The Bettmann Archive. **Chapter 3: 54** The Prinzhorn Collection, University of Heidelberg; **57** Historical Pictures Service, Chicago; **59** Bouchard's Univ. of Minn. study/*Time* Magazine; **63** Painting/Wellcome Institute for the History of Medicine; **64** The Bettmann Archive; **65(l)** UPI/Bettmann; **65(r)** Culver Pictures; **66** Courtesy, Clark University Archives; **67** Laura Dwight/Peter Arnold, Inc.; **70(l)** UPI/Bettmann; **70(r)** Courtesy Dr. Margaret S. Mahler; **71** The Bettmann Archive; **72(l)** UPI/Bettmann; **72(c)** The Granger Collection, New York; **72(r)** Courtesy of Dr. B. F. Skinner; **76** Courtesy of John Dollard; **77(l)** Courtesy of Neal Miller; **77(c)** Photograph by Ralph Norman, courtesy of Brendan Mahler; **77(r)** Dr. Albert Bandura; **80(l)** The Bettmann Archive; **80(c)** Harvard University News Office; **80(r)** The Bettmann Archive; **81(tl)** The Bettmann Archive; **81(tr)** Hugh L. Wilkerson; **81(b)** Peter Frank/Tony Stone Worldwide; **82(l)** AP/Wide World; **82(c)** New York University; **82(r)** Association for the Advancement of Psychoanalysis of the Karen Horney Psychoanalytic Institute and Center, New York; **83(l)** Jon Erikson; **83(r)** William Alanson White Psychiatric Foundation, Washington, D.C.; **84** Henley & Savage/Tony Stone Worldwide; **85** Tom Campbell/Tony Stone Worldwide; **88** Institute for Intercultural Studies Inc., photo by Theodore Schwartz. **Chapter 4: 94** Hill Gallery, Birmingham, Michigan; **97** The Image Works; **98** Robert Brenner/Photo Edit; **100** D. W. Fawcett/Photo Researchers; **105** Myrleen Ferguson/Photo Edit; **106** Charles Gupton/Stock Boston; **109(all)** Patrick Ward/Discover Publications/Family Media; **110** Wallace Kirkland/*Life* Magazine Time Warner Inc.; **111(t)** Anthony Suau/Black Star; **112** AP/Wide World; **115** AP/Wide World; **116** George Goodwin/The Picture Cube; **117** Tony Freeman/Photo Edit; **120** Carol Palmer/The Picture Cube; **121** Abigail Heyman; **123** Robert Brenner/Photo Edit; **124** Mike Mazzaschi/Stock Boston; **128** Elizabeth Zuckerman/Photo Edit; **129** Don Smetzer/Tony Stone Worldwide; **131** Liane Enkelis/Stock Boston; **132** Michael O'Brien. **Chapter 5: 138** Collection de l'Art Brut, Lausanne; **140(l)** Jean-Claude LeJeune; **140(r)** Baldev/Sygma; **141** The Image Works; **144** Richard G. Shaw; **146** NYT Pictures; **148** R. Maiman/Sygma; **153** Ellis Herwig/The Picture Cube; **154** Michael Grecco/Stock Boston; **157** AP/Wide World; **160** R. Maiman/Sygma; **163** Rhoda Sidney/Photo Edit; **164** United States Coast Guard; **167** Larry Burrows/*Life* Magazine Time Warner Inc.; **170** Ira Wyman/Sygma; **172** U.S. Army Photo; **175** Ledru/Sygma; **176** Charles Crowell/Black Star. **Chapter 6: 180** Collection de l'Art Brut, Lausanne; **180** David C. Bitters/The Picture Cube; **184** Alvin H. Perlmutter Inc.; **186(l)** Rick Friedman/Black Star; **186(r)** The Image Works; **193** Alan Carey/The Image Works; **199** Custom Medical Stock Photo. All Rights Reserved; **201** The National Archives; **207** Susan Greenwood/Gamma-Liaison; **212** Carolyn Brown; **216** McCarten/Photo Edit; **222** Dr.

Albert Bandura. **Chapter 7: 228** Collection de l'Art Brut, Lausanne; **231** Robert Frerck/Odyssey Productions, Chicago; **233** Jim Olive/Peter Arnold, Inc.; **235** Lennart Nilsson/Boehringer Ingelheim Zentrale GmbH; **238** David Lissy/The Picture Cube; **240** Robert Frerck/Odyssey Productions, Chicago; **241** Lou Lainey/Discover Publications/Family Media; **244** William Thompson/The Picture Cube; **248** Katrina Thomas/Photo Researchers; **250** Michael Philip Manheim/Picturesque formerly Southern Light; **257** Alvin H. Perlmutter Inc.; **258** Dan McCoy/Rainbow; **259** John Chiasson/Gamma-Liaison. **Chapter 8: 262, vi** Collection de l'Art Brut, Lausanne; **264** Michael Patrick/Picture Group; **266** Richard Hutchings/Photo Researchers; **270** Sandy Herring/The Picture Cube; **272** AP/Wide World; **273** Alvin H. Perlmutter Inc.; **275** Ari Mintz/*New York Newsday;* **279** Alvin H. Perlmutter Inc.; **282** Louis Fernandez/Black Star; **283** UPI/Bettmann; **287** J. Ross Baughman/Visions. **Chapter 9: 294, vii** Collection de l'Art Brut, Lausanne; **297** Paul Conklin/Photo Edit; **299** Alvin H. Perlmutter Inc.; **303** Mike Zerby/*Star Tribune;* **304** Jerry Waxhter/Focus On Sports; **307** Bob Daemmrich/Tony Stone Worldwide; **310(all)** Courtesy of Mrs. Francis M. Erdmann; **312** Leif Skoogfoors/Woodfin Camp & Associates; **318** D&I MacDonald/The Picture Cube; **325** Pamela Price/Picture Group; **327** Larry Milvehill/Photo Researchers; **332** Michael Abramson/Woodfin Camp & Associates; **335** Focus On Sports. **Chapter 10: 340** Collection de l'Art Brut, Lausanne; **342** Ellis Herwig/The Picture Cube; **347** Joel Gordon Photography; **349** Jim Wilson/Woodfin Camp & Associates; **350** Alvin H. Perlmutter Inc.; **354** Tony Korady/Sygma; **356** Peter Yates/Picture Group; **361** Caccavo; **363** Mary Ellen Mark; **366** U.S. Department of Health and Human Services; **369** Bob Mahoney; **373** Ethan Hoffman; **374** Ronald Sheridan/Ancient Art and Architecture Collection; **376** Laima Druskis/Photo Researchers. **Chapter 11: 380** Henrich Anton Muller/Collection de l'Art Brut, Lausanne; **384** Tim Ribar/StockSouth; **385** Rob Nelson/Stock Boston; **387** Robert McElroy/Woodfin Camp & Associates; **390** Erik Feinblatt/Sygma; **393** Alvin H. Perlmutter Inc.; **398(l)** Kevin Horan/Picture Group/With permission of Constance Weil; **398(c)** Kevin Horan/Picture Group; **398(r)** David R. Frazier Photolibrary; **400** From M. E. Phelps, J. C. Mazziotta. Positron Emission Tomograph: "Human Brain Function and Biochemistry," *Science* 228: 799–809, 1985; **406** Alvin H. Perlmutter Inc.; **409** Sudhir/SIPA-Press; **415** Mike McClure; **421** Mary Kate Denny/Photo Edit; **423** Blake Discher/Sygma. **Chapter 12: 426** Collection de l'Art Brut, Lausanne; **431** NIMH; **441** Al Vercoutere, Malibu, Calif.; **444** Al Vercoutere, Malibu, Calif.; **453** Burt Glinn/Magnum Photos; **458** NIMH; **462** Dick Bell/Insight Magazine; **464** Alvin H. Perlmutter Inc.; **471** Ellis Herwig/The Picture Cube. **Chapter 13: 476, viii** The Prinzhorn Collection, University of Heidelberg; **480** Kindra Clineff/The Picture Cube; **483** Dan McCoy/Rainbow; **485** Lynn Johnson/Black Star; **489** Howard Sochurek; **491** Warren Anatomical Museum, Harvard University Medical School; **493** Alvin H. Perlmutter Inc.; **495** Ira Wyman/Sygma; **498** Philip-Lorca di-Corcia; **499** Alvin H. Perlmutter Inc. **Chapter 14: 502** Collection de l'Art Brut, Lausanne; **505** Lawrence Migdale/Stock Boston; **510** Elaine Rebman/Photo Researchers; **517** Will McIntyre/Photo Researchers; **519** Richard Hutchings/Science Source/Photo Researchers; **523** Alvin H. Perlmutter Inc.; **525** Alvin H. Perlmutter Inc.; **526–27** Courtesy of Dr. Bruno Bettelheim; **530** Will & Deni McIntyre/Photo Researchers. **Chapter 15: 534** Collection de l'Art Brut, Lausanne; **536** Tony Freeman/Photo Edit; **539** Alvin H. Perlmutter Inc.; **545** Alvin H. Perlmutter Inc.; **548** John Maher/Stock Boston; **551** E. Williamson/The Picture Cube; **554** Alvin H. Perlmutter Inc.; **562** Michael Grecco/Stock Boston; **565** M. Siluk/The Image Works; **567** AP/Wide World. **Chapter 16: 572** Collection de l'Art Brut, Lausanne; **577** Hank Morgan/Rainbow; **582** Tony Freeman/Photo Edit; **584** Alvin H. Perlmutter Inc.; **586** Alvin H. Perlmutter Inc.; **591** John Mantel/SIPA-Press; **595** Alvin H. Perlmutter Inc. **Chapter 17: 604** Collection de l'Art Brut, Lausanne; **606(l)** Courtesy of Eastern State Hospital; **606(r)** Courtesy of Bakken Library of Electricity in Life; **609(all)** Alvin H. Perlmutter Inc.; **612(all)** UPI/Bettmann; **614** Louis Fernandez/Black Star; **619** Tony Freeman/Photo Edit. **Chapter 18: 626** Adolf Wolfi/Collection de l'Art Brut, Lausanne; **629** Andy Lewis/Photo Researchers; **639** Jacques Chenet/Woodfin Camp & Associates; **657** Alvin H. Perlmutter Inc.; **661** Alvin H. Perlmutter Inc. **Chapter 19: 672**

Collection de l'Art Brut, Lausanne; 675 Alvin H. Perlmutter Inc.; 677 Alvin H. Perlmutter Inc.; 679 Alvin H. Perlmutter Inc.; 686 Christopher Morris/Black Star; 689 AP/Wide World; 691 Courtesy of Dr. Joseph Wolpe; 692 Trippett/SIPA-Press; 694 Alan Carey/The Image Works; 694 Eeric A. Roth/The Picture Cube; 696 Alvin H. Perlmutter Inc.; 696 Keith Meyers/NYT Pictures; 699 D. Goldberg/Sygma; 703 Alvin H. Perlmutter Inc.

Literary, Figure, and Table Credits

12, 13: Reprinted with permission from the *Diagnostic and statistical manual of mental disorders*, 3rd ed. revised. Copyright © 1987 American Psychological Association. 124: Haley, J. The family of the schizophrenic: A model system. *Journal of Nervous and Mental Disease*, 1959, 129, 357–74. 142: Figure 4, "Changes in anxiety over time," from Niall Bolger, "Coping as a personality process: A prospective study," in *Journal of Personality and Social Psychology* 1990, 59(3),531. Copyright 1990 by the American Psychological Association. Reprinted by permission. 150: Figure 1.3, "Selye's General Adaptation Syndrome," from *Stress* by Tom Cox. Copyright © 1978 by Tom Cox. Reprinted by permission of Macmillan, London and Basingstoke. 153: Janis, I. L., Mahl, G. F., Kagan, J., & Holt, R. R. From *Personality: Dynamics, development and assessment*. Published by Harcourt Brace Jovanovich, Inc., 1969. Reprinted by permission. 166: Stern, R. L. Diary of a war neurosis. *Journal of Nervous and Mental Disease*, 1947, 106, 583–86. Published by the Williams & Wilkins Co. Copyright 1947 and reprinted by permission of The Smith Ely Jelliffe Trust. 169: Archibald, H. C., & Tuddenham, R. D. Persistent stress reaction after combat. *ARCH. GEN. PSYCHIAT.*, 1965, 12(5), 475–81. 170: Shatan, C. F. Stress disorders among Vietnam veterans: The emotional content of combat continues. From *Stress disorders among Vietnam veterans: Theory, research and treatment*, edited by Charles R. Figley, Ph.D. Copyright © 1978 by Charles R. Figley. Reprinted by permission of Brunner/Mazel, Publishers. 171: From "Reactivation of traumatic conflicts" by Randall M. Christenson, John Ingram Walker, Donald R. Ross, and Allan A. Maltric from *American Journal of Psychiatry*, 1981, Vol. 138:7, pp. 984–85. Copyright © 1981, the American Psychiatric Association. 174–75: From Stephen M. Sonnenberg, M.D., "Victims of violence and post-traumatic stress disorder" in *The Psychiatric Clinics of North America*, Vol. 11, No. 4, December 1988, Case Study No. 1. Copyright 1988 W. B. Saunders Company. Reprinted by permission. 184–85, 213–14, 439–40: Excerpts from "Anxious Anne," "Paralyzed," and "Another dimension" from *Psychopathology: A case book* by Robert L. Spitzer et al. Copyright © 1983 by McGraw-Hill, Inc. Reprinted by permission. 195: From *Anxiety disorders and phobias: A cognitive perspective*, by Aaron T. Beck and Gary Emery with Ruth Greenberg. Copyright © 1985 by Aaron T. Beck, M.D. and Gary Emery, Ph.D. Reprinted by permission of Basic Books, Inc., Publishers. 198: Reprinted with permission from the *Diagnostic and statistical manual of mental disorders*, 3rd. ed. revised. Copyright © 1987 American Psychiatric Association. 200: Menninger, K. A. *The human mind* (3rd ed.). New York: Knopf, 1945. From pages 139–40 in *The human mind*, by Karl Menninger. Copyright 1930, 1937, 1945, and renewed 1958, 1965 by Karl Menninger. Reprinted by permission of Alfred A. Knopf, Inc. 206: From Ross A. Colin, M.D., *Multiple personality disorder: Diagnosis, clinical features and treatment.* Copyright © 1989 by John Wiley & Sons, Inc. Reprinted by permission. 207–208: Spitzer, R. L., Sdodol, A. E., Gibbon, M. and Williams, J. B. W., *DSM-III-R case book*. Washington, D.C.: American Psychiatric Association, 1989. Reprinted with permission. 209–10: From *Sybil* by Flora Rheta Schreiber. Copyright © 1973 by Flora Rheta Schreiber. Published by Warner Paperback Library, 1974. Reprinted by permission. 236: Adapted with permission of Macmillan Publishing Company from *Principles of immunology*, 2nd edition by Rose, Milgram and Van Oss. Copyright © 1979 by Macmillan Publishing Company. 241: Robert A. Wallace, *Biology: The world of life*, 4th ed., pp. 372–73. Copyright © 1981, 1987 Scott, Foresman and Company. 243: From *American Journal of Epidemiology*, Vol. III, No. 1, Jan. 1980 by Haynes, Feinleib and Kannel. Reprinted by permission of *The American Journal of Epidemiology*, The Johns Hopkins University School of Hygiene and Public Health. 244: Nemiah, J. C. The case of Mary S., from *Foundations of psychopathology*. Copyright © 1961 by Oxford University Press, Inc. Reprinted by permission. 246–47: Reproduced from *Bulimarexia: The binge/purge cycle* by Marlene Boskind-White, Ph.D., and William C. White, Jr., Ph.D., by permission of W. W. Norton & Company, Inc. Copyright © 1987 by Marlene Boskind-White and William C. White, Jr. 258: From *Treating eating disorders* by Gloria Leon. Copyright © 1983 The Lewis Publishing Company. Reprinted by permission. 265: Reprinted with permission from the *Diagnostic and statistical manual of mental disorders*, 3rd ed., revised. Copyright © 1987 American Psychiatric Association. 267–68: Spitzer, R. L., Skodol, A. E., Gibbon, M. and Williams, J. B. W., *DSM-III case book*. Washington, D.C.: American Psychiatric Association, 1981. Reprinted by permission. 270: Spitzer, R.

L., Skodol, A. E., Gibbon, M. and Williams, J. B. W., *DSM-III case book*. Washington, D.C.: American Psychiatric Association, 1981. Reprinted by permission. 271–72: Spitzer, R. L., Skodol, A. E., Gibbon, M. and Williams, J. B. W., *DSM-III case book*. Washington, D.C.: American Psychiatric Association, 1981. Reprinted by permission. 273–74: Spitzer, R. L., Skodol, A. E., Gibbon, M. and Williams, J. B. W., *DSM-III case book*. Washington, D.C.: American Psychiatric Association, 1981. Reprinted by permission. 284–85: Excerpt from *Psychopathy: Theory and research* by Robert D. Hare. Copyright © 1970 by John Wiley & Sons, Inc. Reprinted by permission. 300: "Alcohol levels in the blood," from *TIME*, April 22, 1974. Copyright © 1974 Time, Inc. All rights reserved. Reprinted by permission. 308: From "TV news anchor tells story of recovery from alcoholism," by Frances Burns in *Bloomington Sun Current*, June 16, 1986, p. 7A. Reprinted by permission. 325: From "Crack" in *TIME*, June 2, 1986 by Jacob V. Lamar, Jr., p. 18. Copyright © 1986 Time, Inc. All rights reserved. Reprinted by permission from *TIME*. 353: Adaptation of "Bob, Mae and Susan: Story of a new life," by Eric Black and Jacqui Banaszynski, from *Minneapolis Tribune*, May, 1983, pp. 1A, 4A–6A. Reprinted by permission of Minneapolis Star and Tribune Company. 357: Stoller, R. J. *Sex and gender (Vol. 1): The development of masculinity and femininity*. Published by Jason Aronson, New York. Copyright © 1968, 1974, by Robert J. Stoller. Reprinted by permission of the author. 371: *Why men rape* by Sylvia Levine and Joseph Koenig © 1980, International Cinemedia Centre Ltd., Toronto. Based on the film of the same name produced by the National Film Board of Canada. 371: From Juliet L. Darke, "Sexual aggression: Achieving power through humiliation," by W. L. Marshall et al., in *Handbook of sexual assault* (Plenum Press, 1990), p. 64. Reprinted with permission from Plenum Publishing Corporation. 386–87: Spitzer, R. L., Skodol, A. E., Gibbon, M. and Williams, J. B. W., *DSM-III case book*. Washington, D.C.: American Psychiatric Association, 1981. Reprinted by permission. 387–88: Spitzer, R. L., Skodol, A. E., Gibbon, M. and Williams, J. B. W., *DSM-III case book*. Washington, D.C.: American Psychiatric Association, 1981. Reprinted by permission. 395: From "The stages of mania: A longitudinal analysis of the manic episode," by G. Carlson and F. K. Goodwin, from *Archives of General Psychiatry*, February 1973, Vol. 28, No. 2, 221–28. Copyright © 1973 American Medical Association. Reprinted by permission. 396: Spitzer, R. L., Skodol, A. E., Gibbon, M. and Williams, J. B. W., *DSM-III-R case book*. Washington, D.C.: American Psychiatric Association, 1989. Reprinted by permission. 402: Leff, M. J., Roatch, J. F. and Bunney, W. E., Jr. Environmental factors preceding the onset of severe depressions. *Psychiatry*, 1970, 33(3), 298–311. Reprinted from *Archives of General Psychiatry*, June 1971, 24(6), 515–23. Copyright © 1971, American Medical Association. 420: Tuckman, J., Kleiner, R. and Lavell, M. Emotional content of suicide notes. Reprinted from *The American Journal of Psychiatry*, Vol. 1, pp. 59–63, 1959. Copyright © 1959, the American Psychiatric Association. 420: Darbonne, A. R. Suicide and age: A suicide note analysis. *J. CONS. CLIN. PSYCHOL.*, 1969, 33, 46–50. 435: Reprinted with permission from the *Diagnostic and statistical manual of mental disorders*, 3rd. ed., revised. Copyright © 1987 American Psychiatric Association. 436: Lewinson, T. S. Dynamic disturbances in the handwriting of psychotics; with reference to schizophrenic, paranoid, and manic-depressive psychoses. Reprinted from *The American Journal of Psychiatry*, 1940, 97, 102–35. 442: From *Psychopathology: A case book* by Robert L. Spitzer, et al. Copyright © 1983 by McGraw-Hill, Inc. Reprinted by permission. 445–46: Spitzer, R. L., Skodol, A. E., Gibbon, M. and Williams, J. B. W., *DSM-III case book*. Washington, D.C.: American Psychiatric Association. Reprinted by permission. 450: Reprinted with permission from *Journal of Psychiatric Research*, 21(1), Pekka Tienari et al., "The Finnish adoptive family study of schizophrenia." Copyright 1987, Pergamon Press plc. 469–70: Rosen, E. and Kiene, H. E. Paranoia and paranoiac reaction types. *Diseases of the nervous system*, 1946, 7, 330–37. Reprinted by permission of Physicians Postgraduate Press. 484: From "Diagnosis of dementia" by Charles E. Wells, in *Psychosomatics*, August 1979, 20(8). Copyright © 1979 The Academy of Psychosomatic Medicine. Reprinted by permission. 488: Fetterman, J. L. *Practical lessons in psychiatry*. Courtesy of Charles C. Thomas, Publisher, Springfield, Illinois. 526: Bettelheim, B. "Joey: A 'Mechanical Boy'," *Scientific American*, 1959, 200, 116–27. From "Joey: A 'Mechanical Boy'" by Bruno Bettelheim. Copyright © March 1959 by Scientific American, Inc. All rights reserved. 529: From Charles Wenar, *Developmental psychopathology: From infancy through adolescence*, 2nd ed. (McGraw-Hill, 1990), p. 197. Reproduced with permission of McGraw-Hill, Inc. 541–42: Kendall, P. C. and Finch, A. J. A cognitive-behavioral treatment for impulse control: A case study. *Journal of Consulting and Clinical Psychology*, 1976, 44, 852–57. 557–58: Reprinted from Cynthia R. Pfeffer, "Self-destructive behavior in children and adolescents," in *The Psychiatric Clinics of North America*, Vol. 8, No. 2, June 1985, pp. 218–19. Copyright 1985 W. B. Saunders Company. Reprinted by permission. 569: Figure 1, from Arnold Sameroff, Ronald Seiler et al.,

"Early indicators of developmental risk: Rochester longitudinal study," in *Schizophrenia Bulletin,* 13: 383–94, 1987. Reprinted with permission from American Psychiatric Association. **598–99:** "Semantic interpretation of the Rorschach protocol utilizing the comprehensive system," by John E. Exner, Jr. Copyright © 1985, 1976 by John E. Exner, Jr. Reprinted by permission. **609:** McCall, L. *Between us and the dark* (originally published in 1947). Summary in W. C. Alvarez, *Minds that came back,* 1961. Reprinted by permission of Gladys A. Muirhead, executor. **614–15:** Grinspoon, L., Ewalt, J. R. and Shader, R. I. *Schizophrenia: Pharmacotherapy and psychotherapy.* Copyright © 1972, The Williams and Wilkins Company, Baltimore. Reprinted by permission. **619:** Cade, J. F. J. Lithium salts in the treatment of psychotic excitement. *Medical Journal of Australia,* 36 (part II): 349–52, 1949. Reprinted by permission. **642–43:** Wolf, M., Risley, T. and Mees, H.

"Application of operant conditioning procedures to the behavior problems of an autistic child." *Behavior Research and Therapy,* 1964, *1,* 305–12. **649:** Rush, A. J., Khatami, M. and Beck, A. T. Cognitive and behavior therapy in chronic depression. *Behavior Therapy,* 1975, *6,* 398–404. Copyright © 1975 by Academic Press, Inc. Reprinted by permission. **651–52:** Rogers, C. R. *Client-centered therapy* (Boston: Houghton-Mifflin, 1951). Reprinted by permission of Houghton Mifflin Company and Constable & Company Ltd. **654–55:** Perls, F. S. *Gestalt therapy verbatim* (Lafayette, Calif.: Real People Press, 1969). Reprinted by permission. **694:** From "Psychiatrist-anthropologist: Bag ladies in isolated cultures, too" by Joseph Westermeyer in *Behavior Today* Newsletter, 13(21), May 31, 1982. Reprinted by permission of Atcom, Inc., 2315 Broadway, New York, NY 10024.

Name Index

Quinsey, V. L., 370
Quinton, D., 544
Quitkin, F., 382, 397

Rabin, A. I., 433, 453
Rabinovich, H., 554–55
Rabkin, J. G., 14
Rachman, S., 190, 640
Rachman, S. J., 159
Radnitz, C. L., 251, 256, 257
Rado, S., 270
Radosevich, M. J., 546
Raeburn, S. D., 256
Ragland, D. R., 242
Rahe, R. H., 143, 146, 231, 253
Raifman, L., 400, 692
Rakoff, V., 172
Ramey, C. T., 514
Ramsey, B. K., 520
Ramsey, E., 544
Randall, O., 249
Rao, A. V., 408
Rapagna, S., 519
Rapaport, K., 369, 372
Rapee, R. M., 219
Rapoport, J., 525
Rapoport, J. L., 189, 539, 540
Rapoport, S. I., 498, 525
Raps, C. S., 22
Raskin, A., 555
Raskin, D. E., 75, 409–10
Rathbun, J. M., 554
Ray, M., 101
Razani, J., 462
Rea, W. S., 318
Read, P., 555
Reagan, R., 692
Redlich, F. C., 255
Redmond, D. E., 218
Reed, S. D., 257
Reeders, S., 398
Rees, J., 116
Rees, T. P., 45
Regier, D. A., 16, 183, 264, 281, 429, 695
Reice, S., 110
Reich, J., 264, 288
Reich, R., 118
Reich, T., 59, 304, 398
Reid, A. H., 510
Reid, J. B., 582
Reid, J. C., 555
Reider, R. O., 568
Reimherr, F. W., 620
Reinhardt, R. F., 203, 204
Reinisch, J. M., 59, 107, 352
Reisberg, B., 498
Reiser, D., 458
Reiser, M. F., 249
Reiss, D. J., 462
Rentzel, L., 360
Renvoize, E. B., 498, 607
Reposa, R. E., 564
Reshetnikov, V. I., 237
Resick, P. A., 163
Resnik, H. L. P., 678
Retterstøl, N., 417
Retvedt, A., 558
Revenson, T. A., 142
Revitch, E., 364
Reynolds, D. K., 418
Reynolds, W. M., 410
Reznick, J. S., 275
Reznick, R. J., 106
Rhoades, L. J., 684
Rhodes, N., 395
Ribble, M. A., 117
Rice, B. D., 529, 531
Rice, J., 237, 283
Rice, J. P., 616

Rice, R. D., 106
Rich, B. E., 582
Rich, C. L., 297, 412
Richards, A., 614
Richards, C., 389
Richardson, C. T., 252
Richardson, S. A., 516
Richmond, J. B., 254
Rickels, K., 193
Rieder, R. O., 449, 450
Riessman, F., 134
Rimm, D. C., 75
Rimmer, J., 398
Rimoin, D. L., 252
Rinear, E. E., 155
Ring, K., 462
Risch, S. C., 400
Risley, T., 642–43
Ritchie, J. C., 400
Ritchie, P. L., 462
Ritvo, A., 521–22, 524
Ritvo, E., 521–22, 523, 524, 528
Ritzler, B. A., 433, 445
Roatch, J. F., 402, 403
Roberts, A. H., 645
Roberts, E., 498
Roberts, M. C., 566
Robins, L. N., 16, 183, 264, 281, 283, 408, 438, 545, 695
Robinson, D., 554–55
Robinson, H. B., 106, 504, 505, 506, 507, 509, 517, 518
Robinson, L. N., 650
Robinson, N. M., 106, 504, 505, 506, 507, 509, 517, 518
Robinson, P. W., 540
Robinson, S., 111
Rock, D., 20, 451
Rockley, G. J., 467
Rodger, S., 690
Rodichok, L. D., 252
Rodin, J., 230, 255, 330
Rodman, D. H., 518
Rodnick, E. H., 459
Roff, J. D., 108, 117, 120, 125, 128, 457, 458
Roffman, R. E., 377
Rogers, C. R., 78, 651, 652, 653, 670
Rogers, M. P., 235, 237
Rogers, S. L. B., 400
Rogers, T., 562
Roitch, J. C., 287
Rokeach, M., 444
Rolf, J. E., 450
Rolfs, R. T., 324
Rolider, A., 75
Rolnick, N., 506
Ronningstam, E., 271
Roose, S. P., 394
Rooth, G., 359, 360
Rorvik, D. M., 326
Rose, R. J., 59
Rosen, A. J., 614, 621
Rosen, D. H., 418
Rosen, E., 252
Rosen, H., 469–70
Rosen, N., 517–18
Rosen, R. C., 346, 348, 349–50
Rosenbaum, G., 453, 454
Rosenberg, M., 297
Rosenberg, R., 286
Rosenblatt, A., 44
Rosenblum, M., 486
Rosenman, R., 240
Rosenman, R. H., 240, 242
Rosenstein, M. J., 429

Rosenthal, D., 269, 397, 429, 432, 449, 568
Rosenthal, N. E., 399–400
Rosenthal, R., 105
Rosenzweig, M. R., 111
Rosman, B., 660
Ross, A. O., 538, 539
Ross, C. A., 206, 208, 209, 210, 212
Ross, D. R., 171
Ross, J. M., 330
Ross, M., 414–15
Ross, S., 555
Rossi, P. H., 695
Rosso, P., 110
Rosten, R. A., 334, 335
Roth, L., 330
Roth, M., 389
Roth, S., 141, 162, 369
Rothbart, M. K., 106
Rotter, J. I., 252
Rouleau, J. L., 364, 369, 372
Rounsaville, B. J., 312, 319, 320, 324, 629, 664
Routh, D. K., 553
Rovner, S., 297
Rowse, G. L., 416
Roy, A., 127, 403, 454
Rozin, P., 245
Ruben, H. L., 305
Rubenstein, J., 311
Rubenstein, J. L., 558
Rubert, M. P., 406
Rubin, B., 689
Rubin, C., 558
Rubin, K. H., 129
Rubin, R. T., 59, 107, 352
Rubin, S. P., 102
Rudestam, K. E., 419
Ruedrich, S. L., 454
Rumbaut, R. G., 91
Rumsey, J. M., 525
Runcie, J., 331
Rush, A. J., 409, 648, 649
Rush, B., 44, 51, 52
Russell, A. T., 414
Russell, G. F. M., 242
Russell, S., 525
Russell, S. F., 249
Russo, D. C., 642
Russo, M. F., 567
Russon, A., 366
Rustin, S., 171
Rutter, M., 106, 116, 127, 521–22, 524, 525, 528, 530, 531, 544, 555
Ryan, J. J., 614
Ryan, N. D., 403, 554–55
Ryckoff, I. M., 459
Ryle, A., 413
Rynard, D., 568

Saba, G., 660
Sacco, W. P., 406
Sachar, E. J., 451–52
Sacher-Masoch, L. V., 362
Sack, D. A., 399–400
Sack, R. L., 362, 400
Sacks, M., 148
Sacuzzo, D. P., 328
Sade, Marquis de, 360
Sadock, B. J., 116
Safer, D. J., 540
Safran, J. D., 223, 632
St. Lawrence, J. S., 377
Sakheim, D. K., 162
Salbaum, J. M., 498
Salkovskis, P. M., 409
Salonen, J., 259
Salter, A., 73
Salzberg, H. C., 311
Salzman, L., 221

Sameroff, A., 555, 568, 569
Samloff, I. M., 252
Sanborn, K. O., 463
Sandberg, D., 218
Sanders, D. H., 686
Sanders-Woudstra, J. A. R., 558
Sanderson, W. C., 219
Sandhu, H. S., 252
Sandler, J., 650
Sanislow, C. A., III, 102, 438, 449, 451, 474, 629
Sanson, A. V., 539
Sansone, R. A., 273
Santiago, J. M., 163
Santisteban, D., 677
Sanua, V. D., 463, 524
Sapolsky, R. M., 401
Saracoglu, B., 529, 531
Sarbin, T. R., 14, 40, 438, 453
Sargeant, J. K., 392
Sargent, M., 432
Sartorius, N., 90
Sarvis, M. A., 471
Sasaki, M., 510
Satir, V., 659
Satterfield, B. T., 542
Satterfield, J. H., 542
Saunders, N. L., 645
Savasir, I., 88
Sawyer, J. B., 422
Scalf-McIver, L., 245
Scanlon, W., 697
Scaravilli, F., 486
Scarr, S., 116
Schaar, K., 414
Schachtel, D., 565
Schaefer, A. B., 101, 105–12, 118, 122
Schaefer, J. M., 305
Schaeffer, B., 525
Schaeffer, M. A., 144
Schalock, R. L., 505
Schapiro, M. B., 498
Scharfman, M., 549
Schaumann, H., 528
Schechter, G., 409, 621
Scheck, A. C., 486
Scheff, T. J., 133
Scheier, M. F., 231
Scherl, D. J., 162
Scherr, P. A., 495
Schild, S., 511
Schilling, R. F., 677
Schladenhauffen, J., 303
Schleifer, S. J., 237
Schlesinger, L. B., 689
Schlesinger, M., 697
Schmaling, K. B., 658
Schmauk, F. J., 286
Schmauss, C., 454
Schmid, H., 544
Schnedler, R. W., 542
Schneider, J. A., 256
Schneider, S., 174
Schnurr, P., 16
Schoeneman, T. J., 35, 38, 52
Schofield, W., 456, 629
Schonfeldt-Bausch, P., 454
Schoonover, S. C., 221, 408, 618, 619, 620
Schopler, E., 120, 523, 528
Schork, M. A., 249
Schowalter, J. E., 559
Schreber, D. P., 445–46
Schreiber, F. R., 209
Schreibman, L., 521, 524, 528
Schroeder, D. H., 146
Schroeder, H. E., 554
Schrut, A., 412, 414
Schubert, J. P., 318
Schuckit, M. A., 337
Schuerman, J., 564

Sudak, H. S., 422
Suddath, R. L., 447
Sue, D., 90
Sue, S., 90
Suematsu, H., 255
Sugar, C., 359
Sugita, M., 255
Sulkunen, P., 307
Sullivan, H. S., 83–84, 115, 129, 384, 637
Sullivan, J. L., 618
Sullivan, J. P., 518
Sullivan, S., 318
Sum, G., 540, 541
Summers, D., 524
Summers, F., 600
Summit, R., 366
Sundberg, N. D., 652
Sunderland, T., 498
Surwit, R. S., 257
Sussex, J. N., 398
Suter, B., 412, 418
Sutherland, S., 5, 162
Sutker, P. B., 110, 285, 287, 291
Svanum, S., 303
Svrakic, D. M., 271
Swadi, H., 677
Swain, B. J., 155
Swanson, D. W., 468, 470, 471, 473
Swayze, V. W., 433
Swedo, S. E., 189
Sweetland, H. L., 143
Sweillam, A., 688
Swenson, C. R., 281
Switzer, E., 348
Switzky, H. N., 519
Symonds, M., 162
Szapocznick, J., 677
Szasz, T. S., 14, 423, 462
Szmukler, G. I., 242
Szulecka, T. K., 690

Tacke, U., 616, 622–23
Takahashi, N., 255
Takalo, T., 259
Takayama, D. L., 510
Talbott, J. A., 624, 684
Talbott, J. H., 101, 510
Talley, P. F., 631
Tamarkin, L., 399–400
Tanke, E. D., 104
Tanney, A., 275
Taraldson, B., 564
Tarasoff, T., 691
Tardiff, K., 688
Targum, S., 454
Tarjan, G., 515, 517
Tarler-Beniolo, L., 645
Tarter, R. E., 337
Tarver, S. G., 506
Tassinari, R., 223, 640
Tassone, E. P., 453
Tasto, D. L., 257
Tatum, E. L., 158, 159
Tavel, M. E., 303
Taves, I., 559
Taylor, A. J. W., 678
Taylor, J. O., 495
Taylor, P. D., 558
Taylor, P. J., 163
Taylor, S. E., 162, 163
Teasdale, J. D., 392, 410
Teasdale, T. W., 20, 338, 451, 456
Teders, S. J., 252, 645
Teed, D., 329
Teevan, R. C., 252
Telch, M. J., 664
Tellegen, A., 589

Templer, D. I., 370
Teplin, L. A., 707
Teresa of Avila, 40, 51
Tesiny, E. P., 382, 555
Teska, J. A., 506
Teti, D. M., 115, 123, 567
Thacher, M., 517, 518
Thaler, M., 249
Thase, M. E., 399, 400, 401
Theodor, L. H., 202
Thibaut, J. W., 84
Thivierge, J., 107
Thomas, A., 544
Thomas, C. B., 498
Thompson, C. L., 540
Thompson, D., 305
Thompson, J. A., 272
Thompson, J. C., 249
Thompson, J. K., 245
Thompson, K., 371
Thompson, K. J., 245
Thompson, N. L., Jr., 376
Thompson, R. J., 214, 215
Thompson, T. J., 331
Thorndike, E. L., 72
Thornton, C. C., 311
Tiefer, L., 344
Tien, A. Y., 328
Tienari, P., 449, 450
Timmer, F. C., 558
Timmers, K. I., 111
Tinbergen, N., 524
Tinkcom, M., 311
Tischler, G. L., 183
Tizard, B., 116
Tizard, J., 106
Tobena, A., 184, 219
Tobler, N. S., 678
Todd, T., 324, 660
Todd, T. C., 660
Toffler, A., 134
Tole, J., 452
Tollison, C. D., 343, 345, 347, 349, 375
Tollison, J. W., 375
Tomarken, A. J., 186, 219
Tonomura, A., 511
Toohey, M. I., 459
Torrey, E. F., 130, 447, 463, 624
Tortu, S., 677
Treece, C., 266
Treiber, F. A., 287
Trickett, P. K., 520
Tripp, C. A., 363
Trock, G. K., 660
Tronick, B. E., 555
Troughton, E., 305
True, W. R., 165
Truffant, F., 515
Trull, T. J., 269, 274
Tseng, W. S., 35
Tsuang, M. T., 102, 399, 433
Tuason, V. B., 452
Tuckman, J., 419, 420
Tuddenham, R. D., 169
Tuke, W., 44, 51, 52
Tulis, E. H., 278
Tuma, J., 566
Tune, L. E., 454
Tuomiehto, J., 259
Tupin, J., 447, 459
Turk, D., 650
Turner, R. K., 558
Turner, S., 510
Turner, S. M., 190, 567
Twomey, J., 403, 554–55
Tyler, L. E., 652
Tyor, P. L., 517, 518
Tyrer, P., 265, 266
Tyron, W. W., 505
Tyrrell, G., 433

Uchida, I. A., 510
Uhde, T. W., 400
Uhlenhuth, E., 156
Ulleland, C. N., 302
Ullmann, L. P., 7
Ulmer, D., 240
Ulrich, R. F., 614
Umana, R. F., 680
Unterbeck, A., 498
Upfold, D., 370
Ursano, R. J., 159, 160

Vaillant, G., 128
Vaillant, G. E., 16, 286–87, 291
Valdimarsdottir, H., 237
Valenstein, E. S., 60, 610–11
Valentine, G. H., 101
Vallacher, R. R., 113
Van Broeckhoven, C., 498
Vandecreek, L., 691
Vandenberghe, A., 498
VandenBos, G. R., 22, 466
Vandereycken, W., 255, 349–50
Van Der Lee, J. H., 558
Vandiver, R., 400
Van Elburg, A., 564
Van Hoose, T. A., 686
Van Houten, R. V., 75
van Kammen, D. P., 432, 454
Varah, C., 422
Vargas, L., 297
Vasiljeva, O. A., 237
Vaughn, C. E., 462
Vega, W. A., 91
Velez, C. N., 558
Vellutino, F. R., 530
Venables, P., 20, 451
Venzke, R., 555
Verhulst, J. H., 558
Vermilyea, B. B., 193
Vermilyea, J., 193
Vetter, X. X., 669–70
Viglione, D. J., 585
Villanova, P., 21
Vincent de Paul, St., 41
Viney, W., 47
Virtamo, J., 259
Visçott, D. S., 507
Visscher, B., 378
Volkmar, F. R., 523–24
Vollmer, W. M., 158, 159
von Haller, A., 57
von Knorring, A. L., 59, 305
Von Meduna, 607
Vonnegut, M., 4
Vorters, D. F., 558

Wachtel, P. L., 660
Waddell, M. T., 185
Wadden, T. A., 257
Wagener, D. K., 447
Wagner, G., 344
Wahlberg, K. E., 449, 450
Wahler, R. G., 549
Walder, L. O., 118, 122, 548, 549
Walinder, J., 352
Walker, J. I., 171
Walker, L. J., 567
Wallace, R. A., 241
Wallach, M. A., 462
Wallerstein, J. S., 127, 562
Wallerstein, R. S., 637
Walsh, J. H., 252
Walsh, T. B., 246
Walters, R. H., 548–49
Wampold, B. E., 656
Wang, Y. T., 318
Ward, A. J., 525
Ward, M. J., 5

Warner, A., 320
Warner, L., 273
Warner, V., 567
Warnes, H., 172
Warrack, G., 413–14
Warrington, E. K., 484
Warshauer, D., 540
Wasylenki, D., 695
Waterman, J., 563
Watkins, C., 424
Watkins, J. T., 382, 409, 664, 665
Watson, J. B., 72
Watson, S., 318, 401
Watt, N. F., 450
Waxler, N. E., 458
Weakland, J. H., 556
Weary, G., 13, 85
Wechsler, D., 583
Weekes, J. R., 209
Wegner, D. M., 113
Wehr, T. A., 399–400
Weinberg, M. S., 352, 374, 376
Weinberger, D. R., 447, 454, 478, 483
Weinberger, L., 691
Weiner, H., 238, 247
Weiner, H. F., 249
Weiner, I. B., 536
Weiner, R., 608
Weingartner, H., 432
Weinrott, M. R., 372
Weinstein, A. S., 464
Weinstein, L., 414
Weintraub, M., 120
Weintraub, S., 437
Weisenberg, M., 257
Weisfeld, G., 550
Weiskrantz, L., 484
Weiss, B., 505
Weiss, D. S., 143
Weiss, G., 540, 542, 620
Weiss, J. M., 249, 329, 392, 404
Weiss, R. G., 364
Weiss, R. L., 658
Weiss, S. M., 230, 255
Weiss, T., 645
Weissenburger, J., 409
Weisshar, M., 647
Weissman, M. M., 16, 183, 264, 281, 305, 320, 394, 397, 408, 409, 414, 421, 567, 629
Weisz, J. R., 505, 537–38
Wekstein, L., 411, 413, 414, 421, 422
Welch, C., 177
Welker, R., 406
Welkowitz, J., 106
Wellisch, D. K., 660
Wells, C. E., 484
Wells, C. F., 412
Wells, K. C., 549, 562
Wells, L. A., 256
Welner, J., 568
Welsh, R. J., 312, 313
Wenar, C., 523, 529, 556
Wender, P. H., 269, 397, 449, 568, 620
Wener, A., 542
Wennerholm, M., 592
Werner, M., 459
Werry, J. S., 521, 555, 620
Wertham, F., 362
Wesley, J., 44
Wessels, H., 639
West, J. A., 110
West, K. L., 459
West, M., 274
Westbrook, D., 409
Westbrook, T., 258

Subject Index

Abnormal behavior: assessing, 571–603; biological factors in (*see* Biological factors); causes of, 7–8; classification of, 9–16; defining, 7–8; and dementias of aging, 493–500; incidence of, 15; and mental retardation, 503–33; misconceptions about, 6; models of, 18, 55–93; neurological factors (*see* Neurological factors); prevalence of, 15; popular views of, 4–6; psychosocial factors (*see* Psychosocial factors); research in, 16–23, 25–27; sociocultural factors in (*see* Sociocultural factors); treatment of, 605–71
Abnormal psychology, **8**
Abortion, 508, 511, 674
Absolutistic thinking, 648
Abstinence viewpoint, and alcoholism, 312, 313
"Abstinence violation effect," 314
Abusiveness, 264, 267, 275, 278, 284
Academic skills disorders, 506, 509, 528
Accidental deaths: alcohol, 297; and mood disorders, 394; and stress, 155, 173, 237–38
Accommodation, **113**
Acetylcholine, 497, 614
Acrophobia, 185
Acting out behavior, 68–69, 264, 280, 282, 283, 286, 293, 549
Actualization, 112–15; and normalcy, 8; through therapy, 653–55
Actuarial procedure, and assessment, **590–91**
Acupuncture, 256
Acute disorders, **11**
Acute posttraumatic stress disorder, 156
Acute schizophrenia, 433, 439
Addictive disorders: alcohol abuse, 296–314; assessing for, 588; drug abuse, 314–29; gambling, 333–37; hyperobesity, 329–33; and personality disorders, 266
Adequacy, sense of, 405
ADHD (*see* Attention-deficit hyperactivity disorder)
Adipose cells, 330
Adjustment disorders, 151–56, 179, 384; vs. mood disorders, 384; bereavement, 153–55 (*see also* Grief); divorce, 155–56; forced relocation, 175–76; unemployment, 151–53
Adjustment disorder with depressed mood, 383, 388–89, 425
Adolescence, 263, 642; and antisocial personality, 116, 264, 282, 287, 293, 543, 545, 546, 548; and anxiety-based disorders, 551–54; and delinquency in, 264, 545–51; disorders in, 535, 544 (*see also* Childhood disorders); drug usage in, 297, 314, 327, 548, 676–78; and faulty development, 116; faulty parental relationships in, 121, 125–27, 548–49; and hyperactivity, 538, 542; mental retardation in, 505, 517; mood disorders in, 386, 410; and personality disorders, 265; psychogenic disorders in, 242–48, 252; and runaways, 368, 546, 547, 549; schizophrenia in, 428, 456, 459; sexual variants in, 360, 362, 368, 374; suicide in, 412–13, 415

Adoption strategy of genetic research, 397, 448–49, 450
Adoptive homes, 562
Adults, young: and child abuse, 563–65; and crime, 369; and drug abuse, 297, 314, 323, 327; and hyperactivity, 542; and schizophrenia, 429, 455; and sexual conflicts, 201; and sexual variants, 357–58, 369; and suicide, 410–11, 412–13
Advocacy, **566**
Advocacy programs: for children, 566–67; for mentally retarded, 566–67; for patients, 687, 698
Affect (*see* Emotions)
Affection, 288, 660
"Affectionless psychopathy," 288
Affective disorders (*see* Mood disorders)
African Americans: and hypertension, 248; and IQ tests, 532
Aftercare, 313, 465, 620, 673, 684–86, 698
Aggression: alcohol or drug abuse, 305–6; and antisocial personality, 272, 282, 289, 290; and childhood disorders, 538, 539, 543, 545, 549, 550, 569; and "dangerousness," 688–91; and delinquency, 545, 549; and faulty development, 116, 121, 122, 123, 126; and frustration, 254; imitating, 123; and mental retardation, 506; and neurotic style, 215; by parents (*see* Child abuse); and peer groups, 127–130, 550; and personality disorders, 272, 276–77, 278; and posttraumatic stress, 170–71; and psychoses, 456; and sexual variants, 358–59, 365, 371, 377–78, 379
Aggression/assertion inhibition, 215
Aging: and brain pathology, 108, 493–500; and chromosomal anomaly, 511; and depression, 401; stress as, 149, 237–38; stresses of, 499; and suicide, 413
Agoraphobia, **184,** 185, 221
Aid to Dependent Children (ADC), 520
AIDS, 234–35, 318, 349, 362, 376–77, 378, 379, 486–87, 501
AIDS dementia complex (ADC), **486**
AIDS-related complex (ARC), **487**
Al-Anon family groups, 312
Alarm reaction, 149, 233
Alaska Native Medical Center, 307
Ala-Teen, 312
Albertson's Inc. v. *Workers' Compensation Appeals Board of the State of California,* 178
Alcohol abuse and dependency, 238, 296–314, 549, 553; in anxiety disorders, 185, 193, 221; and brain disorders, 483, 484, 485, 488, 493, 577; and child abuse, 553, 564; controlled drinking vs. abstinence, 312–13; and crime, 297; with drugs, 321, 322; factors in, 304–7, 337–38; and fetus, 302, 507–8; and health, 238, 301; incidence of, 296, 298, 312; misconceptions about, 298; and mood disorders, 381, 387; and personality disorders, 264, 275, 283, 335; and posttraumatic stress, 172, 173; and primary prevention, 676–78; and

psychogenic disorders, 229, 255; psychoses from, 303–4; and sexual variants or dysfunctions, 346, 365, 366; stages of dependency in, 300–3; and suicide, 297, 413, 416; treatment and prognosis in, 257, 307–14, 338–39, 649, 685–86; view of, from different perspectives, 86
Alcohol amnestic disorder, 296, 304
Alcoholic and alcoholism, **296;** (*see also* Alcohol abuse and dependency)
Alcoholic psychoses, 303–4
Alcoholics Anonymous (AA), 309, 311–12, 336, 338, 698–99
Alcohol idiosyncratic intoxications, 338
Alcoholism, Drug Abuse, and Mental Health Administration, 308, 566, 697
Alcohol- or drug-abuse counselor, 630
Alcohol withdrawal delirium, 303, 338
Algophobia, 185
Alienation, 651, 653
Aloofness, 265, 274, 276
Alprazolam, 622–23
Alzheimer's disease, 10, 57, 108, 478, 480, 481, 484, 486, 493–500, 501
Ambivalence, about suicide, 417–20, 423, 425
Amented retardation, 507, 532
American Association for the Advancement of Science (AAAS), 701
American Association of Behavior Therapists (AABT), 700
American Association on Mental Deficiency (AAMD), 504, 505, 701
American Medical Association (AMA), 302, 323, 326, 614, 700
American Nurses Association (ANA), 700
American Occupational Therapy Association (AOTA), 700–701
American Orthopsychiatric Association (AOA), 701
American Psychiatric Association (APA), 10, 265, 373, 435, 504, 505, 509, 555, 591, 600, 601, 610, 700, 702
American Psychoanalytic Association (APA), 700
American Psychological Association (APA), 24, 520, 669, 700
American Public Health Association, 304
American Sociological Association (ASA), 700
Amish, and bipolar disorder, 398
Amitriptyline, 616, 622–23
Amnesia and fugue: and alcoholism, 301, 304; and brain disorders, 478, 481, 483, 484–85, 486, 489, 492, 496, 501; in dissociative disorders, **205–8;** from ETC, 408; in trauma or combat reactions, 157, 634–35
Amnestic syndrome, **484–85,** 486, 492, 501
Amniocentesis, 508, 511
Amok, 89
Amorphous thinking, 459
Amoxapine, 616
Amphetamine psychosis, 323, 485
Amphetamines, 295, 314, 316–17, **321**–23, 331, 485, 540, 569, 620
Amyloid, 498
Anaclitic depression, 554
Analgesia, 202
Analogue studies, **21**

Intimacy/trust inhibition, 215, 216, 227
Intracerebral hemorrhage, 492
Introductory Lectures on Psychoanalysis, 65
Introjection, **68**
Introversion, 59, 588
Inventories (*see* Self-inventories)
In vitro sensitization, 638–39
In vivo procedures, 554, 639–40, 641
Irradiation effect, 682
Irresistible impulse doctrine, 692
Irresponsibility, 279, 282, 283
Irritability: in anxiety-based disorders, 193, 196; and brain disorders, 387, 393; and severe stress, 152, 153, 155, 172, 218
Isocarboxazid, 616, 622–23
Isolation: effect of, 129–30; and Genain sisters, 429–32; and mental retardation, 513, 514–15, 519; in old age, 422; and paranoia, 435, 471; and personality disorders, 269, 274–75, 594; and posttraumatic stress, 174; in schizophrenia, 429–32, 435; and suicide, 422; in therapy, 258–59
Israeli-NIMH High-Risk Study, 450

Japan: and psychogenic illness, 255; and suicide, 417
Jealous-type disorders, 466
Jenkins Activity Survey for Health Prediction, 240
Job: dissatisfaction with, 134, 140, 145, 550; and personnel screening, 591–92; and stress, 141–43; and suicide, 413
Joey, a mechanical boy, 526–27
Joint Commission on the Mental Health of Children, 561, 566
Jonestown murder-suicides, 562
Journal of Abnormal Psychology, 50
Judgment impairment: and alcoholism, 298, 299, 301; assessing, 579; in brain disorders, 479; in senile and presenile dementia, 494, 495
Juvenile delinquency, 546 (*see also* Delinquency)

Kaiser Foundation, 104
Kamikaze, 417
Kenyans, and depression, 407
Killer cells, 234–35
Killing, trauma of, 165, 166, 168
Kitsunetsuki, 89
Klinefelter's syndrome, 101, 509
Korean War, 164–65
Koro, 89
Korsakoff's syndrome, 295, 304

Labeling, 14–15, 541, 684, 685
La Bicêtre, 41, 44
La Maison de Charenton, 41
Language difficulties: in autism, 524, 525; and brain damage, 481; and deprivation, 116; and learning disabilities, 528; and mental retardation, 505–6, 513, 516; in schizophrenia, 434, 439
"Last straw" response, 143, 149
Latah, 89
Latency stage, 67
Latent content of dreams, 635
Latent schizophrenia, 269
Leaders and leadership, 168
Learned drives, 73–76
Learned helplessness, 131, 404
Learning: in anxiety-based disorders, 214–15, 218–19, 227; in autonomic nervous system, 255, 257, 645; in behavioristic model, 73–76; and behavior techniques, 75, 638–46; and brain disorders, 479, 482; and cognitive-behavioral therapies, 646–52; and development, 113–15; and drug

abuse, 306; and environment, 513–16; and hyperobesity, 330–31; immunosuppression as, 237; and mental retardation, 505–7, 514–15, 516; observational, 642; and personality disorders, 264–65, 278, 286; and sexual behavior, 346–47, 379; vicarious, 219 (*see also* Faulty learning)
Learning disabled, **528**, 533
Learning disabilities, 528–31, 539
Legal issues: and the mentally ill, 686–97, 705; and suicide, 422–24
Legalized gambling, 337
Lehrbuch der Psychiatrie, 57
Length: of captivity, and stress, 173–74; of combat duty, and stress, 168
Lesbians, 374
Lethality scale for suicide, 416
Lethargy, 315, 321, 328, 618
Leukocytes, 234
Librium, 316–17, 618, 622–23
Life change units (LCU), 146
Life events: and mood disorders, 383–84, 401, 402; and schizophrenia, 462; and stress, 230, 235, 243–44
Life instincts, 65
Life stress, 145, 146, 147–51, 151–56, 319, 462–63
Life-style: and disease, 230, 238–39, 255–56, 257, 259–60, 261, 675; and suicide, 421–22
Life support retarded, 507
Light, effect of, on mood, 400
Limbic system of brain, 482, 610
Lithium carbonate, 399, 408, 595, 612, 618–19, 622–23, 625, 649
Localized amnesia, 206
Lolita, 363
Loneliness, 126, 254; in personality disorders, 274
Loners, 267, 269, 272, 274
Lonesome Dove, 216
Longitudinal studies, 21, 107, 120, 125, 459, 540, 564, 678
Los Angeles Suicide Prevention Center, 416, 422, 679
Los Angeles Times, 356
Loss: and grieving process, 384–85, 401, 412–13; parental, and abnormal development, 288, 403, 459, 548–49; as stress, 143, 153–55
Love: expression of, in suicide notes, 420; need for, 117–18; and personality disorders, 117–18, 269
Lovemaps, **342**, 351, 354, 358, 360, 364, 365, 368, 370, 374
Ludiomil, 616
Lunatics' Tower, 41
Luria-Nebraska battery, 578–79
Lycanthropy, **36**
Lymphokines, 234
Lysergic acid (LSD), 314, 325–27, 316–17, 451

MacAndrew addiction scale, 588
Macbeth, 299
Macrocephaly, **512**
Macrophages, 234, 236
Mainstreaming, **519**
Maintenance therapy, 257, 410, 422
Major depression, 381, **382**, 383, 384, 389–92, 394, 397, 400, 408, 425
Major tranquilizers, 464 (*see also* Antipsychotic drugs)
Male erectile disorder, **343–44**
Malingering, 197, **199**, 204, 205, 493
Malleus Maleficarum, 40
Malnutrition, 259, 700; among alcoholics and drug abusers, 301, 304, 318, 338; and brain disorders, 484; in combat or POW camps, 109–11, 167; and retardation, 110–11, 508

Mania, 32, 34, 35, 360, **382,** 389, 393, 395, 403, 405, 406, 425, 452, 484, 588, 608, 613, 618, 622–23
Manic bipolar disorder, 392, 394
Manic-depressive psychoses, 392 (*see also* Bipolar disorder)
Manifest content of dreams, 635
Manipulative behavior, 279, 281, 283, 284, 290, 293, 335
Maprotiline, 616
Marathon desensitization procedures, 641
Marijuana, 295, 316–17, 327–28
Marital schism, **126, 458**
Marital skew, **126, 458**
Marital therapy, 276, 280, 655–58, 671
Marplan, 616, 622–23
Marriage: and alcoholism or drug abuse, 297, 306, 338; and anxiety-based disorders, 187–88, 191–92, 194–95, 201, 217; communication in, 85, 123–25; and faulty family structures, 123–27; folie á deux in, 467; and gambling, 334, 336; and mood disorders, 408; and sexual variants, 356, 357, 358, 359, 367–68; as a source of stress, 145, 276; and stress, 143, 144–45, 155–56, 276, 280, 402; and therapy, 655–58, 671
"Mask of insanity," 461
Masochism, 351, **362–63,** 379
Mass madness, 35–37, 205
Mass media and modeling programs, 677–78
Masturbation, 121, 201, 347, 355, 358, 359, 360, 548
Maudsley Hospital, 525
Mayo Clinic, 259, 590
McKenna v. *Fargo,* 592
Meaning, need for, 79, 220, 418, 653–54
Medical Inquiries and Observations upon the Diseases of the Mind, 44
Medical Model (*see* Biological viewpoint)
Medulla of brain, 482
Melancholia, 4, 32, 34
Melancholic type of major depression, 391
Mellaril, 595, 613, 615, 622–23
Memmel v. *Mundy,* 687
Memory impairment: and alcohol, 301, 303; and autism, 523; and brain disorders, 478, 481, 483, 486, 489, 491–92, 495, 496; and depression, 610; and drugs, 321, 327; and ECT, 408; and posttraumatic stress, 156
Memory strategies, 531
Men and boys: and alcohol or drug abuse, 16, 183, 297–98, 304, 324; and antisocial personality, 281; and anxiety-based disorders, 220; and behavior genetics, 59–60; and child abuse, 368, 563; and childhood disorders, 521, 535, 538, 543, 552, 558, 560; and delinquency, 546, 548–49, 550; and depression, 384, 394; and mental retardation, 509, 511; and mood disorders, 382, 385, 394, 398; and neuroses, 186; and paresis, 488; and primary reaction tendencies, 106–7; and psychogenic disorders, 242, 245, 249, 254; and schizophrenia, 456–60; and senile and presenile dementia, 494; and sexual dysfunction, 343–45; and sexual variants, 353, 355, 356, 358, 359, 361, 364, 368–72; and suicide, 411, 416, 419; and unemployment, 152
Meningitis, 484
Menopause, 306
Menstruation, 198
Mental age, 505
Mental health: early concern for, 35, 43–46; and the future, 702–4; and government aid, 673, 697; international

Feedback, please!

We need your reactions and ideas if *Abnormal Psychology and Modern Life* is to serve you and others better. What did you like best and least? What would you like to have more or less of? How could it have been handled better? Please jot down your suggestions, cut out this page, fold and tape or staple it, and mail it to us. No postage is needed.

Many thanks!
The authors

For every chapter that you read, please make a check mark on each line to indicate your evaluation of it. It is ideal if you can do this as soon as you finish reading each chapter.

Chapter	Informational Value			Interest		
	high	average	low	high	average	low
1 Abnormal Behavior in Our Times						
2 Historical Views of Abnormal Behavior						
3 Biological, Psychosocial, and Sociocultural Viewpoints						
4 Causal Factors in Abnormal Behavior						
5 Stress and Adjustment Disorders						
6 Anxiety-based Disorders						
7 Psychological Factors and Physical Illness						
8 Personality Disorders						
9 Substance-Use and Other Addictive Disorders						
10 Sexual Disorders and Variants						
11 Mood Disorders and Suicide						
12 The Schizophrenias and Delusional Disorders						
13 Organic Mental Disorders						
14 Mental Retardation and Developmental Disorders						
15 Behavior Disorders of Childhood and Adolescence						
16 Clinical Assessment						
17 Biologically Based Therapies						
18 Psychologically Based Therapies						
19 Contemporary Issues in Abnormal Psychology						

What did you like best/least about *Abnormal Psychology and Modern Life?*

Your name and address (if you wish)

_____

_____

Male _____ Female _____ Age _____

Your course grade _____

Will you take more psychology? _____

Your probable major _____

School _____

Size of your psychology class _____

Were you in a discussion section? _____

Besides the text, did you use:

Study Guide to accompany *Abnormal Psychology and Modern Life 9th?* _____

Other supplementary material? _____

_____

fold here

How could *Abnormal Psychology and Modern Life* be improved?

All things considered, how does *Abnormal Psychology and Modern Life* compare to texts you have used in other courses?

much better	*better*	*about average*	*worse*	*much worse*

fold here

BUSINESS REPLY MAIL
FIRST CLASS   PERMIT NO. 247   NEW YORK, NY

POSTAGE WILL BE PAID BY ADDRESSEE

HarperCollins*Publishers*

Attn: Developmental Group—Abn Psy 9
College Division—24th Floor
10 East 53rd Street
New York, NY 10022-5299

cut page out